BY THE SAME AUTHOR

BOOKS

The Battles of Coxinga
The Japanese Discovery of Europe
Japanese Literature: An Introduction for the Western Reader
Living Japan
Bunraku: The Art of the Japanese Puppet Theatre
Nō: The Classical Theatre of Japan
Landscapes and Portraits
World Within Walls: Japanese Literature of the Pre-Modern Era, 1600–1867
Dawn to the West: Japanese Literature of the Modern Era
Some Japanese Portraits
The Pleasures of Japanese Literature
Travelers of a Hundred Ages: The Japanese as Revealed Through 1,000 Years of Diaries

TRANSLATIONS

The Setting Sun (by Osamu Dazai)
No Longer Human (by Osamu Dazai)
Five Modern Nō Plays (by Yukio Mishima)
Major Plays of Chikamatsu
The Old Woman, the Wife, and the Archer (by Shichiro Fukasawa, Chiyo Uno, and Jun Ishikawa)
After the Banquet (by Yukio Mishima)
Essays in Idleness (by Yoshida Kenkō)
Chūshingura (by Takeda Izumo, Miyoshi Shōraku, and Namiki Sōsuke)
Madame de Sade (by Yukio Mishima)
Friends (by Kobo Abe)
Twenty Plays of the Nō Theatre (edited and translated)
The Man Who Turned into a Stick (by Kobo Abe)

ANTHOLOGIES

Anthology of Japanese Literature
Modern Japanese Literature

Seeds IN THE Heart

Japanese Literature from Earliest Times to the Late Sixteenth Century

DONALD KEENE

HENRY HOLT AND COMPANY
NEW YORK

Henry Holt and Company, Inc.
Publishers since 1866
115 West 18th Street
New York, New York 10011

Henry Holt ® is a registered
trademark of Henry Holt and Company, Inc.

Published in Canada by Fitzhenry & Whiteside Ltd.,
91 Granton Drive, Richmond Hill, Ontario L4B 2N5.

Library of Congress Cataloging-in-Publication Data
Keene, Donald.
Seeds in the heart : Japanese literature from earliest times to the late sixteenth century / Donald Keene.
p. cm.
Includes bibliographical references and index.
1. Japanese literature—To 1600—History and criticism.
I. Title.
PL726.115.K44 1993
895.6′09—dc20 93-1082
CIP

ISBN 0-8050-1999-5

Henry Holt books are available for special promotions and premiums. For details contact: Director, Special Markets.

First Edition—1993

Book design by Claire Naylon Vaccaro

Printed in the United States of America
All first editions are printed on acid-free paper. ∞

10 9 8 7 6 5 4 3 2 1

Offered to
Ted and Fanny de Bary
in Celebration of
Fifty Years of Friendship
1942–1992

ACKNOWLEDGMENTS

Grateful acknowledgment for permission to print excerpts from their translations is made to:

Edward Seidensticker for *The Tale of Genji* (Alfred A. Knopf) and *The Gossamer Years* (Tuttle); to Helen Craig McCullough for *Yoshitsune* (Stanford University Press); and to Royall Tyler for *Japanese Tales* (Pantheon)

Columbia University Press for Steven D. Carter, *Waiting for the Wind*; Yoshito S. Hakeda, *Kūkai*; *The Manyōshū*; Ivan Morris, *The Pillow Book of Sei Shōnagon*; and Burton Watson, *Japanese Literature in Chinese*

Doubleday for Karen Brazell, *The Confessions of Lady Nijō*

Georges Borchardt, Inc., for Ivan Morris, *As I Crossed a Bridge of Dreams* and *The World of the Shining Prince*

Harvard University Press for Edwin O. Cranston, *The Izumi Shikibu Diary*

Princeton University Press for Helen Craig McCullough, *Ōkagami*; Ian Hideo Levy, *Man'yōshū*; and Richard Bowring, *Murasaki Shikibu: Her Diary and Poetic Memoirs*

Scholars Press for David Pollack, *Zen Poems of the Five Mountains*

Stanford University Press for Helen Craig McCullough, *Kokin Waka Shū* and *Tales of Ise*; William H. and Helen Craig McCullough, *A Tale of Flowering Fortunes*; and Phillip Tudor Harries, *The Poetic Memoirs of Lady Daibu*

State University of New York Press for Robert E. Morell, *Sand and Pebbles*

Tokyo University Press for Thomas J. Cogan, *The Tale of the Soga Brothers*

University of Hawaii Press for Mildred Tahara, *Tales of Yamato*; and Jennifer Brewster, *The Emperor Horikawa Diary: Sanuki no Suke Nikki*.

CONTENTS

THE MIDDLE AGES

PREFACE

Twenty-five years ago I conceived the plan of writing a history of Japanese literature. At that time the only existing history in English had been published in 1899, and the shortcomings of this pioneer volume by W. G. Aston were all too obvious. I reasoned that it would not take me more than two years to write such a history. After all, for a decade I had been giving a survey course at Columbia University on Japanese literature from ancient times to the present, and all that was needed was to put down on paper the kinds of information I had already delivered orally. I would write in the same manner as my lectures—subjectively and enthusiastically, in the hopes of stimulating others to love Japanese literature as I did. I would not bore readers with useless dates or summaries of the contents of books.

With this resolution in mind, I began to write. I started at the beginning, in the normal manner, and wrote quickly, seldom bothering to look up anything I did not already know. I had reached a point somewhere in the fourteenth century when, in the course of a trip around the world, I visited the University of Leningrad and met the professor of Japanese, Evgenia Pinus. I mentioned what I had been writing. "But what if your readers *need* to know dates?" she asked. I answered, "There are other books with dates and information of that sort." "Which other books?" she asked, and I had to admit that there were none in English.

This conversation had the effect of changing my mind about my history. I decided that the manuscript of some three hundred pages would have to be scrapped. But, having reached the fourteenth century in the discarded draft, I found it psychologically difficult to start again at the beginning. I decided to write instead on the literature of the Tokugawa period (1600–1867). My doctoral dissertation had treated Chikamatsu Monzaemon, the outstanding dramatist of the period, and I had spent years reading the poetry of Bashō. If I had followed my original plan, the volume devoted to Tokugawa literature would have consisted mainly of my impressions of these two great writers, plus a few others I could not overlook such as the novelist Ihara Saikaku or the haiku poet Buson. But, having changed my stance to one of greater informativeness, I felt obliged to read plays by second-rate and even third-rate dramatists. I am glad that I did so. Not only did it increase my admiration for Chikamatsu, but I often found even in lesser works scenes or subjects of such interest that I wanted to tell readers about them.

I followed the Tokugawa volume, *World Within Walls*, with two on modern Japanese literature, *Dawn to the West*, and finally with this book, the one with which I should have started, since it is the first in chronological sequence. With the completion of this history I now feel for the first time qualified to teach the courses I have taught for over forty years. If nothing else, I have now read almost all of the works of Japanese literature that the Japanese themselves have selected as the best of their literary tradition.

I have benefited by translations, which were certainly easier to read than the originals, but I have always gone back to the original texts to make sure that the translations conveyed the sense of the original; when they did not, I retranslated. Fortunately, there are now many excellent translations, making my task much easier than it would have been thirty or forty years ago.

I have given in the bibliographies appended to each chapter the books I have consulted. In some cases, a new translation or study appeared after I had completed writing the chapter. Ideally, I should have rewritten the chapter in each instance, but if I had, the writing of the whole would have taken not twenty-five but thirty years, and even then it might not be complete.

When I began to publish my history of Japanese literature there was no other work worthy of the name in a European language, but the first volumes of Professor Jin'ichi Konishi's scholarly *A History of Japanese Literature* have since appeared. It is fortunate that readers can now consult not one but two histories.

In preparing this first and last volume of my history I have had the benefit of the criticisms of Professor Susan Matisoff, to whom I here extend my thanks. I thank also Karen Kennerly, my editor throughout, who has enormously improved the text with her suggestions. And finally, I thank all the friends in Japan and elsewhere who have encouraged me in a task that seemed quite literally endless.

DONALD KEENE

INTRODUCTION

The Genres of Japanese Literature

Japanese literature has a history about as long as that of English literature, and the two share other similarities. Both begin with works of the eighth century that were based on even older materials, and both, reflecting the changes in the language brought about by the intrusion and acceptance of a foreign language—Chinese in the case of Japan, French in the case of England—became vastly richer as the result of the large-scale importation not only of the vocabulary of a more advanced civilization but also of its literary heritage.

Poetry developed earlier than prose in both countries, and some of the finest examples of poetry are to be found in works for the theater. Perhaps the most striking difference between the two is that Japanese literature never experienced a "dark age"; when one genre suffered a period of protracted inactivity, another flourished. Even during times of warfare when conditions made the composition of literature difficult, there were always some people who went on composing poetry or writing accounts of themselves and their time.

Some genres, well known in Europe, never developed at all in Japan—for example, the epic poem or the long narrative poem—and others, such as biography, were of only peripheral significance. On the other hand, genres such as the diary and the travel account achieved a greater literary importance in Japan than in most other countries. One genre that has no close European counterpart, *zuihitsu*, literally "following [the impulses of] the brush," and consisting of brief essays on random topics, has also had a sustained development; a bookstore in Tokyo today is likely to have a large section devoted to such writings. Finally, mixed genres have also been important in Japan—novels interspersed with poetry, plays that are partly in a literary and partly in a colloquial language, and poems whose meaning can be fully appreciated only in conjunction with long prose prefaces.

Poetry

The *Kokinshū*, an anthology of poetry compiled by an imperial commission in 905, contains two prefaces that gave classic definitions of the ideals of Japanese poetry. The preface by Ki no Tsurayuki opened, "Japanese poetry has its seeds in the human heart." The poems in this anthology are by no means artless, but regardless of the degree of poetic technique that went into the composition of a poem, the avowed purpose was to express what lay in the poet's heart, not to display his virtuosity. Truthfulness to experience was prized in these early poems as in much of later Japanese literature; the seeds had to be rooted in the heart, or the flowers, however brilliant, would be meretricious.

The inspiration for composing a poem often came from the experiences of a love affair—anticipation of a meeting, grief over parting, remembrances of someone who is now remote—but it could equally come from a momentary perception of nature: morning dew on flowers growing on a fence, the cry of a deer heard from a distant forest. The real message of a poem describing the fall of cherry blossoms might be the poet's realization that her beauty is fading with the years, but this was usually not spoken. In any case, the brevity of the classic verse form, the *waka*, a poem in 31 syllables arranged in lines of 5, 7, 5, 7, and 7 syllables, limited the range to intuitively perceived subjects. A waka could not tell a story, nor enunciate moral truths, nor could it fully convey religious devotion; but by a meticulously exact choice of words the poet could enable the reader to recontruct the world from which the precious few drops were distilled in the poem's brief compass.

Japanese poetry would be confined largely to lyrics, and the most characteristic subjects would be the changes in the flora and fauna of the seasons and the griefs or (much less often) joys of love. The poems in the *Kokinshū* and later anthologies are arranged not by author, nor chronologically, but by the seasons described, by love, and by a few other topics that were thought worthy of poetic composition. The situations described by Tsurayuki as being likely to inspire men and women to compose poetry were for the most part elegiac—the loss of beauty, the coldness of those who were once dear friends. One theme is dominant, sorrow over the passage of time.

Japanese poetry did not begin with the *Kokinshū*. Indeed, it is generally accepted that many of the finest poems of the language are found in the *Man'yōshū*, a collection compiled well over a century earlier; but the secret of how to read the complicated script in which the poems of the *Man'yōshū* were transcribed was not unlocked until the seventeenth century, and during the nine hundred years after the completion of the *Man'yōshū*, poets looked back to the *Kokinshū* as the finest flowering of court poetry, a model that they sought to emulate in language, subjects, and above all its typical form, the waka.

Allusions to the poetry of the *Kokinshū* are found in countless poems that borrowed its themes and wording, always with the expectation that the reader, familiar with the original *Kokinshū* poems that had inspired the later poet, would admire the skill with which he created variations on the original. *Kokinshū* poems also figure conspicuously in fiction, especially of the Heian period (795–1185), the high point of classical Japanese literature. A phrase quoted from a *Kokinshū* poem could substitute in a conversation for the overt expression of a sentiment, and a failure to recognize an allusion might be cause for humiliation.

Poets who felt the urge to express more than was possible within the thirty-one syllables of a waka had the option of writing poetry in Chinese, and some availed themselves of this possibility. But for most poets the waka was the ideal length for the melancholy thoughts aroused by the first cold winds of autumn, or an expression of despair when one realized one would never again meet one's beloved, or a farewell to the world. There was little that Japanese poets of the past really wished to say that could not be expressed in this form. When, a millennium later, the Japanese first came into contact with European poetry, many poets were bewildered, and supposed that *anything* might be made into a poem of this new style, unlike the old poems that drew their materials from nature and the human heart. Even the principles of sociology were turned into a long poem by an earnest young Japanese scholar of the late nineteenth century who had been reading Darwin and Herbert Spencer.

The waka poets of the *Kokinshū* did not attempt to cram as many meanings into their poems as possible in order to overcome the limitations of the thirty-one syllables allowed them, nor did they free themselves of their Procrustean bed by sneaking in an extra syllable here and there; their chief desire was to make their poems perfect. Perfection was attainable in a poem as short as the waka or the even shorter seventeen-syllable haiku, and this may be why the Japanese poets so seldom expressed themselves in the *chōka*, or long poem, that had been the glory of the *Man'yōshū*, and was still occasionally practiced by poets of the age of the *Kokinshū*.

A knowledge of the kind of poetry that was composed at the Japanese court was not confined to the aristocracy. As education gradually spread from the court and the monasteries to the military and eventually even to the peasantry, so did the cult of cherry blossoms and the other aspects of the stylized worship of nature that had inspired the court poets. Today the progress of the blossoming of the cherry is breathlessly reported on radio and television—60 percent open in one place, only 40 percent in another—and even persons not normally interested in flowers will go off to share in what the poets have made a national experience.

But despite its pervasion of all classes of society, Japanese literature as a whole is prevailingly aristocratic when compared to the literatures of Europe. There are, of course, folk songs and folktales, some of considerable interest, but the main body of the literature from the eighth to the seventeenth century was composed by members of the nobility or else by persons who had adopted its language and manners. Unlike the nobles of medieval Europe, the Japanese aristrocrats rarely took part in the pleasures of the hunt or of war. They of course had rivalries, political as well as amorous, and they were by no means flawlessly behaved at all times, but the ideal courtier was known for his elegance and his ability to compose a well-turned poem, and he had above all to obey the rules of good taste. The poetry composed by the courtiers (and by others writing in their manner) was melancholic, rather than tragic, and avoided the jagged edges of openly expressed emotions.

Even the most refined courtiers on occasion turned for inspiration or amusement to the literature and entertainments of the common people. The Retired Emperor Goshirakawa compiled a massive collection of folk and popular songs in the twelfth century. In the fourteenth century, *dengaku*, the dances and songs that had been performed by peasants at their festivals in honor of the gods of the soil, became a craze at the court, and contributed to the development of the aristocratic Nō drama. Literary preferences tended to move upward: even after the composition of literature by and for the common people became normal in the seventeenth century, the tastes displayed in this literature soon showed unplebeian refinement. Haiku poetry, which had originated as salacious quips at after-dinner festivities, was transformed into a noble art by Bashō, just as the ukiyo-e prints, begun as pornography, blossomed in the flawless combinations of lines and colors that conquered the artistic world of nineteenth-century Europe. Good taste seems to be endemic in the Japanese.

Of course, a new art was not likely to be in impeccable taste from its inception. In between the first, crude beginnings and the elevation of the art to its final form, a process of refinement occurred, generally marked by the evolution of rules intended to purge the new genre of its original earthiness. When dengaku was taken over by the court of the shogun, the simple peasant costumes of the performers were replaced with robes of magnificent brocades, lest ugliness distract the attention of spectators from the plays. Another art of the middle ages, *renga*, or linked verse, had originated as a kind of game, a test of wits that required a man to add a couple of lines to a poem another man had made. The best links composed on a given occasion were rewarded with prizes, and bets might be placed on the likely winners. But before long, codes of composition, similar to (but even more demanding than) those that had evolved for the art of the waka, were applied to renga with the intention of raising a mere diversion to the level of art. Eventually, so many rules were created by renga practitioners, who sought philosophical justification for every aspect of their art, that specialists in the rules were required to preside over each renga session, and what had been a game became a life-and-death matter to participants.

Fiction

Although poetry was considered to be of greater importance than prose, fiction was by no means neglected. The novel developed earlier in Japan than in the West. Some Japanese critics have denied that *Genji Monogatari* (The Tale of Genji), the greatest work of Japanese fiction, should be called a novel, noting its lack of overall structure or a pervading philosophy of life. They may be right, but it is difficult to define what constitutes a novel, and perhaps we may be permitted to use the word loosely, as a designation for any extended work in prose that describes people living in a believable society. The Japanese term *monogatari* means a "telling of things," a neutral term as compared to the later, originally pejorative, *shōsetsu* ("little talk"), a term borrowed from China, where the novel had traditionally not been considered to be of literary importance.

The first and perhaps most effective defense of the monogatari is found in *The Tale of Genji*, written early in the eleventh century. In a famous passage of her novel, the author, Murasaki Shikibu, speaking through Prince Genji, the hero of the work, insisted that works of fiction have a legitimate function, preserving the memory of experiences that the author cannot bear to let pass into oblivion. The official histories recorded the principal events of a reign, but they provided no clue to how people actually lived, or what their emotional lives were like. This was the function of the monogatari.

The Tale of Genji, arguably the first novel written anywhere in the world, was given the benefit of learned commentaries in the middle ages and we know that even emperors did not scorn to read it. Under Buddhist influence, disdain was expressed at times for the "lies" of fiction, and the author was consigned to hell for the offense of having described people who had never actually lived; but in terms of the enormous importance of *The Tale of Genji* in Japanese culture, this was no more than a momentary aberration. *Genji*'s influence can be traced not only in later works of court fiction, but all the way through the modern novel. Tanizaki Jun'ichirō's masterpiece, *Sasameyuki* (The Makioka Sisters), has often been compared to *The Tale of Genji*.

Fiction in the manner of *The Tale of Genji* continued to be composed at the court during the medieval period, but more important than such works of the imagination were the stories based on actual events, notably *Heike Monogatari* (The Tale of the Heike), an account of the rise and fall of the Taira clan and of the battles fought between this clan and its enemy, the Minamoto clan. The recitations of professional storytellers helped to spread the tale throughout the country, creating heroes whose fame has not diminished with time.

A revival of fiction occurred in the seventeenth century, notably with the works of Ihara Saikaku, and his novels have continued to inspire writers who wish to depart from the mainstream of naturalist or autobiographical writing. An equally important revival occurred in the twentieth century, this time winning the attention not only of the Japanese public but of the entire world.

Drama

Drama developed rather late in terms of the whole literature. Crude playlets existed as far back as the twelfth century, but our first texts of plays date from the fourteenth century. These Nō plays include the masterpieces of Zeami, one of the great dramatists of the world. Zeami was by no means the only distinguished playwright of the Nō theater, and some of the works of his successors and rivals are even more popular. The stories of the Nō plays were drawn mainly from works of literature familiar to the audiences at the shogun's court, such as *The Tale of Genji* or *The Tale of the Heike*, and their interest did not lie in unexpected developments in the plots or the piquancy of recent events reenacted before the eyes of the spectators. The chief characters are often dead even before the plays open, and appear as ghosts who recall the bitterness of defeat in battle or the pangs of an unrequited love. In performance the plays combine the magnificent poetry of the texts with a musical delivery of the lines, and the climax is generally a dance that epitomizes the action. It was not customary in the past to consider the plays as literature, despite the unquestionable merit of the texts, largely because the elements of performance counted for so much in the total effect. Yet the plays are not only of literary importance in themselves but exerted a significant influence on later literature.

In the seventeenth century other forms of drama were created specifically for plebeian audiences, notably the plays of the Jōruri (puppet) and Kabuki theaters, and these, too, are often of considerable literary value. The plays of Chikamatsu Monzaemon, the outstanding dramatist of the Jōruri theater, can be divided into two main categories: those that treat, however freely, the heroes of the past (sometimes the same heroes who appear in the Nō plays) and those that portray realistically the lives of the commoners of Chikamatsu's own day. His are perhaps the earliest tragedies written anywhere in the world that have as their heroes members of the bourgeoisie who demonstrate by the intensity and purity of their emotions that their stories are worthy of our tears and our admiration.

The theater was the part of Japanese literature least affected by the changes brought about by the introduction of Western literature in the nineteenth century. Although modern drama eventually developed, some dramatists, even of the twentieth century, have continued to write for the traditional theaters, and performances of Nō and Kabuki plays are still better attended than most works written for the modern stage. For anyone accustomed to the brilliance of a Kabuki play—sets, costumes, offstage music, bravado acting and dancing—the typical interior of a modern play is likely to seem drab and unsatisfying.

Special Features of Japanese Literature

Japanese literature, especially when compared with that of China and other countries of East Asia, is notable for the major role of women among the writers of poetry and prose. This was true especially from the eighth to the fourteenth century, but even during the periods of relatively little activity by women writers there were generally a few who maintained the tradition, which has been revivified in the twentieth century. The importance of the women writers to the literature as a whole was not confined to their own works; the influence of such masterpieces as *The Tale of Genji* or *Makura Sōshi* (The Pillow Book of Sei Shōnagon) affected male writers, who adopted the tone and sometimes even the content of typical writings by women.

Another striking contribution of women to Japanese literature was the literary diary. The earliest such diary, *Tosa Nikki* (The Tosa Diary), was in fact written by a man, but it was in the persona of a woman, and *Kagerō Nikki* (The Gossamer Years), the finest work of the genre, was written by a woman late in the tenth century. There has been an unbroken tradition of keeping diaries ever since, many of high literary value. *The Gossamer Years* opens with the author's declaration of her dissatisfaction with existing accounts of court, and her resolve to describe what the life of a court lady was really like. Her insistence on narrating truthfully and in detail the unhappy circumstances of her married life creates a rare intimacy between herself and her readers. The diary genre includes some of the most beloved works of Japanese literature, by men as well as women, including *Oku no Hosomichi* (The Narrow Road of Oku) by Matsuo Bashō, his account of a journey to the north of Japan in 1689.

In a society where it was not easy for anyone (but especially for a woman) to speak her feelings openly, the diary provided an outlet for thoughts that could not be uttered aloud. Not all diaries are of equal interest. Those written by women of the Heian period seem extraordinarily close to us because they describe emotions that have not changed over the centuries, but the diaries of men of the same period, devoted mainly to events at court, often reveal little of the diarists' feelings.

A diary was sometimes a confession so intimate that a diarist might on his deathbed ask the family to burn the diary, but (like any other kind of confession) it had to be heard to be effective: the diarists seldom burned their diaries themselves. The confession in writing assumed a new form in modern literature with the development of the "I novel," in which the author often described in the utmost detail acts and thoughts that most people normally prefer to keep to themselves. The autobiographical novel is found in every literature, but in Japan the "I novel" has at times taken precedence over works that were dismissed as being no more than the fabrications of storytellers.

The popularity of the diary or the "I novel" with Japanese writers may perhaps be attributed to the difficulty they otherwise experienced in organizing long works of prose or poetry. The natural tendency when composing Japanese prose is to write long sentences, and to devote one's greatest efforts to maintaining an unbroken flow of expression. The transition from one sentence to the next, like the transition from one link to the next of a renga sequence, was carefully considered, but the need for an overall structure was often neglected. A Nō play, thanks to its brevity and its formal requirements, could be flawlessly organized, but the longer plays of the eighteenth and nineteenth centuries tended to break down into only casually related scenes, and Kabuki plays are for this reason seldom performed in their entirety today. In the case of a diary, the succession of the days or the stages of a journey provided a ready-made format, and this may be why the Japanese found this genre so congenial.

The difficulty of organizing material into satisfying wholes may account also for the continuing popularity of the books of essays known as zuihitsu. The observations and reflections of the writer are presented with stylistic grace in such works, but above all, it is the personality of the writer that is likely to attract readers. An essay in a book of zuihitsu may be no more than an intriguing sentence or two, or it may extend over several pages. In the end, after reading a series of seemingly unrelated anecdotes or impressions, we may nevertheless feel a great sense of intimacy with the writer, much as if we had read his diary or perhaps an "I novel" in which he laid bare the joys and sorrows of his life.

Another distinctive feature of Japanese literature as a whole is its conservatism. The waka has been composed for well over a thousand years, much of this time as the chief if not the sole poetic form. The poetic diction established in the tenth century was respected by waka poets until late in the nineteenth century, and although many changes had in the meanwhile occurred in the vocabulary of contemporary speech, the form retained its popularity, even among poets of an untraditional outlook. The haiku, developed into a major poetic form in the seventeenth century, is today even more popular than the waka; it has been estimated that the haiku "population" of Japan—that is, the number of people who actively compose haiku, generally as members of a group centered on a professional poet—is well over a million. The plays of the Nō theater are regularly performed every week by different groups of professional actors, and hundreds of thousands of amateurs learn the singing and dancing of the roles. Kabuki and Jōruri plays are performed almost every night of the year, to large audiences. And the major works of traditional Japanese fiction, beginning with *The Tale of Genji*, have been translated again and again into modern Japanese, and adapted for use on the stage and in films.

The Japanese Language

Twentieth-century purists constantly rage over the corruption of language, and there is no shortage of prophets of doom who predict that it cannot survive tampering with its very nature; but it is curious how little in fact the Japanese language has basically changed. A poem in the *Kokinshū* is obviously not in the same Japanese as a contemporary conversation, but some waka poets still express themselves in the diction of the *Kokinshū*, and their poems are understood without much trouble by educated Japanese. The chief differences between the classical and modern languages are in verb and adjectival endings rather than in basic sentence structure or even vocabulary (though the modern language is incomparably richer).

Although the profusion of words of foreign origin is constantly bewailed, they amount to hardly 3 percent of the words found in a newspaper and to an even smaller proportion of the words in most works of literature. It would be simple, moreover, for the government, if it were ever so inclined, to command that all foreign words be suppressed and thereby restore overnight the purity of the Japanese language. In English, a foreign word that has entered the language quickly loses its original nationality. There can hardly be anyone, for example, who is aware when he uses the word "robot" that it was originally Czech; but *robotto* in Japanese, written in *katakana* script, not in the *hiragana* script reserved for words of Japanese origin, remains forever alien and can instantly be detected.

The special features of the Japanese language as it has developed over the centuries affect even the most cosmopolitan writers today. Some struggle to defy the old prescriptions, others take advantage of the idiosyncracies of Japanese expression. A sentence as neutral as "The weather is nice today" is normally expressed in a manner that makes it immediately recognizable as the utterance of a man or a woman, and the relative social statuses of the speaker and the listener will also be apparent. An author may amuse his readers by having a character express this sentence at an inappropriate level of politeness, creating a comic effect without altering the meaning in any way. A novel in which men and women spoke the same language or in which there was no distinction of levels of politeness would not seem like Japanese.

The nature of the Japanese language has affected the poets most. None of the devices most commonly employed in the European languages to distinguish prose from poetry is effective in Japanese. Rhyme is so easy as to be without interest because every word ends with one of five open vowels (or an "n") and there are no consonant clusters; critics in the past even condemned the accidental use of rhyme at the ends of the lines of a waka because it produced unattractive overtones. Again, the clearly defined meters of an English or Russian poem cannot be approximated in Japanese because there is no stress accent. Finally, the patterns of long and short syllables, typical of Greek and Latin poetry, were not possible in classical Japanese because all the vowels were short. Modern Japanese possesses long and short vowels, but no one, as far as I am aware, has taken advantage of them to compose poetry or to create formal poetic structures. Poets do use them for effect.

The Japanese distinguished poetry from prose by syllabics: that is, the number of syllables in a line. The lines of the earliest surviving poems were irregular in the number of syllables, but by the seventh century a preference had emerged for lines of five or seven syllables. Chinese poems were often written in lines of five or seven characters, and this may have affected Japanese usage, but there is a great difference between the five syllables of a single word (like *hototogisu*, the name of a bird) and five characters each with its own meaning. In any case, an alternation of lines of five and seven syllables became the normal rhythm of poetry, not only in the waka and other verse forms but in the lyrical sections of the Nō plays and later works for the theater. There are even passages in the most prosaic novels of the nineteenth century that observe this rhythm.

Although the Japanese for centuries worshiped Chinese culture and absorbed Chinese literary influences without a struggle, they remained surprisingly conservative with respect to the language of poetry. With rare exceptions, no words of Chinese origin (even those that had long since been taken into daily speech) were permitted in traditional poetry, perhaps because imported words did not seem to come from the heart. Japanese poets made do with words of purely Japanese origin, words that had the affective strength of such English words as *blood*, *sweat*, and *tears*, even when they were phonetically soft and melodious. The classical language remained more or less frozen from the tenth century, and the poetic diction was restricted to the some two thousand words found in the poems of the *Kokinshū*.

The haiku poets of the Tokugawa period, it is true, demonstrated their independence of the old poetic diction by using slang or words of Chinese origin. Most of these "new" words had long since been used in daily speech, and using them in poetry was thus an affirmation of the present, as opposed to the more usual nostalgia for a golden age of long ago; and the haiku poets took advantage of the expanded vocabulary to resort to elaborate wordplay and allusion; but Bashō, the greatest of the haiku poets, returned in his last period to the simplicity of the old expression.

The poetry and prose written by Japanese in classical Chinese, long neglected by most scholars of Japanese literature, have in recent years been given respectful attention. Unquestionably these writings were heavily influenced by Chinese predecessors, but they are by no means mere imitations or of negligible value. At certain periods (for example, the ninth century) this literature was so highly regarded as even to threaten the survival of poetry and prose in Japanese. The Japanese who chose to write their compositions in Chinese (like the Englishmen who chose to write in Latin) were implicitly expressing their belief in the universality of literature; no less than the Chinese (or Koreans), they could voice their feelings in a literary language that not only was highly developed but was read throughout the known world. The option of writing in Chinese when they found Japanese expression inadequate or constricting remained open to the Japanese until the twentieth century, when the need to study other languages (and sciences) made it increasingly difficult to maintain the old facility in a language that seemed increasingly remote.

Even after the Japanese began, under the influence of translations of European poetry, to write longer forms than the waka or the haiku, the lines often consisted of units of five and seven syllables, and the vocabulary was usually traditional. But the appeal of European forms of expression was irresistible, and it would have been reasonable to predict in 1900 (as a few Japanese critics did) that before long the traditional verse forms would be abandoned as having outlived their functions. This did not happen, in part because of the general conservatism of Japanese culture, but mainly because the shorter forms better suited the nature of the language.

Colloquialisms are found in the novels of Saikaku and the plays of

Chikamatsu. This does not necessarily make these works easier for modern readers; ephemeral colloquialisms are more obscure than anything in the standard poetic diction. In the case of plays staged for plebeian audiences, the use of the colloquial in the dialogue was probably inevitable, but the passages that set the scene of the action and the *michiyuki*, or "journey," an important part of many plays, were composed in the classical language and contained much the same kind of verbal dexterity one encounters in the Nō texts. Saikaku's novels, even at their raciest, never deserted the classical language completely.

The struggle between the classical and the colloquial languages as the medium of literature continued until the end of the nineteenth century. The first novel composed wholly in the colloquial appeared in the 1880s, but it did not immediately sweep all before it; some writers who experimented with the colloquial went back to the classical language, finding that the colloquial lacked the shades of expression that had been built up over the years by compositions in the classical language. More than that, writers of the time considered themselves to be craftsmen, much like painters or potters, and it was in the nature of each craft to use its special tools. For them the colloquial was no more than a camera that anyone could operate, but the classical language demanded a control like that of an artist's brush.

It took a number of successful novels in the colloquial, mainly realistic accounts of ordinary daily life, before the writers who prided themselves on their craft were induced to give up the badge of their professionalism. Poets of the waka (now called the *tanka*) and the haiku went on using the classical language because its concision permitted them to say more in the same number of syllables. Poets of the free or modern style generally used the colloquial, but sometimes both; for example, Miyoshi Tatsuji, one of the finest of modern poets, used the classical language for his subjective poems, the colloquial for his meditations on a scene before him.

The modern prose writer almost never uses the classical language for whatever purpose, but he may vary his expression with dialect, current slang, or turgid phrases that sound as if they had been translated from some foreign language. Readers are surprisingly tolerant of departures from normal Japanese, but the attempts to change the nature of Japanese expression have rarely been transmitted to a second generation of writers. The modernists of the 1920s, for all their brave insistence on the need to create a new Japanese, in the end returned to the old patterns; and the typographically daring writings of the Dadaists are today totally forgotten.

Philosophic Background to the Works

The general conservatism of the language does not mean, however, that the Japanese have been reluctant to borrow from foreign literature. Quite to the contrary, the Japanese, ever since they first came in contact with the civilizations of the Asian continent, have never hesitated to borrow themes, forms of expression, and intellectual and religious backgrounds. Buddhism, introduced to Japan from Korea, probably in the sixth century A.D., was perhaps the strongest influence on Japanese literature, coloring every form of expression. It is impossible to understand the literature of premodern Japan without at least a modicum of knowledge of Buddhism. The conviction that the things of this world are evanescent and are not to be relied on; that one's position in this life (whether as a human being or an animal, a king or a slave) is determined by the actions of a previous life, and that one's actions in this life determine the form of one's next reincarnation; and the necessity of cultivating the seeds of Buddhahood within one are some of the Buddhist beliefs that recur innumerable times in all manner of writing.

Confucian ethics, introduced from China, also deeply affected the writing of literature, sometimes in the form of rather heavy-handed sermons that interrupt the narration of a historical tale, sometimes in dramas that depict the extraordinary lengths to which men and women go to display their filial piety or some other Confucian virtue. Confucian principles do not lend themselves as easily to poetic expression as the basic Buddhist beliefs, but they have colored the attitudes of the society as a whole, especially since the seventeenth century, and they have provided the scale by which people and their deeds are judged.

The influence of Shintō, the indigenous religion, on literature is harder to demonstrate, but it is unquestionably present. The nature worship that is so conspicuous a feature of Shintō probably accounts for the attention paid in all forms of literature to the seasons and their flowers and animals. A haiku without a seasonal word is not considered to be a haiku but merely a "miscellaneous verse." Even the plays of the Nō theater are classified by season, and it would seem strange to perform an "autumn play" in any other season. Nature, in all of its aspects, has always comforted the Japanese and been their refuge. This is partly because the climate itself (at least in the parts of the country where literature has traditionally been composed) is comparatively mild and agreeable. The summers are hot but short, the winters chilly but seldom freezing. The poets traditionally wrote not about these seasons but about the spring and autumn, when the landscapes of Japan are especially beautiful. Of course, the poets of many countries have celebrated the beauty of spring, but in no other country that I know of is the awareness of the seasons so acute. Even today a business letter opens with greetings of the season.

The Shintō thinkers insisted also on the importance of the spontaneity of the emotions, contrasting this belief with the intellectuality they associated with Confucianism. In Japanese literature, too, the purity of a person's motives is more important than reasoned considerations. The samurai in a Kabuki play who slits open his belly is demonstrating that he is free of impurity; it was a privilege, not allowed to criminals, to die in this way. Purity in love was equally important: the lovers in the plays of Chikamatsu who commit suicide together prove in this way the sincerity of their love. Although status was seldom forgotten in Japan, a shop clerk and a prostitute who died together for their love were as worthy of commemoration (and even envy) as any prince or princess in the old literature.

Though a mixture of Buddhism, Confucianism, and Shintō can be found running through much of the literature, one does not read of people who were torn between conflicting religions—in spite of glaring contradictions. After the seventeenth century, a person's duties to society were regulated by Confucianism, his spiritual concerns by Buddhism, and his joy in the world—over the beauty of the seasons or love or children—came from Shintō beliefs, not from textual prescriptions in any sacred book but seemingly from the ambience of the land itself.

In addition to recognized religions or systems of philosophy, Japanese authors also adhered to what they called the *michi* or "way" particular to their art. This represented more than a poet's or dramatist's normal devotion to his craft; it was consecration to what were believed to be the highest principles of the art. Often this was reinforced by a conviction that the art could be effectively transmitted only from teacher to chosen disciple, for it was feared that if the teacher allowed the secrets of the art to pass to an unworthy vehicle, they would be distorted or even totally corrupted. Esoteric, or secret, transmission was a basic belief of Shingon Buddhism, but it was also congenial to Japanese Confucianists, who were sure that intensive study of the orthodox texts was not enough to make a person wise; the physical experience of sitting at the feet of a revered master was also essential.

In the past the *Kokin Denju*, the transmission of the secrets of the *Kokinshū*, was a rare privilege accorded to extremely few disciples; even a member of the imperial family might be refused if the possessor of the secrets judged that he was too young or otherwise insufficiently qualified to receive the teachings. The esoteric transmission of the secrets of each art remains an important consideration even today, when most secrets are likely to find their way into print. For example, the techniques of performing certain roles in the Kyōgen farces are taught by a master to only one of his sons, not necessarily the eldest but the one who has demonstrated that he is especially qualified to receive this precious knowledge. The most esteemed novelist of the twentieth century, Natsume Sōseki, held weekly audiences for his disciples, who gathered around him seeking not so much his guidance in writing literary works as his wisdom. The novelist and poet Satō Haruo is said to have had three thousand disciples.

The Professional Writer

It is difficult to say when writing first became a profession. The great Kakinomoto no Hitomaro (fl. 689–700) served as a kind of poet laureate to the Empress Jitō, commemorating her excursions to various places and other felicitous occasions, but he presumably also fulfilled his regular duties as an official, and probably did not receive any special reward for composing magnificent poetry. However, at a somewhat later date it became the practice to promote officials on the basis of their demonstrated poetic ability, whether at composing poetry in Japanese or in classical Chinese, the language of official court documents. The father of Murasaki Shikibu, dissatisfied with his appointment as governor of an unimportant province, obtained a better governorship as the result of one particular poem he wrote expressing his grievance. But normally the most concrete reward to which a court poet could aspire was the inclusion of one or more poems in an imperial anthology. Twenty-one such anthologies were compiled between the first, the *Kokinshū* of 905, and the last, a little-remembered collection completed in 1439. Inclusion of even one poem in an imperial anthology was a guarantee of a kind of immortality, and that, rather than financial reward, was undoubtedly what the court poets desired most.

It can hardly be imagined, for that matter, that Murasaki Shikibu benefited materially from having written *The Tale of Genji*. No doubt her company was even more eagerly sought than before by admirers of her book, and presumably she had no trouble in obtaining paper for the continuation of her manuscript, but there was no possibility of royalties. Contrary to usage in China, where the printing of works of literature was normal by the eleventh century, the Japanese did not print books of poetry or prose until the end of the sixteenth century. This was not because the Japanese were ignorant of the art of printing. Some of the oldest examples of printing are from Japan, and Buddhist books continued to be printed during the medieval period. We do not know why the Japanese chose not to print works of literature, but the reason may have been aesthetic rather than practical: a manuscript was not only a text but a work of art, inscribed in beautiful calligraphy and sometimes embellished with paintings. A printed edition, no matter how elegantly carved the woodblocks, could not match the beauty of a manuscript, especially if it was in the hand of some well-known person.

The cost of having a copy made of an existing manuscript must have been considerable. The scribe would have had to be paid for his labors and his sustenance during the period when he was making the copy. Paper was expensive and sometimes scarce—manuscripts were sometimes copied on the backs of other manuscripts. It would not have occurred to anyone who had incurred these expenses to offer money to an author (or to the descendants of the author) for the privilege of making a copy. Not until books were printed in editions of five hundred or more copies would royalties become feasible.

The first persons to make a living from works of literature were probably not authors but performers. Such works as *The Tale of the Heike*, the superb account, first composed in the thirteenth century, of the battles fought between the Taira and Minamoto clans, were recited by professional storytellers all over the country, and these people were no doubt given monetary or other compensation. The troupes of actors who staged plays at temples and shrines from the fourteenth century (or even earlier) were definitely professionals. Some of the actors, notably Kanze Kannami and his son Zeami, wrote the plays they performed, which made them professional authors as well as actors.

In the fifteenth century a new kind of professional author appeared, the renga master. The composition of linked verse normally required the participation of several poets, the different poets taking turns at supplying successive "links" to form a single long poem. At first, the composition of renga was a pastime, but gradually poets began to see the literary possibilities in fusing the poetic expressions of different people. By the fifteenth century a few renga poets had established themselves as masters of the art and were idolized. The greatest of them, Sōgi, though a man of obscure origins, rose to exceptional authority and wealth, and was fawned over by nobles who sought introductions to his distinguished acquaintances. Sōgi lived through the Ōnin War that devastated the capital in the fifteenth century, forcing him, like various other renga masters, to take refuge in the provinces, where they were welcomed by local potentates eager to acquire the culture of the capital. Sōgi seems to have been generously rewarded for the guidance he gave in renga composition and for his patience as he listened gravely to the inept attempts of his hosts to compose poetry in the manner of professionals. The dispersal of Sōgi and other literary men to the provinces had the further effect of spreading culture to the hinterland.

After his return to the capital, Sōgi derived income from lectures he delivered on the Japanese classics. No doubt he was also well paid for correcting the manuscripts of would-be renga poets. Although his income from various sources enabled him to live comfortably, he was not living off his writings in a modern sense. The transcriptions of the renga sessions in which he participated were copied but not sold, and his works of renga criticism and instruction were part of his teaching, not independent literary productions. This remained true of poets until the nineteenth century. Even Bashō, the worshiped master of haiku, earned no money from the sale of his poetry. Apart from the monetary presents made by his adoring disciples, he seems to have depended on selling examples of his calligraphy and paintings.

The introduction of movable-type printing presses in the wake of the Japanese military invasions of the Korean peninsula toward the close of the sixteenth century brought about a dramatic change in the situation of writers of fiction. Although the Japanese had long known how to print books from woodblocks, they were unfamiliar with movable types, and, perhaps at first as a curiosity or a private extravagance, splendid editions of various classics of Japanese literature were printed from these types. Among them the most famous are the texts of the Nō plays designed by the painter, calligrapher, and potter Honnami Kōetsu. These books appeared in several editions. The most elaborate was printed on special paper of different colors with stenciled mica patterns in many designs. These were probably intended as gifts, but there were also texts printed from the same movable types on ordinary paper, and these no doubt were sold.

The first example of a work of Japanese literature printed from movable type had, however, different origins. The Portuguese, who had come to Japan in the middle of the fifteenth century, eventually brought to Kyūshū, the center of early missionary efforts, a printing press. Initially they printed only texts of Christian doctrine, but in 1592 a version of *The Tale of the Heike* in romanized Japanese appeared. This book was probably intended to help Portuguese and other non-Japanese to learn the language and something of Japanese culture, but the text of *Aesop's*

Fables (also in romanized Japanese), published in the following year, may have been intended instead for Japanese converts. The publications of the Jesuit Mission Press were not numerous, and they are today of great rarity, but they provide an interesting sidelight to the first printing of the classics of Japanese literature.

In terms of the emergence of the professional writer, the publication in 1612 of *Uraminosuke*, a story by a contemporary author, represented a significant development. Although *Uraminosuke* itself is of little literary importance, it was apparently the first new work to have been printed and published in the hope of earning a profit. From this time on, books of a clearly commercial nature were frequently published in the main cities of Kyoto, Osaka, and Edo. The names of over a thousand publishers of the Tokugawa period are known. Most of these companies were short-lived, but they produced a large number of books, and by the middle of the seventeenth century there were authors who made their living entirely by their writing. Asai Ryōi is often said to have been the first professional writer in Japanese history. The great popularity he enjoyed in his time did not outlive him, but his success paved the way for Ihara Saikaku, one of the major Japanese novelists.

Saikaku was a thorough professional who could easily compose works to meet the tastes of his seventeenth-century audiences. One can imagine him writing his amorous tales for Kyoto, his tales of commercial life for Osaka, and his tales of the samurai for Edo, corresponding to the prevailing atmosphere of each of the three great cities of Japan. He may not actually have planned his books so schematically, but he never failed to take into consideration his probable audiences and the likely sales of his books. Saikaku's popularity was such that some of his works include his name in the title: *Saikaku's Tales of the Provinces*, *Saikaku's Parting Gift*, *Saikaku's Final Words of Advice*. Publishers commissioned Saikaku to write his stories, and paid him on the basis of the anticipated sales. A thousand or more copies made up the original printing, which could easily be supplemented by running off additional copies from the same woodblocks. There was no protection against pirated editions. Saikaku's first successful novel, *Kōshoku Ichidai Otoko* (The Life of an Amorous Man), printed in Osaka, was soon pirated by an Edo bookseller and published with illustrations by the great Moronobu.

In the eighteenth century the publication of all varieties of literature became commercially plausible, though the short life of most publishing firms suggests that the market was capricious. The general increase in literacy during the eighteenth century naturally led to an expanded audience for books, whether fiction in the manner of Saikaku, works of practical guidance, or beautifully illustrated books that were bought as much for the pictures as for the texts. By the late eighteenth century authors were being paid by the page of manuscript paper, the same kind of ruled paper still used by Japanese authors today. Books included advertisements for other publications of the same author or for works on similar subjects. There were publication parties at which books were launched. Hardly an aspect of contemporary publication in Japan is without roots in the traditions of the eighteenth and early nineteenth centuries.

By the end of the Tokugawa period, book publishing was a major business with a large audience. In particular, the growth of literacy among women resulted in many well-known books of the time being specifically addressed to women readers. New editions of the classics and of commentaries on the classics (which had become difficult to understand even for the best educated) are evidence that the rise in the cultural level of readers did not stop at contemporary fiction. One problem that had existed earlier became a distinct menace to writers of the early nineteenth century—censorship by agencies of the government. During the seventeenth and eighteenth centuries it was understood that references to politics or contemporary events of potential political significance would not be tolerated in works of literature. Some authors (especially dramatists) got around the censorship by transposing the story to a former age: for example, the vendetta carried out by the forty-seven retainers of the Lord of Akō in 1703 was disguised as an event of the fourteenth century, and the characters were either given the names of historical persons of that period or else had their names slightly altered in order to circumvent the edict prohibiting the representation of actual people on the stage.

The prohibition did not at first extend to plays or stories about members of the *chōnin*, or townsman, class, no doubt because the government deemed them to be of so little importance that they could be freely portrayed without giving offense. Chikamatsu Monzaemon, the foremost playwright of the theater of puppets, scored his greatest successes with plays that dealt directly with the lives of commoners of his time, especially the men and women who ended their lives in love suicides. Chikamatsu's heroes and heroines in these plays are most often shopkeepers and prostitutes. At first sight, nothing could be farther removed from the characters who appear in the Nō plays of Zeami than these mundane characters, but their emotions were equally pure.

The audiences for Chikamatsu's plays consisted largely of people from the same milieus he wrote about. He demonstrated that their tragedies, though unheroic and about people whose only way of controlling their fates was to kill themselves, were as worthy of tears as the griefs of the Heian court ladies or the bitter chagrin of the defeated warriors of the middle ages.

The elevation of Tokubei, a clerk who works in a shop that sells soy sauce, and Ohatsu, a low-ranking prostitute, into the hero and heroine of tragedy in *Sonezaki Shinjū* (The Love Suicides at Sonezaki) reflected the great changes that had occurred in society. In the Heian period such people (if their professions had existed) would not even have been noticed by the members of the court who wrote the poetry and prose that are the glory of Japanese literature. In the middle ages they might have figured in some peripheral capacity in the telling of a war tale—a merchant who, despite his demeaning profession, is a human being, or a prostitute who, despite her calling, is faithful to the soldier she loves. But now they have become the central figures of tragedy.

If members of the upper classes chose to attend the theater, they had to accommodate themselves to the tastes of the rest of the audience, just as a samurai who visited the licensed quarter forfeited his privileges and might be outbid for the favors of a prostitute by a lowly merchant with more money.

Japanese Literature During the Period of Isolation

During most of the Tokugawa period, from the middle of the seventeenth to the middle of the nineteenth century, the country was cut off from almost all contacts with the outside world by deliberate policy of the shogunate. The government, fearing that the European powers might attempt to colonize Japan, as they had already done in the Philippines and elsewhere, and that Japanese converts to Christianity might ally themselves with the foreigners, decreed that no Japanese might go abroad and that no foreigners might enter Japan. Certain exceptions were made: five or six Dutch traders were permitted to reside on a small island in Nagasaki Harbor, and in the town of Nagasaki a few thousand Chinese engaged in trade. A trickle of information about recent developments in the West came into Japan through this one window on the world, but the Japanese authorities were at pains to keep out works containing Christian doctrine. A series of edicts, at first aimed at reducing the strength of Christianity in Japan, culminated in a total prohibition of the religion under penalty of death.

In rare instances Japanese who had been shipwrecked abroad when storms drove their ships to foreign shores were allowed to reenter Japan; but their foreign rescuers, who had hopes that their generosity in returning the castaways would be rewarded by the Japanese opening the country to trade, went home disappointed. Only after strong pressure had been exerted by the American and Russian fleets in the 1850s were the first cautious steps taken toward ending isolation.

It has long been a matter of debate as to whether the long isolation of the country benefited or harmed Japan. When one reads the literature of the late seventeenth century (known in Japan as the Genroku era), it is clear that a new and vital kind of literature had been created in the poetry of Bashō, the novels of Saikaku, and the plays of Chikamatsu, and it can be argued that the period of isolation, by turning Japanese writers on their native resources, promoted this new literature. But it would be hard to pretend that the poetry, novels, and plays of the next century equaled the writings of the Genroku masters, suggesting that the isolation lasted too long. The end of the Tokugawa period was a particularly dismal time for Japanese literature with the sole exception of the plays written for the Kabuki stage. One gets the impression that Japanese writers had exhausted the possibilities of the traditional literature and needed an infusion of foreign influence—of the kind that has fertilized every literature at one time or another—if it was to survive.

During the years following the Japanese defeat in World War II in 1945, it was normal for Japanese to speak of *sakoku*, the period of seclusion, as a "tragedy." Examples were given of how, as the result of the refusal of the government to import grain from abroad, many thousands of Japanese starved to death when volcanic eruptions and other natural disasters destroyed the harvests. Again, the virtual lack of contact with Europeans meant that Japan did not benefit from the industrial and scientific revolutions that took place in Europe at the time. At the beginning of the Tokugawa period, to judge by the reports of European visitors, the level of the material life of the Japanese was higher than that enjoyed in the countries of Europe. The literacy rate was also higher, and European visitors frequently commented on how little misery was to be seen in the cities or the countryside. Above all, the protracted peace under the Tokugawa régime contrasted with the innumerable wars that afflicted Europe during the same period. But by the middle of the nineteenth century Japan had fallen far behind the European countries.

The cost of isolation was the ordeal that the Japanese suffered during the Meiji period, when they were forced to absorb in a few years the material advances achieved by the Europeans in the course of two centuries. Young Japanese learned Western languages so as to acquire the necessary European science and technology. The government devoted immense efforts to bringing compulsory education to all children. With the help of foreign advisers, the Japanese laid railway tracks and telegraph lines. Not all Japanese benefited from the changes: the samurai class, established by the Tokugawa régime as the foundation of the social order, was deprived of its special privileges. For reasons of state, Buddhism and Shintō, which had coexisted harmoniously for a millennium, were wrenched apart. The Japanese at times seemed determined to destroy everything of their past in the name of civilization.

It is difficult to draw up an objective balance sheet of the merits and demerits of sakoku. In reaction to the publications of the immediate postwar era, the writings of more recent Japanese scholars tend to praise, rather than condemn, the policy of isolation, pointing out the many achievements of the Tokugawa period. But the literature created after the Meiji Restoration of 1868 would in effect represent a rejection of the achievements of Bashō, Saikaku, Chikamatsu, and the lesser masters of the recent past, in favor of the newly introduced European literature. Translations of European literature began to be made soon after the country was "opened" to the world.

The Japanese sent abroad to study in the late Tokugawa and early Meiji periods were expected to acquire practical learning. For a time the officially advocated formula was "Eastern morality and Western science," meaning that Japanese who studied in foreign countries should not, in their eagerness to master the knowledge of the West, forget their own spiritual traditions. Young Japanese scholars, whether they went abroad or attended mission schools in Japan, were often subjected to the well-intentioned efforts of foreigners to save their souls by converting them to Christianity. Many intellectuals were converted, but most subsequently lost interest in their new faith and turned instead to socialism or some other intellectual rather than religious system of thought.

European Literature and the Return to Japan

Translations of European literature, begun chaotically in the 1870s, soon became a systematic enterprise. The Japanese have over the years since then translated most of the important works of the Western tradition. It has been said that if one could read no language but one's own, one could read more of the world's literature in Japanese than in any other language. The translations made in the Meiji period were eagerly read by young people especially, and some of them began to write in a manner conspicuously influenced by foreign example. Romantic love, probably the most familiar theme in Western literature, was celebrated for the first time by Japanese poets in the 1880s. Political matters, hitherto banned by the censors, could be discussed with relative freedom, and this encouraged intellectuals who were concerned for the future of Japan to express their thoughts in novelistic form, as a means of reaching readers who might not respond to political tracts.

The new literature of Japan originated in the opening decade of the twentieth century. Even in the late nineteenth century, before European influence could be fully digested, a few important novels and poems, some of them pioneering efforts in the new manner, others charming survivals of the old literature, were published, but the works for which the Meiji period is admired came later.

Many Japanese if asked to name the two greatest writers of modern Japan would respond with Natsume Sōseki and Mori Ōgai. Both men were well acquainted with foreign languages—Sōseki with English, Ōgai with German. Both men, initially at least, were much influenced by the works of European authors. Sōseki's early works are marked with a humor that surely owes something to the British, Ōgai's with the romantic coloring of the nineteenth-century Germans. But both writers in their different ways returned to Japan in later years. This return was by no means total: the "oriental" thought in Sōseki's late works is not so prominent as to obscure his even greater indebtedness to the European novel; and the "nonfictional novels" of Ōgai's last period, though tributes to the men and women of traditional Japan, do not resemble any earlier Japanese novels. The two men belonged to a generation that was perhaps the last to have absorbed Tokugawa-period literature in boyhood, and nostalgia for that lost world sometimes came to the surface, but they never forgot that they were modern men and that their concerns were shared by writers all over the world.

The next generation of Japanese writers, typified by Nagai Kafū and Tanizaki Jun'ichirō, was familiar from childhood with European books and objects. When Kafū left Japan in 1903 for America (and, later, France) he seems to have desired nothing more than to live the rest of his life abroad. Yet Kafū in fact returned to Japan, and he would become known especially for his elegies evoking the fading beauty of old Tokyo.

Tanizaki related in a story published in 1915 that he had come to realize that "I would have to seek from the West objects to satisfy my craving for beauty, and I was suddenly overcome with passionate admiration for the West.... Everything labeled as coming from the West seemed beautiful and aroused my envy. I could not help looking at the West in the same way that human beings look up to the gods. I felt sad that I had been born in a country where there seemed to be no possibility that any first-rate art could ever be nurtured. . . . And I made up my mind that the only way to develop my art fully was to come into ever closer contact with the West, if only by an inch closer than before, or even by totally assimilating myself into the West."

Tanizaki never visited the West, and less than twenty years after writing this story he had made his return to Japan. His own stories of the 1930s were mainly set in the Japanese past, and at that time he made the first of his three modern-language translations of *The Tale of Genji*, a laborious undertaking that entailed the loss to the world of the original works that Tanizaki would otherwise have written.

With each succeeding generation of Japanese authors the return to Japan seems less and less probable. A successful writer of the 1990s would surely have traveled abroad not once but several times, and would have at least a nodding acquaintance with writers in half a dozen countries. He would not be surprised to learn that translations of his books had been published in the principal languages of Europe and perhaps in Chinese and Korean as well. He might believe that he was competing with writers in other countries in developing new narrative techniques; and he might even have the pleasure of learning that some American or French writer had been influenced by his works. He would not be astonished to hear rumors that he was being considered for the Nobel Prize in Literature.

Perhaps for the latest generation of writers the return to Japan is meaningless. "Japan" does not mean classical literature (which they probably have not glanced at since passing their university admission examinations), and they are indifferent to traditional art and architecture. They are apt to be better acquainted with the music of Stravinsky and Bartók than with any Japanese classical music, old or new. Foreign readers of their novels may be distressed that they are not more Japanese, but these writers feel no need to cater to a craving for exoticism. They have a market for their writings, a hundred million and more Japanese, and although they are grateful for praise from abroad, it is not essential to their work or their livelihoods. Their return to Japan, if it occurs, is likely to take the form of the discovery in middle age that they really like Japanese food better than even the most perfectly prepared French cuisine.

During the "fifteen-year war" that began with the invasion of China and developed into the conflict with America and Britain in the Pacific, some Japanese intellectuals, especially those of the left wing, felt profoundly upset by the actions of the military, but extremely few attempted to escape abroad. There was no tradition of Japanese taking refuge in a foreign country rather than living under a hated régime at home, and it was far more difficult for Japanese to escape from their islands than for a German or Italian to cross into Switzerland. Above all, the fact that the only language they spoke was Japanese, a language understood nowhere else but in Japan, inhibited them. Nagai Kafū abandoned his dreams of spending the rest of his life in America or France when he realized that if he wished to become a writer, Japan was the only country where that was possible.

The postwar writers, especially those born after 1945, have often shown impatience with the Japanese language. They introduce into their works innumerable foreign words, mainly English but also some French and German, and in extreme cases have adopted the sentence structures of foreign languages. Poets, bored by the imagery of traditional Japanese poetry, have rigorously excluded cherry blossoms and maple leaves from their works, preferring hyacinths or gloxinia. Some women authors, resisting the normal distinctions between men's and women's language, have chosen to cast their writings into a completely masculine style. But revolutions in style have rarely lasted even the length of the originator's career, and some writers in middle age have rejected the changes they once advocated and returned to prewar spelling or found Japanese equivalents for the foreign words that had seemed the only ones that truly conveyed their thoughts.

Japanese Literature in the World

In the modern period connections with the Japanese past have been more commonly made by poets than novelists. For the latter, reading Stendahl or Dostoyevsky or Kafka is likely to be a far more memorable experience than what they can recollect of *The Tale of Genji*. Some writers have denied that they learned *anything* from traditional Japanese writings. Those who speak in this vein also tend to reject the belief, shared by many of their countrymen, that the Japanese are a special people whose literature cannot be understood by foreigners.

In the past the Japanese often cited Chinese examples to impart greater importance and resonance to their works by insisting on their affinity with those recorded in China. On the first page of *The Tale of Genji*, for example, after giving a brief account of how the love of the emperor for Kiritsubo, a woman not of the highest rank, had stirred criticism at court, Murasaki Shikibu wrote, "In China just such an unreasoning passion had been the undoing of an emperor and spread turmoil throughout the land."[1] In historical tales like the *Taiheiki* (Record of Great Peace) the narration is interrupted again and again by the recitation of parallel examples in Chinese history, much as the Romans found parallels between the Greeks and themselves, or the French revolutionaries saw themselves as Romans. Similarly, when a Japanese wrote a poem in Chinese he believed he was rising above the trivial matters of his daily life and associating himself instead with grand traditions that stretched back a thousand years or more. He was also being cosmopolitan in rejecting the insularity of Japanese who insisted on maintaining the purity of their language.

This cosmopolitanism has been extended to works of European literature. The Japanese child who reads *Treasure Island* does not think of it as a foreign book that relates events of a world he cannot understand. There are no national boundaries to the appreciation of Long John Silver, Mickey Mouse, or Cinderella. Influence in the opposite direction has begun: books and television programs designed originally for Japanese children have acquired popularity in many countries.

With respect to the major literary works of Japan, acceptance and admiration have required more time than picture books. Until the advent of the translations of Arthur Waley in the 1920s, Japanese literature tended to be treated in the West in terms of the miniature, the unintellectual, the exquisite. Poems more or less in the form of haiku were written by the Imagist poets, some quite pretty but so pallid and wispy as to create the impression that Japanese poetry was no more substantial than evocations of dragonflies and cherry blossoms.

The translations by Waley of *The Tale of Genji* and *The Pillow Book of Sei Shōnagon* changed this impression. When the first volume of his translation of the former work appeared in 1923, the stunned reviewers groped for suitable comparisons with European literature. The comparisons they chose were farfetched, suggesting how difficult they found it to accept the idea that a major work of fiction had been created in Japan. Further translations of Japanese literature, both classical and modern, were made into the principal European languages during the 1930s and 1940s, a few published commercially, others buried in learned journals.

It has only been since the 1950s, however, that translations of Japanese literature have made an impact on the readers of the West. When the Japanese learn of new translations, they are pleased, but they are apt to attribute the choice of works translated to their exotic charm. Exoticism has without question attracted some readers to translations from the Japanese, just as the worst examples of Japanese art, those said by the Japanese to be in foreign taste, actually do find customers among foreigners. But the pleasures of exoticism are quickly exhausted, and this has been only a minor factor in the appreciation of modern Japanese literature.

The lasting appeal of Japanese writing, whether classical or modern, is surely in its subjectivity and universality. A European or American who knows nothing about Japanese culture in the tenth or eleventh centuries can nevertheless read such works as *The Tale of Genji*, *The Pillow Book of Sei Shōnagon*, *The Gossamer Years*, or *Sarashina Nikki* (The Sarashina Diary) without once feeling baffled. The experiences of the author of *The Gossamer Years* may seem disturbingly modern, almost too easily comprehended in terms of unhappy marriages known to the reader. It is no accident that the authors of the four works I have mentioned were all women. They were court ladies who seldom left the palace except for visits to temples and shrines. They almost never described in their works political events at court and they displayed extremely little interest in people outside the court. But these women studied their own hearts, and from their perceptions of themselves and their surroundings they created works of literature that defy time.

It is not easy to agree with Japanese writers of the twentieth century when they insist that they share more with their contemporaries in foreign countries than with their literary ancestors. Almost any modern novel, for all its modernity, is likely to contain passages that embody the immediate, intuitive response to nature that is so much a part of the older literature. A passage like the following, written in 1954 by Kita Morio, a novelist who is known as a comic writer, rather than as a "poet of nature," may suggest how contact with nature still has the power to invigorate and inspire the Japanese:

> Something should be said about the seasonal changes in this region. The air in winter is bitterly cold, actually hurting one's bare skin. The mountains soar up high, with a unique sense of weight in their rise and fall; sometimes a range of black shapes with a mere scattering of snow on them, sometimes white peaks blindingly reflecting the sun's rays. Blends of the most subtle shades occasionally appear, then bursts of pure light to dazzle the eyes.
>
> Spring comes, the snow melts on the banks of streams, and with the sound of it falling into the water below, one looks out toward

> the distant Alps to find their shapes floating now behind a finespun haze. Clouds of a thicker mist drift along the valleys, and in the hollows the fuchsia's delicate flowers are already in bloom. But in the mountains spring is inevitably late, and when the upper snows have finally melted every valley is filled with the roar of floodwater, turbid, thudding against the banks which collapse in places, while paths are destroyed as trees borne down by the current are cast up and left lying across them.[2]

Kita's novel *Yūrei* (Ghosts), the account of a boy's growth to manhood, is filled with such passages, not as an exercise in imitating the Japanese of the past who lived much closer to nature than anyone of the twentieth century, and certainly not as a mere pastiche, but as a depiction of what he actually experienced during the period he was growing up. He wrote even more vividly in the same book:

> Then, from deep inside my body an ominous, unknown force seemed to rise in me, and I threw myself facedown on the grass. And so, under a downpour of high summer light, in the stifling odor of the plants, to the erotic buzzing of the gadflies' wings, and savoring the endless warmth and comfort of the earth I had my very first emission.
>
> I suppose people will probably laugh if I say that the object of my desire was nature itself.[3]

Despite such expressions of a characteristically Japanese response to nature, we know that this particular writer was deeply influenced by Thomas Mann, and the novel *Ghosts* as a whole recalls a *Bildungsroman* by some German master. Without such influence, Kita probably could not have written what is likely to strike us as an unusually Japanese work of modern literature. In this sense, his novel is faithful at once to the past and to the literature of other countries.

The private world of the isolated, alienated Japanese of the twentieth century, another feature of modern literature, may also remind us of the diaries of the past, even though the concerns are likely to be specifically modern. Japanese literature has indeed become modern, a part of world literature. If some new movement in literary criticism or politics or philosophy affects writers in the West, it will probably affect the Japanese, too, and often very quickly. It is by no means impossible, for that matter, that some major new conception of literature affecting the whole world will originate in Japan. However, as long as writers continue to express themselves in the Japanese language, there is little danger that their literature will turn into a faceless component of some future Earth literature; language and inherited traditions will probably continue to distinguish modern Japanese writings.

The Japanese language is probably what gives the literature its most conspicuous identity, but the marked differences between the Japanese language—especially the written language with its combination of Chinese characters and Japanese phonetic symbols—and other major languages of the world is likely to continue to restrict direct knowledge of Japanese literature outside Japan to the handfuls of persons who can read the language easily. The rest of the world will have to depend on translations that, however consciously executed, tend to obscure differences. But, rather than bewail what must inevitably be lost in translation, we in the West should rather be grateful that Japanese literature has at last been accepted as a full-fledged member of the literature of the world.

Notes

1. Translation by Edward G. Seidensticker in *The Tale of Genji*, I, p. 3.
2. Kita, Morio, *Ghosts*, trans. Dennis Keene, p. 138.
3. *Ibid.*, p. 134.

Bibliography

Kita, Morio. *Ghosts*, trans. Dennis Keene. Tokyo and New York: Kodansha International, 1991.

Seidensticker, Edward G. (trans.). *The Tale of Genji*, 2 vols. New York: Alfred A. Knopf, 1976.

Early and Heian Literature

1. THE *KOJIKI*

The *Kojiki* (Record of Ancient Matters),[1] presented to the court in A.D. 712, is the oldest Japanese book. The preface mentions even older records, most of which were destroyed in a fire of 645, and other early documents are preserved in the *Nihon Shoki* (Chronicles of Japan),[2] compiled in 720. Both histories contain materials that probably antedate the introduction of writing, notably the many songs. The *Kojiki* is of great importance in the history of Japanese culture not only because of its antiquity but because it has served, especially since the eighteenth century, as the sacred book of the Shintō religion, and because it is our best source of information about the beliefs of the Japanese at the dawn of their civilization.[3] The work opens with the primeval matter of the universe congealing and dividing into heaven and earth; continues with an account of the creation of Japan (traditionally dated 660 B.C.) and the reigns of the first emperors; and finally, in the last of the three books, approaches the realm of history. It is considered today to be not only a basic religious text but an important literary work, a reputation it owes largely to the many poems and the engaging myths and fables scattered throughout the text.

The first question confronting anyone who studies the *Kojiki* is how the text was written down. The only system of writing known to Japanese of the early eighth century was the Chinese characters. These had been devised to represent Chinese words, most of them monosyllabic, and they were therefore unsuited to the polysyllabic Japanese language; but the Japanese had no choice. If, perhaps in conjunction with the arrival of Buddhism in the sixth century, the Japanese had learned the Sanskrit alphabet and used it for their own language, the writing of Japanese would have been vastly simpler; but by the time some Japanese monks acquired a knowledge of Sanskrit (late in the eighth century), the writing of Japanese had been irrevocably linked to the Chinese characters.

The preface to the *Kojiki*, written by Ō no Yasumaro (d. 723), briefly explained the difficulty of writing Japanese with Chinese characters. It was possible to treat them as phonograms, using them solely for their sounds and disregarding their meanings, so as to represent the sounds of the Japanese language—this, in fact, was how the Chinese themselves had rendered Sanskrit terms when translating the Buddhist classics—but the objection to this method of writing Japanese was that it was cumbersome, necessitating a Chinese character for each syllable of a long Japanese word. When the pronunciation was particularly important, as in the names of gods who might be offended if their names were improperly pronounced, Chinese characters were used as phonograms despite the nuisance. They were used also in the transcriptions of songs, presumably because these songs were not mere literary embellishments but the utterances of gods and emperors. The actual sounds of the words were often more important than the meanings of the poems, which retained their ritual significance even when their meanings had been lost.

A second method was to use the Chinese characters as ideograms, taking their meanings into consideration. The character *to*, meaning "rabbit," might be pronounced as *usagi*;[4] in this instance, a single character sufficed instead of the three phonograms needed to represent the syllables *u-sa-gi*. Regardless of the pronunciation, an ideogram communicates its meaning directly to the eye, rather as the number 125 is immediately intelligible, whether one pronounces it as "one hundred twenty-five," "cent vingt-cinq," or "hyakunijūgo."

Almost all modern editions of the *Kojiki* supply "pure Japanese" pronunciations for every character in the text, usually following the reconstruction made by the great scholar Motoori Norinaga (1730–1801), who devoted over thirty years of his life to this task. Motoori determined the Japanese readings by first establishing the Japanese words that were known to have existed in ancient Japan, relying mainly on the phonetic renderings in songs and similar texts, and then matching the characters with the known vocabulary. It was a brilliant though not always convincing achievement, but even the rare persons who have questioned particular readings have usually accepted the basic premise that the *Kojiki* was composed throughout in pure Japanese. This thesis is tenable when discussing places in the text where Japanese constructions can be detected, or where there is a use of honorifics in the Japanese style, but elsewhere, especially in the latter parts of the book, hackneyed Chinese phrases frequently appear, and attempts to read them as pure Japanese are bound to seem arbitrary.[5]

In 1957 a scholar of the Japanese language suggested that the prose parts of the *Kojiki*—that is, the parts where Chinese characters are almost always used for their meanings—were written down so as to convey a message directly to the eye, without respect to pronunciation.[6] Others have doubted that it will ever be possible to reconstruct definitively the pronunciation of the *Kojiki* because the system of punctuating Chinese texts so that they could be read as Japanese was not developed until some two hundred years after the compilation of the *Kojiki*.[7] Any reconstruction is likely to be no more than guesswork. Motoori's version continues to be preferred to more modern renderings because of its great dignity and beauty, appealing to the Japanese much as the King James version of the Bible does to English-speaking peoples.

Motoori's reconstruction has also been popular with those who would like to think of bards reciting and singing the old stories long before Japanese was written down or any Chinese influence was felt. The term *kataribe* (guild of narrators) does not occur in the *Kojiki*, but it appears in documents of 702 and 739. The kataribe were traditionally believed to have recited the myths and legends found in the *Kojiki*, but the nature of their role in the compilation of the work has been questioned by many.[8] It is clear that the kataribe recited songs, perhaps including some contained in the *Kojiki*, during the ritual observances accompanying such important occasions as the celebration of the Daijō-sai (Great Harvest Festival) after an emperor's accession to the throne; but there is no evidence that it was their task to preserve the old legends or to recite them to villagers.[9] The existence of bards among the Ainu, the indigenous people of Japan, may have helped to confirm a belief that the kataribe fulfilled their functions and were repositories of the old traditions, an impression strengthened by the bardic flavor of Motoori's reconstruction of the language of the ancient texts.

If the *Kojiki* was not based on the poetry and prose recited by bards (as was true of the epics of various other countries), what were its sources? The preface mentions *teiki* (imperial chronicles) and *honji* (fundamental dicta), written documents that probably recorded the ancient myths, legends, and songs.[10] The emperor, the preface informs us, was distressed to discover in 681 that many errors and unjustifiable accretions had seriously distorted the facts, marring the offical history, and he was determined to correct these errors while the truth was still remembered.

This was not merely a matter of historical accuracy: the emperor considered that these documents were "the framework of the state, the great foundation of the imperial influence."[11]

These written materials may have been based on the records compiled in 620 by the Crown Prince Shōtoku and the Great Imperial Chieftain Soga no Umako. With the fall from power of the Soga family, the last chieftain, Soga no Emishi, burned in 645 almost all the records compiled by his father and Prince Shōtoku. A few volumes are said to have been rescued from the flames, but nothing now survives of this history. Perhaps a corrupt version of the text still existed in 681, and the emperor, perusing it, was upset by the mistakes he noticed. At any rate, he commanded the court attendant (*toneri*) Hieda no Are, then twenty-eight years old, to memorize the teiki and *kuji* (ancient dicta).[12] Are, it was said, "could repeat orally whatever met his eye, and whatever struck his ears was indelibly impressed in his heart."[13]

The sex of Hieda no Are has been a matter of dispute since Hirata Atsutane opined in 1819 that Are was a woman, basing this conclusion on an early Heian period record which stated that the descendants of the goddess Ame-no-uzume lived at a place called Hieda, and that *sarume* (women dancers) were sent from this place to the court in 920. Are, he declared, was none other than a descendant of the goddess who had tempted Amaterasu, the sun goddess, from the cave in which she had hidden herself.[14] This theory, adopted by various authorities over the next hundred years, was given the powerful support of Yanagita Kunio (1875–1962), who not only repeated Hirata's arguments but suggested that the choice of materials included in the *Kojiki*—songs and love stories, rather than dryly factual deeds—reflected feminine tastes.[15] More recent scholars have declared that it is not merely of antiquarian interest whether or not Hieda no Are was a woman, but a matter that affects our understanding of the entire *Kojiki*.[16]

The uncertainty about the sex of Hieda no Are is compounded by the statement in the preface that the Emperor Temmu commanded Are to "recite and repeat"[17] the two source documents. The significance of these words has been much debated. Those who believe Hieda no Are was a man interpret "recite and repeat" as meaning that Are learned the texts in the traditional manner of recitation aloud and repetition in order to rectify, on the basis of prior knowledge of the old legends, any errors they contained.[18] If we accept this interpretation, it means that Are read through documents (two are specified in the preface) whose meaning had become obscure, supplying Japanese pronunciations for the Chinese characters.[19] It may be wondered why he should have been obliged to memorize materials that already existed in manuscripts, but (considering the loss of the manuscripts in the fire) it was providential that he did.

Those who believe that Hieda no Are was a woman not only cite the importance given in the *Kojiki* to Ame-no-uzume, the ancestress of the Hieda family, but deduce from the words "recite and repeat" that Are intoned the *Kojiki* in accordance with the traditions of her family—hereditary shamans who performed songs, dances, and other rites in order to communicate with the dead and succour the living.[20] They consider, moreover, that the style of the *Kojiki* and the construction of its most memorable episodes were dictated by shamanistic traditions; Are did not merely read the manuscripts but recited them in accordance with a prescribed intonation in order to preserve their magical properties.[21]

These theories are intriguing, but a more prosaic approach to the sex of Hieda no Are concluded that he was a man, on the basis of names in eighth-century registers, where Are appears always as a man's name (the similar name for women was Areme).[22] On the other hand, an even more recent theorist contended that the *Kojiki* was compiled by a woman for recitation in the palace of the princess who later reigned as the Empress Jitō (685–697).[23] The efforts that have been devoted to clarifying this point, and the importance attached to the conclusions, suggest the immensity of the task involved in explicating the *Kojiki*. A lifetime has not been considered an excessive amount of time to consecrate to elucidating details of this most basic text.

The importance of the *Kojiki* as the repository of Japanese myths and legends can hardly be overestimated. During such periods of nationalism as the years of the Greater East Asia War (1941–1945), the *Kojiki* was exalted as the embodiment of "Japanese spirit," and its simple, "masculine" grandeur was praised at the expense of *The Tale of Genji* and other works of the "feminine" tradition. But even those who were in no sense committed to the nationalistic ideals of the war years praised the *Kojiki* not only for its historical significance but also for its high artistic value.[24] A reader who is not Japanese may experience difficulties concurring with such praise. The stories related in the *Kojiki* contain attractive passages, and the poems, though primitive by the standards of later Japanese poetry, have a certain rough-hewn charm, but the work as a whole is marred by the absence of a shaping hand; much seems to have been included simply because it was believed to be true, without regard to artistic effect.

The difficulty a modern reader is likely to experience in trying to evaluate the artistic worth of the *Kojiki* stems largely from the lack of unity even in relatively brief narratives, the internal contradictions, and, above all, the prolixity. Many deities, we can assume, had local importance and were venerated by certain families as their ancestors, but the narration often suggests that the imagination of the ancient Japanese, though fertile, lacked sustained intensity.

The preface to the *Kojiki* by Ō no Yasumaro forms a marked contrast with the rest of the work: it is almost ostentatious in its fluent use of Chinese rhetoric.[25] He summarizes, in language that is indebted especially to Taoism, the events of the three books of the *Kojiki*. Next follows an account of the Emperor Temmu's decision to rectify the existing documents. We are told of Temmu (in pompous language, making due references to instances in Chinese history), "In the Way he excelled the Yellow Emperor; in Virtue he surpassed the king of Chou."[26] However, for unstated reasons, the compilation of the corrected history—that is, the *Kojiki*—was not carried out until the reign of the Empress Gemmei (707–715). Ō no Yasumaro served as the scribe while Hieda no Are, the infallible, dictated the history of Japan from the most ancient times up to the reign of the Empress Suiko (592–628), whose name means "conjecture of the past."

The first book of the *Kojiki* proper opens as three gods come into existence in Takama-no-hara, the High Plain of Heaven. The land below resembles floating oil and drifts like a jellyfish. The first signs of life in this amorphous world look "something like reed-shoots." The philosopher Watsuji Tetsurō (1889–1960) was struck with admiration by this vivid image for the beginning of life, and contrasted its vitality and wonder with the abstract language used for the Creation in the Book of Genesis or in the Chinese legends.[27]

Various other deities are presently created, including the god Izanagi[28] and his spouse Izanami, who are commanded by the original three deities to "create and solidify" the fluid land. Standing on the Bridge of Heaven, Izanagi lowers a jeweled spear[29] into the fluid, stirring it until it curdles to form an island. This island, which cannot be identified with any existing island, is necessary to what follows: the business of procreating the islands of Japan has to be carried out on solid land. Izanagi and Izanami descend to this island and, after inspecting each other's body, decide it would be fitting for Izanagi to join what was excess in his body to what was lacking in Izanami's. By way of preliminaries, they ceremonially circumambulate a pillar on the island, whereupon Izanami greets her mate. Izanagi is disturbed that a woman should have spoken ahead of a man, but they proceed with their task anyway. Their first offspring is a "leech-child," which is so grotesquely formed that they make a little boat and "float it away." Their next attempt yields an island, but it is no more impressive than the leech-child and is promptly disowned.

The couple consult the heavenly deities, who decide that the fault (as Izanagi correctly guessed) lay with Izanami's having spoken first. The pair descend once more to the island and walk around the pillar, but this time the man speaks first and the offspring are all well made. The first group of progeny are islands, beginning with the Great Eight Islands—Awaji, Shikoku, Oki, Kyūshū, Iki, Tsushima, Sado, and Honshū—and are followed by six of lesser importance. The insistence on the number eight, in the total of islands begotten or of gods who sprang into being, suggests that it was a magic number. Perhaps "eight" was originally a vaguely large number that was later justified by specifying the names of eight islands, eight gods, or eight mountains; in any case, it constitutes a conspicuous exception to the preference for odd numbers that characterizes much of Japanese culture.[30]

Once they had completed the business of procreating the land, Izanagi and Izanami moved on to create the deities of land and sea, of the winds, mountains, and other aspects of nature. However, Izanami's genitals were burned when she gave birth to the fire deity, and she fell mortally ill. From her vomit, feces, and urine various deities were born before she died of the aftereffects of the burns. Although Izanami had already given birth to thirty-five deities, Izanagi was enraged that the fire deity has caused her death, and cut off the head of this child. The blood adhering to the top of his sword produced three more deities, and before the procreative power of the blood was lost, five additional deities came into existence. Another eight deities were born from various parts of the slain fire god.

After the death of Izanami, her husband journeyed to Yomi, the land of the dead, in search of his beloved. She came as far as the entrance to the underworld to meet him. Izanagi urged her to return so that they might finish the business of procreating islands, but Izanami regretfully informed him that she could not return because she had eaten the food of Yomi. She went off to beg the gods to permit her to return to earth, but failed to reappear. The impatient Izanagi searched for her, using as his torch in the darkness a tooth from the comb he wore in his hair. To his horror he discovered the corpse of Izanami "squirming and roaring" with maggots, and there were eight thunder gods in various parts of her body. Izanagi fled in alarm. Izanami, crying out that she had been shamed, dispatched the "hags of Yomi" to pursue him. Izanagi, as he ran, threw down first the vine binding his hair, which turned at once into grapes that distracted the hags. Next, he threw down his comb, which turned into bamboo shoots, and while the hags were pulling them up and devouring them, he made his escape. Izanami sent in pursuit the eight thunder gods who had just sprung from her body, but Izanagi fended them off with his sword, and later threw three peaches at them, effectively repelling them. Finally, Izanami herself came in pursuit, but Izanagi with a huge boulder sealed the pass between the world of the dead and the world of the living. Izanami vowed that she would kill one thousand people each day to take vengeance for the humiliation, but Izanagi replied that he would see to it that fifteen hundred people were born each day.

Leaving the cave, Izanagi went to a river where he cleansed himself of the pollution of Yomi. Each part of his body or clothes touched by the water instantly turned into a deity, the most important being the last three: to Amaterasu, born of his left eye, he assigned rule of the High Plain of Heaven; to Tsukiyomi, born of his right eye, he gave the realm of night; and to Susano-o, born from his nose, he delegated the ocean.

The visit of Izanagi to the world of the dead recalls the journey of Orpheus to the underworld where he, like Izanagi, is forbidden to look at his wife's face; the misfortune of Izanami in having eaten the food of Yomi is similar to Persephone's; and Izanagi's stratagem for eluding his pursuers brings to mind Atalanta's. Japanese scholars have examined these and other *Kojiki* myths and detected many resemblances with the mythologies of other countries.[31] Comparisons, however, tend to be disadvantageous to the *Kojiki*. If Izanagi had experienced the torments of Orpheus when, importuned by Eurydice to look on her face, he finally looked, knowing he would lose her, he might seem more worthy of compassion; but the object of the narrator of the *Kojiki* was not to win sympathy but to tell the unvarnished truth. There is a kind of logic in a vine turning into grapes or a bamboo comb into bamboo shoots, but Izanagi's powers are never defined, and it is unclear why he cannot disperse his pursuers with a simple gesture. Again, the three peaches make unconvincing weapons, even if one knows that the Chinese attributed magical properties to this fruit; and when Izanagi, addressing the peaches as if they were sentient beings, bestows on them the name of a god and urges them to save mortal men, it is not only strange but confusing. As yet there has been no mention of mortal men, and a modern reader may feel that the inconsistency of viewpoint weakens the literary effect.

Some passages of the *Kojiki*, such as the creation of the world by copulating deities, are probably unique in world mythology. Many Japanese commentators have remarked on the "innocence" of this sexual encounter, typical of many in the *Kojiki*, but as a result of the curious ability of the divine couple to produce not only other gods but islands, the ruler of Japan is considered the blood relative of the land he governs, an unanswerable claim to sovereignty. (The political implications of the myths become even more apparent in the *Nihon Shoki*.) It is surprising that Izanagi and Izanami never developed into popular objects of worship, as did their numerous progeny, and that (apart from the islands) the deities produced through copulation were of much less importance than those created when Izanagi washed away the pollution of Yomi. It is also puzzling that deities should have been born from Izanami's feces and urine, though one writer attributed this to the importance of excreta as fertilizers in ancient agriculture.[32]

The first pages of the *Kojiki* are likely to produce in the Western reader a bewilderment that is not simply the result of unfamiliarity with the materials. Why should so many deities have been produced only to disappear instantly? Or why, considering the great attention paid to the sun deity and the sea deity, should the third of the triplets, the moon deity, not be heard of again? There is also a mystifying lack of interest in the *Kojiki* in plants or trees, and only anecdotal mentions of animals and fish, despite the importance of agriculture to the ancient Japanese. It is obvious from the descriptions of the barbarians encountered by the progeny of Izanagi and Izanami when they descended from the High Plain of Heaven to the Japanese islands that the Yamato people were not the only inhabitants. The existence of Koreans was also known to the Japanese from remote antiquity, but no explanation is offered for them either. The contradictions in the narrative have induced some to discard sections of the *Kojiki* as "later accretions."[33] However, the lack of unity may have been due less to tampering with the text than to the absence of a central divinity or hero. This is perhaps the most disappointing aspect of the *Kojiki* to those who search for resemblances to epic poetry composed in other parts of the world. Heroic traits are found in some of the gods and godlike mortals, but no one merits the name of hero in the sense that Achilles or Beowulf is a hero, and the stories of these putative heroes are marred by disquieting inconsistencies of characterization; heroic and extremely contemptible qualities are not infrequently found in the same person.

The first "hero" is the god Susano-o who, when charged by Izanagi to rule the seas, bursts into tears that "caused the verdant mountains to wither and the seas to dry up."[34] The puzzled Izanagi asks why Susano-o weeps and howls instead of ruling the seas as directed, to which Susano-o replies that he wishes to go to the land of his mother underground. It will be recalled that Susano-o was born when Izanagi washed his nose; it is therefore not clear who his mother was. Perhaps, as one version of the story in the *Nihon Shoki* has it,[35] Susano-o was the child of Izanagi and Izanami; in that case, he was weeping because he wished to visit his mother in Yomi, a perilous undertaking as we know from the account of Izanagi's visit. The request enrages Izanagi, who banishes Susano-o. When the latter takes leave of his sister, Amaterasu, he insists that his intentions were not evil, and to prove this, he suggests that they should swear oaths and beget children; if the children are good, it will demonstrate that his motives were unblemished.

The test is bizarre. Amaterasu takes Susano-o's sword, breaks it into three pieces, chews the pieces, and spits them out in a misty spray, producing three female deities. Susano-o takes the beads wrapped around Amaterasu's hair, rinses them, chews them, and spits them out, producing five deities. The question at once arises as to whether the deities Susano-o spat out should be considered his progeny or those of Amaterasu, whose beads he used in this experiment. In any case, he claims victory, and is so intoxicated by success that he breaks down the ridges separating Amaterasu's rice paddies, defecates and strews the feces around a sacred hall, and (to crown his indignities) opens a hole in the roof of Amaterasu's weaving hall and drops through it a piebald horse that he has flayed backward.[36]

None of these actions is heroic except in scale. Indeed, the *Nihon Shoki* characterizes Susano-o as a cruel and fierce-tempered god who delights in destruction.[37] The standards of behavior are not the same for gods as for human beings, but Susano-o's wanton acts are in no sense godlike. Amaterasu is so appalled by her brother that she hides herself in a cave, plunging the world into darkness. She is tempted out of the cave when she hears the mighty laughter of the other gods as they watch the lascivious dance of Ame-no-uzume. Susano-o is obliged by the gods to pay a fine, cut off his beard and nails, and to be exorcised before he is finally expelled from the High Plain of Heaven.

Once in the realm of mortals, however, Susano-o becomes a hero in a more normal sense of the word, slaying the dragon who afflicted the people of Izumo and marrying various ladies of the region. His character has changed so completely that it is hard to believe that he is the same Susano-o whom we have previously encountered. The association with Izumo suggests that he may originally have been an Izumo god, adopted into the Shintō pantheon when the Yamato court extended its authority to the Izumo region, but never forgiven his alien origins.

A poem attributed to Susano-o, on the occasion of his building a palace for his bride, is traditionally considered to be the first Japanese poem ever composed:

yakumo tatsu	Eightfold rising clouds
Izumo yaegaki	Build an eightfold fence,
tsumagomi ni	An eightfold Izumo fence
yaegaki tsukuru	Wherein to keep my bride—
sono yaegaki wo	Oh, splendid eightfold fence!

The poem has been variously interpreted as a marriage song, a work song chanted by people building a new house, or as a ritual song that asks the protection of the Izumo gods for a newly wed couple.[38] The poem is noteworthy in that it observes exactly the metrics of what would become the classic verse form, the waka, written in five lines of 5, 7, 5, 7, and 7 syllables. Many poems in the *Kojiki* are irregular both in their length and in the number of syllables in a single line, and it is difficult to imagine that the very first poem would be absolutely regular. Perhaps it was refashioned from an earlier, irregular form when it was set to music,[39] or when Hieda no Are declaimed it to Ō no Yasumaro. The repetition of phrases, typical of primitive poetry but uncommon in later waka, lends this poem the rhythm of an incantation, as does the insistence on the number eight. The first line, literally "eight clouds rise," is a *makurakotoba* or "pillow word," a fixed epithet usually placed before the names of provinces, mountains, and various other nouns, not only in the *Kojiki* but in much later poetry. Perhaps a makurakotoba was originally intended to invoke the magic of a place by mentioning its special attribute. Even when the significance of the makurakotoba was forgotten, it continued to be used, no doubt as a mark of respect. *Yakumo tatsu* (eight clouds rise) was the makurakotoba for Izumo, a region on the Japan Sea coast whose name was derived by folk etymologists variously as "producing clouds," "producing seaweed," and "abundant seaweed."[40]

The most interesting of the *Kojiki* tales are in the mode of folktales or fables. Immediately after the story of the adventures of Susano-o, for example, we have the fable of the white rabbit of Inaba who, wishing to cross over a body of water, tricks a pack of crocodiles into letting him scamper over their backs. The last crocodile in the line, realizing that he and his fellows have been tricked, skins the rabbit and leaves him lying in the sun. Eighty deities, all brothers of Ōkuninushi, a god associated with Izumo, appear and, feigning sympathy for the rabbit, urge him to bathe in saltwater and lie in the wind. The rabbit takes the advice, only to have his skin blister. He is in agony until Ōkuninushi offers a soothing remedy. The grateful rabbit prophesies that Ōkuninushi will wed the Princess Yagami, despite the hostility of his eighty brothers. The story lacks the kind of conclusion that might have imparted universal interest to this fable, but it provides a welcome break in the narration of wars and copulation.[41]

The story of Ōkuninushi is continued in successive episodes. His eighty evil brothers torment him and even twice manage to kill him, but he is revived both times by his mother. He goes to Izumo where, he is assured, the great deity Susano-o will protect him. Susano-o does indeed invite him to stay in his palace, but the bedroom where Ōkuninushi is put up for the night is full of snakes. Ōkuninushi emerges unscathed by this trial thanks to Susano-o's daughter, who has provided him with a snake-repellent scarf. The next night Susano-o offers a bed in a chamber full of centipedes and bees, but the love-smitten daughter again gives Ōkuninushi a scarf, this one an insect repellent. Susano-o, abandoning his chamber of horrors, subjects Ōkuninushi to a new trial: he shoots an arrow into a plain and orders Ōkuninushi to retrieve it. When the latter reaches the middle of the plain, Susano-o encircles him with fire. There seems to be no escape, but a mouse appears before Ōkuninushi and delivers the cryptic message: "The inside is hollow-hollow; the outside is narrow-narrow."[42] Ōkuninushi, solving this riddle at once, responds by stamping his feet until he opens a hole in the ground into which he disappears while the flames pass overhead. Later, the mouse brings him Susano-o's arrow as a souvenir.

Susano-o supposes that Ōkuninushi has been burned alive, and is much surprised when he reappears with the arrow. Not vouchsafing a word of thanks, Susano-o orders Ōkuninushi to pick the lice and centipedes from his head. Ōkuninushi, in collusion with Susano-o's daughter, whom he has by now taken as his wife, cracks acorns in a convincing imitation of a man biting open and spitting out centipedes. Touched by his son-in-law's obedience, Susano-o for the first time entertains affectionate thoughts about him. He falls asleep, whereupon Ōkuninushi ties strands of Susano-o's hair to the rafters and blocks the entrance to the chamber. He steals Susano-o's sword, bow, and arrows, as well as a musical instrument, and escapes with his bride. Unfortunately, he bumps the instrument against a tree and the sound wakens Susano-o. But it is too late to apprehend the fleeing couple, so Susano-o, gazing into the distance, bestows his blessing on them, and predicts that they have a great future awaiting them. He concludes with a derogatory remark that suggests his blessing may have been made under duress. Ōkuninushi is victorious over his eighty malevolent brothers, and he and his wife set about the serious business of creating the land of Izumo.[43]

Ōkuninushi's contribution to literary history consists of some songs he exchanged with a princess from a neighboring land and, later, with his jealous wife. These songs, especially the reply made by Princess Nunakawa, have an erotic quality that is typical of the *Kojiki* at its most beguiling:

aoyama ni	Come in the dark,
hi ga kakuraba	When the sun has disappeared
nubatama no	And the night emerges
yo wa ide nan	Behind the green hills.
asahi no	Come smiling, like the morning sun
emisakaekite	In all its glory,
takuzono no	And take in your embrace
shiroki tadamuki	My arms white as
awayuki no	Ropes of Taku fiber,
wakayaru mune wo	My breasts, young and soft
sodataki	As the first fall of snow;
tatakimanagari	Clasp me in your arms.
matamade	Then you will sleep,
tamade sashimaki	Your legs stretched out,
momonaga ni	Your head pillowed on
i wa nasan wo	My jewellike hands;
aya ni	So do not press your love
na koikikoshi	Too importunately,
yachihoko no	Great divinity
kami no mikoto	Of eight thousand spears.[44]

Ōkuninushi receives help from the deities of Yamato in building his country, but when Amaterasu, who has decided that her son shall rule the Central Land of the Reed Plains, sends two deities to Izumo to ask Ōkuninushi's intentions, he is at first evasive. Only when his sons have reluctantly accepted Amaterasu's command does he yield the land to her, on condition that he be worshiped in Izumo.[45]

Following the collapse of Izumo resistance, Amaterasu commands not her son but her grandson, Ninigi for short, to descend from the Bridge of Heaven and rule the land. She presents him with the three imperial regalia—the *magatama* beads, the mirror, and the sword—and he makes his way through the clouds to the peak of Takachiho, where he builds his palace.

The land is already inhabited, under circumstances that remain obscure, and Ninigi soon finds a lovely maiden whom he wishes to marry. The girl, however, has an elder sister, and their father has his heart set on Ninigi marrying both daughters. Ninigi is reluctant to marry the elder daughter, who is exceedingly plain, and the irate father pronounces a terrible curse on him, vowing that Ninigi and his descendants will henceforth be mortal. The *Kojiki* comments, "For this reason, until this day, the emperors have not been long-lived."[46]

The curse of mortality foreshadows the end of the Age of the Gods, and with Book II we enter the world of men (though their activities remain superhuman). We are told in Book II how the Emperor Jimmu, the great-grandson of Ninigi, extended his sovereignty over the land of Japan from Kyūshū to Yamato. His progress was leisurely, involving stops of seven or eight years at various places, and Jimmu's conquests were abetted by strange creatures he met on the way. At one point he was accosted by a person "riding on a tortoise's back, fishing and flapping his wings as he came."[47] This creature, after identifying himself as an earth deity, offered to accompany Jimmu on his journey. Jimmu was also helped by a giant crow and by men with tails, but he was opposed by others, including eighty mighty Tsuchigumo (pit dwellers), also with tails. Victory over the eighty mighty men was achieved not in open combat but during the course of a banquet to which the men were invited. At a signal, the singing of an ode to the men of Kume, the food servers struck down the guests.

Jimmu lived to the ripe old age of 137. The life-spans of his descendants were more in keeping with their status as mortals, but extremely little is related about them until we reach the tenth emperor, Sujin. He is credited with having initiated various political and social changes, and some *Kojiki* specialists claim that Japanese history begins with Sujin; the events of the Age of the Gods may have been added later in order to enhance the antiquity of the Japanese past.[48] With Sujin, the compilers of the *Kojiki* began to give the dates of the deaths of the successive emperors. These dates are stated in terms of the Chinese cycle of sixty years, but it is difficult in the early periods to be sure just which cycle was intended. Sujin probably died in either A.D. 258 or 318.

The second hero of the *Kojiki* appears in Book II. He is Yamatotakeru, the legendary son of the equally legendary Emperor Keikō.[49]

Mishima Yukio contrasted the prudence of the emperor, typical of mortal men, with the godlike indifference to human conventions of Yamato-takeru.[50] Perhaps so, but the Emperor Keikō was hardly a run-of-the-mill sovereign: he had eighty children and, late in life, married his own great-great-granddaughter.[51]

Yamato-takeru was asked one day by the emperor why his elder brother had failed to appear for morning and evening meals. The emperor commanded the prince to admonish his brother, but still the laggard brother failed to come to meals. The emperor sternly asked if Yamato-takeru had in fact admonished his brother. Yamato-takeru replied that indeed he had, but his admonition took a curious form: early one morning when the brother was in the privy, Yamato-takeru caught him, crushed him, then dismembered his body, wrapping the pieces in straw matting and throwing them away.[52]

The emperor, taken aback by such ferocity, thought it expedient to send the bloodthirsty prince far from the court to Kyūshū, with the mission of subduing the Kumaso, an alien people. Yamato-takeru arrived shortly before a feast was held to celebrate the completion of a new pit dwelling. Dressing himself like a woman, he went into the dwelling, where he attracted admiring comments on his appearance. When the feast was at its height, he took a sword from his bosom and stabbed the elder chieftain. The younger chieftain demanded to know who he was, whereupon Yamato-takeru revealed his identity. The Kumaso warrior, impressed, bestowed on him the name Yamato-takeru (Brave Man of Yamato). The newly named warrior at once slew his godfather and sliced him up like a melon. On his return to the capital Yamato-takeru profited by the opportunity to subdue various mountain and river dignitaries.[53]

The next episode of Yamato-takeru's career is marked by the deceit he employed in killing the Izumo chieftain Izumo-takeru. After pledging his friendship, he made an imitation sword of wood, then invited his new friend to bathe in the river. After their bath, Yamato-takeru, putting on the wooden sword, proposed that they exchange swords as a mark of trust and friendship. The gullible Izumo-takeru put on the wooden sword, whereupon Yamato-takeru slashed him down with the real sword. Yamato-takeru celebrated his victory with this song:

yatsume sasu	The sword worn at the side
Izumo-takeru ga	Of Izumo-takeru
hakeru tachi	From the land of eightfold seaweed

tsuzura sawa maki Is wrapped with splendid vines,
sa-mi nashi ni aware But has no blade, ha ha![54]

The emperor was not pleased to have Yamato-takeru back at court, and wasted no time in ordering him to leave, this time to subdue and pacify the unruly deities and people of the East. This was too much even for the audacious Yamato-takeru, and when he stopped at the Ise Shrine to visit his aunt, the High Priestess Yamato-hime, he asked, "Is it because the emperor wishes me to die soon? . . . Why did he dispatch me once more after only a short while, without giving me troops to subdue the evil people of the twelve regions to the East?"[55] This does not sound like the ruthless conqueror of the Kumaso, but is definitely more appealing. His aunt gave him the sword Kusanagi (Grass-cutter) and a bag to be opened in case of emergency.

When Yamato-takeru arrived in the East he was deceived by an official of the land, who trapped him in the middle of an indefensible plain and set fire to the grass. This was precisely the kind of emergency Yamato-hime had in mind. Her nephew opened the bag, which proved to contain flints, and started a counterfire. Eventually, Yamato-takeru killed the deceitful official and all his clan. He continued his victorious march to the East, subduing demons wherever he went. In the land of Shinano he met Miyazu-hime, the princess he had promised his aunt he would marry. They exchanged songs, including:

hisakata no	A white swan crosses,
Ama no Kaguyama	Like a sharp-honed sickle
tokama ni	Across the far-spreading sky
sawataru kubi	By heavenly Kagu Mountain;
hiwaboso	I would pillow my head
tawayagaina wo	On your slender white arm,
makan to wa	Delicate as a swan's neck,
are wa suredo	I would sleep with you—
sanen to wa	But on the hems of the veil
are wa omoedo	That you are wearing,
na ga keseru	The moon has risen.[56]
osuhi no suso ni	
tsuki tachinikeri.	

The veil mentioned in the poem was a garment that concealed not only the face but the whole head and came down to the knees; and the mysterious reference in the last line refers, commentaries inform us, to the fact that Miyazu-hime's menstrual blood adheres to the long veil. The triple image of the curving sickle, the swan's neck, and the lady's slender arm brings us to the borders of poetry, but the last line is disconcerting.

Following this pleasant interlude, Yamato-takeru had other adventures, notably an encounter with a white boar that was as big as a cow. The boar was in fact the transformed deity of a mountain, and was powerful enough to arouse a storm that dazed Yamato-takeru. From this point on he was fatigued and lonely, a mere shadow of his former self. Worn out by his exertions, he fell ill and, after composing several poems that are more attractive than most in the *Kojiki*, he died. His family came for the funeral, only to discover that he had been transformed into a great white bird. His wives and children ran after the bird, over land and sea, but it eluded them and finally soared off into the heavens.

Ivan Morris placed the story of Yamato-takeru at the head of his book *The Nobility of Failure* and treated him as the prototype of the typical Japanese hero, a man who, though triumphant when young, is deserted and defeated at the end of his life.[57] Unlike Susano-o, who is last seen surrounded by his large and happy family, Yamato-takeru's career ends in lonely death, far from home. In his last hours, he is a poet, rather than a martial hero, and perhaps his best-known poem expresses nostalgia for Yamato, the place where he was born.

Yamato wa	Yamato,
kuni no mahoroba	Fairest of provinces,
tatanazuku	Encircled by mountains
aogaki	Like green fences,
yama komoreru	Layer on layer—
Yamato shi uruwashi	How lovely is Yamato![58]

Morris wrote persuasively, and the poems in the *Kojiki* attributed to Yamato-takeru lend him a romantic aura, but his victories were less those of a hero than of a trickster, and his final transformation is not a defeat but a victory over human limitations. His story, even if we combine the different versions in the *Kojiki* and the *Nihon Shoki*, is not sufficiently detailed for us to form an impression of him as a human being, but the fact that his name (as distinct from those of most figures in the *Kojiki*) lingers in the memory suggests why he has been elevated to the ranks of the heroes. This hero is not like any in the West nor in Japan in later times. He behaves outrageously, indulging in acts of inexplicable brutality, and is redeemed only by his moments of weakness, as when he turns to his aunt for comfort. The poetry composed by Yamato-takeru does not rank high among the poems of the Japanese language, but it may have helped to form the ideal of the soldier-poet, a familiar figure in later Japanese literary history.[59]

The poetry of Yamato-takeru is not closely linked to what we are otherwise told about the man. Indeed, the same poems are attributed in the *Nihon Shoki* to other persons, and their content is often so unspecific that they could be placed in almost any episode of the *Kojiki* and not clash with the text. All the same, the poems were treated as historical facts, along with the deeds of prowess. The inclusion of poetry in historical works was rare in China, though it is found intermingled with prose in works of Buddhist inspiration. Probably these texts influenced the compilers of the *Kojiki*.[60] The prominence given in the *Kojiki* to poetry would be followed in later historical works for good reason: the poem a man composed on a particular occasion, heard or read by people around him, was more likely to be accurate than accounts of deeds known only by report.

The reign of the fourteenth emperor, Chūai, brings us much closer to history, though the supernatural continues to play an important role. A divine oracle, speaking through the mouth of Chūai's empress, informed him of a land to the west that abounded in treasures and was destined to pass into his hands. The emperor did not trust the oracle because the only thing he could see when he looked westward was the ocean. His disbelief so annoyed the deity that he struck Chūai dead. Great rites of exorcism were held, during which another oracle was heard, declaring that it was Amaterasu's will that the land to the west be subjugated. The Empress Jingū, assuming the duties of commander-in-chief of the expeditionary force in the place of her late husband, set off at the head of a fleet of ships, taking the precaution to delay the birth of the child in her womb by attaching stones to her girdle. The conquest of Korea was swift, and the empress presently returned to Japan, where she gave birth to her child.

The invasion of Korea, though described in terms of a great conquest, may have been little more than a raid, on the order of one in A.D. 364 mentioned in Korean records. From this time on it is occasionally possible to verify facts in the *Kojiki* by consulting Korean or Chinese records, and the tone of the *Kojiki* changes imperceptibly from legendary to historical, though prodigies are not uncommon.

The reign of the fifteenth emperor, Ōjin, is dated by the *Nihon Shoki* as 270–310. Probably these years are two cycles (120 years) early. Some historians have therefore identified Ōjin as the "Japanese king" who sent emissaries to China in 421 and 425.[61] Ōjin's reign was marked by the arrival of immigrants from Shiragi (Silla), one of the three Korean kingdoms. The emperor also received gifts from the king of Kudara (Paekche), another Korean kingdom. Ōjin asked this king for a learned man, and the king sent Wani-kishi, along with ten volumes of the *Analects* of Confucius and the one volume of the *Thousand Character Classic*,[62] marking the beginning of literacy in Japan. Other immigrants from Korea included a blacksmith, a weaver, and a sake brewer. This account probably should not be accepted literally, but it indicates that Ōjin's reign was distinguished by the cultural influences that reached Japan from the Asian continent, especially Korea.[63]

Book III of the *Kojiki* is more solidly anchored in the world of men. The first emperor described, Nintoku, is depicted as a Confucian ruler who, when he sees that no smoke is rising from the chimneys of his people, remits taxes and allows his palace to fall into disrepair. Only when smoke once again rises from hearths across the land does he reinstate taxes and conscription. Nintoku was also involved in various romantic intrigues, one of which aroused the jealousy of his consort. She ran away, ostensibly in order to have a look at a strange insect that starts life as a worm, then becomes a cocoon and finally a flying insect—presumably an oblique reference to the importation of silkworms.

The most interesting section of Book III is the romance between Crown Prince Karu and his sister, also named Karu. Marriages between half-brothers and sisters were tolerated, but they were full brother and sister, and their love was forbidden. Prince Karu was attacked by a brother, who enlisted the support of the populace, and Karu was exiled to Iyo on the island of Shikoku. The princess followed him there, and after he composed two love songs they committed suicide together, the earliest example of the double suicide that is featured so prominently in the Japanese literature of the seventeenth and eighteenth centuries.[64]

The younger brother of Prince Karu ascended the throne as the Emperor Ankō (454–456). One day, in the privacy of his bedroom, he confessed to his empress that he had killed her former husband, the father of her son. The son, who was playing nearby, overheard these words and, waiting until the emperor was asleep, crept into the bedchamber and slit his throat. It is hard to imagine a child capable of killing a man that way, but perhaps this murder was intended as background for the reign of the next emperor, a brother of Ankō named Yūryaku (457–479), who stands out, even in the *Kojiki*, for his violence and cruelty.

Yūryaku had a tender side, however.[65] Once, when he saw a girl washing clothes by a river, he was so struck by her beauty that he begged her not to marry until he sent for her. The girl waited eighty years. Then, at last yielding to despair, she went to visit the emperor. Touched by her fidelity, he considered marrying her, but presented her with two songs instead, including:

Hiketa no	In Hiketa
wakakurusubara	Young chestnut trees grow;
wakaku he ni	If only we had slept together
inete mashi mono	When you were still young—
oinikeru kamo	But now you have become so old![66]

Yūryaku lived to be 124, according to the *Kojiki*. We are not told about political or cultural developments during his reign, but much about his brutal efficiency in disposing of heirs presumptive to the throne. His son Seinei (reigned 480–484), one of the few spared by Yūryaku, died without issue, and at first it seemed as though there was no one left to succeed him. Two princes were at length discovered, and they reigned one after the other, to be succeeded by the Emperor Buretsu (498–507), whose wicked deeds are lovingly enumerated in the *Nihon Shoki*. Buretsu, no doubt as punishment for his crimes, died without heirs. A descendant in the fifth generation of the Emperor Ōjin was called to the throne, the most remote instance of succession. The remaining sovereigns treated in the *Kojiki* are passed over with bare accounts of their families, down to the thirty-third sovereign, the Empress Suiko.

The third book of the *Kojiki* is of conspicuously less literary interest than the previous two. It contains poetry that is sometimes attractive, but more often puzzling, as the following waka may suggest:

miyahito no	Because the little bell
ayui no kosuzu	On the nobleman's garter
ochiniki to	Has fallen off,
miyahito toyomu	The nobles raise a clamor;
satobito mo yume	Country folk, don't do the same![67]

Many interpretations have been offered for this poem. One commentator suggested that it meant that a noble had seduced a woman of the commoner class, arousing the jealousy of other nobles; commoners were therefore urged to be careful lest similar relations be forced on them.

Another commentator, taking the poem more literally, opined that the poem implied the nobles were silly to have made a fuss over anything so trivial; commoners were urged not to follow the nobles' example.[68] Other explanations, equally disparate, have been offered, but one can only conclude sadly that whatever the poem may have meant to people of the distant past, it is now, like many *Kojiki* poems, hopelessly obscure.

The prose sections of Book III are also less enjoyable than the myths and fables of the two previous books. Book III is largely given over to accounts of how members of the imperial family were murdered by close relations, often for incomprehensible reasons. The murders become monotonous, and the book ends with a tedious series of names of the wives and children of successive emperors.

The *Kojiki* as a whole is unlikely to satisfy readers who search its pages for the emotional sensitivity that typifies later Japanese literature. Enthusiasts of the *Kojiki* do not agree with this judgment. Kurano Kenji, who devoted much of his life to elucidating the *Kojiki* text, declared, "Today it is normal for the *Kojiki* to be treated as a single, coherent literary work that enjoys an equal footing with the *Man'yōshū*, *The Tale of Genji*, and similar works."[69] Kurano summarily dismissed the views of those who questioned the literary worth of a work written for non-literary purposes and which contains sections totally devoid of literary interest. He insisted on the artistic integrity of the *Kojiki*, regardless of the purposes of the compilers, and pointed out that other literary classics, such as *The Tale of the Heike*, were also marred by dull catalogues of opposing forces in battle and similar factual materials. But, as Kurano admitted, it was not until 1925 that the *Kojiki* was first treated as a work of literature, rather than as a history;[70] he reached the conclusion that it could be considered either as historical literature or else as history composed with literary intent.[71]

Regardless of whether or not one agrees with Kurano, it can hardly be denied that in the years since 1925 the *Kojiki* has become established as a literary classic. It is no longer treated (as the *Nihon Shoki* continues to be) as a work of mainly historical and religious significance. The adulation offered the *Kojiki* in the 1930s and early 1940s, when militarism and emperor worship colored scholarship relating to Japanese classical literature, did not produce any reaction against the *Kojiki* after the war ended. Far from it: scholars of every variety of political belief began to reexamine the *Kojiki*, now free of constraints. The historians attempted to penetrate the obscure language of the text and to piece together from fragmentary information a coherent picture of ancient Japan. Linguists ventured to reconstruct the original pronunciations of the text.[72] The relations between Japanese and Korean historical materials were studied without fear of reaching "wrong" conclusions. Folklorists traced survivals in contemporary Japan of rituals described in the *Kojiki*, and related the poems to similar songs still known in remote regions of the country. Comparative studies of Japanese and non-Japanese myths, begun well before the war years, were carried out by experts in Ainu, Okinawan, Korean, Burmese, Javanese, and other cultures.[73] Finally—but for our purposes most importantly—scholars of literature attempted to fit the *Kojiki* into the history of Japanese literature, not simply as the oldest surviving Japanese book, but as a work that contains seeds of future literary developments.[74]

The *Kojiki* stands close to the sources of Japanese literary expression. For centuries it, together with the *Nihon Shoki*, provided Japanese with all they knew about their ancient past, and there are innumerable references in later literature to its myths and legends.[75] Although the poems are for the most part primitive in conception and expression, they pointed the way to the development of the waka; and the origins of renga, the characteristic poetic form of the medieval period, are traditionally traced back to the completion of a single poem by two persons, Yamato-takeru and an old man, as recorded in the *Kojiki*.[76] More important still, we can see in the *Kojiki* the essential role that poetry played not only in commemorating heroic events but at every moment that called for heightened expression. The inclusion of poetry in prose narratives would be a feature of the literature of the next millennium.

A small band of convinced scholars insists that the *Kojiki* as a whole, or the preface at any rate, is a forgery of Heian times, but their arguments, however persuasively presented, seem to have affected the mainstream of *Kojiki* scholarship very little.[77] Still others have used the *Kojiki* as source material in their quest of the homeland of the Japanese in Southeast Asia, the Himalayas, Central Asia, or elsewhere. The mystery of Japan, a subject of passionate interest to the Japanese, begins with the *Kojiki*.

Notes

This chapter, in a somewhat different form, appeared originally in *Transactions of the Asiatic Society of Japan*, Third Series, vol. 18, 1983.

1. Contrary to my usage elsewhere in these volumes, I shall refer to this work by its Japanese title, rather than by a translation, because the existing translations are called *Kojiki*.
2. The translation by W. G. Aston is called *Nihongi*. Although some scholars believe that this is the correct title, the work is almost universally known as *Nihon Shoki*.
3. In this chapter emphasis will be placed on the literary significance of the *Kojiki*. This does not do justice to a work that has more often been studied for nonliterary reasons, and some details of the narrative are likely to seem ludicrous when deprived of their religious aura; but the interest of the *Kojiki* lies in its remarkable combination of disparate elements.
4. I have given throughout the modern pronunciations, rather than the ancient pronunciations as reconstructed by linguists. The translation of the *Kojiki* by Donald L. Philippi uses the reconstructed pronunciations.
5. For example, the phrase *yōshi tansei*, found in the account of the reign of the Emperor Nintoku, was rendered by Motoori as *kao yoshi*. (*Motoori Norinaga Zenshū*, XII, p. 63.) Kurano Kenji read the same characters as *katachi uruwashi* (in *Kojiki Zenchūshaku*, VII, p. 19), but did not explain why he had departed from Motoori. The renderings by Kanda Hideo and Ōta Yoshimaro (in *Kojiki*, II, p. 199) abandoned "pure" Japanese readings and gave the mixed Chinese-Japanese pronunciation of *sugata katachi tanjō*. Differences in honorifics range downward from Motoori's lavish use to Kanda and Ōta's rather begrudging addition of honorific endings. For example, the sentence "Thereupon the emperor, climbing a high hill, looked in all four directions and said . . ." was rendered by Motoori as "*Koko ni sumeramikoto takayama ni noborimashite yomo no kuni wo mishitamaite noritamaitsuraku*. . . ." Kurano read the passage as "*Koko ni sumeramikoto takayama ni noborite yomo no kuni wo mitamaite noritamaishiku*. . . ." Kanda and Ōta gave "*Koko ni sumeramikoto takayama ni nobori yomo no kuni wo mite noritamawaku*. . . ."
6. Kamei Takashi, "Kojiki wa yomeru ka," in *Kojiki Taisei*, III, pp. 97–154.
7. Kanda Hideo, *Kojiki no Kōzō*, p. 7.
8. Tsuda Sōkichi in *Kojiki oyobi Nihon Shoki no Kenkyū*, p. 57, stated (in 1924), "One can say quite positively that there is not the smallest scrap of evidence that the kataribe of ancient times recited and transmitted the old stories." More recent scholarship has tended to confirm Tsuda's findings.
9. Saigō Nobutsuna, *Kojiki Kenkyū*, pp. 158–61. For a different view, see Mitani Eiichi, *Kojiki Seiritsu no Kenkyū*, pp. 244–59. Mitani believed that records plainly indicate that the kataribe recited legends about the gods or about the origins of particular provinces or villages. He deduced this

mainly from the *norito* religious chants and from documents transcribed long after the compilation of the *Kojiki*.

10. Philippi, *Kojiki*, p. 41. The teiki contained basic information about the Imperial Family, and the honji were of a more general nature.
11. *Ibid.*
12. *Ibid.*, p. 42. The term *kuji* (or *kyūji*) seems to have been used interchangeably with *honji*. The "pure Japanese" rendering of the preface gives *furugoto*.
13. *Ibid.*, pp. 41–42.
14. Saigō, *Kojiki Kenkyū*, pp. 10–11.
15. *Teihon Yanagita Kunio Shū*, IX, p. 310.
16. Saigō, *Kojiki Kenkyū*, pp. 40–41.
17. There are various translations of these two key words. Philippi (*Kojiki*, p. 42) translated them as one word, "learn," but explained in a footnote that the Chinese expression meant to familiarize oneself with a document and to memorize it so that it can be recited without reference to a written text. Kurano (*Kojiki Zenchūshaku*, I, p. 187) insisted on the importance in the old method of learning of repeating aloud and reciting. This is the interpretation I have followed.
18. Kurano, *Kojiki Zenchūshaku*, I, p. 196.
19. This theory of Takagi Toshio is quoted by Kurano, *Kojiki Zenchūshaku*, I, pp. 193–94.
20. Saigō, *Kojiki Kenkyū*, pp. 34–41.
21. *Ibid.*, p. 40.
22. Mizuno Masayoshi, "Kojiki to Kōkogaku," in Ueda Masaaki, *Kojiki*, pp. 113–17.
23. Mitani, *Kojiki*, pp. 2–54.
24. See *Watsuji Tetsurō Zenshū*, III, pp. 189–202. Watsuji, contrasting the *Kojiki* with the *Iliad*, admitted that the latter possessed a unity of time, place, and psychological development that was lacking in the *Kojiki*, but praised the intuitive freshness of the perceptions in the *Kojiki*. These comments appeared in his *Nihon Kodai Bunka*, originally written in 1920, revised in 1939, and further revised on several occasions before being included in his *zenshū* (complete works).
25. However, a "pure Japanese" rendering has been made of even this preface, proof (if proof was needed) that one can read almost *any* Chinese text as ancient Japanese. Kurano (*Kojiki*, *Norito*, pp. 59–60) left some words in Sino-Japanese pronunciations, rather than insist on "pure Japanese" throughout.
26. Philippi, *Kojiki*, p. 40.
27. *Watsuji Tetsurō Zenshū*, III, pp. 191–94.
28. The name is read as Izanaki by some scholars, as Isanaki by others, but I have used the most common pronunciation.

29. Hirata Atsutane believed that the jeweled spear represented a phallus.
30. It seems likely that *ya* (eight) was derived from *iya*, meaning "more and more," "flourishing," and so on.
31. See especially Matsumura Takeo, *Nihon Shinwa no Kenkyū* (A Study of Japanese Myths) in three volumes. In III, pp. 425–96, he considered myths relating to visits to the world of the dead.
32. Matsumura, *Nihon*, III, pp. 370–71.
33. See Tsuda Sōkichi, "Isanaki Isanami Nishin ga Kokudo wo Uminashita Monogatari," p. 19, where he expressed the belief that the begetting of the Eight Islands was the original opening of the *Kojiki*, and that the earlier doings of the gods, related in present texts of the *Kojiki*, were accretions. On p. 22 he also dismissed the circumambulation of the pillar prior to copulation as another accretion, perhaps reflecting religious or magical practices of the ancient Japanese. The existence of a central pillar in the creation myths of Europe, Central Asia, and elsewhere was discussed by Mircea Eliade in *The Sacred and the Profane*, pp. 34–39, 53.
34. Philippi, *Kojiki*, p. 72.
35. Aston, *Nihongi*, pp. 19–20.
36. Philippi, *Kojiki* pp. 79–80.
37. Aston, *Nihongi*, pp. 19–20.
38. Yamaji Heishirō, " 'Yakumo tatsu Izumo yaegaki' uta-kō," pp. 5–7.
39. *Ibid*., p. 5.
40. Ogihara Asao and Kōnosu Hayao, *Kojiki, Jōdai Kayō*, p. 90.
41. Matsumura, *Nihon*, III, pp. 330–33, links this fable with similar stories in Indonesia and other regions of Southeast Asia. Tokugawa Yoshichika in his article "Inaba no Shiro-usagi Kō," published in 1931, first drew attention to these similarities. Various animals appear in the different versions of the fable, but the main lines of the story, up the point where the rabbit (or deer or monkey) crosses to the opposite shore over the backs of lined-up crocodiles, are identical. Crocodiles are not known to have existed in Japan. Perhaps the word *wani* should be translated as "shark."
42. Philippi, *Kojiki*, p. 99.
43. This apparent contradiction with the story of Izanagi and Izanami seems to reflect Izumo traditions.
44. My interpretation follows Ogihara and Kōnosu, *Kojiki*, p. 102. For another translation see Philippi, *Kojiki*, pp. 106–7; also Robert H. Brower and Earl Miner, *Japanese Court Poetry*, p. 64, where this and related poems are treated unconventionally (but effectively) as a "quasi-dramatic sequence."
45. Philippi, *Kojiki*, p. 99.
46. *Ibid*., p. 145. The statement that the emperors have not been long-lived is puzzling in view of the extraordinary longevity of several emperors, beginning with Jimmu.

47. Philippi, *Kojiki*, p. 164.
48. *Ibid.*, p. 208.
49. According to the *Nihon Shoki*, he was the twelfth sovereign and reigned from A.D. 71 to 130.
50. *Mishima Yukio Zenshū*, XXXIV, p. 130.
51. Philippi, *Kojiki*, p. 229.
52. See Saigō, *Kojiki Kenkyū*, pp. 231–35, for an explanation of Yamato-takeru's action: misunderstanding the emperor's words, or deliberately twisting their meaning, he "patiently explained" to the brother that the emperor was disturbed by his failure to appear at mealtime; the "patient explanation" took the form of dismembering him. Perhaps the emperor pronounced the words "patiently explain" with a meaningful leer.
53. Philippi, *Kojiki*, pp. 234–35.
54. I have followed Ogihara and Kōnosu, *Kojiki*, p. 216, in making this translation. Ōkubo Tadashi, *Kojiki Kayō*, p. 68, also interpreted the final word, *aware*, as a burst of mocking laughter. For a different interpretation, see Philippi, *Kojiki*, pp. 236–37. The *Nihon Shoki*, as Philippi points out, connects the narrative and song with entirely different people.
55. Philippi, *Kojiki*, p. 238.
56. My translation follows the interpretation of Ogihara and Kōnosu in *Kojiki*, p. 222. See Philippi, *Kojiki*, pp. 244–45.
57. Ivan Morris, *The Nobility of Failure*, pp. 12–13.
58. Text and interpretation in Ogihara and Kōnosu, *Kojiki*, p. 138. For other translations, see Philippi, *Kojiki*, p. 248, and Morris, *Nobility*, p. 12.
59. See Philippi, *Kojiki*, p. 248. One of Yamato-takeru's last songs is a *kata-uta*, or half-song, consisting of three lines of 5, 7, and 7 syllables. A little earlier (Philippi, p. 242) he and an old man who is tending a fire together compose one waka. This joint effort, which describes how long it has taken Yamato-takeru to pass Tsukuba, was traditionally cited as the beginning of renga, or linked verse, and the art itself was often referred to as "the Way of Tsukuba." For further details on the traditional history of renga, see below, pp. 921–26.
60. Kanda, *Kojiki no Kōzō*, pp. 104–20.
61. Philippi, *Kojiki*, p. 573.
62. *Ibid.*, p. 285.
63. For an up-to-date, brilliantly reasoned study of this period, see Gari Ledyard, "Galloping Along with the Horseriders."
64. Philippi, *Kojiki*, p. 340.
65. He is credited with having composed the first poem in the *Man'yōshū*. See below, p. 93.
66. Ogihara and Kōnusu, *Kojiki*, p. 320. For another translation, see Philippi, *Kojiki*, p. 354.
67. Text in Ogihara and Kōnosu, *Kojiki*, p. 190. See also Philippi, *Kojiki*, p. 335.

68. See Philippi, *Kojiki*, pp. 335–36, for these and other interpretations.
69. Kurano Kenji, *Kojiki, Norito*, p. 23.
70. He referred specifically to the publicaton in that year of Takagi Toshio's *Nihon Shinwa Densetsu*.
71. Kurano, *Kojiki*, p. 25.
72. The vowel system of eighth-century Japanese is mentioned by Philippi in *Kojiki*, pp. 21–22. It is discussed at much greater length by Roy Andrew Miller in *The Japanese Language*, pp. 174–91, and by Roland Lange in *The Phonology of Eighth-Century Japanese*. The existence of eight vowels in ancient times, as opposed to the present five, was first postulated by Hashimoto Shinkichi in 1917.
73. See, for example, Ueda, *Kojiki*, or Matsumura, *Nihon Shinwa*.
74. Tsuchihashi Yutaka, "Kojiki to Uta Monogatari," in Ueda, *Kojiki*.
75. For example, Susano-o's slaying the dragon (*orochi*) is the subject of the Nō play *Orochi*. The combat between Susano-o and the dragon is the climax also of the play by Chikamatsu Monzaemon, *Nippon Furisode no Hajime* (1718), which has Susano-o as its principal character. References to Susano-o and the other main deities of the *Kojiki* occur frequently in later literature. To cite one example: we are told of the hero of Chikamatsu's *The Battles of Coxinga* that he "shows the divine strength of the god Susano-o when he flayed the piebald colt of Heaven." See Donald Keene, *Major Plays of Chikamatsu*, pp. 226, 452.
76. See above, note 59, also below, p. 921.
77. Many doubts have been expressed since the time of Kamo no Mabuchi (1697–1769) about the authenticity of the preface to the *Kojiki*, and some twentieth-century scholars have questioned the authenticity of the whole work. However, the theory that the *Kojiki* was a forgery of the Heian period was refuted by the eminent linguist Hashimoto Shinkichi in his study of the phonetics of the songs. There still remains the matter of the preface. Ikada Isao, in his article "Kojiki Gisho-setsu wa Konkyo Hakujaku de aru ka: Jōhyō to Jo to no Kembetsu," argued that the so-called preface to the *Kojiki* is actually not a preface but a memorial, as Chinese examples demonstrate. Umezawa Isezō in *Kojiki, Nihon Shoki* argued that the *Kojiki* was written *after* the *Nihon Shoki*; the latter represents the Chinese actually written by Japanese early in the eighth century, while the *Kojiki* represents a transitional style between pure Chinese and the *Man'yōshū*. Torigoe Kenzaburō, in *Kojiki wa Gisho ka*, subscribed to the theory that the *Kojiki* was written early in the ninth century, rather than in the eighth century. Many other examples in this vein might be cited, but none of these theories has significantly shaken the edifice of *Kojiki* studies.

Bibliography

Note: All Japanese books, except as otherwise noted, were published in Tokyo.

Aston, W. G. *Nihongi*. London: Kegan Paul, 1896.

Brower, Robert H., and Earl Miner. *Japanese Court Poetry*. Stanford, Calif.: Stanford University Press, 1961.

Bungei Tokuhon: Kojiki. Kawade Shobō Shinsha, 1980.

Chamberlain, Basil Hall, *Ko-Ji-Ki*, 2nd ed. Kōbe: J. L. Thomson, 1932.

Eliade, Mircea. *The Sacred and the Profane*. New York: Harper Torchbooks, 1961.

Ikada Isao. "Kojiki Gisho-setsu wa Konkyo Hakujaku de aru ka: Jōhyō to Jo to no Kembetsu," *Kokugo to Kokubungaku*, June–July, 1962.

Kanda Hideo. *Kojiki no Kōzō*. Meiji Shoin, 1959.

Kanda Hideo and Ōta Yoshimaro. *Kojiki*, 2 vols., in Nihon Koten Zensho series. Asahi Shimbun Sha, 1962.

Kato, Shuichi. *A History of Japanese Literature: The First Thousand Years*. Tokyo: Kodansha International, 1979.

Keene, Donald. *Major Plays of Chikamatsu*. New York: Columbia University Press, 1961.

Kojiki Taisei, 8 vols. Heibonsha, 1956–58.

Kurano Kenji. *Jōdai Nihon Koten Bungaku no Kenkyū*. Ōfūsha, 1968.

———. *Kojiki, Norito*, in Nihon Koten Bungaku Taikei series. Iwanami Shoten, 1958.

———. *Kojiki no Seiritsu*. Yamato Shobō, 1977.

———. *Kojiki Zenchūshaku*, 7 vols. Sanseidō, 1973–80.

———. *Nihon Shinwa*. Kawade Shobō, 1952.

Lange, Roland A. *The Phonology of Eighth-Century Japanese*. Tokyo: Sophia University, 1973.

Ledyard, Gari. "Galloping Along with the Horseriders," *Journal of Japanese Studies* 1:2, Spring 1975.

Masuda Katsumi. *Kiki Kayō*. Chikuma Shobō, 1972.

Matsumura Takeo. *Nihon Shinwa no Kenkyū*, 3 vols. Baifūkan, 1954–55.

Miller, Roy Andrew. *The Japanese Language*. Chicago: The University of Chicago Press, 1967.

Mishima Yukio Zenshū, 36 vols. Shinchōsha, 1973–76.

Mitani Eiichi. *Kojiki Seiritsu no Kenkyū*. Yūseido, 1980.

Morris, Ivan. *The Nobility of Failure*. New York: Holt, Rinehart and Winston, 1976.

Motoori Norinaga Zenshū, 21 vols. Chikuma Shobō, 1968–77.

Ōbayashi Taryō. "The Origins of Japanese Mythology," *Acta Asiatica* 31, 1977.

Ogihara Asao and Kōnosu Hayao. *Kojiki, Jōdai Kayō*, in Nihon Koten Bungaku Zenshū series. Shōgakukan, 1973.

Ōkubo Tadashi. *Kojiki Kayō*, in Kōdansha Gakujutsu Bunko series. Kōdansha, 1981.

Philippi, Donald L. *Kojiki*. Tokyo: University of Tokyo Press, 1968.

———. *This Wine of Peace, This Wine of Laughter*. New York: Grossman Publishers, 1968.

Reischauer, Robert Karl. *Early Japanese History*, 2 vols. Princeton: Princeton University Press, 1937.

Saigō Nobutsuna. *Kojiki Chūshaku*, I. Heibonsha, 1975.

———. *Kojiki Kenkyū*. Miraisha, 1973.

Teihon Yanagita Shū, 36 vols. Chikuma Shobō, 1962–71.

Tokugawa Yoshichika. "Inaba no Shiro-usagi Kō," *Minzokugaku* 3:5, 1931.

Tokumitsu Kyūya. *Kojiki Kenkyū Shi*. Kasama Shoin, 1977.

Torigoe Kenzaburō. *Kojiki wa Gisho ka*. Asahi Shimbun Sha, 1971.

Tsuchihashi Yutaka and Konishi Jin'ichi. *Kodai Kayō Shū*, in Nihon Koten Bungaku Taikei series. Iwanami Shoten, 1957.

Tsuda Sōkichi. "Isanaki Isanami Nishin ga Kokudo wo uminashita Monogatari," in *Bungei Tokuhon: Kojiki*.

———. *Kojiki oyobi Nihon Shoki no Kenkyū*. Iwanami Shoten, 1933.

Ueda Masaaki. *Kojiki*. Shakai Shisō Sha, 1977.

———. *Nihon Kodai Kokka Ronkyū*. Hanawa Shobō, 1968.

Umezawa Isezō. *Kojiki, Nihon Shoki*. Kyoto: San'ichi Shobō, 1957.

Watsuji Tetsurō Zenshū, 20 vols. Iwanami Shoten, 1961–63.

Yamaji Heishirō. "'Yakumo tatsu Izumo yaegaki' uta-kō," *Kokubungaku Kenkyū* 12:33.

2. WRITINGS IN CHINESE OF THE NARA PERIOD

The establishment of a permanent capital in 710 at Nara marked the beginning of a period of extraordinary cultural developments. Previously, the capital had been moved after the death of each sovereign, probably because of the belief that his death had defiled the site.[1] The perishable nature of the materials of native Japanese architecture had also made it easier to abandon an old capital than if the wealth of the nation had been poured into buildings. The decision to break with precedent and to build at Nara an imposing capital was probably occasioned by the desire to emulate China, and this sense of rivalry proved stronger than the claims of native traditions.[2] The choice of the site was influenced by Chinese geomancy: the hills and rivers were in the right places for a capital. The new city, as Sir George Sansom put it, became "the metropolis, the centre of administration, the home of the arts and the Holy See of Buddhism."[3]

The new capital was laid out along the lines of Ch'ang-an, the Chinese capital at the time, and the buildings were in Chinese styles of architecture. A palace of impressive dimensions was constructed, and various Buddhist temples, notably the Kōfuku-ji (associated with the Fujiwara clan), were moved here from elsewhere in the region. Many Chinese administrative and legal institutions were taken over bodily, in the belief that conformity to Chinese models was the best way to prove that the Japanese were truly civilized. The language of the official documents was Chinese, and members of the court, from the emperor down, took pride in their calligraphy and in their ability to compose poetry and prose in Chinese.

It would be hard to exaggerate either the suddenness or the brilliance of the flowering in Japan of Chinese culture that occurred during the six decades of the Nara period, from 710 to 774. The profusion of architecture and sculpture produced at this time would never be surpassed. The literary monuments include the *Man'yōshū*, the finest collection of Japanese poetry, but the works in prose are less impressive, perhaps because the Chinese language enjoyed such prestige at the time that literary expression in Japanese was largely confined to lyric poetry. The writing in Chinese, though mainly of interest because of the historical information it transmits, is not without literary value, and it created the necessary background for the superior works written in Chinese during the Heian period.

The Fudoki

In 713, the year after the *Kojiki* was presented to the court, various provinces were commanded to compile *fudoki*[4] (gazetteers) which would include old tales, records of places, and descriptions of the crops, mineral resources, topography, and wildlife of each region. The fudoki were written mainly in Chinese, though some passages are in the mixed Sino-Japanese style typical of the *Kojiki*, and the poems are phonetically transcribed. Only five of the gazetteers compiled in response to this imperial command have been preserved more or less intact, but some forty others exist in fragments. The most complete is the *Izumo Fudoki*, prepared between 713 and 733 by a group of scholars headed by Miyake no Omi Kanatari.[5]

The *Izumo Fudoki* is not a book for browsing. With the exception of two or three legends, notably the account of how the god Yatsukamizu Omizuno added various islands and promontories to the territory of Izumo by tugging (*kunihiki*) them to him with the aid of a rope,[6] the work consists of brief accounts of villages, mountains, rivers, islands, and other geographical features, often with a folk etymology for each place-name. There seems to have been hardly any attempt to achieve literary distinction, as a typical section will suggest:

> Community of Shitsunu. It is located two miles east of the district office. The alternative name for Amatsu Kichikamitakahiko, a son of Kami Musubi, is Komomakura Shitsunichi. The god resides in this community. Therefore the community is called Shitsunu.[7]

We get very little idea of how the people of Izumo lived, though the names of plants, animals, and the like at least indirectly reveal what they ate. In the more elegantly written *Hitachi Fudoki*,[8] we also find folk etymologies:

The place where he is said to have killed them brutally (*itaku*) is now the district of Itaku; the place where he is said to have slashed them down swiftly (*futsu ni*) is now the village of Futsuna; the place where he killed them easily (*yasuku*) is now the town of Yasukiri; and the place where he killed them well (*yoku*) is now the hamlet of Esaki.[9]

A passage more typical of the style of the *Hitachi Fudoki* reveals obvious Chinese influence:

> In the season of fragrant blossoms or the time of crimson leaves people flock to Takahama in palanquins and boats to enjoy the scenery. In spring the cherry trees along the shore are a thousand hues; in autumn, the leaves on the banks are tinted a hundred shades. The warbler's song is heard in the fields; cranes can be seen dancing on the dried strand. Farmer boys and fisher girls throng the shore; merchants and peasants pole boats to and fro. Especially on hot summer mornings or on evenings when the sun broils down, people invite friends and take along servants to sit along the beach, gazing out at the sea. When a breeze begins to stir the waves bit by bit, people escaping the heat shake off oppressive cares; as the shade of the hills gradually lengthens, those who seek the evening cool express their pleasure.[10]

These lines, written in Chinese phrases of four or six characters each, in an approximation of *p'ien wen*, or parallel prose, are followed by two waka, transcribed with Chinese characters used as phonograms:

takahama ni	The waves off the shore,
kiyosuru nami no	The waves that come approaching
okitsunami	Takahama beach
yosuru to mo yoraji	Come close, but I don't go near
kora ni shi yoraba	Because I am close to you.

takahama ni	Down Takahama beach
shitakaze sayagu	The wind blows tumultuously,
imo wo koi	Like my love for you;
tsuma to iwabaya	I wish I could call you "wife,"
shiko to meshitsu mo[11]	Though you said I was ugly.

The combination of elegant Chinese prose with humble Japanese poetry is characteristic not only of the *Hitachi Fudoki* but of the *Nihon*

Shoki, presented to the court in 720. It would be natural to assume that materials in the fudoki that existed before 720 would have been used by the compilers of the *Nihon Shoki* when tracing local history, but they do not seem to have contributed much to the first official history of Japan.[12]

Nihon Shoki

The *Nihon Shoki* (Chronicles of Japan) was completed in 720, just eight years after the *Kojiki*. It is uncertain whether its original name was *Nihon Shoki* or *Nihongi*,[13] but in the Heian period it was most often called *Nihongi*, as we know from the nickname *Nihongi no Tsubone* (the lady of the *Nihongi*) bestowed on Murasaki Shikibu in recognition of her learning. In later times the name *Nihon Shoki* was almost always used, though some nationalists objected to calling the work "Chronicles of Japan" because that seemed to suggest that if "Japan" did not appear in the title the book might be mistaken for the chronicles of some other country; such men spoke simply of "The Chronicles." Less committed scholars insisted that it was precisely in order to affirm Japan's position in the world that the *Nihon Shoki* was compiled.[14]

The *Nihon Shoki* lacks a preface, and the circumstances of composition are obscure. A section in the work, dated the tenth year of the Emperor Temmu (681),[15] relates how the emperor commanded various nobles to commit to writing a chronicle of the emperors and matters of antiquity.[16] It is not clear whether or not this represented a first step in the compilation of the *Nihon Shoki*, but most authorities agree that the task of gathering materials for this history probably began about that time. In any case, the circumstances of composition were strikingly unlike those of the *Kojiki*. In place of one man (or woman) who memorized the old traditions, a dozen noblemen recorded historical facts. The final compilation was delayed for years at a time, whenever more pressing matters arose, and the laborious preparations for an official national history (as opposed to the unofficial *Kojiki*) did not bear fruit for almost forty years.

It has long been a question, nevertheless, why the court felt it necessary to produce *two* histories of Japan within the space of eight years. Some believe that the *Kojiki* was intended for domestic consumption, but the *Nihon Shoki* for Chinese and Koreans, with the hopes it would impress them with the great antiquity of Japan. That may have been the original intent, but this does not explain why the *Kojiki* disappeared for centuries after it was compiled but the *Nihon Shoki* was revered by the Japanese as the most authentic account of their past. Others have suggested that the *Nihon Shoki* was compiled because of dissatisfaction with the crude style of the *Kojiki*; but if this was so, the compilation of the *Nihon Shoki* could not have been started until after the *Kojiki* was completed in 712. We know from an entry in *Shoku Nihongi*, the continuation of the *Nihon Shoki*, that in 714 two low-ranked officials, Ki Kiyondo and Miyake Fujimaro, received an imperial command to compile a national history. The problem is that the ranks of the two men (junior sixth rank and senior eighth rank) seem too humble for so important an undertaking, and it has also been doubted that they could have finished the work of assembling and editing the necessary documents between 714 and 720.[17] In the absence of firm information, scholars have had no choice but to resort to guesswork.

The chief editor of the *Nihon Shoki* seems to have been Prince Toneri (d. 735), the third son of the Emperor Temmu, a nobleman who filled important positions during the reigns of Temmu and his daughter, the Empress Gemmei. Probably a number of writers took part in the composition of the thirty books of the *Nihon Shoki*. Perhaps some of the discrepancies in style can be attributed to the participation of immigrant Chinese and Koreans in the writing of the final text.[18]

The most striking difference between the *Kojiki* and the *Nihon Shoki* is evident on any page: the former is in crude though generally intelligible Chinese, the latter in the polished language typical of histories written in China itself. Indeed, whole passages in the *Nihon Shoki* were taken bodily from Chinese sources, and the narrative as a whole was embellished with phrases and allusions drawn from such compendia as *I-wen Lei-chü* (Literary References, 624) by Ou-yang Hsün (557–641).[19] The writer of any given sentence of the *Nihon Shoki* had only to consult this work to find appropriate locutions on his subject by the great stylists of the past. The use of time-tested phrases strengthened the overtones of the events described and gave them additional dignity. A few literary works, such as the *Wen Hsüan*, a collection of Chinese poetry composed before the Six Dynasties by Prince Chao-ming of the Liang dynasty (501–31), were also tapped for stylistic decorations, as were a few Buddhist works.

With the exception of the songs, recorded in a system similar to that of the *Kojiki* but with more complicated characters, the *Nihon Shoki* was written throughout in unmistakable Chinese, but there were traditions, going back even to the Nara period, of how words or phrases might be read in pure Japanese pronunciations.[20] By the early Heian period—the ninth century—lectures were delivered to the court on the *Nihon Shoki*, making necessary a rendering of the text into a language that was aurally intelligible to Japanese listeners.[21]

Nihon Shoki and *Kojiki*

The *Nihon Shoki* is by no means as interesting to read as the *Kojiki*. The historical—as opposed to religious or literary—intent of the compilers is everywhere apparent. Unlike the *Kojiki*, which gives only one version of each legend, the editors of the *Nihon Shoki* painstakingly supplied as many as eleven variant traditions concerning a single event. Though these additional materials are of considerable interest to students of the text, they interrupt the narrative flow and are sometimes repetitious. There is a distinctly scholarly attitude evident in the composition, especially in the accounts of historical times, where one sometimes finds cautious recommendations that urge further investigation of the facts. The use of foreign sources, notably from the Korean kingdom of Paekche (known as Kudara to the Japanese), also distinguishes the *Nihon Shoki* from the *Kojiki*, which relies only on native materials. Unfortunately, the Paekche records are not preserved in Korea. The use in these records of *Nihon* for Japan (a name not officially adopted until the Taika Reform of 645) and of *tennō* for emperor (a title adopted during the reign of the Empress Suiko, 593–628) as well as other bits of internal evidence, suggest that the Paekche historical materials may have been compiled by refugees in Japan after the fall of Paekche to the rival Korean kingdom of Silla in 663.[22]

By this time the Japanese court possessed a fairly extensive acquaintance with Chinese historical and literary materials. Some men, especially those who had served a tutelage under various emigrés, could write Chinese with confidence, rather in the manner of Europeans writing Latin during the Middle Ages, and ostentatiously displayed their learning by using unusual characters in writing the *Nihon Shoki*, perhaps in the hopes of impressing the Chinese and Koreans.

A concern over what readers abroad might think may also be detected in the precision with which events are dated in the *Nihon Shoki*. Unlike the *Kojiki*, which seldom supplies a date of any kind, the *Nihon Shoki* is quite specific not only on the years but on the months and even the days when events occurred, starting with the legendary coronation of the Emperor Jimmu in 660 B.C. The accuracy of the dating is hardly credible, but the Japanese were evidently determined to impress foreigners with their historiography.[23]

Although the *Nihon Shoki* makes no reference to the *Kojiki*, its account of the creation of the Japanese islands is similar, and various memorable episodes—the outrages of Susano-o and the withdrawal of Amaterasu into the cave, for example—are much in the same vein; these traditions appear to have become firm, though the names of other deities and their achievements vary considerably between the two works. In the opening description of the creation of the worlds, the *Kojiki* states that three divinities were created even before the reed shoot sprang from the floating oil, but in the *Nihon Shoki* one god called Kunitokotachi was transformed from the primordial reed shoot, followed by two more who were "spontaneously developed by the operation of the principle of Heaven."[24] After its main account of these events, the *Nihon Shoki* gives six variant accounts, the name of the chief god depending on the source.

The creation of Izanagi and Izanami, their circumambulation of the central pillar, and their begetting of the islands of Japan are similar in the two histories, but with one difference: in the *Kojiki* the female deity Izanami speaks first and the couple consequently have imperfect children; but in the main text of the *Nihon Shoki* Izanagi, annoyed that Izanami has spoken first, insists on going around the pillar once more and giving his greeting first, even before they set about procreating islands.[25] One version states that when Izanagi and Izanami decided to copulate they did not know how until a friendly wagtail bird demonstrated the process.[26]

The first god—as opposed to islands—produced by the divine ancestors was Amaterasu, who seemed too glorious and resplendent for the earth. The text states, "At this time heaven and earth were still not far separated, and therefore they sent her up to Heaven by the ladder of heaven."[27] This was certainly a more befitting manner of birth for the chief of the heavenly gods than the description given in the *Kojiki*, stating that Amaterasu was born from Izanagi's left eye when he washed away the pollution of hell.[28] One senses even in this early section of the *Nihon Shoki* a political awareness that guided the composition: it was not sufficient to record the old legends, confused and contradictory as they were; the legends had to make sense, especially in terms of the unbroken ancestry of the emperor and the uniqueness of his relationship to the land.

Some traditions quoted in the *Nihon Shoki* explain matters overlooked by the *Kojiki*—for example, the origins of fish, animals, and plants.[29] The moon god (Tsukiyomi) plays a slightly more important role than in the *Kojiki*: he was so reluctant to see the goddess of food vomit rice, fish, and furred animals that he slew her. This action distressed his sister, Amaterasu, and she arranged the movements of the celestial bodies in such a way that the sun and moon would never meet again.[30]

On the whole, the *Nihon Shoki* is more rational, less apt than the *Kojiki* to relate with wide-eyed wonder the miracles wrought by the gods. This perhaps is why it is less entertaining as literature.[31] Yamato-takeru is credited with some of the heroic deeds he performs in the *Kojiki*, including the subjugation of the Kumaso chieftains; but his entrapment in the middle of a moor is the doing not of a hostile official but of some brigands, and the specifically human touch in the story—the bag his aunt gives the despondent Yamato-takeru to open in an emergency—is missing from the prosaic *Nihon Shoki* account.

For centuries the *Nihon Shoki* was the work to which educated persons turned for a knowledge of their country's early history and the even earlier Age of the Gods, but ever since the rise of National Learning (*kokugaku*) in the Tokugawa period,[32] the *Kojiki* has displaced the *Nihon Shoki* in the affection of the Japanese, and has exerted greater influence on works of literature that touch on the ancient past.

Prince Shōtoku

Among the historical personages described in the *Nihon Shoki*, none is more impressive than Prince Shōtoku (574–622), one of the major cultural figures of Japanese history. Shōtoku was the son of the short-lived Emperor Yōmei and, on his mother's side, a grandson of the Emperor Kimmei. His personal name, Umayado, meaning "stable," was explained by the *Nihon Shoki* in this manner:

> The empress-consort, on the day when her pregnancy was to come to an end, went round the forbidden precincts, inspecting the different offices. When she came to the horse department, and had just reached the door of the stables, she was suddenly delivered of him without effort. He was able to speak as soon as he was born, and was possessed of wisdom. When he grew up he could listen to the suits of ten men at once and decide them all without error. He could foresee what would happen in the future. Moreover he learned the Inner Doctrine [Buddhism] from a Korean priest named Eji

> [Hyo-cha], and studied the Outer Classics [Confucianism] with a doctor called Kakuka. In both of these branches of study he became thoroughly proficient.[33]

Shōtoku, his posthumous name, means "supreme virtue," and the man himself was not only revered as a founder of Japanese civilization, but became an object of worship to whom miracles were attributed.[34] The *Nihon Shoki* informs us that when he died at the age of forty-eight

> The princes and grandees, and indeed, the entire populace of the realm grieved so greatly the streets were filled with the sounds of their lamentation; the old wept as over the death of a dear child, and the food in their mouths lost its savor, the young as if they had lost a beloved parent. The farmer cultivating his fields let fall his plow, and the woman pounding rice laid down her pestle. They all said:—"The sun and moon have lost their brightness; Heaven and Earth must surely soon crumble—from this time forth, in whom shall we place our trust?"[35]

Shōtoku was the first Japanese to be made the subject of a biography, and a portrait, said to be of him, is the oldest Japanese work of this genre.[36] Although he was not credited with martial exploits in the manner of Yamato-takeru, he succeeded in establishing a state on Chinese models, in fostering Buddhism with his commentaries on three sutras, and, most celebrated of all, in expressing the ideals of the Japanese state in his "Seventeen Article Constitution." The text of the Consitution is given in the *Nihon Shoki*. Some scholars have questioned the attribution to Shōtoku, but the ideas accord with what we know of the man.[37]

The opening article of the Constitution[38] is the best-known section: "Harmony is to be prized,[39] and an avoidance of wanton opposition to be honored. All men are influenced by partisanship, and few are intelligent. That is why some disobey their lords and fathers, or maintain feuds with neighboring villages. But when those above are harmonious and those below are friendly, and there is concord in the discussion of business, right views of things spontaneously gain acceptance. Then, what is there which cannot be accomplished?"[40]

Shōtoku's insistence on "harmony" (*wa*) has been reiterated many times ever since as the most essential feature of a well-run society. It has even been cited as the secret of the success of Japanese industry in the years since 1945. The wording of this section of Shōtoku's Constitution was largely derived from the *Analects* of Confucius, but he employed the language freely to epitomize his thoughts on the necessity of harmony in a country that was in fact torn by warfare.[41]

The second article of the Constitution enjoined all to "sincerely reverence the three treasures of Buddhism"—the Buddha, the Buddhist law, and the monastic orders. In other words, Shōtoku was urging in the same document reverence for both Confucian and Buddhist teachings. The two philosophies were not mutually compatible in every respect, as we can gather from the bitterly anti-Buddhist attitudes displayed by many Confucian scholars over the centuries; but Shōtoku was attempting to embrace both systems of thought, Confucianism for the affairs of this world and Buddhism for the world of eternity. No reference to Shintō is made in the Constitution, an indication that Shōtoku desired to build a state on Chinese rather than Japanese lines. He was determined to strengthen the central régime, following Chinese models, rather than accept the more traditional Japanese concept of "eight million deities," each with its sphere of activity.

The twelfth article of the Constitution commanded the provincial authorities "not to levy exaction on the people," and declared, "The sovereign is the master of the people of the whole country. The officials to whom he gives charge are all his vassals. How can they, as well as the Government, presume to lay taxes on the people?"[42] This article, too, seems to indicate that at the time the sovereign was *not* recognized as the master of the people of the whole country.

The last of the seventeen articles states, "Decisions on important letters should not be made by one man alone. They should be discussed with many." Although this article surely reflected Shōtoku's distress over the existing situation—arrogant and dictatorial decisions reached and carried out by some powerful member of the court—it has been linked with the preferences of the Japanese of a much later day for decisions reached by consensus.

Little attention has been paid to the purely literary qualities of Shōtoku's writings,[43] but it is evident from his Constitution and from his commentaries on three Buddhist sutras that he was completely conversant in the Chinese language appropriate for discussing Confucian and Buddhist philosophy. Doubts have been expressed about the attribution to Shōtoku of the Buddhist commentaries,[44] but minor mistakes in Chinese (among other stylistic features) suggest that a Japanese, quite likely Prince Shōtoku, wrote these commentaries at the beginning of the seventh century.

Early Accounts of Japan in the Chinese Dynastic Histories

The most valuable historical information in the *Nihon Shoki* is found in its description of events during the century immediately preceding its compilation,[45] but the foreign sources it quotes are also of special interest. For example, the description of the reign of the Empress Jingū[46] in the *Nihon Shoki* quotes from the *Wei Shih* (The History of the Wei Dynasty), the earliest account of Japan in any language. It is the narrative of a Chinese traveler who visited the land of Wa in the third century A.D. The traveler went by sea to the islands of Tsushima and Iki, and from there to Kyūshū. He eventually reached the land of Wa, also known as Yamatai, a country ruled by Queen Pimiko. Over thirty localities have claimed the honor of being the site of Wa, the two leading contenders being northern Kyūshū and the Yamato plain around Nara. It is not clear how large a territory Pimiko governed, nor whether Wa was the seat of central authority in the country later known as Yamato (or Japan), or merely a local domain; but, as the first description of Japan, the Wei history has long appealed to the imagination of the Japanese.

The account of Wa and of an embassy from Wa that visited China is found in the section of the Wei history devoted to barbarian neighboring countries. The *Nihon Shoki* did not cite the description by the Chinese visitor of the customs of the people of Wa, but only the part of the history that concerns the Japanese embassy:

> In the sixth month of the third year of Ching-ch'u [A.D. 238] in the reign of the Emperor Ming Ti, the queen of the Wa [Pimiko] sent the grandee Nashonmi and others; they visited the prefecture and asked permission to proceed to the emperor's court and present tribute. The governor, Teng Hsia, dispatched an official who escorted them to the capital.[48]

The *Nihon Shoki* at points misquoted the *Wei Shih*,[49] but the inclusion of this extract in the section of the work devoted to the Empress Jingū makes clear the purpose of the Japanese compilers: it was to identify Pimiko, the queen of Wa, with Jingū, and thereby impart greater historicity to its account of a legendary figure. The activities of Jingū in Japan and Korea, described at length in the *Nihon Shoki*,[50] took place about the time of Pimiko (at least according to the traditional chronology), but surely there was no connection between the two women. The compilers of the *Nihon Shoki*, faced with the task of filling up the great expanse of time from the coronation of Jimmu in 660 B.C. to the seventh century A.D. with a scant number of historical facts, eagerly sought substantiating evidence in the Chinese and Korean histories.

The Chinese court encouraged amicable relations with the queen of Wa, and when the Japanese sent an embassy to China, the emperor bestowed on her the title "Queen of Wa, Friendly to Wei," together with a gold seal.[51] The gifts sent by the Wei court to Pimiko included swords, bronze mirrors, and beads; these perhaps were the origins of the Japanese imperial regalia.

The subsequent accounts of Japan in the Chinese dynastic histories often repeat the information found in the Wei history, suggesting a lack of contact or perhaps of interest.[52] Not until the *Sui Shu* (History of the Sui Dynasty, 629–636) was fresh information incorporated in the Chinese descriptions of Japan. In its account of the K'ai-huang era (581–600) it states that "the king of Wa" sent an envoy to the Chinese court. This date, corresponding to the reign of the Empress Suiko, is of special significance because it marked a period when many Chinese customs—for example, distinguishing court ranks by headgear—were being adopted in the hopes of making Japan appear a civilized country in the eyes of the Chinese.

Other information recorded in the *Sui Shu* is invaluable because it describes in detail aspects of Japanese life that the Japanese histories pass over in silence. Here, for example, is its account of crime and punishment in sixth-century Japan:

> Sometimes pebbles are put in boiling water and both parties to a dispute made to pick them out. The hand of the guilty one is said to become inflamed. Sometimes a snake is kept in a jar, and the accused ordered to catch it. If he is guilty, his hand will be bitten. The people are gentle and peaceful. Litigation is infrequent and theft seldom occurs.[53]

The *Sui Shu* also contains mention of the Japanese adoption of Buddhism, and of the transmission of Buddhist scriptures from Paekche. It adds, "This was the first time that they came into possession of characters."[54] The statement was untrue, as we know from inscriptions (as well as from the *Kojiki* account of Wani-kishi), but this no doubt was the impression formed by the Chinese who had met Japanese Buddhist priests.

There is also a description of the Japanese embassy of 607 to the Sui court. This embassy was sent to pay the respects of the Japanese court to the Chinese emperor as a protector of Buddhism, and it included "several tens of monks" who had come to study Buddhism in China.[55] The good impression produced on the Chinese by the Buddhist piety of the Japanese visitors was impaired, however, by a message delivered by the envoy. It bore the superscription: "The Son of Heaven in the land where the sun rises addresses a letter to the Son of Heaven in the land where the sun sets. We trust you are in good health." When the Chinese emperor saw this letter, he was exceedingly displeased, and told the chief official of foreign affairs that "this letter from the barbarians was discourteous, and that such a letter should never again be brought to his attention."[56] The Chinese emperor did not easily brook another monarch addressing him in terms of equality, and he was no doubt annoyed to be called the ruler of the land of the setting sun. The superscription is given in less provocative terms in the *Nihon Shoki*,[57] but in later centuries it was often praised by Japanese nationalists, as affording proof that Prince Shōtoku maintained a spirit of independence toward China; it may be, however, that the prince was simply unfamiliar with the proper form of address to be used by the sovereign of a small country when sending a communication to the Chinese emperor.

By the time of the *Sung Shih* (History of the Sung Dynasty), which treats the period 960–1229, the account of Japan was not only much fuller than before but it cited at some length the *Nihon Shoki*.[58] There was also a short biography of Prince Shōtoku that included this praise:

> It is said that when he was three years of age, he could understand the words of ten persons speaking at the same time. At the age of seven, he understood Buddhism. While he was giving lectures in the temple . . . lotus flowers rained down from Heaven.[59]

Kaifūsō

The first work of unmistakable literary intent to be composed by Japanese in the Chinese language was the collection of 120 poems[60] called *Kaifūsō* (Fond Recollections of Poetry), compiled in 751. Some of the poems go back eighty years, to within a half-century of Prince Shōtoku's death.

The belief that the composition of poetry was an essential accomplishment of a gentleman, long held by the Chinese, was adopted by the Japanese, always eager to emulate their mentors. Gentlemen of the court as a result composed poetry in a foreign language that none of them spoke, and whose tonal patterns had constantly to be verified in tables. The tradition of composing *kanshi*, as poems in Chinese were called, continued until late in the nineteenth century, and even in the twentieth century a few kanshi poets maintained the dignity of the medium.

The poems in the *Kaifūsō* have often been dismissed as being little more than exercises in which members of the Japanese court demonstrated their ability to cope with the rules of Chinese prosody. For the most part, the poems are cast in the style of elegance favored in China during the eighth century, particularly among the poets of the Liang and Ch'en dynasties to the south.[61] In content, too, they tend to celebrate banquets or excursions of the court, rather than treat the poet's deepest feelings; but there are a few poems of greater urgency, such as one composed by Prince Ōtsu (662–687) when he faced execution on the charge of attempted rebellion:

> The golden crow lights on the western huts;
> evening drums beat out the shortness of life.
> There are no inns on the road to the grave—
> Whose is the house I go to tonight?[62]

It is likely that Prince Ōtsu composed this poem in Chinese not because he wished to display his erudition, but because he felt emotions that he could not fully express in Japanese. This would be true of the best kanshi poets of later times. Prince Ōtsu, like eighteen other *Kaifūsō* poets, was also represented in the *Man'yōshū*, compiled later in the eighth century. His Japanese poem on his impending death was in quite a different vein:

momozutau	Today, taking my
iware no ike ni	Last sight of the mallards on
naku kamo wo	The pond of Iware,
kyō nomi mire ya	A hundred times familiar,
kumogakurinan[63]	Must I vanish into the clouds?[64]

Prince Ōtsu's kanshi not only employed such Chinese terms as "golden crow" for the sun, but attempted to impart philosophical overtones to his experience. The Japanese poem more directly suggests an intimate identification with his surroundings even in the moments before his death.

The *Kaifūsō* poetry reveals how closely the Japanese poets of the eighth century followed Chinese models, as in this example by Ki no Suemochi:

> I built my hut by the southern woods;
> I dropped my hook from the northern lake-bank.
> Someone came and sporting birds disappeared;
> A boat crossed, and green duckweed sank.
> The moss, trembling, tells me where the fish are;
> My line, being paid out, I know the depths of the pool.
> Vainly I sigh, and under the tempting bait
> Alone I watch the presence of greedy hearts.[65]

The unrelenting parallelism of this poem is typical of Chinese, though not of Japanese, expression; and the poem itself was derived almost verbatim from "Poem on my Fishing Pole," by the sixth-century Chinese poet Chang Cheng-chien.[66] But even in poems that are less obviously derived from Chinese originals, mechanical parallelism is often at work, as in a poem by Uneme Hirafu, a court official of the early eighth century. The poem opens:

> When he discusses the Way, he is the equal of T'ang;
> When he speaks of Virtue, he is neighbor to Yü.
> He caps the charity of Chou who buried the corpse;
> He outdoes the goodness of Yin who opened the nets . . .[67]

These lines, in praise of a Japanese emperor, reveal less of his character than the familiarity of the poet with the proper Chinese literary allusions. When composing a kanshi it was not enough to write grammatically accurate and metrically correct Chinese, difficult though this was for a Japanese; the poet had to allude to Chinese poetry of the past and demonstrate also his knowledge of Chinese history. Uneme Hirafu's poem refers to the command of King Wen of Chou who, after the corpse of an unknown man had been dug up in the process of enlarging a pond, ordered that it be reinterred in a deeper place; and to the mercy of King T'ang of Yin who opened the bird nets to permit the birds to escape. There is something contrived about these efforts, bringing to mind an English schoolboy painfully including in his Latin poem mention of Philomel or of the wise Cato. Yet for Japanese courtiers of the eighth century composing poetry in Chinese was no mere affectation; if the poem won approbation at the court, it might even lead to a promotion.

Few poems described specifically Japanese scenes, though one by Fujiwara no Fuhito (659–720), a high-ranking courtier, told of a visit to Yoshino, the site of a summer palace, and even incorporated legends of two Japanese ladies of the past.[68] Other poems refer in their titles to banquets given in honor of visitors from Korea or to excursions to various places, but most of the *Kaifūsō* poems are hardly more than pastiches of familiar Chinese imagery.

One distinctly Japanese aspect of the collection, however, is the title itself, an early expression of the nostalgia for the past that typifies not only these poems but much of Japanese literature. The unsigned preface nostalgically described the glorious reign of the Emperor Tenji in these terms:

> The great dignitaries had surcease from their labors; the palace galleries knew much leisure. At times the emperor summoned men of letters; often great banquets were held. On these occasions the imperial brush let fall prose; the courtiers offered their eulogies in verse. Many more than a hundred were the pieces of chiselled prose and exquisite calligraphy. But, with the passage of time, disorders reduced all these writings to ashes. How heart-rending it is to think of the destruction!
>
> In later times men of letters occasionally appeared. A prince, a dragon apparent, made cranes soar in the clouds with his brush; an emperor, phoenix-like, floated his moonlit boat on misty waters. . . .
>
> My minor position at the court has permitted me the leisure to let my fancy wander in the garden of letters and to read the works left by the men of former days. When I recall now those sports with the moon and poetry, how blurred are my remembrances—yet the words left by old brushes remain. As I go over the titles of the poems my thoughts are carried far away, and the tears flow without my being aware. As I lift the lovely compositions, my mind searches the distant past, and I long for those voices that now are stilled. . . .
>
> Since my reason for compiling this anthology was to save from oblivion the poetry of the great men of former days, I think it proper to call the collection *Kaifū*—Fond Reminiscences.[69]

By the middle of the eighth century Chinese civilization had come to exert immense influence over Japan. Native traditions seemed incapable of resisting the overwhelming prestige of the older culture. A rough parallel can be drawn with the situation in the 1870s and 1880s, when the Japanese manifested an almost indiscriminate fascination with European ways. In both instances a reaction set in, but the reaction was not so great as to sweep away the received foreign influences. Indeed, for the next eleven hundred and more years after the founding of the capital at Nara, the model remained China, and although some writers insisted on the importance of indigenous institutions, they continued to use Chinese characters, and they never forgot what they had learned from China. Even Shintō, the native religion, was bolstered with Chinese concepts and terminology (largely Taoist) in order to help it survive the competition offered by Buddhism and Confucianism. The Japanese, having undergone the baptism of Chinese culture, would not return to their primeval state.

Notes

1. The frequent shifting of the capital may also have been occasioned by the custom that required the crown prince, who lived with his mother (the chief of the emperor's many wives), to establish his capital at his mother's residence when he succeeded to the throne.
2. See Robert Karl Reischauer, *Early Japanese History*, I, pp. 169–70.
3. George Sansom, *A History of Japan to 1334*, p. 82.
4. The three characters are normally pronounced *fūdoki*, but the *Go-on* pronunciation was followed in this instance. The word means, literally, "account of winds and earth."
5. Nothing is known about this man, but it has been conjectured on the basis of his surname that he may have been of Korean extraction. See Michiko Yamaguchi Aoki, *Izumo Fudoki*, p. 145.
6. Aoki, *Izumo Fudoki*, pp. 82–83.
7. Aoki, *Izumo Fudoki*, p. 115.
8. The gazetteer for the province of Hitachi was compiled between 718 and 723. See Akimoto Kichirō (ed.), *Fudoki*, p. 27.
9. *Ibid*., p. 61. Although *yoku* and *Esaki* do not seem much alike, the same character was used to begin both words, and the old pronunciation of *e* and *yo* was probably closer than it is today.
10. Akimoto, *Fudoki*, p. 49.
11. *Ibid.*
12. Some quotations in the *Nihon Shoki* may have come from the *Tsukushi Fudoki*, which survives today only in fragments. See Kojima Noriyuki, "Kaisetsu," in Sakamoto Tarō et al. (eds.), *Nihon Shoki*, I, p. 15.

13. For an explanation in English of the difference between the two names, see Sakamoto Tarō, *The Six National Histories of Japan*, 30–33. A fuller account is given in Kojima, "Kaisetsu," in Sakamoto et al., *Nihon Shoki*, I, pp. 3–6. The oldest references to the work are to *Nihongi*, and the continuation was called *Shoku Nihongi*, but the old manuscripts uniformly bear the title *Nihon Shoki*. The difference would seem to have been based on which type of Chinese historical writing was being followed: those called *shu* (*sho* in Japanese), exemplified by the *Han Shu* or *Hou Han Shu*, were more comprehensive than the chronicles known as *chi* (*ki* in Japanese). The *Nihon Shoki*, whose name combined both *shu* and *chi*, is in thirty books like the *Han Chi* or *Hou Han Chi*, suggesting that they, rather than the *Han Shu*, were the models; but perhaps the compilers desired to make their books more than a mere chronology and therefore called it *Nihon Sho*. This was the theory of Kanda Kiichirō, who believed that someone, noticing that the *Nihon Sho*, despite its title, had failed to include biographies in the manner of a standard Chinese history, added the word *ki* to make *shoki*. See Kojima, "Kaisetsu," p. 5; also Yamada Hideo, *Nihon Shoki*, pp. 48–50.
14. Kojima, "Kaisetsu," p. 6.
15. Some reference works give the date as 682, presumably because of confusion over exactly when Temmu's reign began. Sakamoto (*The Six National Histories*, p. xi) favored the 681 date.
16. Sakamoto et al., *Nihon Shoki*, II, pp. 445–46. Translation by Aston, *Nihongi*, II, p. 350. See also Sakamoto, *The Six*, p. 34.
17. Yamada, *Nihon Shoki*, p. 28.
18. Kojima Noriyuki, on the basis of stylistic mannerisms, such as the use of Chinese particles of speech, believed he could distinguish at least ten "groups" among the compilers of the *Nihon Shoki*. He felt sure that some authors were responsible for a single book, others for as many as ten of the total of thirty books. Certain books combine the stylistic features of several different hands, suggesting a division of labor. See Kojima, "Kaisetsu," p. 11.
19. Kojima, "Kaisetsu," p. 20.
20. Ōno Susumu, "Kaisetsu," in Sakamoto et al., *Nihon Shoki*, I, p. 35. (The "Kaisetsu" to the volumes of *Nihon Shoki* in the Nihon Koten Bungaku Taikei series, edited by Sakamoto Tarō, Ienaga Saburō, Inoue Mitsusada, and Ōno Susumu, was written by three men—Kojima Noriyuki, Ōno Susumu, and Ienaga Saburō.)
21. We know that such lectures were given in 812, 843, 878, 904, 936, and 965, and memoranda (*shiki*) were prepared for each session on how the texts should be read. The 843 lectures apparently had as their chief purpose the establishment of authoritative Japanese readings. See Ōno, "Kaisetsu," p. 36.
22. Yamada, *Nihon Shoki*, p. 56; Kojima, "Kaisetsu," pp. 16–17. The Paekche

works quoted in the *Nihon Shoki* are (in Japanese rendering) *Kudara Ki*, *Kudara Shinsen*, and *Kudara Hongi*. See Sakamoto, *The Six*, pp. 48–49, for further information on these sources.

23. The dating was by cyclical characters. According to the *yin-yang* divination, practiced in Japan from early times, there were two "revolutionary" years in the cycle of sixty when great changes were likely to occur, the first and the fifty-seventh. No doubt that was why the "coronation" of the Emperor Jimmu was recorded as having occurred on the first day of the first month of a *shin-yū* year, the fifty-seventh of the cycle, corresponding to 660 B.C. This became the starting point for calculating dates of early Japanese history. See Ryusaku Tsunoda et al., *Sources of the Japanese Tradition*, pp. 57–59.
24. Sakamoto et al., *Nihon Shoki*, I, pp. 76 and 547. These three gods were created by the *yang* spirit only, with no admixture of *yin*. See also Aston, *Nihongi*, I, p. 4.
25. A variant text (Sakamoto et al., *Nihon Shoki*, I, p. 82; also Aston, *Nihongi*, I, p. 15) mentions the leech child, and the main text also mentions his birth, unexplained, soon afterward.
26. Sakamoto et al., *Nihon Shoki*, I, p. 84. The translation by Aston in *Nihongi*, I, p. 17, is in Latin.
27. Sakamoto et al., *Nihon Shoki*, I, p. 87. Aston, *Nihongi*, I, p. 18.
28. The *Kojiki* version is given as a variant tradition in the *Nihon Shoki*. See Sakamoto et al., *Nihon Shoki*, I, p. 95; also Aston, *Nihongi*, I, pp. 27–28.
29. Sakamoto et al., *Nihon Shoki*, I, p. 101. Also Aston, *Nihongi*, I, pp. 32–33.
30. Sakamoto et al., *Nihon Shoki*, I, p. 102. Aston, *Nihongi*, I, p. 32.
31. One of the rare attempts to consider the *Nihon Shoki* and five other early histories composed in Chinese—the *Rikkokushi*—as literature was made by Sakamoto Tarō in *Koten to Rekishi*, pp. 1–17. Sakamoto insisted that the separation between works of literary and historical intent observed today did not exist in the past, and that works of obvious literary intent, such as the *Shih Ching* (Book of Poetry), were read as historical sources. On the other hand, the compilers of the *Nihon Shoki* and the five later histories were trained not only in Chinese historiography but in works that we consider literary, and incorporated both aspects of their training when writing these histories. Sakamoto's point is well taken, but this is still a far cry from claiming that, say, the *Montoku Jitsuroku*, the fifth of the six histories, is of literary interest.
32. For the *kokugaku* movement see my *World Within Walls*, pp. 301–3, 310–30.
33. Sakamoto et al., *Nihon Shoki*, II, p. 173. Takeda Yūkichi, *Nihon Shoki*, IV, p. 221. Translation adapted from Aston, *Nihongi*, II, p. 122. Eji arrived in Japan from the Korean kingdom of Koguryo in 595, and remained there for twenty years before returning to his country, where he transmitted the text of Shōtoku's commentary on the Lotus Sutra. He died in

622. Nothing is known about Kakuka, but his name and rank of *hakase* (doctor) indicate he was either Chinese or Korean.

34. See Ogura Toyofumi, *Shōtoku Taishi to Shōtoku Taishi Shinkō*, pp. 1–104.

35. Takeda, *Nihon Shoki*, IV, pp. 264–65. See also Aston, *Nihongi*, II, p. 148.

36. Ogura, *Shōtoku*, pp. 57–60, discusses the origins of the cult of Shōtoku, which he places in the Hakuhō era in the latter part of the seventh century. The famous portrait of Shōtoku and two attendants (nephews?), now in the Imperial Household collection, dates from the same period, but may be a generalized portrait of a nobleman, rather than specifically a portrait of Shōtoku. See *ibid.*, p. 59.

37. Yokota Ken'ichi, in "Jūshichijō Kempō no Ichi Kōsatsu," compared the frequency of certain key words used in the Constitution with their appearances in other sections of the *Nihon Shoki*, and also compared the view of the state as expressed in the Constitution. Although he reached no definite conclusions, Yokota demonstrated that the language and thought of the Constitution were distinctive, and that they did not resemble those of the periods of the alleged forgers. He called attention (p. 216), moreover, to the somewhat similar edict in six articles proclaimed in 544 by Yu-wen T'ai (505–556) of the short-lived Western Wei dynasty, a document that Prince Shōtoku might have seen. However, an examination of this edict, written by Su Ch'o (498–546), reveals only casual similarities; it consists mainly of moral injunctions on the necessity for the ruler to put into practice the Way of Confucianism. See Chauncey S. Goodrich, *Biography of Su Ch'o*, pp. 16–36.

38. The word *kempō*, which was used also for the Meiji Constitution, obviously had a different meaning in Shōtoku's time. Perhaps Aston's "moral maxims" (*Nihongi*, II, p. 128) is closer than "constitution" to the meaning of the word, though *ken* and *hō*, from which *kempō* is formed, both mean "law."

39. Text in Sakamoto et al., *Nihon Shoki*, II, pp. 180–82; Takeda, *Nihon Shoki*, IV, pp. 232–36. Translation adapted from Aston, *Nihongi*, II, p. 129, and Tsunoda et al., *Sources*, p. 50.

40. From *Analects*, I, 12. The passage is also found in *Li Chi*, but in neither case does it specifically refer to harmony among men. Arthur Waley, in his translation *The Analects of Confucius*, p. 86, gives: "In the usages of ritual it is harmony that is prized; the Way of the Former Kings from this got its beauty." Waley supplied a note on harmony, stating that it meant harmony between man and nature, as exemplified by playing the musical mode that harmonized with the season, wearing seasonal clothes, eating seasonal food, and the like. The difference in usage between *wa* in Shōtoku's Constitution and in the *Analects* has suggested to some scholars that Shōtoku used this Confucian term in a Buddhist sense. See Sakamoto et al., *Nihon Shoki*, II, p. 181.

41. Tsunoda, *Sources*, pp. 39–44, gives a selection of passages from the *Nihon Shoki* that reveal the civil strife in Japan at the time.
42. Sakamoto et al., *Nihon Shoki*, II, p. 184. Translation in Tsunoda, *Sources*, p. 52; also Aston, *Nihongi*, II, p. 131.
43. Shuichi Kato, in *A History of Japanese Literature*, translated by David Chibbett, p. 33, states, "The Seventeen Articles . . . even when read in the Japanese as opposed to the Chinese style, must be regarded as a splendid piece of prose."
44. For example, one passage in his commentary to the Vimalakïrti Sutra has been traced to a Chinese work composed thirty-six years after Shōtoku's death, evidence that he could not have written it; but this passage may have been a later interpolation. Other evidence has been adduced that strengthens the likelihood of his authorship. See Nakamura Hajime, "Shōtoku Taishi to Nara Bukkyō," pp. 73–74.
45. The *Kojiki* ends with the barely stated account of the reign of the Empress Suiko (588–628), but the *Nihon Shoki* continues until the abdication of the Empress Jitō in 697.
46. The Empress Jingū is officially known as a *kōgō* (empress consort), rather than as a *tennō* (emperor or empress), but the *Nihon Shoki* treats her in every respect as an empress regnant.
47. *Wei Shih* was compiled by Ch'en Shou (233–297).
48. Translation based on Sakamoto et al., *Nihon Shoki*, I, p. 351. See also Ryusaku Tsunoda and L. Carrington Goodrich, *Japan in the Chinese Dynastic Histories,* p. 14, and Aston, *Nihongi*, I, p. 245.
49. For example, the date should be the second year of Ching-ch'u, and the name of the governor was Liu Hsia and not Teng Hsia.
50. See Aston, *Nihongi*, I, pp. 224–53. Aston, following Japanese practice of his time, refers to her as Jingō, but Jingū is now preferred.
51. Tsunoda and Goodrich, *Japan*, pp. 14–15. An even older gold seal, apparently presented by the Han emperor to the king of Wa in A.D. 57, was unearthed in northern Kyūshū in 1784.
52. This is true of the accounts in the *Tsin Shu*, *Liang Shu*, and *Nan Shih*. (See Tsunoda and Goodrich, *Japan*, p. vi.) The *Han Shu*, though it describes a dynasty earlier than the Wei, was actually written 150 years later, but contains no original information about Japan.
53. Tsunoda and Goodrich, *Japan*, p. 31.
54. *Ibid.*, p. 31.
55. *Ibid.*, p. 32.
56. *Ibid.*
57. Sakamoto et al., *Nihon Shoki*, II, p. 192. Aston, *Nihongi*, II, p. 139. The *Nihon Shoki* text states: "The Emperor of the East respectfully addresses the Emperor of the West." The Japanese emperor is called *tennō*, and the Chinese emperor *kōtei*. In the letter, as given in the Chinese source, both emperors are called *tenshi* (son of heaven).

58. Tsunoda and Goodrich, *Japan*, p. 50.
59. *Ibid*., p. 51. See also Aston, *Nihongi*, II, p. 122.
60. So stated in the preface, but extant texts lack several poems.
61. See Burton Watson, *Japanese Literature in Chinese*, I, p. 9.
62. *Ibid*., I, p. 18. The text in the Nihon Koten Bungaku Taikei series edited by Kojima Noriyuki, *Kaifūsō, Bunka Shūrei Shū Honchō Monzui*, p. 77, has a somewhat different last line.
63. Poem 416 (Book III) of the *Man'yōshū*. See Takagi Ichinosuke et al., *Man'yōshū*, I, p. 199.
64. Translation adapted from *The Manyōshū* (Nippon Gakujutsu Shinkōkai translation), p. 19.
65. Kojima, *Kaifūsō*, p. 95. See also Watson, *Japanese*, I, p. 20.
66. Watson, *Japanese*, I, p. 20. Kojima, *Kaifūsō*, p. 95, also labels the poem a plagiarism. The first two lines of the poem by Chang Cheng-chien will suggest the similarities: *I built my hut by the long river; / I dropped my hook from the wide river bank*. . . . Apart from minor changes in vocabulary, the only difference between the two poems is that Suemochi's poem omits four lines of the source. (See Kojima, *Kaifūsō*, p. 454.)
67. Kojima, *Kaifūsō*, pp. 109–10.
68. *Ibid*., pp. 100, 455–56.
69. Tsunoda et al., *Sources*, pp. 91–92.

Bibliography

Note: All Japanese books, except as otherwise noted, were published in Tokyo.

Akimoto Kichirō (ed.). *Fudoki*, in Nihon Koten Bungaku Taikei series. Iwanami Shoten, 1958.

Aoki, Michiko Yamaguchi. *Izumo Fudoki*. Sophia University, 1971.

Aston, W. G. (trans.). *Nihongi*, 2 vols. London: Kegan Paul, 1896.

Goodrich, Chauncey S. *Biography of Su Ch'o*. Berkeley: University of California Press, 1961.

Ichikawa Mototarō. *Nihon Kambungakushi Gaisetsu*. Daian, 1969.

Inoue Mitsusada. "Nihon Shoki no Seiritsu to Kaishaku no Rekishi," in *Nihon Shoki*, Nihon no Meicho series. Chūō Kōron Sha, 1971.

Kasai Masaaki. "Jōdaishi Kenkyū Nempyō oyobi Kaisetsu," *Nihon Shoki Kenkyū* 3, 1968.

Kato, Shuichi. *A History of Japanese Literature*, translated by David Chibbett. Tokyo: Kodansha International, 1981.

Kojima Noriyuki. *Jōdai Nihon Bungaku to Chūgoku Bungaku*, 2 vols. Hanawa Shobō, 1962–65.

———. *Kaifūsō, Bunka Shūrei Shū, Honchō Monzui*, in Nihon Koten Bungaku Taikei series. Iwanami Shoten, 1964.

———. "Kaisetsu," in Sakamoto Tarō et al., *Nihon Shoki*.

Kurumisawa Ryūkichi. *Wayaku Shishū Kaifūsō*. Gakutōsha, 1972.

The Manyōshū, translation of the Nippon Gakujutsu Shinkōkai. New York: Columbia University Press, 1965.

Nakamura Hajime. "Shōtoku Taishi to Nara Bukkyō," in *Shōtoku Taishi*, Nihon no Meicho series. Chūō Kōron Sha, 1970.

Ogura Toyofumi. *Shōtoku Taishi to Shōtoku Taishi Shinkō*. Kyoto: Sōgeisha, 1972.

Okada Masayuki. *Ōmi Nara Chō no Kambungaku*. Tamba-shi: Yōtokusha, 1946.

Ōno Susumu. "Kaisetsu," in Sakamoto Tarō et al., *Nihon Shoki*.

Reischauer, Robert Karl. *Early Japanese History*. Princeton: Princeton University Press, 1937.

Sakamoto Tarō. *Koten to Rekishi*. Yoshikawa Kōbunkan, 1977.

———. *The Six National Histories of Japan*, trans. John S. Brownlee. Vancouver: University of British Columbia Press, 1991.

Sakamoto Tarō, Ienaga Saburō, Inoue Mitsusada, and Ōno Susumu (eds.). *Nihon Shoki*, 2 vols., in Nihon Koten Bungaku Taikei series. Iwanami Shoten, 1967.

Sansom, George. *A History of Japan to 1334*. Stanford, Calif.: Stanford University Press, 1958.

Takagi Ichinosuke, Gomi Tomohide, and Ōno Susumu, *Man'yōshū*, I, in Nihon Koten Bungaku Taikei series. Iwanami Shoten, 1957.

Takeda Yūkichi. *Nihon Shoki*, 6 vols., in Nihon Koten Bungaku Zensho series. Asahi Shimbun Sha, 1948–57.

Tanaka Tsuguhito. "Hasseiki Zempan ni okeru Shōtoku Taishi Shinkō no Jittai," *Koten Kenkyū* (Gangōji), ii, 1977.

———. "Shōtoku Taishi-den no Seiri," *Nihon Shoki Kenkyū*, 11, 1979.

Tomoda Kichinosuke. *Nihon Shoki Seiritsu no Kenkyū*. Kasama Shoin, 1969.

Tsunoda, Ryusaku, Wm. Theodore de Bary, and Donald Keene. *Sources of Japanese Tradition*. New York: Columbia University Press, 1958.

Tsunoda, Ryusaku, and L. Carrington Goodrich. *Japan in the Chinese Dynastic Histories*. South Pasadena, Calif.: P. D. Perkins, 1951.

Ueda Masaaki. *Fudoki*. Kyōto: Shakai Shisō Sha, 1975.

Waley, Arthur. *The Analects of Confucius*. London: George Allen and Unwin, 1938.

Watson, Burton. *Japanese Literature in Chinese*, I. New York: Columbia University Press, 1975.

Yamada Hideo. *Nihon Shoki*. Kyōikusha, 1979.

Yamagishi Tokuhei. *Nihon Kambungakushi Ronkō*. Iwanami Shoten, 1974.

Yokota Ken'ichi. "Jūshichijō Kempō no Ichi Kōsatsu," *Nihon Shoki Kenkyū* 3, 1968.

3. THE *MAN'YŌSHŪ*

The *Man'yōshū*[1] is the first and, in the opinion of most who have written about Japanese literature, the finest collection of Japanese poetry. It is the richest in terms of the variety of poetic forms and subjects, and the poets included members of different social classes, though later collections consisted almost exclusively of poetry composed at the court. Above all, it is the intensity of the emotions expressed that imparts immediacy and strength to the poetry. Later Japanese poets often relied on suggestion to amplify what could be explicitly stated in verse forms as short as the waka or the haiku. A combination of statement and suggestion gives the *Man'yōshū* its unique place among anthologies of Japanese poetry.

The level of accomplishment of even the early poems is so much higher than that of the songs in the *Kojiki*, the *Nihon Shoki*, and other early works[2] that it comes rather as a shock to realize that many were composed well before the compilation of the *Kojiki* in 712. Indeed, connections between the poetry in the *Kojiki* and the *Nihon Shoki* and those in the *Man'yōshū* have been demonstrated.[3] Probably the *Man'yōshū* poems, like those in the *Kojiki*, were originally sung; the word *uta* meant both "song" and "poem."[4] Again, the *Kojiki* and *Man'yōshū* poems have both been praised for their simple, "masculine" style. There is, however, a world of difference between the two: many *Man'yōshū* poems were silently absorbed into later collections without disturbing the prevailing "feminine" mood, but few *Kojiki* poems could be introduced into the *Man'yōshū*, let alone later collections, without jarring. Unquestionably, the forms of the waka[5] and *sedōka* poems in the *Kojiki* also exercised influence on the composition of *Man'yōshū* poetry, but we are likely to be more aware of the dissimilarities separating the primitive utterances of the *Kojiki* from the magnificent poetry of the *Man'yōshū*, notably the long poems by Kakinomoto no Hitomaro, whose entire oeuvre was completed before the compilation of the *Kojiki*.

Political and social developments within the country, as well as new conceptions of the functions of poetry, help to explain the differences between the poetry of the *Kojiki* and of the *Man'yōshū*. The beginnings of the *Man'yōshū* have been traced by some scholars to a political event, the Taika Reform of 645–46,[6] an attempt to put into practice in Japan the systems of land tenure, provincial government, and taxation then in operation in China.[7] The elimination of the power of the chieftains, who had hitherto ruled almost independently of the emperor, and the establishment of an absolute monarchy along Chinese lines were part of a massive effort to strengthen the country. The rise of the powerful T'ang dynasty (618–907) represented a threat to Japanese security, the magnitude of which was fully perceived in 660, fifteen years after the Taika Reform, when the Chinese conquered the Korean kingdom of Paekche.

The Reform was a desperate attempt to "modernize" the country by political and social measures, but the Japanese were aware that it was not enough to consolidate the administration; they would have to establish themselves in the eyes of the Chinese as a civilized country. The Japanese, though proud of their own traditions, were well aware that unless they absorbed Chinese civilization they would be considered to be no better than barbarians and as such would be subject to "civilizing missions" that might even take the form of invasion. Fortunately for the Japanese, the Chinese conquest of Paekche led to a flood of refugees making their way to Japan. These refugees included men who were educated in Chinese learning, and they became tutors to the Japanese upper class.[8] It has been suggested that Yamanoue no Okura, one of the finest *Man'yōshū* poets, was originally a refugee from Paekche.[9]

The absorption of Chinese learning, which may in the first instance have been undertaken largely in the hopes of strengthening the country, enormously enriched Japanese poetry. The parallelism typical of Hitomaro's major poems was almost certainly inspired by Chinese poetry, and his realization of the importance of imparting a unified meaning to a poem, not a matter of much concern to the *Kojiki* poets, marked the change from folk poetry to the poetry of individual poets who had mastered their craft.

New themes, new modes of expression, and new uses of poetry were quickly naturalized, but the Japanese remained reluctant to borrow Chinese words for use in Japanese poetry.[10] When, for example, the Japanese came to celebrate the Chinese festival commemorating the two stars that meet once a year, the seventh night of the seventh moon, they called the occasion by a Japanese name, Tanabata, and carefully avoided terminology that might suggest the festival had foreign origins.

The oldest surviving texts of the *Man'yōshū* indicate that Japanese pronunciations were intended throughout, even when the underlying conceptions of poems were directly borrowed from China. With two exceptions, the only words pronounced in approximations of Chinese sounds are found in the heavily Buddhist Book XVI.[11] The fact that almost all the dozen or so words in the *Man'yōshū* given Sino-Japanese pronunciations were related to Buddhism does not mean, however, that they were always used in pious contexts. The following "poem of ridicule," addressed to a priest, and his reply, both in Book XVI, demonstrate the contrary:

hōshira ga	Do not tether a horse
hige no sorikui	To the stubble
uma tsunagi	Of my new-shaven priest's chin,
itaku na hiki so	And pull too hard!
hōshi wa nakan	For, poor priest, he will cry.[12]

THE PRIEST'S REPLY

dan'ochi ya	Oh, say not that!
shika mo na ii so	You too will cry,
sato osa ga	Good parishioner,
edachi hataraba	When the village master comes
imashi mo nakan	To collect the taxes.[13]

In the above poems the words *hōshi* (priest) and *dan'ochi* (parishioner) are given in Sino-Japanese pronunciation. Such Chinese material things as "incense" or "pagoda" occur in several poems of humorous intent where the intrusion of an unfamiliar foreign word may have contributed a comic note to an otherwise purely Japanese context.[14] In any case, only a tiny fraction of the 6,343 different words in the *Man'yōshū* were pronounced in Sino-Japanese fashion, though many poems, whether secular or Buddhist, reveal Chinese influence.[15] A few words such as *ume* ("plum," Chinese *mei*) and *yanagi* ("willow," Chinese *yang*) represent earlier borrowings that by this time had been assimilated into the Japanese language.

The fact that (with extremely few exceptions) the words of the poems were intended to be pronounced in Japanese meant that, in the absence of a native Japanese system of writing, Chinese characters were used to transcribe Japanese sounds. Characters were sometimes used as phonograms, in the manner of the poems in the *Kojiki*, but often also for their meaning. The use of two essentially different systems of writing was mercifully superseded with the invention of the *kana* in the ninth century, but the change in writing meant that *Man'yōshū* poems that were not known orally tended to become obscure or even indecipherable. For centuries not even the most learned scholars could read the *Man'yōshū*, and some poems have yet to be given definitive pronunciations.[16] Moreover, even when the individual words of a poem can be ascertained, the sense of the whole is sometimes elusive. Certain poems that seem to be no more than lyrical cries from the poet's heart have been analyzed with such care (and imagination) that to read all the researches on a single poem may take weeks of study.

The meaning of even the title has engaged specialists for centuries. The three ideograms used to represent *man-yō-shū* mean literally "Ten Thousand Leaves Collection," and it has often been stated that this was a figurative way of referring to the large number of poems in the collection (*shū*), some 4,516 poems in all.[17] "Ten thousand" (*man*), like the English word "myriad," was used to express an indefinitely large number. Another theory is that "leaf" (*yō*) stood for *kotoba* or the earlier *koto no ha*, meaning "leaves of words," and yielding the similar meaning of a "collection of ten thousand words," but the term *koto no ha* seems not to have existed at the time of the compilation of the *Man'yōshū*.[18]

Still another theory, advanced originally by scholars of Chinese literature, was that "ten thousand leaves" was used to mean "ten thousand ages," an expression found not only in numerous Chinese works but in the *Nihon Shoki* and other early Japanese texts composed in Chinese.[19] This seems the most probable explanation, but it does not entirely solve the problem of the title: should the title be interpreted as a "collection of ten thousand ages" (that is, an exaggerated description of the perhaps four hundred years of poetry included in the *Man'yōshū*) or as a "collection to last ten thousand years," a somewhat immodest claim? The great authority on Japanese literature, Origuchi Shinobu (1887–1953), offered still another interpretation: that "ten thousand years" represented a conventional prayer that the sovereign would enjoy a reign of that duration.[20]

The compiler and the time of compilation of the *Man'yōshū* have also been much debated. The work lacks a preface or similar document describing the compilation, and scholars have therefore had to rely on old records or else on clues within the poems themselves in their efforts to determine even the most basic facts. The earliest theory concerning the compiler was given in the eleventh-century chronicle *Eiga Monogatari* (A Tale of Flowering Fortunes), where it is reported that the Empress Kōken in 753 commanded Tachibana no Moroe, the minister of the Left, to compile the *Man'yōshū*.[21] In the thirteenth century the priest Senkaku (c. 1200–1272), who devoted much of his life to the study of the *Man'yōshū*, accepted Moroe as the compiler. However, scholars of the Tokugawa period decided on the basis of internal evidence that the compiler was the poet Ōtomo no Yakamochi.[22]

The most positively worded opinion was that of the priest and National Learning scholar Keichū (1640–1701), who wrote,

> This was not an imperially sponsored collection (*chokusenshū*), nor was Moroe the compiler. Yakamochi, aged twenty-seven or twenty-eight at the time, chose and determined the contents of volumes I to XVI by about 744–45, transcribing poems that he had read and heard since the days of his youth. He brought together the legacy of the past, ending with the poem in Book XVII dated the fifth day of the fifth moon of 744. . . . He continued his work of gradually assembling poems until he reached the end of Book XX. . . . It was not until 759 that he completed his compilation.[23]

The last dated poem in the *Man'yōshū* was indeed composed in 759, and the identification of Ōtomo no Yakamochi as the chief compiler is generally accepted today; but the compilers of individual volumes and the time that the text assumed its present form are still disputed.[24] Origuchi reached the conclusion that the final compilation took place during the reign of the Emperor Heizei (806–809), who was known as the "Nara emperor" because of his attachment to the old capital. Origuchi placed the compilation at this point because Yakamochi, who died in the eighth moon of 785, was stripped of his rank in the following month when members of his family were implicated in the murder of the Middle Councillor Fujiwara no Tanetsugu. Yakamochi was not involved in the crime, but he was posthumously dishonored all the same, and not until 806, when the Emperor Kammu on his deathbed pardoned him and restored his rank, could a work so closely associated with Yakamochi be publicly recognized.[25]

The vast majority of the more than 4,000 poems in the *Man'yōshū* are waka, but the masterpieces of the collection are the 265 chōka, or long poems. There are also 62 sedōka and some poems in nontraditional forms, including 4 in Chinese. The oldest poem in the collection, if we can accept the attribution, is the first, said to have been composed by the Emperor Yūryaku (reigned 457–79).

The *Man'yōshū* is unique, first of all, in its variety of poetic forms. It is true that the chōka was vestigially preserved in the *Kokinshū*, but in the *Man'yōshū* this form attained its highest development, and it would never again serve as the medium of the best poetry of its time. The sedōka, which soon became obsolete, was still functional in the hands of the *Man'yōshū* poets but would later become merely a curiosity. There is also one poem in the *Man'yōshū* in the distinctive *bussokuseki-tai* or "style of the footprint of the Buddha," referring to the poems in 5, 7, 5, 7, 7, and 7 syllables carved into the stone representation of the footprint of the Buddha consecrated in 749 at the Yakushi-ji in Nara.[26] The variety of poetic forms contributes to the appeal of the *Man'yōshū*, especially to the Western reader who is likely to be daunted by the more normal collections of thousands of poems, all in the form of the waka.

The diversity of forms is emphasized by the exceptionally rich vocabulary of the *Man'yōshū*. Some words occur in no later poetry; it would seem that the court poets found many items of vocabulary insufficiently elegant to be employed in their compositions. The meanings of some items of vocabulary, notably the makurakotoba, words or phrases that often function as fixed epithets before the names of places, can also be obscure.[27] The syntax is likely to be involved, perhaps necessarily so: a chōka that is less than tightly constructed quickly drops into prose.

The subject matter of *Man'yōshū* poetry is also more varied than in later collections. There are many poems about love (as was true also of the *Kojiki*), others describe nature and the passing of the seasons, and many poems relate to travel. These themes would recur in all collections, but certain subjects are unique to the *Man'yōshū*. The amplitude of expression, possible in a poem of thirty or forty lines, as opposed to the five of a waka, enabled the poets to compose narratives, elegies for deceased princes or princesses, congratulatory poems on events of national importance, or poems expressing grief over parting from one's family for the frontier in some distant province. These poems give the *Man'yōshū* its special cachet.

Many chronologically early poems in the *Man'yōshū* seem to be purely Japanese in origin, but the later poems reveal unmistakable influence from abroad: Taoist influence in the poems in praise of sake, Buddhist influence in the specifically religious poems, Confucian influence in the poems of Yamanoue no Okura, as well as a general influence of Chinese literature, which became increasingly familiar to Japanese.

The authorship of the poems is also more heterogeneous than that of the later anthologies. Many of the poets served at the court, but there are also poems by frontier guards, by people of the eastern provinces, and by many unidentified persons. It is possible that some poems, ostensibly by commoners, were actually composed by courtiers in the guise of farmers or soldiers, but the poems seem genuine.

These factors distinguish the *Man'yōshū* from later collections of poetry, but perhaps its chief distinction is that—unlike the poems in later collections that may be marvels of mood and suggestion but are too brief to state much—the *Man'yōshū* poems are usually direct in their statements of the poet's emotions. The scholars of National Learning characterized the pervading tone of the *Man'yōshū* as *masuraoburi* ("manliness"), as opposed to the *tawayameburi* ("femininity") of the later collections. Modern scholars tend to reject such characterization as oversimplification, but the "manliness" of the *Man'yōshū*—real or imagined—undoubtedly contributed to its popularity during the war years of 1941–45, when the "spirit of the *Man'yōshū*" was frequently invoked and the "femininity" of the *Kokinshū* fell into disfavor. It is by no means difficult to find *Man'yōshū* poems that anticipate the "femininity" of later poetry, but the distinctive tone of the collection, sometimes also called its "simplicity" in contrast to the effete elegance of the Heian courtiers, is not wholly imagined. The combination of masculine and feminine, direct and indirect, stated and suggested, contributes importantly to the richness and universality of the *Man'yōshū*.

The particular strength of the *Man'yōshū* lies in the ability of the poets to treat the truly tragic, as opposed to the melancholic, the harshly dramatic, as opposed to the touching. There is a whole repertory of poems, for example, on such subjects as the poet's reflections upon seeing a dead body by the side of the road or on the shore. Dead bodies do not appear in the *Kokinshū* or *Shin Kokinshū*. The rules of good taste had come to dominate poetic composition, and if the falling of the cherry blossoms could stir an awareness of transcience similar to the sight of a corpse, it was clearly in better taste to write about cherry blossoms. Some poems on cherry blossoms do indeed convey so poignant a sense of the passing of time as to bring tears to the reader's eyes, but the dramatic impact of falling cherry blossoms is different from that of the sight of a corpse.

The *Man'yōshū* is in twenty books. The significance of this number is not known. Some believe it was an accidental result of a patchwork compilation appended at various times to an "*Ur-Man'yōshū*." The first two books may have been compiled by imperial commission and the later books added as the editor or editors thought appropriate.[28] The eventual format of twenty books would be arbitrary, but this accident determined the number of books in almost all subsequent imperially sponsored collections.[29]

The Early *Man'yōshū* (645–672)[30]

Nakanishi Susumu characterized the first period of the *Man'yōshū* as one dominated by *kotoba no onna* (women of words), a term he used to designate women, probably in their thirties or older, whose duties at court consisted chiefly of composing poetry on formal occasions, either in their own voices or as surrogates. They may also have been charged with preserving and reciting the poetry and tales of the past, in the manner attributed to Hieda no Are.[31] It may seem paradoxical that the *Man'yōshū*, usually treated as the most "masculine" of the anthologies of court poetry, should have been given its characteristic tone by women, but Nakanishi insisted that they were the central *Man'yōshū* poets during most periods;[32] the love poems that make up the bulk of *Man'yōshū* poems were either written by or to women, and male poets excelled only in the public poems. This suggests the danger of contrasting the *Man'yōshū* and later collections by using the convenient but inexact terms "masculine" and "feminine"; it might be better to speak in terms of "public" and "private" or perhaps (remembering masuraoburi and tawayameburi) in terms of "strong" and "sensitive."

The poems in the first book of the *Man'yōshū* are classified as *zōka* (miscellaneous poems) and those of the second book as *sōmon* (mutual inquiries) and *banka* (elegies). These remained the three principal categories of poetry throughout the collection. The most important category was the "mutual inquiries," an oblique way of referring to love poetry. Over half the poems in the *Man'yōshū* are about love. The love affairs described are generally unhappy and frustrated, and this would be true of most love poetry in the later anthologies. The elegies, often public poems that treat the deaths of members of the court, were presumably written in response to requests from the emperor or a high-ranking official; but some elegies are private, mourning the death of members of the poet's own family. The remaining poems—those that dealt neither with love nor death—were classified as "miscellaneous."[33] The term *zōka* seems to have been derived from the Chinese term *tsa-shih*, also meaning "miscellaneous poems," found in the *Wen Hsüan* and other collections of Chinese poetry.[34]

It is curious that Book I should have opened with "miscellaneous poems," suggesting that it consisted of leftovers that belonged to no category. Perhaps, as Nakanishi suggested, it was only after Book II had been classified into love poems and elegies that the compilers decided that the poems in Book I should also have a designation, and "miscellaneous" was the only term applicable to all.[35]

The poems in Book I are arranged in chronological order, beginning with a poem attributed to the Emperor Yūryaku. This poem, like the first in Book II, stands apart from others in the book. Yūryaku's is immediately followed by one by the Emperor Jomei (reigned 629–42), and the remaining poems of Book I (with the exception of a few late works appended at the end) were composed in the second half of the seventh century.

It is puzzling that a poem by the Emperor Yūryaku, described in the *Kojiki* mainly in terms of his brutality, and who lived 150 years before the other poets of Book I, should have been given such a prominent place. It has been suggested that Yūryaku's poem, in the irregular meter typical of *Kojiki* poetry, represented antiquity to the compilers of the *Man'yōshū*, and that they chose a work by an emperor who, if not admirable in his behavior, was both a warrior and a poet and, above all, a man successful in his love affairs.[36] The Emperor Jomei, the author of the second poem, was the successor to the Empress Suiko, the last sovereign mentioned in the *Kojiki*; the *Man'yōshū* can thus be interpreted as opening with a bow toward antiquity, after which it takes up where the *Kojiki* left off, presenting poems composed in the following reigns.[37]

The poem by Yūryaku at first glance seems to offer no problems of interpretation:

komo yo mikomochi
fukushi mochi mibukushi mochi
kono oka ni natsumasu ko
ie kikana nanorasa ne
sora mitsu Yamato no kuni wa
oshinabete ware koso ore
shikinabete ware koso imase
ware kosoba nanorame
ie wo mo no wo mo

Your basket, with your pretty basket
Your trowel, with your little trowel,
Maiden, picking herbs on this hill—
I would ask you: Where is your home?
Will you not tell me your name?
Over the spacious land of Yamato
It is I who reign so wide and far,
It is I who rule so wide and far.
I myself, as your lord, will tell you
Of my home and my name.[38]

A close examination of this pastorale reveals a number of complexities. Why, for example, does the emperor use honorifics when addressing the girl? We might suppose that he was just being polite, or that he was attempting to ingratiate himself with the girl, but scholars insist that there must be some special significance: the girl is either a priestess, to whom even an emperor must be polite, or else she is the daughter of a powerful chieftain whose lands the emperor covets. Those who believe that the girl is a priestess interpret the act of picking greens as one of ritual significance. The places where greens were picked, the time of day, and the amount picked were all ritually determined. Picking greens was an act of *tamafuri*, or summoning of the souls of the dead, and it was performed in the hopes of bringing back a loved one who had died; the emperor used honorifics because the girl was engaged in a sacred duty.[39]

Those who believe that the girl was the daughter of a chieftain must explain why the ruler of Yamato—of all Japan, one might suppose—should have felt obliged to dally with a mere chieftain's daughter in order to consolidate his territories. One authority's response to this challenge was to aver that Yamato was *not* another name for Japan or even for any well-defined administrative area, but merely designated the visible surroundings, or possibly some particular province.[40]

We proceed next to the questions the emperor asks the girl. Here the reconstruction of the original pronunciations presents special problems. The usual reconstruction from the Chinese characters is *ie norase, na norasane* ("Tell me your home, tell me your name"); but some prefer *ie kikan, na norasane* ("I would hear of your home, tell me your name.")[41] Apart from the academic interest in the correct pronunciation, there is the question of why the emperor wants to know the girl's name. This may seem so obvious as to require no explanation. But we are informed that primitive peoples show extreme reluctance to divulge their names because it is tantamount to giving other persons control over themselves.[42] Asking the girl's name was a bold, perhaps even an intimidating action.

At this point a break occurs. So far, the emperor has been addressing the girl, but the rest of the poem is concerned with who he is. This, again, offers no special problems for the casual reader; it is natural that the speaker, having asked the other person's name, should identify himself. But the fact that the poem consists of two parts has suggested to some commentators that it was originally a dance, perhaps even an embryonic drama.[43] The nature of this drama was explained at some length by Itō Haku, who believed that recognition by the reader of the break between the two parts of the poem was the most important factor in understanding the whole. According to Itō, the emperor asked the girl's name as an act of courtship, and if she had given her name it would have meant she had consented. In that case, Yūryaku would not have needed to continue his poem; but the fact that he felt it necessary to identify himself is an indication that she must have hesitated or refused outright to divulge her name. The emperor proclaimed his importance in order to persuade her to reconsider. He also implied that even if the girl were unwilling to reveal who she was, he was ready to make the first move. At this point, the girl acceded. The poem ends with the promise that the emperor and the girl will be united.[44] Itō interpreted the poem as a "primitive, ancient opera with Emperor Yūryaku for its hero."[45] The purpose of the opera was to celebrate the union of the emperor with the land (personified by the girl) and thereby to assure prosperity and a bountiful harvest.

Even if one accepts this interpretation, the final lines are still puzzling. Why should the emperor, having already identified himself as the ruler of the land, promise to tell the girl his name? Commentators, long troubled by this point, have attempted to find alternative readings for the Chinese characters that would permit a more logical conclusion to the poem. The linguist Ōno Susumu proposed the reading *ware ni koso wa norame ie wo mo* (Tell me, your lord, about your home).[46] This rendering of the final lines makes the poem read more logically, but it destroys the break which Itō, writing twenty years after Ōno, thought was the key to understanding the real meaning of the poem. Some specialists, going even further than Itō, have asserted that the poem not only contains a hiatus but was originally two independent poems. They argue that if the poem had been a unified expression of courtship, it would have been included among the "mutual inquiries" poems; but its place at the head of a book of "miscellaneous poems" indicates that the compiler did not consider it to be a love poem. Perhaps the original poem consisted of only the first half, in which the emperor addresses a girl who is picking sacred herbs; but in the process of oral transmission the second half, originally unrelated to the first, was appended, transforming the nature of the poem.[47]

Many *Man'yōshū* poems have been studied with all but fanatical care by scholars who have gladly consecrated their lives to elucidating troublesome points. The slightest variation in readings has been deemed worthy of a learned article, and there are specialized studies of the plants mentioned in the *Man'yōshū*, biographies (though firm facts are scarce) of the major poets, and detailed considerations of the religious and philosophical background.[48] Such publications sometimes provide new insights into the meanings the poems might have had for Japanese of the seventh and eighth centuries, but they seldom increase the literary enjoyment of modern readers. One further example from the early *Man'yōshū* will make this even clearer. It is the second poem, attributed to the Emperor Jomei.[49]

CLIMBING KAGU-YAMA AND LOOKING UPON THE LAND

Yamato ni wa	Countless are the mountains
murayama aredo	in Yamato,
toriyorou	but perfect is
Ame no Kaguyama	the heavenly hill of Kagu:
noboritachi	When I climb it
kunimi wo sureba	and survey my realm,
kunihara wa	Over the wide plain
keburi tachitatsu	the smoke wreaths rise and rise,
unahara wa	over the wide sea
kamame tachitatsu	the gulls are on the wing;
umashi kuni zo	a beautiful land it is,
Akitsushima	Akitsushima,
Yamato no kuni wa	the Land of Yamato.[50]

Even in translation one can sense the wonder and delight in the land; and the forward movement of the poem to the climax in *Yamato no kuni wa* may recall John of Gaunt's enumeration of the glories of his country, concluding with "This England!" Most readers will probably not feel the need of explanations, but commentators have not let this poem pass without scrutiny. Apart from a few questions of pronunciation, the meaning of the makurakotoba *toriyorou*, a hapax legomenon, has variously been defined as "sheathed" (as with armor) by vegetation, or as "perfect."[51] There are also several problems of interpretation. First, how was it possible for the emperor to observe the sea from the top of Mount Kagu, a hill only 148 meters high? Not only is the sea distant, but there are tall mountains intervening and blocking the view. It has been suggested that perhaps the emperor was referring not to the sea but to one of several ponds in the vicinity; alternatively, it has been opined that the emperor did not actually have to catch a glimpse of the sea in order to enter the mood of having seen it.[52] But if he saw a freshwater pond and not the sea, what of the gulls? The word *kamame* is usually interpreted as being a variant on *kamome*, the seagull. If the emperor had been looking at a pond, ducks would be more appropriate than seagulls; but *Man'yōshū* scholars, stopping at nothing in their passion for accuracy, report that seagulls have been sighted as far as twenty-five miles inland, and there is no reason why they could not have found their way to a pond at the foot of Mount Kagu.[53]

Again, the smoke seen by the emperor has often been interpreted as a reference to hearth fires, on the analogy of the passage from the *Kojiki* where the Emperor Nintoku, having climbed a tower, notices that no smoke is rising from the hearths of his people, and he remits taxes until he sees smoke rising once again. However, another theory has it that the "smoke" refers to mist hovering in pockets of the hills.[54] Even more recently, a scholar has suggested that the smoke is not from hearths but from campfires built in the fields by people celebrating the spring festival at which greens were gathered and made into a soup; the meal was followed by singing and an orgy. In support of this interpretation, reference is made to the poems written by Takahashi no Mushimaro on climbing Mount Tsukuba the day of a *kagai* (or *utagaki*), an exchange of amorous poems by men and women that was often followed by sexual intercourse:

washi no sumu	On Mount Tsukuba
Tsukuba no yama no	where eagles dwell,
Mohakitsu no	By the founts
sono tsu no ue ni	of Mohakitsu,
adomoite	Maidens and men,
odome otoko no	in troops assembling,
yukitsudoi	Hold a *kagai*, vying in poetry;
kagau kagai ni	I will seek company
hitozuma ni	With others' wives,
wa mo majirawan	Let others woo my own. . . .
wa ga tsuma ni	
hito mo kototoe[55]	

An anonymous poem also seems to refer to the ceremony:

Kasuga no ni	Yonder on the plain of Kasuga
kemuri tatsu miyu	I see wreaths of smoke arise—

otomera shi Are the young girls
harano no uwagi Boiling the starworts,
tsumite nirashi mo Plucked from the fields of spring?[56]

Apart from the different interpretations of details, there is the question of the meaning of Jomei's poem as a whole. Specialists believe that the key word is *kunimi*, "looking at the land," a religious rite performed by the emperor in the spring, anticipating autumn harvests.[57] Perhaps the mention of the smoke that fills the mountains and the birds that fill the air over the sea were an augury of the crops that would fill the fields.[58]

The various theories that have been advanced concerning the meanings of individual words and of the ritual background do not help us much to grasp what is really memorable about Jomei's poem, his exultant joy over the landscape, but most commentators seem to derive no more pleasure from poems of this surpassing loveliness than from others, of no literary importance, that offer equally demanding problems of analysis. The use of the *Man'yōshū* (and other early poetry) as a means of understanding ancient Japanese society and customs is of course not only valid but important, but burdening each poem with such interpretations tends to obscure its interest as poetry.[59]

The third and fourth poems of Book I of the *Man'yōshū* are both chōka in eighteen verses followed by a *hanka*, a poem in the same form as a waka. From this point on we find one or more hanka appended to each chōka. The meaning of the word *hanka* has been much debated. Some believe that it was derived from the short poems appended by Chinese poets to the *fu*, a long prose-poem; but this has been disputed, and no one has come up with a convincing explanation of why the Japanese used the term. The *han* of *hanka* can mean "repeat" or "respond," and as early as Nijō Yoshimoto's *Tsukuba Mondō* (Questions and Answers on Renga, 1372) it was stated that the function of the hanka was to repeat the content of a chōka within thirty-one syllables.[60] It has also frequently been claimed that the narrative chōka was complemented by the lyric hanka.[61]

These theories contribute to our understanding of how the hanka has been understood over the centuries, but perhaps the English translation "envoy" conveys as much as we really know. In some instances the hanka are called *tanka*[62] either by the poet himself or the compiler. It is hard to explain why Hitomaro referred to some "envoys" as tanka and to others as hanka. Perhaps this represented no more than a change in his vocabulary over the years, though it has been suggested that he intended the word *tanka* to indicate that the appended poem did not merely repeat the themes of the chōka but was to be read as an independent work.[63] Regardless of whether the "envoys" are called hanka or tanka, they are usually more personal than the chōka they follow, and point the way to the future development of the waka as a lyrical, non-narrative poem. In the case of Hitomaro's hanka especially, the mutual relationships of the two or more hanka appended to a chōka seem to have been considered as carefully as the relationship of each to the chōka.

The hanka to Poem 3 of Book I, a chōka describing the emperor's hunt in the fields of Uchi, effectively resumes the chōka. This poem bears the headnote: "Poem which Princess Nakatsu had Hashihito Oyu present when the Emperor went hunting in the fields of Uchi."[64] The identity of Princess Nakatsu is disputed; one rather confusing theory is that she was also called Hashihito. Such problems need not detain us; the headnote is important because it provides evidence that poetry was sometimes composed by one person in place of another. We therefore cannot always accept at face value attributions of authorship. Members of the court were at times obliged to compose poems, whether in response to some event or to another person's poem. Obviously, not all at the court were gifted as poets, and it was natural for some other member of the court, someone of proven poetic ability, to compose a poem in that person's stead. Nakanishi suggested (as noted above) that much early *Man'yōshū* poetry was composed by a group of court ladies who were charged with this task.[65] Chief of these ladies was Princess Nukata,[66] who emerged as the first poet of distinction of the collection even though she is credited with relatively few poems—eight waka and three chōka, all but two of which are "public" poems. Poem 8 of Book I was composed by Nukata in 661 after the Empress Saimei had left for Kyūshū from where she was to dispatch a fleet to relieve the kingdom of Paekche, an ally, from the attacks of the combined armies of Silla and China. Nukata's poem describes one stage of the voyage to Kyūshū:

Nigitazu ni	At Nigitazu
funanori sen to	We have waited for the moon
tsuki mateba	To board ship and leave.
shio mo kanainu	At last the tide favors us—
ima wa kogiide na[67]	Now let us row out our boats!

The *Man'yōshū* credits this poem to Nukata, but a footnote adds that it was also attributed to the Empress Saimei. Modern scholars divide on whether to believe the text or the note. Hisamatsu Sen'ichi stated, without further elucidation, "Certain points in both the content and tone of the poem make it seem more appropriate to take it as a work by the Empress Saimei, rather than by Princess Nukata, but I prefer to think of it as a poem by Princess Nukata."[68] Others argue that the lost collection by Okura no doubt intended it to be understood that the author of the poem was officially the Empress Saimei although Princess Nukata actually wrote it. One authority called Nukata the first ghost-writer![69] *Ruijū Karin* (Forest of Classified Poems) credited two others of Nukata's *Man'yōshū* poems to sovereigns, evidence that she served as a surrogate poet during several reigns.[70]

The Japanese expedition ended in disastrous defeat. The Emperor Tenji, Saimei's successor, fearing an invasion by the victorious Silla forces, hurriedly carried out reforms of the government in an effort to strengthen the country, and moved the capital from Yamato to the more easily defended Ōmi region.[71] Princess Nukata, who had been married to Tenji's brother, the future Emperor Temmu, and borne him a daughter, later became Tenji's wife and wrote, substituting for him, the lovely chōka and hanka on looking back on Mount Miwa after the capital had been removed to Ōmi.[72] After Tenji's death in 671, poems of mourning were composed by various women, including Nukata, who contributed not only a waka in which she conveyed her private grief but a chōka expressing the public grief of the court.[73] This chōka anticipates those of Hitomaro, who soon would fufill the function of a poet laureate mourning the deaths of members of the imperial family.

The best-known poem by Princess Nukata was composed in 668 during the course of a hunt staged by the Emperor Tenji. Fearing that the crown prince, her former husband, might attract attention by waving at her, she wrote:

akane sasu	On your way to the fields
murasakino yuki	Of crimson-tinted lavender,
shimeno yuki	The royal preserve,
nomori wa mizu ya	Will not the guardian notice
kimi ga sode furu[74]	If you wave your sleeve at me?

The crown prince (later Emperor Temmu) replied:

murasaki no	If I had cruel thoughts
nioeru imo wo	About you, radiant as
nikuku araba	Lavender blossoms,

hitozuma yue ni	Would I have fallen in love
ware koimeya mo[75]	With you, another man's wife?

Temmu's poem, though he does not directly answer Nukata's fears that his love will be noticed, implies that only extreme love could have made him transgress social conventions to the extent of loving the wife of another man, his brother.

Nukata's poem and Temmu's response, though they make perfect examples of sōmon, mutual inquiries, appear among the miscellaneous poems of the first book of the *Man'yōshū*, presumably because they were composed on the occasion of an imperial hunt rather than under more private circumstances. Some commentators interpret Nukata's poem as expressing fear that the guardian of the fields will notice if the prince enters a forbidden hunting preserve, but although this interpretation is grammatically possible, it destroys the interest of the poem.[76]

Another well-known poem by Princess Nukata bears a headnote stating that when the Emperor Tenji commanded the prime minister to judge which was superior, the blossoms on the spring hills or the glory of the autumn tints, Nukata settled the issue with this poem:[77]

fuyugomori	When, loosened from the winter's bonds,
haru sarikureba	The spring appears,
nakazarishi	The birds that were silent
tori mo kinakinu	Come out and sing,
sakazarishi	The flowers that were prisoned
hana mo sakeredo	Come out and bloom;
yama wo shimi	But the hills are so rank with trees
irite mo torazu	We cannot seek the flowers,
kusabukami	And the flowers are so tangled with weeds
torite mo mizu	We cannot take them in our hands.
akiyama no	But when on the autumn hill-side
ko no ha wo mite wa	We see the foliage,
momiji woba	We prize the yellow leaves,
torite so shinou	Taking them in our hands,
aoki woba	We sigh over the green ones,
okite so nageku	Leaving them on the branches;
soko shi urameshi	And that is my only regret—
akiyama so are wa[78]	For me, the autumn hills![79]

The debate over the relative merits of spring and autumn and the parallelism in the expression plainly indicate Chinese influence, as does the salonlike atmosphere surrounding the composition. The poem starts promisingly, but is curiously intellectual in its enumeration of the good and bad qualities of the two seasons, and the reason Nukata states for preferring autumn is not persuasive. The poem was rated by Tsuchihashi Yutaka as the champion (*yokozuna*) among the obscure poems of the *Man'yōshū* because of its seeming illogicality: one expects from the penultimate line, expressing regret that some leaves remain green even in autumn, that Nukata will choose spring as her favorite season, only to be told that autumn is her choice.[80] Aoki Takako, on the other hand, imagining that the poem was recited before listeners who eagerly awaited the revelation of which season Nukata would choose, complimented her on her skill in keeping them guessing until the very last line, after presenting in rapid succession six merits and four demerits of spring, and four merits and three demerits of autumn.[81] The poem is as a whole unsuccessful, but it provides evidence of the degree to which Chinese literary influence had reached women of the court, though Chinese learning is often said to have been confined to the men.[82] Chinese influence became even more striking during later periods of *Man'yōshū* poetry.

The Second Period (673–701)

The chief distinction of the poetry of the second of the four periods of the *Man'yōshū* is that it includes all the datable works of Kakinomoto no Hitomaro, the greatest poet represented in the collection. The decade of his poetic activity falls within the reign of the Empress Jitō, who succeeded to the throne after the death of her husband, the Emperor Temmu, in 686, and continued to reign in fact until her death in 702, though she formally abdicated in favor of her grandson in 697. Jitō's relationship to her husband, Temmu, was complicated by her being the daughter of Temmu's enemy, his half-brother, the Emperor Tenji. Temmu had come to the throne in 673, following the Jinshin no Ran (Disturbance of 672), a dispute over succession to the throne between Temmu and Tenji's son, the Emperor Kōbun. In the seventh month of that year a battle was fought in the province of Ōmi. Kōbun suffered a humiliating defeat and committed suicide.[83]

These political developments are of importance to an understanding of the *Man'yōshū*. For example, the longest chōka in the collection, Hitomaro's elegy on the death of Prince Takechi, consists largely of a vivid description of the prince's valiant conduct during the fighting in

672. Takechi himself in 679 composed three poems of lamentation for the Princess Toochi, the daughter of Temmu and Nukata, who was the consort of the ill-fated Emperor Kōbun. The complicated relationships of the participants in the Disturbance of 672 occasioned conflicting emotions, reflected in some of the *Man'yōshū* poems.[84]

Jitō was obsessively devoted to the memory of her husband and to his efforts to implement the Taika Reform and build a strong monarchical state. She made no fewer than thirty-one pilgrimages to Yoshino, apparently because of the connection with the memory of her late husband, who had entered orders there.[85] Confucian and Buddhist learning, imported earlier from China, were given great attention during the reigns of Temmu and Jitō, but there was also renewed devotion to Shintō, especially to the belief in the divinity of the sovereign. The deep religious overtones that contribute to the grandeur of the chōka by Hitomaro and others owe much to the piety displayed by Jitō and her court.

Not much is known about Hitomaro's life[86] apart from his activity as a kind of poet laureate to the Empress Jitō. He commemorated in his poetry her visits to Yoshino and other sites, and he also composed eulogies for deceased members of her court. His devotion to Jitō and the imperial family was absolute. Many poems open with such words as "Our Great Sovereign, a goddess," and it cannot be doubted that he believed in the divinity of the empress he served.[87] The following chōka by Hitomaro, acclaimed by the modern tanka poet Itō Sachio as one of his two supreme masterpieces, suggest the depth of Hitomaro's faith:[88]

yasumishishi	Our great Sovereign, a goddess,
wa ga ōkimi	Of her sacred will
kamu nagara	Has reared a towering palace
kamu sabi sesu to	On Yoshino's shore,
Yoshinogawa	Encircled by its rapids;
tagitsu kōchi ni	And, climbing, she surveys the land.
takadono wo	The overlapping mountains,
taka shirimashite	Rising like green walls,
noboritachi	Offer the blossoms with spring,
kunimi wo seseba	As godly tributes to the Throne.
tatanawaru	The god of the Yū River, to provide the
aokaki yama	royal table,
yamatsumi no	Holds the cormorant-fishing
matsuru mitsuki to	In its upper shallows,
haru he ni wa	And sinks the fishing-nets

hana kazashimochi	In the lower stream.
aki tateba	Thus the mountains and the river
momiji kazaseri	Serve our Sovereign, one in will;
yukisou	It is truly the reign of a divinity.[90]
kawa no kami mo	
ōmike ni	
tsukaematsuru to	
kami tsu se ni	
ukawa wo tachi	
shimo tsu se ni	
sade sashi watasu	
yamakawa mo	
yorite tsukauru	
kami no miyo kamo[89]	

Saitō Mokichi, the finest of modern tanka poets and an important *Man'yōshū* scholar, urged readers not to examine the poem analytically but to recite it again and again and in this way to absorb its message.[91] But Saitō himself provided a valuable analysis of the sounds—the repetitions of *kamu* (god) at the heads of the third and fourth lines, the repetitions of the syllable *ta* later on, and the combination of such sounds as *yama*, *matsu*, *tsumi*, *mitsu* toward the end—as a key to understanding the musical quality of this chōka.

As far as the content of the chōka is concerned, Hitomaro is saying not only that the Empress Jitō is a goddess, but that other gods—of the mountains and rivers—pay homage to this supreme deity. The act of "surveying the land" (*kunimi*) takes on special significance if one believes in the blood relationship between the sovereign and the land.

Hitomaro's earliest dated work is his lament for Prince Kusakabe, composed in 689, and his last dated work a lament for Princess Asuka, composed in 700. Quite possibly some—or many—of the undated poems in what is known as the *Hitomaro Kashū* (Hitomaro Poetry Collection)[92] were composed by Hitomaro in his youth, before he attained eminence as a court poet.

Hitomaro displayed from his first datable chōka the magnitude of his artistry. The eulogy of Prince Kusakabe opens typically, with a statement of the Shintō cosmogony:

ame tsuchi no	At the beginning of heaven and earth
hajime no toki no	The eight hundred, the thousand myriads of gods

hisakata no	Assembled in high council
ama no kawara ni	On the shining beach of the Heavenly River,
yaoyorozu	Consigned the government of the Heavens
chiyorozu kami no	Unto the Goddess Hirumé,[94] the Heaven-
kamu tsudoi	Illuminating One,
tsudoi imashite	And the government for all time,
kamu hakari	As long as heaven and earth endured,
hakarishi toki ni	Of the Rice-abounding Land of Reed Plains
amaterasu	Unto her divine offspring,
hirume no mikoto	Who, parting the eightfold clouds of the sky,
ame wo ba	Made his godly descent upon the earth.[95]
shirashimesu to	
ashihara no	
mizuho no kuni wo	
ametsuchi no	
yoriai no kiwami	
shirashimesu	
kami no mikoto to	
amakumo no	
yae kakiwakete	
kami kudashi[93]	

This proclamation of the divine descent of the Japanese imperial family was certainly not new, but it was expressed with the syntactic tautness typical of Hitomaro, and with the matchless cadences of his language. The translation given above comes to a full stop with "upon the earth," but the original text continues without break for another twelve verses. Some of Hitomaro's chōka are held together by a single syntactic construction from beginning to end, the profusion of the imagery held in tight control.

The central part of the eulogy for Prince Kusakabe describes the speaker's profound regret that the prince, who seemed destined to rule the country, should have died young, and the aimless frustration that this tragedy has brought to all who served him:

wa ga ōkimi	Alas, our mighty lord and prince,
miko no mikoto no	On whom the folk everywhere in the
ame no shita	land leaned,
shirashimeshiseba	Trustful as one riding a great ship,

haru hana no
tōtokaran to
mochizuki no tatawashiken to
ame no shita
yomo no hito no
ōbune no
omoitanomite
ama no mizu
aogite matsu ni. . . .[96]

And to whom they looked up as
eagerly
As to heaven for rain, hoping
That if he came to rule the under-
heaven
He would bring to his reign
A glory of the spring flowers
And such perfection as of the full moon!

Many commentators have noted the stiffness of this eulogy as compared to the immediacy and personal involvement of Hitomaro's later poems in this form, but certain images would often recur: the great ship as a symbol of security; rain as a blessing from heaven; the perfection of the full moon. These images did not necessarily originate with Hitomaro, but he gave them his personal imprint. But there is an element of confusion in this eulogy: if one did not know that Hitomaro was describing in the first section of the poem the myth of Amaterasu's bestowing of rulership of the land on her grandson Ninigi, one might suppose (as some have) that it was the Emperor Temmu who had made his "godly descent" from heaven.[97] Ninigi and Temmu seem to have fused in Hitomaro's mind. Worship of this emperor as a god seems to date back only to Temmu's efforts to consolidate power after coming to the throne. Affirmations in poetry of the divinity of the sovereign were not confined to Hitomaro, but such phrases become scarcer in the generation after his, no doubt reflecting a diminution in the intensity of their belief. Hitomaro's worship of the imperial family gave his poetry special strength even for us who do not believe in its divinity.

Hitomaro has been called a "professional court poet,"[98] but there is no mistaking the genuineness of his grief over the death of Prince Kusakabe. In other eulogies he would relate with equal conviction the desolate feelings of a prince or princess after the death of a wife or husband, mentioning details of their bedchamber that he could not possibly have known. Writing, as it were, on an assigned topic about people he did not know might have resulted in the conventional sentiments that one associates with the poet laureate who is obliged to produce poems on matters of public interest even if they are no concern of his; but it seems that Hitomaro did not feel the sharp difference between public and private, the individual and the group, that many later poets would feel, and the exactness of his images when describing the grief of a princess persuades us—against reason at times—that he somehow shared her grief.[99] Ironically, Hitomaro is so convincing in poems that were not based on personal experience that doubts have been expressed about the truthfulness of poems that ostensibly describe his own emotions.[100] But surely, no one reading Hitomaro's great poems on the death of his wife could doubt the reality of the emotions portrayed.

Regardless of the degree of literal truth in Hitomaro's poems, the poetic truth is incontestable. Even in his first eulogy, the stiffness of manner does not prevent the reader from becoming vividly aware of the terrible confusion that swept over the court after the prince's death. Prince Kusakabe, the son of Temmu and Jitō, should have succeeded his father on the throne, but the crisis that arose immediately after Temmu's death—the conspiracy of Prince Ōtsu against Kusakabe—seems to have persuaded Jitō to serve temporarily as the sovereign. It was she who gave the order for the execution of Prince Ōtsu on the grounds of treason.[101] Perhaps Jitō intended to abdicate in Kusakabe's favor after Temmu was ceremonially buried, but Kusakabe died only five months after his father. His death meant that the direct successor to the throne would not be Kusakabe's son, a boy of six, but a son of Temmu by another consort. Jitō's grief over Kusakabe's death was intensified by her apprehension over the succession.

Hitomaro's chōka was written during the temporary enshrinement of Prince Kusakabe. The practice at the time was to place the body of a deceased member of the imperial family in a temporary shrine (*arakinomiya*)[102] for an indeterminate period of time. During this time the person was considered not to be dead but in a kind of limbo from which he might be called back to life. The reluctance of the Empress Jitō to admit that Temmu was truly dead probably accounted for the extraordinarily long period (two years and two months) of his temporary interment.[103] The adoption of cremation as the official form of interment obviated the need for the eulogies in the form of chōka that had customarily been sung during a temporary enshrinement; this was undoubtedly one reason for the disappearance of the chōka as a poetic form. Hitomaro's eulogies were all composed before 702, when the Empress Jitō became the first sovereign to be cremated rather than buried.

The finest of his eulogies describing deaths in the imperial family was the one composed during the temporary enshrinement of Prince Takechi, who died in 696 at the age of forty-two.[104] This poem, in 151 verses not including the hanka, is the longest in the *Man'yōshū*. The first 138 verses are syntactically unbroken, bound together by a power of expression unique in Japanese poetry. It required a genius like Hitomaro to maintain the poem at maximum intensity throughout, though he could not resort to the devices used by European poets to keep long poems recognizable as poetry—rhyme, patterns of stress accents, quantity. The demise of the chōka after the *Man'yōshū* is attributable to other causes as well,[105] but surely a major factor was the difficulty poets experienced in maintaining poetic tension over an extended work.

Hitomaro's eulogy for Prince Takechi opens with a panegyric of the Emperor Temmu, and the central section is devoted to an account of the fighting during the Disturbance of 672, when Prince Takechi distinguished himself. Temmu commanded Takechi to subjugate his enemies, whereupon:

Forthwith our prince buckled on a sword,
And in his august hand
Grasped a bow to lead the army.
The drums marshalling men in battle array
Sounded like the rumbling thunder,
The war-horns blew, as tigers roar,
Confronting an enemy,
Till all men were shaken with terror.
The banners hoisted aloft, swayed
As sway in wind the flames that burn
On every moorland far and near
When spring comes after winter's prisonment.
Frightful to hear was the bow-strings' clang,
Like a whirlwind sweeping
Through a winter forest of snow.
And like snow-flakes tempest-driven
The arrows fell thick and fast.
The foemen confronting our prince
Fought, prepared to a man to perish,
If perish they must, like dew or frost;
And vying with one another like birds upon the wing,
They flew to the front of battle—
When, lo, from Watarai's holy shrine
There rose the God's Wind confounding them,

By hiding the sun's eye with clouds
And shrouding the world in utter darkness.[106]

Hitomaro was probably too young to have witnessed the warfare he so vividly described. The language he used is strikingly similar to the account of the battle in the *Nihon Shoki*, in turn borrowed from the Chinese dynastic history of the Latter Han.[107] Hitomaro doubtless had access to this work, and its phraseology helped to give his account strength and concreteness. This does not mean that Hitomaro merely "translated" into Japanese an existing Chinese text; there is a specifically Japanese "truth" in what he reports, down to the mention of the God's Wind (*kamikaze*) that places the action firmly in a Japanese setting. However, the existence of a Chinese model enabled Hitomaro to leave behind the badly organized descriptions that were typical of the *Kojiki* and other early Japanese poetry.

The final section of the eulogy describes the palace built by Prince Takechi on Mount Kagu. The poet asks rhetorically if this palace, built to last "ten thousand generations," will ever disappear, implying that although Takechi is gone, his works will last forever. This seems to have been a function of the eulogies in the *Man'yōshū*: to reassure the dead person that his works will not be forgotten, thereby calming his soul (*chinkon*) and persuading him that he need not return to this world as an angry ghost.

Stressing the permanence of worldly things was by no means typical of Hitomaro. A conviction that the world was transitory, a deceit, was a Buddhist belief shared by Hitomaro with most other *Man'yōshū* poets,[108] and the impermanence of even the most splendid works of man was nostalgically lamented again and again. The first poem by Hitomaro in the *Man'yōshū* (number 29 in the collection) describes his feelings as he passed the ruined palace at Ōmi, the site of the Emperor Tenji's capital:

But now, though I am told his royal palace towered here,
And they say here rose its lofty halls,
Only the spring weeds grow luxuriantly
And the spring sun is dimmed with mists.
As I see these ruins of the mighty palace
My heart is heavy with sorrows!

Hitomaro, a worshiper of Temmu's memory, surely did not regret the destruction of Tenji's capital. He regretted instead the changes brought about by the passage of time. This theme runs through Hitomaro's poetry: a yearning for the past, for whatever has disappeared. A sense of contrast between eternal nature and the transcience of man and his works gives poignancy to his observations and universality to his sorrow. The capital at Ōmi, which many men had labored to build, and which had seemed to epitomize the grandeur of an emperor, was now in ruins. It did not matter if the ruins were beautiful (like the Gothic ruins in Europe) or merely some foundation stones and a few stray roof tiles; the irretrievable past could excite the tears not only of Hitomaro but of all who visited the ruins. The changes effected by time would become one of the grand themes of Japanese poetry.

Hitomaro's most moving elegies were not those he composed for members of the imperial family, splendid though they are, but one on an unknown man whose corpse he saw on a distant island, and another about his own wife. The elegy on the death of a man on the small island of Samine in the Inland Sea is deservedly one of Hitomaro's most admired works. It consists of three parts: an invocation to the beautiful province of Sanuki on the island of Shikoku; a description of Hitomaro's voyage over the Inland Sea to Samine;[109] and, finally, a description of the corpse. Perhaps Hitomaro felt obliged to calm the soul of the unhappy man who had died far from home, but there was already a tradition of composing poetry about men who had died by the roadside. The earliest is attributed to Prince Shōtoku:

ie naraba	Had he been at home,
imo ga tamakan	he would have slept
kusamakura	Upon his wife's dear arm;
tabi ni koyaseru	Here he lies dead, unhappy man,
kono tabito aware	On his journey, grass for pillow.[110]

Hitomaro on another occasion composed a waka describing his grief on seeing a corpse on Mount Kagu:

kusamakura	Grass for his pillow,
tabi no yadori ni	His lodgings on this journey—
ta ga tsuma ka	Whose husband is this?
kuni wasuretaru	Has he forgotten his homeland
ie matamaku ni[111]	Where his wife must be waiting?

The death of a man, far from home and abandoned by the world, caused the poet to reflect on the man's fate, the wife vainly waiting at home for the husband who would not return—and perhaps his own mortality, though this is not openly expressed.[112]

The third section of the Samine poem exercised the greatest influence over later *Man'yōshū* poets:

> There I found you, poor man!—
> Outstretched on the beach,
> On this rough bed of stones,
> Amid the busy voices of the waves.
> If I but knew where was your home,
> I would go and tell;
> If your wife but knew,
> She would come to tend you.
> She, not knowing the way hither,
> Must wait, must ever wait,
> Restlessly hoping for your return—
> Your dear wife—alas![113]

Perhaps the most affecting of the poems on this subject in the *Man'yōshū* is found in a group of thirty-one poems known as the Tanabe Sakimaro collection:[114]

> He lies unloosened of his white clothes,
> Perhaps of his wife's weaving
> From hemp within her garden-fence,
> And girdled threefold round
> Instead of once.
> Perhaps after painful service done
> He turned his footsteps home,
> To see his parents and his wife;
> And now, on this steep and sacred pass
> In the eastern land of Azuma,
> Chilled in his spare, thin clothes,
> His black hair fallen loose—
> Telling none his province,
> Telling none his home,
> Here on a journey he lies dead.[115]

This poem is an example of how Hitomaro's themes would affect later *Man'yōshū* poets, sometimes inspiring no more than pastiches of his imagery, occasionally (as in the above example) resulting in poems that rivaled their source. Perhaps Hitomaro's most seminal poems were the two chōka on parting from his wife and two other chōka composed after her death. The latter two are not only Hitomaro's finest achievement but are the most impressive extended poems in the Japanese language. Here is a translation of the first of the two elegies:

> Since in Karu lived my wife,
> I wished to be with her to my heart's content;
> But I could not visit her constantly
> Because of the many watching eyes—
> Men would know of our troth,
> Had I sought her too often.
> So our love remained secret like a rock-pent pool;
> I cherished her in my heart,
> Looking to after-time when we should be together,
> And lived secure in my trust
> As one riding a great ship.
> Suddenly there came a messenger
> Who told me she was dead—
> Was gone like a yellow leaf of autumn.
> Dead as the day dies with the setting sun,
> Lost as the bright moon is lost behind the cloud,
> Alas, she is no more, whose soul
> Was bent to mine like the bending seaweed!
>
> When the word was brought to me
> I knew not what to do nor what to say;
> But restless at the mere news,
> And hoping to heal my grief
> Even a thousandth part,
> I journeyed to Karu and searched the market-place
> Where my wife was wont to go!
>
> There I stood and listened,
> But no voice of her I heard,
> Though the birds sang in the Unebi Mountain;
> None passed by who even looked like my wife.
> I could only call her name and wave my sleeve.[116]

Mention of "watching eyes" refers to the custom among members of the aristocracy of keeping their marriages secret; men visited their wives, especially women who were not legal consorts, stealthily and by night. The imagery is familiar from other poems by Hitomaro—the great ship as a symbol of trustworthiness, the yellow leaves of autumn to indicate the passage of time, the bending seaweed that suggests the wife snuggling against her husband, the hidden moon that deprives the world of light—but the effect is new because the grief is so intense. The unforgettable passage where the poet, even though he knows his wife is dead, goes to look for her at places where she often went is almost unbearable in its truth. At the end, he calls her name and waves his sleeve, a familiar gesture of summoning the dead.[117] The poem's intensity owes much to its unremitting tension: all fifty-three verses form a single syntactical unit.[118] Even the different makurakotoba (not rendered in the translation above)[119] add to the relentless, incantatory effect, suggesting a nightmare from which there is no awakening.

The imagery of this poem would be borrowed by later poets even in quite dissimilar contexts. For example, Lady Ōtomo of Sakanoue's "Lover's Complaint" (*enkonka*), relating a woman's annoyance at the lover who has failed to pay a promised visit, also mentions swaying seaweed, her trust in her love as in a great ship, the messenger with an unwelcome letter, the setting sun.[120] Again, an anonymous poem, possibly by the wife of a frontier guard, describes a woman's grief on learning from a messenger that her husband was "gone like the autumn leaf."[121]

The later poems are no match for Hitomaro's elegy in literary quality, but they bear witness to the pervasive influence of his poetry, even in remote parts of the country.

The second of Hitomaro's poems on the death of his wife also forms a single syntactical unit almost to the end, when it stops, only for Hitomaro to add a final five verses, as if an additional memory of his wife, too strong to suppress, had surged back at this point. Some scholars have opined that the two eulogies describe different women. They point out, for example, that only in the second poem is there mention of a child. More likely, however, both poems refer to the same woman, though the second, clearly set in the past from its opening lines, may have been written later, recalling a now distant sorrow.[122] It is possible that neither poem was actually inspired by Hitomaro's grief, and that he composed both at the request of some man who was himself incapable of expressing his sorrow, but nothing in the poem suggests this.

Apart from the poetry attributed to Hitomaro by the compilers of the *Man'yōshū*, there are also 364 poems, including 2 chōka and 35 sedōka, that are said by the editors to have come from the *Hitomaro Kashū*.[123] These poems are scattered over nine books of the *Man'yōshū*, wherever the editors found an appropriate place for them. The *Hitomaro Kashū*, it is clear, was a source of a large number of poems in the *Man'yōshū*, but the authorship of the poems is a matter of dispute.[124] Some scholars have insisted that none of the poems is by Hitomaro and that the collection was compiled by him from poems by other men. Others have credited all of the poems, except those specifically attributed to other poets, to Hitomaro.[125]

Nakanishi Susumu took a middle ground, expressing the belief that some poems were by Hitomaro but others were added later. He found it difficult, for example, to accept the possibility that the thirty-eight poems on the Tanabata Festival could have been composed by Hitomaro, if only because this festival, imported from China, did not take hold in Japan until at least twenty years after Hitomaro's death.[126] Similarly, themes such as deer crying in the forest were not used in Japanese poetry until after Hitomaro's time.

Regardless of who wrote these poems, some seem worthy of a master, like the following:

mizu no ue ni	I have pledged my life,
kazu kaku gotoki	Insubstantial as numbers
wa ga inochi wo	Written on water,
imo ni awan to	Asking the gods for a sign
ukeitsuru kamo[127]	That I may meet my sweetheart.

Other poems in a lighter mood have charm, like these dialogue poems:

narukami no	Will not the thunder
sukoshi toyomite	Roll for a little while,
sashikumori	The sky cloud over,
ame mo furanu ka	And the rain come pouring down?
kimi wo todomen	Then I can keep you with me.

narukami no	Even if the thunder
sukoshi toyomite	Rolls just a little bit,
furazu tomo	And no rain falls at all,

ware wa todomaran	I will stay beside you,
imo shi todomeba[128]	If you only ask me to.

A prominent feature of the Hitomaro Collection is the body of poems in the form known as sedōka, poems in six lines with a total of thirty-eight syllables. The exact meaning of the term is not clear. According to the theory advanced by Hisamatsu Sen'ichi in 1928, *sedō* meant a "repetition" of the first three lines (5, 7, and 7 syllables) in the second three lines of a single poem. (The "repetition" was not of the words but of the thought, expressed in different words.) This theory was later modified by the suggestion that the two halves of a sedōka (each known as a kata-uta) were originally in the form of a question and answer, as in the earliest example of the form, the exchange between Yamato-takeru and an old man concerning the distance to Tsukuba, found in the *Kojiki*. However, Nakanishi Susumu, noting that sedōka in the form of a question and answer were rare, considered that the main factor in the composition of the second half of a sedōka was a continuation of the original thought, rather than a response to a question. He believed that the original inspiration for composing sedōka was the existence of similar poetry in China, notably linked-verse poems (*renkushi*); and he detected a popular, even folkish tone in many sedōka that suggested to him that Hitomaro might have collected them on his travels around the country as a member of the entourage of the Empress Jitō.[129] A typical example of a "folkish" sedōka is Poem 1281:

kimi ga tame	I have exhausted
tajikara tsukare	The strength of my hands weaving
oritaru kinu zo	This robe for you, my lord;
haru saraba	When spring has come,
ika naru iro ni	What color would you like me
suriteba yoken[130]	To print and dye it for you?

This sedōka is not in the form of a question and answer, but there is a definite caesura between its two halves. A caesura could occur at the end of any line of *Man'yōshū* waka, or even more than once in a single waka, but the break in a sedōka always occurs after the third line.[131]

If, as Nakanishi suggested, Hitomaro collected this poem on his travels, the poem would not be of his own composition (at least according to modern standards of authorship) even if he polished a line or two. But, regardless of who wrote the thirty-four sedōka in the *Hitomaro*

Kashū, their prominence is noteworthy: they constitute more than half of the sixty-two sedōka in the *Man'yōshū*, and about a tenth of the poems in the entire *Hitomaro Kashū*.

One other matter concerning Hitomaro has been the subject of unusually acrimonious debate—the place and circumstances of his death. It was long assumed that he died in the province of Iwami on the Japan Sea coast, but whether in the mountains, by a river, or in the sea has been much contested. Saitō Mokichi felt so sure that he had identified the site of Hitomaro's death that he erected a monument on an otherwise unremarkable mountain and proclaimed it to be the Kamoyama of Hitomaro's valedictory poem:

Kamoyama no	All unaware, it may be,
iwane shi makeru	That I lie in Kamoyama,
ware wo kamo	Pillowed on a rock,
shira ni to imo ga	She is waiting now—my wife—
machitsutsu aruran	Waiting for my return.[132]

The poem, regardless of the location of Kamoyama, strongly suggests death in the mountains. Saitō conjectured that Hitomaro might have died in 707 when an epidemic, especially severe in the provinces of Izumo and Iwami, claimed many victims.[133]

Two poems by Hitomaro's wife, Yosami, given in the *Man'yōshū* immediately after Hitomaro's last poem, cast doubt on the place of his death:

kyō kyō to	Day in, day out,
wa ga matsu kimi wa	I wait for my husband—
Ishikawa no	Alas! he lies buried, men say,
kai ni majirite	In the ravine of the Stone River.
ari to iwazu ya mo	

tada ni awaba	There can be no meeting
ai katsu mashiji	Face to face with him.
Ishikawa ni	Arise, O clouds,
kumo tachiwatare	Hover above Stone River
mitsutsu shinowan	That I may watch and remember.[134]

No river near the present Kamoyama is known as the Ishikawa ("stone river"). Saitō thought that Ishikawa might be an old name for the upper reaches of another river. The text speaks of *kai*, meaning shells, in the river, appropriate only if the river is near the sea, but Saitō and others adopted the variant (also given in the *Man'yōshū*) of *kai*, meaning "ravine." Scholars who reject this explanation and accept the meaning of "shell" have interpreted the poems as meaning that Hitomaro died near the mouth of a large river, not in the mountains. Finally, there is a poem by Tajihi no Mabito, replying to the wife in the persona of Hitomaro:

aranami ni	Who will tell her
yorikuru tama wo	That I lie here,
makura ni oki	My head pillowed
ware koko ni ari to	On the stones brought to shore
tare ka tsugeken[135]	By the rough waves?

The scene of this poem seems definitely to be the sea. "Rough waves" would not fit a mountain stream, but the distinguished scholar Omodaka Hisataka, unwilling to abandon Saitō's theory that Hitomaro died in the mountains, decided that Tajihi no Mabito had mistakenly supposed that *kai* meant "shell," rather than "ravine," and had therefore written in terms of death at sea.[136] But Umehara Takeshi decided, on the contrary, not only that Hitomaro had perished at sea but that he was put to death by drowning. He interpreted Kamoyama as the name of an island off the Iwami coast, and declared that Hitomaro's last poem was his farewell to the world, just before he was executed.[137] Itō Haku, adopting an even more controversial position, argued that Hitomaro's valedictory poem and the wife's responses were part of "The Play of Iwami," a story of love and death in Iwami enacted by Hitomaro and a court lady who took the part of Yosami, the wife in the country. Itō believed that this formed part of a "salon drama" in which participants composed poetry befitting the roles that had been assigned them. Itō insisted on the close relationship between Kamoyama and the Ishikawa, found in other sources, and was sure that the poem of Tajihi no Mabito was originally an unrelated poem that the compilers of the *Man'yōshū* tacked on to the "salon drama" of death in the country.[138]

These different explanations will suggest the insatiable interest aroused by the life and death of the greatest of the *Man'yōshū* poets, and the never-ending persistence of scholars who attempt to make extremely scarce facts yield pertinent information. It is possible that the poems attributed to Yosami and Tajihi no Mabito, around which such complicated theories have evolved, did not even refer to Hitomaro.[139] Tsuchihashi also doubted the authenticity of Hitomaro's death verse, finding it too self-indulgent for such an occasion, and concluded that someone else, imagining Hitomaro's feelings as he was about to die in some remote part of the country, had composed the poem in Hitomaro's voice.[140]

We are left in that case with almost nothing in the nature of biographical information. Hitomaro's name does not appear in any official documents, presumably because he was not of sufficiently high rank to be mentioned,[141] and no family records or memorabilia survive. It will make little difference to lovers of Hitomaro's poetry even if the enigma is never solved. Other poets of the *Man'yōshū* command our admiration and respect, but Hitomaro became a god.

The Third Period (702–729)

It has often been stated that with the death of the Empress Jitō in 702 a marked change occurred in the nature of the poetry composed by the *Man'yōshū* poets. Certainly, a dramatic break occurred in the tradition of court poets celebrating the visits of the sovereign to different parts of the country. With only one exception (a private rather than a public poem), no poems were composed between 702 and 720 on the subject of imperial progresses, though this had been a frequent theme of earlier poems, and we know from the official history of the period, *Shoku Nihongi*, that there were many excursions.[142] Quite possibly the break in tradition reflected the preference of the statesman Fujiwara no Fuhito (659–720) for poetry in Chinese. Fuhito first rose to prominence in 700 when he was commanded to compile the legal code *Taihō-ryō*. When he completed this task in the following year he was given the rank of major counsellor, and in 708 he became minister of the Right. One daughter was the consort of the Emperor Mommu, and another of the Emperor Shōmu. Fuhito was the leading political figure of his age and the chief architect of the move to the new capital at Nara in 710. His contribution to the creation of a centralized state authority functioning under a legal code was his most outstanding achievement, but he also laid the foundations for Fujiwara control of the successive emperors by the marriages of his daughters.

Fuhito studied Confucianism and was a devout Buddhist. His cultural interests were directed almost exclusively toward China, and he became a proficient writer of kanshi (poetry in Chinese). Four of his kanshi were included in the *Kaifūsō*. The Emperor Mommu, who was much under his influence, also contributed three poems to the *Kaifūsō*. Fuhito's poetry does not appear in the *Man'yōshū*,[143] and it is clear that while he lived the court favored Chinese rather than Japanese poetry. After his death in 720, poems describing the visits of the sovereign to Yoshino and other well-known sites resumed, most of them plainly in the tradition of Hitomaro.

During the ten or twelve years before 720, while Fuhito's power was at its height, there occurred a marked decline in the quality of *Man'yōshū* poetry. The only new poet of importance was Takechi no Kurohito. His extant poems consist of eighteen waka, all of them on travel and devoted to scenic descriptions. Despite the scarcity of his poems, their distinctive tone and atmosphere have won for him a secure place among the major *Man'yōshū* poets, and several waka have been acclaimed as masterpieces. Ikeda Yasaburō chose the following waka by Kurohito as one of especially high literary value, a poem that not only confirmed his importance as a poet but enhanced the whole *Man'yōshū*:

izuku ni ka	Where, I wonder,
wa ga yadori sen	Shall I find shelter tonight
Takashima no	Now that the day is ending
Katsuno no hara ni	Over the fields of Katsuno
kono hi kurenaba[144]	In Takashima?

Discussions of this poem, whose surface meaning seems to present no problems, have revolved around matters of relatively slight interest to persons other than *Man'yōshū* specialists. One point of somewhat wider interest is whether the final line of the original—"now that the day is ending"—signifies that it in fact has already become dusk or that the poet is imagining what it will be like after it grows dark. Ikeda, as a scholar of folklore in the tradition of Origuchi Shinobu, favored the former interpretation: twilight for Japanese of the *Man'yōshū* period had sinister overtones, a time of day when people were most susceptible to the evil spirits that rose from their surroundings. Even if Kurohito did not consciously inject such overtones into his poem, he may have had at the back of his mind the spells that were recited to ward off ghosts that wandered in the twilight hour, and people who heard his poem would also remember them. But Tsuchihashi Yutaka, who admired Kurohito because he showed a curiously modern sensibility, believed that the poem was an imagined experience, described in order to convey in the most poignant manner the poet's feelings of forlornness.[145]

Regardless of the interpretation, it is noteworthy that all of Kurohito's poems in the *Man'yōshū* are about travel, and the importance of travel to the poets is attested by many other examples throughout the collection. All but one of Kurohito's poems contains a place-name. This in itself is not surprising in poems about travel, but it suggests the fascination that place-names continued to exert over the Japanese. Thirteen poems in the *Man'yōshū*, most of them in the manner of folk songs, describe Katsuno in Takashima, evidence of the associations that this place-name evoked.[146]

Kurohito's poems are melancholy, establishing a mood for travel poems that were quite unlike the cheerful descriptions of journeys by the earlier *Man'yōshū* poets. Tsuchihashi described Kurohito as a poet whose theme was the disappearing things of the world, whether a ship over the horizon, a bird in the clouds, or a season with the passage of time.[147] In five of his extant poems Kurohito describes a boat seen from a distance, imparting a feeling of poignancy that goes beyond mere observation. In other poems Kurohito himself is aboard the boat:

wa ga fune wa	Our boat will surely
Hira no minato ni	Soon be rowed to safe shelter
kogihaten	In Hira Harbor;
oki e na sakari	Let it not stray far from shore,
sayo fukenikeri[148]	Night is already upon us.

This poem is of special interest because a close variant, believed by Ikeda to be a folk song, is found elsewhere in the *Man'yōshū*:

wa ga fune wa	Our boat will surely
Akashi no mito ni	Soon be rowed to safe shelter
kogihaten	In Akashi Harbor;
oki e na sakari	Let it not stray far from shore,
sayo fukenikeri[149]	Night is already upon us.

Ikeda was convinced that Kurohito's poem, known orally, had "traveled" to different localities in the manner of a folk song, with only the place-name altered to suit the particular circumstances. Many poems in the

Man'yōshū have "doubles"—variants that sometimes (as in this example) differ by only a few words.

This poem is one of a group of eight travel poems by Kurohito that seem to form a poetic sequence—a series of poems intended to reinforce one another. Sometimes the poet himself composed the poems with this intention, at other times it was the compiler who arranged independently composed poems to form a sequence. A sequence could overcome the limitations imposed by the shortness of an individual waka to expand on the expressive possibilities of the opening poem, rather in the manner of a theme and variations.[150] It was possible for *Man'yōshū* poets to write chōka if what they wished to say did not fit into the thirty-one syllables of a waka, but the chōka form was generally reserved for public, and generally solemn, circumstances. Kurohito seems not to have composed any.

Some poems by Kurohito were so admired by later poets that they openly borrowed from him;[151] the *Man'yōshū* poets did not believe that a poem belonged exclusively to its creator. They seemed to think instead that poems on the same subject and even using the same language as existing poems represented attempts by successive generations of poets to touch the core of the sentiments expressed. The following poem by Kurohito has a twin in a poem by Yamabe no Akahito:

Sakurada e	To Sakurada
tazu nakiwataru	The cranes cross, crying.
Ayuchi-gata	At Ayuchi Lagoon,
shio hinikerashi	The tide seems to have ebbed:
tazu nakiwataru[152]	The cranes cross, crying.

The daring repetition of the second line at the end of the poem is particularly effective. Akahito's poem is more conventional, but is also lovely:

Wakanoura ni	At Wakanoura
shio michikureba	The tide, rising to the full,
kata wo nami	Has engulfed the strand;
ashihe wo sashite	Heading for the reedy store,
tazu nakiwataru[153]	The cranes cross, crying.

Adaptation of earlier poetry, frequent in the *Man'yōshū*, would be elevated in later times into the principle of poetry known as *honka-dori*, or allusive variation.[154] This was by no means plagiarism; the later poet not only expected that readers would be familiar with the poem on which he made variations but also hoped that his skill in borrowing some materials unaltered but changing others would convince people that he had improved on the original poem.

Kurohito often broke his waka into three parts, with caesuras after the second and fourth lines as in the Sakurada poem, or after the third and fourth lines as in the poem about Hira Harbor. This poetic device seemed to have originated with Kurohito,[155] perhaps as a part of the melody to which it was sung.[156] The repetition of lines two and five in the Sakurada poem contributes to the rhythm, suggesting a refrain. Akahito's poem, on the other hand, consists of a single syntactical unit: "Because the tide has come to the full at Wakanoura and obliterated the beach, the cranes [deprived of their usual perches] head for the reeds on the shore, crying."

The poet from whom Kurohito learned the most was undoubtedly Hitomaro, but they were quite dissimilar in both poetic techniques and attitudes. Nothing better illustrates their differences than the poems each composed on visiting the ruins of the capital in Ōmi. Hitomaro, after first describing the decision of the Emperor Tenji to break precedent by establishing his capital not in Yamato but in Ōmi, related what he now saw: weeds growing where once a palace stood, and the spring sun dimmed by mist. He concluded:

ōmiya tokoro	As I see these ruins of the mighty palace
mireba kanashimo	My heart is heavy with sorrows![157]

Kurohito wrote three waka describing his visit to the ruins. Unlike Hitomaro, who wanted to see the former capital, even though he knew the ruins would make him sad, Kurohito says that he would have preferred not to see the ruins:

kaku yue ni	That's precisely why
miji to iu mono wo	I never wished to see the place,
sasanami no	But you insisted
furuki miyako wo	On showing me the old capital
misetsutsu motona[158]	Of little waves—for no reason.

Hitomaro was moved by the ruins and the profusion of spring weeds to remember the days, not so long ago, when this was the capital; but Kurohito reproaches someone—probably a friend—for having insisted that he look at a place which, he knew in advance, would make him sad. In another poem composed at the site of the old capital, he asks rhetorically if he feels so sad because he himself is a relic of the past.[159] Obviously, he is not; but if not, why should the ruins depress him so? For Hitomaro the question would not have arisen: he was an elegist of the past—of the palaces and people of former times—but Kurohito was an elegist of the fugitive moment, of his own mortality.

Kurohito's name is often linked with those of two other poets who were probably his contemporaries. The first, Naga no Imiki Okimaro, an obscure figure, may have been of foreign origin.[160] He and Kurohito apparently traveled together in the imperial progresses of 701 and 702, but their ranks were not high enough for their names to be preserved in official records. Okimaro's most distinctive poems are on assigned words or topics. For example, in one poem he was obliged, as part of a poetic game played at the court, to include the words *kō* (incense), *tō* (pagoda), *kawaya* (privy), *kuso* (excrement), *funa* (carp), and *yakko* (servant).[161] The resulting poem is more notable for its ingenuity than its sense. On a similar occasion Okimaro was assigned the subject of "a white heron pecking at a tree, then flying away." The poems composed in response to such tests of ingenuity are not of much literary interest, but they prefigure the *butsumei* poems (in which a word is hidden in the text) in the *Kokinshū* and the poems on set topics (*dai*) at poem competitions. Not all of Okimaro's poems were displays of wit, but most were inspired by a particular event or a request for a poem. Perhaps his most affecting poem is atypical, the description of a bleak day without shelter:

kurushiku mo	How sad and dismal
furikuru ame ka	The rain that comes pouring down;
Miwa no saki	At the Sano ford
Sano no watari ni	On the headland of Miwa,
ie mo aranaku ni[162]	There is not even a house.

The second poet with whom Kurohito's name has been linked was far more celebrated than Okimaro; indeed, Yamabe no Akahito (fl. 724–737) has often been ranked alongside Hitomaro. For centuries when the *Man'yōshū* was little read, Hitomaro and Akahito were the only two *Man'yōshū* poets whose names were generally known. The Japanese preface to the *Kokinshū* asserted that Hitomaro could not be ranked above Akahito, nor Akahito below Hitomaro, an indirect way of saying that the compilers considered Akahito to be even superior to Hitomaro.

A curious legend developed that Hitomaro, having been exiled because of a love affair with an empress, was forgiven so that he might write more poetry, but when he returned to the court he took the name Akahito.[163]

Akahito's name is today more often linked with Kurohito's, rather than Hitomaro's, because critics no longer rank Akahito nearly so high as Hitomaro; in fact, he is given considerably less attention than either Yamanoue no Okura or Ōtomo no Yakamochi, and some authorities rank him lower than Kurohito.[164] The two men are linked for another reason: unlike Hitomaro, Okura, or Yakamochi, whose best poems were their chōka, Akahito (like Kurohito) excelled at the waka. Although no fewer than thirteen of the total of fifty poems by Akahito in the *Man'yōshū* are chōka, scholars as far back as Kamo no Mabuchi have shown relatively little interest in these poems, reserving their praise for Akahito's waka.[165] Akahito's chōka are competent, but his talent was best displayed in his waka and hanka. The hanka appended to Hitomaro's chōka are always of interest, but they never cause the reader to feel that these encapsulations of the content of the chōka make the chōka unnecessary; but that is exactly true of Akahito, as the following chōka and two hanka will suggest:

yasumishishi
wa go ōkimi no
taka shirasu
Yoshino no miya wa
tatanazuku
aokakigomori
kawanami no
kiyoki kōchi so
haruhe ni wa
hana sakioori
aki sareba
kiri tachiwataru

Here in a beautiful dell where the
river runs,
The Yoshino Palace, the high
abode
Of our Sovereign, reigning in
peace,
Stands engirdled, fold on fold,
By green mountain walls.
In spring the flowers bend the
boughs;
With autumn's coming the mist
rises and floats over all.
Ever prosperous like those
mountains,
And continuously as this river
flows,
Will the lords and ladies of the
court
Come hither.

sono yama no
iya masumasu ni
kono kawa no
tayuru koto naku
momoshiki no
ōmiyahito no
tsune ni kayowan

mi Yoshino no
Kisayama no ma no
konure ni wa
kokoda mo sawaku
tori no koe kamo

Oh, the voices of the birds
That sing so noisily in the treetops
Of the Kisa Mountain of Yoshino,
Breaking the silence of the vale!

nubatama no
yo no fukeyukeba
hisagi ouru
kiyoki kawara ni
chidori shiba naku.[166]

Now the jet-black night deepens;
And on the beautiful river beach,
where grow the *hisagi*-trees,
The sanderlings cry ceaselessly.

The chōka is pleasant, but it has little content, and the images with their heavy parallelism seem stale. In Hitomaro's chōka on a similar subject, the visit of the Empress Jitō to Yoshino, the most striking features of the Yoshino scenery, the mountains and clear streams, are given reality by concrete details,[167] but in Akahito's chōka the mountains are reduced to being symbols of permanence and prosperity. However, in the envoys Akahito expressed everything that is missing from its chōka; in them he captured the essence of Yoshino superbly.

It may be that modern readers fail to appreciate the full significance of Akahito's mention of birds in the envoys. The ancient Japanese considered birds to be messengers from the world of the dead. The folklorist Ikeda Yasaburō described them in these terms:

> Birds were not simply fauna. They were the keepers and conveyors of souls (*reikon*). They were also creatures who tempted forth the tranquil souls of people by calling and singing to them. That is why there were periods when birdsong, longed for and prized in later times, was dreaded. People listened to the singing of birds less with appreciation than with awe. This awe, differing according to the time and place, originated in the fear and deference paid the gods or birds as the messengers of the gods.[168]

The approach of night, the twilight hour when souls wandered, was perhaps also intended to convey an ominous note in the second of the envoys. But is is almost impossible for a modern reader, even one acquainted with the beliefs of the ancient Japanese, to read Akahito's envoys as expressions of dread and awe. Even if Akahito himself derived no pleasure from the cries of birds he so magically described, we cannot but interpret these poems in the way that makes sense to us; surely no one after reading the chōka is likely to detect frightening messengers from the world of the dead in the exquisite words of the envoys.

Akahito's reputation is as a poet of nature, but he wrote poems on many other subjects. All the same, even when a chōka is a narrative of events that took place in the past or is the description of a journey, the parts one is likely to remember are the evocations of nature. Sometimes Akahito even seems to exaggerate:

haru no no ni	Forth to the field of spring
sumire tsumi ni to	I went to gather violets—
koshi ware so	Enamoured of the field
no wo natsukashimi	I slept there all night through.
hito yo nenikeru[169]	

It is hard to imagine a grown man actually spending the night in the open because he was enchanted with a field of violets. This doubt has given rise to the suggestion that the violets were a euphemism for the fleshpots of the day.[170] Perhaps so, but even if Akahito indulged in hyperbole, he may well have felt reluctant to tear himself away from so lovely a place. One commentator went so far as to liken Akahito's worship of nature—not only of flowers but rivers and mountains—to Hitomaro's emperor worship.[171] Akahito belonged to the same court-poet tradition as Hitomaro, but his poems, even those intended to celebrate the glories of the sovereign, are mainly concerned with sights before the poet's eyes.

Hitomaro's poetry possesses elusive depths, and there will always be room for fresh commentaries, but Akahito's poetry seems to be clarity itself. If there is a mystery surrounding him, it is why for so long he was ranked as Hitomaro's peer. A half-dozen of his waka are extremely beautiful, and perhaps that is enough to win poetic immortality, but it is puzzling that Akahito, rather than Okura or Yakamochi, should have been paired with Hitomaro by the *Kokinshū* and later poets. It is also possible that the diminution of Akahito's reputation in the twentieth century says more about that century than about the ultimate value of his poetry.

We know very little about Takahashi no Mushimaro, apparently a contemporary of Akahito. Only one poem, composed in 732, is dated. It has been conjectured that both Akahito and Mushimaro died in the smallpox epidemic of 737. Mushimaro's best poems, included in the "Mushimaro Collection," are not specifically identified as his, but they are stylistically and atmospherically similar to the known works. The "Mushimaro Collection" includes thirty chōka, some on legendary subjects like the story of Urashima Tarō, the man who returned to the world after sojourning what he supposed was three years with the daughter of the sea god in their palace under the sea, only to discover that (like Rip van Winkle) he had actually spent many years away from home.[172] Other chōka tell of the unhappy Maiden Tekona, or the even unhappier Maiden Unai, who was loved by two youths and killed herself because she was unwilling to choose between them. (The two young men also committed suicide.)[173]

The chōka dated 732 that Mushimaro presented to his protector Fujiwara no Umakai on his departure as inspector general of the Saikaidō is of interest not only because it is one of the rare facts we know about Mushimaro but because it is an occasional poem of the kind often found in collections of Chinese poetry but relatively unusual in Japan:

shirakumo no	At this time of year when the white-clouded
Tatsuta no yama no	Tatsuta Hill
tsuyu shimo ni	Begins slowly to crimson with dew and
irozuku toki ni	frost,
uchikoete	You cross it to go on a journey.
tabi yuku kimi wa	Over five hundred hills you will tramp your
ioeyama	way
iyuki sakumi	Till you reach the land of Tsukushi
ata mamoru	Where men guard the shore against the
Tsukushi ni itari	alien foes.
yama no soki	There, despatching your subordinates for
no no soki miyo to	inspection
tomo no he wo	To the extremities of hill and plain,
akachitsukawashi	You will survey the land's defenses
yamabiko no	everywhere,

kotaen kiwami *taniguku no* *sawataru kiwami* *kuni kata wo* *meshitamaite* *fuyugomori* *haru sariyukaba* *tobu tori no* *hayaku kimasana* *Tatsutaji no*	Even in that far place where Echo makes reply And at the remotest nook whither creeps the toad. But with the approach of spring time, Come back swiftly like a bird on the wing!
okabe no michi ni *ni tsutsuji no* *niowan toki no* *sakurabana* *sakinan toki ni* *yamatazu no* *mukaemaiden* *kimi ga kimasaba*	Yes, when the red azaleas glow by the wayside Amid the knolls along the Tatsuta road, And when the cherry-trees are in bloom, I will come to meet you—to greet you on your return.[174]

Mushimaro gave new life to the chōka by using it for themes that, although they lack the elegiac grandeur with which Hitomaro filled the form, sustain the reader's interest with a content easily recognizable to Chinese (or European) poets; but the chōka had not much longer to live, and Mushimaro's efforts, though interesting in themselves, led nowhere. Splendid chōka would be composed by some later *Man'yōshū* poets, but the Japanese had made the presumably unconscious decision that poetry must be completely poetic. Narrowly interpreted, this could only lead to short poems in which poetic perfection was attainable. Legends like that of Urashima did not disappear from literature but survived in the folktale, and the chōka came to seem an inappropriate and constricting form for the content.

One other important *Man'yōshū* poet is thought to have died in the epidemic of 737, Kasa no Kanamura, who composed mainly chōka, including several commemorating visits of the sovereign to Yoshino. These chōka, composed between 723 and 733, would seem to be a reversion to the manner of Hitomaro, but a comparison of Kanamura's most striking chōka, composed in 725, with celebrated ones by Hitomaro on similar subjects, quickly reveal the differences:

Though the land of wave-bright Naniwa
Regarded by all men as a ruined place
No better than an old reed-fence,
Was left all forgotten and unfriended—

Now that our Sovereign is pleased to dwell
Here at the Palace of Nagara,
Pillared stout and high,
Thence to rule his wide domain,
And the courtiers of the eighty clans
Have built their cottages on Ajifu Field,
This place has become an Imperial City,
If for but the time of their sojourn.[175]

This chōka suffers when compared with poems on ruined capitals by Hitomaro and Kurohito if only because it is so cheerful. One expects melancholy reflections, and instead Kanamura rejoices that the old capital is once more the scene of imperial pomp, if only briefly. It would take a more skillful poet than Kanamura to make this subject exciting.

It is tempting to put Kanamura down as a sycophantic court poet who could turn out a poem on commission without difficulty and without much distinction, but some of his poems do not fit this description. His chōka composed on the occasion of the Emperor Shōmu's visit to Inami in 726, for example, does not even mention the ostensible subject, but laments instead that the poet lacks a boat to convey him to Awaji Island where, he has heard, lovely fisher maids "cut dainty seaweed in the morning calm, and in the evening stillness burn salt-fires." There is something almost Proustian in Kanamura's fascination with girls he knows of only through report, but the poem itself hardly resembles what Hitomaro would have composed on such an occasion.[176]

Kanamura's most affecting poem was composed in 725, during the Emperor Shōmu's visit to the Detached Palace at Mika-no-hara:

A sojourner in Mika's plains
I saw you on the road,
A stranger to me like a cloud of heaven:
The words I could not speak to you,

Quite choked my heart.
Yet we two, by mercy of the gods,
Are now wedded in love and trust,
Lying upon each other's sleeve.
Ah, tonight! Would it were as long
As a hundred autumn nights together!

ENVOY

I have leaned, body and soul,
Towards you, beloved,
From the moment I saw you—
A stranger like a cloud of heaven.[177]

These poems prove that Kanamura was more than a conventionally competent court poet. In his own day he seems to have ranked higher than Akahito.[178] Kanamura certainly wrote many conventional poems, but he may have found the role of the court poet wearying and taken refuge at times in poems that were dictated not by his position but by his heart.

The first major *Man'yōshū* poet whose career can be traced in the official histories was Ōtomo no Tabito (665–731). Of course, we possess considerable information about members of the imperial family and high-ranking court officials who contributed a poem or two to the collection, but Tabito was both a major poet and an important official. His name first appears in an entry of the official history *Shoku Nihongi* for 710, when he was in his forty-sixth year. In his capacity as general of the Left he led a procession of Hayato and Emishi captives in a parade before the Empress Gemmei on New Year's Day. In 720 he was appointed as General of the Hayato Pacification Headquarters in Kyūshū, but was recalled to the capital later in the same year, after the death of the minister of the Right, Fujiwara no Fuhito. Tabito remained in the capital during the period known as "the age of Prince Nagaya," so called because the prince was the central figure in the political world. In 728 Tabito was once again sent to Kyūshū, this time as commanding general of the Dazaifu.[179]

Not long after Tabito left the capital, Prince Nagaya was denounced by the four sons of Fuhito for having resorted to black magic in the attempt to seize control of the country. The death of the infant born to the Emperor Shōmu and his consort Kōmyō (the daughter of Fuhito) was blamed on Nagaya's sinister practices, and the prince was forced to commit suicide. It is not clear whether Tabito was affected by these developments, though it has been suggested that his famous poems celebrating the pleasures of drink were occasioned by his disgust with a world where such events could take place.[180]

Only two poems composed by Tabito before he went to the Dazaifu have been preserved. Perhaps earlier poems were lost, but this is unlikely in view of the great care with which Tabito's son Ōtomo no Yakomochi collected his father's writings. One of the early poems describes the visit to Yoshino of the Emperor Shōmu in 724, just a month after his accession to the throne. This short chōka seems on the surface to be no more than a hackneyed compendium of familiar reactions to the much-admired sights:

mi Yoshino no	At holy Yoshino
Yoshino no miya wa	The palace of Yoshino,
yama kara shi	Thanks to the mountains,
tōtoku arashi	Seems nobility itself;
mizu kara shi	And thanks to the water,
sayakeku arashi	Seems purity itself.
ame tsuchi to	Long as heaven and earth,
nagaku hisashiku	It will last eternal;
yorozu yo ni	Through ten thousand ages
kawarazu aran	It will remain unchanged,
idemashi no miya[181]	This palace of delights.

Tsuchihashi Yutaka pointed out, however, that Tabito, instead of employing the word *kawa* (river), invariably mentioned in connection with the Yoshino landscape, spoke instead of *mizu* (water). He attributed this variation to a passage in the *Analects*: "The wise man delights in water; the good man delights in mountains."[182] A prediction that a place will last as long as heaven and earth was also commonplace in Chinese literature. The exact sources of Tabito's allusions are of less importance than his unspoken attempt to lend depth to familiar Japanese sentiments about that overly familiar place, Yoshino, by referring to Chinese examples. Many Japanese in later centuries would do the same.

The words "through ten thousand ages it will remain unchanged" on the surface seem no more than the usual hyperbole, but Tsuchihashi traced them to the *semmyō* (imperial edict), issued by the Emperor Shōmu at the time of his coronation, in which the same phrases occurred; these words were derived in turn from the semmyō of the Empress Gemmei at her coronation. In context, Gemmei's words apparently meant that she would continue the practice of relying on the Fujiwara family for assistance in governing the country. The unremarkable claim of Tabito's poem, that the palace of Yoshino would last forever, can therefore be interpreted as meaning that Tabito favored perpetual Fujiwara domination of the sovereign. The hanka appended to the chōka, which also seems at first glance to be no more than predictable praise for Yoshino, has also been given a quite different meaning:

mukashi mishi	The stream of Kisa
Kisa no ogawa wo	That I saw long ago,
ima mireba	When seen again now
iyoyo sayakeku	Appears to have become
narikeru kamo[183]	Even more pellucid.

Tsuchihashi interpreted this poem as meaning that at last the Empress Jitō's desire to have on the throne an emperor belonging to the senior line of Prince Kusakabe has been fulfilled, and the delighted Tabito is voicing his praise.[184] However, a note appended to the above chōka and hanka states that the poems were not actually presented. It would seem that Tabito, after all his efforts to impart special relevance to what could easily be taken for hackneyed expressions of praise of Yoshino, never had the pleasure of having his handiwork admired. It is also possible that Tsuchihashi's interpretation was excessively ingenious.

Tabito's other early poem (its date is not known) is a moderately interesting waka expressing his hopes that falling rain will not melt the snow accumulated on the trees on the mountain.[185] The early poems are so few that we cannot but be surprised that Tabito emerged as a major poet in 728, at the age of sixty-three. The first poems of this period were occasioned by the death of his wife, who had accompanied him to Kyūshū from the capital in that year. There is some uncertainty concerning which poems of the sequence Tabito himself composed and which were by his friend Yamanoue no Okura, at the time serving as governor of Chikuzen in Kyūshū. Most editors now believe that Okura wrote all the poems except the first, but in the persona of Tabito.[186] Even if the poems were not by Tabito himself, the tragic experience of his wife's death and the companionship of a poet of about his own age seem to have induced in Tabito the urge to write poetry. Many poems describe his longing for his wife or his yearning to be back in the capital. Among these are "Three poems written in the fifth year of Jinki, the Year of the Dragon, by the Commander of the Dazaifu, Lord Ōtomo, in affectionate remembrance of a dead person":

utsukushiki
hito no makiteshi
shikitae no
wa ga tamakura wo
maku hito arame ya[187]

Will ever there be
Someone else who will rest
Her head on my arms
As once my beloved wife
Made her pillow there?

A note says that the above poem was written "some ten days after being bereaved."

kaerubeku
toki wa narikeri
miyako nite
ta ga tamoto wo ka
wa ga makurakan

The time has arrived
To go back home again;
In the capital
On whose sleeve
Shall I pillow my head?

miyako naru
aretaru ie ni
hitori neba
tabi ni masarite
kurushikarubeshi[188]

When I sleep alone
In that long-forsaken house
In the capital,
It will be much more painful
Than even on my journey.

A note after the above two poems indicates that they were composed as Tabito neared the capital on the return journey. Other poems written along the way contrast his present feelings as he passed various places with those he had when he passed the same places with his wife on the outward journey. For example, here is the poem he composed at Cape Mimune, east of the present harbor of Kōbe:

yukusa ni wa
futari wa ga mishi
kono saki wo

As I go by, alone,
The cape we saw together
On the outward voyage,

hitori sugureba	How it breaks my heart!
kokoroganashimo[189]	

Once back in the capital, his dream for years, the loneliness of his house was even more heartrending:

wagimoko ga	Every time I see
ueshi ume no ki	The plum tree planted
miru goto ni	By my beloved,
kokoro musetsutsu	My heart is choked
namida shi nagaru[190]	And the tears flow.

Tabito's poems on the death of his wife reveal unmistakable grief; yet we know that during his stay at the Dazaifu he was "consoled" by various women of pleasure, notably one Koshima, who wrote two poems that are included in the *Man'yōshū*:

ō naraba	If you were an ordinary man,
kamokamo sen wo	I would behave as I please,
kashikomi to	But out of deference
furitaki sode wo	I keep myself from waving
shinobite aru kamo[191]	The sleeve I would like to wave.

Tabito was not insensible to Koshima's grief, as he revealed in a poem he composed before leaving on the homeward journey:

Yamatoji no	When I pass by
Kibi no Koshima wo	Koshima in Kibi along
sugite yukaba	The Yamato road,
Tsukushi no Koshima	I shall surely remember
omōen kamo[192]	Koshima of Tsukushi.

Shortly before Tabito returned to Nara he presented a Japanese koto (zither) of paulownia wood to Fusasaki, one of the four Fujiwara brothers responsible for the death of Prince Nagaya.[193] The gift was accompanied by an explanation in Chinese of how the koto had appeared in his dream in the form of a girl who expressed joy that she (who had formerly been a tree) had been fashioned into a koto; she had feared that her wood might be put to unworthy use. The girl in the dream composed a poem to celebrate the occasion, and Tabito replied in kind.

Fusasaki acknowledged the gift with a letter in Chinese and an indifferent waka.

Apart from the possible political significance of the gift and what it reveals of Tabito's attitude toward the Fujiwara family, the sources of the Chinese phraseology in his letter of presentation are of interest. Allusions have been traced back to the *Wen Hsüan*, to the celebrated erotic tale *Yu hsien k'u*, and to the philosopher Chuang Tzu.[194] Such borrowings make it plain that works of Chinese literature and philosophy were known to educated Japanese.

Tabito's pleasure in plum blossoms, attested by a series of waka written by him and his friends just before he left the Dazaifu in the first month of 730, are another sign of his Chinese tastes, plum blossoms having traditionally been associated by the Chinese with the scholar.[195] Thirty-two poems, with a preface in Chinese, describe the occasion and bear witness to the hold that the cult of plum blossoms had come to exert over upper-class Japanese, who enjoyed imagining they were Chinese composing poems on the falling blossoms.[196] In later collections of Japanese poetry, cherry blossoms would largely displace plum blossoms in the affections of the poets, as they moved from Chinese to Japanese aesthetic preferences. None of the thirty-two poems on plum blossoms composed by Tabito and his friends is really distinguished, but four appended waka on plum blossoms, apparently by Tabito, are more interesting. Here is the first:

nokoritaru	Plum blossoms
yuki ni majireru	Lingering on the boughs
ume no hana	Amidst the snow—
hayaku na chiri so	Do not fall too quickly.
yuki wa kenu tomo[197]	Even if the snow melts away.

Although unremarkable in conception and simplicity itself in expression, the poem is affecting, largely because the poet addresses the plum blossoms as if they were sentient, recalling the personification in the tale about the koto. The last of the four appended waka gives the response made by the blossoms:

ume no hana	The plum blossoms
ime ni kataraku	Addressed me in a dream:
miyabitaru	"We consider ourselves

hana to are mou	Most elegant flowers—
sake ni ukabe koso[198]	Please let us float on sake."

The blossoms' desire to float in elegance in a gentleman's sake cup, in a manner befitting their special status among the flowers, suggests the degree of refinement that had been attained in emulation of Chinese culture. Another poem by Tabito, composed on this occasion, is explicitly Taoist:

kumo ni tobu	Better than an elixir
kusuri hamu yo wa	For flying in the clouds,
miyako miba	If I saw the capital
iyashiki a ga mi	It would make even a wretch
mata ochinubeshi[199]	Like myself young once again.

Mention of an "elixir" that permits whomever drinks it to soar into the clouds brings to mind the various elixirs consumed by the Taoists. The poem not only expresses Tabito's longing to return to the capital but his profession of Taoist beliefs. Taoism would be given careful presentation by Kūkai in his *Indications of the Goals of the Three Teachings*, but at this time it probably meant mainly a professed indifference to worldly things. It was popular among nobles of the Nara court, as we know from poems in the *Kaifūsō*, but it was generally linked with Buddhism or Shintō and was not itself professed as a religion.[200]

Chinese influence colored not only Tabito's writings but those of the people who exchanged poetry and correspondence with him. The rapid absorption of Chinese culture by the court led at times to an ostentatious display of learning. A letter to Tabito from his friend Yoshida no Yoroshi is a tissue of allusions to Chinese texts, as this excerpt may suggest:

> I entreat you, Lord, to spread virtue like Lu Kung, who tamed the pheasant in the morning, and to leave behind benevolent acts like K'ung Yu, who freed the turtles in the evening—so that your name may be spoken of, like Chang Ch'ang's and Chao Kung Han's, a hundred generations hence, so that your life like Chih Sung Tzu's and Wang Tzu Ch'iao's may extend a thousand years.[201]

More effective than such ponderous attempts to display mastery of foreign literary traditions are the thirteen poems in praise of sake by Tabito, probably composed soon after his return to the capital from the

Dazaifu. The sequence is loosely constructed, though scholars have detected a traditional Chinese pattern in the arrangement.[202] The sequence opens with this poem:

shirushi naki	Instead of fretting
mono wo omowazu wa	Over things of no avail,
hitotsuki no	It would seem better
nigoreru sake wo	To drink a cupful
nomu beku arurashi[203]	Of clouded sake.

"Clouded sake" (*nigoreru sake*) occurs elsewhere in the sequence and means unrefined (or unfiltered) sake.

The specifically Taoist tone of the sequence is most apparent in the third poem:

inishie no	It was true also
nana no sakashiki	Even of the seven sages
hitotachi mo	Who lived long ago:
horiseshi mono wa	What they had a craving for
sake ni shi arurashi[204]	Was very likely sake.

Tabito here was referring to the "Seven Sages of the Bamboo Grove," a group of hermits of the Chin dynasty (265–316) who fled the turbulence of society to live amicably together, their relations cemented by the sake they consumed. They were often held up as perfect examples of how Taoists should behave in this world.

The last poem of the thirteen, though it seems to be much of a piece with the others, has been interpreted rather differently:

moda orite	Keeping glum silence
sakashira suru wa	In the role of a wise man
sake nomite	Is still not as good
ei naki suru ni	As drinking one's own sake
nao shikazukeri[205]	And weeping drunken tears.

This poem seems to refer to the maudlin thoughts that often overtake the drinker late in a party; the poet says that it is better to experience them (and the accompanying tears) than not to drink at all. Tsuchihashi, however, interpreted the poem as an expression of Tabito's disgust with court society, occasioned perhaps by the ruthlessness with which Prince Nagaya was hunted down. Tabito's only escape from brutal realities was in liquor. If true, it means that he had rejected the comfort of Buddhism and did not experience the satisfaction that Confucianism should have instilled of serving the government.[206]

It is hard to know how much credence to give to such an interpretation, but the Taoist tone of the poem is undeniable, and it is possible that the world of the immortals, evoked by plum blossoms and attainable with the aid of drink, became in the end the only real world for Tabito. He died in 731, not long after returning to the capital. One of his last poems was composed in response to some poems that the priest Mansei had sent him:

koko ni arite	Now that I am here,
Tsukushi ya izuchi	I wonder where Tsukushi is.
shirakumo no	It would seem to be
tanabiku yama no	Off by yonder mountains
kata ni shi arurashi[207]	Where white clouds lie in layers.

Tsukushi—the Dazaifu, presumably—where he had spent years of service, had lost reality now that he was back in the capital. Was it perhaps on the other side of those mountains where the clouds trailed? Did it really exist?

Tabito is a memorable poet, though relatively few of his poems appear in the *Man'yōshū*. Chinese influence is manifest, not only in the themes of his poetry but in his attitudes toward his materials; his decision nevertheless to compose his poetry in Japanese, rather than Chinese, indicates that for all the influence and comfort he received from the Chinese poetry of the past, he believed that the appropriate language for the matters he wished to describe in his poetry was his own.

Tabito's name is often linked with that of his friend Yamanoue no Okura (660?–733?). Okura's reputation has sharply risen in the twentieth century until he ranks second only to Hitomaro. The elevation of his reputation can be explained in part by the increased importance now attached to the chōka, as compared to the past, when the waka of the *Man'yōshū* were more highly praised. But the fact that Okura, rather than some other poet known for his chōka, has benefited by this revaluation is due to the content of his poetry. Most Japanese poems, at least those written before the twentieth century, are devoid of intellectual or social concerns, no matter how beautifully they capture the emotional states of the poets or their perceptions of nature. Okura's poetry provides rare examples of such concerns. His poems are often introduced by long prefaces in Chinese that explain not merely the circumstances of composition but the underlying philosophical truths, whether Confucian, Buddhist, or Taoist. Okura's poetry tends to be so earnest in its tone that he has often been contrasted with the lyric Akahito or the sake-loving Tabito, as if they were totally dissimilar. The differences separating Okura and other *Man'yōshū* poets have in fact been exaggerated, but the individuality of his voice is apparent.

Okura's distinctive style has in recent years been attributed not only to his personality but to his birth in Korea. According to this thesis, he fled with his father and others to Japan from Paekche in 663, the year of the disastrous defeat of the Japanese forces in Korea at Hakusukinoe.[208] The main literary significance of Okura's having been of Korean descent and a refugee at the age of three or four is that he probably obtained from his father a better education in the Chinese classics (and possibly also Buddhist texts) than Japanese of equivalent social standing.

We possess almost no information about Okura before he was appointed in 701 as a member of an embassy to China.[209] Although he was only a junior scribe (*shōroku*), an inconspicuous figure, without rank or title, in a large delegation, it was presumably his knowledge of Chinese that had earned him his position. Perhaps, as has been suggested, he served as a copier of sutras before being sent to China.[210] Okura had attended the court and had accompanied imperial progresses, composing poetry in the manner of Hitomaro, but he was not an official and was not required to compose eulogies in the manner of a recognized court poet.

The embassy to China was the seventh sent by the Japanese to the T'ang court (the first was in 630), and the first since the fall of Paekche. Embassies were dispatched at irregular intervals, sometimes as close as a year apart, but sometimes after long periods of time, as became increasingly true toward the end: when the eighteenth and last embassy was supposed to leave for China in 894 after a lapse of sixty years, it was canceled at the insistence of the ambassador, Sugawara no Michizane. The embassy of which Okura was a member probably consisted of five thousand or more men, divided among four ships, but only a small number of Japanese—perhaps no more than thirty-five—were permitted by the Chinese to proceed from the coast to the capital at Ch'ang-an.[211]

Okura probably remained in Ch'ang-an for two years, returning with the other members of the embassy in 704, but there is some reason to think he might have stayed until 707. This was a time when the Japanese were rapidly absorbing many elements of contemporary Chinese civilization: they learned to play kickball (*kemari*), backgammon (*sugoroku*), and go, as well as various musical instruments; they acquired a taste for glutinous rice, tea, and sweets; and they began to celebrate such festivals as Tanabata.[212] The embassies served as the channels through which this knowledge of China passed into Japan. We do not know, however, how Okura spent his time in Ch'ang-an. Perhaps he met literary men,[213] but nothing in his writings reveals his Chinese acquaintances.

One of Okura's earliest poems may have been written in 701, in between the unsuccessful attempt of the embassy to cross the sea to China and the actual departure:

amagakeri	Soaring like a bird
ari ga yoitsutsu	across the sky,
miramedomo	he is present and he sees.
hito koso shirane	Men do not know it,
matsu wa shiruran	but the pine must know.[214]

This cryptic poem, a rejoinder to one by Naga no Okimaro, is believed to refer to the ghost of Prince Arima, executed for treason in 658: Arima's ghost can see the world of men, but they cannot see it; only the pine is aware of the ghost's presence.

About the time that Okura was to leave China and return to Japan he composed what has been called the only poem in the *Man'yōshū* composed in a foreign country:

iza kodomo	Come on, my lads,
hayaku Yamato e	Let's hurry back to Japan—
Ōtomo no	The pines on the beach
Mitsu no hamamatsu	At Mitsu in Ōtomo
machikoinuran[215]	Must wait longingly for us.

Okura was promoted to the lower junior fifth rank in 714 and appointed governor of Hōki in 716. In 721 he became a tutor to the crown prince, the future Emperor Shōmu. It may have been at this time that he compiled *Ruijū Karin*, a classified collection of Japanese poems that survives only in passages quoted in the *Man'yōshū*.

Okura remained in the capital after Shōmu ascended the throne in 724. A postscript states that Okura composed a Tanabata poem at the residence of the minister of the Left, Prince Nagaya.[216] In the twelfth month of 730, at a farewell banquet for Ōtomo no Tabito, who was about to return to the capital, Okura composed this poem:

amazakaru	Now that I have lived
hina ni itsu tose	Five years in the provinces
sumaitsutsu	At the end of the world,
miyako no teburi	I have quite forgotten
wasuraenikeri[217]	The ways of the capital.

If the figure (five years) given in the poem is accurate, Okura's appointment as governor of Chikuzen in Kyūshū took place late in 725 or early in 726. He seems to have returned permanently to the capital in 732.

The post of governor of Chikuzen was by far the most important Okura ever held, not only because Chikuzen was a major province but because many other officials with literary interests were stationed in the area. Okura's friendship and literary association with Tabito in particular inspired some of his finest works. Book V of the *Man'yōshū* is devoted mainly to poems by the two men. They bear prefaces in Chinese that present Buddhist and Confucian doctrine:

> Thus have I heard: that the birth and death of the four modes of life are comparable to the emptiness of all dreams, that the course of life through the three realms is like the endless spin of a cycle. . . . Man's existence is no more than the flash of a white steed across the evening as glimpsed through a crevice in a wall. Oh how painful it is! The maiden's crimson face is gone forever with the woman's three duties to obey, and young white flesh is destroyed forever with the wife's four virtues. . . .[218]

Another poem, with the title "Poem to Set a Confused Heart Straight," opens with this preface in Chinese:

> There is a certain type of man who knows he should honor his father and mother, but forgets to discharge his filial duties with devotion. He does not concern himself with his wife and children, but treats them more lightly than a pair of discarded shoes. . . . Though his spirit may soar free among the blue clouds, his body still remains among the dust of this world. He shows no sign of being a sage who has undergone ascetic discipline and mastered the Way.[219]

The poem itself is an attack on the indifference to worldly obligations taught by the Taoists. Not only does it insist on the importance of family relationships as taught by the Confucianists and on the ascetic discipline expected of Buddhists, but includes such injunctions as:

When you go to heaven,
You can do as you please;
But on the earth
There is the emperor.
Under the sun and moon
That shine in the heavens,
To the ends of the sky
Where the clouds stretch far away,
To the ends of the earth
Where the toads creep about,
He reigns over all.
A wonderful land it is![220]

The import of these lines would seem to be that no man, even a professed Taoist who has renounced worldly ties, can ignore the emperor's claim to his loyal service.

Other poems by Okura with a seemingly simple message are augmented with philosophical prefaces that state their real intent, whether to describe the poet's conviction that nothing is more precious than one's children, or his insistence that provincial governors must familiarize themselves with local customs. He also wrote graceful waka about plum blossoms in the manner appropriate to a gentleman-scholar. But Okura's reputation rests mainly on three or four chōka that are unique among the poems of the *Man'yōshū*. His themes were by no means unique: the impermanence of human life and the sufferings that come with old age are universal themes, and the *Man'yōshū* contains a number of such poems; but Okura's expression is so powerful and compelling that whatever similarities exist with other poems are quickly forgotten. His poem on the "difficulty of living in this world" contains this memorable passage:

Few are the nights they keep,
When, sliding back the plank doors,
They reach their beloved ones,
And sleep, arms intertwined,
Before, with staffs at their waists,

They totter along the road,
Laughed at here, and hated there.[221]

Okura's poems on "suffering from old age and prolonged illness, and thinking of his children,"[222] are preceded by an essay in Chinese that opens with a declaration of abiding faith in the Three Treasures of Buddhism—Buddha, the Law, and the Priesthood. He wonders why he has nevertheless been afflicted for ten years with an illness that has left him debilitated. In vain he has sought some doctor who could cure him. He has considered also the practices followed by the Taoists to achieve immortality, but declares his willingness to forgo immortality, providing he is relieved of his illness. A poem in Chinese resumes these sentiments, and this is followed by a chōka and envoys in Japanese. Unlike the abstract prefatory matter, the poems abound in images drawn from daily life:

So long as lasts the span of life,
We wish for peace and comfort
With no evil and no mourning,
But life is hard and painful.
As the common saying has it,
Bitter salt is poured into the smarting wound,
Or the burdened horse is packed with an upper load,
Illness shakes my old body with pain.
All day I breathe in grief
And sigh throughout the night.
For long years my illness lingers,
I grieve and groan month after month,
And though I would rather die,
I cannot, and leave my children,
Noisy like the flies of May.
Whenever I watch them
My heart burns within.
And tossed this way and that,
I weep aloud.

The most celebrated of Okura's poems is his "Dialogue on Poverty." The dialogue is between two men, the first a poor but proud man who wonders how people worse off than himself manage to survive, the second a destitute man who indirectly answers the first man's questions by describing his misery:

On the night when the rain beats,
Driven by the wind,
On the night when the snow-flakes mingle
With the sleety rain,
I feel so helplessly cold.
I nibble at a lump of salt,
Sip the hot, oft-diluted dregs of saké;
And coughing, snuffling,
And stroking my scanty beard,
I say in my pride,
"There's none worthy, save I!"
But I shiver still with cold,
I pull up my hempen bed-clothes,
Wear what few sleeveless clothes I have,
But cold and bitter is the night!
As for those poorer than myself,
Their parents must be cold and hungry,
Their wives and children beg and cry.
Then, how do you struggle through life?

Wide as they call the heaven and earth,
For me they have shrunk quite small;
Bright though they call the sun and moon,
They never shine for me.
Is it the same for all men,
Or for me alone?
By rare chance I was born a man
And no meaner than his fellows,
But, wearing unwadded sleeveless clothes
In tatters, like weeds waving in the sea,
Hanging from my shoulders,
And under the sunken roof,
Within the leaning walls,
Here I lie on straw
Spread on bare earth,
With my parents at my pillow,
My wife and children at my feet,
All huddled in grief and tears.
No fire sends up smoke
At the cooking-place,

And in the cauldron
A spider spins its web.
With not a grain to cook,
We moan like the "night-thrush."
Then, "to cut," as the saying is,
"The ends of what is already too short,"
The village headman comes,
With rod in hand, to our sleeping-place,
Growling for his dues.
Must it be so hopeless—
The way of this world?

ENVOY

Nothing but pain and shame in this world of men,
But I cannot fly away,
Wanting the wings of a bird.[223]

During the next thousand years not another such poem would be composed in Japanese. Okura's ability to enter into the feelings of two poor men—the first, perhaps the village headman mentioned in the second man's narration, taking bare comfort from the existence of people who are worse off than himself, the second, overcome by the misery of his life—may well have been the product of actual observation during his time as the governor of a distant province. For later poets, farmers or fishermen were usually small figures in a panorama of sky and mountains, much like those depicted in Chinese landscape paintings; and their dwellings, if represented, were picturesque rather than miserable. The poetic diction that would be established at the beginning of the tenth century would not permit the ugliness evoked by Okura's poem either in language or subject matter.

The differences between Okura's "Dialogue on Poverty" and other poems of its time can be demonstrated with numbers: thirty of the words are not found elsewhere in the *Man'yōshū*.[224] Even so common a word as *mazushiki* (poverty-stricken) does not occur in any other *Man'yōshū* poem and certainly not in the *Kokinshū* or the later court anthologies. Okura seems to have decided to eliminate conventional elegance from this poem, whether in the language or the thought.[225] The irregularity in the length of some lines suggests a poetic impulse so powerful it could not be confined by the rules of metrics. The accent of truth in Okura's words owes much to his refusal to beautify his expression. His concern for the cold and hungry of the world undoubtedly reflected his Confucian training, but later Japanese poets, even if they were officials and had passed examinations on the Chinese classics, would not express these concerns, though they are found in the poetry of the great Chinese masters.

Not all of Okura's poetry was composed at this level of intensity. He wrote so many poems on Tanabata, the festival held on the seventh night of the seventh moon to celebrate the meeting of two stars, that some scholars credit him with having first made this Chinese legend popular in Japan.[226] He also wrote many poems at parties, including:

Okurara wa	I, Okura, will leave now;
ima wa makaran	My children may be crying,
ko nakuran	And that mother of theirs, too,
sore sono haha mo	May be waiting for me!
wa wo matsuran so[227]	

This poem has sometimes been cited as evidence of Okura's dislike of parties,[228] an impression that accords with the seriousness of most of his poetry; but the poem was probably a compliment to his host on leaving a party that he had thoroughly enjoyed, a transparent excuse not really meant to convey concern over his wife and children.

But even if Okura enjoyed parties and composing poetry with his friends under the plum blossoms, it is not for such subjects that his poetry is remembered today but for the chōka describing sickness, death, and misery, themes that bespeak his indebtedness to Chinese literature, though Okura lived before the great T'ang poets whom he most resembled.

The Fourth Period (730–759)

The final period of the *Man'yōshū* was dominated by one poet, Ōtomo no Yakamochi (718?–785). His importance was not confined to his poems; he was the editor of the bulk of (if not the entire) *Man'yōshū*, and the last four books in particular are given over so largely to his poetry that they have been referred to as Yakamochi's "poem-diary." His poetry lacks the grandeur of Hitomaro's and the social concern of Okura's, but his voice is distinctive. Anticipating the *Kokinshū*, his poetry is often melancholy rather than tragic, exquisitely phrased rather than explosively intense. This does not mean that his poetry lacks variety; on the contrary, Yakamochi wrote in almost every mode, from highly personal lyrics to public poems composed in response to a command from the court. So many of his poems have been preserved that it is inevitable that some are not of first quality, but the best rank near the summit of *Man'yōshū* expression.

Yakamochi was the son of Ōtomo no Tabito. His mother was not Tabito's legal consort, but Yakamochi seems not to have suffered on that account, presumably because Tabito had no other son. In 727, when Yakamochi was nine years old,[229] he was taken by his father to the Dazaifu. Yakamochi's stepmother, Tabito's consort, accompanied them. After her death in 728, Tabito sent for his half-sister, Lady Ōtomo of Sakanoue (c. 700–c. 750), presumably to aid in Yakamochi's education.[230] It is not clear how much the boy Yakamochi learned about poetry from his aunt, herself a minor yet accomplished poet; but a poem he wrote in 750 seems to echo the poetry composed at a party held at the Dazaifu in 730 to celebrate the plum blossoms, suggesting that the boy had already acquired sufficient competence as a poet to be present on such an occasion.[231]

Tabito died in 731, the year after his return to the capital, but Lady Sakanoue continued to look after her nephew. Before long—perhaps in 732[232]—the precocious Yakamochi was addressing love poetry to her daughter, then aged eleven or twelve. Eventually, about 740, they would be married. This was Yakamochi's first poem of courtship:

haru no no ni	In the springtime field
asaru kigishi no	A pheasant, searching for food,
tsumagoi ni	Lets the hunters know
ono ga atari wo	His hiding place by his cries
hito ni shiretsutsu[233]	Of yearning for his wife.

The pheasant, like ardent young Yakamochi, cannot help but voice his love, even if he is risking danger. Another early poem, dated 733, was apparently written on an assigned topic, as we can infer from a poem composed at that time by Lady Sakanoue on the same subject, the crescent moon.[234] Yakamochi's likening of the crescent moon to an eyebrow, a simile also found in her poem, was familiar from Chinese poetry. A more interesting poem was about the *uguisu*, a kind of song thrush:

uchikirashi	The sky is fogged over
yuki wa furitsutsu	And snow keeps up a steady fall,

shikasugani	Yet all the same,
wagie no sono ni	In the garden of my house
uguisu naku mo[235]	An uguisu is singing.

This poem is indebted to earlier *Man'yōshū* poetry, evidence that he had carefully studied the works of his precedessors. Many poems in the *Man'yōshū* echo older examples, but Yakamochi borrowed more obviously than, say, Tabito or Okura. His poem on the snow and the uguisu presents a familiar contrast between nature and the calendar: the fog and snow seem to say that it is still winter, but the singing of the uguisu proclaims that spring has come. This kind of contrast, at first quite charming, would become hackneyed before long. Yakamochi's poem echoes two others composed in 730 at the Dazaifu on the occasion of plum-blossom viewing. The first was by Tabito:

wa ga sono ni	In my garden
ume no hana chiru	Plum blossoms are scattering;
hisakata no	Or is it snow
ame yori yuki no	That, from the overarching sky,
nagarekuru kamo[236]	Comes pouring down from above?

This was the response by Ōtomo no Momoyo:

ume no hana	Where do you suppose
chiraku wa izuku	Plum blossoms would be falling?
shikasuga ni	Yet all the same,
kono ki no yama ni	Here at Castle Mountain,
yuki wa furitsutsu	The snow keeps up a steady fall.[237]

Two of the five lines of Yakamochi's poem were lifted bodily from Momoyo's poem, and mention of the garden seems to come from Tabito's. The main difference between Yakamochi's poem and the two others is that he does not profess to confuse the snow and white plum blossoms. This most hackneyed of tropes, traceable as far back as the Chinese poetry of the Six Dynasties (220–589), is found in a poem by Tabito in the *Kaifūsō*. Yakamochi substituted for plum blossoms the uguisu, a bird often found in paintings in the proximity of these blossoms, but this was his only contribution. An even more conspicuous example of Yakamochi's borrowing occurs in the poem he composed after the death of his first wife:

imo ga mishi
yado ni hana saki
toki wa henu
wa ga naku namida
imada hinaku ni[238]

Flowers are blooming
In the garden my wife knew.
How time has gone by!
And yet the tears I shed then
Have still not had time to dry.

This poem was obviously borrowed from one by Okura:

imo ga mishi
ōchi no hana wa
chirinubeshi
wa ga naku namida
imada hinaku ni[239]

The bead-tree blossoms
My wife knew
Surely have scattered;
And yet the tears I shed then
Have still not had time to dry.

Yakamochi borrowed three of five lines from Okura's poem and changed the conception very little, but the specific mention of the passage of time points to this being a later work: the passage of time and the changes it brings would be a favorite theme of *Kokinshū* and subsequent poets.

Yakamochi borrowed not only from Okura's poetry but from his prefaces in Chinese in which he described the backgrounds of some important poems. Yakamochi borrowed from other poets too, notably Hitomaro and Kanamura, but the influence of Okura, whom he surely met as a boy, was the strongest. In the preface to one of his poems Yakamochi confessed that he had never "found his way to the gates of Yama and Kaki." For centuries this was interpreted as meaning that he felt inadequate before Yama(be) no Akahito and Kaki(nomoto) no Hitomaro; but some twentieth-century scholars believe that "Yama" referred not to Akahito but to Yama(noue) no Okura.[240]

Yakamochi's adaptations of the writings of Okura were on the level of language, not of intellectual content. He nowhere touched on harsh subjects such as the infirmities of old age or the misery of poverty, and his prefaces lack the Buddhist or Confucian convictions that gave additional depth to Okura's poems. This does not mean, however, that Yakamochi's poems lack individuality, or that his high reputation was undeserved. Modern commentators continue to find new interest in his poetry. Yamamoto Kenkichi, for example, was particularly impressed by the poems in which Yakamochi spoke of his *ibusemi*, a term suggesting a sense of frustration or of melancholy. The word occurs in some of

Yakamochi's best-known waka. One bears the title "Higurashi" (Dusk Cicadas):

komori nomi	Melancholy because
oreba ibusemi	I had been shut up all day,
nagusan to	To divert myself
idetachi kikeba	I went outside and listened:
kinaku higurashi[241]	Locusts had come and were singing.

A second poem at first glance seems quite similar:

amagomori	Melancholy at heart,
kokoro ibusemi	Having been shut in by rain,
ide mireba	I went out and looked:
Kasuga no yama wa	The mountains at Kasuga
irozukinikeri[242]	Had taken on fall colors.

Despite the resemblances between the two poems, the last lines create a different mood: in the first poem, the poet's melancholy is prolonged and confirmed by the monotonous dinning of the locusts, but in the second poem his dissatisfaction is relieved by the discovery that the nearby hills have changed colors. Yamamoto believed that *ibusemi* was a key word in understanding Yakamochi,[243] and contrasted it with *obōshi*, a word of rather similar meaning that occurs in poems by Hitomaro and others: *obōshi* was used to describe a state of depression for which some cause existed, but *ibusemi* referred to a causeless dissatisfaction and lassitude that struck Yamamoto as being specifically modern.[244] These poems of Yakamochi's youth suggest a state of mind reminiscent of the ennui described by nineteenth-century European poets, and the mood is found also in waka of the Heian period and later.

Ibusemi by no means typified Yakamochi's poetry. Apart from his public poems, which are naturally not melancholy, he wrote many love poems that express a positive personality far removed from the languor of ennui:

chidori naku	Over the river ferry at Saho,
Saho no kawato no	Where the sanderlings cry—
kiyoki se wo	When can I come to you

uma uchiwatashi	Crossing on horseback
itsuka kayowan	The crystal-clear shallows?[245]

Another poem in the same group of seven addressed to a woman suggests his irritation at not being able, in a more masculine manner, to control his emotions:

masurao to	How I waste and waste away
omoeru ware wo	With love forlorn—
kaku bakari	I who have thought myself
mitsure ni mitsure	A strong man!
katamoi wo sen[246]	

Although this expression of exasperation over his susceptibility to love seems genuine, Yakamochi enjoyed the company of women. In addition to the many poems he addressed to his wife and aunt, poems were sent to no fewer than fourteen named women as well as a number of unnamed women.[247] Among the women he loved, Lady Kasa was the best poet. All of her surviving twenty-nine poems were addressed to Yakamochi, and all are love poems. If Yakamochi had not decided to include these private poems when he edited the *Man'yōshū*, we would know nothing about this poet of exceptional ability. Her "feminine" expression perfectly balances Yakamochi's masculinity:

wa ga yado no	In the loneliness of my heart
yūkagekusa no	I feel as if I should perish
shiratsuyu no	Like the pale dew-drop
kenugani moto na	Upon the grass of my garden
omōyuru kamo	In the gathering shades of twilight.[248]

Another poem in the same group contains a note of desperation:

omoinishi	If it were death to love,
shini suru mono ni	I should have died—
aramaseba	And died again
chitabi so ware wa	One thousand times over.
shinikaeramashi[249]	

Lady Kasa's love seems to have grown the more intense as she realized that it was not fully reciprocated:

aiomowanu	To love you who love me not
hito wo omou wa	Is like going to a great temple
ōtera no	To bow in adoration
gaki no shirie ni	Behind the back of the famished devil.
nuka tsuku gotoshi[250]	

Kasa in this poem compared with bitter irony her attempt to win Yakamochi's love with the idiotic gesture of bowing one's head to the ground before the statue of a hungry demon, a sinner condemned to hell because of his avarice, and bowing at the image from behind! The word *gaki* (hungry demon) is a rare instance of a word used in its Sino-Japanese pronunciation, and as a metaphor is unique. The last two poems of the sequence bear a note stating that they were sent to Yakamochi after their separation.

Yakamochi seems to have been overwhelmed by Lady Kasa's love, and he tried to escape her.[251] He responded with two poems, in the first declaring that he felt oppressed at the thought they would not meet again, possibly not a sincere statement of his feelings. The second expressed despair over his inability to be successful in love:

nakanaka ni	Silence, actually,
moda mo aramashi wo	Would have been preferable.
nani su to ka	What had I in mind
aimisomeken	When first we began to meet?
togezaramaku ni[252]	There was no chance of success.

These and other poems exchanged with court ladies provide proof of Yakamochi's complicated involvements with women. He responded to their poems with appropriate gallantry, but love was not the most important element in his life. He took his responsibilities as an official seriously, in keeping with the long tradition of Ōtomo family service to the emperor. He seems not to have become involved in court politics, but he was associated with Tachibana no Moroe, and this connection would have unpleasant consequences when the latter's enemy, Fujiwara no Nakamaro, came to power. In 744 Prince Asaka, the heir of the Emperor Shōmu, died under mysterious circumstances. Some think he may have been the victim of a plot by Nakamaro to remove the prince from the succession and to clear the way for Shōmu's daughter, whose mother was a Fujiwara, to follow him on the throne.[253] Yakamochi wrote six elegies for the dead prince, including this stirring hanka:

Ōtomo no	My heart, that bears the fame of Ōtomo
na ni ou yuki obite	My trust to serve, quiver on back,
yorozu yo ni	For a myriad ages,
tanomishi kokoro	Where shall I take it now?[254]
izuku ka yosen	

Yakamochi was proud to allude to his family's ancient reputation as the quiver bearers, or personal guards, of the imperial family. In this poem he asks how he is to carry on family traditions when, because of the prince's death, there will be no legitimate sovereign to serve.

In 745 Yakamochi was appointed as governor of Etchū, a province on the Japan Sea coast. Etchū was remote, but it was an important province, and its area had been increased four years earlier by an imperial decree that joined to it the small province of Noto. The five years that Yakamochi spent in Etchū were the most productive in poetry of his entire life, both in quantity and quality.[255]

A chōka by Yakamochi favored especially during periods of nationalism was composed in 749 after the discovery of gold in the province of Mutsu. This was the first time gold had been found in Japan, and it could not have occurred at a more opportune moment: the great statue of Roshana Buddha, erected in Nara by command of the Emperor Shōmu,[256] could now be given a coating of gold leaf. The delighted emperor declared at the ceremony when the statue was consecrated that he was the servant of the Three Treasures of Buddhism. The reign name (*nengō*) was changed from Tempyō to Tempyō Kampō, *kampō* meaning "gratitude for the treasure."

Shōmu also issued a semmyō to his officials in which he quoted the oath of loyalty to the throne made many years before by the Ōtomo family. Yakamochi was overcome by this imperial recognition of the service of his family which, despite its ancient lineage, had at times suffered eclipse, and was particularly moved by the emperor's reference to the Ōtomo and Saeki families as warriors who directly protected the emperor (*uchinoikusa*).[257] In the chōka celebrating the discovery of gold, Yakamochi, after first describing the event, moved on to an account of his family:

I ponder more deeply than ever
How to the Ōtomo clan belongs a great office
In which served our far-off divine ancestor
Who bore the title of Ōkumé-nushi.

We are the sons of fathers who sang,
"At sea be my body water-soaked,
On land be it with grass overgrown,
Let me die by the side of my Sovereign!
Never will I look back";
And who to this day from olden times
Have kept their warrior's name forever clean.
Verily Ōtomo and Saeki are the clans
Pledged to the maxim, as pronounced
By their ancestors: "Extinguish not, sons,
The names of your fathers! Serve your sovereign!"
O let us grip birchwood bows in our hands,
Wear on our loins double-edged swords,
And stand guard morning and evening!
There are no men but we to defend the imperial gate—
I exclaim with a fervent heart
When I hear His Majesty's gracious words,
That overwhelm me with awe.[258]

The song "At sea be my body water-soaked..." was often quoted in the first half of the twentieth century as a self-sacrificing ideal for the Japanese to emulate. But there is no mention in the poem of the divinity of the imperial family; the Ōtomo and Saeki clans are supremely loyal to the throne, but their ancestry can also be traced back to the Age of the Gods, and the successive emperors have never failed to acknowledge their gratitude for the protection afforded by these ancient guardsmen.

In the fifth month of 756 the Retired Emperor Shōmu, the protector of the Ōtomo family, died. A week later Ōtomo no Kojihi, the governor of Izumo, was accused of having slandered the court. He was later released, probably because of his wife's close connections with the Fujiwara family, but Yakamochi felt impelled to address a chōka of admonition to his clansmen in which, after reciting the deeds of the founder of the clan, who accompanied Ninigi-no-mikoto when he descended onto Mount Takachiho from the High Plain of Heaven, he insisted that absolute loyalty to the imperial house was the sacred duty of members of the clan. They must not permit even the possibility of false reports being circulated at the court to the effect that they have been disloyal. The chōka concluded:

So cherished and clean is the name of our clan.
Neglect it never, lest even a false word

Should destroy this proud name of our fathers,
You clansmen all, who bear the name of Ōtomo.[259]

After the death in 757 of Tachibana no Moroe, another protector of the Ōtomo family, Fujiwara no Nakamaro decided that the time was ripe to deal a mortal blow to the Ōtomo and Saeki clans. In the sixth month an order was issued by the court prohibiting the clans from assembling more than their allotted number of retainers, soldiers, and horses. Two weeks later, word of a plot to surround Nakamaro's residence leaked out, and a week after that a semmyō was proclaimed that blamed the Ōtomo and Saeki clans for failing to perform their traditional duty of protecting the court.[260] On the same day, the principal members of both clans were arrested and later put to death. The glory of the Ōtomo and the Saeki clans was brutally ended.

Yakamochi was not involved in this disaster, and made no overt reference to it in his poetry. At a gathering at the residence of Prince Mikata toward the end of the year he composed this waka:

aratama no
toshi yuḳigaeri
haru tataba
mazu wa ga yado ni
uguisu wa naḳe[261]

The old year has gone
And the new one has come.
If spring is really here,
Sing, uguisu,
At my home first of all.

This poem, though not of much literary interest, may obliquely express Yakamochi's desire to forget the past and turn his thoughts to the future, symbolized by the uguisu, the harbinger of spring.[262]

In the sixth month of 758 Yakamochi was appointed as governor of Inaba, a remote and unimportant province. This was tantamount to exile. On New Year's Day of 759, at his post in Inaba, Yakamochi wrote:

atarashiḳi
toshi no hajime no
hatsu haru no
ḳyō furu yuḳi no
iya shiḳe yogoto[263]

May good things
Pile up more and more
Like the first snow
That falls today,
Beginning the New Year.

This is the last dated poem in the *Man'yōshū*. Yakamochi was in his forty-second year when he composed it. He lived on until 785, but not a single datable poem survives from the last twenty-six years of his life. No doubt he devoted much of his attention to official duties, as we can gather from the belated promotions that he received toward the end of his life, after he had spent twenty-one years in the upper junior fifth rank.

Some have criticized Yakamochi for the lack of the kind of intellectual concern displayed by Okura in his poems of Buddhist or Confucian intent and for his failure to express interest in the people of the provinces he governed,[264] but no poet of the *Man'yōshū* covered a greater range of subjects, whether gallant verses addressed to ladies of the court, the narration of his dream about a stray hawk, his reproaches directed at a man who has been unfaithful to his wife, an elegy on the death of his brother, or poems voicing the emotions of men who must leave their homes to guard the frontier.[265]

Yakamochi's most appealing poems, however, are perhaps three waka he wrote in 753 while in Etchū, and of them the third is the best:

uraura ni	In the tranquil sun of spring
tereru haruhi ni	A lark soars singing;
hibari agari	Sad is my burdened heart,
kokoroganashi mo	Thoughtful and alone.[266]
hitori shi omoeba	

A note is appended to this poem: "In the languid rays of the spring sun, a lark is singing. This mood of melancholy cannot be removed except by poetry: hence I have composed this poem in order to dispel my gloom."[267] In this entirely private mood, when Yakamochi wrote out of internal necessity, rather than in response to some public occasion or in the tone he deemed appropriate for a member of the Ōtomo clan, he is most attractive to modern readers. The melancholy, stemming from frustration and isolation, that colors his best-known waka is closer in tone to the *Kokinshū* poets than to the earlier *Man'yōshū* poets, but for this very reason, readers who prefer the "unsophisticated" expression of more typical *Man'yōshū* poets are apt to be critical of Yakamochi.

Another cause for complaint is the large number of poems by Yakamochi himself included in the collection. His reputation might be higher if he had chosen only his best poems, but instead there are (in addition to the masterpieces) derivative practice pieces and even some downright bad poems.[268] He was a major poet, but perhaps our greatest debt to him is as the chief compiler of the *Man'yōshū*. Presumably, this was his chief literary activity after 759. We do not know why he compiled the collection, but it can be surmised that he wished to leave behind a record of the literary achievements of the Ōtomo family, after it had been harshly denied its traditional role as guardian of the emperor.

Apart from the last four books of the *Man'yōshū*, undoubtedly compiled by Yakamochi, it is hard to be sure precisely which volumes he edited. No single principle of compilation was followed by Yakamochi and whatever other persons had a hand in the editing. The poems are generally arranged in chronological order within each book, but there are also divisions of the poems (as mentioned above) into such categories as "mutual enquiries" and so on.

Several books of the collection are devoted almost exclusively to anonymous poems. It is possible that some of these poems may have been written by poets who are otherwise represented in the collection, even the poems attributed to frontier guards or composed in the Azuma (Eastland) dialect. But such poems cannot *all* have been written by courtiers playing at being shepherds. The two "beggar poems,"[269] for example, seem to have been written by professional entertainers who improvised poems in the marketplace in the hope of being rewarded by listeners. The poems are written in the personae of a deer and a crab, describing the hardships each suffers in the service of his master. No doubt, as commentators have suggested, the original listeners sympathized with the deer, whose body is converted into ornaments, inkstands, mirrors, bow-ends, writing brushes, leather boxes, mincemeat, and salt pickles for his master's use, or the crab who, when summoned to his lordship's mansion, supposes that he is wanted as a musician only to have his eyes smeared with salt as preparation for being eaten.[270] During the Tokugawa period (and later) these poems were often read allegorically as expressions of selfless devotion to the throne, even at the cost of one's life, but this can hardly have been the original thought behind the poems.

An unmistakable flavor of authenticity also marks many of the rustic poems, making one doubt that a courtier could have composed them, even as a demonstration of virtuosity:

haru no no ni	The mouth of the mare
kusa hamu koma no	Grazing in the spring meadow
kuchi yamazu	Never stops; nor do her lips at home,
a wo shinouran	She talks of me—my wife![271]
ie no koro hamo	

The Azuma poems, of which the above is an example, were collected from the regions east or northeast of the province of Tōtōmi, as far north as Michinoku at the northern tip of Honshū. The poems often provide glimpses into the lives of ordinary people who do not otherwise figure in poetry of the time, like the young woman who wrote:

ine tsukeba	My hands so chapped from rice-pounding—
kakaru a ga te wo	Tonight again he will hold them, sighing,
koyoimo ka	My young lord of the mansion![272]
tono no wakugo ga	
torite nagekan	

Most of the Azuma poems, though not the two examples above, contain place-names, as in this charming example from the province of Kamitsukeno (the later Kōzuke):

Ikaho ne ni	Do not rumble, O Thunder,
kami na nari so ne	Over the mountains of Ikaho!
wa ga he ni wa	Though to me it is no matter,
yue wa nakedomo	You frighten this little darling of mine.[273]
kora ni yorite so	

The poems by frontier guards, many of them contained in Book XIV, mainly describe the hardships of separation from the guards' families and the loneliness of posts in remote parts of the country. They are peculiarly affecting because of the note of truth we seem to hear, even when they are not otherwise memorable. One of the finest does not refer specifically to the hardships of frontier life, but the mood is conveyed:

ashi no ha ni	I will think of you, love,
yūgiri tachite	On evenings when the grey mist
kamo ga ne no	Rises above the rushes,
samuki yūbe shi	And chill sounds the voice
na wo ba shinowan	Of the wild ducks crying.[274]

This poem apparently referred to a departure from the harbor of Naniwa, famed for its reeds, for Iki, Tsushima, or one of the other islands at the "frontier" with Korea. It recalls the poem written by Prince Shiki in 706 when the Emperor Mommu visited the Naniwa Palace:

ashihe yuku	I recall Yamato
kamo no hagai ni	In the cold of evenings when
shimo furite	The frost is falling
samuki yūbe wa	On the wings of the wild ducks
Yamato shi omōyu[275]	Heading for a patch of reeds.

The similarity between the two waka suggests that the poem composed at the court had become known to people of humble station who lived far from the circle of aristocrats. Relatively few people would have had access to manuscripts of the poems, but oral transmission was common, as we know from accounts of people reciting or singing well-known poems at banquets and elsewhere. The court poets of the early *Man'yōshū* had borrowed the forms and sometimes the materials of songs in the *Kojiki* and the *Nihon Shoki*, adding to them the imprint of their society and of their own talents. These more refined poems eventually made their way back to the common people. Similar cycles of borrowing would occur in other traditional Japanese literary and performing arts; the court would again and again seek stimulation from the countryside only to return it eventually in a more evolved form. The anonymous poems in the *Man'yōshū*, even if they were really composed by unlettered soldiers or peasants, show a poetic sophistication not to be found in the *Kojiki* poetry; the old poetry had in the meantime passed through the sensibilities of the early *Man'yōshū* poets.

The *Man'yōshū* stands in solitary grandeur at the head of Japanese poetry both in its antiquity and its quality. The submergence of the *Man'yōshū* during the century immediately after its completion was due largely to the overpowering prestige of Chinese literature at the time. The importance of Chinese learning threatened the very existence of literature in Japanese, and only the short poems of the *Man'yōshū* would influence poetry in Japanese when it was revived a century and a half later. Even though the *Man'yōshū* was little known during the Heian period, it was not forgotten.[276] The recovery of the full text of the *Man'yōshū*, begun sporadically in the medieval period and continued in earnest from the seventeenth century, reached fruition in the twentieth century with the preparation of excellent editions with ample commentaries. There are still problems in the interpretation of some poems, but the *Man'yōshū* as a whole has been established as the supreme monument of Japanese lyricism.

Notes

1. Most scholars in the West now prefer to write the name as *Man'yōshū*, though in the past *Manyōshū* was usual. The name is occasionally rendered as *Mannyōshū*, and this in fact is how many people pronounce it.
2. In addition to the *Kojiki* and the *Nihon Shoki*, old songs can be found in the *Shoku Nihongi*, in various of the fudoki, and in such collections of songs as *Kinkafu*. These songs are intensively treated by Jin'ichi Konishi in *A History of Japanese Literature*, I, especially pp. 81–170 and 266–86. For texts of the ancient songs see Tsuchihashi Yutaka and Konishi Jin'ichi, *Kodai Kayō Shū*.
3. See, for example, Nakanishi Susumu, *Man'yōshū Genron*, pp. 143–45. Konishi (in *A History,* I, p. 167–68) gave examples of poems that appear in identical or strikingly similar forms in both the *Nihon Shoki* and the *Man'yōshū*.
4. A tradition of singing poetry still exists. Tanka are sung to a fixed melody at a ceremony in the Imperial Palace each January. There is also a style of singing *kanshi* (poems in Chinese) known as *shigin*, confirming the importance of melodic declamation even of Chinese poems rearranged in Japanese word order.
5. I shall henceforth use the word *waka* for the classical verse form, in thirty-one syllables, though sometimes *uta* would be better, sometimes *tanka*.
6. Nakanishi, *Man'yōshū Genron*, p. 127.
7. George Sansom, *A History of Japan*, I, p. 57. See also Ryusaku Tsunoda, Wm. Theodore de Bary, and Donald Keene, *Sources of Japanese Tradition*, pp. 70–80.
8. I have referred to such men above, p. 66.
9. See Aoki Kazuo, "Okura Kikajin-setsu Hihan," pp. 265–66, for the evidence put forward in favor of this theory. Aoki was perhaps the most articulate opponent, but his summary is useful. The theory, first put forward by Watanabe Kazuo in 1963, was given the strong support of Nakanishi Susumu, who published in the November 1969 issue of *Kokugakuin Zasshi* the article "Okura Kikajin Ron." Nakanishi subsequently expanded his researches in the article "Okura Toraijin Ron" and in his book *Yamanoue no Okura*. See also below, p. 139.
10. This reluctance persisted, especially in the waka, until late in the nineteenth century when foreign words, of not only Chinese but European origins, became acceptable. Words of Chinese origin were, however, commonly used in the haiku.
11. Nakanishi, *Man'yōshū Genron*, p. 318.
12. *Man'yōshū*, XVI:3847. See Kojima Noriyuki, Kinoshita Masatoshi, and Satake Akahiro (eds.), *Man'yōshū* (in Nihon Koten Bungaku Zenshū series, henceforth abbreviated NKBZ), IV, p. 137. Translation from Nippon Gakujutsu Shinkōkai (henceforth abbreviated NGS), *Manyōshū*, p. 287.

13. *Man'yōshū*, XVI:3847. NKBZ, IV, p. 138. Translation in NGS, p. 287.
14. In a few instances scholars disagree as to whether a Japanese or a Sino-Japanese reading is correct. See Nakanishi, *Man'yōshū Genron*, p. 319.
15. *Ibid.*, p. 322. Nakanishi stated that only five words not of Buddhist origin are in Sino-Japanese pronunciation.
16. For an account of the rediscovery of the *Man'yōshū* by the kokugaku scholars during the Tokugawa period, see Peter Nosco, "*Man'yōshū* studies in Tokugawa Japan."
17. The problem in giving a firm figure for the number of poems stems from the duplications or slight variations of certain poems; some scholars count them as separate poems, others do not.
18. Ōkubo Tadashi, *Man'yōshū no Shosō*, p. 17.
19. *Ibid.*, p. 19.
20. *Origuchi Shinobu Zenshū*, IX, p. 124.
21. See the translation by William H. and Helen Craig McCullough, *A Tale of Flowering Fortunes*, I, p. 79.
22. See Itami Sueo, "Man'yōshū no Henja." Itami believed that Tachibana no Moroe probably had at least nominal responsibility for editing the "original *Man'yōshū*," compiled by Yakamochi by 746. He believed that Moroe, defeated politically and deprived of his authority by Fujiwara no Nakamaro, who rose to power in 745, may have looked to future generations for lasting recognition and for this reason planned the "Collection for Ten Thousand Ages." Itami lists (pp. 106–7) reasons why Yakamochi was chosen as the editor, and why he accepted this responsibility.
23. Quoted by Itami, "Man'yōshū," p. 95, from Keichū's *Man'yō Daishōki*.
24. Summaries of the views of various twentieth-century scholars are presented by Itami in "Man'yōshu," pp. 96–99.
25. Origuchi believed that Yakamochi had essentially completed the compilation of the *Man'yōshū*, which had originally been planned as a private collection of poems of the Ōtomo family, relatives, and friends, by the spring of 759, but that because of the unsettled circumstances of his last years he never finished the task of editing the work. The Chinese preface to the *Kokinshū*, written in 905, stated that the compilation of the *Man'yōshū* was completed during Heizei's reign, about a century earlier. (For a translation of this passage, see Helen Craig McCullough, *Kokin Wakashū*, p. 258.) Origuchi decided that Heizei, himself a poet and the ancestor of the celebrated Ariwara no Narihira, must have authorized the compilation of the *Man'yōshū*, and that it was therefore the first imperially sponsored anthology, a distinction normally accorded to the *Kokinshū*. Ōkubo, who quoted Origuchi in *Man'yōshū*, p. 267, did not believe that the role of Heizei was of great importance, and was unwilling to accept Origuchi's use of the term *chokusenshū*.
26. These poems constitute a unique document of eighth-century poetry because, having been carved in stone, they have not been subjected to cor-

ruptions of the text, but their literary interest is limited. Seventeen of the twenty-one poems describe the footprint. For a study and translation of the poems, see Roy Andrew Miller, *"The Footprints of the Buddha": An Eighth-Century Old Japanese Poetic Sequence*.

27. The makurakotoba (literally, "pillow word") is a word or phrase that occupies the short line in a short-long alternation of waka prosody. It may be composed of a noun, a verb, or a phrase and may function as either an adjective or adverb. See Edwin A. Cranston, "Toward a Reconsideration of *Makurakotoba*," p. 18.
28. See Narahashi Zenji, "Man'yōshū no Hensan Nendai," p. 125.
29. Nakanishi Susumu, however, believed that the final compilation of the *Man'yōshū* did not occur until long after the *Kokinshū* was completed in 905, and that the number of books in the *Man'yōshū* conformed to the pattern of the *Kokinshū*, rather than the other way round. He offered evidence from the writings of Sugawara no Michizane that the *Man'yōshū* may originally have consisted of "tens of books" instead of the present twenty. See Nakanishi, *Man'yōshū Genron*, p. 158. Nakanishi's opinion is as yet not widely shared.
30. In dating the periods of the *Man'yōshū* I have followed Nakanishi Susumu, *Man'yō no Sekai*, p. 101. The Taika Reform took place in 645, and 672 was the year of the Jinshin Rebellion. It should be noted that the poems in the *Man'yōshū* are not arranged in strict chronological order. Notes specifically stating that poems have come from "an old collection" (*koshū*) are found in Books VII and IX (after poems 1246 and 1771), rather than in the first books. On the other hand, poems by Ōtomo Yakamochi occur as early as Book III. The period division I have followed is based on known biographical and other historical data, not on the position of poems within the collection.
31. Nakanishi, *Man'yō no Sekai*, pp. 20, 47–50, 53–54, 101.
32. *Ibid*., pp. 170–71. See also Nakanishi, *Man'yō no Shi to Shijin*, p. 19.
33. Nakanishi, *Man'yō no Shi to Shijin*, p. 27. But see also his *Man'yō no Sekai*, p. 15, where he interpreted the zōka as "public poems"; and Narahashi, "Man'yōshū," p. 127, where he stated that the original meaning of zōka was poems with a historical background.
34. Nakanishi, *Man'yōshū Genron*, p. 117.
35. *Ibid*., p. 118.
36. Itō Haku, "Yūryaku Gyosei no Seikaku to sono Ichi," pp. 8–9.
37. *Ibid*., pp. 7–8.
38. *Man'yōshū*, I:1. NKBZ, I, p. 63. Translation from NGS, p. 3. For another translation, see Ian Hideo Levy, *Man'yōshū*, I, p. 37.
39. Shirakawa Shizuka, *Shoki Man'yō Ron*, pp. 40–66. Shirakawa quoted at length the writings of Origuchi Shinobu, especially his *Man'yōshū Kōgi*. Origuchi was also followed in general by Yamamoto Kenkichi in *Man'yō Hyakka*, pp. 7–8. Yamamoto believed, however, that the girl was the

daughter of a powerful Yamoto chieftain who, in order to acquire full qualifications for marriage, went into the mountains with other girls of her age to perform the sacred rite of picking greens. Origuchi believed that the ultimate significance of the poem had to be considered in the light of what is known about the quick-tempered Yūryaku. The poem was composed in order to restrain his normally tempestuous feelings; it was therefore at once a poem of self-restraint and of spiritual calm for other people. (*Origuchi Shinobu Zenshū*, IX, p. 158.)

40. Saigō Nobutsuna, *Man'yō Shiki*, p. 20.
41. Omodaka Hisataka, *Man'yōshū Chūshaku*, I, p. 12, and Aoki Takako et al., *Man'yōshū*, I, p. 43, emended the text to read *ie norase, na norasane*. Kojima in NKBZ, I, p. 63, gave *ie kikana, na norasane*. Hisamatsu Sen'ichi, *Man'yō Shūka*, I, p. 50, gave *ie kikan, na norasane*.
42. Saigō, *Man'yō Shiki*, p. 19.
43. *Ibid*., pp. 15, 21.
44. Itō, "Yūryaku," pp. 2–3.
45. *Ibid*., p. 5. See also Aoki et al., *Man'yōshū*, I, p. 43.
46. Ōno Susumu, "Man'yōshū Kaikan Daiichi no Uta," pp. 65–67. Yamamoto, reluctant to accept this emendation, interpreted the lines of the emperor as meaning, "I'll tell you my name if you tell me yours." (*Man'yō Hyakka*, p. 11.)
47. Shirakawa, *Shoki*, p. 66.
48. Many of these studies are disappointing. For example, Furuya Akira in "Man'yōshū Hensan no Dōki to Mokuteki" (The Motivation and Purpose of the Composition of the *Man'yōshū*) ambles along to the last page only to reveal he has nothing to contribute on the subject of his article.
49. Nakanishi in *Man'yō no Sekai*, p. 25, states, without expanding his view, that the poem was probably not by the emperor himself but by some "appropriate" court poet. Hisamatsu, *Man'yō Shūka*, I, pp. 58, 63, expressed confidence that Jomei himself had written the poem.
50. *Man'yōshū*, I:2. NKBZ, I, p. 64. Translation from NGS, p. 3. Another translation in Levy, *Man'yōshū*, I, p. 38.
51. See Omodaka, *Man'yōshū Chūshaku*, I, pp. 40–44. See also Kawaguchi Katsuyasu, "Jomei Gyosei no Kunimi-uta no Genryū," pp. 15–18.
52. Nakanishi, *Man'yō no Sekai*, p. 26.
53. Omodaka, *Man'yōshū Chūshaku*, I, pp. 47–48.
54. Hisamatsu, *Man'yōshū Kōza*, I, pp. 61–62.
55. *Man'yōshū*, IX:1759. NKBZ, II, pp. 418–19. Translation in NGS, p. 222.
56. *Man'yōshū*, X:1879. NKBZ, III, p. 60. Translation in NGS, p. 268.
57. For a discussion in English of kunimi, see Gary L. Ebersole, *Ritual Poetry and the Politics of Death in Early Japan*, pp. 23–29. Ebersole listed (p. 23) three ordered parts: "the sovereign or some other ritual functionary (1) climbed a hill, (2) then visually surveyed the countryside below, and (3) recited words of praise of the specific site." See also Ian Hideo Levy, *Hitomaro and the Birth of Japanese Lyricism*, p. 25.

58. See Yamaji Heishirō, "Kunimi no uta futatsu." Also *Origuchi Shinobu Zenshū*, IX, pp. 165–67, 176–79.
59. Ebersole's *Ritual Poetry* provides an excellent example of how the early poetry illuminates ancient practices that are not recorded elsewhere.
60. Kidō Saizō and Imoto Nōichi, *Rengaron Shū, Hairon Shū*, p. 90.
61. See Nakanishi Susumu, *Man'yōshū no Hikaku Bungakuteki Kenkyū*, pp. 598–602.
62. "Short poem," in contrast to *chōka*, or "long poem." Tanka was used at this time (and also in modern times) as another name for the waka.
63. Inaoka Kōji, "Hitomaro 'hanka' 'tanka' no Ron," pp. 183–239.
64. Translation in Levy, *Man'yōshū*, I, p. 38.
65. Nakanishi, *Man'yō no Sekai*, pp. 47–49.
66. The name is also read as Nukada.
67. *Man'yōshū*, I:8. NKBZ, I, p. 69. The pronunciation Nigitatsu is preferred by some scholars. I have followed Omodaka, *Man'yōshū Chūshaku*, I, p. 103. For another translation see Levy, *Man'yōshū*, I, p. 42. Levy translates Nigitazu as Nigita Harbor.
68. Hisamatsu, *Man'yō Shūka*, I, p. 75.
69. Tsuchihashi Yutaka, *Man'yō Kaigan*, I, p. 78. The first scholar to consider Nukata as a "substitute poet" (*daisaku kajin*) was apparently Origuchi Shinobu in his essay "Nukata no Ōkimi" (*Origuchi Shinobu Zenshū*, IX, pp. 444–60).
70. *Ruijū Karin* was the title of a now-lost waka collection by Yamanoue no Okura. Remarks from this work are quoted in the text of the *Man'yōshū*.
71. The Empress Saimei died in Kyūshū before the fleet could sail for Korea. She was succeeded as commander of the expedition by the crown prince, the future Emperor Tenji (the name is also read Tenchi), who did not officially assume the crown until 668. In 663 the Japanese forces in Korea and those of their Paekche allies were dealt a crushing defeat in the naval engagement of Hakusukinoe (Hakusonkō). The Japanese survivors, together with many Paekche refugees, fled back to Japan on the remaining ships. Fearing a Silla invasion, the Japanese fortified the area of the Dazaifu in Kyūshū, and in 667 Tenji moved the capital to the area of Ōtsu in Ōmi. The feared invasion did not materialize, but Tenji went ahead with planned reforms of the government.
72. *Man'yōshū*, I:17. NKBZ, I, pp. 73–74. Translations by NGS, p. 11, and Levy, *Man'yōshū*, I, p. 47. Omodaka (*Man'yōshū Chūshaku*, I, p. 186) expressed the belief that the poem was actually written by Tenji, as the note to the poem in *Ruijū Karin* stated, but Tsuchihashi (*Man'yō Kaigan*, I, p. 87) treated it as another substitutional poem.
73. *Man'yōshū*, II:155. NKBZ, I, pp. 145–46. Translations by NGS, p. 12, and Levy, *Man'yōshū*, I, p. 109.
74. *Man'yōshū*, I:29. NKBZ, I, p. 75. Another translation by Levy, *Man'yōshū*, I, p. 48. The meaning of Tenji's gesture of waving the sleeve has been

variously interpreted as one of affection (Omodaka, *Man'yōshū Chūshaku*, I, p. 203, and Aoki et al., *Man'yōshū*, I, p. 55); of calling attention to his presence (Hisamatsu, *Man'yōshū Shūka*, I, p. 96); or as a magic gesture to summon the soul of the beloved (Nakanishi Susumu, *Man'yō no Jidai to Fūdo*, pp. 54–79). Itō Haku, in *Man'yōshū Sōmon no Sekai*, p. 119, stated that Nukata's profession of embarrassment over the prince's sleeve-waving was coquetry, and that she was actually pleased.

75. *Man'yōshū*, I:21. NKBZ, I, p. 75. Another translation in Levy, *Man'yōshū*, I, p. 49.
76. Saigō, *Man'yō Shiki*, p. 125. Nakanishi, who believed that Nukata was of Korean (Silla) extraction, found it significant that the prince should have associated her with *murasaki*, a plant whose use as a dyestuff had been taught to the Japanese by Koreans. (Nakanishi, *Man'yō no Jidai*, pp. 109–12, 122–27.)
77. *Man'yōshū*, I:16. NKBZ, I, pp. 72–73. I shall not give the romanized texts of every chōka.
78. *Man'yōshū*, I:16. NKBZ, I, pp. 72–73.
79. Translation in NGS, pp. 10–11. Another translation in Levy, *Man'yōshū*, I, p. 46.
80. Tsuchihashi, *Man'yō Kaigan*, I, pp. 91–93.
81. Aoki et al., *Man'yōshū*, I, p. 53.
82. See Nakanishi Susumu, *Man'yō no Utabitotachi*, p. 39. Also his *Man'yō no Jidai*, p. 111, where, in the course of argumentation to prove that Nukata was of Silla origins, he mentions that although disputes on the relative merits of spring and autumn appeared in Chinese writings as far back as the *Huai-nan Tzu* (compiled under Liu An, prince of Huai-nan, d. 122 B.C.), this was the first mention of them in Japan before *The Tale of Genji*.
83. The events leading up to the Jinshin no Ran are confusing. The Emperor Tenji's younger brother, the future Temmu, had been appointed as crown prince in 668 as a reward for his services at the time of the Taika Reform, but Tenji really wanted his son, Prince Ōtomo (the future Kōbun), to succeed him instead. As a first step, he appointed Ōtomo as the prime minister in 671. Soon afterward, he fell ill and, summoning Temmu to his bedside, asked him to carry on after his death. Temmu, who apparently wanted to assume power on his own terms, refused and, resigning his position as crown prince, entered Buddhist orders. After Tenji died, his son accordingly succeeded, and was known as the Emperor Kōbun. Six months later, Temmu left his monastery and raised an army, which (with the help of local rulers, who opposed the reforms of Tenji) defeated Kōbun's forces.
84. For a brief description of the connections between the Jinshin no Ran and the *Man'yōshū*, see Kanda Hideo, "Jinshin no Ran to *Man'yōshū*," in *Bungei Tokuhon: Man'yōshū*, pp. 141–45.

85. See Yamamoto Kenkichi, *Kakinomoto no Hitomaro*, pp. 106–7, for a different explanation of Jitō's many visits to Yoshino: she was desperately desirous of becoming young again, and believed that visiting Yoshiro was an act of purification (*misogi*) that could bring about the desired result. Tsuyuki Noriyoshi, in "Temmu Gyosei no Seikaku," pp. 114–15, presents the more conventional explanation that Jitō visited Yoshino as a mark of devotion to Temmu.
86. Everything known about his life can be found in Levy, *Hitomaro*.
87. See Nakanishi Susumu, *Kakinomoto no Hitomaro*, pp. 14–17.
88. For Itō's comment, see Omodaka, *Man'yōshū Chūshaku*, I, p. 295.
89. *Man'yōshū*, I:38. Text in Kojima et al., *Man'yōshū*, I, pp. 84–85.
90. Translation from NGS, p. 29. Another translation in Levy, *Man'yōshū*, I, pp. 57–58.
91. Quoted by Omodaka in *Man'yōshū Chūshaku*, I, p. 295.
92. For more on this collection, see below, notes 123 and 124.
93. *Man'yōshū*, I:167. Kojima et al. *Man'yōshū*, I, pp. 150–51.
94. Another name for Amaterasu Ōmikami, the sun goddess.
95. *Man'yōshū*, II:167. Text in NKBZ, I, pp. 151–52. Translation in NGS, p. 34. Another translation in Levy, *Man'yōshū*, I, pp. 114–15.
96. *Man'yōshū*, II:167. Text in NKBZ, I, p. 162. Translation in NGS, p. 35. Another translation in Levy, *Man'yōshū*, I, p. 115.
97. See Sasaki Yukitsuna, *Kakinomoto no Hitomaro Nōto*, p. 163.
98. For example, by Yoshida Yoshitaka in "Shikokka no Tenkai," p. 81.
99. See, for example, *Man'yōshū*, II:194–95. Text in NKBZ, I, pp. 159–160. Translations in NGS, pp. 36–37, and Levy, *Man'yōshū*, I, pp. 123–24.
100. For example, Nakanishi (in *Kakinomoto*, p. 152) expressed uncertainty as to whether Hitomaro's poems about Iwami were truthful accounts of personal experiences.
101. Sakamoto Tarō et al., *Nihon Shoki*, II, pp. 486–87. Translation in W. G. Aston, *Nihongi*, II, p. 383.
102. Also called *araki* and *mogari* (or *mogarinomiya*). For a good account of these shrines, see Ebersole, *Ritual Poetry*, pp. 127–29.
103. Temmu died in the ninth month of 686, but the ceremonial burial did not take place until the eleventh month of 688. This was an exceptionally long period of temporary burial. The practice of temporary burial of members of the imperial family was discontinued during the reign of Tenji's daughter, the Empress Gemmei. The first recorded cremation (that of the priest Dōshō) took place in 700.
104. Hitomaro's eulogies were almost all composed for persons who had died young. Prince Takechi was the longest-lived person he eulogized. See Sasaki, *Kakinomoto*, p. 138.
105. Notably, the discontinuance of ceremonies at the arakinomiya mentioned above.
106. *Man'yōshū*, II:199. Text in NKBZ, I, pp. 164–66. Translation in NGS, pp.

39–40. Another translation in Levy, *Man'yōshū*, I, pp. 128–29. See also the analysis of the poem in Ebersole, *Ritual Poetry*, pp. 72–78.

107. Nakanishi, *Kakinomoto*, p. 76.
108. See Yamamoto Kenkichi, *Ōtomo no Yakamochi*, pp. 72–73.
109. The island, now called Shami, has been joined to the "mainland" and boasts recreational facilities. By carefully positioning oneself, one can obtain a view of the Inland Sea similar to the one Hitomaro saw.
110. *Man'yōshū*, III:415. Text in NKBZ, I, p. 259. Translation in NGS, p. 8. Another translation in Levy, *Man'yōshū*, I, p. 212.
111. *Man'yōshū*, III:426. NKBZ, I, p. 264. See also Levy, *Man'yōshū*, I, p. 218.
112. See Kōnoshi Takamitsu, "Kōro Shinin no Uta," pp. 174–87.
113. *Man'yōshū*, II:220–21. Translation from NGS, pp. 46–47. Another translation in Levy, *Man'yōshū*, I, pp. 142–43.
114. Twenty-one poems in Book VI and another ten in Book IX are described in notes to the original text as existing in the Tanabe Sakimaro (or Tanabe no Sakimaro) collection. The rest of the collection has been lost, and the dates of the poet are unknown.
115. *Man'yōshū*, IX:1800. NKBZ, II, p. 435. Translation from NGS, pp. 233–34.
116. *Man'yōshū*, II:35. Text in NKBZ, I, pp. 136–37. Translation from NGS, p. 33. See also Levy, *Man'yōshū*, I, pp. 132–33.
117. Nakanishi, *Kakinomoto*, p. 143. But see also Hisamatsu, *Man'yōshū Shūka*, I, p. 96, and Omodaka, *Man'yōshū Chūshaku*, I, p. 203, where the waving of the sleeve is interpreted merely as a gesture of affection.
118. Nakanishi, *Kakinomoto*, p. 119.
119. For makurakotoba, see above, note 27. Levy made the effort to include in his translations the makurakotoba, and they are often effective, as the following section of his version of the same poem will suggest (Levy, *Man'yōshū*, I, pp. 134–35):

I stood at the Karu market
where often she had gone,
and listened,
but could not even hear
the voices of the birds
that cry on Unebi Mountain,
  where the maidens
  wear the strands of jewels,
and of the ones who passed me
on that road,
  straight as a jade spear,
not one resembled her.

In translating the makurakotoba (given in italics above) there is a danger of overemphasis. For example, the makurakotoba *tamahoko no*, translated here as "straight as a jade spear," may conceivably have meant just that, but spears made of jade probably never existed. "Jeweled spears" (another possible rendering of *tamahoko*) may have been a way of praising the beauty or strength of a spear, but this makurakotoba does not in itself imply straightness. In later times the word came to be used as a synonym for "road," without implication either of beauty or straightness. One must admire Levy's honest attempt to make sense of words that are usually passed over in silence by Japanese commentators as meaningless ornaments to the text, but such phrases tend to confirm the atmosphere of a line rather than add to its meaning.

120. *Man'yōshū,* IV:619. Text in NKBZ, I, pp. 342–44. Translation in NGS, p. 125; also, Levy, *Man'yōshū* I, p. 289.
121. *Man'yōshū*, XIII:3344. Text in NKBZ, III, pp. 436–37. Translation in NGS, p. 313.
122. Nakanishi, *Kakinomoto*, pp. 123–25.
123. The *Hitomaro Kashū* does not now exist independently of the *Man'yōshū*, though such a collection probably existed at the time of the compilation of the *Man'yōshū*.
124. A major problem in determining the authorship of the *Hitomaro Kashū* is caused by the two distinct systems of orthography used in recording the poems. The first system used an absolute minimum of Chinese characters, suggesting to various scholars that these were notes made by Hitomaro in order to remember other people's poems. The second system, which indicates postpositions and other grammatical features of Japanese, would have been used for Hitomaro's own poems. This theory was first advanced by Aso Mizue in 1956. It is described by Umehara Takeshi in *Uta no Fukuseki*, I, pp. 219–24. See also Kōnoshi Takamitsu, "Kakinomoto no Hitomaro Jiten," in *Man'yōshū Hikkei*, II, pp. 125–33, for a summary of scholarship on the *Kakinomoto no Hitomaro Kashū*. See also Aso Mizue, "Kakinomoto no Hitomaro no Sakuhin," pp. 238–46.
125. Umehara, in *Uta no Fukuseki*, I, pp. 113–15, rejecting the evidence adduced by other scholars, insisted that poems written in the persona of a woman or in other guises can be explained as literary conventions, and that poems in a romantic manner that contrasts with the Hitomaro of the chōka can be understood as works of his youth. Hisamatsu Sen'ichi had advanced similar arguments as long before as 1925, as Umehara acknowledges (I, pp. 178–81 and 185). He believed that Hitomaro was the same man as Kakinomoto no Saru, who died in 708. Kamo no Mabuchi had suggested dates of c. 660–709 for Hitomaro, but Umehara rejected these dates, insisting that Hitomaro did not die before he was fifty but (as medieval tradition had it) in his sixties. This necessitates pushing back his birthdate to about 645. See Umehara Takeshi, *Minasoko no Uta*, I, p. 209, and II, p. 108.
126. Nakanishi, *Kakinomoto*, pp. 215–16; also, Nakanishi, *Man'yōshū Genron*,

p. 129. The Tanabata poems are dated with cyclical characters that indicate they were composed either in 680 or 740. Hitomaro was certainly not alive in 740, so if he wrote the poems, it must have been in 680, long before the festival was observed in Japan. However, various scholars have adduced evidence that the festival was in fact known to the Japanese before 680. See Umehara, *Uta*, I, p. 239.

127. *Man'yōshū*, XI:2433. Text in NKBZ, III, p. 190. Another translation in NGS, p. 57.

128. *Man'yōshū*, XI:2513–14. Text in NKBZ, III, pp. 207–8. Another translation in NGS, p. 58.

129. Nakanishi, *Man'yōshū Genron*, p. 125. See also Inaoka Kōji, "Hitomaro Kashū Sedōka no Bungakuteki Igi," pp. 56–58.

130. *Man'yōshū*, VII:1281. Text in NKBZ, II, p. 251. Another translation in NGS, p. 54. "My lord" is rather an overtranslation of *kimi*, a pronoun often used by a woman to a man. The verb *suru*, translated as "to print," refers to the practice of rubbing cloth against an inked surface, rather in the manner of a stencil, to obtain a pattern.

131. See Ōoka Makoto, *Tachibana no Yume*, pp. 65–66.

132. *Man'yōshū*, II:223. Text in NKBZ, I, p. 181. Translation from NGS, p. 51. Another translation in Levy, *Man'yōshū*, I, p. 143.

133. Quoted by Omodaka, *Man'yōshū Chūshoku*, II, p. 504.

134. *Man'yōshū*, II:224–25. Text in NKBZ, I, pp. 181–82. Translation from NGS, p. 52. Other translations in Levy, I, p. 144.

135. *Man'yōshū*, II:226. Text in NKBZ, I, p. 182. Another translation in Levy, *Man'yōshū*, I, p. 144.

136. Omodaka, *Man'yōshū Chūshaku*, II, p. 509.

137. Umehara, *Minasoko*, I, pp. 179ff. Umehara referred to old traditions that Kamoyama was an island off the Iwami coast that was submerged in the tidal wave of 1026, and he identified the river Ishikawa with one called Takatsugawa in old accounts. He cited evidence that islands were traditionally places of exile (*ibid*., p. 185), and cited medieval works that stated Hitomaro died at Kamoshima (an island), not Kamoyama (*ibid*., pp. 196–97). Umehara interpreted the headnote to the poem, which describes Hitomaro as "grieving over his death," as evidence that he did not die of sickness, and certainly not by suicide, but by another person's hand (*ibid*., p. 203). Umehara was led to believe that Hitomaro must have been drowned by the fact that no site has ever been identified as the place where he died (*ibid*., p. 210). The special reverence offered to Hitomaro in the preface to the *Kokinshū*, where he is referred to as a *hijiri* (sage), also suggested to Umehara that his vengeful spirit had been appeased by elevating him to the rank of a god.

Umehara's conclusions were not widely accepted by *Man'yōshū* scholars. Tsuchihashi (*Man'yō Kaigan*, I, p. 175) sharply disagreed with Umehara's reconstruction of the death of Hitomaro.

138. Itō Haku, *Man'yōshū no Kajin to Sakuhin*, I, pp. 333–36.
139. Tsuchihashi, *Man'yō Kaigan*, I, p. 185.
140. *Ibid.*, p. 180.
141. Umehara, who believed that Hitomaro was of at least the fifth rank (and therefore should have been mentioned in official documents), identified him with Kakinomoto no Saru, whose name does appear. The name Saru (meaning "monkey") would have been imposed on Hitomaro when he fell into disgrace.
142. Tsuchihashi, *Man'yō Kaigan*, I, pp. 190–93.
143. Mommu is represented by one poem (I:74), which may well have been written by someone in his entourage. See Tsuchihashi, *Man'yō Kaigan*, I, pp. 193–94.
144. *Man'yōshū*, III:275. Text in NKBZ, I, p. 213. Other translations in NGS, p. 63, and Levy *Man'yōshū*, I, p. 165. Omodaka, *Man'yōshū Chūshaku*, III, p. 127, gives a somewhat different reading: "Izuku ni ka / ware wa yadoran / Takashima no / Kachino no hara ni / kono hi kurenaba."
145. Ikeda Yasaburō, *Takechi no Kurohito, Yamabe no Akahito*, p. 8; Tsuchihashi, *Man'yō Kaigan*, I, p. 199.
146. Ikeda, *Takechi*, pp. 22–27.
147. Tsuchihashi, *Man'yō Kaigan*, I, p. 196.
148. *Man'yōshū*, III:274. Text in NKBZ, I, pp. 212–13. Other translations in NGS, p. 63, and Levy, *Man'yōshū*, I, p. 165. Ikeda's explanation of the dread aroused in *Man'yōshū* poets by the coming of night is found in *Takechi*, pp. 7–10.
149. *Man'yōshū*, VII:1229. Text in NKBZ, II, p. 239. See also Ikeda, *Takechi*, pp. 42–43.
150. Ikeda, *Takechi*, pp. 35–36. See also Roy Andrew Miller, "The Lost Poetic Sequence of the Priest Mansei," in which he reconstructed seven poems, scattered in the *Man'yōshū*, to form a single, cohesive sequence.
151. For a discussion of poems by Kurohito and their later adaptations, see Tanabe Yukio, "Takechi no Kurohito," in *Bungei Tokuhon: Man'yōshū*, pp. 89–94.
152. *Man'yōshū*, III:271. Text in NKBZ, I, p. 212. Other translations in NGS, p. 63, and Levy, *Man'yōshū*, I, p. 164.
153. *Man'yōshū*, VI:919. Text in NKBZ, II, p. 134. Another translation in NGS, p. 191.
154. I have borrowed this translation of *honka-dori* from Robert H. Brower and Earl Miner, *Japanese Court Poetry*. For further discussion of honkadori, see below, pp. 644–647.
155. Omodaka, *Man'yōshū Chūshaku*, III, p. 127.
156. Ikeda, *Takechi*, p. 109. Seven varieties of songs are given in the *Nihon Shoki* and nineteen in the collection *Kinkafu* (Songs to Koto Accompaniment), probably compiled in the ninth century. In the latter work there are indications of how vowels were prolonged to fit an existing piece of

music. Seven of the twenty-two poems in *Kinkafu* were taken from the *Nihon Shoki*, *Shoku Nihongi*, and other early texts, but the orthography is not the same, suggesting that the *Kinkafu* versions more closely fitted the music to which the poems were at that time sung. See Konishi, *A History*, I, pp. 266–67.

157. *Man'yōshū*, I:29. Text in NKBZ, p. 81. Translation from NGS, p. 27. See also Levy, *Man'yōshū*, I, p. 54.

158. *Man'yōshū*, III:305. Text in NKBZ, I, pp. 221–22. Other translations in NGS, p. 63, and Levy, *Man'yōshū*, I, p. 174. See also Ikeda, *Takechi*, pp. 17–83, and Tsuchihashi, *Man'yō Kaigan*, I, p. 204. The poem has an appended note saying that in one text the poem is attributed to another man, but modern commentators accept this as a poem by Kurohito.

159. *Man'yōshū*, I:32. Text in NKBZ, I, p. 82. Translations in NGS, p. 62, and Levy, *Man'yōshū*, I, p. 55.

160. Itō, *Man'yōshū no Kajin*, I, p. 363.

161. *Man'yōshū*, XVI:265. Text in NKBZ, IV, p. 130. Translation by Paula Doe in *A Warbler's Song in the Dusk*, p. 81. The poem occurs in Book XVI, which is strongly Buddhist in tone; this explains the use of Sino-Japanese readings.

162. *Man'yōshū*, III:265. Text in NKBZ, I, p. 210. Other translations in NGS, p. 61, and Levy, *Man'yōshū*, I, p. 162.

163. Umehara Takeshi, *Samayoeru Kashū*, pp. 26–30.

164. For example, Ikeda in *Takechi no Kurohito to Yamabe no Akahito*, ostensibly devoted to both poets, devoted conspicuously more space to Kurohito than to Akahito.

165. This opinion, echoed over the centuries, was disputed by Umehara in *Samayoeru Kashū*.

166. *Man'yōshū*, VI:923–95. Text in NKBZ, II, pp. 136–37. Translation from NGS, p. 192.

167. Hitomaro's poem is I:36. Text in NKBZ, I, pp. 83–84. Translations in NGS, p. 28, and Levy, *Man'yōshū*, I, pp. 56–57.

168. Ikeda, *Takechi*, p. 205. See also Umehara, *Samayoeru*, pp. 37–40.

169. *Man'yōshū*, VIII:1424. Text in NKBZ, II, p. 301. Translation from NGS, p. 196.

170. See Tsuchihashi, *Man'yō Kaigan*, I, p. 253, for various interpretations of "violets."

171. *Ibid*., I, p. 233.

172. *Man'yōshū*, IX:1740. Text in NKBZ, II, pp. 407–8. Translation in NGS, pp. 216–18. Urashima is called Mizunoe no Urashima in the title of the poem.

173. *Man'yōshū*, IX:1809. Text in NKBZ, pp. 440–42. Translation in NGS, pp. 224–25.

174. *Man'yōshū*, VI:971. Text in NKBZ, II, pp. 156–57. Translation from NGS, pp. 214–15.

175. *Man'yōshū*, VI:938. Text in NKBZ, II, p. 138. Translation from NGS, pp. 101–2.
176. *Man'yōshū*, VI:935. Text in NKBZ, II, pp. 141–42. Translation in NGS, p. 102.
177. *Man'yōshū*, IV:546–47. Text in NKBZ, I, pp. 323–24. Translation from NGS, p. 99. Another translation in Levy, *Man'yōshū*, I, pp. 267–68.
178. See NKBZ, I, p. 434.
179. His title was *dazai no sochi*.
180. Tsuchihashi, *Man'yō Kaigan*, II, pp. 16, 44.
181. *Man'yōshū*, III:315. Text in NKBZ, I, p. 225. Other commentators read *mizu* as *Kawa* (river), ruining Tsuchihashi's interpreption.
182. *Analects*, VI:21. Translation from Arthur Waley, *The Analects of Confucius*, p. 120.
183. *Man'yōshū*, III:316. Text in NKBZ, I, p. 225. Other translations by NGS, p. 116, and Levy, *Man'yōshū*, I, p. 177.
184. Tsuchihashi, *Man'yō Kaigan*, II, p. 22.
185. *Man'yōshū*, III:299. Aoki et al., *Man'yōshū*, I, p. 184, noting that the prefatory note seems uncertain about which member of the Ōtomo family wrote the poem, suggested instead that it might have been Ōtomo no Yasumaro, but Tsuchihashi (*Man'yō Kaigan*, II, p. 16) showed no hesitation in crediting it to Tabito. The text in NKBZ, I, p. 220, leans toward Yasumaro. Translation in Levy, *Man'yōshū*, I, p. 172.
186. The poems are *Man'yōshū*, V:793–99. Text in NKBZ, II, pp. 47–52. Translations in NGS, pp. 380, 605–10, and in Levy, *Man'yōshū*, I, pp. 343–47. On the authorship, see Aoki et al., *Man'yōshū*, II, p. 49; Hisamatsu, *Man'yō Shūka*, III, pp. 27–31; Kojima et al., *Man'yōshū*, II, p. 50; and Levy, *Man'yōshū*, I, p. 343.
187. *Man'yōshū*, III:438. Text in NKBZ, I, p. 268. Other translations in NGS, p. 118, and Levy, *Man'yōshū*, I, p. 370.
188. *Man'yōshū*, III:439–40. Text in NKBZ, I, pp. 268–69. Other translations in NGS, p. 119, and Levy, *Man'yōshū*, I, p. 222.
189. *Man'yōshū*, III:450. Text in NKBZ, I, p. 273. Other translations in NGS, p. 120, and Levy, *Man'yōshū*, I, p. 226. A variant in the last line, *mi mo sakazu kana*, means that the poet is so unhappy that he does not even glance at the cape as he passes it now.
190. *Man'yōshū*, III:453. Text in NKBZ, I, p. 274. Other translations in NGS, p. 120, and Levy, *Man'yōshū*, I, p. 227.
191. *Man'yōshū*, VI:965. Text in NKBZ, II, p. 154. See also Nakanishi, *Man'yō no Sekai*, pp. 96–97.
192. *Man'yōshū*, VI:967. Text in NKBZ, II, p. 155.
193. Fusasaki was apparently the most respectable of the brothers and had least to do with the killing of Nagaya. (Tsuchihashi, *Man'yō Kaigan*, II, p. 33.) Nevertheless, Tabito's present of the koto suggests he wished to ingratiate himself with the powerful Fujiwara family. His promotion to

dainagon (major counselor) in the following year and his recall to the capital indicate that this stratagem was effective.

194. See Aoki et al., *Man'yōshū*, II, pp. 57–58. For example, the tree maiden's fear that her wood might be put to an unworthy use echoes the passage in Chuang Tzu describing a tree that refused to serve any useful purpose. (For an English translation of the passage, see Burton Watson, *The Complete Works of Chuang Tzu*, pp. 63–65.)

195. The Dazaifu is still known for its many plum trees. They were planted because of their associations with the scholar Sugawara no Michizane, who is worshiped at the shrine.

196. *Man'yōshū*, V:815–46. Text in NKBZ, II, pp. 68–75. Partial translation in NGS, pp. 241–42; complete translation in Levy, *Man'yōshū*, I, pp. 358–59.

197. *Man'yōshū*, V:849. Text in NKBZ, II, pp. 76. Another translation in Levy, *Man'yōshū*, I, pp. 358–59.

198. *Man'yōshū*, V:852. Text in NKBZ, p. 76. Other translations in NGS, p. 242, and Levy, *Man'yōshū*, I, p. 271.

199. *Man'yōshū*, V:848. Text in NKBZ, II, p. 75. Other translations in NGS, p. 242, and Levy, *Man'yōshū*, I, p. 370.

200. A good introduction to the relations between Taoism and Japanese culture can be found in Fukunaga Mitsuji, *Dōkyō to Nihon Bunka*.

201. Preface to *Man'yōshū*, V:864. Translation from Levy, *Man'yōshū*, I, p. 376. Text in NKBZ, II, p. 81. This preface is (naturally) in kambun.

202. See Tsuchihashi, *Man'yō Kaigan*, II, p. 39. He referred to the "open, follow, change, conclude" sequence observed in the lines of a traditional quatrain.

203. *Man'yōshū*, III:338. Text in NKBZ, I, p. 234. Other translations in NGS, p. 117, and Levy, *Man'yōshū*, I, p. 186.

204. *Man'yōshū*, III:340. Text in NKBZ, I, p. 324. Other translations in NGS, p. 117, and Levy, *Man'yōshū*, I, p. 187.

205. *Man'yōshū*, III:350. Text in NKBZ, I, p. 237. Other translations in NGS, p. 117, and Levy, *Man'yōshū*, I, p. 189.

206. See Tsuchihashi, *Man'yō Kaigan*, II, pp. 40–42.

207. *Man'yōshū*, IV:574. Text in NKBZ, I, pp. 332–33. Other translations in NGS, p. 122, and Levy, *Man'yōshū*, I, p. 277.

208. This theory, first published in 1963 (see above, note 9), was given the support of the *Man'yōshū* scholar Nakanishi Susumu, who in 1969 published an article expressing his conviction that Okura was an immigrant. The unusual name Okura suggested to him a foreign connection, and his researches revealed that two Koreans mentioned in the *Nihon Shoki* had names beginning with the character *oku*; one, a physician, may have been Okura's father. See Nakanishi, *Yamanoue*, p. 41.

209. The embassy first attempted in 701 to make the voyage to China, but the ships were driven back by storms. The next attempt, made in 704, was

successful. It seems likely that in between the two attempts the members of the embassy returned to the court.

210. Nakanishi, *Yamanoue*, p. 68.
211. *Ibid.*, pp. 93–94.
212. *Ibid.*, p. 101.
213. Nakanishi (*Yamanoue*, pp. 120–21) listed Chinese men of letters whom Okura might have met in Ch'ang-an.
214. *Man'yōshū*, II:145. Text in Omodaka, *Man'yōshū*, II, pp. 192–93. Translation from Levy, *Man'yōshū*, I, p. 105. NKBZ (I, p. 141) gives for the first line *tsubasa nasu*.
215. *Man'yōshū*, I:63. Text in NKBZ, I, p. 97. Another translation in Levy, *Man'yōshū*, I, p. 70.
216. Text in NKBZ, II, p. 330. The note is to Poem 1519.
217. *Man'yōshū*, V:880. Text in NKBZ, II, p. 89. Other translations in NGS, p. 203, and Levy, *Man'yōshū*, I, p. 282.
218. *Man'yōshū*, V:793. Text in NKBZ, II, pp. 48–49. Translation by Levy, *Man'yōshū*, I, p. 344.
219. *Man'yōshū*, V:800. Text in NKBZ, p. 53. Translation from Levy, *Man'yōshū*, I, p. 347.
220. *Man'yōshū*, V:800. Text in NKBZ, p. 54. Translation from NGS, p. 200. Another translation in Levy, *Man'yōshū*, I, 349.
221. *Man'yōshū*, V:804. Text in NKBZ, II, pp. 58–59. Translation from NGS, p. 202. See also Levy, *Man'yōshū*, I, pp. 392–401.
222. *Man'yōshū*, V:897. Text in NKBZ, II, pp. 100–114. Translations in NGS, pp. 208–9; Levy, *Man'yōshū*, I, pp. 392–401.
223. *Man'yōshū*, V:892–93. Text in NKBZ, II, pp. 95–97. Translation from NGS, pp. 205–7. Another translation in Levy, *Man'yōshū*, I, pp. 387–89.
224. Takagi Ichinosuke, *Bingū Mondōka no Ron*, p. 45.
225. Takagi, *Bingū*, p. 51. See also Watanabe Kazuo, "Kuso no aru Uta," for a discussion of what Japanese poetry lost when coarse language was forbidden.
226. See Kume Tsunetami, "Okura Bungaku ni okeru Kayōsei," p. 204.
227. *Man'yōshū*, III:337. Text in NKBZ, I, p. 234. Translation from NGS, p. 198. Another translation in Levy, *Man'yōshū*, I, p. 186.
228. See Kume, "Okura," pp. 214–16.
229. The date of Yakamochi's birth has been much disputed. Yamamoto (in *Ōtomo*, pp. 5–9), after examining the evidence and the various traditions, concluded that Yakamochi was born in 720. Tsuchihashi (*Man'yō Kaigan*, II, p. 178) stated unequivocally that Yakamochi was born in 718. For a brief review of the evidence, see Doe, *A Warbler's Song*, pp. 13–14.
230. Other theories have been advanced as to why Tabito sent for Lady Sakanoue, including one that she became his mistress. I have accepted Tsuchihashi's view (*Man'yō Kaigan*, II, p. 200) that she was charged with his

education. Yamamoto (*Ōtomo*, p. 12) expressed the belief that she replaced Tabito's late wife in performing rites of the Ōtomo clan.

231. Tsuchihashi, *Man'yō Kaigan*, II, p. 200.
232. *Ibid.*, p. 203.
233. *Man'yōshū*, VIII:1446. Text in NKBZ, II, p. 307. Another translation by Doe, *A Warbler's Song*, p. 70.
234. *Man'yōshū*, VI:993. Text in NKBZ, II, p. 164. Translation by Doe, *A Warbler's Song*, p. 67. Yamamoto (in *Ōtomo*, pp. 39–40) dates the poem before 732.
235. *Man'yōshū*, VIII:1441. Text in NKBZ, II, p. 306. Another translation in Doe, *A Warbler's Song*, p. 69.
236. *Man'yōshū*, V:822. Text in NKBZ, II, p. 70. Other translations by NGS, p. 242; Levy, *Man'yōshū*, I, p. 362; and Doe, *A Warbler's Song*, p. 31.
237. *Man'yōshū*, V:823. Text in NKBZ, II, p. 70. Another translation by Levy, *Man'yōshū*, I, p. 362.
238. *Man'yōshū*, III:469. Text in NKBZ, I, p. 281. Other translations by NGS, p. 131; Levy, *Man'yōshū*, I, p. 347; and Doe, *A Warbler's Song*, p. 47.
239. *Man'yōshū*, V:798. Text in NKBZ, II, p. 52. Other translations by NGS, p. 199; Levy, *Man'yōshū*, I, p. 347; and Doe, *A Warbler's Song*, p. 47.
240. See, for example, Tsuchihashi, *Man'yō Kaigan*, II, p. 225. This opinion is not, however, unanimous. Some insist that Yakamochi would not have shown such deference toward Okura, who was, after all, a subordinate of his father. Tsuchihashi, on the other hand, thought that when Yakamochi spoke of "Yama" and "Kaki" he *really* only meant Okura, and that Hitomaro was mentioned for the sake of parallelism in a preface written in Chinese.
241. *Man'yōshū*, VIII:1479. Text in NKBZ, II, p. 318. Another translation in NGS, p. 135.
242. *Man'yōshū*, VIII:1568. Text in NKBZ, II, p. 344.
243. The word *ibusemi* is used only ten times in the *Man'yōshū*. Five examples appear in poems by Yakamochi, four others are in anonymous poems, and one is in the Takahashi Mushimaro Collection. See Tsuchihashi, *Man'yō Kaigan*, II, p. 207.
244. Yamamoto, *Ōtomo*, pp. 50–51.
245. *Man'yōshū*, IV:715. Text in NKBZ, I, p. 371. Translation from NGS, p. 134. Other translations in Levy, *Man'yōshū*, I, p. 317; and Doe, *A Warbler's Song*, p. 83.
246. *Man'yōshū*, IV:719. Text in NKBZ, I, p. 372. Translation from NGS, p. 134. Other translation in Levy, *Man'yōshū*, I, p. 319. Kojima (in NKBZ) pointed out that the poem was modeled on one by Tabito (VI:968) and that it borrowed unaltered three lines from the anonymous poem XI:2584.
247. See Yamamoto, *Ōtomo*, p. 151.
248. *Man'yōshū*, IV:594. Text in NKBZ, I, p. 338. Translation from NGS, p. 106. Another translation in Levy, *Man'yōshū*, I, p. 283.

249. *Man'yōshū*, IV:603. Text in NKBZ, I, p. 340. Translation from NGS, p. 107. Another translation in Levy, *Man'yōshū*, I, p. 285.
250. *Man'yōshū*, IV:608. Text in NKBZ, I, p. 341. Translation from NGS, p. 108. Other translations in Levy, *Man'yōshū*, I, p. 286; and Doe, *A Warbler's Song*, p. 86.
251. Yamamoto, *Ōtomo*, p. 157.
252. *Man'yōshū*, IV:612. Text in NKBZ, I, p. 342. Other translations in Levy, *Man'yōshū*, I, p. 287; and Doe, *A Warbler's Song*, p. 68.
253. See Tsuchihashi, *Man'yō*, II, p. 216. The daughter ascended the throne as the Empress Kōken.
254. *Man'yōshū*, III:480. Text in NKBZ, I, p. 285. Translation from NGS, p. 133. Other translations in Levy, *Man'yōshū*, I, p. 239; and Doe, *A Warbler's Song*, p. 114. Aoki (*Man'yōshū*, I, p. 253) reads the second line as *na ou yuki obite*.
255. Tsuchihashi (*Man'yō Kaidan*, II, p. 219) gave these statistics: during the thirteen years before Yakamochi went to Etchū he composed 5 chōka and 153 waka. While in Etchū he composed 35 chōka, 187 waka, and 1 sedōka. During the eight years after his return to the capital from Etchū he composed 6 chōka and 86 waka.
256. The proclamation, made in 743, is translated in Tsunoda et al., *Sources*, pp. 106–7.
257. For a short account of the Ōtomo family, see Doe, *A Warbler's Song*, pp. 14–15; also Yamamoto, *Ōtomo*, pp. 93–106.
258. *Man'yōshū*, XVIII:4094. Text in NKBZ, IV, pp. 262–63. Translation from NGS, pp. 151–52. Another translation in Doe, *A Warbler's Song*, p. 185.
259. *Man'yōshū*, XX:4465. Text in NKBZ, IV, p. 432. Translation from NGS, p. 179. Another translation in Doe, *A Warbler's Song*, p. 225.
260. The semmyō is quoted by Yamamoto in *Ōtomo*, p. 240.
261. *Man'yōshū*, XX:4490. Text in NKBZ, IV, p. 441.
262. Tsuchihashi, *Man'yō Kaidan*, II, p. 251.
263. *Man'yōshū*, XX:4516. Text in NKBZ, IV, p. 450. Another translation in Doe, *A Warbler's Song*, p. 231.
264. See, for example, Tsuchihashi, *Man'yō Kaidan*, II, pp. 226–27.
265. See especially poems VIII:1507; XVII:3957; XVII:4011; XVIII:4106; XX:4331; and XX:4408.
266. *Man'yōshū*, XIX:4292. Text in NKBZ, IV, p. 362. Translation from NGS, p. 172. Another version in Doe, *A Warbler's Song*, p. 214.
267. Translation from NGS, p. 172. See also Doe, *A Warbler's Song*, p. 214.
268. For example, XIX:4160. Text in NKBZ, IV, p. 304. Translations by NGS, p. 163, and by Doe, *A Warbler's Song*, pp. 180–81. The poem is a tissue of clichés on the uncertainty of life.
269. *Man'yōshū*, XVI:3885–86. Text in NKBZ, IV, pp. 151–55. Translation in NGS, pp. 275–77.
270. See Tsuchihashi, *Man'yō Kaidan*, I, p. 222.

271. *Man'yōshū*, XIV:3532. Text in NKBZ, III, p. 494. Translation from NGS, p. 282.
272. *Man'yōshū*, XIV:3459. Text in NKBZ, III, p. 476. Translation from NGS, p. 281.
273. *Man'yōshū*, XIV:3421. Text in NKBZ, III, p. 466. Translation from NGS, p. 280.
274. *Man'yōshū*, XIV:3570. Text in NKBZ, III, p. 503. Translation from NGS, p. 283.
275. *Man'yōshū*, I:64. Text in NKBZ, I, p. 97. Other translations in NGS, p. 20, and Levy, *Man'yōshū*, I, p. 71.
276. Nakanishi, *Man'yōshū Genron*, p. 158, stated his belief that the *Man'yōshū* was given its present form late in the Heian period.

Bibliography

Note: All Japanese books, except as otherwise noted, were published in Tokyo.

Aoki Kazuo. "Okura Kikajin-setsu Hihan," in Gomi and Kojima, *Man'yōshū Kenkyū*, II.

Aoki Takako, Ide Itaru, Itō Haku, Shimizu Katsuhiko, and Hashimoto Shirō. *Man'yōshū*, in Shinchō Nihon Koten Shūsei series, 5 vols. Shinchōsha, 1976–84.

Aso Mizue. "Kakinomoto no Hitomaro no Sakuhin," in *Man'yōshū Kōza*, V.

Aston, W. G. *Nihongi*. Tokyo: Tuttle, 1972.

Brower, Robert H., and Earl Miner. *Japanese Court Poetry*. Stanford, Calif.: Stanford University Press, 1961.

Bungei Tokuhon: Man'yōshū. Kawade Shobō Shinsha, 1979.

Cranston, Edwin A. "Toward a Reconsideration of *Makurakotoba*," in Gomi and Kojima, *Man'yōshū Kenkyū*, V.

Doe, Paula. *A Warbler's Song in the Dusk*. Berkeley: University of California Press, 1982.

Ebersole, Gary L. *Ritual Poetry and the Politics of Death in Early Japan*. Princeton, N.J.: Princeton University Press, 1989.

Fukunaga Mitsuji. *Dōkyō to Nihon Bunka*. Kyoto: Jimbun Shoin, 1982.

Furuya Akira. "Man'yōshū Hensan no Dōki to Mokuteki," in *Man'yōshū Kōza*, I.

Gomi Tomohide and Kojima Noriyuki (eds.). *Man'yōshū Kenkyū*. Hanawa Shobō, 1972—.

Gotō Toshio. "Man'yōshū no Seiritsu," in *Man'yōshū Kōza*, I.

Hisamatsu Sen'ichi. "Man'yōshū no Meigi," in *Man'yōshū Kōza*, I.

———. *Man'yō Shūka*, 5 vols., in Kōdansha Gakujutsu Bunko series. Kōdansha, 1976.

Ikeda Yasaburō. *Takechi no Kurohito, Yamabe no Akahito*. Chikuma Shobō, 1970.

Inaoka Kōji. "Hitomaro 'hanka' 'tanka' no Ron," in Gomi and Kojima, *Man'yōshū Kenkyū*, III.

———. "Hitomaro Kashū Sedōka no Bungakuteki Igi," in Gomi and Kojima, *Man'yōshū Kenkyū*, III.

Inukai Takashi Hakushi Koki Kinen Rombunshū Kankō Iinkai (ed.). *Man'yō sono go*. Hanawa Shobō, 1959.

Itami Sueo. "Man'yōshū no Henja," in *Man'yōshū Kōza*, I.

Itō Haku. *Man'yōshū no Kajin to Sakuhin*, 2 vols. Hanawa Shobō, 1975.

———. *Man'yōshū Sōmon no Sekai*. Hanawa Shobō, 1959.

———. "Yūryaku Gyosei no Seikaku to sono Ichi," in Itō Haku and Inaoka Kōji, *Man'yōshū wo manabu*, I.

Itō Haku and Inaoka Kōji. *Man'yōshū wo manabu*, 8 vols. Yūhikaku, 1977–78.

Kawaguchi Katsuyasu. "Jomei Gyosei to Kunimi-uta no Genryū," in Itō and Inaoka, *Man'yōshū*, I.

Kidō Saizō and Imoto Nōichi. *Rengaron Shū, Hairon Shū*, in Nihon Koten Bungaku Taikei series. Iwanami Shoten, 1961.

Kitazumi Toshio. *Man'yō no Sekai*, in Kōdansha Gakujutsu Bunko series. Kōdansha, 1979.

Kojima Noriyuki. "Utawanu Okura," in *Man'yōshū*, III.

Kojima Noriyuki, Kinoshita Masatoshi, and Satake Akahiro (eds.). *Man'yōshū*, 4 vols. in Nihon Koten Bungaku Zenshū series. Shōgakukan, 1971–75.

Konishi, Jin'ichi. *A History of Japanese Literature*, I. Princeton, N.J.: Princeton University Press, 1984.

Kōnoshi Takamitsu. "Kōro Shinin no Uta," in Itō and Inaoka, *Man'yōshū*, VI.

Kume Tsunetami, "Okura Bungaku ni okeru Kayōsei," in Gomi and Kojima, *Man'yōshū Kenkyū*, V.

Levy, Ian Hideo. *Hitomaro and the Birth of Japanese Lyricism*. Princeton, N.J.: Princeton University Press, 1984.

———. *Man'yōshū*, I. Princeton, N.J.: Princeton University Press, 1981.

Man'yōshū, 3 vols., in Nihon Bungaku Kenkyū Shiryō series. Yūseidō, 1969–77.

Man'yōshū Hikkei, ed. Inaoka Kōji, 2 vols. Gakutōsha, 1979–81.

Man'yōshū Kōza, ed. Hisamatsu Sen'ichi, 7 vols. Yūseidō, 1973.

McCullough, Helen Craig. *Kokin Wakashū*. Stanford, Calif.: Stanford University Press, 1985.

McCullough, William H. and Helen Craig. *A Tale of Flowering Fortunes*, 2 vols. Stanford, Calif.: Stanford University Press, 1980.

Miller, Roy Andrew. *"The Footprints of the Buddha": An Eighth-century Old Japanese Poetic Sequence*, in American Oriental Series, vol. 58. New Haven: American Oriental Society, 1975.

———. "The Lost Poetic Sequence of the Priest Mansei," *Monumenta Nipponica* 36: 2, 1981.

Nakanishi Susumu. *Kakinomoto no Hitomaro*. Chikuma Shobō, 1970.
———. *Man'yō no Jidai to Fūdo*. Kadokawa Shoten, 1980.
———. *Man'yō no Sekai*, in Chūkō Shinsho series. Chūō Kōron Sha, 1973.
———. *Man'yō no Shi to Shijin*. Yayoi Shobō, 1972.
———. *Man'yōshū Genron*. Ōfūsha, 1976.
———. *Man'yōshū no Hikaku Bungakuteki Kenkyū*. Nan'undō Ōfūsha, 1963.
———. *Man'yōshū no Utabitotachi*. Kadokawa Shoten, 1980.
———. "Okura Kikajin Ron," *Kokugakuin Zasshi*, November 1969.
———. "Okura Toraijin Ron," in *Man'yōshū*, III.
———. "Yakamochi Uta Nikki no Hitsuroku," in *Man'yōshū*, III.
———. *Yamanoue no Okura*. Kawade Shobō Shinsha, 1973.
Narahashi Zenji. "Man'yōshū no Hensan Nendai," in *Man'yōshū Kōza*, I.
Nippon Gakujutsu Shinkōkai. *Manyōshū*. New York: Columbia University Press, 1965.
Nosco, Peter. "*Man'yōshū* Studies in Tokugawa Japan," in *Translations of the Asiatic Society of Japan,* 4th series, 1, 1986.
Ōhama Itsuhiko. *Man'yō Genshi Kō*. Shūeisha, 1978.
Ōkubo Tadashi. *Man'yōshū no Shosō*. Meiji Shoin, 1980.
Omodaka Hisataka. *Man'yōshū Chūshaku*, 20 vols. Chūō Kōron Sha, 1957–68.
Ōno Susumu. "Man'yōshū Kaikan Daiichi no Uta," in *Bungaku*, April 1956. The article is reprinted in *Man'yōshū*, III.
Ōoka Makoto. *Tachibana no Yume*. Shinchōsha, 1972.
Origuchi Shinobu Zenshū, 32 vols. Chūō Kōron Sha, 1976.
Philippi, Donald L. *Kojiki*. Tokyo: Tokyo University Press, 1966.
Saigō Nobutsuna. *Man'yō Shiki*. Miraisha, 1970.
Sakamoto Tarō, Ienaga Saburō, Inoue Mitsusada, and Ōno Susumu (eds.). *Nihon Shoki*, 2 vols., in Nihon Koten Bungaku Taikei series. Iwanami Shoten, 1967.
Sansom, George. *A History of Japan*, 3 vols. Stanford, Calif.: Stanford University Press, 1958–63.
Sasaki Yukitsuna. *Kakinimoto no Hitomaro Nōto*. Seidosha, 1982.
Satake Akahiro. *Man'yōshū Nukigaki*. Iwanami Shoten, 1980.
Satō, Hiroaki, and Burton Watson. *From the Country of Eight Islands*. New York: Doubleday, 1981.
Shirakawa Shizuka. *Shoki Man'yō Ron*. Chūō Kōron Sha, 1979.
Takagi Ichinosuke. *Bingū Mondōka no Ron*. Iwanami Shoten, 1974.
———. *Ōtomo no Tabito, Yamanoue no Okura*. Chikuma Shobō, 1972.
Tsuchihashi Yutaka. *Man'yō Kaigan*, 2 vols. Nihon Hōsō Shuppan Kyōkai, 1978.
Tsuchihashi Yutaka and Konishi Jin'ichi. *Kodai Kayō Shū*, in Nihon Koten Bungaku Taikei series. Iwanami Shoten, 1957.
Tsunoda, Ryusaku, Wm. Theodore de Bary, and Donald Keene. *Sources of Japanese Tradition*. New York: Columbia University Press, 1958.

Tsuyuki Noriyoshi. "Temmu Gyosei no Seikaku," in Itō and Inaoka, *Man'yōshū*, I.

Umehara Takeshi. *Minasoko no Uta*, 2 vols. Shūeisha, 1973.

———. *Samayoeru Kashū*. Shūeisha, 1974.

———. *Uta no Fukuseki*, 2 vols. Shūeisha, 1979.

Waley, Arthur. *The Analects of Confucius*. London: George Allen & Unwin, 1938.

Watanabe Kazuo. "Kuso no aru Uta," in Gomi and Kojima, *Man'yōshū Kenkyū*, VIII.

Watson, Burton (trans.). *The Complete Works of Chuang Tzu*. New York: Columbia University Press, 1968.

Yamaji Heishirō. "Kunimi no Uta Futatsu," in *Man'yōshū*, III.

Yamamoto Kenkichi. *Kakinomoto no Hitomaro*. Shinchōsha, 1962.

———. *Ōtomo no Yakamochi*. Chikuma Shobō, 1971.

Yamamoto Kenkichi and Ikeda Yasaburō. *Man'yō Hyakka*. Chūō Kōron Sha, 1963.

Yoshida Yoshitaka. "Shikokka no Tenkai," *Bungaku* 16:7, 1948.

Yoshino Hiroshi. *Sakimoriuta no Kiso Kōzō*. Ochanomizu Shobō, 1956.

4.

POETRY AND PROSE IN CHINESE OF THE EARLY HEIAN PERIOD

In 784, fifteen years after the last dated poem in the *Man'yōshū*, the capital was moved from Nara. There must have been compelling reasons behind the decision to desert a city where culture had flourished, a city not only filled with magnificent temples and palace buildings but surrounded by the lovely scenery of Yamato. Most modern historians seem to think that the probable cause for abandoning Nara was the determination of the court and the Fujiwara family, then in its ascendancy, to move the capital away from the center of Buddhist authority.[1] The unsuccessful attempt of the priest Dōkyō, the favorite of the Empress Shōtoku, to have himself named as her heir had aroused widespread consternation, and after Shōtoku's death in 770, Dōkyō was forced into exile by Fujiwara officials. A grandson of Tenji was brought to the throne, the ineffectual but harmless Kōnin (reigned 770–781), exactly the kind of ruler the Fujiwaras desired. His son Kammu (reigned 781–806), a far more considerable figure, would be intimately involved in the founding of the new capital.

The site chosen for the capital was Nagaoka in the province of Yamashiro, and the move took place in 784. However, before the lavishly planned city could be completed, the crown prince (Kammu's younger brother) was implicated in the murder of Fujiwara no Tanetsugu and deprived of his position. This calamity, auguring ill for the new capital, induced the government to abandon Nagaoka and to choose a new site with the utmost care. In terms of geomancy, there were mountains in three directions (a yang number) and rivers on two sides (a yin number). The city, planned on the model of the Chinese capital at Ch'ang-an, was laid out with nine east-west and eight north-south streets, again observing principles of yin-yang divination. The imperial palace was situated in the north, where the emperor faced south, in the traditional position of authority. And, as if to protect the capital from evil influences emanating from the northeast, the "demon gate" (*kimon*), a Buddhist monastery was founded on Mount Hiei in 788 by the priest Saichō. This monastery developed into the center of Tendai Buddhism, which gradually acquired the importance of a state religion. All these precautions proved to be effective: the city of Heian—"Peace and Tranquillity"—would remain the imperial capital of Japan with minor interruptions for over a thousand years, until 1868, when a new capital was established in Tokyo. The capital city, Heian, lent its name to the literature composed between 793 and 1185, the most glorious period of Japanese literature (with the possible exception of the twentieth century). Heian, or Kyoto as it is now called, continued to be the residence of the emperors after 1185 when the shoguns established their capital at Kamakura.

The surviving literature of the early Heian period is in Chinese. The prestige of composing poetry and prose in Chinese, already evident during the Nara period (as the compilation of the anthology *Kaifūsō* demonstrated), was further enhanced at the end of the eighth century. Some Japanese Buddhist priests who had studied in China acquired such proficiency in Chinese that they were able to express their thoughts freely and gracefully, often with an almost ostentatious display of their familiarity with Chinese literature and philosophy. The predilection of the early Heian court for Chinese learning occasioned the compilation of the first imperially sponsored anthologies—not of Japanese but of Chinese poetry. For a time, indeed, there was a danger that Chinese might wholly supplant Japanese as the medium of literary expression, rather as Norman French overwhelmed Anglo-Saxon; but instead the Japanese language, and especially Japanese literature, benefited immensely from this intensive exposure to the riches of the older literature.

Kūkai (774–835)

The preeminent figure in the creation of the literature in Chinese during the early Heian period was the priest Kūkai, familiarly known by his title, Kōbō Daishi, the Great Teacher who Promulgated the [Buddhist] Law. He was born in 774 on the island of Shikoku into the Saeki family.[2] He himself believed that he belonged to the old Saeki-Ōtomo clan,[3] but recently it has been suggested that the Saeki clan of Sanuki province was quite different from the Saeki of the capital, and may originally have been of Ainu stock.[4] It has also been argued that Kūkai may have chosen to become a Buddhist monk because the normal path of advancement for a bright young man, service in the government, was blocked by the implication of the Saeki family in the murder of Fujiwara no Tanetsugu.[5]

Even as a boy Kūkai demonstrated such promise that his maternal uncle, a Confucian scholar, gave him special instruction in the Confucian classics and Chinese poetry. The uncle took the boy to the capital, and in 791 entered him in the Confucian college in Nagaoka. In 797, when Kūkai composed the first draft of *Sangō Shiiki* (Indications of the Goals of the Three Teachings), he mentioned in the preface that while he was at the Confucian college a Buddhist monk showed him a text of Esoteric Buddhist meditation that so impressed him he decided to follow the prescribed technique of reciting a formula one million times in order to be able to "memorize passages and understand the meaning of any scripture."[6] The technique apparently worked: Kūkai recorded that when he later wandered around Shikoku "the valley reverberated to the sound of my voice as I recited, and the morning star appeared in the sky."[7] Turning his back on worldly fame and wealth, he resolved to become a Buddhist priest. He recalled, "My relatives and teachers opposed my entering the priesthood, saying that by doing so I would be unable to fulfill the Five Cardinal Virtues or to accomplish the duties of loyalty or of filial piety."[8]

But Kūkai, after weighing the merits of Buddhism, Confucianism, and Taoism, reached the conclusion that, though they differed in profundity, all three were the teachings of sages, and therefore an individual who chose to follow any one of them would "not necessarily repudiate loyalty and filial piety."[9] It was partly to refute the Confucian arguments of his relatives, and partly also to enlighten a wayward nephew who indulged in drink and women, that Kūkai wrote *Indications*.[10]

Indications is in the form of a discussion among a Confucianist, fancifully named Kimō (Tortoise Hair), a Taoist named Kyobu (Nothingness), and a Buddhist named Kamei Kotsuji (Nameless Mendicant).[11] The presentation is intentionally dramatic, and the work has been called the first Japanese drama, or even the first Japanese novel. The form has been traced to the dramatic and novelistic elements in the Chinese erotic story *Yū-hsien ku*,[12] but the similarities are not obvious. The dramatic elements in *Indications* are not central to the argumentation, but they lend interest to what would otherwise be a dry recitation of philosophical doctrines. Near the beginning, for example, Kimō visits his friend Tokaku (Rabbit Horn), and they talk about Tokaku's profligate nephew Shitsuga (Leech Tusk), who is "dishonest by nature." We learn that he refuses to listen to other people's advice, indulges in gambling and hunting, and is arrogant and untrustworthy.[13]

The arguments of Kimō, the Confucianist, are put forward in the pedantic manner typical of Japanese members of his school, with numerous references to Chinese precedents, as in this exhortation to Shitsuga:.

> Shitsuga, if you change your heart and devote yourself to filial piety, you could be among those who are well known for this virtue. Think of the men who shed tears of blood; of the man who struck a jar of gold; of Men Tsung; of the man who caught carp; or of Ting Lan.[14]

Loyalty, also urged on Shitsuga, elicits allusions to such paragons as the man who broke the railing, the man who broke a window, the man who exchanged his liver with his lord's, and the man who was stabbed through the heart—all examples drawn from Chinese tradition.[15] The persuasiveness of the Confucian arguments breaks down—at least for a Buddhist—when Kimō, having enumerated a man's duties to his parents and country, stresses the importance of happiness in this world in terms of the pleasures of married life and of friendship. These pleasures are made to sound attractive, but after one has read what the Taoists, and especially the Buddhists, have to say about worldly delights, they are likely to seem hollow and delusory.

Kūkai does not state that he prefers Taoism to Confucianism, but the language of his Taoist is at times quite close to Buddhist belief. Kyobu says, for example, "To an unfit person, we do not open our mouths; unless a man be a proper vessel, we hide our book in a wooden box deep down in the earth. When the occasion comes, we open the box and transmit the secret to those who have been selected."[16] The insistence on finding the proper vessel for the highest teachings was congenial to Kūkai, a believer in Esoteric Buddhism. The rejection of "worldly pollutions" is as absolute with the Taoist as the Buddhist: "You must surrender wealth as if it were a thorn, and an emperor's position as if you were casting off your straw sandals. When you see a beautiful girl with a slender waist, think of her as a devil or a ghost."[17] But the goal of the Taoist was not enlightenment but magical powers: "After you have followed these practices, you will be able to make your shadow vanish, even when out under the sun, and to write in darkness during the night; you will be able to see through the earth and walk on water. . . . You will be able to swallow swords and fire, stir winds, and produce clouds."[18] The ultimate aim of the Taoist, unlike the Buddhist, was to prolong life: "You will live as long as the heaven and earth; enjoy life for an eternity together with the sun and moon."[19]

The third speaker, the Buddhist, is apparently a Japanese. He says of himself, "I have no permanently fixed birthplace or parents. However, in the present temporal existence, the visionlike being you see before you is residing at a bay in Japan, where a large camphor tree spreads its shadow. Having yet to attain what I am searching for, I have already reached the age of twenty-four."[20] Twenty-four (by Japanese reckoning) was Kūkai's age when he wrote most of *Indications*, and there still stands a huge camphor tree in the precincts of the Zentsū-ji, the temple in Shikoku most intimately associated with Kūkai, perhaps the very tree he mentioned. These and several other correspondences lend additional interest to the utterances of the Buddhist, who otherwise betrays few personal touches in his views. He quickly disposes of the arguments of the Confucianist and the Taoist, and recites two prose-poems on impermanence and transcience, reducing his opponents to abject submission. *Indications* concludes with a poem in ten rhymes clarifying the three teachings. The Buddhist, after giving credit to what is admirable in Confucianism and Taoism, affirms his conviction that Mahayana Buddhism is the highest of truths.

Kūkai did not state why he chose to express philosophical beliefs in a literary form—parallel prose with interspersed poems and rhyme-prose—but there were precedents in the Buddhist tradition. Kūkai's mastery of the different styles of Chinese poetry and prose is apparent throughout. He most frequently employed the variety of parallel prose known as *p'ien wen*, perfected in China during the Six Dynasties (220–589). In this style, units of four or six characters are balanced against similar units in succeeding lines. The use of so constricting a medium for conveying philosophical truths that were more normally expressed in unmistakable prose may recall Lucretius or perhaps Pope in *An Essay on Man*. Kūkai, far from considering that formally regulated language impeded the free communication of ideas, evidently assumed that an artistic presentation would lend additional authority to the context. His style, even in this early work, has been praised as unusually beautiful p'ien wen.

Kūkai's journey to China in 804 was probably the chief formative experience of his life. While in Ch'ang-an visiting the famous temples, as he related in *Shōrai Mokuroku* (A Memorial Presenting a List of Newly Imported Sutras), he met the great priest Hui-kuo, the abbot of the Ch'ing Lung (Green Dragon) Temple. As soon as Hui-kuo laid eyes on the young Japanese he intuitively recognized that here was the successor he had long awaited, and he immediately asked Kūkai to prepare for ordination. Part of this ceremony consisted of throwing a flower from a distance onto each of two mandalas, representations of the cosmos under the two aspects of potential entity and dynamic manifestations; the flower's fall, beyond the control of the thrower, revealed which of the many Buddhas represented in the mandala was the one with which he had special affinity. The flower Kūkai threw on the Matrix Mandala fell on Vairochana (Dainichi in Japanese), the supreme Buddha, confirming Huo-kuo's intuition that Kūkai was destined to be his successor. A month later, when Kūkai was initiated into the rites of the Diamond Mandala, his flower once again fell on the image of Vairochana, to the amazement of all.

While Kūkai was in China he studied the mantras (chants) and mudras (accompanying hand movements) necessary to esoteric practices and also learned Sanskrit. The abbot Hui-kuo, satisfied with Kūkai's progress, informed him that "the Esoteric scriptures are so abstruse that their meaning cannot be conveyed except through art."[21] He ordered various painters to execute scrolls of the two mandalas and a bronzesmith to cast ritual implements for Kūkai to take back to Japan. Kūkai not only emphasized the importance of art in religious experience but he is popularly regarded today as the supreme Japanese calligrapher, and many paintings and sculptures are dubiously credited to him. Irrespective of Kūkai's personal contributions to Buddhist art, Shingon Buddhism always placed enormous importance on the mandalas, to the degree that it might be said to be a religion that explains the mandalas.

Another aspect of Shingon Buddhism described in Kūkai's *Memorial* is the importance of the line of transmission of the teachings from Vairochana Buddha to the present. The emphasis given to pedigree was congenial to the Japanese, as we can infer from the unbroken line of emperors or, in later times, the insistence on the fiction that actors or musicians are direct descendants of the founders of their arts. Hui-kuo had received instruction from the Indian master Amoghavajra, but he had been unwilling to transmit the teachings to his Chinese disciples because none of them seemed to be an adequate vessel for such profound and recondite philosophy. The Esoteric teachings were not for everybody, and secrecy in the transmission was essential if unworthy recipients were not to corrupt or pervert the truths of Buddha. The insistence on secret teachings was not confined to Shingon; in time almost all the secular arts in Japan also came to possess secret traditions that were transmitted only to chosen disciples, and usually only on payment of established fees.

Hui-kuo died soon after he had completed the necessary transmission of teachings to Kūkai. The night after he died, he appeared in Kūkai's dream, urging him to return to Japan and propagate the Esoteric teachings there. His last words were, "If I am reborn in Japan, this time I will be your disciple."[22]

Kūkai's *Memorial* is not, as a whole, of literary interest. It consists mainly of the names of sutras and commentaries that Kūkai had obtained in China; but the sections describing the relationship between Hui-kuo and his Japanese disciple are beautifully expressed, suggesting the universality of a religion that had been transmitted from India to China and from China to Japan.

Kūkai owes his place in literary history to his poetry and prose in Chinese, found mainly in *Seirei Shū* (Collected Inspirations).[23] Most of his poems are specifically Buddhist. He describes in one poem, for example, maggots and bluebottle flies infesting the corpse of a once beautiful woman, an allegorical statement of the transitory nature of worldly joys.[24] In other poems or prose-poems Kūkai suggested the Buddhist teachings more obliquely:

Valley water—one cup in the morning sustains life;
Mountain mist—one whiff in the evening nurtures the soul.
Hanging moss, delicate grasses suffice to clothe my body;
Rose leaves, cedar bark—these will be my bedding.
Heaven's compassion spreads over me the indigo canopy of the sky;
The Dragon King's devotion passes round me curtains of white clouds.
Mountain birds sometimes come, each singing its own song;
Mountain monkeys nimbly leap, displaying incredible skill.
Spring flowers, autumn chrysanthemums smile at me;
Dawn moons, morning winds cleanse the dust from my heart.[25]

Kūkai believed that poetry, even the difficult Chinese poems he himself composed, provided a valuable means of teaching Buddhist doctrine. Poetry was also prized by Confucian scholars because they believed it helped in governing a country; this would be the chief justification for composing poetry in Chinese during the early part of the Heian period. A statement of this principle is given in Kūkai's preface to *Bunkyō Hifu Ron* (Secret Treasure-house of the Mirrors of Poetry), a massive study of Chinese poetics compiled by Kūkai in 820. The preface opens:

> The basis of the Buddha's teachings to sentient beings was in his words. Literary composition was fundamental also to the Confucian scholars who sought to remedy the conditions of their time. This is why the truths of the former were revealed in writing that appeared spontaneously in the sky and in this world of dust, and of the latter as writing that formed of itself on the backs of tortoises and dragons.[26] Their observations of changes in the sun, moon, and stars enabled them to discover how to enlighten and nurture the people of the entire world, and harmonies of gold and jade, melodies of pipes and reeds, ornamented their compositions, enabling them to guide the people. What elegance and what brilliance illuminated the compositions that brought them dominance over the mass of men! Just as one marks the beginning of numbers, so writing is the fountainhead of instruction. If we accept instruction by means of words as the first principle, literary compositions constitute the keystone of order within the nation. How can anyone, layman or priest, neglect literary composition?[27]

Kūkai's justification for ornamented language, notably the parallel Chinese prose he wrote with effortless mastery, was that it made truths more palatable than bare statement, rather as Lucretius justified his poetry as honey on the lip of a cup of medicine. Even the man of shallow intelligence will be attracted to pleasingly phrased truths; and the educated man will be repelled by ugly language, even if he is capable of accepting the content. Kūkai quoted the passage in the *Analects* where Confucius, rebuking his disciples for not being interested in poetry,[28] declared that the expressive possibilities of poetry are conducive to the performance of acts of filial piety and loyalty.

The value of poetry had often been affirmed by the Chinese. The anthology of Six Dynasties poetry, *Wen Hsüan*, compiled about 530, contained this statement by the Wei emperor Wen-t'i (Ts'ao P'i, 187–226): "Literature is without doubt a great enterprise for ruling the country, as well as an imperishable glory. The years of a man's life are finite, and with the passage of time reach their end; the joys of wealth and rank terminate with the person. Life and worldly fame both clearly have allotted spans, and are not to be compared to the inexhaustible nature of literature."[29] This opinion—familiar to the West in the formula "art is long, life is short"—was not a glorification of art but a Confucian justification of its value. It was known in Japan by the end of the eighth century and is mentioned in Kūkai's *Indications*, but it did not develop into a theory of literature until the reign of the Emperor Saga (809–23), when it became a fashionable cliché.[30]

Kūkai's contributions to Japanese culture extended to many fields. He was the founder in Japan of Shingon, one of the most important sects of Buddhism, and contributed not only to the arts but to the scholarship associated with this sect. He is credited with the invention of the kana syllabary, a reasonable conjecture in view of his knowledge of Sanskrit; but there is no evidence for this ascription. Nor is it possible to accept the attribution to Kūkai of the *iroha*, a poem that uses each of the forty-seven kana symbols only once.[31]

Such traditions, though of dubious authenticity, reflect popular awareness of the magnitude of Kūkai's achievements. In any case, Kūkai's contributions to Japanese literature were written not in Japanese but in Chinese. Indeed, just before the triumph of the kana literature of the tenth century, there was almost a century during which Chinese writings predominated.[32]

The literature in Chinese of the ninth century was often neglected by historians of Japanese literature, perhaps because they resented the fact that Kūkai and others of his time wrote in what was, after all, a foreign language; but the *kanshi* and *kambun* composed at this time have gradually gained acceptance as part of the Japanese literary heritage, and they are no longer dismissed as being mere exercises in imitation of Chinese models. The works of Kūkai, composed in difficult Chinese, have been translated into Japanese and given the benefit of commentaries, assuring him of a place in the literary as well as the religious history of Japan.

The Emperor Saga (786–842)

The Emperor Saga, who succeeded his brother Heizei on the throne in 809, was a passionate admirer of Chinese culture. He was also a skilled poet of kanshi and a superb calligrapher. Under his guidance the administration of the country was reorganized on Chinese lines, and he encouraged the composition of literary works in the Chinese language. Three anthologies of poetry bear witness to the flourishing state of writing in Chinese during his reign.[33]

The first of the three collections, *Ryōun Shinshū* (New Collection Soaring Above the Clouds), more commonly known as *Ryōunshū*,[34] was completed in 814. It contains ninety-one poems composed by twenty-four poets between 782 and 814. The poets, with one exception, were all members of the imperial family or the high-ranking nobility, and the poems were arranged in descending order of rank, rather than chronologically or by subject.[35] The collection is headed by two poems by Heizei, followed by twenty-two poems by Saga, the largest number of poems by any single poet.[36] Unlike the eighth-century collection *Kaifūsō*, in which poems with lines of five characters predominated, half the poems in the *Ryōunshū* are in seven-character lines, suggesting that poets felt more assurance in handling poems of longer lines and also probably reflecting literary tendencies in China during the middle of the T'ang dynasty.[37]

The preface to the *Ryōunshū* by Ono no Minemori (777–830)[38] opens with the statement by the Wei emperor Wen-t'i (quoted above) on the important role literature plays in good government, and is otherwise devoted mainly to an encomium of Emperor Saga, who is praised equally for his benevolence and literary genius. The immediate occasion for the compilation of the *Ryōunshū*, we are told, was the emperor's regret that so many poetic compositions had been lost. Minemori accepted with gratitude the emperor's request that he compile a collection, though he was well aware of his incompetence and sure that he would fail to do justice to the task. More than once, overwhelmed by the magnitude of the assignment, he had thought of resigning, but the emperor would not permit this. Now that the compilation had been completed, it was possible to see how the poems by the Emperor Saga spread light through the whole collection, as jewels in a pond make the waters bright. Minemori declared that he had not chosen the poems arbitrarily, but only after consultation with other officials, and when no decision could be reached, the emperor himself was consulted.

The collection opens with the two poems by Emperor Heizei, the first on peach blossoms, the second on cherry blossoms. These conventionally pretty compositions are unimpressive, but it is worth noting the prominence of cherry blossoms; they would be as typical of the Heian capital as plum blossoms were of Nara. Despite the assertion in the preface that literature is of service to the government, the poetry of this collection is prevailingly of the kind that was composed at banquets and similar occasions. A typical poem, by the Emperor Saga, is entitled "Going Deep into the Mountains of an Autumn Day":

In my wanderings I encountered the sadness of autumn's coming;
As I went deep into the mountains, I recalled Sung Yü's words.
Midway in the sky, over a steep summit, the fog hovered;
Silent valleys on the dark side were slow to receive the sun.

I listened: monkeys' cries sounded shrill in the old trees;
I looked: crows crisscrossed desolately in the cold wind.
Here even in the steamy summer heat the wind is chilly;
How much more so after sunset at the height of autumn![39]

Apart from one mistake in the tones,[40] the poem is formally unexceptionable. The allusion to Sung Yü, who was famous for having described the sadness of autumn in his "Nine Arguments,"[41] had already been made by *Kaifūsō* poets and would be made many times again. There is not much either to praise or condemn in Saga's poem, and the same is true of most in the *Ryōunshū*. Occasionally a poem will have an intriguing title, promising something that goes beyond gallant or self-consciously noble thoughts, but one is likely to be disappointed by the poem itself. The poem that Saga addressed to Kūkai when he bestowed on him a gift of silk floss is no exception.

You, serene priest, have long dwelled on a peak in the clouds;
My thoughts travel to those distant mountains where the spring is still cold.
The pines and oaks can guess the profound silence of your life;
But the clouds and mist do not know how many years you have eaten coarse food.
Of late word has not reached us from your meditation retreat;
Now the blossoms and willows are at their height in the capital.
Do not scorn, oh bodhisattva, this paltry gift,
But for the donor's sake, deliver the people from hardship.[42]

Kūkai's response, in a similar vein, is preserved, though not in this collection.[43] There are no poems by Buddhist priests in the *Ryōunshū*, but some poems by Kūkai found their way into *Bunka Shūrei Shū*, the second imperially sponsored collection.

Perhaps the tone of the *Ryōunshū* is best suggested by the poem by Fujiwara no Fuyutsugu (775–826) entitled "Hearing Flutes Along the Road in the Autumn Night: To Match a Poem by the Director of the Imperial University Sugawara no Kiyotata":

A feel of autumn in the tall sky of dusk;
hastening officials, through at court, descend from the palace.
In the new night strolling players sound their flutes,
the long notes, the short notes, that stir men's thoughts.

Wind from the willows bears the cry of a luan bird,
the moon in the ash tree lights the figure of a phoenix:
soon we'll hear such music as they played for the sage Shun
when the birds and beasts danced in his royal city.[44]

This poem, like many others in the *Ryōunshū*, was written to "match" a poem by another person. The poem by Sugawara no Kiyokimi which inspired Fuyutsugu's has not been preserved, but another poem, by the Emperor Saga, included in the *Ryōunshū*, "matches" the same poem:

Now that autumn is ending, I hear a strange sound:
The strains of flutes capture the phoenix's song.
Melodies issue from the flute, a plaintive, foreign strain;
Woodwinds send forth tunes, harmonizing with elegant strings.
Fresh voices, ever changing, tremble in the long night;
Wondrous echoes, long drawn out, fade in the wind from afar.
I listened a while on the road and felt my heart would break;
But how much more profoundly the music would have stirred
your heart.[45]

The poems of the *Ryōunshū* are far more accomplished than those in the *Kaifūsō*, but the range is still limited. Poets were restricted both by the circumstance of composing at the court and by their reliance for inspiration on Chinese poetry of the Six Dynasties. Extremely few of these Japanese had ever visited China, and this, no doubt, is why they depended on such old models. Their poetry tended to be allusive, rather than direct, carefully turned, rather than forceful, elegant, rather than sincere. Quite apart from the basic factor of individual talent, these conditions made the kanshi of the early ninth century less affecting than even minor *Man'yōshū* poems. Although one can recognize the poet's skill in handling Chinese metrics, the poems seem curiously distant. It is difficult to believe that the poet could not have found subjects that might be successfully treated in his own language.

The second of the imperially sponsored collections of kanshi, *Bunka Shūrei Shū*, was compiled in 818. The title means something like "Collection of Masterpieces of Literary Flowers."[46] Unlike the *Ryōunshū*, the *Bunka Shūrei Shū* does not insist that literature is of service in governing the country; the collection is aesthetic both in its tone and professed aims. The poems are superior to those in the *Ryōunshū*, perhaps because in the four years since the earlier collection was prepared the poets had gained greater confidence in their ability to describe their emotions, as opposed to flowering trees or the sounds of distant flutes. The poems are arranged by categories, all but one adopted from the *Wen Hsüan*.[47] The occasions for composing poetry, however, remained much the same as for the *Ryōunshū*.

Many poems commemorate excursions by the emperor to hillsides or lakes or describe other courtly matters. The visits of envoys from the country of Po-hai, a kingdom in northern Korea and Manchuria that lasted from 698 to 926, inspired many works, chiefly in the nature of mutual compliments; these poems were naturally in Chinese, the cultural language of all of East Asia, but there are more poems in *Bunka Shūrei Shū* about Japan than in the *Ryōunshū*. The importance of Chinese traditions was reflected in the poems that describe Chinese (but not Japanese) historical events. Although the Emperor Saga was still the central poet of the collection, and most of the other poets were members of his court, a few poems are by Buddhist priests. The style, prevalently that of the *Wen Hsüan*, reveals some influence from early T'ang poetry.

Bunka Shūrei Shū reflects closely the activities of the circle of kanshi poets surrounding the Emperor Saga. The first poem, by Saga himself, set the tone of the collection, opening a section devoted to excursions. It is called "Spring Dawning on the River":

> The pavilion on the river turns its back on worldly things;
> As I lie, propped on my pillow, I hear only cockcrows from the old fort.
> I know from the mist dampening my robe how close I am to the peak;
> I realize from the spring's murmur, rousing me from sleep, how near the valley is.
> The lone moon at the sky's edge swiftly disappears on the water it rides;
> Hungry monkeys in the mountains cry till the dawn's approach.
> The landscape and the weather have yet to take on warmth and mildness, it is true,
> But the spring grasses in the river shallows are all but bursting with buds.[48]

By no means all of the poems in the collection are in the voice of the *bunjin*, the man of letters, though this poem is typical. The following work by Prince Nakao, from the section "Presentations and Replies," bears the prefatory note, "Banished from the Palace, I have recorded something of my feelings and respectfully present them with a letter to the Palace Guard Yoshimine no Yasuyo."

Wine and feasts I followed with a host of officials;
Unworthy, yet I stood in the Court of the Emperor.
With reverence I received the rites of investiture—
Next day I was banished from the council chamber.
On that noble ground, no room for my anxious feet;
From high heaven came accusations, to whom could I cry?
I left the company of the virtuous, the ranks of the adorned;
To me alone the sea-encircling dew came not.
I listened outside the palace to the sound of singing;
Below the stairs, apart, I watched the ladies on the terrace.
I returned at dusk to face my wife in shame;
Through the night I lay talking with my children in bed.
Great faults and small merits were mine, I know.
For mercy and light penalty I am forever grateful.
Though I may never again enter the gate of my lord,
I shall speak from this far land and Heaven may hear me.[49]

We do not know the nature of the accusation against Prince Nakao, but the poem is in a familiar Chinese mood: the slandered (or possibly justly accused) courtier is obliged to leave "the company of the virtuous" and is deprived of the imperial favor ("the sea-encircling dew"). The speaker trusts, however, that the emperor, in his mercy, will forgive the offender and admit him once more to the circle of the elect. Perhaps Yamanoue no Okura could have conveyed similar content in a chōka, but by now it was easier for educated Japanese to express such thoughts in Chinese, relying on the existence of Chinese traditions of poetry in this vein. As the Japanese became familiar with T'ang poetry of greater social and intellectual content, the tendency to use Chinese for their public convictions became even more pronounced, and Japanese poetry was reserved for private emotions.

One more imperially sponsored anthology of poetry in Chinese appeared at this time, the *Keikokushū* (Collection for Governing the Country), completed during the reign of Saga's successor, Junna, in 827.[50] This was by far the biggest of the three anthologies, consisting of twenty books (*kan*) and containing over one thousand poems and prose selections by 178 poets. However, only six of the twenty books have survived, and the ambitious compendium of compositions in Chinese between 707 and 827 is unfortunately incomplete. As the title of the collection indicated, the compilers emphasized the role of poetry in "governing the country"; but the poems that move us are personal rather than instructional. A poem by the Emperor Saga about a lady on a swing is particularly engaging:

As the jewellike hands take turns in pushing her,
Her slender waist, encircled, flies off like a bird.
Her shoes, treading the clouds, graze the trees;
Her long skirts, trailing the ground, brush the flowers.[51]

Several woman poets, including Princess Uchiko, a daughter of Saga who served as the high priestess of the Kamo Shrine, are represented in the three imperial collections of kanshi. A century later it would be considered unladylike for a woman to learn Chinese, as we know from the diary of Murasaki Shikibu, but at this time some women of the court read Chinese collections of poetry and composed kanshi themselves. Their poems are more like the kanshi composed by men than the poetry in Japanese by other women, if only because of the common dependence on Chinese sources; but occasionally we hear a personal note, as in Princess Uchiko's poem expressing joy over a visit from her father,[52] or Lady Ōtomo's poem "Late Autumn Thoughts":

This is a time of loneliness, the year past its prime;
The doors of the women's palace are silent, the autumn day chill.
In the cloudy sky, distant geese, their cries easily heard;
On the tree by the eaves a late cicada—its voice is spent.
At the chrysanthemum pool the remaining blossoms, dew-laden, are
cold;
By the lotus basin old leaves, frost-stricken, look like broken sake
cups.
Solitary and lonely, I grieve over the seasons' insistent rush;
I cannot bear to look at the fluttering, falling leaves.[53]

Reference to the women's palace is evidence that this poem was composed by a woman, but men sometimes also wrote in the persona of a woman. For example, the lost poem by Emperor Saga on "Spring Sorrow in the Women's Quarters" inspired replies from several courtiers, the men writing as if they were court ladies. The poem by Asano no Katori opened, "I grew up in Ch'ang-an, accustomed to every luxury I desired; / My clothes were perfumed, my face like a flower." Kose no Shikihito's response opened, "When I was a winsome sixteen years old / My face was bright as blossoms, my appearance fair as peach or damson."[54] Such poems obviously could not be wholly sincere, but the practice of men writing from a woman's point of view would be carried over into the composition of waka in the *Kokinshū*.

Hakushi Monjū

The single most important event in the development of Chinese poetry and prose in Heian Japan was the introduction of *The Collected Works of Po Chü-i*, known in Japan as *Hakushi Monjū* or sometimes simply as *Monjū* (Works) because of its great celebrity. An envoy to China who returned in 837 brought with him the collection, which he had received from the priest Ennin, then studying in China. When Ennin himself returned to Japan in 847 he brought other copies. No doubt he had heard of the popularity in China of Po Chü-i (772–836) and felt it was important that his countrymen be acquainted with the most admired Chinese poet of the time. There was generally a time lag of fifty or more years between the creation of works of literature in China and their transmission to Japan, but Po's poetry was known in Japan while he was still alive. Within a few years *The Collected Works of Po Chü-i* all but made the Japanese forget the existence of *Wen Hsüan*.

The success of the poetry of Po Chü-i in Japan has been variously explained. The primary reason, it need hardly be said, was the intrinsic quality of the poetry, though this does not explain why the poetry of Tu Fu, usually rated even higher by the Chinese themselves, was relatively little read in Japan.[55] The simplicity of Po's style undoubtedly contributed to his popularity in Japan, and the Japanese felt they knew him from his poetry in a way that it was hard to know the *Wen Hsüan* poets. Finally, as Burton Watson pointed out, the social concerns of Po Chü-i and the attention he devoted to the sufferings of the common people struck a responsive chord in the Heian nobles and inspired them to write similar poems about their own country.[56]

The poems of Po Chü-i were popular almost from the day they were introduced to the Japanese, but their special importance is generally traced to the reign of the Emperor Nimmei (833–850). The Fujiwara clan was then in its ascendancy, and family lineage, rather than skill at composing poetry, became the chief qualification for promotions at the court. The best kanshi poet of the time, Ono no Takamura (802–852), was admired not for his poetry but for the preface he wrote to the legal code, *Ryō no Gige*, an excellent example of Chinese prose but hardly of literary interest. At such a time of disappointment, it was natural that poets should have turned from the festive manner of the earlier kanshi compositions to the more serious, sometimes tragic tones of Po Chü-i's works. Takamura straddled the two styles of Chinese poetry: his early poetry was in the *Wen Hsüan* tradition, but his later poetry shows the influence of Po Chü-i. A new age had begun in the history of the kanshi.

Sugawara no Michizane (845–903)

Sugawara no Michizane was by far the most important kanshi poet of the second half of the ninth century, and in the opinion of many he was the most distinguished kanshi poet of all time. He came of a scholarly background. His grandfather, Sugawara no Kiyokimi (770–842) had served as a Confucian scholar and tutor to the future Emperor Heizei when he was crown prince. Kiyokimi journeyed to China on the same ship as Saichō as a member of the ambassadorial delegation, and after his return to Japan he established himself as the leading Confucian scholar of the day. Works by Kiyokimi appeared in all three imperially sponsored anthologies of kanshi and kambun.[57]

Kiyokimi's son (and Michizane's father), Sugawara no Koreyoshi (812–880), was also a distinguished scholar.[58] We know how his learning inspired Michizane from the latter's long poem "Hardships of a Professor."[59] His most illustrious service to the court was as an editor of *Montoku Jitsuroku* (The Chronicles of the Emperor Montoku), the fifth of the Six Dynastic Histories.[60]

Michizane far eclipsed his grandfather and father in scholarly accomplishments and poetic skill, but he demonstrated his pride in the House of Sugawara by editing three collections of writings in Chinese—one by his grandfather, one by his father, and the third by himself—and presented all three to the Emperor Daigo in 900.[61] His own collection, *Kanke Bunsō*, consists of six books of poetry and six of prose. Michizane's late poems, most of them written in exile, were collected in *Kanke Kōshū*. In addition to the Chinese poetry contained in these collections, Michizane also composed some well-known waka.[62]

Michizane's schooling began when he was four.[63] When he was ten his father appointed his disciple Shimada no Tadaomi (828–891) as Michizane's teacher. Tadaomi was then twenty-eight, but despite the difference in age, he and Michizane became lifelong friends, and at fourteen Michizane married Tadaomi's daughter, who was apparently only nine at the time.[64] Michizane, who had composed his first kanshi at the age of ten,[65] was fortunate to have the opportunity also to study with a Chinese emigrant from whom he learned to read the texts in the original pronunciations and word order.[66]

Michizane entered the university at the age of seventeen, younger than most other students.[67] He remained at the university as a graduate student, and did not take the civil service examinations until 870, when he was twenty-five. He was examined by the Confucian scholar and poet Miyako no Yoshika (834–879), one of the compilers of *Bunka Shūrei*

Shū. He was asked to write on two subjects, Chinese surnames and earthquakes.[68] He passed, but Yoshika rated him as only "above average." Yoshika was a severe marker, and he seems to have given all the candidates he examined the same poor mark. Michizane was nevertheless qualified for an official career. He was promoted in court rank and given a secretariat position. In 871 he was chosen to receive the ambassadors from Po-hai, but his chief duty at the time was drafting documents. For the next six years he served as a minor bureaucrat and wrote little poetry. A poem written in the second month of 874, entitled "Through the Snow to Early Duty at the Office," suggests his routine at the time:

Wind wafts palace bells sounding the hour of dawn;
I hurry along the road through tumbling flurries of snow.
Clad in my three foot coat of fur,
mouth nicely warmed with two portions of wine.
I wonder if the chilly groom has daubed willow fluff on his collar,
amazed to see my tired horse tramping through drifting clouds.
At the office, no time for a moment's rest;
huffing on my hands a thousand times, I scribble official drafts.[69]

Michizane's poems, however, were by no means restricted to descriptions of his public life. His most affecting poems are private, notably "Dreaming of Amaro," written in 883. Amaro was the nickname for Michizane's eldest son, who died that year at the age of six.

Since Amaro died I cannot sleep at night;
if I do, I meet him in dreams and tears come coursing down.
Last summer he was over three feet tall;
this year he would have been seven years old.
He was diligent and wanted to know how to be a good son,
read his books and recited by heart the "Poem on the Capital."
Medicine stayed the bitter pain, but only for ten days;
then the wind took his wandering soul off to the Nine Springs.
Since then, I hate the gods and buddhas;
better if they had never made heaven and earth! . . .[70]

Michizane in his private poems showed how much he had learned from Po Chü-i and other T'ang poets. He was not consciously imitating any particular Chinese poem when he described his yearning for his dead son, but what he had read surely affected his expression. He had discovered that poetry, even if it failed to aid good government and even if it was not couched in elegant language, could convey the profoundest emotions of the poet. This lesson may seem transparently obvious, but it was rare for earlier kanshi poets to accomplish more than to voice appropriately graceful sentiments. Michizane's poetry is most affecting when most personal. Even when he modeled himself directly on Po Chü-i, he wrote not about China but about places he had visited and people he knew.[71]

In 880 Michizane was appointed as a professor at the university, but as he related in the poem "Hakase Nan" (Hardships of a Professor, 881), he had taught only three days when some students he had failed in an examination accused him of having marked them unfairly. Michizane insisted in this poem that he had been absolutely fair, and that no fault could be found with his teaching, but he was nevertheless dismissed from his post.[72] The complaints of the students alone could not have caused his dismissal unless they had been backed by jealous rivals of Michizane.[73] Michizane described this rivalry among scholars in various writings.[74] Anger, like the grief he experienced over the death of his son, gave his poetry an intensity not found in earlier kanshi.

In 882 an anonymous poem criticizing the minister Fujiwara no Fuyuo was circulated at court. It was so skillfully composed that people attributed it to Michizane, but he indignantly denied authorship, and in a long poem called on the gods to clear him of this accusation.[75] Once again, irritation spurred Michizane into writing a poem of exceptional power.

Michizane wrote various other poems in anger. A particular target was the constant bickering among scholars. He was so carried away by his wrath over insults and false accusations that he failed to mention that it was a particularly brilliant time for literature, the "golden age" of the kanshi and kambun in Japan. One of his chief grievances was that nobody seemed to recognize the true worth of his poetry, as he complained in a poem written a year after he was accused of being the author of the anonymous poem:

Last year everybody was amazed how clever the poem was;
This year people abuse the clumsiness of my poems . . .
A signed poem is not necessarily contemptible, nor an anonymous
  poem a treasure;

And even if one's early works were splendid, it doesn't mean the later ones are bad.
One man opens his mouth and ten thousand join the chorus;
When a clever man starts a rumor, the fools happily chime in.
Ten miles, a hundred miles, a thousand miles it flies;
A carriage with four horses, fast as a dragon, is no match for a tongue . . .
My enemies slander me solely as a scholar and a poet;
Last year's row seems to have died a natural death.
My detractors have finally decided I really wrote the unsigned poem;
That's why I cannot take their criticism this year for truth.[76]

In 886 Fujiwara no Tokihira (871–909, also known as Shihei), the son of the chancellor, Fujiwara no Mototsune, had his coming-of-age ceremony in the palace. The occasion was lavishly celebrated, the Emperor Kōkō himself placing the ceremonial hat on the youth's head. Two weeks later orders were issued transferring twenty-eight high-ranking officials, including Michizane, to posts away from the capital, suggesting that the ceremony may have had political implications. Tokihira would one day emerge as Michizane's archenemy, but the decision to send Michizane to the province of Sanuki was obviously the work not of the boy but of his father, the chancellor. Sanuki was by no means a disagreeable post, but it nevertheless was tantamount to an exile for Michizane. The four years he spent in Sanuki, 886–890 with two short breaks in the capital, were frustrating to a man who had hitherto lived at the heart of Heian intellectual life, but they imparted a new dimension to his poetry. We are told that Michizane first saw poverty, old age, and human suffering while in Sanuki. This legend, reminiscent of the stories told of the Buddha's experiences on first leaving his palace, cannot have been literally true, but it is undeniable that such themes first appear in his poetry at this time.

The works of Michizane's years in Sanuki include a sequence of ten poems on "early cold" in which he described how the approach of winter afflicted various unfortunates—a peasant who has fled from another province, an old man who has lost his wife, a packhorse driver, a fisherman, a vagrant, an orphan, an herb gardener, a sailor, a salt peddler, and a woodcutter.[77] He was able in these poems to come close to the essence as well as the expression of the poetry of Po Chü-i because he had become personally acquainted with the kind of misery that his great predecessor had so often described. Michizane, though profoundly influenced by Po Chü-i, referred in such poems as "On the Road I Met a White-haired Old Man" to his experiences in Sanuki. The old man of the poem related unhappy events of the past in these terms:

> In the late years of Jōgan, beginning of Gangyō,
> the government had no mercy or love, laws too often unjust.
> Though drought plagued us, no word of it went to the capital;
> though our people died of contagion, no one pitied or cared.
> 40,000 homesteads or more overrun with thorns and brambles,
> eleven districts where no smoke of cooking fires rose.[78]

The tone of concern recalls Yamanoue no Okura, the only previous Japanese poet to write in such terms, but Michizane had derived his expression from Po Chü-i and probably did not know Okura's poems which, in any case, were in Japanese—not the classical Chinese in which Michizane wrote. Another poem composed in Sanuki, "Written on the Twenty-sixth Day of the Third Month of 888," described his feelings in a way that transcended imitation:

> With whom can I discuss the smallest part of my griefs?
> This distant place has made them all the more unbearable.
> Only four days left to the spring of my fourth year here;
> This will be the third end of spring away from home.
> I'll wait for the summer clothes my wife sends;
> Last year's sake is ready to drink, I'll invite the old men
>   of the village.
> Goodbye song thrushes, blossoms—from today on
> Indifferent to spring, I'll devote myself to crops and
>   silkworm cultivation.[79]

This poem opens with an expression of Michizane's frustration at being cut off from his friends, people with whom he could discuss his thoughts freely. He waits for the clothes made by his wife, rather than wear locally made garments. He will pass the last days of spring not with other poets but with old men of the village. Their celebration will not last long; in the capital he and his friends had regretted the passing of spring, but here the governor is too busy with agricultural matters to dally over such elegant concerns.

Michizane's absence from the capital at least spared him involvement in the *akō* incident that created bitter divisions among the nobility in 887. In that year the Emperor Uda ascended the throne. He was not the son of a Fujiwara mother, but Fujiwara no Mototsune had recommended him as Kōkō's successor, and the grateful Uda commanded the official Tachibana no Hiromi (837–890) to draft a rescript appointing Mototsune as the chancellor. Instead of using the familiar term *kampaku* for "chancellor," Hiromi used *akō*, an archaic word with the same meaning. Some scholars at court asserted that *akō* in China had signified a purely honorary title. Mototsune himself before long accepted this interpretation and withdrew from the government, to the emperor's consternation. The incident was resolved by making Tachibana no Hiromi bear responsibility (though only for a few days), and Mototsune, who had proved himself to be the strongest man in the government, graciously accepted the office of kampaku.[80]

Michizane made two brief visits to the capital during the period of the *akō* incident. The first was at the time of the coronation of Uda, before the full force of the dispute had made itself felt, the second was in response to a request for help from Tachibana no Hiromi, who had seen all of his other friends and students turn against him. In between the two visits, while in Sanuki, Michizane sent a poem to Shimada no Tadaomi titled "Thinking of Various Poet-Friends":

Not many first-class poets are left in the capital;
And those still left are exhausted with arguing about akō . . .
Nothing can be done about the drought in this southern province;
What feelings inspire the ferocity of eastern barbarians?
Now that your duties have ended, you will have ample leisure;
Days and months, misty landscapes, will be yours to command.[81]

This poem alludes to the disputes in the capital over the word *akō*. Those who prefer poetry to arguments have left the capital. But life is difficult for a provincial governor, too: Michizane had to cope with a drought in Sanuki, and governors in the eastern provinces with barbarians on the frontier. Finally, Michizane says with a touch of envy, Tadaomi has completed his service as a governor and can spend his days as he pleases, admiring misty landscapes.

Michizane while visiting the capital in support of Tachibana no Hiromi wrote a letter to Mototsune insisting on the correctness of the term *akō* as used by Hiromi. The letter had no effect on the incident, which had already been settled, but brought Michizane to Uda's attention as someone who could stand up against the powerful Fujiwara family.

After Michizane returned to the capital in 890 he resumed his official duties. He was granted several promotions by Uda, who favored him, especially after Mototsune's death in 891. A new chancellor was not appointed, and the emperor reigned without one until his abdication in 897. The most conspicuous mark of Uda's favor was his appointment of Michizane in 894 as ambassador to China, with Ki no Haseo as his second in command. No doubt Uda imagined that Michizane would be overjoyed to follow in the footsteps of his grandfather as ambassador, but about a month before the emperor ordered the mission Michizane learned from a Buddhist priest who had been studying in China that the country was in disorder and pirates infested the seas. Soon after he was appointed as ambassador, Michizane petitioned the court to reconsider its decision to send an embassy, declaring that there was strong reason to believe that the T'ang dynasty was coming to an end, and that there was nothing now to be learned from the Chinese.[82] Two weeks later the order was rescinded. The decision, objectively considered, was correct: the T'ang dynasty was faltering, and it was hardly a time propitious for Japanese to learn (as so often in the past) of new developments in Chinese civilization. But it is possible that Michizane's reluctance to go to China stemmed from fear that in his absence jealous rivals might undermine his position at court.

The atmosphere at the court was gradually becoming hostile toward poets. Confucianists denounced the breed as "useless" to the nation.[83] Michizane in a famous poem of 901, "On Lo-t'ien's Poem on the Three Friends of the Northern Window,"[84] declared that although Po Lo-t'ien (Po Chü-i) could count on three friends—his lute, wine, and poetry—he himself had only one, poetry. Michizane had a powerful protector in the Emperor Uda, but Uda abdicated in 897 in favor of his twelve-year-old son, Daigo. Uda had named two men, Fujiwara no Tokihira and Michizane, as advisers to the boy emperor. Tokihira was appointed minister of the Left in 899 and Michizane became minister of the Right. Michizane three times attempted to decline the honor, but each time his request was refused. In any case, Tokihira's position was superior,[85] and before long he would take advantage of it to get rid of Michizane. Others in the government, resenting Michizane's success, refused to attend meetings of the council of state if he was present. Michizane sent a letter to the Retired Emperor Uda in 898 complaining of their behavior and asking him to order the others to attend the council.[86] Uda's intervention was effective in this instance, but he himself had sincerely turned toward Buddhism, and showed himself increasingly reluctant to become entangled in such troublesome matters.[87]

In 900 Michizane presented the youthful Daigo with collections of poetry by successive generations of his family. Daigo expressed his thanks with a poem stating that, although he had always been a devoted reader of the *Works* of Po Chü-i, he realized now that the writings of the Sugawara family were superior, and the *Works* would henceforth be stored at the back of his bookcase.[88] Six months later the emperor would send Michizane into exile. People at the court seem to have foreseen that this might happen: the scholar Miyoshi no Kiyoyuki (847–918) sent Michizane a letter late in 900 urging him to "know where to stop, where to be satisfied with honors already received." He used these words of Lao Tzu as part of his concluding recommendation that Michizane withdraw to the mountains and be revered by people of future generations.[89] Michizane ignored this counsel.

In the first month of 901 Tokihira and Michizane were both promoted to the junior second rank, but ten days later, without warning, an imperial edict was issued that banished Michizane to Kyūshū on the grounds that he was ambitious, had attempted to seize undivided power, and intended to disrupt the imperial succession by replacing Daigo on the throne with a younger brother.[90] All the charges were false,[91] but the last accusation was slanderous, originating with Tokihira, who played on the fears of the inexperienced young emperor. Michizane was not given the chance to defend himself. Uda, in monk's attire, went to the palace in the hope of getting the decree rescinded, but guards refused to admit him. Michizane was ordered to leave for exile the same day and placed under heavy guard.

Michizane was sent to the Dazaifu. In the Nara period and earlier this had been a place of importance, the site of the governor generalship of Kyūshū. Ōtomo no Tabito and Yamanoue no Okura had served there as officials and gathered around them a circle of poets. But the place was now deserted, the buildings derelict, and roving gangs of bandits made it dangerous. A poem in two hundred lines by Michizane vividly described the physical hardships of life at the Dazaifu.[92] He also suffered the mental anguish of being separated from his wife and most of his many children; only the two youngest were allowed to accompany him. His poem "To Comfort My Little Son and Daughter," written in 901, described without irony how much worse off some people were than themselves, enumerating the various disasters that had struck others.[93] "Rainy Night," written in the following year, revealed that he suffered from malnutrition:

> . . . When the heart is cold, the rain too is cold;
> nights when you can't sleep are never short.
> The gloss is gone from my skin, my bones dry up;

tears keep coming to sting my eyes;
boils and rash, beriberi in my legs—
shadows of sickness darken my body. . . .[94]

A few months before his death he composed two poems with the title "The Lamp Goes Out." This is the first:

It was not the wind—the oil is gone.
I hate the lamp that will not see me through the night.
How hard—to make ashes of the mind, to still the body!
I rise and move into the moonlight by the cold window.[95]

Questions of sincerity or of received influences dwindle into insignificance in the face of the real grief and hardships that inspired these poems. No court poet, protected by the decorum of his surroundings, could have achieved the intensity of Michizane's last poems. These were not mental exercises, the poet imagining what it must be like to be hungry or an exile, but truth shaped by talent and sensitivity.

Michizane died in exile in the spring of 903. Not long after his death the Great Audience Hall (Shishin-den) of the palace was struck by lightning, and the capital was flooded by rain and shaken by thunderbolts.[96] People wondered if these calamities were not the work of Michizane's wrathful spirit (*onryō*), and when Tokihira died in 909 at the early age of thirty-eight, they were sure of this. In order to pacify Michizane's vengeful spirit, shrines to his memory were erected at various places, notably at Kitano in the capital and at the Dazaifu. He was worshiped at these shrines as a god with the name Tenjin (Heavenly Deity).[97] This tradition continues: students still pray to him and make offerings in the hopes of passing their examinations. The shrines to Tenjin are marked by groves of plum trees because of the association (imported from China) of plum blossoms with scholars. Tokihira, on the other hand, is portrayed in Kabuki plays as a sadistic, lecherous villain without a redeeming feature.

Regardless of the degree of historicity in the legend of Michizane, the importance of his poetry cannot be doubted. Other Japanese before him, notably Kūkai, had demonstrated a mastery of the techniques of Chinese poetry and prose, but Michizane ranks as a major Japanese poet, though his preference for Chinese as a medium of expression had the unforeseeable consequence of estranging him from future generations of readers whose education did not extend to the subtleties of Chinese prosody. There are Japanese touches in Michizane's Chinese, as scholars have pointed out.[98] Such departures from normal Chinese usage were unintentional, but they pointed the way to a freer use of Chinese by later kanshi poets and eventually to a specifically Japanese style of Chinese prose.

Other Writers

Michizane was not the only important writer in Chinese of the early Heian period. Perhaps he has enjoyed a disproportionate prominence because so much of the writing of his contemporaries has been lost. Of the fourteen volumes of the collected poems of Ki no Haseo (845–912) only one survives, though he was much esteemed in his own time.[99] Perhaps the best-known writer of Chinese after Michizane was Miyoshi no Kiyoyuki, who is said to have been of royal Paekche descent.[100] Although Kiyoyuki also wrote kanshi, his forte was prose, an example of which is the letter of advice to Michizane mentioned above. His composition "Iken Hōji Jūnikajō" (Opinions in a Sealed Document in Twelve Articles) has been praised as the finest example of Heian kambun.[101] The Twelve Articles are recommendations to the government concerning prayers to aid agriculture, the dangers of extravagance, the necessity of increasing the food allowance to students at the university, and so on. Not all the articles are important, and the work as a whole lacks literary significance, but the document is admired for its mastery of balanced prose, its clarity of expression, and its objective manner of presenting historical facts.[102] None of Michizane's contemporaries rivaled him as a literary figure, but the level of accomplishment in kanshi and kambun at the court was impressive.

Account of Miracles in Japan

Both Ki no Haseo and Miyoshi no Kiyoyuki wrote stories about ghosts and prodigies. We know the titles of their collections, though the works themselves have been lost.[103] They were not the oldest Japanese examples of miracle stories: one older collection survives, *Nihon Ryōiki* (Account of Miracles in Japan) or, to give the work its full title, *Nihonkoku Gempō Zennaku Ryōiki* (Account of Miracles in Response to Good and Evil Deeds of the Land of Japan). The collection of 116 stories was compiled by the priest Kyōkai (also known as Keikai) of the Yakushi Temple in

Nara, probably soon after 822, the date of the last story in the collection. Unlike the works of poetry and prose in Chinese considered above, *Account of Miracles* was not written at the court for the pleasure of courtiers but by a priest, probably of humble status, for other priests. The stories of the collection, though composed in Chinese, seem to have been intended to serve as the framework for sermons to be delivered in Japanese, with suitable elaborations, by priests to their congregations.[104] *Account of Miracles*, the oldest collection of *setsuwa*,[105] had an undoubtedly didactic purpose: to demonstrate that good or bad deeds performed in this world are appropriately rewarded.

We know almost nothing about Kyōkai except for the fragmentary bits of information he scatters in the prefaces to the three books that make up the work. In addition, in one story (III:38) he relates two dreams and identifies himself as a monk of the Yakushi Temple, but his connection with the temple is unclear.[106] It has been conjectured on the basis of materials in the book that Kyōkai was born between 750 and 770 and died after 822.

Many stories describe miracles performed by Kannon, the bodhisattva of compassion, in response to some act of piety such as copying the Lotus Sutra or daily worship of Kannon. Strong emphasis is given to the fact that these miracles occurred not in distant India or China but in Japan, at clearly identified places, and not in some distant age of miracles but recently, during the reigns of specified emperors or empresses. Unlike the writings in Chinese composed at the court, *Account of Miracles* does not give weight to Chinese precedents for the events related; it was far more important to establish that miracles had actually happened in Japan than to dignify these miracles by alluding to similar Chinese examples. The stories are mainly Buddhist in orientation, though some (including the first, about a man who caught the thunder and kept it under his control) are secular and belong to a folk tradition.

Many stories relate how a man or a woman who has long offered special devotion to Kannon is threatened with death, only to be saved by Kannon's intercession. Here is one such tale:

> Oma Yamatsugi of the upper senior sixth rank was a native of the village of Ogawa in the district of Tama in Musashi Province. His wife belonged to the Shirakabe clan. Yamatsugi became a military official and was despatched to conquer the hairy men in the land of the bandits. While he was traveling in enemy territory, his wife fashioned a wooden statue of Kannon, hoping that it would preserve him from harm at the hands of the bandits. She prayed to it devoutly,

making suitable offerings. When her husband returned safely from the land of the bandits, he joyfully joined his wife in worship, filled with gratitude.

Several years passed. In the twelfth month of the eighth year of Tempyō Hōji [764], during the reign of the Empress Abe [Shōtoku], Yamatsugi took part in the rebellion of the traitorous minister Nakamaro, and was one of thirteen men condemned to death. The other twelve men were beheaded, and Yamatsugi was in a state of panic. At this juncture the wooden statue of Kannon that his wife had carved and worshiped asked Yamatsugi reprovingly, "Oh, what are you doing in such a dirty place?" She raised her foot and stamped into Yamatsugi's body from the neck down, then wrapped his body around her waist. Just as the executioner had stretched out Yamatsugi's neck and was about to behead him, an imperial messenger rode up and asked, "Is Oma Yamatsugi among those here?" "Yes," was the reply, "we are about to cut off his head." The messenger commanded, "Do not kill him. He is to be exiled to Shinano Province."

Yamatsugi was exiled, but after not too long a time he was recalled and given an official position as second-in-command of the district of Tama. The marks of the time when he had been so unfortunate as to have his neck stretched out for the executioner remained on his neck to remind him of the occasion. Yamatsugi escaped death and lived out his full allotment of years because of the intercession of Kannon. Whoever performs such meritorious deeds as making and worshiping an image of Kannon and, awakening to the faith, serves the Buddha with all his heart will enjoy great happiness forthwith and, with the help of the Buddha, escape all harm.[107]

The story is crudely told, and some passages, notably the actions of Kannon in stamping on the man's body and wrapping it around her waist, are mystifying because nothing indicates this was either a dream or a vision. But the story is noteworthy because it is clear that Yamatsugi was punished for taking part in the rebellion of Fujiwara no Nakamaro against the priest Dōkyō in 764, and that he was restored to his rank after Dōkyō's downfall in 770. Mention of the "hairy men" seems to refer to a campaign against the Ainu. The story is given reality by these specific connections with events of history known to all who might hear it. The moral at the end of the tale, that the Buddha rewards those who pray to him, is repeated again and again throughout *Account of Miracles*;

no doubt it was to make this moral lesson more engrossing that the story was set down to help priests making sermons on a time-honored theme.

The ninth century has often been dismissed as a "dark age" of Japanese literature because the memorable works are not in the Japanese language. Only in recent years have the writings in Chinese been accorded a place in the Japanese literary heritage, and the term "dark ages" has come to be used ironically. The real irony, however, is that five years after 900, when Sugawara no Michizane presented to the Emperor Daigo collections of poetry that demonstrated Chinese writing had come of age, the *Kokinshū*, the anthology that defined the nature and scope of classical Japanese poetry and ended the domination of writings in Chinese, was offered to the same emperor.

Notes

1. This is not, however, the opinion of several non-Japanese scholars who have studied the question. Ronald P. Toby in "Why Leave Nara?" called attention to Kammu's descent from Tenji; this might explain his desire to move the capital away from the power base of the Temmu line in Yamato to Yamashiro, near Tenji's old palace site at Ōtsu and close to his tomb in Yamashina. Toby discounted the factor of hoped-for escape from the Buddhist authority in Nara, pointing out the continued importance of the Buddhist clergy in Kyoto.
2. Ueyama Shumpei in his *Kūkai* exhaustively examined all the evidence relating to the date of Kūkai's birth, and decided (p. 61) that 774, rather than 773 (as many people believed), was correct.
3. See Yoshito S. Hakeda, *Kūkai*, p. 14.
4. Shiba Ryōtarō, *Kūkai no Fūkei*, I, pp. 3–6, made this suggestion. He referred to the following passage in the *Nihon Shoki*: " 'The Emishi who were placed beside the sacred mountain have by nature the hearts of beasts. They cannot be allowed to dwell in the inner country.' So he caused them to be stationed without the home provinces, in any places which they pleased. They were the ancestors of the present Saeki Be of the five provinces of Harima, Sanuki, Iyo, Aki, and Awa." (Translation by W. G. Aston, *Nihongi*, I, p. 212.) Shiba also likened (p. 5) the sound of foreigners jabbering (*saeku*) to the name Saeki.
5. See Hakeda, *Kūkai*, pp. 18–19.
6. *Ibid.*, pp. 19, 102.
7. *Ibid*, p. 102.
8. *Ibid.*

9. *Ibid.*
10. The first title of the work was *Rōko Shiiki* (Indications of the Goal for the Deaf and Blind). See Hakeda, *Kūkai*, p. 15.
11. Translation by Hakeda in *Kūkai*, pp. 101–39.
12. Kawaguchi Hisao, *Heian-chō no Kambungaku*, p. 45.
13. Hakeda, *Kūkai*, p. 104.
14. *Ibid.*, p. 109. Hakeda identified all these models of filial piety.
15. Hakeda (*Kūkai*, p. 109) identifies these men. The most interesting is Chu Yun of Han who "while being dragged away by an official to be put to death, broke the railing of the Imperial Palace in his earnest effort to give advice to the Emperor Ch'eng." Remonstrating with one's lord, regardless of whether or not he wanted advice, was a duty incumbent on Confucian advisers. Shih Ching of Wei, the man who broke the window, "tried to hit Marquis Wen with a harp in order to correct the marquis's fault of not listening to another's advice."
16. *Ibid.*, p. 115.
17. *Ibid.*, p. 117.
18. *Ibid.*, p. 118.
19. *Ibid.*, p. 119.
20. *Ibid.*, p. 129.
21. Ryusaku Tsunoda, et al., *Sources of Japanese Tradition*, p. 145.
22. *Ibid.*, p. 146.
23. The full name of this work is *Henjō Hakki Seirei Shū* (there are also alternative pronunciations), but it is usually referred to by the short title, *Seirei Shū*. The compilation was probably made between 827 and 835 by Shinzei (800–860), a disciple of Kūkai.
24. Watanabe Shōkō and Miyasaka Yūshō, *Sangō Shiiki, Seirei Shū*, pp. 462–63. For a translation into modern Japanese of the same poem, see Harada Ken'yū, *Nihon Kanshi Sen*, p. 14.
25. Watanabe and Miyasaka, *Sangō*, pp. 174–75. The translation is part of a work of mixed poetry and prose called "What Pleasure is There in the Mountains?" See Kawaguchi, *Heian-chō no Kambungaku*, p. 18. Kawaguchi, in "Kōbō Daishi no Bungaku ni tsuite," pp. 249–55, makes comparison between this work by Kūkai and a ninth-century Chinese poem found at Tun Huang.
26. According to one Chinese tradition about the origin of writing, in ancient times a dragon emerged from the Yellow River with patterns on its back that inspired the Chinese characters. Another tradition has it that a tortoise emerged from the Lo River with similar patterns on its carapace. (See Richard Wainwright Bodman, *Poetics and Prosody in Early Medieval China*, p. 164.) References are being made to *I-ching* (The Book of Changes), *Wen Hsüan*, the *Analects*, and various Buddhist texts. Almost every word is an allusion to one of these books, and the writing is extremely dense.

The allusions are patiently explained by Fukunaga Mitsuji in *Saichō, Kūkai*, pp. 480ff.

27. Text (original Chinese and Japanese translations) given in Fukunaga, *Saichō, Kūkai*, pp. 303–5. For a more literal translation, see Bodman, *Poetics*, p. 162.
28. He was speaking specifically about *Shih Ching*. The passage occurs in *Analects* XVIII:9, the *Yang Ho* chapter. See Arthur Waley, *The Analects of Confucius*, p. 212.
29. Quoted in Kojima Noriyuki, *Kokufū Ankoku Jidai no Bungaku*, II. pp. 1326–27.
30. Ichiko Teiji (ed.), *Nihon Bungaku Zenshi*, II, pp. 30–31.
31. For a series of articles for and against the attribution to Kūkai, see Hisaki Yukio and Oyamada Kazuo, *Kūkai to Iroha Uta*.
32. See also p. 221.
33. The third of the anthologies was in fact completed during the reign of Saga's successor, but included many poems from Saga's reign.
34. For an explanation of the title, see Kojima, *Kokufū*, II, pp. 1248–52.
35. The same arrangement was found in *Kaifūsō*, the first collection of kanshi.
36. For a list of poets, number of poems, and number of poems by the same men in the next imperially sponsored collection, *Bunka Shūrei Shū*, see Kojima, *Kokufū*, II, pp. 1240–41.
37. *Ibid.*, p. 1283.
38. See *ibid.*, pp. 1849–50, for a biographical notice of the man, derived from official sources.
39. *Ryōunshū* 9. See Kojima, *Kokufū*, II, pp. 1413–18.
40. Chinese "regulated verse" (*lü-shih*) required tonal parallelism (see Burton Watson, *Chinese Lyricism*, pp. 111–12.) However, Japanese is not a tonal language, and Japanese poets writing in Chinese were apt to make mistakes on the tones.
41. For *Chiu pien* or "Nine Arguments," see Burton Watson, *Early Chinese Literature*, pp. 251–52.
42. *Ryōunshū* 24. See Kojima, *Kokufū*, II, pp. 1487–92.
43. See also the poem written by Saga lamenting the death of the priest Gempin in Burton Watson, *Japanese Literature in Chinese*, I, p. 45.
44. *Ryōunshū* 31. See Kojima, *Kokufū*, II, pp. 1520–24. Translation by Watson in *Japanese*, I, p. 47. Watson said of Sugawara no Kiyotata (770–842), the grandfather of Sugawara no Michizane, that his personal name may also be read Kiyotomo (the reading given in *Nihon Koten Bungaku Daijiten*, V, p. 364.) The name is even more frequently pronounced Kiyokimi, and that is how I shall call him except when directly quoting Watson. (For an account of Kiyokimi's life, see Robert Borgen, *Sugawara Michizane and the Early Heian Court*, pp. 30–50.) The *luan* bird mentioned in the poem, like the phoenix, was one of the auspicious birds and beasts that gathered

in the capital of the ancient Chinese ruler Shun to acclaim his enlightened reign; by extension, Saga's reign is also being praised.

45. *Ryōunshū* 17. Kojima, *Kokufū*, II, pp. 1458–62.
46. This is an allusion to the preface to the *Wen Hsüan*. *Bunka Shūrei Shū* contains 143 poems by twenty-eight poets, mainly works composed during the four years since the compilation of the *Ryōunshū*. The chief compiler, Fujiwara no Fuyutsugu, was assisted by Sugawara no Kiyokimi and others.
47. The one category not adopted was Buddhist poems. See Kojima Noriyuki, *Kaifūsō, Bunka Shūrei Shū, Honchō Monzui*, p. 22, for a comparison of the Chinese and Japanese names for the different categories.
48. *Ibid.*, pp. 196–97.
49. Translation by Burton Watson in Donald Keene, *Anthology of Japanese Literature*, pp. 163–64. For the original, see Kojima, *Kaifūsō*, pp. 220–22.
50. The editors included Shigeno no Sadanushi, Yoshimine no Yasuyo, and Sugawara no Kiyokimi.
51. Japanese translation by Kawaguchi in *Heian-chō no Kambungaku*, p. 41.
52. See the translation by Watson in Keene, *Anthology*, p. 164.
53. Kojima, *Kaifūsō*, p. 237. Nothing is known about Lady Ōtomo except her poem and the response by Kose no Shikihito, an early ninth-century poet. See Kojima, *Kaifūsō*, p. 512.
54. *Ibid.*, pp. 241, 243.
55. See Kawaguchi Hisao, *Hana no Utage*, pp. 183–84.
56. Watson, *Japanese*, pp. 79–80. The tradition of writing poetry in Japanese about social conditions began and ended with Yamanoe no Okura, as we have seen, but poems of social content continued to be composed in Chinese, in large part because of the associations with Confucianism.
57. Poems by Kiyokimi are given by Borgen in *Sugawara*, pp. 44, 47.
58. An excellent account of his life (including translations of some of his poems) is given in Borgen, *Sugawara*, pp. 50–67.
59. Kawaguchi Hisao, *Kanke Bunsō, Kanke Kōshū*, pp. 175–76. The original title is "Hakase Nan." See above, p. 199, for further reference to this poem.
60. Kiyokimi tutored Montoku (reigned 850–858) while he was the crown prince, and after Montoku ascended the throne served him in various important positions. See Kawaguchi Hisao, *Heian-chō Nihon Kambungaku-shi no Kenkyū*, pp. 111–22.
61. See Borgen, *Sugawara*, p. 222–23, for the circumstances of compilation.
62. Translations are given by Watson in *Japanese*, I, pp. 125–30.
63. In giving Michizane's age at various times in his life I have followed the Western rather than the traditional Japanese count.
64. Kawaguchi, *Kanke*, p. 27.
65. It is given in translation by Borgen in *Sugawara*, p. 89. The title is "Viewing the Plum Blossoms on a Moonlit Night." The text is given in Kawaguchi,

Kanke, p. 105, with Michizane's note that this was his first poem, composed at the age of eleven (Japanese count).

66. Kawaguchi, *Kanke*, p. 28. See also Borgen, *Sugawara*, pp. 97–98, for mention of Michizane's study with Wang Tu. Michizane wrote an affectionately satirical poem about Wang Tu's manner of playing go, translated by Borgen on p. 98; original text in Kawaguchi, *Kanke*, p. 129. Almost nothing is known about Wang Tu apart from his having taught the *Analects* to Michizane's father before he became Michizane's tutor.
67. The university and the examination system, taken over from China by the Japanese, is illuminatingly discussed by Borgen in *Sugawara*, pp. 71–80. Only sons of the aristocracy were eligible for admission to the university, and the purpose of study at the university was to prepare candidates to take the civil service examinations. While at the university students studied specific Confucian texts and their commentaries. At the end of a year there were final examinations, and those who passed were eligible to take the civil service examinations. In later times these examinations largely lost their meaning as offices tended to become hereditary, but at this time they seem to have been carefully and fairly conducted.
68. Borgen discusses Michizane's responses to the two questions in *Sugawara*, pp. 107–11.
69. Translated by Watson in *Japanese*, I, p. 88.
70. *Ibid.*, I, pp. 90–91. (The poem is about three times as long as I have quoted.) For the original, see Kawaguchi, *Kanke*, pp. 200–201. For another poem describing a dream of Amaro, see Watson, *Japanese*, I, p. 92, and Kawaguchi, *Kanke*, p. 207.
71. An example of a poem by Michizane directly modeled on one by Po Chü-i is "On the Road I Met a White-haired Old Man," written in 887 in Sanuki, when Michizane was the governor there. It is based on Po Chü-i's "New *Yüeh-fu*" ballads. However, the poem deals entirely with events in Sanuki. See Watson, *Japanese*, I, pp. 96–98. Text in Kawaguchi, *Kanke*, pp. 274–77.
72. For a translation of the poem, see Borgen, *Sugawara*, p. 133. Text in Kawaguchi, *Kanke*, pp. 175–77.
73. See Imai Gen'e and Gotō Akio, "Tōfū Oka," in Ichiko, *Nihon Bungaku Zenshi*, II, p. 45. But see also Borgen, *Sugawara*, p. 134, for an explanation of why Michizane might not have got along with his students.
74. See, for example, the preface to some poems composed in 883 during the visit of the Po-hai ambassadors. After describing the lively exchanges of poetry and the relaxed atmosphere that prevailed, Michizane expressed fear that if other men of letters found out about the poems they would deride them, in the manner typical of scholars making light of rivals. Text in Kawaguchi, *Kanke*, p. 543.
75. The poem is translated by Borgen in *Sugawara*, pp. 137–38. The original text is in Kawaguchi, *Kanke*, pp. 184–87.

76. Text in Kawaguchi, *Kanke*, pp. 202–3. Borgen gives a complete translation in *Sugawara*, p. 139.
77. Text in Kawaguchi, *Kanke*, pp. 259–64. See Watson, *Japanese*, I, pp. 93–94, for translation of four of these poems under the title of "Who Does the Cold Come Early To?" Six of the poems are translated by Borgen in *Sugawara*, pp. 187–88.
78. Translation in Watson, *Japanese*, I, p. 96. The Jōgan era (859–876) was followed by the Gangyō era (877–84).
79. Kawaguchi, *Kanke*, pp. 301–2.
80. The *akō* incident is discussed at much greater length by Borgen in *Sugawara*, pp. 173–81.
81. Text in Kawaguchi, *Kanke*, p. 313. A complete translation in Borgen, *Sugawara*, pp. 178–79. Tadaomi was completing a term of service as governor of Mino; perhaps Michizane is referring to Tadaomi's former subjects as "eastern barbarians," though what he really means is the ferocity not of eastern barbarians but of nobles in the capital.
82. A translation of "A Request That the Members of the Council of State Determine Whether or Not to Send a Mission to the T'ang" is translated by Borgen in *Sugawara*, pp. 242–43. The text is given by Kawaguchi in *Kanke*, p. 568.
83. Imai and Gotō, "Tōfū Oka," pp. 46–47.
84. Translated by Watson in *Japanese*, I, pp. 108–10.
85. According to traditional Chinese (and Japanese) beliefs, left ranked higher than right; minister of the Left (*sadaijin*) therefore was superior to minister of the Right (*udaijin*). Minister of the Left ranked second only to the prime minister (*dajōdaijin*) in the bureaucracy.
86. Text in Kawaguchi, *Kanke*, p. 572.
87. *Ibid.*, p. 34.
88. The poem (together with Michizane's modest reply) is translated by Borgen in *Sugawara*, p. 223. See also Kawaguchi, *Kanke*, pp. 34–35.
89. The text of Kiyoyuki's letter is included in *Honchō Monzui*. See Kojima, *Kaifūsō*, pp. 382–83. The letter is translated by Borgen in *Sugawara*, pp. 275–76.
90. The edict is translated by Borgen in *Sugawara*, p. 278.
91. Michizane was indeed ambitious, but in the manner that men of great talent are apt to be ambitious, and not in the sense of the two other charges.
92. Text in Kawaguchi, *Kanke*, pp. 486–99. "Recording My Feelings: A Hundred Couplets" is translated by Borgen in *Sugawara*, pp. 296–300.
93. Translated by Watson in *Japanese*, I, p. 113.
94. *Ibid.*, p. 118. Text in Kawaguchi, *Kanke*, pp. 514–15.
95. Kawaguchi, *Kanke*, p. 521. Translation by Watson in *Japanese*, I, p. 122.
96. George Sansom, *A History of Japan*, I, p. 215.

97. For a study of the process of deification, see Borgen, *Sugawara*, pp. 308–36.
98. These departures from standard Chinese are indicated in great detail by Kawaguchi in *Heian-chō no Kambungaku*, pp. 76–96. Most of these are difficult to communicate in English translation. For example, a line of poetry that according to orthodox Chinese interpretation should mean "Why should anyone grieve over it?" was used by Michizane to mean quite the opposite—"What a grievous thing it is!" (Kawaguchi, p. 80.) Michizane's mistake was in the use of a Chinese word used properly only when asking a rhetorical question. At other times, Chinese auxiliary particles that were quite clearly distinguished by the Chinese were used by Michizane (and other Japanese) as if they were interchangeable, probably because such distinctions did not exist in the Japanese language. (Kawaguchi, p. 91.)
99. See Kawaguchi, *Heian-chō Nihon*, I, p. 263.
100. *Ibid.*, pp. 245–70.
101. Kawaguchi, *Heian-chō no Kambungaku*, pp. 66, 99.
102. Kawaguchi, *Heian-chō Nihon*, I, p. 263.
103. Kawaguchi, *Heian-chō no Kambungaku*, p. 67. Kiyoyuki's devotion to "occult science" was otherwise manifested in the letter he wrote Michizane in 900, warning him of danger ahead. See the translation by Borgen in *Sugawara*, pp. 275–76.
104. See Nakada Norio, *Nihon Ryōiki*, III, p. 102.
105. Moral tales; for a fuller treatment, see below, chapter 15.
106. Nakada, in *Nihon Ryōiki*, p. 307, suggests various possibilities: he was a monk at the Yakushi Temple; he received ordination there; or he received the title of *dentō jūi* from the temple in return for a donation. Kyoko Motomochi Nakamura, in *Miraculous Stories from the Japanese Buddhist Tradition*, p. 3, explains the title *dentō jūi*, which she translates as "Junior Rank of Transmission of Light."
107. This is story 7 in Book III. I have followed the text given by Nakada in *Nihon Ryōiki*, III, pp. 71–75. See also Endō Yoshimoto and Kasuga Kenzō, *Nihon Ryōiki*, pp. 334–37. For another translation see Nakamura, *Miraculous*, pp. 231–32. Other stories from *Nihon Ryōiki* are translated by Watson in *Japanese*, I, pp. 27–39.

Bibliography

Note: All Japanese books, except as otherwise noted, were published in Tokyo.

Bodman, Richard Wainwright. *Poetics and Prosody in Early Medieval China: A Study and Translation of Kūkai's Bunkyō Hifuron*. Ann Arbor, Mich.: University Microfilms, 1978.

Borgen, Robert. *Sugawara no Michizane and the Early Heian Court*. Cambridge, Mass.: Harvard University Press, 1986.

Endō Yoshimoto and Kasuga Kazuo. *Nihon Ryōiki*, in Nihon Koten Bungaku Taikei series. Iwanami Shoten, 1967.

Fukunaga Mitsuji. *Saichō, Kūkai*, in Nihon no Meicho series. Chūō Kōron Sha, 1977.

Hakeda, Yoshito S. *Kūkai*. New York: Columbia University Press, 1972.

Harada Ken'yū. *Nihon Kanshi Sen*. Kyōto: Jimbun Shoin, 1974.

Hisaki Yukio and Oyamada Kazuo. *Kūkai to Iroha Uta*. Kyōto: Shibunkaku, 1984.

Ichiko Teiji (ed.). *Nihon Bungaku Zenshi*, II. Gakutōsha, 1978.

Inoguchi Atsushi. *Nihon Kambungaku Shi*. Kadokawa Shoten, 1984.

Katō Junryū. *Kōgoyaku Sangō Shiiki*. Sekai Seiten Kankō Kyōkai, 1977.

Kawaguchi Hisao. *Hana no Utage*. Yoshikawa Kōbunkan, 1980.

———. *Heian-chō Nihon Kambungaku-shi no Kenkyū*, third ed., 3 vols. Meiji Shoin, 1975–88.

———. *Heian-chō no Kambungaku*. Yoshikawa Kōbunkan, 1981.

———. *Kanke Bunsō, Kanke Kōshū*, in Nihon Koten Bungaku Taikei series. Iwanami Shoten, 1966.

———. "Kōbō Daishi no Bungaku ni tsuite," in Nakano Gishō (ed.), *Kōbō Daishi Kenkyū*. Yoshikawa Kōbunkan, 1978.

Keene, Donald. *Anthology of Japanese Literature*. New York: Grove Press, 1955.

Kojima Noriyuki. *Kaifūsō, Bunka Shūrei Shū, Honchō Monzui*, in Nihon Koten Bungaku Taikei series. Iwanami Shoten, 1964.

———. *Kokufū Ankoku Jidai no Bungaku*, II. Hanawa Shobō, 1979.

Konishi Jin'ichi. *Bunkyō Hifuron Kō*, 3 vols. Kyōto: Ōyashima Shuppan, 1948–52.

McCullough, Helen Craig. *Brocade by Night*. Stanford, Calif.: Stanford University Press, 1985.

Nakada Norio. *Nihon Ryōiki*, 3 vols., in Kōdansha Gakujutsu Bunko series. Kōdansha, 1978–80.

Nakamura, Kyoko Motomochi. *Miraculous Stories from the Japanese Buddhist Tradition*. Cambridge, Mass.: Harvard University Press, 1973.

Sansom, George. *A History of Japan*, 3 vols. Stanford, Calif.: Stanford University Press, 1958–63.

Shiba Ryōtarō. *Kūkai no Fūkei*, 2 vols. Chūō Kōron Sha, 1975.

Toby, Ronald P. "Why Leave Nara?" *Monumenta Nipponica* 40:3, Autumn 1985.

Tsunoda, Ryusaku, Wm. Theodore de Bary, and Donald Keene. *Sources of Japanese Tradition*. New York: Columbia University Press, 1958.

Ueyama Shumpei. *Kūkai*. Asahi Shimbun Sha, 1981.

Waley, Arthur. *The Analects of Confucius*. London: George Allen & Unwin, 1938.

Watanabe Shōkō and Miyasaka Yūshō. *Sangō Shiiki, Seirei Shū*, in Nihon Koten Bungaku Taikei series. Iwanami Shoten, 1965.

Watson, Burton. *Chinese Lyricism*. New York: Columbia University Press, 1971.

———. *Early Chinese Literature*. New York: Columbia University Press, 1962.

———. *Japanese Literature in Chinese*, I. New York: Columbia University Press, 1975.

5. THE TRANSITION FROM THE *MAN'YŌSHŪ* TO THE *KOKINSHŪ*

The Invention of the Kana

The literature in Japanese of the Heian period could not have existed without the two kana syllabaries, the script that took the place of the cumbersome *Man'yōgana*. Although Kūkai was traditionally given credit for having invented the kana, the process of replacing Chinese characters with symbols that represented the sounds of the Japanese language took at least a century, and many people were surely involved.

The first step toward the creation of the kana was the transcription of Japanese poems in the *Kojiki*, where Chinese characters were used as phonograms to indicate the sound of each Japanese syllable.[1] However, as the preface to the *Kojiki* mentioned, it was tedious spelling out with characters, syllable by syllable, a long Japanese name. A line of Japanese poetry in five syllables, such as *o-shi-na-be-te*, might have a meaning that could be expressed with a single Chinese character, and the line obviously had far less content than a line of Chinese poetry written with five characters, each of which contributed meaning to the poem. Chinese characters, moreover, often consist of many strokes, and it was wasted labor to write such characters when a simple mark or two would suffice to indicate the pronunciation of a syllable.

Even in China abbreviations derived from the cursive forms of the characters were commonly used by this time, and though they were still far more complicated than the kana would be, they may have suggested to the Japanese the possibility of using simplified forms of the characters to represent Japanese sounds. It might have been preferable to jettison the characters altogether, but the prestige of Chinese writing was so great that, even if the Japanese had learned of the existence of alphabets elsewhere, they would have been reluctant to sever their contacts with the mainstream of East Asian traditions.[2]

Abbreviated forms of the phonograms used to represent Japanese sounds are found as early as a letter written in Japanese toward the end of the eighth century.[3] These abbreviations suggest the beginnings of both *hiragana* and *katakana*, the two forms in use today. At first, there was no consistency as to which Chinese characters would be abbreviated and used for their sounds, and uniformity would not be achieved until 1900 when the 973 different kana symbols that had been used over the centuries (though not all at the same time) were reduced and standardized into two sets of forty-eight symbols each.[4]

The hiragana originated in the cursive forms of the characters. This script, swift-moving and graceful in its shapes, would be well suited to the poetry and prose written by the Heian court ladies, who attached as much importance to the appearance of a composition as to its content. The katakana consisted of elements of formally written characters, in some cases the same ones that were also used as the basis of the hiragana. Katakana did not lend itself to elegant calligraphy, but its easy legibility made it appropriate for official or religious documents. The many variant forms for each hiragana symbol were occasioned chiefly by calligraphic considerations: each symbol had to fit smoothly into the flowing contours of a line and, depending on the shape of the previous symbol, the writer would choose one rather than another kana to represent *ka* or *su* or whatever the syllable might be.

During the Nara period men and women alike had used Man'yōgana, a mixture of Chinese characters used both as phonograms and ideograms, but the Man'yōgana gave way during the Heian period either to writings by men (and a few ladies of the court) in Chinese, or else to compositions in Japanese that were mainly in kana.[5]

The kana (originally *kari-na*, or "temporary names," as opposed to the *mana* or "true names," meaning Chinese characters used as ideograms)[6] had at first served as a mere convenience, a quick way to write the characters used as phonograms. Women may have been earlier than men to use the kana for literary purposes; but by the end of the ninth century the hiragana, the script associated with writing by women (it was long known as *onnade*, or "woman's hand") was also being used by men. In 1984 a tracing from the original manuscript of *The Tosa Diary* was discovered, affording proof that by 935, when Ki no Tsurayuki wrote the manuscript, hiragana had already attained a superb artistic level. Presumably the *Kokinshū*, compiled in 905, was written in a similar script.

The special place that calligraphy enjoyed among the arts of China accounted for the importance attached to this art by Japanese of the

Heian period and later. Persons of taste were expected to be proficient in at least one of the scripts in use at the time, and writing practice was a part of daily life at the palace. At first, the texts most often copied by court ladies were old poems, especially the two mentioned in the preface to the *Kokinshū* as being of special antiquity, the "parents of the *uta*."[7] Later, special exercises in penmanship were invented in the form of waka in which each of the forty-seven syllables of the language appeared once, apparently on the analogy of the Chinese *Thousand Character Classic*. The best-known of such poems (not composed, however, until late in the tenth century) was the *iroha*, so named from the first three syllables:[8]

iro ha nihoedo	Though the color is bright,
chirinuru wo	The blossoms scatter;
wa ga yo tare zo	Who in this world of ours
tsune naramu	Will last forever?
ui no okuyama	As today I cross the deep
kefu koete	Mountains of *ui*,[9]
asaki yume miji	I shall have no shallow dreams,
wehi mo sezu	Nor shall I be drunk.

The scholar of the Japanese language Ōno Susumu associated the creation of the kana with similar occurrences elsewhere in the orbit of Chinese culture. At the end of the tenth century the Khitan, a people of Inner Asia, devised a script that resembled the Chinese characters but represented their own language.[10] In the twelfth century the Tangut, a Tibetan people, invented an extremely complicated script that was also based on the Chinese characters. A similar development occurred in Vietnam during the thirteenth century.[11] These events seem to represent a gradual shift on the part of the peoples of East Asia from unconditional emulation of China to an assertion of the importance of their own languages and cultures. Perhaps the creation of the kana should be viewed against the background of this general tendency; but it was also true that the rise of Fujiwara hegemony during the early Heian period led to an emphasis being given to the preservation of Japanese traditions and to the Japanese language as a medium of court poetry.

Shinsen Man'yōshū

The ninth century has often been described as a "dark age" of poetry in Japanese. The central importance of literary Chinese, reflected in the sponsorship by the court of three anthologies of kanshi, has given rise to the impression that the waka survived only vestigially during the period, but this was clearly not true. Two celebrated waka poets, Ariwara no Narihira and Ono no Komachi, wrote all of their poetry in the middle of the ninth century, and the poems of many others active about the same time, both known and anonymous, are represented in the *Kokinshū*. The darkness of the "dark age" is attributable more to the decline of interest at the court in poetry in Japanese rather than to any real dearth of waka.

A few examples of court sponsorship of waka composition date from the end of the "dark age" that preceded the compilation of the *Kokinshū* in 905. The title of the first anthology of waka compiled during the Heian period, *Shinsen Man'yōshū* (Newly Compiled *Man'yōshū*), reveals a knowledge of the existence of the original *Man'yōshū*, though there are not many obvious influences.[12]

The standard text (*rufubon*) of the anthology consists of two books (*kan*) of waka with a kanshi on a related theme given after each waka.[13] The waka in the *Shinsen Man'yōshū* were transcribed in the archaic Man'yōgana, though this was done barely a dozen years before the compilation of the *Kokinshū*, in which the poems were all given in hiragana. Perhaps (considering the name of the collection) it was thought appropriate to continue the tradition of transcribing the texts in the manner of the *Man'yōshū*, though surely by this time the use of hiragana was known.

The orthography represented a backward look to the past, but the organization of the *Shinsen Man'yōshū* looked to the future: the poems were arranged by the four seasons, followed by a section of love poetry. There had been no consistent organization of the poems in the *Man'yōshū*, but from this time on all court-sponsored anthologies would be arranged into books of spring poetry, followed by books of summer poetry and so on. There was no precedent either in Japan or China for this arrangement, but it was perfectly suited to the subjects about which Japanese poets usually composed waka.

The circumstances of the compilation of the *Shinsen Man'yōshū* have long puzzled scholars. There are two prefaces; the one for the first book is dated 893, and the one for the second book, 913. Neither preface gives specific details on the compilation, the identity of the compilers, the purpose of the collection, or the source of the poems; in fact, the prefaces say almost nothing of interest.[14]

The attribution of the compilation of the *Shinsen Man'yōshū* to Sugawara no Michizane, first made in the eleventh century, is accepted by most but not all scholars.[15] However, even if Michizane edited both volumes and wrote all the kanshi (as was traditionally believed), he could not have written the preface to the second book, dated ten years after his death.

Many of the waka included in the *Shinsen Man'yōshū* had originally been composed for poetry competitions (*uta-awase*), especially one known by the rather overpowering title of *Kampyō no ontoki Kisai no Miya Uta-awase* (Poem Competition at the Empress's Palace During the Kampyō Era).[16] This competition, staged in 893 under the auspices of the Empress Dowager Hanshi, was the source of 140 of the 228 waka in the shorter verson of the text.[17] At this time, poem competitions were chiefly social events, and the poetry composed tended to be less important than the presentations, but ninety-two poems in the *Kokinshū* are identified as having been composed at competitions.

The prevailing manner of both Japanese and Chinese poems in the *Shinsen Man'yōshū* is courtly. The poets attempted to create graceful and elegant compositions that would be appropriate to the occasion of a poetry competition held in the palace. A typical pair of waka and kanshi is the second in the collection. The waka was by the priest Sosei (fl. 859–897), a major *Kokinshū* poet and the son of the Archbishop Henjō (816–890), an important waka poet of the ninth century:

chiru to mite	If only I had
arubeki mono wo	Merely watched as they fell—
ume no hana	The plum blossoms—
utate nioi no	But, alas, their fragrance
sode ni tomareru[18]	Lingers still on my sleeve.

The anonymous kanshi follows:

Whatever the spring breeze touches gives delight.
In the upper garden, plum blossoms open and fall.
A lady secretly reaches to pick a spray for her hairpin.
The lingering fragrance scenting her sleeves cannot be brushed away.

Although the kanshi was based on the waka and was intentionally imitative, the two poems display some of the differences separating

Japanese and Chinese poetry. Sosei's poem does not mention the central action, the breaking of the branch of flowering plum by the poet, the reason why his (or her) sleeve is scented. This reliance on suggestion is typical of the waka, but even the reader who can take this unspoken action in his stride may be surprised that the waka says precisely the contrary of what one would expect. A poet was normally happy to have his sleeve scented by plum blossoms, if only because the scent was believed to bring back memories of people of long ago; but this particular poet regrets that his sleeve is scented because it will recall his sadness that the blossoms have fallen. The kanshi is much fuller in expression; the whole of the waka usually did not convey even as much as two lines of a Chinese poem. It is also more romantic, introducing the lady's embarrassment that the scent of plum blossoms, clinging to her sleeve, will reveal that she has secretly broken off a spray.

Neither poem is distinguished (though Sosei's would be included in the *Kokinshū*), but the tone was exactly right for the occasion. Matching Japanese and Chinese poems, like matching shells, pictures, or perfumes, was an elegant pastime, but it seldom resulted in the creation of poetry of importance. Indeed, the kanshi in the *Shinsen Man'yōshū* are of such poor quality as to suggest to some scholars that they were not by the great Michizane but by some much later poet who wrote at a time when the art of composing kanshi had seriously deteriorated.[19] Among the waka, those in Book I were judged superior to those in Book II by the compilers of the *Kokinshū*, who borrowed many more poems from the former for their collection.[20]

Kudai Waka

In 894, a year after the compilation of Book I of the *Shinsen Man'yōshū*, the Emperor Uda commanded the poet Ōe no Chisato[21] to compile a collection of his waka, a clear sign that after the long "dark age" the waka was coming into its own again. Chisato thought of himself mainly as a kanshi poet, but this mark of recognition from the emperor no doubt pleased him. He compiled a collection of 110 of his waka, on the seasons and on such topics as "Wind and Moon," and presented them together with individual poems by Po Chü-i that had inspired them. He gave the collection the name *Kudai Waka* (Waka on Themes of Lines), referring to the practice of taking one line from a Chinese poem and recasting it in the form of a waka. This was the first collection of poems to be avowedly inspired in this way, though Japanese poets had long since borrowed themes and images from the Chinese poetry known to them.

The poets of the *Kaifūsō* had borrowed especially from the *Wen Hsüan*, the sixth-century collection of poetry compiled at the court of the Emperor Wu of the short-lived Liang dynasty. This collection, known in Japan as *Monzen*, influenced not only kanshi but waka poets. The influence cannot be said to have been wholly fortunate: the *Wen Hsüan* contains highly finished, elegant poems, but is known more for its artifice than for its poetic truth, and artifice would be the bane of the poetry of the *Kokinshū* especially. The many poems professing uncertainty as to whether the poet sees snow or plum blossoms, clouds or mountains covered with cherry blossoms, and so on clearly are indebted to the *Wen Hsüan*.[22] The ideal of courtliness observed by poets who wrote in this style meant that nothing indecorous could be allowed to mar the expression. Helen Craig McCullough wrote after presenting some examples of *Wen Hsüan* poetry, "There are no paeans of joy, explosions of indignation, despairing cries, or satirical thrusts"[23] in these compositions. This would be true not only of waka written specifically in the tradition of the *Wen Hsüan* but of much Japanese poetry of the next millennium; overt expression of the emotions was usually shunned.

Ōe no Chisato's borrowings from Po Chü-i, a poet of an entirely different stamp from the *Wen Hsüan* poets, did not result in paeans of joy or explosions of indignation either. He chose only the elements that could be assimilated into the court waka. His versions of lines from Po Chü-i were no more than moderately successful, but they showed the way to more effective borrowing which would enrich the content and expression of the waka throughout the Heian period and long after.[24]

The Six Immortals of Poetry

More important examples of ninth-century waka are found among the surviving poems of the *rokkasen*, the Six Immortals of Poetry. The distinction that these six poets shared was that they were all mentioned by Ki no Tsurayuki in his preface to the *Kokinshū* as important poets of an earlier day. Two, Ariwara no Narihira (825–880) and the Archbishop Henjō, were men of high birth (Narihira was a grandson of the Emperor Heizei) and served at the court, but are known mainly as poets. Ono no Komachi is even better known today, mainly because of the legends that grew up around her. The other three "immortals," Fun'ya no Yasuhide, the priest Kisen, and Ōtomo no Kuronushi, were minor poets who are remembered mainly because Tsurayuki mentioned them.

Narihira and Komachi are celebrated not only as poets but as archetypes of the beautiful man and woman of the Heian court, and they figure frequently in this capacity in literary works of later times, notably the Nō plays.[25] Thirty waka by Narihira were included in the *Kokinshū*. Many other poems in later court anthologies were attributed to him mainly because they appeared in *Ise Monogatari* (Tales of Ise), a collection of stories focused on waka by an unnamed courtier who is assumed to be Narihira.[26] Not all of these poems (some of them composed after Narihira's death) could have been written by him, but even on the basis of the limited number of poems in the *Kokinshū* it is possible to form a distinct impression of his characteristic manner. The preface by Tsurayuki to the *Kokinshū* said of Narihira that his poems contained "too much feeling and insufficient words. They are like faded flowers whose color has been lost but which retain a lingering fragrance." This unsympathetic appraisal may reflect a change in the poetic preferences of the generation after Narihira; the poetry of the period of the compilation of the *Kokinshū* was nothing if not accomplished in language, though it sometimes lacked emotional content. Tsurayuki's comments nevertheless suggest the prevailingly melancholy tone of Narihira's poetry.

A third of the poems by Narihira included in the *Kokinshū* describe his various loves. Even in his own day he was known as a great lover, and after he died the national history *Sandai Jitsuroku* (True Records of Three Reigns, 901) said of him, "Narihira was elegant and of handsome appearance, but he was unrestrained in his self-indulgence."[27] This reputation grew, largely as the result of the popularity of *Tales of Ise*. The following poem is typical of Narihira's style:

aki no no ni	My sleeves are wetter
sasa wakeshi asa no	On a night spent without meeting
sode yori mo	Than when one morning
awade koshi yo zo	I made my way through fields of
hichi masarikeru[28]	Autumnal growths of bamboo.

The second line might have been faulted by Tsurayuki for its extra syllable, and he might also have objected to the ambiguity caused by insufficiently precise language. The renowned scholar of Japanese literature Keichū (1640–1701) wrote of this waka, "Dew is not mentioned in the first three lines, but they nonetheless refer to dew; tears are not mentioned in the last two lines, but tears are present all the same."[29] The association between the dew brushed off onto the poet's sleeves by the bamboo grass of an early morning and the tears that he shed into his sleeves over his failure to meet his beloved is fairly obvious, and later poets would regularly use dew as a metaphor for tears, but there is ambiguity in the poem: does mention of his making his way through bamboo grass one morning refer to a morning after a night spent with his beloved, and if so, are his sleeves wet not only with dew but with tears of parting?[30] Each syllable in a waka was carefully considered by old-fashioned scholars for clues as to what the poet was trying to imply in the few words allowed by the form.

The *Kokinshū* is probably the least ambiguous of the anthologies of court poetry,[31] but Narihira's waka pose special problems. Perhaps that is why the compilers of the *Kokinshū* provided relatively long prefaces to his poems, the only poet represented in the collection who received such attention. His best-known waka is particularly perplexing:

tsuki ya aranu	Is that not the moon?
haru ya mukashi no	And is the spring not the spring
haru naranu	Of a year ago?
wa ga mi hitotsu	This body of mine alone
moto no mi ni shite[32]	Remains as it was before.

Two quite incompatible interpretations of this poem were proposed by eminent scholars. Motoori Norinaga interpreted the particle *ya* in the first and second lines as indications of rhetorical questions, yielding the meaning, "Of course, the moon and the spring are the same as last year's." This interpretation, however, gives rise to a logical contradiction: if the moon and the spring are the same as before, why does the poet claim that he alone remains the same? Motoori explained this by adding an "implied" conclusion: though I am exactly the same as I was before, everything somehow seems different.[33] Kagawa Kageki, interpreting *ya* as an exclamatory particle rather than the sign of a rhetorical question, took the poem to mean: "That is not the moon! The spring is not the spring of long ago! I alone am exactly the same as before."[34] A more recent authority, Kyūsojin Hitaku, offered this explanation for the final two lines: "I alone am the same, but the woman I love is not."[35] Finally, Ozawa Masao believed that the poet was asking questions of the moon and the spring: "Moon, are you not the same moon as last year? Spring, are you not the spring of last year? I who ask these questions am definitely the same person as before, and yet. . . ."[36]

The ambiguity of this poem, probably a fault in the eyes of Ki no Tsurayuki and the other compilers of the *Kokinshū*, contributed to the high reputation it has enjoyed in later times; its obscurity, which affords the reader's imagination free play, has been more highly valued than the clarity of other poems. But, of course, the popularity of this poem is not ascribable simply to its vagueness; as often in the poetry of the *Kokinshū*, the rhythm and the atmosphere evoked by the words are as important as the meaning.[37]

Apart from their stylistic difficulties, the waka of Narihira are marked by distinctive poetic devices. He frequently resorted to inversion in the logical order of the thought, as in the following waka which is headed in the *Kokinshū* by an introduction:

> In the days when Narihira attended Prince Koretaka, the prince became a monk and went to live at Ono. Narihira set out to call on him there in the first month. Since Ono was at the foot of Mount Hiei, the snow was very deep, but he managed to struggle on to the hermitage, where he found the prince looking bored and forlorn. After returning to the capital, he sent the prince this poem:
>
> *wasurete wa* If perchance I forget
> *yume ka to zo omou* I wonder, "Was it a dream?"
> *omoiki ya* Could I have supposed
> *yuki fumiwakete* I would make my way through snow
> *kimi wo min to wa* To see my lord in such a place?[38]

Not only does the thought require the first two lines to follow the rest, but according to normal Japanese syntax the third line should follow the fifth. Narihira may in his way have been suggesting feelings of confusion and incredulity. His use of the rhetorical particle *ya* ("could I have supposed") also occurred in his poem about the moon and the spring. The extra syllable in the second line, the repetition of the particle *wa* at the ends of the first and fifth lines, and of the verb *omou* in the second and third lines, might all be considered faults if an amateur had composed this poem, but they impart a particular rhythm and conviction typical of Narihira.

These stylistic features undoubtedly contribute to the effectiveness of the poem, but Narihira's intent has been debated by the critics. Most interpret it as an expression of Narihira's grief at finding the prince, with whom he had often composed poetry, in a lonely monk's cell that he has reached only after tramping through drifts of snow; but an entirely different interpretation has been proposed according to which the poem is no more than a greeting to an old friend along the lines of, "Sorry not to have written. Never expected to find you in a place like this . . ."[39]

A satisfactory interpretation of a given waka by Narihira usually depends on a knowledge of the circumstances under which it was composed. His poems not only benefit from extended prefaces in the *Kokinshū* but from the even fuller descriptions in *Tales of Ise*; sometimes the explanations of the circumstances clash, as in the following instance:

nuretsutsu zo	Even if I got wet,
shiite oritsuru	I was resolved to pick them,
toshi no uchi ni	Remembering that
haru wa ikuka mo	Hardly any days of spring
araji to omoeba[40]	Were still remaining this year.

The preface (*kotobagaki*) in the *Kokinshū* states, "On the last day of the third month, while it was raining, I picked some wisteria and sent it to someone." McCullough interpreted the poem as an expression of elegant Heian sensibility: "I have not minded getting wet, because I wish very much for you to share my enjoyment of the fragile, ephemeral beauty that, like the spring—and indeed like men and his works—vanishes all too soon."[41] However, in *Tales of Ise* the poem is presented with a different preface: "Once there was a man, rather down on his luck, who owned a flowering wisteria vine. On a drizzly day late in the third month, he decided to pluck some of the blossoms and send them off as a gift to a certain personage. He composed this poem." In the light of *this* preface, McCullough interpreted the poem as meaning: "At my humble house there is nothing of value except these flowers, which I have plucked for you, getting myself soaked in the process, in the hope that you may remember my plight and be moved to help me."[42] Both explanations, though they vary greatly, are accommodated by the words of Narihira's poem.[43]

The brevity of the waka was the main cause of its ambiguity. The poet sought to suggest as much as possible because he was not free to add another stanza in the manner of a European poem. Sometimes, as in Narihira's case, the poet failed to supply all the information that was necessary for understanding the meaning. The Japanese language, which normally omits subject pronouns but conveys much through particles and verb endings, abetted the poets who sought to communicate an experience in a mere thirty-one syllables. The ambiguity resulting from the omission of such prosaic matters as the circumstances of composing a waka was compounded by the imprecision of the language itself; but the Japanese, far from considering the poem unworthy of attention, have mulled over its every possible connotation, relishing the multiple meanings.

Quite apart from the ambiguity of the poem and its two introductions, its possible inspiration has also been much discussed. Some scholars believe that Narihira's source was two lines from a poem by Po Chü-i:

I grieve that I cannot prevent spring from departing;
Under purple wisteria blossoms day gradually draws to an end.[44]

If Narihira was indeed borrowing from Po Chü-i, he was one of the first Japanese poets to derive inspiration from this source, but the worship of Po's poetry soon became general at the Heian court. Many *Kokinshū* poems have been traced not only to Po Chü-i but to other Chinese poets of his time.[45]

Narihira may have mentioned the wisteria simply because wisteria were actually in bloom in his garden, but the pale color and drooping lines of wisteria blossoms would later be used in poetry to evoke the languor of late spring days. Wisteria appears in the *Man'yōshū*, but first acquired special associations in Narihira's time. The same is true of chrysanthemums (not mentioned at all in the *Man'yōshū*) and cherry blossoms (overshadowed by plum blossoms in the *Man'yōshū*).[46] The change in the attitudes toward different flowers suggests the degree to which the aesthetic preferences of Narihira and other courtiers of the early Heian period influenced the tastes of later Japanese.

Narihira's use of *engo* (related words)[47] and *kakekotoba* (pivot words)[48] would also be observed by later poets. In the following exchange of poems between Fujiwara no Toshiyuki and Narihira the imagery is unified by engo on water. Toshiyuki was courting a girl—traditionally, the younger sister of Narihira's wife. According to *Tales of Ise*, Narihira composed a poem for the girl to send by way of reply to Toshiyuki who (supposing the girl had written it herself) was much impressed. He answered her:

tsurezure no	Lost in idle brooding,
nagame ni masaru	That swells with the long rains
namidagawa	A river of tears

sode nomi nurete	That soaks only my sleeves:
au yoshi mo nashi[49]	There is no way to meet you.

Narihira once again replied for the girl:

asami koso	How shallow must be
sode wa hizurame	A river of tears that soaks
namidagawa	No more than your sleeves;
mi sae nagaru to	If I hear that you yourself
kikaba tanoman[50]	Are adrift, I'll believe you.

In these poems the engo are images relating to water, including *nagame* (brooding, but the near homophone of *naga-ame*, long rain); *namidagawa* (a river of tears); *nurete* (is soaked); *asami* (shallows of a river); *hizurame* (may be soaked); and *nagaru* (to drift). *Namidagawa*, the River of Tears, does not occur in the *Man'yōshū*, but appears all too often in the *Kokinshū*.

The use of engo, though not unknown in the *Man'yōshū*, became a conscious poetic device with Narihira, and represented one aspect of the emphasis on technique that is so conspicuous in his poetry. Perhaps the most brilliant example of his virtuosity was the acrostic poem he composed at a place called Yatsuhashi, or Eight Bridges, in the province of Mikawa. Along the river spanned by these bridges *kakitsubata* (irises) grew, and for this reason he composed a waka, each line of which begins with a successive syllable of *ka-ki-tsu-ba-ta*:

karagoromo	Because my dear wife
kitsutsu narenishi	Is familiar as the skirt
tsuma shi areba	Of a well-worn robe,
harubaru kinuru	I feel as if I have come
tabi wo shi zo omou[51]	A long distance on my way.

Not only is this poem an acrostic (*oriku*), but it also contains engo and also kakekotoba. *Karagoromo kitsutsu narenishi* means "my robe has become soft with repeated wearings," and *narenishi tsuma* means both "hems that have become familiar" and "beloved wife." *Haru* means "distant," but its homonym *haru* means to "full" clothes, and is therefore an engo for articles of clothing. The first eight syllables of the poem are a *joshi*[52] (preface) for the remainder. Finally, the repetition of the emphatic particle *shi* is typical of Narihira's poetic syntax.

The poem became so popular that the irises at Eight Bridges came to be an *utamakura*, or "topic of poetry," that continued for a thousand years to fascinate travelers. Almost everyone who passed through Mikawa felt the urge to see with his own eyes the site of the Eight Bridges and to comment sadly that no irises grew there anymore. It was not the meaning of the waka, hardly remarkable in itself, but the dazzling skill with language that earned it such popularity.

One other travel poem by Narihira became almost equally celebrated. It appears in the *Kokinshū* immediately after the acrostic. Narihira and his companions had been traveling a long time, and when they reached the Sumida River they were homesick for the capital. The bleakness of the landscape before them made them realize just how far from home they were. As they boarded a ferry, they noticed an unfamiliar river bird and asked the ferryman its name. He replied that it was a "capital bird" (*miyakodori*), and this inspired Narihira's poem:

na ni shi owaba	If you are faithful
iza koto towan	To your name, I would ask you,
miyakodori	Bird of the city,
wa ga omou hito wa	Is the woman I think of
ari yo nashi ya[53]	Alive, or is she no more?

This poem, often quoted in later works of literature, figures prominently in the Nō play *Sumida-gawa*. The use of personification—addressing the bird as if it were capable of answering—may have been borrowed from Chinese poetry,[54] but it was a poetic conceit to ask the bird (simply because its name was "capital bird") about his wife in the capital. The implied longing for the wife is nevertheless affecting. The reversal of the normal order of the lines, typical of Narihira, contributed to the popularity; of all Narihira's poems it was the most often quoted in later literature.[55]

The Japanese tradition of traveling to "famous places" in order to experience for oneself their special attractions, described in poetry composed about these places, may have originated in Narihira's travels. But Narihira was even more celebrated as a lover. *Tales of Ise* consists largely of accounts of various affairs attributed to him, including one with the most inaccessible of women, the high priestess of the Ise Shrine, who was strictly forbidden to have relations with men. The *Kokinshū* gives poems exchanged by Narihira and the priestess together with the prefatory note, "When Narihira was in Ise he met in absolute secrecy the woman who was serving as the high priestess. The morning after, while he was puzzling what to do, there being no way to send her a messenger, this poem came from her."

kimi ya koshi	Did you come to me,
ware ya yukiken	Or did I go to you?
omōezu	I have no idea
yume ka utsutsu ka	A dream or reality?
kanete ka samete ka[56]	Was I asleep or awake?

Narihira replied:

kakikurasu	In the utter dark
kokoro no yami ni	Of a mind that obscures all
mayoiniki	I have long wandered.
yume utsutsu to wa	A dream or reality?
yohito sadame yo[57]	Let other people decide.

The affair between Narihira and the high priestess of Ise figures so prominently in *Tales of Ise* that it may have occasioned the title of the work. The genuine or feigned uncertainty as to whether or not a meeting actually took place would be typical of many poems in the *Kokinshū*, where "elegant confusion"[58]—a professed inability to distinguish between white blossoms and snow or between dream and reality—is frequent.

Exchanges of poetry between men and women not only typified the waka of the ninth century but may account for the waka's survival. Since women usually did not learn Chinese,[59] men who normally wrote their poetry and prose in Chinese, the language of the court literature of the ninth century, had no choice but to address their poems to women in Japanese. This presumably is why the preface to the *Kokinshū* gives as a function of the waka "making sweet the ties between men and women." The poems exchanged were often witty, in the manner of the gallant verses of seventeenth-century Europe, but they could also be tragic, especially when lovers represented their awareness that an affair was ending.

Narihira's last poem ranks among his most moving:

tsui ni yuku	Long ago I heard
michi to wa kanete	That this is the road we must all

kikishikado	Travel in the end,
kinō kyō to wa	But I never thought it might
omowazarishi wo[60]	Be yesterday or today.

The line *kinō kyō to wa* (that it might be yesterday or today) presents a problem: would it not have been more natural to say instead "today or tomorrow"? Some scholars suggest that the line actually means "until yesterday I never thought it might be today"; others believe that it was merely an elaborate way of saying "right about now."[61] But beyond such quibbling is the emotion that Narihira has described: the speaker has known all along, of course, that some day he must die, but it shocks him that the day has arrived unexpectedly soon.

Narihira was not a profound poet. His surviving poems are mainly occasional, and even when the expression suggests deeply felt emotion, its worldly manner keeps his poetry from attaining the grandeur of the best *Man'yōshū* poems in the same vein. He is nevertheless of historical importance as one who maintained the traditions of the waka during the long night of the dominance of poetry in Chinese.

Ono no Komachi was another of the Six Immortals of Poetry. Almost nothing of her life is known apart from the names of various men with whom she exchanged the poems included in the *Kokinshū*. The absence of facts about a poet who so captured the imagination of people of later times led to the creation of legends about her, most of which have some justification in her poetry.

Komachi was probably born between 820 and 830, at a time when the popularity of composing poetry in Chinese was at its height, and her period of greatest poetic activity seems to have occurred about the middle of the ninth century. It has been conjectured that she was a *kōi*, a lady-of-the-bedchamber, who served the Emperor Nimmei. After Nimmei's death in 850, she entered into liaisons with other men.[62] Much scholarship has been devoted to attempts to ascertain her place of birth, her family, and other basic information, but without conclusive results. Arai Hakuseki (1657–1725) advanced the theory that many women, not just one, were known as Komachi, and that the legends therefore referred to different people. A later expansion of this theory came up with four Komachis.[63] For the student of literature, however, it is easiest to assume that the legends had formed about a single Ono no Komachi.

The legends can be classified into four categories. First, there are those that describe Komachi, the peerless beauty desired by all men of the court. The perhaps accidental placing in the *Kokinshū* of a poem by Komachi next to one by Narihira may have been the source of the legend that the two matchlessly beautiful people were lovers.[64] The second group of legends concerns Komachi's heartless treatment of her lovers, especially Fukakusa no Shōshō. She insisted that he visit her a hundred nights before she would yield her favors. He accepted, and faithfully made his way to her house each night, regardless of the weather. On the ninety-ninth night he died. The third group of legends portrays Komachi in old age, when she was doomed to wander in rags, her beauty lost and her appearance so wretched that she was mocked by all who saw her, her punishment for her cruelty to lovers. Finally, there were legends of Komachi's death, and of her skull lying in a field; when the wind blew through her eye sockets the mournful sound evoked her anguish. These legends proliferated and were used by the Nō dramatists and other writers. Most of the legends about Komachi existed as early as the eleventh century.[65]

The surviving poems of Komachi are almost all in a melancholy vein, typified by her most famous waka:

hana no iro wa	The flowers withered
utsurinikeru na	Their color faded away,
itazura ni	While meaninglessly
wa ga mi yo ni furu	I spent my days in brooding,
nagame seshi ma ni[66]	And the long rains were falling.

This is the only poem by Komachi included among the seasonal poems of the *Kokinshū*; the rest are all love or miscellaneous poems. For this reason, some commentators interpret the poem as an objective description of the passing of spring: but this does not take into account the phrase *wa ga mi*, "my person," a clue that a subjective meaning was also intended. The poem can also be interpreted as referring solely to the speaker: the color of my springtime faded while meaninglessly I spent my time in affairs with men and brooded over my fate. The possibility of two such different interpretations results from double meanings to some of the words. *Furu* in the line *wa ga mi yo ni furu* is a form of the verb *fu*, meaning to pass time; but with *nagame*, a shortened form of *naga-ame* (long rains), it can also be the verb *furu*, meaning to fall (of rain), or else *furu*, to become old. *Nagame* is not only "long rain," but also "brooding" or "staring at." Such verbal dexterity was characteristic of Komachi, and enabled her to say a great deal in thirty-one syllables. But the expression is so elliptical that there have been many disputes about the meaning of the poem.[67]

It is easy to imagine how such a poem might give rise to the legend of Komachi in old age, bewailing the loss of her beauty. In another waka, seemingly from the early part of her life, Komachi expressed despair over not being able to meet a lover:

hito ni awan	This night of no moon
tsuki no naki ni wa	There is no way to meet him.
omoiokite	I rise in longing:
mune hashirihi ni	My breast pounds, a leaping flame,
kokoro yakeori[68]	My heart is consumed in fire.

This poem is filled with word-play. The word *tsuki* means both "moon" and "means" (to meet). *Omoi* was written in the historical spelling of *omohi*, which includes the word *hi*, "fire." *Okite* means "to rise (from bed)" but also "to stir up (a fire)." *Mune hashiri* refers to the pounding of the chest with excitement or anxiety, but *hashirihi* is a flying spark. This use of language might be dismissed as a mere toying with words, but the poem carries conviction, suggesting a woman who is so distraught that her mind leaps from one verbal association to another.

The intensity of emotion expressed in Komachi's poetry not only was without precedent but would rarely be encountered in later years. The poetry of the *Kokinshū* was usually pitched in a lower key, and the ingenious use of language was a mark not of overpowering emotion but of a kind of intellectuality. Komachi's poetry, however extravagant in expression, always seems sincere. Another poem suggests how the legends concerning her old age may have originated:

wabinureba	So lonely am I
mi wo ukikusa no	My body is a floating weed
ne wo taete	Severed at the roots.
sasou mizu araba	Were there water to entice me
inan to zo omou[69]	I would follow it, I think.

This poem bears the headnote: "Written by way of reply when Fun'ya no Yasuhide, after his appointment as assistant governor of Mikawa, sent word to her, 'Won't you come and inspect my new post?' " It is not known when (or even if) Yasuhide was appointed as assistant governor (*jō*) of Mikawa, but the presence of his name gives Komachi's poem a reality in time and place apart from the legends. The imagery of the poem is unified by engo related to water, but the effect is less one of powerful emotion than of resignation. Komachi indicates that she would go if invited, but she really does not believe in the possibility.[70]

The poems of Narihira and Komachi are the most memorable of those composed during the "dark age" of the ninth century, but there were other waka of importance. There is reason to believe that many of the best were incorporated into the *Kokinshū* with the notation "author unknown" (*yomibito shirazu*).

The Anonymous Poems

Most of the ninth-century poems collected in the *Kokinshū* are anonymous. They often show close kinship with the *Man'yōshū*, and some may even have been composed in the eighth century, while the capital was still in Nara. Others nostalgically recall the old capital, referring to it as *furusato*, "old home."[71] It is generally not clear when anonymous poems were composed, but sometimes they are so closely related in theme to signed and datable poems that we can safely assume they existed by a certain time. The following poem is anonymous:

oiraku no	If only I knew
kon to shiriseba	When Old Age was approaching,
kado sashite	I would bolt the door
nashi to kotaete	And, calling out "Not at home!"
awazaramashi wo[72]	Bluntly refuse to meet him.

Keichū suggested that this poem was the source of the waka composed by Narihira in 875 in honor of the fortieth birthday of Fujiwara no Mototsune:

sakurabana	You cherry blossoms—
chirikaikumore	Cloud the sky with falling petals
oiraku no	And blot out the path
kon to iu naru	Along which, they say, Old Age
michi magau gani[73]	Is likely to travel on.

The most striking feature of both poems is the use of personification, not only for old age but for the cherry blossoms. Personification was relatively rare in Japanese poetry, and it may be that Narihira found the conceit of approaching "Old Age" so striking that he borrowed it.

Some anonymous poems in the *Kokinshū* also appeared in *Tales of Ise*, where they were elucidated by prose descriptions. The following poem is in the *Kokinshū*:

Kasugano wa	Do not set fire to
kyō wa na yaki so	Kasuga Fields today,
wakakusa no	Fresh as the spring grass
tsuma mo komoreri	My wife is lingering there,
ware mo komoreri[74]	And I too wish to linger.

Commentators agree that this is an old folk song.[75] The speaker is apparently a man from the capital who asks the people who are about to burn some old fields (in order to promote new growth) to refrain this day because he and his wife are enjoying their spring outing in the fields of Kasuga. However, the word *tsuma*, translated above as "wife," meant "spouse," and therefore could also refer to a husband. In *Tales of Ise* the same poem, with one word changed, acquired a quite different meaning:

Musashino wa	Do not set fire to
kyō wa na yaki so	Musashi Plain today,
wakakusa no	Fresh as spring grass,
tsuma mo komoreri	My husband is hiding there,
ware mo komoreri	And I too wish to hide.[76]

The prose passage that accompanies this poem in *Tales of Ise* tells how a man once abducted another man's daughter. He was on his way to Musashi Plain with the girl when he was caught and arrested by provincial officials. He hid the girl in a clump of bushes and attempted to make his escape. His pursuers decided to set fire to the plain so as to catch him, but the abducted girl, who seems to have fallen in love with her kidnaper, begged the officials not to start a fire. The officials subsequently caught the man and took both man and woman away.[77] The fact that a single change in wording could permit a poem to be interpreted so differently suggests how freely the surviving poems of the ninth century were used by later poets.

The waka poetry of the ninth century may be said to mark a transition between one great anthology and the next, but it is of exceptional appeal in its own right. The passionate accents of the waka of Komachi and Narihira would never be surpassed, and the poetry as a whole is of such charm as to make the appearance of the *Kokinshū* seem less a brilliant dawn after a dark night than the culmination of a steady enhancement of the expressive powers of the most typical Japanese poetic art.

Notes

1. See above, p. 34.
2. Kūkai while in China learned Sanskrit, a tradition still preserved by Shingon monks. It is possible that his knowledge of the Sanskrit alphabet affected the ordering of the kana along the lines of *a, i, u, e, o, ka, ki, ku, ke, ko,* and so on. This may be why Kūkai was credited with the invention of the kana. However, Kūkai, as we know from his literary works, was far too attached to Chinese literary expression to consider adopting an alphabet that, in effect, would have cut Japan off from Chinese writings.
3. Komatsu Shigemi, *Kana*, pp. 148–51. See also Ōno Susumu, *Nihongo no Seiritsu*, pp. 283–85.
4. Komatsu, *Kana*, p. i.
5. A combination of characters and kana, similar to that found in books and newspapers today, became normal in the late Heian period both in the tale literature and in works that described historical events.
6. See Komatsu, *Kana*, p. 65; also Ōno, *Nihongo*, p. 299. The term *hiragana*, meaning "simple kana," apparently dates from the late Muromachi period; the earliest mention is in the *Arte da Lingoa de Iapam* by João Rodrigues, published in 1604. (See Komatsu, *Kana*, p. 65. See also Michael Cooper, *Rodrigues the Interpreter*, p. 224.) The term *katakana*, meaning "partial kana," and referring to the use of only a part of a Chinese character, is much older; the word is found as early as the tenth-century *Utsubo Monogatari* (The Tale of the Hollow Tree).
7. The two poems, known as the "Naniwazu" and "Asakayama" from place-names mentioned in each, were popular from early times. The opening of the "Naniwazu" poem is found in a graffito on a wall of the Hōryū-ji pagoda, probably written in the eighth century. The "Asakayama" poem is included in the *Man'yōshū* (no. 3807). For use of the poems in calligraphy practice, see Komatsu, *Kana*, pp. 142–43. See also Edward Seidensticker's translation of *The Tale of Genji*, I, p. 98.
8. Normally pronounced, however, as *iro wa*. The final *n* of Japanese does not appear in the poem because this syllable was usually written as *mu*.
9. *Ui* is a Buddhist term that refers to all phenomena that are produced through cause and effect. The phrase *ui no okuyama* has been rendered as "the difficulty of escaping from this inconstant world."
10. For a brief account of the Khitan script (and of the Jurchen script, a modified form of the Khitan), see S. Robert Ramsay, *The Languages of China*, pp. 224–27.
11. Ōno, *Nihongo*, p. 304, mentions the invention of the Khitan and Vietnamese scripts and (in the fifteenth century) of the Korean alphabet. The Tangut script (not discussed by Ōno or by Ramsay) was also known as Hsi Hsia.

12. For a much more detailed consideration of the *Shinsen Man'yōshū* see Helen Craig McCullough, *Brocade by Night*, pp. 261–75.
13. A shorter text, perhaps the older of the two, does not include kanshi in the second book. This text also differs from the rufubon in having a preface only for the first book.
14. Asami Tōru, "Kaisetsu," in his edition of *Shinsen Man'yōshū*, p. 227. McCullough (*Brocade*, pp. 261–62) briefly quotes the preface to Book I.
15. Kyūsojin Hitaku (*Shinsen Man'yōshū to Kenkyū*, pp. 139–40), Takano Taira (*Shinsen Man'yōshū ni kansuru Kisoteki Kenkyū*), and Yamaguchi Hiroshi (*Ōchō Kadan no Kenkyū*, p. 86) accept Michizane as the compiler, but Asami Tōru, writing after all these scholars, insisted that there is no firm evidence to support this traditional attribution. (Asami, "Kaisetsu," p. 229.) See also McCullough, *Brocade*, pp. 274–75, for a consideration of arguments for and against Michizane's authorship. She concludes (p. 291) that because of the impersonality of the poems it is impossible to verify the traditional association of Michizane with the collection.
16. For a study of the poetry composed at this uta-awase, see Takano Taira, *Kampyō no Kisai no Miya no Uta-awase ni kansuru Kenkyū*. See also McCullough, *Brocade*, pp. 241–52.
17. This figure is from McCullough, *Brocade*, p. 262. Ichiko Teiji (ed.), *Nihon Bungaku Zenshi*, II, p. 79, gives 150.
18. See Ichiko, *Nihon*, II, p. 80. The poem by Sosei was included in the *Kokinshū* (poem 47). See also Takano, *Shinsen Man'yōshū*, pp. 63–64.
19. See Kyūsojin, *Shinsen*, pp. 117, 157.
20. McCullough (*Brocade*, p. 263) gives a table of poems from the *Shinsen Man'yōshū* in the *Kokinshū*, showing that 48 of the 119 poems in Book I were taken, as opposed to 27 from the 134 in Book II. McCullough translates (pp. 264–74) more than 30 waka from the collection and also several of the kanshi.
21. The dates of birth and death of Ōe no Chisato are not known.
22. See McCullough, *Brocade*, p. 67.
23. McCullough, *Brocade*, p. 63. She also gives (p. 62) a list of themes missing from the "salon corpus" of this Chinese court poetry: "poems of protest, elegies, laments, celebrations of the pleasures of reclusion, nature poetry in the Xie Lingyun [Hsieh Ling-yün] tradition, and, in general, topics of an eccentric, private, or controversial nature." Hsieh Ling-yün (385–433) was a poet of Buddhist and Taoist interests who wrote mainly of the beauty and grandeur of mountain landscapes.
24. McCullough gives (*Brocade*, pp. 255–59) some examples of poems by Po Chü-i from which Ōe no Chisato borrowed lines to create his waka. One well-known example, though not included in the *Kokinshū*, was chosen three hundred years later for the *Shin Kokinshū*. Other examples of waka by Chisato on lines of Po and Yüan Chen (779–831) are given by Konishi Jin'ichi in *A History of Japanese Literature*, II, pp. 212–14.

25. Kuronushi also appears in several Nō plays, notably *Sōshi Arai Komachi*, where he appears as Komachi's rival in an uta-awase. Unable to compose a poem of his own, he decides to accuse Komachi of having copied her poem from the *Man'yōshū*. When his machinations are exposed, he attempts to commit suicide, but is stopped by Komachi, who forgives him.
26. For *Tales of Ise*, see below, pp. 452–457.
27. Mezaki Tokue, *Ariwara no Narihira, Ono no Komachi*, p. 24.
28. *Kokinshū* 622. The poem also appears in *Tales of Ise*. I have translated *sasa*, a kind of low bamboo grass, as "bamboo." A variant, found in *Tales of Ise* and elsewhere, gives for the fourth line *awade nuru yo zo*, "a night that I slept without meeting her."
29. Quoted by Mezaki in *Ariwara*, p. 25.
30. See Ozawa Masao, *Kokin Waka Shū*, p. 256.
31. Okumura Tsuneya, "Kokinshū no Seishin," p. 23.
32. *Kokinshū* 747. For a sampling of opinions on this poem written during the Tokugawa period, see Koizumi Hiroshi, *Shochū Shūsei Kokin Waka Shū Sen*, pp. 157–59.
33. Mezaki, *Ariwara*, p. 64.
34. *Ibid*., p. 64. Mezaki accepted this interpretation. Helen Craig McCullough, *Tales of Ise*, p. 53, presented four different interpretations of the poem.
35. Kyūsojin Hitaku, *Kokin Waka Shū*, III, pp. 257–58.
36. Ozawa, *Kokin*, p. 92. See also Robert H. Brower and Earl Miner, *Japanese Court Poetry*, p. 193, for a particularly interesting analysis of Narihira's poem.
37. See Mezaki, *Ariwara*, p. 11, where she discusses a poem by Ariwara no Narihira which, if literally translated into modern Japanese, would have a meaning something like, "If there weren't any cherry blossoms in the world, we would probably feel calm and collected in spring." This is the banal, surface meaning of the poem, but the language Narihira actually used makes it convey much more.
38. *Kokinshū* 970. The translation of the prose introduction is from McCullough, *Tales of Ise*, p. 181. See also op. cit., pp. 127–28. Another translation by McCullough in *Kokin Wakashū*, p. 212.
39. This is the interpretation of Kanda Hideo, as quoted by Mezaki in *Ariwara*, pp. 112–13.
40. *Kokinshū* 133. Other translations by McCullough in *Tales of Ise*, p. 123, and *Kokin Wakashū*, p. 38.
41. McCullough, *Tales of Ise*, p. 236.
42. *Ibid*., p. 236. McCullough quoted Arai Mujirō, *Hyōshaku Ise Monogatari Taisei*, pp. 676–78, as a source for this interpretation.
43. These strikingly different interpretations of the poem stem primarily from two words, *otoroe taru ie*, in the prefatory passage in *Tales of Ise*, "a house that has seen better days," and *tatematsuru*, "to present to a superior." The *Kokinshū* text says that the wisteria blossoms were sent to *hito*, mean-

ing a person but generally the woman with whom the poet is in love. The poet's emotions on offering the blossoms would differ considerably if the recipient were his sweetheart, rather than a superior official. Again, the words *haru wa ikuka mo araji* (surely, not many days are left to the spring) might, if the flowers were offered to a woman, refer to the springtime of the poet's own life; he would be saying that he picked the wisteria blossoms despite the rain because there was so little time left to enjoy the spring and his own youth. This does not dispose of all the problems in the poem. The kotobagaki in the *Kokinshū* states that the poem was composed on the last day of the third month, which was the last day of spring according to the lunar calendar; but the waka itself says that there are not many more days left to the spring. Commentators since the eighteenth century have voiced their worries over this apparent contradiction. Kyūsojin, *Kokin*, I, pp. 183–84, adopted a variant text of the *Kokinshū* that gave as the final lines *haru wa kyō wo shi kagiri to omoeba* (when I realize that today is the last day of spring). He believed that some editor tampered with the poem, giving rise to the contradiction.

44. Mezaki, *Ariwara*, p. 116, quoting Kaneko Hikojirō, *Heian Jidai Bungaku to Hakushi Monjū*.
45. In this connection, see especially Konishi Jin'ichi, "The Genesis of the *Kokinshū* Style."
46. See Mezaki, *Ariwara*, pp. 14, 119.
47. *Engo* are found in English writing, both consciously and unconsciously. An example of the former is Shakespeare's Sonnet 137, where imagery drawn from courts of law runs through the poem:

    When to the *sessions* of sweet silent thought
    I *summon* up remembrance of things past. . . .

    Unconsciously used "related words" are often found in such statements as "The Post Office Department urged cancellation of the contract," or "The airlines initiated a crash program."
48. The meaning of a kakekotoba changes with what follows. A crude English equivalent would be something like: "What do I seaweed on the shore?" Joyce's *Finnegans Wake* abounds in portmanteau words that have a similar effect, such as, "Sir Tristram, violer d'amores, fr'over the short sea, had passencore rearrived from North Armorica." Perhaps the best known example in Japanese is *sen kata namida,* where *sen kata nami* means "there is nothing I can do" and *namida* is "tears," the situation described in the first part of the statement leading to the tears.
49. *Kokinshū* 617.
50. *Kokinshū* 618.
51. *Kokinshū* 410. The fourth line begins with *ha* rather than *ba*, but this was

unavoidable because no Japanese words at that time began with a voiced consonant.

52. *Joshi* (also called *jo* and *jokotoba*) are introductory phrases connected to what follows not by syntax but by a play on a word, suggesting a train of thought that has been diverted into an unexpected direction by word associations.
53. *Kokinshū* 411.
54. Mezaki, *Ariwara*, p. 89. See also McCullough, *Brocade*, pp. 70–71.
55. See Kyūsojin, *Kokin*, II, p. 260, for a list of twenty-one texts in which it is quoted.
56. *Kokinshū* 645. Another translation by McCullough in *Kokin*, p. 144.
57. *Kokinshū* 646. See also translation by McCullough, *Kokin*, p. 144.
58. McCullough traces this feature of *Kokinshū* poetry to the Chinese poetry of the Six Dynasties. See, for example, her *Brocade*, pp. 66–67.
59. There were exceptions. See above, p. 195.
60. *Kokinshū* 861.
61. See Mezaki, *Ariwara*, p. 152.
62. Katagiri Yōichi, *Ono no Komachi Tsuiseki*, pp. 23–24.
63. *Ibid.*, pp. 59–60.
64. *Ibid.*, pp. 12, 155.
65. *Ibid.*, p. 66.
66. *Kokinshū* 113.
67. Some commentators insist that it is a mistake to interpret the last three lines of the poem as a comment on the first two: that is, to interpret the whole poem as a lament on the poet's loss of beauty. Mezaki, *Ariwara*, p. 169, quotes Keichū and Motoori Norinaga to this effect. Okumura Tsuneya, *Kokin Waka Shū*, p. 61, says that if the first three lines were intended to refer to the poet's appearance, the poem should have been included in the "miscellaneous" section of the anthology. Fujihira Haruo, Ueno Osamu, and Sugitani Jurō, *Kokin Waka Shū Nyūmon*, pp. 63–64, argue the opposite: the placement of this poem among other poems on falling blossoms was intended to indicate the poet's loss of her beauty. They also contend that *itazura ni* refers both to the fading flowers and to the manner in which Komachi spent her life in the world.

    The poem was also used by Egoyama Tsuneaki (in "Kakekotoba," p. 272) as an example of one of two varieties of kakekotoba. Poems containing this kind of kakekotoba can be understood from beginning to end with either or both surface meanings. Poems containing the second kind of kakekotoba have no overall continuity: the meaning up to the kakekotoba and the meaning after it remain distinct.
68. *Kokinshū* 1030. See also the discussion in Brower and Miner, *Japanese*, p. 206.
69. *Kokinshū* 938.
70. This is not the interpretation of every scholar. Okumura (in *Kokin*,

p. 319) suggested that Komachi meant she would like to cut her roots and drift as she pleased.

71. See Abe Akio, *Nihon Bungaku Shi: Chūko-hen*, pp. 74–76.
72. *Kokinshū* 895.
73. *Kokinshū* 349.
74. *Kokinshū* 17.
75. See Ozawa, *Kokin*, p. 68; Okumura, *Kokin*, p. 32.
76. Helen Craig McCullough, *Tales of Ise*, p. 12.
77. *Ibid.*, p. 78.

Bibliography

Note: All Japanese books, except as otherwise noted, were published in Tokyo.

Abe Akio. *Nihon Bungaku Shi: Chūko-hen*. Hanawa Shobō, 1966.

Asami Tōru. "'Kaisetsu' to *Shinsen Man'yōshū*," in Kyōto Daigaku Kokugo Kokubun Shiryō Sōsho series. Kyōto: Rinsen Shoten, 1979.

Brower, Robert H., and Earl Miner. *Japanese Court Poetry*. Stanford, Calif.: Stanford University Press, 1961.

Cooper, Michael. *Rodrigues the Interpreter*. New York: Weatherhill, 1974.

Egoyama Tsuneaki. "Kakekotoba," in Nihon Bungaku Kenkyū Shiryō Sōsho series, *Kokin Waka Shū*. Yūseidō, 1976.

Fujihira Haruo, Ueno Osamu, and Sugitani Jurō. *Kokin Waka Shū Nyūmon*. Yūhikaku, 1978.

Hirshfield, Jane, and Mariko Aratani. *The Ink Dark Moon*. New York: Vintage Books, 1990.

Ichiko Teiji (ed.). *Nihon Bungaku Zenshi*, II. Gakutōsha, 1978.

Katagiri Yōichi. *Ono no Komachi Tsuiseki*. Kasama Shoin, 1975.

Koizumi Hiroshi. *Shochū Shūsei Kokin Waka Shū Sen*. Yūseidō, 1970.

Komatsu Shigemi. *Kana*, in Iwanami Shinsho series. Iwanami Shoten, 1968.

Konishi, Jin'ichi. "The Genesis of the *Kokinshū* Style," trans. Helen McCullough, *Harvard Journal of Asiatic Studies* 37:1, 1978.

———. *A History of Japanese Literature*, II, trans. Aileen Gatten, Princeton, N.J.: Princeton University Press, 1986.

Kyūsojin Hitaku. *Kokin Waka Shū*, 4 vols., in Kōdansha Gakujutsu Bunko series. Kōdansha, 1979–83.

———. *Shinsen Man'yōshū to Kenkyū*. Toyohashi: Mikan Kokubun Shiryō Kankōkai, 1958.

McCullough, Helen Craig. *Brocade by Night*. Stanford, Calif.: Stanford University Press, 1985.

———. *Kokin Wakashū*. Stanford, Calif.: Stanford University Press, 1985.

———. *Tales of Ise*. Tokyo: Tokyo University Press, 1978.

Mezaki Tokue. *Ariwara no Narihira, Ono no Komachi*. Chikuma Shobō, 1970.

Okumura Tsuneya. *Kokinshū no Kenkyū*. Kyōto: Rinsen Shoten, 1980.

———. "Kokinshū no Seishin," *Bungaku* 43:8, 1975.

———. *Kokin Waka Shū*, in Shinchō Nihon Koten Shūsei series. Shinchōsha, 1978.

Ōno Susumu. *Nihongo no Seiritsu*, in Nihongo no Sekai series, I. Chūō Kōron Sha, 1980.

Ozawa Masao. *Kokin Waka Shū*, in Nihon Koten Bungaku Zenshū series. Shōgakukan, 1971.

Ramsay, S. Robert. *The Languages of China*. Princeton, N.J.: Princeton University Press, 1989.

Seidensticker, Edward G. (trans.). *The Tale of Genji*, 2 vols. New York: Alfred A. Knopf, 1976.

Takano Taira. *Kampyō no Kisai no Miya no Uta-awase ni kansuru Kenkyū*. Kazama Shobō, 1976.

———. *Shinsen Man'yōshū ni kansuru Kisoteki Kenkyū*. Kazama Shobō, 1970.

Yamaguchi Hiroshi. *Ōchō Kadan no Kenkyū*. Ōfūsha, 1973.

6.
THE *KOKINSHŪ*

The *Kokin Waka Shū* (Collection of Waka, Old and New), usually referred to as the *Kokinshū*, was the first imperially sponsored collection of poetry in Japanese. This recognition of the importance of the waka seems to reflect the attitude adopted toward China by Sugawara no Michizane when he urged the suspension of embassies to China on the grounds that the Japanese no longer needed to look abroad for guidance. The *Kokinshū* represented not a rejection of Chinese influence—much is evident even in these exquisitely turned Japanese lyrics—but a shift from close imitations of Chinese models to a freer use of Chinese poetic sources as a means of enriching the waka. The poems in the collection, whether those of the era of Narihira and Komachi or more recent, display such skill and grace in conveying within the bare thirty-one syllables of the waka the elegance of the Japanese court during a golden age that the *Kokinshū* may be said to have established the canons of Japanese poetic taste. For a thousand years the *Kokinshū*, more than any other anthology, would be revered as the acme of Japanese poetry.

Imperial sponsorship of the anthology imparted a special character. The compilers were court officials, charged with preparing a collection that would meet with the emperor's approval and redound to the glory of his reign.[1] Some of the circumstances of the compilation are described in the two prefaces to the collection, one in Japanese by Ki no Tsurayuki (868?–945) and the other in Chinese by Ki no Yoshimochi (d. 919).

The Two Prefaces

The Japanese preface to the *Kokinshū* is one of the earliest and best-known documents of Japanese poetic criticism. It opens with a declaration of the nature of Japanese poetry:

> Japanese poetry has its seeds in the human heart and burgeons into many different kinds of leaves of words.[2] We who live in this world are constantly affected by different experiences, and we express our thoughts in words, in terms of what we have seen and heard. When we hear the warbler that sings among the blossoms or the voice of the frog that lives in the water, we may ask ourselves, "Which of all the creatures of this world does not sing?" Poetry moves without effort heaven and earth, stirs the invisible gods and demons to pity, makes sweet the ties between men and women, and brings comfort to the fierce heart of the warrior.[3]

Yoshimochi in the Chinese preface expressed similar views, and these sentiments, like much else in both prefaces, have been traced back to China.[4] The major preface to the *Shih Ching* (Book of Poetry) had declared, "Nothing approaches the *Book of Poetry* in maintaining correct standards for success or failure [in government], in moving Heaven and Earth, and in appealing to spirits and gods."[5] The resemblances with Chinese works of criticism are no more than intermittent, but Tsurayuki and Yoshimochi shared the belief of the Chinese that human feelings were the ultimate source of all poetry. This was not a truism: the miracles of the gods, the battles fought by heroes, the communication of moral and political truths, and other subjects that do not stem immediately from the emotions have inspired great poetry elsewhere in the world; but the strengths and limitations of the waka, as it developed over the years, were anticipated by Tsurayuki's definition of its origin and purpose.

The word that Tsurayuki used both for poetry and for song was *uta*, and he seems not to have made a clear distinction between the two. Whether the song was melodious like that of the springtime warbler amid the blossoms or as harsh as the croaking of an autumnal frog, it proved that every living creature has its song. Birds and beasts, and human beings, too, sing in response to stimulation, whether external—things seen and heard—or internal, like the pangs of love. The stimulus tends to be short-lived, and for this reason may be more easily turned into a brief lyric that distills the poet's experience than developed into an extended poem.[6]

Although Tsurayuki says in his preface that poetry can stir the gods, in the West it was more common for the poet to think of himself as the instrument of the gods, whose aid he might invoke in making his song. In Japan divine help was not necessary; the poet, unaided, could move the spheres and make even supernatural creatures feel the poignancy of *aware*, the touching things of this world. Poetry was also important in the relations between men and women; as we have seen, the necessity of writing love poetry in Japanese to women who could not read Chinese may have saved the Japanese language as a medium of literary expression. And, as we know from *The Tale of Genji* and other works of the Heian period, poetry was an indispensable element of courtship, at least among the nobility.

Finally, the composition of poetry could calm the hearts of warriors whose profession obliged them to kill. The Japanese warrior was expected to be able to compose poetry, at the very least a farewell poem to the world (*jisei*) when he was on the point of death. The poems composed by the Heian warriors were not hymns to the Lord God of Battles or shouts of triumph over the fallen foe, but drew their imagery from flowers, and their surface meaning was often virtually indistinguishable from the evocations of nature of poets who had never once heard a battle cry. The imperially commissioned collections contain many poems by soldiers. Taira no Tadanori (1144–1184) was so eager to have a poem in such a collection that he risked death to return to the capital, then in the hands of enemies, in order to ask the poet Fujiwara Shunzei to include one of his poems. He realized that the fortunes of his family were at an end, but if even one of his poems was included in an imperial anthology, it would be sufficient glory for a lifetime.

Tsurayuki went on to describe the circumstances under which people of the past had turned to composing poetry:

> When they saw blossoms fall on a spring morning, or heard the leaves fall on an autumn evening; when they grieved over the new snow and ripples reflected with each passing year by their looking glasses; when they were startled, seeing dew on the grass or foam on the water, by the brevity of life; when they lost their positions, though yesterday they had prospered; or when, because they had fallen in the world, even those who had been most intimate treated them like strangers.[7]

These springs of poetry can be resumed under a single general heading, regret over the changes brought about by the passage of time. This is, indeed, a dominant theme of the collection, and perhaps the quality that distinguishes the *Kokinshū* most conspicuously from the Chinese anthologies of poetry that were especially admired by the Japanese. Nostalgia for the past, known even to the kanshi poets of the *Kaifūsō*, is one of the keys to the understanding of Japanese lyricism.

The diminution of the scale of the *Kokinshū* poetry, when compared to that of the *Man'yōshū*, was not solely a matter of the virtual disappearance of the chōka and with it the kind of themes that could not be expressed in the thirty-one syllables of a waka. The vocabulary was also much shrunken (even allowing for the smaller number of poems in the *Kokinshū*);[8] the compilers especially avoided poems that included the kind of coarse or obscure words that gave pungence to many *Man'yōshū* poems. The poets of the *Kokinshū* grieved over the loss of beauty, of love, of trusted friends, but they rarely permitted the rough edges of emotions to pierce the elegant surface of their compositions.

Both Japanese and Chinese prefaces to the *Kokinshū* described the six styles of poetry found in the collection, naming them according to the categories that had been used for the different varieties of Chinese poetry.[9] The Japanese preface gives an example of each category, but the attempt to dignify waka composition by clothing it in the borrowed robes of Chinese poetry was no more than halfhearted.

The most persuasive defense of the waka was given in the first line of Tsurayuki's preface: Japanese poetry has its seeds in the human heart. Regardless of the imagery or techniques of a particular poem, the avowed purpose of composition was to express what lay in the poet's heart, not to display virtuosity in the handling of language. The literary sophistication in Chinese poetry was professedly rejected in favor of an unaffected, sincere expression of the poet's emotion; but in fact, even the most artless-seeming cry from the heart of a *Kokinshū* poet was likely to bear the marks of Chinese influence. So great was the prestige of the foreign literature, so pervasive were its modes of expression, that a court poet who insisted on following only pure Japanese traditions of poetry would have seemed hopelessly out of date, despite the lip service paid to Hitomaro and Akahito in the prefaces.

The prefaces both present a brief history of the waka from its inception, when the god Susano-o composed the first poem in thirty-one syllables, through the great period of *Man'yōshū* poetry, to the recent past. The preface writers insisted that the poets of the past—specifically, those of the *Man'yōshū*—had no equals in modern times. Even the Six Immortals of Poetry of the ninth century were dismissed with a sentence or two characterizing their faults. The poetry of Ono no Komachi was described in these terms: "Her poetry is beautiful but weak, like an ailing woman wearing cosmetics."[10] Of Ōtomo no Kuronushi it was stated: "His style is extremely crude, as though a peasant were resting in front of a flowering tree."[11] Contemporary poetry fared even worse: not a single poet of the recent past was praised, and the compilers even expressed fear that the modern poems they had included might expose them to ridicule. But we should not accept at face value such examples of editorial modesty. In spite of their protestations, the preface writers were not only sensible of the great honor they had received in being asked by the emperor to edit a collection of waka but confident that the poems they had chosen were of eternal value. "Hitomaro is dead, but poetry lives," Tsurayuki declared, and he prophesied, "Time may pass and circumstances may change, pleasures and sorrows may succeed one another, but these poems will endure."[12]

Compilation of the Collection

The four compilers of the *Kokinshū* were all of modest court rank. Ki no Tsurayuki and Ki no Tomonori both belonged to the once-illustrious Ki family. At the beginning of the Heian period it had provided empresses to the court, but it had lost influence with the rise of the Fujiwara family. Mibu no Tadamine and Ōshikōchi no Mitsune were of even less distinguished families. The humble ranks of the compilers, when compared to those of the official history *Sandai Jitsuroku* (True Records of Three Reigns), the *Engishiki* (Institutes of the Engi Period), and other works in Chinese sponsored about the same time by the court, may reflect a lingering attitude of condescension toward the waka.[13]

All four compilers had been represented in the poem competitions of 892 and 893, when Tsurayuki was little more than twenty years old. Perhaps the scarcity of capable waka poets (after a century of official neglect of the form) accounted for the participation of men of minor court rank in these gatherings. As greater importance came to be attached to waka composition, competent poets enjoyed new favor at the court. Tomonori was over forty at the time he received his first court office, but his poetic skill enabled him to associate with such powerful statesmen as Fujiwara no Tokihira. After the abdication of the Emperor Uda in 898, Tokihira began to show active interest in promoting a revival of the waka, and staged poetry gatherings at his residence where the future compilers of the *Kokinshū* joined in poetic competition with members of the highest nobility.[14]

The selection of the compilers of the *Kokinshū* was probably made four or five years before its completion. The *Kokinshū* scholar Murase Toshio believed that Tokihira's approval was the paramount factor behind the final choice of compilers.[15] Although Tokihira (also known as Shihei) is now remembered mainly for his plotting against Sugawara no Michizane, he not only was a competent administrator but also was capable of recognizing poetic talent.

The date of the presentation of the completed text of the *Kokinshū* to the Emperor Daigo is traditionally given as 905. Scholars as far back as Fujiwara no Kiyosuke (1104–1177) suggested, in view of ambiguity in the wording of the Japanese preface,[16] that the collection, though ordered in that year, was not presented until some later date; but an examination of the evidence leads to the conclusion, not accepted by everyone, that 905 was the year of both the completion of the selection of poems and the formal presentation to the emperor.

The circumstances of the compilation are not known, but it has been conjectured, on the basis of procedures followed when compiling later anthologies, that the work was done in secret.[17] The editors apparently chose for inclusion mainly works that had appeared in private collections of poetry by both recognized and unknown poets of the previous century. Poems by 127 poets were included, 70 of them represented by only one poem, and another 22 by only two. Not surprisingly (considering the large number of poems by Ōtomo no Yakamochi in the *Man'yōshū*), the best-represented poets were the compilers themselves—Tsurayuki with 102 poems, Mitsune with 60, Tomonori with 46, and Tadamine with 35.[18] Although the Japanese preface stated that the policy was to exclude poems that had already appeared in the *Man'yōshū*, fifteen of these poems nevertheless found their way into the collection, possibly because they were thought of as folk songs of an indeterminate period.

It was naturally out of the question to include in the *Kokinshū* poems by persons of humble station, of the kind prominent in the *Man'yōshū*, though some of the unusually large number of anonymous poems may in fact have been by commoners. Most of the poems by known authors were by members of the lower ranks of the aristocracy.[19] Regardless of the ranks of the contributors, the poetry was selected to display the degree of sophistication that the waka had attained during the brief period since the form was revived twenty or thirty years before.

Neither in the prefaces nor elsewhere in the collection was the claim made (as in the prefaces to ninth-century collections of kanshi) that poetry helped to promote good government. Tsurayuki declared that he and his colleagues had chosen not only seasonal poems but poems that prayed that the emperor would enjoy "the lifespan of the crane and the tortoise," and other poems that prayed the gods of travel to preserve travelers from harm.[20] No mention was made of poems of courtship, though they are far more numerous than poems of prayer. Perhaps the compilers were somewhat embarrassed by the large number of love poems, a category that had not been recognized by the Chinese.

It is not known what principles of selection (other than conspicuous excellence) guided the compilers. Probably they started off with the plan of putting together an anthology in twenty books, like the *Man'yōshū* or the *Keikokushū*. Perhaps (as Tsurayuki's preface states) they also originally intended to include no more than a thousand poems, but another hundred or so were added in the course of compilation. The next step was to decide the contents of each of the twenty books and their order.

Arrangement of the Poems

Seasonal poems make up the first six of the twenty books of the *Kokinshū*. The placing of seasonal poetry at the head of the collection may have been in keeping with the example of the *Shinsen Man'yōshū*, but otherwise reflected the importance given to the seasons at poetry competitions at the court. Poems describing the seasons (and especially the flowers and birds associated with each) had not figured prominently in the *Man'yōshū*; it was only with the poem competitions and the *Shinsen Man'yōshū* of the late ninth century that seasonal poetry acquired special importance, and with the *Kokinshū* this became definitive. A large proportion of the waka composed at this time and during the next millennium would describe the seasons, either directly or as revealed by some characteristic such as mist, haze, fog, and so on. In time, some seasonal words became arbitrary: the moon, unless qualified by some other seasonal word, always referred to the autumn moon, when its light was most appreciated.

The Japanese have sometimes explained their absorption with the seasons in terms of the distinctive nature of each of the four seasons in Japan. This explanation implies that in other countries the seasons are less clearly differentiated, a claim that might be difficult to prove. Probably it is wisest not to search for reasons, but to content oneself with noting that Japanese poets have been unusually responsive to the seasons.

Two books each were devoted to spring and autumn poetry, but only one each to summer and winter. In terms of the number of poems, the disproportion is even greater: the *Kokinshū* contains 145 autumn poems as against only 34 summer poems. This marked preference among the seasons may reflect the peculiarities of the climate of the capital—the modern Kyoto—where spring and autumn are delectable, but the summers stifling and the winters bitterly cold. Perhaps the choice of birds and flowers mentioned in the poems also was influenced by the flora and fauna of Kyoto. The preferences of the capital have always spread to other regions, and even poets who lived where a hototogisu was never heard dutifully mentioned this bird in their summer poems.

The six books of seasonal poems are followed by one each of congratulatory, parting, travel, and *butsumei* (names of things) poems. The latter, though written in various moods on different subjects, all contain some word concealed in the text. In the following poem by Mibu no Tadamine (*Kokinshū* 462), the place-name *Katano* is concealed:

natsukusa no	Like the marsh water,
ue wa shigereru	Covered with a thick growth
numamizu no	Of summer grasses
yuku kata no *naki*	That leaves it nowhere to go
wa ga kokoro kana[21]	So too is my choked-up heart.

Apart from the ingenuity of fitting Katano into the text, the poem is gloomy and not at all in the self-consciously droll manner we might expect of a poem fashioned around a pun. Perhaps, however, the "hidden word" poems were private and the concealed word had a special meaning for one person. This might explain why the book of butsumei poems immediately precedes the five books of love poetry, the most private of the *Kokinshū* poems.

The *Kokinshū* contains 360 love poems, the largest number in any category. The prominence given to love poetry reflects its importance during the "dark age" of poetry in the Japanese language. However, the fact that the love poetry was placed in the second half of the collection suggests that the compilers were anxious to avoid giving the impression that the main function of the waka was to serve as an adjunct to lovemaking.

The love poems are followed by a book of poems of mourning, two books of miscellaneous poems (that is, poems that are neither seasonal nor related to love), a book of poems in forms other than the waka (including some chōka and sedōka, as well as a selection of *haikai*, or comic poetry), and finally a book of waka associated with palace ceremonies. The last two books contain such a scrappy assortment of materials that they create the impression of having been appended mainly to fill out the intended twenty books.[22]

The assignment of the poems to the different books was in many ways subjective and even arbitrary; the editors had to decide, for example, whether a love poem that mentions the flower of a certain season should be classified as a love or seasonal poem. A whole book was devoted to travel poems, although there were only sixteen poems in this category. The compilers evidently believed that poems composed on a journey formed a distinctive class of waka, even though there were just a few of merit.

Once the poems had been assigned to the various books, the compilers arranged the poems within each book. They could have followed the precedent of the *Kaifūsō* and arranged the poems in descending order of rank of the authors, or they could have followed the *Man'yōshū* in largely disregarding order of rank and instead clustering together poems by the same author. Instead, the compilers elected to arrange the poems in terms of temporal progression. In the case of spring poems, those that described the early haze over the landscape appeared first, followed by poems on the plum blossoms, then on cherry blossoms (in the bud, in full glory, and finally scattering). A similar pattern can be traced in other seasonal poetry, and in the love poems the first tremors of love were followed by poems describing hidden love, the anguish of a love affair, and lastly, resignation over the end of the affair.

Many poems are provided with introductions or followed by notes. The introductions usually describe the circumstances that occasioned the poems, as in an unusually detailed example:

> Poem respectfully composed after the retired emperor had written a poem on the subject of a picture on a screen at the Teiji Palace that shows a traveler reining in his horse and pausing under a tree from which red leaves fall as he prepares to cross a river.[23]

In other instances the preface makes clear some point in the waka that might puzzle readers. For example, the following poem by the priest Sosei does not specify what kind of flowers he has in mind:

hana chirasu	Does anyone know
kaze no yadori wa	The residence of the wind
tare ka shiru	That scatters the blossoms?
ware ni oshie yo	Anyone who knows, tell me!
yukite uramin[24]	I will go there and complain.

In later court anthologies the word *hana* (flowers) alone designated cherry blossoms, but in the *Kokinshū* it might designate any flower. That, no doubt, is why the preface to this poem plainly states, "Composed on seeing scattered cherry blossoms."[25]

The appended notes (*sachū*) are generally brief, along the lines of: "Some say that this poem was composed by the Nara emperor."[26] However, an exceptionally long and interesting note follows the poem composed by Abe no Nakamaro. The poem bears the prefatory note: "Composed while gazing at the moon in China." The appended note states, "It is related of this poem, 'A long time ago, Nakamaro was sent to China to study. After he had spent many years there, he was not allowed to return home, but on one occasion, when an ambassador arrived from Japan, Nakamaro joined his party, hoping to return to Japan together with the ambassador. At a place on the coast called Mingchou, the Chinese offered a farewell banquet. That night, Nakamaro, gazing at the moon, which had risen most beautifully, composed this poem.' "[27] The prefaces and notes seem to have been considered by the compilers to be integral parts of the poems, a tradition that went back to the *Man'yōshū*.

Poetic Diction of the *Kokinshū*

The themes of the *Kokinshū* poets were those of a court of great refinement. The poets sought perfection in the language, the order of the words, the music of the successive syllables, even more perhaps than in the meaning of the poems.[28] Many subjects could not be treated because they were considered to be unattractive, but the *Kokinshū* poets did not feel frustrated. It was only in certain moods, especially those mentioned in the Japanese preface, that they felt impelled to express themselves in poetry, and none of their themes required a muse of fire.

The conventions of life at the court favored artificiality and even insincerity in poetic composition. Perhaps, as some *Man'yōshū* scholars have suggested, there was artificiality in that collection, too, despite its reputation for plainspoken sentiments; but the memorable poems persuade us of their sincerity. The composition of poetry to assigned topics, as on the occasion of an uta-awase, inevitably involved some insincerity; poets had to compose on these topics whether or not they were of personal relevance. Similar conditions seem to have governed the composition of many poems in the *Kokinshū*, as a love poem by the priest Sosei suggests:

ima kon to	"I'll be coming soon"
iishi bakari ni	You said, and all because of that

nagatsuki no	I waited until
ariake no tsuki wo	The moon at dawning appeared,
machiidetsuru kana[29]	The longest month of the year.

Not only would it be highly inappropriate in real life for a priest to write a love poem, but this one was written in the persona of a woman.[30] The poem is nonetheless charming and deserves its popularity.

Perhaps none of the poems composed by Ki no Tsurayuki and his generation were sincere in the manner that *Man'yōshū* poetry or the poems of Narihira and Komachi strike us as being sincere. The love poetry no longer seems to have formed a part of real courtship, but rather restated variations on the theme of the impossibility of enjoying happiness in love.[31] Such poems most often describe the unresponsiveness of the beloved, the failure of the beloved to pay a visit, the difficulty of meeting the beloved except in dreams, the acceptance of death as the only resolution to an unhappy affair.[32] Rarely is there a suggestion of the joys of love; the poets apparently did not consider that joy could inspire poetry. The narrowness of the court society provided another theme, the fear of gossip.[33] The imagery in the love poems is often lachrymose, whether in the many mentions of tears (or dew, by now a hackneyed metaphor) or in the comparison of the poet's tears to the surge of a river of tears or even to an ocean of tears.[34] The pathetic fallacy is much in evidence: birds, deer, insects, and even plants join in the sufferings of the poet.[35]

The images in *Kokinshū* poetry, whether seasonal, amorous, or miscellaneous, tended to be repeated again and again. There are many poems on cherry blossoms at all stages of their flowering, but few or none on other flowers (such as the chrysanthemum) that would inspire later poets.[36] Poets usually reacted more to other poets' poems than to personal experiences. Even if a poet happened to be deeply moved, say, by the beauty of peach blossoms, he was likely to describe instead in his poetry the clouds of white cherry blossoms, if only because peach blossoms had rarely figured in the poetry of his predecessors. Again, the moon was always described in the *Kokinshū* in terms of its brightness, not in terms of misty nights nor of the moon on nights when it showed itself only once in a while from beyond the clouds.[37]

Probably the compilers rejected poems that contained unexpected imagery or employed words that did not meet their standards of good taste. Their choices were so exact and the *Kokinshū* so admired that they succeeded in establishing a poetic diction—some two thousand words in all—waka poets would observe for the next thousand years with only minor additions. Words that did not appear in the *Kokinshū* were frowned on as neologisms, and the associations of most flowers, trees, and birds were permanently established.

For all the adulation the *Kokinshū* poets offered to Chinese poetry, they did not seek to expand their poetic vocabulary by borrowing words of Chinese origin. Instead, they attempted to make each poem perfect, considering every syllable in terms of syntax and sound as well as of meaning. It has been argued[38] that the subject, predicate, modifiers, and modified words are clearer in the *Kokinshū* than in any later work of poetry or prose, but the reader must be extremely attentive: the change of a single particle may alter the meaning of an entire work, as the following much-admired poem by Tsurayuki will suggest:

musubu te no	Unsatisfied as
shizuku ni nigoru	Someone who scoops water from
yama no i no	A spring so shallow
akade mo hito wo	It clouds with drops from her hands—
wakarenuru kana[39]	She went away and left me.

The poet observes a woman scooping water from a stream so shallow that her hands disturb the bottom and drops from her hands cloud the water. She goes away unsatisfied, not having been able to get enough to drink; the poet is also unsatisfied because they have parted after so little time together.[40] Although the translation specifies "her hands" and "she went away," the original text does not state from whose hands the water dripped, nor who went away. I have followed the interpretation of Okumura Tsuneya, who was convinced that if one reads the *Kokinshū* poems carefully they become absolutely clear. For example, Tsurayuki's use of the particle *wo* instead of *ni* (as one would expect) after the word *hito* plainly indicated who had left whom. Examining many texts of the period, Okumura had discovered that whenever *wo* was used in such cases, it always meant that it was the other person who went away, not the speaker. The subject of this poem (the person who scooped up water) must also be the person who went away. Okumura's interpretation has not been adopted by every commentator, an indication that perhaps the poem is not so clear, but it suggests the extreme care poets took in their choice of words.[41]

The prestige of the *Kokinshū* was so great in later centuries that poets who lived long afterward—and under quite different conditions from those of the Heian court—felt obliged to restrict themselves to the *Kokinshū* vocabulary. One might suppose that poets of, say, the eighteenth century would have fretted over such restrictions, but in fact, most of them not only worshiped the *Kokinshū* but had no desire to deviate from its themes. Maple leaves were as lovely in the eighteenth century as in the tenth, and the colors they turned with the first frost gave just as much pleasure even if the poet lived in Edo, a city that did not exist in Tsurayuki's time, and was a *chōnin* (townsman), a class that Tsurayuki would not have believed capable of poetic utterance. If a chōnin poet had wished to describe convincingly in the waka his daily life, he would certainly have had to violate the standard poetic diction, which lacked words for the food he ate, the clothes he wore, the tobacco he smoked, the business in which he was engaged, and the licensed quarter which he sometimes visited. Of course, if a chōnin found the poetic diction of the *Kokinshū* confining, he could write haiku or kanshi instead, neither bound by the old vocabulary; but most waka poets were content to treat eternal themes in eternal languge.

Poetic Techniques of the *Kokinshū*

Tsurayuki's preface mentioned that poets were moved to compose waka not only on seeing the sights of nature but by the signs of old age reflected in their looking glasses. Tsurayuki wrote a poem inspired by this revelation:

ubatama no	Is it possible
wa ga kurokami ya	My hair that was once jet black
kawaruran	Has changed so much?
kagami no kage ni	Reflected in the looking glass
fureru shirayuki[42]	A recent fall of white snow.

The snow was, of course, a metaphor for white hair. Seeing the snow in the mirror, like seeing cherry blossoms as they fell, was not merely an act of observation, but led to a revelation of the havoc wrought by time. The falling blossoms, like the decay in his own appearance, revealed to the poet his mortality, the loss of the joys of youth. The indirectness of this statement is typical of the *Kokinshū*, and its melancholy note is sounded again and again in other poems, even those with conventionally pretty imagery.

Despite the shortness of the *Kokinshū* poems and the restrictions on the vocabulary, the existence of meanings on more than one level gave richness to the poetry. In the following poem by Tsurayuki a makurakotoba and a kakekotoba impart complexity:

hatsukari no	The early wild geese
naki koso watare	Cry as they cross overhead.
yo no naka no	They are sorrowful
hito no kokoro no	Because there is in this world
aki shi ukereba[43]	Autumn in the hearts of men.

This translation gives only part of the meaning of the poem. The first wild geese, as they head south, keep up their unending cries of grief because of the sadness of autumn; but "cry" refers also to the poet, who weeps at the thought that someone—probably the woman he loves—has grown weary (*akishi*) of him; it is the autumn of their love. Or perhaps he has discovered boredom in his own heart. *Hatsukari* (the first wild geese) was a makurakotoba that modified *naki*; *naki* refers here both to the cries of the wild geese and to the poet's weeping; *hito* is not merely "person" but also the beloved; *aki* is both "autumn" and "satiety" or "weariness."

The obliqueness of expression in the *Kokinshū* was traced by Konishi Jin'ichi to the poetry in *Wen Hsüan* and other Six Dynasties collections. Some of the techniques borrowed by the *Kokinshū* poets from the Chinese poets of those times may seem artificial, especially the many examples of feigned ignorance as to whether mountains are not clouds or cherry blossoms not snow, as in this poem by Ki no Tomonori:

mi Yoshino no	In fair Yoshino,
yamabe ni sakeru	Blossoming in the mountains.
sakurabana	Were cherry flowers.
yuki ka to nomi zo	I thought that they must be snow
ayamatarekeru[44]	But how mistaken I was!

On first reading one may be struck by the improbability of anyone really confusing even masses of cherry blossoms for snow, especially at Yoshino, famed for its cherry blossoms. However, Okumura Tsuneya noted that it was not until the age of the *Shin Kokinshū* that Yoshino acquired its reputation as a place to admire cherry blossoms; in the time of the *Kokinshū* it was known above all for its deep falls of snow.[45] This gives greater plausibility to this particular example of *mitate*, taking one thing for another. Other examples of mitate are not merely more convincing but contribute to the beauty of poems like this one by Fujiwara no Okikaze:

shiranami no	Autumn leaves floating
aki no konoha no	On the white-crested waters:
ukaberu wo	I thought they might be
ama no nagaseru	Boats like those fishermen ply,
fune ka to zo miru[46]	Adrift on the river waves.

Of course, the difference in scale between leaves and fishing boats is too great for the poet *really* to have been deceived; but for a moment the comparison flashed into his head, and he captured that moment exquisitely.

The device of mitate was convincingly traced back to the Six Dynasties poets by Konishi,[47] but other scholars have found Japanese sources, notably in certain poems of the *Man'yōshū*. In these the first part consists of observations by the poet, and the remainder the inferences drawn from those observations.[48] Some anonymous poems in the *Kokinshū* follow this pattern, including:

yū sareba	When evening arrives
koromode samushi	The cold penetrates my sleeves.
mi Yoshino no	At fair Yoshino,
Yoshino no yama ni	In the Yoshino Mountains,
mi yuki fururashi[49]	Surely it must be snowing.

It was a relatively short step from experiencing the cold and imagining it must be snowing in Yoshino (an even colder place) to the device of mitate, seeing something and imagining it is something else.

Mitate was only one of many technical devices used by the *Kokinshū* poets that would recur in later Japanese literature. The engo and kakekotoba, already in use by the ninth-century poets,[50] were given greater authority in the *Kokinshū* as a technique of expanding the meaning. An anonymous poem contains both engo and kakekotoba. It is technically highly complex, yet read in the original it flows effortlessly. The poem bears the note, "Long ago a woman's husband ceased to visit her. She went to the Mitsu Temple in Naniwa where she became a nun. She composed this poem which she sent to her husband."

ware wo kimi	Because you left me
Naniwa no ura ni	At the Bay of Naniwa
arishikaba	Where fishermen cut
ukime wo mitsu no	Weeds that float in the water,
ama to nariniki[51]	I have become a nun at Mitsu.

The poem is filled with word-play. The noun *ura*, meaning a "bay," with *Naniwa no ura* means "the Bay of Naniwa," but it is used as a kakekotoba, suggesting the verb *uramu*, "to resent," a meaning necessary in order to fill out the meaning of the first line: "because you resented [or bore ill will toward] me." The noun *ukime* means "floating seaweed," but (by a pun) also means "painful experience." Mitsu was the name of a temple near Naniwa, but also meant "harbor," continuing the marine engo, and with *ukime* it means "to have a painful experience." *Ama* means both "fisherman" and "nun," the context usually determining which. The engo in the poem are *Naniwa, ura, ukime, mitsu,* and *ama*, all words referring to fishermen who gather seaweed in Naniwa Bay. A second set of engo, consisting of *ura, ukime, mitsu,* and *ama* relates to the painful experience that has induced the woman to forsake the world and become a nun at the Mitsu Temple.

The technical virtuosity in such a poem may seem obtrusive, even if one admires the skill, but the use of engo and kakekotoba can be justified in terms of the unconscious associations of words.[52] Few poems are quite as complicated as this example, but engo and kakekotoba occur in many *Kokinshū* poems. Such virtuosity would become a major cause of modern poets' dissatisfaction with the *Kokinshū*; they doubted poems so contrived could contain emotional truth.

Another feature of the *Kokinshū* poetry that deserves attention is the use of personification. Perhaps the closeness with which the poets empathized with the flowers and birds they described induced them to write as if these flowers and birds could be addressed, reasoned with, persuaded not to fall or not to sing, in order to spare the poet anguish. Scholars have established a contrast between emotional and intellectual personification,[53] the latter usually inspired by Chinese examples in the *Wen Hsüan* and elsewhere; but it is difficult to find a poem where the personification is purely emotional or purely intellectual. The *Kokinshū* poets attributed human characteristics even to the sound of the wind or the murmur of a mountain stream, but personification was most common with reference to birds and beasts.[54] The following poem by Ki no Tomonori is typical:

yo ya kuraki	Is the night so dark?
michi ya madoeru	Or has it wandered on its way?
hototogisu	The hototogisu,
wa ga yado wo shimo	Reluctant to leave my house,
sugigate ni naku[55]	Sings as it circles the sky.

Personification occurs also when the poet addresses flowers as if they could understand his words, as in this poem by Ki no Tsurayuki:

kotoshi yori	You cherry blossoms
haru shirisomuru	Who this year for the first time
sakurabana	Have learned what spring is,
chiru to iu koto wo	Do not learn from the others
narawazaranan[56]	What makes the blossoms scatter.

Personification could be used to convey the poet's feelings by attributing them to another creature, as in the waka by Ōshikōchi no Mitsune entitled "On Hearing the Wild Geese Cry":

uki koto wo	As one unhappy
omoitsuranete	Memory succeeds the next,
karigane no	The chains of wild geese
naki koso watare	Cry out as they cross the sky
aki no yona yona[57]	Night after night in autumn.

Sometimes personification intrudes on the world of reality as in this anonymous poem:

nakiwataru	Are those the tears shed
kari no namida ya	By the wild geese crying out
ochitsuran	As they cross the sky?
mono omou yado no	In this garden, where I brood,
hagi no ue no tsuyu[58]	Dew on the clover blossoms.

In this poem personification intensifies the expression of the poet's emotions: the dewdrops on flowers in the garden look like tears that could only have come from above, perhaps from the wild geese in the autumn sky. Poems addressed to cherry blossoms were also at times melancholy, as in this example by the priest Sōku:

iza sakura	Yes, cherry blossoms,
ware mo chirinan	I will fall along with you!
hito sakari	When once brief glory
arinaba hito ni	Is past, better thus than let
ukime mienan[59]	Others see one's ugliness.

The ideal of perishing in the prime of one's life would be especially cherished by warriors, but courtiers of this time normally lamented the speed with which cherry blossoms (as opposed to, say, plum blossoms) scattered after only a few days of glory. This poetic conceit confirmed the intimate connections between the *Kokinshū* poets and their natural surroundings.

Topics and Themes of Poetic Composition

As we have seen, the poetry in the *Kokinshū* owed much to the Chinese poetry of the Six Dynasties. Not only were many poetic images taken over bodily, but the Chinese practice of composing poems on assigned topics, first observed in Japan by participants in the uta-awase competitions, was also followed by the *Kokinshū* poets, though the practice was not known to the *Man'yōshū* poets.[60] Waka on Chinese topics were apparently composed as early as 898, on the occasion of the visit of the Emperor Uda to Miyadaki. These poems have been lost, but poems composed to commemorate an imperial excursion to the Ōi River in 907 are still extant.[61] The Chinese topic, stated at the head of each poem, was generally along the lines of "gazing at the autumn hills," or "cranes standing on the riverside." The anthology *Kokin Waka Rokujō* (Six Volumes of Japanese Poetry, Old and New), compiled toward the end of the tenth century, contains some 4,370 poems by 193 poets, classified according to 517 topics. It was probably conceived along the lines of a similar compendium edited by Po Chü-i.[62] The practice of composing in accordance with fixed topics, some of them used repeatedly over the years, would inhibit the creation of entirely new poems, but at the time of the *Kokinshū* the topics were still relatively fresh and capable of inspiring graceful compositions.[63]

In a similar manner, the themes of the *Kokinshū* poems would be borrowed by later poets who would change the imagery or emphasis, sometimes very slightly, in attempts to attain the essence of the theme. The practice of *honka-dori*, borrowing from an original poem, became general in the centuries after the compilation of the *Kokinshū*. Borrowing one or more lines of a *Kokinshū* poem was a mark of the later poet's respect for the *Kokinshū* and of his desire to participate in the never-ending search for poetic perfection. A poem without ancestry in the *Kokinshū* was considered to lack resonance.[64] The influence of the *Kokinshū* style remained so pervasive, even as late as the beginning of the twentieth century, that many waka composed centuries afterward could have been slipped into the text of the *Kokinshū* without clashing.

An ability to compose waka on a prescribed topic became an indispensable accomplishment of members of the court, as the uta-awase developed from pleasant diversions into stately court functions. The popularity of folding screens painted with Japanese-style pictures (*Yamato-e*) created a demand for poems that could be inscribed on the screens, next to the scenes portrayed. The *Kokinshū* includes, for example, three waka (one by Tsurayuki and two by the priest Sosei) composed for the screen that was offered to Prince Motoyasu on his seventieth birthday.[65] The depicted scenes sometimes directly inspired the poems, but at other times a screen poem merely touched on the painting and was mainly an expression of congratulations or something similar. Screen paintings fostered the growth of the *utamakura*, places that inspire poetry, and in some cases resulted in *rensaku*, sequences of poems that continued from one panel of a screen to the next.

Poems on prescribed topics or on the scenes depicted on screens were often beautiful but rarely personal. The *Kokinshū* poets seldom attempted to be personal, except perhaps in the love poetry, but even that was usually written only about conventionally prescribed moments in the course of an affair, and tended to consist of variations on established themes and expressions. For example, the pun on *aki* (autumn) and *aki* (satiety) occurred again and again, often as a woman poet detected signs of the lover's loss of interest, presaging a long autumn of loneliness. The dread that an affair might be discovered, another familiar topic of love poetry, was often suggested by the word *hitome* (people's eyes) or by *mirume*, the name of a kind of seaweed but also, by a pun, "watching eyes." A list of conventional expressions could be prolonged to such lengths as to make one doubt that freshness could be achieved in the love poetry, but this was a test that the *Kokinshū* poets willingly underwent.

Stereotyped phrases and themes occur in many *Kokinshū* poems, especially by known authors. The anonymous poems, on the other hand, are often appealingly direct and fresh. These examples may suffice to suggest their characteristics:

tane shi areba
iwa ni mo matsu wa
oinikeri
koi wo shi koiba
awarazame ya mo[66]

Because there was a seed
A pine has grown even here,
On these barren rocks.
If we really love our love,
What can keep us from meeting?

kome ya to wa
omou mono kara
higurashi no
naku yūgure wa
tachimataretsutsu[67]

Although I wonder
If he really will be coming,
In the twilight hour
When the evening locusts call
I stand by the gate and wait.

The expression of such poems is more appealing to most modern readers than the elegance of language and intricate poetic devices of more typical *Kokinshū* poetry, but the latter would form the mainstream of Japanese tradition.

The Poetry of Ki no Tsurayuki

The most important of the *Kokinshū* poets was undoubtedly Ki no Tsurayuki. His views on the nature of Japanese poetry, stated in his preface to the *Kokinshū*, and the many poems he contributed to the collection would make him the most influential Japanese poet for a period of at least three hundred years—until the rise to prominence of Fujiwara Teika—and the *Kokinshū* would form part of the basic education of every Japanese. His poems are seldom startling, but that is mainly because they later became a part of poetic orthodoxy and were so often imitated. In their own time, many were praised not because of their ingenuity but because of their freshness; and a poem that a reader might today pass over quickly as no more than a mildly interesting observation may contain unexpected complexities that account for its appeal. The following love poem bears the prefatory note, "Sent to someone in Yamato":

koenu ma wa
Yoshino no yama no
sakurabana
hitozute ni nomi
kikiwataru ka na

Until I go there,
I must continue merely
to hear from others
word of the cherry blossoms
in the hills of Yoshino.[68]

This translation, though accurate and graceful, conveys little of what a Japanese reader would have found in the poem. The note says the poem was sent to someone (*hito*) who lived in Yamato, but it would have been clear to readers that the person was a woman. The unexpressed meaning of the poem is that Tsurayuki is unable to go to Yamato and see the woman he loves; he can only hear about her from others' reports. But this interpretation does not cancel out the surface meaning: remembrances of the woman and of the cherry blossoms evoke a twofold yearning for beauty he cannot enjoy. The use of cherry blossoms as a symbol of beauty soon became the most hackneyed of Japanese tropes, but Tsurayuki's phrase was by no means hackneyed at this time; and it started, rather than repeated, the vogue.[69]

Of the surviving 1,614 waka by Tsurayuki, 539 were composed for inscription on screens. These poems by their very nature were public, and Tsurayuki can be thought of as a professional poet who could be counted on to produce a poem whenever one was needed. While such poems were not the place to display private emotions, sometimes the words yielded additional meanings that hinted at some unspoken sadness or joy. The screen poems and others composed in response to a request from the emperor or some great official were deliberately bland in tone, and were praised for their technical excellence rather than for individuality or depth of feeling. These are the poems by Tsurayuki most generously represented in the *Kokinshū*; to obtain a fairer picture of him as a poet one must also consult the poems in his private collection, *Tsurayuki Shū*,[70] or those found in later imperial collections. This highly personal poem is found in the *Gosenshū*, the next imperial collection after the *Kokinshū*:

ikade ware	There is something
hito ni mo towan	I would like to ask of you:
akatsuki no	What is it resembles
akanu wakare ya	A parting at break of day
nani ni nitari to[71]	Before one has had one's fill?

Perhaps Tsurayuki was embarrassed to include this poem, obviously addressed to a woman with whom he had spent the night, in the *Kokinshū*, the collection he himself edited, but the editors of the *Gosenshū*, under no such constraint, "rescued" it. The poem is free of the obvious technical virtuosity of his most typical *Kokinshū* poems, though it does not openly express Tsurayuki's belief that nothing is more painful than parting at dawn. A poem closer to Tsurayuki's *Kokinshū* manner bears the prefatory note, "Composed and offered when I was commanded to offer a poem."

wa ga seko ga	I full my husband's
koromo harusame	Winter clothes, and every time
furu goto ni	The spring rains fall,
nobe no midori zo	The green of the meadows
iro masarikeru[72]	Turns an ever deeper hue.

This poem was considered, even during Tsurayuki's lifetime, to be one of his best works.[73] The first eight syllables of the poem are a *jo*, or preface, connected to the remainder of the poem by the kakekotoba on *haru*, meaning with what precedes to "full" the winter clothes before putting them away, and with what follows means the "spring" rain. On first reading the two halves of the poem may seem to be unrelated, but the poem was probably written in the persona of a young wife whose attention is drawn to the scenery each time a spring shower falls on the clothes she is beating. So interpreted, the poem has charm, and the masterful use of the kakekotoba earns it a place in the collection.

The momentary glimpse of someone who is not of the aristocracy is also refreshing and rare in a work written by members of the court about one another. But Tsurayuki's poem is not likely to have been composed after actual observation of a scene. The same is largely true of his poems on the seasons. The sensitivity of Tsurayuki and the other *Kokinshū* poets to the changes of the seasons was probably responsible for the extraordinary attention paid by Japanese poets during the next millennium to the sights and sounds of the four seasons, but the *Kokinshū* poets were responding not to nature itself but to a conceptualization. Nature was less important to these poets than the calendar. They knew the appropriate natural phenomena to describe in their poems not only with respect to the season but at every point within a given season. Some years, surely, the weather was unusual, even in the glorious Heian age. It must have happened at times that leaves, instead of turning a brilliant crimson, dropped brown and sodden from the autumn trees. This made no difference to the poets, who composed their seasonal poems as if nature was as sensitive to the calendar as they were. If a heavy fall of snow blocked their view of the supposedly springtime mountains, they were able to filter out the snow with the aid of the poetry composed by many predecessors and see the mists that *should* have been there.[74]

The artificiality of the poetry of Ki no Tsurayuki and most of his *Kokinshū* colleagues may make us equally suspicious of the sincerity of their observation of the seasons and their sighs of love. Their elaborate poetical devices—engo, kakekotoba, jo, and the like—also may make us doubt that anyone who really felt the emotions described would have been able to write in such an involuted manner. It might be argued that these stylistic features represented Japanese resistance to the kanshi: if they could not surpass the great Chinese poets in the grandeur of their themes, they could at least demonstrate what the Japanese language did better than the Chinese language: create an unbroken thread of beaten gold.[75]

The poems of Tsurayuki's late years—found in two later imperial collections, the *Gosenshū* and the *Shūishū*, rather than the *Kokinshū*—are more straightforward and compelling, perhaps because he had acquired greater familiarity with the *Man'yōshū*.[76] Two of his last poems are particularly moving. The first bears a prefatory note, "Written on the last day of the third month at the end of a letter in which I complained that someone had not visited me for a long time."

mata mo kon	I suppose you will
toki zo to omoedo	Visit me again sometime,
tanomarenu	But I can't depend
wa ga mi ni shi areba	On my body holding up—
oshiki haru kana[77]	That's what made the spring so sad.

Regret over the passing of the spring was a familiar trope, but it is given conviction here by the poet's doubt that he will ever see another spring. There was still one day left to the season, and he was urging his friend to come that day to share it with him. An appended note states that Tsurayuki died in the same year that he composed the poem.

Tsurayuki's farewell poem to the world, written just before he died, bears the prefatory note, "Feeling depressed and not my usual self, I composed this poem and sent it to Minamoto no Kintada. Of late my sickness has grown more severe."

te ni musubu	The world turned out
mizu ni yadoreru	To be as uncertain as
tsukikage no	The moonlight shining
aru ka naki ka no	In water cupped in my hands—
yo ni koso arikere[78]	Was it there, was it not there?

It is hard to doubt in reading these poems that Tsurayuki was a major poet. The circumstances of the composition of most of his poems—poetry competitions, poems to be inscribed on screens, poems to be offered at palace ceremonies—made it almost impossible for him to express what we want most to hear from him, the unmistakable accents of a particular human being. The public poems were sometimes miracles of deft composition, and occasionally Tsurayuki permitted a personal note to be heard, but in his last poems, when he no longer thought to please some potential patron and did not fear to cast an unseemly gloom over some palace festivity, he was able to communicate, without the aid of the linguistic devices in which he was so proficient, his exceptional poetic gifts. Tsurayuki's importance in the history of Japanese literature is first of all as the compiler of the *Kokinshū*, secondly as the author of *The Tosa Diary*, and only thirdly as a poet, though under other circumstances he might well have ranked among the two or three greatest masters of the waka.

The Other *Kokinshū* Poets

The most memorable poets of the *Kokinshū* are probably those like Ariwara no Narihira or Ono no Komachi who belonged to the previous generation of waka poets. Ise (877?–938?), the consort of the Emperor Uda, also left some notable poems in the passionate vein of Komachi. The first has a prefatory note, "Composed on seeing fires in the fields when she was going somewhere at a time when she was grieving over an unhappy love."

fuyugare no	If I could compare
nobe to wagami wo	My body to these fields
omoiseba	Withered by winter,
moete mo haru wo	I would hope, though I was burned,
matamashimono wo[79]	That spring might come again.

yume ni dani	Not even in dreams
miyu to wa mieji	Would I wish him to see me—
asa na asa na	My glass each morning
wa ga omokage ni	Reveals a face so wasted
hazuru mi nareba[80]	I turn away in shame.

The poems of Komachi, Ise, and other passionate women are certainly more striking than the screen poems, but they had far less influence on later poets. Other poets, even among those who are well represented in the *Kokinshū*, are remembered for their one poem included in *Hya-*

kunin Isshu (A Hundred Poems by a Hundred Poets), the celebrated thirteenth-century anthology.

One poem by Ki no Tomonori (d. 905?), chosen for the *Hyakunin Isshu*, stands out among his compositions because of its aural effects:

hisakata no	This perfectly still
hikari nodokeki	Spring day bathed in the soft light
haru no hi ni	From the vaulted sky,
shizu kokoro naku	Why do the cherry blossoms
hana no chiruran[81]	So restlessly scatter down?

It will be noted that four of the five lines begin with an *h*, and the fifth with *sh*. This surely was not accidental; each line seems to begin with a sigh. The first words *hisakata no* were a makurakotoba for *hikari*. It does not contribute much to the meaning, but the aural effect is particularly lovely.

Some scholars argue that the finest *Kokinshū* poet was Ōshikōchi no Mitsune (fl. 898–922). The exceptional number of his poems included in this and other imperial collections testifies to his reputation in his own day, but his official rank was extremely modest, strongly suggesting how impressed even rank-conscious members of the court were with his poetry. His poems, especially those on love, are often given complexity by the use of a full range of makurakotoba, engo, and kakekotoba, but his best poems are probably the simplest:

wa ga koi wa	My love
yukue mo shirazu	Knows no destination
hate mo nashi	And has no goal;
au wo kagiri to	I think only
omou bakari zo	Of meeting as its limit.[82]

natsumushi wo	Why did I suppose
nani ka iiken	Summer insects were foolish?
kokoro kara	Of my own free will
ware mo omoi ni	I, too, have plunged into the flame
moenubera nari[83]	And now must be seared by love.

This poem contains a kakekotoba on *omohi* (the traditional spelling of *omoi*, meaning love) and *hi*, or fire. It is not this ingenious use of language but the conviction the poem carries that earned it a place in the collection.

Conclusion

It is by no means difficult to find beautiful poems in the *Kokinshū*, though reading it through is not as satisfying an experience as reading through the *Man'yōshū* or the *Shin Kokinshū*, largely because of the great number of courtly poems of little emotional intensity. But the *Kokinshū* formed aristocratic taste during the Heian period and later, as we know from the innumerable variations on *Kokinshū* poems by later poets and from the equally numerous allusions to *Kokinshū* poems in works of fiction, from *The Tale of Genji* on down. The tastes of the aristocrats were passed on to the entire Japanese people. One would have to search for a Japanese who is indifferent to cherry blossoms and tinted autumn leaves, or who cannot see equivalents between the events of nature and those of human life.

Toward the end of the Japanese preface, Ki no Tsurayuki declared with unmistakable confidence, "We rejoice that we were born in this generation and that we were able to live in the era when this event [the compilation of the *Kokinshū*] took place.... Those of future times who know poetry and who understand the heart of things will look up to old poetry as they look up to the moon in the great sky, but will they not also cherish our poems?"[84]

The self-assurance manifested by Tsurayuki was richly merited, but perhaps the compilers of the *Kokinshū* were overly successful. The poetic vocabulary that they handled so skillfully was not merely a legacy to future generations but a Procrustean bed on which poems would be stretched; and any poem whose vocabulary or themes did not meet its measurements would be mercilessly rejected. Nevertheless, the best of the poets of the later collections, building on the achievements of the *Kokinshū* poets, would be able to create poetry as representative of their age as the *Kokinshū* was of the early Heian period.

The *Kokinshū* style was evolved by a relatively small number of people, the members of the Japanese court at a particularly brilliant period. The courtiers spent their days largely in dealing with court business—matters of administration, precedence, and decorum. Promotion was their most ardent wish, and some perfected their poetry in the hopes that it might enable them to obtain superior rank. Only a few were truly talented as poets, but many more were skillful enough to participate in an uta-awase and to have one of their poems included in an imperial anthology. Even at their least impressive, the *Kokinshū* poems have grace, clarity of diction, and elegance of tone that would be the object of emulation of countless later poets.

Notes

1. Murase Toshio in *Kokinshū no Kiban to Shūhen*, p. 68, linked the compilation of the *Kokinshū* with the efforts of the youthful Emperor Daigo to increase imperial prestige, otherwise revealed by the compilation of the history *Sandai Jitsuroku* in 901, the prohibition on manors (*shōen*) the following year, the commencement of lectures on the *Nihon Shoki* in 904, and the command to compile the *Engishiki* and *Engikaku* in 905. These undertakings reflect Daigo's absorption with the past as well as his desire to restore the dignity the throne had earlier enjoyed.
2. *Koto no ha*, which can be translated simply as "words," means literally "leaves of words," and here continues the metaphor of seeds growing into the leaves of a plant.
3. Text in Okumura Tsuneya, *Kokin Waka Shū*, p. 11.
4. Notably the major preface to the *Shih Ching*, usually ascribed to a disciple of Confucius named Pu Shang (also known as Tzu-hsia), though many scholars now believe it was written by Wei Hung of the first century A.D. See James J. Y. Liu, *Chinese Theories of Literature*, p. 64. For a study specifically of the influence of Chinese literary theory on the prefaces to the *Kokinshū*, see John Timothy Wixted's essay "Chinese Influences on the *Kokinshū* Prefaces" in Laurel Rasplica Rodd, *Kokinshū*, pp. 387–400. But one should bear in mind also the strictures of Okumura, *Kokin*, pp. 404–6, who questioned whether the Japanese meant the same things as the Chinese even when they used the same characters.
5. Translation by Liu in *Chinese Theories*, pp. 111–12.
6. This might seem to limit the possibilities of poetic expression, but a thousand years later the tanka poet Ishikawa Takuboku would write, "People say the tanka form is inconvenient because it's so short. I think its shortness is precisely what makes it convenient. . . . We are constantly being subjected to so many sensations, coming from both inside and outside ourselves, that we forget them soon after they occur, or even if we remember them for a little while, we end up by never once in our whole lifetimes ever expressing them because there is not enough content to sustain the thought. . . . Although a sensation may last only a second, it is a second that will never return again. I refuse to let such moments slip by." See *Dawn to the West*, II, pp. 43–44.
7. Okumura, *Kokin*, p. 18. I have used Okumura's text and notes throughout in making my translation. Other editions are given in the Bibliography. Other translations in Helen Craig McCullough, *Kokin Wakashū*, p. 5, and Rodd, *Kokinshū*, p. 41. The "snow and ripples" seen in the looking glass are, of course, white hair and wrinkles.
8. See Takizawa Sadao, "Kokinshū no Yōgo," in Nihon Bungaku Kenkyū

Shiryō Kankōkai (ed.), *Kokin Waka Shū*, pp. 295–96, for tables showing comparative numbers of nouns, verbs, and so on, in the *Man'yōshū*, *Kokinshū*, and *Shin Kokinshū*.

9. The six styles were those mentioned in the "Major Preface" to the *Shih Ching*. See Helen Craig McCullough, *Brocade by Night*, pp. 304–5. The meaninglessness of this division of the waka into six styles is discussed by Ōoka Makoto in *Ki no Tsurayuki*, pp. 111–12, 123–24.
10. Translation from Yoshimochi's Chinese preface by McCullough in *Kokin*, p. 258. For a Japanese version of the Chinese text, see Okumura, *Kokin*, p. 382.
11. *Ibid.*.
12. Translation by McCullough (*Kokin*, p. 8) from Tsurayuki's preface.
13. Murase, *Kokinshū*, p. 93.
14. *Ibid.*, p. 73. In a similar manner, talented renga poets, even if they were of the humblest birth, were accepted in court circles of the middle ages.
15. *Ibid.*, p. 79.
16. The Chinese preface by Ki no Yoshimochi is dated the fourth month of that year. The Japanese preface states only that in the fourth month of 905 the emperor commanded four men to present to him old poems that had not previously appeared in the *Man'yōshū*, as well as more recent poems, including works by the compilers themselves.
17. Murase, *Kokinshū*, p. 96.
18. Sosei, one of the Six Immortals of Poetry, was represented by thirty-six poems, but other Immortals even more famous than Sosei were less well represented—Narihira by thirty poems and Komachi by eighteen. See Murase, *Kokinshū*, pp. 100–1.
19. See Murase, *Kokinshū*, pp. 147–48, for a table by rank of both living and dead contributors to the *Kokinshū*.
20. For text see Okumura, *Kokin*, p. 25. Other translations by McCullough (*Kokin*, pp. 7–8) and Rodd (*Kokinshū*, p. 47.)
21. Other translations by McCullough, *Kokin*, p. 109, and Rodd, *Kokinshū*, p. 248. These two translations of the *Kokinshū* are both complete, but the styles of the translations are quite different. Although I shall not give references to these translations in subsequent notes, it should be remembered that they provide alternate versions to mine.
22. Murase, *Kokinshū*, p. 115.
23. Preface to *Kokinshū* 305 by Ōshikōchi no Mitsune. The retired emperor, who lived at the Teiji-no-in, was Uda.
24. *Kokinshū* 76.
25. See Okumura, *Kokin*, pp. 396–97, for a discussion of the use of prefaces to designate particular flowers.
26. Note to *Kokinshū* 283.
27. *Kokinshū* 406. For a translation of the poem itself, see below, p. 362.
28. Okumura, *Kokin*, p. 393.

29. *Kokinshū* 691. *Nagatsuki* is the poetic name of the ninth month; the name contains *naga*, or "long," because autumn nights were always said to be long.
30. Poems in the persona of a woman are found in Chinese poetry of the Six Dynasties. See McCullough, *Brocade*, p. 59, for one such poem. As far as I know, women did not write poems in the persona of a man.
31. See Masuda Shigeo, "Kokinshū no Chokusensei," p. 36, in Nihon Bungaku Kenkyū Shiryō Kankōkai (ed.), *Kokinshū*.
32. See poems 522, 520, 521, 540, 516, 552, 506 and 551 for a sequence approximating the one I have given.
33. See poems 629, 630, 631, 651, 653, 659, 673, and 674.
34. See poems 617, 618, 573, 511, and 595.
35. See poems 578, 579, 581, 582, 584, and 520.
36. Masuda, "Kokinshū," p. 38, pointed out that there is only one poem each on the *unohana* and *tokonatsu*, flowers often mentioned in later poetry.
37. Okumura (in *Kokin*, pp. 398–99) describes how a famous poem by Ōe no Chisato, a poet of the generation immediately before Tsurayuki's, was not included in the *Kokinshū* because it described the misty moon of a spring night. The poem was, however, chosen by the editors of the *Shin Kokinshū* because they preferred mistiness to an unclouded moon.
38. Notably by Okumura in *Kokin*, pp. 394–95.
39. *Kokinshū* 404. The poem also appears in *Shūishū* (poem 1228), with a somewhat different headnote. See Okumura, *Kokin*, pp. 391–95, for a discussion of the poem. Another translation by McCullough in *Kokin*, p. 96. McCullough takes the traveler mentioned in the headnote as the water scooper, and her translation concludes: "so, unsatisfied, I part from you." The poem was praised by Fujiwara Shunzei (in *Korai Fūteishō*) for its mastery of syntax and its simplicity.
40. The word *akade*, "unsatisfied," applies to both what precedes (the woman who does not get enough water to drink) and what follows (the man who has not yet had his fill of the company of the woman who leaves him). The first three lines of the poem have been interpreted as a *jo*, or preface, to the remainder of the poem, but unlike some prefaces, this one has a full meaning.
41. For the importance of the particles in *Kokinshū* poetry, see Ōoka, *Ki no Tsurayuki*, p. 103.
42. *Kokinshū* 460. This is a butsumei poem with the name Kamiyagawa "concealed" in the text.
43. Poem 804 in the *Kokinshū*. Text in Okumura, *Kokin*, p. 273. Another translation in McCullough, *Kokin*, p. 176. McCullough includes both meanings of *aki* in her translation. See also her comments in *Brocade*, p. 336.
44. *Kokinshū* 60.
45. Okumura, *Kokin*, p. 45.
46. *Kokinshū* 301. The poem does not specify the waves are in a river (rather

than the sea), but this can be inferred from the familiar image of red autumn leaves floating on the blue waters of a river.

47. Konishi Jin'ichi, "The Genesis of the *Kokinshū* Style," pp. 135–47.
48. See Ozawa Masao, *Kokinshū no Sekai*, pp. 114–16.
49. *Kokinshū* 317. Okumura, *Kokin*, p. 124, calls attention to the *Man'yōshū* poem (no. 2319) that has the same two opening lines, and suggests this is a response.
50. See above, pp. 229–230.
51. *Kokinshū* 973.
52. Similar examples of word associations are found, of course, in James Joyce's *Finnegans Wake*.
53. See Ozawa, *Kokinshū no Sekai*, pp. 104–13, for a discussion of personification. See also Andō Teruyo, "Kokinshū Kafū no Seiritsu ni oyobaseru Kanshibun no Eikyō ni tsuite," in Nihon Bungaku Kenkyū Shiryō Kankōkai (ed.), *Kokin Waka Shū*, pp. 183–85. Andō estimated that 130 *Kokinshū* poems employ the device of personification of natural objects.
54. Ozawa, *Kokinshū no Sekai*, p. 105. On p. 106 he gives a table of eighty-five examples of personification involving hototogisu, cherry blossoms, uguisu, wild geese, the wind, the *ominaeshi* (a kind of flower), haze, and *kirigirisu* (crickets), plus a listing of thirty-six instances of these natural objects being addressed by the poet.
55. *Kokinshū* 154.
56. *Kokinshū* 49.
57. *Kokinshū* 213.
58. *Kokinshū* 221.
59. *Kokinshū* 77. The priest's name is also pronounced Zōku.
60. Ozawa, *Kokinshū no Sekai,* p. 225.
61. See E. B. Ceadel, "The Ōi River Poems and Preface."
62. Ozawa, *Kokinshū no Sekai*, p. 236. For a brief discussion in English of *Kokin Waka Rokujō*, see Konishi Jin'ichi, *A History of Japanese Literature*, II, pp. 205–6.
63. The topics were generally stated in four Chinese characters. This remained true even of the later anthologies, but the topics became rather more complicated. One finds, for example, in the *Shin Kokinshū* such topics as "mist obscures the distant trees" (number 72) or "in a mountain hut to await the blossoms" (number 79).
64. The same was true of Chinese poetry as well; a poem that did not allude to a work by some great predecessor seemed insubstantial and flat.
65. Poems 352–54. During the festivities, the screen was placed behind the seat of the person whose birthday was being celebrated. The three poems are translated by McCullough in *Kokin*, p. 85.
66. *Kokinshū* 512. Okumura (*Kokin*, p. 190) takes the subject to be "I" rather than "we."
67. *Kokinshū* 772.

68. *Kokinshū* 588. Translation from McCullough, *Kokin*, p. 217.
69. According to Kaneko Motoomi (*Kokin Waka Shū Hyōshaku*, I, p. 621), this was the first poem ever to mention the cherry blossoms of Yoshino. Earlier poets had written about the clear-flowing rivers and the beauty of the mountains, or about the snow, but not about cherry blossoms.
70. The most convenient edition of *Tsurayuki Shū* is included in Hagitani Boku, *Tosa Nikki*, in Nihon Koten Zensho series.
71. *Gosenshū* 719. Text in Katagiri Yōichi, *Gosen Waka Shū*, p. 220. For a discussion of the poem, see Ōoka, *Ki no Tsurayuki*, pp. 57–59.
72. *Kokinshū* 25.
73. See Ōoka, *Ki no Tsurayuki*, p. 95.
74. See *ibid.*, pp. 171–74, for similar observations.
75. See the interesting observations by Yoshikawa Kōjirō, the great Japanese scholar of Chinese literature, considered by Ōoka in *ibid.*, pp. 109–11.
76. *Ibid.*, p. 194.
77. *Gosenshū* 146. See Katagiri, *Gosen*, p. 47.
78. *Shūishū* 1322. See Komachiya Teruhiko, *Shūi Waka Shū*, p. 387.
79. *Kokinshū* 791. Fields were burned to improve the fertility of the soil before a new crop was planted.
80. *Kokinshū* 681. Mention of "each morning" has suggested to some commentators that she and her lover have been spending their nights together, and that is why she looks bedraggled. I prefer the interpretation that she fears that, having grown old, she has lost her beauty. (See Kyūsojin Hitaku, *Kokin Waka Shū*, III, p. 197.)
81. *Kokinshū* 84. See Robert H. Brower and Earl Miner, *Japanese Court Poetry*, pp. 192–93, for further discussion of this poem. See also McCullough, *Brocade*, pp. 396–400, for a discussion of Tomonori.
82. *Kokinshū* 611. Translation, by Arthur Waley, is from my *Anthology*, p. 77. See McCullough's discussion of Mitsune in *Brocade*, pp. 401–8. See also Brower and Miner, *Japanese*, pp. 175–76. The most extensive discussion of Mitsune's poetry is found in Minegishi Yoshiaki, *Heian Jidai Waka Bungaku no Kenkyū*, pp. 11–149.
83. *Kokinshū* 600.
84. Text in Okumura, *Kokin*, p. 26. Other translations in McCullough, *Kokin*, p. 8, and Rodd, *Kokinshū*, p. 47.

Bibliography

Note: All Japanese books, except as otherwise noted, were published in Tokyo.

Abe Akio. *Nihon Bungaku Shi, Chūko-hen*. Hanawa Shobō, 1966.

Akiyama Ken. *Ōchō Bungaku Shi*. Tōkyō Daigaku Shuppankai, 1984.

Brower, Robert H., and Earl Miner. *Japanese Court Poetry*. Stanford, Calif.: Stanford University Press, 1961.

Ceadel, E. B. "The Ōi River Poems and Preface," *Asia Major* 3:1, 1952.

Hagitani Boku. *Tosa Nikki*, in Nihon Koten Zensho series. Asahi Shimbun Sha, 1950.

Kaneko Motoomi. *Kokin Waka Shū Hyōshaku*, 2 vols. Meiji Shoin, 1927.

Katagiri Yōichi. *Gosen Waka Shū*, in Shin Nihon Koten Bungaku Taikei series. Iwanami Shoten, 1990.

Keene, Donald. *Anthology of Japanese Literature*. New York: Grove Press, 1955.

Kojima Noriyuki and Arai Eizō. *Kokin Waka Shū*, in Shin Nihon Koten Bungaku Taikei series. Iwanami Shoten, 1989.

Komachiya Teruhiko. *Kokin Waka Shū*, in Ōbunsha Bunko series. Ōbunsha, 1982.

———. *Shūi Waka Shū*, in Shin Nihon Koten Bungaku Taikei series. Iwanami Shoten, 1990.

Konishi Jin'ichi. "The Genesis of the *Kokinshū* Style," trans. by Helen C. McCullough, *Harvard Journal of Asiatic Studies* 37:1, 1978.

———. *A History of Japanese Literature*, II, translated by Aileen Gatten. Princeton, N.J.: Princeton University Press, 1986.

Kubota Shōichirō, Sugitani Jurō, and Fujihira Haruo. *Kokin Waka Shū*, *Gosen Waka Shū*, *Shūi Waka Shū*, in Kanshō Nihon Koten Bungaku series. Kadokawa Shoten, 1975.

Kyūsojin Hitaku. *Kokin Waka Shū*, 4 vols., in Kōdansha Gakujutsu Bunko. Kōdansha, 1979–83.

Liu, James J. Y. *The Art of Chinese Poetry*. London: Routledge and Kegan Paul, 1962.

———. *Chinese Theories of Literature*. Chicago: University of Chicago Press, 1975.

McCullough, Helen Craig. *Brocade by Night*. Stanford, Calif.: Stanford University Press, 1985.

———. *Kokin Wakashū*. Stanford, Calif.: Stanford University Press, 1985.

Minegishi Yoshiaki. *Heian Jidai Waka Bungaku no Kenkyū*. Ōfūsha, 1965.

Murase Toshio. *Kokinshū no Kiban to Shūhen*. Ōfūsha, 1971.

Nihon Bungaku Kenkyū Shiryō Kankōkai. *Kokin Waka Shū*. Yūseidō, 1976.

Okumura Tsuneya. *Kokinshū, Gosenshū no Shomondai*. Kazama Shobō, 1971.

———. *Kokinshū no Kenkyū*. Kyōto: Rinsen Shoten, 1979.

———. *Kokin Waka Shū*, in Shinchō Nihon Koten Shūsei series. Shinchōsha, 1978.

Ōoka Makoto. *Ki no Tsurayuki*. Chikuma Shobō, 1971.

———. *Shiki no Uta Koi no Uta*. Chikuma Shobō, 1979.

Ozawa Masao. *Kokinshū no Sekai*. Hanawa Shobō, 1978.

———. *Kokin Waka Shū*, in Nihon Koten Bungaku Zenshū series. Shōgakukan, 1971.

Rodd, Laurel Rasplica. *Kokinshū*. Princeton, N.J.: Princeton University Press, 1984.

Yasuda Akio. *Ōchō no Kajintachi*. Nihon Hōsō Shuppankai, 1975.

7. LATE HEIAN COLLECTIONS OF WAKA POETRY

Sequels to the *Kokinshū*

Six collections of waka compiled by imperial command (chokusenshū) and many private collections were set down on paper between the presentation of the *Kokinshū* in 905 and the *Shin Kokinshū* in 1205.[1] Many poems from these collections would be remembered, and some were included in *Hyakunin Isshu*, the basic body of waka poetry known to every literate Japanese; but the six collections have not generally been read as artistic wholes, and relatively little scholarship has been devoted to them.[2] Even their titles seem to suggest leftovers from the *Kokinshū* rather than new developments in poetry by people of later times. Each nevertheless revealed to some extent the changed spirit and the poetic principles of succeeding ages and contributed to the formation of the waka tradition.

The Gosenshū

The second imperial collection, *Gosen Waka Shū* (Later Selection of Waka) is generally known by the abbreviated title *Gosenshū*. It was compiled in response to a command issued by the Emperor Murakami in 951, but the date of the presentation of the completed manuscript is not certain. Most probably it was between 953 and 958.[3] None of the five compilers was a distinguished poet; in fact, whether because of modesty or objective considerations of poetic worth, the compilers did not include a single poem by themselves, a rare instance of self-restraint. The Cloistered Emperor Juntoku in his book of poetics *Yakumo Mishō* (c. 1221) declared that the only qualification of two of the compilers was that they were sons of famous poets.[4] It should be borne in mind, however, that the compilers were not chosen specially for the task of preparing the *Gosenshū*, but carried out this work as part of their duties at the Poetry Bureau (*waka dokoro*) established in 951 by the Emperor Murakami primarily for the purpose of deciphering the text of the *Man'yōshū*. Perhaps the two men were chosen as scholars of the *Man'yōshū* rather than as poets; but the prestige of their fathers' names undoubtedly enhanced their position in the world of poetry.

In any case, the compilers of the *Gosenshū* displayed little aptitude for their task; the unusually large number of variants in the texts suggests either haste or incompetence. Depending on the particular text, the total number of poems varies between 1,396 and 1,426, and there are numerous discrepancies both in the poems and in the prose prefaces (kotobagaki). The arrangement of the poems is peculiar: poems that obviously should be included in the books of love poetry are found among the seasonal poems.[5]

The *Gosenshū* has long suffered from comparisons with its immediate predecessor, the *Kokinshū*. The nun Abutsu stated in her thirteenth-century book of poetics *Yoru no Tsuru* (The Crane at Night) that the *Gosenshū* was marred by an unevenness that she attributed to the unequal abilities of the compilers.[6] The scholars of National Learning (kokugaku) of the seventeenth and eighteenth centuries were even harsher in their appraisals of the *Gosenshū*: Kamo no Mabuchi declared that good poems were "very, very scarce," and Motoori Norinaga felt so dissatisfied with the wording of the prose prefaces that he rewrote them himself. Twentieth-century critics have not hesitated to dismiss the *Gosenshū* as the dregs of the *Kokinshū*.[7]

Despite these severe criticisms, the *Gosenshū* is of exceptional interest, perhaps less because of the intrinsic quality of the poems than because of what they reveal about the daily composition of waka during the Heian period. The poems in the *Gosenshū* were largely composed by amateurs writing under informal, usually private circumstances, rather than the polished works of "professional" poets intended for "publication" at the court. The collection contains many waka by poets who figured prominently in the *Kokinshū*, including seventy-six by Ki no Tsurayuki, but the new poets—the contemporaries of the compilers—differed from the *Kokinshū* poets not only in their tastes but in their social positions.[8] They included emperors and princes as well as officers of the highest ranks, evidence that waka composition was now being practiced even by the kind of persons who at the time of the compilation of the *Kokinshū* preferred to express their poetic thoughts in kanshi.

Many poems in the collection are occasional, and the events that inspired the composition are often explained in prose prefaces. The poems tend to describe minor, even trivial events of daily life, and seldom have the "public" character of the poems that were inscribed on screens or composed at uta-awase competitions. Many poems take the form of dialogues between men and women. Both parts of the dialogue are given, though this was not true of any other imperial collection. They show every sign of having been poems that were actually composed by lovers the morning after a tryst or by friends at a party, and what they lack in literary value they possess as documents of an era. The poems in the *Gosenshū* are all in the form of waka, without even the token representation of chōka and sedōka found in the *Kokinshū*.

Following the example of the *Kokinshū* (and the *Man'yōshū* before it), the *Gosenshū* was in twenty books, but the divisions were different, as was the arrangement of poems within each book. Eight (instead of six) books were devoted to seasonal poems; six (instead of five) to love poems; and four (instead of two) to miscellaneous poems.[9] The seasonal poems are arranged temporally, like those in the *Kokinshū*: the first poem is dated the first day of the first month, and similar notations before other poems give the impression that the march of the seasons was carefully observed. In a sense the *Gosenshū* is even more rigorous than the *Kokinshū* in its attention to the progress of the seasons: in the *Kokinshū*, for example, each flower is treated through its cycle of early blossoming, full bloom, and scattering before moving on to the next flower, but in the *Gosenshū* flowers that blossom at the same time are treated together.[10]

The other books of the *Gosenshū* show no signs of systematic arrangement. Unlike the love poems in the *Kokinshū*, which are arranged to trace the course of a love affair, the *Gosenshū* love poems open with one composed *after* the first meeting, and there is no chronological progression, though poems on related themes are sometimes grouped together.

About half the poems in the *Gosenshū* are anonymous. Some twenty were borrowed from the *Man'yōshū* and others came from the *Shinsen Man'yōshū*, but the bulk probably originated in the same body of uncollected poetry that supplied many anonymous poems to the *Kokinshū*. The anonymity of some poems may have been deliberate, as when a high-born lady revealed in her poem a secret love affair. Some anonymous poems may antedate the *Kokinshū*, and others no doubt were composed shortly before the compilation of the *Gosenshū*, but the stylistic differences between two poems on a similar subject, even poems composed a century apart, are generally not sufficiently pronounced for us to decide which was composed earlier. The retention of the forms of classical grammar and a restricted vocabulary would continue to produce this kind of anonymity for almost a millennium, in disregard of the changes that had occurred in the spoken language. The relative neglect of the *Gosenshū* can be understood in terms of the scarcity of distinctive voices among the poets, whether named or anonymous.

Few poets are known specifically as "*Gosenshū* poets." Fujiwara no Kanesuke (877–933) had had four poems included in the *Kokinshū*, but he was more generously represented in the new collection with thirty-two poems, most in the uncomplicated manner that was favored by the *Gosenshū* compilers. One affecting poem, composed after the death of his wife, was sent to his friend Tsurayuki on the last day of the year. It bears the prose preface "Composed on the last day of the last month of the year in which my wife died, while telling tales about the old days."

naki hito no	If only the year
tomo ni shi kaeru	Would return together with
toshi naraba	She who is no more,
kureyuku kyō wa	This day that draws to an end
ureshikaramashi	Would fill me with happiness.

Tsurayuki responded:

kouru ma ni	If, while you still love,
toshi no kurenaba	The year has come to a close,
naki hito no	Parting from someone
wakare ya itodo	Who is no more must make her
tōku nari nan[11]	Seem all the farther away.

Most of the 227 *Gosenshū* poets (as opposed to only 126 named *Kokinshū* poets) either were minor poets or else were better represented in other collections, and the *Gosenshū* poems tend to be remembered because of the circumstances related in the prefaces.

A small sample of *Gosenshū* poetry may suffice to suggest the characteristics of the collection. The numerous dialogue poems are typified by the exchange between the celebrated Taira no Sadafun (also known as Heichū, c. 870–923)[12] and a court lady whose name is not given in the text, though we know from other sources that she was a granddaughter of Ariwara no Narihira. The preface mentions in vague terms her relationship with Fujiwara no Kunitsune (829–908), the uncle of Shihei (Tokihira), the prime minister. Kunitsune, though much older than the lady, was in fact her husband, and Shihei stole his wife from him.[13] These circumstances provide the background for the most dramatic of the 180 sets of dialogue poems in the *Gosenshū*.[14] It opens with a prose preface:

> Taira no Sadafun was carrying on a clandestine affair with a woman in the household of the Major Counselor Kunitsune. They had gone so far as to exchange promises of marriage when the woman was suddenly carried off as his bride by the late prime minister, and Sadafun had no way even to write her. The woman had a daughter of five, and one day when the girl was playing by the west wing of the prime minister's residence, Sadafun called to her. "Show this to your mother," he said, and wrote this poem on her arm:

mukashi seshi	Solemn promises
wa ga kanegoto no	We made so long ago have
kanashiki wa	Ended in sadness;
ika ni chigirishi	What fault was there in our vows
nagori naruran	That they have ended this way?

> Her reply was:

utsutsu ni te	Who made a promise
tare chigiriken	In the world of reality?
sadame naki	The I who wanders
yumeji ni mayou	An uncertain path of dreams
ware ware ka wa[15]	Is surely not the same I.

Another feature of the *Gosenshū* is the use of words outside the elegant poetic diction established by the *Kokinshū*. In the haikai, or comic, section of the book of miscellaneous poetry in the *Kokinshū* some words that fell outside the approved vocabulary were tolerated, but in the *Gosenshū* (though not in later court anthologies) they might appear in serious contexts, as in the following example.

"A certain man went to the country house of a woman with whom he had been intimate and knocked on her gate, but she seemed not to have heard him. As he waited before the shut gate, he heard frogs croaking in a nearby rice field, and he wept."

ashihiki no	A forlorn scarecrow
yamada no sōzu	Stands in the mountain paddy,

uchiwabite	Difficult to cross;
hitori kaeru no	As I leave, alone, I hear
ne wo zo nakinuru[16]	The cries of frogs, and I weep.

This anonymous poem has for its first line the familiar makurakotoba *ashihiki no* (foot-dragging), the standard, more or less meaningless, epithet for *yama* (mountain), but here it accords with the tone of the whole poem and even seems to characterize the forlorn scarecrow standing in the mountain paddy.[17] There is kakekotoba on *kaeru*: in the phrase *hitori kaeru* it means "I return alone," but *kaeru no ne* means "the cries of frogs." Again, the verb *naku* (in *nakinuru*) refers to the frogs' crying, but also to the speaker's weeping when he must leave without seeing the woman. A word like *kaeru* for "frog" (or like *sōzu* for "scarecrow") might have appeared in a comic verse, though not elsewhere in the *Kokinshū*; in the *Gosenshū* it is not out of place even in an unhappy context.

Another feature of the *Gosenshū* is the exceptionally large number of poems by women. Lady Taifu, though a minor poet, is represented in the collection by sixteen poems, second among women poets only to Ise with seventy. Her lover, Ono no Michikaze (894–966), was renowned both as a calligrapher and a lover. The prose preface tells us, "Sent when Michikaze paid her a secret visit and her parents, hearing of this, forbade her to see him."

ito kakute	Rather than let things
yaminuru yori wa	End in this uncertain way,
inazuma no	I want to see you
hikari no ma ni mo	Even for the brief space of
kimo wo miteshi ga[18]	A lightning flash in the dark.

Perhaps the *Gosenshū* poem most often quoted in later works of literature was by Fujiwara no Kanesuke:

> Once, on a day when the prime minister, then general of the Left, offered a banquet to celebrate victory in the sumō matches, the poet, then a middle general, visited his residence. When the banquet had ended and the guests were leaving, two or three high-ranking noblemen detained him and insisted on their drinking together. After he had consumed a good deal of sake and was quite inebriated, the conversation turned to the subject of children, and he composed this verse:

hito no oya no	The heart of the parent
kokoro no yami ni	Of a child is not shrouded
aranedomo	In the dark of night,
ko wo omou michi ni	But for love of that child
madoinuru kana[19]	How it has strayed from its way!

The tone of the poem may recall the *Man'yōshū* rather than the *Kokinshū*.[20] A special connection between the *Man'yōshū* and the *Gosenshū* can be explained in terms of the work of the Poetry Bureau.[21] Twenty-four *Man'yōshū* poems, all anonymous, were incorporated into the *Gosenshū*, but this could have been less a case of direct borrowing than of choosing songs that were still known orally.[22] It may be that the normal reaction against the work of their immediate predecessors inspired the *Gosenshū* compilers to look beyond the *Kokinshū* to the *Man'yōshū* for inspiration and guidance.[23] In any case, the rejection of the model of the *Kokinshū* made the *Gosenshū* an anomaly among the imperial collections of waka, and this may be why it still engages the attention of Japanese scholars.

The Shūishū

The *Shūi Waka Shū*, commonly known as the *Shūishū*, was the third imperial collection. The title, meaning "Collection of Gleanings," suggests that it was no more than a further mining of a body of poetry that had already been explored by the compilers of the two earlier anthologies. This impression is not altogether mistaken; though new voices were also heard, there was a noticeably generous selection of waka by *Kokinshū* poets (including 106 by Ki no Tsurayuki), as well as 122 poems attributed to Hitomaro and other *Man'yōshū* poets. Some of the *Gosenshū* compilers are represented here (though not in the *Gosenshū*), but that collection as a whole did not exert much influence over the compilation of the *Shūishū*.

The circumstances of the compilation of the *Shūishū* are obscure. The first stage was apparently in the form of a shorter anthology with a similar title, *Shūishō* (Selection of Gleanings), made between 996 and 999 by Fujiwara no Kintō (966–1041), the most admired poet of the day. This work served as the framework for the *Shūishū*, compiled about 1005 by the Retired Emperor Kazan (968–1008).[24] Nothing indicates whether this anthology went through the same stages of preparation as the earlier ones—the issuance of an imperial command to compile an anthology, the selection of texts, the submission of the completed anthology for the emperor's approval, and so on. It may have been considered as the private project of Kazan, who had long demonstrated a passionate interest in waka composition. Indeed, from the time of its completion until the early part of the nineteenth century it was mistakenly believed that the *Shūishō* was a selection of the best poems in the *Shūishū*, and for that reason it was treated with greater respect than the imperial collection.[25]

The present text of the *Shūishū* is divided into the usual twenty books, but the divisions are unconventional. For example, there is only one book for each of the four seasons, in contrast to other collections that give two books for spring and autumn poems.[26] The representation of contemporary poets is meager: Fujiwara no Kintō led the rest with fifteen poems, but there is only one by Izumi Shikibu, and none at all by Murasaki Shikibu or Sei Shōnagon, both of whom were actively writing at the time. The emphasis was definitely on the past, and every attempt was made to link the collection to the *Kokinshū*.

Many poems were composed on public occasions in the manner of the *Kokinshū*, and (like the *Kokinshū*) the collection contains a large number of poems for inscription on screens. The poets of the *Shūishū* were often called upon to enhance the landscapes depicted on screens by describing the emotions of the people in the paintings or else of the poet on contemplating the scenes in the paintings. A screen poem by Ise[27] exhibits the impersonality typical of such poems:

"At a place on the screen at the high priestess's palace showing a man going along a path through the mountains."

chiri chirazu	Have they fallen or not?
kikimahoshiki wo	That is what I would ask if
furusato no	I could meet someone
hana mite kaeru	Who has returned from seeing
hito mo awanan[28]	The blossoms in the old town.

Ise's poem was skillful and fulfilled its purpose as an explanation of the thoughts of the man in the picture, but it reveals nothing of herself, nor does one get the impression that she was addressing the poem to another person. Ise and most of the other *Shūishū* poets, unlike those of the *Gosenshū*, were "professionals," and the chief criterion of Fujiwara no Kintō and the Retired Emperor Kazan in making their selection of poems seems to have been an absence of faults rather than marked individuality.

The seasonal poems in the *Shūishū* are arranged in the usual temporal sequence, opening with:

"Composed at a poem competition held at the house of Taira no Sadafun."

haru tatsu to	Is it only because
iu bakari ni ya	The calendar says spring has come?
mi Yoshino no	Even the mountains
yama mo kasumite	At Yoshino this morning
kesa wa miyuran[29]	Are faintly touched with haze.

This waka by Mibu no Tadamine, one of the *Kokinshū* compilers, was no doubt chosen to head the *Shūishū* because the early spring haze hovering over the mountains at Yoshino was an extremely familiar poetic image for the beginning of spring. Yoshino was remembered as the site of temporary imperial residences in *Man'yōshū* times, and the arrival of spring at so holy a place was therefore of special poetic interest. The poet says he knows that, according to the calendar, spring has officially begun, but that is not all: the haze tells him that the spring has reached even the remote mountains at Yoshino, known for its heavy snows.

Tadamine's waka was extravagantly admired. Kintō, who had originally selected it to head his collection *Shūishō*, declared that the "wording is magical and there are almost too many overtones."[30] Fujiwara Shunzei (1114–1204) called attention to the word *mo* (even), suggesting the poet's surprise on discovering that spring had come to the mountains at Yoshino; he had not expected it would even have reached the village below.[31] Admittedly, Tadamine's poem displays more than usual competence, but it is unlikely to touch the hearts of modern readers. The poem was originally composed at an uta-awase, a public occasion, and this may explain its impersonality. Its position at the head of the collection is unmistakable evidence that this mode of expression was favored by the compiler.

These two poems from the *Shūishū* were both by poets of an earlier generation, chosen because the *Kokinshū* ideal of courtly poetry was still the ideal of the compilers. The newer poems, by men and women active at the time of the compilation, were in much the same mood and style, revealing little that was original even to the extent that the *Gosenshū* poems were original.

A waka by Fujiwara no Tameyori (d. 998), composed at an uta-awase held in 977 at the house of Fujiwara no Yoritada (924–989), the father of Kintō, typifies the contemporary poetry in the *Shūishū*. Like many poems in this and later collections, it was on an assigned topic (*dai*). Yoritada is referred to in the prefatory note as "Rengi," his posthumous title.

"Composed at the house of Prince Rengi on the topic of 'night insects in a grass thicket.' "

obotsukana	It's a mystery—
izuko naruran	Where does that singing come from?
mushi no ne wo	If I should seek out
tazuneba kusa no	Those cries of insects, the dew
tsuyu ya midaren[32]	On the grass might be disturbed.

Tameyori's waka does not seem to satisfy the requirement that it refer to "night insects," but we know from other sources that this poetry competition was held on a night when moonlight illuminated the shrubbery around Yoritada's house, and this may have obviated the need to make a more overt reference to the night than the poet's professed inability to tell where the singing of the insects originates. The poem is innocuous, even agreeable, but the subject seems contrived, and the poet's fear that searching in the thicket for the insects might shake the dew from the grass cannot be taken seriously.

The playful element in courtly verse was emphasized by the revival of poetry containing "hidden words,"[33] a category found in the *Kokinshū* but not in the *Gosenshū*. Such poems were obviously not composed in order to express the poet's emotions but in the hopes of winning the approbation of the court by a display of wit. Fujiwara no Sukemi (d. 956?) was known as the most accomplished writer of poems containing "hidden words." Almost all his surviving poems are in the comic vein, typified by this example:

"After a mouse had given birth to its young on the belly of a koto."

toshi wo hete	Through all the years
kimi wo nomi koso	With you and you alone
nesumitsure	Have I slept and lived;
kotohara ni yawa	How could I have another
ko wo ba umubeki[34]	Woman bear a child of mine?

Sukemi's poem contains two "hidden words." The first, *nesumi* (sleep and live), is a virtual homonym of *nezumi* (mouse); and *kotohara* (different belly) means the womb of another woman but also the "belly" or sounding-board of a koto. The puns are clever, but the interest of the poem, at least for modern readers, lies less in the hidden words than in the crudity of the question addressed the lady; it demonstrates that even at the court that produced this elegant but bloodless anthology not every poet sang the beauty of autumn leaves or worried about disturbing the forest dew.

The most striking of the *Shūishū* poets was undoubtedly Sone no Yoshitada (923?–1003?), though many of his best poems appeared in other collections as well. In his own day Yoshitada was known as an eccentric because his unconventional language at times violated the accepted poetic diction. Some of his vocabulary was new and other words had not been used since the *Man'yōshū*, but even if such deviations sometimes served no other function than to startle, his evocations of real emotions contrasted with the more typical, genteel poetic conceits found in the *Shūishū*. Yoshitada was ostracized by other court poets, and one poem in particular was denounced as the work of a madman by a later critic,[35] largely because he had mentioned a clump of wormwood (*yomogi*), a common weed that grows to a height of four or five feet at most, as if it were a stand of trees being grown for lumber, seeing the wormwood through a cricket's eyes:

nake ya nake	Weep, yes, weep your fill,
yomogi ga soma no	Crickets under the stand
kirigirisu	Of wormwood plants:
kureyuku aki wa	Autumn drawing to a close
ge ni zo kanashiki[36]	Is enough to break one's heart.

Yoshitada never rose above the sixth rank, and he was excluded from many court functions, but his importance as a poet was recognized, as we can infer from the inclusion of nine poems in the *Shūishū*, though they did not accord with the prevailing tone of the collection. The appeal of his poetry to his contemporaries is suggested by the following:

akikaze wa	O autumn wind,
fuki na yaburi so	Do not blow and destroy
wa ga yado no	The spider webs
abara kakuseru	That hide the gaping cracks
kumo no sugaki wo[37]	Of my derelict hut.

Yoshitada's poem is unconventional in its mention of cobwebs and his ramshackle hut, but the image of cobwebs hiding the dilapidated walls has a poetic delicacy that probably pleased even the fastidious compilers of the *Shūishū*. More than ninety poems by Yoshitada appear in this and later imperial collections, reflecting the continued interest in his work; but many excellent poems were not accepted by the editors of any anthology, perhaps because they seemed too controversial. On the other hand, this unconventionality accounts for the freshness that makes Yoshitada's poems stand out among those of his age.

The practice of composing sequences of one hundred poems also seems to have originated (about 960) with Yoshitada. Perhaps dissatisfaction with the brevity of the waka inspired him to compose a series of poems in which each poem, though independent, fitted smoothly into the longer sequence and was linked by spatial or temporal relationships to the preceding and following poems. The content was also distinctive. Yoshitada departed from the customary reliance on utamakura and other familiar waka topics, and included poems that described real scenes in the countryside or on the coast, poems that complained of the poet's misfortunes, and poems of satirical content.[38] The language also violated the normal poetic diction by including archaisms, colloquialisms and neologisms, all in order to keep the one hundred waka from becoming monotonous. Yoshitada's reputation as an enemy of tradition stemmed chiefly from this poetic sequence; most of the poems in his private collection, *Sotan Shū*, are far less striking.[39]

Izumi Shikibu (970–1030) also merits special attention, though only one of her poems appeared in the *Shūishū*. This extraordinary woman, remembered today for her diary and her many poems, of which 240 were included in later imperial collections, was probably only sixteen or seventeen when she composed her best-known poem:

kuraki yori	Coming from darkness
kuraki michi ni zo	I shall enter on a path
irinubeki	Of greater darkness.
haruka ni terase	Shine on me from the distance,
yama no ha no tsuki[40]	Moon at the edge of the mount.

Izumi Shikibu borrowed her imagery from Buddhist writings, but clearly the poem is something more personal than a conventional expression of piety. Perhaps, as has been conjectured on the basis of what we know of her later life, she had already suffered the torment of an unhappy love affair and was seeking guidance (the moon is a familiar Buddhist metaphor for enlightenment) from the priest to whom the poem was offered. Izumi Shikibu's poem stands out in the *Shūishū*, not only from the mass of graceful but impersonal poems but also from the equally unruffled poetry of Buddhist priests.[41]

The most important of the poet-priests of the *Shūishū* was Egyō (1085–1164), represented by eighteen poems. Almost nothing is known about his life, but his poems (with their prefaces) indicate that he associated with leading poets of the late tenth century, notably the compilers of the *Gosenshū*. His acquaintance with Ki no Tokifumi, the undistinguished son of Tsurayuki, was of special importance because Tokifumi lent him the manuscripts of Tsurayuki's complete poems and of *The Tosa Diary*.[42] When Egyō returned the manuscripts, a poetry gathering was held at the Kawara-no-in, a ruined temple that had originally been built as the palace of the statesman and poet Minamoto no Tōru (822–95). The temple, virtually destroyed by a storm and flood in 979, was a suitable place for composing poetry on the transience of worldly things. On this occasion Egyō composed the following poem with its preface: "On returning the volume of the late Tsurayuki's collected poems, which I had borrowed."

hitomaki ni	Into one volume
chiji no kogane wo	A thousand pieces of gold
kometareba	Have been crammed;
hito koso nakare	The man is no longer here,
koe wa nokoreri[43]	But his voice still lingers on.

Ki no Tokifumi replied,

inishie no	There is a limit
chiji no kogane wa	To the thousand pieces of gold
kagiri aru wo	Of long, long ago;
au hakari naki	But no scale can measure
kimi ga tamazusa[44]	The value of your poem.

The poems evoke the atmosphere of an informal gathering of poets, one gracefully complimenting the other.

Although Egyō was a Buddhist priest, he did not shun the world in the manner of the priest-poets of later times. One commentator explained, "At the time Buddhism was more of an academic discipline than a religion, and there was a tendency, even among those who had entered the path of Buddhism, to think of it as knowledge rather than as a faith."[45] Priests who wrote poetry, even poetry that seemed to contradict their vows of chastity or their professed rejection of the beautiful things of this world, were not exposed to criticism; rather, it was accepted that priests, especially those of aristocratic birth, could legitimately participate in the aesthetic life of society.

Egyō's best-known poem, included in *Hyakunin Isshu*, has no obvious religious significance:

"Composed at the Kawara-no-in when people were writing poems on the theme of autumn overtaking a ruined dwelling."

yaemugura	In the loneliness
shigereru yado no	Of a house where rankly grows
sabishisa ni	The prickly goose-grass,
hito koso miene	There is not a soul in sight:
aki wa kinikeri[46]	Autumn has come once again.

The desolation of a once magnificent palace is intensified by the absence of any other person, and the coming of autumn compounds the loneliness.

Egyō's other poems in the *Shūishū* do not leave a strong impression of either the poet or the priest, but his celebrity in his time is attested to by a poem of Ōnakatomi no Yoshinobu, one of the *Gosenshū* compilers:

"Having read the poetry of the priest Egyō, I was wondering how I might arrange a meeting with him when, in the middle of the seventh month, we happened to meet at a certain place."

tanabata no	Imagine meeting
chigereru tsuki no	Someone I have been yearning for
uchi ni shimo	In the very middle
koiwataritsuru	Of the month when the two stars
hito ni au kana[47]	Are pledged to be reunited.

The extravagance of the language (*koiwataritsuru* means "to go on yearning for something for a long time") and the comparison of the meeting of Egyō and himself to the once-a-year meeting of the Herdboy and Weaving Girl stars, conveyed Yoshinobu's immense repsect for Egyō, but it suggests a courtliness more appropriate to Versailles than to Heian Japan.

The most curious feature of Egyō's poems in the *Shūishū* is that they are so little concerned with Buddhism, even in an attenuated form. However, the twentieth book of the *Shūishū* is given over to poems of mourning, a rubric that covers works of specifically Buddhist content, including one attributed to Baramon Sōjō, the Buddhist priest from southern India who took a leading part in the celebration of the dedication of the great Buddha at Nara in 752. But the most famous of the *Shūishū* Buddhist poems is a later version of a famous *Man'yōshū* poem by the priest Mansei:

yo no naka wo	This world of ours—
nani ni tatoen	To what should I compare it?
asaborake	The white wake behind
kogiyuku fune no	A boat that is rowed away
ato no shiranami[48]	In the first light of morning.

This poem, in its *Shūishū* version, marked an important development of Buddhist poems in Japanese because of its alleged influence on the celebrated priest Genshin (942–1017).[49] According to the *Fukuro Zōshi* (Book of Folded Pages, 1159), Genshin had always considered the waka to be no more than *kyōgen kigyo* ("wild words and fancy language"),[50] but one daybreak, as he gazed out over Lake Biwa from the Eshin Temple, he saw a boat being rowed to shore, and someone standing nearby murmured the first two lines of Mansei's waka. The experience so moved Genshin that he realized poetry could assist religious contemplation, and from this time on he himself composed waka.[51]

Similar stories would be recounted during the medieval period,[52] when the composition of literature was justified in terms of the higher truths that it painlessly communicated by means of "wild words and fancy language." Mansei's poem, a comparison of the transience of human life to the wake of a boat dissolving in the waters of a lake, was a perfect example of a poem that, though not didactic in any obvious way, conveyed a truth of Buddhism. Many more Buddhist poems would appear in subsequent imperial collections, beginning with the next one, the *Goshūishū*.[53] In prose, too, an amusing anecdote was often provided with a "moral" that justified the existence of what might seem to be a frivolous tale; literature was considered to be an expedient (*hōben*), like the honey on the lip of a cup that enables the patient to swallow bitter medicine.

The *Shūishū* has not been studied with nearly so much care as the *Gosenshū*, let alone the *Kokinshū*. It contains some beautiful poetry, and in at least one respect—the inclusion of a sampling of renga—it anticipated future developments, but it did not create a distinctive *Shūishū* style. Hardly a poem would be out of place in the *Kokinshū*; indeed, the *Shūishū* has been called the grand summation of the *Kokinshū* style.[54] The first three imperial collections of waka were often considered to form a single unit; critics referred to them as *sandaishū*, "collections of three generations." Subsequent imperial collections would start on a fresh footing.

The Goshūishū

The title of the fourth imperial collection, *Goshūi Waka Shū* (henceforth abbreviated as *Goshūishū*) suggests that it was no more than one further sampling of the poetic heritage of the past, an anthology of waka that had failed to impress the compilers of previous anthologies. In fact, however, it contains poetry of considerably better quality than either the *Gosenshū* or the *Shūishū*, and marks a change in attitude from unconditional reverence for the past and a professed desire to save old poetry from oblivion to an insistence on the worth of contemporary waka. The preface states that the *Goshūishū* would not include poems from the *Man'yōshū* or from previous imperial or private collections that were well known. Some poetry in fact goes back as far as the *Gosenshū*, but the *Goshūishū* consists almost entirely of poems composed during the eighty years since the compilation of the *Shūishū* in 1005.

In 1075 Fujiwara no Michitoshi (1047–1099) received a command from the Emperor Shirakawa to compile a new imperial collection. Michitoshi was only twenty-seven at the time and not particularly famous for his poetry, but he had already established himself as an important figure at the court of Shirakawa, who was about to reassert imperial authority after the long period of domination by the Fujiwara regents. Probably Shirakawa thought that a new imperial collection would bring back memories of the days when the emperor exercised personal rule.[55] Michitoshi's political activities seem to have prevented him from devoting much time to the compilation of the anthology, and it was not completed for nine years. He presented the manuscript to the emperor in 1086 and, after some revisions, it was submitted again the next year.[56]

No sooner was the collection presented than it was subjected to abuse. An account written seventy years later stated, "The *Goshūishū* is a collection that provides a model for us of later times. However, when it was finally completed, it was subjected to criticism of every kind. Some said that the preface did not conform to tradition, others complained that although Minamoto no Yoritsuna's poems are of no great consequence, many were included. I find such criticism peculiar. Four of Yoritsuna's poems are indeed included, but each one of them is profoundly moving. This sort of error arises when one places undue importance on reputation and does not trust one's own critical judgment."[57]

Nan Goshūi (Faulting the *Goshūi*), an anonymous work attributed to Minamoto no Tsunenobu (1016–1097),[58] a leading poet of the day, attacked close to ninety poems in the *Goshūishū* for various faults. Much of Tsunenobu's criticism is hardly more than nit-picking inspired by his resentment over the choice of a younger man (and less competent poet) as the sole editor of the collection.[59] Regardless of the degree of jealousy involved, Tsunenobu's poetic skills enabled him to make some telling points. Undoubtedly, the collection has its weaknesses, but the faults to which Tsunenobu drew attention do not alter the importance of the *Goshūishū* as a monument of eleventh-century poetry.

The *Goshūishū* contains 1,218 poems divided into the usual twenty books.[60] The most notable feature of the arrangement of the poetry is the revival of the book of travel poems and the inclusion of haikai (comic) poems for the first time since the *Kokinshū*. There are also many more Shintō and Buddhist poems than in earlier anthologies. The *Goshūishū* is distinguished otherwise by the preponderant role played by woman poets—sixty-eight poems by Izumi Shikibu, forty by Sagami, and thirty-two by Akazome Emon. The most poems by any man were the thirty-one by the priest Nōin. Only six poems by Tsunenobu were included, no doubt a cause for his dissatisfaction. The small number was likely occasioned by his poor relations with the compiler, Michitoshi, but there is also a tradition that Tsunenobu himself deleted poems that failed to meet his standards.[61] The poets included court members of the highest rank, but most were of the *zuryō* class, officials of the fourth or fifth rank who had served as provincial governors.

The fact that eighty years had elapsed since the previous imperial collection did not mean that there was a dearth of good poetry during those years. One group of young poets of the period styled themselves the Waka Rokunin Tō (The Six Poets Group). These men of the zuryō class were so passionately devoted to waka composition that one of them, Minamoto no Yorizane, requested divine assistance from the god of the Sumiyoshi Shrine. He vowed that if he received the inspiration to write a truly great poem he would willingly die in return. Soon afterward, this poem, on the topic "falling leaves like rain," came to him:

konoha chiru	At my house, where leaves
yado wa kikiwaku	Are falling, I cannot be sure
koto zo naki	What sound I hear

shigure suru yo mo	On nights of autumn showers,
shigure senu to mo[62]	On nights when no showers fall.

At first no one seemed impressed by the poem, so Yorizane returned to the shrine and prayed as before. In a dream he was vouchsafed the reply: "Your poem was excellent. Among poems on autumn leaves it ranks as a masterpiece. Don't you agree?" Soon afterward the worth of the poem was widely recognized and Yorizane died.

The Six Poets were the subject of innumerable anecdotes, many describing the difficulties they encountered in composing poetry. Nothing in such works as *Tales of Ise* or *Tales of Yamato* suggests that Narihira or Komachi ever struggled over their poems, but from this time on the theme became familiar.[63] The difficulties experienced by the Six Poets were not confined to expression; they were attempting to create a distinctively new kind of waka, and they turned to Chinese poetry for inspiration.[64] More important than their borrowing from particular Chinese poems was their assumption of such attitudes of the Chinese poets as preferring life in a hermit's cottage or in a mountain village to the comforts of the court, though this was hardly true of their real lives. Their interest in Chinese poetry also inspired their practice of composing poems to topics from Chinese sources. Typical topics were "spring snow by a mountain house," "remaining chrysanthemums by a pond," and "admiring the moon at an old temple."[65] Such natural scenes had often been treated in Chinese painting as well as poetry, and it is easy to visualize them. Human beings rarely intrude on such landscapes except as the tiny figures of travelers set against the vastness of nature. A poem by Minamoto no Yoriie may suggest this Chinese influence:

"Written on the theme of 'autumn evening in a mountain hut' when people went to Zenrin-ji."

kureyukeba	When it grew dark
asaji ga hara no	In the weed-covered fields,
mushi no ne mo	The cries of insects
onoe no shika mo	And the voices of the deer
koe tatetsu nari[66]	Rose from the crest of the hill.

Though the scene appears pastoral, in the manner of the many Chinese poems on hermits, the temple mentioned in the prefatory note (more commonly known as Eikandō) was situated within the city of Kyoto; for all their professed love of lonely retreats, the Six Poets seldom ventured beyond the immediate vicinity of the capital.

The preface to a waka by the priest Dōmyō made overt reference to Chinese poetry: "Written on a painting of the 'Song of Everlasting Regret' depicting Hsüan-tsung after his return to the capital whence he had fled. Insects are dinning, and the whole area has turned to withered grass. The emperor grieves over the scene."

furusato wa	My old home has gone
asaji ga hara to	To rack and ruin and become
arehatete	A wilderness of weeds.
yosugara mushi no	All through the night I can hear
ne wo nomi wo kiku[67]	Nothing but insects crying.

The poem describes the emotions of the Emperor Hsüan-tsung on returning to the destroyed capital at Ch'ang-an, but it could equally well be a description of a Japanese scene, of the kind familiar from waka poetry. However, it would be a more typically Japanese poem if the speaker were recalling someone who once lived in what was now desolation.

Another poem in a similar vein was by the ill-fated Minamoto no Yorizane:

"Composed when, having gone to a mountain village, it grew dark."

hi mo kurenu	The day has ended
hito mo kaerinu	And the visitors have left—
yamazato wa	In the mountain village
mine no arashi no	All that remains is the howl
oto bakari shite[68]	Of storm winds from the peak.

A shift to descriptive poetry, exemplified by Yorizane's poem, was probably the most notable contribution of the *Goshūishū* to the development of Japanese poetry, but the poems in that vein are less moving than the unforgettable poems written by women expressing their passion. Although the *Goshūishū* is generally dismissed as being "conservative,"[69] the intensity of the poems of Izumi Shikibu, Akazome Emon, and Sagami give the collection its distinctive coloring.

Izumi Shikibu is of special interest to us because of her diary, but her poems (with their prefaces) are also marked by an individuality that contrasts with the unassertive elegance of much other waka poetry. In almost any of her poems we hear her voice, which sometimes carries modern overtones:

kurokami no
midare mo shirazu
uchifuseba
mazu kakiyarishi
hito zo koishiki[70]

As I lie prostrate
Indifferent that my black hair
Is all dishevelled,
I recall with yearning how
He always combed and stroked it.

One explanation of the poem, perhaps too modern, is that Izumi recalls with nostalgia, after making love with another man, her first lover.

We can hear Izumi's voice in her seasonal poetry, too, as in this pair of spring poems:

hito mo minu
yado no sakura wo
uetareba
hana mote yatsusu
mi to zo narinuru

Because I planted
A cherry tree at a house
That nobody visits,
I now use the cherry flowers
To beautify myself.

wa ga yado no
sakura wa kai mo
nakarikeri
aruji kara koso
hito mo mi ni kure[71]

The cherry tree
In my garden has blossomed,
But it does no good:
The woman, and not a tree,
Is what draws the visitors.

Izumi Shikibu's most characteristic poetry describes the successive stages of her love affairs, generally in terms of her unhappiness. Often grief turns her thoughts to the perishability of life, as in this poem:

ari totemo
tanomubeki ka wa
yo no naka wo
shirasuru mono wa
asagao no hana[72]

I'm still alive, yes,
But can I depend on it?
The thing that reveals
The true nature of the world
Are morning-glory blossoms.

The phrase *yo no naka* was often used to mean not only "the world in which we live" but "the relations between men and women," and these overtones are also present. The poem is classified among the spring poems, presumably because of the mention of short-lived morning glories, but the season is hardly of consequence. Izumi Shikibu's love poetry used nature imagery to powerful effect:

hito no mi mo
koi ni wa kaetsu

For love I am ready
To change even my human shape;

natsu mushi no	All that distinguishes
arawa ni moyu to	Me from the summer insects
mienu bakari zo[73]	Is that my flame is hidden.

The summer insects Izumi refers to are probably fireflies: she contrasts their visible flames with her internal passion, and supposes that she would prefer to be a firefly, consumed by her own fire, even at the cost of sacrificing the human form which (according to Buddhist belief) she acquired through merit in a previous existence.

Izumi Shikibu in later life was tormented by men who forsook her, but the greatest pain she suffered was caused by the death of her lover, Prince Atsumichi. It led her to consider renouncing the world and becoming a nun.

ima wa tada	Now I can only think—
so yo sono koto to	Yes, that happened, and that, too,
omoiidete	Recalling the past.
wasuru bakari no	I wish I had some memories
uki koto mo gana[74]	So sad I'd want to forget them.

The next poem has the preface "Composed about the same time, when I was thinking of becoming a nun."

sutehaten to	I feel so wretched
omou sae koso	I am ready even to
kanashikere	Abandon the world—
kimi ni narenishi	When I think that I was once
wa ga mi to omoeba[75]	Intimate with such a man!

The third poem of the sequence is titled "Written the Last Night of the Year."

naki hito no	I have heard there is
kuru yo to kikedo	A night when the dead return;
kimi mo nashi	But he is no more,
wa ga sumu yado ya	And the house I live in is
tamanaki no sato[76]	A soulless habitation.

Perhaps the most affecting of Izumi Shikibu's poems is the one included in the collection *Hyakunin Isshu*. It was apparently composed early in her life, though the title and contents suggest otherwise. The title is "Sent to Someone When I Was Not Feeling Well."

arazaran	Soon I shall be dead.
kono yo no hoka no	As a final remembrance
omoide ni	To take from this world,
ima hito tabi	Come to me now once again—
au koto mo gana[77]	That is what I long for most.

Akazome Emon, though far less celebrated than Izumi Shikibu, was also an affecting poet. In addition, she is credited with having written the first part of the historical romance *A Tale of Flowering Fortunes*. The dates of her birth and death are not known, but her poetry indicates that she was alive between 976 and 1041.[78] Akazome was a contemporary of Izumi, and they were apparently friends. When Akazome heard that Izumi had separated from her first husband, she wrote a poem with the prefatory note "Sent on hearing that Izumi Shikibu, having been deserted by Michisada, had become intimate with Prince Atsumichi."

utsurowade	Do not shift your love,
shibashi shinoda no	Be patient awhile longer;
mori wo mi yo	See how in the Wood
kaeri mo zo suru	Of Shinoda the wind twists back
kuzu no urakaze[79]	The leaves of the arrowroot.

The verb *utsurou* in the first line means to change, but also (of blossoms) to fade or scatter. The Wood of Shinoda was in the province of Izumi; mention of this wood surely refers to Izumi Shikibu's husband, the governor of Izumi. Shinoda also suggests the verb *shinobu*, "to endure." The arrowroot (*kuzu*) leaves were often mentioned in poetry in terms of their white undersides, revealed when the autumn wind blows. The heart of the poem is the word *kaeri*, meaning the "turning over" of the leaves and the "return" of the husband. The poem can hardly be said to be typical of Akazome's style, but its involved expression suggests the intellectual cast of her poetry, as opposed to the more highly emotional Izumi. The latter's reply to Akazome was, however, almost equally complicated:

akikaze wa	However fiercely
sugoku fuku tomo	The autumn wind may blow,
kuzu no ha no	I feel sure my face

uramigao ni wa	Will not reveal the underside
mieji to zo omou[80]	Of the leaves of arrowroot.

Plays on words give Izumi's poem their meanings: *aki* is not only "autumn" but "satiety," suggesting that her husband is weary of her and treats her cruelly; but, Izumi insists, she will not show bitterness on her face. *Urami* means both "resentment" and "seeing the underside."

These and other exchanges between the two women indicate that Akazome, more prudent than Izumi, never achieved the poetic intensity of her friend. She was the daughter of one distinguished poet, Taira no Kanemori (d. 990), and the wife of another, the learned Ōe no Masahira (952–1012). The attribution to Akazome of *A Tale of Flowering Fortunes* is proof of the respect that she enjoyed as a scholar of Japanese history. Her poems reveal that she was also well acquainted with Buddhism. The following poem is from the *shakkyō* (Buddhist teachings) section of the *Goshūishū*:

koromo naru	Unknown to me
tama to mo kakete	It was attached as a jewel
shirazariki	To my garment!
eisamete koso	How pleasant to have awakened
ureshikarikere	From my drunken stupor.[81]

The poem refers to the Buddhist parable of the man who sewed a jewel into the lining of his friend's garment. The friend wore the garment unaware of the treasure it contained; the jewel is the Buddha nature within all of us which we must discover. Akazome's Buddhist piety did not, however, prevent her from addressing poems of prayer to the Shintō god Sumiyoshi for her son's recovery from illness.

Akazome's skill as a poet is confirmed by the large number of *daisaku* (poems written in place of another person) she composed, more than any other woman poet. She was repeatedly asked to compose poems even on very private occasions:

"When Michitaka was a lesser captain, he for a time courted my sister. Early one morning, after he had failed to keep his promise to visit her, I wrote this poem in her place."

yasurawade	I suppose you slept
nenamashi mono wo	Soundly, nothing troubling you;
sayo fukete	But late that same night

katabuku made no I stared at the moon until
tsuki wo mishi kana[82] It sank in the sky to the west.

Akazome was also much in demand for "screen poems." Although these poems, because of their public nature, seldom express personal feelings, by imagining the emotions of a woman portrayed in a screen painting Akazome at times suggested she was personally involved:

haru ya kuru	Will there be a spring?
hito ya tou tomo	And will people come to visit?
matarekeri	Then, I can wait.
kesa yamazato no	This morning in my mountain village
yuki wo nagamete[83]	I spent staring at the snow.

Akazome's most personal poems describe such subjects as the death of her husband.

"When I was on my way to Ishiyama after the death of Masahira, I saw a new house that looked extremely dilapidated. I asked what had happened, and was told that it had fallen into this state after the death of the occupant's father two years before. I wrote:"

hitori koso	I had supposed
areyuku toko wa	That I alone lamented
nagekitsure	A neglected bed,
nushi naki yado wa	But here was another house
mata mo arikeri[84]	Bereft of its master.

Akazome's last poems, however, were cheerful, celebrating the birth of her great-grandson Ōe no Masafusa. Here is the first of the series:

"Composed after the birth of Masafusa, on asking someone to sew baby clothes for him."

kumo no ue ni	I wish I could live
noboran made mo	Long enough to see him soar
miteshi gana	High above the clouds
tsuru no kegoromo	When his cloak of crane feathers
toshi fu to nareba[85]	Has grown out with the years.

Ōe no Masafusa (1041–1111), a brilliant scholar, would live up to Akazome's expectations; in his case, likening the baby to a crane who will soar above the clouds was not mere hyperbole.

The third of the important women poets of the *Goshūishū*, Sagami, belonged to the generation after Izumi Shikibu and Akazome Emon. She was the contemporary of Izumi's daughter, Koshikibu no Naishi, and of Murasaki Shikibu's daughter, Daini no Sammi, both of whom had a few poems in the *Goshūishū*.

Sagami's poetry acquires its special intensity from what we know of her life. She was married first to Ōe no Kin'yori (d. 1040), a scholar and poet whose career was largely spent as a provincial governor. It was apparently after their return to the capital that Sagami had an affair with Fujiwara no Sadayori (995–1045). A poem by Sagami bears the prefatory note, "While I was married to Kin'yori, the Middle Counselor Sadayori secretly visited me on occasion, but he seems to have found it increasingly difficult to arrange meetings, and his visits threatened to cease altogether. I wrote":

au koto no	Even in the days
naki yori kanete	Before we became lovers
tsurakereba	You were often cold;
samo aramashi ni	My sleeves are soaked with tears,
nururu sode kana[86]	The future seems so bleak.

Sagami's husband was furious when he learned of the affair. She related in the preface to another poem that the husband searched out all the poems and works of fiction in her possession and burned every one.[87] This extraordinary action may have been intended to spite Sagami by burning works of her composition, but Kin'yori may also have blamed her infidelity on her readings in amorous literature. He seems to have considered that their marriage was ended, but Sagami complained in another poem, "When Ōe no Kin'yori was governor of Sagami, I went to his province with him, but when he became governor of Tōtōmi, he forgot about me and took another woman with him. When I learned this, I sent him this poem."

Ōsaka no	Although I do not hope
seki ni kokoro wa	In my heart to see again
kayowanedo	Ōsaka Barrier,
mishi azumaji wa	I still recall with longing
nao zo koishiki[88]	The road we took to the east.

Sagami did not attempt to excuse her infidelity, nor even the cruelty she sometimes showed her lovers:

"When the Middle Counselor Sadayori came on horseback to visit me, he called, 'Open the gate!' but I put him off with one excuse after another and refused to open the gate. He went away. The next day I sent this poem."

samo koso wa	Just as I supposed—
kokoro kurabe ni	In any contest of wills
makezarame	You won't be outdone.
hayaku mo mieshi	Your horse certainly looked fast,
koma no ashi kana[89]	But you needn't have rushed away!

Another lover of Sagami's, Tachibana no Norinaga, was the son of Sei Shōnagon and her first husband, Tachibana no Norimitsu. This affair must have taken place after Kin'yori went off to Tōtōmi with his new wife. A touching poem is a souvenir of that affair.

"I saw Tachibana no Norinaga pass by one day on horseback. It was while his father was governor of Michinoku. Norinaga seemed to be completely unaware he had been noticed, so I sent this poem early the next day."

tsuna taete	Yesterday I saw
hanarehatenishi	A horse from Obuchi
Michinoku no	In Michinoku;
Obuchi no koma wo	His reins had been broken
kinō mishi kana[90]	And he ran completely loose.

The poem describes Norinaga as he rides by, but it indirectly refers to Sagami herself: now that their affair has ended, she too has been cut adrift, like a horse without reins.

Such glimpses make us want to know more about Sagami, but there are only scraps of information to satisfy one's curiosity. Her poems lack the intensity that make Izumi Shikibu's so memorable, but they stand out among the poems of passionate women in the *Goshūishū*.

The most important male poet of the collection was the priest Nōin, who figures in almost as many anecdotes as the Six Poets. One poem became particularly famous because of its alleged untruthfulness.

"Composed at the Shirakawa Barrier when I traveled to Michinoku."

miyako wo ba	I left the capital
kasumi to tomo ni	Together with the rising
tachishikado	Mists of spring, but

akikaze zo fuku	Autumn winds are blowing now
Shirakawa no seki[91]	At Shirakawa Barrier.

Despite Nōin's statement that he composed the poem while on his travels in the north, rumors insisted that he had actually remained in his house in the capital, sunning himself in order to give the impression that he had been exposed to the elements. It makes little difference to us whether or not Nōin composed the poem at Shirakawa Barrier, but it is noteworthy that Nōin inspired such gossip; it proves that he was of exceptional interest to his contemporaries. Another travel poem by Nōin was less controversial.

"On the way to the province of Tsu."

Ashinoya no	Day draws to a close
Koya no watari ni	At the crossing of Koya
hi wa kurenu	Near Ashinoya.
izuchi yukuran	Which direction should I take?
koma ni makasete[92]	I will let my horse decide.

One other poem by Nōin in the *Goshūishū* illustrates the practice, increasingly common from this time, of borrowing the language or conception from a predecessor's poem. The practice of honka-dori did not originate with the poets of the *Goshūishū* (as we have seen)[93] but from this time on it became typical of poetry composed at the court. Ōe no Yoshitoki, later governor of Tsushima, had composed this poem on wild pinks:

kokoro aran	I should like to show,
hito ni misebaya	To someone who understands them,
asatsuyu ni	Blossoms of the pink
nurete wa masaru	Lovelier than ever when
nadeshiko no hana[94]	Moistened with morning dew.

Nōin's poem was:

kokoro aran	I should like to show,
hito ni misebaya	To someone who understands it,
Tsu no kuni no	The beauty of spring

Naniwa watari no	In the Naniwa region
haru no keshiki[95]	Of the province of Tsu.

Nōin obviously borrowed the first two of his five lines from Yoshitoki's poem. His admiration for Yoshitoki's poetry was no secret: he had become a disciple of a certain poet after hearing the latter recite, as an example of how a waka should be composed, a poem by Yoshitoki which he himself had long admired.[96] It was precisely because Nōin revered the poetry of Yoshitoki that he chose to pay him the compliment of borrowing, rather as Beethoven borrowed a melody from Mozart for his variations—not because he had run out of original tunes, and certainly not in the hopes that nobody would suspect he had borrowed Mozart's music, but because the melody had moved him so deeply that he paid it the homage of allowing it to develop within his own imagination.

In this instance, the "variation" is clearly more impressive than the original theme. The poem by Nōin was likened to a piece of writing in kana by a master calligrapher: it shows no special artifice but achieves with a minimum of words an indescribably poetic effect.[97] Nōin's poems were in turn borrowed by later poets. For example, his poem on Shirakawa Barrier,[98] (see above, p. 302) inspired this variation by Minamoto no Yorimasa (1104–1180):

miyako ni wa	In the capital
mada aoba nite	The leaves were still green
mishikadomo	When I saw them last,
momiji chirishiku	But red leaves are falling in drifts
Shirakawa no seki[99]	At Shirakawa Barrier.

When Yorimasa's poem was submitted at an uta-awase on the topic of "fallen leaves on the barrier road," Shun'e said of it, "This poem resembles the famous one by Nōin, 'Autumn winds are blowing / At Shirakawa Barrier.' All the same, the poem is sure to make quite an impression. It is not the same as Nōin's, but demonstrates that the materials can be used in another way. It should not be criticized for the resemblances."[100] Yorimasa's poem reads so well that it was included in the seventh imperial anthology, *Senzaishū*, but it may strike modern readers as being excessively close to its source. It makes a good example of how much greater importance Japanese critics attached to perfection of language than to originality.

The many anecdotes about Nōin are likely to whet the reader's appetite for poems in an eccentric vein, but Nōin's eccentricity in poetry rarely goes beyond conceits such as the following:

kōri to mo	I should like to think
hito no kokoro wo	Her heart was made of ice:
omowabaya	The warm breeze blowing
kesa tatsu haru no	Since this first morning of spring
kaze ya toku beku[101]	Would surely liquefy it.

The poem probably was not inspired by Nōin's heartfelt love for some woman, but composed on the stated topic of a poetry gathering. On such occasions even Buddhist priests wrote of love, and Nōin was no exception, but he was happiest in descriptive poetry:

yamazato no	An evening in spring
haru no yūgure	In a mountain village—
kite mireba	Just as I arrived,
iriai no kane ni	To the sound of a vesper bell,
hana zo chirikeru[102]	Cherry blossoms were falling.

Other poets of the *Goshūishū* might be mentioned, but the strongest impression is left by those whose poetry was most generously selected. Izumi Shikibu, Akazome Emon, Sagami, and Nōin are memorable not only for their poetry but for the legends that surround them. The *Goshūishū* is the best of the imperial collections between the *Kokinshū* and *Shin Kokinshū* both because of the intrinsic quality of the poetry and because it set the direction of future collections away from the past and toward the present.

The Last Heian Imperial Collections

The Kin'yōshū

Some forty years elasped between the compilation of the *Goshūishū* and the fifth imperial collection, *Kin'yō Waka Shū* (Collection of Golden Leaves), usually known as the *Kin'yōshū*. During this period conceptions of poetry changed, largely in response to changes in the political situation. As long as control of the country was in the hands of the Fujiwara regents and chancellors, poetry had tended to be considered mainly as an elegant accomplishment that ornamented the public and private lives of members of the court. Such poems were most often intended to serve as go-betweens in love affairs or to perform other social functions, and were not expected to display profundity or the complexities of the poet's intelligence. A poem was praised to the degree that the author had succeeded in conveying his emotions and perceptions with the utmost sensitivity.

A change in attitude occurred late in the eleventh century as the Fujiwara family was gradually displaced as the de facto rulers of Japan by retired emperors who ruled after taking the tonsure, a system of government known as *insei*, or "cloister government." The first attempt to free the throne of Fujiwara domination had occurred when the Emperor Gosanjō abdicated in 1072 in favor of his son, Shirakawa, intending that the boy serve as a ceremonial figurehead while he himself exerted actual power. Gosanjō's death in the following year prevented him from carrying out this plan, but Shirakawa, who abdicated in 1086, was to reign as the cloistered emperor for forty-three years until his death in 1129.

Shirakawa and his counselors thought of poetry not merely as a pleasant adjunct to life but as a manifestiation of a well-governed state; waka poetry was to be the Japanese equivalent of the rites and music described in Confucian texts.[103] Such an attitude threatened to inhibit waka composition by burdening this poetic form with an ideology that it was too frail to bear, but Shirakawa, who still exercised power during the reign of the Emperor Horikawa (1086–1107), seems to have allowed Horikawa to indulge his dilettantish tastes in poetry and music. This affected the composition of poetry at the court, but it did not signify a return to the *Kokinshū*.

The outstanding poetic achievement of Horikawa's reign was the compilation of the collection of poetry known as *Horikawa-in Ontoki Hyakushu Waka* (One Hundred Waka Composed in the Time of the Cloistered Emperor Horikawa). The time of the compilation was 1105 or 1106. This was not an imperial collection (chokusenshū), and has therefore been given comparatively little attention, but most of the leading poets of the day participated, regardless of whether they were "progressive" or "conservative," and the collection represents an important development between the *Goshūishū* and the *Kin'yōshū*.

Poetic sequences were composed from time to time during the century and a half after Sone no Yoshitada produced his sequences of one hundred waka, and there were numerous uta-awase at which participants composed poems on set topics. The Horikawa sequence combined the variety of Yoshitada's with the competitiveness of the uta-awase.

The title of the sequence composed under the aegis of the Cloistered Emperor Horikawa mentions "one hundred waka"; this meant that sixteen poets each composed waka on one hundred set topics, for a total of 1,600 poems. The sequence was on the scale of an imperial collection, and the quality of the participants ensured that the poetry would be exceptionally skillful. Ōe no Masafusa was traditionally credited with having set the hundred topics,[104] but this claim has been disputed by recent scholars who believe that Minamoto no Toshiyori (1055?–1129?, also known as Shunrai) more probaby provided them.[105] Many topics were borrowed from *Wakan Rōei Shū* (see pages 341–344).

The Horikawa sequence contains poems in the most advanced style practiced at the court, but it was squarely in the traditions of the imperial collections; over 40 percent of the 1,600 poems were variations on waka in the *Kokinshū*, *Gosenshū*, or *Shūishū*.[106] The topics were also familiar, giving special attention to meteorological phenomena (mist, fog, wintry showers, and so on); flowers, insects, and birds of the four seasons; and the stages in a love affair from the first amorous thoughts to the bitterness of parting. A group of miscellaneous topics included mountains, rivers, bridges, and dreams. Composing one hundred poems on topics that may not have been of special interest to a particular poet must have been a strain, but the compiler had a far more difficult task—to ensure that the poems remained at a high level of proficiency and to keep the sixteen poems on any given topic (whether hail, mosquito incense, or reeds) from becoming tedious. If Toshiyori was in fact the compiler, it gave him good practice for the next imperial collection, the *Kin'yōshū*.

The *Kin'yōshū* was compiled by command of the Cloistered Emperor Shirakawa in 1124.[107] The first draft of the collection was rejected by Shirakawa, as was the second. Only on Minamoto no Toshiyori's third attempt did he obtain the cloistered emperor's approval. The grounds for Shirakawa's rejection of the first two versions are not clear. Some critics have suggested that he disapproved of Toshiyori's overly "radical" tastes in waka,[108] but surely he must have known Toshiyori's tastes when he appointed this third son of the disgruntled Tsunenobu as the sole compiler. Perhaps Shirakawa himself had changed during the years since he commanded the compilation of the *Goshūishū* and had moved over to the "radical" camp, at least to the extent of wishing to create a collection that would not be one more sounding of the themes of the *Kokinshū*.

All three versions of the *Kin'yōshū* have been preserved, but although there are differences in the contents (and the total number of poems), it is not obvious why Shirakawa preferred the third to the earlier versions. According to a theory that goes back to *Imakagami* (The New Mirror), a historical work completed in 1170, Shirakawa objected to the prominence of a poem by Ki no Tsurayuki at the head of the first version.[109] If this was true, Shirakawa, far from opposing the radical tendencies of his editor, expected to see an even more decisive rejection of old poetic traditions; but there is contradictory evidence. The first version included many poems by authors represented in the *Kokinshū*, *Gosenshū*, and *Shūishū* that were pruned in the second version to present a distinctly more modern impression; however, the inclusion in the third version of eighty-one poems by Nōin and twenty-one additional poems from the archconservative collection *Shūishū* suggests that editorial policy had shifted in the opposite direction. In any case, the second rather than the third version of the *Kin'yōshū* gained recognition as the definitive text.

The *Kin'yōshū* was in ten rather than the customary twenty books, perhaps on the model of the *Shūishō*.[110] The total number of poems was small, only 691 waka in even the most ample version. The title was the first to depart from the practice of naming imperial collections by referring to the *Kokinshū*; instead of describing itself as a "later" collection or as a collection of "gleanings" missed by the *Kokinshū* compilers, this collection boldly proclaimed itself to be the "Collection of Golden Leaves," meaning glorious poems. Some critics, however, recalling the story that on the day of Buddha's death flowers with golden petals fell from the sky, insisted that the title was inauspicious.[111] Other, less complimentary, nicknames were soon given to the collection. Fujiwara no Moritsune called it *hijitsuki aruji* (the master who leans on an armrest), mocking the self-assurance of the compiler.[112] Certainly, self-confidence was evident not only in the title but in the unusually generous selection of poems by Toshiyori and his father Tsunenobu: Toshiyori led all contributors with thirty-seven poems, and his father came next with twenty-seven, but the "enemy," the conservative Fujiwara no Mototoshi, had only three poems included. Izumi Shikibu, who figured so prominently in the *Goshūishū*, was also represented by a bare three poems.[113]

The "radical" tendencies of Toshiyori should not be interpreted as a rejection of the courtliness that had been the most conspicuous feature of waka composition since the *Kokinshū*; indeed, from our point of view the *Goshūishū*, thanks to the startlingly passionate poetry of Izumi Shikibu and Sagami, is much more immediate than the poetry of Toshiyori and his group. His radicalism consisted mainly in his advocacy of the poetry of contemporaries. This was generally true also of the *Goshūishū*, but that collection had covered a much longer period of time than the

Kin'yōshū.[114] The *Goshūishū* had also included a greater variety of poetic styles than the *Kin'yōshū*, in which the poetry is largely descriptive. The poetry in the *Kin'yōshū* is fresh mainly in terms of its contrasts with the first three imperial collections, but at times its "light" manner threatens to become superficial.[115]

The emphasis in the *Kin'yōshū* on contemporary poetry accounts for another distinctive feature, the inclusion of sixteen renga in the last book. This was the first collection to designate a renga section, though examples of renga were also found in the *Shūishū*. These examples of linked verse, unlike the extended "chains" of the medieval period, consisted of a single waka composed by two persons, the first supplying the opening seventeen syllables, and the second completing the poem with an additional fourteen syllables. The renga would achieve far greater complexity in later times, but it may have been as a mark of contemporaneity that Toshiyori included in his collection samples of an incipient development in court poetry.

The *Kin'yōshū* cannot be said to be strikingly new; indeed, it contains many poems that bear no relationship to the theories of poetry that Toshiyori had elsewhere voiced.[116] The collection opens, for example, with this waka by Fujiwara no Akisue:

"Composed on the theme 'the beginning of spring' when, in the time of the Cloistered Emperor Horikawa, I offered one hundred poems."

uchinabiki	Mists all pervading,
haru wa kinikeri	Spring has at last arrived.
yamakawa no	Has the ice between
iwama no kōri	The rocks in the mountain streams
kesa ya tokuran[117]	Started to melt this morning?

This poem, with its observation of one natural phenomenon leading to a conjecture about another,[118] would not have been out of place in the *Kokinshū*. Akisue's place in the history of Japanese poetry is as the founder of the conservative Rokujō school, the first real poetic "house,"[119] and definitely not as an innovator. It is strange that a poem by a man who was the literary enemy of the compiler—a conservative who opposed Toshiyori's innovations—should have been honored by having his poem head an imperial collection, but perhaps the Cloistered Emperor Shirakawa imposed this choice.

Another poem that appears early in the collection was by Shirakawa himself. It is on the topic "willow threads follow the breeze." "Willow threads" was a familiar term for the slender branches of the weeping willow.

kaze fukeba	When the breezes blow
yanagi no ito no	The threads of willow branches
katayori ni	Incline to one side;
nabiku ni tsukete	And with each rippling response
suguru haru kana[120]	The spring is disappearing.

Much of the poetry is charming in the courtly manner of this poem by Fujiwara no Tsunetada (1075–1138) on the topic "the mountains are cold and the blossoms late":

yamazakura	Mountain cherry flowers—
kozue no kaze no	The wind through the treetops
samukereba	Is still so chilly
hana no sakari ni	That the flowers hesitate
nari zo wazurau[121]	To burst into full bloom.

The freshness of tone in the collection was not necessarily due to Toshiyori's iconoclasm. Fujiwara no Mototoshi (1056–1142), who has been described as the "outstanding representative of the ultraconservative group,"[122] could write no less strikingly. One of three poems by Mototoshi included in the *Kin'yōshū* is on the topic "facing the water, I await the moon":

natsu no yo no	While I waited for
tsuki matsu hodo no	The moon of a summer night,
tesusabi ni	To distract my hands
iwa moru shimizu	I dipped again and again
iku musubishitsu[123]	The pure water through the rocks.

The heart of this poem is in the words *tesusabi ni* ("to distract my hands"), suggesting the pleasure of letting cool water trickle from the rocks onto his hands. Mototoshi's poem was much admired, even though rivals had denied him adequate representation in the *Kin'yōshū*. His overbearing self-confidence probably explains why he never rose above the junior fifth rank, but he ultimately gained a niche in the history of the waka as the teacher (in his old age) of the young Fujiwara Shunzei, to whom he transmitted the secrets of the *Kokinshū*. These teachings, later known as the *Kokin Denju*, were to be the most prized credential of a waka poet for the next five hundred years.

Still, it cannot be doubted that the characteristic tone of the *Kin'yōshū* was imparted by the poems of Toshiyori and his father, Tsunenobu. The latter had a villa in the country he often visited and unlike the many poets who, scarcely stirring from the capital, imagined the loveliness of the autumn mountains, he had actually seen them. The difference can be detected in such descriptions of nature as the following poem on the beginning of autumn:

onozukura	Without any fanfare,
aki wa kinikeri	Autumn has made its way to
yamazato no	The mountain village
kuzu wa hikakaru	Where arrowroot vines enlace
maki no fuseya ni[124]	The peasants' wooden shanties.

Another poem, on "autumn wind by a house in the fields," describes the mountain hamlet of Umezu where a friend had a villa:

yū sareba	When it becomes dusk,
kadota no inaba	The autumn wind blows against
otozurete	The huts thatched with reeds
ashi no maroya ni	And pays its respects to leaves
akikaze zo fuku[125]	Of rice plants before the gate.

For the most typical *Kin'yōshū* style we must turn to the poems of Toshiyori, the chief "radical" poet. One may not be immediately struck, however, by his daring. The following poem bears the heading "Composed on the theme of 'the wind is calm and the blossoms fragrant' at the palace of the empress during the reign of the Cloistered Emperor Horikawa."

kozue ni wa	Though nothing suggests
fuku to mo miede	Wind blowing in the treetops,
sakurabana	The cherry blossoms
kaoru zo kaze no	Are fragrant—surely a sign
shirushi narikeru[126]	That wind is stirring today.

The novelty of the poem comes from the conceit that even cherry blossoms (which have no odor) are as fragrant as plum blossoms when the spring breeze caresses them.

Freshness in Toshiyori's poetry is likely to be found in a particular image rather than in the basic conception. The topic of the following poem is "the wind over the water is cool at eventide."

kaze fukeba	When the wind blows
hasu no ukiha ni	Jewels leap from the water to
tama koete	Floating lily pads,
suzushiku narinu	And now it has become cool—
higurashi no koe[127]	The voice of the cicada.

There is some uncertainty about the meaning of this poem. One commentator believed that drops of water (jewels) are blown off the lily pads into the water; but another (whose version I have followed) interpreted the line as meaning that the wind caused drops of water from the stream to jump onto the lily pads where they looked like jewels. Whichever meaning was intended, the image is appealingly unconventional, and the last line successfully transfers the impression of coolness from the water lilies to the sound of an evening cicada (*higurashi*), a harbinger of autumn.

Another poem, on the theme of "grasses of the field after the rain," displays Toshiyori's careful observation of nature:

kono sato mo	In this village, too,
yūdachi shikeri	There has been an evening shower;
asajiu ni	In the clump of weeds
tsuyu no suguranu	There is not a blade of grass
kusa no ha mo nashi[128]	Without its clinging dewdrop.

The poet has arrived in a village. The sky is clear, but when he closely examines the grasses in the field he notices drops of water that tell him it has rained here recently, just as in the place from which he has come.

Toshiyori became prominent as a poet rather late in life; the earlier part of his career was apparently devoted to official duties, though he remained to the end humble in rank. The bitter feelings aroused by his unluckiness are revealed again and again in his poetry; he may have been the first waka poet to employ the form to express grievances.[129] The last poem in the *Kin'yōshū* bears the prefatory note: "Not having obtained office until the age of seventy, my mind, as a result, has been constantly occupied with disagreeable thoughts about everyone."

nanasoji ni	Seventy years old—
michinuru shio no	The rising tide has engulfed
hamabisashi	The sand castle:
hisashiku yo ni mo	What a terribly long time
uzumorenuru kana[130]	I have been buried in this world!

Toshiyori communicated the same resentment in another poem without being so specific:

yo no naka wa	Is this world of ours
ukimi ni soeru	A shadow somehow attached
kage nare ya	To my luckless self?
omoisutsuredo	Although I try to shake free,
hanarezarikeri[131]	It refuses to let me go.

Another poem by Toshiyori (not in the *Kin'yōshū*) is in essentially the same vein but has a note of humor:

tsukuzuku to	After much careful
hitori emu wo mo	Pondering I could not but
shitsuru kana	Smile to myself
aramashigoto wo	As I reviewed once again
omoitsuzukete[132]	All the things I had once planned.

Many of Toshiyori's best poems are in the descriptive mode, and the *Kin'yōshū* is often said to mark a turning point in the development of the waka from the conceptually viewed nature of the *Kokinshū* poets to nature as actually observed. However, Toshiyori also wrote some Buddhist poems of interest. One bears the prefatory note "Written on a place on a painting that depicts a priest boarding a boat at the West Gate of the Tennō-ji, where it is rowed westward away from the shore."

Amida butsu to	My voice invoking
tonauru koe wo	The name of Amida Buddha
kaji nite ya	Shall be my rudder
kurushiki umi wo	And I will row away across
kogihanaruran[133]	The sea of unhappiness.

The misery of life in this world has often been likened to a sea of pain (*kukai*), and the Buddhist Law was compared to a boat that enabled the believer to traverse that sea. There was also a belief that if anyone rowed a boat from the great temple Tennō-ji in Naniwa (Osaka), where it was customary to gaze at the sun as it set in the sea, and jumped into the sea and drowned, he would go directly to Amida's paradise.[134] Elsewhere, Toshiyori declared his belief that poetry could not fail to be a help in gaining salvation (*uta mo yomiji wo tasukezarame ya*), a first sounding of the medieval justification for the existence of literature.[135]

Many *Kin'yōshū* poems by Toshiyori and his collaborators could be cited to illustrate their skill at composing descriptive poetry or to demonstrate their other interests. The lasting impression left by the collection is nevertheless likely to be of poems of middling interest whose chief appeal is their anticipation of the greatly superior poetry of the *Shin Kokinshū*.

The Shikashū

The *Shikashū* (Collection of Verbal Flowers) is the smallest and least interesting of the six imperial collections compiled between the *Kokinshū* and *Shin Kokinshū*. In 1144 the Retired Emperor Sutoku (1119–1164) commanded Fujiwara no Akisuke (1090–1155) to compile a new imperial collection. Less than twenty years had elapsed since the final version of the *Kin'yōshū* had been approved by the Retired Emperor Shirakawa, but most of the major *Kin'yōshū* poets were dead, and Akisuke, who was not only a distinguished poet but an uncle of Sutoku, was an appropriate choice for the compiler. He presented the completed collection for imperial approval (probably in 1151), and it was accepted with minor revisions the next year.[136]

Akisuke seems to have modeled the *Shikashū* on the *Kin'yōshū*: it is in ten rather than the customary twenty books, and the title, literally "Collection of Flowers of Words," echoes the "golden leaves" of the earlier collection.[137] The title aroused adverse criticism from the start: unfriendly critics pointed out that *shi* (words) was the homophone of *shi* (death), a most unsuitable association for a collection that bore the emperor's imprimatur.[138] This criticism was not taken seriously, but there were more fundamental objections: even at the time, it was recognized that little new poetry of worth was being composed, reflecting the deteriorating fortunes of the court during the late Heian period. It was alleged, moreover, that not enough time had elapsed since the compilation of the *Kin'yōshū* for sufficient poetry to accumulate from which a reasonable selection could be made.[139] Anti-*Shikashū* collections were compiled to demonstrate the inadequacy of Akisuke's,[140] but most of them, unlike the imperial collection, have been lost.

The *Shikashū* contains 415 poems.[141] Its character is apparent from the poets who were best represented: Sone no Yoshitada (seventeen poems), Izumi Shikibu (sixteen poems), and Ōe no Masafusa (fourteen poems). The *Kin'yōshū* had favored contemporary poets, but the *Shikashū* definitely looked back to the past. One might attribute this to Akisuke's conservative tastes, but Yoshitada and Izumi Shikibu were hardly academic poets, and their poems in the *Shikashū* are especially unconventional. Again, the "radical" Toshiyori was represented by eleven poems, but there was not one poem by his conservative rival Mototoshi. These contrary tendencies have induced commentators to describe the *Shikashū* as a "middle-of-the-road" anthology; it is conservative in its preference for relatively recent poems, but daring in its choice of old works. A spirit of compromise characterizes the *Shikashū*, and although the attempt to achieve a "middle way" between old and new did not lead to distinctive poetry, more successful attempts along the same lines would be made in the future.[142]

Akisuke, following the Retired Emperor Sutoku's explicit directions, searched for neglected superior poems from as far back as "middle antiquity," meaning the *Gosenshū* period, but not including the *Kokinshū*. The dissatisfaction of Shirakawa with the preponderance of new poets in the *Kin'yōshū* probably also induced Akisuke to choose new poems sparingly. He included in *Shikashū* some old poems that had been added to the third version of the *Kin'yōshū*, and also poems that had originally appeared in such prose works as *Tales of Yamato, The Gossamer Years,* and *A Tale of Flowering Fortunes*.[143] Forty-five poems were derived from uta-awase sessions held between 970 and 1150.[144]

The chief contribution of the *Shikashū* to the development of Japanese poetry may have been Akisuke's arrangement of the poems. Ever since the *Kokinshū* it had been the practice to arrange seasonal poems in the order in which the described natural events occurred. Akisuke observed this pattern, but he also took account of the language and imagery of the poems in an attempt to make a collection of poems that were originally unconnected read like a single flowing "chain" of poetry.

The opening three poems of the *Shikashū* illustrate Akisuke's method.

(1)	*kōriishi*	At Karasaki
	Shiga no Karasaki	In Shiga the sheet of ice
	uchitokete	Has begun to melt,

sazanami yosuru	And the spring breeze is blowing
harukaze zo fuku	The little waves to the shore.

ŌE NO MASAFUSA

(2) *kinō kamo*	Was it yesterday
arare furishi wa	That hailstones beat down on us?
Shigaraki no	The mist hovering
toyama no kasumi	At Shigaraki over
harumekinikeri	The nearby hills is springlike.

FUJIWARA NO KORENARI

(3) *furusato wa*	The old capital
harumekinikeri	Is given over to spring;
mi Yoshino no	At fair Yoshino
Mikaki ga hara wo	The meadows of Mikaki
kasumikometari	Are covered over with mist.

TAIRA NO KANEMORI[145]

Masafusa's poem had originally appeared in *Horikawa-in Ontoki Hyakushu Waka*, Korenari's in an uta-awase of 986, and Kanemori's in an uta-awase of 960. Needless to say, a great many poems on the beginning of spring had been composed at the court between 960 and 1151. Akisuke chose from among countless examples these particular three because he wished to display from the outset the variety of his collection: Masafusa was a *Goshūishū* poet, Korenari a *Shūishū* poet, and Kanemori a *Gosenshū* poet. The smoothness of the transitions from one poem to the next must also have been in his mind. Masafusa's poem, describing the early spring scenery over Lake Biwa, led naturally to mention of Shigaraki in the province of Ōmi which borders the lake; and the mountains of Shigaraki in turn led naturally to mention of Yoshino in the mountains. If the first two poems had been presented in reverse order, the transition between Lake Biwa and Yoshino would have been difficult, and that was probably why Akisuke favored this arrangement, though in terms of content or chronology either poem could have been first. The connections between poems 2 and 3 are further strengthened by mention in both of mists and by the long word *harumekinikeri* (it has become springlike). The poems are independent, but they are linked in a manner that would be true of later collections of Japanese poetry, creating the impression of a hand scroll being unrolled to disclose continuous but new scenes.

The fourth poem of the *Shikashū*, on the uguisu, is not linked by content to either the preceding or the following poem, though it fits into the general progression of spring. Presumably Akisuke wished to have the "chain" of poetry shift from a general description of the new season to a cluster of poems on a specific sight, the young shoots, and he needed a "neutral" poem to help the transition, much as landscapes in a hand scroll that do not easily merge together are separated by clouds. This technique would be perfected by the masters of renga. Again, in the sequence of late-spring poems, those describing the flowering and falling of the cherry blossoms were separated by two poems on wild geese returning to the north. The first wonders if the geese are leaving because the cherry blossoms are even lovelier in the north, the second suggests that the geese are leaving in order not to be saddened by the fall of the blossoms,[146] the two poems combining to make a perfect transition between the major clusters of poems on the cherry blossoms.

The two books of love poems in the *Shikashū* were arranged, much as in earlier collections, in the order of a love affair from beginning to final separation and forgetting the once beloved. The last two of the ten books consist of poems on a variety of subjects—the seasons, travel, congratulations, mourning, love, and Shintō and Buddhism. The arrangement of the seasonal poems within these books is similar to the pattern in the first four books, but it proved harder to join the other, miscellaneous topics into a seamless sequence. Akisuke's efforts to integrate even these poems may have influenced the more successful compilers of later collections.[147]

There are no poets (whether men or women) who are known primarily as *Shikashū* poets. The lack of any dominant figures is suggested by the fact that the 415 poems were composed by 192 poets, of whom 122 were represented by only one poem. Among the contemporary poets, Akisuke, though only four of his poems appear, was probably the best, as his poem on the topic "relating my feelings to the moon" may suggest:

Naniwae no	As I watch the moon
ashima ni yadoru	Lingering between the reeds
tsuki mireba	Of Naniwa Bay,
wa ga mi hitotsu wa	I am not the only one
shizumazarikeri[148]	To sink into obscurity.

A poem composed in 1135 by the chancellor and former prime minister Fujiwara no Tadamichi (1097–1164) bears the prefatory note

"Composed when His Majesty, the new retired emperor, commanded me to describe a distant view over the sea."

wata no hara	When I row over
kogiidete mireba	The plains of sea and gaze,
hisakata no	Far in the distance
kumoi ni magau	The white waves of the offing
okitsu shiranami[149]	Merge with the clouds of the sky.

One poem that stands out by its individuality is said to have been composed by the obscure Koremune Takayori, but some commentators believe it was really by Minamoto no Toshiyori. Its topic is "falling leaves have no voices."

kaze fukeba	When the storm winds blow
nara no kareha no	The withered leaves of the oak
soyo soyo to	Murmuring, one to
iiawasetsutsu	The other, *soyo, soyo,*
izuchi chiruran[150]	They fall—in which direction?

The use of personification is particularly effective in this winter poem. Another poem, this one definitely by Toshiyori, has the prefatory note "Written on seeing women gathering spring greens in a marsh."

shizunome ga	Thin ice glazes over
egu tsumu sawa no	The marsh where peasant women
usu kōri	Gather watercress;
itsu made fubeki	How much longer can it
wa ga mi naruran[151]	And I remain unbroken?

The fragility of the ice, soon to be broken by the coming of spring (if not by the peasant women), seems to the poet to suggest his own fate. The poem is made vivid by the surprisingly realistic scene and the note of urgency.

A few other poems attract attention because of their authors: one is by the priest Shun'e, the son of Toshiyori and teacher of Kamo no Chōmei; another (identified, however, as anonymous) is by the young Saigyō; another was written by the martial hero and poet Minamoto no Yorimasa; but none is distinctive enough to warrant quotation.

In 1156 a struggle broke out between the Retired Emperor Sutoku and his younger brother, the reigning Emperor Goshirakawa, for control of the court. In the struggle, known as the Hōgen Rebellion, Goshirakawa with the aid of the Taira family overcame Sutoku, who was supported by the Fujiwara.[152] The long domination of the country by civil administrators was broken, leading to the feudal rule of the Taira and the Minamoto, the two great military clans. Sutoku, because of his part in the rebellion, was exiled to the island of Shikoku where he died. A poem in the *Shikashū* by Sutoku expressed hopes for a reconciliation after estrangement. The poem is about a love affair, but it is curiously prophetic of his situation after the unsuccessful rebellion:

se wo hayami	The current is fast
iwa ni sekaruru	And the valley stream is blocked
tanikawa no	By the river rocks;
warete mo sue ni	It divides, but at the end
awan to zo omou[153]	Surely it will reunite.

Two years after the Hōgen Rebellion, in 1158, Goshirakawa abdicated in favor of his son Nijō, but continued to rule as the retired emperor. About 1165 Nijō commanded Fujiwara no Kiyosuke,[154] the son of Akisuke, to compile a new imperial collection of waka. The *Shoku Shikashū* (Continued *Shikashū*), as it was called, was much larger than the *Shikashū*, consisting of 998 poems in twenty books. Kiyosuke presented the manuscript to Nijō, expecting that it would be recognized as the seventh imperial collection, but the emperor died in the same year, 1165. Lacking his approval, the *Shoku Shikashū* ranks only as a private collection.[155]

The poets of the *Shoku Shikashū* were chosen from the period between the *Gosenshū* and Kiyosuke's day. That was about the same range for the *Shikashū*, but Kiyosuke gave preference to recent poets, including the unhappy Sutoku. The selection of poets was fair, with no noticeable prejudice directed against schools other than the compiler's, but the Rokujō poets were prominent all the same.[156] The poems, unlike those written in happier times, when the atmosphere of the Heian court was tranquil and the falling of the cherry blossoms might have been the most dramatic incident in the poets' lives, included some that seem to have had for their background the warfare of the mid-twelfth century.

During the years after the Hōgen Rebellion, the Taira family established its supremacy. Taira no Tadamori had composed poems that were included in the *Kin'yōshū* and *Shikashū*, but his son Kiyomori exhibited no interest in poetry. The next generation of Taira made up for Kiyomori's indifference by the eagerness with which it adopted the cultivated ways of the court aristocracy, including the composition of waka. The Taira continued to hold poetry gatherings and uta-awase competitions in the capital until they were driven from the city by the Minamoto warriors in 1183. Four months before the Taira fled, Goshirakawa commanded Fujiwara Shunzei to compile the imperial collection that would be known as the *Senzaishū*.

The Senzaishū

There could hardly have been a less propitious time for planning a new imperial collection than the spring of 1183. Kyoto had been afflicted during the previous year by a terrible famine, and soon the city would be the scene of warfare. The work of compilation nevertheless continued through the years until the final defeat of the Taira in 1185. When Shunzei submitted the manuscript of the *Senzaishū* (Collection of a Thousand Years) to Goshirakawa in 1188, so many changes had occurred in the country since the command to compile a collection was issued that whatever the original intent may have been, the circumstances were now much altered.

It is rather strange that Goshirakawa sponsored a collection of waka. He was known for his exceptional interest in folk poetry, especially in the *imayō*[157] and *saibara* included in the great collection of popular songs he edited, *Ryōjin Hishō* (Secret Selection of Dust on the Beams), but he was not a waka poet. His reasons for ordering the collection are unclear, but many conjectures have been made. It has been suggested, for example, that he may have been inspired by dread of the vengeful spirit of Sutoku, whose wrath in exile is described in many literary works. Those who were in some way responsible for the exile naturally feared the vengeance of his *onryō*, or vindictive spirit, and the famine had been attributed to this cause. In 1184 a shrine was erected in the hope it would calm Sutoku's anger. The learned priest Jien, writing in 1219, stated that the shrine was necessary because people had come to feel terror over what Sutoku's onryō might do next.[158] It would have made sense (in view of Sutoku's love of poetry) to dedicate a collection of poetry to his memory and thereby placate his spirit.[159]

Goshirakawa's choice of Shunzei as the compiler of the new collection was appropriate not only in terms of his reputation as a poet but because Shunzei had some ten years earlier compiled a private anthology which he had hoped might be promoted to the status of an imperial collection. The abdication of the Emperor Takakura had frustrated this plan, but Shunzei seems not to have abandoned his ambition of being named as the compiler of an imperial collection. Perhaps he even persuaded Goshirakawa to authorize the collection at a time when he was trying to think of some way of assuaging the turbulent ghost of Sutoku.

Goshirakawa may also have been motivated initially by a desire to ingratiate himself with the Taira family. Naturally, he could not have foreseen the future collapse of the Taira, and he may have wished to demonstrate that he could discriminate between the Taira, who by this time had become so aristocratic in their tastes that they could appreciate the waka, and the uncouth Minamoto warriors who were their enemies. Even though Kiyomori showed no interest in poetry, other members of his family were eager poets. Shunzei, as the leading poet of the day, had given instruction to Taira poets, and Goshirakawa had reason to think that appointing him as the compiler would be welcome to them.[160]

Finally, Goshirakawa may have hoped that the old court aristocracy, deprived of its traditional functions by the rise of the military, would be comforted by the appearance of a new imperial collection of waka, the art most intimately associated with them. At a time when their country estates were devastated, and their very survival threatened, an anthology of poetry obviously could not materially improve the situation, but it might at least provide some solace.

Goshirakawa's command for an anthology was issued in the second month of 1183. In the fourth month an expedition set out from the capital to put down an uprising in the provinces, but the Taira army was crushed two months later by the fierce warrior Kiso no Yoshinaka, who followed up his victory by occupying the main temple buildings on Mount Hiei, overlooking the capital. The Taira, realizing that they could not successfully defend the city, fled with the child Emperor Antoku and the imperial regalia. In the eighth month of 1183, the three-year-old Gotoba, a younger brother of Antoku, was crowned in Kyoto, though without the regalia. The Taira were denounced as enemies of the throne.

During this time Shunzei continued to work calmly on the *Senzaishū*, unruffled by the catastrophic changes around him. Dissatisfied with the policy followed by the compilers of the previous two imperial collections, he determined to include as many poems as he deemed fitting, though little new poetry was available. The uta-awase sessions at the palace, which so often had supplied poems for the imperial collections, had been discontinued because of the tense situation. Shunzei had no choice but to depend largely on poems already assembled for his private anthology.[161] Needless to say, the flight of the Taira supporters from the capital brought about a sharp change in editorial policy. Far from attempting to please the Taira family, Shunzei was now obliged to restrict the number of poems by Taira adherents or else to conceal the names of the authors.[162]

The final defeat of the Taira family took place at the Battle of Dannoura in 1185. The Emperor Antoku drowned, and his mother, Kiyomori's daughter, was taken prisoner. Soon afterward, in the seventh month of 1185, a great earthquake struck Kyoto. Not surprisingly, it was ascribed to the vengeful spirits of Antoku and the defeated Taira warriors. Goshirakawa had no love for the Taira, but he was worried about the harm their unquiet ghosts might wreak. In the fourth month of 1186 he ordered services to be held on Mount Kōya for the Taira dead, declaring that although they had been rebels, he no longer felt any animosity toward them.[163] Further memorial services were held the next year for all those who had died since warfare began in the Hōgen era. It might have been expected that the poetry composed by enemies of the court would automatically be excluded from the new collection, but this gesture on the emperor's part was understood by Shunzei, who was emboldened to include in the *Senzaishū* poems by adherents of the Taira.

In later years Shunzei in his important book of poetics *Korai Fūteishō* (Notes on Poetic Style Through the Ages, 1197–1201) would write of the compilation of the anthology, "The poems in the *Senzaishū* were selected entirely by myself, incompetent though I am. I considered only the poetry and forgot who the poets were."[164] His professed disregard for the politics of the poets was most unusual, especially in view of the disorder of the times, but it is hard to believe that he was quite that unaffected; surely there would have been more poems by Tairas if they had not been declared enemies of the state. But Shunzei's basic impartiality cannot be gainsaid. He included twenty-three poems by Sutoku, a number that went beyond the strict necessity of appeasing his ghost, but only six by Goshirakawa. He also included more poems by Toshiyori than by Mototoshi, though the latter was his revered teacher and Toshiyori his teacher's most bitter enemy.

The date of the formal presentation of the completed collection is usually given as 1188.[165] We know of at least one change that occurred in the contents of the *Senzaishū* before it attained its final form. When Shunzei first submitted the manuscript to Goshirakawa, the latter thought Shunzei had included too few of his own poems, and directed him to add another thirty or forty. Shunzei in fact added twenty-five, for a total of thirty-six poems.[166] The present text contains 1,287 poems arranged in twenty books, a return to the scale and format of earlier imperial collections.

Shunzei's selection of poems revealed his astuteness as a judge of poetry, but he has been taken to task for minor faults of editing, such as having included twelve poems that had already appeared in imperial collections. The preface to the next collection, *Shin Kokinshū*, no doubt referring to such lapses, mentioned the likelihood of mistakes when one person, unassisted, compiled a collection; but we should marvel instead that Shunzei, at a time of great turbulence in which he was to some degree involved, persevered and carried his task to completion. Shunzei was sixty-nine years old when he received the command to compile the collection, and seventy-four when the work was done. Some years earlier (in 1176) he had been afflicted with an illness so severe that he had taken the tonsure, supposing he had not much longer to live, but he was now at the height of his powers. He seems to have thrown himself into the editing of the *Senzaishū* as a refuge from thinking about the terrible disorders that ravaged the country, resolved to preserve from the destruction of war the great poetry of his own and earlier times.

Shunzei was the most eminent poet since Tsurayuki to have been charged with the compilation of an imperial collection. His skill was displayed not only in the choice of poems but in their arrangement. Following the method of Akisuke in the *Shikashū*, he arranged the poetry of the *Senzaishū* so that one poem would flow into another by its themes or images. Shunzei, not content with arranging outstanding poems in a suitable order, at times deliberately included inferior poems that served the function of transitions from one masterpiece to the next.[167] It is at first puzzling why the poetry of Dōin, a priest of mediocre poetic talent, should have been generously represented in the *Senzaishū*, but Shunzei seems to have found his poetry particularly useful as neutral "links" in the chains of poetry he had strung together.[168]

Shunzei chose for the *Senzaishū* poems that went back even before the *Shūishū*, but more than half were culled from private anthologies that had appeared since the compilation of the *Shikashū* in the middle of the twelfth century, or had figured in uta-awase of the same period. The emphasis Shunzei gave to poetry of the recent past contrasted with the reverence for old poetry exhibited by the compilers of the *Shikashū*. Sixty-one percent of the *Senzaishū* poets made their first appearance in any imperial collection. The most generously represented poets were Toshiyori (52 poems), Shunzei (36 poems), Mototoshi (26 poems), Sutoku (23 poems), Shun'e (22 poems) and Izumi Shikibu (21 poems). When Shunzei did choose old poems, it was not as a gesture of piety to his poetic ancestors but because these poems possessed a special appeal for him. Some poems composed a century earlier seemed to acquire new overtones when placed in the company of the poetry of Shunzei's contemporaries.[169] A further sign of Shunzei's independence of judgment was his decision to include poems by thirty-three women poets, the largest number of women represented in the six collections between the *Kokinshū* and *Shin Kokinshū*, and a sharp contrast with the *Shikashū* which included the work of only one woman poet.

Perhaps the most striking, though definitely not the best, poet was the unfortunate Sutoku. It is hard to ignore the authorship of his poems, and there is always a danger of reading too much into the expression. The following poem may have meant no more than it says, but it is possible to catch from the words a note of despair in the voice of a man whose every plan had been frustrated.

hana wa ne ni	Flowers have returned
tori wa furusu ni	To their roots and birds have gone
kaeru nari	Back to their old nests;
haru no tomari wa	But no one knows where the spring
shiru hito zo naki[170]	Will find its final haven.

The poem seems to suggest the loneliness of the man with no home to which he can return. Another poem reflects his despondency:

momijiba no	When I looked to see
chiriyuku kata wo	Where the fallen maple leaves
tazunureba	Could have disappeared,
aki mo arashi no	Autumn itself had vanished,
koe nomi zo suru[171]	Leaving the voice of the storm.

In such poems one senses Sutoku's bitterness, though it is not overtly expressed. The spring, unlike the flowers or birds, has nowhere to return once its time has passed. When the fallen leaves, the last remnant of autumn, are gone, nothing except the howl of the winter wind remains—an apt metaphor for his desolation. Another poem, listed in the *Senzaishū* as anonymous but elsewhere attributed to Sutoku, is more outspoken:

uki koto no	While I was dozing
madoromu hodo wa	I was able to forget
wasurarete	My unhappiness,

samureba yume no	And when I woke up I felt
kokochi koso sure[172]	Sure that I must be dreaming.

Minamoto no Yorimasa is closely associated with the *Senzaishū*. The priest-poet Shun'e said of him,

> Lord Yorimasa was a superb waka poet. He threw himself completely into each poem he wrote, from the bottom of his heart, never wavering in his attention and bearing the object constantly in mind. The cry of a bird, the murmur of a breeze—and, of course, the fall of the cherry blossoms, the dropping of the autumn leaves, the rising and setting of the moon, the coming of rain and snow—were all associated with his daily life, and he never failed to make them occasions for poetry. Indeed, it is only natural that he created splendid poems under such circumstances. . . . When he participated at ordinary poetry gatherings and read his poems aloud, or when he criticized other people's compositions, he seemed entirely absorbed by the poetry. He was so impressive that every gathering he attended always had a special éclat.[173]

Yorimasa was a soldier to the end, dying by his own hand at the age of seventy-six after suffering defeat at a battle fought near the Phoenix Hall in Uji. Japanese commentators have pointed out the spaciousness and grandeur in the poems of this soldier-poet, especially in this waka on the theme of "returning wild geese":

amatsusora	Wild geese returning
hitotsu ni miyuru	Make their way through the breakers
Koshi no umi no	Of the Koshi Sea
nami wo wakete mo	That appears to be one with
kaeru karigane[174]	The canopy of the sky.

Many other *Senzaishū* poems merit being quoted, but the central figure of the collection, not only as editor but as a poet, was undoubtedly Shunzei. His poetry had already appeared in the *Shikashū*, and he would have a total of 455 poems in the various imperial collections, but his name is most closely associated with the *Senzaishū*. The tone of his poems pervades the entire collection. Perhaps his most celebrated waka was the following:

yū sareba	When evening comes
nobe no akikaze	Autumn winds across the fields

mi ni shimite Bite into my flesh;
uzura naku naru And the quails are crying now
Fukakusa no sato[175] At Fukakusa Village.

The time is dusk—not the brightness of noon nor the dark of night but the melancholy hour when light and dark mingle. The place is Fukakusa, whose name means "deep grass," suggesting stillness. It is autumn, and the loneliness of the season is augmented by the forlorn cries of the quails.

The imagery in the *Senzaishū* is more often aural than visual, and the sounds evoked are melancholy. The much-admired song of the uguisu had figured prominently in earlier collections, but in the *Senzaishū* the sad notes of the hototogisu figure five times as often as the song of the uguisu. There are more poems than in any previous imperial collection on deer crying dolefully for their mates. The marked increase in the number of poems that mention temple bells tolling has been attributed to the enhanced importance of religion in a period of warfare and disaster.[176]

Shunzei's poem on the quails typifies the *Senzaishū* also in the importance of the melody of the poem. He had written, "It is only on reading a poem aloud that one can tell whether it is good or bad."[177] Shunzei's reverence for the *Kokinshū* was probably occasioned not by its intellectual manner but by the mellifluous lyricism. The emphasis on sound in the *Senzaishū* is thrown into relief also by the scarcity of poems that mention color, the fewest of any imperial collection up to this time. The poets' world had become monochromatic, perceived in the twilight hour more by sound than by sight.

Princess Shokushi was a major poet who made her debut in the *Senzaishū*. She was already in command of her characteristic manner in this poem composed on the last day of spring.

nagamureba As I stare, brooding,
omoiyaru beki There is no way to dispel
kata zo naki My melancholy;
haru no kagiri no In the evening sky lingers
yūgure no sora[178] The last remnant of spring.

Her melancholy thoughts at dusk typify the collection as a whole. Fujiwara no Sanesada (1139–1191), who also made his debut in the *Senzaishū*, composed this waka on hearing the hototogisu at dawn:

hototogisu	When I gaze far off
nakitsuru kata wo	In the direction where
nagamureba	A nightingale sang,
tada ariake no	All that is left in the sky
tsuki zo nokoreru[179]	Is the moon at break of day.

Of course, there are more cheerful poems, too, but they do not alter the prevailingly dark tone of the collection. This darkness is confirmed by the creation for the first time of separate books of Shintō and Buddhist poetry. Although poems in these categories were often composed on specifically religious subjects, they are aesthetic rather than doctrinal in expression. In many cases one would not know without the prefatory notes that a poem had a religious meaning:

furusato wo	When, at dusk of day,
hitori wakaruru	All alone, I take my leave
yūbe ni mo	Of the place I lived,
okuru wa tsuki no	I have been told that moonlight
kage to koso kike[180]	Will guide me on my way.

The surface meaning of this poem by Princess Shokushi is that she trusts that moonlight will enable her to find her way in the dark, but the prefatory note mentions the vow of Fugen[181] not to desert the believer until he or she reaches the Pure Land of Amida Buddha. The poem refers to the speaker's last hours, not simply to an evening's journey.

The *Senzaishū* was the most important of the imperial collections during the century following the compilation of the *Goshūishū*, and it served as the prelude to the *Shin Kokinshū*, edited by Shunzei's son, Fujiwara Teika.

The great differences between the two best collections of waka poetry, the *Kokinshū* and *Shin Kokinshū*, can be explained in terms of the three hundred years separating them. Even the most conservative poetic expression is bound to change as the political and social life of a country changes with the years; but seen in terms of the six collections compiled by imperial command during the period, the changes become intelligible as literary phenomena. The conflicting attractions of the old and the new, between what most poets believed to be the incomparable tradition of the *Kokinshū* and their desire to convey something of the darker world in which they themselves lived, were not easily resolved, but the advantage (as it became increasingly evident) lay with those whose poetry was responsive to the changes in their world.

The practice of honka-dori, the borrowing of the language and images of earlier poetry, especially the *Kokinshū*, had the effect of keeping the old poems constantly in the minds of the poets of even several hundred years later, and gave the *Kokinshū* all the greater authority; but the borrowing inevitably altered the original poems, usually in the direction of greater depth and often of greater sadness. Some *Kokinshū* poems, even those not intended to be humorous, tend to create an effect of frivolity by their repeated expressions of feigned ignorance of whether blossoms are snow or clouds; but these mitate poems became rarer in the later collections; again and again the poems strike to the heart with a poignance that goes beyond technique.

On the other hand, the increasing use of topics sometimes made the poems seem like ingenious responses to "problems" posed by an examiner rather than heartfelt utterances. The best poets were nevertheless able to make the topics seem an integral part of their natural and even inevitable expression.

These six collections are marked also by a tendency toward unifying the poems into a progression of thoughts, rather than a presentation of a number of excellent poems by different authors. This tendency, at first apparent in the *Shikashū*, would reach its apogee in the *Shin Kokinshū*.

Each of the six "in-between" collections has at least a few notable poems that would be remembered and paraphrased by later poets, and the collections as a whole merit far greater attention than they have customarily been given. There was no break in the traditions of the waka after the *Kokinshū*; indeed, each of the six collections helped in some way to make possible the finest of all anthologies of waka poetry, the *Shin Kokinshū*.

Notes

1. I am provisionally accepting these dates, though I am aware that they have been challenged by authorities.
2. The publication in 1983 of Fujimoto Kazue's annotated edition of *Goshūi Waka Shū* in the Kōdansha Gakujutsu Bunko series, followed in 1989 by the publication in the Shin Nihon Koten Bungaku Taikei series of annotated editions of *Kin'yō Waka Shū* and *Shika Waka Shū*, marked dra-

matic steps forward in understanding of the texts, and they have been followed by similar editions of the remainder of the six collections.

3. Sugitani Jurō, "Gosen Waka Shū," in Kubota Shōichirō, Sugitani Jurō, and Fujihira Haruo, *Kokin Waka Shū, Gosen Waka Shū, Shūi Waka Shū*, p. 215. The dating of the *Gosenshū* is discussed at length by Okumura Tsuneya in *Kokinshū, Gosenshū no Shomondai*, pp. 375–409. Okumura decided on the basis of uses of the title *ason* that the years 955 to 958 were the only ones when the titles of people cited in the text of the *Gosenshū* were valid. However, Okumura's findings were questioned by Katagiri Yōichi in *Gosen Waka Shū*, pp. 474–77. Katagiri was inclined to follow Yamaguchi Hiroshi in believing that the compilation was completed in 953, two years after the emperor commanded it.

   The eleventh-century historical *Tale of Flowering Fortunes* states that Murakami himself gave the collection its name, *Gosenshū*, because he considered it to be a sequel to the *Kokinshū*. It also reports that it was by Murakami's command that the collection was arranged in twenty books. See William H. and Helen Craig McCullough, *A Tale of Flowering Fortunes*, I, p. 79. The same source explains the lack of a preface to the *Gosenshū* in these terms: "The Emperor had wanted it to contain something comparable to Ki no Tsurayuki's splendid Preface to the *Collection of Early and Modern Times*, but he had reluctantly concluded that the great Tsurayuki had evoked the past, mused on the present, and predicted the future with such skill that nobody at his Court could equal the performance." It is not known whether or not this account, written long after the events, accurately conveys the circumstances of the composition of the *Gosenshū*.

4. Kyūsojin Hitaku, *Kōhon Yakumo Mishō to sono Kenkyū*, p. 231. The two men were Ki no Tokifumi, the son of Ki no Tsurayuki, and Sakanoue no Mochigi, the son of Sakanoue no Korenori.
5. See Katagiri, *Gosen*, pp. 481–85.
6. See Morimoto Motoko, *Izayoi Nikki, Yoru no Tsuru*, p. 212. One of the oldest commentaries on the collection, *Gosenshū Seigi* by Fujiwara Tameie (1198–1275), described it as "shavings" left after the editors had polished the *Kokinshū*. See Sugitani Jurō, "Gosen Waka Shū," in Kubota Shōichirō et al., *Kokin*, p. 222.
7. Sugitani, "Gosen," p. 222.
8. Kikuchi Yasuhiko, *Kokinteki Sekai no Kenkyū*, pp. 300–13, gives detailed figures on the number of poets and poems, listed according to category and sex of the poets.
9. This left only two books for categories that had been allotted a book each in the *Kokinshū*—congratulations, separation, travel, and mourning. Congratulatory and mourning poems were combined in one book as were separation and travel poems.
10. Sugitani, "Gosen," p. 220. However, Katagiri in *Gosen*, p. 482, pointed out conspicuous lapses in the temporal arrangement.

11. *Gosenshū* 1425 and 1426. Text in Katagiri, *Gosen*, p. 434. These are the last two poems of the collection. Tsurayuki's poem implies that with the new year the anniversary of the wife's death will make her seem even farther away. See also Hisamatsu Sen'ichi, *Kodai Waka Shi*, p. 159.
12. For more on Heichū, see below, pp. 459–61
13. Reference to this celebrated incident is found in *Tales of Yamato*. See the translation by Mildred Tahara, *Tales of Yamato*, p. 76. The wife of the episode is the central character in the novel *Shōshō Shigemoto no Haha* by Tanizaki Jun'ichirō.
14. There are only fourteen such sets in the *Kokinshū*.
15. *Gosenshū* 710 and 711. Text in Katagiri, *Gosen*, pp. 206–7.
16. *Gosenshū* 806. Text in Katagiri, *Gosen*, p. 236.
17. The first two lines of this poem were taken over from poem 1027 in the haikai section of the *Kokinshū*, where they are used to a quite different, comic effect.
18. *Gosenshū* 883. Text in Katagiri, *Gosen*, p. 259. See also Sugitani, "Gosen," pp. 268–69.
19. *Gosenshū* 1102. Text in Katagiri, *Gosen*, p. 327. See also Sugitani, "Gosen," p. 276.
20. I am thinking especially of the poems of Yamanoue no Okura, including *Man'yōshū*, V:802–3 and V:897.
21. A detailed discussion of the relations between the *Man'yōshū* and the *Gosenshū* is found in Satō Takaaki, *Gosen Waka Shū no Kenkyū*, pp. 160–99.
22. Satō, *Gosen*, pp. 110, 161. Other scholars (e.g., Matsuda Takeo, quoted by Satō on p. 162) were sure that direct borrowings from the text of the *Man'yōshū* had occurred.
23. Satō, *Gosen*, p. 953, conjectured that Minamoto no Shitagō, the best known of the *Gosenshū* compilers, was dissatisfied with the "artificiality" of the *Kokinshū*.
24. Although scholars now agree (for the most part anyway) that Kazan himself edited the collection, it is not clear whether or not he had any collaborators. See Komachiya Teruhiko, *Shūi Waka Shū*, p. 472.
25. The first person to correct this misapprehension and to affirm that the *Shūishō* was older but that the *Shūishū* was the definitive text was Hanawa Hokinoichi (1746–1821), the celebrated compiler of the *Gunsho Ruijū* (Classified Collection of Japanese Classics), an immense compendium of works of literature and history, published between 1779 and 1819. See Komachiya, *Shūi*, p. 472.

    Fujiwara Teika discovered a manuscript of the *Shūishū* at the beginning of the thirteenth century, but even he believed that the *Shūishō* was the superior text. Teika's text of the *Shūishū* contained 1,351 poems, as contrasted with the 590 poems in the *Shūishō*. The additions consisted partly of poems derived from the *Man'yōshū*, but partly also of undated, anonymous poems.

26. The seasonal poems are followed by single books of congratulatory and parting poems, five books of love poetry , seven books of miscellaneous poems, and three others devoted to poems composed during court ceremonies and entertainments.
27. For Ise, see above, p. 268.
28. *Shūishū* 49. Text in Komachiya, *Shūi*, p. 16. The blossoms are of course cherry blossoms, and the "old town" (*furusato*) is probably Nara, the old capital, still fondly remembered.
29. *Shūishū* 1. Text in Komachiya, *Shūi*, p. 4. See also Fujihira Haruo, "Shūi Waka Shū," in Kubota Shōichirō et al., *Kokin Waka Shū, Gosen Waka Shū, Shūi Waka Shū*, p. 307.
30. The quotation is from Kintō's *Waka Kuhon* (Nine Grades of Waka). Tadamine's poem was placed at the very top of all the poems discussed, in the category *jōhon jō* (highest grade, top) along with the anonymous *Kokinshū* 409, which has been attributed to Kakinomoto no Hitomaro. See Hisamatsu Sen'ichi and Nishio Minoru, *Karon Shū, Nōgakuron Shū*, p. 32.
31. Quoted by Fujihira in "Shūi," p. 308.
32. *Shūishū* 178. Text in Komachiya, *Shūi*, p. 52. See also Fujihira, "Shūi," pp. 320–21.
33. Variously known as *butsumei* and *mono no na*, meaning "names of things."
34. *Shūishū* 421. Text in Komachiya, *Shūi*, p. 119. See also Fujihira, "Shūi," pp. 330–32.
35. The critic was Fujiwara no Nagatō. See Ozawa Masao et al., *Fukuro Zōshi Chūshaku*, I, pp. 366–69.
36. *Goshūishū* 273. Text in Fujimoto, *Goshūi*, II, pp. 60–61. See also Kansaku Kōichi and Shimada Kyōji, *Sone no Yoshitada Shū Zenshaku*, pp. 223–24. Also Ozawa et al., *Fukuro*, I, p. 368. Another translation in Robert H. Brower and Earl Miner, *Japanese Court Poetry*, pp. 179–80.
37. *Shūishū* 1111. Text in Komachiya, *Shūi*, p. 318. See also Fujihira, "Shūi," pp. 357–58. The poem exists in several variant forms; see Kansaku and Shimada, *Sone*, pp. 220–21.
38. Hashimoto Fumio and Takizawa Sadao, *Horikawa-in Ontoki Hyakushu Waka to sono Kenkyū*, p. 334.
39. *Ibid.*, p. 335.
40. *Shūishū* 1342. Text in Komachiya, *Shūi*, p. 394. See also Fujihira, "Shūi," pp. 370–72; also Brower and Miner, *Japanese*, p. 218.

    The poem is credited in the *Shūishū* to "Shikibu, the daughter of Masamune," evidence that she had not yet married Michisada, the governor of Izumi. The prose preface to the poem states that it was sent to the High Priest Shōkū. This occasioned tales that Izumi composed the poem at the end of her life, when she had repented over her dissolute ways and entered Buddhist orders; however, this is her earliest, not her last surviving poem. The first two lines paraphrase a passage in the Lotus Sutra.

41. For a fuller treatment of Izumi Shikibu, see pp. 295–98.
42. Kumamoto Morio, *Egyō Shū*, pp. 139–43.
43. *Goshūishū* 1085. Text in Fujimoto, *Goshūi*, IV, pp. 249–50. Reference is apparently being made to a passage in *The Collected Works of Po Chü-i*, in which the poet, after referring to a deceased poet's "voice of gold and jade," declared that "though they have buried your bones, they have not buried your fame." See Fujimoto, *Goshūi*, p. 250.
44. *Goshūishū* 1086. See Fujimoto, *Goshūi*, IV, p. 251.
45. Kumamoto, *Egyō*, p. 134.
46. *Shūishū* 140. Text in Komachiya, *Shūi*, p. 42. See Shiraishi Mitsukuri, "Shūi Waka Shū," in Hisamatsu Sen'ichi, *Hachidaishū Hyōshaku*, p. 180. For the poem in the *Hyakunin Isshu*, see Odaka Toshio and Inukai Yasushi, *Ogura Hyakunin Isshu Shinshaku*, p. 113.
47. Kumamoto, *Egyō*, p. 141, from *Nishihonganji-bon Yoshinobu-shū*.
48. *Shūishū* 1327. Text in Komachiya, *Shūi*, p. 389. See also Yamagishi Tokuhei, *Hachidaishū Zenchū*, I, p. 616.
49. Genshin was a celebrated popularizer of Amida Buddhism. He conveyed its truths in easily understood form in *Ōjō Yōshū* (The Essentials of Salvation), a basic text of Amida Buddhism.
50. For more on *kyōgen kigyo*, see below, p. 1030.
51. Ozawa et al., *Fukuro*, I, pp. 333–34. Genshin is referred to in this text as Eshin Sōzu.
52. I use the term "medieval period" to refer to the Kamakura and Muromachi periods, from 1185 to 1573, though I am aware that the appropriateness of using for a discussion of literature a term based on political developments has been questioned.
53. See the article with translations by Robert E. Morrell, "Buddhist Poetry in *Goshūishū*."
54. Kikuchi, *Kokinteki*, pp. 453–54, gave a summary of the respects in which the first three collections were related and quoted two authorities who agreed that the *Shūishū* was a grand summation of the *Kokinshū* style.
55. See Ueno Osamu, *Goshūishū Zengo*, p. 36.
56. Fujimoto, *Goshūi*, IV, p. 442, gives an exact chronology.
57. Ozawa et al., *Fukuro*, I, pp. 224–25.
58. The attribution to Tsunenobu was made in *Fukuro Zōshi*. See *ibid.*, pp. 50, 187.
59. Hisamatsu in *Kodai*, pp. 191–92, discusses and discounts Tsunenobu's criticism. Sekine Yoshiko's *Nan Goshūi Shūsei* collates existing texts.

The first poem Tsunenobu singled out for attack was the ninth in the *Shūishū*, by Ōnakatomi no Yoshinobu:

tazu no sumu	The roots have melted free
sawabe no ashi no	Along the mountain gully
shitane toke	Where the cranes dwell,

migiwa moeizuru And the banks have budded forth:
haru wa kinikeri The spring has come at last!

Tsunenobu commented, "It is with great trepidation that I criticize a poem that has been described as a masterpiece. I realize that I should look up to it in reverence, but the word *sawabe* (along the gully) has the same meaning as the word *migiwa* (banks). In addition, one should say 'budded forth on the banks.' The poem says instead 'the banks have budded forth,' and I felt that *ni* (on) was missing." (Fujimoto, *Goshūi*, I, pp. 52–53.)

Modern critics agree that this criticism misses the mark. The poem is a good one, made so especially by the unconventional expression "the banks have budded forth."

60. The preface states that there are 1,218 poems, but there are slight discrepancies in surviving texts. See Fujimoto, *Goshūi*, I, p. 23.
61. Fujimoto, *Goshūi*, I, p. 85. The tradition goes back at least as far as *Fukuro Zōshi*. See Ozawa et al., *Fukuro*, I, p. 271.
62. *Goshūishū* 382. Text in Fujimoto, *Goshūi*, II, pp. 192–93. The anecdote that follows is found in Ozawa, *Fukuro*, I, p. 246.
63. Ueno, *Goshūishū*, p. 23.
64. *Ibid.*, p. 86. Ueno quotes *Ōgishō*, which gave Chinese sources (e.g., *Shih Chi* and poems by Po Chü-i) for thirteen poems.
65. *Ibid.*, p. 96, gives a list of these four-character topics. Brower and Miner in *Japanese*, pp. 185, 197–98, and 140–41, discuss *kudai waka*, "poems on the topics of quotations from Chinese poems." They connect such poetry with the acceptance in Japan of descriptive poetry of the kind practiced by Chinese poets.
66. *Goshūishū* 281. Fujimoto, *Goshūi*, II, p. 69.
67. *Goshūishū* 270. Text in Fujimoto, *Goshūi*, II, p. 56.
68. *Goshūishū* 1146. Text in Fujimoto, *Goshūi*, IV, p. 335.
69. Hisamatsu, *Kodai*, p. 180.
70. *Goshūishū* 755. Text in Fujimoto, *Goshūi*, III, pp. 213–14.
71. *Goshūishū* 101 and 102. Text in Fujimoto, *Goshūi*, I, pp. 173–75. The two poems constitute an early example of rensaku, poems composed in sequence and meant to be read together.
72. *Goshūishū* 317. Text in Fujimoto, *Goshūi*, II, p. 113.
73. *Goshūishū* 820. Text in Fujimoto, *Goshūi*, III, pp. 293–94.
74. *Goshūishū* 573. Text in Fujimoto, *Goshūi*, II, p. 436.
75. *Goshūishū* 574. Text in Fujimoto, *Goshūi*, II, p. 437.
76. *Goshūishū* 575. Text in Fujimoto, *Goshūi*, II, pp. 438–39.
77. *Goshūishū* 763. Text in Fujimoto, *Goshūi*, III, p. 223.
78. McCullough and McCullough, *A Tale*, I, p. 43.
79. *Shin Kokinshū* 1820. Text in Kubota Jun, *Shin Kokin Waka Shū*, p. 272. See Uemura Etsuko, *Akazome Emon*, p. 109.

80. *Shin Kokinshū* 1821. Text in Kubota Jun, *Shin*, p. 272.
81. *Goshūishū* 1196. Text in Fujimoto, *Goshūi*, IV, p. 405. Translation from Robert E. Morrell, "The Buddhist Poems in the *Goshūishū*," p. 188.
82. *Goshūishū* 680. Fujimoto, *Goshūi*, III, pp. 108–9. Another poem composed by Akazome as a daisaku for her daughter rebuked the daughter's lover, major captain of the Right Michitsuna, known as the son of the author of *The Gossamer Years*.
83. *Goshūishū* 410. Text in Fujimoto, *Goshūi*, II, pp. 226–27.
84. *Goshūishū* 594. Text in Fujimoto, *Goshūi*, II, pp. 461–62.
85. *Goshūishū* 438. Text in Fujimoto, *Goshūi*, II, p. 262.
86. *Goshūishū* 640. Text in Fujimoto, *Goshūi*, III, p. 56.
87. Yasuda Akio, *Ōchō no Kajintachi*, p. 154. The original source is given in Wakashi Kenkyūkai (ed.), *Shikashū Taisei*, II, p. 257.
88. *Goshūishū* 916. Text in Fujimoto, *Goshūi*, IV, pp. 28–29.
89. *Goshūishū* 952. Text in Fujimoto, *Goshūi*, IV, pp. 79–80.
90. *Goshūishū* 955. Text in Fujimoto, *Goshūi*, IV, pp. 83–84.
91. *Goshūishū* 518. Text in Fujimoto, *Goshūi*, II, p. 365.
92. *Goshūishū* 507. Text in Fujimoto, *Goshūi*, II, pp. 352–53.
93. See above, pp. 262–63.
94. See Fujimoto, *Goshūi*, I, p. 103.
95. *Goshūishū* 43. Text in Fujimoto, *Goshūi*, I, p. 102.
96. Ozawa et al., *Fukuro*, I, pp. 352–53. The poet under whom Nōin studied was Fujiwara no Nagatō, a nephew of the author of *The Gossamer Years*. See Fujimoto, *Goshūi*, p. 56.
97. Kamo no Chōmei, *Mumyōshō*. Text in Hisamatsu and Nishio, *Karon Shū*, p. 89. See also Yanase Kazuo, *Mumyōshō Zenkō*, p. 404.
98. *Goshūishū* 518. See Fujimoto, *Goshūi*, II, p. 365.
99. Quoted in Hisamatsu and Nishio, *Karon Shū*, pp. 41, 240.
100. *Ibid*., p. 42.
101. *Goshūishū* 624. Text in Fujimoto, *Goshūi*, III, pp. 36–37.
102. *Shin Kokinshū* 116. Text in Kubota Jun, *Shin*, I, p. 57.
103. See Hashimoto and Takizawa, *Horikawa-in*, pp. 342, 382.
104. It is so stated in *The New Mirror*. See *ibid*., p. 341.
105. *Ibid*., p. 342.
106. An analysis of the *honka* (source poems) of 679 poems in the sequence shows that 106 were derived from the *Man'yōshū*, 174 from the *Kokinshū*, 40 from the *Gosenshū*, 64 from the *Shūishū*, and 26 from the *Goshūishū*. Others were drived from poems in such prose works as *The Tale of Genji*. See Hashimoto and Takizawa, *Horikawa-in*, p. 363.
107. This was the second chokusenshū that he commanded. The first was compiled during his reign, the second after he entered Buddhist orders. Three other emperors (Gosaga, Gouda, and Gokōgon) also commanded two chokusenshū.
108. Brower and Miner, *Japanese*, p. 483.

109. Hisamatsu, *Kodai*, p. 194.
110. *Shūishō*, it will be remembered, was the first version of the imperial collection *Shūishū*. It was Fujiwara Teika who suggested that the *Shūishō* was the model for the *Kin'yōshū*.
111. Ozawa et al., *Fukuro*, I, pp. 227–28.
112. *Ibid*., pp. 227–29.
113. The numbers of poems given here are from the second version, the rufubon. The numbers vary somewhat according to the version. See Ikeda Tomizō, *Minamoto no Toshiyori no Kenkyū*, p. 208.
114. The *Goshūishū* was compiled eighty-one years after the *Shūishū*, but the *Kin'yōshū* was compiled forty-one years after the *Goshūishū*.
115. See Kubota Jun, "Chūsei waka e no michi," in Akiyama Ken, *Ōchō Bungaku Shi*, p. 316. He contrasted *keikai* (light) with *keichō* (superficial).
116. Toshiyori's best-known criticism is in *Toshiyori Zuinō* (1129?).
117. *Kin'yōshū* 1. Text in Kawamura Teruo, Kashiwagi Yoshio, and Kudō Shigenori, *Kin'yō Waka Shū, Shika Waka Shū*, p. 4. The poem originally appeared in *Horikawa-in Ontoki Hyakushu Waka*. The opening line, *uchi-nabiki*, was taken by Kawamura (and also by Masamune Akio in *Kin'yō Waka Shū Kōgi*, pp. 35–38) as a makurakotoba of uncertain meaning; but Fujisaki Kazushi, "Kin'yō Waka Shū," in Hisamatsu, *Hachidaishū*, p. 239, interpreted it as "wide-spreading" (of mists), the meaning I have followed here.
118. See above, p. 259.
119. Brower and Miner, *Japanese*, p. 242.
120. *Kin'yōshū* 23. Text in Kawamura et al., *Kin'yō*, p. 10. See also Masamune, *Kin'yō*, pp. 87–88. Masamune commented, "We can infer that the poet was describing his regret over the passing spring in terms of this late spring scene; but the language is overly ingenious, and the emotions it arouses are not very profound. However, at the time this kind of exhibition of poetic craft was much admired. The poem enables us to see how the style of *Kin'yō* and *Shika* developed into that of the *Shin Kokin*."
121. *Kin'yōshū* 667. Text in Kawamura et al., *Kin'yō*, p. 202. Also Masamune, *Kin'yō*, pp. 115–16; Fujisaki, "Kin'yō," p. 241.
122. Brower and Miner, *Japanese*, pp. 237, 249.
123. *Kin'yōshū* 154. Text in Kawamura et al., *Kin'yō*, p. 44. Also Masamune, *Kin'yō*, p. 259.
124. *Kin'yōshū* 170. Text in Kawamura et al., *Kin'yō*, p. 50. See also Masamune, *Kin'yō*, p. 281.
125. *Kin'yōshū* 173. Text in Kawamura et al., *Kin'yō*, p. 50. See also Masamune, *Kin'yō*, p. 283; Fujisaki, "Kin'yō," p. 249.
126. *Kin'yōshū* 59. Text in Kawamura et al., *Kin'yō*, p. 19. Also Masamune, *Kin'yō*, p. 142; Fujisaki, "Kin'yō," p. 242.
127. *Kin'yōshū* 145. Text in Kawamura et al., *Kin'yō*, p. 42. See also Masamune, *Kin'yō*, pp. 250–51; Fujisaki, "Kin'yō," p. 247.

128. *Kin'yōshū* 150. Text in Kawamura et al., *Kin'yō*, p. 43. See also Masamune, *Kin'yō*, pp. 255–56; Fujisaki, "Kin'yō," p. 247.
129. From this time on, poems on the topic of *jukkai* (personal grievances) appear in the imperial anthologies and also in poem competitions.
130. *Kin'yōshū* 665. Text in Masamune, *Kin'yō*, pp. 943–44. See also Kawamura et al., *Kin'yō*, p. 201; Fujisaki, "Kin'yō," p. 268. *Hamabisashi*, translated here as "sand castle," is variously explained as a house on the beach, a part of the shore washed by waves, a cliff that has been eaten away by the waves, or (if it is an error for *hamahisagi*, given in Kawamura's text), a plant that grows on the shore. In any case, it was probably used as a makurakotoba, the sound of hama*bisashi* being repeated in *hisashi*ku.
131. *Kin'yōshū* 595. Text in Kawamura et al., *Kin'yō*, p. 173. Also Masamune, *Kin'yō*, pp. 840–43.
132. Yasuda Akio, *Ōchō no Kajintachi*, p. 179.
133. *Kin'yōshū* 647. Text in Kawamura et al., *Kin'yō*, p. 191. Also Masamune, *Kin'yō*, pp. 919–20.
134. Ikeda, *Minamoto*, p. 387. There is a celebrated tale describing an event of 1140 when the priest Sainen rowed his boat westward until he was guided to Amida's Western Paradise.
135. Ikeda, *Minamoto*, p. 371. The quoted words are the last two lines of a poem by Toshiyori.
136. The dates are not certain. I have followed Matsuda Takeo, *Shikashū no Kenkyū*, pp. 29–30. See also Kawamura Teruo and Kashiwagi Yoshio, "Kaisetsu," in Kawamura et al., *Kin'yō*, pp. 449–50.
137. See Matsuda, *Shikashū*, pp. 18–19.
138. Ozawa et al., *Fukuro*, I, pp. 227–28.
139. *Ibid*., pp. 193–95.
140. Kubota Jun, "Chūsei," pp. 317–18, briefly describes these collections.
141. Ozawa et al., *Fukuro*, I, p. 193, stated that it contained 409 poems. Other editions give 411 poems. The figure I have used is from Kawamura et al., *Kin'yō*.
142. See Inoue Yutaka, "Shika Waka Shū," in Hisamatsu, *Hachidaishū*, p. 272.
143. Matsuda, *Shikashū*, p. 61.
144. *Ibid*., pp. 103–4. Matsuda gives a list of all the uta-awase that were sources of poems in the *Shikashū*.
145. *Shikashū* 1–3. See Kawamura et al., *Kin'yō*, pp. 220–21.
146. *Shikashū* 33–34. Kawamura et al., *Kin'yō*, p. 229. Poem 33 is by the Mother of Nagazane, and poem 36 by Minamoto no Takasue. I have borrowed my analysis of the relationship of one poem to the next largely from Matsuda, *Shikashū*. Writing in 1960, he insisted that he was the first ever to analyze the arrangement of poems in a chokusenshū (see especially pp. 4–6, 345). However, two years earlier Konishi Jin'ichi had published an article on the subject, "Association and Progression: Principles of Inte-

gration in Anthologies and Sequences of Japanese Court Poetry, A.D. 900–1350." Because this article appeared in the English translation of Robert H. Brower and Earl Miner, it probably had not come to Matsuda's attention.

147. Konishi's article treated in special detail a selection of the *Shin Kokinshū* where the practice of "association and progression" is seen to best advantage. See also Robert H. Brower and Earl Miner, *Fujiwara Teika's Superior Poems of Our Time*.

148. *Shikashū* 347. Text in Kawamura et al., *Kin'yō*, p. 328. See also Sugane Nobuyuki, *Shika Waka Shū Zenshaku*, pp. 460–62. The poem was composed at an uta-awase held in 1128. It echoes one by Ōe no Chisato in the *Kokinshū* (no. 193), which also contains the line *wa ga mi hitotsu no*. It is also associated with the anonymous *Kokinshū* poem (no. 878) on the moon at Obasuteyama.

149. *Shikashū* 382. The "new retired emperor" was Sutoku. Text in Kawamura et al., *Kin'yō*, p. 340. See also Sugane, *Shika*, pp. 508–10. The poem was included in *Hyakunin Isshu*. See Odaka and Inukai, *Ogura*, pp. 189–91.

150. *Shikashū* 146. Text in Kawamura et al., *Kin'yō*, p. 262. *Soyo soyo* is onomatopoetic, usually suggesting the sound of a gentle wind, though here used for the rustling of falling leaves. It also suggests the leaves are saying to one another, "That's right! That's right!" (*sō yo, sō yo*). Text in Sugane, *Shika*, pp. 179–80. The text given in Kawamura et al., *Kin'yō*, p. 262, has *uraha* instead of *kareha*.

151. *Shikashū* 349. Text in Kawamura et al., *Kin'yō*, p. 329. See also Sugane, *Shika*, pp. 464–65.

152. See below, p. 616.

153. *Shikashū* 229. Text in Kawamura et al., *Kin'yō*, p. 288, who gives *takikawa*, rather than *tanikawa*. See also Sugane, *Shika*, pp. 298–99. The poem was included in *Hyakunin Isshu*. See Odaka and Inukai, *Ogura*, pp. 192–94.

154. Kiyosuke, a mediocre poet of the conservative Rokujō school, is known primarily as the author of *Fukuro Zōshi* and *Ōgishō*, compendia of poetic lore.

155. For the text and a study of this collection, see Suzuki Norio, *Shoku Shika Waka Shū no Kenkyū*.

156. See Kubota Jun, "Chūsei," p. 318.

157. *Imayō* (meaning "new style") were popular songs of the middle and late Heian period, generally in eight or twelve lines of seven plus five syllables each. See below, pp. 777–78.

158. See Delmer M. Brown and Ichirō Ishida, *The Future and the Past*, p. 142.

159. Taniyama Shigeru. *Senzai Waka Shū to sono Shūhen*, p. 22.

160. *Ibid.*, p. 24.

161. This collection, *Sangoshū*, has been lost.

162. See above, p. 247, for the account of Tadanori.

163. Taniyama, *Senzai*, p. 33.
164. Hashimoto Fumio, Ariyoshi Tamotsu, and Fujihira Haruo, *Karon Shū*, pp. 295, 464.
165. Taniyama, *Senzai*, p. 41. The preface states 1187, but an even more reliable source, *Meigetsuki* (Chronicle of the Bright Moon), the diary of Fujiwara Teika, gives 1188. The discrepancy has been explained in terms of a first and final version of the text.
166. Taniyama, *Senzai*, p. 71.
167. Matsuno Yōichi, "Senzaishū," in Waka Bungaku Kai, *Man'yōshū to Chokusen Waka Shū*, pp. 212–13.
168. Taniyama, *Senzai*, pp. 144–46.
169. *Ibid*., p. 136.
170. *Senzaishū* 122. See also Taniyama, *Senzai*, p. 139.
171. *Senzaishū* 380.
172. *Senzaishū* 1122. See also Yasuda, *Ōchō*, p. 186.
173. Yanase, *Mumyōshō Zenkō*, p. 280.
174. *Senzaishū* 38. See also Taniyama, *Senzai*, p. 141, for adverse comments on Yorimasa's reliance on such stylistic devices as engo and kakekotoba.
175. *Senzaishū* 258. For analysis of the poem, see Brower and Miner, *Japanese*, pp. 17, 266, 298, 475.
176. Taniyama, *Senzai*, p. 222.
177. Hashimoto, *Karon Shū*, p. 276.
178. *Senzaishū* 124.
179. *Senzaishū* 161.
180. *Senzaishū* 1219. See also Manaka Fujiko, *Senzaishū Shin Kokinshū Shakkyōka no Hyōshaku*, p. 20.
181. Fugen is the Japanese name for the bodhisattva Samantabhadra, who made ten vows to follow the Buddha's teachings and work for the salvation of all sentient beings.

Bibliography

Note: All Japanese books, except as otherwise noted, were published in Tokyo.

Akiyama Ken. *Ōchō Bungaku Shi*. Tōkyō Daigaku Shuppankai, 1984.

Ariyoshi Tamotsu. *Senzai Waka Shū no Kisoteki Kenkyū*. Kasama Shoin, 1976.

Brower, Robert H., and Earl Miner. *Fujiwara Teika's Superior Poems of Our Time*. Stanford, Calif.: Stanford University Press, 1967.

———. *Japanese Court Poetry*. Stanford, Calif.: Stanford University Press, 1961.

Brown, Delmer M., and Ichirō Ishida. *The Future and the Past: A Translation and Study of the "Gukanshō."* Berkeley: University of California Press, 1979.

Fujimoto Kazue. *Goshūi Waka Shū*, 4 vols., in Kōdansha Gakujutsu Bunko series. Kōdansha, 1983.

Hashimoto Fumio. *Inseiki no Kadanshi Kenkyū*. Musashino Shoin, 1966.

———. *Ōchō Wakashi no Kenkyū*. Kasama Shoin, 1972.

Hashimoto Fumio, Ariyoshi Tamotsu, and Fujihira Haruo. *Karon Shū*, in Nihon Koten Bungaku Zenshō series. Shōgakukan, 1975.

Hashimoto Fumio and Takizawa Sadao. *Horikawa-in Ontoki Hyakushu Waka to sono Kenkyū*. Kasama Shoin, 1976.

Hirasawa Gorō. *Kin'yō Waka Shū no Kenkyū*. Kasama Shoin, 1976.

Hisamatsu Sen'ichi. *Chūsei Waka Shi*. Tōkyōdō, 1961.

———. *Hachidaishū Hyōshaku*. Daimeidō, 1954.

———. *Kodai Waka Shi*. Tōkyōdō, 1960.

Hisamatsu Sen'ichi, Matsuda Takeo, Sekine Yoshiko, and Aoki Takako. *Heian Kamakura Shikashū*, in Nihon Koten Bungaku Taikei series. Iwanami Shoten, 1964.

Hisamatsu Sen'ichi and Nishio Minoru. *Karon Shū, Nōgakuron Shū*, in Nihon Koten Bungaku Taikei series. Iwanami Shoten, 1961.

Ikeda Tomizō. *Minamoto no Toshiyori no Kenkyū*. Ōfūsha, 1973.

Imai Gen'e. *Kazan-in no Shōgai*. Ōfūsha, 1968.

Inoue Muneo. *Heian Kōki Kajin no Kenkyū*. Kasama Shoin, 1978.

Inukai Yasushi. "Waka Rokunin Tō ni kansuru Shiron," *Kokogu to Kokubungaku*, Sept. 1956.

Kansaku Kōichi and Shimada Kyōji. *Sone no Yoshitada Shū Zenshaku*. Kasama Shoin, 1975.

Katagiri Yōichi. *Gosen Waka Shū*, in Shin Nihon Koten Bungaku Taikei series. Iwanami Shoten, 1990.

———. *Ōchō Waka no Sekai*. Kyōto: Sekai Shisō Sha, 1984.

Kawamura Teruo. *Nōin Hōshi Shū, Gengenshū to sono Kenkyū*. Miyai Shoten, 1979.

Kawamura Teruo, Kashiwagi Yoshio, and Kudō Shigenori. *Kin'yō Waka Shū, Shika Waka Shū*, in Shin Nihon Koten Bungaku Taikei series. Iwanami Shoten, 1989.

Kikuchi Yasuhiko. *Kokinteki Sekai no Kenkyū*. Kasama Shoin, 1980.

Komachiya Teruhiko. *Shūi Waka Shū*, in Shin Nihon Koten Bungaku Taikei series. Iwanami Shoten, 1990.

Konishi Jin'ichi. "Association and Progression: Principles of Integration in Anthologies and Sequences of Japanese Court Poetry, A.D. 900–1350," *Harvard Journal of Asiatic Studies*, XXI, 1958.

Kubota Jun. *Shin Kokin Waka Shū*, 2 vols., in Shinchō Nihon Koten Shūsei series. Shinchōsha, 1979.

Kubota Jun and Matsuno Yōichi. *Senzai Waka Shū*. Kasama Shoin, 1969.

Kubota Shōichirō, Sugitani Jurō, and Fujihira Haruo. *Kokin Waka Shū, Gosen Waka Shū, Shūi Waka Shū*, in Kanshō Nihon Koten Bungaku series. Kadokawa Shoten, 1965.

Kumamoto Morio. *Egyō Shū*, Ōfūsha, 1978.

Kyūsojin Hitaku. *Kōhon Yakumo Mishō to sono Kenkyū*. Kōseikaku, 1939.

Manaka Fujiko. *Senzaishū Shin Kokinshū Shakkyōka no Hyōshaku*. Daiichi Shobō, 1956.

Masamune Akio. *Kin'yō Waka Shū Kōgi*. Jichi Nippō Sha, 1968.

Matsuda Takeo. *Ōchō Wakashū no Kenkyū*. Hakuteisha, 1968.

———. *Shikashū no Kenkyū*. Shibundō, 1960.

Matsuno Yōichi. *Fujiwara Shunzei no Kenkyū*. Kasama Shoin, 1973.

McCullough, William H. and Helen Craig McCullough. *A Tale of Flowering Fortunes*, 2 vols. Stanford, Calif.: Stanford University Press, 1980.

Minegishi Yoshiaki. *Heian Jidai Waka Bungaku no Kenkyū*. Ōfūsha, 1965.

Morimoto Motoko. *Izayoi Nikki, Yoru no Tsuru*, in Kōdansha Gakujutsu Bunko series. Kōdansha, 1979.

Morell, Robert E. "Buddhist Poetry in the *Goshūishū*," *Monumenta Nipponica* 28:1, 1973.

Odaka Toshio and Inukai Yasushi. *Ogura Hyakunin Isshu Shinshaku*. Hakuyōsha, 1954.

Okumura Tsuneya. *Kokinshū, Gosenshū no Shomondai*. Kazama Shobō, 1971.

Ōoka Makoto. *Ki no Tsurayuki*. Chikuma Shobō, 1971.

Ozawa Masao. *Heian no Waka to Kagaku*. Kasama Shoin, 1979.

———. *Sandaishū no Kenkyū*. Meiji Shoin, 1981.

Ozawa Masao, Gotō Shigeo, Shimizu Tadao, and Higuchi Yoshimaro. *Fukuro Zōshi Chūshaku*, 2 vols. Hanawa Shobō, 1976.

Satō Takaaki. *Gosen Waka Shū no Kenkyū*. Nihon Gakujutsu Shinkō Kai, 1970.

Sekine Yoshiko. *Nan Goshūi Shūsei*. Kazama Shobō, 1975.

Sugane Nobuyuki. *Shika Waka Shū Zenshaku*. Kasama Shoin, 1983.

Suzuki Norio. *Shoku Shika Waka Shū no Kenkyū*. Ōsaka: Izumi Shoin, 1987.

Tahara, Mildred. *Tales of Yamato*. Honolulu: University of Hawaii Press, 1980.

Taniyama Shigeru. *Senzai Waka Shū to sono Shūhen*. Kadokawa Shoten, 1982.

Uemura Etsuko. *Akazome Emon*. Shintensha, 1984.

Ueno Osamu. *Goshūishū Zengo*. Kasama Shoin, 1976.

Waka Bungaku Kai. *Man'yōshū to Chokusen Waka Shū*, in Waka Bungaku Kōza series. Ōfūsha, 1970.

Wakashi Kenkyūkai (ed.). *Shikashū Taisei*, 11 vols. Meiji Shoin, 1973–76.

Yamagishi Tokuhei. *Hachidaishū Zenchū*, 3 vols. Yūseidō, 1960.

Yanase Kazuo. *Mumyōshō Zenkō*. Katō Chūdōkan, 1980.

Yasuda Akio. *Ōchō no Kajintachi*. Nihon Hōsō Shuppan Kyōkai, 1975.

8. LATE HEIAN POETRY AND PROSE IN CHINESE

None of the courtiers or priests who wrote kanshi or kambun during the latter part of the Heian period could compare with Sugawara no Michizane in the quality of their compositions. This should not suggest that the Japanese had lost interest in writing Chinese; on the contrary, the composition of kanshi and kambun was more popular than ever at the Heian court despite the absence of outstanding practitioners. The compilation at this time of anthologies of Chinese poetry and prose written by Japanese earlier in the Heian period may even have been given impetus by the scarcity of new writers of distinction, but it also reflected the undiminished enthusiasm.[1]

Wakan Rōei Shū

The best known of these anthologies is undoubtedly *Wakan Rōei Shū* (Collection of Japanese and Chinese Poems for Singing), compiled in 1013 by Fujiwara no Kintō. The collection was intended to serve as a wedding present offered on the occasion of the marriage of his daughter to Fujiwara no Norimichi, the third son of the *nairan* (Imperial Examiner) Michinaga. The work consists of 588 couplets in Chinese, chosen from works composed by fifty Japanese and thirty Chinese poets. These couplets are arranged by seasonal and other topics, and are matched with 216 waka on related themes. The compilation of a collection that was intended to be sung, rather than merely read, was occasioned by a new vogue at the court.

Rōei, as the singing of poetry to a fixed melody was called, originated in China as an entertainment offered at banquets where poets sang poems of impromptu composition. This after-dinner entertainment spread to Japan as early as the eighth century, but did not become popular for another three centuries. At first rōei was performed at the Japanese court only on especially festive occasions, but it gradually became an indispensable feature of all court gatherings. In theory the poems that were sung were supposed to be composed on the spot (as was true in China), but it was obviously more difficult for Japanese than for Chinese to compose impromptu kanshi, so they usually prepared themselves in advance with "spontaneous" compositions of their own or with suitable quotations from other poets. Probably it was not until the middle of the tenth century that it became customary to sing only two lines, rather than whole poems.[2] A passage in *The Tosa Diary* mentions people "lifting up their voices to deliver Chinese poems,"[3] evidence that the singing of Chinese poetry goes back at least to that period. The music to which the poems were sung was strongly influenced by Buddhist chanting.[4]

The choice of Chinese and Japanese poems in his *Wakan Rōei Shū* probably reflected less Kintō's personal preference than those of the court as a whole. Naturally, the great favorite, Po Chü-i, was well represented; it has even been said that the collection is virtually an anthology of his poems.[5] The other Chinese poets represented were mainly from the mid and late T'ang periods. Most of the couplets were extracted from works that might be described as nature poems, understandable in a collection edited by a Japanese, and they are almost all in seven-character lines of "regulated verse," the preferred form of Chinese poetry during the Heian period. This style of poetry attached special importance to parallelism; the skill demonstrated in finding for the second line of a couplet exact parallels to the meanings and grammatical forms of the words of the previous line was considered to be at the heart of poetic accomplishment, and the reputation of a poem was more likely to be established by the deftness of its parallels than by its originality.[6]

A tradition in China of compiling anthologies of couplets with especially choice parallels can be traced back to the T'ang dynasty, and such collections were imported into Japan, as we know from the writings of Kūkai.[7] The earliest Japanese collection of Chinese couplets was probably *Senzai Kaku* (Splendid Verses of a Thousand Years) compiled about 950 by Ōe no Koretoki (888–963). This collection consists of 1,083 couplets in seven-character lines by 149 Chinese and 4 Korean poets, arranged under some 250 headings. Po Chü-i (as usual) is by far the best-represented poet; about half of the selections (507 in all) were drawn from his works. The poet with the next highest total, his intimate friend Yüan Chen, was represented by 65 couplets, followed by another 147 poets, many with only a couplet or two each. The special importance of *Senzai Kaku* is that two thirds of the Chinese couplets in *Wakan Rōei Shū* came from this source.

The general method followed by Kintō in his collection was to present under each of the topics one or more couplets in Chinese, followed by waka on related themes. For example, we find under the theme "spring night" a couplet by Po Chü-i (given in a Japanese rendering), followed by a waka by Ōshikōchi no Mitsune:

Tomoshibi wo somukete wa tomo ni awarebu shin'ya no tsuki	Averting the lamp, together we enjoy the late night moon;
Hana wo funde wa onajiku oshimu shōnen no haru	Treading on blossoms, alike we regret youthtime's spring.

haru no yo no
yami wa aya nashi
ume no hana
iro koso miene
ka ya wa kakururu[8]

It does not make sense
For spring nights to be so dark:
The plum blossoms' color
Cannot be seen, it is true,
But can the dark hide their scent?

Although modern scholars have demonstrated how greatly Chinese poetry influenced the waka of the *Kokinshū* and later Heian collections, Kintō did not pair the Chinese poems with waka they had directly inspired: he preferred to group together kanshi and waka with similar echoes or "perfumes," anticipating the method of "linking" in renga poetry.[9] The exactness of the parallelism between the first and second lines of Po Chü-i's couplet above is apparent even in translation, but parallelism is not a feature of this or any other waka in the collection, and there is not much similarity between the content or mood of the two poems apart from mention of the theme, spring night. The tender regret of Po Chü-i's lines is not echoed by the poetic conceit of this waka; and in other cases the connection between the Chinese and the Japanese poems presented under the same rubric were even more remote. For example, friendship, a frequent theme of Chinese poetry, is so rarely described in waka poetry that one of two waka on the theme (following five kanshi) is actually a love poem appropriated for the purpose, faute de mieux.[10] Themes derived from Chinese history, such as the tragic story of Wang Chao-chün, a court lady who was sent into exile to appease a Tartar chieftain, naturally had no equivalent in the waka, so the seven Chinese couplets on this theme are followed by only one waka, by Fujiwara no Sanekata; its justification was merely that Sanekata had (like Wang Chao-chün) been sent off to a distant place, in his case the province of Mutsu, where he went as governor.[11]

The greatest importance of *Wakan Rōei Shū* was the influence exerted on later Japanese literature by the Chinese couplets, as rendered in Japanese readings. The lines by Po Chü-i on a spring night, translated above, appear in such Nō plays as *Shunzei Tadanori* and *Tsunemasa*, and were the source of the opening phrases of *Sagaromo Monogatari* (The Tale of Sagoromo),[12] evidence of how strongly the lines appealed to the Japanese. The texts of the Nō plays were given their distinctive texture by such quotations of Chinese poetry, which enriched not only the content with Chinese imagery but also the sound of the lines with combinations of consonants and vowels not found in pure Yamato speech. The waka in *Wakan Rōei Shū*, mainly by poets of the *Kokinshū* such as Ki no Tsurayuki and Ōshikōchi no Mitsune, exerted less influence on later literature if only because most of them were already familiar from earlier collections.

The *Honchō Monzui*

The most important collection of poetry and prose composed in Chinese entirely by Japanese of the later Heian period is undoubtedly the *Honchō Monzui* (Literary Essence of Our Country), compiled about 1060 by Fujiwara no Akihira (989?–1066), a Confucian scholar and poet. The title of the work was derived from *T'ang Wen Sui* (Literary Essence of the T'ang), an anthology of T'ang dynasty poetry and prose compiled in 1011 by Yao Hsüan, but the organization itself was modeled on the celebrated *Wen Hsüan*, compiled about 530. The *Honchō Monzui* contains some 430 selections[13] by sixty-nine authors, the works ranging in date of composition from 810 to 1037. The ten most generously represented authors in the *Honchō Monzui* are almost the same as the ten Japanese whose kanshi are most often quoted in *Wakan Rōei Shū*, including Ōe no Masahira, Ōe no Asatsuna, Sugawara no Fumitoki, Ki no Haseo, and Sugawara no Michizane.[14] The list suggests the preponderant importance of two scholarly families, the Ōe and the Sugawara, even though scholars had by this time lost much of the authority they enjoyed before the downfall of Sugawara no Michizane and the seizure of political power by the Fujiwara regents. No member of the Fujiwara clan figures among the important authors of the *Honchō Monzui*. Women and Buddhist priests are also missing. The absence of women is not surprising, in view of the prevalant belief that learning Chinese was unladylike (though some women not only learned Chinese but composed kanshi); but the exclusion of Buddhist priests suggests a Confucian bias to the editorial process.

Not all of the works included in the *Honchō Monzui* are literary. In addition to the poetry and artistic prose, many memorials, prefaces, petitions (*gammon*), and other nonliterary compositions make it evident that the work was intended primarily to serve an educational purpose, providing models of composition for officials to follow when obliged to compose poetry or prose in Chinese.[15] Another reason for compiling the *Honchō Monzui* seems to have been to present the full texts of poems that had been quoted in the *Wakan Rōei Shū* in the form of couplets.[16]

The style of the selections in the *Honchō Monzui*, whether in poetry or prose, tends to be the ornate language and rather crude parallelism favored in China during the period immediately before the T'ang dynasty.[17] The contents are only occasionally marked by any note of strong emotion, as when the author relates hardships he has endured or appeals to his superior for appointment to office. Various letters and memorials by Ōe no Masahira describe the poverty under which literati labored in his day, contrasting their present neglect with the honors they used to receive in the past: "Confucian scholars used to be appointed as provincial governors, evidence of how the wise rulers of the past revered the Way: Confucian scholars are not appointed as provincial governors anymore, evidence of how learning has come to be despised in recent times."[18] Masahira recalled that in the past members of the Sugawara and Ōe families regularly received stipends that enabled them to continue their studies, regardless of whether or not they were talented, and irrespective of their age. He appealed for financial support for his descendants, arguing that the selection and effective employment of Confucian scholars was an act of service to the state; and so, "if rewards are given to their sons and grandsons, who will dare to be envious, who will dare to spread slander?"[19]

One of the best-known selections in the *Honchō Monzui*, "Tokyū no Fu" (*Fu* on Tu-chiu) by Prince Kaneakira (914–87), described in the form of a *fu* (rhyme-prose) how he (like a Chinese who lived long ago at Tu-chiu) attempted to withdraw from an uncongenial world only to be falsely accused of wrongdoing and prevented from carrying out his intent. The fu bears this preface:

> I had a site selected by geomancy for my little retreat at the foot of Kameyama,[20] and intended to resign my office and spend the re-

maining years of old age there. Just when the thatched hut was at last ready, I was falsely accused by someone in the government.[21] The prince was foolish, his ministers sycophantic, and I had nowhere to appeal my innocence. This was my fate, the lot imposed by heaven. Ordinary people in the future will no doubt blame me, saying I have acted as I have because I was unable to carry out my ambitions. However, Duke Yin of Lu wished nothing more than to spend his last years cultivating his land at Tu-chiu, only to be killed by his son, Hui. The principles enunciated in the *Spring and Autumn Annals*[22] had strengthened him and made of him a wise ruler. If some ruler in the future should learn of me, surely he will not hide my true intentions. That is why, in imitation of the fu on the owl by Chia I,[23] I have composed a fu on Tu-chiu to comfort myself.[24]

The special interest of this preface and the fu that follows is the political nature of the content. Chinese scholars as far back as Confucius grieved that they were not suitably employed and that their words of wisdom went unheeded. Complaints by Chinese authors about being neglected were habitual; but in Japan the typical complaints voiced in waka poetry, even by officials, were over the uncertainty of life or the indifference of women they loved, and the standard poetic diction had no place for criticism of foolish rulers. The possibility of expressing not only political grievances but also many other matters that could not be squeezed into the thirty-one syllables of a waka undoubtedly contributed to the appeal of the kanshi for Heian intellectuals. It probably also comforted them to find parallels between their misfortunes and those suffered by great Chinese in the past.

In reading the *Honchō Monzui* we are likely to be struck by the wide divergence between the subject matter and what would be found in contemporary or later collections of poetry composed in Japanese. The best-known selections, translated by Burton Watson, are *Rhyme-prose on the Marriage of Man and Woman* by Ōe no Asatsuna, *A Record of the Pond Pavilion* by Yoshishige no Yasutane, and *Song of the Tailless Ox* by Minamoto no Shitagō.[25]

Although *Danjo Kon'in no Fu* (Rhyme-prose on the Marriage of Man and Woman) includes specific references to Japan—for example, the woman is compared to Ono no Komachi and the man to Ariwara no Narihira—the profusion of flowery language makes one suspect that the poem must be an imitation of some Chinese original. Not only is the expression un-Japanese in its imagery, but the joys of love were usually not celebrated by Japanese poets, who preferred to write about anticipated or else remembered love, shunning the central area of the experience. The successful courtship described in the poem, leading to the shared delights of the nuptial bed, was no doubt as true in Japan as in China, but the tradition of Japanese poetry did not allow for such expression. Love poetry in Japan tended to be so indirect that its erotic aspects might pass unnoticed, but there is no possibility of reading this work without being aware of the poet's subject, suggested by the final lines:

> Should widows and young boys hear of such things,
> None but would be stirred to desire![26]

Chitei no Ki (Record of the Pond Pavilion), in a totally dissimilar mood, tells of an official who, tired of court life, has found a house after his own tastes in a quiet part of the capital:

> So after five decades in the world, I've at last managed to acquire a little house, like a snail at peace in his shell, like a louse happy in the seam of a garment. The quail nests in the small branches and does not yearn for the great forest of Teng; the frog lives in his crooked well and knows nothing of the vastness of the sweeping seas. Though as master of the house I hold office at the foot of the pillar, in my heart it's as though I dwelt among the mountains.[27]

Again and again in *Record of the Pond Pavilion* we find passages that prefigure Kamo no Chōmei's *Hōjōki* (An Account of My Hut). There can hardly be any doubt that Chōmei was influenced by the earlier work, and both works insist that the house is a microcosm of the world; but there is a difference, too: Yasutane declared that he loves his house, even though it is most humble, but Chōmei anxiously wonders if his attachment to his house is not a sin.

Yasutane, too, was a devout Buddhist, but he does not seem troubled by fear of attachment to wordly things; each night after he had said his prayers and eaten his meal he would go to his library to enjoy the company of the great Chinese of the past, notably Po Chü-i, whose prose pieces inspired this work. Yasutane said he feared that even his humble house might appear extravagant, but this thought seems not to have weighed on him unduly. He continued, "I'm like a traveler who's found an inn along the road, an old silkworm who's made himself a solitary cocoon."[28] These words, suggesting the simplicity and impermanence of his dwelling, bring to mind those of Bashō, written some seven hundred years later: "My body, now close to fifty years of age, has become an old tree that bears bitter peaches, a snail which has lost its shell, a bagworm separated from its bag; it drifts with the winds and clouds that know no destination. Morning and night I have eaten traveler's fare, and have held out for alms a pilgrim's wallet."[29] Much of the Japanese literature of the middle ages and later would be devoted not to the quiet pleasure of a house but to the homelessness of the perpetual traveler or the snail that has lost its shell.[30]

The humor of *O naki Ushi no Uta* (Song of the Tailless Ox) distinguishes it from most Japanese poetry of the Heian period and later. It is not that the Japanese were too serious even to compose light verse; it seems more probable that, with rare exceptions, the funny or bawdy poems composed in the past were not considered to be worthy of preservation.[31] In the case of Minamoto no Shitagō's poem on his tailless ox, however, the elaborate presentation in Chinese saved the poem from being dismissed as coarse or crude, though it contains these lines starting the first of the five "virtues" of an ox without a tail:

> First, when it eats tender grass and turds come flopping down,
> it has no tail to swish about and dirty up the shafts.[32]

Composing poetry in classical Chinese, a language that for the Japanese was the equivalent of the Latin with which the Victorian translators clothed the naked descriptions of the *Kojiki*, emboldened the poets of the *Honchō Monzui* to risk the charge, normally anathema to Japanese, of being in poor taste. Fujiwara no Akihira (unlike most anthologists) did not openly include any of his own compositions, but it has been conjectured that *Tettsuiden* (Biography of Iron Hammer), a salacious piece credited to someone with a farcical pseudonym, was by Akihira himself. Burton Watson has characterized this piece as being "one of the most tedious works of pornography in all literature."[33] It is curious that such a poem appeared in a collection otherwise devoted to providing scholars with models for the correct composition of petitions and memorials. The coarseness of *Song of the Tailless Ox* or *Biography of Iron Hammer* suggests not the untutored jests of the stable boy but the prurience of the pedant exchanging leers with his cronies. All the same, even such poems provide a welcome diversion from the excessive decoration of other compositions in Chinese by members of the Heian court.

The *Honchō Monzui* is unified only by the use of Chinese as the medium of expression. Judged in strictly literary terms, very little is memorable, but it provided Japanese not only with models of how to compose various types of Chinese poetry and prose but continued to provide stimulation to writers at times of literary stagnation. Kawaguchi Hisao has pointed out that the creation of a new literature at the beginning of both the Kamakura and Edo periods was signaled by the copying, collation, and study of texts of the *Honchō Monzui*.[34]

A New Account of Sarugaku

Fujiwara no Akihira is remembered also for two other works composed in Chinese: *Shin Sarugaku Ki* (A New Account of Sarugaku) and *Unshū Shōsoku* (Letters by Unshū). *Sarugaku* (literally, "monkey music") was the name given to entertainments that would later develop into the austere Nō, and *A New Account of Sarugaku* has therefore been read mainly by those interested in the history of the Japanese theater. The work opens promisingly with the assertion, "I have been attending performances in both the east and west halves of the capital for twenty and more years, but never have I seen anything in the past or present as splendid as the sarugaku performances tonight." This is followed by a list of the entertainments the author witnessed, including juggling, acrobatics, magic tricks, marionette shows, swordplay, one-man wrestling, playlets, and mimetic dances of various kinds.[35] The performers were so marvellously expressive and the dialogue so funny that, according to the writer, it was impossible not to "split one's intestines and dislocate one's jaw" with laughing. Some of the performers are named and their specialities are briefly mentioned, followed by an account of the enthusiastic reception by the audience.

All the above is merely a prologue—less than a tenth of the whole work—to the real subject of the work, an outing to the theater by Emon-no-jō, an inhabitant of the western sector of the capital, who attended with his entire family, consisting of three wives, sixteen daughters, and nine sons, each of whom is satirically characterized in succeeding episodes. The author devoted the greatest attention to making each of the wives and children distinct; Emon's first wife is older than himself and by now quite ugly; the second is a capable manager of his household; and the third, much younger than the other two, is very beautiful and (naturally) Emon's favorite. The description of the first wife typifies the manner:

> His official consort was already sixty, and her once ruddy face was now much faded. Her husband was barely fifty-eight, and his interest

> in women was as flourishing as ever. Probably when he was a young apprentice he surrendered himself to the blandishments of his father-in-law and mother-in-law, but now in his full maturity he bitterly regretted the difference in age separating him from his wife. When he looked at the hair on her head, it was white as morning frost; when he looked at the wrinkles on her face, they were numerous as the folds of waves at dusk. So many teeth were missing, above and below, that her face resembled a trained monkey's. Her breasts, left and right, hung down like the underparts of a bull in summer. However much makeup she applied, no one could love her; she was like a moonlit night in the dead of winter. Whatever coquetry she displayed to endear herself, the number of those who disliked her grew steadily more numerous; she was unwelcome as the sun in midsummer. She was unaware of her own failings, but was constantly annoyed by her husband's neglect. She made offerings to the gods of conjugal happiness, but always without result.[36]

The parallels in the prose, as relentless as in compositions of old-fashioned elegance, are here exploited for their comic effects. Emon's other two wives and all sixteen daughters are given equally unsentimental treatment. Most of the daughters are described in terms of an unusual occupation (one is a medium) or avocation (one is a glutton whose favorite dishes are enumerated) or attribute (the ugliness of one is evoked in great detail), and each, with the exception of a widow, is provided with a husband or lover of a different profession, ranging from gambler and sumo wrestler to master of *yin-yang* divination and physician. The nine sons are also provided with a full gamut of professions. Akihira presented a marvellous cross-section of Heian society which, for all its humorous exaggeration, carries conviction.

Letters by Unshū

Letters by Unshū is a collection of 209 letters, most of them in the form of a request or query to which a response is given in the next letter. The name "Unshū" was apparently a reference to Akihira's service as governor of the province of Izumo,[37] and the book was intended to provide models of epistolary composition.[38] A fair number of the letters have to do with the lending and borrowing of manuscripts, an important feature of intellectual life at a time when only religious books were ever printed.[39] Other letters contained invitations to poetry gatherings or kemari matches, congratulations on promotions, gifts and acknowledgments, and queries on scholarly matters. Letter 23 is a request for corrections to some waka composed by the writer, who declared in inflated language that "even one word of correction would be worth a thousand pieces of gold." The recipient declared in his response that the poems are so superb "they would not be unworthy of the poets of old, and in the present day they are quite beyond compare"; he is incapable of correcting them.[40] One gets the impression that such locutions were typical of letters of this nature. Although *Letters by Unshū* lacks the humor and the incisive details of *A New Account of Sarugaku*, it, too, contributes interesting sidelights to our knowledge of life in Heian times.

The Last of the Heian Writers of Literary Chinese

The dates of *A New Account of Sarugaku* and *Letter by Unshū* have yet to be established, but probably Akihira wrote them in old age, between 1053 and 1065.[41] *Honchō Zoku Monzui* (Japanese Monzui, Continued), compiled sometime after 1140, contains a selection of poetry and prose in Chinese, patterned after the first *Honchō Monzui*, but only about two-thirds as long. The lack of influence of this collection on later literature is probably accounted for largely by the conspicuous falling off of the literary quality. Only one new writer of importance emerges, Ōe no Masafusa, but his contributions to the collection are less impressive than his own *Gōdanshō* (Selection of Ōe's Conversations).[42]

Perhaps the most important work composed in Chinese prose during the last century of the Heian period was *Chūyūki*, the massive diary kept by the statesman Fujiwara no Munetada.[43] Among the kanshi poets, two stand out: Ōe no Masafusa and Fujiwara no Tadamichi.

Masafusa, the great-grandson of Masahira, was (by his own testimony[44]) a boy prodigy who, before he was eight, was familiar with such Chinese classics as *Shih Chi* and *Han Shu*. By eleven he was composing kanshi that were acclaimed as the work of a genius. Indeed, his poems were so skillful that some people doubted they could possibly have been composed by a mere boy. The acting major counselor, Fujiwara no Morofusa, deciding to test him, asked little Masafusa to compose a poem in his presence. The boy took up a brush and dashed off a poem that profoundly impressed Morafusa. In the following year, 1052, the regent, Fujiwara no Yorimichi (990–1074), decided to convert his villa at Uji into a temple with the name Byōdō-in. That year was believed to mark the beginning of *mappō*, the last stage of degeneration of the Buddhist law, and the temple was dedicated in the hope of forestalling disaster. Yorimichi, eager to make sure that nothing would go amiss, asked Morofusa if there were earlier examples of temples with their front gates to the north. Morofusa said that he did not know, whereupon Masafusa (who was attending him) piped up, "In India the Nalanda Monastery, in China the Hsi-ming Temple, and in our country the Rokuhara Temple all face north." Needless to say, Yorimichi was astonished by this display of precocious knowledge. Masafusa, at Morofusa's recommendation, received a special scholarship in 1056 from the Emperor Goreizei, and went on to enjoy an important career as an official. He compiled a personal collection of waka, but his most important poetry and prose was composed in Chinese. His kanshi are found in various collections including the *Honchō Zoku Monzui* and *Honchō Mudai Shi*,[45] compiled about 1163. Among these poems is a series written toward the end of his life when he was suffering from illness, including:

Close to death—how shameful still to grieve over illness;
My life shrinks together with the fall.
My head is like frost and snow, but the white will soon be gone;
Tears, red as phoenix-tree leaves, inexorably drop.
Wordly success scatters pell-mell like blossoms, slowly;
My life has gradually turned into a rushing stream.
Who, unless he's Wang Tzu-ch'iao, can enjoy longevity?
The Nine Saints and Seven Sages have all disappeared.[46]

The disillusion that marks this and other examples of Masafusa's late poetry probably reflected his depressed state in old age when he was beset by illness and sensed that his life must soon end; but perhaps he also grieved over the decline in the art of a Chinese poetry and prose to which he had consecrated his life.

Fujiwara no Tadamichi has been described as "the last monumental presence" in the literature written by aristocrats of the late Heian period.[47] Perhaps his best-known poem is *The Puppeteers*:

Ceaseless wanderers from of old, the puppeteers,
over countless miles always seeking a new home.
They set up camp and sing alone in the night to the autumn moon;
restless, they seek new paths in the midst of spring fields.
Youth in the bright capital, their women pampered favorites;

the years of age alone, watching over a hut of thatch.
The traveler passing far off casts suspicious eyes
at the white hair, the vacant, wrinkled face.[48]

The puppeteers were gypsylike people who traveled around Japan, the men operating puppets and the women working as prostitutes. Although they themselves were not Japanese (they apparently originated somewhere on the continent, perhaps the Near East), they formed an element of ordinary Japanese life, unlike the historical figures known only from Chinese literature, and the touches of realism in Tadamichi's description, contrasting with the ornamental language of earlier Heian kanshi, suggest that he was using the form for purposes unlike those of his predecessors. The end of the Heian period was a period of decline of the kanshi, but it was also the time when Chinese loanwords, hitherto hardly employed in works written in Japanese, greatly enriched the language and the literature.

Notes

1. This suggestion was made by Inokuchi Atsushi in *Nihon Kambungaku Shi*, p. 175.
2. See Ōsone Shōsuke and Horiuchi Hideaki, *Wakan Rōei Shū*, p. 306, where an account is quoted stating that the practice began during the reigns of Daigo and Suzaku. According to the same account (*Rōei Kyūjisshu Shō*), two traditions of rōei were created from the start, the Fujiwara and the Minamoto, but no details are given. A more reliable account states that Minamoto no Masanobu, the Minister of the Left, asked Sugawara no Fumitoki to compose music for the couplets and made them the "secret tradition" (*hikyoku*) of the Minamoto family. This event is said to have occurred during the reign of the Emperor En'yū (969–84).
3. Hagitani Boku, *Shintei Tosa Nikki*, p. 88. The text reads: *"kara-uta koe agete iikeri."*
4. Ōsone and Horiuchi, *Wakan*, p. 307.
5. Kawaguchi Hisao, *Wakan Rōei Shū Zen'yakuchū*, p. 628.
6. Ōsone and Horiuchi, *Wakan*, p. 305. Parallelism of a simpler nature was found earlier in China, and had echoes in Japanese prose composition.
7. *Ibid.* Kūkai refers to such works in his *Bunkyō Hifu Ron*, and he also made arrangements of *ren*, as he called couplets notable for their parallels, under the four seasons and nine other headings.
8. These are poems 27 and 28 of the collection. For the texts, see Ōsone and Horiuchi, *Wakan*, p. 20. The lines by Po Chü-i are given in the customary Japanese rendering.

9. Kawaguchi Hisao believed that the origins of *Wakan Rōei Shū* were the kanshi and waka inscribed on squares of paper called *shikishi* and pasted on screens, some decorated with Chinese scenes and others with Japanese scenes. See his *Zen'yakuchū*, pp. 625–26.
10. This is poem 738. See the explanation to this waka given by Ōsone and Horiuchi in *Wakan*, pp. 276–77.
11. This is poem 704. For the explanation, see Ōsone and Horiuchi, *Wakan*, p. 264.
12. Kawaguchi, *Zen'yakuchū*, p. 38.
13. The number ranges from 427 to 431, depending on the particular text.
14. For a list of the ten best-represented writers and the number of works by each, see Kawaguchi Hisao, *Heian-chō Nihon Kambungaku Shi no Kenkyū*, III, p. 782.
15. The proportions allotted to different genres by the *Wen Hsüan* and *Honchō Monzui* suggests the dissimilarity of their aims. For example, there are 435 *shi* (Chinese poems) in *Wen Hsüan* as opposed to only 28 in *Honchō Monzui*. On the other hand, *Wen Hsüan* contains only 19 *hyō* (memorials) and 9 *jo* (prefaces) as opposed to 46 *hyō* and 156 *jo* in *Honchō Monzui*. There are 27 *gammon* (petitions) in *Honchō Monzui* and none at all in *Wen Hsüan*. See Kawaguchi, *Heian-chō*, III, p. 779.
16. It has been estimated that 88 percent of the Japanese kanshi extracted in *Wakan Rōei Shū* are presented in full in *Honchō Monzui*. See Kojima Noriyuki, *Kaifūsō*, *Bunka Shūrei Shū*, *Honchō Monzui*. p. 32.
17. Burton Watson contrasted the parellelism of the Six Dynasties poets with that practiced by the T'ang poets in these terms: "Handled with skill and imagination, the device of parallelism is capable of conveying a kind of profound verbal, even philosophical wit. But in Six Dynasties times its use is seldom as subtle as even the example cited above, which is still a far cry from what the device was to become in the hands of the T'ang masters, and more often the reader is bored or irritated by the mechanical way in which it clanks along" (*Chinese Lyricism*, p. 103).
18. Quoted in Ōsone Shōsuke, "Honchō Monzui no Sekai," p. 125.
19. *Ibid*, p. 126.
20. A mountain in the Saga area of Kyoto overlooking the Ōi River.
21. Apparently he is referring to the kampaku, Fujiwara no Kanemichi. See Kojima, *Kaifūsō*, p. 333, note 6.
22. *Ch'un ch'iu* is a chronicle of events from 722 to 481 B.C. According to tradition, it was compiled by Confucius from records preserved in his native state of Lu. Although the narration itself is spartan and possesses little obvious philosophical interest, elaborate explanations have been given to the language in the attempt to deduce whether Confucius approved or disapproved of the events described. For a description, see Burton Watson, *Early Chinese Literature*, pp. 37–40.
23. For *Fu on the Owl* by Chia I (201–169 B.C.), see Watson, *Early*, pp.

25–58. Watson (p. 255) wrote of this work, "The poet, deeply troubled by his estrangement from the emperor and the thought of impending death . . . attempts to console himself with the Taoist view of life and death as a process of endless and ineluctable change."

24. Kojima, *Kaifūsō*, pp. 334–35.
25. Translation by Burton Watson in *Japanese Literature in Chinese*, I, pp. 53–67.
26. *Ibid*, p. 56. For the original text, see Kojima, *Kaifūsō*, pp. 340–44.
27. Watson, *Japanese*, I, p. 62. Watson points out in a footnote, "At this time Yasutane held the post of *naiki* or secretary in the Nakatsukasa-shō, a bureau of the government which handled edicts, pensions, and other documents. 'Clerk at the foot of the pillar' was the Chinese term for such a secretary." For the original text, see Kojima, *Kaifūsō*, p. 424.
28. Watson, *Japanese*, I, p. 64. For the original, see Kojima, *Kaifūsō*, p. 428.
29. Matsuo Bashō, *Genjūan no Fu*, translated as "Prose Poem on the Unreal Dwelling" in my *Anthology of Japanese Literature*, p. 374.
30. The poetry of the Six Dynasties, a period of strife and disorder, was called by Watson "the poetry of reclusion"; the prose of *Record of the Pond Pavilion* is in a similar mood.
31. Some of the earliest surviving comic verses were accidentally preserved in the notebooks of the renga poet Sōchō.
32. Watson, *Japanese*, I, p. 65. Original in Kojima, *Kaifūsō*, p. 359.
33. Watson, *Japanese*, I, p. 53.
34. Kawaguchi Hisao, *Seiiki no Tora*, p. 203.
35. See Shigematsu Akihisa, *Shin Sarugaku Ki*, *Unshū Shōsoku*, pp. 8–12, for a *yomikudashi* (Chinese arranged in Japanese word order) reading of the text plus detailed notes on each of the entertainments presented. See also chapter 26, p. 1002.
36. Shigematsu, *Shin*, p. 14.
37. Because of the character *kumo* ("cloud") in the name Izumo was also read *un*, the province of Izumo had the alternative name of Unshū. Fujiwara no Akihira had served as governor of Unshū and was therefore sometimes called by that name.
38. There has been some discussion about the difference between *shōsoku* and *ōrai*, both terms for letters, and both used in manuals of correspondence. The distinction originally seems to have been that *shōsoku* were letters in general, and *ōrai* were exchanges of letters (as the word literally means). In later times, however, *shōsoku* was used to designate real letters that had actually been sent, whereas *ōrai* were only models. See Shigematsu, *Shin*, pp. 276–77. In still later times *ōraimono*, as manuals of letter writing came to be called, were an important element in education.
39. The Japanese were familiar with the art of printing from the eighth century, as surviving documents prove, but the only works printed before the late sixteenth century were Buddhist sutras and other religious works.

No explanation was offered for the failure to print works of literature or history, for example, but it may have been because of the aesthetic preference for handwritten and illustrated books.

40. Shigematsu, *Shin*, pp. 96–98.
41. This is the opinion of Shigematsu, in *Shin*, p. 270.
42. For further information on this work, see below, p. 580.
43. See below, pp. 399–402, for an account of this diary.
44. In his memoir *Bonenki* (Account of Twilight Years); quoted by Inokuchi, *Nihon*, p. 180.
45. The title means literally "Poems of This Country Without Titles." In fact, most of the poems have titles, but "without titles" may be a technical term designating titles of more than six characters. (See *Nihon Koten Bungaku Daijiten*, V, p. 495.) The collection is dated after 1162, when Fujiwara no Tadamichi took the priestly name by which he is called in the collection, and 1164, when he died. Thirty poets of kanshi are represented including Ōe no Masafusa and Fujiwara no Tadamichi.
46. *Honchō Mudai Shi*, p. 271. "Phoenix tree" is a translation of the Chinese *wu-tung* or Japanese *aogiri*. The red tears refer to the "tears of blood" that frequently figure in Chinese poetry. Wang Tzu-ch'iao (called Wang Tzu-chin in this poem, an alternate name) was a Taoist immortal, said to have lived in the sixth century B.C. See Kenneth J. DeWoskin, *Doctors, Diviners, and Magicians of Ancient China*, p. 174. The "Nine Saints" (or "Nine Bright Ones") were legendary figures of antiquity. The "Seven Sages of the Bamboo Forest" were third-century Chinese poets and scholars who turned their backs on worldly endeavor.
47. Kawaguchi, *Heian-chō*, III, p. 916. Kawaguchi used the word *insei*, meaning government by the retired emperor, to designate the late Heian period. The insei period is usually considered to have lasted from 1087 to 1192.
48. Translated by Watson in *Japanese*, I, p. 69.

Bibliography

Note: All Japanese books, except as otherwise noted, were published in Tokyo.

Brewster, Jennifer. *The Emperor Horikawa Diary*. Honolulu: University of Hawaii Press, 1977. The original Australian edition of this translation was called *Sanuki no Suke Nikki*.

DeWoskin, Kenneth J. *Doctors, Diviners, and Magicians of Ancient China*. New York: Columbia University Press, 1983

Hagitani Boku. *Shintei Tosa Nikki*, in Nihon Koten Zensho series. Asahi Simbun Sha, 1969.

Honchō Mudai Shi, in Shinkō Gunsho Ruijū series, kan 126. Naigai Shoseki, 1931.

Inokuchi Atsushi. *Nihon Kambungaku Shi.* Kadokawa Shoten, 1984.

Kawaguchi Hisao. *Heian-chō Nihon Kambungaku Shi no Kenkyū*, 3 vols. Meiji Shoin, 1975–88.

———. *Ōe no Masufusa*, in Jimbutsu Sōsho series. Yoshikawa Kōbunkan, 1968.

———. *Seiiki no Tora.* Yoshikawa Kōbunkan, 1974.

———. *Wakan Rōei Shū, Ryōjin Hishō*, in Nihon Koten Bungaku Taikei series. Iwanami Shoten, 1965.

———. *Wakan Rōei Shū Zen'yakuchū*, in Kōdansha Gakujutsu Bunko series. Kōdansha, 1982.

Keene, Donald. *Anthology of Japanese Literature.* New York: Grove Press, 1955.

———. *Travelers of a Hundred Ages.* New York: Holt, 1989.

Kojima Noriyuki. *Kaifūsō, Bunka Shūrei Shū, Honchō Monzui*, in Nihon Koten Bungaku Taikei series. Iwanami Shoten, 1964.

Nihon Koten Bungaku Daijiten, 6 vols. Iwanami Shoten, 1983–85.

Ōsone Shōsuke. "Honchō Monzui no Sekai," *Kokubungaku Kaishaku to Kyōzai no Kenkyū* 26:12, Sept. 1981.

Ōsone Shōsuke and Horiuchi Hideaki. *Wakan Rōei Shū*, in Shinchō Nihon Koten Shūsei series. Shinchōsha, 1983.

Shigematsu Akihisa. *Shin Sarugaku Ki, Unshū Shōsoku.* Gendai Shichō Sha, 1982.

Watson, Burton. *Chinese Lyricism.* New York: Columbia University Press, 1971.

———. *Early Chinese Literature.* New York: Columbia University Press, 1962.

———. *Japanese Literature in Chinese*, 2 vols. New York: Columbia University Press, 1975.

Yamanaka Hiroshi. "Ōe no Masafusa," *Kokugo to Kokubungaku* 35:10, October 1957.

9. HEIAN DIARIES

The beginnings of literary prose in the Heian period can be traced back to Ki no Tsurayuki's preface to the *Kokinshū*. Thirty years later, in 935, Tsurayuki wrote *Tosa Nikki* (The Tosa Diary), a monument in the development of Japanese prose and the first example of an important genre, the literary diary.

The diaries composed in Japanese, beginning with *The Tosa Diary*, tended to be personal rather than public, and the best-known examples were written by ladies of the Heian court who rarely went anywhere and knew little of court politics. What they wrote therefore tended to be introspective, evoking their thoughts and emotions as they passed long days in the semidarkness of their palace apartments. The tradition of court ladies keeping diaries would continue until the fourteenth century and would be revived by other women, not members of the court, during the Tokugawa period. Their intuitive, sometimes ambiguous style would affect the writing of many kinds of literary prose over the centuries.

Officials at the Heian court and Buddhist priests also kept diaries recording their daily activities, but they wrote not in Japanese but in kambun. Such diaries were definitely not literary in purpose, and they figure in histories of literature mainly because of the factual information they supply on events described in more literary but less systematic works. The diaries of the Heian courtiers were of great value not only to the persons who actually wrote them but to their descendants, as records of precedents; such information was of crucial importance at a court where precedents were venerated. The diaries in kambun often extended to volumes that are filled with the minutiae of daily life at the court, but it probably never occurred to the diarists to seek literary distinction. Those who kept diaries in Japanese, on the other hand, recorded only matters of personal importance, but they expressed themselves with poetic beauty.

The differences in the usage of the word *nikki*, or diary, were not confined to the language employed by the diarist. The dry accounts of the male diarists were kept from day to day in the usual manner of diaries in other countries, but those by court ladies were sometimes written years after the events they described. The latter variety of nikki resemble autobiographies, but there is a critical difference: the writer of an autobiography, situating himself in the present, recalls the past, and sometimes compares events to those in the present; but the diarist, even when writing long after the events, never compares them to the present or anticipates later developments. The Heian literary diarist generally relied on her memories, but even when relating half-forgotten events, she never stepped outside the chronology to suggest her awareness of the distance between the act of writing and those events.

Diaries composed in Japanese usually contain poems, not as embellishments of the texts but as "facts." Indeed, the only documents a woman was likely to possess when writing a diary were the poems composed on a given occasion and noted at the time. Diaries sometimes even took the form of a collection of poems arranged chronologically and presented with explanatory materials.

Sometimes diaries were written in the third person, blurring the distinction between a diary and a work of fiction. Such diaries are known by several titles, depending on the manuscript; the same work may have been termed a diary by one scribe and a tale (monogatari) by another. The diary was closely linked to almost every variety of literature composed during the Heian period, and its importance would extend even to the literature of our own day: the "I novel" of the twentieth century, in which the author closely describes events of his own life, can be considered as a development of the techniques of the literary diary.

Ennin's Diary

By far the most detailed of the surviving diaries by Japanese monks who traveled to China is *Nittō Guhō Junrei Gyōki* (Travel Diary of a Pilgrimage to China in Search of the Law), an account written in kambun by the Tendai[1] priest Ennin (793–864), who traveled to China as a member of a Japanese embassy, from the time of his departure in 838 until his return to Japan in 847. The voyage was dangerous because ships were completely at the mercy of the winds, and the sailors lacked compasses to guide them. Only after three attempts did the ships succeed in reaching China, and no sooner had they arrived than the ships ran aground and had to be ditched. Ennin and the others would experience innumerable hardships throughout their stay. Famine conditions prevailed in northern China because of a plague of locusts that devoured the crops, and almost as bad as the locusts were the officials, who seemed determined to frustrate Ennin in his plans to study at the great Tendai monasteries.

Ennin spent much of his time in China waiting to be allowed to visit Mount Tien-t'ai, where he hoped to hear the Tendai teachings at their fountainhead. He was unable to the end to obtain permission, but did manage to reach Mount Wu-t'ai, another important Tendai center. Ennin's account of his visit to Mount Wu-t'ai records in detail legends associated with Monju (Mañjuśri in Sanskrit), the object of a cult there. Typical of his account is the description of a solemn and majestic statue of Monju riding on a lion. He wrote of the lion, "It seems to be walking, and vapors come from its mouth. We looked at it for quite a while, and it looked just as if it were moving."[2] Ennin related the difficulties encountered by the sculptor while fashioning this statue. Six times he cast it, and six times it cracked to pieces. At last, realizing that his failure must be due to Monju's dissatisfaction, he prayed to Monju, begging him to appear before him, so that he might know his true appearance and copy it more faithfully. Hardly had he finished this prayer than he saw Monju before him, riding on a golden lion. When he made the statue for the seventh time, it did not crack.[3]

During the latter part of Ennin's stay in China the Emperor Wu-tsung initiated a persecution of Buddhism. For a time Ennin had no choice but to let his hair grow out and to put aside his Buddhist robes. He was eager to return to Japan, but permission was not forthcoming. For a time he was even faced with contradictory orders—to remain in China until given permission to leave, and to leave China as soon as possible as an undesirable foreign Buddhist. With the death of Wu-tsung in 846 the persecution of Buddhists ended, and an amnesty was proclaimed.[4] Ennin was now free to return to Japan, but only after experiencing many hardships and delays was he able in 847 to board an eastbound Korean ship. Aboard ship he prayed not only to the Buddha but to the Shintō deities for a safe crossing.[5]

The ship traveled along the Korean coast, then crossed over to Kyūshū by way of Tsushima. Ennin landed at Hakata Bay, where he had set sail for China over nine years earlier. His exertions in China were rewarded after his return: he was honored by the court and eventually rose in 854 to become the abbot of Enryaku-ji on Mount Hiei. Ennin died in 863 and three years later was given the posthumous title of Jikaku Daishi, the Great Teacher of Compassionate Awareness.

Edwin Reischauer, who made a complete translation and a study of Ennin's diary, stated that neither the diary itself nor the biographies of Ennin written by other men conveyed anything of his personality: "He was a scrupulously accurate and delightfully detailed diarist, but he was no Boswell determined to make posterity his confidant."[6] Even Boswell might have had difficulty in making good reading out of the life of a man of irreproachable virtue who was so resolutely matter-of-fact in his expression. Reischauer commented, "While he was not a mind of brilliant originality and creativeness, he must have possessed extraordinary ability." Unfortunately, Ennin's ability, especially his skill at writing difficult classical Chinese, has kept most Japanese from reading the diary in which he narrated his travels.

Ennin's diary is notable for his vivid descriptions of Chinese inns, New Year celebrations, and life within the monasteries, but the reader seldom feels in contact with the man. He does not even voice the admiration for the great Chinese cities we might expect in a traveler from Japan. He was absorbed by a single purpose, to seek the Buddhist Law, and nothing else was of more than passing interest. Only occasionally did he even mention the hardships he suffered, as in the letter he sent to a Chinese official in which he described himself in these terms: "He makes his home anywhere and finds his hunger beyond endurance, but, because he speaks a different tongue, he is unable to beg for food himself. He humbly hopes that in your compassion you will give the surplus of your food to a poor monk from abroad."[7]

This is about as close as Ennin came to voicing a cry from the heart, but it would be against the sober background of kambun diaries such as Ennin's that the far more personal diaries in Japanese would be created.

The Tosa Diary[8]

Tosa Nikki, though written in the third person, is just such a personal diary, and it too describes a journey, during the years 934 and 935. It is the first example of *nikki bungaku* (diary literature), a genre that would constitute an important element of Japanese literature for centuries to come. Such diaries were not simply records of daily experiences, but usually revealed the personality of the diarist in a manner seldom encountered in the prose writings of the time.

The author, the poet Ki no Tsurayuki, had been appointed as governor of Tosa (on the island of Shikoku) in 930, and the diary relates his return to the capital after completing his duties in 934. Tsurayuki, as an official, undoubtedly knew kambun, and, like other men of his day, could have kept his diary in Chinese if he had wished, but there may have been emotions he could not fully convey except in his own language. He probably also wished to include in the diary waka that had been composed on the way; *The Tosa Diary* can even be read as a defense of Japanese poetry. One passage recalls how, when Abe no Nakamaro was about to leave China for Japan, his Chinese friends offered a banquet and composed Chinese poems in honor of the occasion:

"Nakamaro responded, 'In my country, poetry of this kind has been composed ever since the age of the gods, even by the gods themselves, and people of all classes, regardless of their standing in the world, also compose poetry when they grieve over parting, as we grieve now, or when moved by joy or sadness.' So saying, he composed this poem."

aounabara	Gazing out over
furisake mireba	The blue meadows of the sea,
kasuga naru	I think: that must be
mikasa no yama ni	The same moon that rose above
ideshi tsuki kamo	Mount Mikasa in Kasuga![9]

At first, the diary relates, the Chinese could not understand the poem, but after Nakamaro had supplied a rough approximation in Chinese characters of the meaning, and a Chinese who knew a little Japanese explained the poetic qualities, the other Chinese seemed surprisingly appreciative. If this account is to be trusted, the Chinese, who were so proud of their own poetic traditions that they were reluctant to admit that others existed, had been moved by the special powers of the waka (described by Tsurayuki in the preface to the *Kokinshū*) "to move without effort heaven and earth, and stir to pity the invisible gods and demons." It may in fact have been Tsurayuki's purpose when writing the diary to demonstrate that the waka was a fair match for Chinese poetry.[10] *The Tosa Diary* contains fifty-six poems, variously attributed to "the present governor," "a certain person," "a certain woman," and so on, though quite possibly they were all composed by Tsurayuki himself.

This note of fiction suggests how flexibly the term *nikki* might be used by authors who wrote in this mode.

The journey took fifty-five days, much of it by sea. Events are related by month and day from the farewell banquets in Tosa to Tsurayuki's return to his old house in Kyoto. The diary opens with the statement, "Diaries are things written by men, I am told. Nevertheless, I am writing one to see what a woman can do."[11] The author was *not* a woman; Tsurayuki probably wrote this falsehood to explain why the diary was composed in kana, or *onna-moji* (women's writing). He kept up throughout the pretense that the diary had been written by a woman, but there is nothing specifically feminine about either the style or the subjects treated.

Although there is no absolute proof that Tsurayuki wrote the diary, we have strong evidence for accepting this traditional attribution. The imperially sponsored anthology *Gosenshū*, compiled after 951, contains two poems from *The Tosa Diary* that are identified as by Tsurayuki, and the poems are described in prose prefaces as having been composed on a ship going from Tosa to the capital. Tsurayuki's son, Ki no Tokifumi, was a compiler of this anthology, and the attributions are therefore likely to be correct. Other early references also identify Tsurayuki as the author of the diary; but even if such evidence did not exist, we might guess from the diary itself that the author was not, as is professed, the work of a gentlewoman in the entourage of an official who was returning to the capital.

Near the beginning we are told, "A certain person, having completed four or five years at his post in the provinces, disposed of the usual formalities and received his certificate of clearance, left the official residence, and proceeded to the place where he was to board ship." The preparation of a "certificate of clearance" (*geyujō*), a document inscribed by the incoming official attesting that no fault had been found in his predecessor's accounts, was unlikely to have been known to a lady in the governor's party. Again, although we are reminded that the author was a woman by the statement that she could not understand poetry composed in Chinese, the language of men, there is unmistakable Chinese influence in the style, notably in the use of parallel constructions.

The Tosa Diary is as much a daily record of occurrences in the diarist's life as the account of a journey. Various scholars have pointed out, however, that *The Tosa Diary* is not a good example of travel literature. Much less is said about the journey than about poetry; names of places passed are sometimes mistaken; and there is hardly any description of the scenery. The following entry, for the thirtieth day of the first moon, is typical:

> Thirtieth. The wind and rain have let up. There are reports that the pirates do not operate at night, so we rowed out our boats about midnight and crossed the strait of Awa. It was the middle of the night, and we could not tell east from west. Men and women alike prayed frantically to the gods and buddhas, and we safely made it across the strait.[12]

It is hard to imagine any diarist passing the whirlpool of Naruto in the Awa Strait without making a comment about it. Even supposing it was too dark too see anything, surely Bashō, the saint of haiku, might have lied to the extent of saying that the starlight was so bright he could see the swirling waters. But Tsurayuki seems to have been uninterested in scenery. His chief concern while on the water was with the danger of pirates, and his attention was frequently distracted from the journey itself. But unlike most other Heian diarists, he was at pains to maintain the pretense that he faithfully made an entry in the diary each day, if only to say, "The same place as yesterday."

One unusual aspect of *The Tosa Diary* is the diarist's division of himself into various persons. He is not only the gentlewoman who supposedly kept the diary but other people as well. *The Tosa Diary* has even been referred to as an "embryonic drama" with a cast of characters, though it lacks dramatic tension.[13]

Hagitani Boku, a distinguished scholar of Heian literature, suggested that Tsurayuki intended the diary primarily as a book of poetics for children of the nobility, and listed twenty topics concerning poetic theory that are mentioned in the course of the work. He believed that Tsurayuki related such episodes as the near encounter with pirates in order to make his discussions appealing to young readers, and suggested that Tsurayuki, assuming that the parents of the children would also examine the "diary," included materials of a satiric nature for their amusement, making fun of bribe-taking officials or mocking people in the capital who expect presents from officials returning from posts in the provinces.[14]

Intriguing though this theory is, there is a much simpler explanation of why Tsurayuki wrote *The Tosa Diary*, one first proposed almost two hundred years ago:[15] the underlying theme is Tsurayuki's grief over the death of his daughter in Tosa. This theme surfaces at critical points in the narrative, and is stated most movingly in the final poem and comments. Perhaps it was because Tsurayuki considered this theme to be "unmanly" that he chose to write the diary in the persona of a woman.

Tsurayuki was apparently sixty-six years old when he left Tosa, homeward bound to the capital. References in *The Tosa Diary* to his daughter suggest that she was probably born when he was in his late fifties. A child of old age may seem even more precious than earlier ones, and that may be another reason why the author wished to express his grief in writing. The diary form itself could have been learned from Ennin or someone else who kept a diary in Chinese, though there was naturally no similarity in content. Despite the precise dating of the events, the diary was not written day by day but after Tsurayuki's return to the capital, and may have been inspired by the desolation he felt when he saw his house again. For years he had been anticipating this moment, but instead of the beautiful garden he remembered, he found an untended wilderness. The sight in turn recalled the daughter who had been born in this house but whose grave was in Tosa. The ending of the diary is poignant:

> Nothing but stirred old memories, and most affecting of all were those of the girl who had been born in this house but has not returned with us, to our immeasurable sorrow. Other people who were with us on the ship all have their children swarming noisily around them, and their happy cries make the sadness all the more unbearable. This was the poem I exchanged privately with someone who understands my feelings.

mumareshi mo	Though she was born here,
ḳaeranu mono wo	She has not returned with us;
wa ga yado ni	How sad it is, then,
ḳomatsu no aru wo	To see the little pine trees
miru ga ḳanashisa[16]	That have grown in my garden.

The theme of the daughter who died gives underlying unity to the diary even when poetry is discussed or drunken parties described. The diary literature that would develop after *The Tosa Diary* would be extremely personal, not at all like Ennin's massive journal or the later diaries kept in Chinese by men of the court. Tsurayuki's decision to write *The Tosa Diary* in the persona of a woman deprived it of some of the directness and truth that characterizes the diaries kept by real women during the following century, but surely no one who reads *The Tosa Diary* will doubt that he has come closer to Tsurayuki. The diary abounds in references to poetry, but not necessarily because Tsurayuki intended it to serve as a textbook for young people. Rather, he loved the waka and wanted to persuade others that it could be used to express the most poignant feelings. Writing about the death of his daugher probably helped assuage his grief, and his expressions of sorrow, though indirectly presented, have the power to move us as individual evocations of a universal theme.

The Gossamer Years

The Tosa Diary was written by a man pretending to be a woman, but *Kagerō Nikki* (The Gossamer Years) was written by a real woman. It is the record of a woman's unhappy life, written without a thought to objectivity. She was convinced that no one had ever suffered as much as she, and was determined that readers be fully aware of her misery.

Events in *The Gossamer Years* are not recorded by year, month, and day. Only one year, the third of the Tenroku era (972), is plainly stated, and other dates (from 954 to 974) must be calculated from this point of reference. The first two of the three volumes were probably written considerably after the events described, but in the third volume the author seems to be writing about the recent past. The gap between the time of the events and of the narration makes *The Gossamer Years* seem more like an autobiography than a diary, but the genre is hard to define. The work, in any case, is one of the masterpieces of diary literature, a stunning account of the life of an intelligent and passionate woman who refused to accept the conditions of a Heian marriage. The author, a daughter of the governor of Mutsu, was the second wife of Fujiwara no Kaneie (929–990), a highborn statesman who became regent in 986 and chancellor in 989. Because the author's own name is not known, she is referred to as the Mother of Michitsuna (955–1020), her son by Kaneie. She probably lived from 936 to 995.

Considering the importance of her husband's position at court, we might expect that the diary would contain political gossip picked up from Kaneie, but the author shows hardly a trace of interest in anyone except members of her immediate family. The only political event she mentions is the banishment to Kyūshū of the minister of the Left for allegedly plotting an insurrection in 969.[17] Moved by sympathy for this prince and his sons, all of whom were exiled to distant places, she expressed her grief, adding, "These are matters that have no place in a diary which describes only things that have happened to me, but since the person who felt this grief was none other than myself, I have set down what I experienced."[18]

This passage provides evidence that the Mother of Michitsuna considered her account to be solely a vehicle for describing personal experiences. At the very opening of *The Gossamer Years* she stated her reasons for writing the diary. She described herself as being below average in looks, a woman who has profitlessly spent her life in the world. She had read old romances, presumably to lighten the monotony of her days, and as she read these books she could not help but contrast the passionate love affairs they recounted with her own dreary life. Such books were wholly fictitious, but she thought that perhaps an account of what the life of a well-born lady was really like, without the addition of fantasies, might be of interest. Her purpose in writing the diary was not to divert, but to evoke the sadness and the loneliness of the life led by a woman such as herself.

We need not accept her statements at face value. She was so obsessed with her suffering that even her inborn gifts and the love she was offered brought no pleasure. We know from other sources that, far from being a plain and undistinguished person, she was admired both as one of the three most beautiful women of her time and as a poet.[19] But from the outset she chose to picture herself not as an envied woman but as a suffering wife.

The Gossamer Years describes the author's life from the time when Kaneie first sent her love notes until, twenty years later, she had resigned herself to never seeing him again. As a second wife, she should not have expected him to spend more than occasional nights with her, but she could not accept this convention: her diary is filled with mentions of nights and days spent waiting for him in vain, and of the frustration each of his visits caused by providing evidence that he could never love her as completely and intensely as she loved him. Her New Year's wish for 969 was that "he may be with me thirty days and thirty nights a month."[20] But when Kaneie visited and attempted to placate her, she was often unresponsive, seemingly unable to resist her craving for pain.

The work is colored throughout by mentions of the author's grief. Some scholars have suggested that, although she constantly complained of her unhappiness, she was actually very fortunate.[21] In a sense this is true. She was never deprived of Kaneie's material assistance even when he was least attentive, and despite his affairs with other women, he did not forget her. There is no suggestion in the diary, however, that she rejoiced in the comforts with which she was provided. In keeping with the persona she had assumed, she related extremely few moments of joy and many of desolation. She declared, "I concluded that my unhappiness was part of my inescapable destiny, determined from former lives, and must be accepted as such."[22] After one visit from Kaneie she recorded, "Eventually he appeared, but our interview was as unpleasant as before. There seemed no relief from the gloom that had become the dominant tone in my life."[23]

The author bitterly resented Kaneie's affairs with other women, though it seems not to have occurred to her that when Kaneie took her as his second wife, the first wife may well have experienced the kind of anguish that she considered to be her private disaster. She had little compassion to spare for others. At one point, after Kaneie had been describing something that bothered him, she admitted, "I was absorbed in my grief and paid no attention to him."[24] The title of her diary came from the statement of her unhappiness at the close of the first book: "And so the months and the years have gone by, but my grief over the fate of having nothing turn out as I hoped prevents me from feeling joy over the coming of a new year. This depressing life is likely to continue, as I fully realize, so I have thought it appropriate to call this the diary of a woman whose life was insubstantial as the summer haze (*kagerō*)."[25]

The most striking feature of *The Gossamer Years* is its incredible honesty. No author has ever engaged in self-revelation more candidly or appeared in a less attractive light. One night, when Kaneie announced his intention of visiting the author,

> I sent back word that I would not see him, but presently he appeared, cool and nonchalant as ever. His playful manner I found most irritating, and before I knew it I had begun pouring out all the resentment I had stored up through the months. He said not a word, pretending to be asleep, and after I had gone on for a time he started up and exclaimed, "What's this? Have you gone to bed already?" It may not have been entirely gracious of me, but I behaved like a stone for the rest of the night, and he left early in the morning without a word.[26]

The author could not have expected that such a passage would win the reader's sympathy, but she writes so vividly and with such awareness of her self-inflicted wounds, that we feel that we have all but participated in her life. Even if we do not approve of her behavior, we can understand it.

Perhaps the most shocking part of the diary describes the author's exultation over the misery of a rival. Kaneie had a paramour who lived in a narrow lane. The author was acutely aware of his visits to her rival because his carriage passed her house on the way. She was enraged when she learned that the other woman had given birth to Kaneie's child, but soon afterward, as she related,

> It began to appear that the lady in the alley had fallen from favor since the birth of her child. I had prayed, at the height of my unhappiness, that she would live to know what I was then suffering, and it seems that my prayers were being answered. She was alone, and now her child was dead, the child that had been the cause of that unseemly racket.... For a moment she had been able to use a person who was unaware of her shortcomings, and now she was abandoned. The pain must be even sharper than mine had been. I was satisfied.[27]

The normal reaction to the death of the child of a hated rival would have been expressions of sympathy, real or feigned, and perhaps even of contrition over the prayers that had yielded such a result, but the writer proclaims her satisfaction. No Japanese male writer up to this time—or even much later—had described his feelings with such honesty. As we have seen, various poems in the *Man'yōshū* by men describe their emotions on seeing a dead body by the roadside or on a beach. They wonder who the man is and imagine the grief of the man's wife who waits in vain for his return. Their compassion is moving but probably was inspired less by what they actually felt than by what they considered to be appropriate sentiments for the occasion. When the author of *The Gossamer Years*, on her way to Ishiyama, saw a dead body by the river, her only comment was, "I was quite beyond being frightened by that sort of thing."[28] And, at the sight of beggars at a temple, each with his bowl, she "recoiled involuntarily at being brought so near the defiling masses."[29]

Such outspoken expressions of feelings are not endearing, but their honesty is unmistakable. Other parts of the diary, notably her descriptions of places she saw on the way to various temples, are wonderfully evocative and as beautifully written as anything in the literature of the time, reminding us that she was admired as a poet. In such passages we see another side to the author, no less true to herself than her more frequent, unhappy reflections on her fate:

> The moon flooded through the trees, while over in the shadows of the mountain great swarms of fireflies wheeled about. An uninhibited cuckoo made me think ironically of how once, long ago when I had no worries, I had waited with some annoyance for a cuckoo that refused to repeat his call. And then suddenly, so near at hand that it seemed almost to be knocking on the door, came the drumming of a moor hen. All in all it was a spot that stirred in one the deepest of emotions.[30]

Although she responded to the beauty of the scene, it inevitably awakened bittersweet memories of the past. When a thrush, late for the season, surprised her with its song, she noticed that it sang in a dead tree.

The diary breaks off with the account of how, at the end of 974, the author heard a knocking at the gate. Scholars conjecture that the knocking came from exorcisers who went around from house to house on the last night of the year driving away demons. Even if the knocking was not that of exorcisers, it surely was not from Kaneie. The last third of the diary, in fact, contains comparatively little mention of Kaneie and treats instead the efforts of Kaneie's younger brother to marry the girl whom the diarist has adopted.

Many critics have opined that the last volume of *The Gossamer Years*, written soon after the events actually occurred, is literarily superior to her recollections of the more distant past, but it is hard to concur in this view. Like most autobiographical works, the earlier sections are the most compelling, perhaps because the imagination of the author was not blocked by quotidian concerns. The first two of the three books of *The Gossamer Years*, filled with half-remembered conversations and emotions, create an unforgettable portrait of a woman who, though sensitive and intelligent, little noticed her good fortune and was aware only of what she lacked.

The diary contains over three hundred poems. None is of the highest quality and most, at least for modern readers, tend to interrupt the narrative; but because they were written down immediately after being composed, they are probably more accurate than the author's recollections.

The most notable poem is Kaneie's chōka. Kaneie naturally did not keep a diary in which he described his relations with the Mother of Michitsuna, but if he had, he surely would not have revealed even as much of himself as in this poem, the only version of the affair from his side. It opens, "True, the newly gathered red leaves will fade. Love is but love. Each autumn is the same." These words suggest he was aware of the impossibility of keeping love burning at the same intensity forever. But, he insists, he has never forgotten his wife or son: "I did not forget, my purpose was as always. I sought to see the child and was turned away." The wife, even by her own testimony, often refused to see him and, driven from her house, he sought solace in "other, kinder places. But sometimes still I came, and I slept alone. And when I awoke in the middle of the night, I found the friendly moon, quite unreserved. And not a trace of you. Thus one may find that love has lost its flavor and left one inattentive. . . ."[31]

The reader of *The Gossamer Years* is likely to be struck by its unusual modernity, so much so that one is tempted to conjecture that if the Mother of Michitsuna were writing today, her book would probably be much the same. *The Tosa Diary* led to many other travel diaries, but *The Gossamer Years* led to *The Tale of Genji* by the truth and refinement of its expression.[32] It would be agreeable to report that Kaneie grieved as much over the death of the Mother of Michitsuna as Genji grieved over Murasaki, but if he died before her, and even if he had lived, his grief would have been tempered by relief that the demands of a woman who had loved him too much had at last ended.

The Tale of the Tōnomine Captain

A recurrent theme in both the diaries and the works of fiction of the Heian period is the desire to "leave the world" and become a Buddhist priest. Most people who expressed this desire, like Genji himself, were unable—because of worldly connections, expecially to the people who depended on them—to take so drastic a step, but some Heian noblemen did precisely that. Although blessed with everything their society prized—distinguished ancestry, rank, wealth, children—they gave these up in favor of a monk's somber habit.

The surviving diaries of the period reveal that when a man entered Buddhist orders this decision in no way altered the affection his family felt for him, and the "great step," which persons who had already become priests recommended to those who were disillusioned with the world, was often the cause of bitter lamentation. *Tōnomine Shōshō Monogatari* (The Tale of the Tōnomine Captain), though not always discussed as a diary, seems to be free of fictitious elements; it has, moreover, been known also as *Takamitsu Nikki* (The Takamitsu Diary). The work consists almost entirely of episodes relating the grief of members of the family of Fujiwara no Takamitsu (939–94) over his decision to abandon the world and become a monk.

The work seems to have been written about 962, while Takamitsu was living in a monastery on Mount Hiei. Soon afterward, Takamitsu moved from Hiei, where he had first taken the tonsure, to remote Tōnomine, where he spent the rest of his life; hence the title by which the work is most often called. The author is unknown, but it has been suggested that it was a woman in the service of Takamitsu's wife.[33] The period of the diary is more or less the same as that of *The Gossamer Years*, and scholars have debated which work came first.[34]

Takamitsu was a grandson of the Emperor Daigo and a brilliant waka poet. He was acclaimed as a genius when he was barely fifteen, and was later chosen as one of the thirty-six immortals of poetry; but at the age of twenty-three he suddenly left his wife and daughter to become a monk. He had previously, on many occasions, announced his intention of taking this step, though probably only half in earnest; but once his father, who had forbidden him to enter orders, died in 960 he felt free to carry out this long-cherished plan. One day he informed his wife of his decision to go to Mount Hiei and become a priest. The wife, having heard similar declarations before, thought it was just his usual joke, but he insisted, "This time I really mean it." She was sure that he would return home that night and merely laughed. He repeated his intention, at which she grew angry, imagining he was trying to provoke her. But after he had left home forever he sent a poem reassuring her:

wa ga iran	Keep your faith always
yama no ha ni nao	In the mountains in whose depths
kakaritare	I soon shall go:
omoi na ire so	Do not think too much of this;
tsuyu mo wasureji	I never shall forget you.

Apparently he found it hardest to leave his sister,[36] Aimiya. He visited her a final time, but refused to enter her house, saying, "I'm going somewhere in a hurry." He went on to Mount Hiei and, going directly to the cell of his younger brother, who had already become a priest, he commanded, "Shave my head!" The brother, unable to believe his ears, asked Takamitsu if he had forgotten his promise to their father not to leave the world. The abbot of the monastery, Zōga, was also in tears and refused to shave Takamitsu's head, whereupon Takamitsu himself calmly cut off his topknot. Zōga, realizing that there was no way to change Takamitsu's resolve, finally shaved his head.

The remainder of *The Tale of the Tōnomine Captain* is given over largely to descriptions of the grief caused by Takamitsu's decision. Both his wife and his sister Aimiya declared their intention of entering Buddhist orders, but opposition from members of their family prevented them. Aimiya repeatedly wrote doleful letters to Takamitsu's wife, expressing her never-ending sorrow. Attempts made by Aimiya's sister to cheer her with flowers had no effect. Another sister wrote Aimiya,

> How have you been of late? I have felt so terribly unsettled that I haven't been able to write for some time. I can easily imagine just how upset you must be over what has happened. Why haven't you come to see me? Have you had any word from the mountain? Nothing can be done about his decision to turn his back on the world, but it shouldn't be impossible for him to make his way here in secret and pay a visit to you, if nobody else. If it were a place where women could go, I would want nothing more than to go there myself, but this is one more instance of how helpless a woman is. I'm sure that you, too, when everything seems to be going contrary to your wishes, would like to go to the mountain, but that's one thing you must not even think of doing. I'm told you talk of wanting to become a nun. What a dreadful thing! Is it true? Never, never let that thought into your head.

urami koshi	After all your grief
somukamahoshiki	You'd like to turn your back on
yo nari tomo	This sad world of ours,
mirume kazukanu	But don't become a diver
ama ni naru na yo[37]	Who fails to gather seaweed

The expressions of grief get monotonous with repetition, and the poems are undistinguished; but it is striking that nobody even pretended to be glad that Takamitsu had entered the path of the Buddha. Takamitsu's late father, Fujiwara no Morosuke,[38] appeared in a dream to demand to know what grief had induced his son to become a priest.[39] He recognized that the priesthood was a holy profession, but was heartbroken over Takamitsu's decision, even though the son's prayers might help the father to gain salvation. Not only do people deplore Takamitsu's action, but they remind his wife and sister that even if they enter orders they will not be able to join him. Takamitsu himself opposed his wife's becoming a nun, as this poem indicates:

ama nite mo	Even as a nun
onaji yama ni wa	You surely could not remain
e shimo araji	On the same mountain;
nao yo no naka wo	Still spend your days in this world
uramite zo hen[40]	Bitterly though you hate it.

Takamitsu was by no means indifferent to what happened to his wife, sister, and daughter, but he was inflexible in his determination to remain secluded from all worldly ties. Other people of the day, such as the cloistered sovereigns or the mother of the author of *The Sarashina Diary* (see page 383), remained at home (or in a palace in the city) even after entering Buddhist orders, and changed their lives only to the extent of trimming their hair or wearing dark clothes; but Takamitsu had found his vocation and he refused to temporize, despite the ties to his family.

Perhaps the most interesting part of the diary concerns a former suitor of Takamitsu's wife, who sends her a letter reminding her that when, long ago, she refused him, he also considered, "living in the mountains." Then, with startling unpleasantness, he declares that she should consider her present grief as her punishment for having made him suffer in the past. He is sure that the wife, left to spend sleepless nights alone, now suffers more than Takamitsu, who has cut himself off from those he loved.[41]

The wife for a time considered suicide, but refrained, out of love for her small daughter. She sent Takamitsu a chōka describing the plight of the child. His reply showed he was also worried, and being unable to see his daughter in waking hours was attempting to see her in dreams. When his longing became desperate, he took comfort even from daytime visions.[42]

The Tale of the Tōnomine Captain, despite the lugubrious tone, is affecting, particularly because it describes an aspect of Heian court life that was seldom mentioned by the writers of fiction; a character who had really "left the world" would simply disappear from a novel.[43] The diary lingers in the mind as a convincing account of the loneliness of those left behind when a man chose the path of salvation.

The Izumi Shikibu Diary

The first question to be asked about *Izumi Shikibu Nikki* (The Izumi Shikibu Diary) is whether or not it should be considered a diary, and some scholars not only refuse to call it a diary but doubt that Izumi Shikibu wrote it. It certainly does not resemble a diary: the entries are undated; it is written throughout in the third person, with Izumi Shikibu always referred to simply as *onna*, "the woman"; and the author enters into the thoughts of other people in a manner customary in works of fiction but not in diaries. Because of such departures from the normal form of a diary, some scholars have insisted that the work must have been written by another person,[44] but at present most authorities accept the attribution to Izumi Shikibu.

Regardless of whether or not she wrote the work, the term "diary" seems inappropriate.[45] Perhaps the work might best be called a romance,[46] related in short sections of prose and interspersed with over 140 waka. Both prose and poetry are of high literary quality. The work as a whole suggests a fragment of a longer monogatari, but its closeness in tone and content to the diaries by Heian court ladies accounts for its being treated as a diary.

The Izumi Shikibu Diary covers a little less than a year between the early summer of 1003, when Prince Atsumichi made his first overture to Izumi Shikibu, a spray of orange blossoms he sent with a messenger, and the spring of the following year, when Atsumichi's wife, enraged by his infidelity, left his home to go live with her sister. Prince Atsumichi (980–1007), the son of the Emperor Reizei by a secondary consort, was twenty-three at the beginning of the work; Izumi Shikibu was probably a few years older. She had been married to the governor of Izumi (a title from which she derived part of her name) and had borne him at least one daughter, but her affair with Atsumichi's brother seems to have broken up the marriage.

The messenger who bears Atsumichi's gift at the opening of the work is a page who was formerly in the service of Atsumichi's elder brother, Tametaka (977–1002). Izumi and Tametaka had been lovers until the year before, when he suddenly died at the age of twenty-five. According to some sources, Tametaka was so assiduous in his wooing of Izumi that he paid no attention to a raging epidemic, but made his way through streets filled with rotting corpses to her house.[47] Perhaps he died of a disease contracted at that time.

When Izumi received the orange blossoms she was still so wrapped in memories of Tametaka that she was reluctant to reply. Finally, however, she sent Atsumichi a poem, and the ensuing correspondence, at first intended by Izumi to be no more than a distraction from "the listless boredom of her existence,"[48] before long led to their becoming lovers. They remained so until his death in 1007. Izumi, who was probably twenty-nine at the time, composed a hundred poems after Atsumichi's death attesting to her extreme grief. The prevailing tone of the diary, the poetry especially, is dark. For all her reputation as a creature of the senses, Izumi seems to drift rather than leap into her relationship with Atsumichi: "What she really wanted was to live 'in a cavern deep within the crags.' But how would she cope with the melancholy that might come to haunt her?"[49] She seems to have sought in her affair with Atsumichi not so much pleasure as an escape from a heaviness of spirit.

Despite the general atmosphere of melancholy that infuses the diary, some passages have unusual charm:

> He came to her as usual in his carriage. Because of having changed his residence temporarily due to the directional taboo,[50] he was now living in a highly secluded place, he said. She went with him, deciding that this time she would simply do whatever he asked of her. They talked together to their hearts' content from morning till night, rising or sleeping as they pleased. She felt relieved of the bitter tedium of her days and wished to go and live with him. But the period of his taboo passed, and she returned to her own home.
>
> Today she felt more than ever overpowered with love and longing, until, unable to endure her emotions any longer, she wrote:

tsurezure to	Today I discovered,
kyō kazōreba	On carefully counting up
toshitsuki no	All the months and years,
kinō zo mono wo	That yesterday was the first
omowazarikeru	I did not spend in
	brooding.[51]

Such happy days, however, were few. Perhaps the most frequently reiterated theme in the diary is the fear of gossip. Atsumichi feared what not only his wife but also his servants might say if he went out night after night. "And further, he reflected, it was because of his infatuation with this woman that his brother, the late Prince, had been made the subject of vicious gossip until the day of his death."[52] Izumi also worried about gossip, but "she resigned herself to the thought that this was the inevitable consequence of her continued existence in society."[53]

The fear of gossip is mentioned on almost every page. When Atsumichi decided to visit Izumi, his old nurse tried to dissuade him by saying that "people are talking about this affair."[54] He later heard rumors that Izumi was unfaithful to him, and for a time believed them. Izumi was distraught that Atsumichi had listened to this gossip, but even after they were reconciled, he told her, "I have been made the object of much vexing criticism. Perhaps because my visits to you are few and far between, I have never been discovered: yet people are saying most distressing things."[55]

It is hard to understand why a man of Atsumichi's rank should have been afraid that waiting women in the palace might gossip about him, but one recalls the opening of *The Tale of Genji* where, we are told, "The emperor's pity and affection quite passed bounds. No longer caring what his ladies and courtiers might say, he behaved as if intent on stirring up gossip."[56] The Heian aristocrats, regardless of their position, dreaded gossip, and only the bravest or most love-stricken dared to ignore what people might think. The one sure way to avoid comment was to withdraw completely from society, either by entering a religious order or else by secluding oneself and becoming known as a hermit or eccentric. Gossip and concern over what other people think often appear obsessive in works of Heian literature, despite the general air of permissiveness. The court society was limited to some one or two thousand people who had the leisure to observe and spread tales about one another's behavior. The necessity of preserving dignity (or "face") no doubt inspired such acute fear.

Izumi Shikibu and Prince Atsumichi tried for a long time to keep their affair a secret, but, at last realizing that it was impossible to keep tongues from wagging, Atsumichi took the bold step of installing Izumi under the same roof with his wife. We know from *Ōkagami* (The Great Mirror) the historical work that describes this period, that at the Kamo Festival of 1005 Atsumichi defiantly placed Izumi in his carriage, from which her long sleeves and *hakama* (divided skirts) trailed to the ground. *The Great Mirror* reports, "Everyone seemed to be looking at them instead of watching the procession."[57]

The last we hear of Izumi Shikibu is that "she decided simply to go on serving the Prince as before, but she knew that after all she was destined never to be free of sorrows."[58]

The Murasaki Shikibu Diary

Our expectations when we open a copy of *Murasaki Shikibu Nikki* (The Murasaki Shikibu Diary) are likely to be higher than for any other diary written by a Japanese, certainly one written by a Japanese literary figure. We turn to it, above all, for clues as to how a rather obscure court lady, known to us only by her nickname of Murasaki Shikibu, managed to create one of the masterpieces of world literature, *The Tale of Genji.*

The diary consists of three main sections: an account of the birth of Prince Atsuhira, the first child of the Empress Shōshi,[59] the daughter of Fujiwara no Michinaga; a description of life at the court in the form of a letter to a friend; and, finally, a collection of seemingly unrelated anecdotes concerning court life. *The Murasaki Shikibu Diary*, like other diaries by women of the time, is not a diary in the normal sense. The entries are dated casually or not at all, occasioning speculation as to the years of some events, such as Murasaki Shikibu's first appearance at court.

Needless to say, every scrap of information that Murasaki Shikibu provides about herself is of unique importance to scholars of Japanese literature, whether her description of her early education, when she read the Chinese classics so much more quickly than her brother (for whose sake the lessons had been arranged) that her father regretted she had not been born a boy, or her expressions of admiration or disapproval for various ladies of the court. There are also passages that recall the manner of *The Tale of Genji*. But the diary as a whole is a disappointment because it reveals so little of how she worked as a writer. Did she begin with the first chapter or (as tradition has it) with the chapters describing Genji's life at Suma and Akashi? Was the order of chapters the same as in the present text, or did she later interleave chapters? These and similar questions intrigue everyone who has ever studied *The Tale of Genji*, but the diary remains silent on such matters.[60]

Of the few mentions of *The Tale of Genji*, perhaps the best-known is: "When His Majesty had *The Tale of Genji* read to him he was pleased to say, 'This person surely must have read the *Nihongi*. She certainly has a good knowledge of Chinese.' [Saemon no Naishi], quick to make inference, spread word among people at the court to the effect that I am terribly proud of my learning, and she bestowed on me the nickname of The Lady of the *Nihongi*."[61]

The malice of the court lady Saemon no Naishi in spreading word that Murasaki Shikibu enjoyed showing off her knowledge of writings in Chinese recalls Murasaki Shikibu's own criticism of Sei Shōnagon, and again reminds us of the power of gossip in a closed society like that of the Japanese court. But it is puzzling that his reading of *The Tale of Genji* should have suggested to the emperor that Murasaki Shikibu was well versed in the *Nihon Shoki*. Surely the impression a modern reader receives from *The Tale of Genji* in no way resembles the effect of reading the accumulation of legendary and historical materials that make up the *Nihon Shoki*. Perhaps people of her day read *The Tale of Genji* in a different manner from our own, as a kind of veiled commentary on actual events at the court, but the clues in the diary are too incomplete to enlighten us.

In other respects *The Murasaki Shikibu Diary* is an excellent source of information on what life was like at the Heian court during its period of greatest glory. In the "Fireflies" chapter of *The Tale of Genji* Murasaki Shikibu, speaking through the character Genji, set forth the importance of the art of fiction, contrasting it with the materials found in the official histories. Genji at first had made light of the old romances, but he concluded by admitting that the *Nihon Shoki* gives an incomplete picture of what life in the past was like, and it was the romances that filled in the details.[62] In much the same way, the diaries of the court ladies, especially *The Murasaki Shikibu Diary*, supply materials that are found nowhere else. If, for example, *The Gossamer Years* did not exist, the portrait of Kaneie that could be pieced together from other sources would be so incomplete that only a specialist in Heian history would be likely to remember his name. But who could forget Kaneie after reading *The Gossamer Years*?

It has been suggested that Fujiwara no Michinaga (966–1027) served as the model for Genji. Little in *The Murasaki Shikibu Diary* substantiates this theory; in fact, it would be easier to conclude that Genji was an anti-Michinaga, a diametrical opposite in every sense. The bulk of the diary is given over to an account of the celebrations attending the birth of Michinaga's grandchild, the son of his daugher Shōshi. At all stages Michinaga, rather than the infant's father (the Emperor Ichijō), is in command. "His Excellency was shouting everything in such a loud voice that the intoning of the priests was drowned out and could not be heard."[63] His joy after the safe delivery was not merely that of a grandfather, but of the grandfather of a future emperor. He was so delighted that he could not resist the impulse to visit his daughter and the baby every morning and evening for the pleasure of taking his grandchild in his arms, though on one occasion the baby responded by wetting Michinaga's cloak.

Genji experienced few such joys. His first son, the fruit of his secret union with his father's consort Fujitsubo, could not be recognized as his, and thoughts of this son stirred feelings of shame rather than pride. His other son, Yūgiri, was born while the mother, Aoi, was in a state of demonic possession; and hardly is the baby born before Aoi is killed by the living ghost of Lady Rokujō. The woman Genji loves most, Murasaki, is childless. It is true that his daughter by the Lady of Akashi marries an emperor, but Genji derives no advantage from this.

There are even more important differences between Genji and Michinaga. The latter not only never seems to have heard of *mono no aware* (sensitivity to things), but behaves on occasion with a crudity that would be unimaginable in Genji. But there is no need to belabor the point. Whether or not it was Murasaki Shikibu's intent to describe in *The Tale of Genji* what a truly civilized court was like, the account in her diary of the court she actually knew is disillusioning.

On reading *The Murasaki Shikibu Diary* one quickly becomes aware of the differences separating the world of *The Tale of Genji* and Murasaki's life at the court. However, it is not a totally different world. The opening of the diary is permeated with an awareness of beauty that demonstrates that the novel was not wholly fictitious:

> As autumn deepens, the beauty of the Tsuchimikado mansion defies description. The trees by the lake and the grasses by the stream become a blaze of color that intensifies in the evening glow and makes the voices in ceaseless recitation sound all the more impressive. A cool breeze gently stirs, and throughout the night the endless murmur of the stream blends with the sonorous chanting.[64]

For all the court's beauty, Murasaki Shikibu was only intermittently happy there. She stated in her diary that her loneliness was quite unbearable. This was not the loneliness of isolation but of having no one with whom to share her thoughts. It was also the loneliness of the artist who craves companionship but also rejects it, knowing that work requires solitude. There were times when court life gave Murasaki Shikibu unmistakable pleasure, as she reveals in her description of the entertainments offered to celebrate the birth of the prince; and she was especially sensitive to music, especially music heard over water.[65]

More often, however, Murasaki Shikibu wrote of her displeasure or even dismay. She related at one point how the celebrated poet Fujiwara no Kintō asked a group of court ladies, "I wonder if young Murasaki is in attendance here?" Murasaki murmured to herself, "Why should that lady have come when there is nobody here who even suggests

Genji?"[66] Perhaps it was at this time that Murasaki acquired the nickname by which she would henceforth be known.[67] But there are even more striking contrasts between the world of the novel and that of the Heian court, as the following passage (which occurs immediately after the above) suggests:

> "Assistant Master of Third Rank Sanenari!" shouted His Excellency. "Take the cup!" He stood up and, because his father the Minister of the Center, Kinsue, was present, he came up the steps from the garden. Seeing this, his father burst into tears. Provisional Middle Counsellor Takaie, who was leaning against a corner pillar, started pulling at Lady Hyōbu's robes and singing dreadful songs, but His Excellency said nothing. I realized that it was bound to be a terribly drunken affair this evening, so, once the formal celebrations were over, Lady Saishō and I decided to retire.[68]

Murasaki Shikibu's diary portrays not the flawlessly behaved courtiers of *The Tale of Genji* but drunken men who make obscene jokes and paw at the women. Some modern readers may find that such proofs of the coarseness of the real (as opposed to the fictional) Heian courtiers make them seem more "human" and closer than the peerless Genji, but that was obviously not Murasaki Shikibu's point of view. Weary of such excessively human men, she took refuge in the world she had created.

Murasaki Shikibu's loneliness was occasioned also by her exceptional powers of discernment. The "letter" section of her diary contains thumbnail sketches of some fifteen court ladies. She was not always critical; indeed, she praised several women without qualification and generally found something to praise even in women she disliked. But her barbed criticisms are what we remember of her comments, and an ability to see through seeming perfection to hidden flaws, though valuable in a novelist, is a sure way to lose friends. At one point Murasaki Shikibu restrained herself, saying that if she went on describing people in so unflattering a manner she would certainly acquire the reputation of being a gossip; but having said this, she immediately launched into a description of Lady Saishō that concluded with her judgment that Saishō was by no means perfect.

The most interesting of Murasaki Shikibu's comments on court ladies of her time refer to women we know from their own works, Izumi Shikibu and Sei Shōnagon. Murasaki Shikibu wrote of the former, "She does have a rather unsavory side to her character but has a genius for tossing off letters with ease and can make the most banal statement sound special. . . . I cannot think of her as a poet of the highest quality."[69] Sei Shōnagon fared even worse. She is described as being dreadfully conceited, and Murasaki Shikibu was unimpressed either by her wit or her familiarity with Chinese characters. Her final comment was the characterization of Sei Shōnagon and people like her as "ridiculous and superficial."

Such sharp observations demonstrated how mistakenly people at the court judged Murasaki Shikibu. At first her reluctance to join in general gossip was attributed to her shyness. Later, they concluded that she must be stupid, despite her literary accomplishments. Murasaki's own estimation of herself was more astute:

> Do they really look upon me as such a dull thing, I wonder? But I am what I am and so act accordingly. Her Majesty too has often remarked that she had thought I was not the kind of person with whom she could ever relax, but that now I have become closer to her than any of the others. I am perversely standoffish; if only I can avoid putting off those for whom I have genuine respect.[70]

This is not only a successful self-portrayal but helps to explain how Murasaki Shikibu was able to keep writing her lengthy novel while serving at the court. She had to preserve her distance from the intrigues and rivalries that occupied the other court ladies, and only with a few chosen friends did she reveal her true nature.

Apart from the emperor's praise (in which he likened the work to the *Nihon Shoki*), there are only indirect references to *The Tale of Genji*. For example, Murasaki Shikibu's mention of ladies in the empress's entourage choosing paper of various colors and asking skillful calligraphers to make copies of monogatari has been interpreted as meaning that the empress had asked for copies of *The Tale of Genji*. But, even if this is what the passage signifies,[71] it is not clear whether or not the work had already been completed.

Murasaki Shikibu soon afterward in her diary noted that one day, while she was busy serving at the court, Michinaga sneaked into her room and found the copy of *The Tale of Genji* she had brought along for safekeeping. He gave this manuscript to his second daughter. Murasaki Shikibu expressed her distress that an inferior copy (presumably, not the final version) might harm her reputation. It is unclear in what way the manuscript was inferior to the final version, but the statement is evidence that she worried about the future reception of her book.

Murasaki Shikibu was far more ambitious than the writers of the old tales had been. She put into her novel not only romantic elements of the kind that had appeared in earlier works of fiction, but also her experience of life. As time passed, it was natural that her outlook changed, necessitating revisions. She wrote at one point, "I tried re-reading the Tale, but it did not seem to be the same as before, and I was disappointed."[72] Perhaps she was not in fact referring to *The Tale of Genji* but to some other work, but the meaning remains the same: she had outgrown her former tastes and was no longer satisfied with what had once pleased her.

The final reference in the diary to *The Tale of Genji* consists of the banter and poems exchanged by Murasaki Shikibu and Michinaga after he happened to notice a copy of the work near where the empress had been sitting.[73] The manner of presentation of this incident suggests that Murasaki Shikibu felt quietly confident in the value of her novel. The diary is also of high literary distinction, but it survives only in a sadly mutilated state, and of course lacks the magnitude of *The Tale of Genji*. Even in its present state, unfortunately incomplete, it is still a high point in the Japanese tradition of diary literature.

The Sarashina Diary

Sarashina Nikki (The Sarashina Diary) is even less like a diary than *The Murasaki Shikibu Diary*. Hardly an entry is dated, and the work covers not a limited number of years but, like an autobiography, virtually the entire life of the writer. It is most unlike a true diary in its implicit denial of reality. Diaries usually insist on verisimilitude—whether or not it rained on a certain day, who came to visit, from whom letters were received, and so on—but in *The Sarashina Diary* the place of reality is taken by fiction or dreams. The world of the monogatari, especially *The Tale of Genji*, bulked larger in the writer's mind than everyday existence, and the people of the novel were not merely characters in literature but her most intimate friends and the object of her emulation. Her greatest desire as a child was not that she would lead a happy life as a wife and mother, or as a member of the court, but that she would be able to immerse herself to her heart's content in the old romances.

The opening paragraph of her diary set the tone for the entire work:

> I was brought up in a part of the country so remote that it lies beyond the end of the Great East Road. What an uncouth creature I must have been in those days! Yet even shut away in the provinces

I somehow came to hear that the world contained things known as Tales, and from that moment my greatest desire was to read them for myself. To idle away the time, my sister, my step-mother, and others in the household would tell me stories from the Tales, including episodes about Genji, the Shining Prince; but since they had to depend on their memories, they could not possibly tell me all I wanted to know and their stories only made me more curious than ever. In my impatience I got a statue of the Healing Buddha built in my own size. When no one was watching, I would perform my ablutions and, stealing into the altar room, would prostrate myself and pray fervently, "Oh, please arrange things so that we may soon go to the Capital, where there are many Tales, and please let me read them all."[74]

To have the statue of Yakushi Buddha built was an extraordinary undertaking for a girl not yet twelve years old, and it demonstrates the strength of her determination to read every last monogatari.

One can easily imagine that a well-educated girl who had grown up in a distant part of the country would yearn to go to the capital, the only place in Japan where she could lead the kind of life for which her education had prepared her. She craved not the social life that actually existed at the court but the vicarious pleasure of reading about imaginary people who had once populated it. Manuscripts were scarce and expensive, and it was most unlikely that a complete set of *The Tale of Genji* would turn up in remote Kazusa, so the only way this sensitive, introverted girl could be sure of being able to read all that had been written about Prince Genji was by living in the capital. If she could have obtained in the country all the books she wanted, perhaps she would not have desired to leave.

No sooner did she and her family arrive at their destination than she let it be known that she was eager to read some tales immediately. Her house, set in uncultivated grounds, in no way suggested the refinement of a great city, and the household was in confusion as people tried to make the place livable, but the girl could not wait for things to settle down. She wrote in her diary, "I begged my mother, 'Please, please look for some tales and show them to me.' "[75]

From the time she left Kazusa in 1020 at the age of twelve until she was invited at the age of thirty-one to serve at the court, the author of *The Sarashina Diary* seems to have done nothing except read monogatari. In addition to *The Tale of Genji*, which she read again and again, she read such works as *Tōgimi*, *Serikawa*, *Shirara*, and *Asauzu*, all of which have disappeared without a trace. Granting that there were many more romances for her to read than still survive, it was still a most unusual way to spend what are considered to be the most precious years of a woman's life. She was by no means unhappy to have spent her life in this way. On the contrary, she related what immense joy she felt when an aunt presented her with all fifty-odd volumes of *The Tale of Genji*, making it possible for her to read the whole work for the first time. She declared, "I wouldn't have changed places with the Empress herself."[76]

She spent every day reading until late at night. Apparently no suitors came to distract her from her readings—the young men of the court were probably not even aware that she existed. She told herself, "I was not a very attractive girl at the time, but I fancied that, when I grew up, I would surely become a great beauty with long flowing hair like Yūgao, who was loved by Genji, the Shining Prince, or like Ukifune, who was wooed by the Captain of Uji. Oh, what futile conceits!"[77]

It is by no means strange for a plain girl to imagine that, like the ugly duckling of Andersen's fairy tale, she will one day turn into a swan; but she continued to entertain such hopes long after the time when that transformation should have occurred. Her life at home was monotonous. Her father was an official of the zuryō class, a man who is remembered only because the author of the diary is known as the daughter of Takasue. It is true that Sugawara no Michizane was a distant ancestor, and that she was a niece of the author of *The Gossamer Years*, but she does not mention this. She took refuge from her humdrum life in books and also in the world of dreams.

She recorded her dreams faithfully, many times in the course of the diary. Often a dream had religious significance, but initially at least she paid scant attention to such dreams. "One night I dreamt that a handsome priest appeared before me in a yellow surplice and ordered me to learn the fifth volume of the Lotus Sutra as soon as possible. I told no one about the dream, since I was much too busy with my Tales to spend any time learning sutras."[78]

Some time later, the author's mother, worried about what would happen to a girl who lived so secluded from the world, ordered a mirror to be made for the Hase Temple, and asked the priest to stay in retreat for three days and pray for a dream about her daughter's future. The priest did as requested, and had a dream in which a beautiful lady appeared, dressed in splendid robes, who asked if there was a document presented with the mirror. The priest replied that there was none. The lady seemed surprised, but she showed the priest what was reflected on both sides of the mirror. On one side a figure was seen tossing with weeping and lamentation; on the other was reflected a beautiful springtime scene.[79] Years later the author would decide that the unhappy figure tossing with grief was a prophetic vision of herself, but at the time she paid no attention to the dream. "So indifferent was I to such matters that when I was repeatedly told to pray to the Heavenly Goddess Amaterasu I wondered who this deity might be and whether she was in fact a Goddess or a Buddha. It was some time before I was interested enough to ask who she actually was."[80]

Unlike other educated Heian women, she did not study the Lotus Sutra or the mysteries of Shintō. At first, she was so involved with reading tales that she had no time to spare even for dreams, though she accepted the contemporary belief that they reveal the future. Her mind was filled not only with the dreams that come during the hours of sleep but with daydreams that made her life as uncertain and unreal as the future. This is how she described her thoughts when she was about twenty-four:

> I lived forever in a dream world. Though I made occasional pilgrimages to temples, I could never bring myself to pray sincerely for what most people want. I know there are many who read the sutras and practice religious devotions from the age of about seventeen; but I had no interest in such things. The height of my aspirations was that a man of noble birth, perfect in both looks and manner, someone like Shining Genji in the Tale, would visit me just once a year in the mountain village where he would have hidden me like Lady Ukifune. There I should live my lonely existence, gazing at the blossoms and the autumn leaves and the moon and the snow, and wait for an occasional splendid letter from him. That was all I wanted; and in time I came to believe that it would actually happen.[81]

She dreamed of herself as Ukifune (the unhappiest woman portrayed in *The Tale of Genji* and the only one who attempted suicide), finding it easier to identify with this tragic character than with Murasaki, who was favored with Genji's love. She had no hopes that a Genji of her own would install her in a wing of his palace, with a garden that reflected her preference among the seasons, but only that he would keep her in some lonely mountain village. This was a modest ambition, but this vision of Genji to which she clung was of a perfect man who did not resemble anyone she had actually seen. She was sure that even if such a man visited her only once a year she would be satisfied. And if between his visits he favored her with a lettter—of course, it would be a splendid letter—she would be happy while she waited. Like many children, but not like most women of twenty-four, she was sure that if she wished hard enough she would obtain whatever she wanted. There is something at once childish and extremely affecting in the frankness with which she expressed these desires.

About this time her father was appointed as the governor of a distant province. He did not take his daughter with him, for fear she might turn into a mere country woman. He told her, "The provinces are terrible places. . . . I may not be long for this world and I can think of all too many examples of girls who have lost their fathers and then gone to seed in the Capital."[82] He did not openly refer to the fact that she was still unmarried, though this must have been on his mind.

After her father left for Hitachi fewer visitors than ever came to her house. By way of distracting herself from her loneliness, she made a pilgrimage to Uzumasa. Her prayers were not for her own salvation but for her father's return. During another pilgrimage, this one to the Kiyomizu Temple, she dreamed that a priest approached and scolded her: "Engaged in senseless trifling, you are risking your future salvation."[83] She noted in the diary that she told no one about this dream, and left the temple without giving it further thought.

We may admire her for her indifference to dream warnings, and may even interpret this as proof that she was a sceptic, or at any rate immune to superstitions, but this is probably a misinterpretation. The diary was written in later years, after she had turned to religion, and her account of her indifference may have been intended as a warning to others who, like herself, thought only of happiness in this dreamlike world.

When the daughter of Takasue was invited to court for the first time, her father, who had returned from Hitachi, urged her to decline, no doubt reluctant to be deprived of her company, but other people persuaded him to yield. She wrote laconically, "My first period of service lasted exactly one night."[84] The statement may suggest that she spent one night in the arms of some courtier, but in fact nothing of interest occurred. The only people she knew at court were those from whom she had borrowed books, and she was accustomed to the old-fashioned ways of her parents with whom she used to gaze, in the conventional manner, at the spring blossoms or the autumn moon. She wrote,

> During my cloistered years I had often imagined that life in the Palace would offer all sorts of pleasures which I never encountered in my monotonous routine at home. As it turned out, my first experience at court suggested that I would feel extremely awkward and unhappy in these new surroundings. Yet what could I do about it?[85]

Her youth had been spent mainly alone. She probably lacked the conversational ability that enabled other court ladies to pass their days amusingly, and she was so unaccustomed to the presence of others that when she went to court again later that year (1039) she could not sleep at night with strangers in the same room. When she returned home this time her parents begged her not to go to court again because it made them so lonely. She accordingly ceased, but she seems to have undergone a change, perhaps at the sudden realization that her childhood dreams would never be fulfilled. She wrote,

> Things now became rather hectic for me. I forgot all about my Tales and became much more conscientious. How could I have let all those years slip by. . . . I began to doubt whether any of my romantic fancies, even those that had seemed most plausible, had the slightest basis in fact. How could anyone as wonderful as the Shining Genji or as beautiful as the girl whom Captain Kaoru kept hidden in Uji really exist in this world of ours? Oh, what a fool I had been to believe in such nonsense![86]

The author says almost nothing about her marriage, which took place in her thirties, an advanced age for a Heian lady. Her husband was older than herself, perhaps a widower, and they had several children, including a boy who is briefly described. The marriage seems to have been happy, but nothing suggests that it was like the romantic love affairs chronicled in the tales of which she was so fond.

The only time in her life when she came close to realizing her dream of meeting a Prince Genji was when she was serving at court. One night she and another lady were listening to priests intone a sutra when a gentleman approached and exchanged a few words with the author's companion. "He talked in a quiet, gentle way and I could tell that he was a man of perfect qualities."[87] The reader is likely to hope that, in the manner of romances, the man will detect her unusual nature even in the dark and despite her unassertiveness, so we are pleased when he asks her companion who she is. The author commented, "There was none of the crude, lecherous tone in his voice that one would expect from most men who asked this sort of question. Then he started speaking about the sadness of the world and other such matters, and there was something so sensitive about his manner that, for all my usual shyness, I found it hard to stand stiff and aloof."[88] We sense that something has occurred between the two and imagine for a moment that miracles are possible.

The gentleman who addressed the daughter of Takasue and her companion described the contrasting beauties of spring and autumn, in language suitable to this familiar theme of Japanese poetry, then related a memorable experience he had at Ise when he went there one winter as an imperial envoy. The moonlight on the snow and the otherworldly atmosphere had so profoundly affected him that he had ever since been moved particularly by snowy winter nights. He predicted that in the future, as the result of this unforgettable encounter, he would no doubt be moved also by dark, rainy nights. The author added, "After he had finished speaking and had left us, it occurred to me that he still had no idea who I was."[89]

Some ten months later, when the author accompanied the princess she served to the palace, a concert was being held. The gentleman whom she had met on the rainy night was present, but she did not learn this until afterward. Later that night he passed by her room and for a few moments, until his companions joined him, they spoke together. He said, "I have never forgotten that rainy night, not for a moment." She murmured in reply a waka asking why he should remember a night when nothing happened except for the rain falling on the leaves.[90]

One quiet spring evening she heard that he was visiting the palace. She made up her mind to go to him, but the place was so crowded that she was intimidated and withdrew to her room. He was equally upset by the commotion and left without seeing her. This was the last time she attempted to see him. The girl who yearned to be like Yūgao, who died the victim of Rokujō's jealousy, or like Ukifune, who was torn between two men who loved her, achieved a pathos of her own.

At this point, without any transition, the author declared that the time had come for her to think of her future salvation. Perhaps the failure of the one romance of her life had wakened her from her dreams of happiness in this world. There are increasing mentions of religious devotions and of visits to distant temples. She must have realized the effect this would produce on readers of the diary. She wrote, "Anyone reading this account of visits to one temple after another might well imagine that I was forever going on pilgrimages. In fact there were long intervals, often several years, between my retreats."[91] After her marriage she became even more religious, and went on a number of pilgrimages, apparently without her husband. This section of the diary is less interesting than earlier ones, no doubt because the reader is sorry to see the romantic girl turn into a pious woman of no special distinction, but the writing remains beautiful. At the Ishiyama Temple she had a dream. In the past she probably would have ignored it, but now she wrote, "Thinking it might be an auspicious omen, I spent the rest of the night in prayer."[92]

The daughter of Takasue nowhere stated why she wrote *The Sarashina Diary*. Perhaps it was intended to persuade readers, especially young persons deluded by dreams of worldly happiness, that real happiness is possible only through religion. After her husband died she wrote, "If only I had not given myself over to Tales and poems since my young days but had spent my time in religious devotions, I should have been spared this misery."[93] She could have avoided some of her grief, but the portrait of a young woman who lived entirely in books is strangely touching.

The last passage in the diary has been dated tentatively as describing an event of 1059, when the author was in her fifty-second year, but nothing is known about her later years or when she died. She has often been credited with having written two surviving monogatari,[94] as well as several lost works, and her poems figure in several anthologies. If these attributions are correct, she must be counted as the most important prose writer of the late Heian period.

The Poems of the Mother of the Ajari Jōjin

In 1071 an old lady, probably eighty-four at the time, began to write a diary which would have as its central theme her yearning for her son, a man over sixty years old. This old lady was the granddaughter of Takamitsu's sister Aimiya, and the great-granddaughter of the Emperor Daigo. She enjoyed the highest rank of any of the Heian court ladies who kept diaries, and had no doubt received a suitable education. However, it was not until she was in her eighties that she decided to relieve the stress of great emotional agitation by writing the work known as *Jōjin Ajari Haha no Shū* (The Poems of the Mother of the Ajari Jōjin).[95] At the outset of the work she related why she felt impelled to write down her thoughts:

> Over the years that have fleetingly passed, so many things, both delightful and strange, have happened to me that I can no longer count them all. I have decided to write them down, not in the hopes that anyone will see them, but because, at the age of eighty, I have had a most extraordinary experience. I have kept it to myself for some time, but I thought that I would try setting it down on paper.[96]

She was convinced, as she relates many times in the diary, that no one had ever suffered as much as she. On the surface, at least, this was patently untrue. After the death of her husband she had decided that the best way of providing for her two sons was to have them enter the priesthood. Both men did so and gained extraordinary distinction, the elder becoming a *risshi*[97] who served in the imperial palace, the younger the *ajari* Jōjin. The old lady always wrote respectfully of the risshi, but she clearly preferred Jōjin. For years her fondest dream had been that when she was about to die her two sons, one seated on either side of her pillow, would read the holy sutras, and with the sound of their voices in her ears, she would breathe her last. She seems to have lived quite happily, comforted by this dream, until the day when Jōjin informed her of his intention of going to China to study at Mount Wu-t'ai, the same center of Tendai Buddhism where Ennin had lived two hundred years earlier. From this time on the mother became obsessed with her griefs, and she wrote a diary in the hope that someday, doubtless after her death, Jōjin would read of all the suffering he had caused her.[98]

The mother evinced not the slightest interest in why Jōjin should have felt it necessary to make the dangerous journey to China; she was aware only of his seeming indifference to her. She vacillated between the desire to die as quickly as possible and the desire to live at least until Jōjin's return. Again and again she blamed herself for the sin of having lived too long. If only she had not committed this sin, she would have been spared the agony of separation from her beloved Jōjin.

She did not doubt the special ties that bound her to her son. In an unusually outspoken passage she insisted: "A mother's love for her child, regardless of whether she is noble or humble in birth, differs entirely from a father's. While the child is still in her womb she is constantly in pain, whether she is up or lying down, but she never thinks of her own comfort. She prays that the child will be superior to others in looks and in every other respect, and this hope is so strong that even the agony of giving birth to the child is as nothing to her."[99] She recalled how, when Jōjin was an infant, he would cry if anyone else picked him up, but that he stopped crying the instant she took him in her arms. And, she insisted, her love for him had not changed to that day. It is hard to remember that she was writing not about an adolescent but about a man in his sixties who was an outstanding cleric of his day.

Jōjin's mother was so distraught over being separated from her son that she did not feel it was impious to compare her situation with those of the sacred figures of Buddhism. She declared, for example, that Maya, the mother of Shakyamuni Buddha, had been fortunate because she died before experiencing the anguish of parting from her son. At moments in the diary the mother seems to have realized that the bitterness engendered in her by Jōjin's decision to go abroad might do him harm, but she was powerless to restrain her emotions. After describing Shakyamuni Buddha's awakening to the sorrows of human life on seeing old age, sickness, and death, she (as usual) applied the parable to Jōjin and herself: "He has seen that I suffer from two of these griefs, that I am old and sick. I should think that, under the circumstances, he might postpone his departure." She realized that Jōjin would suffer hardships and even danger on his journey, but she insisted that she would suffer even more, as she stated in a poem written at this time:

morokoshi e	More than he
yuku hito yori mo	Who departs for China,
todomarite	I who remain behind
karaki omoi wa	Am subject to
ware zo masareru[100]	The bitterest sorrow.

She used the verb *uramu*, "to bear a grudge" or "to feel bitterness toward," when describing her feelings about the son who left her. She even wrote, after recovering from an illness which she hoped would be fatal, "I am bitter above all toward Buddha and Buddha alone. I prayed to him wholeheartedly that he would let me die quickly, and I recovered! I thought I had lived shockingly long."[101]

It is rare in the literature of the world for any woman in her eighties to keep a diary devoted almost exclusively to her son, who occupies her thoughts not only in waking hours but in dreams. No one could comfort her in her distress, though many people (including her other son) made the attempt. She dwelled on the past, recalling how she worried over the health of her sons during an epidemic, and wondered why such love had been so poorly repaid. She accused Jōjin of being "a child whose enmity was sworn in a previous existence."[102] She regretted that she had not screamed and howled to keep him from leaving, and could not restrain her indignation over his failure to write. Her griefs made her wonder if Buddha himself did not hate her.[103]

Apart from the solace it gave her to record her misery, Jōjin's mother seems to have been trying in her diary to understand the irony of her life. She recalled that she was sickly as a child and marvels at how long she had nevertheless lived.[104] Her mother had died young and the early death of her husband had cut short her married life. After reviewing her life, she concluded, not unexpectedly, that hers had been a life of unparalleled hardships, and among the hardships none had been more painful than separation from Jōjin.

Jōjin (1011–81) is not an easy man to understand. After he left the capital, bound for China, he returned and informed his mother that he had been unable to proceed farther than Kyūshū because he had not secured official permission to go abroad. But why, during the months while he waited in Kyūshū for permission, could he not have sent his mother a note? Probably he was convinced, as he often informed his mother, that meetings in this world were of little importance when compared to the true joy of long, uninterrupted meetings in paradise. Gaining admission to paradise, not only for himself but for his mother (and others) took precedence over conventional manifestations of solicitude. But even his brother could not help but express surprise that Jōjin was so unlike everyone else in the world.[105]

Jōjin eventually made his way to China. Soon afterward a certain priest brought word to Jōjin's mother that he would return to Japan in the autumn of the next year. She was not comforted, having abandoned all hope of ever seeing him again. Her premonitions proved to be correct: Jōjin was so highly esteemed by the Chinese that they refused to let him return to Japan.[106] His mother died, as she had feared, without her beloved son to give last words of comfort.

The relationship of mothers and sons is of dominant importance in Japan. The diary of the mother of Jōjin can be viewed as an early, extreme expression of this pervasive strain in Japanese life. Apart from *The Tosa Diary*, the love of a father for his daughter does not figure prominently in the diaries or other works of Japanese literature of this time. This is true not only of works written by women, such as *The Tale of Genji*, in which Genji's love for his lost mother, Kiritsubo, and for her substitute, Fujitsubo, is an important theme. The insistence of Jōjin's mother that mothers are closer than fathers to their children probably found a responsive chord among her readers. But at the end of her complaints about a son who seemed to have forgotten his mother, the last poem of her diary contained a note of hope:

asahi matsu	If the dew that waits
tsuyu no tsumi naku	The sunrise disappears, leaving
kiehateba	No trace of its guilt,
yūbe no tsuki wa	Surely the evening moon
sasowazarameya[107]	Will not fail to guide me forth.

For all her expressions of despair, she seems to have felt confident that she would indeed meet her son again in paradise.

THE SANUKI NO SUKE DIARY[108]

Sanuki no Suke Nikki (The Sanuki no Suke Diary) is a short account written by the court lady Fujiwara no Nagako (1079–c. 1120) soon after the death of the Emperor Horikawa in 1107. Unlike most diaries written by women of the Heian period, it offers few psychological insights into her own character, but is focused instead on her recollections of Horikawa, whom she had served for eight years. He is hardly mentioned in works of history, but emerges in this diary as an unusually appealing man.

At times, especially when his long illness worsened, Horikawa was capricious or irritable, but he was normally so affable and so gifted as to inspire love among all who served him. Horikawa is remembered today mainly for his interest in poetry.[109]

The author of *The Sanuki no Suke Diary* considered it her duty to preserve the memory of a sovereign whose death she mourned. Probably she had no specific readers in mind, but the diary was definitely intended to be read by others. It suggests a gesture of gratitude rather than a formal tribute, and that no doubt accounts for its poignant charm. Nagako figures very little in literary history apart from this diary. She was not a gifted poet, though one waka was included in an imperially sponsored anthology.

We know, from the diary kept in kambun by a courtier,[110] exactly when Nagako was summoned for service at the court; it was recorded on New Year's Day of 1102 that Nagako, who had been appointed the previous night, offered the emperor the traditional spiced wine.

Horikawa was sickly through most of his reign until his death at the age of twenty-eight. It was widely believed that this was the work of an evil spirit,[111] who showed himself as Horikawa lay on his deathbed. Nagako makes no reference to supernatural influence. Her reminiscences of Horikawa tend instead to be of little gestures of affection that lingered in her memory. One such gesture was so vivid that she described it twice. It happened at a time when she was obliged to lie beside the emperor during his final illness in case he should need her. She recalled,

> The Regent approached from behind. I rose, and was about to withdraw, as I felt it would be ill-mannered and unseemly to remain lying where I was, when the Emperor, realising that I must be feeling that I should not be seen, said, "Stay where you are. I shall make a screen." He bent up his knees and hid me behind them. I recalled this considerate action as if it had only just happened.[112]

Nagako was not a skillful writer, and her diary has been dismissed by many as being inferior to others of the Heian period, but it is affecting to be present and so close at the death of an emperor, described not in conventional phrases but in small details:

> Nobody slept a wink, but kept a watch over the Emperor. He seemed to be in great pain and rested his foot on me. "Could anything ever equal this total lack of concern over the probable death, tomorrow or the next day, of somebody of my position? What do you think?" he asked.[113]

During the last stages of his illness Horikawa had begun to imagine that the people who served him, even the woman who gladly acted as his footstool, were all indifferent to his imminent death. He turned his gaze to another waiting woman and rebuked her for slacking. When dawn came and Nagako thought she might take a few moments of rest, "the Emperor saw me pulling an unlined robe over myself, and pulled it back. I understood this to mean that I was on no account to sleep, so I arose."[114]

If the emperor had been portrayed as a despot, such an action would hardly seem admirable, but we sense that Horikawa's fear of approaching death, and especially of dying alone, is so extreme that he behaves for a moment not like an emperor but like a most ordinary human being. At the end, after a violent spell of coughing, the emperor declared,

> "I am going to die now. May the Ise Shrine help me. I put my faith in the Lotus Sutra which tells of the Buddha of impartial benevolence

and great wisdom." These and similar truly reverent phrases fell from his lips. "It's agonizing. I can't bear it. Hold me up," he cried.[115]

But when Nagako took his hands, they felt cold to the touch. Soon afterward the lips of the emperor, who had put all of his remaining strength into saying the *nembutsu*, the invocation of the name of Amida Buddha, finally stopped moving. Nagako was inconsolable after the death of the Emperor Horikawa. She wrote in her diary,

> I must find some way of becoming a nun. But then, I seem to remember that even in old romances, people who capriciously have their heads shaved are criticised by the world in general as being "superficial." And that in fact is how I myself feel about the matter. And so I could not in all conscience opt for that way out.[116]

In the meanwhile, messengers arrived from the court asking her to be present at the accession ceremony of the new emperor. Much against her inclinations, she finally agreed, and visited the palace again. Seeing the new emperor, a boy of four, seated on the imperial throne was almost more than Nagako could bear. She wrote, "The Emperor was decked out very prettily, but the sight of him seated upon the Imperial Throne was a severe shock to me. A haze swam before my eyes, and, I am ashamed to admit, I felt so distressed that I could not look at him directly."[117]

Some weeks later she was again summoned to the palace on a snowy morning. She heard a child singing as he played in the snow and wondered whose child it might be. Then she realized it was the emperor! She thought, "If this is the master whom I am to regard as my lord and protector, I am certainly not filled with a sense of security, I thought desolately."[118]

Eventually the boy emperor won her affection, not because he was the emperor but because he was a lovable child. Nagako decided to remain with him, touched to see how eagerly he ate when she brought his meal. She had come to realize that the best way to cherish the late emperor's memory was to serve his son.

Her memories add a movingly human touch to her portrayal of Horikawa. Nagako recalled his love of poetry and especially of music. One day when the boy emperor Toba asked her to lift him up so that he could see the pictures on the sliding doors in the imperial dining room, she noticed on the walls the tattered remains of musical scores that Horikawa had copied and pasted there in the hope that by constantly seeing the scores he would memorize them. Regardless of the festivals she now attended, or the service she offered to the Emperor Toba, her thoughts dwelled constantly on the past. She realized that readers might be puzzled by her insistence on old memories, but wrote that if they had known the late emperor they would understand her attachment.

Nagako always kept future readers of the diary in mind. She defended herself against possible criticism of excessive partiality to Horikawa. She wrote,

> This will all seem of no consequence to those who do not cherish the memory of the late Emperor. However, I feel so unworthy of, and so lost without, the tenderness of my late master the Emperor—one might have expected such attentions from a mistress—that I just had to record it so that it would live in people's minds and never be forgotten.[119]

The death of Horikawa seems to have affected everyone who knew him just as deeply. *Taiki*, the kambun diary kept by Fujiwara no Yorinaga (1120–56), relates that a member of Horikawa's bodyguard named Sadakuni, distraught over the emperor's death, decided he must have become a dragon king living in the northern sea. In the hope of rejoining his late master, he built a "dragon-head boat" and set sail for the north. He was never seen again.[120] Nostalgia and longing for Horikawa inspired even such preposterous actions. Nagako's diary, though less extreme, was no less an expression of unremitting love.

Even without Nagako's diary, Horikawa's name and the principal events of his reign would of course be preserved in official documents but, like Murasaki Shikibu justifying the existence of monogatari in terms of what they, but not the *Nihon Shoki* or other official histories, reveal about the past, Nagako believed that it was essential to preserve not only the facts of Horikawa's reign but his humanity. In the epilogue to the diary she wrote, "I pondered how I would like to show this record to someone who shared my feelings. But is there anyone who does not yearn for the late Emperor?"[121] She decided in the end to show the manuscript to another court lady. The last sentence of the diary states, "We spent the rest of the day talking." No doubt their reading of the diary was many times interrupted by memories of an emperor who had inspired great affection.

Diaries in Kambun

Although, as we have seen, *The Tosa Diary*, the earliest diary kept in Japanese, was written by a man, not another such diary survives from the Heian period. Instead, there are a number of diaries by men written in kambun, some of voluminous length. These diaries contain daily entries dealing with court religious ceremonials, customs and precedents, and state business, though they sometimes touch on more personal matters. Their chief interest to scholars of Japanese literature lies in the background materials they supply for events related more impressionistically in the diaries of the court ladies.

The earliest of the kambun diaries kept by Heian courtiers is *Teishinkō Ki* by the sometime regent Fujiwara no Tadahira (880–949).[122] It is without literary interest, but *Gonki*, the kambun diary of Fujiwara no Yukinari (972–1027), is somewhat more interesting if only because the author is mentioned in *The Murasaki Shikibu Diary* and was known in his time (and much later) as a master calligrapher.[123] The style, rather than the content, of this diary suggests Yukinari's literary inclinations.

Records of the Midō Chancellor

Fujiwara no Michinaga, the son of Kaneie, was the most important political figure of his time. He kept a voluminous diary titled *Midō Kampaku Ki* (Records of the Midō Chancellor) between the years 995 and 1021.[124] The diary, written in an uningratiating style of kambun and devoid of literary merit, is important to the student of Japanese literature not only because of its factual information on court life, but because it occasionally provides information on the cultural life of the time. There is an entry for every day, even if it is only a single brief sentence such as, "In the evening I went to the palace." If Michinaga had had the slightest intent of imparting literary interest to the diary, surely there were many incidents he could have included, but he was concerned solely with recording accurately the events of the day. It is almost impossible to divine anything of the personality of the writer.

A well-known example of Michinaga's private behavior, naturally not mentioned in his own diary, occurs in *The Murasaki Shikibu Diary*: "One night as I lay asleep in a room in the corridor, there came the sound of someone tapping at the door. I was so frightened that I kept quiet for the rest of the night."[125] The unannounced visitor, we discover, was none other than Michinaga.

If *Records of the Midō Chancellor* contained even a few such passages it might be read today, despite the problems of the style, but Michinaga obviously had no intention of reporting such undignified behavior. Perhaps, too, his knowledge of kambun, though adequate for noting who attended New Year festivities at the palace, did not extend to describing the subtleties of his amorous activities. But his diary contains such crumbs of interest as the entry for the twenty-first day of the first month of the second year of Kannin (1018), where he described how kanshi and waka were chosen to be inscribed on a screen that would be displayed at a banquet given by the Regent Yorimichi. The waka poets on that occasion included Izumi Shikibu.[128] Michinaga's diary in this manner provides a scrap of hard information on someone whose diary was not simply a record of daily events but a work of diary literature.

Chūyūki

The most important kambun diary of the Heian period is *Chūyūki*, the huge diary kept by Fujiwara no Munetada (1062–1141) between 1087 and 1138, during the reigns of three emperors—Horikawa, Toba, and Sūtoku.[127] It is the kind of diary that has often been termed "public," but it was by no means public in the modern sense: the diary was a closely guarded secret that Munetada intended to transmit only to his eldest son. In 1120, after he had been keeping the diary for thirty-four years, Munetada made a classification of the materials for the benefit of his son, Muneyoshi, and gave an indirect explanation of why he had kept the diary:

> I have completed today the classified selection of entries from my diary. The diary covers a period of thirty-four years from the first of Kanji [1087] to the fifth month of this year. It comes altogether to fifteen volumes containing 160 chapters. I began the classification two years ago, and with the assistance of household retainers who were assigned such tasks as copying or cutting and pasting, the work has been completed today. I have made these extracts from my diary in order to help Muneyoshi perform his public duties if he succeeds in his aspirations of being appointed to an official post. . . . For this reason, I have felt impelled to exert all my efforts, not sparing my aged bones, to make this classified selection. It must under no circumstances be made public. In general, it should not be shown to outsiders under any circumstances.[128]

Munetada elsewhere stated that his purpose in keeping the diary had been to enable his descendants to carry on family traditions.[129] A knowledge of what happened in the past was invaluable in determining whether or not precedents existed for actions contemplated by the court, and this was a matter of the utmost importance to traditionalists. Most of the annual rites, customary observances, religious ceremonies, and so on that Munetada described are no longer of much interest, but Munetada believed that keeping this diary was the most important task of his life.

His attachment to the diary increased with the years. For example, Munetada described in a diary entry of 1133 how he had spent one rainy day filling in gaps in his records for the sake of future generations who would consult them. He was seventy-two at the time and *naidaijin* (minister of the interior), but his concern for the diary never faltered. In the following year he had a dream in which his ancestor Fujiwara no Morosuke showed Munetada his diary.[130] Munetada interpreted this as a favorable augury.

The most affecting parts of *Chūyūki* are those describing the Emperor Horikawa, whom Munetada served for twenty years. Horikawa selected him to be a chamberlain in 1094, passing over the heads of seniors. This promotion naturally aroused jealousy, but Horikawa never wavered in his support. Munetada refused one particularly spectacular promotion, but Horikawa insisted, referring to Munetada as an "intimate."[131] Munetada's gratitude was unbounded, and it carried over into his descriptions of Horikawa's life and death.

Unlike most other entries in *Chūyūki*, those describing the death of Horikawa are filled with emotion. The diary entry for the nineteenth day of the seventh month of 1107 relates how the illness of the emperor had taken a turn for the worse. Masters of divination (*onyōji*) were consulted, but they reported that the imperial destiny had reached its last extremity and nothing could save the emperor.[132] A thousand Buddhist monks intoned sutras and chanted spells, it being feared that evil spirits were at work. Later, the chancellor emerged and whispered to Munetada that the emperor had lapsed into a profound sleep after invoking the Sutra of Great Wisdom and the deity Fudō and Amida Buddha, then facing west.[133] The chancellor ordered those in attendance not to waken the emperor, for fear of evil spirits.

During the hour of the sheep it was announced that the emperor had died. As the report spread through the palace, people wept uncontrollably, all but deprived of their senses by the shock. Members of the court were allowed one last look at the emperor. Munetada reported that his features were unaltered, and that he looked as if he were asleep. Though overwhelmed by grief, Munetada could not forget his official responsibilities, and he described the arrangements he had made for the transference to the new emperor of the imperial regalia. The following was his résumé of Horikawa's life:

> He became emperor at the age of eight. When he was nine he could read the *Shih Ching* and the *Shu Ching* [Book of Documents]. He was by nature compassionate, and the Buddhist Law was engraved on his heart. He reigned for twenty-one years. During this time he was reluctant to punish and quick to reward. He dispensed benevolence and radiated his gracious favors. He did not reveal joy or anger on his countenance, nor his likes and dislikes. From the princes and ministers down to all classes of men and women, each and every one was touched by his benevolence. . . . This occasion was for them like losing a father or mother. His Majesty was extremely intelligent, and he was already an expert in the various kinds of learning. His natural ability, particularly as concerns laws, ordinances, and regulations, and his pleasure in wind and stringed instruments could stand comparison with any examples from antiquity.[134]

Despite the sometimes stilted kambun of *Chūyūki*, it is clear that Munetada, no less than Nagako, was haunted by the memory of the sovereign he had served. *Chūyūki* is not normally discussed as a literary work, and Munetada would have been much surprised to think he had written one. But here and there in this long work, so full of boring details, we find the qualities that move us in literature.

One other Heian diary in kambun merits notice: *Taiki*, kept by Fujiwara no Yorinaga between 1136 and 1155. Although this diary, like most in kambun, is given over largely to descriptions of ceremonies, the irascible personality of the diarist comes through the conventional wording, giving individuality to some sections of a long work.

Various other kambun diaries of the second half of the twelfth century recorded activities at the court. They are not considered to be works of literature, though sometimes one finds passages that shed light on more literary diaries.[135] Not a single diary by a woman, the kind of writing that established the genre of diary literature and contributed so much to the creation of the fiction of the Heian period, survives for the period of over one hundred years after the completion of *The Sanuki no Suke Diary* in 1109. This may be due merely to the accident of what happened to be preserved. In any case, the introspective tradition established by these diaries would give a distinctive coloration to much of Japanese literature to come.

Notes

1. Tendai is the Japanese reading of the Chinese name T'ien-t'ai. The Tendai sect is based on the Lotus Sutra, as taught by the philosopher-monk Chih-i, and was established in Japan by Saichō (767–822) after his return from China in 805. The Tendai monastery on Mount Hiei overlooking the capital was the strongest religious establishment during the Heian period, and continued to be a major center of religious learning until it was destroyed in 1571 by the forces of Oda Nobunaga. Ennin, the disciple of Saichō, introduced esoteric practices into Tendai Buddhism. For an account of these developments, see Ryusaku Tsunoda, Wm. Theodore de Bary, and Donald Keene, *Sources of Japanese Tradition*, pp. 116–20, 157–59.
2. Edwin O. Reischauer, *Ennin's Travels in T'ang China*, p. 199.
3. *Ibid*., p. 200.
4. *Ibid*., p. 270.
5. *Ibid*., p. 298.
6. *Ibid*., p. 37.
7. *Ibid*., p. 117.
8. There are several translations into English and other languages, the most recent by Helen Craig McCullough in her *Kokin Wakashū*.
9. Text in Hagitani Boku, *Tosa Nikki Zenchūshaku*, p. 223–24, 232. Hagitani states (p. 232) that the final *kamo* indicates a combination of uncertainty and emotional response; the poet wonders if it can possibly be the same moon he saw at the mountain in Kasuga, then decides that it really is. See also Hasegawa Masaharu et al., *Tosa Nikki, Kagerō Nikki, Murasaki Shikibu Nikki, Sarashina Nikki*, p. 17. Another translation by McCullough, *Kokin*, p. 277.
10. Higuchi Hiroshi, "Tosa Nikki ni okeru Tsurayuki no Tachiba," p. 52.
11. Translation by G. W. Sargent in Donald Keene, *Anthology of Japanese Literature*, p. 82. Text in Hagitani Boku, *Tosa Nikki Zenchūshaku*, p. 51.
12. Hagitani, *Tosa*, p. 293. Hasegawa, et al., *Tosa*, p. 22. Translation by McCullough in *Kokin*, p. 281.
13. For the theory that *The Tosa Diary* is a drama, see Hagitani Boku, "Kaisetsu," in *Shintei Tosa Nikki*, pp. 18–21; also Higuchi, "Tosa Nikki," p. 45.

14. Hagitani, "Kaisetsu," in *Shintei Tosa*, pp. 24–29.
15. The theory was presented by the poet Kagawa Kageki in *Tosa Nikki Sōken*, written in 1823.
16. Text in Hagitani, *Tosa Nikki Zenchūshaku*, p. 399, 401, 425; also Hasegawa et al., *Tosa*, pp. 32–33. Another translation in McCullough, *Kokin*, p. 290.
17. The minister of the Left at this time was Minamoto no Takaakira (914–982), a son of the Emperor Daigo. See below, p. 487.
18. Muramatsu Seiichi et al., *Tosa Nikki, Kagerō Nikki*, p. 207; also, Hasegawa et al., *Tosa*, p. 98. See also Edward Seidensticker, *The Gossamer Years*, p. 73.
19. Uemura Etsuko, "Kagerō Nikki Sakusha, Seiritsu, Dempon," p. 143. Tamai Kōsuke, in *Nikki Bungaku no Kenkyū*, pp. 115–16, quotes Sei Shōnagon's praise for the author's poetry. Praise for the author's beauty is found in *Sompi Bummyaku* (1399) and various later works. Her poetry appeared in chokusenshū beginning with *Shūishū*. Praise for her poetry is found in *Fukuro Zōshi* (c. 1158) and *The Great Mirror*. For a translation of the relevant passage in the latter work, see Helen Craig McCullough, *Ōkagami*, p. 166.
20. Translation in Seidensticker, *Gossamer*, p. 71. Text in Muramatsu, et al., *Tosa*, p. 203. Also Hasegawa et al., *Tosa*, p. 95.
21. This theory was advanced by Shimizu Yoshiko among others; see Akiyama Ken, "Kodai ni okeru Nikki Bungaku no Tenkai," p. 20.
22. Seidensticker, *Gossamer*, p. 48. Muramatsu et al., *Tosa*, p. 156; also Hasegawa et al., *Tosa*, p. 61.
23. Seidensticker, *Gossamer*, p. 61. Muramatsu et al., *Tosa*, p. 184; also Hasegawa et al., *Tosa*, p. 81.
24. Seidensticker, *Gossamer*, p. 53. Muramatsu et al., *Tosa*, p. 168; also Hasegawa et al., *Tosa*, p. 70.
25. Muramatsu et al., *Tosa*, p. 202; see also Seidensticker, *Gossamer*, p. 69.
26. Seidensticker, *Gossamer*, p. 95. Muramatsu et al., *Tosa*, pp. 250–51; also Hasegawa et al., *Tosa*, p. 131.
27. Seidensticker, *Gossamer*, p. 44. Muramatsu et al., *Tosa*, pp. 149–50; also Hasegawa et al., *Tosa*, pp. 56–57.
28. Seidensticker, *Gossamer*, p. 88. Muramatsu et al., *Tosa*, p. 237; also Hasegawa et al., *Tosa*, p. 120.
29. Seidensticker, *Gossamer*, p. 67. Inukai Kiyoshi, *Kagerō Nikki*, p. 81.
30. Seidensticker, *Gossamer*, p. 103. Text in Uemura Etsuko, *Kagerō Nikki*, II, p. 204.
31. Seidensticker, *Gossamer*, pp. 46–47. Muramatsu et al., *Tosa*, pp. 151–55; also Hasegawa et al., *Tosa*, pp. 57–60.
32. There is no proof that Murasaki Shikibu or anyone else at the court in her day actually read *The Gossamer Years*, but it seems likely. An entry dated 1269 in the diary of Asukai Masaari mentions being lent *The Gos-*

samer Years along with *The Tosa Diary* and other diaries of the period, indicating that it had acquired the status of a classic. See Donald Keene, *Travelers of a Hundred Ages*, pp. 141–42.

33. Tamai Kōsuke, *Tōnomine Shōshō Monogatari*, p. 135.
34. For a summary of the discussions, see Nitta Takako, *Tōnomine Shōshō Monogatari no Yōshiki*, pp. 79–84. At one time some scholars believed that *The Tale of the Tōnomine Captain* was composed long after the events, perhaps as late as the Kamakura period; but linguistic evidence has made it clear that it is unquestionably a work of the early Heian period. See *ibid*., pp. 36–37.
35. Tamai, Tōnomine, p. 50.
36. They were the children of Fujiwara no Morosuke and Princess Gashi (Masako), the daughter of the Emperor Daigo and a high priestess before her marriage. Their mother had died seven years earlier, and their father had also died recently. Aimiya was a half-sister (by a different mother) of Fujiwara no Kaneie, and was friendly with the author of *The Gossamer Years*, who sent her a chōka condoling with her over the exile of Minamoto no Takaakira, her husband. (See above, note 17; see also Seidensticker, *Gossamer*, pp. 75–76; text in Inukai, *Kagerō*, pp. 96–97.) Accounts of Aimiya in contemporary sources are gathered in Uemura Etsuko, *Kagerō Nikki no Kenkyū*, pp. 517–21.

    There is some confusion about the relationship of Takamitsu and Aimiya. A passage in *The Great Mirror* identifies Aimiya as the fifth daughter of Fujiwara no Morosuke. (Quoted by Uemura in *Kagerō Nikki no Kenkyū*, p. 523.) Takamitsu (like Kaneie) was a son of Morosuke. The mother of both Aimiya and Takamitsu was Princess Gashi (Nitta, *Tōnomine*, pp. 206, 208). It seems clear that Takamitsu and Aimiya were full brother and sister, but various studies state that they were born of a different mother.
37. Nitta, *Tōnomine*, p. 67. Despite the sister's wish, nothing suggests that Takamitsu ever left the mountain to visit his family. The word *ama* in the poem means both a "nun" and a "diver" who gathers seaweed at the bottom of the sea. A "diver who fails to gather seaweed" is a failure; it is an indirect rebuke to someone who has pointlessly become a nun.
38. See below, note 122.
39. Nitta, *Tōnomine*, p. 106. The text states that Takamitsu relates this dream to his younger brother. The author of the text presumably heard the story from the brother.
40. *Ibid*., p. 73. The meaning of the poem is that if the wife wishes to become a nun under the mistaken impression that this will bring her closer to Takamitsu, she will be disappointed; monks and nuns did not reside on the same mountain.
41. *Ibid*., p. 85.
42. *Ibid*., p. 96.

43. Attempts have been made to show the influence of this work on later fiction. Nitta, in her voluminous *Tōnomine*, pp. 659–80, discusses possible influences on *The Tale of Genji* and *The Tale of the Hollow Tree*. The resemblances are not obvious. For example in the "Tenarai" (Writing Practice) chapter of *The Tale of Genji* there is mention of a captain, the son-in-law of a nun, who visits a younger brother who is in seclusion on Mount Hiei. (Seidensticker translation, *The Tale of Genji*, II, p. 1054.) This conceivably recalled to readers the somewhat similar episode of Takamitsu going to Hiei where his younger brother is a priest. But if any influence existed, it was more likely to have come from the actual event—a celebrated young poet who forsook the world—than from the diary.
44. It was the theory of Kawase Kazuma that Fujiwara Shunzei, two hundred years later, pieced together a "diary" from the *kotobagaki* to the collection of poems by Izumi Shikibu. (See Edwin A. Cranston, *The Izumi Shikibu Diary*, p. 45.) The theory was developed by Yamagishi Tokuhei, who advanced six different arguments why Izumi Shikibu could not have written the diary.
45. For centuries it was more commonly referred to by an alternative title, *Izumi Shikibu Monogatari* (The tale of Izumi Shikibu). Some other works with alternative titles (one as a diary and the other as a work of fiction) include *Ise Monogatari*, also known as *Zaigo Chūjō Nikki*; *Takamura Nikki*, also known as *Takamura Monogatari*; and *Heichū Nikki*, also known as *Heichū Monogatari*. See Cranston, *Izumi*, pp. 70–71.
46. Cranston adopted as the subtitle of his translation "A Romance of the Heian Court." See also Janet A. Walker, "Poetic Ideal and Fictional Reality in the *Izumi Shikibu Nikki*."
47. See Cranston, *Izumi*, p. 8. His source is *A Tale of Flowering Fortunes*.
48. *Ibid*., p. 133. Text in Nomura Seiichi, *Izumi Shikibu Nikki, Izumi Shikibu Shū*, p. 87.
49. Translation in Cranston, *Izumi*, p. 175. Text in Nomura, *Izumi*, p. 65.
50. Japanese of the Heian period believed that, depending on the positions of the stars, people who traveled or stayed in "forbidden directions" would suffer harm. This was sometimes used as an excuse for staying in one place rather than another.
51. Translation of prose from Cranston, *Izumi*, p. 178. The translation of the poem is mine, following Enchi Fumiko and Suzuki Kazuo, *Zenkō Izumi Shikibu Nikki*, p. 288.
52. Translation in Cranston, *Izumi*, p. 136. Text in Nomura, *Izumi*, p. 18. This is an example of how the diary on occasion enters the thoughts of persons other than the diarist, one of the reasons given by Yamagishi (see note 44) for rejecting the attribution of the work to Izumi Shikibu.
53. Cranston, *Izumi*, p. 140. Nomura, *Izumi*, p. 22.
54. Cranston, *Izumi*, p. 142. Nomura, *Izumi*, p. 25.
55. Cranston, *Izumi*, p. 163. Nomura, *Izumi*, p. 51. The passage is ambiguous,

and other interpretations have been made. Following Cranston, Atsumichi is complaining about gossip that has nothing behind it; he has not even been seen visiting Izumi, but people are nevertheless gossiping.

56. Translation by Seidensticker in *Genji*, I, p. 3.
57. McCullough, *Ōkagami*, p. 166.
58. Translation in Cranston, *Izumi*, p. 191. Text in Nomura, *Izumi*, p. 85.
59. Because of the difficulty of determining the correct pronunciations of the names of empresses, it is now customary to use the Sino-Japanese pronunciations, about which there is usually no dispute. However, this empress's name was probably pronounced Akiko.
60. The extant text of the diary is clearly incomplete. It is possible that in the lost portions of the work Murasaki Shikibu touched on such questions.
61. Yamamoto Ritatsu, *Murasaki Shikibu Nikki, Murasaki Shikibu Shū*, p. 96. See also Richard Bowring, *Murasaki Shikibu*, p. 137.
62. See Seidensticker, *Genji,* I, p. 437.; also Ivan Morris, *The World of the Shining Prince*, p. 309.
63. Yamamoto, *Murasaki*, p. 20. See also Bowring, *Murasaki*, p. 53.
64. Translation in Bowring, *Murasaki*, p. 43. Text in Yamamoto, *Murasaki*, p. 11.
65. See Bowring, *Murasaki*, pp. 77–83; also Yamamoto, *Murasaki*, pp. 40–45.
66. Yamamoto, *Murasaki*, p. 52. See also Bowring, *Murasaki*, p. 91.
67. For other theories concerning the origin of the name, see Bowring, *Murasaki*, p. 12; also Yamamoto, *Murasaki*, p. 167.
68. Translation in Bowring, *Murasaki*, p. 91. Text in Yamamoto, *Murasaki*, p. 52.
69. Bowring, *Murasaki*, p. 131. Yamamoto, *Murasaki*, p. 88.
70. Bowring, *Murasaki*, p. 135. Yamamoto, *Murasaki*, p. 94.
71. See the explanation by Bowring in *Murasaki*, p. 92. He states that the "monogatari" mentioned in the text is almost universally assumed to be *The Tale of Genji*. Yamamoto (*Murasaki*, p. 55) does not identify the "monogatari," but Itō Hiroshi (in Hasegawa et al., *Tosa*, p. 284) accepts the identification of the "monogatari" as *The Tale of Genji*.
72. Translation in Bowring, *Murasaki*, p. 95. Text in Yamamoto, *Murasaki*, p. 57. Here, too, it is not absolutely certain that "Tale" (monogatari) refers to *The Tale of Genji*, but the context makes it seem likely.
73. In this instance the text gives *Genji no monogatari*, so there can be no question of the work to which she refers. Bowring, *Murasaki*, p. 143; Yamamoto, *Murasaki*, p. 57.
74. Translation in Ivan Morris, *As I Crossed a Bridge of Dreams*, p. 41. Morris gave *Sarashina Nikki* this evocative English title, and referred to the author not in the customary manner as the Daughter of Takasue, but by a name of his own coining, Lady Sarashina. For text, see Sekine Yoshiko, *Sarashina Nikki*, I, p. 13.

75. Morris, *As I Crossed*, p. 53. Sekine, *Sarashina*, I, p. 87.
76. Morris, *As I Crossed*, p. 55. Sekine, *Sarashina*, I, p. 105.
77. Morris, *As I Crossed*, p. 55. Sekine, *Sarashina*, I, pp. 105–6.
78. Morris, *As I Crossed*, p. 55. Sekine, *Sarashina*, I, p. 105.
79. Morris, *As I Crossed*, pp. 78, 80. Sekine, *Sarashina*, I, p. 204.
80. Morris, *As I Crossed*, p. 80. Sekine, *Sarashina*, I, p. 208.
81. Morris, *As I Crossed*, pp. 71–72. Sekine, *Sarashina*, I, p. 174.
82. Morris, *As I Crossed*, p. 72. Sekine, *Sarashina*, I, p. 175.
83. Morris, *As I Crossed*, p. 78. Sekine, *Sarashina*, I, p. 199.
84. Morris, *As I Crossed*, p. 82. Sekine, *Sarashina*, II, p. 13. The original text of this statement is: *Mazu hitoyo mairu.*
85. Morris, *As I Crossed*, p. 84. Sekine, *Sarashina*, II, p. 14.
86. Morris, *As I Crossed*, p. 87. Sekine, *Sarashina*, II, p. 35.
87. Morris, *As I Crossed*, p. 91. Sekine, *Sarashina*, II, p. 50.
88. *Ibid.*
89. Morris, *As I Crossed*, p. 95. Sekine, *Sarashina*, II, p. 59.
90. *Ibid.*
91. Morris, *As I Crossed*, p. 107. Sekine, *Sarashina*, II, pp. 99–100.
92. Morris, *As I Crossed*, p. 98. Sekine, *Sarashina*, II, p. 74.
93. Morris, *As I Crossed*, p. 119. Sekine, *Sarashina*, II, p. 135.
94. *Yoru no Nezame* (Wakefulness at Night) and *Hamamatsu Chūnagon Monogatari* (The Tale of the Hamamatsu Middle Counselor).
95. *Ajari* (*ācārya* in Sanskrit) was the title of a high-ranking priest of the Tendai and Shingon sects of Buddhism. Jōjin (1010–1081) belonged to the Tendai sect.
96. Miyazaki Sōhei, *Jōjin Ajari Haha no Shū*, p. 13. Translation from my *Travelers*, p. 62.
97. *Risshi* means "master of the *vinaya* (discipline)," but was also the third-highest ranking of priest. It is generally accepted that the risshi was Jōjin's elder brother because the mother refers to him first (Miyazaki, *Jōjin*, p. 17). Jōjin also used honorifics when referring to the brother. However, the brother was identified by one scholar as a priest named Jōson of the Ninna-ji who was a year younger than Jōjin. (*Ibid.*, p. 23.)
98. *Ibid.*, p. 73.
99. *Ibid.*, p. 74. Translation from *Travelers*, p. 63.
100. *Ibid.*, p. 76.
101. *Ibid.*, p. 90. Translation from *Travelers*, p. 65.
102. *Ibid.*, p. 100.
103. *Ibid.*, p. 112.
104. *Ibid.*, p. 209.
105. *Ibid.*, p. 152.
106. Jōjin kept a diary in kambun describing his life in China, *San Tendai Godaisan Ki* (Record of a Pilgrimage to T'ien-t'ai and Wu-t'ai Mountains). The work, in the tradition of Ennin's diary, is unliterary, but it is of great

importance to students of Buddhism during the Sung dynasty. Jōjin died in China and was buried on Mount T'ien-t'ai.

107. Miyazaki, *Jōjin*, p. 230. Translation in *Travelers*, p. 67. Hirabayashi Fumio, *Jōjin Ajari Haha no Shū no Kisoteki Kenkyū*, p. 96, suggests that the place to which the mother expects to be led by the moon is Ryōjusen, or Eagle Mountain, mentioned in her previous poem. Eagle Mountain is where Shakyamuni Buddha taught the Lotus and many other sutras. The implication, however, is that she will be guided to paradise.
108. The translation of the diary by Jennifer Brewster when first published in Australia bore this original title; however, the American edition (from which citations have been made) bears the title *The Emperor Horikawa Diary*.
109. See above, pp. 306–307.
110. *Chūyūki* by Fujiwara no Munetada. See above, p. 399.
111. See my *Travelers*, p. 69, for the details of the curse placed on Horikawa before he was born by the priest Raigō, who was furious that Horikawa's father had not fulfilled a promise. According to the diary, Raigō's ghost manifested itself while Horikawa lay dying.
112. Translation in Brewster, *Horikawa*, p. 100. Text in Ishii Fumio, "Sanuki no Suke Nikki," in Fujioka Tadami et al., *Izumi Shikibu Nikki*, p. 421.
113. Brewster, *Horikawa*, p. 60. Ishii, "Sanuki," p. 376.
114. Brewster, *Horikawa*, p. 62. Ishii, "Sanuki," p. 379.
115. Brewster, *Horikawa*, p. 72. Ishii, "Sanuki," p. 395.
116. Brewster, *Horikawa*, p. 82. Ishii, "Sanuki," p. 408.
117. Brewster, *Horikawa*, pp. 87–88. Text in Tamai Kōsuke, *Sanuki no Suke Nikki*, p. 150.
118. Brewster, *Horikawa*, p. 88. Ishii, "Sanuki," p. 418.
119. Brewster, *Horikawa*, p. 112. Ishii, "Sanuki," pp. 453–54.
120. Brewster, *Horikawa*, p. 22.
121. Brewster, *Horikawa*, p. 114. Ishii, "Sanuki," p. 456.
122. This diary, which covers the period 907 to 948, survives only in the extracts made by Tadahira's son Saneyori, probably about ten years after Tadahira's death. *Kyūreki*, the diary of Fujiwara no Morosuke (908–60), another son of Tadahira's, is also preserved only in extracts.
123. The title of the work (like that of other kambun diaries of the period) is derived from a title, *gon dainagon*, or acting major counselor, the highest office Yukinari attained. There are several references to Yukinari's calligraphy, with the name pronounced as Kōzei, in *Essays in Idleness*. See Donald Keene, *Essays in Idleness*, pp. 26, 195–96.
124. There is a complete translation of this work into French by Francine Hérail, *Notes journalières de Fujiwara no Michinaga*. The translation is augmented by an important introduction, extraordinarily rich annotations, and superb indices that make this by far the best edition of the work in any language.

125. Translation in Bowring, *Murasaki*, p. 145. Text in Yamamoto, *Murasaki*, p. 103.
126. See Hérail, *Notes*, III, p. 461.
127. The name *Chūyū* was the abbreviation of *Naka*mikado *U*daijin, read in Sino-Japanese pronunciation. *Ki* means "record."
128. Toda Yoshimi, *Chūyūki: Yakudō suru Insei Jidai no Gunzō*, p. 276.
129. *Ibid.*, p. 278.
130. See above, note 122.
131. Toda, *Chūyūki*, p. 59. The phrase in the *kundoku* reading of the Japanese is *shinjitsu wo nasu hito*.
132. *Ibid.*, pp. 74–75.
133. *Ibid.*, p. 76. See the translation in Brewster, *Horikawa*, p. 18.
134. Toda, *Chūyūki*, p. 296.
135. For example, Bowring in *Murasaki*, pp. 183–98, translated passages from two kambun diaries, *Fuchiki* and *Shōyūki*, that describe the birth of Prince Atsuhira, given such prominent attention in *The Murasaki Shikibu Diary*.

Bibliography

Note: All Japanese books, except as otherwise noted, were published in Tokyo.

Akiyama Ken. "Kodai ni okeru Nikki Bungaku no Tenkai," in *Heian-chō Nikki*, I, in Nihon Bungaku Kenkyū Shiryō Sōsho series. Yūseidō, 1961.

Bowring, Richard. *Murasaki Shikibu: Her Diary and Poetic Memoirs*. Princeton, N.J.: Princeton University Press, 1982.

Brewster, Jennifer. *The Emperor Horikawa Diary*. Honolulu: The University Press of Hawaii, 1977.

Cranston, Edwin A. *The Izumi Shikibu Diary*. Cambridge, Mass.: Harvard University Press, 1969.

Enchi Fumiko and Suzuki Kazuo. *Zenkō Izumi Shikibu Nikki*, rev. ed. Shibundō, 1971.

Fujioka Tadami, Nakano Kōichi, Inukai Yasushi, and Ishii Fumio. *Izumi Shikibu Nikki, Murasaki Shikibu Nikki, Sarashina Nikki, Sanuki no Suke Nikki*, in Nihon Koten Bungaku Zenshū series. Shōgakukan, 1975.

Hagitani Boku. *Shintei Tosa Nikki*, in Nihon Koten Zensho series. Asahi Shimbun Sha, 1969.

———. *Tosa Nikki Zenchūshaku*, in Nihon Koten Hyōshaku Sōsho series. Kadokawa Shoten, 1967.

Hasegawa Masaharu, Imanishi Yūichirō, Itō Hiroshi, and Yoshioka Hiroshi. *Tosa Nikki, Kagerō Nikki, Murasaki Shikibu Nikki, Sarashina Nikki,* in Shin Nihon Koten Bungaku Taikei Series. Iwanami Shoten, 1989.

Hérail, Francine. *Notes journalières de Fujiwara no Michinaga*, 3 vols. Genève-Paris: Librairie Droz, 1987–91.

Higuchi Hiroshi. "Tosa Nikki ni okeru Tsurayuki no Tachiba," in *Heian-chō Nikki*, I, in Nihon Bungaku Kenkyū Shiryō Sōsho series. Yūseidō, 1961.

Hirabayashi Fumio. *Jōjin Ajari Haha no Shū no Kisoteki Kenkyū*. Kasama Shoin, 1977.

Inukai Kiyoshi. *Kagerō Nikki*, in Shinchō Nihon Koten Shūsei series. Shinchōsha, 1982.

Keene, Donald. *Anthology of Japanese Literature*. New York: Grove Press, 1955.

———. *Essays in Idleness*. New York: Columbia University Press, 1967.

———. *Travelers of a Hundred Ages*. New York: Henry Holt, 1989.

Koyano Jun'ichi. *Sanuki no Suke Nikki Zenchūshaku*. Kazama Shobō, 1988.

McCullough, Helen Craig. *Kokin Wakashū*. Stanford, Calif.: Stanford University Press, 1985.

———. *Ōkagami*. Princeton, N.J.: Princeton University Press, 1980.

Miyazaki Sōhei. *Jōjin Haha Ajari no Shū*, in Kōdansha Gakujutsu Bunko. Kōdansha, 1979.

Morimoto Motoko. *Sanuki no Suke Nikki*, in Kōdansha Gakujutsu Bunko. Kōdansha, 1977.

Morris, Ivan. *As I Crossed a Bridge of Dreams*. New York: Dial Press, 1971.

———. *The World of the Shining Prince*. London: Oxford University Press, 1964.

Muramatsu Seiichi, Kimura Masanaka, and Imuta Tsunehisa. *Tosa Nikki, Kagerō Nikki*, in Nihon Koten Bungaku Zenshū series. Shōgakukan, 1973.

Nitta Takako. *Tōnomine Shōshō Monogatari no Yōshiki*. Kazama Shobō, 1987.

Nomura Seiichi. *Izumi Shikibu Nikki, Izumi Shikibu Shū*, in Shinchō Nihon Koten Shūsei series. Shinchōsha, 1981.

Reischauer, Edwin O. *Ennin's Diary: The Record of a Pilgrimage to China in Search of the Law*. New York: Ronald Press, 1955.

———. *Ennin's Travel's in T'ang China*. New York: Ronald Press, 1955.

Seidensticker, Edward. *The Gossamer Years*. Tokyo: Charles E. Tuttle, 1964.

———. *The Tale of Genji*, 2 vols. New York: Alfred A. Knopf, 1976.

Sekine Yoshiko. *Sarashina Nikki*, 2 vols., in Kōdansha Gakujutsu Bunko series. Kōdansha, 1977.

Shioiri Yoshimichi. *Nittō Guhō Junrei Ki*, 2 vols., in Tōyō Bunko series. Heibonsha, 1970.

Tamai Kōsuke. *Nikki Bungaku no Kenkyū*. Hanawa Shobō, 1965.

———. *Sanuki no Suke Nikki*, in Nihon Koten Zensho series. Asahi Shimbun Sha, 1953.

———. *Tōnomine Shōshō Monogatari*. Hanawa Shobō, 1960.

Toda Yoshimi. *Chūyūki: Yakudō suru Insei Jidai no Gunzō*. Soshiete, 1979.

Tsunoda, Ryusaku, Wm. Theodore de Bary, and Donald Keene. *Sources of Japanese Tradition*. New York: Columbia University Press, 1958.

Uemura Etsuko. *Kagerō Nikki*, 3 vols., in Kōdansha Gakujutsu Bunko series. 1978.

———. *Kagerō Nikki no Kenkyū*. Meiji Shoin, 1972.

———. "Kagerō Nikki Sakusha, Seiritsu, Dempon," in *Heian-chō Nikki*, I, in Nihon Bungaku Kenkyū Shiryō Shū series. Yūseidō, 1961.

Walker, Janet A. "Poetic Ideal and Fictional Reality in the *Izumi Shikibu Nikki*," *Harvard Journal of Asiatic Studies* 37, 1977.

Yamamoto Ritatsu. *Murasaki Shikibu Nikki, Murasaki Shikibu Shū*, in Shinchō Nihon Koten Shūsei series. Shinchōsha, 1980.

10. *THE PILLOW BOOK OF SEI SHŌNAGON*

The most brilliant example of the *zuihitsu* genre ("following the brush") is undoubtedly *Makura Sōshi*[1] (The Pillow Book of Sei Shōnagon), a collection of prose pieces ranging in length from a line or two to several pages, in which the author recounted her experiences at the court and her observations of nature and of other people's behavior. She made no attempt to unify or arrange in order these sparkling short essays, but her style—flashing with witty perceptions—gives a consistency to the work as whole. Her voice is heard distinctly in each of the some three hundred episodes, a voice that proved to be inimitable, though works in the zuihitsu tradition that she established would be written by innumerable Japanese over the centuries. Sei Shōnagon's observations were expressed in prose rather than poetry, but they are so acute as to defy any poet to surpass her.

Not much is known about the life of Sei Shōnagon.[2] Even her name is something of a mystery: Sei is obviously the Sino-Japanese pronunciation of the first character in Kiyohara, the surname of her family, but we do not know why she was known as *shōnagon*, or lesser counselor. It was the practice at the Heian court to call a woman by the title of either her father or her husband, but Sei's father was not a shōnagon, nor was either of the two men she married. It has been suggested, mainly out of desperation, that it was the title of a third husband.[3]

Sei Shōnagon was born in or about 966.[4] Her father, Kiyohara no Motosuke (908–990), was a distinguished waka poet, one of the five members of the "Pear Court" who compiled the imperial anthology *Gosenshū*. His own poetry, preserved in a private collection, included one poem that was made immortal by being chosen for the *Hyakunin Isshu*. His grandfather, Kiyohara no Fukayabu, was an even more distinguished poet; forty-one of his poems appeared in imperially sponsored anthologies. Sei Shōnagon's extraordinary literary gifts have been attributed to this heritage.

Extremely little is known about Sei's life before she took up service at the court in 993. She herself gives in *The Pillow Book* a touching (and rather uncharacteristic) account of her emotions on first becoming a waiting woman:

> When I first went into waiting at Her Majesty's Court, so many different things embarrassed me that I could not even reckon them up and I was always on the verge of tears. As a result I tried to avoid appearing before the Empress except at night, and even then I stayed hidden behind a three-foot curtain of state.[5]

Seeing court ladies perform their duties with the effortlessness born of long practice, she wondered when (if ever) she would be able to conduct herself with equal confidence and grace. She listened with admiration to the banter exchanged by the empress and her brother, commenting that it resembled the elegant conversations she had hitherto known only from romances. When Korechika, the empress's brother, addressed Sei, she was overcome with embarrassment and tried to hide her face with a fan, but Korechika snatched it away, then proceeded to tease Sei by alluding to her reputation for knowing absolutely everything. The arrival of another gentleman, even more splendidly attired than Korechika, made her wonder what creatures from another world such courtiers must be:

> Yet, after some time had passed and I had grown accustomed to Court service, I realized that there had been nothing very impressive about their conversation. No doubt these same ladies, who talked so casually to Lord Korechika, had been just as embarrassed as I when they first came into waiting, but had little by little become used to Court society until their shyness had naturally disappeared.[6]

This passage is especially striking because virtually every other entry in *The Pillow Book* depicts Sei Shōnagon as a woman of matchless wit who again and again demonstrates her intellectual superiority to any man who ventures to engage her in conversation. Her initial shyness seems to have melted away in record time, but on one occasion she was reprimanded by the empress for a thoughtless word. This took place early in Sei's service at court. She had spent a period of abstinence (*monoimi*) away from the court. The empress sent Sei a poem describing how much she missed her, and received this response:

kumo no ue mo	On these days in spring
kurashinikanekeru	So hard for you to endure
haru no hi wo	Even above the clouds—
tokorogara tomo	How I am lost in brooding
nagametsuru kana	In this humble place below.[7]

The empress was apparently offended by the word *kurashinikanekeru*, "which have been difficult to live through." Her ladies also criticized the poem severely. No reason is given for their annoyance, but it may have been because they thought Sei had been presumptuous in accepting as literal truth the empress's conventional expression of loneliness during Sei's absence. The empress probably resented the implication that (regardless of what she had written in her poem) anyone could *ever* be bored or lonely at her brilliant court situated "above the clouds."[8] But in the end the empress found Sei's presence indispensable.

The empress on whom Sei Shōnagon waited was Teishi[9] (976–1001), the daughter of Fujiwara no Michitaka (953–995) and the consort of the Emperor Ichijō. She was appointed *chūgū*, or empress, at a time when her father enjoyed the favor of the emperor. When the father died in 995, it was assumed that Teishi's brother Korechika would succeed him as chancellor, but to Korechika's disappointment, his elderly uncle was appointed instead. The uncle died a week after the appointment was made, and Korechika once again expected to be named as chancellor, but this time another uncle, Michinaga, received a position which, though not that of chancellor, gave him effective control over the court, and he was ill-disposed toward Korechika. In the following year, 996, Michinaga succeeded in having Korechika exiled to Kyūshū for a variety of offenses, including that of having shot an arrow at a retired emperor.[10]

In 999 Michinaga arranged for his daughter Shōshi (Akiko) to be taken into the emperor's household, and in the following year, at his insistence, she was named chūgū. Teishi, supplanted in that position, was given the title of *kōgō*, which also designated an empress.[11] This was the first time that two empresses reigned at the same time. The rivalry between Korechika and Michinaga was reflected in the courts of the two empresses: Sei Shōnagon served Teishi and Murasaki Shikibu served Shōshi. Judging from Murasaki Shikibu's diary, the two great writers were not on the best of terms.

It has long been a tradition to contrast the two women—Sei Shōnagon the brilliant conversationalist and Murasaki Shikibu the sensitive and retiring observer of court life. The clearest evidence of rivalry is found in Murasaki Shikibu's diary, where she wrote,

> Sei Shōnagon, for instance, was dreadfully conceited. She thought herself so clever, and littered her writings with Chinese characters, but if you examined them closely, they left a great deal to be desired.[12]

Despite this criticism, Murasaki Shikibu had without question read *The Pillow Book*, and she borrowed imagery and even scenes when writing *The Tale of Genji*.[13] The diary of Murasaki Shikibu has been tentatively dated 1006. Her use of the past tense when referring to Sei Shōnagon suggests that the latter was no longer at the court or perhaps no longer even in the capital. It is not certain that the two women ever met; Murasaki Shikibu may have formed her opinions of Sei Shōnagon on the basis of rumors or gossip picked up from the rival court, or perhaps they were mainly derived from a reading of *The Pillow Book*. It may even be that she was induced by Shōshi to write *The Tale of Genji* as an "answer" to the masterpiece produced at the other court. The rivalry between the two empresses ended in 1001 with the death of Teishi. Shōshi died at the age of eighty-six in 1074, having become empress dowager in 1012 and grand empress dowager in 1018. She is known also as Jōtō Mon'in, her title after entering Buddhist orders in 1026.

The first question that suggests itself when we take up *The Pillow Book* is the meaning of the title. Probably Sei Shōnagon did not give her book this or any other title, but some scholar or copyist of later times, searching for an appropriate designation for the manuscript, may have found it in the epilogue:

> One day Lord Korechika, the Minister of the Centre, brought the Empress a bundle of notebooks. "What shall we do with them?" Her Majesty asked me. "The Emperor has already made arrangements for copying the Records of the Historian."
>
> "Let me make them into a pillow," I said.
>
> "Very well," said Her Majesty. "You may have them."[14]

The translation conveys the words exchanged by the empress and Sei Shōnagon, but the meaning of "pillow" remains unexplained. Surely it was not a pillow in the usual sense of the word; paper was far too precious at that time to be used for making pillows. Nor is it likely that the meaning was a *livre de chevet*, or "bedside book," in the normal sense of these words: Sei would hardly have been so conceited as to keep at her bedside for repeated reading a book that she herself had written. Ivan Morris suggested that it was a "notebook or collection of notebooks kept in some accessible but relatively private place, and in which the author would from time to time record impressions, daily events, poems, letters, stories, ideas, descriptions of people, etc."[15] Other scholars, whose interpretation of the word "pillow" is essentially the same as Morris's, have suggested that the book was kept in the drawer of one of the wooden pillows on which ladies of the court at that time rested their elaborately coiffured heads when they slept. No aspect of *The Pillow Book* has given rise to as many different theories as the meaning of "pillow" in this passage.

Perhaps, as has been plausibly suggested, Sei Shōnagon meant by "pillow" a writer's notebook in which she intended to record topics for poetry and prose composition. The word *utamakura*, literally "poem pillow," had at this time the meaning of a handbook in which the essentials of literary composition were transmitted,[16] and Sei's "pillow" might have been a shortcut for designating this kind of book, though in later times utamakura generally referred to sites that were famous because of mentions in poetry.[17] It is also possible that Sei had this more restricted use of utamakura in mind when she announced her intention of making a "pillow"; the lists of waterfalls, rivers, bridges, villages, and so on that are a conspicuous feature of *The Pillow Book* were perhaps intended as a thesaurus to be consulted when composing poetry. It may be also that Sei's many lists, whether bare enumerations of place-names and the like or brief essays, represent the original form of *The Pillow Book*. The celebrated opening of the work is a kind of catalogue describing the time of day for best admiring each of the four seasons:

> In spring it is the dawn that is most beautiful. As the light creeps over the hills, their outlines are dyed a faint red and wisps of purplish cloud trail over them.
>
> In summer the nights. Not only when the moon shines, but on dark nights too, as the fireflies flit to and fro, and even when it rains, how beautiful it is!
>
> In autumn the evenings, when the glimmering sun sinks close to the edge of the hills and crows fly back to their nests in threes and fours and twos; more charming still is a file of wild geese, like

specks in the distant sky. When the sun has set, one's heart is moved by the sound of the wind and the hum of the insects.

In winter the early mornings. It is beautiful indeed when snow has fallen during the night, but splendid too when the ground is white with frost; or even when there is no snow or frost, but it is simply very cold and the attendants hurry from room to room stirring up the fires and bringing charcoal, how well this fits the season's mood! But as noon approaches and the cold wears off, no one bothers to keep the braziers alight, and soon nothing remains but a pile of white ashes.[18]

Perhaps this marvelous opening originated as a simple series of notations such as "Spring: dawn. Summer: night. Autumn: evening. Winter: early morning." Even such laconic observations would testify to an exceptionally perceptive mind and would have provided poets with valuable reference points for their compositions, as we can surmise from the well-known spring poem by the Emperor Gotoba (1180–1239) in the *Shin Kokinshū:*

miwataseba	When I gaze far off
yamamoto kasumu	The mountain slopes are misty—
Minasegawa	Minase River:
yūbe wa aki to	Why did I ever suppose
nani omoiken[19]	Evenings are best in autumn?

Gotoba denies Sei Shōnagon's claim that evenings are best in autumn; evenings in spring can be even more affecting. Another poem from the same collection, this one by Fujiwara no Kiyosuke (1104–1171), also took exception with Sei Shōnagon:

usugiri no	The morning dampness
magaki no hana no	On flowers along a fence
asajimeri	Swathed in a thin mist:
aki wa yūbe to	Who was it claimed that autumn
tare ka iiken[20]	Was best enjoyed at evening?

Here, the poet insists that mornings in autumn are even more beautiful than autumn evenings, despite what *The Pillow Book* says.

Regardless of whether a poet accepted or rejected Sei's ratings of the times of day best suited for appreciating the different seasons, she was not ignored. But this first "list" in *The Pillow Book* goes far beyond providing useful pointers for persons who are about to compose seasonal poems. The characteristics of, say, a frosty winter morning had been evoked in many poems, but the greater amplitude of prose enabled Sei to extend her comments to human beings in wintry landscapes, and finally, to note how much less beautiful the scene becomes when once the morning sun melts the frost.

The Pillow Book contains two varieties of "catalogues." The first consists of places, plants, and objects familiar from their use in poetry, such as "peaks," "plains," "markets," "ferries," and so on;[21] the second, much richer in content, consists of "things" to which Sei Shōnagon has some individual reaction, such as "awkward things," "things that should not be seen by firelight," or "things that look pretty but are bad inside."[22] The difficulty of compiling lists of the latter variety that are both amusing and psychologically true is known to anyone who has ever tried to make one in emulation of Sei Shōnagon.

Scholars have searched, thus far in vain, for convincing antecedents for the lists in *The Pillow Book*. Arthur Waley in his translation compared Sei Shōnagon's lists, notably those of the "things" variety, to the somewhat similar lists in the short text called *I-shan tsa-tsuan* (I-shan's Miscellany) attributed to the late-T'ang poet Li Shang-yin (812?–858?); but nothing indicates that Sei Shōnagon ever saw this book or, indeed, that it was known to Japanese of her time.[23] Passages have been traced to Chinese poetry, especially the poetry of Po Chü-i,[24] but few of the discoveries are convincing. For example, Sei need not have turned to Po Chü-i for a revelation that mist is particularly beautiful in spring or that sunsets are lovely in autumn.[25] This is not to say that she absorbed absolutely no influence from her readings in Japanese and Chinese literature, but that *The Pillow Book* was probably an original conception. It is possible that Sei, having at first nothing more ambitious in mind than drawing up lists of utamakura, was led to compile lists of amusing and other "things" she had observed during her life at the court, and finally to descriptions of the life itself, which she related in a manner similar to that of the Heian court lady's diary.

Sei Shōnagon served at the court from 993 to 1001.[26] During this time the only "events" of her life that we know about were her visits to various Buddhist temples (such as Kiyomizu-dera and Hase-dera) and Shintō shrines (such as Inari-jinja and Kamo-jinja). Most of the rest of her time was spent, it would seem, conversing with men and women of the court, attending palace ceremonies, or writing her book. Although she was officially married at least twice, she evidently had affairs with several other men of the court and, though not notorious as a promiscuous woman (in the manner of Izumi Shikibu), she discussed her love affairs openly in such passsages as:

> In the winter, when it is very cold and one lies buried under bedclothes listening to one's lover's endearments, it is delightful to hear the booming of a temple gong, which seems to come from the bottom of a deep well. The first cry of the birds, whose beaks are still tucked under their wings, is also strange and muffled. Then one bird after another takes up the call. How pleasant it is to lie there listening as the sound becomes clearer and clearer![27]

She did not neglect to describe disappointing lovers, as in the section "Hateful Things":

> A lover who is leaving at dawn announces he has to find his fan and his paper. "I know I put them somewhere last night," he says. Since it is pitch dark, he gropes about the room, bumping into the furniture and muttering, "Strange! Where on earth can they be?" Finally he discovers the objects. He thrusts the paper into the breast of his robe with a great rustling sound; then he snaps open his fan and busily fans away with it. Only now is he ready to take his leave. What charmless behaviour! "Hateful" is an understatement.[28]

This episode shows Sei Shōnagon at her best. Perhaps the key to her mastery of psychology is most apparent in the words "he snaps open his fan and busily fans away with it." The lover, we can be sure, did not fan himself because he felt hot; and this was the least felicitous gesture he could make as he took leave of his lady. Why did he use the fan, then? Because that was his—and everyone else's—conditioned reflex on picking up a fan, as surely as salivating was the reaction of Pavlov's dog to the sound of a bell. We, readers of a thousand years later, smile as we recognize a universal, somehow endearing though foolish, human action.

Sei Shōnagon must have realized, even as she wrote, that some day her words would be read by other people. She certainly anticipated that the Empress Teishi would read the "pillow" for which she had supplied the paper. But only in the last section of the work does Sei reveal that her manuscript was already in circulation. After expressing surprise and regret that people had found out what she had been writing, she mentions her fear that she would be harshly judged on the basis of the unflattering observations she has made about various people.

The final section of the work otherwise provides the only information we have about the circumstances under which Sei commenced writing the book and how the book was evaluated in its own time.[29] Though hardly a page long, its importance is such that scholars have generally treated it separately as an "epilogue" (*batsubun*), and the most exhaustive scrutiny has been given to its every word.[30] Toward the conclusion of the epilogue Sei wryly referred to those who had expressed admiration for her book as "persons who like what other people detest, and dislike what they praise." She claimed to be able to see through such people, perhaps because she suffered from the same defect. *The Pillow Book* concludes with this passage:

> When the middle general of the Left was still the governor of Ise,[31] he came to visit me at my home. I put out for him the mat closest to hand, only to notice to my horror that this notebook was on top. In confusion, I pulled back the mat, but he kept his grip on the notebook and took it off with him. It did not come back until a considerable time later. That, I imagine, is when it first began to circulate.[32]

If we can accept this as literal truth, Sei Shōnagon must have composed the first draft of *The Pillow Book*—the manuscript that the middle general carried off—between 994 and 996. The last datable event recorded in the work is the visit of the empress to the Sanjō residence of Taira no Narimasa in 1000.[33] Probably Sei continued to work on the manuscript for at least another two years.[34]

There remains, however, a textual problem: if, as most authorities agree, the Sankan text (which lacks the passage about the middle general) is the best,[35] should this passage be regarded as an interpolation by a later hand and therefore worthless as a source of information about Sei Shōnagon and her work?[36] The problem is compounded by the fact that there is no discernible order in the successive episodes, not even as much order as has been found in *Tsurezuregusa* (Essays in Idleness), a later example of zuihitsu often compared with *The Pillow Book*. Even if Sei Shōnagon wrote every word of the fullest text, there is nothing to indicate that she personally arranged the materials, and at any stage in the process of editing her manuscript, a copyist's errors, glosses, and intrusions might have crept into the text.

Another passage in the epilogue, found only in the Nōin text, expresses Sei's concern over what the Empress Teishi will think on reading the book: "I greatly fear that because I have not only told people about things that have impressed me but written them down in this way, I may seem frivolous to Her Majesty."[37] Sei seems to be saying that even people who enjoyed her repartee at court might disapprove of her decision to commit her observations to paper. It is clear, in any case, that she expected people to read and comment on her work.

Sei Shōnagon also revealed in the epilogue the circumstances under which she first began to write *The Pillow Book*:

> I wrote and collected these notes at home, when I had nothing better to do, setting down things I had noticed and thoughts that had occurred to me, wondering all the while if someone would see them.[38] Unfortunately, there are places here and there which other people might consider to be deplorable exaggerations. I thought I had hidden away the manuscript quite successfully, only to learn to my great surprise that the contents had leaked out and were now public.

This passage leads without transition[39] into the one, already quoted, in which the empress gives paper to Sei Shōnagon, who says she will use the paper to make a "pillow." The next section seems to resume the train of thought interrupted by the anecdote. Sei describes the kinds of materials she included in her work:

> I chose lines of poetry that people find amusing, and things that everybody is apt to admire. I am sure that if I started out by discussing poems or writing about trees, plants, birds, and insects, I would be maligned in terms of "It's even more boring than we expected. One can see just how shallow she is." As a matter of fact, I wrote down, in a spirit of fun and without help from anyone else, whatever happened to suggest itself to me. I thought it most unlikely my book would ever be considered in the same breath with other people's or that I should ever hear it discussed on their level; but, strange as it may seem, people who have read it say such things as, "You put us all in the shade!"[40]

The most striking aspect of this passage, viewed in the light of other writings of the time, is Sei Shōnagon's insistence that she wrote "for fun" (*tawabure ni*). Indeed, the adjective she most frequently used in the course of her work is *okashi*; it appears 445 times in *The Pillow Book* out of a total of some 3,660 adjectives.[41] This adjective can often be translated as "amusing" or "funny," but it is always used in a good sense, not with the meaning of "ridiculous."[42] Sometimes the word can be effectively rendered in translation as "splendid," "adorable," "interesting," and so on, but regardless of the nuance, *okashi* always indicated a reaction of pleasure and usually of amusement. The literary ideal of *okashi* is often contrasted with *aware*, a word that typified Murasaki Shikibu's writings, used to evoke the moving and touching aspects of human experience. *Aware* would occur many times more frequently in the Japanese literature to come than Sei Shōnagon's *okashi*, suggesting the rarity of the kind of humor found in her writings.

Again and again in *The Pillow Book* Sei Shōnagon relates with evident self-satisfaction her amusing or learned spontaneous comments. Such episodes generally end with the empress's laughing with pleasure or else expressing her admiration for Sei's unique learning, as in the following:

> One day, when the snow lay thick on the ground and it was so cold that the lattices had all been closed, I and the other ladies were sitting with Her Majesty, chatting and poking the embers in the brazier.
>
> "Tell me, Shōnagon," said the Empress, "how is the snow on Hsiang-lu Peak?"
>
> I told the maid to raise one of the lattices and then rolled up the blind all the way. Her Majesty smiled. I was not alone in recognizing the Chinese poem she had quoted; in fact all the ladies knew the lines and had even rewritten them in Japanese. Yet no one but me had managed to think of it instantly.
>
> "Yes indeed," people said when they heard the story. "She was born to serve an Empress like ours."[43]

Such examples of self-praise risk irritating the reader, but they were intended perhaps to arouse admiration for the rare intelligence and discrimination of the empress, rather than of the author. Indeed, *The Pillow Book* can be interpreted as an act of homage toward the empress, possibly written after her death, as a means of expressing Sei Shōnagon's conviction that never before and probably never again would there be so gifted and delightful a royal personage.

The Pillow Book is famous, above all, for its many lists. There are seventy-seven of the type that gives examples of famous mountains, birds, dances, and so on; and another seventy-eight along the lines of "things that make one impatient" or "things that fall from the sky."[44] The following list of "Hateful Things" suggests how items of a list could develop into vignettes:

> One is in a hurry to leave, but one's visitor keeps chattering away. If it is someone of no importance, one can get rid of him by saying, "You must tell me about it next time"; but, should it be the sort of visitor whose presence commands one's best behaviour, the situation is hateful indeed. . . .
>
> To envy others and complain about one's own lot; to speak badly about other people; to be inquisitive about the most trivial matters and to resent and abuse people for not telling one, or, if one does manage to worm out some facts, to inform everyone in the most detailed fashion as if one had known all from the beginning—how hateful!
>
> One is just about to be told some interesting piece of news when a baby starts crying.
>
> A flight of crows circles about with loud caws.
>
> An admirer has come on a clandestine visit, but a dog catches sight of him and starts barking. One feels like killing the beast.
>
> One has been foolish enough to invite a man to spend the night in an unsuitable place—and then he starts snoring.[45]

Sei's wit (like all wit) has a cruel side, especially for modern readers, as the following will suggest:

> It is very annoying when one has visited the Hase Temple and has retired into one's enclosure, to be disturbed by a herd of common people who come and sit outside in a row, crowded so close together that the tails of their robes fall over each other in utter disarray. I remember that once I was overcome by a great desire to go on a pilgrimage. Having made my way up the log steps, deafened by the fearful roar of the river, I hurried into my enclosure, longing to gaze upon the sacred countenance of Buddha. To my dismay I found a throng of commoners had settled themselves directly in front of me, where they were incessantly standing up, prostrating themselves, and squatting down again. They looked like so many basket-worms as they crowded together in their hideous clothes, leaving hardly an inch of space between themselves and me. I really felt like pushing them all over sideways.[46]

No doubt this reaction was not confined to Sei Shōnagon but true of the aristocrats of her day. One can imagine an art lover of our own day feeling similar irritation when local people who have gone to a church to worship, rather than admire the paintings, obstruct his view. But even people who would really like to push the peasants out of their line of view hesitate to commit such undemocratic thoughts to writing.

An even more unpleasant example of how Sei Shōnagon and her friends treated the lower classes is found in the section describing a man whose house has just been destroyed in a fire. He tells Sei, the first person he meets on coming into the palace, that the fire started in a hayloft belonging to the imperial stables and spread to his house. "There is only a fence between the two buildings, and one of the lads in the bedroom just escaped being burnt alive. They didn't save a single object."

"We all burst out laughing at this," Sei reports, and then relates how she wrote a poem and asked a servant to give it to the man. The servant threw the poem at the man who (being unable to read) supposed the paper was a list of rice and other food he was to receive by way of charity, and asked how much she had given. He was told to get someone to read it. Then, we are informed,

> Roaring with laughter, we set off for the Palace. "I wonder if he's shown it to anyone yet," said one of my companions after a while. "How furious he will be when he hears what it really is!"
>
> When we saw Her Majesty, Mama [the nurse of the Lord Bishop] told her what had happened, and there was a lot more laughter. The Empress herself joined in, saying, "How can you all be so mad?"[47]

It is difficult for a modern reader to join in the laughter. The ladies of the court, and even the empress, seem heartless. Perhaps, as one commentator suggested, the laughter originated in the unabashed way the man referred to the bedroom of his house and to his wife; he used for "bedroom" the elegant *yodono*, hardly suitable for a man of his humble station, and for "wife" the affectionate *warawabe*.[48] The court ladies, always sensitive to nuances of language, were amused by the man's inappropriate choice of words, and Sei composed a poem, full of puns and other types of word-play, teasing the man for having used such a word as *yodono*. But even if one accepts this explanation, it still does not make the behavior of the court ladies any more endearing; in the end, one has to accept the fact that for members of the court at this time the illiterate mass of Japanese did not belong to the same species as themselves.

The epilogue continues: "It is getting so dark that I can scarcely go on writing; and my brush is all worn out. Yet I should like to add a few things before I end."[49] This translation by Ivan Morris follows the standard interpretation of the words and suggests at the same time a well-known figure in European literature, the aged chronicler who has come to the end of his tale. But unless one assumes that Sei Shōnagon wrote *The Pillow Book* at one sitting, it is curious that, if it was too dark for her to write on that particular night, she did not consider resuming the next morning. Moreover, if her brush was actually worn out, she could easily have obtained another.

An intriguing new interpretation of this passage was given by Mitani Kuniaki.[50] He believed that Sei Shōnagon wrote these words at the age of thirty-seven (thirty-six by Western count), a year that was considered to be peculiarly ill-omened for women. He gave examples of various Heian court ladies who, when they reached this unlucky age, entered orders as Buddhist nuns and others (like Murasaki Shikibu) who found this an appropriate time to reflect on their life and write about it. We are told in *The Tale of Genji* that Murasaki died at thirty-seven though her age, if calculated by information previously given about the character, should actually be thirty-nine. Both Genji's wife Aoi and his beloved Fujitsubo also die at thirty-seven, evidence of how strong the belief was in the danger of this year to a woman.

The revised meaning of the opening of the epilogue, following this new explanation, would be close to: "Everything has become so dim I cannot write any more. I have worn out my brushes and it is time to put an end to my writing." The translation is similar to Morris's, but the implications are different. If we accept Mitani's theory, Sei Shōnagon completed *The Pillow Book* in 1002, at the age of thirty-seven. Heian women often made a break at this point in their lives (though thirty-seven was not considered to be an advanced age even in the Heian period), and in Sei's case, it followed by just a year the death of her beloved Empress Teishi.

The Pillow Book did not enjoy in later centuries the popularity of two other masterpieces of the Heian period, the *Kokinshū* and *The Tale of Genji*, and for this reason old manuscripts are comparatively scarce.[51] It was imitated from time to time, notably in *Essays in Idleness*, but no zuihitsu author ever equaled her achievement. It is the wittiest book in the Japanese language, one that brings to mind George Meredith's statement in *Essay on Comedy* that only in societies where men and women associate as equals is wit possible. Sei Shōnagon, like the other ladies of the Heian court, spent most of her time in dimly lit rooms, protected from the eyes of male visitors by silken hangings; but we know from her book that she never hesitated to engage men in conversation. She not only associated with them as equals, but did not hesitate to assert her superiority when a man seemed an unworthy adversary. She enjoyed this aspect of life at the court so much that she felt contempt for women whose lives were bound up with their families:

> When I make myself imagine what it is like to be one of those women who live at home, faithfully serving their husbands—women who have not a single exciting prospect in life yet who believe that they are perfectly happy—I am filled with scorn. Often they are of quite good birth, yet have had no opportunity to find out what the world is like. I wish they could live for a while in our society, even if it should mean taking service as Attendants, so that they might come to know the delights it has to offer.[52]

In later times, such thoughts would be frowned on by the military rulers, and relations on an equal footing between men and women were definitely not advocated by the Confucian philosophers. Even today, when the position of women in society has risen very considerably, *The Pillow Book* still remains rather on the fringe of studies of classical Japanese literature. Scholars, uncomfortable with humor and unable to extract from *The Pillow Book* a social message to their tastes, have sometimes defamed it, but it is impervious to their attacks. It is the work of an extraordinary woman whose writings have maintained their freshness and individuality a millennium after they were first conceived.

Notes

1. The pronunciation of the title is uncertain. *Makura Zōshi* is also found, and *Makura no Sōshi* is even more common than *Makura Sōshi*, perhaps because *makura-zōshi* (with which it is easily confused) came to designate pornographic books, left by the pillow of an inexperienced bride, that were intended to teach her what to expect. The original pronunciation seems to have been *Makura Sōshi*. See Kuwabara Hiroshi, "Makura Sōshi no Shomei ni tsuite," p. 63; also Masuda Shigeo, *Makura Sōshi*, p. 10.

2. The biography by Kishigami Shinji, *Sei Shōnagon*, gives all the known facts of her life, together with the writer's speculations on materials of possible biographical interest in her works and those of her contemporaries.
3. By Tsunoda Bun'ei in "Sei Shōnagon no Shōgai," pp. 30–32. Tsunoda's candidate was Fujiwara no Nobuyoshi, who became a shōnagon in 984. The marriage would have taken place about 985. Nobuyoshi died in 993. Tsunoda believed that Fujiware no Muneyo, the governor of Settsu, usually identified as her second husband, was actually her third. It has often been stated that Muneyo married Sei Shōnagon after she left court service in 1000, but as Hagitani Boku demonstrated (in "Sei Shōnagon wo meguru Dansei," p. 86), if we accept the data given about Muneyo in *Sompi Bummyaku*, he must have been over seventy at that time, presumably too old to be the father of Sei's daughter. Hagitani believed that there was an error in *Sompi Bummyaku* about the order of birth of Muneyo and his brothers, and that Muneyo was in fact born in 937, which would have made him sixty-three in 1000. (Sei Shōnagon was thirty-four that year.) Hagitani was still not too happy about a man of sixty-three being the father of a child, and suggested that the marriage probably took place in 991 when Muneyo was fifty-five and Sei Shōnagon twenty-five, and that they were divorced soon after the birth of their daughter. (Hagitani, "Sei Shōnagon," pp. 87–88.) This still does not take care of the problem of why she was known as shōnagon, even if that was the office of her second husband.
4. Four theories, giving dates that range from 964 to 971, are discussed by Tsunoda in "Sei Shōnagon," pp. 15–16. Most scholars are inclined to accept the date 966 proposed by Kishigami in *Sei Shōnagon*, pp. 38ff.
5. Translation by Ivan Morris in *The Pillow Book of Sei Shōnagon*, I, p. 178. Morris dates her arrival at court as 990, but states (II, pp. 141–42) that 993 is more widely accepted by Japanese specialists.
6. *Ibid.*, I, pp. 181–82.
7. Cf. *ibid.*, pp. 244–45. The passage is found in section 280 of the text Morris used (the Shunsho Shōhon text); in other texts it is section 286 (Yōmei Bunko text) or 284 (Sankan text).
8. See Kishigami Shinji, "Sei Shōnagon Kenkyū e no Shōtai," p. 11.
9. The name is normally read as Sadako.
10. For an account of these developments, see Francine Hérail, *Notes journalières de Fujiwara no Michinaga*, I, pp. 8–9, 185, 290. The retired emperor was Kazan.
11. Although *chūgū* had up to this time been used for the consort of the emperor, Teishi's promotion to *kōgō* indicates that this rank was considered to be somewhat higher in prestige. In other words, there were two empresses, a senior and a junior.
12. Richard Bowring, *Murasaki Shikibu: Her Diary and Poetic Memoirs*, p. 131.
13. Shimizu Yoshiko, a specialist in *The Tale of Genji*, declared that in places *The Pillow Book* gives the impression of having served as a "writer's note-

book" (*sōsaku nōto*) for *The Tale of Genji*. (In "Sei Shōnagon to Murasaki Shikibu," p. 151.) Shimizu cited several examples of close parallels, both in conception and wording, between the two works.

14. Ivan Morris, *Pillow*, I, p. 267. A quite different interpretation of the passage is given by Hagitani Boku in *Makura Sōshi*, II, pp. 1276–77. He believed that Sei's mention of a "pillow" was no more than a clever response to the news that the emperor was having *Shiki* (Records of the Historian) copied. She pretended to interpret *shiki* as "horse blanket," and declared she would place a "saddle" (*ma-kura*) atop the blanket. The two words suggested by Hagitani are so rare that they do not appear in dictionaries of old Japanese. The more usual meaning of *shiki* as "bedding," and *makura* as "pillow," would also make a suitable play on words, but surely the meaning given in Morris's translation was uppermost in Sei's mind.
15. Ivan Morris, *Pillow*, II, p. 195.
16. See Masuda, *Makura Sōshi*, pp. 11–12.
17. For an excellent guide to these utamakura, see Katagiri Yōichi, *Utamakura Kotoba Jiten*. Katagiri gives not only place-names but many other nouns and verbs that were frequently employed when composing poetry.
18. Ivan Morris, *Pillow*, I, p. 1.
19. *Shin Kokinshū* 36. The poet is saying that this particular evening in spring is so lovely that he wonders why evening in autumn should be so celebrated.
20. *Shin Kokinshū* 340.
21. An exhaustive analysis of such lists is given by Sugiyama Shigeyuki in "Makura Sōshi no Ruijūteki Shōdan," pp. 293–96.
22. Japanese scholars when discussing these lists refer to the former as the *wa* type and the latter as the *mono* type; the headings or first statements of any list conclude with one or the other word. For example, the section on mountains is headed *yama wa* and consists mainly of the names of mountains worthy of being celebrated in poetry. The section "things that make one's heart beat faster" begins *kokoro tokimeki suru mono*. For a discussion in English of the two kinds of lists, see Mark Morris, "Sei Shōnagon's Poetic Catalogues," pp. 8–28.
23. See Arthur Waley, *The Pillow-Book of Sei Shōnagon*, pp. 22–23. For a discussion of different theories about possible literary antecedents of Sei Shōnagon's lists, see Mark Morris, "Sei Shōnagon," pp. 42–50.
24. See Yahagi Takeshi, "Makura Sōshi no Gensen—Chūgoku Bungaku," pp. 149–50, where he tabulates possible Chinese sources for individual phrases in *The Pillow Book*. His conclusion (p. 150) was that "apart from *The Collected Works of Po Chü-i* and *Wakan Rōei Shū*, Sei Shōnagon's knowledge of Chinese literature was rather restricted." *Wakan Rōei Shū*, discussed above, pp. 341–344, was compiled about 1013; if Sei Shōnagon was actually influenced by Chinese poetry apart from the poems of Po Chü-i, she must have had access to the manuscript of *Wakan Rōei Shū* or else her book was written after 1013.

25. See Yahagi, "Makura Sōshi," pp. 133–34, for poems by Po Chü-i that are alleged to have influenced the opening section of *The Pillow Book*. He believed that Chinese influence was responsible for deepening Sei's conception of the beauty of the seasons beyond the usual Japanese mentions of cherry blossoms in the spring and colored leaves in autumn; but the poems by Po Chü-i that he quotes do not in the least resemble the opening of *The Pillow Book*.
26. The Empress Teishi died in the twelfth month of 1000, or in 1001 by the solar calendar. Sei Shōnagon is presumed to have served at the court until the death of the empress.
27. Ivan Morris, *Pillow*, I, p. 64. This is in section 69 in the text known as the second variety of the Sankan text. See Masuda, *Makura Sōshi*, p. 55.
28. Ivan Morris, *Pillow*, I, p. 29. This passage is found in different sections of *The Pillow Book*, depending on the text. In the Shunsho Shōhon version, which Morris used, it is in section 27; in the Nōin-bon it is section 28; and in the Sankan-bon it is section 60.
29. The contents of the epilogue depend to a considerable extent on the manuscript. The Sankan (Three-Volume) text, accepted as the most authentic by the majority of scholars, gives a disappointingly meager account. For what seems to be the full version, one must turn to one of the two Nōin texts, as Ivan Morris did in his translation. For a comparison of the two Nōin and the Sankan texts, see Mitani Kuniaki, "Makura Sōshi no Batsubun wo megutte," pp. 84–87.
30. Hayashi Kazuhiko, the author of the monumental *Makura Sōshi no Kenkyū*, which runs to nearly one thousand pages, devoted the second half of this book entirely to a consideration of the batsubun. See also Mitani "Makura Sōshi," pp. 74–75.
31. A reference to Minamoto no Tsunefusa, who was governor of Ise from 995 to 997 and became middle general of the Left (*sachūjō*) in 998. He remained in this office until 1000. This passage must therefore have been written between 998 and 1000.
32. Hagitani, *Makura Sōshi*, II, p. 278; Matsui Satoshi and Nagai Kazuko, *Makura Sōshi*, p. 465; Ikeda Kikan and Kishigami Shinji, *Makura Sōshi*, p. 332. Morris did not translate this passage, possibly because he found it anticlimactic.
33. See Ishida Jōji, "Makura Sōshi no Seiritsu," p. 30. Translation by Ivan Morris, *Pillow*, I, p. 199. Text in Hagitani, *Makura Sōshi*, II, p. 135; Matsui and Nagai, *Makura Sōshi*, p. 360; and Ikeda and Kishigami, *Makura Sōshi*, pp. 262–63.
34. The unusual number of textual variants may represent different stages of the text, but scholars are by no means agreed as to which texts represent the earlier and which the later stages.
35. The text prepared by Hagitani Boku for the Shinchō Nihon Koten Shūsei series opens with the editor's declaration that he has tried, insofar as hu-

manly possible, to eliminate the "arbitrary emendations" in popular editions, and to find instead the "stylistic psychology" of the original author, as revealed in the Sankan text, where alone it can be discovered.

36. The problem of the various texts is not confined to this one example. The marvelous account of the lover who ineptly takes his leave at dawn is not found in all texts. It has been suggested that the Sankan text may be earlier than the Nōin text. In that case, assuming Sei Shōnagon wrote the Nōin text, the latter should be preferred. See Matsui and Nagai, *Makura Sōshi*, pp. 39–41, for a summary of the opinions of various scholars who have considered the order of composition of the two main lines of text. Mitani (in "Makura Sōshi," p. 95) expressed categorically the opinion that the Sankan text is *later* than the Nōin text.
37. Matsuo and Nagai, *Makura Sōshi*, p. 465. Mitani ("Makura Sōshi," p. 93) believed that the word *kimi*, translated here as "Her Majesty," meant not only Teishi but the people immediately around her.
38. My translation follows the interpretation of Hagitani in *Makura Sōshi*, II, p. 276. Matsui and Nagai (in *Makura Sōshi*, p. 465) interpret the same words *hito ya wa min to suru* as meaning "I thought it unlikely anyone would see them."
39. That is, in the Sankan text. In the Nōin text there is an additional sentence that Morris rendered as "I now had a vast quantity of paper at my disposal, and I set about filling the notebooks with odd facts, stories from the past, and all sorts of other things, often including the most trivial material." (Ivan Morris, *Pillow*, I, p. 267.) Morris's translation is far clearer than the original; see Matsui and Nagai, *Makura Sōshi*, p. 464, for a discussion of some of the problems.
40. This passage contains a number of thorny points that some commentators pretend not to notice and others more candidly describe as unclear. The frankest discussion of such points is in Matsui and Nagai, *Makura Sōshi*. Despite the problems, however, the verve of Sei Shōnagon's prose keeps the reader's attention.
41. Kikuta Shigeo, "Makura Sōshi no Biishiki (1)," p. 237. Kikuta gives (on p. 249) two other calculations of the number of times the word appears: one scholar put it at 461 and another at 466. Ivan Morris (*Pillow*, II, p. 195) gave 439 times. Obviously, when different texts are used, there will be a different number of occurrences of the word.
42. The adjective *okashi* has been derived from the obsolete verb *oku*, "to invite," or "to beckon to." The original meaning seems to have been to invite closer to the speaker something that had pleased him.
43. Translation in Ivan Morris, *Pillow*, I, p. 243. This is episode 278 in his text. It is episode 280 in the text prepared by Hagitani, episode 278 in the text of Matsui and Nagai, and episode 299 in the text of Ikeda and Kishigami. The allusion is to a poem by Po Chü-i: "Pushing aside the blind,

I gaze upon the snow of Hsiang-lu peak. . . ." (Ivan Morris, *Pillow*, II, p. 180.)

44. The figures are from Sugiyama, "Makura Sōshi," p. 291. Sugiyama included (pp. 293–96) a table comparing the lists as they appear in four different texts.
45. Translation in Ivan Morris, *Pillow*, I, pp. 25–26. This is episode 25 in Hagitani and in Matsui and Nagai, but episode 28 in Ikeda and Kishigami.
46. Translation in Ivan Morris, *Pillow*, I, p. 258. This is episode 308 in the text of Matsui and Nagai. It is variant edition (*ippon*) 26 in Hagitani and variant edition 28 in Ikeda and Kishigami.
47. Translation in Ivan Morris, *Pillow*, I, pp. 252–53. Text is given by Hagitani in II, pp. 249–52; by Matsui and Nagai, pp. 441–44; and by Ikeda and Kishigami, pp. 320–21.
48. The word *warawabe* usually meant a child (Morris's "lad"), but recent commentators agree that it means here the wife of the man, *warawabe* having been used affectionately of one's wife, suggesting she is still a childlike creature.
49. Ivan Morris, *Pillow*, I, p. 267. The Japanese text is: *mono kurō narite, moji mo kakarezu narinitari. Fude wo tsukaihatete, kore wo kakihatebaya.* Text in Matsui and Nagai, *Makura Sōshi*, p. 463.
50. Mitani, "Makura Sōshi," pp. 89–91.
51. See Masuda, *Makura Sōshi*, p. 17.
52. Free (and effective) translation in Ivan Morris, *Pillow*, I, p. 20. Text in Hagitani, I, p. 61; Matsui and Nagai, p. 91; Ikeda and Kishigami, p. 63.

Bibliography

Note: All Japanese books, except as otherwise noted, were published in Tokyo.

Bowring, Richard. *Murasaki Shikibu: Her Diary and Poetic Memoirs.* Princeton, N.J.: Princeton University Press, 1982.

Hagitani Boku. *Makura Sōshi*, 2 vols., in Shinchō Nihon Koten Shūsei series. Shinchōsha, 1977.

———"Sei Shōnagon wo meguru Dansei," in *Makura Sōshi Kōza*, I.

Hayashi Kazuhiko. *Makura Sōshi no Kenkyū*. Yūbun Shoin, 1964.

Hérail, Francine. *Notes journalières de Fujiwara no Michinaga,* 3 vols. Genève-Paris: Librairie Droz, 1987–91.

Ikeda Kikan. *Kenkyū Makura Sōshi*. Shibundō, 1963.

Ikeda Kikan and Kishigami Shinji. *Makura Sōshi*, in Nihon Koten Bungaku Taikei series. Iwanami Shoten, 1958.

Ishida Jōji. "Makura Sōshi no Seiritsu," in *Makura Sōshi Kōza*, II.

Katagiri Yōichi. *Utamakura Kotoba Jiten.* Kadokawa Shoten, 1983.
Kikuta Shigeo. "Makura Sōshi no Biishiki (1)," in *Makura Sōshi Kōza*, I.
Kishigami Shinji. *Sei Shōnagon.* Yoshikawa Kōbunkan, 1962.
———"Sei Shōnagon Kenkyū e no Shōtai," in *Makura Sōshi Kōza*, I.
Kuwabara Hiroshi. "Makura Sōshi no Shomei ni tsuite," in *Makura Sōshi Kōza*, II.
Makura Sōshi Kōza, 4 vols. Yūseidō, 1975.
Masuda Shigeo. *Makura Sōshi.* Osaka: Izumi Shoten, 1987.
Matsui Satoshi and Nagai Kazuko. *Makura Sōshi*, in Nihon Koten Bungaku Zenshū series. Shōgakukan, 1974.
Mitani Kuniaki. "Makura Sōshi no Batsubun wo megutte," in *Makura Sōshi Kōza*, II.
Morris, Ivan. *The Pillow Book of Sei Shōnagon*, 2 vols. New York: Columbia University Press, 1967.
Morris, Mark. "Sei Shōnagon's Poetic Catalogues," *Harvard Journal of Asiatic Studies*, Spring 1980.
Nakano Kōichi. "Makura Sōshi no Dokusha Ishiki," in *Makura Sōshi Kōza*, I.
Sawada Masako. *Makura Sōshi no Biishiki.* Kasama Shoin, 1985.
Shimizu Yoshiko. "Sei Shōnagon to Murasaki Shikibu," in *Makura Sōshi Kōza*, I.
Shimotamari Yuriko. *Makura Sōshi Shūhen Ron.* Kasama Shoin, 1986.
Sugiyama Shigeyuki. "Makura Sōshi no Ruijūteki Shōdan," in *Makura Sōshi Kōza*, I.
Tsunoda Bun'ei. "Sei Shōnagon no Shōgai," in *Makura Sōshi Kōza*, I.
Waley, Arthur. *The Pillow-Book of Sei Shōnagon.* Boston: Houghton Mifflin, 1929.
Yahagi Takeshi. "Makura Sōshi no Gensen—Chūgoku Bungaku," in *Makura Sōshi Kōza*, IV.

11. THE BEGINNINGS OF FICTION

For over a thousand years works of fiction composed in Japanese were known as *monogatari*, a term that means "telling of things." The word still exists as a general designation for a story, but no one today would call a work of literature a monogatari without being aware that he was employing an archaism. The earliest use of the word occurs in a poem in the *Man'yōshū*, where it seems to have the meaning of a "legend."[1] Instances in old writings where *mono* was used to mean the gods or the souls of the dead have suggested to some that monogatari were originally narrations about supernatural beings, both gods and the deified ancestors of the different clans.[2]

No doubt there were Japanese from ancient times who were known for their ability to tell stories that entertained the members of their family or their village, quite apart from priests whose business it was to relate the deeds of the gods, but the first examples of written fiction date no further back than the Heian period. The earliest examples were probably crude and implausible, as we can infer from pejorative references in *The Gossamer Years* or *The Tale of Genji*, but with time they acquired greater polish, as we know from the different stages of some surviving works. The ladies of the court read monogatari to pass the time on a long summer's day or while waiting for nightfall and the possibility of a lover's visit. Many of the books they read have been totally lost or are known today only by the title and a few poems. Paper was scarce and expensive, and since a single manuscript sufficed for the limited number of readers, a minor fire could destroy a work of literature forever.

Two varieties of monogatari were composed in Japan, beginning in the late ninth century. The first, known as *tsukuri monogatari*, or "invented tale," like similar stories told elsewhere in the world, relate the actions of unusually good or bad people. They sometimes included realistic details, but they were generally marked by elements of fantasy or the supernatural, and they also drew inspiration from folklore. The second variety, the *uta monogatari*, or "poem-tale," a more specifically Japanese development, consisted mainly of poems and accounts of the circumstances of the composition of the poems; these tales, prevailingly realistic in content, for the most part described life at the court, and were usually short, unconnected anecdotes rather than single stories. The two streams of fiction converged in the late tenth century and made possible the composition of the major works of Heian fiction of the eleventh and twelfth centuries.

The Invented Tale

The Tale of the Bamboo Cutter

The oldest surviving monogatari is *Taketori Monogatari* (The Tale of the Bamboo Cutter).[3] Its date of composition is unknown, but on the basis of both internal and external evidence it seems likely the work was completed no later than 909. An episode in the poem-tale *Yamato Monogatari* (Tales of Yamato) includes this verse:

taketori no	The Bamboo Cutter
yoyo ni nakitsutsu	Sadly weeping every night,
todomeken	Tried to detain her:
kimi wa kimi ni	But tonight you are about
koyoi shimo yuku[4]	To go to His Majesty.

The poem, addressed by the courtier Minamoto no Yoshitane to Princess Katsura, compares the speaker to the Bamboo Cutter who tearfully attempted to dissuade Kaguya-hime from leaving him. Yoshitane was trying to persuade the princess not to go to the palace of her father, the Cloistered Emperor Uda, for a moon-viewing party. The party took place in 909;[5] *The Tale of the Bamboo Cutter* must have existed in some form by this date.

Mention at the end of *The Tale of the Bamboo Cutter* of smoke rising from Mount Fuji indicates that the volcano was still active at the time of composition, but the kana preface to the *Kokinshū*, written in 905, stated that smoke no longer rose from the mountain; it has therefore been conjectured that *The Tale of the Bamboo Cutter* must have been written prior to 905. Other evidence suggests a date of composition between 871 and 881.[6]

The author of *The Tale of the Bamboo Cutter* is not known, but scholars (with varying degrees of confidence) have attributed it to Minamoto no Shitagō, to the Abbot Henjō, to a member of the Imbe clan, to a member of a political faction opposed to the Emperor Temmu, and to the kanshi poet Ki no Haseo (845–912).[7] It is not clear whether one or several persons had a hand in the text.[8] The original language of the tale has also been much debated.[9] In short, nothing is certain about the date, author, or original literary style of the work.

The Tale of the Bamboo Cutter has been known as "the ancestor of all romances" ever since Murasaki Shikibu described it as such in *The Tale of Genji*. She added, "The story has been with us a very long time, as familiar as the bamboo growing before us, joint upon joint."[10] There is little dispute about *The Tale of the Bamboo Cutter* being the oldest monogatari, but some scholars characterize *Sangō Shiiki* (Indications of the Goals of the Three Teachings) by Kūkai as the first Japanese "novel."[11] This work, however, is a philosophic dialogue with some literary flourishes, rather than a novel, and it exercised no influence on the development of the monogatari.

The Tale of the Bamboo Cutter is the story of the beautiful Kaguya-hime and not of the old Bamboo Cutter, who serves mainly to open and close the tale. The poverty-stricken Bamboo Cutter and his wife were unhappy because they were childless. One day the Bamboo Cutter found a stalk of bamboo that gave forth light, and he discovered inside a tiny little girl whom he took home. Within three months she grew to full adult height and word spread of her extraordinary beauty. Various suitors came to woo her, but she refused even to appear before them. In the end, only five men persisted, and at the Bamboo Cutter's urging (he reminded Kaguya-hime that in this world men and women customarily marry) she agreed to marry one of the suitors, provided he performed whatever service she asked of him. The suitors gladly accepted this condition, but were dismayed when they learned the tasks involved bringing to her some unobtainable object, such as the begging bowl the Buddha himself had used or a jewel from the head of a dragon. All five men nevertheless attempted to meet her demands, but each ultimately failed, to the boundless delight of Kaguya-hime, who had no intention of marrying.

The emperor heard of Kaguya-hime's beauty and, with the connivance of the Bamboo Cutter, called at her house while out on a hunt.

Unable either to refuse or accept him, she turned herself into a shadow.[12] The emperor regretfully abandoned his suit.

After three years had gone by, Kaguya-hime became increasingly pensive, spending much of her time gazing at the moon. One night she burst into tears and revealed to the Bamboo Cutter that she was not a creature of this world but had come from the Palace of the Moon. Soon, she predicted, people from the moon would come to fetch her. The Bamboo Cutter vowed to prevent them from taking away his daughter, but when the flying chariot arrived from the moon he was powerless to resist. One of the celestial beings gave Kaguya-hime a jar of the elixir of immortality. She offered some of it to the old man and his wife, but now that Kaguya-hime was lost to them, life itself had lost its pleasure, and they refused to taste it. The elixir was offered to the emperor, who also refused because he could not see Kaguya-hime again. He commanded a messenger to take the elixir to the top of the highest mountain and set it afire. The tale concludes, "Ever since they burnt the elixir of immortality at the crest of the mountain, people have called the mountain Fuji, meaning immortal. Even now the smoke still rises into the clouds."[13]

Each of the main elements of this tale has precedents or parallels in the folklore and other literature of Asia.[14] Clues not only to the time of composition but to the work's purpose have been sought in the names of the five suitors.[15] All five suitors were adherents of the Emperor Temmu, and this suggested that the author of *The Tale of the Bamboo Cutter* was indirectly expressing his dislike for Temmu and his line by these satiric portraits.[16] One of the suitors, Kuramochi, was the ancestor of Fujiwara no Yoshifusa (804–872), the dominant political figure of the day, and the ridicule directed at Kuramochi may reflect the author's dislike of Fujiwara rule or possibly of the entire nobility.[17]

Perhaps the suitors originally included the Bamboo Cutter. Although he describes himself at the beginning of the tale as being over seventy years old (and therefore disqualified as a suitor), toward the end of the work he is said to be just fifty. This means that when he found Kaguya-hime some twenty years earlier,[18] he might well have been a suitor, though his wife represented something of an obstacle.[19] It is puzzling why the work was named after the Bamboo Cutter, rather than Kaguya-hime, the central figure, but some have called attention to the sacred nature of the profession of gathering bamboo.[20]

No fewer than twenty-two theories have been advanced concerning the purpose of the author in writing *The Tale of the Bamboo Cutter*.[21] The two main interpretations are those that see the work as being essentially a realistic portrayal of life among the Heian courtiers, and those that insist it is a fairy tale from the world of make-believe with few realistic elements.[22] The great folklore scholar Yanagita Kunio divided *The Tale of the Bamboo Cutter* into fixed and free elements, the former being parts of oral tradition that had to be incorporated in any retelling of the story, the latter the parts that storytellers could add or drop as the inspiration moved them. Yanagita believed that the sections of the work of greatest interest to the authors were those devoted to the fruitless quests of the five suitors.[23]

A study of the use in the work of the suffix *-keri*, found after verbs to indicate reported action, revealed that *-keri* occurred almost exclusively in the "frame" story, the parts of the work derived from earlier accounts. One does not find *-keri* in the "free" sections of the work (those not borrowed from predecessors).[24] The additions, departing from the familiar tale, presumably appealed to readers who were rather bored with the overly familiar "fixed" elements, and it was in the "free" sections that the author demonstrated his attitude toward the materials.

Perhaps the least discussed aspect of the work has been its literary appeal, though a somewhat less than startling "moral" has been extracted to the effect that nobility of spirit transcends wealth or poverty.[25] Nothing in the text indicates for whom *The Tale of the Bamboo Cutter* was written, but it must have been for educated readers. The style, however, is astonishingly simple and straightforward; it is perhaps the easiest to read of all Heian texts. The simplicity of style suggests that its language was close to the colloquial of the time (the text contains an unusually high proportion of dialogue), but it may also be attributed to the complete absence of the kind of introspective elements that contributed to the complexity and difficulty of the major works of Heian prose, notably those by women. The high percentage of words of Chinese origin (for a work written in kana) also suggests that the author was a man.[26] The most likely reason for anyone's writing such a story was to please or amuse people at the court.

The humor in the work certainly suggests that the author's main intent was to divert. The satire directed at the unlucky suitors has frequently been noted, but there is also humor in the characterization of the Bamboo Cutter and Kaguya-hime. The Bamboo Cutter is a dim-witted man who, by the accident of having found Kaguya-hime, rises to a position of importance. His knowledge is commonsensical: Kaguya-hime, when she is fully grown, should get married like every other girl. It does not occur to him that a girl found in a stalk of bamboo might be an exception to this general rule. He is also so guileless that he is unable to realize what is happening even as Kaguya-hime systematically disposes of one suitor after another. When workmen accost the second suitor, Prince Kuramochi, and demand their wages for having fashioned the "jeweled branch from paradise," the old man shakes his head in perplexity, wondering what they are talking about.

Again, he is so impressed by the robe of fire-rat fur offered by the minister of the Right, the third suitor, that the Bamboo Cutter insists on inviting him into the house. Kaguya-hime attempts to restrain him, pointing out that they have not yet tested the robe and made sure that it will not burn in fire, but he answers, "That may be so, but I'll invite him in anyway. In all the world there is not another such fur robe. You'd best accept it as genuine. Don't make people suffer so." The contrast in personality between the Bamboo Cutter and Kaguya-hime is graphically expressed: the old man is foolish but good-hearted, but Kaguya-hime, for all her charm, is icy.

The Bamboo Cutter's foolishness is most clearly depicted in the section describing the imminent arrival of the celestial beings who have come to escort Kaguya-hime back to the moon. He insists that he is a match even for supernatural creatures: "If anyone comes after you, I'll tear out his eyes with my long nails. I'll grab him by the hair and throw him to the ground. I'll put him to shame by exposing his behind for all the officers to see!" But when the celestial horde actually appears, the old Bamboo Cutter is unable to resist: "The old man, who had assumed such an air of defiance, prostrated himself before the strangers, feeling as though he were in a drunken stupor." His last resource is peasant cunning: when the king demands to see Kaguya-hime, saying she was condemned to live for a short while in humble surroundings on earth because of a sin committed in the past, the old man answers, "I have been watching over Kaguya-hime for more than twenty years. You speak of her having come down into this world for 'a short while.' It makes me wonder if you are not talking about some other Kaguya-hime living in a different place."

The Bamboo Cutter may seem foolish, but he is treated with affection by the author. Kaguya-hime, on the other hand, is far from eliciting our sympathy, let alone affection. She is portrayed as a woman who delights in making men suffer. From the first, when many men come to court her, she shows not a flicker of compassion, and she is not impressed by the five suitors who, without the least encouragement, persist in their courtship "undaunted by hindrances, whether the falling snows and the ice of midwinter or the blazing sun and the thunderbolts of summer." The old man urges Kaguya-hime to choose one of the five suitors. She agrees, but insists on testing the men to make sure they really love her. "I am not asking for anything extraordinary," she says, but after she has enumerated the five tests, the stunned old man replies, "How shall I break the news of such difficult assignments?" "What's so difficult about them?" asks Kaguya-hime. When the suitors are informed, they exclaim, "Why doesn't she simply say, 'Stay away from my house'?" They leave in disgust.

The suitors' ardor is presently revived, however, and they set about performing their tasks. No one could fulfill such assignments honestly, but each man attempts in his own way to achieve the impossible. The failure of the first suitor, the highest-ranked noble, excites no pity, and he is given short shrift not only by Kaguya-hime but by the author. The second suitor, who like the first resorts to deceit in his effort to win Kaguya-hime, is equally unsuccessful, but his fabrication is at least interesting. The remaining three men each try to obtain by legitimate means the object Kaguya-hime has demanded. For a while she fears that the minister of the Right has been successful in his quest of a robe that will not burn in fire, but when she tests it, the robe burns brightly. The minister turns the color of leaves of grass, but Kaguya-hime is enchanted.

The fourth suitor, the grand counselor, sends his men to get the five-colored jewel from a dragon's neck, but when they fail to return he sets off himself, only to encounter a terrible storm at sea. The grand counselor, terrified that he might lose his life, solemnly vows that he will never again attempt to harm a dragon, and the storm subsides. He returns home, more dead than alive, only to be informed that his men have been equally unsuccessful. He is pleased, rather than grieved: "If you had actually caught a dragon, it would certainly have meant the death of me! I'm glad you didn't catch one! That cursed thief of a Kaguya-hime was trying to kill us! I'll never go near her house again."

The last suitor, attempting to get the easy-delivery charm carried by mother sparrows, falls from a height just as he takes the charm in his hand; the charm proves to be bird droppings. Kaguya-hime vouchsafes to send a poem of inquiry about his health to which he feebly replies before he expires. We are told that Kaguya-hime was somewhat moved.

The cold-heartedness of Kaguya-hime is evoked with humor, but over the centuries her character has been subjected to a process of sentimentalization in the later versions of the tale, and she is now generally depicted as a lovable creature come from another world who is unsullied by base human emotions. However, the author of the thirteenth-century diary *Kaidōki* (Journey Along the Seacoast Road) characterized her as a "poisonous, transformed woman"[27] who troubled the emperor's heart, a reference to her refusal to yield even to the emperor when he courted her, and an apt evocation of how she treated all her suitors.

The visit of the emperor is the least successful episode of the work. In it Kaguya-hime's refusal to marry is given the ultimate test, a request for her hand by the one person she cannot refuse; but instead of presenting this as the climax of the account of the unlucky suitors, the author emphasizes her nonhuman nature by transforming her into a shadow.

The final part of the tale describes the arrival of people from the moon who, in defiance of the Bamboo Cutter and a body of soldiers sent by the emperor, carry off Kaguya-hime. In order that she may ascend to the moon, they give her a robe of feathers, a familiar element in Japanese folktales dealing with women who come from another world and, after a sojourn on earth, return to their original homes. In Kaguya-hime's case, the robe is really not necessary since a chariot has come to escort her to the moon, but putting on the feather robe symbolizes her breaking her ties with this world; we are told that anyone who wears this robe instantly forgets all earthly attachments. Kaguya-hime delays putting on the robe in order to write a final poem to the emperor, then departs with the celestial beings for the moon.

The Tale of the Bamboo Cutter shares "fixed" elements with Japanese and other folktales that describe the miraculous births of tiny human beings inside a stalk of bamboo, a song thrush's egg, or a peach, or that relate how a celestial being, deprived of the robe of feathers that permits her to ascend to heaven, becomes the wife of a human being (usually the man who found and hid the robe), but returns to heaven when she finds the missing garment. Variations on the thematic material are found in the folklore of the world and even within Japanese traditions, but *The Tale of the Bamboo Cutter* is distinguished from other accounts by the presence of literary intent.

Perhaps the intent of the author was to satirize the idle and ineffectual aristocrats, as many commentators have suggested, but he may have had in mind nothing more ambitious than an urbane retelling of a childish tale. In variants of this and similar tales of suitors who are assigned tasks, the lady marries either the man who first found her or else the last of the many men she tests, but Kaguya-hime does not yield, avoiding lèse-majesté by the expedient of vanishing. The suitors are treated with humor, but we are likely to sympathize with at least two of them. The author's detachment from his materials made it possible for him to tell a children's tale in a manner that appeals to adults, rather like Jean Cocteau's retelling of the story of Beauty and the Beast.

The manner of *The Tale of the Bamboo Cutter* was perhaps too sophisticated for most readers of the time. It does not seem to have led to other works in the same mode, though it undoubtedly helped to create the tsukuri monogatari. The birth of Kaguya-hime and her final ascent to the moon were surely not taken as literal truth even in the tenth century; but despite the elements of fantasy contained in *The Tale of the Bamboo Cutter*, it is also rich in realistic detail of a kind not often found in the elegant poem-tales, as in the description of the grand counselor's seasickness or of the bird droppings clutched by the unfortunate middle counselor. It also contains fifteen waka; the inclusion of poetry would be typical of all future monogatari.[28]

Various underlying assumptions and attitudes of the Heian court society revealed in this work, perhaps unconsciously, would also be prominent in later monogatari. The dread of what people might think (which obsesses the unlucky victims of Kaguya-hime's wild-goose chases), for example, would be typical of other Heian works of fiction. The repeated mention of tears, notably in the account of the Bamboo Cutter's grief over the loss of Kaguya-hime, prepared the way for the rivers of tears and pillows floating in tears of later works.[29] But the chief contribution of *The Tale of the Bamboo Cutter* to the development of Japanese fiction lay in its success in using the Japanese language as a medium of artistic expression.

The Tale of the Hollow Tree

Almost all of the works of fiction composed during the tenth and eleventh centuries have been lost or survive only in later reworkings. Two "invented tales," *Utsubo Monogatari*[30] (The Tale of the Hollow Tree) and *Ochikubo Monogatari* (The Tale of Ochikubo), are all that remain. The dating and authorship of these tales have been much disputed, but both seem to antedate *The Tale of Genji* and provide in their different ways a transition between the fairy tale (represented by *The Tale of the Bamboo Cutter*) and the complex masterpiece of Murasaki Shikibu.

The dating of *The Tale of the Hollow Tree* presents many problems, but it is probably safe to say that it was written between 970 and 983, though the last chapter may have been added after 1000.[31] The work has most often been ascribed to the scholar and poet Minamoto no Shitagō (911–983), though the evidence is by no means conclusive.[32] The title of the work is derived from the hollow tree where Nakatada (the chief male character) and his mother live after the death of his grandfather, Toshikage.

The chief distinction of *The Tale of the Hollow Tree* is that it was the first work of fiction of book length to have been composed in Japan and possibly in the world. It is clear, however, that the author or authors did not commence the work with this intention. Although an attempt was made, presumably at some late stage, to unify the disparate chapters, they hang together poorly. Numerous contradictions within the text confirm the impression that the work originally consisted of perhaps four or five independent stories that were arranged in chronological order and otherwise given unity by having characters make brief appearances in previously unrelated stories.[33] The texts of *The Tale of the Hollow Tree* contain an exceptionally large number of variants, providing many happy hours for industrious collators. Even the order of the chapters is uncertain: for example, the chapter "Tadakoso," a story complete in itself that refers very little to any other section of the tale, appears as the second, third, or fourth chapter, depending on the manuscript tradition.[34] The hoarding of texts by collectors (whether members of the aristocracy in the past or merely rich men today) has ensured a seemingly never-ending supply of new variants as the manuscripts are gradually published. This is true not only of *The Tale of the Hollow Tree* but also of a large part of the literature composed before printing became general in the seventeenth century.

The longest sequence of stories is devoted to the courtship of the beautiful Princess Atemiya by a variety of suitors.[35] Unlike Kaguyahime, she does not deign to set tasks for these men, but stonily refuses even to acknowledge their letters. When one suitor, the Chancellor Sanetada, seems about to expire because of unrequited love, Atemiya at first feels pity and considers writing him a note, but decides against it, for fear of what other people might think.[36] She finally marries the crown prince, who is captivated by her superb playing of the koto; but there is not the slightest indication that she prefers him to the other suitors or, indeed, that she has any preferences.

The story of Atemiya and her suitors seems to have been the central episode around which the other stories in *The Tale of the Hollow Tree* were grouped, but the book as a whole is given unity by the theme of music, which runs through every episode. The work (in its present form, though there is reason to suspect that the original form was different) opens with the account of Toshikage, a brilliant young prince who is sent to China with an embassy. Two of the three ships of the embassy sink, and the third, with Toshikage aboard, drifts southward until it reaches the land of Hashi, a country that has been identified variously as Persia or Malaysia.[37] The ship founders off the coast of Hashi, and Toshikage is the only survivor. He prays to the *bodhisattva* Kannon, whom he has worshiped ever since he was a child, and a miracle occurs: a white horse, saddled and ready to be mounted, suddenly appears on the deserted beach, prancing and whinnying. Toshikage, recognizing the source of this miracle, bows in thanks to Kannon. (This intrusion of the supernatural is typical of the early sections of *The Tale of the Hollow Tree* and links it with Buddhist tales of the same era.) Toshikage is carried by the horse to an enchanted realm where he learns the secrets of playing the koto.

Toshikage's tutors are three men who spend their entire days playing the koto, and he shares their simple meals of dew from the flowers and drops of water from the red maple leaves. In the spring of the following year he hears the sound of a tree being felled far off to the west, and the echoes continue to reverberate for three years. It occurs to Toshikage that wood from this reverberative tree would make a marvelous koto. He leaves his three teachers and travels westward for three years until he finds the tree at the crest of a mountain. The tree is guarded by a fierce being called an *asura* who intimidates Toshikage by announcing that he devours every creature, be it tiger, wolf, or merely bug, that falls into his trap. He rolls eyes that are like wheels and gnashes his rapierlike teeth.

The asura is not, however, devoid of feelings: when he learns that Toshikage is from Japan, he offers to guide him back to his country, provided Toshikage promises to hold a Buddhist service for him. Toshikage, emboldened by this show of compassion, asks for a piece of the tree in order to make a koto. The asura angrily refuses, whereupon the sky grows dark, a torrential rain falls, lightning flashes, and a boy riding on a dragon's back descends from heaven with a golden tablet inscribed with the words: "Give the bottom third of the tree to Toshikage, a mortal from Japan!" The terrified asura bows seven times before Toshikage, and, in obedience to the command, he cuts the tree into three portions and gives Toshikage the bottom third, the best part. The celestial boy, hearing the sounds of the asura's axe, descends once again from heaven and fashions thirty kotos from the wood. He is followed by celestial maidens who lacquer and string the kotos.

Toshikage tests the thirty kotos. Twenty-eight produce similar sounds, but when the remaining two are played, mountains crumble, the earth is sundered, and the "seven mountains" sway together.[38] A band of celestial ladies riding on a purple cloud reveals to Toshikage that it is the will of heaven that he found a line of great koto players. He is informed that he must go to the Buddha's paradise for instruction in the ultimate secrets of the koto.

Toshikage proceeds to paradise, as directed, with the help of a peacock and an elephant who carry him over difficult stretches of the terrain. Obliging whirlwinds carry the thirty kotos all the way. In paradise Toshikage receives the promised instruction from seven immortals. The sound of their music reaches the ears of the Buddha himself, who expresses admiration for Toshikage and promises that one of the seven immortals will be reborn as his grandson.

Soon afterward Toshikage, having mastered the secrets of the koto, leaves paradise and sets off on the homeward journey to Japan. He has been away for twenty-three years and is worried about his parents. He catches a ship going in his direction, and before long reaches home. He learns that his parents are dead, and goes into mourning for three years. When his period of mourning is completed, he attends court, where he is cordially received by the emperor, who appoints him vice-minister of ceremonies.[39]

From this point on the story of *The Tale of the Hollow Tree* becomes more or less realistic. The narration, with the exception of the account of prodigies attributed to the two miraculous kotos, is devoted chiefly to activities at the court. In some ways the descriptions of life at the court are more realistic than those in *The Tale of Genji*: at the banquets the nobles get drunk and boisterous; they eat food that sounds most unappetizing (though nobody in *The Tale of Genji* does anything so vulgar as eat); they stake bets on the outcome of games of go. The world is altogether more believable than the peerless one in which Genji moved, but it is also boring, as court life tends to be. Only the insistence on the beauty of music imparts an intermittent elegance of the kind that abounds in *The Tale of Genji*.

The last chapter is devoted to the account of a concert attended by two former emperors at which Nakatada, the grandson of Toshikage and the successor to his knowledge of the secret traditions of the koto, Nakatada's mother, and his daughter all play. The two magical kotos Toshikage brought back to Japan are played by Nakatada's mother to such powerful effect that the earth trembles, stars veer from their courses, and the waters of a nearby lake overflow. As the melody changes, the foolish become wise, the wrathful are calmed, the sick are cured, and invalids who have been unable even to move leap with joy.[40]

It can hardly be doubted that the author loved music, but he was ineffectual in describing its charms, and the innumerable accounts of amazing performances of koto music become tedious. The first time we read of playing so magnificent that snow falls even in midsummer, we may be impressed, but in the absence of more internal descriptions of the pleasures of music, it is difficult to take these prodigies seriously. Little besides the mentions of music can be said to unify this badly organized work; and there are still many loose ends when we reach the last chapter, despite the author's efforts to round off the story by returning to the kotos Toshikage acquired abroad. The prophecy of the Buddha that one of the seven immortals would be reborn as Toshikage's grandson is not specifically fulfilled, though Nakatada's musical talent may be attributed to this heritage.

Like all of the "invented" tales, *The Tale of the Hollow Tree* was set in the past. The world portrayed seems to be that of the early tenth century, when music enjoyed unequaled popularity at the court and the waka, long subservient to the kanshi, had come into its own with the compilation of the *Kokinshū*. Close to a thousand waka are scattered among the twenty books of *The Tale of the Hollow Tree*, as opposed to 794 in *The Tale of Genji*, which is almost twice as long, suggesting the importance of poetry in the life of the court. None of the poems in *The Tale of the Hollow Tree* is memorable, but one is quoted in *The Gossamer Years*, proof that the work circulated at court.

It is not clear for whom *The Tale of the Hollow Tree* was written. Konishi Jin'ichi offered the theory that various "sponsors" commissioned a man who was known for his literary skill to write stories for them.[41] It is unlikely that anyone, even at the court, would have written a work of fiction for his own diversion or for literary practice unless someone provided at least the paper. The expected audience was probably very small, no more than the sponsors and members of their circle. Stories may have been written for several sponsors at the same time, perhaps describing the same characters, though with different plots. The stories might be broken off if their sponsors found them insufficiently interesting, or might be prolonged by request of a satisfied sponsor. When the original writer or his literary executor decided to assemble under one title the various stories, he undoubtedly tried to give the work greater consistency. Later on, a sleepy scribe might introduce textual errors, or he might unwittingly eliminate passages, or (when less sleepy) add flattering references to the family of whoever had asked him to copy the original manuscript.

One unusual feature of *The Tale of the Hollow Tree* is the presence in the texts of descriptions of illustrations, sometimes merely the notation "There is a picture here" or "This is Chikage's palace" but sometimes more lengthy. It is not clear who wrote these passages or what their purpose might have been, but it has been suggested that they were written by the author himself, perhaps to describe illustrations contained in a separate volume (or scroll). One can imagine a gentlewoman's reading aloud the text while ladies of the court followed the illustrations. But it is not necessary to accept this particular interpretation: we do not know why *The Tale of the Hollow Tree* contains notations on the illustrations, but literature and illustrative paintings were closely identified at this time.

The Tale of the Hollow Tree has attracted favorable attention in the twentieth century because it included such political materials as the description of an abdication or the account of a rivalry over succession to the throne. Such elements are undoubtedly present, but they occupy a very small part of the author's attention. Similarly, the presence among the characters of persons who do not belong to the upper ranks of the nobility has been contrasted favorably with *The Tale of Genji*. For example, the indigent student Tōei makes a pleasant contrast with the flawlessly costumed, exquisitely scented nobles who were more often treated in Heian fiction. Three of Atemiya's suitors are comic—an eccentric rich man, a miser, and a rustic widower—and the people in their service are at least momentarily interesting because gamblers, mediums, diviners, and the riffraff of the capital do not otherwise appear in early fiction. But the book is long, and these brief sketches of unfamiliar members of Heian society do not compensate for the ineptitude of the whole. The most memorable feature of *The Tale of the Hollow Tree* is perhaps its length. It suggested to more talented writers new possibilities in the art of fiction.

The Tale of Ochikubo

The Tale of Ochikubo is a far more successful work, and may have been the first full-length tale planned as such. It is the story of a good and beautiful girl harshly treated by her stepmother, who favors her own daughters. She poisons her husband's mind against his daughter and keeps him from interfering. Luckily for the girl, a handsome young prince rescues her from the dungeon where her stepmother had confined her, and they live happily ever after. The wicked stepmother is humiliated and her daughters, who treated poor Ochikubo as a servant, have no choice but to depend on her kindness.

The story corresponds so closely to that of Cinderella that the Western reader may miss the presence of a fairy godmother, but the tale is firmly anchored in this world and has none of the fantasy of *The Tale of the Hollow Tree*. It is also resolutely unpoetic both in the narration and in the scarcity of waka. The last of the four books may be by a later hand, but even so, the work as a whole is a sustained and effective story.

The author of *The Tale of Ochikubo* is not known, though Minamoto no Shitagō has traditionally been credited with this work.[42] Apart from a few allusions to Chinese literature that suggest the author had a reasonably good education, there is little to substantiate this attribution. If the dates most commonly accepted for the composition of the work, between 990 and 998, are correct, Shitagō, who died in 983, obviously could not have played an active part in the final version.

The heroine of *The Tale of Ochikubo* derives her name from the room where her stepmother compelled her to live: *ochikubo* means a room at one level lower than others in the house. The cruel stepmother insists that Ochikubo sew all the clothes for the large household though she herself is given only threadbare old clothes to wear. One day, however, the handsome young nobleman Michiyori, who had heard rumors about the beautiful young woman kept a prisoner in the house of her senile father, pays her a visit with the connivance of Akogi, her waiting woman. At first his intentions seem to have been frivolous, but he gradually falls in love with Ochikubo and decides to make her his wife. The wicked stepmother, learning from an intercepted letter that Ochikubo has a gentleman visitor, is enraged to think that her useful little seamstress may be stolen from her, and shuts Ochikubo in a locked storeroom. She further arranges to humiliate the girl by inducing a lecherous old man to visit her at night. Ochikubo and Akogi contrive to frustrate the old man, and finally Michiyori smuggles Ochikubo out of the dungeon and takes her to his house.

Not satisfied with having secured his prize, Michiyori is determined to make Ochikubo's family suffer for all the cruelty they had inflicted on her. By one device or another he manages to bring misery to all of Ochikubo's tormentors, tricking one sister into accepting as her husband a grotesque half-wit, depriving Ochikubo's father of the house he had furnished at great expense, and finally stealing all the good servants.

His greatest severity is naturally reserved for the stepmother, whom he humiliates in numerous ways. Only when Ochikubo's family has been reduced to misery and is utterly at his mercy does he relent and display (in the last of the four books) his filial piety, enabling his father-in-law to realize his lifetime ambition of becoming a major counselor by yielding his post to the old man. And when the wicked stepmother, now contrite save for rare flashes of her old nastiness, finally dies, Michiyori provides a splendid funeral.

We are likely after reading *The Tale of Ochikubo* to remember Michiyori's sadistic treatment of his wife's family more vividly than the cause of his anger. But it is unfair to treat *The Tale of Ochikubo* as if it were a novel with believable characters whose actions can be analyzed; although the setting is realistic, it is a tale in which the good people are absolutely good, and the bad people very bad indeed. Ochikubo is patient and long-suffering, but we learn little about her emotions. Her only reaction after spending her first night with Michiyori is shame that her clothes are so shabby. She is a poor-spirited creature who does nothing to stop her husband from persecuting her father, though she does not actually encourage him in his vengeance. She has no trace of the introspective character that would be typical of later monogatari. Michiyori is a model Heian husband and, that great rarity, a confirmed monogamist who is so faithful to Ochikubo that he refuses the hand of the prime minister's daughter. His rise to power is nonetheless spectacular, and at the end of the book he is the most powerful man in the realm.

The most effectively drawn character in *The Tale of Ochikubo* is Ochikubo's waiting woman and confidante, Akogi. Persons like Akogi are found in the literatures of other countries—the quick-witted servant who foils the enemies of her mistress (too frail and too well behaved to resist their machinations)—but it is surprising to find the type so well developed in an early Heian work of fiction. Strangest of all is the last sentence of the work, which proclaims that Akogi (and not Ochikubo or Michiyori) "lived until the age of two hundred." The prominence of Akogi is such that the first translator into English found "more autobiographical feeling" in the portrait of Akogi than of the rest of the characters, adding, "Many details of style and expression certainly do point to a man as the author, yet still I feel reluctant to give up my first impression that a woman of the same station in life as Akogi was the author, even though the whole weight of the opinions of all the experienced commentators is against this conjecture."[43] Some Japanese have since given this theory serious consideration,[44] but it is hard to avoid the conclusion that the author was probably a man. It was not a prototype of Akogi who wrote the book; rather, the book seems to have been written in the hope of pleasing women readers of the same station as Akogi, though we cannot be sure who actually read the manuscript.

The coarseness and even scatological humor that characterize *The Tale of Ochikubo*, distinguishing it from most of the Heian monogatari, suggest an author who lacked refinement, but he might have been a "professional" who judged that such touches would capture the attention of his audience. Readers like Akogi would have found it easier than their mistresses to accept not only the lapses from good taste but the childishness of the story itself.

The theme of the stepmother's cruelty toward her stepdaughter, which first appears in *The Tale of Ochikubo*, would become prominent among the works of fiction of the Kamakura and Muromachi periods. Origuchi Shinobu for this reason doubted that the work could have been composed during the Heian period,[45] and many later scholars accepted his view; but others insisted that the theme of the cruel stepmother was found in Heian literature long before *The Tale of Ochikubo*. They pointed out, for example, that in *The Tale of the Hollow Tree* Tadakoso, a young man, is accused by his stepmother of a theft of which he is entirely innocent, irreparably harming his relations with his father. It is true that the woman is Tadakoso's stepmother, but only by a technicality: Tadakoso's father felt so sorry for the old hag that he condescended to visit her for three nights, in that way establishing marital relations. The father avoided the woman afterward and she sought comfort from Tadakoso. Her cruelty was caused not by eagerness to advance her daughters' prospects (she is childless) but by fury that Tadakoso had spurned her—not surprising, considering she is old enough to be his stepmother. Tadakoso's nearest equivalent in Western literature is not Cinderella but Hippolytus, the stepson of Phaedra.[46]

A more likely predecessor of this story of a stepmother's cruelty is *Sumiyoshi Monogatari* (The Tale of Sumiyoshi). Unfortunately, the only surviving texts are revised versions made during the Kamakura period or later, and it is difficult to be sure of the contents of the original *Tale of Sumiyoshi* mentioned in *The Tale of Genji*. Probably it was similar in general outline to the present text. The story, as we now have it, concerns a major counselor who had two wives, one the daughter of an important official, the other a member of the imperial family. His union with the former produces two daughters, and with the latter one daughter whose mother dies when the girl is still a small child. The major counselor decides to assemble his entire family under one roof, but this leads to the stepmother's ill-treatment of the motherless girl. Unlike most versions of the Cinderella tale, the girl gets along well with her half-sisters, but her stepmother prevents an eligible young man from visiting the girl and contrives to have him marry one of her daughters instead. The stepmother attempts to foist an old man on the girl as her husband, but she escapes to Sumiyoshi. The gentleman who had married the girl's half-sister is unable to forget the girl, and eventually he learns her whereabouts in a dream and takes her to his house. At the conclusion the stepmother's wickedness is revealed. She is disgraced and reduced to penury.[47]

The most striking difference between *The Tale of Ochikubo* and *The Tale of Sumiyoshi* is the divine intercession in the latter, which takes the form of a dream revelation vouchsafed to the gentleman. This religious element perhaps crept into the story when it was retold in the Kamakura period; it would become even more conspicuous in medieval stepmother stories, and perhaps its absence in *The Tale of Ochikubo* is the strongest evidence for assigning the work to the Heian period.

Heian Japan was not a likely place for the creation of stories about wicked stepmothers. The Heian gentleman usually did not live even with his chief consort (*kita no kata*) until a considerable time had elapsed after the "wedding," which consisted of visits to the future wife on successive nights, the third distinguished by the consumption of certain traditional foods. There was no religious ceremony and sometimes, at the convenience of the groom, the "wedding" was kept secret. Secondary wives lived in separate establishments and their children lived with them. If the mother of the children of a second or third wife died, the children were reared by grandparents rather than by the chief consort. In *The Tale of Ochikubo* the author carefully noted that Ochikubo's grandmother had also died, and that was why she was subjected to the cruelties of a stepmother. But such cases seem to have been relatively rare. The spate of original and revised works on the theme of the mistreated stepdaughter did not stem from any special abundance of such cases in Japanese society; rather, having been harshly treated by a stepmother seems to have enhanced a girl not only in the eyes of her Prince Charming but of the readers as well. Perhaps stories about wicked stepmothers were also read to children in order to make them better appreciate their own parents.[48]

The transition from *The Tale of the Hollow Tree* and *The Tale of Ochikubo* to *The Tale of Genji* involves a staggering leap: the earlier works make little appeal to a mature mind, but *The Tale of Genji* stands with the great creations of prose of the world. The genius of Murasaki Shikibu made this possible, but not even she could have moved from the "invented stories" described above to her masterpiece had there not already been another tradition of fiction, the poem-tale, and another tradition of prose (as we have seen), the diary.

The Poem-Tale

The second variety of monogatari developed during the late ninth or early tenth century, the *uta monogatari*, a name first given to the genre during the Meiji period.[49] Even works of straightforward narration like *The Tale of the Bamboo Cutter* contained poetry, included as an integral part of the experiences of the persons described, but in the poem-tales the poems form the core of successive episodes, and the accompanying prose may consist of no more than brief evocations of the circumstances that inspired the poems. There may be no apparent connection between one episode and the next, or they may be linked by their having been composed by members of the same court society.

The authors of the poems in these tales are generally unidentified, but it is sometimes possible to determine who wrote them because the same poems were also included (with the authors' names) in court anthologies. It was long believed that the poem-tales originated in the prefaces that introduce waka in the anthologies and private collections; but recent scholars of Japanese literature have categorically rejected this theory.[50] The kotobagaki usually state no more than basic information about the time and place of composition of the poems, but occasionally there is a fairly lengthy description of the background. The prefaces in the *Man'yōshū* were at times longer than the poems, and those in the *Gosenshū* were also exceptionally detailed.

The ambiguity of many poems probably necessitated such prefaces. The Japanese preferred blurred outlines to hard clarity. But the readers at times wanted to know which of various possible meanings the poet actually had in mind, and this may have been the origin of the *utagatari* (talks on poetry),[51] sessions when friends related their knowledge of the backgrounds of poems. The narrative style of such conversations led more naturally into the poem-tales than the dryly factual prefaces of the poetry collections.

Tales of Ise

The most celebrated of the uta monogatari is *Ise Monogatari* (Tales of Ise). Together with the *Kokinshū*, it probably exercised the greatest influence on later literature of any work of the Heian period.[52] It may seem strange that a collection of 125 casually connected episodes,[53] sometimes hardly more than bare explanations of the circumstances behind the poems, should have possessed such enormous appeal for later generations. Perhaps the length of *The Tale of Genji*, a far superior work, militated against its being widely circulated and imitated; the brief episodes of *Tales of Ise*, taken individually or all together, made fewer demands on the reader's attention. It was also less expensive to copy a short text. In an age when literary works were not printed, anyone who wished to read a work of fiction or a collection of poetry had first to borrow someone else's manuscript, buy the paper, then pay for a copyist's services during the weeks or months it took him to complete the task. But probably the chief reason why *Tales of Ise* was so popular was that it presented in encapsulated form the glamour of the Heian court and was therefore irresistibly attractive to members of later generations who yearned for that golden age.

We do not know the author of *Tales of Ise*. Probably there was no single author who at a particular time sat down to write the work.[54] The central figure, Ariwara no Narihira (825–880), may himself have written the earliest version, presenting the poems that he and people around him had composed on various occasions along with explanations (not necessarily truthful) of what had inspired the poems. It is easy to imagine that someone, finding such a manuscript after Narihira's death, decided to expand it with other poems by Narihira, together with related anecdotes. It may have been at this point that various unconnected episodes were first arranged in a roughly chronological order from the time of Narihira's coming of age until his death.

Not all of the 125 episodes concern Narihira, and the period of many is vague, but readers over the centuries have accepted *Tales of Ise* as a kind of biography. If the expanded version of the original text was made not long after Narihira's death, there may still have been people who were present when the poems were composed or who had heard of the circmstances from the poet himself. When the backgrounds of the poems had been clarified and recorded in a style of high literary quality, whatever ephemeral interest that they possessed as gossip was forgotten, and these evocations of court life aroused nostalgia and envy.

The pervading quality of *Tales of Ise* is conveyed by the word *miyabi*, translatable as "elegance," though it referred specifically to the refined ways of the capital, as opposed to rustic inelegance.[55] The word itself occurs only once in the work, at the conclusion of the first episode: *Mukashi hito wa kaku ichihayaki miyabi wo nan shikeru.* (People in the past displayed in this manner remarkable elegance.) The elegance in *Tales of Ise* is epitomized by the behavior of the hero, who is usually referred to simply as *otoko* (the man). The "man" has always been identified by readers as Narihira, though some events in the work occur fifty years before his birth and others long after his death. Many episodes open with the short sentence *Mukashi otoko arikeri* (Long ago, there was a man). This repeated association of the hero with the past no doubt helped to establish Narihira as the emblematic figure of a glorious but vanished age.[56]

Narihira combined all the qualities most admired in a Heian courtier: he was of high birth (a grandson of the Emperor Heizei), extremely handsome, a gifted poet, and an all-conquering lover. He was probably also an expert horseman, adept in arms, and a competent official. These aspects of his life are not emphasized in *Tales of Ise*, but they distinguish Narihira from other heroes of Heian literature, including Genji.

The repetition of the word *mukashi* (long ago) at the beginning of many episodes suggests that *Tales of Ise* was written long after the events described, but the work, in more or less its present form, probably existed by the middle of the tenth century and perhaps earlier.[57] The process of evolving the present text of *Tales of Ise* probably took seventy years, beginning with Narihira's death in 880.[58]

Surviving texts follow the same order, opening with the story of a young man who, shortly after coming of age, goes hunting on his estate near Nara, and concluding with the poem the man composed when he was ill and sensed that he was dying. However, the Buddhist monk Kenshō (c. 1130–c. 1210) mentioned that some texts began with episode 69 of the present version.[59] The fact is of more than usual interest because episode 69 describes the visit of "the man" to the Great Shrine of Ise where he has a brief romance with the high priestess. It has often been suggested that the title of the work was derived from this especially striking example of the man's audacious lovemaking. If this episode stood at the head of the work the theory would be convincing, but even if it did not (no such text survives), the episode is central, both in its characterization of Narihira and its description of a love affair that took place despite the strict prohibition on the high priestess, an imperial princess, having relations with men. The notoriety of the affair might well have given its name to *Tales of Ise*. This explanation of the title seems more plausible than most that have evolved over the centuries.[60]

The first readers of *Tales of Ise* were surely aware that if Narihira had actually had an affair with the high priestess it was not an occasion for poetic commemoration: they would both have been severely punished. The episode must be largely fictitious, but as time went on, most readers probably lost sight of historical fact and assumed that the account of the legendary hero was true. Medieval scholarship did not dwell on such points, but concentrated instead on identifying the many anonymous men and women who appear in the work. Sometimes this scholarship was incorporated into the text itself, as the following episode (number 79) suggests:

> Long ago a prince was born to a certain family, and at the ceremonies afterward people composed poetry. Here is the poem written by an old gentleman who was the baby's relative on its grandfather's side:

wa ga kado ni	By the gate of our house
chihiro aru take wo	Bamboo, a thousand cubits high
uetsureba	Has now been planted;
natsu fuyu tare ka	In summer and in winter
kakurezarubeki	Who will not take shelter here?

> This refers to Prince Sadakazu. Gossip at the time had it that the baby's father was the middle captain. The baby was born to the daughter of his elder brother, Middle Counselor Yukihira.[61]

The identification of the baby as Prince Sadakazu and the rumor that Narihira ("the middle captain") was its father was undoubtedly added later, after Narihira had established his reputation as a great lover. Yukihira, Narihira's brother, died in 893 thirteen years after Narihira. His daughter was a consort of the Emperor Seiwa. The allegation that Narihira was the child's father thus reflected adversely on Yukihira, his daughter, and the Emperor Seiwa. Such a remark could hardly have been committed to writing while the persons involved were still alive. Perhaps Prince Sadakazu's remarkable beauty as a child inspired the rumor that the father was actually Narihira, and the rumor was incorporated into the text.[62] A recent commentator, after noting that the lines after the poem were a later addition, commented, "A vulgar note, and probably not true."[63]

A key episode in *Tales of Ise* (number 9), describing Narihira's journey to Azuma, opens:

> Long ago, there was a certain man. Convinced that he could serve no useful function if he remained in the capital, he decided to set out for the East in search of a suitable place to live in that region.[64]

The interest of this passage lies in Narihira's characterization of himself as *yōnaki mono*, meaning a "useless," or superfluous, man. The philosopher Karaki Junzō believed that the term indicated that Narihira was a new phenomenon in Japanese history, a man who did not fit into his society. It was lonely to be cut off from other men and their aspirations, but by removing himself from the busy capital, where he was doomed to be always a stranger, Narihira discovered a world of his own of true miyabi and of mono no aware, a sensitivity to things.[65] Karaki termed Narihira the first of the Japanese bunjin, men of letters, who chose to remain aloof from the ambitions that occupy most men and who eschewed a profession as being unworthy of a gentleman. An odor of decadence clings to such men, but they are more attractive than the successful courtiers of their day.

Narihira's journey to Azuma—to the region around modern Tokyo and to the mountainous districts of central Japan—inspired innumerable later travelers. Few of them missed the opportunity when they traveled in that part of the country to examine the Eight Bridges that Narihira had described, even after generations of diarists had reported that the bridges were all down and the irises by the bridges (also mentioned by Narihira) had long since withered. Yatsuhashi became perhaps the most celebrated of all *utamakura*, places that inspired poetry.

However, for centuries there was a tradition that Narihira never actually visited Azuma. The whole of the ninth episode, it was averred, consisted of elaborate allegories that hid the central fact that Narihira was in disgrace because of an affair with Takaiko, the consort of the Emperor Seiwa. Narihira may have had such an affair, as commentators for centuries insisted, but nothing in *Tales of Ise* suggests that he was in disgrace. The medieval commentators, reluctant to accept surface meanings, indulged in speculation:

> When it says he felt reluctant to remain in the capital and went to the East, this refers to his having been left in the custody of the Chancellor Yoshifusa of Higashiyama. When it says he pursued his journey to the province of Suruga, it means he went to the house of Sadaiben Takatsune, then the governor of Suruga. When it says he looked at the peak of Fuji, it is referring to the Emperor Seiwa. He was comparing the rank of the sovereign to Mount Fuji and his

> own rank to Mount Hiei. . . . The boatman of the Sumida River was the Horikawa Chancellor Mototsune.[66]

As proof of the truth of their elaborate (but unconvincing) "explanations," the commentators asserted that if Narhira had really traveled all the way to the east he would surely have produced more than five poems about his journey.[67] Perhaps Narihira really had some other reason for making the journey than his conviction that he was a "useless" member of society; one scholar has suggested that he may have been in mourning for his mother, a time when he was excused from official duties.[68] But, far from being in disgrace, he probably made the journey at government expense for reasons of health, and chose the east, rather than some other part of the country, because he had close friends and relatives there.[69]

Almost any extended episode of *Tales of Ise* is worthy of detailed examination. Although the sentences are generally simple, little is plainly stated, and the commentators have felt obliged to explain at length almost every phrase. For example, the frequent use of the verb ending *-ḳeri* has suggested to some that *Tales of Ise* was originally narrated, perhaps to a small circle at the court, in the manner of the utagatari. Scholars have also pointed out the influence of earlier works: episode 14 contains a poem that is a reworking of one from the *Man'yōshū*, and the celebrated episode 69 (describing Narihira's tryst with the high priestess of Ise) seems to have been inspired by a short story of the T'ang poet Yüan Chen (779–831).[70] The existence of such literary influences confirms the belief that *Tales of Ise* should not be considered, as often in the past, a factually truthful account of Narihira's life. In the process of creating a literary work from what originally may have been little more than gossip about the events behind Narihira's poems, the compilers did not hesitate to "improve" the text with materials of their own or other people's invention.

Even recognizing that *Tales of Ise* contains fanciful, sometimes implausible elements, this is by no means the kind of fantasy we find in *The Tale of the Bamboo Cutter*. With the exception of a strange passage in episode 6 that relates how an abducted woman was swallowed "in one gulp" by a demon, the supernatural does not figure in the stories, and even this episode was provided with a rationalistic explanation that the woman was not in fact swallowed by a demon but rescued from her abductors by her brothers, who happened to pass by and hear her weeping. The need the reviser felt to explain the demon is evidence of his understanding that it had no place in the world of *Tales of Ise*.

The poems in the work benefit immensely from their prose settings. Even poems that seem perplexingly obscure when read in isolation become intelligible in the light of the prose; and both poetry and prose create a picture of a nostalgically remembered world.

An awareness of the passage of time and the sad changes it causes colors much of Heian poetry and prose. *Tales of Ise* can even be interpreted as a desperate attempt to halt the flow of time by preserving from oblivion poignant moments from the past.[71] The successful evocation of such moments, even though no thread joins them, no doubt accounts for the extraordinary popularity over the centuries of a work that might seem to persons born outside the tradition to be too delicate and wispy to fully engage the reader's interest. The overtones of *Tales of Ise* are not easy to catch on first reading, but they are definitely present and detectable to anyone who takes the trouble to read slowly and with the attention befitting a work whose every word has excited admiration for a millennium.

Tales of Yamato

The best known of the other poem-tales of the Heian period is a collection of 173 episodes, each containing one or more waka. *Tales of Yamato*, like *Tales of Ise*, probably attained its present form only after various additions had been made to an original text, but the period of compilation was shorter. Dates of 951–953 have been proposed for the compilation.[72] Perhaps a group of people at the court was involved from the outset in the compilation, and one person's story about the background of a poem was followed by another's, linked to the first by a poem related in theme or imagery.[73] More specific theories of authorship have also been proposed, including the suggestion that Ise, the noted court lady and waka poet, was the principal author and that the work was completed by her daughter, Nakatsukasa, another well-known poet.[74]

The problem of authorship is complicated by the dissimilarity between the two parts into which *Tales of Yamato* divides. The first 146 episodes are devoted to life at the court of the Emperor Uda (867–931). Over one hundred members of the court are named, and their poems gave rise to the anecdotes related in this first part.

With episode 147, however, the work changes character and treats a world remote from the palace. This is the story of a girl who was courted by two men. She could not choose between them, so her mother set the men a task: whichever of them succeeded in shooting a waterfowl in the Ikuta River would be given her daughter. Unfortunately, the arrows of both men hit the target, and the girl, despairing of ever deciding which man to marry, threw herself into the river, whereupon both young men jumped in after her, and all three drowned. The story relates how the three were buried, the poems composed by other people imagining the emotions that had occasioned the deaths of the three people, and finally the appearance as a ghost of one of the suitors.[75] Not only is this episode unrelated to life at the court, but it is much longer than earlier episodes, and the inartistic trailing off of the conclusion suggests an authentic folktale. The later episodes of *Tales of Yamato* are nevertheless far more interesting than the often pointless anecdotes in the miyabi manner of the first 146 episodes, and some provided material for the Nō plays and other works of literature.[76]

The stories in the first part of *Tales of Yamato* are not nearly so interesting as those in *Tales of Ise*. They lack a central figure to bind together the disparate anecdotes, and it is hard to keep one's attention focused on the large cast of characters. Episode 45, which contains a well-known poem, typifies the first part:

> When Tsutsumi no Chūnagon first sent his daughter, who would later become the mother of the thirteenth prince, to serve in the palace, he was quite anxious about her and asked himself: "I wonder what the Emperor thinks of her?" Very much concerned, he wrote this poem which he sent to His Majesty:
>
> | | |
> |---|---|
> | *hito no oya no* | Though it is not lost |
> | *kokoro wa yami ni* | In darkness, a parent's heart, |
> | *aranedomo* | For love of a child, |
> | *ko wo omou michi ni* | Is apt to lose its bearings |
> | *mayoinuru kana* | And know not which way to turn. |
>
> The Emperor was deeply moved by this poem. Although he sent Tsutsumi no Chūnagon a return poem, no one remembers the lines.[77]

Tsutsumi no Chūnagon (the Tsutsumi middle counselor) is better known by his name, Fujiware no Kanesuke. He figures prominently not only in *Tales of Yamato* but also in the imperial anthologies, where fifty-five of his waka are found. At the beginning of the tenth century (from about 900 to 930) the salon in which he and Fujiwara no Sadataka (873–932) were the central figures dominated waka poetry, and various poems emanating from that salon were included in *Tales of Yamato*. The waka by Kanesuke given above also appeared in the imperial anthology *Gosenshū*, but with an entirely different preface.[78]

The *Tales of Yamato* version of the circumstances of the composition of the poem is more artistic and may even be construed as evidence that the work has a literary intent absent from the *Gosenshū*.[79] The poem itself rises above either set of circumstances to become the expression of a universal sentiment. Probably that is why it was quoted in *The Tale of Genji* more often than any other waka and appears again and again in other literary works.

Kanesuke does not emerge distinctly as a person in the passages introducing his poems. Indeed, only one person in *Tales of Yamato* is memorable, and that mainly because of her name. Toshiko, the wife of the official Fujiware no Chikane, appears in a number of episodes, and scholars, intrigued by her prominence, have fantasized about her relations with her husband, other lovers, and so on.[80] The special interest of Toshiko lies in the fact that she is referred to by her personal name rather than by her father's or her husband's title. In general, we know the personal names only of women of the imperial family,[81] but Toshiko is an exception. Why was she singled out for this honor? Perhaps she was so prominent (or so lively) a member of a salon that the members always referred to her in an affectionate manner.

Another figure of more than casual interest is the celebrated lover Taira no Sadafun, whose exploits are recounted in greater detail in *Tales of Heichū*, another poem-tale. The people who appear in the legends and folktales that make up the second part of *Tales of Yamato* are distinctly more memorable than the courtiers of the first part, but many of them would be treated even more effectively in the tale literature (*setsuwa bungaku*) of later times.

Tales of Heichū

Heichū Monogatari (Tales of Heichū) seems to have been completed between 960 and 965, but there is reason to believe that much of the work existed during the lifetime of Taira no Sadafun, and it is possible that he himself was the author.[82] It contains only thirty-nine episodes, a third as many as *Tales of Ise*, but they are longer, making the whole about three quarters the length. The greater amplitude of the stories again and again arouses hopes that something memorable is about to happen, but each time the reader is sadly let down by the ordinariness of the narration and the feebleness of the conclusions. Perhaps that is why *Tales of Heichū* was all but unknown when the unique manuscript was discovered in 1931.

Very little is known about the historical Taira no Sadafun, not even why he was known by the nickname of Heichū (the Taira middle general),[83] though it has been suggested that it was by way of parallel to Zaichū (the Ariwara middle general), a name by which Narihira was known. Sadafun, however, never rose to a position as exalted as middle general. His father, Taira no Yoshikaze, was a middle general, and was also known for his romantic exploits; it has therefore been suggested that the careers of father and son were confused. Sadafun's career as an official was in fact so undistinguished that he is not even mentioned in the historical records of the time, though nine of his waka were included in the *Kokinshū*, and the poem competitions (uta-awase) held at his house were attended by outstanding poets of the day. He was widely known as a great lover, but before long this reputation was supplanted by the caricature portrait of Heichū as a comically inept suitor. He does not appear in this guise in *Tales of Heichū*, but this work might easily have given him such a reputation: he is unsuccessful three times as often as successful in his love affairs.

Tales of Heichū, in the poem-tale tradition, contains 153 poems, 99 of them attributed to Sadafun. The quality of these poems is not high. Probably they were the poems actually composed extemporaneously on the occasions described, rather than the much-polished products that found their way into anthologies. The everyday nature of these poems provides us with glimpses of court life not found in *Tales of Ise* or *The Tale of Genji*. Of course, we are aware, even as we read *Tales of Ise*, that it is improbable that such splendid waka could have been composed impromptu, but only on reading *Tales of Heichū* do we realize just how great the difference was between the first versons of poems composed at the court and the versions that brought the authors fame.

The traditions of the poem-tale were intimately connected with the pursuit of love affairs. The poems given in the course of these works are almost all of courtship, together with the ladies' responses. Heichū was an appropriate choice as the hero of a poem-tale, but he is far less attractive a lover than Narihira. We never feel we get inside his thoughts or emotions, and the women he pursues are equally characterless.

Episode 25 is perhaps the most disappointing because it promises at first to be of real interest. A woman, a friend of some court ladies who accidentally met Heichū on a journey, recognizes him from their description as the former lover who abandoned her, and she warns the other ladies not to trust him. For a moment we may imagine that she will prove to be a Donna Elvira who denounces her Don Giovanni even though in her heart she still loves him. But this Donna Elvira is so effective in her denunciation of her faithless lover that the other ladies, after a few exchanges of poems, contrive to elude him completely. The episode concludes lamely, "I wonder what happened afterwards [*ikaga nariniken*]?"[84]

Apart from the fleeting character glimpse, the episode is noteworthy for its details. We are told, for example, that when the ladies in their carriages proceeded down the main avenue of the capital, Heichū followed on horseback, singing to the tune of a popular song a poem composed by one of the ladies. It is hard to imagine Genji on a horse, and impossible to imagine him bawling out a popular song. The poems composed jointly by Heichū and the ladies on this occasion are also intriguing:

aki no yo no	Insubstantial
yume wa hakanaku	As dreams of an autumn night,
au to iu wo	The meeting we shared.

When the ladies said this, the man replied,

haru ni kaerite	When the spring returns again,
masashikaruran[85]	Perhaps the dream will come true.

The conventional gallantry behind this early instance of linked verse is closer to the compliments exchanged by European courtiers and their ladies than to the world portrayed in *The Tale of Genji*. In this sense the inartistry of *Tales of Heichū* gives the work greater verisimilitude than the perfect beauty of the court described by Murasaki Shikibu.

The Tale of Takamura

The most affecting of the poem-tales is *Takamura Monogatari* (The Tale of Takamura). Unlike the poem-tales considered above, it tells essentially a single story and does not break down into episodes. This is probably why some manuscripts call it *The Takamura Diary*, though it is a diary only in the sense that it relates in chronological order the events of a man's life. The man in question was the distinguished scholar Ono no Takamura, famed especially as a kanshi poet. *The Tale of Takamura* consists of two parts, the first describing the unhappy love affair of Takamura and his half-sister, the second (separated from the first by an awkward break in the manuscript) concerns Takamura's happy marriage, after the death of his half-sister, to the daughter of the minister of the Right. The two parts were probably composed by different people, perhaps a century apart; the first part dates from the tenth century, the second as late as the thirteenth century. Dating is difficult because the work was written throughout in a stylized literary language that provides almost no clues to the period of composition. There are not even the titles of officials or names of buildings that often provide clues to the period of a work. The author (or authors) is unknown.

The justification for calling *The Tale of Takamura* a poem-tale is the large number of waka it contains. These poems serve as the principal vehicles for the sentiments of the characters. It has long been doubted that Takamura wrote the waka attributed to him in the work, but nine of them were later included in imperial collections, beginning with the *Shin Kokinshū*, and attributions in these collections were not made irresponsibly. Perhaps the poems were originally contained in a private collection of Takamura's waka, but if such a collection existed it has been lost.

Despite all the problems concerning the text and the unsatisfactory fusion of the two parts, the story is unusually moving and the poems, if not of first quality, fit perfectly into the narration. The work opens,

> There was once a girl whose parents had lavished every care on her education. When she had mastered all the accomplishments expected of a young lady, her parents decided that the next step was to teach her the Chinese classics. "It would be best," they thought, "if we could find someone close to our family as her teacher." They finally settled on the girl's half-brother, a student at the university.[86]

It was unusual, in view of the title, for the author to have opened the work with a description of the half-sister, rather than of Takamura, who is sent for by the girl's parents (though neither Narihira nor Heichū would have waited for an invitation). The girl was not eager to have lessons from her half-brother, whom she scarcely knew, but her parents persuaded her by asking, when she showed signs of resisting their decision, "Wouldn't he be better than a total stranger?"

The two fall in love without realizing it. At first the girl is protected from Takamura's gaze not only by the usual reed blinds but by curtains. One day, however, she inadvertently allows him to catch a glimpse of her face and she also sees his. The text informs us, "They could not long remain distant in a world where everything conspired to bring them together." They exchange poems and he scribbles notes to her during her Chinese lessons.

Had the girl's parents not considered her to be quite remarkable, they would not have arranged for Chinese lessons, and the rare court lady who learned to read Chinese normally did not have the benefit of a private tutor. The parents presumably chose Takamura because of his reputation as a brilliant student. They may also have supposed that Takamura would not make advances to his half-sister.

Marriages between children of the same father but different mothers were tolerated at the Heian court. *The Tale of the Hollow Tree* even describes a man who is so passionately eager to marry his full sister that he pines away and dies when he is refused. The fury of the girl's mother in *The Tale of Takamura* when she suspects that her daughter may be having an affair with her tutor is occasioned by indignation that advantage has been taken of her precious daughter, but also by annoyance that the daughter, who has been given the best possible education in the hope that she might be chosen as a maid of honor (*naiji*) at the court, is about to make an unworthy match. Takamura is portrayed as a penniless student, not the kind of person who usually appears in a poem-tale.[87] The girl also has a distinct personality and is not a mere stereotype like most of the court ladies in *Tales of Ise* and other early fiction.

A revealing passage occurs not long after the girl's return from a visit with Takamura and some attendants to the Inari Shrine, where she had caught the attention of a handsome young officer who later sent her several notes, most of which Takamura managed to intercept. The girl was surprised when the officer, who had started the correspondence with great ardor, suddenly stopped writing. One day the jealous Takamura confronted the girl:

> "I gather you've been corresponding with a perfect stranger you merely happened to pass on the street and now you've fallen in love with him. It's true, isn't it? I suppose he'd like to marry you, the quicker the better. Oughtn't you to consult a matchmaker? But don't forget, you can't get married without your parents' consent."
>
> The girl replied, "Why should I want to marry him? And what exactly have you found out that makes you ask so many questions?"
>
> Takamura countered, "Someone who knows as little about love as you do should refrain from making such remarks. You seem to

have no conception of what is involved. You worry me. I should never have expected anything like this."[88]

The sarcasm of Takamura and the swiftness of the girl's rejoinder are unlike anything in the earlier poem-tales. The seeming harshness of Takamura's rebuke is a first indication of his love, which he soon declares more overtly. But, we are told, even after he and the girl confessed their love to each other, they could not speak freely for fear of what her parents might think. One night, unable to endure being alone, Takamura secretly made his way to the place where his half-sister was sleeping. From then on he occasionally visited her quarters, though this was exceedingly difficult. "Seeing each other constantly by day, though only rarely at night, was more unsettling for Takamura than if they had never met at all, and he wondered dejectedly what remedy he could obtain for his grief."[89]

Not long afterward the girl discovered she was pregnant. She was no longer in a mood to study Chinese, and her maids, noticing that she had missed her periods, were soon gossiping. Takamura, not realizing the cause of her lassitude during lessons, ascribed it to the spring weather. The girl refused all usual food and asked for nothing but oranges and other citrus fruit. Her innocent parents ordered the fruit, and when Takamura gave a dinner for friends at the university, he set aside two or three pieces of fruit for her, wrapping them in paper he carried in his kimono. He offered the fruit to his half-sister with this poem:

ada ni chiru	Finer than the scent
hanatachibana no	When orange blossom petals
nioi ni wa	Idly flutter down,
midori no kinu no	The perfume emanating
ka koso masarame	From my silken robe of green.

"I thought you might like this fruit," he said. The girl replied, "Because it lay next to your chest,"

nitari to ya	I wondered as I sniffed
hanatachibana wo	The flowering citrus fruits
kagitsureba	If they resembled you;
midori no ka sae	But I could not detect
utsurazarikeri[90]	Even the scent of the green.

The green of Takamura's robe associated it with the fruit he gave his half-sister. It also indicated the humbleness of his rank: it was prescribed in the legal code *Ryō no Gige* that officers of the sixth rank wear dark green and those of the seventh rank wear light green robes.

The girl's mother happened to overhear these poems (which were recited aloud) and for the first time her suspicions were aroused. While Takamura was giving his lessons the mother entered, took the girl by the hand, and dragged her off to her room. She ordered the servants never to allow "that gentleman from the university" to set foot in the house again and, to make sure that Takamura would not get even a furtive glimpse of his half-sister, she had the keyhole of the girl's room filled in with plaster.

It was impossible for the lovers to meet, but Takamura one night discovered a crack in the wall of the girl's room through which they could talk until dawn. The girl, in despair, refused all nourishment and a few days later she died. That night Takamura lay weeping in his room, lit only by a dim candle, when he sensed something stirring nearby. It was an apparition that spoke with his half-sister's voice, telling of her griefs. The apparition disappeared at dawn, but for twenty-one nights it returned. Afterward, it appeared only occasionally and its form became indistinct. When three years had passed Takamura no longer saw his half-sister even in dreams.

The first part of the tale concludes with the statement "He did not marry but remained single."[91] The second part opens without transition: "He composed a clever poem in Chinese asking for the hand of a daughter of the minister of the Right." Soon afterward, he is described as he appeared before the minister, dressed in a tattered gray gown and carrying a battered old set of books. He wins the minister's daughter, but is unable to forget his half-sister. One night he goes to the house where she had lived and sleeps there; she appears in his dream and recites this poem:

mishi hito ni	Is that really the man
sore ka aranu ka	I used to know long ago?
obotsukana	I cannot be sure.
mono wasureji to	How certain I was that he
omoishi mono wo[92]	Would never forget the past!

Takamura was so much moved by this experience that he did not return to his new wife for some days. When he reappeared, she asked what had happened, and he told her the whole story. She was not only sympathetic but expressed fear that she could never replace the woman he had lost. The tale concludes with a brief account of Takamura's subsequent career and the successes of his descendants. The last words are: "Can we imagine a prime minister today choosing a university student for his son-in-law? The difference must be that university students nowadays are by no means the equal of their predecessors in mind, appearance, or ability. And surely there will never be another man like Takamura who, when he wished to marry a minister's daughter, addressed her a poem in Chinese."[93]

The Tale of Takamura is the first Japanese work of fiction that can be said to be "modern" in that it engages the attention of modern readers without requiring any concession for its time.[94]

Looking backward, we may get the impression that each of the early Heian works of fiction contributed to the creation of *The Tale of Genji*. *The Tale of the Hollow Tree* may have suggested to Murasaki Shikibu the possibility of writing an extended work of fiction; *The Tale of Ochikubo*, the importance of a unified plot; *Tales of Ise*, the manner of incorporating poems, as events of daily life, in the narration of a story; and *The Tale of Takamura*, the grown-up nature of the conversations. This by no means explains everything in the formative process of *The Tale of Genji*—the diaries probably contributed even more—but helps to make intelligible the creation of the great masterpiece of Japanese literature.

Notes

1. *Man'yōshū* VII: 1287. See Aoki Takako et al., *Man'yōshū*, II, p. 243.
2. Mitani Eiichi, *Monogatari Bungaku no Sekai*, pp. 4–5. Neither the legends of the *Kojiki* nor the edifying Buddhist stories contained in *Account of Miracles in Japan* were known as monogatari. Perhaps because of their close association with Shintō or Buddhist priests, these tales were not transmitted by ordinary storytellers though they included materials drawn from the oral folklore of Asia as well as from written Chinese and Indian sources.
3. My complete translation of this work is included in J. Thomas Rimer, *Modern Japanese Fiction and Its Traditions*, pp. 275–305.
4. Katagiri Yōichi et al., *Taketori Monogatari*, p. 320. The passage occurs in section 77. See also the translation by Mildred Tahara in *Tales of Yamato*, p. 44, and her explanation of this poem on pp. 224–25.
5. See Sakakura Atsuyoshi et al., *Taketori Monogatari, Ise Monogatari, Yamato Monogatari*, p. 267.
6. Mitani Kuniaki, *Monogatari Bungaku no Hōhō*, I, p. 212, expressed his belief

that the work was written between "the end of Jōgan and the fifth year of Gangyō." The Jōgan era ended in 876 and the fifth year of Gangyō was 881. I have given 871 (ten years before 881) because on p. 213 he also states that "it is inconceivable that it could have been composed except during the period of ten years between the end of Jōgan and the fifth year of Gangyō."

7. Itō Seiji, *Kaguya-hime no Tanjō*, pp. 85–88, summarizes the major theories. Mitani Eiichi (*Monogatari*, pp. 42–46) presents at length the theory of Mitani Kuniaki, first advanced in 1969, that the author was Ki no Haseo; but Mitani Kuniaki himself, in his more recent *Monogatari*, does not identify the author.
8. Mitani Eiichi expressed (*Monogatari*, p. 36) his conviction that one man had written the work, but Itō declared (*Kaguya-hime*, p. 11) that *The Tale of the Bamboo Cutter* was not the work of a single author writing at a particular time but the product of revisions by many hands over the years.
9. The original language has been much discussed ever since Kanō Morohira (1806–1857) offered the theory that it was composed about 700 in kambun, as is evidenced by the use in the text of the names of members of the court of that time. Kanō also theorized that the intent of *The Tale of the Bamboo Cutter* was satiric, and for this reason it was originally kept a secret. About a century later, someone uncovered the manuscript and rewrote it in the form of a picture book. Finally, Kanō suggested, the work was translated from Chinese into Japanese. See *Nihon Koten Bungaku Daijiten*, IV, p. 151, for a summary of *Taketori Monogatari-kō* by Kanō Morohira. Kanō's thesis that the work must have been composed about 700 is no longer accepted, but some scholars admit the possibility that it was originally composed either in kambun or else in a mixture of kambun and Japanese like the *Kojiki*. Scholars who believe *The Tale of the Bamboo Cutter* was written before the kana preface to the *Kokinshū* generally agree that it must have been written in kambun; otherwise, it is unlikely that a first attempt at writing kana prose would be so successful. (Itō, *Kaguya-hime*, p. 91, quotes Takeda Yūkichi to this effect.) The use in the text of close to one hundred words of Chinese origin and the Chinese style of the numbers lend credibility to this theory. But not all scholars agree: one authority, admitting that some Japanese legends (such as the tale of the fisherman Urashima Tarō) were first recorded in kambun during the ninth century, insisted that no Japanese of the time was capable of writing in kambun a work of the length of *The Tale of the Bamboo Cutter*. He believed that the hundred or so words of Chinese origin had already entered the speech not only of the author but also of his expected readers (Noguchi Motohiro, *Taketori Monogatari*, pp. 177–78). This implies that the author was an intellectual, writing for other intellectuals, and not a purveyor of tales for women and children who could read only kana. (Noguchi, *Taketori*, pp. 170–73.) Parts of the work, notably the waka and the word-play, could not have been

conceived of except in Japanese, but unless kana had come into general use earlier than the last decades of the ninth century or, alternatively, *The Tale of the Bamboo Cutter* was composed later than now supposed, the work must originally have been written entirely in Chinese characters.

10. Translation by Edward Seidensticker in *The Tale of Genji*, I, p. 311.
11. For an account of this work, see pp. 183–85.
12. Or perhaps a pool of light, depending on how the word *kage* is interpreted.
13. In making my translation of the work I followed the Kohon version because I thought it makes the best sense, but most commentators prefer the oldest datable text, known as the Mutō text. According to the Mutō version, the mountain is called Fuji because a large party of soldiers (*shi*) climbed it, making it rich (*fu*) in soldiers.
14. The most striking of the parallels is with a Tibetan folktale, first recorded by a Chinese scholar in 1954 and introduced to the Japanese reading public in a book published in 1971. The text is given by Noguchi in *Taketori*, pp. 201–20, in a Chinese rendering of the original Tibetan, together with a Japanese translation.

The parallel Tibetan tale opens with the discovery of a tiny little girl inside a bamboo stalk, though in this case the discoverer is a young man rather than an old bamboo cutter. When the girl is fully grown, a process that requires considerably more time than in the Japanese version, the young man's mother urges Bamboo Girl (as she is known) to marry the young man, but the girl begs for three years in which to make a decision. In the meantime, five other young men, all of well-to-do families but lazy and without talent, happen to get a glimpse of Bamboo Girl while they are enjoying an excursion. Each of the five men falls desperately in love with Bamboo Girl.

Unfortunately for the girl, her fiancé has gone off to visit relatives, and she has no one to help her fend off the young men's importunate requests for marriage. She sets tasks for each of them, giving them three years in which to prove their worth by bringing her what she has asked for. The tasks assigned by Bamboo Girl are not exactly the same as those imposed by Kaguya-hime, but they are strikingly similar and in two cases identical. The five suitors naturally fail in their assignments, and at the end Bamboo Girl marries the young man who first found her.

The "birth" of the girl in a bamboo stalk and the similarities in the tasks she sets the suitors created a sensation when the Tibetan text was published in Japan. Many scholars unhesitantly accepted the evidence that the oldest Japanese tale had originated on the border between Tibet and China; but the lack of a similar tale elsewhere in China, and the excessively close resemblances between a Japanese text of the ninth century and a Tibetan folktale narrated over one thousand years later suggested to others that some Japanese—perhaps one of the military who infiltrated the area during the 1920s—had passed the story on to the Tibetans. See the article

"Taketori Monogatari" by Mitani Eiichi in *Nihon Koten Bungaku Daijiten*, IV, p. 149. Doubts about the authenticity of the Tibetan tale were also voiced by Katagiri Yōichi in "Taketori Monogatari wa Chūgoku-dane ka." Other doubts about the direct influence of foreign folktales on *The Tale of the Bamboo Cutter* were expressed by Shinoda Kōichirō in *Taketori Monogatari to Ukigumo*, pp. 20–21, 43–44. Shinoda's main point was that, unlike written texts that are intentionally modified when copied, folktales are subject to constant, unintentional changes. Different versions of essentially the same story are found in unrelated parts of the world, and it is impossible to trace the direction in which influences may have gone.

15. Some are identical with those in official records, others were matched with difficulty to historical names.
16. Mitani Eiichi, *Monogatari*, p. 37. Mitani Kuniaki (*Monogatari*, I, pp. 216ff) also called attention to the identity of the five suitors with men who had distinguished themselves during the Jinshin War of 672. He considered *The Tale of the Bamboo Cutter* to be an "allegory" directed against extravagance at the court, and cited (pp. 214–15) the petition against extravagance made by the scholar-statesman Miyoshi Kiyotsura (847–918) as evidence of the prevalence of luxurious habits at the court.
17. See Mitani Eiichi, *Monogatari*, p. 37, and Imai Takuji, *Monogatari Bungaku Shi no Kenkyū*, p. 224, who characterized the author as someone "fiercely critical" of the upper-class aristocrats in the work. Tanaka Gen, *Taketori, Ise Monogatari no Sekai*, pp. 174–81, discussed the ridicule to which the aristocrats were subjected.
18. The Bamboo Cutter says this to the celestial horde who have come for Kaguya-hime, but the story itself does not suggest so long a period of time.
19. Shinoda, *Taketori*, p. 65.
20. Mitani Eiichi, *Monogatari*, pp. 22–23. Also Itō, *Kaguya-hime*, p. 196.
21. See Tanaka, *Taketori*, for summaries of the main theories.
22. The former theory is associated with Tsuda Sōkichi, the latter with Watsuji Tetsurō, both eminent historians. See Tanaka, *Taketori*, pp. 153–58.
23. Yanagita Kunio, "Taketori no Okina," in *Teihon Yanagita Kunio Zenshū*, VI, pp. 173–74.

D. E. Mills, "*Soga Monogatari*, *Shintōshū* and the Taketori Legend," is a study of parallel accounts of the Taketori legend. The oldest considered, the *manabon* of *Soga Monogatari* (The Tale of the Soga Brothers), contains the story of the old couple who find a little girl in the bamboo of their garden and rear her. She later becomes the wife of a provincial governor, but after five years of life with him reveals that she has come to earth from the Immortal's Abode on Mount Fuji and must return there. The suitors do not appear in this prosaic version of the tale (translated by Mills, in "*Soga*," pp. 38–40). The version in the fourteenth-century *Shintōshū* (Mills, pp. 40–42) is very similar. The emphasis in both accounts is on Kaguya-hime's return to Mount Fuji, mentioned only incidentally in *The Tale of the Bamboo Cutter*, an indication perhaps that the story was used as a *honjimono* (a story that tells the history of a shrine) for the Sengen Shrine on Fuji.

Mills gives various later versions of the story of Kaguya-hime, some of them associated with particular shrines, and on pp. 66–67 he presents in the form of a chart the main themes found in sixteen texts, showing which themes appear in which works. He is inclined to believe that the account of Kaguya-hime in *Kaidōki* (Journey Along the Seacoast Road) was not derived directly from *The Tale of the Bamboo Cutter* because Kaguya-hime is described as having been born from the egg of an uguisu. But the text of *The Tale of the Bamboo Cutter* was widely disseminated, and it is hard to imagine that the author of *Journey Along the Seacoast Road* was ignorant of its existence.

24. Sakakura et al., *Taketori*, pp. 14–18. Sakakura believed that the additions to the basic tale were in a style associated with translations from the Chinese that the author (as an intellectual) would have found most congenial. In this style *-keri* is not used for this purpose.
25. Shinoda, *Taketori*, p. 97.
26. In support of the theory that the author was male, it has been claimed that the work reveals a fairly detailed knowledge of Buddhism and familiarity with the inner workings of court society. See Imai, *Monogatari*, p. 224.
27. See Donald Keene, *Travelers of a Hundred Ages*, p. 119.
28. Noguchi, *Taketori*, p. 147, made this distinction between monogatari and other forms of fiction such as the setsuwa or shōsetsu.
29. Tanaka, *Taketori*, p. 201.
30. The original pronunciation was more like Utsuho, and for centuries (until the late Tokugawa period) it was known as Utsuo. Utsubo is, however, normally used today.
31. Fujikawa Fumiko, *A Study of the Dates and Authorship of the Tale of the Hollow Tree*, pp. 468–69. These pages give the author's conclusions, after over four hundred pages of detailed consideration of earlier theories and available evidence. Konishi Jin'ichi in "Utsubo Monogatari no Kōsei to Seiritsu Katei," pp. 91–92, suggested a time lapse of twenty to thirty years between the first and second halves of the work, the first half having been written during the reign of the Emperor En'yū; however, he believed that the last chapter was written still later. Kōno Tama (in *Utsubo Monogatari*, III, p. 39) suggested earlier dates, 952 to 965.
32. See Fujikawa, *A Study*, pp. 467–74, for her presentation of the evidence both for and against the attribution of authorship to Minamoto no Shitagō. Konishi, "Utsubo," p. 85, expressed his belief that the work was written by one man over a considerable period of time. Noguchi Motohiro in *Kodai Monogatari no Kōzō*, p. 301, stated, "Minamoto no Shitagō has long been suggested as the author of the tale, and in recent times this possibility has been increasingly stressed. Some critics still hesitate to attribute the work

to a single person, Shitagō, but no one seems to deny that the work was written for his own amusement by a Confucianist who had consecrated his life to the art of letters."

33. See Konishi, "Utsubo," p. 93.
34. See Kōno, *Utsubo*, I, p. 5, for a comparison of texts. Most scholars, noting references within this chapter to persons and events not previously described, believe that the chapter "Fuji no Kimi" should precede "Tadakoso." See Konishi, "Utsubo," pp. 79–80.
35. There is a translation of this section of the work by Edwin A. Cranston entitled, "Atemiya: A Translation from the *Utsubo monogatari*."
36. Kōno, *Utsubo*, II, p. 86.
37. *Ibid.*, I, p. 451, denies that Hashi could have been used in its normal meaning of Persia because the work seems to situate it between India and China.
38. *Ibid.*, p. 42. The "seven mountains" are not identified by Kōno. In some manuscripts the word "seven" does not appear, suggesting that the author had no particular mountains in mind.
39. *Ibid.*, p. 51.
40. *Ibid.*, III, p. 519.
41. See Konishi, "Utsubo," especially pp. 65–68 and 82–83.
42. Inaga Keiji, writing in 1977, suggested that Shitagō wrote the first three books and Sei Shōnagon the fourth (Inaga Keiji, *Ochikubo Monogatari*, p. 319).
43. Wilfrid Whitehouse, *The Tale of the Lady Ochikubo*, p. 261. His translation was first published in 1934.
44. See, for example, Mitani Eiichi and Inaga Keiji, *Ochikubo Monogatari*, pp. 19–20.
45. *Origuchi Shinobu Zenshū*, XII, p. 245.
46. For a study of the theme of the stepmother who unsuccessfully attempts to seduce her stepson, see my article "The Hippolytus Triangle."
47. For a description of the Kamakura period version of the same tale, see below, pp. 814–17.
48. Ikeda Yasaburō, *Bungaku to Minzokugaku*, pp. 52, 114.
49. Fukui Teisuke, "Kaisetsu," in Katagiri Yōichi et al., *Taketori Monogatari*, p. 118.
50. Sakakura Atsuyoshi published in 1953 a study of uses of the particle *nan* called "Utamonogatari no Bunshō—nan no kakarimusubi wo megutte," in which he contrasted the frequent use of *nan* in the poem-tales, as an integral part of the narration, with the absence of this particle from the prefaces. He concluded, "The prose style of the poem-tales could not have been created directly from that found in the kotobagaki, regardless of whether one believes it developed more or less directly from the existing model or was to some degree elaborated." (Quoted by Masuda Katsumi in *Setsuwa Bungaku to Emaki*, p. 119.) Katagiri Yōichi, approaching the question from a different angle, demonstrated that the first version of *Tales of*

Ise antedated the compilation of the *Kokinshū*, and that borrowing must have gone in the opposite direction. (Katagiri Yōichi, *Ise Monogatari*, *Yamato Monogatari*, p. 15.) He conceded, however, that some second-stage or third-stage material in *Tales of Ise* was probably borrowed from the *Kokinshū*.

51. The word occurs in the "Sakaki" (Sacred Tree) chapter of *The Tale of Genji*, though in this instance only two persons—Genji and his father, the old emperor—participate in the utagatari.
52. Katagiri, *Ise*, p. 9.
53. The standard text (in the hand of Fujiware Teika) has 125 episodes, but other texts have as many as 143.
54. Katagiri Yōichi declared he did not believe *anyone* still supposed that there was a single author and time of composition. See his "Ise Monogatari no Hōhō," p. 14.
55. See Tanaka, *Taketori*, p. 276. Also, Kawaguchi Hisao, *Hana no Utage*, pp. 2–20, for a discussion of miyabi, especially in reference to Genji.
56. In time the words *mukashi otoko* were run together to form the noun *mukashiotoko*, meaning "a man of long ago," referring (as in the Nō play *Izutsu*) specifically to Narihira.
57. Fukui, "Kaisetsu," p. 115. Katagiri (in *Ise* pp. 15–23) distinguished three stages in the composition of the work. The first stage was based directly on Narihira's poems though the background events do not necessarily conform to the facts of his life. The second stage contains many poems that were probably not by Narihira, and the proportion of fiction to fact is higher. In the third stage the writer, standing at some remove from Narihira, mentions him by name (instead of referring to him merely as "the man") and treats him as a legendary figure of the past rather than as a particular person who wrote certain poems. Katagiri cites many incidents in the text that confirm his division into three stages.
58. For a discussion in English of the different texts of *Tales of Ise*, see Helen Craig McCullough, *Tales of Ise*, pp. 187–93. Her translation includes not only the 125 episodes of Teika's text but an additional 18 episodes culled from other sources.
59. McCullough, *Tales*, pp. 183–84. Also Fukui, "Kaisetsu," pp. 121–22.
60. See Katagiri, *Ise*, pp. 10–11, and Fukui, "Kaisetsu," pp. 115–17, for other explanations of the name. The most fanciful was the theory that *i* meant "woman," and *se* meant "man," and that the title revealed the amatory nature of the work. Katagiri felt sure that a text of *Tales of Ise* headed by episode 69 existed in the late Heian period. See Katagiri, *Ise*, p. 26.
61. I have followed the text given by Katagiri in *Ise*, p. 183, but other texts give *kage* (shadow) rather than *take* (bamboo) in the second line. The meaning—that the family will in the future depend on the newborn babe for "shelter"—is much the same.
62. See Katagiri, *Ise*, p. 184.
63. Watanabe Minoru, *Ise Monogatari*, p. 94. For a general discussion of the

appended remarks, see Yamada Seiichi, "Ise Monogatari no Kōsei Ishiki ni okeru Mondai," pp. 92ff.

64. Text in Katagiri, *Taketori*, pp. 140–41. See also McCullough, *Tales*, pp. 74–75. The acrostic poem in this section is discussed above, p. 230.
65. Karaki Junzō. *Muyōmono no Keifu*, pp. 16–20.
66. Tsunoda Bun'ei, "Narihira no Azuma-kudari," p. 37. See also Katagiri Yōichi, *Ise Monogatari no Shinkenkyū*, pp. 44–51, for equally ludicrous examples of medieval commentaries on the work.
67. Tsunoda, "Narihira," p. 38.
68. *Ibid.*, p. 41.
69. *Ibid.*, pp. 43–46.
70. See Katagiri, *Ise*, pp. 168–69, for this theory, first advanced by Mekada Sakuo. The story in question was contained in *Huai-chen-chi*, known in English as "The Story of Ying-ying."
71. Katagiri, *Taketori*, p. 97.
72. Katagiri, *Ise*, p. 238. The most recent datable event occurred in 951.
73. *Ibid.*, p. 247.
74. This is the suggestion of Yamazaki Masanobu, presented in Amagai Hiroyoshi et al., *Yamato Monogatari no Hitobito*, pp. 141–60.
75. For a translation, see Tahara, *Tales*, pp. 93–98.
76. Episode 147 is the source of the Nō play *Motomezuka*, one of the most somber of the entire repertory.
77. Translation from Tahara, *Tales*, p. 26. Text in Katagiri, *Taketori*, pp. 298–99. See also Katagiri, *Ise*, pp. 285–90.
78. For this preface (and a different translation of the poem) see above, p. 283.
79. This is the opinion expressed by Katagiri in *Ise*, p. 290.
80. See, for example, the theories of Suzuki Kayoko in Amagai et al., *Yamato*, pp. 7–26.
81. The pronunciations of these names are so uncertain that scholars today usually refer to these ladies by the Sino-Japanese readings of their names; Toshiko's name, however, is given in kana.
82. Mekada Sakuo, *Heichū Monogatari*, p. 230, advanced this theory and suggested that the work can be read both as a diary and as a collection of poetry.

    For detailed information about Sadafun in English, see Susan Downing Videen, *Tales of Heichū*, pp. 8–11.
83. Videen (*Tales*, p. 9) states that there is no evidence that Sadafun ever used the name Heichū during his lifetime.
84. The episode is translated by Videen in *Tales*, pp. 61–66.
85. Text in Endō Yoshimoto and Matsuo Satoshi, *Takamura Monogatari*, p. 84. Another translation in Videen, *Tales*, p. 65.
86. Text in Endō and Matsuo, *Takamura*, p. 25.
87. It has been suggested that the student Tōei in *The Tale of the Hollow Tree* was the model for Takamura. See Tsumoto Nobuhiro, "Takamura Mo-

nogatari no Seiritsu wo megutte," in Ishihara Shōhei et al., *Takamura Monogatari Shinkō*, pp. 132–36.

88. Text in Endō and Matsuo, *Takamura*, p. 30. I have, however, accepted some of the interpretations by Ishihara et al. in *Takamura*, pp. 40–44. For another translation, see Ward Geddes, "*Takamura Monogatari*," p. 285.
89. Endō and Matsuo, *Takamura*, p. 31.
90. *Ibid.*, p. 32. See also Ishihara et al., *Takamura*, pp. 49–52.
91. Endō and Matsuo, *Takamura*, p. 35.
92. *Ibid.*, p. 36.
93. *Ibid.*, p. 37.
94. Tanizaki Jun'ichirō, after retelling the story of *The Tale of Takamura* in "Ono no Takamura Imoto ni koi suru koto" (1950), expressed his regret that he had not turned the material into a novel of his own. See *Tanizaki Jun'ichirō Zenshū*, XVI, p. 459. Not long before (1949–50) he had written *Shōshō Shigemoto no Haha*, a novel set in the Heian period in which Heichū appears.

Bibliography

Note: All Japanese books, except as otherwise noted, were published in Tokyo.

Akiyama Ken (ed.). *Ōchō Bungaku Shi*. Tōkyō Daigaku Shuppankai, 1984.

Amagai Hiroyoshi, Yamazaki Masanobu, and Suzuki Kayoko. *Yamato Monogatari no Hitobito*. Kasama Shoin, 1979.

Aoki Takako et al. *Man'yōshū*, II, in Shinchō Nihon Koten Shūsei series. Shinchōsha, 1977.

Cranston, Edwin A. "Atemiya: A Translation from the *Utsubo monogatari*," *Monumenta Nipponica*, 24:3, 1969.

Endō Yoshimoto and Matsuo Satoshi. *Takamura Monogatari*, *Heichū Monogatari*, *Hamamatsu Chūnagon Monogatari*, in Nihon Koten Bungaku Taikei series. Iwanami Shoten, 1964.

Fujikawa, Fumiko M.C. *A Study of the Dates and Authorship of the Tale of the Hollow Tree*. Hamburg: Gesellschaft für Natur- und Völkerkunde Ostasiens, 1977.

Fukui Teisuke. "Kaisetsu," in Katagiri Yōichi et al., *Taketori Monogatari*, *Ise Monogatari*, *Yamato Monogatari*, *Heichū Monogatari*.

Geddes, Ward. "*Takamura Monogatari*," *Monumenta Nipponica* 46:3, 1991.

Hakeda, Yoshito S. *Kūkai*: *Major Works*. New York: Columbia University Press, 1972.

Heian-chō Monogatari, 3 vols. in Nihon Bungaku Kenkyū Shiryō Sōsho series. Yūseidō, 1970–79.

Ikeda Yasaburō. *Bungaku to Minzokugaku*. Iwasaki Shoten, 1956.

Imai Takuji. *Monogatari Bungaku Shi no Kenkyū*. Waseda Daigaku Shuppanbu, 1977.

Inaga Keiji. *Ochikubo Monogatari*, in Shinchō Nihon Koten Shūsei series. Shinchōsha, 1977.

Ishihara Shōhei, Nemoto Keizō, and Tsumoto Nobuhiro. *Takamura Monogatari Shinkō*. Musashino Shoin, 1977.

Issatsu no Kōza: Ise Monogatari. Yūseidō, 1983.

Itō Seiji. *Kaguya-hime no Tanjō*. Kōdansha, 1973.

Karaki Junzō. *Muyōmono no Keifu*. Chikuma Shobō, 1964.

Katagiri Yōichi. "Ise Monogatari no Hōhō," in *Issatsu no Kōza: Ise Monogatari*.

———. *Ise Monogatari no Shinkenkyū*. Meiji Shoin, 1987.

———. *Ise Monogatari, Yamato Monogatari*, in Kanshō Nihon Koten Bungaku series. Kadokawa Shoten, 1975.

———. "Taketori Monogatari wa Chūgoku-dane ka," *Kokubungaku* 22:11, 1977.

Katagiri Yōichi, Fukui Teisuke, Takahashi Seiji, and Shimizu Yoshiko. *Taketori Monogatari*, *Ise Monogatari*, *Yamato Monogatari*, *Heichū Monogatari*, in Nihon Koten Bungaku Zenshū series. Shōgakukan, 1972.

Kawaguchi Hisao. *Hana no Utage*. Yoshikawa Kōbunkan, 1980.

Keene, Donald. "The Hippolytus Triangle, East and West," in *Yearbook of Comparative and General Literature*, XI, 1962.

———. *Travelers of a Hundred Ages*. New York: Henry Holt, 1989.

Konishi Jin'ichi. "Utsubo Monogatari no Kōsei to Seiritsu Katei," in *Heianchō Monogatari*, II.

Kōno Tama. *Utsubo Monogatari*, 3 vols., in Nihon Koten Bungaku Taikei series. Iwanami Shoten, 1959–62.

Masuda Katsumi. *Setsuwa Bungaku to Emaki*. San'ichi Shobō, 1980.

McCullough, Helen Craig. *Tales of Ise*. Stanford, Calif.: Stanford University Press, 1968.

Mekada Sakuo. *Heichū Monogatari*, in Kōdansha Gakujutsu Bunko series. Kōdansha, 1979.

Mills, D. E. "*Soga Monogatari*, *Shintōshū* and the Taketori Legend," *Monumenta Nipponica* 30:1, 1975.

Mitani Eiichi. *Monogatari Bungaku no Sekai*. Yūseidō, 1978.

Mitani Eiichi and Inaga Keiji. *Ochikubo Monogatari*, *Tsutsumi Chūnagon Monogatari*, in Nihon Koten Bungaku Zenshū series. Shōgakukan, 1972.

Mitani Kuniaki. *Monogatari Bungaku no Hōhō*, 2 vols. Yūseidō, 1989

Nihon Koten Bungaku Daijiten, 6 vols. Iwanami Shoten, 1983–85.

Noguchi Motohiro. *Kodai Monogatari no Kōzō*. Yūseidō, 1969.

———. *Taketori Monogatari*, in Shinchō Nihon Koten Shūsei series. Shinchōsha, 1979.

Origuchi Shinobu Zenchū, XII. Chūō Kōron Sha, 1966.

Rimer, J. Thomas. *Modern Japanese Fiction and Its Traditions*. Princeton, N.J., Princeton University Press, 1978.

Sakakura Atsuyoshi, Ōtsu Yūichi, Tsukijima Hiroshi, Abe Toshiko, and Imai Gen'e. *Taketori Monogatari, Ise Monogatari, Yamato Monogatari*, in Nihon Koten Bungaku Taikei series. Iwanami Shoten, 1957.

Seidensticker, Edward (trans.). *The Tale of Genji*, 2 vols. New York: Alfred A. Knopf, 1976.

Shinoda Kōichirō. *Taketori Monogatari to Ukigumo*. Shūeisha, 1981.

Tahara, Mildred. *Tales of Yamato*. Honolulu: University of Hawaii Press, 1980.

Tamagami Takuya. *Ōchōbito no Kokoro*. Kōdansha, 1975.

Tanaka Gen. *Taketori, Ise Monogatari no Sekai*. Yoshikawa Kōbunkan, 1982.

Tanizaki Jun'ichirō Zenshū, XVI. Chūō Kōron Sha, 1974.

Tsunoda Bun'ei. "Narihira no Azuma-kudari," *Bungaku* 37:12, no. 12, 1969.

Uraki, Ziro (trans.). *The Tale of the Cavern*. Tokyo: Shinozaki Shorin, 1984.

Videen, Susan Downing. *Tales of Heichū*. Cambridge, Mass.: Council on East Asian Studies, Harvard University, 1989.

Watanabe Minoru. *Ise Monogatari*, in Shinchō Nihon Koten Shūsei series. Shinchōsha, 1976.

Whitehouse, Wilfrid (trans.). *The Tale of the Lady Ochikubo*. Garden City, N.Y.: Doubleday, 1971.

Yamada Seiichi. "Ise Monogatari no Kōsei Ishiki ni okeru Mondai," in Chūko Bungaku Kenkyūkai (ed.), *Shoki Monogatari Bungaku no Ishiki*. Kasama Shoin, 1979.

Yanagita Kunio. *Teihon Yanagita Kunio Zenshū*, VI. Chikuma Shobō, 1963.

12.
THE TALE OF GENJI

Genji Monogatari (The Tale of Genji) is considered to be the supreme masterpiece of Japanese literature. The author, Murasaki Shikibu, borrowed much from earlier monogatari and collections of waka, and especially from the diaries of court ladies, but her novel rises in solitary grandeur like a great mountain over lesser hills. In every age since *The Tale of Genji* was first written and circulated at the court it has been accorded special respect, and it would not be possible to list all the other works of Japanese literature it has inspired. During the centuries after the completion of *The Tale of Genji* the court life it so superbly evoked was overshadowed by the rise to power of the samurai class, and at times its very existence seemed to be imperiled; but the fierce warriors who threatened the way of life at the court generally did not long remain immune to its charms, and they turned with respect and a kind of nostalgia to *The Tale of Genji*. Kawabata Yasunari once wrote that it was impossible to understand the culture of the Muromachi period (though it is often discussed by historians in terms of turbulent forces from below overthrowing the traditional authorities) without a knowledge of the extraordinary influence this supreme product of the aristocratic culture continued to exert.[1] Even today its magnetic attraction persists, as we know from the many translations and adaptations into modern Japanese made by writers who felt they needed to replenish their writings through their culture's central work of literature. And, at the time of the greatest crisis of modern Japan, the wartime bombings and the defeat, Kawabata turned to *The Tale of Genji* for reassurance and comfort. He related that reading it, at a time when the thought of death never left him, persuaded him that he must go on living "along with these traditions that flowed within me."[2] *The Tale of Genji* is not only the quintessence of the aristocratic culture of Heian Japan, but has affected the aesthetic and emotional life of the entire Japanese people for a millennium.

Authorship of the Work

Our best source of information concerning the authorship of the novel[3] is the diary kept by the author, Murasaki Shikibu, herself. An entry for the eleventh month of 1008 mentions the existence of a rough draft of part (or perhaps all) of the work. It has been conjectured from other evidence that Murasaki Shikibu began writing *The Tale of Genji* sometime between 1001, the year her husband Fujiwara no Nobutaka died, and 1005, when she entered the service of the Empress Shōshi (Akiko). Dates ranging from 1005 to after 1013 have been suggested for the completion.[4] We know from mention in *The Sarashina Diary*, written about 1021, that all of *The Tale of Genji* must have been completed by that date.[5]

Murasaki Shikibu's diary reveals unusual gifts of expression, but neither the diary nor any of the earlier monogatari prepares us for the achievement of *The Tale of Genji*. In the past (especially during the Muromachi period) some, reluctant to believe that a woman could have written so grand a work, insisted that it must have been composed by Murasaki Shikibu's father, Fujiwara no Tametoki, who merely left details for his daughter to fill in.[6] No one now denies that Murasaki Shikibu wrote all, or at any rate most, of *The Tale of Genji*, though differences of style, vocabulary, and the manner of waka composition have led critics to question the authorship of some chapters.[7]

The ten chapters at the end were also at one time attributed to another hand, most often to Murasaki Shikibu's daughter, the waka poet Daini no Sammi. This theory[8] is no longer taken seriously, though these chapters have an unquestionably darker, more oppressive tone than the earlier ones. Others have argued that some additional chapters existed before the present text in fifty-four chapters became standard, but little evidence supports such a hypothesis. One missing chapter, entitled "Kumogakure" (Disappearance in the Clouds), is said to have related the death of Genji, not described in any current text; but opinions in the old commentaries are divided between the view that it was so painful for the author to contemplate Genji's death that she could not bring herself to write this chapter (even though she gave it a name), and the contrary assertion that although Murasaki Shikibu wrote the chapter it was destroyed by imperial command because this example of the evanescence of human life had induced an excessive number of readers to "flee the world" and take refuge in Buddhist monasteries.[9] Modifications of the text unquestionably occurred, as we can infer from the numerous variants, but for most purposes it can be assumed that Murasaki Shikibu wrote the entire work.

Murasaki Shikibu

The dates of the birth and death of Murasaki Shikibu have not been established, but 973 is now accepted by many scholars as the year of her birth, and her death occurred sometime after 1013, when she was mentioned for the last time in a contemporary document.

We know from Murasaki Shikibu's own writings as well as other sources that she was the daughter of Fujiwara no Tametoki, an official who, though of highly distinguished ancestry, enjoyed only a mediocre career as a provincial governor. An office he held early in his career, Shikibu no Daijō, accounted for the title *shikibu* (secretariat) in the name by which Murasaki Shikibu is known; it was common for women to be called by the names of the offices held by their fathers or husbands. Murasaki was a nickname, probably derived from the character of the same name in her novel; she seems to have been known, before she acquired her nickname, as Tō (for Fujiwara) Shikibu.[10]

Tametoki was a fourth-generation descendant of Fujiwara no Fuyutsugu, the founder of the "flowering fortune" of the Fujiwara family, and his wife (Murasaki's mother) was a fifth-generation descendant of the same man. By Tametoki's time, however, the glory of this particular branch of the Fujiwara family had been dimmed, and its members belonged to the zuryō class.[11] The most distinguished literary figure among Murasaki's ancestors was her great-grandfather, Fujiwara no Kanesuke, one of the chief *Gosenshū* poets. Later generations of Murasaki's ancestors had been honored by the inclusion of poems in imperial anthologies of waka, but this literary distinction had not brought them political power.

Tametoki was not only an accomplished waka poet but excelled at kanshi composition.[12] Many of his kanshi were included in such collections as the *Honchō Reisō* (c. 1010).[13] In 996, after ten years without office, Tametoki was appointed governor of Awaji, an inferior post. Disappointed, he composed a kanshi describing his grief and presented it to the Emperor Ichijō. The kanshi so impressed the emperor that he directed Fujiwara no Michinaga, who had already appointed a relative governor of Echizen, to cancel this appointment and give the post to Tametoki instead.[14] The anecdote indicates the recognition accorded to Tametoki's kanshi, but it must have been galling for a man of his ancestry to have to depend on a poem for preferment.

Murasaki Shikibu apparently lost her mother when she was a small child. She grew up in her father's house, where she was educated together with a brother, as we know from a passage in her diary, in which she described how much more quickly than her brother she (from her place on the other side of a screen) absorbed the lessons in Chinese given by their father. She recalled, too, that her father regretted that she had not been born a boy: if she had been a man, she might well have developed into a capable, perhaps even brilliant, writer of kanshi and excelled otherwise at the kinds of learning that brought recognition from the court. This, however, would have deprived Japanese literature of its greatest glory, for men scorned to write fiction, and the composition of waka was virtually the only exception to their refusal to use Japanese for literary purposes.

We know little else about Murasaki's early years, though her poems suggest that she fell in love at least once. In 996 she violated custom by accompanying her father to his post in Echizen, apparently in order to avoid marriage with a second cousin, the governor of Chikuzen. The suitor, Fujiwara no Nobutaka, was in his middle forties, had several wives and concubines, and a number of children, the oldest a son of twenty-six. The difference in age and these family circumstances, more than the personality of the man, may have occasioned Murasaki Shikibu's reluctance to marry him; however, life in the unfamiliar, depressing surroundings of Echizen seems to have changed her mind: in the spring of 998, before her father completed his term of office, she returned alone to the capital, and that autumn she and Nobutaka were married.

In the following year the daughter later known as Daini no Sammi was born. Judging from the poems she and Nobutaka exchanged, Murasaki's married life was happy, but in 1001, less than three years after their marriage, Nobutaka died, perhaps a victim of the epidemic that had raged since the previous year. His death deeply affected Murasaki, as we can infer from poems she composed at the time:

"Remembering how I had grieved over my fate and then gradually returned to normal, I wrote:"

kazu naranu	Helpless as I am,
kokoro ni mi wo ba	I cannot lead my life as
makasenedo	My heart desires;

mi ni shitagau wa	I have learned how to submit
kokoro narikeri[15]	My desires to my fate.

kokoro ni wa	I wonder what place
ika naru mi ni ka	In the world could satisfy
kanauran	Such desires as mine?
omoishiredomo	Although I know to hope is vain,
omoishirarezu[16]	I cannot keep from hoping.

It has been conjectured that Murasaki Shikibu began writing *The Tale of Genji* before 1005–1006, when she was appointed lady-in-waiting (*nyōbō*) to Shōshi, the consort of the Emperor Ichijō. A brilliant group of court ladies had been assembled around Shōshi by her father, Michinaga, and Murasaki Shikibu may have been invited to join this group because parts of *The Tale of Genji* had already been circulated and admired. Murasaki Shikibu's activities at Shōshi's court are described in the diary in which she recorded events between the autumn of 1008 and the beginning of 1010. Perhaps Murasaki Shikibu kept the diary at the suggestion of Michinaga, as an "answer" to *The Pillow Book of Sei Shōnagon*, written at the rival court of the Empress Teishi (Sadako).[17]

Composition of the Work

Murasaki wrote little in her diary about the composition of *The Tale of Genji,* but passing references make it clear that the work was already well known, perhaps from having been read aloud before the Emperor Ichijō and Shōshi. Men at the court normally did not read fiction, considering even the best examples to be no more than diversions for women, but perhaps Ichijō, hearing praise of the work from the ladies around him, was curious about the contents. It is recorded that he praised the knowledge of Chinese revealed by allusions in the text, expressing the belief that Murasaki must have read the *Nihon Shoki*. He probably meant that she wrote in a far more coherent and organized manner than earlier writers of fiction, more like a historian than a romancer. Its high reputation among men of the court is also attested by mention of Michinaga's generosity in providing fine paper, ink, and brushes for the scribes who made the copy, though it is unlikely that Michinaga himself read the novel; his readings seem to have been confined to the Chinese classics.

It has been speculated that the first germs of *The Tale of Genji* were probably tales of court life of the past related by some lady to the empress and her entourage. Although this lady may have been guided by a "scenario" written in kambun[18] that gave the essential facts of the tales, she extemporized in "free" sections that were not part of the frame story.[19] Murasaki's act of writing down the text ended the possibility of significantly modifying the story in retelling; but the word *monogatari* (telling of things) itself continued to be used, as if it were still being orally related. Many passages in the present text of *The Tale of Genji* suggest the typical manner of speech of court ladies, though at times Chinese literary influence also seems to be present.[20]

It is difficult to establish sources for *The Tale of Genji,* and equally difficult to determine how Murasaki Shikibu set about writing her book. It would be natural to assume that she began with the first chapter, "Kiritsubo," but there have long been theories to the contrary. One persistent tradition is that Murasaki, gazing from the Ishiyama Temple at the moon reflected in the waters of Lake Biwa, was inspired to write about her hero, Genji, during the period when he was exiled to Suma, a place with a somewhat similar landscape. The title of the best-known text of the work, *Kogetsu-shō,* meaning "lake moon collection," alludes to this legend, and visitors today to the Ishiyama Temple are shown the room (known as *Genji no ma*) where Murasaki Shikibu began writing *The Tale of Genji,* and even the inkstone she used.[21] Another recurrent theory is that Murasaki Shikibu began by writing the chapter "Waka-Murasaki" (Young Murasaki), perhaps by way of imagining in Genji an ideal husband for her own daughter.[22]

Scholars who accept "Kiritsubo" as the first chapter in order of composition are divided between those who express boundless admiration for the skill with which Murasaki adumbrated in this chapter the major themes of the entire work, and those who ask that it be read with indulgence, making allowance for her inexperience.[23]

The order of composition of the chapters is complicated by the fact that some relate events that occur simultaneously to those in earlier chapters instead of advancing the narrative in chronological sequence. These chapters are known as *narabi,* or parallel chapters, as contrasted with the *hon no maki,* or basic chapters.[24] The existence of these "parallel" chapters has suggested that the work was not written in the present order, but that some chapters were inserted into an existing text, even though there was no room for them chronologically.

Basic doubts about the order of composition of the chapters were convincingly expressed by Takeda Munetoshi in 1954.[25] He postulated the existence of an "Ur-text" of *The Tale of Genji* consisting of seventeen chapters in which Murasaki was the principal character. Sixteen chapters in which Tamakazura was the principal character were subsequently inserted at appropriate places to make up the thirty-three chapters of the First Part of the work. The original seventeen chapters ended with Genji acclaimed by all as the foremost man of the land. His son, the Emperor Reizei, whom everyone supposes to be the son of the old emperor, Genji's father, has learned the secret of his birth, and he bestows on Genji a rank second only to a retired emperor. He further insists that Genji sit by his side, sharing with him the place of honor, an unprecedented mark of respect.[26]

The main female characters in the Ur-text, or "Murasaki line" of chapters, apart from Murasaki herself, are Kiritsubo (Genji's mother) and Fujitsubo (the romantic obsession of Genji's life). The "Tamakazura line," named after the daughter of Genji's friend Tō no Chūjō, includes such memorable women as Yūgao and Suetsumuhana. The characters of the "Tamakazura line" are not mentioned in the chapters of the "Murasaki line" because, following Takeda, they had not yet been created; but characters of the "Murasaki line" do appear in the "Tamakazura line" because they already existed. Takeda reinforced this theory with objective evidence, such as the different titles and other appellations used for the characters in the two lines.[27] The characters who first appear in the "Tamakazura line" are more complex, in Takeda's view, than those of the "Murasaki line" and are sometimes treated with a humor not present earlier, suggesting an evolution in the author's manner.[28] Takeda's thesis has not been universally accepted, but it is the most plausible explanation yet offered of the parallel chapters and the many discrepancies of style.

Takeda believed that after Murasaki Shikibu had written the first thirty-three chapters she was persuaded to continue the story. However, her outlook on the world had for some reason changed, and the glory of Genji described in the First Part was much diminished. The chief incident of the Second Part is Genji's marriage to the third daughter of the Retired Emperor Suzaku, who has taken Buddhist orders. Suzaku, worried about the future of his favorite daughter, induces Genji to marry her. Genji accepts, in part because the princess is also a niece of his beloved Fujitsubo.

The marriage has unfortunate consequences for everyone concerned. First of all, it creates a rift between Genji and Murasaki, who is understandably upset over his marriage to a royal princess. Genji assures Murasaki of his unchanging love, and explains why he felt obliged to marry Suzaku's daughter. But Murasaki falls ill and is tormented by the jealous spirit of the late Lady Rokujō, a lover of Genji who has never forgiven Murasaki for having taken Genji from her. Murasaki begs to be allowed to become a nun, but Genji cannot bear to let her go. Before long, she dies. Genji is so distraught over Murasaki's illness and death that he neglects the Third Princess, a childlike creature who, hardly realizing what is happening, has a secret affair with Kashiwagi, the son of Genji's best friend. Genji, like his father before him, is obliged to take in his arms and recognize as his own the child of his wife and another man. His glory no longer seems so radiant.

The Third Part (once again following Takeda) describes events that take place after Genji's death. The characters in this part of the novel are remarkably beautiful and gifted, but their failings are also conspicuous. They are presumably closer to the real people of Murasaki Shikibu's day than those of the First or Second parts, and their lives are colored by griefs and passions that would have been immediately familiar to the people mentioned in her diary. The novel ends in a manner that may strike readers as inconclusive, but it has never occurred to Japanese scholars that the novel may be unfinished. Murasaki Shikibu took leave of her world in the manner of the painters of horizontal scrolls who, after depicting scenes crowded with people, show at the end one last haunting figure disappearing into the dark.

Style of the Work

The Tale of Genji is famous not only because of its beauty but because of the difficulty of its style. In the past, when there were few detailed commentaries and no satisfactory translation into modern Japanese, even highly educated Japanese were not embarrassed to confess that it was easier for them to read Waley's English translation than the original. The main problem is the poetic ambiguity of many sentences that may leave in doubt the subject or the nature of the action performed. The difficulty cannot be explained merely in terms of the antiquity of the text; some works (like *The Tale of the Bamboo Cutter*) which antedate *The Tale of Genji* are far easier for modern readers to understand. The style was unique to Murasaki Shikibu, and she employed it because she felt confident that her anticipated readers at the court would be able to follow even very complicated sentences without difficulty. Any passage would do almost equally well to suggest the complexities, which tend to disappear in fluent translations that eliminate run-on sentences or augment the original with explanations. The following passage occurs near the beginning of the "Yūgao" chapter:

> *Mikuruma irubeki kado wa sashitarikereba, hito shite Koremitsu mesasete, matasetamaikeru hodo, mutsukashige naru ōji no sama wo miwatase shitamaeru ni, kono ie no katawara ni, higaki to iu mono wo atarashū shite, kami wa, hajitomi shigoken bakari agewatashite, sudare nado mo ito shirō suzushige naru ni, okashiki hitaitsuki no sukikage, amata miete nozoku. Tachisamayouran shimotsukata omoiyaru ni, anagachi ni taketakaki kokochi zo suru.*

It is not possible to make an absolutely literal rendering, but the meaning is approximately: "Because the gate through which carriages were admitted was locked, he sent a man for Koremitsu, and while he waited, he ran his eyes along the disreputable-looking street [and noticed] that [someone] in the house next door had newly [put up] what they call a cypress-bark fence, above which [someone] had lifted the row of four or five shutters; the blinds looked very white and cool, and he could dimly see through them many charming foreheads peeping [at him]. When he tried imagining the lower parts [of the figures] that seemed to be wandering around, he had a feeling that they must be very tall."

The translation by Arthur Waley renders this passage:

> [H]e managed to find the house; but the front gate was locked and he could not drive in. He sent one of his servants for Koremitsu, his foster-nurse's son, and while he was waiting began to examine the rather wretched-looking by-street. The house next door was fenced with a new paling, above which at one place were four or five panels of open trellis-work, screened by blinds which were very white and bare. Through chinks in the blinds a number of foreheads could be seen. They seemed to belong to a group of ladies who must be peeping with interest into the street below. At first he thought that they had merely peeped out as they passed; but he soon realized that if they were standing on the floor they must be giants. No, evidently they had taken the trouble to climb on to some table or bed; which was surely rather odd![29]

Edward Seidensticker's translation is closer to the original:

> The carriage entrance was closed. He sent for Koremitsu and while he was waiting looked up and down the dirty, cluttered street. Beside the nurse's house was a new fence of plaited cypress. The four or five narrow shutters above had been raised, and new blinds, white and clean, hung in the apertures. He caught outlines of pretty foreheads beyond. He would have judged, as they moved about, that they belonged to rather tall women.[30]

Waley's amplification of the text—especially his placing the women on "some table or bed," though it is hard to imagine a Heian room containing either—was undoubtedly inspired by his desire to make the text as immediately intelligible as possible to the European reader. Murasaki Shikibu does not explain why the women looked tall, and Waley felt obliged to insert an explanation.[31] Seidensticker evidently preferred not to mention the peeping of the women nor their lower parts (*shimotsukata*), nor did he attempt to explain the tallness of the women. Waley is perhaps closer to the original than Seidensticker in the leisurely pace of the sentences. But probably no translator could be completely faithful both to the original and to the English language.

An even more striking aspect of the style is the presence in the text of almost eight hundred poems. Quickly read in translation, they seem to add little to the narrative, and one is likely to be left merely with an impression that people of the Heian period were able to talk in poetry, and that they beautified their language as they beautified every other aspect of their lives. Closer reading of the poems, however, makes it evident that they contribute not only to the beauty of the style but also to the creation of a lyrical mode of narration.[32]

The style of the prose of *The Tale of Genji,* despite its difficulty, would affect writings in the courtly tradition over the centuries. Passages were incorporated almost word for word in the Nō plays,[33] and certain incidents would be alluded to innumerable times, in poetry as well as prose.[34] The descriptions of nature, whether observed in a palace garden or at some lonelier spot, are without exception lovely, all but poems in themselves. The expressive genius of the Yamato language—Japanese before it was greatly affected by Chinese influence—is nowhere better displayed than in the prose and poetry of *The Tale of Genji*.

Historical Background

The Tale of Genji covers a period of about seventy years. It opens, as we can tell from various clues in the text, during the reign of the Emperor Daigo (897–930), an age that would be recalled as the high point of Heian civilization, and continues up to a time close to Murasaki Shikibu's own day. It has convincingly been suggested that the model for Genji was Minamoto no Takaakira, the tenth son of the Emperor Daigo; not only was he (like Genji) made a commoner with the surname of Minamoto (or Genji)[35] but he too was exiled (in 969) and later recalled to the capital.[36] It is likely that, regardless of whether or not Murasaki Shikibu had Takaakira in mind when she created the character of Genji, her readers, noting the resemblances, associated Genji with the historical figure. Other references within the novel to historical events confirmed the impression that the story had actually occurred. The work is nevertheless fiction, not a literary retelling of history.

The world of the "Shining Prince" may well have been Murasaki Shikibu's refuge from the world in which she actually found herself, a transmutation of the prose of daily life at the court to the poetry of her imagination. We know from her diary that the men of the court were by no means flawlessly decorous. Even the most distinguished among them not uncommonly got drunk and behaved boorishly. She undoubtedly romanticized, attributing to the past a beauty and elegance often missing from the world she observed, but she did not venture into fantasy; the people she described, though incomparably more gifted and beautiful than those she knew at court, were motivated by the unmistakable passions of human beings.

The occasions when supernatural events occur in the novel, notably the appearances of the baleful spirit of Lady Rokujō, have been explained by some modern commentators in terms of the power of hate or jealousy to harm and even to kill, but Murasaki Shikibu, like other Japanese of her time, believed in the literal existence of such spirits.[37] On the other hand, she dismissed as old-fashioned the kind of unreality present in *The Tale of the Bamboo Cutter*—the birth of a little girl inside a stalk of bamboo, or Kaguya-hime's ability to vanish at will—and she looked down on other early works that relied on the supernatural for their plots. The world of *The Tale of Genji* was a sublimation of Murasaki Shikibu's world, not a never-never land.

SOURCES OF *THE TALE OF GENJI*

The Tale of Genji is likely to seem modern, especially if read in a translation, whether one in contemporary Japanese or a foreign language. We believe in the characters of this work in a way not possible in the case of earlier monogatari such as *The Tale of the Hollow Tree* or, for that matter, much Japanese fiction written before the twentieth century. The characters are so distinctly drawn that we could not confuse the utterances of, say, Murasaki and Aoi or Rokujō and Tamakazura, and in the course of the novel the characters develop as they grow older and have new experiences. Indeed, the internal life of the characters, rather than their actions, is the subject of *The Tale of Genji*. In this sense its ancestor is not the early fiction, noticeably lacking in such qualities, but the diaries, especially *The Gossamer Years*. It is hard to imagine Murasaki Shikibu having created *The Tale of Genji* if there had not existed a tradition of women writing down their private thoughts.

With respect to specific literary influences, it is a commonplace of Japanese criticism of *The Tale of Genji* to mention its indebtedness to *Chang-hen-ḳo* ("A Song of Unending Sorrow"), the long poem by the great Chinese poet Po Chü-i that was much admired in Heian Japan. The poem concerns the love of the Emperor Hsüan Tsung for Yang Kuei-fei, a beautiful woman who, in the old phrase, "overturned the country." Murasaki Shikibu was certainly familiar with this poem, and alludes to it at the opening of her novel, where she wrote,

> His court looked with very great misgiving upon what seemed a reckless infatuation. In China just such an unreasoning passion had been the undoing of an emperor and had spread turmoil throughout the land. As the resentment grew, the example of Yang Kuei-fei was the one most freqently cited against the lady.[38]

Although Murasaki was thinking of "A Song of Unending Sorrow" when she wrote the opening of *The Tale of Genji*, it is an overstatement to suggest that Po Chü-i's poem inspired the novel. The poem relates how the Chinese emperor's passionate love for the incomparably beautiful Yang Kuei-fei endangered the state and caused a rebellion during which she was executed by soldiers. It also describes how a priest, by command of the emperor, searched the afterworld for Yang Kuei-fei until he found her. She nostalgically recalled her love and gave the priest keepsakes to take back to the emperor. The poem concludes: "Earth endures, heaven endures; some time both shall end, / While this unending sorrow goes on and on for ever."[39]

The love of the emperor for Kiritsubo occasioned the jealousy of other palace ladies, and she died untimely, her hold on life weakened by unhappiness, but there was never any danger of rebellion, and she was certainly not cut down by soldiers. The most memorable keepsake of her union with the emperor was Genji, and the emperor's sorrow was mitigated by this child. Later he found solace in Fujitsubo, a woman who much resembled Kiritsubo.

The search for literary sources has been inspired largely by the difficulty scholars have experienced in imagining that a work of the magnitude of *The Tale of Genji* could have been created without models. The early commentators found sources in the Tendai Buddhist scriptures, the *Records of the Historian* of Ssu-ma Ch'ien, the *Spring and Autumn Annals,* and other Chinese sources. Other commentators, concerned less with literary sources than with the moral intent of the work, provided a simplistic Buddhist explanation that persists to this day: *The Tale of Genji* is the story of a man who was punished for his affair with his stepmother when his own wife betrayed him with another man.

The best-known and most persuasive interpretation, however, was that of Motoori Norinaga, who denied Buddhist and Confucian intent behind the novel and treated *The Tale of Genji* as a work embodying the principle of mono no aware, a sensitivity to things. Motoori wrote in *Tama no Ogushi* (The Jeweled Comb):

> There have been many interpretations over the years of the purpose of this tale. But all of these interpretations have been based not on a consideration of the novel itself but rather on the novel as seen from the point of view of Confucian and Buddhist works, and thus they do not represent the true purpose of the author. . . . Good and evil as found in this tale do not correspond to good and evil as found in Confucian and Buddhist writings. . . . Generally speaking, those who know the meaning of the sorrow of human existence, i.e., those who are in sympathy and in harmony with human sentiments are regarded as good; and those who are not aware of the poignance of human existence, i.e., those who are not in harmony with human sentiments are regarded as bad. . . . Since novels have as their object the teaching of the meaning of the nature of human existence, there are in their plots many points contrary to Confucian and Buddhist teachings. This is because among the varied feelings of man's reactions to things—whether good, bad, right, or wrong—there are

> feelings contrary to reason, however improper they may be. . . . In the instance of Prince Genji, his interest in and rendezvous with Utsusemi, Oborotsukiyo, and the Consort Fujitsubo are acts of extraordinary iniquity and immorality according to the Confucian and Buddhist points of view. . . . But *The Tale of Genji* does not dwell on his iniquitous and immoral acts, but rather recites over and over again his awareness of the sorrow of existence, and represents him as a good man who combines in himself all good things in men.[40]

Motoori, later in the same essay, declared that the purpose of the author of *The Tale of Genji* was similar to that of a man who collects muddy water in order to have lotuses bloom: "The impure mud of illicit love affairs described in *The Tale of Genji* is there not for the purpose of being admired but for the purpose of nurturing the flower of the awareness of the sorrow of human existence."[41]

If Motoori's explanation is correct, Murasaki Shikibu was inspired by a literary rather than a didactic purpose, and similarities between *The Tale of Genji* and Buddhist or Confucian writings are therefore coincidences or of only minor significance. Other scholars have pointed out the political overtones of the novel; for example, the fact that the hero belongs to the Minamoto clan (Genji), though the Fujiwara family was supreme at the time, surely had importance for her first readers,[42] and may have suggested even that Murasaki disapproved of Fujiwara hegemony. Some critics, especially during the 1950s, insisted that *The Tale of Genji* was an exposé of the contradictions and corruption in the upper aristocracy, written by an embittered member of its lower ranks, but this is hardly the impression received from the novel itself.

It is not clear to what degree Murasaki Shikibu intended her work to convey religious or political meaning. In describing the world around her hero she no doubt drew on the assumptions of her class and particularly of the women at Shōshi's court. At an even more unconscious level, she may have drawn on folklore. For example, Genji's exile to Suma was perhaps derived from the story of the exiled young noble, known in many parts of Asia.[43] This is the story of a young prince who is slandered and forced to go into exile; but eventually, after proving his worth, he returns in triumph to the capital. A knowledge of this tale may have guided Murasaki Shikibu as she wrote about Genji's time of trial at Suma and return, but the historical instance of Minamoto no Takaakira's exile was closer at hand; and Genji's exile at Suma, though a time of trial, was not the occasion for proving his mettle and winning a glorious reputation.

The relations between Genji and his enemy Kokiden, the consort of his father, the old emperor, have also been traced to folkloristic sources, in this case the widely known tales about cruel stepmothers.[44] If Murasaki Shikibu had these tales in mind when she wrote about Genji and Kokiden, she confused the issue by giving contrasting examples of stepmother-stepson relations. Genji's love for his stepmother Fujitsubo is of vastly greater importance to the novel than his suffering at the hands of Kokiden; and the pains Genji takes to ensure that his son Yūgiri will never see Murasaki are occasioned not by fear that Murasaki will mistreat her stepson but by a premonition that one glimpse of Murasaki will be all that Yūgiri needs to fall in love with her. Yūgiri in fact does get a glimpse of Murasaki when storm winds blow down the screens that normally conceal her, and his astonishment over her beauty proves that Genji's fears were well grounded. If one had to judge from these examples, one could only conclude that Murasaki Shikibu, far from intending to write a story in the manner of *The Tale of Ochikubo,* about a cruel stepmother, was warning of the danger that beautiful stepmothers are likely to inspire improper sentiments in their stepsons.

Murasaki's clearest statement on why she wrote *The Tale of Genji* is found in the celebrated account of the "art of fiction" found in chapter 25, "Hotaru" (Fireflies). Genji, going to Tamakazura's room on a summer's day, finds her reading a pile of books, to pass the boredom of the rainy season. At first he teases her over the credulity of women, who are willing to be deceived by the fabricators of romances. But, on second thought, he continues in this vein:

> If it weren't for old romances like this, how on earth would you get through these long tedious days when time moves so slowly? And besides, I realize that many of these works, full of fabrications though they are, do succeed in evoking the emotions of things in a most realistic way. One event follows plausibly on another, and in the end we cannot help being moved by the story, even though we know what foolishness it all really is. . . .

He moves from this somewhat grudging recognition of the value of fiction to a more positive statement:

> It was rather churlish of me to speak badly about these books as I did just now, for the fact is that works of fiction set down things that have happened in this world ever since the days of the gods. Writings like *The Chronicles of Japan* really give only one side of the

picture, whereas these romances must be full of just the right sort of details. . . . The author certainly does not write about specific people, recording all the actual circumstances of their lives. Rather it is a matter of his being so moved by things, both good and bad, which he has heard and seen happening to men and women that he cannot keep it all to himself but wants to commit it to writing and make it known to other people—even to those of later generations. This, I feel sure, is the origin of fiction.[45]

Genji goes on to suggest that fiction may correspond to the "accommodated truths" of Buddhism which, though not strictly the truth, have the same end as the teachings of Buddha: the enlightenment of mankind. Medieval scholars interpreted *The Tale of Genji* as a *hōben*, an expedient for gaining truth painlessly. But Murasaki Shikibu indicates that, quite apart from the possible value her work (or any other example of fiction) may have in enlightening people, it results from the compulsion that authors feel to record events that have so deeply moved them that they cannot bear to think that a time might come when they would be forgotten.

The Story

The novel opens with an account of the birth of its hero, Prince Genji, together with the circumstances preceding his birth. Genji's mother, Kiritsubo, though much loved by the emperor, is of inferior birth and lacks backing at the court. She is accordingly slandered and maltreated by other palace ladies who are jealous of the attentions the emperor showers on her. She dies when Genji is only three years old. A few years later, a Korean physiognomist, asked to tell the boy's fortune, predicts that if Genji should ascend the throne, as his birth (he is the son of the reigning emperor), his intelligence, and his extraordinary beauty seem to prescribe, there will be disaster. On the other hand, Genji's face does not reveal the traits of a minister who can order affairs of state on behalf of the emperor.[46] The emperor, disturbed by the prediction, which seems to rule out the boy's ever occupying a position of importance, decides to preserve the boy from harm by making him a commoner and giving him the surname of Minamoto, or Genji.[47]

After the death of Kiritsubo, apparently a victim of mental torment, the emperor is inconsolable until he hears rumors of the daughter of a former emperor who is said to look exactly like the dead lady. This is the first example of a leitmotiv that runs through the novel: a man will fall in love again and again with the same woman, though her identity may be different. Genji falls in love with Fujitsubo after learning how much she resembles his mother, and later with Murasaki who resembles her aunt Fujitsubo, now a nun and inaccessible. His interest in Yūgao and her daughter Tamakazura stems from a single love. Late in the novel, Genji's supposed son Kaoru loves Ukifune because she resembles Ōigimi.

When the emperor chooses Fujitsubo as his official consort, the women of the palace cannot complain, for she is of the highest birth. Genji, on whom his father dotes so much that he can scarcely bear to let the boy out of his sight, is allowed to play in the presence of his youthful stepmother, and she soon becomes his ideal of beauty. Even after his initiation into manhood at the age of twelve and his marriage to Aoi, six years older than himself, Genji remains under Fujitsubo's spell, which is one reason why his marriage fails. His wife Aoi, ironically, is the only woman in the book who remains impervious to Genji's charm, and Genji first appreciates Aoi's beauty only when she is on her deathbed. Murasaki Shikibu does not attribute this coldness of husband and wife to any specific cause, but leads us to believe that they are incompatible, and that nothing can change this fact.

Genji has a son by Aoi, the intelligent but charmless Yūgiri. He also has a son as the result of his brief, poignant relationship with Fujitsubo. This son, whom the world supposes to be the emperor's, eventually ascends the throne as the Emperor Reizei.[48] Genji is far from exultant over having a son on the throne; he is tormented by the fear that the unusual resemblance between Reizei and himself will be noticed, and filled with shame that he has betrayed his father. After Reizei becomes emperor he discovers the secret of his birth and is appalled to think that he has failed to pay his real father the appropriate homage. The honors he bestows on Genji represent the apogee of Genji's glory and a fulfillment of the prophecy of the Korean physiognomist. (He is neither an emperor nor a surrogate of the emperor but has been given a rank equivalent to that of a retired emperor.) Many scholars believe that the chapter "Fuji no Uraba" (Wisteria Leaves) marked the end of the First Part of the work; Murasaki Shikibu seems originally to have intended to conclude her story of Genji at this point.

At the opening of the Second Part, the Retired Emperor Suzaku, who has taken Buddhist orders, asks Genji to marry his third daughter. For all his many affairs with different women over the years, he unquestionably loves Murasaki best, but she was of insufficiently exalted birth to be designated as his official consort. Genji accedes to Suzaku's request, though without enthusiasm. This marriage upsets the harmony that has hitherto reigned over his Rokujō Palace, where each of Genji's principal ladies occupies a wing with a garden whose flowers reveal her choice of season. The childless Murasaki, though resentful of Genji's alliance with the Lady of Akashi during his exile, never seriously fears this retiring lady as a rival, and (another example of a model stepmother!) gladly rears the lady's child as if it were her own. But the status of the Third Princess makes Murasaki apprehensive, despite Genji's assurances, that she will be supplanted in his affections. The Third Princess's position becomes even more exalted when Reizei abdicates in favor of her brother. The distraught Murasaki expresses the desire to become a nun and "leave the world," but Genji restrains her. She falls ill, and the distressed Genji completely neglects the Third Princess. Kashiwagi, the son of Genji's friend Tō no Chūjō, has fallen desperately in love with the Third Princess after a single glimpse of her. The two have a brief, guilt-ridden affair. Soon afterward Murasaki dies. Genji seriously considers taking vows as a Buddhist priest, but his sense of responsibility to those who depend on him obliges him to postpone this decision. The Second Part ends with a description of Genji, who is appearing in public for the first time after the death of Murasaki. We are told that he seemed more beautiful than ever.

The chapter entitled "Niou," at the beginning of the Third Part, opens with the bleak statement, "Genji was dead, and there was no one to take his place."[49] The last third of *The Tale of Genji* has for its heroes two young princes, Niou, a grandson of Genji, and Kaoru, the son of Kashiwagi and the Third Princess. Both are uncommonly attractive, but each is only a part of Genji: Niou combines Genji's beauty with an impetuous ardor that generally wins any woman, but he lacks Genji's sensitivity; Kaoru has more than his share of Genji's sensitivity, but he lacks self-assurance and fails to win the heart of either of the two women he loves. The flaws in these young men suggest the diminution that has occurred in the world since Genji's death. The absence of a hero who is described only in superlatives has the effect of making the last part of the novel seem more realistic; it may have been for this reason that future readers tended to identify themselves with the characters of this part. Niou and Kaoru are rivals for Ukifune, whose despair at being forced to choose between them induces her to attempt suicide, a development in the plot that would have been inconceivable in earlier sections of the novel.

Characters in the Novel

We tend to remember, even more than the plot of *The Tale of Genji,* the characters created by Murasaki Shikibu. This in itself was an extraordinary achievement: nothing in any of the earlier monogatari prepares us for these characters. Only in the diaries does one come across people with the complexity of real human beings and who can be conceived of as having an existence apart from the book. Genji himself is not especially complex, but on almost every page devoted to him there is some little touch that makes us believe in him. The opening of the chapter "Young Murasaki," where Genji sees Murasaki (then a girl of ten) for the first time, presents numerous effective details that enable us to see Genji with particular clarity. Although he has gone to the hermitage in the mountains hoping to obtain a miraculous cure from the ague that has been bothering him, he is by no means so overcome by fever that he is oblivious to his usual pleasures. A companion tells him about a beautiful spot in the west country where an old man, a former governor, lives with his wife and daughter. At the mention of a daughter Genji's interest is at once aroused and he wants to know more about her. The passage is brief and not especially striking, but it is a first sounding of a theme that will eventually acquire major importance, Genji's exile to the very spot his companion had described, and his romance with the former governor's daughter, the Lady of Akashi.

That evening, though still suffering from his illness ("possessed by a hostile power," according to the holy man who is attempting to cure him), he ventures out to a nearby house and goes up to the fence in order to peep through a crack and get a look at the people inside. Peeping through cracks in fences or hedges was an almost inevitable feature of courtship in a world where young men of the upper classes had few opportunities to see women of their class; there is a special verb, *kaimamiru,* to describe this action. Genji's curiosity is rewarded: he sees inside a little girl who reminds him of "a certain person," another reference to events that have not yet been revealed to the reader, in this case Genji's love for Fujitsubo. Soon afterward Genji is invited to visit a learned cleric who lives nearby. The man, as Buddhist priests are apt to do, speaks of the unreliability of this world and the supreme importance of the world to come, stirring in Genji thoughts of his own sins, though once again the reader does not know what specifically is meant. Genji turns the conversation to the subject of the little girl, and to the priest's great surprise, asks to be allowed to take charge of the girl's education. He alludes briefly to his unhappy marriage with Aoi, saying that he is now living alone.[50] The priest imagines that Genji does not realize the girl is much too young for romance, but Genji waves off this objection: he is not proposing anything improper, but (for reasons he does not disclose) he wants the girl near him. Although he insists that he is not being frivolous, we are inclined to doubt the veracity of his words, remembering his earlier escapades, but he manages to persuade the nun who is Murasaki's guardian that he is earnest, and the girl comes to live with him.

Was Genji sincere in his professions of disinterested concern for the young Murasaki's welfare? Probably he does not himself know, but he clearly is entranced by the girl despite her extreme youth. He behaves toward Murasaki like a tender father or older brother. One day, for example, he asks her if she misses him when he is away. She nods, and he tells her, "You are still a child, and there is a jealous and difficult lady whom I would rather not offend. I must go on visiting her, but when you are grown up I will not leave you ever. It is because I am thinking of all the years we will be together that I want to be on good terms with her."[51] The jealous and difficult lady mentioned by Genji is, of course, Rokujō, but we do not understand just how terrible her jealousy is for several more chapters, when we learn that Rokujō's "living ghost" kills Aoi.

Genji promises to marry Murasaki when she is grown up, but he never suggests when this might be. The scene where he finally decides the moment has arrived is surprisingly brutal. We are given no details, but the implications are unmistakable:

> She was clever and she had many delicate ways of pleasing him in the most trivial diversions. He had not seriously thought of her as a wife. Now he could not restrain himself. It would be a shock, of course.
>
> What had happened? Her women had no way of knowing when the line had been crossed. One morning Genji was up early and Murasaki stayed on and on in bed. . . .
>
> She had not dreamed he had anything of the sort on his mind. What a fool she had been, to repose her whole confidence in so gross and unscrupulous a man.[52]

Murasaki's shock and disillusion are likely to be shared by the reader. For a moment at least Genji's charm is tarnished. Sooner or later this would have had to happen, Genji thought, and perhaps he was right; but even after Murasaki has come to accept this aspect of Genji's love and perhaps to desire it, that day when she thought of him as gross and unscrupulous surely could not have been forgotten. The scene, it may be noted, occurs not long after the death of his wife Aoi at the hands of a malignant spirit even as she is giving birth to Genji's child. After the harrowing experience of seeing his wife being tormented by a vengeful spirit so powerful that exorcism was futile, Genji may well have needed comfort; his violation of Murasaki at this particular time is psychologically true, but not endearing.

That Genji can be discussed in these terms is evidence that he is no cardboard Prince Charming. But it would be wrong to infer from this incident that he was a great lover in the European mold, a Don Giovanni whose conquests were to be recorded in Leporello's catalogue by numbers rather than by names. Once Don Giovanni had conquered a woman he lost all interest in her, and if (like Donna Elvira) she failed to realize that their affair had ended and that it was futile to appeal to his love, he humiliated her openly by asking his servant to make love to her. Genji never forgets any woman he has loved, and even when he discovers to his horror that he has made a dreadful mistake, as when he woos the princess with the red nose, he does not drop her, but sees to it that her needs are taken care of and even continues the pretense of still being her suitor. With each woman he courts he is different, not simply in the manner of Don Giovanni's wooing a peasant girl in a way she can understand, but in satisfying each woman's dreams of a perfect lover.

Genji's most disastrous love affair was with the proud and aristocratic Lady Rokujō. He was attracted to her initially by the very difficulty of approaching such a woman, the widow of a former crown prince. Early in the novel Genji and several friends discuss the ideal wife and they agree that women of the highest rank are to be avoided, but Genji was drawn to Rokujō, who undoubtedly belongs to this class. Once he succeeded in making her his lover, his passion cooled: "He could not deny that the blind intoxicating passion which possessed him while she was still unattainable had almost disappeared. To begin with, she was far too sensitive; then there was the disparity of their ages, and the constant dread of discovery which haunted him during those painful partings at small hours of the morning."[53]

Rokujō falls far more deeply in love with Genji than he with her. Realizing that his love has waned, she decides to accompany her daughter, who has just been named the high priestess, to the Great

Shrine of Ise; she hopes that leaving the capital may help her to forget Genji. Before her departure she attends the festival of the Kamo Shrine, supposing that it would prove a distraction, only to suffer the indignity of having her carriage pushed rudely out of the way by the attendants of the carriage belonging to Genji's wife Aoi. The proud Rokujō feels so humiliated that perhaps at that moment she unconsciously wishes Aoi dead. Soon afterward, unbeknownst to Rokujō herself, her "living spirit" goes to torment Aoi. At first the cause of Aoi's sickness baffles the doctors, but diviners eventually succeed in compelling the spirit that possesses Aoi to speak. The words that issue from Aoi's mouth are not in her own voice but, as Genji realizes to his horror, Lady Rokujō's. Moments later Aoi gives birth to a son, and dies soon afterward.

Rokujō receives the news with mixed feelings. Perhaps she feels secretly pleased that a rival for Genji's affection is now out of the way, but for some time she has noticed a strange scent of incense, the kind used when exorcising demons, clinging to her clothes and hair, no matter how often she bathes, and she has gradually come to realize that she herself has been responsible for Aoi's death.[54]

Rokujō is the most interesting of the many women who figure in *The Tale of Genji*. Not only does her "living ghost" have the power to kill, but after her death her "dead ghost" torments Murasaki; however, she herself is by no means hateful, and Genji, though he realizes she has killed his wife, cannot face leaving her: "And yet, after all, he did not wish to make a final break. He told himself that if she could put up with him as he had been over the years, they might be of comfort to each other."[55] When Genji fails to get in touch with Rokujō after the death of Aoi, she surmises that it is because he blames her, and she is all the more determined to leave the capital and accompany her daughter to Ise. Genji, alarmed at the thought of losing her, visits her at the Shrine in the Fields, a lonely place on the outskirts of the capital. The description of the meeting of Genji and Rokujō contains some of the most beautiful writing of the entire work:

> The autumn flowers were fading; along the reeds by the river the shrill voices of many insects blended with the mournful fluting of the wind in the pines. Scarcely distinguishable from these somewhere in the distance rose and fell a faint, enticing sound of human music. . . . They came at last to a group of very temporary-looking wooden huts surrounded by a flimsy brushwood fence. The arch-

ways, built of unstripped wood, stood out black and solemn against the sky. Within the enclosure a number of priests were walking up and down with a preoccupied air. There was something portentous in their manner of addressing one another and in their way of loudly clearing their throats before they spoke. In the Hall of Offering there was a dim flicker of firelight, but elsewhere no single sign of life. So this was the place where he had left one who was from the start in great distress of mind, to shift for herself week after week, month after month! Suddenly he realized with a terrible force all that she must have suffered.[56]

The meeting of the lovers is tender. They exchange poems. Then, "suddenly he realized with astonishment that though after that unhappy incident he had imagined it to be impossible for them to meet and had so avoided all risk of his former affection being roused to new life, yet from the first moment of this strange confrontation he had immediately found himself feeling towards her precisely as he had before their estrangement."[57] They spend the night together: "At last the night ended in such a dawn as seemed to have been fashioned for their especial delight. 'Sad is any parting at the red of dawn; but never since the world began, gleamed day so tragically in the autumn sky,' and as he recited these verses, aghast to leave her, he stood hesitating and laid her hand tenderly in his."[58]

At this moment it would be impossible to think of Rokujō as the fierce incarnation of jealousy who killed Genji's wife. We sense her beauty, her grief, and, above all, her love for Genji, given special poignance because she is much older than he; she knows that before long she must lose him. That is how she is depicted in the Nō play *Nonomiya,* one of the most moving of the entire repertory. Rokujō's suffering prevents us from passing judgment on her; this, too, is evidence of how much more complex she is than any character of earlier Japanese literature.

For most readers, however, Murasaki is the "heroine" of *The Tale of Genji.* From Genji's first glimpse of her as a little girl, angry because a playmate has released her pet sparrow, until her death, she is never far from his mind, and again and again he reminds himself of her perfection. But we seldom see her except when she is unhappy—first when Genji unexpectedly takes her, later when she resigns herself to never being able to bear a child, and often when she fears that Genji's love has strayed to another woman. Genji, for all his philandering, always insists that Murasaki occupies a unique place in his heart; but when he meets Fujitsubo again after the death of the old emperor he is astonished by her beauty, and he realizes afresh how closely she resembles Murasaki:

> For years Murasaki had served to keep Lady Fujitsubo, to some extent at any rate, out of his thoughts. But now that he saw how astonishingly the one resembled the other he fancied that all the while Murasaki had but served as a substitute or eidolon of the lady who denied him her love. Both had the same pride, the same reticence. For a moment he wondered whether, if they were side by side, he should be able to tell them apart.[59]

How wretched Murasaki would have been if she had thought that perhaps she was no more than a substitute for Fujitsubo! The other ladies in Genji's life expect much less than Murasaki. The Lady of Akashi, for example, is too self-effacing ever to make any demands on Genji, and she even surrenders her daughter to Murasaki to raise as her own. The most striking female characters are those who appear in what Takeda called the "Tamakazura line" of chapters, especially Yūgao, Suetsumuhana, the Lady of Ōmi, and Tamakazura.

Yūgao is terrified of Genji. When he promises to take her "somewhere very nice where no one will disturb us," she cries out, "No, no, your ways are so strange, I should be frightened to go with you."[60] Indeed, he behaves like the hero of some Gothic romance, never revealing his identity or showing his face before the frightened young woman. Yūgao dies after Rokujō has appeared to her in a nightmare she has in the abandoned old house where Genji has taken her. Suetsumuhana, the princess with the red nose, lives in a deserted palace. Genji makes his way through the underbrush, sure that some sleeping beauty must be hidden there, only to find a fantastic creature, living in another world, too shy to appear before others, though she does not suspect how ridiculous she appears. The last thing Genji wishes is to have this fright as his mistress, but he gravely courts her in old-fashioned language, exactly as she most desires, and she responds with musty gifts. The Lady of Ōmi, a minor character, is memorable because of her foolish pretensions; she displays a rather appealing vulgarity, a lone exception to the good taste that rules the court. (She is an unrecognized daughter of Genji's friend Tō no Chūjō.) Tamakazura, the daughter Yūgao bore Tō no Chūjō, is memorable too, if only because it is to her that Genji, speaking for Murasaki Shikibu, gives the famous explanation of the value of fiction.

Genji responds perfectly to each woman. He is a genius at lovemaking, and if he had lived in a society where monogamy was strictly enforced or if, deciding that Murasaki was an ideal wife, he had never looked at another woman, the world would have been the poorer. Unlike Don Giovanni, he not only woos and wins each lady but he makes each feel sure of his love, and each is content with her small part of his life. When Genji lays out the plans for his Rokujō Palace, there are apartments not only for the women he still loves but for Suetsumuhana and even for the Lady from the Village of Falling Flowers, a woman much older than himself who was one of the less important concubines of his father.

Only one woman in the book is intentionally unkind to Genji, his father's consort Kokiden. On learning of Genji's affair with her younger sister Oborozukiyo, she is outraged. She had earlier become Genji's enemy because she feared that the emperor would name the peerless Genji, rather than her own son, as his successor. Even after Suzaku safely ascended the throne, her anger was not appeased, and Genji's scandalous behavior afforded her a perfect opportunity to demonstrate that she wielded greater power than Genji at court, despite his beauty and talent. She creates so unfriendly an atmosphere that Genji finds life at the court intolerable, and he leaves for exile in Suma. Kokiden's unkindness recalls the proverbial cruelty of the stepmother, anxious for the success of her own children, but unlike most stepmothers of fiction, she has real cause for complaint: Genji, after all, has seduced her sister.

The only woman who refuses Genji when he makes advances is the wife of a provincial governor.[61] They accidentally meet again years later at the barrier house on the road to the east as she is returning from the provinces with her aged husband. She and Genji exchange poems referring to the irony of being at the Ausaka Barrier, whose name contains the verb *au,* "to meet," though they are destined never to meet again. Soon afterward the lady's husband dies, and rather than yield to the advances of another man, she becomes a nun. It is hard to think that she does not regret her coldness to Genji years before.

Genji remains an important character in the Second Part, but he does not dominate the action as earlier on. The most memorable figure is Kashiwagi, the son of Tō no Chūjō, who has the affair with Genji's consort, the Third Princess. The overmastering passion that drives him to violate the wife of the man he most admires brings him no joy or even relief. He falls ill, and when he sees Genji he is tormented by the fear that Genji knows his secret. The chapter entitled "Kashiwagi" (The Oak Tree) opens:

> The New Year came and Kashiwagi's condition had not improved. He knew how troubled his parents were and he knew that suicide was no solution, for he would be guilty of the grievous sin of having left them behind. He had no wish to live on.[62]

After the Third Princess has given birth to Kaoru, Kashiwagi's child, she falls into a wasting illness, and in a desperate attempt to save her life the Buddhist rites of ordination as a nun are administered. The next morning the malignant spirit who has afflicted the Third Princess reveals herself, seemingly Rokujō once again, jealous even of so spiritless a creature as this princess.

Soon afterward Kashiwagi dies. The next chapter, devoted to Yūgiri, describes his wooing of Kashiwagi's widow, Ochiba, the second daughter of the Emperor Suzaku. Yūgiri's wife, Kumoinokari, had been his childhood sweetheart, and he married her only after overcoming the opposition of their parents to the match, but Yūgiri's great devotion to Kumoinokari (that had won him praise as a model husband) seems to have made her into something of a termagant. Turning elsewhere to escape from his overbearing wife, he decides to court Ochiba, though she is still in mourning for Kashiwagi. This princess stubbornly refuses to yield to Yūgiri's wooing, her resolve strengthened by the words of her dying mother, who warned her never to take a second husband. Kumoinokari, aware that her husband is spending his nights elsewhere (she does not realize, of course, that Yūgiri has been unsuccessful), becomes obsessively jealous. Yūgiri, puzzled and enraged by his failure to win the princess, pursues her all the more frantically. Ochiba's women urge her not to be so cold to a splendid gentleman, and finally conspire to admit Yūgiri to her chamber. Not until the next morning does he get his first good look at the woman for whom he has risked his reputation as a serious and dignified member of the court.[63] Kumoinokari returns to her father's house, taking her daughters. When Yūgiri appears and demands that she return home, she refuses to listen to him. We are told:

> Lying down among the children, he surveyed the confusion he had managed to create in both houses. The Second Princess must be utterly bewildered. What man in his right mind could think these affairs interesting or amusing? He had had enough of them.[64]

Yūgiri's self-analysis is exact. Although his appearance is described with the usual superlatives, he is a much reduced version of his father, and his pursuit of the reluctant princess is not only undignified but, in the end, ludicrous. It is as if he decided that, being the son of a great lover, he must demonstrate on occasion that he, too, can win a desirable woman. He chooses Ochiba without ever having seen her and knowing nothing about her qualities, a mechanical display of lust devoid of affection. And once he has succeeded by sordid means in having his way with the princess, he realizes that it has given him no pleasure. He comes to his senses, a smaller man even in his own eyes.

Genji allows Yūgiri to see Murasaki's face only after she has died. Yūgiri wept that such beauty was lost to the world, but for Genji the shock was so severe that, as many times before (but much more earnestly), he considered "leaving the world" to become a Buddhist priest. There had always been a good reason for postponing the step, but at the end of the chapter "Minori" (The Law) Genji seems at last to have made up his mind. In the following chapter, "Maboroshi" (Mirage), he destroys old letters (except those from Murasaki), plays with his grandson Niou, visits the uncomplaining Lady of Akashi after a long absence, and reminisces about the two women he loved most, Fujitsubo and Murasaki. One day succeeds another and Genji has still not carried out his resolve. The chapter concludes with Genji's watching Niou scampering around to scare off the devils before New Year and reflecting sadly that soon he would have to say goodbye to this child, too. This is the last we see of Genji.

Chapters 42, 43, and 44 are invariably included in editions of *The Tale of Genji,* but many scholars have expressed doubts concerning their authenticity. Chapter 42, "Niou," is germane to the narration, even though it is literarily inferior to preceding chapters; but chapters 43 and 44, describing respectively a younger son of Tō no Chūjō and a son of Tamakazura and Prince Higekuro, are scarcely more than digressions. Chapter 44, "Takegawa" (Bamboo River) opens in this unpromising fashion:

> The story I am about to tell wanders rather far from Genji and his family. I had it unsolicited from certain obscure women who lived out their years in Higekuro's house. It may not seem entirely in keeping with the story of Murasaki, but the women themselves say that there are numerous inaccuracies in the accounts we have had of Genji's descendants, and put the blame on women so old that they have become forgetful. I would not presume to say who is right.[65]

It is possible that some scribe or commentator, intending to make the story easier to read, added materials in the hope of tying up loose ends; or it may be that a quite independent story was woven into the text of *The Tale of Genji* by someone who thought that the work would profit by expansion.[66] In any case, it is with relief that we reach the last ten chapters; indeed, many people believe that they constitute the finest part of the entire work.

The last ten chapters are known as the Uji chapters. Uji is today a short way from Kyoto, but at the time it seemed distant and was reached with difficulty, as we know from descriptions of the journey such as: "As he came into the mountains the mist was so heavy and the underbrush so thick that he could hardly make out the path; and as he pushed his way through thickets the rough wind would throw showers of dew upon him from a turmoil of falling leaves."[67] There was also a danger of encountering bandits on the deserted trails to Uji. Even the name Uji was depressing: puns were often made on Uji and *ushi*, meaning "sad."[68] The dismal sound of the Uji River is heard again and again in these chapters, and it is associated especially with the unhappiness of the girl Ukifune, torn between two lovers, Niou and Kaoru.

Ukifune is the half-sister of the two princesses who are introduced to us at the opening of the Uji chapters, Ōigimi and Nakanokimi. They are the daughters of a prince, a younger brother of Genji, who was living in retirement as a sage and hermit at Uji. The constant noise of the river was a hindrance to meditation, but he devoted himself to his religious studies with such diligence that he was revered as a saint. Kaoru, who has grown up into a bookish young man much attracted to religion, hears of the prince and visits him. At the prince's house Kaoru encounters an old woman called Bennokimi who hints that she knows something of the secret of his birth. Kaoru has long been tormented by uneasiness about the identity of his real father, and this uncertainty contributes to his inability to act decisively. He eagerly listens as Bennokimi reveals that Kaoru is the son not of Genji but of Kashiwagi, and shows him letters Kashiwagi had received from the Third Princess.

Kaoru returns again and again to Uji, despite the hardship of the journey. His friend and rival Niou suspects that Kaoru's frequent visits to Uji are inspired by a romance, and his suspicions are confirmed when he learns of the two princesses. However, Kaoru is in fact not interested in the princesses, and it is only after their father's death that, more by way of expressing condolences than as a would-be lover, he addresses letters to the sisters. He gradually is attracted to the older sister, Ōigimi. Niou also writes her, but she spurns to answer his letters, aware of his reputation, but Kaoru's letters are so serious that she responds without fear. Kaoru before long shows greater affection, but Ōigimi has resolved never to marry, and she rarely vouchsafes more than a few words or a poem.

Kaoru, attracted by Ōigimi's seriousness, a fair match for his own, hits on the idea of shifting Niou's attention to the younger sister, Nakanokimi, though he is aware of Niou's promiscuity. Ōigimi for her part tries to divert Kaoru's affection for herself to her sister. Bennokimi, sympathizing with Kaoru, admits him to Ōigimi's bedroom, but she senses his approach and flees, leaving her sister alone. When Kaoru discovers Nakanokimi, he feels sorry for her and angry at Ōigimi.

Kaoru's plan is successful. Niou marries Nakanokimi; but this does not alter Ōigimi's resolution not to marry. Worry causes her to lose weight, and she examines with satisfaction her face in the mirror, sure that no man will now be attracted to her. When it becomes clear that Niou is unfaithful to her sister, Ōigimi feels disillusion with Kaoru, who had assured her of Niou's steadfastness. She had trusted Kaoru, but this is no longer possible, and she begins to think of death as the only release from her trials. When she dies not long afterward, Kaoru regrets he did not follow her suggestion and marry Nakanokimi, rather than bring unhappiness both to himself and Ōigimi.

Kaoru learns from Nakanokimi about her half-sister Ukifune, and when he is told that she resembles Ōigimi, his interest is aroused. One day he returns to Uji, where he catches sight of Ukifune through a crack in a door. The resemblance to Ōigimi is indeed astonishing (one recalls Murasaki's resemblance to Fujitsubo), and he is drawn back again and again.

Kaoru is by no means infatuated with Ukifune—even after they have become lovers he cannot help contrasting her unfavorably with Ōigimi—but he is attentive and always behaves correctly. Niou, once again getting wind of a romance, goes to Ukifune's room one night and, mimicking Kaoru's voice, gains admission. He spends the night with her, and pleases her more than the forbidding Kaoru. But she is under no illusions about him.

One snowy day Niou makes his way to Uji and carries Ukifune off to a house on the other side of the river where they spend two days together. Ukifune is torn by mixed feelings—love for Niou, whom she knows she cannot trust, and fear that Kaoru, whom she does not love, will learn of her affair with Niou and abandon her. Kaoru in fact discovers that Niou has been visiting Ukifune and is outraged. He stops writing, and she thinks of suicide.

The girl felt as if she were being cut to shreds. She wanted to die. . . .

And outside the river roared. "There are gentler rivers," said her mother, somewhat absentmindedly. "I'm sure the general [Kaoru] feels guilty about leaving her all this time in this godforsaken place."

Yes, it was a terrible river, swift and treacherous, said one of the women. "Why, just the other day the ferryman's little grandson slipped on his oar and fell in. Any number of people have drowned in it."

If she herself were to disappear, thought Ukifune, people would grieve for a while, but only for a time; and if she were to live on, an object of ridicule, there would be no end to her woes. Death would cancel out the accounts, nothing seemed to stand in the way.[69]

Ukifune's depression is more profound than any described earlier in the novel, and toward the end she resolves to throw herself into the terrible river. She makes preparations for death: "Unobtrusively, she began tearing up suggestive papers, burning them in her lamp and sending the ashes down the river."[70] She disappears soon afterward. Everyone supposes she is dead, but she has not drowned, recalling ironically the meaning of her nickname, "floating (or drifting) boat." This name was derived from the poem she composed and gave to Niou: "Immutable may be / the color of the orange tree / on this small island; / and yet this drifting boat / cannot know where it is bound."[71]

Kaoru's reactions to the news of Ukifune's death are surprisingly cold. His calm seems rather out of character, but perhaps he is deceiving himself: long after Niou has shifted his attentions to other women, Kaoru, though he cannot forgive Ukifune for deceiving him, still searches for her.

Ukifune is found by some priests near the river, incapable of speech, and is nursed back to health. In response to her entreaties, she is admitted to holy orders, and goes to live with some nuns. Kaoru accidentally learns where Ukifune is and asks a boy, one of her brothers, to beg her to see him; but she sends the boy away without an answer. This is where the novel ends.

The Uji chapters are literally the best part of *The Tale of Genji.* There are not many characters, and each is carefully drawn. Genji is so marvelously beautiful and accomplished that it is hard for readers to identify with him. This problem does not arise in the case of Kaoru or Niou, whose beauty is fully described but whose flaws are equally obvious. Both *kaoru* and *niou* are verbs meaning "to be fragrant," and these nicknames suggest their courtliness; but whereas Kaoru's mysterious scent is a natural part of him over which he has no control, Niou resorts to blending perfumes in order to keep up with his rival. Niou is the less attractive of the two men, even though we are told that he is handsomer than Kaoru and can gather from Ukifune's preference that he possesses greater charm; but it is hard to forgive his ruthlessness in pursuing the few women whom Kaoru has loved. There is a bitterness in the relations between the two men absent from Genji's with his rival, Tō no Chūjō, another sign perhaps that they belong to a world in decline in which friendship is unhesitantly discarded for personal advantage.

The doctrine of mappō, the latter days of the Buddhist Law,[72] may have colored Murasaki Shikibu's portrayal of times closer to her own than those of the peerless Genji, times when the sorrow of human existence was no mere phrase. The persons of the Uji chapters live in a world much darker than Genji's. The unhappy Ōigimi has resolved never to marry; her sister Nakanokimi is persuaded by his beauty to trust Niou, only to discover his heartlessness; Ukifune, an unsophisticated girl, finds being courted by two desirable young men so oppressive that she attempts suicide; and the two men, so superlatively gifted, are both frustrated in their desires. The story of these unforgettable persons develops systematically and even inevitably; there is no question here of chapters having been written out of order or later inserted.

Contemporary Appeal of the Work

Murasaki Shikibu devoted her greatest attention to the elements in human life that have changed least over the centuries. Because the emotions of her characters are so easily intelligible, we sometimes obtain a startling impression of modernity, and it is easy to overlook even the aspects of life in Heian Japan that differ most conspicuously from our own. Although we are repeatedly informed that court ladies were normally invisible to men, hidden behind curtains and intervening screens, it is difficult to believe that these people whom we feel we know so intimately could have fallen passionately in love without once getting a proper look at each other, and we may therefore suppress the reality of the curtains and screens, regardless of what Murasaki Shikibu says. It is hard even to keep in mind what the faces of the women must have looked like: women customarily blackened their teeth and shaved their eyebrows (painting false eyebrows on their foreheads); but when we attempt to visualize the women of *The Tale of Genji* we are more likely to think of Japanese women we have actually seen than the lookalikes of the old illustrations.

Arthur Waley, writing in 1933, discussed the resemblances that reviewers had found between *The Tale of Genji* and the works of Proust, Jane Austen, Boccaccio, and Shakespeare, commenting, "Her book indeed is like those caves, common in a certain part of Spain, in which as one climbs from chamber to chamber the natural formation of the rock seems in succession to assume a semblance to every known form of sculpture—here a figure from Chartres, there a Buddha from Yun-Kang, a Persian conqueror, a Byzantine ivory."[73] Waley did not deny the resemblances that reviewers had found between the writings of Murasaki Shikibu and modern writers: "Murasaki, like the novelist of to-day, is not principally interested in the events of the story, but rather in the effect which these events may have upon the minds of her characters. Such books as hers it is convenient, I think, to call 'novels,' while reserving for other works of fiction the name 'story' or 'romance.' "[74]

Critics have questioned the appropriateness of referring to *The Tale of Genji* as a "novel." The lowly reputation of fiction as a whole in the Heian period contrasts with the prestige that novels enjoy today; but Tamagami Takuya, who disliked referring to *any* monogatari as a novel, conceded that *The Tale of Genji* was read and discussed by men as well as women,[75] suggesting that, whether or not modern in any other sense, the work was treated with the respect due a work of high literary value. This contemporary evaluation has not wavered. *The Tale of Genji* is the central work of Japanese literature. It was read and imitated by generations of court writers, and was adapted for use in different forms of drama, not only the aristocratic Nō[76] but the plebeian Bunraku and Kabuki theaters. It was the model (though considerably distorted) for Saikaku's *Life of an Amorous Man* (1682), the work that is considered to mark the birth of the characteristic form of fiction of the premodern period. It furnished the advocates of the Shintō revival of the eighteenth century (notably Motoori Norinaga) with the supreme example of distinctively Japanese expression. In the twentieth century it has been translated into modern Japanese by Tanizaki Jun'ichirō and other important writers, and through these translations has reached an infinitely greater number of readers than ever before. It has been beautifully translated into English, French, and German, bringing it world renown.[77] It occupies in Japanese literature the place of Shakespeare in English literature, of Dante in Italian literature, or of Cervantes in Spanish literature. It is also a monument of world literature, the first novel of magnitude composed anywhere, a work that is at once distinctively Japanese and universally affecting.

Notes

1. *Kawabata Yasunari Zenshū*, XXIII, p. 319.
2. See *Dawn to the West*, I, p. 824.
3. The appropriateness of the term "novel" has been much discussed. I use it as a convenience, rather than "monogatari," "tale," or "romance."
4. *Nihon Koten Bungaku Daijiten*, II, p. 408.
5. See Ivan Morris, *As I Crossed a Bridge of Dreams*, p. 55. The diarist wrote that an aunt presented her with "fifty-odd volumes of *The Tale of Genji.*" She did not date this entry, but it follows close after mention of the death in 1021 of her nurse.
6. See *Nihon Koten Bugaku Daijiten*, II, p. 406.
7. It has been suggested that some other person who was close to Murasaki Shikibu wrote the chapters "Niou," "Kōbai," and "Takegawa."
8. It was advanced by Ichijō Kaneyoshi in his book of *Genji* criticism entitled *Kachō Yojō* (1492).
9. See *Nihon Koten Bungaku Daijiten*, II, p. 406.
10. See Ii Haruki, *Genji Monogatari no Nazo*, p. 137.
11. See Akiyama Ken, *Genji Monogatari*, p. 99.
12. Tametoki's waka were included in imperial collections, notably the *Goshūishū* in which there are three. Poem 147 in this collection is of the *jukkai* variety, a complaint, using the imagery of flowers, over his failure to gain advancement.
13. Akiyama, *Genji*, p. 100.
14. *Ibid.*, p. 100. The story is given in *Tales of Times Now Past* and elsewhere.
15. See Yamamoto Ritatsu, *Murasaki Shikibu Nikki, Murasaki Shikibu Shū*, p. 136. The poem is included in the *Senzaishū*.
16. *Ibid.*
17. Akiyama, *Genji*, p. 108.
18. In kambun, rather than in kana, because of its greater concision, and possibly also on the analogy of *Nihon Ryōiki*, which was composed in kambun as the basic material for sermons to be delivered in Japanese.
19. Tamagami Takuya, *Genji Monogatari Kenkyū*, pp. 147, 150.
20. *Ibid.*, pp. 150–51.
21. Unfortunately for this charming legend, the temple burned to the ground after the time of Murasaki's supposed visit.
22. See Ii, *Genji*, p. 45. Abe Akio, a noted specialist of *The Tale of Genji*, also

believed that Murasaki Shikibu began her work with the "Waka-Murasaki" chapter. See Aileen Gatten, "The Order of the Early Chapters in the *Genji monogatari*," pp. 30–33.

23. See Arthur Waley's translation of *The Tale of Genji*, p. 7, note 1, where he stated, "Murasaki, still under the influence of her somewhat childish predecessors, writes in a manner which is a blend of the court chronicle with the conventional fairy-tale." However, the "Kiritsubo" chapter is singled out for special praise in *Mumyō Zōshi* (Story Without a Name) and in many later works.
24. See *Nihon Koten Bungaku Daijiten*, II, p. 410.
25. Takeda Munetoshi, *Genji Monogatari no Kenkyū*. Gatten, in her absorbing article "The Order," discussed problems in the narration when the work is read in the accepted order. She drew on the theory of Abe Akio, who postulated two lines of composition, the "Wakamurasaki Group" and the "Hahakigi Group." These two lines correspond very closely to Takeda's theory. Abe believed that the "Kiritsubo" chapter was written perhaps at the time of the twenty-first chapter, "Otome," but Gatten decided that the "Kiritsubo" chapter was indispensable to the narration of the early chapters and must *in some form* have existed before the "Wakamurasaki" chapter was written. (Gatten, "The Order," p. 39.)
26. Takeda, *Genji*, p. 34–35.
27. *Ibid.*, pp. 17ff.
28. *Ibid.*, pp. 64–65.
29. Waley, *Genji*, p. 92.
30. Edward Seidensticker, *The Tale of Genji*, I, p. 57.
31. Waley was not the only one to believe that the women must be standing on something. Ikeda Kikan in his edition of *Genji Monogatari* (in Nihon Koten Zensho series), I, p. 234, had the women on *fumidai*, a kind of platform. This is more plausible than Waley's table or bed, but it also requires an explanation of *why* they were on a fumidai. Other commentators have suggested that the floor level was higher than Genji would have expected, and for this reason the women seemed taller than they actually were.
32. Esperanza Ramirez-Christensen wrote, in "The Operation of the Lyrical Mode in the *Genji Monogatari*," p. 39, "What happens in the passages under consideration is that the poetic function is being superimposed upon the narrative progression, slowing it down and transforming its constitutive elements (plot-character-setting) into paradigmatic transparencies of meaning. The paradigm, by reiterating the same message in various reifications, endows the narrative with a certain permanence, and at the same time a certain ambiguity and richness." Her essay is specifically concerned with the first three of the ten Uji chapters, but her illuminating observations are valid for the entire work.

    Another essay in the same book (*Ukifune: Love in The Tale of Genji*, edited by Andrew Pekarik) by Amy Vladeck Heinrich, "*Blown in Flurries:* The Role of the Poetry in 'Ukifune,'" gives further proof of the vital function played by the poems, though they are often overlooked by those who write about *The Tale of Genji.*

33. This is the subject of Janet Goff's *Noh Drama and The Tale of Genji.* See below, pp. 1022–24, for an example of how a passage from the "Suma" chapter of *Genji* was used in the Nō play *Matsukaze.*
34. I am thinking, for example, of the passage in Part One of the "Wakana" chapter in which a cat on a leash upsets the screen protecting the Third Princess from the gaze of outsiders. Kashiwagi gets only a glimpse of the princess, but it is enough to make him fall desperately in love, the commencement of their tragic affair. See Seidensticker, *Genji*, II, pp. 592–93; Waley, *Genji*, pp. 642–43.
35. Akiyama, *Genji*, p. 8.
36. Takaakira's rebellion figures in *The Gossamer Years*, and the Mother of Michitsuna sent a poem to Aimiya, Takaakira's wife, when he was exiled to Kyūshū. Aimiya was the sister of the Tōnomine Captain. See chapter 9, notes 17 and 36 (pages 403–4).
37. The role of ghosts in the work is exhaustively discussed by Mitoma Kōsuke in *Genji Monogatari no Minzokugakuteki Kenkyū.* See also Norma Field, *The Splendor of Longing in the Tale of Genji*, pp. 51–63, where spirit possession is discussed.
38. Translation in Seidensticker, *Genji*, I, p. 3.
39. Translation by Witter Bynner in Cyril Birch, *Anthology of Chinese Literature*, I, pp. 266–69.
40. Translation in Ryusaku Tsunoda, Wm. Theodore de Bary, and Donald Keene, *Sources of Japanese Tradition*, pp. 532–34.
41. *Ibid.*, p. 534.
42. See Haruo Shirane, *The Bridge of Dreams: a Poetics of "The Tale of Genji,"* pp. 10–11, for a discussion of this aspect of the work.
43. Shirane, *The Bridge*, pp. 3–4 considers this theme, and cites (p. 228) the article by the folklore scholar Origuchi Shinobu, "Shōsetsu gikyoku bungaku ni okeru monogatari yōso," in which it is discussed. Field (in *The Splendor*, pp. 33–35) quotes Origuchi and considers the same theme in *Tales of Ise* and similar works. See also Mitani Kuniaki, *Genji Monogatari Shitsukeito*, pp. 24–31.
44. Field (in *The Splendor*, pp. 97–103) considers the stepmother (and stepdaughter) theme in Heian literature with reference to *The Tale of Genji.*
45. Translated by Ivan Morris in *The World of the Shining Prince*, pp. 308–9.
46. Translation in Seidensticker, *Genji*, I, p. 14.
47. Minamoto was one of the two most powerful noble families of the time, the other being the Fujiwara. The Sino-Japanese reading of Minamoto is Gen; hence, the name Genji, or "he of the Minamoto clan." The character Genji is not given a personal name anywhere in the work.

48. The irregularity in the succession was responsible for the action of the prewar militarists in banning publication of the offending chapters of Tanizaki's modern-language translation of *The Tale of Genji.*
49. Arthur Waley, *The Lady of the Boat*, p. 15. The passage occurs in the Seidensticker translation in *Genji*, II, p. 735.
50. See Waley, *Genji*, p. 146. Seidensticker, who was evidently using a different text, omitted this passage.
51. Seidensticker, *Genji*, I, p. 142. See also Waley, *Genji*, p. 227.
52. Seidensticker, *Genji*, I, p. 180.
53. Waley, *Genji*, p. 100. See also Seidensticker, *Genji*, I, p. 63.
54. See Waley, *Genji*, pp. 262–78; also Seidensticker, *Genji*, I, pp. 165–74.
55. Seidensticker, *Genji*, I, p. 183; Waley renders the passage, "He thought with great tenderness and concern of Lady Rokujō's distress; but it was clear to him that he must beware of ever again allowing her to regard him as her true haven of refuge. If however she would renew their friendship in quite new terms, permitting him to enjoy her company and conversation at such times as he could conveniently arrange to do so, he saw no reason why they should not sometimes meet." (*Genji*, p. 294.)
56. Arthur Waley, *The Sacred Tree*, p. 41. See also Seidensticker, *Genji*, I, p. 186.
57. Waley, *The Sacred Tree,* p. 43.
58. *Ibid.,* p. 44.
59. *Ibid.*, p. 61.
60. Waley, *Genji*, p. 106.
61. Waley refers to the lady as Utsusemi, Seidensticker by the translation of this name, the Lady of the Locust Shell. Her rejection of Genji occurs in chapter 2.
62. Seidensticker, *Genji*, II, p. 636. See also Arthur Waley, *Blue Trousers*, p. 230.
63. See Seidensticker, *Genji*, II, p. 708.
64. *Ibid.*, p. 710.
65. *Ibid.*, p. 751. See also Waley, *The Lady,* p. 41.
66. In the absence of firm information about the transmission of the text during the two centuries between Murasaki Shikibu's manuscript and the oldest surviving manuscript, it is impossible to be sure whether or not these three chapters were in the original version. For a brief history of the texts of *The Tale of Genji*, see Aileen Gatten, "Three Problems in the Text of 'Ukifune,'" pp. 87–89. The earliest surviving recension of the entire text with variants was completed by Minamoto Chikayuki in 1255. Four chapters in Fujiwara Teika's handwriting, made early in the thirteenth century, survive, and later manuscripts purport to be copies of his text.
67. Seidensticker, *Genji*, II, p. 772.
68. *Ibid.*, p. 781.
69. *Ibid.*, p. 999.

70. *Ibid.*, p. 1006.
71. Translation by Amy Vladeck Heinrich in Pekarik, *Ukifune*, p. 156.
72. According to the doctrine of mappō, after the death of Shakyamuni Buddha there would be three great periods affecting his teachings: during the first, of five hundred years, they would flourish; during the second, of one thousand years, they would decline; and in the third period, of ten thousand years, they would gradually disappear. In Japan it was widely believed that the third period, that of mappō, would begin in 1052. Once the world entered this phase, it would be impossible for individuals to save themselves; they would have to depend on the saving grace of Amida for salvation.
73. Arthur Waley, *The Bridge of Dreams*, p. 23.
74. Waley, *The Sacred Tree*, pp. 30–31.
75. Tamagami, *Genji Monogatari Kenkyū*, p. 144.
76. See Goff, *Noh Drama*, for an account of how the dramatists borrowed from *The Tale of Genji*.
77. The earliest English and French (partial) translations, made in the nineteenth century, did little to promote the reputation of *The Tale of Genji* abroad, but the translations into English of Arthur Waley (1926–33) and Edward Seidensticker (1976), into French by René Sieffert (1978–85), and into German by Oscar Benl (1966) have been widely read and admired.

Bibliography

Note: All Japanese books, except as otherwise noted, were published in Tokyo.

Akiyama Ken. *Genji Monogatari*, in Iwanami Shinsho series. Iwanami Shoten, 1968.

Benl, Oscar. *Die Geschichte vom Prinzen Genji*, 2 vols. Zurich: Manesse Verlag, 1966.

Birch, Cyril. *Anthology of Chinese Literature*, 2 vols. New York: Grove Press, 1965–72.

Field, Norma. *The Splendor of Longing in the Tale of Genji.* Princeton, N.J.: Princeton University Press, 1987.

Gatten, Aileen. "The Order of the Early Chapters in the *Genji monogatari*," *Harvard Journal of Asiatic Studies*, 41:1, 1981.

———. "Three Problems in the Text of 'Ukifune,' " in Pekarik, *Ukifune.*

Goff, Janet. *Noh Drama and The Tale of Genji.* Princeton, N.J.: Princeton University Press, 1991.

Heinrich, Amy Vladeck. "*Blown in Flurries:* The Role of Poetry in 'Ukifune,' " in Pekarik, *Ukifune*.

Ii Haruki. *Genji Monogatari no Nazo*, in Sanseidō Sensho series. Sanseidō, 1983.

Ikeda Kikan. *Genji Monogatari*, I, in Nihon Koten Zensho series. Asahi Shimbun Sha, 1946.

Kawabata Yasunari Zenshū, 35 vols. Shinchōsha, 1980–83.

Kawaguchi Hisao. *Genji Monogatari e no Michi*. Yoshikawa Kōbunkan, 1991.

Mitani Kuniaki. *Genji Monogatari Shitsukeito*. Yūseidō, 1991.

Mitoma Kōsuke. *Genji Monogatari no Minzokugakuteki Kenkyū*, Ōfūsha, 1980.

Morris, Ivan. *As I Crossed a Bridge of Dreams*. New York: Dial Press, 1971.

———. *The World of the Shining Prince*. London: Oxford University Press, 1964.

Nihon Koten Bungaku Daijiten, 6 vols. Iwanami Shoten, 1983–85.

Oka Kazuo. *Genji Monogatari no Kisoteki Kenkyū*. Tōkyōdō, 1966.

Okada, H. Richard. *Figures of Resistance*. Durham, N.C., and London: Duke University Press, 1991.

Pekarik, Andrew (ed.). *Ukifune: Love in The Tale of Genji*. New York: Columbia University Press, 1982.

Ramirez-Christensen, Esperanza. "The Operation of the Lyrical Mode in the *Genji Monogatari*," in Pekarik, *Ukifune*.

Seidensticker, Edward (trans.). *The Tale of Genji*, 2 vols. New York: Alfred A. Knopf, 1976.

Shimizu Yoshiko, Mori Ichirō, and Yamamoto Ritatsu. *Genji Monogatari Tekagami*. Shinchōsha, 1973.

Shirane, Haruo. *The Bridge of Dreams: a Poetics of "The Tale of Genji."* Stanford, Calif.: Stanford University Press, 1987.

Sieffert, René. *Le dit de Genji*, 2 vols. Paris: Publications Orientalistes de France. 1978–85.

Stinchecum, Amanda Mayer. *Narrative Voice in the Tale of Genji*. Urbana, Ill.: University of Illinois, Center for Asian and Pacific Studies, 1985.

Takeda Munetoshi. *Genji Monogatari no Kenkyū*. Iwanami Shoten, 1954.

Tamagami Takuya. *Genji Monogatari Hyōshaku*, 14 vols. Kadokawa Shoten, 1964–69.

———. *Genji Monogatari Kenkyū* (vol. XIII of *Genji Monogatari Hyōshaku*). Kadokawa Shoten, 1966.

———. *Genji Monogatari no Hikiuta*. Chūō Kōron Sha, 1955.

Tomikura Tokujirō. *Mumyō Zōshi Hyōkai*. Yūseidō, 1952.

Tsunoda, Ryusaku, Wm. Theodore de Bary, and Donald Keene. *Sources of Japanese Tradition*. New York: Columbia University Press, 1958

Waley, Arthur (trans.). *Blue Trousers*. Boston and New York: Houghton Mifflin, 1928.

———. *The Bridge of Dreams*. Boston and New York: Houghton Mifflin, 1933.

———. *The Lady of the Boat*. Boston and New York: Houghton Mifflin, 1932.

———. *The Sacred Tree*. Boston and New York: Houghton Mifflin, 1926.

———. *The Tale of Genji*. Boston and New York: Houghton Mifflin, 1926.

———. *A Wreath of Cloud*. Boston and New York: Houghton Mifflin, 1927.

Yamamoto Ritatsu. *Murasaki Shikibu Nikki, Murasaki Shikibu Shū*, in Shinchō Nihon Koten Shūsei series. Shinchōsha, 1980.

13. COURTLY FICTION AFTER *THE TALE OF GENJI*

The fiction composed at the court during the two centuries after the completion of *The Tale of Genji* is often discussed in terms of the overpowering influence of Murasaki Shikibu's masterpiece. Every similarity in language, plot development, and characterization has been carefully traced, and one is likely to receive the impression that these tales contain nothing new, certainly nothing to suggest how much the world had changed during the years after the completion of *The Tale of Genji.*[1] And yet, anyone who reads these later works with an open mind will surely discover significant differences between them and *The Tale of Genji*, some so striking as to suggest explorations of aspects of fiction that had not been considered by Murasaki Shikibu.

It is obvious that the authors of the later fiction were not only thoroughly acquainted with *The Tale of Genji* but imitated it without constraint. They also shared the tacit assumption of Murasaki Shikibu that the only place worthy of being depicted in a monogatari was the court; hardly a glance was given at life elsewhere in the capital, much less elsewhere in Japan. Again, the central characters of the monogatari, male and female alike, were almost inevitably described in terms of their incomparable beauty, recalling Genji and his ladies. Mundane problems (such as those relating to poverty) were rarely touched on, and were never considered important enough to be treated as a central cause of unhappiness.

The world portrayed by Murasaki Shikibu was not exactly like the Heian court of her day, as we have seen, but it was not altogether remote either; and the last third of her book describes a society that fairly closely resembles the court life of the time as we know it from other accounts. Monogatari written during the latter part of the eleventh and early part of the twelfth century also reflected their times, unconsciously perhaps, especially the changes in the morals and in the way of life of the courtiers—what may, for want of a more precise term, be described as the decadence of the aristocracy.

The courtly fiction composed after *The Tale of Genji* changed in nature even more conspicuously in the middle of the twelfth century, when a series of aborted coups and other military uprisings shook the foundations of the court, depriving the nobles of political power and the means to lead the lives of luxury described in earlier literature. These uprisings would be treated in a series of *gunki monogatari* (martial tales), but the writers of court fiction, disdaining to write about the changes brought about by the shift of power from the aristocracy to the military, continued to write monogatari in the traditional manner, as if nothing had happened. The variety of fiction composed from the late Heian period well into the Kamakura period is known as *giko monogatari*, meaning "archaic fiction." Unlike the courtly fiction of the post-*Genji* era, the giko monogatari were set in the past, during the happy days when the court was the undisputed center of Japanese culture, and they were written not in the language of their own time but in close imitation of the language of the earlier fiction, only inadvertently revealing the changes that had occurred over the years in Japanese speech. The giko monogatari, though they resemble in many ways the fiction composed after *The Tale of Genji*, will therefore be treated in a later chapter.

It is easy to find instances of direct borrowing from *The Tale of Genji* in the later fiction. An obvious example of this tendency occurs in *Torikaebaya Monogatari* (If I Could Only Change Them),[2] where we are told of a certain prince, a man of great religious devotion, who lives in Uji with his two daughters. This description also exactly fits Prince Hachi in the "Hashihime" (Lady of the Bridge) chapter of *The Tale of Genji*. It was not essential to the plot of *If I Could Only Change Them* for the hero to encounter in Uji a prince with two daughters (as opposed, say, to a prince with three daughters who lived near Lake Biwa), but the author undoubtedly expected that readers would accept this borrowing from *The Tale of Genji* in the spirit of honka-dori, the practice of waka poets of borrowing material from the poems of their predecessors.

There can hardly be any disputing the accepted opinion that *The Tale of Genji* is incomparably superior to all other examples of court fiction, and the influence of this towering masterpiece was virtually inescapable; but reading the later works it soon becomes clear that the writers were trying in different ways to create something distinctive in their subject matter or their tone even if they could not hope to surpass the literary quality of *The Tale of Genji*. For example, the beauty of

Prince Genji, repeatedly extolled by Murasaki Shikibu, created a model for the heroes of the later fiction, almost always described in terms not of their skill in running the country, but of their looks. However, the authors of the later court fiction, not content merely with praising the faces of their heroes, insisted that these men were radiantly lovely, sometimes so beautiful that they could easily be mistaken for women. From this it was a short step (which various authors took) to works of fiction in which the sexes were virtually interchangeable. The transvestism in *If I Could Only Change Them*, the sole claim of the work to our attention, is a grotesque exaggeration of an element present in *The Tale of Genji*, but the quantitative difference has become qualitative. Beauty is by no means an inevitable attribute of a hero: it is uncommon to encounter a beautiful man in a European novel, and in Japan neither the martial tales of the thirteenth century nor the much later novels of Saikaku and his successors devoted much attention to the physical appearance of their heroes. One can hardly imagine there would have been such insistence on the beauty of the heroes in fiction of the later Heian period had there not been the model of *The Tale of Genji*, but the authors of these works developed the theme in a manner that would have been inconceivable to Murasaki Shikibu.

The later tales are not dated and their authors remain uncertain despite the most painstaking tracing of the meager clues.[3] Works of fiction were not printed before the seventeenth century, and though we must lament the loss of many, it is a miracle that so many survived the medieval warfare and the burning of libraries, some only in a single manuscript.

Mumyō Zōshi (Story Without a Name, c. 1200),[4] the oldest work of criticism of Japanese fiction, is cast in the form of a conversation among various literary ladies about their favorite books. They all take it for granted that *The Tale of Genji* is the supreme work of fiction. One of them says,

> The more I think of it, the more I am convinced that to have created this *Tale of Genji* was such an extraordinary achievement it could not have been accomplished without divine aid. I believe it was a genuine miracle granted by the Buddha in response to the author's prayers. Fiction composed ever since has obviously been very easy to write. There is no reason why someone who had learned about the art of fiction from *Genji* could not produce an even better book. But, it seems to me, for Murasaki Shikibu to have created such a work, when the only precedents she could consult were *The Hollow*

Tree, The Bamboo Cutter, and *Sumiyoshi*, was not the achievement of a mere human being.[5]

Although the ladies agreed that it should be easy for someone to create a work that was even better than *The Tale of Genji* by skillfully borrowing its techniques and materials, they clearly did not believe that any later tale was in fact superior.

The Tale of Sagoromo

The work to which the ladies of *Story Without a Name* gave the most attention among those composed after *The Tale of Genji* was *Sagoromo Monogatari* (The Tale of Sagoromo). One lady, asked to state her likes and dislikes among the tales she had read, replied, "I think *The Tale of Sagoromo* is next best to *Genji*. From the opening words, 'We regret the passing of the spring of youth,'[6] the language is somehow charming, but although it maintains a wonderfully aristocratic manner,[7] nothing strikes especially deep into one's heart. On the contrary, there are many things in the book that might better not have been there at all."[8] This mixed praise is followed by a more favorable evaluation of various scenes in the work; but the section of *Story Without a Name* devoted to *The Tale of Sagoromo* ends with sharp disapproval of the instances of supernatural intervention, and with condemnation of the resolution of the tale, the ascension to the throne of the hero, Sagoromo.

The lady is remarkably astute in her analysis of the faults of *The Tale of Sagoromo*—its failure to strike deeply into the reader's heart, the various passages that are unnecessary to the development of either the plot or the characters, the implausibility of the intervention of a divine being in a work that is otherwise realistic, and the unconvincing oracle that leads to Sagoromo's becoming the emperor; but her reasons for ranking *The Tale of Sagoromo* second only to *The Tale of Genji* are disappointingly brief and uninformative. The judgment nevertheless is basically sound: with the exception of *Yoru no Nezame* (Wakefulness at Night), the work the ladies rated next highest in order of excellence, *The Tale of Sagoromo* is the finest example of fiction in the tradition of *The Tale of Genji*.

The authorship of *The Tale of Sagoromo* is nowhere mentioned in contemporary writings. Fujiwara Teika, writing more than a century later, expressed the belief that it was the work of a court lady, a daughter of Minamoto no Yorikuni known by her title of Senji,[9] who died in

1092 at an advanced age.[10] This attribution is generally accepted today, and internal evidence suggests that the work was probably written about 1080. One other monogatari[11] and four poems in imperially sponsored collections are also credited to Senji, and we know that she was in the service of Princess Baishi (1039–1096), the fourth daughter of the Emperor Suzaku. Baishi was the high priestess at Ise from 1046 to 1058, but later took orders as a Buddhist nun; perhaps her influence explains the striking combination of Shintō and Buddhist elements in *The Tale of Sagoromo*. The work is little read today except by specialists in Heian literature, but for many years it enjoyed great popularity, as we can infer from the more than a hundred manuscripts that have been preserved, each with its complement of textual variants.

The Tale of Sagoromo is perhaps the first extended work of Japanese fiction to have been conceived from the outset as a single, unified story.[12] The three love affairs that make up the bulk of the work are related more or less independently, but the reader does not get the impression that chapters, unanticipated when the work was begun, were added in response to the demands of readers or to a deepening understanding of the materials on the author's part. Although most manuscripts divide *The Tale of Sagoromo* into four books, each with an elegantly written introductory section, it is from beginning to end an uninterrupted account of ten years in the life of Sagoromo, a prince of the highest rank (the son of the kampaku and the nephew of the emperor). He is blessed with extraordinary beauty and intelligence, as the author frequently reminds us, but to the end is unsuccessful in his love for his cousin, Princess Genji.[13] Other loves or worldly honors, even becoming emperor, give him no pleasure because of this frustration, and as his despair accumulates, his thoughts turn incessantly to "leaving the world" as a Buddhist priest. The work concludes as Sagoromo gazes out over an autumn garden in the deepening twilight, and wonders about the nature of the karma that has caused his life in the present world to be so unsatisfying.

The Tale of Sagoromo opens with the quotation from Po Chü-i praised by the lady of *Story Without a Name*, then abruptly plunges into an account of Sagoromo's secret love for Princess Genji without identifying by name either Sagoromo or his beloved. After a few pages the story begins again, this time in a more conventional manner, suggesting (despite the evidence of *Story Without a Name*) that the present opening may represent a corruption in the text. The second opening is also rather unusual because it sets the story in recent years (*kono koro*), though monogatari generally were set in some vague but distant past. There follows a description of Sagoromo's immediate ancestry. His father, the kampaku, was of impeccable imperial birth, a brother of the present emperor, but he had fallen from the rank of prince and was now a commoner. All the same, he lived in the utmost splendor with his three wives, one the younger sister of the former emperor, the second the daughter of the present prime minister, and the third the younger sister of an empress. His greatest treasure was his only son, born to his favorite wife, the emperor's sister. This son, referred to in the course of the work by his various titles rather than by his name, is otherwise known by the nickname Sagoromo (garment), derived from the last word of a poem he composes:

iroiro ni	I refuse to wear
kasanete wa kiji	Layered robes of many hues;
hito shirezu	At night I shall wear
omoisometeshi	The garment my love first dyed
yo wa sagoromo[14]	When not a soul was aware.

The meaning of the poem is that Sagoromo intends to be true to Princess Genji, his first love, though other women may offer themselves.

After introducing Sagoromo's parents, the narrative moves on to Sagoromo himself, now in his eighteenth year. He is of such flawless beauty and so wondrously talented that his parents fear an early death may await him. Their fears seem confirmed when, one night at the palace, he is asked by the emperor to play the flute. His notes seem to echo to the heavens, and everyone from the emperor down to the lowliest servant is moved to tears. Lightning flashes and music is heard from the sky, harmonizing with the sound of Sagoromo's flute. The music comes closer, and a purple cloud descends bearing a wondrously beautiful child, who catches hold of Sagoromo's sleeve to pull him up into the sky. Sagoromo makes no effort to resist, but the emperor, desolate at the thought of losing Sagoromo, distraughtly clings to him. Sagoromo's unsuccessful love for Princess Genji has deprived him of all attachment to this world, but when he sees the emperor desperately tugging at his sleeve and thinks of how forlorn his parents will be if he leaves them, he sadly refuses to go, composing a poem in Chinese to explain his feelings. Now it is the turn of the child, none other than the god of music Amewakamiko, to weep in disappointment.

The emperor, portrayed with a realism that contrasts with the fantasy of the scene, feels he must do something to overcome Sagoromo's lack of attachment to this world. He knows Sagoromo well enough to realize that promoting him to high office will have no effect, so he decides to offer him his most precious possession, his beloved daughter, the Second Princess.[15] Sagoromo cannot openly refuse this incomparable gift, but he is prevented by love for the Princess Genji from accepting, and gives an ambiguous answer. His strange romance with the Second Princess is the subject of the second of the four books of *The Tale of Sagoromo*.

The criticisms directed by the lady in *Story Without a Name* against this and similar interventions of the supernatural in *The Tale of Sagoromo* were entirely apt. The reader is willing to accept the supernatural in a fairy tale like *The Tale of the Bamboo Cutter*, but this work is otherwise so realistically plotted—even more so than *The Tale of Genji*—that the miracle is an intrusion. The naturalistic, worldly aspects of the novel are found most conspicuously in the conversations; each character seems to speak an appropriate idiom, and there are flashes of excitement, irritation, and even outright anger in the expression, as well as the more usual bittersweet regret.

The reactions of Sagoromo's parents to the miracle are at once characteristic and touchingly human. Sagoromo's father is dismayed, not proud, that his son should have been given so signal a mark of divine recognition: "He was not in the least happy that his son possessed such an excess of talents."[16] His mother, worried by Sagoromo's lateness in returning home after the concert in the palace, herself prepares and serves a meal when he at last gets back, urging him to eat.[17] This is a touch of startling realism for a court romance: it would be inconceivable that any of the ladies in *The Tale of Genji* would have prepared a meal. It is difficult to visualize a woman dressed in twelve layers of robes preparing food in the kitchen, but this glimpse of the sister of an emperor, worrying about her son in the manner of mothers of all times and places, is undeniably appealing. Somewhat later in the story there is a charming scene between Sagoromo and his mother in which, during the exchange of casual, rather witty remarks that suggest a real mother and son, he hints that his thinness, about which the mother worries, is not caused by a loss of appetite induced by the summer heat but by hopeless love.[18]

Sagoromo's unsuccessful courtship of Princess Genji provides the framework for the entire story, but he is involved with other women who distract him, at least momentarily, from his grief. The first is with the daughter of a middle counselor and commandant of the Dazaifu headquarters, a man of consequence but by no means of the highest birth. One night Sagoromo catches a glimpse of a priest through the window of a carriage and notices that there seems also to be a woman inside.[19] His suspicions are aroused and he sends men to investigate.

The priest runs away when they question him, and a page informs the men that the priest has abducted a woman. Not knowing what to do with the woman, barely visible in the dark, Sagoromo offers to take her to his palace for the night. She makes no reply. He then asks if she was accompanying the priest by choice; if so, he will leave her where she is. The woman only weeps for an answer. Unable to elicit a word from her, Sagoromo asks with a touch of exasperation, "I take it then that you have no objection if I leave you here?" She at length controls her tears long enough to inform him where she lives.

The woman (known as Asukai, from the place-name in a poem she composes) much resembles Yūgao in her inarticulateness and in the awe she feels toward her unknown rescuer, but the circumstances of Sagoromo's rescue of Asukai are far more sinister than those of Genji's first meeting with Yūgao. Indeed, one can hardly imagine anything so violent in *The Tale of Genji* as a woman being abducted by a lecherous priest, a reflection perhaps of a deterioration in the morals of Heian society.

Sagoromo's motives in rescuing Asukai are at first disinterested, but gradually he notices her unusual beauty and he feels a sudden, unexpected love for the little creature huddled in terror in her corner of the carriage. In the usual manner, he ascribes these feelings (and, indeed, the whole incident) to causes in a previous existence. But at his first words of endearment she shrinks from him and even tries to leave the carriage. Sagoromo, irritated, asks, "Why can't you even answer my questions? If you're glad I'm seeing you home, you might at least invite me to stay. You're most exasperating." She responds at last with this poem:

tomare tomo	I can't possibly
e koso iwarene	Invite you even to stay:
Asukai ni	In Asukai
yadori hatsubeki	We have no lodgings worthy
kage shi nakereba[20]	Of one who would spend the night.

Despite her objections, he not only sees her home but spends the night with her, without revealing his identity.

At this point there is a flashback, an unusual narrative device for this time, that reveals who Asukai was and how it happened that she and the priest were in the same carriage. After the death of Asukai's parents she was left in the care of a *menoto*, a woman who had at one time been Asukai's wet nurse but had remained in the household as a governess, a person of some importance.[21] Deprived of the financial support of Asukai's family, the menoto asked a priest of the Ninna-ji to look after the girl, not anticipating he would be tempted into abducting her.

Now that the priest has been discredited, the menoto does not know where to turn. The mysterious lover only adds to her problems. She supposes from their disguise that Sagoromo and his escorts must be from the police (*kebiishi*) and complains to Asukai, "Even the maids who help me once in a while are so frightened that of late they haven't come at all. It's most annoying. For all I know, he may be a great noble and a splendid gentleman of the highest rank, but he's not likely to help you, miss. I am old, and it doesn't matter what happens to me. Somebody's invited me to the north, and I'd been thinking I would go there. But when I try to think of who I can ask to look after you when I'm not here, I realize what an encumbrance you are!"

The menoto's remarks have an earthiness that suggests her plebeian background, and a comical quality one does not find in *The Tale of Genji*, where even the menoto speak the language and share the attitudes of the women they serve. Asukai, bursting into tears, declares that she will go wherever the menoto goes. The menoto's irritation gives way momentarily to pity for the helpless girl, but she has no thought of sacrificing herself. She thinks, "I wonder if Asukai would be willing to go as a bride for some fourth-class officer in the depths of Michinoku province?"[22] In these and similar remarks the menoto reveals a nature that would not be out of place in the fiction of Saikaku or even in a modern novel.

The menoto, realizing at last how deeply Asukai has fallen in love with Sagoromo (though she still has no idea of his identity), suggests that Asukai remain in the capital when she goes to the north, but Asukai refuses, threatening to kill herself if she is deprived of the only person she can trust. Sagoromo during his frequent visits constantly assures her of his undying love, but Asukai has trouble believing his words.

As if to confirm her doubts, this scene between Asukai and the menoto is followed by one in which Sagoromo first reveals his love to Princess Genji. Sagoromo's unhappy love for Princess Genji has a complication that distinguishes it from other Heian court tales: he is able to see her freely.[23] Although they are cousins, a relationship distant enough to require a woman normally to keep her face shielded from his gaze, Princess Genji was orphaned as an infant, and raised by Sagoromo's parents. She therefore treats Sagoromo as a real brother and does not bother to hide behind curtains at his approach. He—and we—see her more closely than the heroines of other monogatari, as the following passage may suggest:

> The summer heat was at its most unbearable now and Sagoromo, no less than the "water-loving bird,"[24] burned with a longing that left no room in his heart for anything else, though no one suspected it. About noon one day, visiting the apartments of Princess Genji, he found her dressed in a thin, white unlined robe, reading something written on bright red paper. Her skin seemed translucent, even whiter than her robe, and the hair framing her face spilled over abundantly, the tips twining with the cascade of her back hair. The trimmed ends of her thick locks suggested they might continue to grow for some years to come, though her hair was already so abundant there seemed no room for more; its flow and grace were quite entrancing. The beautiful lines of her body and her arms, visible at gaps in her tresses through a garment that did not fully conceal her form, were so little like those of other women that Sagoromo thought, "I wonder if my love is playing tricks with my eyes?" He gazed at her, his heart pounding, but managed to control his emotions and to ask in a casual manner, "What can you be reading in this terrible heat?"
>
> "A book of pictures the First Princess gave me," she replied. He was dazzled by the bright glow of her face in the shadeless glare of the sun. Her face was somewhat flushed, and the look in her eyes as she avoided his glance, gracefully holding the book to her face as if to protect it from the sun, was quite indescribable. He was all but moved to tears. To distract himself from such thoughts he examined the pictures.
>
> "These illustrations of Narihira's diary[25] really capture the spirit," he said, feeling somehow that he and Narihira shared much the same emotions. So many of the pictures moved him that finally he could control himself no longer. He leaned close to her and asked, "What do you think of this one?" As he pointed, he murmured a poem:

yoshi saraba	Well, then, I'll be plain—
mukashi no ato wo	Examine these instances
tazune miyo	From the distant past!
ware no mi mayou	Am I the only one who's
koi no michi ka wa	Wandered on the path of love?

Hardly had he uttered these words than tears spilled from his eyes. The princess thought this was most peculiar, only for him to take her hand. Though he pressed his sleeve to his face, it seemed too frail a barrier to hold back the tears. The princess, greatly shocked and even afraid, bent her head to weep over the very arm that he was holding. She looked as if she were held captive by some unspeakable monster. His thoughts became all the more turbulent, but he felt incapable of revealing even the smallest part of all that had accumulated in his heart; he could only collapse in tears.

He said, "It was while I was still a child that I first fell in love with you. If I should go to my grave without once telling you all the feelings that have built up within me over the years, I am sure that such silence would do neither of us any good in the world to come. That is why I have blurted out my thoughts, shocking though they are. It would seem from these pictures here that in the past, too, there were men who suffered as I do from a love that was not permitted them.[26] You nonetheless seem to look on me with horror, and this gives me the greatest pain."

kaku bakari	Do you wonder if
omoikogarete	I have spent years in extreme
toshi fu to ya	Yearning, as I say?
Muro no Yashima no	Ask the smoke that rises up
keburi ni mo toe	From Muro no Yashima.[27]

The description of Princess Genji is more sensual than the accounts of beautiful women one finds in earlier fiction. Not only is Sagoromo able to see her face plainly in the glaring light of the summer sun, but her thin garment gives him tantalizing glimpses of the lines of her body. Heian ladies were normally depicted in literature and art as no more than a head and a hank of hair emerging from a tent of many-layered robes. It is disappointing that nothing is said, for example, about the beauty of the eyes, always depicted in paintings of the time as long and narrow, a clear mark of aesthetic preference; but in the descriptions of women in this and later monogatari praise is bestowed exclusively on the hair, not the eyes, the nose, or the mouth. Surely some court ladies, even of the highest birth, had eyes that were displeasingly round, and the exquisite narrowness of the heroine's eyes should have been worthy of comment; but only if there were some departure from the ideal (such as the red-tipped nose of Suetsumuhana in *The Tale of Genji*) would such features be noted.

Princess Genji remains obdurate to Sagoromo's professions of love to the very end, but he does not forget her, even while he is diverting himself elsewhere. This attachment to the one woman who resists his charms may suggest the love of Genji for Fujitsubo in *The Tale of Genji*, but Princess Genji rejects Sagoromo not out of fear of hurting her husband (she is unmarried) but simply because she is unable to think of this man, whom she has respected as an elder brother, as her lover. There is no suggestion, as in the case of Fujitsubo, that she really loves Sagoromo; instead, her response to his confession is that she bewails the fact that she lost her parents when a small child and, being deprived of their guidance and protection, has had to endure humiliation.[28] It concludes with Princess Genji's outraged exclamation that she hopes she will never again hear such talk from Sagoromo. When he returns later to her apartment, he finds not only the princess but his mother, who challenges him to a game of go. As they play, he darts glances at the princess, and again her beauty dazzles him, only for him to recall with regret and embarrassment his promises to Asukai.

That night in the moonlight Sagoromo thinks of Asukai. She is probably gazing at the moon, her shutters still open, hoping he will visit. He has absolutely no doubt about her love. He thinks of her with affection, but his affection does not blind him to the fact that she is in no way a match for Princess Genji. Still, he recognizes, she is easier to get along with and her helplessness is appealing. Then a new thought strikes him: if Princess Genji continues to refuse him but this woman succeeds in consoling him, she may prove to be a hindrance to salvation by preventing him from renouncing worldly ties and becoming a priest. At such moments of calm calculation, rare if not unique in Heian literature, Sagoromo is not endearing.

The rest of the first book of *The Tale of Sagoromo* is devoted mainly to the efforts of the menoto to get Asukai married to a young official named Shikibu no Tayū[29] who has fallen in love with Asukai from having once caught a glimpse of her. Asukai has by this time guessed Sagoromo's identity, and she also discovers she is pregnant. Tayū, who has just been appointed to a post in Tsukushi (Kyūshū), is desperately eager to take Asukai with him as his bride. He knows that she has had an affair with a high-ranking aristocrat (though not that her lover is Sagoromo), but this does not disturb him. He tells the menoto, "It would be better for her if she looked into my offer, rather than remain the kept woman of some little noble."[30] The menoto determines to help Tayū realize his ambition.

The crucial element in the menoto's plan is getting Asukai out of her house and into a carriage that will take her willy-nilly to Tayū. The menoto invents a reason why Asukai must temporarily move. Asukai protests that Sagoromo will not be able to find her if she moves, but the menoto counters that if he really loves her he will find out where she has gone and follow her.[31] The menoto, employing one ruse after another, finally succeeds in getting Asukai into a carriage.

Asukai soon realizes that she has been deceived, and before long she is moved from the carriage to a boat where a man lies down beside her. Tayū is full of self-confidence. Even the highest-born families want him as a son-in-law, and no woman has ever disliked him. He urges Asukai to do what he asks of her and not make a fuss. He repeats his sneering remarks about insignificant little nobles, and boasts about the lord he serves—none other than Sagoromo, though he does not name him.[32]

Sagoromo has had a nightmare in which he saw Asukai throw herself into the sea, but he is prevented by a directional taboo from going to see her. When at last he goes it is too late; she is already on her way to Tsukushi. He is desolate to think he has lost her, and blames himself. However, he does not allow grief to lower his standards; his remembrances of Asukai are excessively objective: "She was not incomparable in every way, not my ideal. She was just sweet and lovable, and I never expected to lose her so suddenly."[33]

Asukai, aboard ship, waits for a chance to jump into the water, but she is closely guarded. Rebuffed by Asukai, Tayū finds a more approachable lady aboard ship. The menoto, who has been royally treated by Tayū as long as he thought his suit was going well, is angry with Asukai. She declares, "I wonder if there is anyone else in the world as childish and as lacking in understanding as you."[34] She storms off. The moment for which Asukai has waited has come. She prepares to throw herself into the sea. Her thoughts are only of Sagoromo: "I wonder where he is now and what he is doing. Perhaps he has gone to bed, not having the least idea of what I am about to do. But even if he has, if he wakes at night, I'm sure he will think again of me."[35] The book concludes as Asukai composes a last poem and looks in terror at the sea into which she is about to throw herself.

I have related at length the plot of the first book of *The Tale of Sagoromo* in order to demonstrate that, contrary to the general assumption, it is not merely a patchwork of elements derived from *The Tale of Genji*. The plot is carefully constructed and better organized than that of *The Tale of Genji*, and the contrasting shifts of scene are particularly effective. The characters are restricted, and each (with the unfortunate exception of Sagoromo) is distinctly drawn. It is possible to find in Fujitsubo the model for the inaccessible Princess Genji, though the two women are quite dissimilar; and the other resemblances discovered between characters in the two works often seem to be products of the tacit conviction that *The Tale of Sagoromo* could not but be derived from *The Tale of Genji* (or, at any rate, from *some* monogatari written earlier in the Heian period).[36]

The most memorable characters in *The Tale of Sagoromo* are unsympathetic. The menoto is not simply a mischievous matchmaker but an evil woman whose momentary feelings of sympathy for Asukai do not last long. There is certainly no model for the menoto in *The Tale of Genji*, and the closest example of an evil woman, the stepmother in *The Tale of Ochikubo*, is hardly more than a cartoon.

Shikibu no Tayū is another disagreeable character, but there is humor in the portrayal. Once he finally realizes his desires and is actually lying beside Asukai he indulges in self-advertisement, presumably in order to persuade her how lucky she is to have found such a splendid man.

A comic interlude (which occurs just before Asukai is abducted) describes Sagoromo's visit to the unsophisticated Princess Imahime. She is a foolish young woman, but she is neither vulgar like the Lady of Ōmi nor hopelessly out of touch with the times like Suetsumuhana. The note of coarseness in this section comes not from Imahime herself but from the ladies of her entourage who gape at Sagoromo, make indecorous comments, and so on. One gets the momentary impression that this was what most court ladies of the time were really like, though such women do not appear in *The Tale of Genji* or other works of the high court tradition.

The resemblances between Sagoromo and Kaoru have often been pointed out. Kaoru was perhaps the figure in *The Tale of Genji* who appealed most to the readers and authors of the later monogatari, and it is not surprising that some of his characteristics should be found in the hero of *The Tale of Sagoromo*. He and Sagoromo are alike in their failure to win the woman they love most, and various other resemblances exist, but they are unalike in the most crucial respect: Kaoru is a memorable creation, a man of complex character who is so tormented by the secret of his birth that he is incapable of achieving even momentary happiness, but Sagoromo is hardly more than an instrument of the plot of *The Tale of Sagoromo*. If Sagoromo had been drawn as effectively as the surrounding characters this would be a monument of Heian literature.

Of the four books of *The Tale of Sagoromo*, the first is the best. The second is concerned chiefly with Sagoromo's secret affair with the Second Princess, a woman he could have married and possessed with the approval of the emperor and the whole court. The theme is intriguing, but the plot becomes unwieldy when the empress, learning of the pregnancy of her daughter by an unknown man, decides the only way to avoid disgrace is to pretend that the baby about to be born is her own. Even amid such improbable plot developments there are passages of startling directness. When, for example, Sagoromo learns for the first time that the Second Princess's baby is his, he "blushes violently,"[37] a reaction one could hardly imagine of any of the men in *The Tale of Genji*. The third and fourth books are built around two oracles, one that forbids Princess Genji to take Buddhist orders (and thereby leads to her becoming the high priestess at the Shintō shrine of Ise), and the second that decrees Sagoromo must become the emperor after the direct succession to the throne has been broken. These books are inferior to the first, but the account of the chilly marriage between Sagoromo and Princess Ippon (likened unconvincingly by the critics to Genji's marriage to Aoi) is excellently evoked.

The style of *The Tale of Sagoromo* was much admired. Like other monogatari of the Heian period, the text is written mainly in kana with only occasional words of Chinese origin written in kanji, particularly words referring to Buddhism. The conversations sometimes seem remarkably close to colloquial speech, and there are even a few coarse words,[38] but little else distinguishes the language from that written by Murasaki Shikibu sixty or seventy years earlier. Among the features it shares with *The Tale of Genji* are the *sōshiji*, the passages in which the author directly addresses the reader. *The Tale of Genji* is referred to several times, as a work of fact rather than fiction, and mention is also made of *The Tale of the Bamboo Cutter*, *The Tale of the Hollow Tree*, and other monogatari, emphasizing the statement made near the opening of the work that this was a story of more recent times than the others.

The more than two hundred poems in the text were highly rated by Fujiwara Teika, and at the time of the composition of the *Shin Kokinshū* the work was considered to be no less essential an object of study for aspiring poets than *The Tale of Genji*.[39] The poetry forms an integral element of the style, epitomizing the action and supplying leitmotivs for the different persons of the book. In addition to the original poems, there are many quoted from the *Kokinshū*, the *Gosenshū*, and other official and private collections. *The Tale of Sagoromo* has a professional competence that is still impressive, but the author could not rise to the supreme test of creating a hero worthy to stand at the side of Prince Genji.

Wakefulness at Night

The monogatari next most highly praised by the ladies of *Story Without a Name* was *Yoru no Nezame*[40] (Wakefulness at Night). The title is a reference to the opening sentence of the work: "Much have I seen of the varied and devious ways of love, but the romance of the lonely, wakeful ones, bound by deep love yet doomed to suffer, seems the strangest of all."[41] The word *nezame* (wakeful) suggests the woman whose anxiety over not being able to meet her lover causes her to wake at night and lie sleepless. It was used in this work also as a kind of nickname for the heroine, whose many worries kept her from sleeping soundly.

Fujiwara Teika attributed this monogatari to the daughter of Takasue, known chiefly for *The Sarashina Diary*.[42] It is the custom of modern scholars to reject such attributions when unsupported by other evidence, but Teika's opinion has been cautiously revived in recent years.[43] If there is little evidence to support the theory, there is equally little reason for rejection.[44] In any case, it is hard to avoid the impression that it was written by a woman, and it has been suggested, on the basis of a study of known facts of the life of the daughter of Takasue, that the work possesses the features of an autobiographical novel.[45] Most authorities believe that *Wakefulness at Night* was written between 1045 and 1068, though the composition is placed considerably later by others.[46]

The completed work, consisting of four parts, was originally perhaps half the length of *The Tale of Genji*, but at some point the second and fourth parts were lost and less than half survives.[47] It is possible to reconstruct the general outlines of the work from later adaptations, but much has been irretrievably lost, and discussion of *Wakefulness at Night* can only properly be made of the two books that remain.

The critical attention bestowed on *Wakefulness at Night* by *Story Without a Name* is more satisfying than its treatment of *The Tale of Sagoromo*, though the author once again seems to enjoy finding fault more than bestowing praise. The section devoted to the work opens,

> There is nothing specially impressive about *Wakefulness at Night*, and no scenes that strike one as being particularly remarkable, but

> from the outset it describes just one person, unwaveringly depicting that person in a most profoundly affecting manner. One can easily imagine what intense feelings inspired the author to create so rare and deeply moving a work.[48]

The accounts of specific parts of the work that were praised or dispraised by the ladies of *Story Without a Name* are valuable because they preserve poems and other excerpts that would otherwise have been lost, but more important than the particulars of their criticism is the high overall ranking they give to *Wakefulness at Night* and their recognition that the work is devoted to only one person, the heroine, Nezame. Although earlier monogatari, including *The Tale of the Bamboo Cutter* and *The Tale of Ochikubo*, have a woman as the central character, this is the first work of fiction to deal in a mature manner with a woman's thoughts and emotions. Again, unlike most earlier monogatari, *Wakefulness at Night* contains very little action, contrasting notably with *The Tale of Sagoromo* in which the author, though rarely entering into the thoughts of the characters, gives a full account of their actions. The style is also reminiscent of the diaries of the court ladies, especially *The Sarashina Diary*. During the course of the narration the names of several historical emperors are mentioned, in this way setting the events about a hundred years before the time of composition, but no attempt was made to contrast the past and the present. Probably the author was merely following the tradition of setting monogatari in the past.

The story is an unbroken account of events in the life of Nezame, especially those relating to her love for the high-ranking courtier Naidaijin. At the opening of the work we are told a little about her family background. Nezame was the daughter of an imperial prince who had relinquished his position in order to serve as a minister. He had four children, and after the death of both his wives he decided not to remarry but to devote himself entirely to their education. His favorite among the children was Nezame, his second daughter, who was the most gifted, especially in music. When she has learned all her father can teach her about playing the biwa, a celestial being appears in a dream on the night of the harvest moon to teach her even more difficult works. He reappears in a dream on the same night of the next year; after teaching her five more pieces, he announces that this is his last visit, and predicts that the life of so unusual a person as Nezame will be filled with grief and anxiety, a prophecy that proves to be all too true.

The celestial being's music lessons may recall the intervention of the supernatural child in *The Tale of Sagoromo*, and both occur early in the work, but he appears in Nezame's dreams only, not before the assembled court.[49] Far from sounding a jarring note of unreality, this prodigy serves to emphasize the internal nature of the work.

The main action of *Wakefulness at Night* begins with an account of the search of Nezame's father for a suitable son-in-law for Ōigimi, his older daughter. He chooses Naidaijin, a man of such outstanding birth, position, and talents that the father regrets only that the custom of daughters' marrying in order of age prevents him from giving Nezame, his second daughter, to such a paragon. Preparations for the wedding are soon under way, but (because this is astrologically an unlucky year for her) Nezame is sent to a house in the south of the capital, for fear that her presence may exert an unfortunate influence on the marriage.

One moonlit night, shortly before the wedding, Naidaijin goes to visit his old nurse in the suburbs and hears from a nearby house the sounds of music so ravishingly played that he peeps into the house from a hiding place in a bamboo grove. He sees a woman of surpassing beauty with whom he instantly falls in love. The house is so far from the section of the capital where the great nobles live that Naidaijin not unreasonably supposes that the woman must belong to the lower ranks of the aristocracy, fair game for someone like himself. He forces his way into the house and succeeds in spending the night with Nezame, though she is terrified of him and has no notion, even when he leaves, who he might be.

The tragedy of the entire novel stems from this single rash act of Naidaijin. His brief encounter with Nezame results in her becoming pregnant; as so often in the fiction of this time, a single meeting leads to the birth of a child. Before long he discovers that the beautiful woman with whom he spent the night was none other than the sister of his bride. It is too late to call off the wedding and, to protect Nezame from gossip, she is sent off to Ishiyama under pretext of a serious illness to have her baby there.

There events are related so realistically as indeed to suggest some autobiographical element in the narration. Less realistic are the descriptions of the beauty of Nezame, but even these passages are not as tedious as in other monogatari, and hardly a word is said about Naidaijin's looks. The work from the start is concerned mainly with the internal meaning of the events related, and such descriptions as are found of peerlessly beautiful women and their magnificent clothes were probably a bow in the direction of monogatari tradition, rather than matters of real concern to the author.[50] There are surprisingly few descriptions of nature.

The second part of the work is devoted largely to the account of Nezame's marriage. Although the emperor himself asks for her hand (as a secondary consort), her father refuses, knowing that without proper backing at court she will be at the mercy of the empress. The father decides instead to marry Nezame to a middle-aged widower, who soon becomes the regent. If this had been a different kind of novel, his action might be interpreted as a sacrifice of Nezame to her father's greed for wealth or power, but the father in fact chose altruistically, and the marriage proves to be unusually happy. Shortly before the wedding, however, Naidaijin again makes his way to Nezame, unable to bear the thought of giving her up completely, and she yields to him once more, and once more a baby is born of a single night's meeting; but the regent, though fully aware the child is not his own, rears it with affection. One is reminded of Tatiana and Prince Gremin in *Eugene Onegin*; marriage to a much older man is not necessarily a disaster if the man shows understanding and love. After the death of the regent and also of Naidaijin's wife, Nezame and Naidaijin are free to marry. He goes to her confident that all obstacles have now been removed, only to meet with an unimagined refusal from Nezame in a scene reminiscent of *La Princesse de Clèves*. The possibility of making such comparisons with masterpieces of European literature is not in itself of great significance, but (apart from *The Tale of Genji*) this is the first monogatari that suggests comparisons of this kind.[51]

The third part of *Wakefulness at Night* was apparently the best in literary terms; its excellence explains why it (rather than the lost second and fourth parts) survived, but the survival is puzzling in other terms. Almost nothing happens during the course of perhaps two hundred pages, and the few incidents are far less dramatic than those of *The Tale of Genji*, let alone earlier monogatari. The appeal of this part of *Wakefulness at Night* for modern readers lies in the subjective and introspective aspects of the narration. Each action, however small or trivial, elicits a complex response from Nezame, Naidaijin, or, less often, the emperor. The work has a curiously modern flavor that is strengthened by such internally directed questions as: "What must her stepdaughters have heard about her, what must they be thinking now?"; "What does he really think? Surely he cannot help despising me"; or "What did it matter now, he wondered, if everyone reproved him, if appearances could not be saved?" The other face of the absence of action is the sensitivity with which internal agitation is depicted.

The principal characters are complicated human beings who cannot easily be classified in the conventional manner as either good or bad;

in general, they are good, but each has an ambiguous side that makes us wonder at times if we really understand them, evidence of the author's success in creating characters who are as self-contradictory as real human beings. The one character who is prevailingly bad—meaning, hostile to the interests of Nezame—is the dowager empress, but her machinations are ultimately inspired by love for her daughter, the unhappy wife of Naidaijin (whom he married after Nezame rejected him), and by her frustration that this young woman is by no means as dazzling as Nezame.

The major characters are even more complex. Nezame loves Naidaijin, but never utters a word of affection, and seems passive or even hostile when they are together. She sometimes has occasion to remember the momentous circumstances of their first meeting, but her thoughts dwell less on Naidaijin than on her late, devoted husband. (She recalls, however, that "when her husband had stayed with her constantly, never looking at another woman, she had found him too tedious. 'If only some business would take him away,' she had thought at times. . . . But his attention had never wavered. He had stayed by her side every moment."[52]) Unable to avow the depths of her feelings for Naidaijin, she tells herself that if they were able to spend the rest of their lives together "he would often cause me unhappiness and I am sure to be disillusioned with him."[53]

Naidaijin's love for Nezame is unconstrainedly expressed, though sometimes with words of reproach. Every contact with Nezame—whether a letter in her superb handwriting or the barest glimpse of her profile in the obscurity of her curtained chamber—renews his passion, but he is not entirely indifferent to his wife. He tells her, "You can be sure that Nezame will never explicitly or openly become my dependent. She dislikes me so intensely you need never fear that I will begin to treat you carelessly."[54] He talks in this manner to reassure the wife, but he is not attempting to deceive her. Probably, while he is actually speaking, he believes his own words.

Like many of the heroes of the Heian monogatari written after *The Tale of Genji*, Naidaijin is in the tradition of Kaoru rather than of Genji. He is more successful with the woman he loves than is Kaoru, but seldom has the satisfaction of feeling that Nezame reciprocates his love. Toward the end of the third part he becomes convinced that Nezame is having an affair with the emperor, and he torments her with his jealousy, though he realizes eventually that she is innocent.

The emperor, though by no means a prominent character, is perhaps the most intriguing. At the opening of the third part he plots with the dowager empress to get a glimpse of Nezame, whose beauty is celebrated at the court though few women and even fewer men have ever seen her face. He peeps at her from a hiding place, and one glance convinces him that her loveliness is indeed unparalleled. Soon afterward he induces the dowager empress to arrange a meeting, and this time he shows himself before the unsuspecting Nezame, who successfully resists his advances. Neither in this scene nor anywhere else in the work is it suggested that the emperor is superior to ordinary men except in the position he occupies. He is ruthless in his pursuit of Nezame and, despite constant rebuffs that wound his pride as an emperor and as a lover, he continues the pursuit, sending her letters in which he pours out his disappointment in the strongest terms. We are told that "he even uttered curses upon her."[55]

Frustrated in his attempt to win Nezame, the emperor takes charge of her son Masako, a boy of eight or nine, and can scarcely be persuaded to let him out of his sight.[56] Masako is described (in the familiar Heian manner) as looking as beautiful and graceful as a girl. The emperor is attracted to him because he looks like his mother: this connection with the woman he loves is so precious that, we are told, the emperor loses interest in his wives and the other ladies around him: "The nights his ladies attended him were far surpassed in number by nights spent with the boy. Yet, no one dared utter a word of criticism or suggest he was acting strangely."[57]

Everyone else in the novel, however, is obsessed with fear about what people will think or, worse, what they will say. The words "rumor" and "gossip" occur again and again. Most of the time the feared rumormongers are faceless, unnamed members of the court society, but they are dreaded even by persons as close to the throne as Nezame and Naidaijin. Nezame is constantly worried lest her honor—one thinks of the heroine of a play by Racine referring to *ma gloire*—be stained by ugly rumors, and the fear of gossip limits the freedom of even the emperor. In the small world of the court, where everyone knew everyone (even if the women's faces were hidden) and the architecture provided few places for privacy, secrets did not last long. Nezame dreads the emperor's overtures, not because he is personally repulsive but because she knows how quickly gossip will spread if she yields. The ladies of most courts desired nothing more than to be favored by the monarch, but here the high opinion of other members of the court was even more important.

False rumors were no less a danger than rumors that originated in what somebody actually saw or heard. When Naidaijin's wife is ill she acts as if she is possessed by the living ghost of Nezame. It seems likely, as Naidaijin thinks, that she is only feigning possession in order to discredit Nezame; but gossip soon reaches the ears of Nezame, who is appalled to think people may believe she is capable of the malice of a living ghost. Much of the third part of *Wakefulness at Night* is devoted to an account of the despair the rumor produces in Nezame, especially at the thought that Naidaijin may believe it. She reflects,

> So he believes it. If such a spirit appeared and said such bizarre things, would he hesitate to tell me about it if he did not think it genuine? He seems to believe it is true. How he must wish to sever completely all ties with me. In this case, his careful politeness is all the more humiliating. If I thought that every time he is with his wife my spirit flees from me and is with him at her side, I would loathe myself. But is it possible I appeared before them?[58]

Nezame's doubts concerning Naidaijin and the self-torture to which she subjects herself are typical of the work and contribute to its specifically modern quality, even though her reflections are occasioned by an unmodern dread of being perhaps a "living ghost." Nezame's fear is so acute that she decides to "leave the world" and take orders as a Buddhist nun, but in this, too, she is frustrated, first by Naidaijin's intervention, then by the discovery that she is once again carrying his child. The prediction made long before by the heavenly being who appeared in her dream, that she would know much suffering, has proven to be all too true.

Wakefulness at Night is deeply affecting, even in its present truncated state. The characters linger in the mind not by what they do but by what they think, and in this sense it represents an advance as a novel over *The Tale of Genji*, though it lacks that work's encompassing vision of the court society and its richness of detail. It is novelistic also in the resolutely prosaic style and in the comparative scarcity of poems. These factors probably militated against its reputation in its own day but contribute to the prevailing impression of modernity. It is an extraordinary work, as close as the Heian storytellers ever came to creating what even purists might call a novel.

The Hamamatsu Middle Counselor[59]

The same postscript to Fujiwara Teika's manuscript of *The Sarashina Diary* that identified the daughter of Takasue as the author of *Wake-*

fulness at Night also credited her with *Hamamatsu Chūnagon Monogatari* (The Tale of the Hamamatsu Middle Counselor).[60] The title of the work, as given by Teika and other early sources, was originally *Mitsu no Hamamatsu* (The Pine on the Beach at Mitsu), derived from a poem by Chūnagon, the hero:

hi no moto no	The pine on the beach
Mitsu no hamamatsu	At Mitsu in the country
koyoi koso	Of the rising sun
ware wo kourashi	Tonight—it seems to miss me—
yume ni mietsure[61]	I could see it in my dream.[62]

Teika's attribution of the work has been bolstered in recent years by comparative analysis of *The Sarashina Diary* and *The Hamamatsu Middle Counselor*, especially the importance of dreams in both. Some scholars are now reluctant to accept the daughter of Takasue as the author of *Wakefulness at Night*, but hardly anyone doubts she wrote *Hamamatsu*.[63] The dating of the two works divides the critics. Those who believe she wrote both works opine that *Wakefulness at Night* came earlier,[64] but those who think she wrote only *Hamamatsu* are sure that *Wakefulness at Night* was written much later. Judged in more subjective terms than Japanese critics have been willing to employ, it is easier to imagine the wonderfully sensitive author of *The Sarashina Diary* as the author of the no less sensitive *Wakefulness at Night* than of the pedestrian *Hamamatsu* but, obviously, the authorship and dating of both works have yet to be determined.

Hamamatsu survives only in texts that lack the first chapter (or, possibly, chapters). Until 1930 it also lacked the concluding chapter, but two manuscripts were discovered at that time. Our knowledge of the lost opening is derived (as so often) from the account in *Story Without a Name* and from poems quoted elsewhere. We can gather that the work began with the unhappiness of the hero, Chūnagon, over his mother's hasty remarriage after his father's death. This sounds like *Hamlet*, but there are no further resemblances. Chūnagon has a dream revelation that his father has been reborn in China, and he decides to travel there. At this point the surviving text begins.

A summary of the plot of *Hamamatsu* is likely to do it more than justice. The prominence of dreams and reincarnation is intriguing; that was what attracted Mishima Yukio to the work when he began to write his final tetralogy, *Hōjō no Umi* (The Sea of Fertility). However, the narration unfortunately does not live up to the promise of the themes.

Chūnagon's voyage to China and the account of the great welcome he receives on arrival are of interest if only because Heian court fiction hardly ever ventured beyond the limits of the capital. The author seems to have had little knowledge of China beyond the standard collections of Chinese poetry and such works of Chinese art as had entered Japan, but the exotic details probably appealed to readers of the time. Chūnagon has no trouble in finding the reincarnation of his father, the third son of the Chinese emperor. Although this prince is only seven or eight years old, Chūnagon recognizes his father in his transformed state. More important than the prince is his mother, called the empress from Ho-yang-hsien. Chūnagon eventually wins the heart of the empress and, before he leaves China to return to Japan, she bears his child.

In the meantime, the entire Chinese court is captivated by Chūnagon. His poems in kanshi in particular are acclaimed. The greatest nobles and the highest officials desire nothing more than to have Chūnagon meet their daughters; but Chūnagon, who left a pregnant lady friend in Japan, declares that he has not come all the way to China for a romance. Such is his attitude until he meets the empress. She is incomparably beautiful, in fact exactly like a beautiful Japanese woman, and he is moved to pledge his love. He later discovers that her mother was Japanese, and her father (a former minister) has spent so much time in Japan that he does not seem at all foreign to Chūnagon when they meet.

Shortly before Chūnagon returns to Japan, the empress bears his baby. He takes the infant back to Japan. The baby does not cry even once during the long journey, persuading Chūnagon that he must be none other than a transformation of the Buddha himself. Chūnagon discovers the empress's mother in Yoshino, and (as we might have predicted) has a romance with her daughter, Lady Yoshino, born of a second marriage. Toward the end of the work Chūnagon has a dream in which the Chinese empress reveals that she has died and is now in heaven. However, she reassures him, she will soon be reborn in Japan as the daughter of Lady Yoshino. At the end of the book Chūnagon receives confirmation from China that the empress has died. He also learns that the old emperor has left the world to become a priest and his third son—the reincarnation of Chūnagon's father—has been named crown prince. At these tidings he dissolves in tears.

Hamamatsu also contains various subplots, most of them involved with dreams and reincarnation. The author seems not to have been disturbed by the complications in family relationships when, say, Chūnagon has a child by the mother of a boy who is actually his father in a transformed state—but probably readers were not expected to pay much attention to such details. Although a belief in reincarnation is basic to Buddhism, it had never before been made the central theme of an extended work of fiction, and must have intrigued readers for that reason. The setting of the second (the present first) book in China also lent exotic charm, though Chūnagon, after initially being surprised by everything he sees, soon realizes there are usually Japanese equivalents; he reaches the conclusion that the two countries are basically the same. If there are differences, they exist not in the material world but in the natures of the people of the two countries: the Chinese are straightforward and honest, whereas the Japanese are more subtle and artistic. Perhaps this was the impression that the author gained from comparing Chinese and Japanese poetry.

Hamamatsu is disappointing as a novel, but it suggests some of the complex feelings entertained by the Japanese toward China, the source of so much of their culture. One recalls Kūkai's account of his first meeting with his teacher Hui-kuo who recognized as soon as he saw the Japanese priest the disciple he had long awaited, a vessel copious enough to hold the whole of the esoteric teachings. After his death, Hui-kuo appeared in Kūkai's dream and informed him that if he was reborn in Japan, this time he would be Kūkai's disciple.[65] In a similar manner, people at the Chinese court immediately recognize Chūnagon's remarkable qualities, even before he has had the opportunity to display them, and we are informed at the end that his father's reincarnation will ascend the Chinese throne.

Although the tone is by no means boastful, the implication is clear that, despite its indebtedness to China, Japan is now in no way inferior. The author seems also to have believed that, for all the attractions of Chinese civilization, the best place for Japanese is Japan. At one point in the narration a Chinese prince, supposing that Chūnagon must be tempted to remain in China, warns him that it is improper for a Japanese to spend his whole life in China. This view was shared by the Japanese priests who actually studied in China; much as they revered the learning of their teachers and the splendor of the Chinese temples, their desire to return to Japan remained constant. When seen against this historical background *Hamamatsu*, for all its imperfections as a work of literature, is not without interest as a cultural document.

If I Could Only Change Them[66]

Torikaebaya Monogatari (If I Could Only Change Them) is difficult to date, and there are no clues to the author. It is clear from the discussion of the work in *Story Without a Name* that it existed in two versions, of which only the second survives. Various dates have been suggested for the completion of the two versions; the most plausible are late in the eleventh century for the earlier, and between 1161 and 1183 for the later one.[67] It has been conjectured that the author of the earlier version was a man, and of the later version a woman.[68]

The title of the monogatari comes from the exclamation uttered by the minister of the Left, the father of two children, as he observes their most peculiar behavior.[69] The boy is so shy that he is happy only behind the curtains of the women's quarter, where he delights in playing with dolls; the girl, on the other hand, enjoys nothing more than participating in such masculine activities as playing kemari and composing poetry in Chinese. The father understandably wishes that he could change the personalities of the children and have the boy behave like a boy and the girl like a girl. The minister deplores this reversal of roles, but he is powerless to change the predilections of his children, and when the time comes for their coming-of-age ceremonies he arranges for each to undergo the ritual prescribed for the apparent rather than the real sex. Eventually the children return to their original sex, and only then does the father learn why they grew up with deviant tastes: in a dream a holy priest informs him that it was the work of a *tengu* (a kind of goblin); but, he says, now that the tengu's power to do malice has been exhausted the children will never again be afflicted by a confusion of their gender roles.[70]

The story might have been more interesting if the sexual preferences of the brother and sister had also been inverted, but the girl, who rises to the position of chūnagon (middle counselor)—for which she is named—and the boy, who is a lady-in-waiting, show no signs of any sexual preference. Chūnagon marries Shi no Kimi, the daughter of the minister of the Right, but she/he never goes beyond holding hands. Regardless of appearances, Chūnagon is physiologically a woman, and for this reason goes off somewhere for a few days every month during her menstrual period. Even if we can accept the possibility of brother and sister carrying on a masquerade for years without anyone's discovering their true sex, or without they themselves feeling any sexual urges, once the discovery has been made (about a quarter of the way through the book) that Chūnagon is really a woman, the work contains little to interest us.

One regrets that *If I Could Only Change Them* is not a psychological study of the decadence of the Heian court. A neuterization of men of the aristocracy became conspicuous from the middle of the Heian period, and by the reign of the Emperor Toba (1107–1123) men powdered their faces, blackened their teeth, used rouge, and painted false eyebrows on their foreheads. On occasion nobles paraded naked through the streets or wearing only red loincloths. In the summer of 1096 many high-ranking nobles roamed the capital on stilts, wearing gaudy clothes that included hats decorated with pheasant feathers.[71] It may be that this atmosphere of decadence engendered *If I Could Only Change Them*, but the work itself does not portray these developments. When Saishō, a typically promiscuous Heian lover (who has already seduced Chūnagon's wife), is stirred by Chūnagon's flawless beauty into making overtures, the latter, far from welcoming such attentions, is outraged; she/he does not wish to have sexual relations with *anyone*. Neither here nor elsewhere in the book are homosexual relations treated.

If I Could Only Change Them was nevertheless given very cold treatment until recent times, not because of stylistic failings but because of its supposed immorality. The distinguished historian of Japanese literature Fujioka Sakutarō (1870–1910) was so appalled by the work that he wrote a denunciation which concluded, "It makes me want to vomit."[72] The ladies of *Story Without a Name*, broader minded perhaps than Fujioka, praised the version we now have, contrasting it with the earlier version, which they found shocking. It is difficult to be sure what this lost version was like, but it may have contained more vivid, or perhaps more immoral, scenes than the present tame, rather tedious text.[73]

The Riverside Counselor's Stories[74]

A single collection of ten short stories in the Heian court tradition survives of what may have been a very large body of works. We know the circumstances of composition of one of the ten stories. In the fifth month of 1055 a story-matching contest was held in the palace under the sponsorship of Princess Baishi, the lady whom the author of *The Tale of Sagoromo* served. Stories were submitted by left and right teams on each of nine topics that had been assigned, and a referee chose the better of the two. The contest was between rival stories, but the topics related to poems contained in the stories, which were supposed to encapsulate the key events.[75] The story "Osaka koenu Gon Chūnagon" (The Provisional Middle Counselor Who Failed to Cross the Divide) was written by a woman named Koshikibu, about whom virtually nothing else is known except that she served Baishi. The authors and dates of the other stories in the collection are unknown, though many guesses, based on enormous research, have been made. Probably all but the last story, a fourteenth-century addition to the collection, were written in the eleventh or early twelfth century. The title, *Tsutsumi Chūnagon Monogatari*, has long been a mystery; the most plausible suggestion is that it is the name of the compiler, rather than that of the author of one or more of the stories.

The stories in the collection are on the whole disappointing. The endings especially are unsatisfactory, often leading the reader to believe that the author simply did not know how to conclude a tantalizing little vignette of court life. Some stories were probably of great interest to people at the court who recognized the models for the characters or who detected under surface disguise an incident with which they were familiar. For modern readers, however, the lack of the introspective qualities that make the great Heian works so memorable and so intelligible deprives these stories of anything more than mildly amusing interest.

One story stands out from the others. "Mushi mezuru Hime" (first translated by Arthur Waley in 1929 under the title "The Lady Who Loved Insects"[76]) is the account of a young woman who dislikes artifice and insists on being natural. She refuses to pluck her eyebrows, does not blacken her teeth (giving rise to ghastly white smiles), and leaves her hair untrimmed. She gives the boys who work for her such names as Mole Cricket, Grasshopper, and Millipede.[77] When her parents tax her for collecting insects that most people would avoid, she replies, "The clothes that people wear by the name of 'silk' are produced by worms before they grow wings, and when they become butterflies, why then they are completely ignored and worthless!"[78] She is clearly no fool, and we may indeed be attracted to a Heian lady who is more than an exquisite, dimly visible object in a curtained chamber. The intent of the author was probably to satirize people who had outlandish tastes, but in the process of describing the eccentric lady he made her so attractive that when, at the end of the tale, some gentlemen come to see the strange spectacle, we cannot help but hope that one of them will recognize the worth of a woman who is so sincere, so little concerned with artifice.

The story "Haizumi" (Lampblack), with prototypes in *Tales of Ise* and *Tales of Yamato*,[79] also stands out. It is the familiar story of a man who decides to abandon his wife in favor of a younger woman. As we hope, he is in the end moved to pity and love for his old wife, and he gives up his plan to acquire a new one. The ending is farcical: the younger woman, hearing that her lover has arrived, hurriedly powders her face, but (because the room is badly lit) she mistakes the pot of eyebrow blacking for powder, and smears her face with black paint. Few modern readers are likely to laugh at this denouement, but our sympathy for the first wife is real.

The other stories in the collection, if read carefully enough, yield passages of interest, but the writing is on the whole jejune, the work of people at the court who have time on their hands. One senses in this and other twelfth-century works that the tradition of courtly fiction is coming to an end, though this may be hindsight. Each of the post-*Genji* monogatari contains something to intrigue and even move us, but only one—*Wakefulness at Night*—is of the quality of *The Tale of Genji*. The courtly tradition would linger on to the Muromachi period, but its glory, intimately associated with the fortunes of the court, had sadly waned.

Quite different kinds of stories, describing the lives of commoners (who rarely figure in the court tales) and written in a language much closer to the colloquial of the time than the faded echoes of *The Tale of Genji*, were already being composed and collected in the late Heian period. These would in time develop into the mainstream of fiction during the medieval era.

Notes

1. An extreme expression of this attitude is found in Kataoka Toshihiro's essay "Heian Makki no Monogatari," pp. 116–17, where he states, "The special features of the monogatari of the late Heian period are almost the same as the special features of *The Tale of Genji*, and it might well be said that with the exception of one respect there is no reason to distinguish the monogatari of the late Heian period from *The Tale of Genji*. That one respect is none other than the fact that the monogatari of the late Heian period were strongly influenced by *The Tale of Genji*."

For a summary of views by various distinguished scholars on the indebtedness of late Heian fiction to *The Tale of Genji*, see Suzuki Hiromichi, *Heian Makki Monogatari Kenkyū*, pp. 227–46. Suzuki also gives some examples of differences.

2. The title is freely rendered as *The Changelings* by Rosette F. Willig in her complete translation of the work.
3. Two works are of special importance in dating fiction before the late thirteenth century: *Mūmyō Zōshi* (Story Without a Name), a book of literary criticism written about 1200, and the *Fūyōshū* (Wind and Leaves Collection), an anthology compiled in 1271 of waka that had originally appeared in works of court fiction. These two works are especially helpful in dating tales of the very late Heian and Kamakura periods, and they are therefore discussed below, in Chapter 19.
4. See above, note 3. "Mumyōzōshi" by Michele Marra is a complete translation of this work.
5. Kuwabara Hiroshi, *Mumyō Zōshi*, p. 23. See also the translation by Marra, "Mumyōzōshi," p. 137. *The Tale of Sumiyoshi* mentioned is not the same as the work of that title which is preserved today.
6. These words, the first of *The Tale of Sagoromo*, were derived from the Japanese versions of lines by Po Chü-i, quoted in such collections as *Wakan Rōei Shū*. See Kawaguchi Hisao, *Wakan Rōei Shū Zen'yakuchū*, pp. 37–38.
7. The words *imijiku jōzu mekashiku nado aredo* were interpreted by Kuwabara in his edition of *Mumyō Zōshi* (p. 59) as meaning something like "it affects a terribly aristocratic manner." I have followed Tomikura Tokujirō (*Mumyō Zōshi Hyōshaku*, p. 142). The question is whether or not the lady is praising the diction of *The Tale of Sagoromo*. Tomikura's interpretation fits in more smoothly with what follows, although *imijiku* more often had a pejorative meaning.
8. Kuwabara, *Mumyō Zōshi*, pp. 58–59. See also the translation by Marra, "Mumyōzōshi," p. 292.
9. The name is also read Seji.
10. So estimated by Suzuki Kazuo in *Sagoromo Monogatari*, I, p. 280. Imai Takuji in *Monogatari Bungaku Shi no Kenkyū*, p. 7, estimated that she was at least sixty-five.
11. The lost *Tamamo ni asobu Gon-dainagon*. Imai (*Monogatari*, p. 7) believed that this work was written in 1055 or earlier. Senji was identified in an uta-awase held in that year as the author of the work. However, the name Senji (or Seji) was in fact a common noun, used of a class of high-ranking court ladies, and the Senji who wrote *Tamamo* may have been another woman with the same rank.
12. This distinction will be questioned by admirers of *The Tale of Ochikubo*, also a single, unified story; but it is far less complex than *The Tale of Sagoromo* and also much shorter.
13. Although the name is the same as that of the hero of *The Tale of Genji*, and for this reason somewhat confusing, there is no connection between the two characters.
14. Suzuki Kazuo, *Sagoromo*, I, p. 41. The word *sagoromo*, though written with characters that mean "narrow robe," means no more than "robe,"

with *sa* as a meaningless prefix. *Omoisometeshi* contains a kakekotoba: with what precedes it means "I began to love," but with what follows *someteshi* means "I dyed," modifying *sagoromo*.

15. Suzuki Kazuo, *Sagoromo*, pp. 30–35.
16. *Ibid*., p. 37.
17. *Ibid*., p. 39.
18. *Ibid*., pp. 51–52.
19. Presumably he makes this deduction because he can see the ends of her trailing robes or her sleeves protruding from the carriage, in the usual manner.
20. Suzuki Kazuo, *Sagoromo*, I, p. 64.
21. The word *menoto* occurs very often in Heian literature, used not only for wet nurses but for women charged with the education of children of the aristocracy. It was even used of the husbands of these women, especially if they were involved in the education of young aristocrats.
22. Suzuki Kazuo, *Sagoromo*, I, p. 68. The province of Michinoku (here called Michinokuni but elsewhere Oku) was at the extreme north of the island of Honshū. For people in the capital Michinoku was the end of the world, but the menoto makes the place seem even more unattractive by specifying that it is to be not merely in Michinoku but in the *depths* of Michinoku. The potential bridegroom is a *sōkan*, a fourth-rank officer of the frontier guard unit.
23. It is true that Genji, as a child, was able to see Fujitsubo freely, but Murasaki Shikibu does not show us Fujitsubo with this clarity.
24. *Mizukoidori*, also known as *akashōbin*, or the Japanese ruddy kingfisher; used here because it was known for its apparent craving for water. Sagoromo's burning thoughts also seem to crave water.
25. The text calls the work usually known as *Ise Monogatari* by an alternative name, *Zaigo Chūjō no Nikki*, *zaigo chūjo* (The Middle Captain of the Fifth Rank) having been an appellation of Ariwara no Narihira.
26. Sagoromo and Princess Genji have been reared as brother and sister (though they are actually cousins), and their love is therefore forbidden. This is why Princess Genji is so horrified to learn of his feelings. Sagoromo seems to have found in *Tales of Ise* scenes that recall his own emotions.
27. Text in Suzuki Kazuo, *Sagoromo*, I, pp. 43–45. Muro no Yashima is mentioned because a goddess, suspected by her husband of having conceived a child by another man, set fire to a *muro*, a doorless room, declaring that if the baby survived the smoke, it would prove she was innocent. The child was safely born. Smoke is always mentioned in the many poems about Muro no Yashima, which also appears in Bashō's *Narrow Road of Oku*. Sagoromo is saying that his word is also true.
28. *Ibid*., p. 47.
29. He is a son of Sagoromo's menoto. See *ibid*., p. 92.
30. *Ibid*., p. 93. His words are so unusual as to merit quotation in the original:

"Sayō no hosokindachi ni kageme nite owasen yori wa, tada kokoromi tamae." The menoto has already referred to Sagoromo as *namakindachi*, a term of contempt with more or less the same meaning as *hosokindachi*.

31. *Ibid.*, pp. 102–3.
32. Tayū does not suspect that Sagoromo is Asukai's lover.
33. Suzuki, *Sagoromo*, I, p. 116.
34. *Ibid.*, p. 120.
35. *Ibid.*, p. 122.
36. A typical such evaluation is given in the article on *The Tale of Sagoromo* in *Nihon Koten Bungaku Daijiten* (III, pp. 56–58) by Nakada Takanao, an authority on the work. He writes, in part, "The author, using the techniques of the story of Yūgao in *Genji*, presents the character Asukai, who is a combination of Yūgao and Ukifune, and, just as Yūgao's child Tamakazura becomes Genji's adopted daughter, Shinobigusa, the child born of Sagoromo and Asukai, is for a time reared by the Princess Ippon, who resembles Aoi no Ue in *Genji*, and this becomes the connection that brings Sagoromo together with Ippon. The author otherwise reveals a fineness of touch in presenting the character Princess Imahime, a combination of the Lady of Ōmi and Suetsumuhana, as an intermediary when Sagoromo is searching for Shinobigusa. But just as Genji again and again shows himself incapable of giving up his love for Fujitsubo, Sagoromo's plans to approach Princess Genji even after she has entered the sacred precincts of the Great Shrine and the Second Princess after she has taken Buddhist orders indicate that both women have been given characteristics similar to those of Fujitsubo."
37. Suzuki, *Sagoromo*, I, p. 185.
38. See Imai, *Monogatari*, p. 31.
39. Suzuki, *Sagoromo*, I, p. 266.
40. The work is often referred to as *Nezame Monogatari*, but the text I have used (in the Kan'yaku Nihon no Koten series) calls it by the more distinctive title *Yoru no Nezame*. Other texts bear the title of *Yowa no Nezame*, meaning about the same.
41. Translation by Carol Hochstedler in *The Tale of Nezame*, p. 4. Text in Suzuki Kazuo and Ishino Keiko, *Yoru no Nezame*, I, p. 11.
42. See above, pp. 383–90. The translation by Ivan Morris is called *As I Crossed a Bridge of Dreams*.
43. Some scholars now accept with enthusiasm the attribition of the authorship to the daughter of Takasue. See Inaga Keiji, "Heian Kōki Monogatari no Atarashisa wa doko ni aru ka," p. 103. Inaga believed that the author probably wrote *The Sarashina Diary* while in mourning after the death of her husband, and followed this (while her memories of life at the court were still fresh) with *Wakefulness at Night*.
44. An attempt was made by Sakakura Atsuyoshi in his study of the vocabulary, especially of the use of the verb *saburau*, to prove that the work was composed after the death of the daughter of Takasue. See his "*Yoru no*

Nezame no Bunshō." This theory does not seem to have changed the minds of those who believe that *Wakefulness at Night* was written by the daughter of Takasue.

45. Suzuki and Ishino, *Yoru*, I, p. 337, quote Ishikawa Tōru, a supporter of the theory that the same woman wrote *The Sarashina Diary* and *Wakefulness at Night.*
46. Some, basing their conclusion on the date of the death of the historical woman who they believe was the model for the character Nezame, believe that the work could not have been written before 1102. See Suzuki Hiromichi, *Heian Makki Monogatari Kenkyū*, pp. 63–64.
47. Another line of manuscripts divides the surviving two books into five *kan*, not leaving space for the lost second part. The Nakamura text, a considerably revised version of the original made in the fourteenth century, stays close to the original in the first part, and there is reason to think that its retelling of the missing second part is in general faithful. However, the Nakamura version of the third part is much abbreviated (as we can tell by comparing it to the surviving original text), and the treatment of the fourth part evidently departed considerably from the original.
48. Kuwabara, *Mumyō Zōshi*, p. 63. See also the translation by Marra, "Mumyozōshi," p. 295.
49. The secret instructions in music given to Nezame by a celestial being also recalls *The Tale of the Hollow Tree* and *The Hamamatsu Middle Counselor*.
50. For a good summary of the plot see Hochstedler, *The Tale of Nezame*, pp. 4–12. Summaries in Japanese are given in many works, notably by Suzuki and Ishino, I, pp. 310–34.
51. I am aware that when Arthur Waley's translation of *The Tale of Genji* first appeared it was compared to *Le Morte d'Arthur*, the writings of Boccaccio, and even to *Tom Jones*, but none of these comparisons is taken seriously today. For that matter, I no longer feel much confidence in the comparison I drew in 1953 between *The Tale of Genji* and Proust's *À la recherche du temps perdu*.
52. Translation in Hochstedler, *The Tale of Nezame*, p. 212.
53. *Ibid.*, p. 196.
54. *Ibid.*, p. 189.
55. *Ibid.*, p. 101.
56. *Ibid.*, p. 80: Suzuki and Ishino, *Yoru*, II, p. 80.
57. Hochstedler, p. 215.
58. *Ibid.*, p. 133.
59. There is a complete translation of this work by Thomas H. Rohlich, *A Tale of Eleventh-Century Japan: Hamamatsu Chūnagon Monogatari*.
60. I shall henceforth refer to this work simply as *Hamamatsu*.
61. Endō Yoshimoto and Matsuo Satoshi, *Takamura Monogatari, Heichū Chūnagon Monogatari*, p. 168. *Mitsu*, originally meaning "anchorage," was the port section of Naniwa, the modern Osaka.

62. The meaning of the poem is that Chūnagon, now in China, has had a dream in which he saw his beloved in Japan. He supposes that he has dreamed of her because she misses him. According to the commentary of Endō and Matsuo (p. 446), the "pine on the beach" (*hamamatsu*) is used for the Taishō no Ōkimi, the lady Chūnagon left in Japan.
63. See Suzuki Hiromichi, *Heian Makki*, pp. 41–64, for a discussion of the authorship of the two works. Suzuki himself believed that the Daughter of Takasue wrote *Hamamatsu* but not *Wakefulness at Night* (p. 64).
64. Suzuki Hiromichi, *Heian Makki*, pp. 54–55, states that *if* both monogatari were written by the daughter of Takasue, (1) *Wakefulness at Night* was written before *Hamamatsu*; (2) *Hamamatsu* was written after 1064, when she was in her fifty-seventh year: and (3) *Wakefulness at Night* was written after 1045, when she was in her thirty-eighth year.
65. See Tsunoda, de Bary, and Keene, *Sources of Japanese Tradition*, pp. 144–46.
66. See above, note 2.
67. This is the suggestion put forth by Tanaka Shin'ichi, Tanaka Kimiharu, and Morishita Sumiaki in *Shinshaku Torikaebaya*, pp. 640–41. Imai Gen'e suggested that the earlier version was written between 1080 and 1105, and the later version between 1105 and 1170. See Imai Gen'e in Mitani Eiichi and Imai Gen'e, *Tsutsumi Chūnagon Monogatari, Torikaebaya Monogatari*, p. 204.
68. See Mitani and Imai, *Tsutsumi*, p. 204; also Tanaka et al., *Shinshaku*, p. 641. Tanaka mentions the theory that Ōe no Masafusa was the author of the old text, and another theory that Fujiwara no Tametsune was the author of the new one, but he does not agree with either.
69. See Kuwabara Hiroshi, *Torikaebaya Monogatari*, I, p. 29; III, p. 237. Also Willig, *The Changelings*, pp. 16, 164.
70. See Kuwabara, *Torikaebaya*, III, p. 181.
71. See Imai Gen'e, "Sōsetsu" in Mitani and Imai, *Tsutsumi*, p. 199.
72. Quoted by Suzuki Hiromichi in "Torikaebaya Monogatari no Sekai," in Mitani and Imai, *Tsutsumi*, p. 403.
73. We know something of the original text of *If I Could Only Change Them* from the account in *Story Without a Name*. For example, the middle counselor in the earlier version gave birth to a child while still dressed in "his" official court costume, and his formally arranged, masculine hair-style became disarrayed under the strain of labor. The same work characterized the descriptions of "his" monthly periods as "extremely dirty." See Kuwabara, *Mumyō Zōshi*, p. 81; also Marra, "Mumyōzōshi," part 3, p. 410.
74. I owe this rendering of *Tsutsumi Chūnagon Monogatari* to Robert L. Backus, whose complete translation, together with enlightening introductions to each story, makes the collection as a whole available for the first time in graceful English. The title is more ordinarily translated as "The Tales of

the Tsutsumi Middle Counselor," *tsutsumi* being either a place-name or a word meaning "river embankment."

75. See Backus, *Riverside*, pp. 89–95, for a discussion of the story-matching contest and of Koshikibu.
76. Two translations of the same story have appeared since then. The first, included in Edwin O. Reischauer and Joseph K. Yamagiwa, *Translations from Early Japanese Literature*, calls the work "The Lady Who Loved Worms," and the translation by Robert L. Backus calls it "The Lady Who Admired Vermin." The objection to translating *mushi* as "insects" is that butterflies are also insects, and it was quite normal to collect them, but the fondness of the lady of the story for caterpillars and suchlike vermin distinguished her from other people. This is no doubt correct, but the Waley title is obviously more pleasing as English.
77. Backus, *Riverside*, p. 59.
78. *Ibid*., p. 55.
79. *Ibid*., p. 185.

Bibliography

Note: All Japanese books, except as otherwise noted, were published in Tokyo.

Backus, Robert L. *The Riverside Counselor's Stories*. Stanford, Calif.: Stanford University Press, 1985.

Endō Yoshimoto and Matsuo Satoshi. *Takamura Monogatari, Heichū Monogatari, Hamamatsu Chūnagon Monogatari*, in Nihon Koten Bungaku Taikei series. Iwanami Shoten, 1964.

Hochstedler, Carol. *The Tale of Nezame: Part Three of Yowa no Nezame*. Ithaca, N.Y.: Cornell University East Asian Papers, 1979.

Ii Haruki. *Monogatari Bungaku no Keifu*. Kyoto: Sekai Shisō Sha, 1986.

Imai Takuji. *Monogatari Bungaku Shi no Kenkyū*. Waseda Daigaku Shuppanbu, 1977.

Inaga Keiji. *Genji Monogatari Zengo*. Osaka: Izumi Shoin, 1980.

———. "Heian Kōki Monogatari no Atarashisa wa doko ni aru ka," *Kokubungaku*, 39:4, 1984.

Kataoka Toshihiro. "Heian Makki no Monogatari," in Ii Haruki, *Monogatari Bungaku no Keifu*.

Kawaguchi Hisao. *Wakan Rōei Shū Zen'yakuchū*, in Kōdansha Gakujutsu Bunko series. Kōdansha, 1982.

Kawai Hayao. *Torikaebaya, Otoko to Onna*. Shinchōsha, 1991.

Kuge Haruyasu. *Heian Kōki Monogatari no Kenkyū*. Shintensha, 1984.

Kuwabara Hiroshi. *Mumyō Zōshi*, in Shinchō Nihon Koten Shūsei series. Shinchōsha, 1976.

———. *Torikaebaya Monogatari*, 4 vols., in Kōdansha Gakujutsu Bunko. Kōdansha, 1978–79.

Marra, Michele. "Mumyōzōshi," *Monumenta Nipponica*, 39:2–4, 1984.

Mitani Eiichi and Imai Gen'e. *Tsutsumi Chūnagon Monogatari, Torikaebaya Monogatari*, in Kanshō Koten Bungaku Zenshū series. Kadokawa Shoten, 1974.

Mitani Eiichi and Inaga Keiji. *Ochikubo Monogatari, Tsutsumi Chūnagon Monogatari*, in Nihon Koten Bungaku Zenshū series. Shōgakukan, 1972.

Nihon Koten Bungaku Daijiten, 6 vols. Iwanami Shoten, 1983–85.

Reischauer, Edwin O., and Joseph K. Yamagiwa. *Translations from Early Japanese Literature*. Cambridge, Mass.: Harvard University Press, 1951.

Rohlich, Thomas H. *A Tale of Eleventh-Century Japan: Hamamatsu Chūnagon Monogatari*. Princeton, N.J.: Princeton University Press, 1983.

Sakakura Atsuyoshi. "*Yoru no Nezame* no Bunshō," *Kokugo to Kokubungaku*, October 1964.

Suzuki Hiromichi. *Heian Makki Monogatari Kenkyū*. Kyoto: Daigakudō Shoten, 1979.

Suzuki Kazuo. *Sagoromo Monogatari*, 2 vols., in Shinchō Nihon Koten Shūsei series. Shinchōsha, 1985–86.

Suzuki Kazuo and Ishino Keiko. *Yoru no Nezame*, 2 vol., in Kan'yaku Nihon no Koten series. Shōgakukan, 1984–85.

Tanaka Shin'ichi, Tanaka Kimiharu, and Morishita Sumiaki, *Shinshaku Torikaebaya*. Kazama Shobō, 1988.

Tomikura Tokujirō. *Mumyō Zōshi Hyōshaku*. Yūseidō, 1954.

Tsunoda, Ryusaku, Wm. Theodore de Bary, and Donald Keene. *Sources of Japanese Tradition*. New York: Columbia University Press, 1958.

Willig, Rosette F. *The Changelings*. Stanford, Calif.: Stanford University Press, 1983.

14. MIRRORS OF HISTORY

As early as the tenth century the Japanese were writing works of literature that owed more to actual events than to the artifice of story-tellers. The distinction between such works and true histories is not easy to make. Almost any history that is written with care for expression and with a sense of dramatic form can be read as literature. The *Kojiki* and even the *Nihon Shoki*, though normally treated as works of history, have often been included in collections of Japanese literature because they contain not only purportedly historical information but myths and poems that evoke the deeds of the gods and ancient monarchs. Even if events in these histories can be demonstrated to be fabrications, or if speeches attributed to a Japanese hero prove to have been copied word for word from some Chinese history, this does not lessen their claim to be considered as literature; indeed, a deliberate alteration of historical fact or a borrowing from Chinese sources may indicate that literary rather than historical concerns were uppermost in the author's mind.

Many gradations exist between works of solely historical interest, such as the diaries kept in kambun by statesmen, and those of purely literary significance, such as the Nō plays based on events of the war between the Taira and the Minamoto.[1] This chapter treats historical works that describe in artistic Japanese prose the Heian court before the wars of the twelfth century ushered in an age of military domination.

A Tale of Flowering Fortunes

The earliest example of the *rekishi monogatari* (historical tale), *Eiga Monogatari* (A Tale of Flowering Fortunes),[2] is a chronicle dealing with the period from the middle of the tenth century to the death of Fujiwara no Michinaga in 1028. This extensive work, in the manner followed even by historians without literary pretensions when they wrote in their native language, presents not only the bare bones of history—births and deaths, promotions and demotions, and the like—but the poetry written on various occasions. *A Tale of Flowering Fortunes* has traditionally been considered to be a work of literature, and some passages are deservedly famous, though a translator described the work as being so prolix that "we are in danger of drowning in a sea of trivia."[3]

It is conjectured that the author was a woman, Akazome Emon, the court lady who married Ōe no Masahira and entered holy orders as a Buddhist nun after his death. Even if she was the principal author, she certainly could not have written *all* of the work unless she lived to be over 120; we know from her poems that she was alive in 976, and the last recorded event in *A Tale of Flowering Fortunes* occurred in 1092. The final ten chapters of the work, conspicuously inferior to the first thirty, have been consigned to "deserved oblivion,"[4] suggesting that another person, not as good a writer as Akazome Emon, continued her chronicle, carrying it down to 1092. Akazome Emon enjoyed a high reputation as a poet, but *A Tale of Flowering Fortunes* is not of literary distinction. The narration, far from being poetic, does not rise much above the bare format of a chronology, as the following passage, relating events at the end of 986, may suggest:

> So time passed. The Crown Prince's Coming-of-Age ceremony was performed around the First of the Twelfth Month, and the Principal Handmaid Suishi at once came to wait upon him, taking up residence in the Reikeiden. The Prince was very young, but Suishi was already fifteen. Since she was Kaneie's daughter, she quickly received permission to ride in a hand-drawn carriage, and people treated her with as much respect and solicitude as though she were a Junior Consort. Her mother, the Lady in the Wing Chamber, was fortunate indeed.[5]

The palace ceremonies described in this passage occurred every year, and there was nothing special about those of 986. In a work of fiction such ceremonies probably would not be mentioned unless it was intended to establish, say, a contrast between the present year, when they were performed brilliantly, and some past or future year when they were badly performed. The brief scene of the coming-of-age ceremony of the crown prince and his acquisition of a "handmaid" brings us to the border of literature; it may remind us of Genji's marriage to Aoi, about whom we are told in *The Tale of Genji*, "The bride was older, and somewhat ill at ease with such a young husband."[6] But instead of alluding to the awkwardness created between the crown prince and Suishi by the difference in their ages, or even of telling us something about the relations between Kaneie (whom we know otherwise from *The Gossamer Years*) and his daughter Suishi, *A Tale of Flowering Fortunes*, in the manner typical of palace chronicles, enumerates the privileges that Suishi came to enjoy at court. This certainly lessens the appeal of the work, but it also imparts authenticity as a "reflection of the rhythm and tone of the life she witnessed."[7] *A Tale of Flowering Fortunes*, even more than *The Tale of Genji*, tells us what it was like to live at the Heian court during a particularly brilliant period.

Most of the events related leave little impression because of the mass of indigestible details, but every so often an incident is literary in its effect. For example, there is the story of Akinobu, a son of Michinaga's who, without telling his family, ran away to become a monk on Mount Hiei. His father sent out search parties in all directions and before long his whereabouts were discovered. Michinaga himself hurried to the mountain and was shocked to see that his son's head was already shaved:

> "What made you decide to do it?" Michinaga asked through his tears. "Were you worried about anything? Did some act of mine seem harsh? Were you impatient for a promotion? Was there a girl you were in love with? As long as my influence lasted, I was ready to get you anything you wanted. I feel utterly miserable. How could you have done such a thing with no consideration for your mother or me?"
>
> Overcome with emotion, Akinobu burst into tears. "I wanted nothing at all," he said. "It is just that always, even as a child, I have had my heart set on being a monk. I was ashamed to tell you, since that was not what you had in mind for me, and while I hesitated you raised me so high that I became involved in Court life against my will. But I am quite, quite sure that I will be most useful to everybody as I am now."[8]

This touching exchange between the most powerful man in the country and his son, each revealing his character in a few words, is a rare testimony to Akazome Emon's literary gifts, made all the more so because no such meeting between Michinaga and Akinobu took place at this time. The conversation was unquestionably invented for dramatic purposes, and succeeded so well we wish she had invented more.

Occasionally Akazome Emon goes beyond her role as the mere

narrator of events she has witnessed and describes her pleasure over some sight or experience:

> The grounds of the mansion were spacious and elegant. The hills in the garden blazed with autumn foliage, and the leaves of the ivy vines on the islands shone with the brilliance of brocade, trailing from the pines in varying hues of crimson, dark red, green, and yellow. The same autumnal colors shimmered on the sparkling waters of the lake, and from the midst of the brocade the boats emerged, their music resounding with a chill beauty.[9]

Akazome's chief purpose in writing *A Tale of Flowering Fortunes* seems to have been to describe the career of the statesman Fujiwara no Michinaga, the father-in-law of three emperors. She was convinced that Michinaga was the most glorious courtier Japan had ever known, "and it was clearly her intention to include in her chronicle nothing that would contradict this view."[10] From the moment when he is first introduced to the reader, along with the other sons of Kaneie, he is idealized. The author mentions his older brothers only to comment,

> One wonders what he must have thought of his older brothers. He was entirely different from them in appearance and character—tactful, manly, pious, and considerate and protective in matters affecting his friends. Indeed, his character was extraordinary and ideal in every respect![11]

Members of the court whom we know from other works of literature occasionally appear, but the author generally did not lavish on them the passion for details found in the portrait of Michinaga. Several poems by Murasaki Shikibu are quoted in the context of the occasions when they were composed, but little else is said about her; and Izumi Shikibu's affairs with Prince Tametaka and his brother Atsumichi are only briefly described. One passage, however, leads us up to the opening pages of *The Izumi Shikibu Diary*:

> Meanwhile, Prince Tametaka, the President of the Board of Censors, had fallen into the dangerous habit of roaming about at night to visit women's houses. It made people uneasy, and there was a good deal of disapproving gossip. As it happened, a pestilence was raging that year with such virulence that no one's life was safe. The streets

> and avenues were clogged with stinking corpses, yet the Prince went blithely ahead night after night, without paying the slightest attention. Perhaps that is why he finally fell ill and died. His recent notorious infatuations with Shinchūnagon and Izumi Shikibu had been unpleasant for his wife, but she took his death very hard, and on the Forty-ninth Day she became a nun.[12]

The death of Tametaka, as readers of the diary will recall, is alluded to in the first sentence of *The Izumi Shikibu Diary,*[13] and serves as the background to her love affair with Tametaka's brother, Atsumichi. If there were more such passages as these *A Tale of Flowering Fortunes* would be an invaluable companion to the reading of the masterpieces of Heian literature.

THE GREAT MIRROR

Ōkagami (The Great Mirror),[14] was the first of the four "mirrors" that reflected Japanese history from the ancient past to the fourteenth century.[15] These "mirrors," unlike the later war stories, reflect not all of society but only the nobility. The use of the word "mirror" was in keeping with the Chinese practice,[16] and is explained by several poems in *The Great Mirror*, including:

akirakeki	Now that I have chanced upon
kagami ni aeba	This clear mirror,
suginishi mo	I can see the past,
ima yukusue no	The present,
koto mo miekeri	And what is to come.[17]

The Great Mirror describes events that took place from 850 to 1025. It opens as two exceedingly old men—Oyake no Yotsugi is 180 and Natsuyama no Shigeki a mere 170—begin their reminiscences about the past. The device of having these ancient gentlemen tell what happened in the old days was intended to impart immediacy to events of long ago by pretending that they lingered in the memories of men who actually witnessed what they describe. In addition to the two old men, three other people appear in the text: Shigeki's wife, a crone with little to say, an attendant from a noble household who occasionally interrupts Yotsugi's monologue to supply the version he has heard of some event, and the narrator, who addresses only the reader. The presence of these figures gives shape and even dramatic interest to the story, and the style is firmer and better suited to the materials than the more typical Heian style of *A Tale of Flowering Fortunes*.

The chief subject of *The Great Mirror*, like that of *A Tale of Flowering Fortunes*, is the life and times of Fujiwara no Michinaga, the dominant presence at the court from 995 until his death in 1027. Yotsugi, the elder of the two venerable narrators, says at one point, "I have only one thing of importance on my mind . . . and that is to describe Lord Michinaga's unprecedented successes to all of you here, clergy and laity of both sexes."[18] As a background to the achievements of the great Michinaga, the reigns of fourteen emperors who ruled between 850 and 1025, from Montoku (the fifty-fifth) to Ichijō (the sixty-eighth) are briefly summarized, followed by more detailed biographies of twenty members of the Fujiwara family who served the emperors as ministers of state.

The resemblances between the structure of *The Great Mirror* and that of Ssu-ma Ch'ien's masterpiece *Shih Chi* (Records of the Historian) are obvious; but even if the author of *The Great Mirror* was influenced by Ssu-ma Ch'ien (145?–90? B.C.) to the extent of describing first the reigns of emperors, followed by biographies of ministers, the final part of *The Great Mirror* (a fifth of the whole) consists of anecdotes about people of the distant past, the origins of festivals, strange happenings and so on, and owes nothing to the structure of the Chinese history. This part has only tenuous connections with Michinaga.

As a work of history, *The Great Mirror* suffers when compared to *Shih Chi*. Its interest, like that of *A Tale of Flowering Fortunes*, lies in its anecdotes and the glimpses it provides of the people and events of the Heian court not found in more formal histories. *The Great Mirror* does not dwell on the failings of the people who appear in its pages, but neither does it attempt to conceal them:

> Hōshi gave birth to a son known as the Eighth Prince—a handsome lad, but excessively slow-witted, or so it was rumored. . . . It was amazing that a son of the Emperor Murakami and grandson of Mototada should have been such a simpleton.[19]

The portrait drawn of another feeble-minded person, the Emperor Kazan, is particularly affecting. Kazan ascended the throne at the age of seventeen and left it to become a monk two years later. Michikane, a son of Fujiwara no Kaneie and brother of Michinaga, was eager to have Kazan abdicate. We are told:

A pathetic thing happened on the night of his abdication. As he was about to leave through the Fujitsubo Apartment's side door, he noticed the late moon flooding the surroundings with light.

"It looks so bright," he said. "What shall I do?"

Michikane urged him forward. "There is no reason why you should stop now. The Necklace and Sword have already been transferred," he said. He had personally delivered the Imperial Regalia to the Crown Prince while the Emperor was still in the Palace, so he knew it would never do for His Majesty to turn back.

While the Emperor hesitated, not wanting to venture into the light, some drifting clouds dimmed the moon's radiance. "I shall be able to take the vows after all," he thought. But as he stepped forward he remembered a note from the Kokiden Consort, something he had saved and read over and over.

"Wait a minute," he said, starting back to fetch it.

"You mustn't think about things like that any more," said Michikane, pretending to weep. "Some obstacle is certain to come up if you don't take advantage of this opportunity."[20]

Each time Kazan hesitates Michikane, with Machiavellian adroitness, insists that he carry through his plan of becoming a monk, and as soon as they reach the Hanayama Temple, Kazan cuts off his hair. At this point Michikane (who had promised Kazan to join him in entering the path of the Buddha) says, "I must leave you now. I want to let my father see me as my old self one last time, and I also have to tell him about my decision to become a monk. But I'll come back."

Kazan is not so dim-witted as to be incapable of seeing through Michikane's wiles:

Tears filled the Emperor's eyes. "You have deceived me, haven't you?" he said. It was a pitiful scene. As far as I can make out, Michikane had been encouraging him for a long time by swearing to serve as his faithful disciple. What a terrible way to act![21]

This episode, told in a minimum of words, is as memorable as any described by Herodotus, and the characters of the two men are perfectly caught. Kazan achieved his wish of becoming a Buddhist monk, but only after the act was irrevocable did he realize that another hand had guided his every move. Michikane may have comforted himself with the thought that he had done no more than help the incompetent Kazan to carry out his deeply desired wish; but when he took ill and suddenly died, just a week after realizing his great ambition and becoming the regent, he may in his final moments have remembered the trick he played on the Emperor Kazan.

Such anecdotes, though of literary interest, are hard to take seriously as history. The narrator, whose own reflections are presented at the end of the excerpt, could not have seen or heard most of what he describes, but perhaps rumors of what happened had become common gossip at the court, a place where it was hard to keep secrets. The narrator tells us, in his account of the career of minister of the Left Tokihira, "I heard it whispered later that Tokihira had arranged the scene with the Emperor in order to make others obey the law."[22] Whispers no doubt were the source of many of the stories related in *The Great Mirror*.

Even in sections of the work that are devoted to other persons, Michinaga's presence can generally be felt. He was, first of all, a "supremely lucky man."[23] If other, senior courtiers had not perished in the pestilence of 995 he would surely not have risen so high. He was lucky also in his offspring: none of his twelve children had died and, we are told, "There is not one who is at all inadequate or open to criticism in disposition or character, or who lacks accomplishments and elegance."[24] Michinaga was named kampaku in his thirtieth year, and served the court until he was fifty-four, when he took Buddhist vows.

Michinaga's first consort shared his amazing good fortune:

> Nobody could possibly be better off than this consort of Michinaga's. Although she is a subject, she is the grandmother of the Emperor and the Crown Prince, and she enjoys the same status as the three Empresses, with annual ranks and offices. She is perfectly free to go about as she pleases in her Chinese carriage—much more so than if she were an Empress. Whenever she wants to witness a public spectacle or Buddhist ceremony, she watches it from her carriage or viewing stand.[25]

The portraits of Michinaga and the people around him make no attempt to present the facts chronologically, let alone analytically. We are therefore apt to remember him as he appears in various unrelated bits of gossip, rather than as the most powerful man in the government. It is hard to forget such moments as when Michinaga hears reports that his sister Suishi is having an affair with Minamoto Yorisada and is pregnant. He goes to find out if this is true:

> Startled by his unexpected visit, Suishi drew her curtain-stand closer, but Michinaga pushed it aside. She was looking even lovelier than usual, her showy beauty enhanced by cosmetics. "When I went to the Crown Prince's palace, he told me about some stories he had heard," Michinaga said. "I have come to see for myself, because it will be very sad for you if he believes false tales." He opened her robes and pinched one of her breasts—and didn't he get a stream of milk in the face? He left without a word.[26]

This anecdote tells us little about Michinaga as a statesmen but it certainly conveys much about his mode of action. *The Great Mirror* concludes with comments by the anonymous narrator of all that has preceded, including: "It is usually tedious and annoying to be forced to listen while old crones and graybeards spin their yarns about the past, but Yotsugi and Shigeki made me feel as though I had stepped back into a bygone age. If only they would go on and on, I thought; if only I might have a chance to bring up all my comments and questions."[27] But the narrator loses sight of the two old men when they get caught up in a crowd of worshipers, and he never hears the resolution of Yotsugi's last tale. The ending confirms the essentially literary purpose of the unknown author of *The Great Mirror*.

The New Mirror

Imakagami (The New Mirror) is a continuation of *The Great Mirror*, describing events that occurred between 1025 and 1170. The work has been dated with some precision: it was probably written between the eighth month of 1174 and the seventh month of 1175.[28] The author, a matter of dispute, was most probably Fujiwara no Tametsune (1113?–1180?).[29] The period covered was one of great turbulence, marked toward its close by the rise of the samurai class and two major revolts, but *The New Mirror* rarely touches on political developments. Its attention is devoted instead to nostalgic recollections of the court in happier days, when poetry and music were the matters of chief concern, and ceremonies were performed with the most careful observance of precedents. The pattern of *The Great Mirror* is followed in that an extremely old person relates events that occurred long ago, but in this case the old person is a woman, the granddaughter of Yotsugi. It has been suggested that the choice of a woman as the narrator was influenced by what the author wished to describe—not affairs of state or military disturbances but the elegance of a vanished age.[30]

Some people on a pilgrimage to the various temples of the Yamato region during the early summer of 1170 have stopped to refresh themselves in the shade of a tree. An old woman approaches, leaning on a stick and accompanied by a girl who carries a basket of fern shoots. They ask the old woman if she lives in the vicinity, and she replies that she spent one hundred years in the capital and another fifty years in the province of Yamashiro; only since then has she lived in Yamato. The pilgrims are astonished to learn her great age, but she modestly cites examples in Japan and China of people who have lived even longer, including her grandfather, Yotsugi, who lived to be nearly two hundred. Her name, she reveals, is Ayame (iris), bestowed on her because she was born on the fifth day of the fifth month, the day of the Iris Festival. In her youth she served Murasaki Shikibu, who (alluding to a poem by Po Chü-i that describes the casting of a mirror on that day) gave her the nickname of Imakagami, the New Mirror.[31]

The rest of this long work consists of the old lady's recollections of the past. *The New Mirror* contains 140 waka and innumerable references to both Chinese and Japanese literature,[32] but as a whole it lacks literary quality. There is even less of an attempt than in *The Great Mirror* to give the narrator individuality or even to keep the reader aware that somebody in particular is telling a story. Only occasionally does the old woman insert a personal comment, as in this passage:

> Yotsugi when writing about the emperors took advantage of the opportunity to describe their mothers. I, too, will take advantage of the same opportunity to tell about this emperor's mother. She was about twenty-one or twenty-two when she gave birth successively to the Cloistered Emperor Goichijō and the Cloistered Emperor Suzaku.[33]

At other times the narrator declines to enter into details about some event because, she says, it has already been fully described in *furuki monogatari* (the old tale), a reference to *The Great Mirror.*[34] Occasionally she also mentions "the lady I served long ago," meaning Murasaki Shikibu, and quotes one of her poems.[35]

The chapters are arranged in more or less the same order as *The Great Mirror*; the first third is devoted to the reigns of the successive emperors, the next third to the Fujiwara family, and the final third partly to the Minamoto family and partly to various unrelated anecdotes.

The New Mirror, unlike *The Great Mirror*, has no central unifying figure. Michinaga appears only in the early sections, and the account of his death is brief, like most of the other vital information.

Only when the author is especially interested in someone do the descriptions blossom into literary prose, usually with the help of allusions to Chinese poetry. For example, the death of the Empress (chūgū) Genshi in her twenty-third year, shortly after her second childbirth, is treated in so much greater detail than the brief notice in *A Tale of Flowering Fortunes* that it is conjectured some personal reason was involved.[36] The passage is heightened by the last sentence, a paraphrase of a line from Po Chü-i's celebrated "Song of Unending Sorrow" describing the grief of the Emperor Hsüan Tsung on being separated from his beloved Yang Kuei-fei:

> His Majesty commanded that monks from the Seven Temples of Nara read the sutras for the repose of the late empress. The emperor wore mourning and, now that court functions had been suspended, he remained in the Pavilion of Pure Cool with the blinds drawn. When offering His Majesty his meals, the heralds refrained from their customary cries at the beginning and end. Sunken as he was in an all-pervasive atmosphere of gloom, even the sight of fireflies at dusk made him brood.[37]

Yang Kuei-fei's name appears on the next page of *The New Mirror*, making the source of the allusion perfectly clear.

The best-known part of *The New Mirror* occurs in the section of miscellaneous anecdotes at the end. It is a discussion of the belief that had sprung up by this time that Murasaki Shikibu had been doomed to suffer in hell because of her sin in writing untruths. An unnamed person asks the narrator,

> I wonder if it's true, as everybody says, that the person of long ago who wove together in her *Tale of Genji* exquisite and charming incidents that had little basis in reality was punished after her death by suffering the tortures of burning hell. If true, it provides an invaluable lesson for us who seek salvation, but how sad she should have come to such an end! I would like to pray for her.[38]

The narrator says she also has heard such tales. She thinks it quite proper that people who lead others astray with their writings should be punished. But, she insists, the author of *The Tale of Genji* had no such sinister intention, and surely does not deserve to suffer in hell. Works of literature can save as well as delude people: Po Chü-i, a very prolific poet who wrote in a most beautiful style, was so successful in inducing his readers to follow the teachings of the Buddha that he was believed to be a reincarnation of Monju, the bodhisattva of wisdom. Moreover, she continues,

> Buddha himself in his parables invented things that did not exist, and left these teachings for later generations. This, as the holy writings inform us, was because no deception was involved. The very fact that Murasaki Shikibu, a woman, was able to write such a long book, would seem to prove that she was no ordinary person. They say Myōon, Kannon, and other holy beings transformed themselves into women in order to preach the Law and guide humankind.

The girl with the basket of fern shoots who accompanies the old woman does not seem convinced by this explanation. She contrasts the actions of the bodhisattvas and other holy beings, who sought only to lead people to the Buddha, with Murasaki Shikibu's intention of arousing the passions of her readers with her vivid accounts of love affairs. "How can this be said to be in keeping with the Holy Law?" she asks. To this the old woman replies that the tale does indeed treat in detail many love affairs, but it nevertheless has always been considered by members of the nobility, from emperors and empresses down, as an incomparable treasure; and although people commonly say it is a sin even to make a manuscript copy of the work, it in fact serves to encourage people to turn to the Buddha. She insists that *The Tale of Genji* is by no means restricted to descriptions of the romantic attachments of men and women, and gives examples of passages in the novel that are specifically intended to guide people to enlightenment. The book accords perfectly with the Way of the Buddha, and even those passages that have been sullied by the impurities of this world promote a yearning for the morning sunlight of the Buddhist teachings.[39]

The New Mirror is less engrossing than its predecessor, *The Great Mirror*, but some of the stories, partly because they recur in later writings, resonate within the reader's memory. An anecdote describing the decoration of roofs with irises on the fifth day of the fifth month may recall Bashō's *The Narrow Road of Oku*, and mention in the same anecdote of the flowering water-oat (*hanagatsumi*) may have inspired his fruitless search for the same plant (which he also knew from poetry).[40] Life at the court is almost always portrayed cheerfully except when relating such things as the deaths of members of the imperial family. There are some delightful passages, such as the account of the time when Ariwara no Narihira wrestled in the palace with the future Emperor Uda. The two men—or rather, the man Narihira (about fifty-two) and the boy Uda (about ten)—knock against a chair and break the armrest. It was left broken in commemoration of the wrestling match, but recently some official, not knowing the history, decided to repair the armrest, a sign of his stupidity![41]

Generally, life at the court is described with no hint that this life would soon come to an end. The Hōgen and Heiji revolts are passed over in a few words, as if such deplorable examples of taste should not be allowed to besmirch the pages of a refined chronicle. One would like to think that Fujiwara no Tametsune (if indeed he was the author) was trying to preserve intact the memory of the glory of the imperial court in the face of the forthcoming triumph of the barbarians, but more probably he simply could not conceive that the society he admired so much would soon be dramatically altered.

The Water Mirror

One other "mirror" of history survives from approximately the same period, *Mizukagami* (The Water Mirror), an account of the reigns of fourteen emperors during the 1,522 years between the coronation of Jimmu, the legendary first emperor, and A.D. 850, the reign of the Emperor Goichijō. The work was obviously intended to complete the history of Japan by narrating what had happened up to the point where *The Great Mirror* begins. The time of compilation and the author have not been firmly established, but it is generally agreed on the basis of internal evidence that it was written at the very beginning of the Kamakura period, probably between 1185 and 1190. Nakayama no Tadachika (1131–1195), a nobleman of some importance, is most frequently suggested as the author.[42] Regardless of who wrote *The Water Mirror*, the literary achievement was small. It is a bare account of the reigns of the successive emperors, and lacks the chapters on members of the noble houses that in the other "mirrors" contain the most interesting anecdotes.

It has been demonstrated, moreover, that when writing *The Water Mirror*, the author used only one source, *Fusō Ryakki* (A Short History of Japan), a work in Chinese compiled between 1094 and 1107. This history is often credited to the Buddhist monk Kōen (d. 1169), but if this is correct it means, in view of the date of composition, that Kōen as a small boy compiled in kambun a thirty-volume history of Japan. Whoever actually wrote the work was undoubtedly a devout and learned Buddhist, but that is about all one can say with confidence. *The Water Mirror* is an incomplete translation of *Fusō Ryakki*, rendered into smoothly flowing Japanese.[43] This in itself was an achievement worthy of a place in the history of translation, but apart from the very beginning and end, where the old nun and the ascetic appear, almost nothing is original with *The Water Mirror*; its obscurity is richly earned.

Four more "mirrors" would be written in the tradition of *The Great Mirror*. *Masukagami* (The Clear Mirror) is in literary terms the most distinguished and a major work of the Muromachi period.[44] It treats events that occurred between 1180, the year of the birth of the Emperor Gotoba, and 1333, the year when the Emperor Godaigo returned from exile. *Akitsushima Monogatari* (A Tale of Akitsushima) is dated 1218, but there is no clue to the author.[45] This "mirror" goes back even farther than *The Water Mirror* to the age of the gods, long before the Emperor Jimmu came into the world, and most of the information it contains originated in the *Nihon Shoki*. The two remaining mirrors were both compiled during the Tokugawa period. *Tsuki no Yukue* (Where the Moon Goes) was written in 1771 in the incredibly brief period of eight days by Arakida Reijo (1732–1806), a learned lady of Ise. The materials were derived mainly from literary sources such as *Kenreimon'in Ukyō no Daibu no Shū* (The Poetic Memoirs of Lady Daibu), and the style harkens back to the Heian period. It opens with the accession to the throne of the Emperor Takakura in 1168 and continues until the death of the Emperor Antoku and the destruction of the Taira family in 1185. Arakida Reijo also wrote in 1771 the last of the mirrors, *Ike no Mokuzu* (Scraps of Waterweed in the Pond), which continues from 1333 to the 1600s the account of Japanese history presented in *The Clear Mirror*. For this work Reijo used as her primary source such works as the *Taiheiki* (1372?), though she chose the style of the Heian romances. These works differ in many ways from the first mirrors of history, but they observe the convention of being the narrations of witnesses of the events they describe, and suggest how congenial later writers found the Heian mixture of history and poetry.

Notes

1. Specialists have divided works that describe historical events, especially warfare, into such categories as *senki monogatari* (battle tales), *rekishi monogatari* (historical tales), and *gunki monogatari* (war tales). A more recent trend is to consider all works relating to warfare as gunki, regardless of their degree of literary content. See for example the article on gunki in *Nihon Koten Bungaku Daijiten*, II, p. 317. The tradition has been to treat as literature works composed in Japanese, but to discuss those in Chinese as histories or works of primarily historical interest. In general, I have followed this practice, though composition in Japanese is not always a guarantee of literary value and some histories in Chinese contain literary elements.
2. I have adopted the translation of the title given by William H. and Helen Craig McCullough in their translation.
3. William H. and Helen Craig McCullough, *A Tale of Flowering Fortunes*, I, p. 15.
4. *Ibid*., p. 42.
5. *Ibid*., pp. 140–41. Text in Matsumura Hiroji and Yamanaka Yutaka, *Eiga Monogatari*, I, p. 108. For more on Suishi, see p. 559.
6. Translation by Edward G. Seidensticker, *The Tale of Genji*, I, p. 18.
7. McCullough and McCullough, *A Tale*, I, p. 49.
8. *Ibid*., p. 344. Text in Matsumura and Yamanaka, *Eiga*, I, pp. 335–36.
9. McCullough and McCullough, *A Tale*, I, pp. 240–41. Text in Matsumura and Yamanaka, *Eiga*, I, p. 225.
10. McCullough and McCullough, *A Tale*, I, p. 23.
11. *Ibid*., p. 138. Text in Matsumura and Yamanaka, *Eiga*, I, p. 106.
12. McCullough and McCullough, *A Tale*, I, p. 249. Matsumura and Yamanaka, *Eiga*, I, p. 234.
13. See the translation by Edwin A. Cranston, *The Izumi Shikibu Diary*, p. 131.
14. The excellent translation by Helen Craig McCullough is called *Ōkagami: The Great Mirror*. Joseph K. Yamagiwa published a section of the work in the volume of translations made by himself and Edwin O. Reischauer. (Edwin O. Reischauer and Joseph K. Yamagiwa, *Translations from Early Japanese Literature*.) Yamagiwa subsequently published a complete translation under the title *The Ōkagami*.
15. The order of composition of the four "mirrors" is not the same as the periods of history they cover. The third, *The Water Mirror*, opens with the most ancient events, those ascribed to the reign of the Emperor Jimmu.
16. See McCullough, *Ōkagami*, p. 3.
17. *Ibid*., p. 85. Text in Hosaka Hiroshi, *Ōkagami Zenhyōshaku*, I, p. 170.
18. McCullough, *Ōkagami*, p. 68. Hosaka, *Ōkagami*, I, p. 40.
19. McCullough, *Ōkagami*, p. 116. Hosaka, *Ōkagami*, I, p. 339.

20. McCullough, *Ōkagami*, pp. 80–81. Hosaka, *Ōkagami*, I, pp. 134–35.
21. McCullough, *Ōkagami*, p. 81. Hosaka, *Ōkagami*, I, p. 135.
22. McCullough, *Ōkagami*, p. 103. Hosaka, *Ōkagami*, I, p. 265.
23. McCullough, *Ōkagami*, p. 185. Hosaka, *Ōkagami*, II, p. 180.
24. McCullough, *Ōkagami*, p. 190. Hosaka, *Ōkagami*, II, p. 239.
25. McCullough, *Ōkagami*, p. 186–87. Hosaka, *Ōkagami*, II, p. 204.
26. McCullough, *Ōkagami*, pp. 164–65. Hosaka, *Ōkagami*, II, p. 29.
27. McCullough, *Ōkagami*, p. 240. Hosaka, *Ōkagami*, II, p. 605.
28. Takehana Isao, *Imakagami*, III, p. 620.
29. *Ibid.*, pp. 620–22. See also Matsumura Hiroji, *Rekishi Monogatari*, pp. 156–61.
30. Takehana, *Imakagami*, I, p. 42.
31. *Ibid.*, pp. 38–39.
32. See Matsumura, *Rekishi*, pp. 168–80, for an account of the allusions to Chinese and Japanese literature.
33. Takehana, *Imakagami*, I, p. 130. The empress in question was Shōshi. Goichijō was born in 1008 and Suzaku in 1009.
34. *Ibid.*, p. 59. At other times (see page 64) the author says the same of *mukashi no monogatari* (stories of long ago), apparently a reference to *A Tale of Flowering Fortunes*.
35. Takehana, *Imakagami*, I, p. 131.
36. *Ibid.*, p. 112.
37. *Ibid.*, p. 108.
38. *Ibid.*, III, p. 595. There is some uncertainty about the meaning of *en ni enaranu tsuma*. Takehana takes *en* to be the familiar "connection" with the Buddha, but other scholars interpret the *en* as "charm," meaning in context that Murasaki Shikibu's writings have such charm as to create a rare occasion for arousing indescibable feelings.
39. *Ibid.*, pp. 591–605. On pp. 605–11 Takehana considers other accounts of Murasaki Shikibu's punishment in hell. The statement in the text that Po Chü-i was a reincarnation of the bodhisattva Mañjuśri has not been found in any earlier texts.
40. *Ibid.*, pp. 522–23.
41. *Ibid.*, pp. 107–10.
42. Nothing in the work either confirms or contradicts this theory. A rival candidate, Minamoto no Masayori (1129–1192), is backed by some scholars. For an account of the conflicting claims, see Matsumura, *Rekishi*, pp. 237–39.
43. For a parallel passage in the two texts, see *ibid.*, pp. 234–35.
44. See below, pp. 899–906. It is so far removed in time of composition and literary style from the earlier mirrors that I have discussed it in a later chapter.
45. See Matsumura, *Rekishi*, pp. 314–15.

Bibliography

Note: All Japanese books, except as otherwise noted, were published in Tokyo.

Cranston, Edwin A. *The Izumi Shikibu Diary*. Cambridge, Mass.: Harvard University Press, 1969.

Hosaka Hiroshi. *Ōkagami Zenhyōshaku*, 2 vols. Gakutōsha, 1979.

Matsumura Hiroji. *Rekishi Monogatari*. Hanawa Shobō, 1979.

Matsumura Hiroji and Yamanaka Yutaka. *Eiga Monogatari*, 2 vols., in Nihon Koten Bungaku Taikei series. Iwanami Shoten, 1964–65.

McCullough, Helen Craig. *Ōkagami: The Great Mirror*. Princeton, N.J.: Princeton University Press, 1980.

McCullough, William H. and Helen Craig McCullough. *A Tale of Flowering Fortunes*, 2 vols. Stanford, Calif.: Stanford University Press, 1980.

Nihon Koten Bungaku Daijiten, 6 vols. Iwanami Shoten, 1983–85.

Reischauer, Edwin O., and Joseph K. Yamagiwa. *Translations from Early Japanese Literature*. Cambridge, Mass.: Harvard University Press, 1951.

Seidensticker, Edward G. *The Tale of Genji*, 2 vols. New York: Alfred A. Knopf, 1976.

Takehana Isao. *Imakagami*, 3 vols., in Kōdansha Gakujutsu Bunko series. Kōdansha, 1984.

Yamagiwa, Joseph K. *The Ōkagami*. London: George Allen and Unwin, 1967.

15. TALE LITERATURE

The compilation of extensive collections of stories, fables, and parables known today as *setsuwa bungaku* (tale literature) was a notable development of the late Heian period. Some of the stories were native folktales that had been transmitted orally, others were derived from Buddhist or Confucian writings of the continent. Although their backgrounds were diverse, many tales were alike in possessing Buddhist or other "lessons" at the close; the compiler generally managed to salvage from even the most mundane or risqué story an edifying moral, unconvincing though it might seem. The stories are brief—usually not more than a few pages in length—and they differ greatly in literary value; but twentieth-century writers and critics have often contrasted the vigor and freshness of these collections with the effete manner of works of courtly fiction written at about the same time.

Tales similar to those contained in these collections may be found as far back as the *Kojiki*, and they also appear in such works of court literature as *Tales of Yamato* and *The Great Mirror*. The major collections of setsuwa date from the twelfth and early thirteenth centuries, but a number of lesser collections were compiled during the three hundred years between the ninth-century *Account of Miracles in Japan*, the oldest collection of setsuwa, and the twelfth-century *Konjaku Monogatari* (Tales of Times Now Past), the principal repository of setsuwa. The word *setsuwa* itself, originally a designation for orally transmitted tales,[1] is now used mainly for written tales, and embraces a wide variety of works, ranging from artless children's stories to intensely serious accounts of awakening to the truths of Buddhism.[2]

The major setsuwa collections contain both religious and secular tales. Some relate incidents from the lives of the successive buddhas; others depict emperors, generals, and similar figures of Japanese history; still others are devoted to humble people who could never have appeared in the aristocratic writings of the Heian period. Naturally, the accounts of Buddhist miracles were clothed in suitably dignified language, but elsewhere the compilers did not hesitate to include crude and even indecent language. Some stories bear resemblances to folktales known all over the world, but others seem to have been created specifically in order to explain the origins of place-names, customs, and unusual features of the Japanese landscape.[3]

Orally Transmitted Tales

Many tales included in the setsuwa collections undoubtedly originated as folktales or, to use the Japanese term, *mukashibanashi*, meaning "stories about long ago." In the past, when literacy was largely confined to members of the court and the priesthood, the narration of tales and poetry possessed for the common people the importance of written texts or visually presented entertainments today. The telling of "stories about long ago" still goes on; collectors continue to discover treasure troves of folktales, remembered by elderly people in villages scattered all over Japan. Few, however, of the folktales currently being told can be shown to be closely related to the tales found in the setsuwa collections; and even in such cases, it is possible that at some time during the intervening centuries these folktales were derived from written accounts.[4] Resemblances to folktales found elsewhere in the world have induced scholars to classify them under rubrics first devised for European tales,[5] but the dissimilarities are no less striking.

Probably the best known of all Japanese folktales is that of the fisherman Urashima Tarō. One day, after hours of unsuccessful fishing, he caught a great tortoise. He did not kill it, and the grateful tortoise took him on its back to the Dragon Palace under the sea, where he spent three happy years with a beautiful princess (in some versions a transformation of the tortoise). Eventually, however, he became homesick, and told the princess he wished to return to his family. She gave him a jeweled casket with the injunction never to open it. When he reached his native village he was astonished by the changes that had occurred in only three years. He recognized no one, but finally encountered a villager who had heard the story of how, three hundred years before, Urashima went out to sea and never returned. Distraught to hear this revelation, Urashima opened the casket, and at once turned into an extremely old man.

This tale was first recorded in the fudoki for the province of Tango in 713,[6] and appeared in many different versions over the centuries, notably in *Kojidan* (Tales About Old Matters), a collection compiled early in the thirteenth century.[7] In each version details differ, but the general outlines remain much the same. Kawai Hayato, a Jungian analyst, discussing the fudoki version, contrasted it with similar European tales:

> In an important process in Western ego development, the male figure tries to separate from Mother (symbolically by killing her) and then to gain a new woman. However, in the *Fudoki* version of "Urashima Tarō," there is no sign of an incident which might symbolize killing the mother. Instead, suddenly, the turtle princess appears and proposes to him. Urashima, not knowing anything about this woman, follows after her. In short, rather than getting a woman after a heroic battle, this hero was captured by her![8]

The passivity of the Japanese hero often leads to endings to the tales that seem incomplete to a Western reader; but even if nothing seems to have happened in the tale, at least according to Western conceptions, a poignant atmosphere at the conclusion is enough for Japanese readers, for whom the silent grief of a woman makes as satisfying an ending as the triumph of a hero.[9]

Probably the manner of narration of the oral tales, as distinct from written ones, added overtones to the meaning. Some orally transmitted tales can be appreciated when committed to paper, but others are fully intelligible only in the context of the culture that produced them. This is the particular interest of the tales to the student of Japanese literature—not as sources of later fiction, nor even as depictions of how people of the past lived, but as embodiments of cultural attitudes that antedate the earliest examples of written literature yet continue to be felt in modern Japan.

Illustrations of the Three Jewels

The beginnings of setsuwa literature (as opposed to orally transmitted tales of uncertain antiquity) are traced back to *Account of Miracles in Japan*.[10] The stories of this collection, as the title indicated, narrated the miracles vouchsafed by various buddhas and bodhisattvas in response to the prayers and virtuous actions of Japanese believers, and this was true of other collections of Buddhist tales.

The first monument of setsuwa literature of the Heian period was also Buddhist in content. The title *Sambō-e* (Illustrations of the Three Jewels)[11] refers to the three treasures (*sambō*) of Buddhism—the Buddha, the Buddhist Law (*dharma*), and the priesthood. The word *illustrations* (*e*), at the end of the title, indicates that the work was originally a combination of text and paintings, probably in the form of a horizontal scroll, but these illustrations have been lost. The collection was compiled in 984 by Minamoto no Tamenori (941–1011) for the Princess Sonshi, who had recently taken vows as a Buddhist nun, to guide her in the Buddhist teachings. Probably Tamenori originally composed the work in Chinese but later (perhaps for Princess Sonshi's benefit) translated it into Japanese.[12]

Illustrations of the Three Jewels contains sixty-two stories, divided into three books, each of which is devoted to one of the "jewels." The tales in the first book were derived from *jātaka* stories told about the previous lives of the Buddha; those in the second book are concerned with the Buddhist Law, as practiced in Japan; and those in the third book describe the origins of Buddhist rites performed by Japanese monks. Tamenori borrowed all but one of the tales in the second book from *Account of Miracles in Japan*, as he himself stated, and closely followed his source.[13] These stories, like many other examples of setsuwa literature, are no more than moderately entertaining. No doubt they helped readers to absorb the lessons taught in the Buddhist scriptures, but they are seldom of literary interest, and generally trail off without reaching an aesthetically satisfying conclusion. Some stories in the first book, especially those in which animals are portrayed more sympathetically than human beings, are pleasantly naive,[14] but Tamenori's main concern in compiling *Illustrations of the Three Jewels* was clearly to enlighten rather than to amuse Princess Sonshi.

COLLECTION OF THINGS HEARD

Two collections of Buddhist tales compiled early in the twelfth century are of special interest: *Hyakuza Hōdan Kikigaki Shō*[15] (Notes on One Hundred Sessions of Sermons) and *Uchigiki Shū* (Collection of Things Heard). The former work consists of notes on twenty of the sermons delivered on different chapters of the Lotus Sutra during a period of a hundred days in 1110.[16] The notes refer mainly to the thirty-five tales incorporated in the sermons, providing a rare glimpse of the language and manner of contemporary preaching. Of the surviving thirty-five tales, eighteen are set in India, sixteen in China, and only one in Japan; the preponderance of tales set outside Japan contrasts especially with *Account of Miracles in Japan*.[17]

Collection of Things Heard gives in outline form the main elements of twenty-seven Buddhist tales set in India, China, and Japan. The brief preface to the work states that it was copied in 1134 by a monk named Eigen—probably a Tendai monk, judging by the attention given to the Tendai sect in the collection. Most authorities believe that Eigen merely copied another priest's manuscript, but it is at least possible that he himself was the author.[18] Only one volume of the original two or three has been preserved, and the contents of all twenty-seven of the surviving tales appear in other collections of setsuwa;[19] but *Collection of Things Heard* is nonetheless important because of its distinctive treatment of the materials. The outlines of the tales found in this work are sometimes written in a mixture of Japanese and Chinese, sometimes in an approximation of Chinese, depending on whether the author was relating the tale at length or merely stating the bare essentials. In the form in which they are presented in *Collection of Things Heard* the tales lack literary interest, but like those in *Notes on One Hundred Sessions of Sermons* they reveal much about the nature of popular Buddhism in their day.[20] The author's purpose in compiling the book seems to have been to provide himself or others with a ready store of Buddhist anecdotes with which to enliven sermons. The sources of the stories are nowhere stated, but they were probably derived from a common pool of tales, and may have appeared in the lost *Uji Dainagon Monogatari* (Tales of the Uji Grand Minister) compiled about 1070 by Minamoto no Takakuni (1004–1077), known as the Uji Grand Minister.[21] Despite the striking similarities in content between *Collection of Things Heard* and other collections, it is clear from the differences among the texts that the compiler did not borrow directly from any surviving work.[22]

Tales of Times Now Past

These early setsuwa collections are not without interest, despite the crudity of the narration and the inadequate characterization of the people who appear in the tales. No apologies need be made, however, for *Konjaku Monogatari* (Tales of Times Now Past), the most important work of setsuwa literature. Neither the date of compilation nor the name of the editor is known, but there is reason to believe that it was compiled between 1130 and 1140. Traditionally, the compilation of *Tales of Times*

Now Past was credited to Minamoto no Takakuni, an enthusiastic collector of folktales, who is reported to have stopped people passing his house to ask if they knew any interesting tales. This may have happened, but no one now believes that Takakuni compiled *Tales of Times Now Past*; not only does the collection contain stories describing events that occurred long after his death, but the stories have been carefully integrated into the whole, strong evidence that the compilation was made by a later man.[23]

Tales of Times Now Past contains over a thousand stories, but even so the text is incomplete: three of the projected thirty-one books bear numbers but no tales, and elsewhere only the titles of tales survive. Such gaps in the manuscipt suggest not that sections of the manuscript were lost, but that the compilation was broken off before the manuscript could be completed.

The books of the collection are arranged in the order of India, China, and Japan, suggesting the path taken by Buddhism as it spread across Asia. The first five books, therefore, are devoted to Buddhist tales from India. They are followed by five books (one of them missing) of tales from China, mostly Buddhist but some Confucian. Finally, the original plan apparently called for twenty-one books of tales from Japan, but only nineteen were completed. The Japanese tales constitute the most interesting segment of the collection, not only because they are far more numerous, but also because many are devoted to the daily lives of Japanese of the time, rather than to repetitious accounts of Buddhist miracles. When contemporary editors make selections from the great corpus of *Tales of Times Now Past*, they almost always choose from the secular Japanese tales about nobles and commoners found in the last ten books.

Within each book the tales are arranged in a manner especially congenial to the Japanese: each tale links to the next by some common theme or association. The style shows a similar pattern, ranging from the somewhat stiff language of the translations from Chinese versions of the sacred texts of Buddhism or from the Confucian classics to the much more relaxed style of the tales of the last ten books, those that treat Japanese people. Except for titles of office and special Buddhist terminology, very few words in the text are of Chinese origin, but the appearance of any given page does not in the least resemble one from any of the Heian classics of courtly literature; Chinese characters are so extensively used to represent the Japanese words and sounds that at first glance one might even suppose that the texts were in Chinese.[24]

Each of the tales opens with the formula *ima wa mukashi*, rather like the "once upon a time" of European fairy tales, but meaning something closer to "now it is long ago." There is also a concluding formula for each tale, *to nan kataritsutaetaru to ya*—"thus it has been told and transmitted." It is not clear whether these formulae were original or borrowed from some existing tradition or why it was felt necessary to include them in each instance. Part of the problem is that many of the conjectured sources for *Tales of Times Now Past* have been lost, and we cannot even be sure of how long the compilation took or when it was finished. The earliest possible date for the completion of the work was 1120, the year when a Chinese book it quotes was first imported into Japan. The latest possible date is more difficult to establish,[25] but stylistic features suggest that the later limit is about 1140.[26]

Many tales of India and China found in *Tales of Times Now Past* have been traced back to two collections of Buddhist tales compiled by Chinese monks: fifty-five came from *San-pao kan-ying yao-lüeh-lu* (Outline Account of Responses of the Three Treasures)[27] by Fei Cho (d. 1063), not only the main source of stories but the model for the entire collection with respect to the arrangement of the tales; and forty-eight tales were drawn from *Ming-pao chi* (Account of Retribution in the Afterworld) compiled about A.D. 650 by the monk T'ang Lin.[28] The editor of *Tales of Times Now Past* did not borrow directly from the sutras or other sacred works of the Buddhist tradition for his religious tales but from these and other secondary Chinese collections.[29] The Confucian tales were similarly borrowed from popular works, rather than the canonical Four Books. The religious tales set in Japan borrowed from *Account of Miracles in Japan*, *The Three Jewels*, and other secondary works. The secular tales came from a greater variety of sources: tales that dealt with military matters were derived from such works as *Shōmonki* (The Story of Masakado) and *Mutsu Waki* (Tales and Records of Mutsu);[30] stories of court life from *Tales of Ise*, *Tales of Yamato*, and various anthologies of poetry; and other tales from lost collections. It was long assumed that many tales must have been based on orally transmitted folktales, but most scholars now believe that the tales were all derived from written sources.[31]

The chief pleasure in reading *Tales of Times Now Past* comes from the glimpses it provides of life during the Heian period. People of every class, from every part of Japan, appear in its pages; even when the work describes persons of the upper class, they are usually specimens we do not encounter in works of the courtly tradition. Consider, for example, the portrait of Goi[32] in the tale "Yam Soup":

> A few days later Toshihito appeared at Sir Goi's lodging and invited him for a bath.
>
> Sir Goi accepted. "I *am* a bit itchy this evening," he admitted. "But I've no conveyance."
>
> "Don't worry," said Toshihito. "I've brought you a nag to ride."
>
> "Wonderful, wonderful!" Sir Goi rose to go. He had on a tattered light-blue outfit with rents and gaps here and there, and not even proper underwear under his trousers. The end of his sharp nose was red, and the drop quivering there showed that he had not wiped it for some time.[33]

This description from *Tales of Times Now Past* is all one needs to visualize the hapless Goi. Even when they are only a few lines long, the portraits of characters high and low, but especially low, make many episodes unforgettable. This is true of such varied figures as the ferocious bandit who is intimidated by the nonchalant flute playing of the nobleman he intends to attack;[34] the female chief of a band of robbers who sadistically whips her adoring underlings;[35] or the woman who turns into a demon and tries to devour her own sons.[36] Many tales are devoted to Buddhist priests. Priests described in the religious tales are for the most part admirable, but those in the secular tales are almost without exception corrupt or licentious men, and some even commit murder.[37] The impression left by these contrasting accounts is not one of contradiction but of a richly varied world.

The interest that the stories in *Tales of Times Now Past* (after their rediscovery in the fifteenth century) aroused in later readers can be inferred from the number that were incorporated into works of fiction and drama. Nō plays were based on tales included in the collection, as were medieval stories. Occasionally a passage seems to anticipate the seventeenth-century novelist Saikaku: "You know the saying, a governor can't stumble without snatching a handful of dirt."[38] Twentieth-century writers have also been tempted into creating works of their own about the people and situations found in *Tales of Times Now Past*, enhancing them with psychological insights and the skill of professional writers.

For all their interest as documents of the past and their intermittent charm, however, few of the original tales can be said to be well crafted. Sometimes even the anonymous narrator seems to be dissatisfied with the resolution of a tale:

> Now think: there's nothing unusual in a fox taking human form; it's happened often since ancient times. But what an impudent trick

> it was, to take him all the way to Toribeno! And then why was it that on the second occasion the guardsman did not see the procession or lose his way? Some have guessed that how a fox behaves depends on the person's state of mind.[39]

At other times a tale may provide unnecessary information, as in the opening to one well-known episode:

> Many years ago there were in the province of Mimasaka two gods, Chūzan and Kōya. Chūzan had the shape of a monkey, and Kōya of a snake. Every year, at the time of the festival, a living creature was offered up to the gods. The victim was an unwedded girl of this province.[40]

Apart from these opening words, there is not a single reference in the story to the snake god. He is mentioned not because he will figure later in the account but because there *was* such a divinity; it seemed more important to mention this truth than to worry about creating a work of art. In other cases, the story is inadequately developed, as we realize immediately when we read a modern version of the same tale. Perhaps the most celebrated tale in the collection (though it is hardly a page long) describes a robber who hides in the upper story of the Rashōmon, the great gate at the southern entrance to the capital. He sees a dim light in the darkness of the windowless room and goes to investigate. An old woman is pulling the hair from the corpse of a young woman. The sight is so appalling that at first the robber wonders if the old woman might not be a demon. He tries frightening her away with a shout, only for the old woman to beg for mercy. He demands to know what she is doing.

> "I lost my mistress, sir," she said, "and as there was no one to bury her, I brought her here. See what nice long hair she has. I'm plucking it out to make a wig. Spare me!"
>
> The thief stripped the corpse and the old woman of the clothes they wore and stole the hair. He ran to the ground and made his getaway.[41]

The crone who pulls out the hair of her dead mistress leaves an indelible, nightmarish impression on the reader, and the incident symbolizes the capital at a time when pestilence and wanton crime had rendered unrecognizable a city that a century earlier had been the loveliest in the world. But, for all its memorable qualities, the tale as narrated here is no match for Akutagawa Ryūnosuke's story based on the same episode from *Tales of Times Now Past.* The man in the original tale is a faceless thief, and his ultimate brutality, snatching the rags from the old woman's back, is no more than one of a series of almost automatically performed acts, all in keeping with his profession. In the Akutagawa story, the man is portrayed as having hitherto resisted somehow the temptation to turn to crime (like so many other desperate men); but the sight of the crone's plucking hair from the head of the dead woman shocks him into brutality. He seizes the dead woman's robe, her hair, and, the final step into the abyss, the worthless rags the crone is wearing. He rushes off into the night, a criminal.

Many similar instances of successful adaptation of tales from the collection could be given, testimony at once to the richness of the material and the inadequacy of the storytelling. When the same story appears both in *Tales of Times Now Past* and in *Uji Shūi Monogatari* (Later Tales from Uji), the later version is almost always literarily superior. It may be that *Tales of Times Now Past* was never intended to be read in the manner in which it is read today, but it is impossible to know what was in the compiler's mind: the book lacks the kind of preface or afterword that often informs us of the intentions of Japanese authors.[42]

Collection of Old Setsuwa Texts

In 1943 the announcement was made that a collection of setsuwa that had never before been carefully examined (it had previously been assumed it was no more than a variant text of *Tales of Times Now Past*) was in fact an independent work. The sole surviving manuscript had been labeled *Konjaku Monogatari* at some time in the past, but it was decided, to avoid confusion, that the work be given a different title. It was uninspiringly called *Kohon Setsuwa Shū* (Collection of Old Setsuwa Texts). Neither the compiler nor the date of composition is known, but it probably dates from the early twelfth century.[43]

Collection of Old Setsuwa Texts consists of two volumes, the first containing forty-six Japanese secular tales, the second twenty-four Buddhist tales, all but three set in Japan. Forty of the tales relate anecdotes similar to ones in *Tales of Times Now Past*, many of them devoted to the circumstances of the composition of waka by members of the court.[44] The resemblances go beyond the subject matter: they all open with the familiar *ima wa mukashi* (now it is long ago), and the style is also very similar, though the stories lack the stereotyped phrases with which each episode in *Tales of Times Now Past* concludes. There are, however, important differences: even when the story treats what is in general the same incident, the structure and the emphasis may be so dissimilar as to obscure any resemblances. For example, tales 4 and 5 in *Collection of Old Setsuwa Texts* are devoted to Ōe no Masahira and his wife, Akazome Emon (the author of *A Tale of Flowering Fortunes*). They parallel tales 51 and 52 in Book XXIV of *Tales of Times Now Past* and even contain some of the same poems; but the *Collection* text emphasizes Akazome's dislike for her ugly husband, whereas the *Tales of Times Now Past* version tells how she won back Masahira's affection after he had had an affair with another woman.[45]

Apart from their importance as sometimes strikingly different versions of tales familiar from earlier collections, some tales in *Collections of Old Setsuwa Texts* are interesting in their own right. One, concerning Murasaki Shikibu, opens intriguingly:

> Many years ago, when Murasaki Shikibu, the celebrated poet, was serving the Empress Shōshi,[46] a note came from the grand high priestess[47] one spring day saying, "I'm bored. Haven't you some story I can read?"
>
> Various books were brought out, and the empress picked her way through them, finally asking, "I wonder which one I should send her?"
>
> Murasaki Shikibu said, "I'm sure she knows them all backward and forward. I think you should have a new one written and send that to her."
>
> "Very well," said the empress, "You write it."
>
> Since this was Her Majesty's command, she wrote *Genji* and the empress sent it along to the grand high priestess.[48]

It is hard to believe that the composition of *The Tale of Genji* originated in so casual an impulse, but the dialogue in this and other episodes is so lively as to suggest it was faithful to the speech of the day.[49] Although *Collection of Old Setsuwa Texts* shares many resemblances with other collections of setsuwa, the style is actually closer to that of court romances and diaries, suggesting that the compiler's intended audience was the readers of court fiction, rather than monks looking for anecdotes with which to enliven their sermons. This impression is confirmed by the appearance of a typical page: very few Chinese characters are used, and no attempt was made to induce the reader to believe he held in his hands a work of Chinese learning.

Tales Written in Chinese

It will be remembered that the first collection of Buddhist tales, *Account of Miracles in Japan*, was written in classical Chinese. It was not surprising, in view of the purpose of the collection—to provide priests with anecdotes for their sermons—that it should have been in the language of the Buddhist texts used in Japan. The tradition of writing anecdotes in Chinese continued long past the end of the Heian period, even when they were not inspired by Buddhism.

Honchō Shinsen Den (Lives of Japanese Spirit Immortals, c. 1097) consists of brief descriptions in Chinese of thirty-seven[50] Japanese "immortals," as related by the Confucian scholar Ōe no Masafusa. The use of the word "spirit immortals" *(shinsen)* plainly indicates Taoist influence,[51] and even though many of the figures treated were Buddhist clerics (like Kōbō Daishi or Jikaku Daishi), emphasis is placed not on their knowledge of the sutras but on their success in achieving immortality or on their ability to perform such feats as flying through the sky. The biography of Yōshō, a monk of the Tendai sect, typifies the collection. It opens:

> Yōshō was a native of the province of Noto. His family name as a layman was Ki. His mother, after having a dream in which she swallowed sunlight, conceived and gave birth. In the third year of Gangyō [879] he climbed Mount Hiei, where he lived at the Hōdō Temple. At the time he was in his eleventh year, and he took the *vinaya* master Kūnichi as his master. He was extremely quick and intelligent, and once he had learned something he never asked about it again. He was versant in the Lotus Sutra, the Yuga Sastra, and the Great Concentration and Insight,[52] and never in all his life did he show joy or anger, nor did he sleep. Although he accumulated no worldly goods, he gave what clothes and food he possessed to the hungry and cold.
>
> Later, he climbed Metal Peak Mountain[53] and stayed at the Muta Temple there. For three years he practiced austerities, and ate no more than a single grain of millet each day. He walked so quickly that, although he had no wings, he flew. Even in the dead of winter he wore no cloak and used no bedding. In the autumn of the first

year of the Engi era [901] he finally climbed the mountain and became an immortal [*hijiri*]. In the eighteenth year of the same era a priest of the Tōdai-ji visited the peak where the spirit immortal lived. He had run out of food and water and was on the point of expiring when he heard a voice chanting the Lotus Sutra. Astonished, he struggled to his feet and searched for the source of the voice, and that was how he happened to meet Yōshō. Yōshō directed spells at the man's bowl and water jug, and soon the bowl was full of delicious food, and the jug overflowed with nectar.[54]

The magical feats of Yōshō belong more to the world of the Taoist practitioners than to Buddhism, despite the references to Mount Hiei, the center of Tendai Buddhism, and to the sacred texts of Tendai. Not all the tales are on this elevated level, however. Here is the entire text of *Saouchi no Hijiri* 'The Tale of the Immortal Beaten with Poles':

The Immortal Beaten with Poles was a native of the province of Yamato. He had mastered the art of becoming an immortal, but his worldly bones were still heavy, and even the medicines used by immortals were powerless to alleviate this condition. He was able to take off from the earth and fly, but he never got more than seven or eight feet from the ground, and little children would all run after him brandishing poles with which to hit him. That is how he acquired his name. It is not known what happened to him afterward.[55]

Ōe no Masafusa is credited with various other collections of setsuwa written in Chinese, including *Zoku Nihon Ōjō Gokuraku Ki* (Sequel Account of Japanese Reborn in Paradise), a continuation of the work by Yoshishige no Yasutane, and *Lives of Japanese Spirit Immortals.*[56] But his best-known work was the *Gōdanshō* (Selection of Ōe's Conversations), a series of short essays taken down from Masafusa's conversations by Fujiwara no Sanekane (1085–1112). Most of the essays are devoted to explanations of couplets in Chinese that appear in *Wakan Rōei Shū*.[57] These explanations are occasionally of interest, but the appeal of the collection lies chiefly in the relatively few stories in the setsuwa vein, like the following account of the dream prophecy vouchsafed to Fujiwara no Kaneie, known as the "Great Lay Priest":

When the Great Lay Priest was a major counselor he dreamt of crossing the Ōsaka Barrier in the falling snow. The barrier was completely white. He was greatly shocked by this dream, supposing that snow was an unlucky omen. He sent for a dream interpreter and related the dream. The man said, "Your dream was a most auspicious one. You have definitely nothing to worry about. Somebody is certain to offer you a mottled ox." Thereupon a man did indeed offer him a mottled ox, and Kaneie rewarded the dream interpreter. When Ōe no Masahira came to call, Kaneie related what had happened. Masahira was astonished. He urged Kaneie to take back the reward from the dream interpreter, and gave his own interpretation of the dream: "The Ōsaka Barrier contains the same character *kan* as used in *kampaku.* The snow is white, written with the character *haku.* It means that you are without question going to become the kampaku." Kaneie was overcome with emotion. In the following year he was appointed as kampaku.[58]

In this and many other passages Masafusa glorified his great-grandfather, the scholar Ōe no Masahira. He never hesitated to refer to the achievements of other members of his family, beginning with Ōe no Otondo (811–877), the founder of the Ōe family. When Otondo was appointed chief of police (*kebiishi bettō)* the prison was in such a bad state of repair that criminals were constantly escaping. Otondo built a new prison wall, which ended the escapes. Shortly before he died, Otondo prophesized that because of this distinguished service to his country, his descendants would rise to high positions in the government. Masafusa had modeled himself on this ancestor and credited him with his own successful career.[59] Autobiographical touches of this kind contribute to the interest of the book.

The text of *Selection of Ōe's Conversations* is mainly in Chinese, but it contains some Japanese, probably because the text originated as notes on actual conversations. This is perhaps the most interesting of the setsuwa collections written entirely or largely in Chinese. Such collections, because they were composed by members of the court and treat only people and events that occurred at the court, lack the variety of the setsuwa tales composed in Japanese. When, moreover, a Japanese conversation was reported in Chinese, the pungency of expression in the original tale tends to be diluted by being translated into what was, after all, a foreign language. In some passages verb endings, particles, and other typical elements of the Japanese language interrupt the Chinese text of this and similar collections, suggesting that the translator at times could not help but use Japanese, especially when a story was concerned with waka composition or some other aspect of court life.

Two similar collections of setsuwa consist of the conversations, recorded mainly in Chinese, of the statesman Fujiwara no Tadazane (1078–1162). Tadazane's life was one of extreme changes of fortune. He rose at one time to the position of kampaku, only to be dismissed after offending the Priestly Sovereign Shirakawa. Reinstated by the Retired Emperor Toba, he was implicated in the Hōgen Rebellion, and confined to the Chisoku-in, a temple whose name meant ironically "to know satisfaction," where he spent the rest of his days. Even though he was living in disgrace, he was nevertheless a repository of information about precedents and court customs, and his reminiscences, both before and after his incarceration, were preserved in *Chūgaishō*, recorded by Nakahara no Moromoto between 1137 and 1154, and in *Fuke Go*, recorded by Takashina no Nakayuki between 1151 and 1161.[60] These two works would exercise considerable influence over later collections of tales, especially those compiled in the Kamakura period.[61]

Tales Translated from Chinese

The setsuwa collections of the late Heian period include a few that are devoted entirely to figures of Chinese history. *Kara Monogatari* (Tales of China),[62] the best known, consists of twenty-seven tales; its title suggests it was intended as a Chinese equivalent to the tales of Japan in *Tales of Yamato*. Recent research indicates that it was probably compiled between 1165 and 1176 by Fujiwara no Shigenori (1135–1177), the son of the priest Shinzei who perished in the Heiji Rebellion.[63]

Tales of China, apparently intended for young Japanese readers (though not all of the tales can be said to be edifying), presents in easy-to-read Japanese the deeds of Chinese of the past. The translator freely chose his materials for each of the stories, and transmuted the original Chinese into effortless prose of the Heian variety, embellished with waka at places where they would naturally appear if the tales had been written from the start in Japanese. Each episode begins with the same formula as in *Tales of Times Now Past*, and if the names of people and places were not all Chinese, it would be hard to distinguish this from a purely Japanese collection. However, *Tales of China*, unlike the Chinese stories in *Tales of Times Now Past*, is usually treated as a translation rather than as an original work. The sources of the tales have been traced to the works of Po Chü-i; to *Meng Ch'iu*, the collection of rhymed epitomizations of the lives of some six hundred famous people of the past by the eighth-century official Li Han; to *Shih Chi*, the great history by Ssu-ma Ch'ien; and to various other works of Chinese history and literature.[64]

In view of the great importance of translation in the development of Japanese literature, especially from the late nineteenth century, *Tales of China* occupies an honored place as the oldest surviving translation into Japanese, but its worth as literature is modest.[65]

Mōgyū Waka (*Meng Ch'iu* Waka), compiled (according to the preface) in 1204 by Minamoto no Mitsuyuki (1163–1244), consists of twenty-five anecdotes translated from *Meng Ch'iu*, each anecdote ending with a waka that epitomizes its essential points. The stories are arranged in the traditional order of waka collections, beginning with poems on the four seasons and continuing with love poems and other poems on the usual topics. The translations are free, taking from the original only what would go smoothly into Heian-period Japanese. Each tale concludes with a waka that is intended as a crystallization of the story as a whole, and is not (as in *Tales of China*) attributed to one of the characters of the story. A comparison of the original Chinese text (in the translation of Burton Watson) of one of the episodes together with the Japanese version may suggest the differences. The story of Li Kuang in the original opens in this manner:

> Li Kuang of the Former Han was a native of Ch'eng-chi in Lung-hsi. The art of archery had been handed down in his family for generations.
>
> Li Kuang was out hunting one time when he spied a rock in the grass which he mistook for a tiger. He shot an arrow at the rock and hit it with such force that the tip of the arrow embedded itself in the rock. Later he discovered that it was a rock, but another day when he tried shooting at it again, he was unable to pierce it.[66]

The above is about one quarter of the anecdote. The Japanese translation is much shorter than the original and does not mention (as the original Chinese text does) Li Kuang's subsequent career or his spectacular suicide, but in the part of his life it describes it gives various details that are not found in the source. Here is the full text from *Mōgyū Waka* (where it is classified as a spring story because of the reference to peach blossoms):

> Li Kuang was a native of Ch'eng-chi in Lung-hsi. He excelled in the art of bows and arrows, and repeatedly won glory in battle. That is how he became a general. The Grand Historian[67] said, "I myself have seen General Li—a man so plain and unassuming that you would take him for a peasant, and almost incapable of speaking a

word. And yet the day he died all the people of the empire, whether they had known him or not, were moved to the profoundest grief. There is a proverb which says, 'Though the peach and damson trees do not speak, the world wears a path beneath them.' "[68] General Li's father was eaten by a tiger. When General Li went into the fields he thought he saw a tiger in the grass, and shot an arrow through it. They say the arrow penetrated as far as the feathers. When he examined it close up, he saw that it was not a tiger but a big rock. Later on, if ever he saw a rock and fired on it, the arrow would never stand in the rock. It was because he was under the impression he was firing on the tiger who had devoured his father that his arrow pierced the rock.

mono iwanu	Even blossoms that
hana mo hitome wo	Say nothing have attracted
sasoikeri	People's attention;
michi mo sariaenu	One cannot avoid the path
momo no shitakage[69]	That leads beneath the peach trees.

The Japanese version of the story of General Li Kuang, though ostensibly a translation of the account in *Meng Ch'iu*, incorporates materials from other sources, and the waka, needless to say, is not found in the Chinese original. The explanation of *why* Li Kuang's arrow penetrated the rock only the first time, not given either in *Meng Ch'iu* or in *Shih Chi*, may have been inspired by the questions of little Japanese boys who were obliged to memorize this edifying tale.

These Chinese tales, though the names of the people and places were probably rather exotic to the first Japanese readers, soon became a part of the Japanese heritage as we can tell from the repeated references to Chinese heroes in the later Japanese literature, especially the war tales. To the modern reader the many citations of Chinese parallels in *The Tale of the Heike* and similar works are likely to seem tedious. The unfamiliar Chinese names add nothing to the narration and serve mainly to interrupt it; but for readers acquainted with *Tales of China* and other stories derived from *Meng Ch'iu*, such references imparted an added dimension to the Japanese deeds of valor, as parallels with the ancient Greeks confirmed the importance of Roman prowess.[70]

Some Later Collections of Tales

During the latter part of the twelfth and early part of the thirteenth centuries a number of setsuwa collections were compiled, but it is often difficult to determine which of two collections came first or (another way of saying the same thing) which collection influenced the other. An identical or virtually identical tale may appear in several collections; and even if we know the name of the compiler, it is by no means clear why he thought it necessary to include in his own collection—even to the point of copying word for word—stories that had already been anthologized. Perhaps, considering the scarcity of manuscripts, he thought that the best way to preserve a story he liked was to include it in his collection, regardless of how many other collections might have included it.

Kojidan (Tales About Old Matters), compiled by Fujiwara no Akikane (1160–1215), is almost entirely derived from earlier collections, and the author hardly ever intrudes in the narration. His chief contribution would seem to have been organizing the 462 tales into six books devoted to (1) members of the imperial family, (2) ministers, (3) priests, (4) warriors, (5) Shintō shrines and Buddhist temples, and (6) buildings and arts. These categories are by no means absolute, but *Tales About Old Matters* is better organized than *Selection of Ōe's Conversations*, also in six books.[71] It is believed that Akikane set about compiling *Tales About Old Matters* soon after he gave up his successful career as an official and became a Buddhist monk in 1211, completing his task sometime after 1213.[72] The language used in narrating the tales ranges from more or less normal Chinese, with no admixture of kana, to stories in Japanese dotted with Chinese Buddhist and technical terms in the manner of *Tales of Times Now Past.* If Akikane wrote the entire text, the changes in style must reflect the different attitudes he assumed toward his materials.

It might be expected that a collection of tales compiled toward the end of his life by a man who had taken vows as a priest would be highly moral and generally boring, but the very first story in *Tales About Old Matters* will disabuse anyone of this notion. Here is how it opens:

> The Empress Shōtoku, dissatisfied with the size of Dōkyō's penis, large though it was, had a dildo fashioned from a mountain potato. It broke off while she was using it, and got stuck inside her. The area became infected and swelled, and her life was imperiled. At this point the Nun of the Small Hands (a doctor from Paekche,

> whose hands were no bigger than an infant's)[73] examined her and said, "Her Majesty's malady is curable." She greased her hands and was about to extract the dildo when Momokawa,[74] the middle contoller of the Right, shouting that she was a fox spirit, whipped out his sword and slashed the nun's shoulder. As a consequence the empress passed away, no cure being possible.[75]

There is certainly no hint of worshipful reverence for the imperial family in this account of the wayward empress whose love for the priest Dōkyō was behind her unsuccessful attempt to seat him on the throne. It is hard to imagine, all the same, why Akikane should have placed this particular anecdote at the head of his collection, unless he was simply hoping that such a story would attract a maximum of attention. Several other anecdotes about reigning sovereigns suggest that Akikane may also have had a prurient interest in what went on behind the curtains of the imperial bedchamber. Two extremely brief tales (translated in full) confirm this impression.

> On the day of the coronation of the Emperor Kazan, Uma no Naishi was serving as noblewoman of the curtains;[76] he pulled her inside the curtains and immediately began to copulate with her.[77]

> After Lord Takakuni became the chief secretary to His Majesty[78] he used to help him on with his clothes. He first of all would grab for His Majesty's penis. His Majesty would respond by knocking off Takakuni's court cap. This did not seem to bother him in the least, and he would continue serving, even though his topknot was exposed.[79] This happened every time.[80]

Similar informal (to say the least) glimpses of life at the court occur elsewhere in *Tales About Old Matters,* but they do not typify the collection as a whole, which devotes most of its pages to anecdotes that are illustrative of court precedents. The following describes an unusual reaction to precedent on the part of Emperor Shirakawa:

> It was because the emperor's love for the Empress Kenshi surpassed his love for anyone else that she died in the palace.[81] Although his grief was extreme, he refused to allow her to be taken from him. When she finally shut her eyes, he still clung to the corpse, and would not get up and leave. Lord Toshiaki[82] came up to him and said, "There is no precedent for a sovereign's being present when

> someone dies. You should leave at once, Your Majesty." The emperor replied, "The precedent will begin from *now.*"[83]

Other anecdotes helped to create legends about celebrated figures of the Heian period. One, describing Sei Shōnagon in old age, when she had gone down in the world and was living in a ramshackle hut, offers evidence that, despite the ravages of time that had destroyed her beauty, she had preserved her wit. When some young noblemen passed by her hut, one of them commented on the wretched state to which she had been reduced. Hearing this, she raised the blinds and, pointing to her emaciated face, cried, "How about buying the bones of a fine horse?"[84] Her reference to an incident described in the ancient Chinese historical work *Chan-kuo Tse* (Intrigues of the Warring States) demonstrated she still retained her vaunted familiarity with the Chinese classics, and the aptness of the comparison of her bony head to the bones of the prize steed mentioned in the Chinese tale showed she still retained her high opinion of herself—and her wit.

Not all the stories were about members of the court, nor were they restricted to the capital, though the court was the locus for most of *Tales About Old Matters.* Some, like the following example, belong to the tradition of strange tales found in earlier collections:

> Along about the fourth month of 1026, a boat carrying a woman over seven feet tall with a face over two feet long called at a bay in the province of Tango. There was food and drink in her boat, but everyone who came close and touched the food fell painfully ill. For this reason the boat was not allowed to dock, and in the meantime the woman died, they say.[85]

Tales About Old Matters also contains some folktales, notably the story of the fisherman Urashima Tarō. There can hardly be a less effective narration of this famous folktale, but literary excellence seems not to have been a concern of the editor. Despite the often inept expression, however, the intrinsic interest of many anecdotes attracted the attention of the compilers of later collections of tales, and a revival of scholarly interest in the work after long neglect began in the 1960s.[86]

Zoku Kojidan (Sequel Tales About Old Matters) is arranged in a similar manner to the original work, but the stories are of conspicuously less interest. The compiler is unknown, but the large number of anecdotes about Sugawara no Michizane have suggested that the compiler may have belonged to the Sugawara family.[87] A postscript is dated 1219, but this may be the date of the sixth and concluding volume rather than of the whole collection, which seems to have been compiled earlier.

The most literary of the collections of tales is undoubtedly *Later Tales from Uji*.[88] The title indicated that the tales of this collection supplemented those in *The Tales of the Uji Grand Minister*: the preface to the collection, after relating how Minamoto no Takakuni had collected the tales of the old days, states that the present work included stories that were omitted from the earlier collection.[89] Unfortunately, that work does not survive, and it is therefore impossible to compare its contents with those of *Later Tales from Uji*.

Considerable scholarship has been devoted to efforts to identify the compiler of *Later Tales from Uji*, but no generally acceptable candidate has emerged, and there is reason to think that more than one compiler was involved.[90] The time of compilation has also been much debated, but it is now generally agreed that it was probably between 1210 and 1220, with some later additions. Regardless of the exact year of compilation, the time was undoubtedly the beginning of the Kamakura period.

One might expect that a collection of anecdotes devoted for the most part to describing Japanese life during the century or so prior to the time of compilation would include many stories about the heroic or villainous deeds that had occurred during the revolts of the middle of the twelfth century and the war between the Taira and the Minamoto, but with one exception there is not a single reference to any of these events. The exception occurs at the end of a tale describing how a mackerel (or perhaps a great many mackerel), brought by an old man to the consecration services of the great temple Tōdai-ji, magically turned into the eighty volumes of the Avatamsaka Sutra.[91] The pole on which the old man carried the mackerel, stuck into the ground by the Hall of the Great Buddha, had developed into a tree, "but recently it was burned down, when the Taira fired the temple."[92]

References to recent happenings are so rare that even this casual mention of Taira wantonness has been a focal point of attempts to date the collection. The question naturally arises as to why the compiler was so careful not to include anecdotes relating to the turbulent years of warfare. Perhaps he felt that the events were still too vividly remembered for him to employ the traditional formula *ima wa mukashi* with which, in the manner of *Tales of Times Now Past*, he began each tale.[93] It is also possible that, as a member of the nobility, he felt that war between military adversaries was no concern of his. Certainly, any overt expression of political opinion would have taken the collection outside the framework of setsuwa literature.

The literary appeal of *Later Tales from Uji* does not stem primarily from the freshness of the materials. Of the 197 tales, 143 may be found in other collections of setsuwa literature, including *Tales of Times Now Past*, *Collection of Old Setsuwa Texts*, and *Tales About Old Matters*.[94] *Later Tales from Uji*, however, omits details that are unnecessary from a literary point of view, unlike *Tales of Times Now Past*, which insists on historical truth even at the expense of literary interest; the aim of the compiler was probably *le vraisemblable* rather than *le vrai*. This is the first setsuwa collection that seems to have been intended to be read rather than delivered aloud, and the style and narrative techniques owe much to the old monogatari, though the tales are not introspective in the courtly manner. Above all, the accomplished prose, a polished Japanese that is considerably simpler and more direct than earlier prose, distinguishes it from the ungracious expression of such collections as *Tales About Old Matters*. Because it is literarily the finest of the setsuwa collections, it continued to be read at the court during centuries to come.[95]

One distinctive feature of the narration of *Later Tales from Uji* is that the tales conclude with an artistically conceived ending, rather than a moral or simply one more line in the same flat tone as what has preceded. Again and again when reading *Tales of Times Now Past* we are let down by a lame conclusion, or absence of any conclusion, but *Later Tales from Uji* generally manages to impart literary point to its stories by a suitable "coda." For example, the tale of the mackerel that turned into eighty volumes of sutras ends this way in *Tales of Times Now Past*:

> The mackerel peddler's pole is still by the entrance to the hall. It hasn't grown, or burst into bloom, or done anything in particular. It's just there.[96]

The version in *Later Tales from Uji* ends:

> Until thirty or forty years ago this "mackerel-pole" tree was green and flourishing. From that time it withered, though it remained standing, but recently it was burned down, when the Taira fired the temple. What a pity it is—so typical of this decadent age![97]

The interest of the *Tales of Times Now Past* version of the tale is exhausted with the account of the old mackerel peddler who, despite his protests, is taken for a great dignitary and ushered to a place of honor; the rest of the tale, down to this tentative ending, is clumsily narrated. The conclusion in the *Later Tales from Uji* text, on the other hand, effectively confirms the claim made earlier in the tale that "as the temple flourishes or declines, so this tree flourishes or withers."[98] It may even have been for the sake of this observation that the tale was included in the collection.

Jikkinshō (A Miscellany of Ten Maxims) is a collection of tales compiled in 1252 by an unknown author.[99] Most of the more than two hundred tales are devoted to anecdotes concerning the aristocracy of the Heian period. The compiler was evidently moved by nostalgia for the glorious days of the Heian court, probably because he sensed they would never return. The purpose of the collection was stated in the preface:

> What I am going to do is make selections from the abundant materials of all kinds of ancient and modern tales, both oral and written, to follow the trail of both the wise and the foolish through history, promoting virtue and reproving vice. This is meant to be a help for the formation of good character in young people who have not yet had proper instruction of this type.
>
> As a start, I have divided it into ten parts, and called it "A Miscellany of Ten Maxims." . . . I have written preferably in the Japanese syllabary and not Chinese characters, without worrying that the sentences will come out too long, so that it will be easy for a person reading it by himself. Similarly, in order to make the examples intelligible to a person having it read to him, I took them mainly from Japanese literature and only secondly from Chinese works, without scouring great numbers of books.[100]

Although the author's purpose was professedly educational, not all the tales accord with conventional morality, and the examples given for each of the ten virtues or vices discussed must have seemed very remote to young people of the mid-thirteenth century, living in a world quite unlike that of the Heian court. Each of the ten sections of the work is introduced by a generally Confucian statement of its intent. The third "maxim" (the word has also been translated as "moral principles"), a warning against despising people, will illustrate the manner. The introduction opens:

> Someone said that a display of haughtiness toward others, whatever form it takes, is an inevitable part of life. Some people look

> down on the poor and humble, others show their contempt for the unwary, and still others, sneering at those less fortunate than themselves, think in response to what these people do or say, "One can't expect any better from them." This is the behavior of ignoramuses.[101]

The tale that immediately follows, though literarily more interesting than most in *A Miscellany of Ten Maxims*, is not a particularly good illustration of the theme "one must not be contemptuous of people," but it typifies the aristocratic orientation of the collection:

> While Izumi Shikibu, the wife of Yasumasa,[102] was off in Tango[103] a poem competition was held in the capital. Koshikibu Naishi[104] was chosen to participate. The Middle Counselor Sadayori[105] went to her room and teasingly called in to her, "Has the messenger you sent to Tango returned? I can imagine how nervous you must be." As he was passing before the room, she leaned halfway out from behind her screen-of-state and held for a moment the sleeve of his robe, reciting:
>
> | | |
> |---|---|
> | *Ōeyama* | The road that goes to |
> | *Ikuno no michi no* | Mount Ōe and Ikuno |
> | *tōkereba* | Is so far away |
> | *mada fumi mo mizu* | I have yet to tread upon |
> | *Ama no Hashidate* | The Heavenly Bridge of Tango.[106] |
>
> Sadayori, taken aback by this unexpected display of wit, could only say, "How did that happen? I never expected anything like that!" Unable even to compose a return poem, he pulled his sleeve free and made his escape. From this time on Koshikibu's reputation as a poet was recognized. It was quite reasonable for Sadayori to have thought as he did, but couldn't he have known in his heart that she was capable of producing on the spot a poem of this quality?[107]

This example of someone's looking down on another person is indeed in accord with the theme; but surely there was little malice behind Sadayori's imputation that Koshikibu could not compose a poem without her mother's help. Unlike the examples of people who despise others, given in the introduction to this section of *Ten Maxims*, Sadayori was merely teasing Koshikibu. For that matter, Koshikibu's poem, in which she denied, under the surface meaning of expressing unfamiliarity with the distant landscapes of Tango, that she had received any help from her mother, is hardly one of bitter resentment at the slur on her reputation as a poet. The poem and the tale itself are a part of the aristocratic tradition that the compiler of *Ten Maxims* nostalgically evoked throughout the work.

Many of the tales given in *Ten Maxims* had already appeared in earlier collections, sometimes in exactly the same language, sometimes with variants, and it would in turn influence later collections, but it is hard to think of anything really distinctive about these tales unless it is the exclusive attention given to life at the court at a time when tales about the military or the common people had come to occupy a prominent place in other setsuwa collections.[108]

Kokon Chomonjū (Collection of Tales Heard, Present and Past, 1254) was the last setsuwa collection in the aristocratic tradition. The compiler was Tachibana no Narisue, a nobleman of the fifth rank about whom little else is known, though it is conjectured that he was about fifty when he completed the collection in 1254. *Tales Heard* contains 726 tales in twenty books, ranking second only to *Tales of Times Now Past* in size. The stories are carefully arranged in chronological order under thirty topics such as "Buddhist Teachings," "Loyal Ministers," "Waka Poetry," "Music and Dance," "Love," "Brave Warriors," "Gambling," "Bandits," "Clever Repartee," "Prodigies," and "Fish, Insects, Birds, and Beasts."

About two thirds of the tales are set in the Heian period, and the tone throughout is one of nostalgic remembrance of a glorious past. Again and again a note of regret is sounded over the disappearance of some old custom, as at the conclusion of the lovingly evoked description of a pleasure excursion of the court in 1092: "In the old days this happened all the time, but the practice died out in middle antiquity. What a lamentable world it is!"[109] This comment by the compiler was not simply an expression of nostalgia, a common theme in Japanese literature, nor was it conventional regret over the devastation wrought by the passage of time, in the all too familiar mood of waka poetry; it was the recognition by a nobleman that he lived in an age when the refined pleasures of the past had been supplanted by the uncouth manners of the military.

We are likely to read *Tales Heard* for the stories set in roughly the same period as that of the compiler, for the contemporary gossip and tales of prodigies that reached Narisue's ears. It is intriguing, for example, that a section each should have been devoted to gambling and bandits; the stories arranged under these and similarly unconventional topics are not only of greater literary interest than those about Buddhist priests or loyal ministers but constitute the principal attraction of the collection for readers today. It is clear, nevertheless, that Narisue's chief concern was his own class, and even the cruder tales of the collection usually represent the nobility in an unbuttoned, "daily" mood, and not the common people.

The division of the work into twenty books recalls the standard number of books in an imperially sponsored collection of waka poetry. This impression is strengthened by the preface and afterword, one in classical Chinese and the other in Japanese (following the precedent of the *Kokinshū*). These two essays provide invaluable background information on Narisue's purpose in compiling the collection. Narisue opened the preface with an acknowledgment of his indebtedness to the setsuwa collections compiled by the Uji Major Counselor (Minamoto no Takakuni) and Ōe no Masafusa. The extent of the influence of the former *(The Tales of the Uji Grand Minister)* on *Tales Heard* cannot be measured because the text has been lost, but *Selection of Ōe's Conversations* is the one earlier collection from which direct borrowing definitely occurred. Perhaps this influence, from a collection composed largely in Chinese, explains the noticeable increase in the use of words of Chinese origin in an otherwise Japanese text.[110]

The main sources of the stories are factual, rather than literary—the diaries and similar records kept in Chinese by noblemen. Indeed, Narisue's stated purpose was not to entertain but to transmit reliable information about people and events of the past. On occasion, when he had no documentary evidence to support a tale, he felt obliged to explain why he nevertheless included it: "I do not know whether or not this matter has been described in any diary, but it is widely reported."[111] Narisue seems to have thought of *Tales Heard* much as the Heian courtiers thought of their diaries—as a repository of important information about the past that would be useful to future generations of their families. In his afterword Narisue warned,

> With respect to this collection, showing it to outsiders is not permitted. If any son or grandson of mine violates this prohibition, and takes the manuscript outside our walls, he is no longer a son or grandson of mine. The gods of our clan will surely punish him with their divine wrath. However, the granting or refusal of permission to examine the text will depend on who wishes to see it, and the decision should depend on the circumstances. If the person in question enjoys the closest intimacy with our family, someone with whom caution is unnecessary, permission may occasionally be granted.[112]

Whatever purpose Narisue may have had in mind when he compiled this enormous grab bag of anecdotes, it serves as a last memento of the nostalgia for the Heian court on the part of aristocrats whose glory had much faded. But even these evocations of the past were couched in a Japanese that was distinctly unlike that of *The Tale of Genji*, and the present—the rise of the military, the loss of prestige of the court, the spread of culture to a much wider segment of the population than before—frequently intruded in the narration, apparently without the author's realizing it. The later tale literature would have a quite different emphasis.

Notes

1. Sugimoto Keizaburō, "Uchigikishū ni okeru setsuwa to setsuwa bungaku," p. 45. The word *setsuwa* is found in Japanese dictionaries going back to the early eighteenth century, but its modern usage dates back to the middle of the nineteenth century, where it occurs in translations (such as Nakamura Keiu's version of *Self-Help* by Samuel Smiles), usually with the meaning of a discourse pronounced for some moral or instructional purpose.
2. The setsuwa collections treated in this chapter are mainly those of the late Heian period. Kamakura period collections, especially those with strong Buddhist coloration, are discussed in chapter 19.
3. Usuda Jingorō, "Setsuwa no Hassei," p. 29, in Usuda Jingorō and Nishio Kōichi, *Nihon no Setsuwa*, I.
4. For example, the tale called "The Sparrow with a Broken Back," collected in Ōita Prefecture and translated by Fanny Hagin Mayer in *Ancient Tales in Modern Japan* (pp. 144–45), is extremely close to tale 48 in *Later Tales from Uji*. (Translation by Douglas Mills in *A Collection of Tales from Uji*, pp. 209–14. Another translation, by Robert H. Brower, is given in my *Anthology of Japanese Literature*.) Elsewhere, Yanagita Kunio said of an abbreviated version of the same tale that "It is distributed widely in Japan and cannot be considered the result of modern books." See Fanny Hagin Mayer, *The Yanagita Kunio Guide to the Japanese Folk Tale*, p. 131. It would seem that the extent of influence from written sources on this and other tales still being recounted has yet to be determined.

   Yanagita Kunio (1875–1962) was recognized in his day as the outstanding authority on Japanese folklore. He collected tales in many parts of Japan, and some of them, notably his earliest collection, *Tōno Monogatari* (The Legends of Tōno, 1910), have been admired not simply as faithful transcriptions of orally transmitted tales but as works of modern Japanese literature. There is an English translation by Ronald A. Morse of *The Legends of Tōno*.

5. See Richard M. Dorson, *Studies in Japanese Folklore*, p. 13.
6. Most of the *Tango Fudoki* has been lost; the Urashima Tarō story is given in one of the surviving fragments. The text of *Urashimako* (as it is called) together with a *kundoku* (Chinese text punctuated for reading in Japanese) version and notes is given in Shigematsu Akihisa, *Urashimako Den*, pp. 8–22. The same work also gives the texts of the accounts of Urashima Tarō in the *Kojiki*, the *Man'yōshū*, and many later works.
7. See Kobayashi Yasuharu, *Kojidan*, I, pp. 24–28.
8. Kawai Hayao, *The Japanese Psyche*, pp. 95–96.
9. *Ibid*., pp. 13–22.
10. See above, pp. 206–9.
11. There is a complete translation with an introduction by Edward Kamens in *The Three Jewels*. I have followed his translation of the title, though the term *sambō* is more commonly rendered as the "three treasures."
12. The question is discussed by Kamens in *The Three Jewels*, pp. 26–30; and on p. 28 he gives samples of three different systems of recording the texts that are found in manuscripts.
13. *Ibid*., p. 65.
14. I am thinking especially of stories 8 ("The Lion Who Held Firmly to His Vows"), 9 ("The Deer King"), and 11 ("Prince Mahāsattva"). See *ibid*., pp. 132–46.
15. The title is variously given. *Nihon Koten Bungaku Daijiten* gives it as *Hokke Shuhō Ippyakuza Kikigaki Shō*.
16. These sermons were delivered at the request of a certain prince, who had made a vow that required such observances. Although it was originally intended to conclude the sermons after the hundred days devoted to the Lotus Sutra, the sermons were prolonged to three hundred days and treated the *Amida-kyō* and the *Hannyashin-kyō* as well.
17. A discussion in English of *Notes on One Hundred Sessions of Sermons*, together with a comparison of one of its tales with the same one as given in *Tales of Times Now Past*, is found in W. Michael Kelsey, *Konjaku Monogatari-shū*, pp. 37–39.
18. Yoneda Chizuko in "Uchigakishū ni okeru Hensha no Shisei," pp. 62–65, cites but rejects earlier authorities who declared there was absolutely no intrusion of the compiler's personality in the text. She believed that she could hear the "faint voice" of the compiler. Kishi Seizō, in "Uchigakishū ni okeru ateji no imi," believed that Eigen had given himself away by his use of mistaken characters (*ateji*), and also mentions (p. 195) without elaborating an erasure in the text that satisfies him that Eigen himself was the compiler.
19. Twenty-one are found in *Tales of Times Now Past*, another five in *Later Tales from Uji*, and the remaining one in *Account of Miracles in Japan*. See

Nakajima Etsuji, *Uji Shūi Monogatari, Uchigiki Shūi Zenchūshaku*, pp. 589–93.

20. Kunisaki Fumimaro, "Uchigikishū," p. 3.
21. See Mori Masato, *Konjaku Monogatari Shū no Seisei*, pp. 11–12. Takakuni was known as the Uji Grand Minister because of his habit of spending his summers at Uji, away from the sweltering capital.
22. See, for example, Miyata Shō, "Konjaku Monogatari Shū kan-roku Buppō to Shintan Dan," p. 66, in *Uchigikishū*.
23. Kunisaki Fumimaro, a lifelong scholar of *Tales of Times Now Past*, reached the tentative conclusion that it was compiled by Minamoto no Toshiyori. In his *Konjaku Monogatari Shū Sakusha Kō* he described (p. 9) the faint clues that had led him to this conclusion. He compared *Tales of Times Now Past* and *Toshiyori Zuinō*, a collection of anecdotes compiled by Toshiyori (pp. 28–51). Kunisaki believed that the anecdotes Toshiyori wrote in Japanese before setting to work on *Tales of Times Now Past* were revised both in style and transcription before being absorbed into that work, but that some stories were left over; these were edited by a later person to create the collection now known as *Collection of Old Setsuwa Texts* (pp. 392–93). Another group of "leftover" stories was combined with *Tales About Old Matters* to create *Later Tales from Uji* (p. 393). Kunisaki, who had published quite different views earlier in his career, now felt sure that the source of the stories in *Tales of Times Now Past* and other collections of setsuwa was not any body of orally transmitted tales but the writings of Toshiyori in Japanese.

    These opinions, though they deserve respectful attention considering their source, do not seem to have changed the conviction of other authorities.
24. Verb endings and case particles are given in katakana, but very much smaller than the Chinese characters, suggesting a text in kambun that has been punctuated for Japanese reading.
25. The earliest reference to the collection occurs in a work of 1449, three centuries after completion.
26. Ōsone Shōsuke et al., *Kenkyū Shiryō Nihon Koten Bungaku*, III, p. 58.
27. This work was introduced to Japan late in the eleventh century, and was widely used in later times in spreading the Buddhist teaching. See *Nihon Koten Bungaku Daijiten*, III, p. 138.
28. See *Nihon Koten Bungaku Daijiten*, V, pp. 698–99, for an account of this work and its importance.
29. See Ōsone et al., *Kenkyū*, p. 53.
30. See below, pp. 614–15.
31. See, for example, Ōsone et al., *Kenkyū*, p. 55. For an exhaustive study of sources of *Tales of Times Now Past*, see Katayose Masayoshi, *Konjaku Monogatari Shū no Kenkyū*, 2 vols.
32. Goi meant "fifth rank," rather too exalted a position, we may feel, for

the scruffy character portrayed in the story. The man is known not by his name but his rank.

33. Translated by Royall Tyler in *Japanese Tales*, p. 118. Tyler's note indicates his translation was made from *Later Tales from Uji*, but the *Tales of Times Now Past* text in this instance is the same, and I could not resist quoting this delightful rendering.
34. The story of the notorious bandit Hakamadare and the imperturbable nobleman Yasumasa is number 27 in Book V. See Sakakura Atsuyoshi et al., *Konjaku Monogatari Shū*, II, p. 54.
35. This is story 3 in Book XXIX. For text, see Sakakura et al., *Konjaku*, IV, pp. 22–32.
36. This is story 22 in Book XXVII, translated by Marian Ury in *Tales of Times Now Past*, pp. 161–63. Original in Sakakura et al., *Konjaku*, III, pp. 72–75.
37. Hiroko Kobayashi in *The Human Comedy of Heian Japan* (p. 77) remarks, "To sum up, there are no tales in the *Konjaku* secular section in which priests are treated with reverence.... For the most part the priests drawn are wicked, covetous, or rather disreputable."
38. Ury, *Tales*, p. 182. This is from tale 38 in Book XXVIII. I am thinking of Saikaku's hero Fujiichi (in *Nippon Eitagura*) about whom he wrote, "Even if he stumbled he used the opportunity to pick up stones for fire-lighters, and tucked them in his sleeve." (See G. W. Sargent, *The Japanese Family Storehouse*, p. 36.)
39. Ury, *Tales*, pp. 170–71. This is story 41 in Book XXVII of *Tales of Times Now Past*. For text, see Sakakura et al., *Konjaku*, III, p. 132.
40. Sakakura et al., *Konjaku*, II, p. 130. This is tale 7 in Book XXVI. A translation of the tale is given in S. W. Jones, *Ages Ago*, pp. 83–87.
41. Translation by Ury in *Tales*, p. 183. For the original text, see Sakakura et al., *Konjaku*, IV, pp. 84–86.
42. Kunisaki Fumimaro in "*Konjaku Monogatari* no Dokusha" attempted to discover what level of reader was anticipated by the compiler of *Tales of Times Now Past*, restricting himself to the last six books, those devoted to secular tales of Japan. His conclusion (p. 120) was that members of the zuryō class of the fifth rank or thereabouts, the people most frequently described in these tales, were the intended readers, and contrasted this with other works of Heian literature, aimed at higher classes.
43. See above, note 23.
44. See Kawaguchi Hisao, *Kohon Setsuwa Shū*, pp. 9–10.
45. See *ibid*., pp. 94–98, and Sakakura et al., *Konjaku*, I, pp. 253–58.
46. The text calls her Jōtōmon'in, her name after taking Buddhist vows. She is also known as Akiko.
47. This is Senshi (964–1035), the tenth daughter of the Emperor Murakami, who became the high priestess *(saiin)* of the Kamo Shrine in 975. Normally, the resident priestess was replaced when the emperor who appointed her

died or retired, but Senshi remained high priestess for five reigns, fifty-six years in all, until she was relieved of her office in 1031. She was known as *daisaiin* (grand high priestess) because of her extraordinarily long tenure in the sacred office. Her "salon" was frequented by many talented poets. Although she was a Shintō priestess, she is best known for her Buddhist poetry. For an account of this poetry, see Edward Kamens, *The Buddhist Poetry of the Great Kamo Priestess*.

48. Kawaguchi, *Kohon*, p. 105. The second part of this tale describes how Murasaki Shikibu encourages a court lady named Ise no Taifu to compose a poem on cherry blossoms that attracts favorable attention and leads to a happy marriage.
49. This point is emphasized by Imai Takuji in *Monogatari Bungaku Shi no Kenkyū: Kōki Monogatari*, pp. 473–77.
50. No more than thirty or thirty-one biographies are still extant, even combining what is preserved in all three surviving texts, but Kawaguchi Hisao in his edition (contained in *Kohon Setsuwa Shū*) managed to piece together the remaining biographies from related sources. See Kawaguchi, *Kohon*, p. 325.
51. The title is borrowed from *Shen-hsien chuan* (Lives of Spirit Immortals), ascribed to Ko Hung of the fourth century A.D. For an account of Taoist "immortals" and other alchemists, magicians, and so on, see Kenneth J. DeWoskin, *Doctors, Diviners, and Magicians of Ancient China*, especially pp. 29–33.
52. These are three basic Buddhist texts, referred to here by shortened titles. The Lotus Sutra (in Sanskrit, *Saddharmapundarīka Sūtra*) the chief text of Tendai Buddhism, was first translated from Sanskrit into Chinese during the third century A.D. Saichō, the founder of Tendai Buddhism in Japan, introduced this sutra from China. The Yuga Sastra (in Sanskrit, Yogācaryabhūmi-sātra) was translated into Chinese by Hsüan-tsang in 646–47. It is more closely associated with the pure idealism of the Hossō sect than with Tendai. Great Concentration and Insight (in Chinese, *Mo-ho chih-kuan*) was a manual of religious practice written by Chih-k'ai (538–597), a Chinese T'ien-t'ai (Tendai) master.
53. *Kane no mitake no yama*, otherwise known as Kimpō-san, one of the mountains of Yoshino, in the general area of Nara. The Muta Temple was at the foot of this mountain.
54. Text in Kawaguchi, *Kohon*, pp. 363–66.
55. *Ibid*., pp. 382–83.
56. The text of this work is found in Kawaguchi, *Kohon*.
57. See above, pp. 341–44.
58. Gōdanshō Kenkyūkai, *Ruijūbon-kei Gōdanshō Chūkai*, pp. 37–38. Kaneie is otherwise remembered as the husband of the author of *The Gossamer Years*. He is referred to as Great Lay Priest *(dainyūdō)* in *The Great Mirror* and elsewhere.

59. *Ibid.*, pp. 57–59. Masafusa also had words of praise for his father, who (though not a distinguished scholar) took meticulous care of the family documents.
60. The titles of these two collections can be freely translated as "Selection of Inner and Outer [Stories]" and "Conversations of Fuke." *Fuke Go* is also known as *Fuke Godan*. Tadazane was known as Fuke-dono because he had a villa at Fuke. For a discussion of *Fuke Go*, see Masuda Katsumi, "*Fuke Go* no Kenkyū," in Jōkō Kan'ichi, *Chūsei Bungaku no Sekai*, pp. 42–67; also Masuda Katsumi, *Setsuwa Bungaku to Emaki*, pp. 210–12. Masuda was able to demonstrate the direct influence of *Fuke Go* on *Tales About Old Matters*.
61. For comparisons of *Fuke Go* and other setsuwa texts (notably *Tales About Old Matters* and *Later Tales from Uji*), see Masuda, "Fuke," pp. 43–44, 51–52. Masuda gives the text of *Fuke Go* as an appendix to his article. It is written in an unattractive mixture of Chinese and Japanese.
62. There is a complete translation, together with a study of the work by Ward Geddes, *Kara Monogatari: Tales of China*.
63. See Hinotani Akihiko et al., *Setsuwa Bungaku Hikkei*, pp. 51–56. See also Geddes, *Kara*, pp. 3–11, where he considers various theories of authorship.
64. See Geddes, *Kara*, pp. 45–68, for a discussion of the sources. He notes (p. 45) that the Chinese sources for all but two of the twenty-seven tales can be easily found; but he also remarked that because the stories in *Tales of China* are so freely rendered, it is impossible to be sure which of various versions of each tale, both Chinese and Japanese, was *the* source for the *Tales of China* text.
65. Probably the most intriguing tale is the last in the collection. It tells of two women (a young lady of good family and the daughter of her nurse) who have "left the world" and are living in separate hermitages deep in the mountains. One day a lively dog appears at the hut of the nurse's daughter, and in her boredom she fondles the dog and holds him to her breast. "Gradually she found her feelings growing more and more involved and difficult to control; all barriers were removed in their relationship." (Geddes, *Kara*, p. 140.) When she finally summons up the courage to tell her mistress about the dog, the mistress, far from disapproving, arranges to meet the dog and finds him "heart-winning." The author comments, "For a human to enter into vows of love with an animal is unexampled, but those who do not know the heart of the matter should not assume an attitude of scorn." (*Ibid.*, p. 141.)
66. Li Han, *Meng Ch'iu*, trans. by Burton Watson, p. 109. For Chinese text with a Japanese translation, see Hayakawa Mitsusaburō, *Mōgyū*, pp. 420–21, in Shin'yaku Kambun Taikei series.
67. Ssu-ma Ch'ien, the author of *Shih Chi*, was known by this title; at this point the Japanese author seems to be borrowing directly from the source of the account in *Meng Ch'iu*.

68. Translation of the quotation (with a few minor changes made so as to fit the Japanese text) by Burton Watson in *Records of the Grand Historian of China*, II, p. 154. The proverb means that even if these fruit trees say nothing, their blossoms and fruit will attract people so numerous that a path will be worn in their shade.
69. *Mōgyū Waka*, in Zoku Gunsho Ruijū series, p. 79.
70. See Ikeda Toshio, "Kara Monogatari, Mōgyū Waka no Sekai," pp. 258–59.
71. See Kobayashi Yasuharu, "Kaisetsu," in Kobayashi, *Kojidan*, I, pp. 211–12.
72. *Ibid.*, pp. 202–3.
73. The note is in the original text.
74. Fujiwara no Momokawa (732–79) was a leader of the faction opposed to Dōkyō. He became middle controller of the Right *(uchūben)* in 767. After his daughter married the Emperor Kammu, he rose to be prime minister *(dajōdaijin)* and held the senior first rank.
75. Kobayashi, *Kojidan*, I, p. 21. The source of this tale is not known, but a similar account is found in an entry dated the eighth month of 770 in *Nihon Kiryaku*, a chronology compiled at some time after 1036 that covers the period from the Age of the Gods to the reign of the Emperor Goichijō. See *ibid.*, p. 23.
76. In the original *kenchō no myōbu*, a noblewoman who lowered or raised the curtains around the emperor's seat in the palace during the coronation ceremony.
77. Kobayashi, *Kojidan*, I, p. 43.
78. Minamoto no Takakuni succeeded to this office in 1029. The emperor at the time was Goichijō. Late in life he lived in retirement in Uji and was known as Uji Dainagon. He was formerly credited with the compilation of *Tales of Times Now Past*. See above, p. 573.
79. Courtiers considered it to be shaming if their hair, not shielded by some kind of hat, was exposed to public view.
80. Kobayashi, *Kojidan*, I, p. 76.
81. A death was considered to pollute the place where it occurred, and anyone who was present when a person died was compelled to remain in seclusion. Shirakawa's insistence that his consort die in the palace bespeaks unusual love.
82. Minamoto no Toshiaki (1044–1114), the son of Minamoto no Takakuni, was at this time the master of the empress's household *(chūgū daibu)* as well as the commander of the Right Palace Guard *(uemon no kami)*. He enjoyed the confidence of the Emperor Shirakawa.
83. Kobayashi, *Kojidan*, I, pp. 167–68. A similar story is found in *A Tale of Flowering Fortunes*.
84. *Ibid.*, pp. 169–70.
85. *Ibid.*, p. 62. This is the full text of episode 40, and the commentary does

not explain, for example, why people should have eaten the food aboard the strange boat. It has been suggested, however, that this story may refer to the arrival in 1004 of a ship from the island called Uruma by the Japanese. References to this island (which was situated off the southeast coast of the Korean peninsula) in the old literature generally emphasize the unintelligibility of the speech of its inhabitants.

86. The eleven-part "Kojidan Kanshō" by Masuda Katsumi, serialized in the magazine *Kokubungaku Kaishaku to Kanshō* from May 1965, marked a new level of scholarly consideration of the work.
87. Shimura Kunihiro, *Setsuwa Bungaku no Kōsō to Denshō*, pp. 153–54.
88. The complete translation by D. E. Mills has the title *A Collection of Tales from Uji*, but in order to bring out the meaning of *shūi* ("gleanings" or, more literally, "picking up what was left out") I have used this revised title here.
89. See the translation of the preface in Mills, *A Collection*, p. 83. Fragments of the preface are found in older editions of *Later Tales from Uji*.
90. See Mills, *A Collection*, pp. 129–30. Miki Sumito in "Uji Shūi Monogatari no Uchi to Soto," pp. 552–53, suggested that the priest Jien (the author of *Gukanshō*) might have been the compiler, but admitted that the matter was far from settled.
91. Known in Japanese as the *Kegon-kyō*. It contains the teachings delivered by Shakyamuni Buddha immediately after attaining enlightenment. There are various texts in sixty, eighty, or forty volumes.
92. This tale is number 103. The burning of the Tōdai-ji by Taira forces under Shigemori's command occurred in the twelfth month of 1180. Translation by Mills, *A Collection*, p. 296.
93. There are slight variations in the opening formula, including *kore mo ima wa mukashi*, and *mukashi* as well as some tales that open without any such phrase. See Mills, *A Collection*, p. 135, for a discussion of the translation of the formula.
94. For years it has been a matter of debate whether influence went from *Tales About Old Matters* to *Later Tales from Uji* or vice-versa, but it is now generally accepted that *Tales About Old Matters* came first. See Mills, *A Collection*, pp. 90–91. The researches of Masuda Katsumi have been particularly important in this area.
95. Diaries kept by courtiers (*Kammon Gyoki* and *Sanetaka-kō Ki*) mention that *Later Tales from Uji* was read at the palace in 1438 and 1475. It is also possible that some Kamakura period references to the reading at the palace of *Tales of the Uji Grand Minister* may actually refer to *Later Tales from Uji*. See Mills, *A Collection*, p. 94.
96. Translation by Tyler in *Japanese Tales*, p. 35. This is tale 7 in Book XII of *Tales of Times Now Past*.
97. Translation by Mills in *A Collection*, p. 296. The text that Mills used gives not "thirty or forty" but "thirty-four." This seems excessively precise, in

the light of the temporal vagueness typical of the collection, so I have chosen the variant from another text and changed the translation. See Miki Sumito et al., *Uji Shūi Monogatari*, *Kohon Setsuwa Shū*, pp. 209–10.

98. Mills, *A Collection*, p. 296.
99. One manuscript bears the name "Rokuhara Jirōzaemon Nyūdō," but the identity of this lay priest has not been established. Various scholars favor Tachibana Narisue (the compiler of *Kokon Chomonjū* [Collection of Tales Heard, Present and Past]), Sugawara Tamenaga, or Yuasa Munenari. See John Brownlee, "*Jikkinshō*, a Miscellany of Ten Maxims," p. 127, and Hinotani Akihiko et al., *Setsuwa Bungaku Hikkei*, p. 178. Nagazumi Yasuaki in *Chūsei Bungaku no Kanōsei* declared (p. 203) his conviction that the editorial policies displayed in *A Miscellany of Ten Maxims* and *Tales Heard* were so dissimilar they could not possibly both have been compiled by Tachibana Narisue. The candidacy of Sugawara Tamenaga, first suggested in *Shōtetsu Monogatari* (Tales of Shōtetsu, c. 1448), was recently backed by Shimura in *Setsuwa*, pp. 167–79 and 194–98, but he does not squarely face the problem of how Tamenaga, who died in 1246, could have compiled the work in 1252. Nagazumi (pp. 205–6) was more favorably impressed than most scholars with the theory, first advanced in 1952 by Nagai Yoshinori, that Yuasa Munenari, a powerful landholder *(gōzoku)* from the province of Kii, was the compiler. But no theory has gained full acceptance.
100. Translation by Brownlee in "*Jikkinshō*," p. 133.
101. I have followed the text given in Okada Minoru, *Jikkinshō Shinshaku*, p. 134. It is somewhat different from that found in Ishibashi Shōhō, *Jikkinshō Shōkai*, p. 131.
102. Fujiwara no Yasumasa (958–1036).
103. Tango was a remote province on the Japan Sea coast. Ōeyama (Mount Ōe) and Ikuno, mentioned in the poem by Koshikibu, were in the depths of Tango.
104. The daughter of Izumi Shikibu by a previous husband, Tachibana no Michisada. *Naishi* was the name of an office, and has been rendered as palace attendant. Koshikibu died in childbirth in 1025 while still in her early twenties.
105. Fujiwara no Sadayori, the son of the distinguished poet and anthologist Fujiwara no Kintō.
106. The translation gives the less interesting of the two possible interpretations of the poem. The fourth line contains the key to the two meanings: *fumi mo mizu* means (as in the translation) "I have not yet tried to tread on," but by puns it can also mean "I have not yet seen a letter," meaning that she has not yet heard from her mother. The poem at once denies Sadayori's assertion that she is receiving help from her celebrated mother and demonstrates that she herself is capable of a clever rejoinder.

107. Okada, *Jikkinshō*, pp. 135–36. See also Ishibashi, *Jikkinshō*, pp. 131–32. For another translation see Brownlee, *"Jikkinshō,"* p. 140.
108. Almost every scholar who has commented on *Ten Maxims* has given as an example of the best in its content the story of the artist Ryōshū who calmly (or even joyfully) watches as his house is enveloped in flames because the sight will enable him to paint the halo of flames around Fudō more accurately. This tale (VI, 35) is interesting in itself and is said to have been the source of *Jigoku-hen*, the celebrated story by Akutagawa Ryūnosuke, but the tale had already appeared, in exactly the same language, in *Later Tales from Uji*.
109. Nagazumi Yasuaki and Shimada Isao, *Kokon Chomonjū*, p. 377.
110. At some point after *Tales Heard* was completed, a number of stories were appended to the collection. Most of these are from *Ten Maxims*, completed two years earlier. See Nagazumi and Shimada, *Kokon*, p. 29.
111. *Ibid*., p. 239. This is the conclusion of tale number 295.
112. Nishio Kōichi and Kishi Shōzō (eds.), *Chūsei Setsuwa Shū*, p. 121.

Bibliography

Note: All Japanese books, except as otherwise noted, were published in Tokyo.

Brownlee, John. *"Jikkinshō*, a Miscellany of Ten Maxims," *Monumenta Nipponica* 29:2, 1974.

DeWoskin, Kenneth J. *Doctors, Diviners, and Magicians of Ancient China*. New York: Columbia University Press, 1983.

Dorson, Richard M. *Studies in Japanese Folklore*. Bloomington, Ind.: Indiana University Press, 1963.

Frank, Bernard. *Histoires qui sont maintenant du passé*. Paris: Gallimard, 1968.

Geddes, Ward. "The Courtly Tradition: Chōmei and Kiyomori in *Jikkinshō*," *Monumenta Nipponica* 42:2, 1987.

———. *Kara Monogatari*: *Tales of China*. Tempe, Ariz.: Center for Asian Studies, Arizona State University, 1984.

Gōdanshō Kenkyūkai. *Ruijūbon-kei Gōdanshō Chūkai*. Musashino Shoin, 1983.

Hayakawa Mitsusaburō. *Mōgyū*, in Shin'yaku Kambun Taikei series, vol. 58. Meiji Shoin, 1973.

Hinotani Akihiko, Kobayashi Yasuharu, and Takahashi Mitsugu (eds.). *Setsuwa Bungaku Hikkei*. Tōkyō Bijutsu, 1976.

Ikeda Toshio. "*Kara Monogatari, Mōgyū Waka* no Sekai," in Ichiko Teiji and Ōshima Tatehiko, *Nihon no Setsuwa*, vol. II, in Nihon no Setsuwa series. Tōkyō Bijutsu, 1974.

Ikegami Jun'ichi. *Konjaku Monogatari Shū no Sekai*. Chikuma Shobō, 1983.

Imai Takuji. *Monogatari Bungaku Shi no Kenkyū: Kōki Monogatari*. Waseda Daigaku Shuppanbu, 1977.

Ishibashi Shōhō. *Jikkinshō Shōkai*, rev. ed. Meiji Shoin, 1927.

Jōkō Kan'ichi (ed.). *Chūsei Bungaku no Sekai*. Iwanami Shoten, 1960.

Jones, S. W. *Ages Ago*. Cambridge, Mass.: Harvard University Press, 1959.

Kamens, Edward. *The Buddhist Poetry of the Great Kamo Priestess*. Ann Arbor, Mich.: Center for Japanese Studies, The University of Michigan, 1990.

———. *The Three Jewels*. Ann Arbor, Mich.: Center for Japanese Studies, The University of Michigan, 1988.

Katayose Masayoshi. *Konjaku Monogatari Shū no Kenkyū*, 2 vols. Geirinsha, 1974.

Kawaguchi Hisao. *Kohon Setsuwa Shū*, in Koten Bungaku Zensho series. Asahi Shimbun, 1967.

Kawaguchi Hisao and Nara Shōichi. *Gōdanshō Shōchū*. Benseisha, 1984.

Kawai, Hayao. *The Japanese Psyche*. Dallas: Spring Publications, 1988.

Kelsey, W. Michael. *Konjaku Monogatari-shū*. Boston: Twayne Publishers, 1982.

Kishi Seizō. "*Uchigikishū* ni okeru ateji no imi," in *Uchigikishū*.

Kobayashi, Hiroko. *The Human Comedy of Heian Japan*. Tokyo: The Centre for East Asian Cultural Studies, 1979.

Kobayashi Yasuharu (ed.). *Kojidan*, 2 vols. Gendai Shichō Sha, 1981.

Kunisaki Fumimaro. "*Konjaku Monogatari* no Dokusha," in Mitani Eiichi, Kunisaki Fumimaro, and Kubota Jun (eds.), *Ronsan Setsuwa to Setsuwa Bungaku*. Kasama Shoin, 1979.

———. *Konjaku Monogatari Shū Sakusha Kō*. Musashino Shoin, 1985.

———. "*Uchigikishū*," in *Uchigikishū* wo yomu Kai (ed.) *Uchigikishū, Kenkyū to Hombun*.

Li Han. *Meng ch'iu*, translated by Burton Watson. Tokyo: Kodansha International, 1979.

Masuda Katsumi. *Setsuwa Bungaku to Emaki*. San'ichi Shobō, 1980.

Mayer, Fanny Hagin. *Ancient Tales in Modern Japan*. Bloomington, Ind.: Indiana University Press, 1984.

———. *The Yanagita Kunio Guide to the Japanese Folk Tale*. Bloomington, Ind.: Indiana University Press, 1986. [This is a translation of *Nihon Mukashibanashi Meii*, compiled under the supervision of Yanagita Kunio and published in Tokyo in 1948.]

Miki Sumito. "*Uji Shūi Monogatari* no Uchi to Soto," in Miki, *Uji Shūi Monogatari*.

Miki Sumito, Asami Kazuhiko, Nakamura Yoshio, and Kouchi Kazuaki. *Uji Shūi Monogatari, Kohon Setsuwa Shū*, in Shin Nihon Koten Bungaku Taikei series. Iwanami Shoten, 1990.

Mills, D. E. *A Collection of Tales from Uji*. Cambridge: Cambridge University Press, 1970.

Miyata Shō. "*Konjaku Monogatari Shū* kan-roku Buppō to Shintan Dan," in *Uchigikishū* wo yomu Kai (ed.), *Uchigikishū Kenkyū to Hombun*.

Mōgyū Waka, vol. 405 in Zoku Gunsho Ruijū series. Zoku Gunsho Ruijū Kanseikai, 1910.

Mori Masato. *Konjaku Monogatari Shō no Seisei*. Osaka: Izumi Shoin, 1986.

Nagano Jōichi. *Setsuwa Bungaku no Sekai*. Meiji Shoin, 1980.

Nagazumi Yasuaki. *Chūsei Bungaku no Kanōsei*. Iwanami Shoten, 1977.

Nagazumi Yasuaki and Shimada Isao. *Kokon Chomonjū*, in Nihon Koten Bungaku Taikei series. Iwanami Shoten, 1966.

Nakajima Etsuji. *Uji Shūi Monogatari, Uchigiki Shū Zenchūshaku*. Yūseidō, 1970.

Nihon Koten Bungaku Daijiten, 6 vols. Iwanami Shoten, 1983–85.

Nishio Kōichi and Kishi Shōzō (eds.). *Chūsei Setsuwa Shū*, in Kanshō Nihon Koten Bungaku series. Kadokawa Shoten, 1977.

Okada Minoru. *Jikkinshō Shinshaku*. Daidōkan Shoten, 1927.

Ōsone Shōsuke et al. *Kenkyū Shiryō Nihon Koten Bungaku*, III. Meiji Shoin, 1984.

Sakakura Atsuyoshi, Honda Giken, and Kawabata Yoshiaki. *Konjaku Monogatari Shū*, 4 vols., in Shinchō Nihon Koten Shūsei series. Shinchōsha, 1979.

Sargent, G. W. (trans.). *The Japanese Family Storehouse*. Cambridge: Cambridge University Press, 1959.

Shigematsu Akihisa. *Urashimako Den*. Gendai Shichō Sha, 1981.

Shimura Kunihiro. *Kojidan*. Kyōikusha, 1980.

———. *Setsuwa Bungaku no Kōsō to Denshō*. Meiji Shoin, 1982.

Sugimoto Keizaburō. "*Uchigikishū* ni okeru setsuwa to setsuwa bungaku," in *Uchigikishū* wo yomu kai (ed.), *Uchigikishū*.

Tyler, Royall. *Japanese Tales*. New York: Pantheon Books, 1987.

Uchigikishū wo yomu kai (ed.). *Uchigikishū*. Kasama Shoin, 1971.

Ury, Marian. *Tales of Times Now Past*. Berkeley: University of California Press, 1979.

Usuda Jingorō and Nishio Kōichi. *Nihon no Setsuwa*, vol. I. Tōkyō Bijutsu, 1974.

Watson, Burton. *Records of the Grand Historian of China*, 2 vols. New York: Columbia University Press, 1961.

Yanagita Kunio. *The Legends of Tōno*, translated by Ronald H. Morse. Tokyo: Japan Foundation, 1975.

Yoneda Chizuko. "*Uchigikishū* ni okeru hensha no shisei," in *Uchigikishū* wo yomu Kai (ed.), *Uchigikishū*.

The Middle Ages

INTRODUCTION

The term *chūsei*, or middle ages, is often used of the period in Japanese history from 1185, the year when the Minamoto destroyed the Taira, to 1600, the year of the Tokugawa victory at the Battle of Sekigahara. These dates are not accepted by all scholars (whether of literature or of history) but almost everyone agrees that Japan had a "middle age," a period whose characteristics differed from those of both earlier and later times. The period is further divided along political lines into the Kamakura, Muromachi, and Azuchi-Momoyama periods, each with distinct features.

It goes without saying that Heian civilization did not break down as soon as the shogun's government was established in Kamakura. Members of the emperor's court led much the same lives as before, as we know from surviving diaries. The court poets continued to produce great quantities of waka evoking the changes of the seasons and their bittersweet memories of love. Monogatari, in the style and language of *The Tale of Genji*, were written for the pleasure of ladies of the aristocracy. Men (not only at the court but in monasteries) pursued the study of classical Chinese with unabated devotion, and left behind many examples of Chinese poetry and prose. If one confined one's attention to the literature created in Kyoto, one would probably get the impression that the literature of the Kamakura period was essentially the same in nature as that of the Heian period, though the literary quality of the prose had noticeably deteriorated.

The interest of medieval Japanese literature lies elsewhere—in the newly created genres, notably the war tales, renga, and the Nō dramas. All three of these genres originated as entertainments performed by and for people who lived far from the court. The war tales, recited by professional entertainers, familiarized people even in remote villages with the deeds of heroes of the twelfth-century warfare; and in time largely extemporaneous recitations solidified into texts that were read as literature. Renga began as a kind of game in which one man composed three of the five lines of a waka and challenged others to complete the poem. In its early stages of development (and even much later) it was popular not only with amateur poets but with gamblers who bet on the winning "solutions" to the problems of the first three lines; but by the fifteenth century this game was elevated into an art based on the philosophical ideal of a communal creation of a work of poetic beauty, and was provided with innumerable rules. Finally, the Nō dramas, the earliest Japanese theater of literary importance, probably began as playlets that enlightened worshipers (many of them illiterate) on the miracles of the deities of the temples and shrines where the plays were performed. The patronage of the Ashikaga shoguns made possible the development of Nō as a highly artistic and literary theater whose texts could be fully comprehended only by connoisseurs; but simpler forms of Nō continued to be performed on crudely fashioned stages throughout the country for the pleasure of people of the vicinity.

Medieval literature reflected the increased importance of places outside the capital. Most of the action of a typical Heian monogatari generally took place in the capital, and descriptions of other places were rare; but a medieval tale was not confined by such restrictions. The battles between the Taira and the Minamoto were fought in various parts of Japan, and the subsequent flight to the north of the hero Minamoto Yoshitsune provided storytellers with still other opportunities to extend the geographical scope of their narrations. No doubt the audiences for recitations wanted most of all to hear about great events that had occurred close to where they lived.

The decision of Minamoto Yoritomo to establish his government—the shogunate—at Kamakura in the east of Japan, a section of the country that inhabitants of the capital had always considered to be uncivilized, led to the building of an imposing second capital whose temples and halls of state rivaled those in Kyoto. The existence of two capitals obliged some people to travel from one to the other on official business, or as litigants at the shogunate courts, or merely as sightseers. The sights of the journey, often recorded in diaries, also became a feature of the new literature.

The diffusion of the culture of the old capital to the hinterland was further accelerated by the warfare of the fourteenth and fifteenth centuries. Kyoto was burned again and again, and the senseless Ōnin War of the 1460s destroyed almost every building. During the Heian period, governors sent from the capital had tried to spend as little time as possible in their provinces; and even those who lived in remote areas did not associate with the local people. The father of the author of *The Sarashina Diary* warned her, "The provinces are terrible places," meaning that the inhabitants were barbarous, and any girl brought up there could never hope to acquire the refined culture of the capital. But once the country was torn by warfare, the castles of provincial warlords became havens to courtiers, learned priests, and other refugees from the capital. In return for the hospitality they gladly instructed their hosts in poetry, painting, and similar pursuits.

It is noteworthy that the warlords, however ferocious they might have been on the battlefield, wanted to acquire the culture of the aristocracy. That is why they welcomed (among others) renga poets and treated them generously for long periods while they attempted to learn the rules governing the art. We may assume that the poets were slow to criticize and quick to praise the literary efforts of their hosts; no doubt many a warrior was delighted to be informed that he, like M. Jourdain, was speaking prose. Kyōgen farces reveal the contempt felt for provincial lords who were persuaded that they possessed the elegance of the courtier.

The seemingly endless warfare gave new meaning to the uncertainty of life, a frequent theme in the writings of the Heian courtiers, who saw death in the fall of blossoms or in a moment of parting. The court lady who brooded over a lover's neglect also had many occasions to consider the fragility of happiness; but the loss of a lover was even more terrible when it was caused by his death in battle. In some of the diaries women tell of their emotions on seeing their lover's head on a pike being paraded through the streets.

The literature also describes natural disasters—earthquakes, typhoons, failures of crops. The capital, where roof had vied with proud roof in splendor, seemingly impervious to calamity, proved to be unexpectedly vulnerable, and aristocrats and commoners alike turned increasingly to religion for support and comfort. New sects of Buddhism arose to meet the needs of people, especially those who could not understand the sacred texts or the symbolism of the older religious art. The most popular of the new sects taught that one's only hope for salvation was to throw oneself on the mercy of Amida Buddha, who had vowed to save everyone who asked his intercession. A believer needed only call Amida's name once in his lifetime, in this way admitting that he was incapable of saving himself. The religious fervor of the middle ages, unlike the learned, prevailingly aristocratic religious practices of earlier periods, affected every segment of the population in every region of the country.

Religious belief in the middle ages tended to be a centrifugal force, sending men from the capital to lonely hermitages in the mountains or to holy sites in distant places. A whole body of medieval literature describes their pilgrimages. On these journeys men from the capital heard the legends associated with the places they passed, and some of them would be developed into works of literature—for example, into Nō plays. The warfare destroyed much of what had survived from the past, masterpieces of architecture as well as unique manuscripts. We know the titles of many works of literature that perished forever in the flames of medieval wars. The only compensation for this loss was the creation of a new culture shared by the entire Japanese people.

The middle ages came to an end with the unification of the country by three celebrated generals—Oda Nobunaga, Toyotomi Hideyoshi, and Tokugawa Ieyasu—during the sixteenth century. These men had to contend not only with the various warlords who fought to maintain possession of their lands, but with the arrival of the first Europeans in the middle of the century. European inventions (notably, the gun) were quickly accepted, and many Japanese were converted to Christianity. The middle ages concluded with a rare period of cosmopolitanism, when Japanese eagerly adopted (or at least tolerated) foreign ways. Not long afterward, Japan was closed to outsiders, and the cosmopolitanism ended in a massacre of surviving Christians; but the wars were over and the country was unified. The culture, including literature, had left the hands of the aristocracy forever.

16. TALES OF WARFARE

The Heian period was brought to a close by the warfare of 1180–1185. The protagonists of this warfare were two clans, the Taira and the Minamoto, also known respectively as the Heike and the Genji.[1] Both clans claimed descent from the imperial family, but over the course of time these connections had become of less significance than their estates in various parts of the country and their military forces. The Taira had their main base in the area of the Inland Sea, and their naval power had accordingly developed. The strength of the Minamoto—or at any rate, the branch of the Minamoto clan that engaged in the fighting of the twelfth century—was centered in the east, especially in Izu and Sagami provinces. The Fujiwara, the other major clan, concerned themselves with political activities in the capital. By the middle of the twelfth century the Fujiwara had lost much of their authority, and even if they possessed such imposing titles as regent (*sesshō*), they were often ineffectual or even grossly incompetent men.[2]

The tales that narrated the fighting of the twelfth century, first committed to paper in the following century, were not the earliest compositions devoted to accounts of warfare. Various uprisings of the early Heian period had previously been described in battle records (*senki*), beginning with *Shōmonki* (The Story of Masakado), the first work of the genre. These precursors of the war tales of the thirteenth century lack their literary interest, and differ also from the later tales in having been composed in Chinese rather than Japanese; but they stand out from other Heian historical works in that they treat events that occurred in the provinces, far from the traditional center of Japanese literature, the court. In this sense, too, they anticipated the great war tales.

BATTLE TALES

The Story of Masakado

Shōmonki (The Story of Masakado) relates how Taira no Masakado (903?–940), a warrior from the eastern provinces, after having defeated many local warlords received in 939 an oracular message from the god Hachiman conferring on him the title of emperor of Japan. He accepted this honor without hesitation, taking for himself the title of *shinkō* (new emperor). The emperor and the nobles in Kyoto, terrified by this development, frantically prayed to the gods and buddhas for deliverance. Their prayers and offerings were answered: Masakado's luck turned, and he was defeated by his archenemy, Taira no Sadamori. "Never in this world had a general actually joined in battle and died at the front like Masakado,"[3] we are told, seemingly without cynicism. His severed head was sent to Kyoto. A message was later received from Masakado's spirit, repenting of his crimes on earth and relating his suffering in the world of the dead. The final words from Masakado's spirit were in the form of a Buddhist injunction: "No matter how good something may taste, you must refrain from eating the flesh of living things, and although you may begrudge it, give alms to the priesthood."[4]

In contrast to Chinese history or to the histories of the various countries of Europe, no hero of Japanese history, with the single exception of Masakado, ever sought to establish himself on the throne. Taira no Kiyomori, Minamoto no Yoritomo, Toyotomi Hideyoshi, or Tokugawa Ieyasu, to name the most celebrated military men, surely could have killed the reigning emperor or forced him to abdicate and seized the imperial regalia, but this did not happen; even the most powerful tyrant appeared afraid to violate the sanctity of the throne and paid at least lip service to the emperor, though usually he was stripped of political power.

Masakado based his claim to the throne not only on his military triumphs but on his descent from the Emperor Kammu. Probably he never sought to rule more than the eastern half of the country; even after he became the "new emperor" he continued to write deferentially to Fujiwara no Tadahira, a noble he had formerly served, and he never commanded the emperor in Kyoto to vacate his throne. The scale of Masakado's battles was very small by modern standards, and if he had not taken the title of "new emperor" he might well have been forgotten along with other warriors of his time. This act made him a unique figure in Japanese history, and the reader is likely to turn to *The Story of Masakado* with high expectations of absorbing literary interest. Such expectations are bound to be disappointed.

The Story of Masakado was written mainly in a documentary kambun that is of interest chiefly because of the occasional intrusions of Japanese honorifics and syntactical forms.[5] There are moments of excitement, it is true, but there are no memorable personalities, and the innumerable references to Chinese history and the moralization make dull reading though, ironically, such passages were no doubt intended to impart literary interest.[6]

We cannot be sure exactly when *The Story of Masakado* was composed, but it was probably soon after the death of Masakado in 940. The unknown author was on the whole sympathetic to Masakado, at least up until the time when he assumed the title of "new emperor." The word "enemy," used of Masakado's foes in the earlier part of the text, is used of Masakado himself toward the close,[7] a shift in attitude that has made some critics suggest that the latter part was by a different author. More likely, however, it represented a changed response of the same author to Masakado's transformation from a brave soldier to a usurper. For all its inadequacy, however, *The Story of Masakado* was the first literary work to be based on recent historical events, and occasionally even anticipates the major war tales of later years.

By contrast, *Sumitomo Tsuitō Ki* (Record of the Punitive Expedition against Sumitomo), describing the suppression of the rebellion led by Fujiwara no Sumitomo (d. 941), is no more than a bare chronicle without literary interest. *Mutsu Waki* (Tales and Records of Mutsu),[8] more in the tradition of *The Story of Masakado* and by an anonymous author, describes in a documentary kambun the successful campaign of Minamoto no Yoriyoshi (988–1075) against rebels in the north of Japan during the Earlier Nine Years' War (1051–1062). The only literary interest of the work is found in the various anecdotes (originally transmitted orally) about the events of the campaign, as related by the unknown author.[9] Other chronicles written in classical Chinese (some with admixtures of Japanese syntax) are even more like official records, and will not be considered here.

These battle records are not in themselves of much literary interest, but they were the predecessors of the war tales, works of exceptional literary importance that described the next period of major warfare, the latter part of the twelfth century.

WAR TALES

Tale of the Disturbance in Hōgen

The earliest of the gunki monogatari is *Hōgen Monogatari* (Tale of the Disturbance in Hōgen),[10] an account of the rebellion staged in 1156, the first year of the Hōgen era. It began as a conflict between the reigning emperor, Goshirakawa, and his half-brother Sutoku, the retired emperor, over possession of the throne. Sutoku had been forced by his father, the Emperor Toba, to abdicate in 1142 so that Toba's son by another consort might ascend the throne. When this son (the Emperor Konoe) died in 1155 Sutoku thought his chance had come to obtain the throne for his own son, if not for himself, only to be frustrated in his hopes by the accession of his brother, Goshirakawa. Furious at this new development, Sutoku joined with the minister of the Left, Fujiwara no Yorinaga, and various members of the Minamoto family, in a conspiracy to capture the throne by force.

The bitterness of the dispute between the two sons of Toba was paralleled by the divisions within the various noble families. The Fujiwara family had long dominated the government, but they were by no means united: Fujiwara no Tadamichi supported Goshirakawa, but his brother Yorinaga was the leader of Sutoku's faction. Similarly, Minamoto no Tameyoshi backed Sutoku, but his son Yoshitomo supported Goshirakawa; Taira no Kiyomori, who would emerge as the most powerful man in Japan, served Goshirakawa, but his uncle Tadamasa was on the side of Sutoku. During the brief conflict that ensued (it was over in a single day), Sutoku's forces were defeated and many of his adherents killed, including the hero Tametomo. Sutoku himself was exiled to the island of Shikoku, where he died. At the very end of the work[11] there is a description of the visit to Sutoku's grave by the traveler-poet Saigyō.[12]

The historical significance of the Hōgen disturbance was not confined to the dispute over the succession. The Buddhist priest and poet Jien (1155–1225), whose *Gukanshō*[13] is considered to be the first work of history to deal critically and interpretatively with the Japanese past, wrote, "After the death of the Cloistered Emperor Toba on the second day of the seventh month of the first year of Hōgen [1156] a rebellion broke out in the land of Japan, and it was from this time that the age of the military began."[14] The losers in the one-day war of 1156 were not so much Sutoku's followers as the whole of the nobility; for over seven hundred years afterward the military and not the emperor or the

Fujiwara regents would rule Japan, though the imperial court and even the old aristocracy continued to maintain a precarious existence.

With *Tale of the Disturbance in Hōgen* a new genre of literature came into being. The war tales, though they treated materials much resembling those of the battle records and the various "mirrors,"[15] differed from them in that they were not written at a particular time by a particular individual. Undoubtedly someone first set down the facts recorded in the war stories, perhaps in the form of the diaries traditionally kept in kambun by members of the nobility, but the bare facts found in such diaries grew into works of literary interest as the events of the wars were embellished by professional storytellers with anecdotes and interpretative comments, and recited to musical accompaniment before audiences all over the country. The narrators of these tales came to be known as *biwa hōshi*, the biwa being an instrument resembling the mandolin, and *hōshi* meaning a priest, or someone who resembled a priest in his costume and shaved head. The war stories continued to grow, perhaps until printing of the texts became common in the seventeenth century, in response to the demand of successive audiences for further details about favorite characters or as the result of the narrator's desire to point out moral truths, whether Buddhist or Confucian.

It is difficult to know at which point in the history of Japanese literature these works should be situated. Probably *Tale of the Disturbance in Hōgen* existed in some form by the beginning of the thirteenth century or even before, but the earliest surviving manuscript dates from 1318.[16] Differences among these and other texts are not restricted to minor variants of language, but extend to whole scenes included or omitted by the different text "families." Under these circumstances, it does not make much sense to search for a single author, and the dating of the work is approximate.

Tale of the Disturbance in Hōgen not only marks the emergence of a new political and social system, based on the central importance of the military, but the emergence of a new literary style of written Japanese.[17] The Heian historical tales were composed in much the same language as the fiction of that era, in part perhaps because they were supposed to be narrations by extremely old men or women for whom it was natural to use the language of the past. The most striking difference in language between the Heian historical tales and the war tales was the great increase in the number of words borrowed from Chinese. Although the spoken Japanese language had been steadily admitting more and more such words, the written language was conservative, generally avoiding words of foreign origin except for terms for which no Japanese equivalents existed, such as the special vocabulary of Buddhism or the names of political offices. The sentences in the various "mirrors" often conclude with a form of the polite verb *tamau*, used by the narrator in referring to the actions of a person of superior social class, but the sentences in the war tales are more likely to conclude (as in the modern Japanese written language) with a neutral verb ending. The copula verb *sōrō*,[18] associated with the military class, also makes its first appearances in the war tales.

The feature of the war tales that most clearly distinguishes them from earlier historical tales is their literary importance. In reading these tales we are likely to be struck especially by the memorable characters. Unlike the account of Michinaga in *The Great Mirror*, for example, which resembles a panegyric more than a portrait, the characters in *Tale of the Disturbance in Hōgen* capture the imagination of the reader, especially the larger-than-life Minamoto no Tametomo (1139–1177) and the wrathful Emperor Sutoku.

Tametomo is perhaps as close as the Japanese ever came to creating a hero in the manner of European epic poetry. He is a man of great stature and overpowering strength who can bend a bow that no other man can bend, and whose arrows easily pass through the stoutest armor. Toward the end of the book he is captured by enemies when stark naked in the bath. The sinews of his right arm are severed to keep him from ever drawing a bow again, and he is exiled to the island of Ōshima. Before long, however, his arm mends, and he proceeds to conquer not only Ōshima but the other islands of the Izu chain. Probably this is where the account of Tametomo originally ended, but the audiences who listened to recitations of the work no doubt clamored for more. A chapter was accordingly added describing Tametomo's conquest of the Island of Devils,[19] inhabited by descendants of the eponymous demons. Although they are more than ten feet tall and their bodies are covered with hair, they are a sorry lot, totally lacking in diabolic magic, and soon surrender abjectly to the great Tametomo.

When Goshirakawa hears of Tametomo's success, he decides to send an army to subdue him. Soon a flotilla of warships is seen off Ōshima, and Tametomo decides the time has come for him to die. He describes his achievements in battle, insisting that he never harmed anyone except enemy soldiers. All the same, he says, killing people (the inevitable task of the warrior) is a sin, and he surely will be punished in the future life. Then, as a last token of his mighty prowess, he fires an arrow at a warship. It passes first through one hull and then the other, and the ship, taking water, keels over and sinks. Tametomo, satisfied, goes into his house and, leaning against a pillar, commits seppuku. His body remains erect (because of the pillar), and the enemy soldiers at first do not realize he is dead. At length one exceptionally brave man approaches the fearsome Tametomo and, recognizing at last that he is dead, cuts off his head.[20]

The death of Tametomo makes an appropriate end for a martial tale. Other versions, however, have a quite different but equally appropriate ending, the death of the Emperor Sutoku at his place of exile. Sutoku, it will be recalled, precipitated the Hōgen disturbance because of his anger over the succession to the throne. After his forces were defeated, he was taken prisoner and sent into exile; his journey is described in a *michiyuki* (travel account) of considerable pathos, each place passed on the way recalling events or poetry of the past.[21]

Sutoku's destination was a small island off the Sanuki coast, and his dwelling there, unspeakably gloomy, was like a prison cell. He passed his time copying in his own blood the texts of five sutras, which he sent to the abbot of the Ninna-ji, the great Shingon temple in Kyoto where he himself had once taken refuge, with the request that if permission was granted they should be placed before the grave of his father, the Emperor Toba.[22] The abbot wept at these words of a once proud man. He tried to induce the kampaku, Fujiwara no Michinori, better known by his Buddhist name, Shinzei (1106–1160), to grant Sutoku's request, but the latter replied, "He is at present detained at a place of exile. It would bode ill for us if His Majesty allowed the writings but not the man to return to the capital. If this request is granted, there is no telling what he may ask for next."[23] The Emperor Goshirakawa, persuaded by Shinzei's argument, refused permission.

When Sutoku learned this, he exclaimed,

> What a heartless thing to say! . . . There have been many instances, past and present, of brothers who fought each other or of uncles who waged wars against nephews; but with the passage of time, their crimes were forgiven and their punishment lightened. This is the mercy befitting the ruler, his boundless compassion. Needless to say, moreover, anyone who has become a Buddhist priest and wished to study the sutras so as to achieve enlightenment has always been given permission; but now I am begrudged even a place to put the Mahayana sutras I have copied out for the sake of future generations. He is my enemy for all time! If that is how things are to be, living longer will do me no good.[24]

Sutoku, we are told, from this time onward neither combed his hair nor trimmed his nails; even while still alive he looked like a goblin. Enraged that the efforts he had devoted during the past three years to copying the sutras had been in vain, he decided to offer them not to the Buddha but to the demons of the Three Evil Realms,[25] and with the power this gave him he would turn into "the great evil demon of the land of Japan, make the emperor a subject, and make a subject the emperor."[26] He bit off the tip of his tongue, and inscribed in his blood at the end of the sutras a prayer to the gods of the supernal and infernal worlds asking them to join their strength to his vow of becoming a demon. He then threw the sutras into the sea.

Sutoku did not die for another nine years. At the time of his death in 1164 he was only forty-five years old, but he is usually pictured in later works as a fearsome old man. He was cremated at Shiramine in the province of Sanuki. The smoke rising from his funeral pyre drifted in the direction of the capital, a sign of his unabating attachment to the throne. In the winter of 1168 the great poet Saigyō visited Shiramine and, making his way to the desolate, overgrown grave, offered a poem to the late emperor. As he soliloquized on the tragic fate of an emperor who had once ruled wisely only to suffer disaster as the result of an ill-judged rebellion, he heard a voice from the grave recite a poem bewailing the empty resolution of his exile. Saigyō, uncertain whether he really heard this voice or if it might be a dream, replied with a poem urging Sutoku to abandon his futile indignation.[27]

In 1177 the court, fearing Sutoku's vengeful spirit, sought to mollify him by granting him a posthumous name, but his wrath was not appeased: the misfortunes that soon afterward afflicted Kiyomori and the others of the Taira clan were attributed to the curse Sutoku had placed on those who had fought him during the Hōgen disturbance.

Tale of the Disturbance in Hōgen can be interpreted as an account of how Sutoku was punished for the crime of plotting against the reigning monarch. One feels sympathy for him when one reads how he was forced to abdicate, but Sutoku was a headstrong and even violent man. He seems fated to be tortured in the realm of angry spirits just as surely as Tametomo, his loyal supporter to the end, will reach paradise. Tametomo fought his heroic battles for an unworthy cause, but perhaps its unworthiness served to make his loyalty all the more absolute. The presence in the narration of these two strongly contrasted men gives dramatic intensity to the *Tale of the Disturbance in Hōgen.*

The events directly relating to Sutoku and Tametomo are not, however, the only ones of literary interest. There is a harrowing account of how Tametomo's elder brother Yoshitomo who, though loyal to Goshirakawa, was sadistically commanded by the latter to cut off the head of his own father, Tameyoshi. He begged the emperor to spare him from commiting the ultimate act of unfilial behavior, but Goshirakawa was adamant. Yoshitomo asked his trusted retainer Kamada Masakiyo which was worse, to kill one's father or to disobey the command of the emperor. Masakiyo advised him to kill Tameyoshi, citing instances in the Buddhist texts of men who for causes of overriding importance had no choice but to kill their fathers. Tameyoshi was doomed in any case as an enemy of the crown and, rather than have some stranger cut off his head, it would be best for his son to do it.

Yoshitomo decides to follow Masakiyo's advice. He first reassures Tameyoshi by telling of the many times he has refused to comply with the command to cut off his father's head. His meritorious achievements during the fighting had earned him special consideration, and he had built for his father a hermitage in the eastern hills where he could live and devote himself to prayer.

Tameyoshi is moved to tears of joy. He says, "Ah, they say no treasure is as great as one's children. Who but my own son would help me at the risk of his own life? I shall not forget this for the rest of my lives in this world and those to come," and he joins his hands in prayer before his son. Yoshitomo, by this time feeling wretched, brushes away the tears and manages to look composed. He calls to Masakiyo and asks for a vehicle to take his father to the eastern hills, but the cart with Tameyoshi aboard heads westward instead.

Masakiyo is waiting, sword in hand, at Suzaku-dōri where Tameyoshi is to transfer from the cart to a palanquin. This is the place where he is to die. Hadano Yoshimichi, another of Yoshitomo's retainers, who has accompanied Tameyoshi this far, remonstrates with Masakiyo, pointing out how much he owes Tameyoshi, who raised him as an adopted child. If his life cannot be spared, he should at least be told what is in store for him and given the time to say his prayers. Masakiyo agrees, but asks Yoshimichi to inform Tameyoshi. Yoshimichi says to Tameyoshi, "Are you still not aware, sir, what is happening? His Excellency [Yoshitomo] received an imperial command, and Masakiyo is to kill you here, between the cart and the palanquin."

Tameyoshi, needless to say, is astonished. He is chagrined that Yoshitomo deceived him, and wishes now that he had heeded Tametomo's advice to flee to the north. "If I and my six sons had fired every last one of our arrows, and had then been killed in the fighting, I would have left a name for future ages. Am I to die like a dog instead?" He declares that he would have given up his life to save Yoshitomo's, but remembers the saying "The host of buddhas think of humankind, but humankind does not think of the buddhas; parents always worry about their children, but children never think of their parents." He urges the men to be quick in their execution. It is still dark, but when day breaks people, high and low alike, will gather around to gape while he is killed. He invokes the name of Amida Buddha again and again in a loud voice as he waits for the executioner's sword; but Masakiyo, appalled to think of killing the master of a family that his ancestors have served generation after generation, asks Yoshimichi to kill Tameyoshi instead. Yoshimichi refuses. A retainer of Masakiyo unsheathes his sword and strikes, but because it is too dark to see properly, he misses the neck, and the blade hits bone instead. Tameyoshi turns and asks, "Why don't you do it, Masakiyo?" He calls the name of Amida Buddha in an even louder voice than before. At the next stroke of the sword his severed head drops to the ground.[28]

The last of the three books opens as Yoshitomo receives another imperial command, this one to kill all of his younger brothers. Once again, he has no choice but to obey. He directs Hadano Yoshimichi to go to the house in the capital where his four youngest brothers live. Yoshimichi is to take them on some pretext to Funaoka Mountain, where he will cut off their heads. He is reluctant to carry out these orders, but cannot disobey his master. The incident is given pathos by the necessity imposed on him of killing small, defenseless children. Tameyoshi with virtually his last words had commended the four boys to Yoshitomo, predicting that each would some day be worth a hundred men.

Yoshimichi tells the four boys that he has come to escort them to their father. The three younger boys are delighted and can hardly wait to get into the palanquin that is to take them to their death, but Otowaka, the oldest boy (he is thirteen), is puzzled because Tameyoshi had not mentioned going to Funaoka. He wants to wait for his mother, but his brothers beg him to hurry.[29]

When their palanquin is set down at a deserted place in the mountains, Yoshimichi takes the smallest boys on his knees and tells them in tears, stroking their hair, that they must die. He tells them that their father was killed at dawn on the previous day. The children cling to him, but Otowaka stands apart. Finally he pulls his brothers away from Yoshimichi, and tells them not to weep. He says that it makes no difference whether they die as children or as adults. They have no reason to go on living, now that their father and brothers have been killed.

Rather than become beggars and have people point at them, they should pray that their father will welcome them to paradise. Otowaka cuts off his brothers' forelocks and his own, as last mementoes for their mother. The three younger boys and then Otowaka are beheaded. When Yoshimichi reports to the palace what has happened, he is coldly informed that it will not be necessary to carry out a head inspection in the usual manner.

These incidents (and there are others almost equally affecting in *Tale of the Disturbance in Hōgen*) have no parallels in the earlier historical tales. They are superbly told and made up of the genuine stuff of tragedy. Although this work was not extensively used as a source for the dramas of later times, the events described are so memorable as to cast shadows over the medieval Japanese world. The "head inspection" (*kubi jikken*), briefly mentioned above, would become a familiar feature of Kabuki plays, and the deaths of children to save the lives of adults also figure prominently in these plays. Above all, the samurai's reluctance to kill, as his profession and his loyalty to his lord command, has many echoes in the literature of later times. Although the court in Kyoto still maintained much of its former elegance and decorum, one senses while reading this work that a world dominated by the military was the shape of things to come. Up until this time no one had been put to death for a crime since 810, the severest penalty being distant banishment, but from now on death by the executioner's sword would be common, even when the offender had taken the tonsure. A harsh world had come into being in which warfare would destroy the treasures of the past and the wishes of soldiers, rather than of courtiers, would prevail.

Tale of the Disturbance in Heiji

In 1160, three years[30] after the abortive coup of the Hōgen era, a similar clash, known by the reign-name Heiji, again divided the court and the military families. The events of the fighting are recorded in *Heiji Monogatari* (Tale of the Disturbance in Heiji), a work that closely resembles its predecessor in length and in its general structure—three books that present respectively the origins, fighting, and resolution of the disturbance. Quite apart from the similarities in several incidents, the tales belong to the same stylistic tradition, and may even have been originally composed by the same person. Both are memorable creations of literature, quite apart from their value as historical sources.

The many surviving texts of *Tale of the Disturbance in Heiji* provide evidence that it, like its predecessor, grew over the centuries as successive storytellers added to the basic historical facts. Five magnificent horizontal scroll paintings (*emakimono*) dating from the late thirteenth century illustrate some of the memorable scenes, further evidence of its popularity. The inscriptions on the paintings constitute the oldest texts of the work.

Both works open with a quarrel among members of the court that soon spreads to the military. Unlike the warfare described in *Tale of the Disturbance in Hōgen*, however, during the Heiji disturbance no clashes occurred between members of the same military family. For three years after the suppression of the Hōgen disturbance the hostility between the Taira and the Minamoto had been growing, in part because Taira no Kiyomori was so much more generously rewarded than Minamoto no Yoshitomo for his role in the war, though (as we have seen) Yoshitomo had been required to make inhuman sacrifices. The disturbance of the Heiji era, when the two great military families clashed, laid the groundwork for the war between the Taira and the Minamoto.

Tale of the Disturbance in Heiji, after an introductory section in a Confucian vein citing various instances from Chinese history to prove that a worthy ruler must possess both literary and military virtues, launches into descriptions of the two men who initiated the disturbance. Unlike the disputants of the Hōgen disturbance, an emperor and a former emperor, the protagonists this time were members of the Fujiwara family, though of relatively humble rank. Fujiwara no Nobuyori (1133–1160) was the son of an unimportant provincial governor and, the text informs us, "he had neither literary nor martial talent, neither intellectual capability nor artistic skill."[31] He had nevertheless managed, by favor of Goshirakawa, to rise with phenomenal rapidity through the hierarchy until at the age of twenty-seven he was a middle counselor and could anticipate appointment as a major counselor, an unprecedented honor for someone of his background. He would ally himself with the Minamoto in his struggle to achieve complete power at the court.

Nobuyori's great enemy was Fujiwara no Michinori (Shinzei). *Tale of the Disturbance in Heiji* describes Shinzei with unconditional admiration: although his family background was modest in terms of rank or office, it boasted a long tradition of Confucian scholarship, and Shinzei himself was conversant with all branches of learning. His position at court was only that of a minor counselor, but he benefited from his wife's relationship to Goshirakawa as his former wet nurse, and he came to be entrusted with affairs of state great and small. He had revived palace ceremonies that had fallen into desuetude, repaired or reconstructed buildings that had been permitted to decay, and sought to return the court to the simple ways of the past. The administration of justice under Shinzei was so fair that no one could complain; and the composition of poetry and performance of music, the two hallmarks of culture at the court, yielded in no way to the glories of the past. People marveled that it had been possible for Shinzei in a remarkably short period of time to revive the dignity and grandeur of the court. He would side with the Taira.

The disturbance began when Nobuyori, seeking to take advantage of the absence from the capital of Taira no Kiyomori, then on a pilgrimage to Kumano, persuaded the embittered Yoshitomo to join forces in a coup against Shinzei and the Taira family. On the night of the ninth day of the twelfth month of 1159 Nobuyori, Yoshitomo, and several hundred mounted warriors attacked the Sanjō Palace, the residence of the Retired Emperor Goshirakawa, alleging that a plot against Nobuyori's life had been discovered. Goshirakawa was taken as a hostage and moved to the Imperial Palace. The small band of Taira soldiers who were guarding the place were slaughtered, and the severed heads of their commanders were taken to the palace and displayed above one of the gates. The Sanjō Palace was set afire and the fleeing inhabitants were relentlessly pursued. Later that night Shinzei's residence was also burned.

Yoshitomo's son, Akugenta Yoshihira, in Kamakura at the time, learned of the disturbance and headed immediately for the capital. He arrived just as Nobuyori, flushed with his victory, was making up a list of promotions. Nobuyori was delighted to see Yoshihira, whose martial prowess was already celebrated, and, asking his help in battles to come, offered Yoshihira a promotion in rank and his choice of province. The flattered Yoshihira replied,

> Now I understand why, at the time of the Hōgen disturbance, my uncle Hachirō Tametomo refused, saying the promotion was too precipitous, when the Uji Minister[32] named him a chamberlain on the spot. What I need now is some soldiers. We should head for Abeno and wait there for the Taira. This is on Kiyomori's way back from the Kumano Shrine and he and his men will probably be wearing nothing more than pilgrim's robes. If we surround them and attack through the middle, he'll probably try to save his precious life by making for the hills or the woods and hiding there. We'll

> pursue and capture him, and we'll hang his head over the scaffold gate. Then we'll destroy Shinzei. Once the country's peaceful, I'll be glad to accept a major province or a superior province and a promotion, too. What sense would it make for me to accept a reward before I've even had the chance to accomplish anything?[33]

Nobuyori, unconvinced by Yoshihira's strategy (which seemed to him excessively crude), decided not to tire his horses by traveling all the way to Abeno to intercept Kiyomori. He preferred to wait until Kiyomori entered the capital, where it would be easier to surround and kill him. The others all agreed, but the narrator tells us, "This marked the end of his good fortune."

Kiyomori would foil Nobuyori's plans, but not before Nobuyori had killed his archenemy Shinzei. We are told that when Shinzei first thought of becoming a Buddhist priest he groomed himself before going to the palace to inform the emperor of his decision. As he dampened his sidelocks he noticed to his astonishment that his head, as reflected in the water, had a sword blade stuck in its throat. It was the face of a man doomed to die by violence. He consulted a physiognomist who confirmed that, for all his learning, Shinzei would probably die by the sword. The only possibility of escaping this fate was to enter orders as a priest, and Shinzei wasted no time in following this advice.

At noon on the day when the Sanjō Palace was to burn Shinzei saw a white rainbow pierce the sun, a portent of calamity. He hurried to the palace to report, but the emperor was listening to music and could not be disturbed. Shinzei went into a nearby temple building to read the sutras and pray, when a spark from burning incense flew onto the page and burned two lines. The same spark then leaped to Shinzei's sleeve and set it afire. He interpreted this prodigy as meaning, as an old text stated, the strong would become weak and the weak strong. This seemed a warning, and Shinzei returned home at once and informed his wife that he was leaving for Nara. He did not explain his actions, but the wife, suspecting some crisis had arisen, begged to be taken along. Shinzei refused, and left for Nara with only four retainers.

Once in Nara, Shinzei observed the stars and planets, and saw signs that a loyal minister would have to die to save the life of the emperor. When word reached him of the burning of the Sanjō Palace and of his own house, he knew that his interpretation of the celestial portents had been correct. Soon men would be coming from the capital to capture him. He had his retainers dig a hole deep in the ground as a hiding place for himself with a bamboo tube inserted for breathing. The pursuers arrived soon afterward and, finding one of Shinzei's men, tortured him until the man revealed where Shinzei was hiding. The men dug him up. He was still breathing, but they cut off his head and, after parading it around the city, intended to expose it over the prison gate. The people of the capital crowded along the Kamo River to gape at the head as it went by. When Nobuyori and Yoshitomo stopped their carriages to have a look at the head, the sky suddenly clouded over, and the head nodded, signifying to the crowd that the enemies of the court would soon be destroyed.

This section of *Tale of the Disturbance in Heiji* is justly celebrated. The oldest surviving text, however, makes no mention of the bamboo tube through which Shinzei breathed, stating merely that he stabbed himself in his hiding place in the ground.[34] Obviously, the story improved in the telling. Similar additions can be traced in other parts of the narrative, elevating what may originally have been no more than a straightforward account of warfare into a work of literature. Departures from strict chronological order helped to impart a dramatic structure, scenes of great intensity being presented in counterpoint to those of a lighter nature. Some sections appear to be deliberately pictorial in their incidents and composition, an impression confirmed by the scroll paintings. One such scene is that when the youthful Emperor Nijō, exasperated by the ineptitude of Nobuyori, leaves the palace and goes to Kiyomori's headquarters at Rokuhara. The carriage bearing the emperor, disguised as a woman, is stopped by Yoshitomo's men as it leaves the palace gate. "Whose carriage is that?" they ask. "Ladies of the court on their way to the Kitano Shrine. Nothing unusual," is the reply. But the leader of the guards, still suspicious, lifts the carriage blinds with the tip of his bow, and by torchlight examines the interior of the carriage. He sees the emperor, dressed in woman's clothes and wearing a wig, and his ladies, all in elaborate costumes, and this country samurai, dazzled by the unfamiliar splendor, lets the carriage pass.

The characters are well drawn, especially the cowardly and corrupt Nobuyori who, even as the emperor is making his escape, is drunkenly amusing himself with court ladies, a scene of grotesque humor that effectively contrasts with the tension of the preceding account of the emperor's escape. During the fighting that ensues between the Taira and the soldiers of Nobuyori and Yoshitomo, it seems at first as if the Taira have been routed and are withdrawing to Rokuhara, but this is only a feint to induce the enemy to come after them, leaving the palace virtually undefended. Yoshitomo and the Minamoto are defeated, and the terrified Nobuyori begs Yoshitomo to take him to safety in the east.

Yoshitomo, enraged by Nobuyori's fecklessness, calls him the worst blunderer in Japan, and lashes him with his whip. Nobuyori manages to escape as far as the Ninna-ji, where he implores Goshirakawa to save him, but to no avail. He is captured and executed by the Taira, a miserable figure in death as in life.

Akugenta Yoshihira, a totally dissimilar figure, is a hero along the lines of Tametomo who fights bravely but on the losing side. In another memorable scene of the work he and Taira no Shigemori, Kiyomori's son, fight within the palace grounds. Shigemori has five hundred men against only seventeen of Yoshihira. The mounted warriors circle the cherry tree and orange tree before the Hall of State ten times before Shigemori realizes that he and his men are no match for Yoshihira and leaves the field. After Yoshitomo, on his way back to the east, is betrayed and killed, Yoshihira goes to Rokuhara alone in a last gesture of resistance. When captured he taunts the Taira and urges them to kill him as soon as possible; he vows to become a thunder god and wreak his vengeance on them. A crowd gathers to watch the execution, only for Yoshihira to order the commoners to stand aside so that he can direct his prayers to Amida Buddha's paradise in the west. He rebukes the Taira for making a public ceremony in broad daylight of his execution, then commands the executioner to do his job well "or else I will bite your face off." The executioner efficiently lops off Yoshihira's head; the text informs us, "He was twenty years old." His head was hung on the prison gate.

The last part of *Tale of the Disturbance in Heiji* is devoted mainly to the account of Yoshitomo's mistress Tokiwa and her sons. Tokiwa attempted to escape to safety in the east, but she and her sons were captured by Kiyomori's men. At first Kiyomori was resolved to kill the three boys, but his stepmother, Ike no Zenni, interceded for them, saying that Yoritomo, the eldest, looked exactly like a son of hers who died young.[35] Kiyomori could not disregard her request. He still intended to kill Yoshitomo's other sons, but his passions were aroused by Tokiwa, described as the most beautiful woman in Japan, and he agreed to spare these sons if Tokiwa became his mistress. Although women naturally played a smaller part in warrior society than they did at the Heian court, these two instances (and there are many others) provide evidence that the role of women in affecting the results of military or political conflicts during the medieval period was by no means insignificant.

As the result of his mother's self-sacrifice in yielding to Kiyomori, Yoritomo was sent into exile in Izu. He promised he would become a priest and pray for the salvation of his father. This is where the work ends. The conclusion is somewhat disappointing, but every reader knows that the story has not ended: Yoritomo will avenge his father's death and the humiliation of his clan, the Minamoto, the story told in *The Tale of the Heike*.

The Tale of the Heike

The supreme example of the martial tale is unquestionably *Heike Monogatari* (The Tale of the Heike), an evocation of, successively, the origins of the conflict between the Taira and the Minamoto clans, the various defeats suffered by the Taira during the warfare that lasted from 1183 to 1185, and finally, the deaths of the last members of the once proud Taira family.

The work was probably set down on paper for the first time early in the thirteenth century. The priest Kenkō in *Essays in Idleness* stated that one Yukinaga, a scholar and official whose name appears in various documents dated between 1181 and 1213, wrote *The Tale of the Heike* and taught a blind man named Shōbutsu to recite it.[36] Kenkō added, "Shōbutsu, a native of the Eastern Provinces, questioned soldiers from his part of the country about military matters and feats of arms, then got Yukinaga to write them down. *Biwa* entertainers today imitate what was Shōbutsu's natural voice."[37] There seems to be some confusion in this passage as to who taught whom; probably Shōbutsu, after having been taught to recite Yukinaga's text, was dissatisfied because it failed to describe the fighting in the eastern provinces, and he himself, after questioning men who had taken part in the warfare, supplied additional materials which he "taught" to Yukinaga.

Although Kenkō's account is not directly substantiated by other evidence, it is now generally accepted.[38] Even if Yukinaga was not the author, Kenkō's description of the manner in which *The Tale of the Heike* was compiled rings true: a written text was probably used as the basis of recitations by professional storytellers who embellished the original narrative, perhaps in response to the demands of listeners who craved to hear more about the heroic deeds of the war. This process resulted in recited texts that were longer and more detailed than the original written text. An epilogue, which movingly recounts the fates of the last of the Heike, was added late in the thirteenth century. The recited texts achieved definitive form by 1371, the year in which the blind priest Kakuichi dictated to a disciple the version of the tale he intoned.[39] This text is generally considered to be the final version, and is included by editors in collections of the Japanese classics, but the storytellers' practice of adding to the text continued long after Kakuichi's labors were completed.[40] Probably no other work of Japanese literature exists in so many different versions.[41]

The central character of *The Tale of the Heike*, though he dies about halfway through the work, is Taira no Kiyomori (1118–1181), and the celebrated opening lines, a statement in Buddhist terms of the transitory nature of worldly fame, seem to refer specifically to Kiyomori's extraordinary career. Perhaps, as has been suggested,[42] *The Tale of the Heike* originally concluded with the death of Kiyomori, described in terms resembling those of the opening:

> Though his name had resounded to every corner of Japan, and the power he wielded was immense, his flesh became no more than a momentary wisp of smoke that rose into the sky above the capital. His ashes lingered a while longer, tossed among the sands of the shore, before they too turned to sterile earth.

The portrait of Kiyomori in *The Tale of the Heike* is by no means favorable. He is a tyrant, merciless in his dealings with men who oppose him or women whom he no longer loves, ready to flaunt his contempt even for Buddha by wantonly destroying temples. So crudely does he behave that it is hard to believe, despite the pedigree provided at the opening of the work, that Kiyomori was a member of the aristocracy; he seems totally lacking in refinement. Conceivably, some modern readers may be attracted by Kiyomori's bold rejection of constricting traditions and precedents, whether expressed in his defiance of religion or his arbitrary decision to remove the capital from Kyoto to his stronghold at Fukuhara on the coast of the Inland Sea. But the author of *The Tale of the Heike* clearly did not intend readers to admire Kiyomori; instead, he emphasized the wanton brutality of this tyrant, and in asides frequently deplored his behavior and contrasted him with more prudent, pious men.

We know from other sources that this was not an entirely faithful portrait of Kiyomori. He was reared not as a soldier, though his recent forebears had been samurai, but as a young prince, lending credence to rumors that he was the illegitimate son of the Retired Emperor Shirakawa.[43] As a grown man, Kiyomori was at first exceptionally affable and eager to please; he seemed to be the kind of man who never made enemies.[44] He and the Emperor Goshirakawa eventually became the bitterest of enemies, but for years they were on cordial terms, united by similar temperaments and by a shared dislike of the rigid code that governed behavior at the court. Of all this *The Tale of the Heike* says nothing; from the first we see of Kiyomori he is a tyrant who employs three hundred young men to spy on people and denounce anyone who dares utter a word against his rule. The Taira were so powerful that one of them boasted, "A man who's not a Taira is not a human being." The sympathies of the author were clearly with the Minamoto.

The first half of the work is devoted to a description of the power and overweening pride of the Taira, and recounts the various outrages perpetrated by Kiyomori and others of his clan; the second half tells of the disasters that humbled and finally destroyed the once mighty Taira clan. Although the author was no doubt glad that the Minamoto warriors were victorious, *The Tale of the Heike* is not a celebration so much as an elegy. Kiyomori is portrayed so harshly that it is impossible to feel sympathy for him even when he suffers an excruciatingly painful death, but the Taira clan in defeat claims our compassion. The fall of a great dynasty is inevitably tragic: *"Et pourtant c'est triste quand meurent les empires."*

The Taira were not all proud and violent men. Kiyomori's antithesis, his son Shigemori, is presented as a model of sound judgment and circumspection. He repeatedly admonishes the wayward actions of his father, and his Confucian sermons on the nature of loyalty to the throne and similar subjects usually succeed in persuading Kiyomori to abandon some precipitous course of action. The depiction in *The Tale of the Heike* of Shigemori as a model of statesmanship owes as much to the storyteller as does its counterpart, the diametrically opposed portrait of Kiyomori. It even seems likely that some of the wicked deeds attributed by the narrator to Kiyomori were in fact the work of his virtuous son.[45] Shigemori is described in nonliterary documents of the time mainly as a bold and skillful warrior,[46] but his martial activities are not mentioned in *The Tale of the Heike*, where the interest of the narrator lies in establishing the contrast between Kiyomori and Shigemori, rather than in depicting Shigemori as a hero.

The first incident in which the opposing natures of father and son are brought to the fore is when the Major Counselor Narichika, bitter that he has been passed over for promotion by Kiyomori, resolves to overthrow the Taira. The author, far from applauding Narichika's courage, expresses horror that he could have forgotten that when Narichika was implicated in Nobuyori's plot during the Heiji disturbance, he was saved from death only by Shigemori. Narichika seems unafraid of the Taira, a foolhardy attitude, as others in the conspiracy are aware, and compounds his folly with ingratitude, an offense that the Confucian author of *The Tale of the Heike* does not forgive.

Shigemori also interceded with his father on behalf of the Retired Emperor Goshirakawa, an egregiously disagreeable man. Shinzei had said of him that he was "one of the rare examples in the history of China and Japan of a truly unenlightened ruler," and Minamoto no Yoritomo later described Goshirakawa as "the biggest *tengu* in all Japan."[47] Little suggests that he had other aspects to his character, although he was a generous patron of Buddhism, and students of literature are grateful to him for having compiled the treasury of *imayō* (popular songs) called *Ryōjin Hishō*. In *The Tale of the Heike* he is a scheming figure ready to do anything that will satisfy his insatiable craving for power. When a coup against the Taira was being hatched at the house of the priest Shunkan in the eastern hills, Goshirakawa paid a visit to the conspirators and smilingly expressed his approval when the Major Counselor Narichika, as a sign to the others that the Taira clan (*heishi*) would be overthrown, knocked over a sake bottle (*heiji*). But when Kiyomori decided to punish Goshirakawa for his role in the abortive coup, Shigemori was inspired to deliver his longest and most impassioned lecture to his father on the absolute requirement of loyalty to the throne.

After Shigemori's death no one can control Kiyomori. Enraged at the report that Goshirakawa was enjoying himself with music even as Shigemori lay dying, Kiyomori orders that the former emperor be removed from his own palace and taken to a ramshackle palace where he is kept under guard. When Kiyomori's men arrive to escort him to his new dwelling, Goshirakawa at first expects to be put to death; but even Kiyomori is not audacious enough to kill a former emperor.

The downfall of the Taira is attributed by the author to their repeated crimes, but the immediate cause is the uprising led by Minamoto no Yoritomo against the Taira power. It will be recalled that Yoritomo's life was spared at the entreaty of Kiyomori's stepmother. On his deathbed Kiyomori asked for only one offering to be made at his tomb: the head of Yoritomo. According to *The Tale of the Heike*, the priest Mongaku, who like Yoritomo was exiled to Izu, urged Yoritomo to rally the anti-Taira forces. At first Yoritomo was reluctant to break his vow of devoting his life to prayers for the repose of his benefactress, but Mongaku convinced him of the sincerity of his devotion to the Minamoto cause by displaying the skull of Yoritomo's father, Yoshitomo, which he claimed to have carried on his person for over ten years. Yoritomo seemed rather dubious about the authenticity of the skull, but Mongaku's determination swept away his objections, and in the end he agreed to lead a revolt against the Taira.

The best-known hero on the Minamoto side was not Yoritomo himself, for all his resolute authority, but his younger half-brother Yoshitsune, the victor at two of the chief battles of the war. Another hero, Kiso no Yoshinaka, like Tametomo before him, was an incomparable fighter but a poor leader of men. Yoshinaka, who grew up in the distant mountains of Kiso, lacked all sense of discipline, let alone refinement, and he allowed his men, after they had wrested the capital from the Taira, to pillage the storehouses and rob the inhabitants. The people of the capital began to complain that the Minamoto were even worse than the Taira had been, and Goshirakawa himself decided that he must destroy this sometime ally.

In the ensuing struggle with the forces of Goshirakawa, which included many armed monks from the monasteries on Mount Hiei, Yoshinaka was at first victorious. His forces burned the palace of the former emperor, and he himself demanded and received as his bride the daughter of a former kampaku. Yoritomo could not permit such actions even on the part of a devoted retainer, and he commanded Yoshitsune to destroy Yoshinaka. At the time, many of Yoshinaka's soldiers were in the west of the country, fighting the Taira, and at the end he was left with only a handful of retainers, including the woman warrior Tomoe. He died alone, thrusting his sword into his mouth and leaping headfirst from his horse. The new order established by Yoritomo had no place for heroes suited to an earlier age.

The dramatic climax of *The Tale of the Heike* is the precipitant abandonment of the capital by the Taira in face of Yoshinaka's attacks, but three battles were even more crucial in the defeat of the Taira by the Minamoto. The first, at Ichinotani, a site ideally situated for defensive action that had been fortified by the Taira in anticipation of a decisive battle, was won by the Minamoto thanks mainly to a daring attack by Yoshitsune. The Taira neglected to protect their rear, a precipice so steep that attack from that quarter seemed impossible, but Yoshitsune led a night charge down the precipice that caught the unprepared Taira by surprise. Soon the heads of numerous fallen Taira warriors were being paraded through the capital, now occupied by the Minamoto. The remnants of the Taira forces gathered at their stronghold of Yashima on the island of Shikoku, fortified by the presence of the boy Emperor Antoku, whom they had brought with them from the capital. For a time they even managed to win minor skirmishes with the Minamoto, but they were defeated during the second major battle of the war at Yashima, where Yoshitsune overcame a large Taira army as much by his wiles as by his bravery.

The third and final battle was fought at Dannoura, near the point where the islands of Honshū and Kyūshū come closest together at the straits of Shimonoseki. The Taira had always counted on their naval supremacy, but in the battle that ensued they were utterly defeated. The Emperor Antoku, in his grandmother's arms, was carried to the depths of the sea.

Kenreimon'in, the mother of the emperor, also jumped into the sea, but she was rescued by the Minamoto and brought back to the capital. She was eventually permitted to go to the Jakkō-in, a small convent to the north of the capital, where she spent the rest of her days. One of the last episodes in *The Tale of the Heike* describes the visit of Goshirakawa, who has survived the warfare unscathed, to the lonely Jakkō-in. The first person he meets there is an old nun dressed in robes so frayed that he cannot even guess from what material they were made. In contrast to her humble appearance, she speaks in learned Buddhist language, and he wonders who she might be. He asks, and she answers in unforgettable words: "I am Awa no Naishi, daughter of the late Shinzei. Once you loved me very deeply, and if now you have forgotten me it must be because I have grown old and ugly." "Yes," the former emperor replies, "it is you, Awa no Naishi. I had forgotten all about you. Everything now seems like a dream." The nun, who had up until this point expressed indifference to present hardships, attributing them to causes from a previous existence, is still a woman, and cannot forget that once she was beautiful and loved; and Goshirakawa's words convey perfectly the callous nature of the man. When he finally meets Kenreimon'in, they exchange reminiscences on the events of the past few years. He leaves as the bell of the Jakkō-in sounds the coming of evening, the work ending as it began with the tolling of a temple bell.

The above is, in general, the plot of *The Tale of the Heike*. The fall of the Taira is a worthy subject of an epic, but even more than the accounts of battles or the speeches by Shigemori or other sections that relate directly to the overarching theme, incidental episodes are apt to stay in the reader's memory—moments in the lives of people, even those on the periphery of the action, who suffer because of causes beyond their control. The story of the priest Shunkan, which occurs early in the narrative, is particularly moving. As one of the leaders of the conspiracy against Kiyomori, he was punished (like two of the others) by being banished to a remote island populated by savages. The other two men were eventually allowed to return to the capital, but Shunkan, by a caprice of Kiyomori's tyranny, was alone condemned to remain on the island. Shunkan has not been portrayed as a worthy man, but we cannot but be moved by his anguish over being left behind, clinging desperately to the hope, voiced by one of his disingenuous companions, that a pardon will be forthcoming. His futile, even childish attempts to persuade the obdurate boatman to take him aboard are pitiful, and in the end the ship disappears over the horizon leaving Shunkan alone on the deserted shore. It is small wonder that this section of the work has been adapted for the theater, and the image of Shunkan, wildly beckoning to a ship that ignores him, has been evoked again and again in works of art.

The death of the Taira general Atsumori is another, wonderfully dramatic episode. The Minamoto warrior Kumagai Naozane sees a Taira horseman fleeing toward a ship in the offing and calls on him to turn around and fight. The Taira warrior responds, and in the ensuing combat Naozane knocks the other man off his horse. He lifts his sword, preparing to deal the final blow, when he notices, tearing off the helmet, that his enemy is a mere youth of sixteen, just about the same age as his own son. Remembering his own shock when he learned earlier that day that his son had been wounded, he can imagine how the parents of this youth would grieve to hear of his death. Naozane decides he will spare him. He addresses the youth politely, asking his name, only to receive the snarled reply, "Take my head and show it to somebody. They'll tell you who I am." At that moment other Minamoto horsemen appear and Naozane realizes that if he does not kill the young general, others will. He explains this, and promises to pray for the youth's salvation, but the latter expresses no gratitude, merely repeating, "Cut off my head!" Naozane steels himself to the act with the bitter reflection that it was only because he was born into a family of warriors that he must commit such cruel acts. When he strips the youth's armor he finds a flute, and he reflects how unlikely it was that anyone on the Minamoto side would have taken a flute to the battlefield. Naozane presents the head to Yoshitsune and learns that this youth was Atsumori, the son of a palace official, and that the flute, once owned by the Emperor Toba, had been a gift to Atsumori's grandfather.

The dramatic contrasts in this episode are superb. Naozane, a grizzled old warrior, fights a young warrior; a rough soldier from the eastern provinces confronts a nobleman from the capital. Naozane, his sword poised over Atsumori's throat, speaks politely, even deferentially to the youth, but Atsumori's replies are short and harsh, as if uttered in contempt of a man from the barbarous hinterland. The Taira themselves had been fierce warriors, but they had adopted the aristocratic ways of the capital, and now they seem to represent the old culture, symbolized by the flute. Naozane, far from exulting over his victory, laments the necessity of killing, and from this time on his heart is turned toward the religious life. None of the various works for the theater based on the story of Atsumori's death is as dramatically affecting as the original episode from *The Tale of the Heike*.

Many other episodes and people live in the reader's memory, and these are the stories that inspired numerous Nō plays—more than any other work of literature. There are also dull sections, at least for modern readers: the least affecting parts are the recitations of Chinese and Japanese precedents for the events described. It is tedious when the action is suspended for, say, a listing of twenty instances of traitors to the throne over the course of Japanese history, followed by a similar description of notable Chinese traitors.[48] No doubt such a roll call resounded impressively when delivered by the storytellers, and the parallels in Chinese history rendered more important the Japanese examples.

The full effect of *The Tale of the Heike* requires that it be read aloud, with the intonation of the biwa hōshi who recited the work, accompanied by the plangent notes of the biwa. In translation the musical effects are inevitably lost, and even the most accurate version is likely to seem inadequate to anyone familiar with the cadences of the original. Some passages follow the standard poetic practice of alternating lines in five and seven syllables, but even those in unmistakable prose are frequently of exceptional aural beauty. For these reasons, *The Tale of the Heike* suffers far more in translation than, say, *The Tale of Genji*, which was intended to be read rather than recited. The language is also more varied than the pure (or nearly pure) Yamato vocabulary of the earlier work; some of the most impressive effects of the recitation are achieved by the greater richness of sound and sharpness of definition made possible by the admixture of words of Chinese or Sanskrit origin. The opening paragraph may suggest the characteristic combination of native and foreign words:

"*Gion shōja* no kane no koe, *shogyō mujō* no hibiki ari. *Shara sōju* no hana no iro, *jōsha hissui* no kotowari wo arawasu. Ogoeru hito mo hisashikarazu, tada haru no yo no yume no gotoshi. Takeki mono mo tsui ni horobinu, hitoe ni kaze no mae no chiri ni onaji." (The sound of the bell of the Gion Temple echoes the impermanence of all things. The color of the blossoms of the twin-trunked sala trees[49] reveals the truth that those who wax must wane. The proud man does not long endure; he is just like the dream of a spring night. The fearless person, too, in the end will perish, exactly like dust before the wind.)

The italicized words (those of foreign origin) stand out when read aloud because of the long vowels, the doubled consonants, such unfamiliar sounds as *sha*, and the final *-n* of the first word. Although the last two sentences contain no foreign words, Chinese influence may be inferred from the rhetorical device of parallelism: the sound of the bell / the color of the flowers; proud man / fearless person; does not long endure / in the end will perish; just like a dream of a spring night / exactly the same as dust before the wind. The foreign words also occur at the same positions in the first and second sentences, each heading a main or subordinate clause. It has been argued that *The Tale of the Heike* is the first and greatest masterpiece of the Japanese language, as opposed to the Yamato language of the Heian period. Although the Kakuichi text was written down six hundred years ago, much of it is still immediately intelligible, an indiction of its importance in the formation of the modern language.

Recitation of *The Tale of the Heike* to biwa accompaniment has lingered into the twentieth century, though it is no longer, of course, a popular entertainment. More than any other single work of classical Japanese literature, *The Tale of the Heike* is in the blood of the Japanese. No one has to explain even to the badly educated who Kiyomori, Shigemori, or Yoshitsune were, and there is much in later literature to recall the unhappy women who figure so prominently in the pages of the work—Giō, Kogō, Kenreimon'in, and the rest. Innumerable works not only of literature but of painting and other arts have been based on the tale of the glory and the downfall of the Taira. Although it was not composed in poetry, in theme and execution *The Tale of the Heike* merits being considered as the Japanese epic.

Notes

1. The Taira were also known as the Heishi. Heike is the Sino-Japanese reading of "Taira family" and Heishi of "Taira clan." The enemies of the Taira, the Minamoto, are usually referred to as Genji, also a Sino-Japanese reading. Except for mentions of the title *The Tale of the Heike*, I have used the names Taira and Minamoto throughout for the two families, in order to avoid confusion.
2. George Sansom in *A History of Japan to 1334* (p. 203) wrote of the Fujiwara

officials of the mid-twelfth century, "The quality of the Fujiwara Regents and ministers naturally began to diminish as their authority waned, until in 1180 we find it recorded by a diarist that the then Regent was utterly ignorant of the literature and history of Japan and China. That was certainly a grave complaint to bring against a statesman at the Heian court, where learning had always been prized and encouraged."

3. Translation by Judith N. Rabinovich in *Shōmonki*, p. 131.
4. *Ibid*, pp. 138–39.
5. For a good discussion of the style, see *ibid.*, pp. 53–62. Rabinovich gives examples of the parallel prose (*p'ien wen*) with which the author attempted to decorate the otherwise dreary text, and of Japanese words or constructions that intruded into the Chinese prose.
6. Nagazumi Yasuaki (in *Gunki Monogatari no Sekai*, p. 195) insisted that *The Story of Masakado* was a gunki monogatari and was indebted to such earlier examples of monogatari as *The Tale of the Bamboo Cutter* and *Tales of Ise*. It is difficult to concur in this attempt to find literary merit in the work.
7. *Ibid.*, p. 204.
8. Translated by Helen Craig McCullough as "A Tale of Mutsu."
9. McCullough characterized the work (p. 186) as "a brief, plodding synopsis of dull official documents, written moreover in Chinese, which can interest the literary critic solely because of the anecdotes inserted as artlessly as sticks disposed in a child's mud pie." A statement appears at the end of the text of *Tales and Records of Mutsu* to the effect that both written and oral accounts have been combined to form the present text. For a brief discussion of the relations between *Tales and Records of Mutsu* and the great collection of setsuwa, *Tales of Times Now Past*, see Ikegami Jun'ichi, "Setsuwa Bungaku kara Gunki Monogatari e," in Nagazumi Yasuaki, *Hōgen Monogatari, Heiji Monogatari* (Kadokawa), pp. 385–88.
10. A more literal translation of the title is the plain "Tale of Hōgen."
11. There are many variant texts of *Tale of the Disturbance in Hōgen*, and the ending differs according to the "family" of text.
12. Saigyō's visit to Sutoku's grave at Shiramine in the province of Sanuki is the subject of the first story in Ueda Akinari's collection *Ugetsu Monogatari* (Tales of the Rain and Moon, 1776).
13. It has been translated by Delmer H. Brown and Ichirō Ishida in *The Future and the Past*. The literal meaning of the title is something like "A Selection of the Opinions of a Fool."
14. Quoted in Nagazumi, *Gunki*, p. 10. See also the translation by Brown and Ishida, *The Future*, p. 89.
15. See Chapter 14.
16. A conspicuously more literary account of the same events appears in the Kotohira Shrine text; and a pirated edition of 1624 is the earliest known example of the rufubon (vulgate) text, the most disseminated. For a concise account of the different texts, see Nagazumi, *Hōgen*, pp. 17–20. A fuller

account is given in Nagazumi Yasuaki and Shimada Isao, *Hōgen Monogatari, Heiji Monogatari*, pp. 11–31.

17. A style similar to that of the gunki monogatari, approaching that of the contemporary colloquial, is found in *Tales of Times Now Past*, the collection compiled about 1120, but *The Tale of the Disturbance in Hōgen* is far more literary in expression than the tales of this collection.
18. The verb *sōrō* was a contracted form of *saburau*, meaning "to serve" (samurai is derived from the same verb). It was an appropriate verb for a society that placed the highest value on service to one's master.
19. This mythical island, known as Onigashima, figures in the story of Momotarō and other Japanese children's stories. It has been identified with Kikai (Devils' Realm) Island, an island east of Amami Ōshima, or with various other islands to the south of Kyūshū. Here, it probably does not designate any geographically known island.
20. This is where most versions of the story end, but in later accounts (presumably, once again, in response to audience demand) Tametomo escapes from Ōshima and makes his way to Okinawa, which he conquers and rules as its first king.
21. For a translation, see William R.Wilson, *Hōgen monogatari*: *Tale of the Disorder in Hōgen*, p. 84.
22. I have followed here the rufubon text (translated by Wilson in *Hōgen*, p. 97). According to the Kompira Shrine text, Sutoku asked that the manuscripts be kept somewhere near the Hachiman (shrine) at Toba. See Nagazumi, *Hōgen*, p. 152.
23. Nagazumi, *Hōgen*, p. 152; also Nagazumi and Shimada, *Hōgen*, p. 180. This passage does not occur in the rufubon.
24. Nagazumi, *Hōgen*, pp. 152–53; also Nagazumi and Shimada, *Hōgen*, p. 180. For another version, see Wilson, *Hōgen*, p. 98.
25. The realms were *jigokudō*, *gakidō*, and *chikushōdō*. The first was a general term for hell, the second the hell of hungry demons, and the third the hell of beasts.
26. Nagazumi, *Hōgen*, pp. 155–56; also Nagazumi and Shimada, *Hōgen*, p. 181. It is not clear what Sutoku meant by his threat of making "a subject the emperor." Perhaps he still entertained hopes of putting on the throne his son Shigehito, who was now a monk at the Ninna-ji.
27. Nagazumi and Shimada, *Hōgen*, p, 183. Both the poem ascribed to Sutoku and Saigyō's reply are included in the collected poems of Saigyō.
28. *Ibid.*, pp. 142–47. I have also consulted the modern-language translation in Nagazumi, *Hōgen*, pp. 116–31. The translation in Wilson, *Hōgen*, pp. 65–68, is from a literarily less interesting text.
29. Nagazumi and Shimada, *Hōgen*, pp. 150–51.
30. The fighting took place mainly in the twelfth month of the first year of Heiji. The year as a whole was 1159 according to the European calendar, but the twelfth lunar month corresponds to January 1160 in the solar calendar.

31. Nagazumi and Shimada, *Hōgen*, p. 190.
32. Fujiwara no Yorinaga was known as the Uji Minister of the Left. The incident to which Yoshihira refers is described in *Tale of the Disturbance in Hōgen*. See Nagazumi and Shimada, *Hōgen*, p. 98. The word "chamberlain" is used to translate the post of *kurando* (or *kurōdo*).
33. *Ibid.*, p. 197.
34. See Nagazumi, *Hōgen*, p. 247. The source is *Gukanshō*, translated by Brown and Ishida in *The Present*, p. 109. See also Edwin O. Reischauer and Joseph K. Yamagiwa, *Translations from Early Japanese Literature*, p. 417, for another rendering of the description of Shinzei's death.
35. The son was called Umanosuke. Ike no Zenni was the second wife of Taira no Tadamori. See Nagazumi and Shimada, *Hōgen*, p. 277. There is a French translation of this passage in René Sieffert, *Le dit de Hôgen*; *Le dit de Heiji*, p. 214.
36. All that is known about Yukinaga, the son of Nakayama Yukitaka, is given by Gomi Fumihiko in *Heike Monogatari, Shi to Setsuwa*, pp. 36–55. He was probably born about 1165. He served as governor of Shimotsuke and later as governor of Shinano before taking vows as a priest. His protector in the priesthood was the eminent Tendai priest Jien, the author of *Gukanshō*.
37. Donald Keene, *Essays in Idleness*, p. 186. Nothing else is known about Shōbutsu.
38. See, for example, Gomi, p. 33. Gomi believed that Kenkō probably obtained this information on the authorship of *The Tale of the Heike* from priests of the Yokawa temples on Mount Hiei.
39. For a detailed examination of the formation of the text of *The Tale of the Heike*, see Kenneth Dean Butler, "The Textual Evolution of the *Heike Monogatari*."
40. The role of the biwa hōshi in the transmission and augmentation of the text of *The Tale of the Heike* is briefly described by Nagazumi in *Gunki*, pp. 60–65. For a fuller description of the growth of the legends of the Gempei War, see Takehisa Tsuyoshi, "Gunki Monogatari no Tassei," in Kitagawa Tadahiko, *Gunkimono no Keifu*, pp. 61–105, or (even fuller) Fukuda Akira, *Gunki Monogatari to Minkan Denshō*.
41. The longest of these versions, about four times the length of *The Tale of the Heike*, is known by a title of its own, *Gempei Seisui Ki* (also read as *Gempei Jōsui Ki*) (A Record of the Rise and Fall of the Minamoto and Taira). This and other variant texts sometimes provide valuable background material for events only briefly mentioned in *The Tale of the Heike* or by rephrasing make clear the intended meaning of obscure passages. For example, the passage in the second chapter *yawara kono katana wo nukiidashi, bin ni hikiaterarekeru ga kōri nando no yō ni zo miekeru* is translated by Helen Craig McCullough in *The Tale of the Heike* (p. 24) as "he drew the weapon with deliberation and held it alongside his head, its blade gleaming

like ice." Neither she nor the original indicates why he should have held the sword by his head. The *Gempei Seisui Ki* version is somewhat clearer: *tachi wo nukiidashi, bin ni suwari suwari to bin ni hikiatekereba, hi no hikari ni kagayakiaite kiramekikereba* ..., which may be rendered as "He drew his sword and touched it lightly to his sidelocks, where [the sword and the sidelocks] mutually glittered in the firelight." See Mizuhara Hajime, *Shintei Gempei Seisui Ki*, I, p. 99. However, I shall be concerned here only with the Kakuichi version of the work.

42. See, for example, Uwayokote Masataka, *Heike Monogatari no Kyokō to Shinjitsu*, I, p. 66. Butler, "The Textual Evolution," pp. 31–33, agrees that it is likely that the earliest version was in six volumes, but they would have treated the full range of materials found in present versions of the work.
43. This rumor was perpetrated, together with the reasons for believing it, at the opening of the "Gion Nyogo" chapter of *The Tale of the Heike*.
44. Se Uwayokote, *Heike*, I, p. 42.
45. See Nagazumi, *Gunki*, p. 80, where he cites a text of *Gempei Seisui Ki* which states that Shigemori, and not Kiyomori, was responsible for the attack on the Regent Fujiwara no Motofusa, in revenge for an insult offered Sukemori, Shigemori's son. The Kakuichi text insists instead on Shigemori's anger with his son, so great that he banished Sukemori to Ise for a time. See McCullough, *The Tale of the Heike*, p. 44, or Hiroshi Kitagawa and Bruce T. Tsuchida, *The Tale of the Heike*, p. 48, for a translation of this passage.
46. See Uwayokote, *Heike*, I, pp. 88–89. The source of this evaluation is *Hyakurenshō*, a history written about 1260 based largely on diaries kept by members of the court.
47. Uwayokote, *Heike*, I, p. 81. A tengu is a long-nosed hobgoblin. The remark of Yoritomo's is found in *Gyokuyō*, the diary of Kujō Kanezane, kept between 1164 and 1200.
48. The similarity of this device to a technique found in *La Chanson de Roland* has been pointed out by Helen Craig McCullough in the essay "The 'Heike' as Literature" appended to her translation of *The Tale of the Heike*, p. 466.
49. These trees bore yellow blossoms which, according to Buddhist texts, turned white in mourning for the death of the Buddha.

Bibliography

Note: All Japanese books, except as otherwise noted, were published in Tokyo.

Butler, Kenneth Dean. "The Textual Evolution of the *Heike Monogatari*," *Harvard Journal of Asiatic Studies* 26, 1966.

Fukuda Akira. *Gunki Monogatari to Minkan Denshō*. Iwasaki Bijutsu Sha, 1972.

Gomi Fumihiko. *Heike Monogatari, Shi to Setsuwa*. Heibonsha, 1987.

Keene, Donald (trans.) *Essays in Idleness*. New York: Columbia University Press, 1967.

Kitagawa, Hiroshi, and Bruce T. Tsuchida. *The Tale of the Heike*, 2 vols. Tokyo: Tokyo University Press, 1977.

Kitagawa Tadahiko. *Gunkimono no Keifu*. Kyoto: Sekai Shisōsha, 1985.

Matsumura Hiroshi. *Rekishi Monogatari*. Hanawa Shobō, 1979.

McCullough, Helen Craig. *The Tale of the Heike*. Stanford, Calif.: Stanford University Press, 1988.

———. "A Tale of Mutsu," *Harvard Journal of Asiatic Studies* 25, 1964–65.

Mizuhara Hajime. *Shintei Gempei Seisui Ki*, 4 vols. Shin Jimbutsu Ōrai Sha, 1988–90.

Nagazumi Yasuaki. *Gunki Monogatari no Sekai*. Asahi Shimbun Sha, 1978.

———. *Hōgen Monogatari, Heiji Monogatari*, in Kanshō Nihon Koten Bungaku series. Kadokawa Shoten, 1976.

Nagazumi Yasuaki and Shimada Isao. *Hōgen Monogatari, Heiji Monogatari*, in Nihon Koten Bungaku Taikei series. Iwanami Shoten, 1961.

Nihon Koten Bungaku Daijiten, 6 vols. Iwanami Shoten, 1983–85.

Rabinovich, Judith N. *Shōmonki: The Story of Masakado's Rebellion*. Tokyo: Sophia University, 1986.

Reischauer, Edwin O., and Joseph K. Yamagiwa. *Translations from Early Japanese Literature*. Cambridge, Mass.: Harvard University Press, 1951.

Sansom, George. *A History of Japan to 1334*. Stanford, Calif.: Stanford University Press, 1958.

Seidensticker, Edward G. *The Tale of Genji*, 2 vols. New York: Alfred A. Knopf, 1976.

Sieffert, René. *Le dit de Hôgen*; *Le dit de Heiji*. Paris: Publications Orientalistes de France, 1978.

———. *Le dit des Heike*. Paris: Publications Orientalistes de France, 1978.

Takagi Ichinosuke, Ozawa Masao, Atsumi Kaoru, and Kindaiichi Haruhiko. *Heike Monogatari*, 2 vols., in Nihon Koten Bungaku Taikei series. Iwanami Shoten, 1959–60.

Uwayokote Masataka, *Heike Monogatari no Kyokō to Shinjitsu*, 2 vols. Hanawa Shobō, 1985.

Wilson, William R. *Hōgen Monogatari: Tale of the Disorder in Hōgen*. Tokyo: Sophia University, 1971.

17. THE AGE OF THE *SHIN KOKINSHŪ*

The three finest anthologies of classical Japanese poetry are, by general consent, the *Man'yōshū*, the *Kokinshū*, and the *Shin Kokinshū*. Each of the *chokusenshū* between the first, the *Kokinshū*, and the eighth, the *Shin Kokinshū* (New Collection of Poems Ancient and Modern), contains poems of exceptional beauty, as we have seen, and they have often been quoted and imitated; but these collections do not maintain a consistently high level, and they are therefore seldom considered as whole works; and the thirteen imperial collections that followed the *Shin Kokinshū*, even more conspicuously neglected, are known only to specialists.[1] The *Shin Kokinshū* represents not only the summit but the end of the glorious tradition of court poetry, though innumerable poems, some of undeniable merit, continued to be composed at the court during the following centuries.

The *Shin Kokinshū* was compiled during the first decade of the thirteenth century, at a time when the rise of the military had deprived the court of most of its real power. This may have given added importance to the functions the court retained, such as the composition of poetry and the compilation of the chokusenshū. The *Shin Kokinshū* stands out among such collections because of the cluster of extraordinary poets whose works ornament its pages. Three—the priest Saigyō, the Retired Emperor Gotoba, and Fujiwara Teika[2]—rank among the supreme masters of the waka, and another half-dozen *Shin Kokinshū* poets are nearly as celebrated.[3] Each of these poets has a recognizably distinct voice, but a general similarity in the tone and syntax of the characteristic poems in the collection has induced commentators to speak of a "*Shin Kokinshū* style." For example, syntactic breaks after the first or third lines of a waka are far more common in the *Shin Kokinshū* than in the *Kokinshū*.[4] A reliance for poetic effect on nouns (especially at the very end of a poem), rather than on the verbal inflections typical of the

Kokinshū, is another feature of *Shin Kokinshū* style, shared by its poets regardless of their subjects.[5]

Apart from such empirically verifiable stylistic features, no one can read the *Shin Kokinshū* without sensing that it is conspicuously more intense and moving that the *Kokinshū*. It is true that the poems by two of the best *Kokinshū* poets, Ono no Komachi and Izumi Shikibu, are full of passion, but more typical of the collection are the many poems that describe intellectual perceptions. Again and again we encounter poetic conceits—for example, the poet's pretense that he cannot be sure if he sees snow or blossoms on the branches of a plum tree; or else logical deductions from natural phenomena—the poet, seeing crimson leaves floating on a river, deduces that it must be colder at the upper reaches of the river than where he stands. Poems in this manner are not absent from the *Shin Kokinshū*, but the prevalent tone is darker and the expression fragmented.

HONKA-DORI

Despite the differences between the two collections, the immense importance of the *Kokinshū* in the creation of the *Shin Kokinshū* can hardly be doubted. Not only do the *Shin Kokinshū* poems possess a technical finish bespeaking generations of composition in the waka form, but many of the poems were openly derived from source poems in the *Konkinshū*. In Europe the borrowing of lines of earlier poetry was relatively uncommon, except when the intention was parody or when the new poem was in a different language from the original; but many *Shin Kokinshū* poets directly borrowed whole sections from poems in the *Kokinshū* and other early collections, as well as from works of courtly fiction.The intent was certainly not humorous. Implicit in such borrowing was the conviction that the poems a poet had read, no less than his perceptions of nature or his direct emotional experiences, can inspire him to compose new poetry; and poems that borrowed elements from the poetry of the past were believed to possess greater depth than poems without allusions.[6] There was also an assumption, quite the opposite of the plagiarist's, that the likely reader of the poem (someone belonging to the same court society) would recognize the source poem and be able to appreciate how the original meaning had been altered to communicate the emotions of a poet who lived hundreds of years later. The practice, known as *honka-dori* (*honka* being "original poem," and *-dori* "borrowing"), did not originate in the *Shin Kokinshū*, as we have seen,[7] but it was here most fully realized.

Two well-known poems will suggest how the process of borrowing could lead to the creation of a distinctively personal new poem. The first, by the priest Henjō, is in the *Kokinshū*:

wa ga yado wa	The weeds grow so thick
michi mo naki made	You cannot even see the path
arenikeri	That leads to my house:
tsurenaki hito wo	It happened while I waited
matsu to seshi ma ni[8]	For my cold-hearted lover.

The poem by Princess Shokushi, though directly based on Henjō's, is not only personal but typical of the *Shin Kokinshū* manner:

kiri no ha mo	Paulownia leaves
fumiwakegataku	Too thick to make one's way through
narinikeri	Have covered the ground.
kanarazu hito wo	It's not necessarily
matsu to nakeredo[9]	That I expect anyone . . .

Henjō's poem, written on a prescribed topic and in the persona of a woman, could hardly have reflected his actual feelings, but it is nonetheless affecting; Shokushi's communicates the despair of a woman who had forbidden herself even the hope that her lover will visit. Her mention of paulownia leaves, more vivid than Henjō's untended garden, is given additional resonance by another poetic source, the lines by Po Chü-i quoted in *Wakan Rōei Shū*: "In my unswept autumn garden, leaning on a rattan stick, / I slowly walk over fallen paulownia leaves."[10]

In this instance of honka-dori the later poem was unusually close to its sources. More frequently, the borrowing poet shifted the emphasis of the poem from, say, the sights of the seasons to those of a journey. Sometimes the new poem departed completely from the sense of the original. The following anonymous poem is from the *Kokinshū*:

wa ga seko ga	How pleasantly fresh
koromo no suso wo	Is the first wind of autumn,
fukikaeshi	That blows back the hems
uramezurashiki	Of the robe my husband wears,
aki no hatsukaze[11]	Showing the fancy lining.

The poem has the grace typical of many *Kokinshū* poems, but surely has no special depth; it seems to be little more than an expression of pleasure that the summer heat has at last ended. The first three lines of the original (the last three of the translation) are considered by most commentators to be an "introduction" (*jokotoba*), not directly related by meaning to the last two lines of the original.The two parts of the poem are linked by *ura*, an intensifying prefix for *mezurashiki*, meaning "fresh" or "unusual," but also the "lining" (*ura*) of the husband's robe. Mention of the lining was probably intended to indicate that the husband had changed this day, the first of autumn, from an unlined to a lined robe. The poem is classified in the *Kokinshū* as a seasonal poem, but the "borrowed" poem in the *Shin Kokinshū* by Fujiwara no Ariie (1155–1216) is a love poem:

sarade dani	Even without this,
uramin to omou	I think I would resent her:
wagimoko ga	The autumn wind blows
koromo no suso ni	In the hems of the garment
akikaze zo fuku[12]	The woman I love is wearing.

Despite the resemblances of vocabulary to the source poem, this poem creates a quite dissimilar effect. The autumn (*aki*) wind here suggests the melancholy atmosphere surrounding the end of a love affair, and there are overtones of the homonym *aki*, "weariness" or "boredom." *Uramin* means "I would resent," but *ura min* is "to see the inside (or lining)," a metaphor for the inner thoughts of the beloved. The poem can be expanded in translation: "Even if this had not happened [even if the autumnal wind had not stirred the hems of my beloved's robe to reveal the lining], I think I should still have detected her inner feelings of apathy and resented them." Although imagery was borrowed from the *Kokinshū*, the poem has been transformed out of recognition.

Such complexity, made possible because of the ease of punning in Japanese, may arouse doubts about the sincerity of the poet's expression, but when honka-dori was successfully employed, the new poem could still be personal, regardless of the extent of the borrowing. The uncovering of source poems has long been a favorite pastime of academics involved with Japanese poetry. Sometimes new light is thrown on a poem by revealing its inspiration, but there is a tendency to imply that once the source poem has been discovered, everything necessary to an understanding of the new poem stands revealed; the use of words and their sounds, the basic concern of any poet, is often passed over without comment.[13] But the fact that the themes of many *Shin Kokinshū* poems were borrowed from earlier collections should not suggest that its poets composed in a claustrophobic atmosphere of rigid conformance with old traditions. The resonance given to a poem by its echoes in the past was more important to these poets than asserting their individuality, but their new use of the old imagery imparted richness and complexity, and that is what makes their poems distinctive.

Borrowings from prose, most often from *Tales of Ise* or *The Tale of Genji*,[14] were also made to enrich the poetic associations, but the sources from which the *Shin Kokinshū* poets most often borrowed were poems that had been composed some three hundred years earlier in what was perceived to have been the golden age of the Heian court. A nostalgic looking back to an age when the court society was untroubled by fears of disorder may account for the "neoclassicism" discernable in the *Shin Kokinshū* poetry,[15] even though the unhappiness overtly voiced in the poems was almost always restricted to the poet's own life. It is difficult, however, to imagine that there was no relation between the emergence of honka-dori as a consciously practiced artistic discipline at the end of the Heian period and the reduced circumstances of the lives of the aristocrats that made many of them yearn for the happier times evoked by the poetry of the past.

Composing allusive variations on the old poetry had long served aspiring Japanese poets as a preparation for expressing themselves in their own voices, but with Fujiwara Teika it became a basic part of poetic praxis, and (as so often in Japan) this involved the creation of rules governing the art. In various critical works he laid down such prescriptions as (1) borrowing should be mainly from the first three imperially commissioned collections, the *Kokinshū*, the *Gosenshū*, and the *Shūishū*;[16] but not more than one or two, or at the most two and a half lines should be taken from the source poem; (2) the borrowed elements should be in a different place within the poem from their position within the source poem; and (3) the main theme of the original poem should be so altered that, for example, a seasonal poem is turned into a love or miscellaneous poem.[17] It was strictly forbidden to borrow from the poets of recent times, let alone contemporaries.[18]

It might seem as if the adoption of honka-dori as an intrinsic part of poetic discipline would have tended to impair the creative imaginations of Japanese poets, but within the limits of the rules for honka-dori laid down by Teika there was still room for entirely personal expression, as the poets of the *Shin Kokinshū* demonstrated again and again.

Uta-awase

As early as the tenth century (as we have seen) members of the Japanese court participated in uta-awase, or poem competitions. These competitions gradually developed into serious literary occasions at which poems on set themes by outstanding poets were matched and judged by experts, but in the early days of uta-awase the literary aspects were overshadowed by the elaborate presentations. Music was an indispensable part of these courtly entertainments, and members of the two teams, left and right, were dressed in elaborate, contrasting costumes.[19] The competing poems were not presented casually but arranged on poem slips set in miniature landscape gardens that were embellished with precious stones. The greatest care was devoted to the impression the competing teams made with their stately entrances to the hall where the competition took place. The poems themselves do not seem to have benefited by the same attention, judging by surviving examples.

As would be true of other, later poetic forms such as renga or haiku, literary importance was imparted to what had originated merely as a game or a diversion by the creation of strict rules governing the art. Fujiwara no Kiyosuke was one of the first to attempt to enhance the dignity of uta-awase sessions by prescribing the manner of choosing the themes, the participants, and the judges. Initially, the judges made only the most perfunctory comments on why they chose as superior the poem submitted by the left team or by the right team, or why they decided to call it a tie, but when the competitions, no longer lavish displays of artistic taste, developed into occasions for the creation of literature, the opinions expressed by the judges became more substantial, and some are still of interest.

The shift from the Heian to the "medieval" style of literary uta-awase has been traced to a period of twenty years during the reigns of the emperors Horikawa and Toba, from about 1100 to 1120.[20] It is not clear precisely why the change occurred, but it has been plausibly linked to the inability of the court to indulge in the extravagance that was typical of the older uta-awase competitions. Certainly this was true of the court during the late Heian and early Kamakura periods, the time when the literary uta-awase flourished most memorably.[21]

The lasting importance of the many sessions of literary uta-awase conducted at the court during the period of greatest activity can be measured in terms of the number of poems composed for such occasions that were later included in the imperially sponsored anthologies: out of a total of 1,981 poems in the *Shin Kokinshū*, 373 originated in uta-awase competitions.[22]

Once the uta-awase had changed from being a court festivity at which the composition of poetry was only one element of an evening's entertainment to a serious contest between individual poets or rival schools, the atmosphere became much less relaxed. Most participants wanted more to win than to create beautiful poems, and this no doubt accounted for the tendency to compose poems that were free of blemishes rather than poems that communicated the poet's deepest feelings. (Of course, it was by no means impossible to communicate deep feelings in a poem without flaws.) A knowledge of the faults of poetry, most of them arbitrarily decided by the compilers of "codes," became as essential as thorough familiarity with the *Kokinshū*.

The judge (*hanja*) of an uta-awase was usually a poet of unquestioned competence. The two best judges during the period when the literary uta-awase first became prominent were Fujiwara no Michitoshi, and Minamoto no Tsunenobu (1016–1097), his bitter rival for recognition as the poet arbiter of the day. Michitoshi headed the conservative faction among the poets of the day, Tsunenobu the faction of innovators. The division between the Ancients and Moderns, which began about this time, would continue to affect the composition of court poetry for centuries to come, though the names of the schools standing on one side or the other of the issue of tradition versus modernity changed from time to time.

Probably the most distinguished judge of the fully developed uta-awase was Fujiwara Shunzei, who served an unprecendented twenty-one times. He owed this distinction both to his reputation as a poet and to his extraordinary longevity. A passage in *Mumyōshō* (Nameless Selection, 1209–1210), the book of poetic criticism by Kamo no Chōmei, quoted the poet-priest Kenshō on the different impressions created by Shunzei and his conservative rival Fujiwara Kiyosuke when they served as judges:

> It is hard to decide who was better as a judge of modern waka, Shunzei or Kiyosuke. Both of them had their prejudices, which assumed different forms in their judgments. Shunzei's expression seemed to say that he was aware that he himself on occasion made mistakes, and he never pronounced a really devastating opinion. He generally would say something like, "This is the usual way of expressing oneself, I'm sure, but would it be wrong to compose the

> poem in some other way?" Kiyosuke seemed, on the surface at least, absolutely beyond reproach, and there was not the faintest suggestion of unfairness in his expression, but if ever anyone looked unconvinced by one of his pronouncements, his expression would invariably change, and he would argue his points fiercely. Eventually people became aware of this, and nobody ever dared voice a word of opposition.[23]

The uta-awase sessions became the occasion for recriminations as judges defended their own decisions or attacked those of other judges;[24] but read today, long after most of the issues brought up by the judges have ceased to be matters of real concern to poets, let alone readers, one is unlikely—even if one plods through the judges' comments appended to the many rounds of uta-awase—to find in them sentiments as perceptive or as universally meaningful as those expressed in the poems they analyze.

The most famous of all uta-awase gatherings took place in 1201 by command of the Retired Emperor Gotoba. Thirty poets were invited to submit one hundred poems each on prescribed subjects, for a total of three thousand poems. These poems were subsequently divided into two matching sets of fifteen hundred "rounds" and judged by a group of ten eminent poets, headed by Shunzei. It was the biggest uta-awase in the history of Japanese poetry.[25]

Even on this famous occasion, the comments made by the judges when revealing their choices of the winning or losing poems (or the reasons for calling a tie) were seldom persuasive and occasionally, no doubt because of the pressure of such a huge competition, the judges seemed to misunderstand the poems.[26] One example, round 221, may suggest the manner in which the poems were judged. It is of special interest because the judge, Shunzei, obliquely refers to his predicament in judging his own son's composition.

LEFT

asahikage	In morning sunlight,
nioeru yama no	Glowing along the mountains,
sakurabana	The cherry blossoms—
tsurenaku kienu	I thought they might be snow that
yuki ka to zo miru	Had stubbornly refused to melt.

ARIIE

RIGHT

sakurabana	The cherry blossoms
utsurou haru wo	Have passed through so many springs,

amata hete	Blooming and fading,
mi sae furinuru	And even I have grown old
asajiu no yado	In my cogon-thatched cottage.[27]

TEIKA

[Judge's comment] The left poem is given great charm by the placement of "morning sunlight" at the head and by the elegance conjured up by the words "had stubbornly refused to melt." As for the right poem, perhaps parental affection has blinded me, or it may be that commiseration induces me to favor "have passed through so many springs" and "even I have grown old"; but all the same, when I think how, if the "evening crane of long ago" were still alive, he might feel about the "morning sunlight" of the left poem, I am at a loss to decide which poem should win, and perhaps the best I can do is to call it a tie.[28]

A modern commentator, if asked to judge the comparative merits of the two poems, might also have trouble deciding the winner, though not for Shunzei's reasons. Ariie's poem, later incorporated in the *Shin Kokinshū*, is the more polished, but the poet's momentary uncertainty as to whether he saw cherry blossoms or snow is all too apt to make the reader recall (without pleasure) a mannerism of the *Kokinshū*, and the first two lines, especially admired by Shunzei, were borrowed virtually unchanged from the *Man'yōshū*.[29] The most memorable part of Shunzei's judgment is his avowal that partiality for his son makes him want to judge that Teika's poem is the winner; but, if Ariie's father, the late Fujiwara no Shigeie,[30] were still alive, he too would want his son to win. The safest policy, then, was to declare the match a draw.[31]

Shunzei's best-known comment made in his capacity as the judge of an uta-awase was pronounced during the competition in six hundred rounds of 1193. He awarded victory to this winter poem by Fujiwara no Yoshitsune:

mishi aki wo	In this grassy field,
nani ni nokosan	What can bring back traces of
kusa no hara	The autumn I saw?
hitotsu ni kawaru	The landscape of the meadows
nobe no keshiki ni	Has turned a single color.

Shunzei of course recognized the allusion to *The Tale of Genji* in the words *kusa no hara* (fields of grass),[32] and declared that it lent

Yoshitsune's poem special charm. He added, "Murasaki Shikibu was even more extraordinary as a writer [of prose] than as a poet,[33] and among the chapters of her book 'The Flower Feast' has special charm. It is shocking for anyone to write poetry without knowing *Genji*."[34] Shunzei's comment is of interest because it reveals his great love for *The Tale of Genji*, but it does not help us much to understand the merits of Yoshitsune's poem. The same might be said of most of the comments made by judges of uta-awase, but they were of great importance to members of the court whose lives were consecrated to the perfection of their poetry.

Poetic Sequences

Another important source of poems for the *Shin Kokinshū* was the series of poetic sequences submitted in response to imperial commands. The practice of individual poets' composing sets of poems, usually one hundred poems (*hyakushu*) on prescribed topics, went back as far as the tenth century, but it first acquired importance—indeed, became something of a craze—as the result of the extremely favorable impression produced by the sets of hundred-poem sequences composed at the court of the Emperor Horikawa early in the twelfth century.[35] These sequences were organized along the lines of the imperially sponsored anthologies: seasonal poems were followed by poems on love and these in turn by poems on various other subjects. The particular novelty of the sequences associated with the Emperor Horikawa was the adoption of set topics for each poem. The poems submitted all bore titles—not merely "Spring Poem" but such topics associated with spring as "Young Shoots," "Remaining Snow," "Plum Blossoms," "Geese Returning Home," and so on.[36]

The arrangement of poems within a given section of a poetic sequence followed the pattern Konishi Jin'ichi called "association and progression."[37] "Association" implied a smoothly flowing series of poems, each independent but linked to the poem before and the poem after by associations of imagery or language; "progression" refers to the temporal progression of the seasons within a sequence, flowers appearing in the order in which they bloom, and love poems being arranged to suggest the course of a love affair, from the first awakening of interest to the bitter realization that the affair is over. Another aspect of the arrangement was the deliberate mixing of poems of greater and lesser degrees of emotional or literary intensity in order to avoid monotony.[38] The principle of "association and progression" would be followed in the arrangement of the poems in the *Shin Kokinshū*.

Gotoba and the Compilation of the *Shin Kokinshū*

Sometime about the middle of the year 1200 the Retired Emperor Gotoba invited some twenty poets to submit for his approbation hundred-poem sequences. Gotoba was only twenty at the time. He was the fourth son of the Emperor Takakura, and there had seemed to be little likelihood that he would ever ascend the throne, but his oldest brother, the Emperor Antoku, and his second brother were both carried off by the Taira when they fled the capital in 1183. As we have seen, Antoku perished at Dannoura; the second brother eventually became a Buddhist priest. A passage in *The Tale of the Heike* relates how, just as Gotoba was being taken from the capital to join his brothers in the western provinces, his escort was stopped by an official who was aware that if the child remained in the capital he might become the next emperor.[39] The official's premonition proved to be correct, but there was another step before Gotoba was chosen: when the Retired Emperor Goshirakawa was debating whether to put on the throne the third or the fourth son of Takakura, he called them to his side. The third son looked reluctant and burst into tears. He was accordingly dismissed, but when the retired emperor called Gotoba, he unhesitantly went to his grandfather and sat on his lap.[40] That (plus some divination) decided Goshirakawa in favor of the fourth prince.

Gotoba was officially proclaimed emperor in 1183 even though his brother Antoku was still alive, and even though for the first time in "eighty-two generations" an accession ceremony was performed without the Three Sacred Treasures of the imperial regalia.[41] There is little to report on the sixteen years of Gotoba's reign, partly because of his youth, partly because power in Kyoto was exercised by Goshirakawa and by Minamoto no Michichika (1149–1202), a poet and high-ranking noble.[42]

It is strange, considering Gotoba's later development as a poet of exceptional ability, that not a single poem survives from his years on the throne. He apparently spent his time mainly at kemari, rather than at composing poetry, and he also enjoyed playing the flute, hunting, cockfights, dog chasing (*inu-oimono*), wrestling, and the songs of women entertainers.[43] Early in 1198 Gotoba named his eldest son, the future Emperor Tsuchimikado, as crown prince, and abdicated on the same day. His abdication was not occasioned by any sudden realization of the meaninglessness of worldly existence; on the contrary, he seems to have found life as emperor disagreeably constricting, and he abdicated in order to devote himself wholeheartedly to his pleasures.[44] Once he was free of official duties he was like "a fish that has found water." Kemari matches were held in his palace, and many other diversions brightened his days. Gotoba's oldest surviving poem, describing a nostalgic visit to the Imperial Palace when the cherry trees were in bloom, was written in 1199, the year after his abdication.[45] His interest in poetry, once ignited, quickly became a consuming passion. This was the background for the two sessions of solo composition of hundred-poem sequences at the retired emperor's palace in 1200.

Gotoba's command to the outstanding poets of the day to submit hundred-poem sequences was the occasion for a display of bitter rivalry between the two main factions in the world of poetry, the Mikohidari school (including Shunzei, Teika, and other "progressive" poets) and their enemies, the Rokujō family of conservative poets. The latter conspired to keep Teika and other junior members of the Mikohidari faction from participating by obtaining a command from Gotaba specifying that only senior persons (*rōsha*) would be asked to submit sequences. Teika was outraged. He declared in his diary, "In all the history of Japanese poetry, I have never heard of age being considered as a factor of competence. This had all been arranged by Suetsune with his bribes in order to get rid of me."[46] Teika had good reason to suspect that Fujiwara Suetsune (1131–1221) had bribed Michichika: a few months earlier Suetsune had been enraged to hear that Teika had refused to participate in a poem competition because "that fake poet" (*ese utayomi*) was to be the judge.

The only way to get Michichika's decision reversed was by a direct appeal to Gotoba himself. Teika's aged father, Shunzei, accordingly wrote a letter to Gotoba pointing out the lack of any precedent for making age a factor in choosing poets for a gathering. He urged that Teika be invited to participate: he was already close to forty (by Japanese reckoning), and he had demonstrated his ability. Teika was attempting to create a new style of poetry,[47] but the self-styled poets who had slandered him were incapable of going beyond the old, hackneyed traditions. Shunzei wrote, "Of late the people who call themselves poets have all been mediocrities. The poems they compose are unpleasant to hear, wordy and lacking in finesse."[48] He denounced by name Teika's enemy Suetsune, calling him an ignoramus, and urged Gotoba not to be misled by his machinations. He asked that not only Teika but two other poets, Fujiwara Takafusa and Fujiwara Ietaka, be added to the list of poets invited to compose hundred-poem sequences. Shunzei's letter concluded with the assurance that he did not make these recommendations because of fatherly love but because he believed that appointing

Teika would prove to be of benefit to the world and to Gotoba in particular.[49]

Gotoba was moved by Shunzei's appeal, both because of its intrinsic merits and because Shunzei was old and respected; he agreed to ask Teika (and the two others) to submit hundred-poem sequences.[50] Needless to say, Teika was overjoyed to learn that he had been included among the participants. He attributed this development not only to his father's intercession but to the gods, and four days later went to worship at the Kitano Shrine, sacred to Sugawara no Michizane, the god of literature, and offered a scroll of his poems by way of thanks.[51]

During the next ten days Teika worked frantically on his poetic sequence. He took eighty of the assigned hundred poems to his father and asked for his suggestions. Shunzei found nothing to correct, and urged Teika to submit the poems as soon as possible. Two days later he presented the hundred poems to Gotoba, who had been impatiently waiting for them. On the following day Teika received a letter informing him that Gotoba had permitted him to enter the imperial presence. Teika wrote in his diary, "It is not surprising, after all, that I should be admitted to the palace at this point, nor is it anything I had my heart set upon. But that the privilege should be conferred on the basis of my hundred-poem sequence—this is a great honor for the art of Poetry and a beautiful and inspiring story to pass on to future generations. My gratification is unbounded. This incident shows better than anything else that a revival of poetry has taken place."[52] The hundred-poem sequences composed in 1200 would prove second only to the uta-awase in 1,500 rounds as a source of poems for the *Shin Kokinshū*.[53]

Recognition by Gotoba was immensely gratifying to Teika, and the latter's counsels fostered Gotoba's burgeoning poetic talent. Teika's hundred-verse sequence reveals him at the height of his powers, although the poems have not enjoyed the popularity of those included in other collections.[54] Teika was not asked to compose poems for the second set of poetic sequences compiled that year, presumably because the number of participants was much reduced. He and Gotoba remained on excellent terms, and Gotoba showed himself to be an unusually apt pupil. He began to attend uta-awase sessions, often those staged before a portrait of Hitomaro, the most revered of the Japanese poets.[55] On such occasions Gotoba regularly concealed the authorship of his poems, signing them with a pseudonym in order to permit free criticism.

In the seventh month of 1201 Gotoba, following the practice of the Emperor Murakami who in 951 had established a Poetry Bureau (*waka dokoro*) by way of preparation for compiling the anthology *Gosenshū*, created a Poetry Bureau in the Nijō Palace, the first step toward compiling the *Shin Kokinshū*.[56] During the next few years fresh excitement was imparted to the regular uta-awase sessions by the possibility that poems composed on these occasions might be included in the new court anthology. In 1202 alone there were a dozen or so major poetry competitions held at Gotoba's palace. Gotoba's progress as a poet was little short of astonishing: in 1202, a bare two years after taking up the composition of poetry, he wrote this poem for a competition:

uguisu no	The uguisu
nakedomo imada	Has begun to sing but still
furu yuki ni	In the falling snow
sugi no ha shiroki	The cedar needles are white
Ausaka no yama[57]	At Ausaka Mountain.

The contrast between the uguisu's song, heralding the spring, and the snow falling on the green cedars is a graceful variation on a *Kokinshū* poem, but superior in its imagery.[58] Gotoba was qualified now not only to command the compilation of a court anthology but to contribute to its contents.

Contents of the *Shin Kokinshū*

The 1,981 poems of the *Shin Kokinshū* are divided in the traditional manner into twenty books of which six are devoted to the seasons; one each to poems of congratulations, condolences, separation, and travel; five to love; three to miscellaneous topics; and, finally, one each to Shintō and Buddhism. Following the model of the *Kokinshū*, the collection has two prefaces, one in Japanese by Fujiwara Yoshitsune, the other in Chinese by the Confucian scholar Fujiwara Chikatsune (1151–1210). The poems included were not restricted to works composed during the period of the compilation: poems that had already appeared in chokusenshū were excluded, but some poems from the *Man'yōshū* (not a chokusenshū) were chosen, as were many works by poets of the *Kokinshū* era. It is nonetheless customary to speak of a "*Shin Kokinshū* style" pervading the entire collection because the compilers chose poetry from the past as well as from the present that best suited the tastes of their generation.

When the Retired Emperor Gotoba toward the end of 1201 officially decided to sponsor a chokusenshū, he appointed an editorial committee of six men: Minamoto Michitomo, Fujiwara Ariie, Fujiwara Teika, Fujiwara Ietaka, Fujiwara Masatsune, and the Buddhist priest Jakuren. Jakuren died in the following year but was not replaced. We know quite a bit about the manner in which the committee went about its task thanks to two diaries, Teika's *Meigetsuki* (Chronicle of the Bright Moon) and the diary of Minamoto Ienaga.[59] We know, for example, that there was debate over the name of the new anthology; it was agreed that the name should refer to the *Kokinshū*, the collection it emulated, but not for several years did the compilers settle on *Shin Kokinshū*. In the meantime, they had made good progress with the task of selecting and arranging poems in the twenty books of the new anthology.

Both Chinese and Japanese prefaces to the *Shin Kokinshū* contain much the same information: a traditional account of the history of the waka, related with the utmost brevity; a statement of the policy followed in selecting poems for inclusion; and an explanation of how it came about that poems by Gotoba, who had commanded the compilation, were included, although the compilers of the *Kokinshū* had not included poems by the emperor, who had issued a similar command. Both prefaces, in describing Gotoba's injunctions to the editors, state that he urged them to choose superior poems without respect to the social status of the poets. Naturally, this was not interpreted as meaning that the editors should search for suitable poems composed by soldiers, artisans, or peasants; in practice, it meant little more than that a small number of anonymous poems (some borrowed from the *Man'yōshū*) and a few more by priests not of the highest social station were included in a collection that otherwise consisted almost entirely of poetry composed by aristocrats of impeccable lineage. Perhaps the *Shin Kokinshū* suffers when compared to the *Man'yōshū* because the backgrounds and experiences of its poets were so similar, but it is the ultimate achievement of Japanese court poetry, and the aesthetic that colors its expression would become that of Japanese poets of future centuries, even those far removed from the world evoked by its poets.

The *Shin Kokinshū*, as its name indicates, stands in the direct line of the *Kokinshū*. Many poems derived their inspiration from honka in the earlier collection, and some of the mannerisms—such as the disproportionate attention given to snow, the moon, and cherry blossoms among the sights of nature—were taken over without question by the *Shin Kokinshū* poets.[60] This meant that the images of many *Shin Kokinshū* poems hardly differ from those in the *Kokinshū*. If the poets had been satisfied with creating no more than an elegant pastiche of poems in the manner of the *Kokinshū*, they no doubt could have done this so skillfully that it would be difficult to tell the new from the old; but although the *Shin Kokinshū* poets invariably spoke with reverence of the *Kokinshū*, they were aware that they lived in times quite dissimilar to the golden age of the emperors Daigo and Murakami and knew that their poetry would inevitably reflect the changes. The differences between their collection and the *Kokinshū* would not be of imagery but of mood, of outlook on the world; the *Kokinshū* poets savored their gentle melancholy, but the *Shin Kokinshū* poets expressed an intensity of grief that sometimes approached despair.

The *Shin Kokinshū* poets might have looked back to the age of the *Kokinshū* with envy, in the manner that Japanese poets often recalled the past, but despite the sadly changed circumstances of their world, they believed that they lived in an age of a great revival of the waka. The Japanese preface concluded,

> If one looks down on what one actually sees with one's eyes and reveres excessively the reports that reach one's ears, one will feel ashamed before the old writings; but we have followed the mainstream of poetry back to its sources, and have striven to revive this never-ending art. Frosts may succeed dews again and again, but this collection will not disappear; no matter how many autumns follow springs, it will remain bright and unclouded as the moon. We who are fortunate enough to be alive for this occasion rejoice that the work is completed. Will not future generations of people who honor the way of poetry envy us today?[61]

This confidence was justified by the extraordinary quality of the collection. The first poem in the *Shin Kokinshū* is by the Regent and Prime Minister Fujiwara Yoshitsune, and this is followed by poems by the Retired Emperor Gotoba, Princess Shokushi, Kunaikyō, Shunzei, and the priests Shun'e and Saigyō—a dazzling array. With the possible exception of the *Man'yōshū*, no collection contains waka poetry of this quality.

In 1205 a banquet was held to celebrate the completion of the *Shin Kokinshū*. Such festivities were a departure from tradition—no banquet was held for the *Kokinshū* or *Gosenshū*—but Gotoba was eager for a celebration, and it was possible to cite as a precedent the banquet that commemorated the completion of the *Nihon Shoki* some five hundred years before.[62] Teika, annoyed that tradition had been violated, did not attend, giving as his excuse that he was still in mourning for his father,

Shunzei, who had died in the previous year. On this occasion Fujiwara Ariie read aloud the Chinese preface for the *Shin Kokinshū*, written as if by Gotoba himself, though it was in fact by Fujiwara Chikatsune.[63] An elaborate ceremony of poetry reading and music followed.

Teika, who learned what occurred from someone who had been present, commented sourly in his diary, "What was the point of holding such a ceremony? It was not in accordance with precedents. It was suddenly arranged and everything was at cross purposes. The poets were not even poets. The choice was most peculiar."[64] Teika's remark that the "poets were not even poets" refers to the circumstance that four of the twenty poets who attended the banquet, members of the defeated Rokujō faction, had not had a single poem included in the *Shin Kokinshū*. The Japanese preface was unfortunately not ready in time for the celebration,[65] but Gotoba composed a poem expressing satisfaction with his achievement in having commissioned such a splendid anthology, likening himself to the Emperor Daigo who "mindful of the past and desiring to revive the ancient ways" had commanded the compilation of the *Kokinshū*.[66]

Although the banquet ostensibly signified the completion of the *Shin Kokinshū*, editorial work continued until late in 1210, and years later, while Gotoba was an exile in the Oki islands, he completely revised the text, eliminating nearly four hundred poems. But it is usual to say that the *Shin Kokinshū* was completed in 1205, if only because that makes it exactly three hundred years after the completion of the *Kokinshū*.

Fujiwara Teika (1162–1241)

One great *Shin Kokinshū* poet, Fujiwara Teika, was missing from the opening cluster of poets, but his first poem, the thirty-eighth in the collection, set the tone of the entire work and typifies the waka of its age:

haru no yo no	When the floating bridge
yume no ukihashi	Of dreams of a night in spring
todae shite	Was interrupted,
mine ni wakaruru	In the sky a bank of clouds
yokogumo no sora	Was taking leave of the peak.

Teika's poem is found in a section of the first book of the *Shin Kokinshū* devoted to sights of early spring, but commentators agree that, despite the imagery drawn from nature, the poem is not about the seasons but about love. The poet awakes at dawn from a dream. We are not told the content of the dream, but the tone of the poem strongly suggests that it was romantic. Awakening, he feels a poignant sense of separation (perhaps from a woman he met in the dream), and when he looks outside he sees in the dawn sky a bank of clouds separating from the peak, an echo in nature of his own experience. The "floating bridge of dreams" was the name of the last chapter in *The Tale of Genji*, in which the lovers Kaoru and Ukifune are separated forever. The term appears elsewhere in literature of the time, with overtones of an important experience coming to an end, causing the writer to reflect on the transience of the world. It is twice used in this sense by Minamoto Michichika in his diaries to describe his feelings, once when the Emperor Takakura abdicated after a short reign, and later when he saw the emperor lying on his deathbead.[67]

The last two lines of Teika's poem borrowed from earlier poems. The *honka* is believed to be the poem by Mibu no Tadamine in the *Kokinshū*:

kaze fukeba	Like a white cloud that
mine ni wakaruru	Has been cut loose from the peak
shirakumo no	By the blowing wind,
taete tsurenaki	Has your heart, cut off from me,
kimi ga kokoro ka[68]	Turned completely unfeeling?

The second line of this poem is identical with the fourth line of Teika's. A poem by Fujiwara Ietaka on the theme of "a spring dawning" (also included in the *Shin Kokinshū*) is even closer:

kasumi tatsu	Swathed in the spring mist
Sue no Matsuyama	Mount Pine-to-the-End is now
honobono to	Faintly visible,
nami ni wakaruru	In the sky a bank of clouds
yokokumo no sora[69]	Is taking leave of the waves.

It seems probable that Teika derived the last line and a half of his poem from the above poem by his friend Ietaka. Although his practice of borrowing from the poetry of contemporaries violated his own prohibition,[70] this is not only Teika's most famous poem, but the best known of all *Shin Kokinshū* poems.[71] The two source poems are both of exceptional quality, but read in conjunction with Teika's it is at once apparent why they never acquired its fame: for all their beauty, they lack the mysterious depth in Teika's waka that for centuries has intrigued readers and induced scholars to supply explanations. The contemporary poet Tsukamoto Kunio wrote about the poem,

> The clouds of a spring night that lie on the peak are at once a landscape and a bridge joining the worlds of the dream and of reality. No harm is done by inferring that the poem hints at a lovers' parting at dawn, but one should keep this at a barely perceptible level, the last of the last. . . . With respect to the neologism "the floating bridge of dreams," it is customary to cite the name of the last chapter of *The Tale of Genji*, but more theories than one can count on the fingers of both hands have been advanced concerning the term; in this instance, too, it is quite sufficient if, with the utmost caution, one bears this theory in mind. Of greater importance than the sources is the question of how the words of the poem have been given life, and how the image of the bridge has always been used to symbolize the route connecting this shore to the far shore. The figure of speech "the floating bridge," necessitated by "clouds," resonates mutually with *todae shite* [was interrupted].[72]

Tsukamoto provided a necessary corrective to the tendency to "explain" *Shin Kokinshū* poems in terms of their sources or their hidden meanings. As a poet, Tsukamoto was especially sensitive to the effects created by the placement of words and their sounds, quite apart from their ultimate sources. Even if Teika had borrowed every single word in this poem, the combination of images and sounds was uniquely his own; and the epiphany he experienced on seeing the bank of clouds in the dawn sky, rather than any hidden reference to a lovers' parting, gave immortality to his poem.

Another poem by Teika conveys, perhaps even better than his poem on the "floating bridge of dreams," the lonely beauty evoked by the word *sabi*,[73] an aesthetic ideal that became prominent from this time:

miwataseba	In this wide landscape
hana mo momiji mo	There are no cherry blossoms
nakarikeri	And no colored leaves;
ura no tomoya no	Evening in autumn over
aki no yūgure[74]	A straw-thatched hut by the bay.

The source of Teika's poem is the "Akashi" chapter of *The Tale of Genji*. Genji, staying at the house of the former governor of Akashi after his lonely exile at Suma, is delighted by the landscape, which suits his mood exactly.

> In the wide, unbroken view over the seacoast, the exuberant foliage under the trees seemed even more captivating than the full brilliance of cherry blossoms in the spring or colored leaves in the autumn.[75]

Although Teika probably had this passage in mind when he composed his poem, the effect is diametrically dissimilar. Genji is enchanted by a brilliance of color that seems to him (at least at this moment) even more captivating than the conventionally admired sights of nature; but Teika's attention is caught not by foliage that rivals in color the sights of spring and autumn but by a monochrome landscape—a wretched hut in the growing dark of an autumn day. The intent was certainly not parody of *The Tale of Genji*, but there could not be a more striking contrast between the charm of the original and the sabi of Teika's poem.[76]

Teika was one of the handful of undoubtedly great Japanese poets, but he does not inspire the affection we feel toward Hitomaro, Saigyō, or Bashō, an affection that makes us want to know every detail of their lives. He was unwaveringly aristocratic in his tastes and (especially in later years) extremely conservative in his views on poetry.[77] His famous declaration (found in his diary, *Chronicle of the Bright Moon*) that "the red banners and the expeditions against the traitors are no concern of mine"[78] has been interpreted as an expression of the poet's determination to maintain his integrity in the face of sordid conflicts, but it is hard not to catch overtones of aristocratic disdain for matters (like warfare) that concern only the lower classes.

Although Teika's diary abounds in mentions of sickness, suggesting that he suffered from a delicate constitution, he was unusually long-lived, and evidently had a fierce temper.[79] In 1185 he had a quarrel with a junior official named Minamoto Masayuki whom he accused of having insulted him. The quarrel is described in *Gyokuyō* (Jeweled Leaf), the diary kept between 1164 and 1200 by Fujiwara Kanezane (1149–1207): "It has been reported that on the night of the rehearsal of the Gosechi dances in the presence of His Majesty,[80] a quarrel took place between the lesser general Masayuki and the chamberlain Teika. In the course of making some sneering remarks, Masayuki became quite disorderly. Teika, unable to control his indignation and disgust, struck Masayuki with a lantern. Some people say he hit him in the face. Because of this incident, Teika's name was removed from the palace register.[81] Teika was restored to the ranks of those permitted to present themselves at the palace the next year, after his father, Shunzei, had written a letter pleading that Teika be forgiven because of his youth.

Among the earliest surviving poems by Teika are hundred-verse sequences he contributed in 1189 to two poetry gatherings. He was also selected to compose poems to ornament the screens presented to Ninshi, the daughter of Fujiwara Kanezane, when she became the consort of the Emperor Gotoba. Clearly, his talent as a poet had been recognized, but he was slow in rising in the hierarchy. His disappointment when he discovered in 1187 that, once again, he had been passed over for promotion in the spring list is suggested by this poem:

toshi furedo	Another year gone by
kokoro no haru wa	And still no spring warms my heart,
yoso nagara	It's nothing to me
nagamenarenuru	But now I am accustomed
akebono no sora[82]	To stare at the sky at dawn.

This kind of poem was called jukkai, a poem complaining about some personal grievance, a subject for poetry first admitted to poetry competitions in the twelfth century. As this example suggests, the grievance is not baldly stated. The "sky at dawn" probably refrs to the statement at the opening of *The Pillow Book of Sei Shōnagon* that "in spring it is the dawn that is most beautiful," but the coming of spring brings Teika no joy. The cause of Teika's discontent is not mentioned, but failure to gain promotion was a typical theme of jukkai poems.

In 1190 Teika was promoted for the first time in ten years. His joy was short-lived: in the following month the great poet Saigyō, who had always encouraged Teika, died on his travels. Teika wrote a poem of mourning:

mochizuki no	Just as he desired,
koro wa tagawanu	A full moon was in the sky
sora naredo	When he passed away,
kieken kumo no	But how sad to trace the cloud
yukue kanashi na[83]	To the place where it vanished.

That autumn the regent and prime minister, Fujiwara Yoshitsune, summoned poets to a gathering at which hundred-verse sequences were to be presented. In a marked departure from tradition, there were only two topics of poetry for each sequence—fifty poems each on the moon and on cherry blossoms—and the sequences were accordingly known as *Kagetsu Hyakushu* (One Hundred Poems on Blossoms and the Moon). The choice of these topics indicated that the poems composed at this gathering were dedicated to the memory of Saigyō, whose greatest joy was cherry blossoms, and who never wearied of celebrating the beauty of the moon. Some of the best of Teika's early poetry is found among the poems composed on this occasion, including:[84]

hana no ka wa	Only the fragrance,
kaoru bakari wo	Still pervasive, indicates
yukue tote	Where the blossoms went:
kaze yori tsuraki	The dark of the evening sky
yūyami no sora	Is harder to bear than the wind.

This poem presents problems at different levels.[85] The first is that cherry blossoms have no scent. Since the variety of blossoms is not specified, some critics have assumed that Teika was describing plum blossoms, whose scent is the subject of innumerable poems.[86] This is plausible, but if the flowers mentioned in only one poem of the sequence of fifty were plum blossoms rather than cherry blossoms, it would distrupt the harmony of the sequence and run counter to the underlying theme of the poems. This poem must also be about cherry blossoms, even though they have no scent; a poetic, rather than a botanical, logic is involved. The importance of the scent to the poem is underlined by the repetition (contrary to normal waka practice) of near synonyms, *ka*, meaning "scent," and *kaoru*, meaning "to be fragrant," in successive lines. The statement that the evening sky is "harder to bear than the wind" is puzzling, especially since we have been told nothing about the wind. The poem might be spelled out: "The cherry blossoms have all been blown away by the wind, leaving only their scent to suggest the direction in which they were carried off. The sky has grown dark, making it even harder to see where the blossoms might have gone; this darkness is harder to bear than the wind."

The poem is certainly beautiful, evoking through sight (the falling blossoms in the twilight), touch (the wind), and smell (the fragrance of the blossoms) a late-spring scene. But was that all Teika had in mind? The poet Andō Tsuguo was the first to suggest that the flowers in the poem referred to Saigyō;[87] in that case, it describes Teika's loneliness after Saigyō "disappeared," blown off by the wind of death, leaving only the fragrance of his poetry in the dark. Interpreted in these terms, the poem becomes doubly interesting. But was that in fact Teika's intent? We shall probably never know.

The difficulty of the poems Teika wrote as a young man earned them the nickname of *daruma-uta*, or Zen poems, implying that they were as arcane as the sayings of the Zen masters. Later in his career, after Teika had become conspicuously more conservative, his poems were much easier to understand, but the daruma-uta, long deplored by critics, have a special appeal for poets today because they convey philosophical ideas within the thirty-one syllables of a waka by means of symbolist imagery.[88]

Teika's experiments at this time included an enlargement of the subject matter of the waka to include themes that hitherto had been treated only in Chinese poetry: toward the end of 1191 Fujiwara Yoshitsune convened a poetry gathering at which poets were asked to compose one hundred poems on ten themes including "animals," "birds," and "insects." These themes had hitherto been treated by Chinese poets, who were not restricted in their subject matter, but rarely appear in the waka;[89] so it was natural for Teika to have turned to Chinese poetry for precedents when composing poetry about such unpoetic animals as bears, monkeys, wild boars, and sheep. His poem on a tiger, the last of the sequence of ten animal poems, had a double meaning:

takayama no	The path taken by
mine fuminarasu	The tiger cub as it climbs
tora no ko no	With powerful tread
noboran michi no	To the mountain peak stretches
sue zo harukeki[90]	Far out into the distance.

This is definitely not one of Teika's masterpieces, but it does suggest an attempt to expand the horizons of the waka poet. It also has an allegorical meaning: Teika is congratulating the tiger cub (his host, Yoshitsune) on his success in climbing up the high mountain (the ranks of the nobility) to his present position, and is further predicting that his prospects are limitless.[91]

Another of Teika's experiments inspired by Yoshitsune involved expanding the vocabulary of the waka. In later years Teika would be known as an uncompromising exponent of the traditional poetic diction—essentially, the vocabulary of the poetry in the *Kokinshū*—but when a messenger came from Yoshitsune with the request that Teika compose a set of poems each of which began with a different member of the kana syllabary, he immediately rose to the challenge, though this involved using words not sanctioned by earlier poetic practice. The main problem was the need to begin poems with the *ra, ri, ru, re, ro* of the syllabary. No native Japanese word begins with these sounds, and Teika therefore had to use words of Chinese origin, some of them technical terms of Buddhism. These poems were hardly more than a display of virtuosity, and the non-native elements of vocabulary did not figure in Teika's later works, but he had demonstrated that a few words of foreign origin did not destroy the lyric beauty of a waka.[92] Teika's later opposition to untraditional language would, however, be one of the causes of the establishment of a poetic diction that was observed by most waka poets until well into the nineteenth century.

Yoshitsune seems to have enjoyed testing Teika's powers of improvisation. In 1192, when Teika visited his house, Yoshitsune suddenly asked him to compose thirty-three poems, each one beginning with a syllable from a certain poem by the priest Sosei in the *Kokinshū*.[93] Teika not only complied without hesitation, but composed all thirty-three poems about autumn, since that was the season, and many of these poems are of exceptional pictorial beauty.[94] In 1196 Yoshitsune asked Teika to compose 128 poems, each of which concluded with one of the 128 characters used for rhymes in Chinese poetry. It goes without saying that Teika responded brilliantly to the challenge.[95]

Of greater lasting importance than these experiments was the uta-awase held at Yoshitsune's house in 1193. Late in 1192 Yoshitsune asked twelve poets each to compose a hundred-verse sequence. Teika's mother died in the spring of the next year, and Teika attempted to withdraw, but Yoshitsune insisted. The twelve hundred poems were all assembled by the autumn of that year and were then paired off into the six hundred rounds of a poem competition. The poets included the host, Yoshitsune, his uncle Jien, Teika, Jakuren, and various younger poets of the Mikohidari school as well as poets of the rival Rokujō school. Shunzei was the judge, and the standards set by the competition were unusually high.[96]

Teika's success as a poet seemed assured when he and the others of the Mikohidari school suffered a setback from a quite unexpected quarter. Minamoto Yoritomo, the shogun, had a daughter called Ōhime whom he decided he would marry off to the finest man in Japan—that is, the emperor himself. It occurred to him that the best way of approaching the youthful Emperor Gotoba (who was sixteen at the time) was through the poet and courtier Minamoto Michichika, whose wife had been Gotoba's wet nurse. Up until this time Yoritomo had been friendly with Fujiwara Kanezane, the kampaku,[97] but he now seemed to favor Michichika, Kanezane's bitter rival. This gave Michichika the chance to persuade Gotoba that Kanezane was incompetent and to replace him in 1196 with a man of his own faction. The repercussions of political change were extended to the world of poetry: the Mikohidari school, associated with Kanezane's family, was displaced at the court by the conservative Rokujō school, and the brilliant gatherings at Fujiwara Yoshitsune's salon ended. Only two poems by Teika survive from 1197, unmistakable evidence of the difficulty he experienced in composing in the hostile atmosphere of the new régime.

At the end of 1197 Teika was summoned from this spiritual banishment by a request from the Cloistered Prince Shukaku, who was resident at the Ninna-ji, a Shingon temple in the northwest of the capital. Teika recorded in his diary,

> Jakuren came. He had gone to see the prince at the Ninna-ji at the latter's request on the first. The prince informed him that he would like to have a session of fifty-poem sequences and asked him to inform Teika and his father that he wished them to participate. Although I felt very hesitant, considering the times, once I heard this request I accepted without condition. A request from the prince is not at all like a request from a stranger.[98]

A manuscript of the poems in Teika's hand survives, together with corrections in another hand, presumably Shunzei's. Most of the poems were submitted more or less in their original form, but some were replaced, suggesting that Teika had taken adverse criticism to heart. The quality is remarkably good: six of his fifty poems would be incorporated in the *Shin Kokinshū*, including:

ōzora wa	The wide heavens are
ume no nioi ni	Misted over with the scent
kasumitsutsu	Of the plum blossoms:
kumori mo hatenu	The moon of a night in spring
haru no yo no tsuki[99]	Not quite obscured by the clouds.

and

shimo mayou	Spring rain is falling
sora ni shioreshi	On the wings of the wild geese
karigane no	As they return north,
kaeru tsubasa ni	Wings that drooped when they struggled
harusame zo furu[100]	Through a sky laden with frost.

The poem on the "floating bridge of a spring night," discussed above, was also included.

The poetry gathering at the Ninna-ji, like the hundred-poem sequences of 1200, was a direct predecessor of the *Shin Kokinshū*. In between the two events an important political change occurred, Gotoba's abdication in favor of his three-year-old son, Tsuchimikado. This should have given even greater power to Michichika, who was related to the new emperor on his mother's side (and who himself was often referred to as Tsuchimikado Michichika); but Gotoba intended to rule as a retired emperor, and showed himself increasingly independent of Michichika, finally restoring Yoshitsune to power by appointing him as regent in 1202. In the meantime, as has been related, Gotoba had begun to manifest an extraordinary interest in composing poetry. The celebrated uta-awase in fifteen hundred rounds was held in 1201. Teika, whose poetic genius had been recognized by Gotoba in 1200, the year of the hundred-poem sequences, was now a constant companion to the retired emperor. Fundamentally, however, the two men were not alike in their tastes. Gotoba still enjoyed an evening with prostitutes and *shirabyōshi* (women entertainers), but on such occasions Teika apparently sat in a corner sulking.[101]

Shunzei died in 1204, ninety-one years old by Japanese reckoning. Teika, who wrote many poems mourning the death of his mother, left no poems about Shunzei's death,[102] but remained absorbed with the task of compiling the *Shin Kokinshū*. The sudden death of Yoshitsune in the spring of 1206 seems to have affected Teika more; he composed a number of poems of mourning, including:

tsukihi hete	The months and days pass,
aki no konoha wo	And in the wind that blows through
fuku kaze ni	The leaves of autumn,
yayoi no yume zo	The dream of the third month slips
itodo furiyuku[103]	Farther and farther away.

From this time until about 1220 Teika was at the height of his creative powers. His relations with the imperial court continued to be excellent even though no poem competitions or similar gatherings were held at the court of Tsuchimikado (reigned 1198–1210). Gotoba, who had never much liked his eldest son, replaced him on the throne with his second son, the Emperor Juntoku (reigned 1210–1221). It was a time of unusual poetic activity: although Gotoba himself seemed to have lost interest in composing poetry, Juntoku was an enthusiast for the waka and eagerly participated in poetry sessions held at the palace.[104] Teika and his friend Ietaka were the leading spirits of poetry of the day, and Teika was especially heartened when (in 1207) Minamoto Sanetomo (1192–1219), the youthful shogun, sent him thirty poems for correction. Two years later, in response to Sanetomo's questions about poetry, Teika composed for his benefit *Kindai Shūka* (Superior Poems of Our Time), his first work of criticism.[105] Although Teika and Sanetomo wrote in entirely different manners, Teika recognized the unusual ability of his pupil, as we know from the large number of Sanetomo's poems included by Teika in the court anthology he edited, *Shin Chokusen Waka Shū* (known as the *Shin Chokusenshū*). The contacts that Teika made in this way with the Kamakura shogunate would prove beneficial to his official career in later years.[106]

Sanetomo's natural poetic bent led him back to the *Man'yōshū*, rather than to the more courtly *Kokinshū* or the *Shin Kokinshū*. Teika (perhaps imitating his pupil) turned to the *Man'yōshū* for honka in the poetry he composed at this time, though he did not always seek to emulate the simple strength that Sanetomo found in the old collection. A particularly complex poem among the hundred he composed in 1215 on "famous places" drew on the *Man'yōshū*:

Ikoma yama	At Mount Ikoma
arashi mo aki no	Even the storm winds blow
iro ni fuku	The color of autumn:
tezome no ito no	How sad to twist together
yoru zo kanashiki[107]	Thread I have dyed with my hands.

The honka is this anonymous *Man'yōshū* poem:

Kōchime no	The Kōchi girl
tezome no ito wo	Again and again twists the thread
kurikaeshi	She herself has dyed;
kataito ni aredo	Although the thread is single,[108]
taen to omoeya[109]	There is no fear it will break.

Teika's poem incorporates the imagery of the *Man'yōshū* poem, but changes the mood and the implications. The "color of autumn" is the crimson of autumn leaves, and this leads to the color of the thread spun by the speaker; but *aki* is not only "autumn" but "satiety," suggesting that the speaker fears her lover is weary of her. Again, *yoru* is at once the verb "to twist together" and the noun "night," yielding for the last line the additional meaning "the nights are sad (now that he is weary of me and I am alone)." Perhaps Teika, planning to write about Mount Ikoma, famous for its autumn leaves, thought of Kōchi (more commonly, Kawachi), the general area of the mountain, a place where crafts were early introduced from the continent, and then recalled the *Man'yōshū*.[110]

A poem written in 1216 which also has a honka in the *Man'yōshū*[111] is of similar complexity:

kono hito wo	Waiting for someone
Matsuho no ura no	Who does not come, my heart burns
yūnagi ni	Like seaweed fires
yaku ya moshio no	Smoldering in the calm of dusk
mi mo kogaretsutsu[112]	On the shore of Matsuho.

These poems are unusual in that Teika was describing women of the peasant or fisherfolk class, unlike his usual aristocratic subjects. He rarely left the surroundings of the Imperial Palace and probably knew of such people mainly through the poetry of the *Man'yōshū*.

Teika continued to compose poetry at the palace and seems to have been on unusually good terms with Juntoku, but his relations with Gotoba steadily deteriorated. On the thirteenth day of the second month of 1220 there was an uta-awase at the palace. Teika was invited to participate, but he declined because it was the anniversary of his mother's death and he always spent that day in prayer. Gotoba insisted that he attend, regardless of the circumstances, sending a messenger three times. Teika finally yielded and went to the palace with two poems for the competition. The first bore the title "Moon over the Spring Mountains":

sayaka ni mo	The mountain should be
mirubeki yama wa	Brilliantly clear, but tonight
kasumitsutsu	It is mist-covered;
wa ga mi no hoka mo	The moon of a night in spring
haru no yo no tsuki[113]	Has no connection with me.

It is not difficult, in view of the background, to deduce what Teika had in mind: the mountain, which should be clearly visible on this moonlit night, is blurred because of his tears, and has nothing to do with someone who at heart is in mourning. There is an allusion to a poem by Nakatsukasa in the *Shūishū* in which she says that the moon, which should be brilliantly clear that night, seems blurred because of her tears, a poem very similar to Teika's. It may well be imagined that this poem did not please Gotoba, but Teika's second was even less to his liking. It was called "Willows Beyond the Fields":

michinobe no	Alongside the road,
nohara no yanagi	The willows of the meadows
shita moenu	Have sprouted below.
aware nageki no	Alas, which of us will win
kemuri kurabe ni[114]	This test of burgeoning grief?

The poem compares the willow shoots rising from the ground to the "smoke" (*kemuri*) rising from his breast because of his grief. The poem contains allusions to two poems attributed to Sugawara no Michizane, one included in the *Shin Kokinshū* and the other in *The Great Mirror*. Michizane, it will be remembered, was sent into exile though blameless, and the poems convey his grief. This is the first of the two poems:

michinobe no	The withered willow
kuchiki no yanagi	Standing alongside the road
haru kureba	When spring at last comes
aware mukashi to	Surely must think with longing,
shinobare zo suru[115]	"Ah, how I long for the past!"

The second of Michizane's poems to which Teika alluded appears in *The Great Mirror* with a prefatory note, "On an evening when everything conspired to deepen his gloom, he noticed plumes of smoke here and there in the distance."[116]

yū sareba	The day has ended,
no ni mo yama ni mo	And in the fields and mountains
tatsu keburi	Plumes of smoke arise;
nageki yori koso	Fires burn ever more intense
moemasarikere[117]	Because they feed on my griefs.

By quoting these two poems Teika was in effect comparing himself to Sugawara no Michizane, who was exiled to Kyūshū by a scheming politician. It may easily be imagined how Gotoba reacted to Teika's poems. The diary of the Emperor Juntoku describes the wrath of the retired emperor: at first, Gotoba asked only that Teika be forbidden to appear for the time being at poetry sessions in the palace, but his anger mounted, and he never forgave Teika. Quite different explanations of

Gotoba's anger were given by the novelist Maruya Saiichi. First, he cited the opinion of the *Shin Kokinshū* authority Ishida Yoshisada that the real cause of Gotoba's anger with Teika was the latter's friendly relations with the Kamakura shogunate; the poems merely served to ignite his hostility. Maruya, disagreeing, recalled an incident that appears in Teika's diary for 1213. Because the willows planted in the previous year at Gotoba's Kaya-in Palace had withered, he requisitioned two willow trees that were in Teika's Reizei garden. This angered Teika (as he relates in the diary), and when asked seven years later to compose a poem on willows he may have recalled the incident. The word *keburikurabe* (literally, "a comparison of [the degree of] smoldering") could well apply to the two willows, comparing their unhappiness over being transplanted. This reference may have annoyed Gotoba, but Maruya, after considering these possibilities, concluded that what Gotoba really disliked was not so much any implied meanings to the poems but their gloomy tone, so at variance with the auspicious nature of the occasion.[118]

In 1221 the Jōkyū disturbance, a rebellion headed by Gotoba against the Kamakura shogunate, broke out. The forces of the shogunate easily defeated the imperial rebels in two months of fighting, and the emperors involved (Gotoba, Juntoku, and Tsuchimikado) were exiled to Oki, Sado, and Tosa respectively—the more serious the crime, the more distant the banishment. Teika, though a member of the Kyoto aristocracy, was delighted by the results of the fighting: not only was his enemy Gotoba defeated, but his wife's family, the Saionji, rose to the highest power in Kyoto, and he himself prospered as never before.

Despite this worldly recognition, Teika's activity as a poet markedly diminished; during the ten years following the Jōkyū Rebellion, Teika composed a total of fewer than eighty poems. Early in 1232 he was at last promoted to the position of middle counselor as he had long desired. In the sixth month he was commanded by the emperor to compile singlehandedly a new court anthology, *Shin Chokusenshū*, and subsequently resigned his post as middle counselor to devote himself entirely to the selection of poems for the collection. His final flowering as a poet is found in the hundred-poem sequence he composed in the same year for presentation at the house of the chancellor and minister of the Left, Kujō Norizane. In the poems of this sequence Teika wrote in a simpler style than in his better-known works, as the following may suggest:

niou yori	As soon as it blooms
haru wa kureyuku	The spring approaches its end:
yamabuki no	The yamabuki

hana koso hana no	Flowers are the most disliked
naka ni tsurakere[119]	By all the other flowers.

The poem says that the yamabuki (a yellow flower sometimes called a kerria rose) is disliked by the other flowers because, being the last to bloom, it presages the end of spring. The use of personification gives the comparatively simple conception a certain piquance, but it would be hard to pretend that this was one of Teika's masterpieces.

The editing of the *Shin Chokusenshū* was far from being completed when, in the tenth month of 1232, Teika presented a list of the contents to the Emperor Gohorikawa for his approval. Probably he was aware that the emperor intended to abdicate two days later in favor of his son, the Emperor Shijō, and wished to make the formal presentation while Gohorikawa, who had ordered the collection, was still on the throne. Work continued for another three years, and Teika was besieged by people who wanted their poems included. The completed collection was in any case a disappointment; despite the brilliance of the individual poets, the *Shin Chokusenshū* is in the rather bland manner of Teika's late poetry and has never enjoyed wide popularity.[120] In the next year, following the death in childbirth of the lady she served, Teika's daughter entered orders as a nun. Teika seems to have been shocked by this development; at any rate, he himself took vows as a priest the same year. People flocked to express their grief that Teika had "left the world." Minamoto Ienaga wrote a poem "on hearing of your retreat from the world":

sumizome no	Sleeves layered on sleeves
sode no kasanete	All of them dyed inky black—
kanashiki wa	How sad that the world,
somuku ni soete	Deserted by one, is now
somuku yo no naka	Deserted by another.

Teika replied,

ikeru yo ni	I am delighted
somuku no mi koso	I could desert the world while
ureshikere	I was still alive.
asu to mo matanu	A old man's life is so unsure
oi no inochi wa[121]	He cannot wait the morrow.

During his last years Teika seems to have composed little poetry, but he was otherwise engaged in copying manuscripts, especially of the major works of Heian literature. It is not much of an exaggeration to say that what we know of the literature of Teika's day and earlier is mainly what he thought was worthy of preservation.[122]

One compilation made by Teika about this time (c. 1235) is of special importance, *Hyakunin Isshu*. It was long a matter of debate among scholars whether Teika in fact compiled the collection or whether it was a forgery attributed to him because of his great fame; but it now seems definite that Teika was the compiler, though perhaps one of his sons (or some later person) modified his selection somewhat.[123] These poems constituted the basic knowledge of classical Japanese poetry for most people from the early Tokugawa period until very recent times. Innumerable editions have been published, and a knowledge of the poems was essential in order to play the New Year's game of *karuta* (poem cards).[124] This meant, in a real sense, that Teika was the arbiter of the poetic tastes of most Japanese even as late as the twentieth century. The poems themselves conform in manner and vocabulary to the prescriptions laid down by Teika in *Superior Poems of Our Time*, and for this reason have been subject to attacks by those who feel that the poems insufficiently represent the vast majority of people who lived in Teika's time or that the elegant language conceals a poverty of intellectual content. It can hardly be pretended that all the poems deserve the immortality Teika bestowed on them, but many are fine poems, and his choices do no harm to his reputation as a critic.[125] But, regardless of the merits of the poems, Teika's selection of one hundred poems influenced the aesthetic preferences of Japanese for seven centuries after his death.

Teika's reputation as a poet would not have been much different even if all the poems of the last twenty years of his life had been lost. Gotoba, on the contrary, seems to have attained full maturity as a poet only after suffering the shock of exile. It will be remembered that during the years after the compilation of the *Shin Kokinshū* Gotoba lost interest in poetry, but when he was sent into exile on one of the lonely Oki islands, composing poetry became his greatest distraction and comfort. In the postscript he added to the version of the *Shin Kokinshū* he edited in exile, he wrote that it was easier for him now, when he was a priest and leading a quiet life, to devote himself to poetry than when he was occupied by the business of the court.[126] The poems he wrote during the twenty years of his exile are preserved mainly in such historical works as *The Clear Mirror*. On the way to exile he composed this poem:

tōyamaji	Distant mountain road—
ikue mo kasume	Hide yourself in layers of mist!
sarazu tote	Even if you don't,
ochikatabito no	It's not likely anyone
tou mo nakereba[127]	Will visit me from afar.

The note of self-pity is sounded often, but it is not objectionable because we feel that Gotoba really had reason to feel sorry for himself. When he wrote that he wept, we can be sure that this was no mere figure of speech:

shiokaze ni	More and more distraught
kokoro mo itodo	By the sound of the salt wind,
midare ashi no	My sobs burst from me
ho ni idete nakedo	Like ears on a reed stalk, but
tou hito mo nashi[128]	Nobody comes to ask why.

Most of all, he suffered by being deprived of suitable company, and it made him bitter to think that, for all the professions of loyalty and devotion in the past, nobody came to Oki to see him:

towaruru mo	Getting a letter
ureshiku mo nashi	Does not bring any pleasure—
kono umi wo	It's merely empty
wataranu hito no	Consolation from someone
nage no nasake wa[129]	Who does not dare cross the sea.

Gotoba must have been aware how dangerous it would have been for anyone to attempt to visit him, but this poem (striking in its lack of imagery) seems an unpremeditated outcry of resentment.

While in exile Gotoba also composed a work of poetic criticism, *Gotoba-in Gokuden* (Oral Instructions of the Cloistered Emperor Gotoba), probably about 1225–27. The work was ostensibly intended for beginners in waka, but its most interesting sections are not those concerned with techniques but those that relate Gotoba's opinions of other poets, both predecessors and contemporaries. About half of the second part of the work is devoted to a criticism of Teika. Gotoba recognized that Teika possessed unusual talent, but he dwelt particularly on the serious faults that marred Teika's works. Gotoba's criticism is of interest because of the light it sheds on his relations with Teika, but his accusations are vaguely worded and the essay as a whole does not contribute much to our understanding of poetic practice at the time of the *Shin Kokinshū*.

Saigyō (1118–1190)

At least a half-dozen other *Shin Kokinshū* poets are remembered for their mastery of the waka. The most affecting poems in the collection were perhaps those of Fujiwara Shunzei, but his work has already been discussed in connection with the *Senzaishū*, the imperial collection he edited. The Prime Minister and Regent Fujiwara Yoshitsune (1169–1206), the priest Jien, Princess Shokushi (d. 1201), and Fujiwara Ietaka[130] all composed memorable poems; but one more poet must be treated in detail, Saigyō. Although Saigyō belonged to a somewhat earlier generation than most of the poets of the *Shin Kokinshū*, this is the imperial collection in which he was most fully represented.[131]

Saigyō was born into a distinguished family of the military class, and was known by his lay name, Satō Norikiyo, during the early part of his career, when he served in the guard of the retired emperor. He seems to have won a reputation for martial ability: when (in 1186), long after Saigyō abandoned his lay career and entered orders as a priest in 1140, he met Minamoto Yoritomo, the shogun asked him not only about the art of poetry but about "bows and horses,"[132] evidence that Saigyō was still considered to be an authority on martial matters, despite his long years as a priest.

It is not known why Saigyō, at the early age of twenty-two, decided to abandon a promising career as a soldier and take the vows of a Buddhist priest. It often happens when scholars attempt to explain why men of letters or artists have given up the careers for which they seemed to be intended that they attribute these decisions to disappointed love, most often love for a woman of a higher social station.[133] This explanation of Saigyō's renunciation of the world is found as early as *Gempei Seisuiki*, an account of the warfare between the Taira and the Minamoto compiled about 1250,[134] and is still supported by some scholars.[135] Other sources state that the sudden death of a relative shocked Saigyō into an awareness of the uncertainty of life;[136] and still other evidence suggests that he may have "left the world" out of disgust with the state of the country or perhaps out of sympathy for the Retired Emperor Sutoku, who was forced to abdicate in 1142.[137]

Saigyō was by no means the only young man with a promising future to turn his back on the world. A series of six poems written before he entered the path of the Buddha indicates that his decision was made not in the wake of any one particular disappointment but after long consideration. The first bears the preface, "Along about the time when I made up my mind not to remain in the world, there was a gathering of people at Higashiyama and poems were composed on the theme of 'relating one's griefs in terms of mist.'" Higashiyama referred to the hills in the east of Kyoto where there were (and still are) many Buddhist temples; "mist" was an image associated with spring, but it was sometimes used also with the melancholy overtones of the "mist" rising into the sky after someone has been cremated.

sora ni naru	My mind, uncertain,
kokoro wa haru no	Rises like the mists of spring
kasumi nite	Up into the sky;
yo ni araji to mo	It seems it has decided
omoitatsu kana[138]	Not to remain in this world.

The third poem of the sequence bears the preface, "A long time ago, when I visited the retreat on Higashiyama of the holy man Amida-bō, I composed this poem, feeling moved somehow."

shiba no io to	A hut of brushwood—
kiku wa kuyashiki	The term is unappealing
na naredomo	To hear, but in fact
yo ni konomoshiki	I discovered a dwelling
sumai narikeri[139]	That was truly to my taste.

It is likely that the life of a hermit, secluded from the world in a lonely hut, attracted the young Saigyō (still known as Satō Norikiyo) more than any religious teaching, and induced him to "leave the world." From this time on, the writings of recluses (*inja*) form an important genre, and in this sense Saigyō is closer to the literature of the medieval era than any other *Shin Kokinshū* poet.[140] The particular qualities of his poetry are known by a term that is often mentioned as being characteristic of all Japanese literature and even of all Japanese artistic creation, though it evolved as a touchstone of poetry about this time, and is less typical of Heian civilization—*mujō*, the awareness of the impermanence of all things, a basic Buddhist doctrine. For people of Saigyō's and later times mujō referred especially to the perishability of the works of man; an awareness of this sad truth impelled people to flee human society and take refuge in the mountains and forests where they lived in hermitages. Some, like Saigyō, refused even the comfort of a familiar hut, and spent much of their lives traveling as mendicants to distant parts of the country. Yet even the loneliness of such an existence afforded the possibility of finding beauty, especially in nature. This beauty was often called by another term, wabi,[141] a word related to sabi—the discovery of beauty within the old, the faded, the forlorn.[142] The following poem by Saigyō suggests the quality of wabi:

tou hito mo	A mountain village
omoitaetaru	Where there is not even hope
yamazato no	Of a visitor—
sabishisa nakuba	If not for the loneliness,
sumiukaramashi[143]	How painful life here would be!

Saigyō was a Shingon priest and spent considerable time on Mount Kōya, but he was not attached to any temple; he appears to have lived as a hermit even in such surroundings, rejecting the comfort of joining with others in prayer or of studying together the sacred texts.[144] Kōya seems to have attracted Saigyō especially because of its remoteness from the cities. Each of the ten poems in a series he composed on Kōya and sent to his friend, the priest and poet Jakuzen,[145] opens with the words *yama fukami*, "deep in the mountains." The second of the series is perhaps the most memorable:

yama fukami	The mountains are so deep
maki no ha wakuru	The moonlight as it pierces
tsukikage wa	The black pine needles
hageshiki mono no	Has a fierce intensity
sugoki narikeri[146]	So cold it sends chills through me.

Saigyō seems not to have been interested in the doctrinal differences that separated Shingon from other varieties of Japanese Buddhism; but it was perhaps because of an equation he made in his mind between Dainichi, the central divinity of Shingon Buddhism, and Amaterasu, the chief Shintō goddess, both sun deities, that he was attracted to Ise, where he spent over five years. His first visit to Ise took place soon after he entered the priesthood, and there are scattered references to conversations with Shintō priests in his later poems. Saigyō lamented the sadly deteriorated state of the shrine buildings and the failure of the court for many years to send a princess to serve as the high priestess. His identification with the two religions is most clearly conveyed in a poem that bears the preface, "Composed at the Great Shrine when I visited Ise":

sakakiha ni	By sakaki leaves
kokoro wo kaken	I offer a heartfelt prayer
yū shidete	With cotton streamers,
omoeba kami mo	And the thought occurs to me,
hotoke narikeri[147]	The gods were also buddhas.

In other poems Saigyō revealed even more openly his conviction that the gods of Ise were manifestations in Japan of Dainichi, or Vairochana, the cosmic Buddha. A poem included in the *Senzaishū* bears the preface, "I had grown restless living on Mount Kōya, and went to stay at the Futami Bay in Ise. I was told that the mountain behind the Great Shrine is known as Kamiji, the Path of the Gods. I composed this poem, bearing in mind that the god here is the manifested trace of Dainichi."[148]

Saigyō is known as a great traveler.[149] His journeys seem to have been inspired mainly by the desire to see utamakura, the places that had been described in old poetry, rather than (as one might expect of a priest) the celebrated temples of the country. One journey stands out because it was inspired by a different reason. In 1168, as we have seen, he traveled to the island of Shikoku, mainly to pay his respects at the grave of the former emperor Sutoku. The opening story of Ueda Akinari's celebrated collection *Tales of the Rain and Moon* recounts how Saigyō made his way to the grave and attempted to mollify the ghost of the emperor, still furious over the indignities to which he had been subjected. This story was an invention, but it is true also that for Saigyō, who was close to the exiled emperor, the rebellion marked the end of the world of the Heian aristocrats and the beginning of the domination by the military; when he spoke of the past (*mukashi*), he normally meant the happy days before the rebellion.[150]

Saigyō is known especially for his many poems on cherry blossoms and on the moon,[151] and for his famous last wish (which was ultimately granted) that he might die on a night of the full moon when the cherry blossoms were in bloom. Although both cherry blossoms and the moon were sometimes used allegorically in his poems, it can hardly be doubted that Saigyō delighted in their beauty, and in this respect he may seem disappointingly like the mass of court poets who praised cherry blossoms and the moon as if there were no other attractive sights of nature. However, some of Saigyō's finest poems describe the winter, a season especially conducive to expressions of sabi because its beauty is not of the conventionally admired kind. The following poem appears in the *Shin Kokinshū*:

Tsu no kuni no	Spring in Naniwa
Naniwa no haru wa	In the province of Tsu—
yume nare ya	Was it just a dream?
ashi no kareha ni	The wind crosses over
kaze wataru nari[152]	The withered stalks of rushes.

The desolate wintry scene made Saigyō wonder if this could be the same landscape he had seen in spring sunlight. The scene is lonely, epitomized by the withered stalks, not at all like the fresh green of the reeds for which Naniwa was famous, but it is not devoid of a melancholy beauty. What may be Saigyō's most famous poem describes a lonely scene in autumn:

kokoro naki	Even to someone
mi ni mo aware wa	Free of passions, this sadness
shirarekeri	Would be apparent;
shigi tatsu sawa no	Evening in autumn over
aki no yūgure[153]	A marsh where a snipe rises.[154]

The "someone free of passions" of the poem is probably Saigyō himself, a man who has renounced worldly passions; and the moment when the snipe rises from the marsh, though meaningless in itself, stirs within him a profound emotion that is a response to the essential nature of the scene.

Saigyō himself believed that this was his finest poem, but it was not recognized as such in his time. Fujiwara Shunzei refused to include it in the imperial collection he edited, the *Senzaishū*, to Saigyō's great disappointment. When Saigyō later asked Shunzei to judge a series of thirty-six pairs of his poems, arranged in the form of a poem competition, Shunzei decided that the "rival" poem was superior to this masterpiece.[155] Perhaps the expression of sabi was too far in advance of the tastes of the time; it was not until the commentary on the *Shin Kokinshū* by Tō no Tsuneyori (1401?–1484?) that the deeply moving nature of the poem was fully appreciated,[156] but from that time on it was ranked at the top of Saigyō's oeuvre.

Although his poetry may not have been fully understood in his lifetime, Saigyō's reputation at the time of the compilation of the *Shin Kokinshū* is attested to by the inclusion of more poems by him than by any other poet. Early in his career Teika was encouraged and influenced by Saigyō, and Gotoba praised him more than any other recent poet. Saigyō was also blessed with friends, especially the priests Saiju and Jakuzen. Poems on friendship, so common in China, were rare in Japan, but Saigyō, though at times obsessively desirous of solitude, needed friends, as we can infer from a well-known poem:

sabishisa ni	I wish there were a man,
taetaru hito no	Someone else who can endure
mata mo are na	Loneliness, nearby—
iori naraben	I would build my hut beside his:
fuyu no yamazato[157]	A mountain village in winter.

Saigyō kept acquiring new friends in the centuries that followed. When Bashō in *Oi no Kobumi* (Manuscript in My Knapsack) chose one waka poet to represent the genius of the genre, it was Saigyō; and his journey to the north of Japan in 1689, immortalized by his *Narrow Road of Oku*, was inspired by the travels of Saigyō to that part of the country.[158] All during the journey, Saigyō was never far from Bashō's mind, and he did not overlook a sight mentioned in his poetry. Saigyō's reputation has continued to grow, and many books have been devoted to an appreciation of his poetry and, above all, of the man. The technical excellence of his poetry is generally passed over in silence, as if it were too obvious to merit consideration or else irrelevant to the true importance of Saigyō.[159] His poetry is not typical of the *Shin Kokinshū* as a whole, and admirers of Teika sometimes express no more than condescending interest in Saigyō,[160] but he unquestionably contributed to making the *Shin Kokinshū* the finest of the imperially sponsored collections of poetry.

Notes

1. Kibune Shigeaki, in the afterword to his *Shoku Gosen Waka Shū Zenchūshaku*, p. 458, stated that there were absolutely no commentated editions of the chokusenshū between the *Shin Kokinshū* and the thirteenth. His edition marked a first step at remedying this deficiency. The second to seventh chokusenshū were almost as badly neglected, but the Shin Nihon Koten Bungaku Taikei series has conspicuously changed this situation.
2. I shall refer from this point on to members of the aristocracy without the particle *no* between the surname and the personal name. In the case

of Teika and his father, Shunzei, there is a further problem, the rendition of the name in romanized form. Teika probably referred to himself as Sadaie, and his father probably called himself Toshinari, but the Sino-Japanese versions of their names were used by their contemporaries, and this practice is still observed.

3. Kubota Jun, in *Shin Kokin Kajin no Kenkyū*, pp. 4–5, related why he decided to devote his lengthy book on the *Shin Kokinshū* poets to six men—Fujiwara Teika, his father Shunzei, Fujiwara Ietaka, the priests Saigyō and Jien, and Fujiwara Yoshitsune, the regent and prime minister. He recognized that the Retired Emperor Gotoba, the priest Jakuren, the daughter of Shunzei, and others should not be ignored, but believed that the six poets he had chosen deserved prior treatment. Most other critics who have treated the *Shin Kokinshū* have included Gotoba among the chief poets, but presumably Kubota was evaluating his importance only as a *Shin Kokinshū* poet and not taking into consideration the poems he wrote in exile, his best.

   Princess Shokushi (or Shikishi), though certainly celebrated, figures in surprisingly few of the lists of the "best poets" of the *Shin Kokinshū*.

4. See Robert H. Brower and Earl Miner, *Japanese Court Poetry*, pp. 277–85, for a discussion of rhetoric and syntax in the *Shin Kokinshū*. On p. 278 they give statistics: "only 19 poems in the *Kokinshū* have full stops at the end of the first line and 160 at the end of the third, whereas the *Shinkokinshū* has 108 poems with full stops at the end of the first line and 476 at the end of the third." Even allowing for the fact that the *Shin Kokinshū* contains 1,981 poems as opposed to the 1,111 poems in the *Kokinshū*, the tendency of the former to have breaks at the ends of the first and third lines is unmistakable.
5. See *ibid.*, p. 274.
6. This was true of Chinese poetry too. A poem that lacked the extra dimension provided by allusions to the poetry of the past was likely to be criticized for this reason.
7. See above, pp. 303–4.
8. *Kokinshū* 770. Text in Okumura Tsuneya, *Kokin Wakashū*, p. 262; other English translations by Laurel Rasplica Rodd, *Kokinshū*, p. 270, and by Helen Craig McCullough, *Kokin Wakashū*, p. 169.
9. *Shin Kokinshū* 534. Kubota Jun, *Shin Kokin Waka Shū*, I, p. 185.
10. Ōsone Shōsuke and Horiuchi Hideaki, *Wakan Rōei Shū*, p. 119. In the poem by Po Chü-i the leaves are identified not as *tung* (*kiri* in Japanese), the paulownia, but as *wu-tung* (*aogiri* in Japanese), the Chinese parasol tree. However, the association between *kiri* and *aogiri* would have been clear to Japanese of the time.
11. *Kokinshū* 171. Okumura, *Kokin*, p. 80. Other translations of the poem may be found in Rodd, *Kokinshū*, p. 47, and McCullough, *Kokin Wakashū*, p. 97.

12. *Shin Kokinshū* 1305. Kubota, *Shin Kokin Waka Shū*, II, p. 108.
13. The poet Tsukamoto Kunio (in his *Teika Hyakushu*, p. 93) noted that although many commentaries had explained the honka-dori in one of Teika's poems (*Samushiro ya / matsu yo no aki no / kaze fukete / tsuki wo katashiku / uji no hashihime*), he had yet to come across a commentary that took cognizance of the extraordinary inversions in language (such as *yo no aki* instead of the usual *aki no yo*), and the ellipses that make this poem memorable.
14. The term used to describe borrowing from works of prose (as opposed to borrowing from earlier poetry) was *honsetsu*, meaning "original version."
15. See, for example, Kubota, *Shin Kokin Waka Shū*, I, pp. 376–77.
16. Teika also stressed the importance to poets of his time of *Tales of Ise*, *Sanjūrokkasen* (Poems of the Thirty-six Immortals), and the first two fascicules of *The Collected Works of Po Chü-i*. See his *Eiga no Taigai* (Essentials of Poetic Composition, c. 1216), p. 115, in Hisamatsu Sen'ichi and Nishio Minoru, *Karon Shū, Nōgakuron Shū*. See also Robert H. Brower and Earl Miner, *Fujiwara Teika's Superior Poems of Our Time*, p. 44, where Teika says, "With regard to preferring the old, the practice of taking the words of an ancient poem and incorporating them into one's own composition without changing them is known as 'using a foundation poem.' However, I feel that if one uses, say, the second and third lines of such a foundation poem, just as they are, in the first three lines of one's own poem, and then goes on to use the last two lines of it in the same fashion, it will prove impossible to make something that sounds like a new poem. Depending on the style, it may be best to avoid using the first two lines of the foundation poem."
17. Kubota, *Shin Kokin Waka Shū*, I, pp. 376–77. Teika's original text is given in *Essentials of Poetic Composition*; see Hisamatsu and Nishio, *Karon*, pp. 114–15. The relevant passage from *Eiga no Taigai* is translated by Brower and Miner in *Superior*, p. 44, note 10.
18. Kubota, *Shin Kokin Waka Shū*, I, p. 377. The original statement is found in Teika's *Superior Poems of Our Time*, included in Hisamatsu and Nishio, *Karon*, pp. 102–3. The manner in which these rules were interpreted by later poets and theorists of poetry is the subject of an exceptionally interesting article by Kubota Jun, "Honka-dori no Imi to Kinō." A similar statement is found in Teika's *Superior Poems*; for a translation, see Brower and Miner, *Superior*, pp. 45–46.
19. For a description in English of the early uta-awase, see Setsuko Ito, "The Muse in Competition," pp. 204–6.
20. See Minegishi Yoshiaki, *Uta-awase no Kenkyū*, p. 15. Minegishi states that the Heian-style uta-awase came to an end during the reign of Horikawa. I have adopted his term *chūseiteki* ("medieval") to describe the literary variety of uta-awase that developed in the twelfth century.

21. Taniyama Shigeru, "Kaisetsu," in Hagitani Boku and Taniyama Shigeru, *Uta-awase Shū*, pp. 286–87.
22. Minegishi, *Uta-awase*, p. 115. This is the total number of *Shin Kokinshū* poems that were derived from uta-awase. However, only 233 of these poems are specifically identified within the collection itself as having originated in uta-awase.
23. Takahashi Kazuhiko, *Mumyōshō Zenkai*, pp. 171–73.
24. An example is the book of poetic theory *Kenshō Chinjō*, in which Kenshō expressed his dissatisfaction with the judgments pronounced by Shunzei at the *Roppyakuban Uta-awase* (Poem Competition in Six Hundred Rounds) of 1194. Most of the points of disagreement are trivial (at least to a modern reader) and are involved with such matters as the correct pronunciations for ancient words. See the article in *Nihon Koten Bungaku Daijiten*, II, p. 446.
25. It is known in Japanese as *Sengohyakuban Uta-awase*.
26. For example, the left poem of round 186 was criticized because the first line, *hana zo miru*, was difficult to understand, but as Taniyama pointed out, it was easily intelligible as an example of poetic inversion. The poem, by Fujiwara Sueyoshi (1153–1211), was subsequently included in the *Shin Kokinshū* (poem 97), despite the unfavorable criticism during the competition. See Hagitani and Taniyama, *Uta-awase Shū*, p. 484; also Kubota, *Shin Kokin Waka Shū*, I, pp. 50–51.
27. I have translated *asaji* as "cogon," the name of a tropical grass used for thatching.
28. Hagitani and Taniyama, *Uta-awase Shū*, p. 484. For Ariie's poem (*Shin Kokinshū* 98), see Kubota, *Shin Kokin Waka Shū*, I, p. 51. For Teika's poem, see Kubota Jun, *Yakuchū Fujiwara Teika Zenkashū*, I, p. 156. Teika's poem also appeared in the imperial anthology *Shoku Kokinshū*, compiled in 1265.
29. The source poem (honka) is *Man'yōshū* IV, 495: *Asahikage / nioeru yama ni / teru tsuki no / akazaru kimi wo / yamagoshi ni okite*. It is one of four poems composed by Tabe no Imiki Ichihiko when he was appointed to a post at the Dazaifu in Kyūshū. The four poems are written in two voices: the first and fourth are a woman's and the second and third a man's. Poem 495 is the fourth of the sequence. The first three lines (including the two borrowed by Ariie) are usually considered to constitute a more or less meaningless *jo* (preface) to the remainder of the poem, and as such are often omitted from modern-language versions. The expanded meaning of the poem is: "On the mountains the early morning sunlight is bright, and the shining moon, though it would linger, must disappear behind the mountain, even as I, who have never tired of you, must leave you and go beyond the mountain." See the translation by Ian Hideo Levy in *Man'yōshū*, I, p. 248–49.
30. Shunzei did not call Shigeie by name or title. Instead, he referred to him

as "the evening crane of long ago," a reference to a line from a poem by Po Chü-i: "The evening crane remembers the little crane chirping in the nest." See Hagitani and Taniyama, *Uta-awase Shū*, p. 484.

31. In principle, the names of the authors of the poems submitted to an uta-awase were concealed, but the judges generally knew who the poets were; otherwise they might commit the grave lapse of giving bad marks to compositions by members of the imperial family. See Kubota Jun, *Fujiwara Teika*, p. 28. In this instance, Shunzei made no pretense of being ignorant of the identity of the poets.

32. The allusion is to a poem of Oborozukiyo in the "Hana no En" chapter of *The Tale of Genji*: *Ukimi yo ni / yagate kienaba / tazunete mo / kusa no hara woba / towaji to ya omou.* (Text in Ishida Jōji and Shimizu Yoshiko, *Genji Monogatari*, II, p. 58.) The poem means something like: "If I, the unfortunate woman, were to disappear, even if you searched for me, would you look in these fields of grass?" The words *kusa no hara*, repeated in Yoshitsune's poem, meant not only "fields of grass" but also a grave. The poem is rendered in Edward Seidensticker's translation (*The Tale of Genji*, I, p. 153):

   Were the lonely one to vanish quite away,
   Would you go to the grassy moors to ask her name?

33. The meaning of this passage has been disputed. I have followed the interpretation of Taniyama Shigeru, but he admitted that it was also possible to construe the passage as meaning "Murasaki Shikibu was more accomplished as a writer than any poet." See Hagitani and Taniyama, *Uta-awase Shū*, p. 539.

34. Hagitani and Taniyama, *Uta-awase Shū*, p. 442. The poem was in the thirteenth round of the first book of winter poems.

35. For an account of the background of the hundred-poem sequence of 1200, the most important in terms of its contribution to the *Shin Kokinshū*, see Robert H. Brower, *Fujiwara Teika's Hundred-Poem Sequence of the Shōji Era, 1200*, pp. 3–8.

36. See Brower, *Fujiwara*, p. 4, for a complete list of the twenty spring topics found in the Horikawa sequence.

37. Konishi's "Association and Progression: Principles of Integration in Anthologies and Sequences of Japanese Court Poetry," translated by Robert H. Brower and Earl Miner, pp. 67–127.

38. Konishi, "Association," p. 111. In later poetic criticism, especially of renga, a distinction was made between *ji no uta*, or background poems of lesser intensity, and *mon no uta*, or "design" poems of greater intensity.

39. See Helen Craig McCullough, *The Tale of the Heike*, p. 258. The official was Norimitsu, the governor of Kii. Gotoba was being taken from the capital by the wife of Nōen, who was the second brother of Kiyomori's

wife, Nii-dono. Nōen's wife was Norimitsu's sister. Text in Takagi Ichinosuke et al., *Heike Monogatari*, II, p. 122.

40. McCullough, *The Tale of the Heike*, p. 257.
41. *Ibid.*, p. 354. The Three Sacred Treasures were the sacred mirror, the *magatama* jewels, and the sacred sword. The sword was lost when the Emperor Antoku drowned in the sea at Dannoura.
42. Michichika left two diaries, one describing the Emperor Takakura's visit to Itsukushima (*Takakura-in Itsukushima Gokō Ki*), and the other relating the death of the same emperor (*Takakura-in Shōka Ki*). His poetry is not highly rated, but six of his poems were included in the *Shin Kokinshū*. He is remembered chiefly because of his bad relations with Teika, but also because he was the father of the great Zen monk Dōgen. For Michichika's diaries, see Keene, *Travelers of a Hundred Ages*, pp. 107–13.
43. See Higuchi Yoshimaro, *Gotoba-in*, p. 23, for a list of Gotoba's favorite diversions. An entry for 1214 in Teika's *Chronicle of the Bright Moon* mentions Gotoba's continued interest in kickball, horse racing, and cockfights. Teika reported that Gotoba went day and night, incognito, to places where such entertainments were held.
44. Higuchi, *Gotoba-in*, p. 21, quotes Jien's *Gukanshō* and also *The Clear Mirror*, both of which state that this was why Gotoba yielded the throne.
45. There is some disagreement about the dating: the diary of Minamoto no Ienaga dates Gotoba's visit to the imperial palace and his poem as 1200, but Teika's *Chronicle of the Bright Moon* and other sources make 1199 seem more probable. See Higuchi, *Gotoba-in*, p. 28. However, Kubota Jun in his "Kaisetsu" (*Shin Kokin Waka Shū*, I, p. 353) states that Gotoba's earliest poems were three composed in 1200.
46. Imagawa Fumio, *Kundoku Meigetsuki*, I, p. 209.
47. The term used by Teika's enemies to describe his poems was *shingi hisho daruma uta*. *Shingi* meant "new," in the sense of newfangled; *hisho* meant "without sources," an offense in a society governed by precedents; *daruma* was the Buddhist dharma or law, but was used in this instance to signify something incomprehensible. See Kubota, *Fujiwara Teika*, p. 126.
48. *Ibid.*, p. 125.
49. *Ibid.*, p. 127.
50. Fujiwara Takafusa (1148–1209) was not an important poet, but forty-three poems by Fujiwara Ietaka (1158–1237) were included in the *Shin Kokinshū*.

    Robert Brower wrote of Gotoba's change of heart: "The decision was vital to the position and future status of Teika in particular, affording an opportunity to establish contact and ingratiate himself with the powerful ex-sovereign and to demonstrate his poetic prowess to the discomfiture of his enemies. One hesitates to make such a sweeping statement as that the course of Japanese classical poetry would have been forever altered had Teika been shunted aside at this juncture to eke out the remainder of his days in wretched obscurity." (Brower, *Fujiwara*, p. 10.) Brower goes on to indicate why "one may be excused for thinking his [Teika's] inclusion in the Shōji sequences more than a mere ripple on the surface of literary history."

51. Kubota, *Fujiwara Teika*, p. 127. See also Brower, *Fujiwara*, p. 15.
52. Translation by Brower in *Fujiwara*, p. 16. The entry is from *Meigetsuki*, Shōji 2 (1200) 8/26. For text, see Imagawa, *Kundoku Meigetsuki*, I, p. 215.
53. Ninety poems came from *Sengohyakuban Uta-awase*, and seventy-nine from *Shōji Ninen Shodo Hyakushu*. See Kubota Jun, "Shōji Ninen Shodo Hyakushu ni tsuite," p. 235.
54. Brower's *Fujiwara* gives a complete translation of all one hundred poems, together with translations of the honka on which many were based. His translation of the sequence was based on "a completely bare, unannotated text of the poems," an indication of the extent of his achievement but also of the relative indifference of Japanese scholars to this important sequence.
55. Such sessions were known as *eigu uta-awase*. *Eigu* meant an offering placed before the portrait of a god or of a deceased person; Hitomaro was honored in this manner because of his reputation.
56. He also appointed fifteen poets as *yoryūdo*, or contributing members, including Fujiwara Yoshitsune, Minamoto Michichika, Jien, Shunzei, Teika, and Jakuren. Minamoto Ienaga was chosen to be the secretary of the committee. Later, three poets (including Kamo no Chōmei) were added to the original members.
57. *Shin Kokinshū* 18. The topic of the poem is *sekiji no uguisu*, or "uguisu on the barrier road," but instead of mentioning the barrier (*seki*) of Ausaka (Ōsaka) in the usual manner, Gotoba spoke instead of the mountain (*yama*) at the barrier. Maruya Saiichi, in an interesting analysis of the poem and its relation to the honka in the *Kokinshū*, suggested that Gotoba concluded the poem with the word *yama* because he wished to avoid having too many words begin with the sound of s. If he had ended the poem with *seki*, the key words *sugi*, *shiroki*, Au*saka*, and *seki* would all have contained the sound. (Maruya Saiichi, *Gotoba-in*, p. 29.)
58. The poem is the anonymous fifth poem of the collection: *Ume ga e ni / kiiru uguisu / haru kakete / nakedomo imada / yuki wa furitsutsu*. The second line of Gotoba's poem is the same as the fourth line of the *Kokinshū* poem. His mention of snow lying on the bare cedar boughs is more effective than the more conventional snow on the bare branches of the plum trees.
59. Minamoto Ienaga (1170?–1234) was a statesman who participated in various poetry gatherings associated with Gotoba, such as the second of the two hundred-poem sequences of 1200. He was chosen to take charge of the secretarial work connected with the compilation of the *Shin Kokinshū*, and was therefore privy to the discussions. His diary, kept from 1197 to 1207, is an invaluable source of information about the activities of the court at this time. The text of the diary is given, together with good notes,

by Ishida Yoshisada and Satsugawa Shūji in *Minamoto Ienaga Nikki Zenchūkai*. See also Keene, *Travelers*, pp. 103–6.

60. Comparative statistics on the number of poems in the *Kokinshū*, the *Shin Kokinshū*, and other imperial collections in which the poet mistook cherry blossoms for snowflakes or, alternatively, thought snowflakes were cherry blossoms, are given by Kusuhashi Hiraku in "Ōchō Waka to Yuki," p. 205. This essay is devoted to snow in the imperial collections; two other essays in the same volume (Katagiri Yōichi, *Ōchō Waka no Sekai*) take up the important roles played by the moon and cherry blossoms. No fewer than 305 poems in the *Shin Kokinshū* describe the moon. See Ōtori Kazuma, "Ōchō Waka to Tsuki," in Katagiri, *Ōchō*, p. 218.
61. Text in Kubota, *Shin Kokin Waka Shū*, I, pp. 19–20. I have, following Kubota, pruned away the decorative language with which Fujiwara Yoshitsune embellished his prose. Hardly a phrase is without a jo, a makurakotoba, or at least an engo, but the overall meaning is more or less as given in the translation. The contrast made between the eyes and the ears at the beginning of the quotation is essentially that between contemporary poetry, easily available to prospective readers, and poetry of the past, known mainly by repute.
62. Higuchi, *Gotoba-in*, p. 109. When Gotoba took as a precedent the party that celebrated the completion of the *Nihon Shoki*, he was in effect indicating that he believed the compilation of the *Shin Kokinshū* to be no less important than that of a national history.
63. Gotoba's command for a preface in Chinese was issued to Chikatsune in the seventh month of 1204. He completed the preface in the second month of 1205. After reading the manuscript, Gotoba turned it over to Fujiwara Yoshitsune, who made some emendations. See Kubota, *Shin Kokin Waka Shū*, I, p. 13.
64. Imagawa, *Kundoku*, II, p. 170. See also Higuchi, *Gotoba-in*, pp. 110–11.
65. A rough draft of the kana preface was completed three days after the banquet.
66. See Higuchi, *Gotoba-in*, p. 111, for the poem. The quoted passage is from the Japanese preface to the *Kokinshū*. I have given the translation by Rodd in *Kokinshū*, p. 46.
67. Kubota, *Fujiwara Teika*, p. 114. For the relevant passages in the diaries of Minamoto Michichika, see Mizukawa Yoshio, *Minamoto Michichika Nikki Zenshaku*, pp. 211, 467. Michichika's diaries are also described in Keene, *Travelers*, pp. 107–13.
68. *Kokinshū* 601.
69. *Shin Kokinshū* 37.
70. See Brower and Miner, *Fujiwara Teika's Superior*, pp. 45–46, where Teika says, "Next, with regard to poems by one's fellow poets, even if they are no longer living, if they have been composed so recently that they might be said to have been written yesterday or today, I think it essential to

avoid using any part of such a poem, even a single line, that is distinctive enough to be recognized as the work of a particular poet."

71. Kubota, *Fujiwara Teika*, pp. 113, 115.
72. Tsukamoto, *Teika Hyakushu*, p. 164.
73. The word *sabi*, related to the modern *sabishii*, meaning "lonely," and also to its homonym *sabi*, meaning "rust," was used to suggest the unobtrusive, unassertive beauty that was the ideal of Japanese poets, especially during the turbulent decades of the Japanese middle ages. The "discovery" of sabi as an aesthetic ideal has often been attributed to Saigyō. See below, p. 678; also Ishida Yoshisada, *Inja no Bungaku*, p. 46. For a discussion of sabi, together with the related aesthetic ideal of *wabi*, especially in connection with the tea ceremony, see Paul Varley and Kumakura Isao, *Tea in Japan*, pp. 239–41.
74. *Shin Kokinshū* 363. It was composed in 1186, when Teika was twenty-four.
75. Ishida Jōji and Shimizu Yoshiko, *Genji*, II, p. 276.
76. Tsukamoto (in *Teika Hyakushu*, p. 78) called attention to the "slashing, fierce" tone of the third line, which he contrasts with the gentle, pliant tone of the passage in *The Tale of Genji*.
77. See the essay by Kubota Jun, "Fujiwara Teika ni okeru Koten to Gendai," in his *Chūsei Bungaku no Sekai*, p. 221, where he says of Teika, "He was a conservative, and even among the nobles, whose ranks included many conservatives, his way of thought was the most aristocratic."
78. For a consideration of this statement, see Keene, *Travelers*, pp. 95–96.
79. For an account of Teika's illnesses, see Kubota, *Fujiwara Teika*, pp. 18–19. Kubota was aware of the possibility that Teika might have exaggerated his illnesses, but that he was often ill seems to have been a fact.
80. A reference to the *gosechi no kokoromi*, dances staged on the second Day of the Tiger of the eleventh month of each year in the presence of the emperor. The term *gosechi* referred to the five seasonal ceremonies held in the palace, the high points of which were dances; *kokoromi* were the rehearsals performed before the emperor on the night before the official viewing of the dances. For a brief acount of such an occasion, see William H. and Helen Craig McCullough, *A Tale of Flowering Fortunes*, pp. 146–47.
81. Quoted by Kubota in *Fujiwara Teika*, p. 53. The term *joseki*, which I have translated as "removed from the palace register," referred to the practice of inscribing wooden tags with the names of nobles permitted to present themselves at the palace (*shōden*). If, for some reason, a noble was punished by not being allowed to present himself any longer, his tag was removed from the Seiryōden, the private residence of the emperor.
82. Kubota, *Yakuchū*, I, p. 54. See also Kubota, *Fujiwara Teika*, p. 68.
83. Kubota, *Yakuchū*, II, p. 446. See also Kubota, *Fujiwara Teika*, p. 72. The "cloud" in the poem is, of course, Saigyō. In a famous poem, Saigyō

had expressed the hope that he would die when there was a full moon in the sky; hence, the reference to the full moon in the poem.

84. Seven of the one hundred poems by Teika discussed in Tsukamoto, *Teika Hyakushu*, were from *Kagetsu Hyakushu*.
85. However, Yoshida Hajime began his discussion of the poem with, "There surely is no special need to attempt an explication of the poem. The language presents no problems worth mentioning. It is the kind of poem for which it is quite sufficient to savor quietly, slowly, after one's own fashion." Yoshida Hajime, *Fujiwara Teika*, p. 66.
86. Both Tsukamoto Kunio (in *Teika Hyakushu*, p. 89), and Yoshida (in *Fujiwara Teika*, p. 66) state that Teika was writing about plum blossoms, though Tsukamoto immediately afterward expressed a preference for a general "fragrant thing" as an explanation of *hana*, rather than any particular blossom. Kubota (in *Yakuchū*, I, p. 97) did not commit himself on the identity of the blossoms, but perhaps he assumed that readers would understand without his help that *hana* meant cherry blossoms, as so often in Japanese poetry.
87. Andō Tsuguo, *Fujiwara Teika*, p. 102.
88. This was the view of Tsukamoto, expressed in his *Teika*, pp. 28–29; but Konishi Jin'ichi, in "Teika wa Shōchō Kajin ka," expressed doubts about the appropriateness of referring to Teika as a symbolist poet.
89. Kubota, *Fujiwara Teika*, p. 77.
90. Kubota, *Yakuchū*, I, p. 117.
91. *Ibid.* Yoshitsune was at the time *sakon'e no daishō* (general of the left bodyguard), a position of considerable importance normally filled only by nobles of the highest rank. Kubota pointed out in a note that in China generals were sometimes likened to *ryōko* (dragon-tigers); hence, the "tiger cub." Teika was correct in his prophecy: Yoshitsune was destined to climb to the very top of the mountain—in other words, to become the regent and prime minister, the highest position to which a noble could attain.
92. Teika composed several sets of poems that began with each of the forty-seven syllables of the *iroha* poem. The texts are given in Kubota, *Yakuchū*, II, pp. 36–49. Teika not only observed the order of the *iroha* poem but imposed a second kind of order, that of the chokusenshū, with seasonal poems followed by love poems. It was a remarkable feat, but the poems have only minor intrinsic importance.
93. Sosei's poem (*Kokinshū* 691) was irregular, consisting of thirty-three rather than the standard thirty-one syllables.
94. The poems are given in Kubota, *Yakuchū*, II, pp. 56–60.
95. The 128 "rhyme poems" are given in Kubota, *Yakuchū*, I, pp. 235–52. They are arranged in order of the seasons, followed by jukkai poems, poems on mountain dwellings, and poems on travel. The Chinese rhymes are given in Japanese pronunciations; thus, the *feng*, *k'ung*, *lung*, *meng*,

etc. of the Chinese rhymes turn in Teika's poems into *kaze*, *sora*, *komoreru*, and *yume*.

96. For further details, see Kubota, *Fujiwara Teika*, p. 93; also Andō, *Fujiwara Teika*, pp. 130–44.

97. Fujiwara Kanezane (1149–1207) was also known as Kujō Kanezane. His brother, Jien, was not only a prominent Tendai abbot but an important poet and the author of *Gukanshō*. Fujiwara (or Kujō) Yoshitsune was his son. Kanezane had been appointed kampaku in 1186 because his candidacy was supported by Minamoto Yoritomo.

98. Quoted in Kubota, *Fujiwara Teika*, p. 111. A somewhat different *kundoku* (kambun punctuated for reading as Japanese) version of the kambun text (the entry in *Chronicle of the Bright Moon* for the fifth day of the twelfth month of 1197) is given in Imagawa, *Kundoku*, I, p. 72. There are only two entries in the diary for the year 1197 (the eighth year of Kenkyū).

99. The poem is number 40 in the *Shin Kokinshū*. See Kubota, *Shin Kokin Waka Shū*, I, p. 33. The honka by Ōe no Chisato, a poet of the *Kokinshū* era, is also found in the *Shin Kokinshū* (poem 55): *Teri mo sezu / kumori mo hatenu / haru no yo no / oborozukiyo ni / shiku mono zo naki*. (Nothing can compare with a misty moon on a spring night when it is neither shining nor completely clouded over.) Chisato's poem was in turn based on lines by Po Chü-i: "A misty moon that is neither bright nor dark, / A gentle wind that is neither warm nor cold." Kubota states, further, that a similar description occurs in Teika's work of fiction, *Matsuranomiya Monogatari* (The Tale of the Matsura Palace), and suggests (in *Fujiwara Teika*, p. 112) that Teika had in mind a romantic passage in the "Hana no En" chapter of *The Tale of Genji* where Oborozukiyo quotes part of Chisato's poem. Teika probably expected that people would recognize the antecedents of his poem but also his particular contribution, the explanation of the mistiness of the moon in terms of the scent of plum blossoms, a superb example of synesthesia.

100. *Shin Kokinshū* 63. Teika contrasts the wild geese's painful flight south through the frosty sky of late autumn with their present appearance as they head back north through the warm spring rain. Andō (*Fujiwara Teika*, p. 157) suggested that the poem may be a prayer for the revival of the fortunes of Teika's family, now in sad decline.

101. Kubota, *Fujiwara Teika*, p. 165.

102. *Ibid.*, p. 175. Kubota, trying to guess why Teika failed to mention his father's death in his poetry, suggested it might be because he thought of Shunzei with awe, rather than affection.

103. Kubota, *Yakuchū*, I, p. 454. See also Kubota, *Fujiwara Teika*, p. 182. Although the poem does not specifically refer to Yoshitsune's death in the third month, surely it must be the "dream" to which he alludes. The poem was written in the third month of 1206. It bears the title "Nostalgic Remembrances of the Past Addressed to the Moon." There is a pun in

the last line between *furu*, "to fall" (as of leaves), and *furu*, "to grow old."

104. Later in his life, while in exile on the island of Sado, he compiled one of the important works of medieval poetic criticism, *Yakumo Mishō*.
105. The work was translated by Robert H. Brower and Earl Miner under the title *Fujiwara Teika's Superior Poems of Our Time: A Thirteenth-Century Poetic Treatise and Sequence*.
106. Two poems by Minamoto Yoritomo, the founder of the Kamakura shogunate but not an important poet, were included in the *Shin Kokinshū*. Further evidence of the good relations prevailing between the court in Kyoto and the Kamakura shogunate may be found in Yoritomo's choice of Gotoba as Sanetomo's godfather (*nazuke no oya*).
107. Kubota, *Fujiwara Teika*, p. 203.
108. It was usual to twist two threads together; only one (*kataito*) would have been considered likely to break.
109. *Man'yōshū* 1316. See Aoki Takako et al., *Man'yōshū*, II, p. 251.
110. For a discussion of Teika's poem, see Andō, *Fujiwara Teika*, pp. 220–21; also Kubota, *Fujiwara Teika*, pp. 203–4.
111. The poem, VI:935, is by Kasa no Kanamura. For an English translation, see Nippon Gakujutsu Shinkōkai, *The Manyōshū*, p. 102.
112. Kubota, *Yakuchū*, I, p. 404. See also Kubota, *Fujiwara Teika*, pp. 208–9; also Andō, *Fujiwara Teika*, pp. 232–33. There is a kakekotoba on *matsu*, "to wait," and the place-name Matsuho. The burning of the seaweed (to obtain salt) is at the same time the burning anguish the woman feels at the thought her lover has deserted her.
113. Kubota, *Yakuchū*, I, p. 437. See also Kubota, *Fujiwara Teika*, p. 214; also Tsukamoto, *Teika Hyakushu*, pp. 219–21.
114. Kubota, *Yakuchū*, I, p. 438. See also Kubota, *Fujiwara Teika*, pp. 214–16.
115. *Shin Kokinshū* 1448. See Kubota, *Shin Kokin Waka Shū*, II, p. 152.
116. Translated by Helen Craig McCullough in *Ōkagami*, p. 97. She also gives another version of Michizane's poem.
117. Quoted by Kutoba, *Fujiwara Teika*, p. 214.
118. Maruya, *Gotoba-in*, pp. 225–29.
119. Kubota, *Yakuchū*, I, p. 218. See also Andō, *Fujiwara Teika*, pp. 270–71, and Tsukamoto, *Teika Hyakushu*, pp. 145–47. Tsukamoto wrote (p. 146) of this poem that it was vibrantly alive, quite unlike the other poems on the yamabuki found in the *Shin Kokinshū*, "eight or nine out of ten of which are empty poems intended to be inscribed on screens depicting the celebrated Tama River of Ide, dead descriptions of nature in the manner of picture postcards. The use of personification is not in the least offensive."
120. The major contributors included Ietaka (47 poems), Yoshitsune (36 poems), Shunzei (35 poems), Saionji Kintsune (30 poems), Jien (27 poems), and Sanetomo and Michiie (25 poems each). The conservative manner of the collection appealed to the Nijō school of poets, who considered that it (rather than the *Shin Kokinshū*) represented the finest flowering of Teika's

genius as a compiler. The *Shin Chokusenshū*, together with Shunzei's *Senzaishū* and *Shoku Gosenshū* (compiled by Teika's son Tameie) were especially admired as the work of three generations of poets of conservative tendencies.

121. Both Ienaga's poem and Teika's response are given in Kubota, *Yakuchū*, I, p. 474.

122. In this connection, there is special significance in the note Teika appended to the manuscript of the *Gosenshū* he was copying in 1221, when the Jōkyū Rebellion broke out; he wrote that, despite the infirmities of old age, he continued to copy manuscripts for the sake of future generations. (Maruya, *Gotoba-in*, p. 230; Maruya was quoting Ishida Yoshisada, "Shin Kokin Kadan to Kafū no Bunretsu.")

123. A scholarly account of the various theories relating to the compilation of the *Hyakunin Isshu* (also known as the *Ogura Hyakunin Isshu*) is found in Shimazu Tadao's "Kaisetsu" to his edition of *Hyakunin Isshu* in the Kadokawa Bunko series. There is reason to think that the poems of Gotoba and Juntoku included in the hundred were added after Teika's death.

124. The word *karuta* is of Portuguese origin, and was introduced to Japan along with Portuguese card games in the late sixteenth century, but the New Year's game, though played with foreign-inspired cards, much resembled the traditional game of *kai-oi*, or matching shells. A reader intones the first part of one of the hundred poems, and the two players (sometimes more), who have memorized all hundred poems, search on the board for a card inscribed with the second part of the same poem, eager to sweep the card off the board before the other player. An accomplished player will recognize a poem from the first couple of syllables.

125. Arthur Waley, early in his career as a scholar of Japanese literature, said of *Hyakunin Isshu*: "It is so selected as to display the least pleasing features of Japanese poetry. Artificialities of every kind abound, and the choice does little credit to the taste of Sadaiye [Teika] to whom the compilation is attributed. These poems have gained an unmerited circulation in Japan, owing to the fact that they are used in a kind of 'Happy Families' card-game." (Arthur Waley, *Japanese Poetry*, p. 7.)

126. See Kubota, "Kaisetsu," in his *Shin Kokin Waka Shū*, I, p. 367, for the original text (in extremely convoluted language) and for a modern-language paraphrase.

127. Higuchi, *Gotoba-in*, p. 191.

128. *Ibid.*, p. 197. The expression *ho ni idete* means something like "revealing on one's face," but *ho* means literally an ear (of rice or other grain), and *ashi* a reed. There is thus a double set of meanings, one describing the speaker's grief, the other a desolate scene by the shore.

129. *Ibid.*, p. 199.

130. A generous selection of poems by Ietaka is found in Steven D. Carter, *Waiting for the Wind*, pp. 32–42.

131. The *Shin Kokinshū* contains 94 poems by Saigyō, 92 by Jien, 79 by Yoshitsune, 72 by Shunzei, 49 by Princess Shokushi, 46 by Teika, 43 by Ietaka, 35 by Jakuren, and 34 by Gotoba.
132. The original description of this encounter is found in *Azuma Kagami* (Mirror of the East). (See Ozawa Akira, *Shinshaku Azuma Kagami*, II, pp. 59–62, for a modern-language version of the account in *Mirror of the East*.) Saigyō's answers to Yoritomo's questions were curt to the point of rudeness, and *Mirror of the East* relates that he gave the present he had received from Yoritomo, a cat made of silver, to some children he saw playing by a bridge. See Takagi Kiyoko, *Saigyō no Shūkyōteki Sekai*, p. 107; Yasuda Ayao, *Saigyō*, p. 15; also Burton Watson, *Saigyō*, p. 6.
133. I am thinking, for example, of the popular explanations for the decision of Kenkō to become a priest, or of Bashō to leave the domain of the Tōdō family for Edo.
134. The relevant passage is quoted by Kubota Jun in *Sankashū*, pp. 72–73. It opens quite unambiguously: "If one looks into the reasons why Saigyō had an awakening of faith, one will discover that it originated in love." See also Yasuda, *Saigyō*, pp. 21–22.
135. Kubota (in *Sankashū*, p. 72) indicates that he is unwilling to discard this theory out of hand, and in fact produces evidence that suggests that the theory is tenable. Yasuda (*Saigyō*, p. 27) seems to believe that the person (*yukari no hito*) to whom Saigyō sent a poem just before entering orders may have been a woman he loved.
136. Yasuda, *Saigyō*, p. 22. The story is related in *Saigyō Monogatari*, a fictionalized account of Saigyō's life written in the late Kamakura period.
137. Kubota, in *Sankashū*, pp. 78–79, gives evidence from Saigyō's poetry of his disenchantment with the world. See Yasuda, *Saigyō*, p. 23, for the opinion that he sympathized with Sutoku. (Sutoku abdicated two years *after* Saigyō took Buddhist vows.) It is clear that Saigyō was eager to free himself from the dust of the world, but he himself does not indicate whether this was because he was upset over some specific matter or if he was moved by the usual Buddhist rejection of the world.
138. *Sankashū* 723. I have in general followed the interpretation of the poem given by Kubota in *Sankashū*, pp. 90–91. The poem was quite differently explained by Gotō Shigeo (in *Sankashū*, pp. 194–95). He took *sora ni naru* to mean that the speaker's mind was traveling up into the sky out of yearning for the Pure Land. Kubota gave examples of the use of *sora ni naru* in the *Man'yōshū* and *Kokinshū* with the meaning of "to be distracted" or "to be absentminded." The mist is only barely perceptible, but it rises into the sky, leaving this world behind; in a similar manner, the speaker's mind, uncertain precisely what it wants to do, rises into the sky, now that it is sure it does not wish to remain in this world. Another translation (including the preface) by William R. LaFleur in *Mirror for the Moon*, p. 34.

139. *Sankashū* 725. Gotō, *Sankashū*, p. 195.
140. See Ishida Yoshisada, *Inja*, p. 12.
141. See Varley and Kumakura, *Tea*, p. 76, where the use of wabi as an aesthetic ideal is said "to express religious discipline as a life on the bare edge of survival in a thatched hut in the midst of nature."
142. See above, note 73.
143. *Sankashū* 937. Text in Kazamaki Keijirō and Kojima Yoshio, *Sankashū, Kinkai Waka Shū*, p. 167. Other translations by Watson (*Saigyō*, p. 144), LaFleur (*Mirror*, p. 47), and Brower and Miner (*Japanese*, p. 261).
144. Takagi Kiyoko, *Saigyō*, p. 104. Takagi gives on pp. 99–102 many of the poems composed by Saigyō on Mount Kōya.
145. For Saigyō's relations with Jakuzen (whose name is read as Jakunen by some scholars), see Kubota, *Sankashū*, pp. 123–31.
146. *Sankashū* 1199. I have followed Gotō's interpretation of this difficult poem, given by him in *Sankashū*, p. 342. For translations of other poems of this series, see Watson, *Saigyō*, pp. 169–74; also LaFleur, *Mirror*, p. 56.
147. *Sankashū* 1223. See Kubota, *Sankashū*, p. 255, and Gotō, *Sankashū*, p. 349, for different interpretations of this poem.
148. Kubota, *Sankashū*, p. 257. The poem does not appear in *Sankashū* itself, but is found in other collections of Saigyō's poetry.
149. Yasuda (in *Saigyō*, p. 37) lists the places to which Saigyō traveled; they include the provinces of Michinoku, Dewa, Sanuki, and Awa, as well as places closer to Mount Kōya.
150. Kubota, *Sankashū*, p. 60. For Saigyō's relations with the unhappy Sutoku, see *ibid.*, pp. 56–57.
151. Some of these poems are translated by LaFleur in *Mirror*.
152. *Shin Kokinshū* 625. Kubota, *Shin Kokin Waka Shū*, I, p. 213. Other translations by Watson (*Saigyō*, p. 90) and LaFleur (*Mirror*, p. 88).
153. *Shin Kokinshū* 362. It is preceded by a poem by the priest Jakuren and followed by a poem by Teika, each ending with the same last line, *aki no yūgure*. All three poems are considered to be masterpieces. Kubota, *Shin Kokin Waka Shū*, I, p. 133.
154. I have followed the interpretation of Kubota, but there is another tradition concerning the meaning of the verb *tatsu* (which I have translated as "rises"). Gotō (in *Sankashū*, p. 129) interprets *tatsu* as meaning "stands." Other translations by Watson (*Saigyō*, p. 81) and LaFleur (*Mirror*, p. 24).
155. See Ishida, *Inja*, p. 90; also Takagi Kiyoko, *Saigyō*, p. 165. The poem by Saigyō that Shunzei preferred (*Sankashū* 294) is an unimpressive example in the manner of the *Kokinshū*; the speaker asks what the source might be of the dew that covers the landscape and decides it must be the tears he has shed into his sleeve. Gotō, *Sankashū*, p. 86.
156. Ishida, *Inja*, pp. 90–91, gives the text of Tō no Tsuneyori's evaluation of the poem.
157. *Shin Kokinshū* 627. Kubota, *Shin Kokin Waka Shū*, I, p. 213; it is also

poem 513 in *Sankashū*. See Yasuda, *Saigyō*, pp. 63–64, for other poems in which Saigyō expressed the wish he had friends with whom to share the pleasures of solitude.

158. Saigyō made at least two journeys to Michinoku, the provinces at the northern end of Honshū. His poems on such sites as the Shirakawa Barrier seem to have been inspired by the priest Nōin, who visited the same places about 1025. See Kubota, *Sankashū*, pp. 210–16.

159. An interesting exception to this generalization is found in Yasuda, *Saigyō*, where he discusses such matters as the vowel patterns in Saigyō's poetry, notably on pp. 57, 61, 66, 68–69.

160. See, for example, Tsukamoto, *Teika Hyakushu*, p. 24.

Bibliography

Note: All Japanese books, except as otherwise noted, were published in Tokyo.

Andō Tsuguo. *Fujiwara Teika*. Chikuma Shobō, 1977.

Aoki Takako, Ide Itaru, et al. *Man'yōshū*, 4 vols., in Shinchō Nihon Koten Shūsei series. Shinchōsha, 1976.

Brower, Robert H. *Fujiwara Teika's Hundred-Poem Sequence of the Shōji Era, 1200*. Tokyo: Sophia University, 1978.

Brower, Robert H., and Earl Miner. *Fujiwara Teika's Superior Poems of Our Time*. Stanford, Calif.: Stanford University Press, 1967.

———. *Japanese Court Poetry*. Stanford, Calif.: Stanford University Press, 1961.

Carter, Steven D. *Waiting for the Wind*. New York: Columbia University Press, 1989.

Gotō Shigeo. *Sankashū*, in Shinchō Nihon Koten Shūsei series. Shinchōsha, 1979.

Hagitani Boku and Taniyama Shigeru. *Uta-awase Shū*, in Nihon Koten Bungaku Taikei series. Iwanami Shoten, 1965.

Higuchi Yoshimaro. *Gotoba-in*. Shūeisha, 1985.

Hisamatsu Sen'ichi and Nishio Minoru. *Karon Shū, Nōgakuron Shū*, in Nihon Koten Bungaku Taikei series. Iwanami Shoten, 1961.

Imagawa Fumio. *Kundoku Meigetsuki*, 6 vols. Kawade Shobō Shinsha, 1977–79.

Ishida Jōji and Shimizu Yoshiko. *Genji Monogatari*, II, in Shinchō Nihon Koten Shūsei series. Shinchōsha, 1977.

Ishida Yoshisada. *Inja no Bungaku*. Hanawa Shobō, 1969.

Ishida Yoshisada and Satsugawa Shūji. *Minamoto Ienaga Nikki Zenchūkai*. Yūseidō, 1982.

Ito, Setsuko. "The Muse in Competition," *Monumenta Nipponica* 37:2, Summer 1982.

Katagiri Yōichi (ed.). *Ōchō Waka no Sekai*. Kyoto: Sekai Shisō Sha, 1984.

Kazamaki Keijirō and Kojima Yoshio. *Sankashū, Kinkai Waka Shū*, in Nihon Koten Bungaku Taikei series. Iwanami Shoten, 1961.

Keene, Donald. *Travelers of a Hundred Ages*. New York: Henry Holt, 1989.

Kibune Shigeaki. *Shoku Gosen Waka Shū Zenchūshaku*. Kyoto: Daigakudō Shoten, 1989.

Konishi Jin'ichi. "Association and Progression: Principles of Integration in Anthologies and Sequences of Japanese Court Poetry," *Harvard Journal of Asiatic Studies* 21, 1958.

———. "Teika wa Shōchō Kajin ka," *Kokubungaku Gengo to Bungei* 43, November 1965.

Kubota Jun. *Chūsei Bungaku no Sekai*. Tōkyō Daigaku Shuppankai, 1972.

———. *Fujiwara Teika*. Shūeisha, 1984.

———. "Honka-dori no Imi to Kinō," *Nihon no Bigaku* 3:12, 1988.

———. *Sankashū*. Iwanami Shoten, 1983.

———. *Shin Kokin Kajin no Kenkyū*. Tōkyō Daigaku Shuppankai, 1973.

———. *Shin Kokin Waka Shū*, 2 vols., in Shinchō Nihon Koten Shūsei. Shinchōsha, 1979.

———. "Shōji Ninen Shodo Hyakushu ni tsuite," in Akiyama Ken (ed.), *Chūsei Bungaku no Kenkyū*. Tōkyō Daigaku Shuppan Kai, 1972.

———. *Yakuchū Fujiwara Teika Zenkashū*, 2 vols. Kawade Shobō Shinsha, 1985.

Kuriyama Riichi. *Teika Den*. Furukawa Shobō, 1974.

LaFleur, William R. *Mirror for the Moon*. New York: New Directions, 1978.

Levy, Ian Hideo. *Man'yōshū*, I. Princeton, N.J.: Princeton University Press, 1981.

Maruya Saiichi. *Gotoba-in*. Chikuma Shobō, 1973.

McCullough, Helen Craig. *Kokin Wakashū*. Stanford, Calif.: Stanford University Press, 1985.

———. *Ōkagami, The Great Mirror*. Princeton, N.J.: Princeton University Press, 1980.

——— (trans.). *The Tale of the Heike*. Stanford, Calif.: Stanford University Press, 1988.

McCullough, William H., and Helen Craig McCullough (trans.). *A Tale of Flowering Fortunes*, 2 vols. Stanford, Calif.: Stanford University Press, 1980.

Minegishi Yoshiaki. *Uta-awase no Kenkyū*. Sanseidō, 1954.

Miya Shūji. *Saigyō no Uta*. Kawade Shobō Shinsha, 1977.

Mizukawa Yoshio. *Minamoto Michichika Nikki Zenshaku*. Kasama Shoin, 1978.

Morris, Ivan. *The Pillow Book of Sei Shōnagon*, 2 vols. New York: Columbia University Press, 1967.

Nihon Koten Bungaku Daijiten, 6 vols. Iwanami Shoten, 1983–85.

Nippon Gakujutsu Shinkōkai (trans.). *The Manyōshū*. New York: Columbia University Press, 1965.

Okumura Tsuneya. *Kokin Wakashū*, in Shinchō Nihon Koten Shūsei series. Shinchōsha, 1978.

Ōsone Shōsuke and Horiuchi Hideaki. *Wakan Rōei Shū*, in Shinchō Nihon Koten Shūsei series. Shinchōsha, 1983.

Ozawa Akira. *Shinshaku Azuma Kagami*, 2 vols. Senjūsha, 1985.

Rodd, Laura Rasplica, with Mary Catherine Henkenius (trans.). *Kokinshū*. Princeton, N.J.: Princeton University Press, 1984.

Seidensticker, Edward G. *The Tale of Genji*, 2 vols. New York: Alfred A. Knopf, 1976.

Shimazu Tadao. *Hyakunin Isshu*, in Kadokawa Bunko series. Kadokawa Shoten, 1969.

Takagi Ichinosuke et al. *Heike Monogatari*, 2 vols., in Nihon Koten Bungaku Taikei series. Iwanami Shoten, 1959–60.

Takagi Kiyoko. *Saigyō no Shūkyōteki Sekai*. Taimeidō, 1989.

Takahashi Kazuhiko. *Mumyōshō Zenkai*. Sōbunsha, 1987.

Tsukamoto Kunio. *Teika Hyakushu*. Kawade Shobō Shinsha, 1977.

Varley, Paul, and Kumakura Isao. *Tea in Japan*. Honolulu: University of Hawaii Press, 1989.

Waley, Arthur. *Japanese Poetry: the Uta*. London: Lund Humphries, 1946.

Watson, Burton. *Saigyō: Poems of a Mountain Home*. New York: Columbia University Press, 1990.

Yasuda Ayao. *Saigyō*. Yayoi Shobō, 1973.

Yoshida Hajime. *Fujiwara Teika*. Hōsei Daigaku Shuppankyoku, 1986.

18. WAKA POETRY OF THE KAMAKURA AND MUROMACHI PERIODS

The *Shin Kokinshū* was by far the finest collection of poetry compiled during the Kamakura period, and many of its poets remained active during the first decades of the new era, but its roots were in the past. The fusion of nostalgia for the golden age of the *Kokinshū* and awareness of the dark uncertainty of the present gave the poetry particular depth and resonance. More characteristic poetry of the age of the Kamakura shoguns is not found until the court anthologies of the 1220s, as well as in contemporary private collections.

The poetry that faithfully conveys the special atmosphere of the Kamakura period may strike Western readers as being less memorable and certainly less beautiful than the poetry of the *Shin Kokinshū*. It is true that the poems of the third Kamakura shogun, Minamoto Sanetomo, have been accorded extraordinary praise by Japanese critics, especially since the Meiji period. The qualities most often admired in Sanetomo's poetry—the unaffected simplicity or the masculinity in the vein of the *Man'yōshū*—appealed especially to those who deplored what they consider to be artificiality or overrefinement in earlier waka poetry.

The Kamakura period is otherwise important in the history of the waka because of the emergence at this time of bitterly opposed schools of poetry. The differences between these schools are likely to seem, at our distance from the protagonists and their concerns, somewhat less than cataclysmic; the most "conservative" and the most "radical" waka poets used essentially the same vocabulary to evoke essentially the same scenes or states of mind, and all paid homage to Teika. But to members of the court in Kyoto (and their pupils everywhere) even slight differences in literary principles seemed enormously important, and the various schools fought for supremacy, especially for recognition in the form of a command to compile a chokusenshū. Poetry became by default the chief concern of the aristocrats in an age when the court had lost most of its other powers to military men in Kamakura and elsewhere in the east.

Minamoto Sanetomo[1]

The first distinctive new voice in the waka poetry of the Kamakura period, however, was that of a military man. Minamoto Sanetomo was the second son of Minamoto Yoritomo who, after his victory in the war with the Taira, had founded the Kamakura shogunate. Yoritomo died under mysterious circumstances in 1199 and was succeeded as shogun by his elder son, Yoriie, who was in turn forced by the Hōjō, his mother's family, to yield the office of shogun to his younger brother Sanetomo in 1203.[2] Sanetomo was eleven when he became shogun, and during the sixteen years of his reign—until 1219 when he was assassinated by his nephew—he was unable to free himself from the domination of the Hōjō regents. His short life has nevertheless appealed to the imagination of later Japanese writers, especially those who have lived during times of war, perhaps because he seemed to embody the ideal of the soldier-poet.[3]

According to *Mirror of the East*, the semiofficial history of the Kamakura shogunate, Sanetomo began composing waka when he was thirteen.[4] These poems have not survived, but we know that Sanetomo's first acquaintance with the poetry in the *Shin Kokinshū* dates from about this time. Four years later he obtained a copy of the *Kokinshū*. Study of the poetry in these two collections probably inspired him to compose poems of his own. When he was seventeen (in 1209) he sent thirty of his waka to Teika for his appraisal, presumably because Teika's reputation as the finest poet of the age extended even to distant Kamakura. Teika, in return (as has been mentioned), sent Sanetomo *Superior Poems of Our Time*, a collection of eighty-three waka, mainly from the period from the *Kokinshū* through the *Shūishū*, that was intended to provide models for Sanetomo's future poetic composition.[5] Teika's prefatory essay to *Superior Poems* mentioned that he had been "asked by a certain person how poetry should be composed," no doubt a guarded reference to Sanetomo.[6] The best-known part of Teika's advice relates to the proper diction and treatment in the waka: "If in diction you admire the traditional, if in treatment you attempt the new, if you aim at an unobtainably lofty effect, and if you study the poetry of Kampei and before—then how can you fail to succeed?"[7] Probably Teika was referring in general to the poetry of the *Kokinshū* and especially to such ninth-century poets as Ariwara no Narihira and Ono no Komachi.

Teika was sure that in order to compose superior waka it was necessary to be thoroughly familiar with the poetry of the past. Sanetomo, obeying the advice to adopt the old poems as his models, tried to make up for his youth and lack of poetic experience by imitation; many early poems hardly differ either in language or manner from their models, as the following poems on the topic "nightingale in the depths of the night" may suggest:

satsuki yami	Rainy season dark:
obotsukanaki ni	And in the uncertain light,
hototogisu	A nightingale,
fukaki mine yori	Emerging from a distant peak,
nakite izu nari[8]	Sings as it approaches.

At least four poems could have served as sources, but one by Fujiwara no Sanekata in the *Shūishū* is especially close:

satsuki yami	Rainy season dark:
Kurahashi yama no	And from Black Bridge Mountain
hototogisu	A nightingale
obotsukanaku mo	Uncertainly makes its way,
nakiwataru kana[9]	Singing as it passes by.

The great twentieth-century waka poet Saitō Mokichi expressed his admiration for Sanetomo's poem, insisting that Sanetomo had completely absorbed influences from the source poems and made them a part of himself; in this way, Saitō said, he created a splendid new poem that was entirely his own.[10] A contemporary reader's evaluation of this and many other poems by Sanetomo is likely to be measured in terms of whether or not he agrees that Sanetomo had imparted something distinctive to the borrowed imagery; if not, many of the poems will seem egregiously unoriginal. It is clear, in any case, that heavy reliance on the poetry of predecessors has not kept Sanetomo's poetry from enjoying a high reputation. A private anthology of Sanetomo's collected poems (known as *Kinkai Waka Shū*),[11] regularly appears in sets devoted to the classics of Japanese literature, a distinction he shares only with Saigyō.[12]

Sanetomo's poetry is often praised in terms of its successful absorption of influence from the *Man'yōshū*, but this influence came late in his short life as a poet. He was twenty-one when Teika first sent him a volume of *Man'yōshū* poetry, and all the poems in *Kinkai Waka Shū* were written between the ages of seventeen and twenty-two. Indeed, only about a tenth of the poems in *Kinkai Waka Shū* reveal *Man'yōshū* influence,[13] but these poems, rather than the nine tenths in the manner of the *Senzaishū* or *Shin Kokinshū*, account for the esteem that poets and critics have expressed for Sanetomo's poetry. Unfortunately, the *Man'yōshū* diction—the *makurakotoba*, the archaic vocabulary, the particles that suggest states of mind—is the least communicable part of his poetry. Even if a reader recognizes that *ashihiki no* (sometimes translated as "foot dragging") is a makurakotoba used as a fixed epithet before the names of mountains, the term is unlikely to induce an emotional reaction. This would not matter if the poem were as long as the famous chōka of Hitomaro in the *Man'yōshū*, but when one of the five lines of a waka consists of an essentially meaningless makurakotoba, it inevitably reduces what an already short poem can communicate. Only a poet or critic who for some reason dislikes the indirectness and unspoken overtones that characterize later poetry is likely to display enthusiasm for Sanetomo's poems in the heroic mode.

Kamo no Mabuchi (1697–1769), one of Sanetomo's early admirers, went through the text of *Kinkai Waka Shū* bestowing one star[14] on exceptionally good poems and two on masterpieces. Mabuchi was a good poet, and he was well versed in the *Man'yōshū*, but it is not always easy for a modern reader to concur in his judgments of Sanetomo's poetry. Here is a poem to which Mabuchi gave two stars:

ama no hara	When I lift my head
furisake mireba	And gaze at the firmament,
tsuki kiyomi	The moon is so pure;
aki no yo itaku	How terribly far along
furinikeru kana[15]	This autumn night has advanced!

The poem may bring to mind a more famous one, composed in China by Abe no Nakamaro (d. 770):

ama no hara	When I lift my head
furisake mireba	And gaze at the firmament,
Kasuga naru	The moon is the same
Mikasa no yama ni	That rose over Mikasa,
ideshi tsuki kamo[16]	The mountain in Kasuga.

The last three lines are different, it is true, but Sanetomo's were not wholly original, as a poem by Fujiwara no Tametoki in the *Shin Kokinshū* makes clear:

yama no ha wo	As I wait for the moon,
idegate ni suru	So reluctant to appear
tsuki matsu to	Over the mountain edge,
nenu yo no itaku	How terribly far along
furinikeru kana[17]	This sleepless night has advanced!

Comparing Sanetomo's poem with these two source poems, it is apparent that three of the five lines of his waka were borrowed in toto from the two earlier works, and parts of the two remaining lines were also borrowed. What, then, did Sanetomo contribute to his poem, and why was it so highly rated by Kamo no Mabuchi? Presumably, Mabuchi was attracted by the simple, straightforward expression in the manner of the *Man'yōshū*, and perhaps by the archaic phrase *ama no hara*, "the plain of heaven," for the sky; Sanetomo's contribution, Mabuchi might have argued, consisted in joining two waka, one old and one relatively recent, to form a new poem that combined the language of one with the greater poetic sensitivity of the other. Another poem by Sanetomo, written on the same topic, the moon, probably about the same time, shows even more conspicuous *Man'yōshū* influence:

tsuki kiyomi	The moon is so pure:
aki no yo itaku	How terribly far along
fukenikeri	The autumn night advances;
Saho no kawara ni	On the Saho river beach
chidori shiba naku[18]	The sanderlings keep crying.

This poem was derived from one by Yamabe no Akahito in the *Man'yōshū*:

nubatama no	Now, as the jet black
yo no fukeyukeba	Of the night deepens over
hisagi ouru	The lovely river beach
kiyoki kawara ni	Where the *hisagi* trees grow
chidori shiba naku[19]	The sanderlings keep crying.

Mabuchi gave Sanetomo's poem one star, though he surely was aware how much inferior it was to Akahito's, no doubt because he was always ready to welcome unmistakable influence from the *Man'yōshū*.

Saitō, who preferred poems by Sanetomo that stemmed directly from personal experience, praised especially the miscellaneous (*zatsu*) section of *Kinkai Waka Shū*, which includes those composed during Sanetomo's travels to various shrines. One especially celebrated travel poem bears this prefatory note: "When I crossed over the Hakone mountains and surveyed the scene, I could see a small island where the waves broke. I asked my companion the name of this bay, and he replied that it was the Izu Sea. Hearing this, I wrote:

Hakone-ji wo	When I crossed the pass
wa ga koekureba	By the road through Hakone,
Izu no umi ya	There was the Izu Sea;
oki no kojima ni	I could see the waves approach
nami no yoru miyu[20]	A little offshore island.

The poem was awarded two stars by Mabuchi, who commented, "I never cease to wonder how anyone could have composed such a poem. In the *Man'yōshū* there is the poem 'When this morning I crossed over Ōsaka Pass, in the Sea of Ōmi waves were rising like cotton flowers,' but this poem is even better."[21] Sanetomo's poem will probably strike most contemporary readers as a pleasant evocation of an actual experience, but not as a poem of such extraordinary beauty as to make one wonder how it could have been created with merely human powers. Yet even Japanese critics who are known for their high standards have expressed particular admiration for this poem,[22] seeing in the lonely little island a symbol for Sanetomo himself.

The greatest disappointment that Western readers experience with Sanetomo's poetry comes not from inadequacies in his collection but from the absence of poems that suggest his life as a shogun. Only a few, like the following, reveal that he was a military man:

mononofu no	As the warrior
yanami tsukurou	Rearranges his arrows,
kote no ue ni	Hail falls and bounces
arare tabashiru	Off his upraised sleeve of mail,
Nasu no shinohara[23]	In the bamboo plain of Nasu.

This poem seems to present a personal recollection of Sanetomo, not filtered through the images of other people's poetry. And even if Sanetomo himself was not the warrior described, the poem surely was based on an actual experience. This kind of direct involvement with his subject is so rare in Sanetomo's poetry as to lend special interest to the poem. If the scene had been written in the *Shin Kokinshū* style, unspoken implications might have added complexity; but although the poem lacks depth, it is exceptionally effective. The reader will search in vain for other poems that so memorably evoke the life of the third of the Kamakura shoguns, the last of Yoritomo's line.

The *Shin Chokusenshū*

In 1232 the Emperor Gohorikawa commanded Fujiwara Teika to compile the ninth chokusenshū. Teika had of course played a prominent role in the compilation of the *Shin Kokinshū*, but he had been obliged to accommodate himself to the views of the other compilers, especially those of the Emperor Gotoba. It might have been expected that the new collection, of which Teika was the sole editor, would, even more than the *Shin Kokinshū*, embody his aesthetic preferences, especially his advocacy of the principle of *yūgen*, or mysterious depths, something that cannot be expressed in words; but the *Shin Chokusenshū* (New Imperial Collection) contains few poems comparable to those in the *Shin Kokinshū*, and suggests that the court in Kyoto had lost its self-assurance after the ill-fated Jōkyū Rebellion. If the *Shin Chokusenshū* truly reflected Teika's tastes, one can only conclude that they had changed conspicuously since the time of the compilation of the *Shin Kokinshū*.[24]

The compilation of the *Shin Chokusenshū* did not go smoothly, even though Teika was not obliged to take other people's views into consideration. Toward the end of 1232 he formally presented for imperial approval a preface in kana and a table of the proposed contents. Two years later he offered the court a fair copy of the anthology, but soon afterward the Emperor Gohorikawa unexpectedly died. Teika, grieved by this loss, burned his copy of the manuscript. Fujiwara Michiie later found the copy that had been presented to Gohorikawa and returned it to Teika, who was induced to re-edit the work. The final draft was delivered to Michiie in 1235.[25]

The *Shin Chokusenshū* has sometimes been praised as the "fruit" of which the *Shin Kokinshū* was the flower, but if this is so, the fruit has never been enjoyed as much as the flower.[26] When the contents first became known, the prominence of poems by members of the military gave rise to sarcasm and even hostility at the court in Kyoto.[27] Teika had been friendly with Sanetomo ever since the latter sent him poems to correct, and his bitter quarrel with Gotoba strengthened his ties to the shogun's court.[28] Gotoba's defeat and exile in 1221 had enabled Teika to regain his eminence in the world of poetry. Not surprisingly, political considerations affected his choice of poems for the new collection. But although Teika included poems by Sanetomo and others of the shogunate, the collection as a whole was dominated as before by the poets of the aristocracy.

Fujiwara Ietaka was the most generously represented contributor to the *Shin Chokusenshū* with forty-four poems, two more than in the *Shin Kokinshū*. However, most other well-known poets of the *Shin Kokinshū* were represented by a drastically reduced number of poems—Saigyō with fourteen instead of ninety-four, Jien with twenty-seven instead of ninety-one, and Teika himself with fifteen instead of forty-seven.[29] Twenty-five poems by Sanetomo (whose poems do not appear in the *Shin Kokinshū*) were chosen. Even if Sanetomo had not happened to be a good poet, some of his poems would probably have been included anyway;[30] but apart from Sanetomo, the military men were represented with two or three poems each, rather in the manner that a few poems by Minamoto Yoritomo had appeared in the *Shin Kokinshū*.

Not all of the changes in the representation in the new anthology can be explained in terms of politics. Ietaka and Teika were friends, but Ietaka remained faithful to Gotoba even after he was sent into exile, and if Teika had invariably punished people who were sympathetic to Gotoba by reducing the number of their poems in the *Shin Chokusenshū*, Ietaka should have been the first to suffer. No doubt it was the notably clear and pure expression of Ietaka's poems that won them such generous representation despite his political unreliability. In place of his ideal of *yōembi*, or "ethereal beauty," Teika now preferred a simpler style that was exemplified by Ietaka's poems.

The blandness of the poems in the *Shin Chokusenshū* distressed poets who still clung to the typical *Shin Kokinshū* style. The daughter of Shunzei, one of the most accomplished poets of the yōembi style, complained that the collection was artistically inferior, and declared that if it had not been compiled by Teika she would have refused even to take it in her hands.[31] There was from the outset a division of opinion concerning the worth of the collection: Fujiwara Tameie (1198–1275), who would compile two imperial anthologies, praised the "unaffected configuration and felicitous conception" (*sugata sunao ni kokoro uruwashiki uta*) of the poems in the *Shin Chokusenshū*;[32] and his high opinion was shared by his wife, the nun Abutsu, in her work of poetic criticism *The Crane at Night*.[33]

Tameie was a scholar of Heian literature and a not inconsiderable poet. Over three hundred of his poems were included in the imperial collections, beginning with the *Shin Chokusenshū*. The following poem is typical:

oto tatete	With a mournful sound
ima hata fukinu	It is blowing once again—
wa ga yado no	The first autumn wind
ogi no uwaba no	Over the upper leaves of
aki no hatsukaze[34]	The *ogi* by my dwelling.

There is nothing wrong with this poem, but it fails to produce much of an impression. The upper leaves of the *ogi*, a reedlike plant, were the first to change color in the autumn, a fact that had been duly noted by innumerable poets before Tameie. If Tameie had mentioned some normally overlooked plant, or had situated the blowing wind in a somewhat more unusual place than his own garden, the poem might linger a bit longer in the memory, but as it is, nothing distinguishes it from countless other poems on the upper leaves of the ogi in the first autumn wind, save perhaps the rather unusual words *ima hata* for "again." But, it should be noted, poets of the age were quite content if their waka were free of faults (*yamai*) of the kind that might be reproved by the judge of an uta-awase session or the author of a text of poetic criticism.

Regardless of its absolute merits, the *Shin Chokusenshū* never attained anything like the popularity of the *Shin Kokinshū*. Even its excellent poems, by masters of the waka, have been largely forgotten. Motoori Norinaga, as always a model of sound judgment, attributed the relative failure of the collection to the fact that the best poems by the poets of the previous generation had already appeared in the *Shin Kokinshū*, and there simply were not any outstanding poets in the next generation.[35]

Four Nijō School Collections

Four imperially sponsored collections were compiled between the *Shin Chokusenshū* of 1235 and the *Gyokuyōshū* of 1313. These collections all have titles beginning with either *shin* (new) or *shoku* (sequel), suggesting in a depressingly accurate manner that the compilers looked back to past glories rather than ahead to new developments in poetry. The central figures behind these collections were all poets of the conservative Nijō school.

The creation of schools of waka poetry began with the sons by different wives of Tameie, who contested the possession of Teika manuscripts that were believed to embody the true traditions of the waka. The eldest son, Tameuji (1222–1286), founded the Nijō school (named, like the other schools, after his place of residence in the capital); another son, Tamenori (1226–1279) established the more innovative Kyōgoku school; and a much younger son named Reizei Tamesuke (1263–1328) founded the Reizei school which, though generally on good terms with the Kyōgoku poets, had its own horde of manuscripts and poetic traditions.

The style of Tameie's most characteristic poetry was perpetuated by the conservative Nijō school, and the tenth and eleventh chokusenshū, which he compiled, represented this school at its most typical. Naturally, there were good poems among the thousands in the four collections, but to read all the poems in these collections might persuade one that they contained not one individual voice or original image in this poetry. This is not true, but much poetry was composed in the manner of a virtuoso spinning out variations on established themes—not attempting to surprise but to impress the reader with some slight modification of a honka that came closer, even very slightly closer, than the original poem to the heart of the perception or emotion described.

The *Gyokuyōshū*

The next major imperial collection, the fourteenth, was called the *Gyokuyōshū* (Jeweled Leaves Collection).[36] The name itself, probably an allusion to the *Man'yōshū*, was a departure from the dreary titles of the four previous collections, and indicated the desire of the compiler to return to the roots of Japanese poetry in the *Man'yōshū*, rejecting the normal insistence on fidelity to the orthodox line of descent of waka composition from the *Kokinshū*.[37] The *Gyokuyōshū* and the *Fūgashū* (Collection of Elegance), the seventeenth anthology, were the only two compiled by poets of the Kyōgoku-Reizei school; Nijō school poets edited all the other Kamakura and Muromachi period chokusenshū down to the twenty-first, the *Shin Zoku Kokinshū* (New Collection of Ancient and Modern Times Continued) of 1439.

The background to the compilation of the *Gyokuyōshū* was as much political as literary. The division between the two main schools of poetry paralleled the division in imperial authority from the middle of the thirteenth century until late in the fourteenth century. In 1246 the Emperor Gosaga abdicated in favor of his elder son Gofukakusa, who reigned from 1246 to 1259. Gofukakusa was in turn obliged by his father, the *in* (cloistered emperor), to abdicate in favor of his younger brother Kameyama, his father's favorite son. Gosaga lived on until 1272, acting as long as he lived as the power behind the throne, insofar as it is possible to speak of imperial "power" at a time when the Hōjō family ruled the country as regents for the shoguns, who at this time were themselves merely figureheads. Relations between Gofukakusa and Kameyama remained friendly, at least on the surface,[38] until the death of Gosaga. Two years later, in 1274, Kameyama abdicated in favor of his son, the Emperor Gouda, much to the annoyance of the partisans of Gofukakusa, who believed that the throne should have gone to the senior line of the older brother. Open antagonism over the succession broke out between followers of the two retired emperors, and it could be subdued only by the shogunate.

State policy was controlled in almost every instance by the shogunate officials. It was by their decree that the crown came to alternate more or less regularly between the senior line (Gofukakusa) and the junior line (Kameyama), beginning with the successor to Gouda, who abdicated in 1287, and continuing until the accession to the throne of Godaigo in 1318.[39] In the capital the *in* continued to exercise greater authority than the reigning emperor, leading to further conflicts between senior and junior lines. The office of *in* was discontinued by Gouda in 1321, but the dynastic dispute, far from subsiding, soon erupted into open warfare.

It may seem surprising that these political events should have had a direct bearing on the composition of poetry. It was not that poets used the waka for obviously political ends, composing poetry that would in some way further the cause of whichever branch of the imperial family they supported. Regardless of the faction, the poets continued to celebrate in their poetry not some political cause but the first mist of early spring or the first cool breeze of autumn. The permissible subjects of waka had been established at the time of the *Kokinshū*, and no one was so indecorous as to compose a waka with openly political content.

All the same, a connection was established between the political and poetic factions. The bitter disputes among the sons of Tameie for his estates and treasured documents of poetic lore resulted, as we have seen, in the creation of schools of poetry. Tameie was of a naturally conservative bent, although his poetic stance apparently changed in late years under the influence of his wife Abutsu. She was not only a diarist and poet,[40] but a resolute woman who was unswervingly determined to obtain the inheritance from Tameie for her son Reizei Tamesuke.[41] Her suit for possession of two of Tameie's estates, placed before the courts in Kamakura, was eventually successful (in 1289, after her death) and Reizei Tamesuke subsequently established close relations with the shogunate.

The Nijō school, headed by Nijō Tameyo (1251–1338), supported the junior line (Kameyama's), and both the Reizei and Kyōgoku schools the senior line (Gofukakusa's).

The command for the compilation of a new imperial collection—the future *Gyokuyōshū*—was issued in 1293 by the Emperor Fushimi (1265–1317), a member of the senior line and a gifted poet who had been impressed by the poetry and poetic theory of Kyōgoku Tamekane (1254–1332). Fushimi chose four poets of different schools to compile the collection, but clashes between Kyōgoku Tamekane and Nijō Tameyo, over such matters as whether or not *Man'yōshū* poems should be included, made it almost impossible for the editors to collaborate.

In 1296 Tamekane, who then held the office of acting middle counselor, suddenly resigned. He had been accused by rivals of having used his poetry as a means of insinuating himself into political activity. The shogunate, accepting the truth of these rumors, placed Tamekane under house arrest.[42] In 1298 he was imprisoned at the shogunate headquarters in Kyoto, and two months later was sent into exile on the island of Sado. In the following month the Emperor Fushimi abdicated in favor of his son, Gofushimi. The cause of his abdication is not known, but it may be that he felt chagrined over his inability to prevent the shogunate from exiling the poet he so much admired.

The Nijō poets were delighted to learn of the exile of Tamekane and abdication of Fushimi. Although Tamekane had made considerable progress with the compilation of the *Gyokuyōshū*, this project was dropped, and the Nijō poets, by command of the Cloistered Emperor Gouda (and not Gofushimi, the reigning emperor), set about preparing an imperial collection that accorded with their conservative preferences, the *Shin Gosenshū*, the fourth of the Nijō collections that immediately preceded the *Gyokuyōshū*. This collection, compiled by Nijō Tameyo, has so dismal a reputation that critics claim that the poems of his own that Tameyo chose for the *Shin Gosenshū* are inferior to those in the *Gyokuyōshū*, proof that he not only lacked poetic talent but was incapable of judging even his own work.[43]

Once again, however, it is necessary to stress that not all the poems even in a collection with as poor a reputation as the *Shin Gosenshū* were inept. Here is one on a spring day by Tameyo, composed on the theme of "dawn moon in late spring":

tsurenakute	O moon at dawn,
nokoru narai wo	prolonging your stay in the sky
kurete yuku	with such indifference—

haru ni oshie yo won't you teach your ways to spring
ariake no tsuki before it draws to a close?[44]

Perhaps this poem shows no great originality, but the personification of the moon and the spring makes it appealing. Other examples of agreeable Nijō poetry are easily found,[45] but ultimately, the value of a waka lies in the individual voice of the poet and not in undifferentiated charm.

In 1301 Gofushimi abdicated and was succeeded by Gonijō of the junior line. This development boded even worse days ahead for the Kyōgoku school; but although the change led immediately to the compilation of the *Shin Gosenshū* by the Nijō school, it did not result in any diminution of activity by the Kyōgoku poets. At the time there were five retired emperors,[46] each with a small court of his own. Gouda, as the *in*, had the greatest power, but Fushimi, the best poet among the retired emperors, gathered around him poets of the Kyōgoku school and frequent uta-awase sessions were held at his palace.[47]

The shogunate relented in 1303 and allowed Tamekane to return to the capital from his place of exile in Sado. This heralded a period of even greater activity by the Kyōgoku school poets, and when Gonijō died in 1308 and was succeeded by Hanazono of the senior line, the stage was set for the Kyōgoku poets to compile an imperial collection of their own. But first there was a clash between Nijō Tameyo and Kyōgoku Tamekane. It will be recalled that Fushimi in 1293 had asked four poets to compile a new imperial collection. During the years of Tamekane's exile, two of the other poets died, and Tameyo himself had withdrawn. It seemed that the *Gyokuyōshū* had died a natural death, but Tamekane, back from exile, insisted that he still had a mandate to compile the collection. The rumor spread at the court that Tamekane had been appointed as the sole compiler. Tameyo, much upset by the rumor, sent his son to ask Tamekane his intentions. Tamekane replied that he did indeed consider himself to be the only one in a position to make the compilation, and he suggested that if Tameyo did not like this arrangement he should make representations at once to the shogunate.[48]

When Tameyo received this news, he was furious. He sent a messenger to the shogunate and also formally protested to the court alleging that Tamekane was not fit to be the compiler because he had been exiled and, further, was an illegitimate son. Tamekane responded in equally acrimonious terms. He admitted that he was illegitimate, but gave precedents for illegitimate sons' having been designated as the compilers of imperial collections; moreover, he insisted, he had received personal instruction from Tameie (the grandfather of both men), unlike Tameyo, who had been taught by another man and had received neither written nor oral instruction from Tameie. He declared that it would be intolerable if a man of no poetic ability were chosen to edit a collection, solely on the basis of his seniority.[49]

The recriminations continued between the two men. During the course of these heated exchanges there was hardly a mention of poetic practice. Fushimi, in his capacity as the original sponsor of the collection, was the recipient of these letters. His inclination was to appoint Tamekane as the sole compiler, but he feared this might upset the shogunate: Tameyo was the poetry tutor of both the shogun and the Hōjō regent. However, word was received from Kamakura in the summer of 1311 that there was no objection to Tamekane's compiling the collection by himself.[50]

The *Gyokuyōshū* was presented to the ex-Emperor Fushimi by Kyōgoku Tamekane in 1312.[51] Of all the imperially sponsored collections, it contains the largest number of waka, 2,796 in all. Perhaps, as has been suggested,[52] Tamekane feared that the Kyōgoku and Reizei poets might never again have the chance to compile a collection, and for this reason included as many poems from these schools as possible.

The choice of poets for inclusion in the *Gyokuyōshū* provided a clear indication of the change in the poetical preferences of the editors: of the 182 poets, 113 were published in an imperial collection for the first time.[53] Among the poets most generously represented, the majority were affiliated with the Kyōgoku school, including the Retired Emperor Fushimi with 93 poems, Saionji Sanekane (1249–1322) with 62 poems, Tamekane's sister Kyōgoku Tameko (1252?–1316?) with 60 poems, the Empress Eifukumon'in (1271–1342) with 49 poems, and (modestly) Tamekane with 36 poems. Teika, Shunzei, and Saigyō were also favored, but there was only a token selection of poems of the Nijō school.

The *Gyokuyōshū* has never been studied with the care accorded the *Kokinshū* or the *Shin Kokinshū* or even the *Gosenshū*, but it has had its admirers. Toki Zemmaro (1885–1980), an important tanka poet[54] who published several studies devoted to Kyōgoku Tamekane, wrote about the *Gyokuyōshū*:

> Seen against the background of the history of the waka from ancient times to the middle ages, there is something truly startling about the freshness of the *Gyokuyōshū*. A desire to break through the traditional methods of the chokusenshū is apparent at every turn. It is distinguished among the twenty-one collections by its rare pas-

sion, evidenced by the number of the poems (the largest of any collection), the grandness of its scale, the abundance and vividness of its nature poetry, the respect offered the *Man'yōshū* in both quality and quantity, its unique manner of carrying on the *Shin Kokinshū* traditions; and again, by the boldness of its selection of works by unknown poets and its policy of excluding compositions on stereotyped set topics. With respect to the division of the collection into books, love poems (always difficult for Kyōgoku poets) have been reduced to five books, while the miscellaneous poems have been increased to five books, in place of the traditional four books or fewer, making it possible to include many poems on freely chosen topics. Again, the category of travel poems was freshly considered. A great many poems devoted to the contemplation of nature—about twice the number of poems on love—were selected with the intent of employing the vivid Kyōgoku style of portraying nature as the framework for a new and real fusion between place and nature.[55]

It may be wondered why, if this praise is to be believed, the *Gyokuyōshū* has left so little impression on the history of Japanese literature. In part this can be explained in terms of the overwhelming strength of the Nijō school during the following centuries. Not only were all but one of the subsequent imperial anthologies compiled by Nijō poets but most of the important waka poets of the fourteenth, fifteenth, and sixteenth centuries were conservative in their poetic tastes even if not formally associated with the Nijō school. Again, the innovations of the Kyōgoku poets, though important historically, have long since ceased to startle readers, and it takes a certain effort to remember that some poems that today seem innocuously attractive were interpreted in their day as acts of defiance.

The lasting attraction of the *Gyokuyōshū* can be measured in terms of the successful works composed by a very few poets. Three of the many poets were outstanding—Kyōgoku Tamekane, the Emperor Fushimi, and Fushimi's consort, the Empress Eifukumon'in.

Of all the *Gyokuyōshū* (and *Fūgashū*) poets, surely Kyōgoku Tamekane was the best. He not only excelled in poetic composition but his book of criticism, *Tamekanekyō Wakashō* (Lord Tamekane's Notes on Poetry),[56] was the most important expression of the theoretical basis of Kyōgoku school poetry. In this work Tamekane insisted above all on the *kokoro*, or feeling, expressed by a poem, and he accorded less importance to the diction. As a matter of fact, most of his poems were on topics that had claimed the attention of waka poets ever since the days of the *Kokinshū*, and his poetic vocabulary hardly differed from Tsurayuki's, but his close observation of nature enabled him to impart freshness even to hackneyed themes:

eda ni moru	Sifting through branches,
asahi no kage no	the rays of the morning sun
sukunaki ni	are still very few—
suzushisa fukaki	and how deep is the coolness
take no oku kana	back among the bamboos![57]

There is nothing startling in the material of the poem, but two words stand out: *sukunaki* (few) and *fukaki* (deep). These ordinary adjectives are peculiarly effective because unexpected: it was unusual to speak of morning sunlight as *sukunaki*, and evokes an image of a bamboo grove so thickly overgrown that only a few rays of sunlight find their way inside. Because the sunlight cannot penetrate very far into the bamboos, the coolness has a "depth" that is not easily dissipated. The adjective *fukaki* is used with both what it follows and precedes: "the cool is deep" "deep within a bamboo grove." The poem as a whole conveys with a minimum of words and images a convincing picture of an early morning scene that suggests actual observation. Another outstanding poem by Tamekane has even more vivid imagery:

neya no ue wa	It makes no sound
tsumoreru yuki ni	On the snow piled on the roof
oto mo sede	Of my bed chamber;
yokogiru arare	But the hail, slashing sideways,
mado tataku nari[58]	Rattles against the window.

The poem creates an impression of novelty with two words, the first the verb *yokogiru*, meaning to cut slantwise, and the second *mado*, a window—words that were unexpected in the context of Kamakura poetry.[59] The contrast between the heavy blanket of snow on the roof, absorbing every sound, and the volatile hail beating against the window exemplifies the antithesis between the still and the moving often found in *Gyokuyōshū* poems.[60] Mention of snow, needless to say, was in no way unusual in a winter poem, but snow at night (indicated by the mention of the bed chamber) is typical of the attention given to dawn, twilight, and night by the Kyōgoku poets.[61]

One other feature of this poem is worthy of note: the extra syllable in the first line. Poets as far back as the *Kokinshū* had occasionally written lines containing an extra syllable (though never a line with one syllable too few), but the Kyōgoku poets wrote such lines so often as to make *ji-amari*, as the practice is known, a typical feature of their school.[62] To add a single syllable to a poem is hardly revolutionary, even when measured by the yardstick of traditional court poetry, but it serves to distinguish Kyōgoku poetry from the poetry of the Nijō poets, who rarely permitted themselves such liberty.

The most interesting poems in the *Gyokuyōshū* are complex and sometimes obscure, in contrast to the easy intelligibility of the poems by the Nijō poets. Even when a poem seems to be no more than a straightforward description of a natural scene, it may "conceal" a Buddhist text, as various allegorical poems (more in the *Fūgashū* than in the *Gyokuyōshū*) demonstrate. Again, Chinese poetic practice of the Sung dynasty seems to have inspired the preference for hazy or dimly lit landscapes, rather than for the more conventionally admired brilliance of cherry blossoms or tinted maple leaves. In the following poem by Kyōgoku Tamekane the brightness of the crimson plum blossoms is seen through the mistiness of spring rain:

ume no hana	On an evening
kurenai niou	aglow with the crimson
yūgure ni	of plum flowers,
yanagi nabikite	the willow boughs sway softly;
harusame zo furu	and the spring rain falls.[63]

Tamekane was arrested again in 1315. He had been denounced to the shogunate by Saionji Sanekane, formerly his disciple in waka poetry. This time Tamekane was accused of having flaunted his wealth and prosperity during a visit to Nara, where he conducted himself like a reigning emperor, surrounded by a great entourage of nobles, court ladies, and priests. A passage in *Essays in Idleness* recalls the scene of his arrest:

> When the Major Counsellor and Lay Priest Tamekane had been arrested and led off to Rokuhara surrounded by soldiers, Lord Suketomo saw him near Ichijō. He exclaimed, "How I envy him! What a marvellous last remembrance to have of this life!"[64]

Suketomo's envy would be ironically satisfied in 1324 when he was exiled to Sado and put to death. Tamekane also died in exile, but the place of his last exile had been moved closer to the capital; he died in Kawachi in 1332 at the age of seventy-eight.

The large number of poems by the Emperor Fushimi included in the *Gyokuyōshū* was not a sign of sycophancy; he was a distinguished and exceptionally prolific member of the Kyōgoku school whose poems would have ornamented any collection. Perhaps his best-known poem is on the unusual topic of "lightning":

yoi no ma no	All through the evening,
murakumozutai	From one cloud bank to the next,
kage miete	The flashes travel:
yama no ha meguru	Circling the edge of the hills,
aki no inazuma[65]	The bursts of autumn lightning.

Not only is this poem unconventional, but it seems to be the poet's actual perception, rather than a variation on a set theme. Fushimi was also prominently represented in the *Fūgashū*, which contains another of his poems on lightning:

nioi shirami	The glow is so white
tsuki no chikazuku	That flashes of lightning
yama no ha no	Pale in its brilliance
hikari ni yowaru	By the edge of the mountains
inazuma no kage[66]	At the approach of the moon.

There is more artifice than truth in this description of a moonrise that dims even the lightning flashes. The poem is a tour de force: three different words are used for "light" to suggest the different qualities of the light of the sky, the moon, and lightning. Another *Fūgashū* poem by Fushimi also contains striking imagery:

sayo fukete	As the night grows late
yado moru inu no	The barking of a watchdog
koe takashi	Noisily echoes
mura shizuka naru	Far beyond the moon over
tsuki no ochikata[67]	A village wrapped in silence.

The evocation of the silence of a village with the sound of a dog's barking recalls Bashō's haiku on the noisy cicadas at Yamadera: "How still it is! / Stinging into the stones, / The locusts' trill."[68]

Konishi Jin'ichi, in the course of an illuminating essay on the characteristics of *Gyokuyōshū* poetry, mentioned the frequent use of one particular poetic device—a momentary external stimulus that causes the speaker to become aware of something that might otherwise have remained unnoticed, as in another poem by Fushimi:

fukenu to mo	The hour grew late,
nagamuru hodo wa	yet so intent was my gaze
oboenu ni	I didn't know it—
tsuki yori nishi no	until I saw so little left
sora zo sukunaki	of the sky west of the moon.[69]

Even those who have praised the poetry of the Kyōgoku school generally admit that love poetry was not their forte. Konishi took exception to this commonly accepted view, insisting that of all the poems in the *Gyokuyōshū*, the love poems most clearly exhibit the characteristic features of the collection.[70] These poems seem bare because (unlike the love poetry typical of other collections) they often contain not a single image;[71] but sometimes they are effective precisely because the impression of direct, even unliterary expression of feelings is not weakened by conventionally pretty imagery. This poem by Fushimi illustrates such an instance:

koyoi toe ya	Come to me tonight—
nochi no ikuyo wa	and if all your promises
ikutabi no	on nights to come
yoshi itsuwari to	should turn out to be lies,
naraba naru tomo	then let them be lies.[72]

Konishi discovered a strain that runs through many of the love poems—an attempt to analyze the speaker's emotions by addressing them or by keeping them, as it were, at arm's length so as to better discern them, instead of outspokenly declaring one's feelings in the manner of earlier waka. In the following by Kyōgoku Tamekane's sister, Tameko, the speaker addresses her heart, which personifies her emotions:

wa ga kokoro	O my heart,
urami ni mukite	If you are turning to resentment,
uramihate yo	Do so to the limit,
aware ni nareba	For if you turn to weaker sorrow,
shinobigataki wo	It will be impossible to bear.[73]

Sometimes, too, love and other emotions are spoken of as if they possess visible form, as in a poem (written in the persona of a woman) by the statesman Saionji Sanekane:

koishisa wa	My yearning for him
nagame no sue ni	After endless pondering
katachi shite	Has taken on shape:
namida ni ukabu	Floating in a blur of tears,
tōyama no matsu[74]	A pine on a distant hill.

The pine into which the speaker's longing has been transformed is blurred by her tears, but seems to be a symbol of her grief over a lover who no longer visits. It was unusual for poets to speak of emotions taking on shape or for a pine to be used as a symbol of this kind (though the pun on *matsu*, meaning both "pine" and "wait for," frequently appeared in poetry). The *Gyokuyōshū* is notable for the number of poems with unexpected perceptions expressed in unusual combinations of language. Konishi pointed out examples in the *Gyokuyōshū* and *Fūgashū*: the adjective *omoki* (heavy) used to characterize the sound of a vesper bell, or "the deep color of autumn" mentioned in a poem by the Princess Yūgimon'in (1270–1307), the daughter of Gofukakusa and sister of Fushimi.[75]

Eifukumon'in, Fushimi's consort, had the melancholy distinction of being the last important woman waka poet from the fourteenth until the twentieth century. She was a member of the Saionji family at a time when the Saionji were emulating the Fujiwara of the Heian period in marrying their daughters to emperors.

In the sixth month of 1288 Sanekane sent his eldest daughter, the future Eifukumon'in, to the palace as a *nyogo* (imperial concubine) in the service of the Emperor Fushimi, who was then twenty-three. Two months later she was proclaimed as his official consort. Although Eifukumon'in was childless, the marriage was happy, and the royal couple both excelled at composing waka in the style of the Kyōgoku school. In 1298 she resigned her position as consort to enter Buddhist orders with the name Eifukumon'in.

Her earliest-known poems date from 1297, but she did not display any special competence for another twenty years. Shortly before Fushimi died in 1317, he bade his son, the Emperor Gofushimi, to consult with Eifukumon'in and the former kampaku Takatsukasa Fuyuhira in the event he planned to command the compilation of a new imperial collection. Fushimi's high opinion of her poetic ability was otherwise demonstrated by his deathbed gifts to her of manuscripts of the *Kokinshū*, *Gosenshū*, and *Shūishū* in his own hand. At the time Kyōgoku Tamekane was in exile, and Eifukumon'in became in effect the central figure of the Kyōgoku school.[76]

The first poems by Eifukumon'in to appear in an imperially sponsored collection were three included in the *Shin Gosenshū* (1303), compiled by the Nijō school. This was only token participation, but forty-nine of her poems were chosen for the *Gyokuyōshū*, and in the *Fūgashū* sixty-nine of her poems appear, second only to Fushimi with eighty-five. A few of her poems were also included in three of the last four imperial collections.

Little is especially striking in the poems of Eifukumon'in, but as one reads it is difficult not to be moved by the felicity of expression and the suggestion of genuine emotion (*kokoro*) behind the words. One of the first poems to reveal her poetic talent (composed in 1303, when she was thirty-two) was the following:

kaku bakari	If even now
uki ga ue dani	in the midst of rejection
aware naru	I still love him so,
aware nariseba	then what would be my feelings
ikaga aramashi	if he were to love me back?[77]

This poem, typically for a love poem in the style of the Kyōgoku school, contains no imagery; indeed, there is hardly an image in any of Eifukumon'in's many love poems. The echoing of the words *aware naru* of the third line in the *aware nariseba* of the next line is also characteristic of her poetry; Brower and Miner said of her that among the Kyōgoku poets she was "the fondest of the various balances, contrasts, and parallelisms possible in Japanese."[78] Her adherence to the Kyōgoku school is also suggested by her use of ji-amari:

tsune yori mo	At the very moment
namida kakikurasu	When, more depressed than usual,
ori shimo are	I yielded to tears,
kusaki wo miru mo	I saw the grasses and trees
ame no yūgure[79]	Soaked in the rainy twilight.

The second and third lines of this poem have an extra syllable each, a suggestion perhaps of griefs too great to squeeze into the normal structure. The division in the poem between the first three lines that describe the speaker's grief and the last two lines concerning the scene outside is typical of Kyōgoku poetry.[80] The time of day of the poem—the twilight hour—is also characteristic, as is the use of the pathetic fallacy of imagining that the grasses and trees are also weeping in the rain even as she weeps in her room.

kawachidori	The river plovers—
tsuki yo wo samumi	Are they unable to sleep
inezu are ya	This cold moonlit night?
nesamuru goto ni	Every time I wake from sleep
koe no kikoyuru[81]	I can hear their voices call.

The empathy between the speaker and the subject is typical of Eifukumon'in's poems. The season, winter, was also well suited to the lonely quality of her poetry, though she naturally composed even more poems about spring and autumn.

The *Fūgashū*

Eifukumon'in did not live to see the completion and presentation of the *Fūgashū*. In between the *Gyokuyōshū* and *Fūgashū* there were two collections compiled by the Nijō school, neither of much literary distinction. In 1308 the Emperor Hanazono (1297–1348), a son of Fushimi, came to the throne as a boy of eleven and reigned until 1318 when he was obliged to abdicate in favor of Godaigo. It was during his reign that the *Gyokuyōshū* was compiled, though he was too young to participate in the editing. After his abdication he spent much of his time in literary and scholarly pursuits. His diary in kambun, *Hanazono-in Shinki* (Diary of the Cloistered Emperor Hanazono),[82] which covers the years 1310–1322, is an important source of information on poetic activity during the late Kamakura and early Muromachi periods.

Hanazono lived for thirty years after his abdication, a period when the country was repeatedly torn by warfare.[83] As a member of the senior line, he suffered particularly during the Kemmu Restoration of 1333–1336, when Godaigo of the junior line established a government in Kyoto intended to assert imperial authority after centuries of rule by surrogates.[84] Godaigo was no friend of the senior line, and Hanazono, along with the ex-Emperor Gofushimi and the Emperor Kōgon, was forced to flee the capital. He took refuge in a remote monastery in Mino province and did not return to the capital until after Ashikaga Takauji had restored the senior line of emperors to the throne in 1336. Hanazono lived in retirement until his death in 1348.

In 1343 work was begun on the compilation of a new imperial collection, the *Fūgashū*. Hanazono took an active part in the work and contributed both the Japanese and Chinese prefaces,[85] but (as recent research has shown) it was not Hanazono, as long believed, but another former emperor, Kōgon (1313–1364) who actually compiled the *Fūgashū*.[86] This was the first imperial collection compiled by an emperor.

Kōgon, the son of Gofushimi, was the favorite nephew of Eifukumon'in and had taken part in various poetry gatherings at her palace. He first emerged into prominence in 1331, when the shogunate officials in Kamakura, getting wind of Godaigo's plans to overthrow their government, sent a strong force to the capital. Godaigo fled, and by command of the shogunate Kōgon was proclaimed the emperor. His enthronement ceremony was, however, postponed until the next year in the hope that Godaigo would be captured and with him the imperial regalia. Godaigo refused to abdicate or surrender the regalia, and two emperors ruled at the same time. Godaigo was captured and banished to the Oki islands in 1332, but he escaped the next year and returned in triumph to the capital. Kōgon had no choice but to abdicate; he had officially ruled for less than a year. Kōgon is known as the first of the Northern Court emperors, the term referring to the period from 1336 to 1392 when there were two courts, one in Kyoto (the senior or Northern Court) and the other in Yoshino (the junior or Southern Court). After three years in power, Godaigo was forced in 1336 to abandon the capital and take refuge in Yoshino.

In 1352 Kōgon took the Buddhist tonsure and during the following years devoted himself chiefly to religion. Many sovereigns had entered orders without noticeably changing their way of life, but Kōgon was deeply religious and, especially toward the close of his life, devoted himself to prayers for the repose of those who had died in the wars. In 1362 he visited the Southern Court emperor, perhaps in the hope that this might bring about peace. In the following year he founded the Zen temple Jōshō-ji to the north of Kyoto and lived there in the utmost simplicity. Shortly before he died in 1364 he gave instructions that there be no elaborate funeral ceremony, but that he be buried in the earth without any other marker than the trees that might of themselves grow upon his grave.[87]

Kōgon was an accomplished poet. His waka were included not only in the *Fūgashū*, but in several collections edited by the Nijō school.[88]

Among his poems the most affecting are those with religious or humanitarian overtones.

terikumori
samuki atsuki mo
toki toshite
tami ni kokoro no
yasumu ma mo nashi[89]

Burning sun or clouds,
Frigid cold or searing heat,
Each has its season;
In the hearts of my people
There is no time even to rest.

This poem has no specific religious background (it is included among the "miscellaneous" poems in the *Fūgashū* rather than those devoted to Buddhism), but it expresses compassion for the common people who, afflicted by heat and cold by turns, have no time to think of anything else. Kōgon in his wanderings saw more of the life of the people than emperors who never left the capital, and this may have inspired his compassion. The chiasmus in the first and second lines provides a welcome poetic touch. Another poem of social concern is even more effective:

samukarashi
tami no waraya wo
omou ni wa
fusuma no naka no
ware mo hazukashi[90]

How cold they must be!
When I think of my people
In their huts of straw,
I feel ashamed of myself
As I lie under blankets.

Such poems make up only a small part of the poems in the *Fūgashū*, but specialists in the poetry of this period claim that they can sense under the surface of poems on the usual set topics—flowers, birds, the moon, snow—a tension intimated sometimes in the prefatory notes, sometimes in the words themselves.[91] The prominence of poems on mountain retreats, not true of the *Gyokuyōshū*, also suggests an even darker and lonelier world. On the whole, however, the poems much resemble not only those in the *Gyokuyōshū* but often the *Shin Kokinshū*:

yūhi sasu
ochiba ga ue ni
shigure sugite
niwa ni midaruru
ukigumo no kage

The evening sun shines
over fallen leaves still wet
from a passing shower;
in the garden, a confusion
of shadows from floating clouds.[92]

One of the casualties of the warfare was the Kyōgoku school. In 1351 the general Ashikaga Takauji, who had hitherto backed the Northern Court, ostensibly surrendered to the Southern Court. Gomurakami, the Southern Court emperor, thereupon invalidated the offices of Sukō, the Northern Court emperor, and his crown prince, Naohito. In the following year Southern Court troops occupied Kyoto. When they left, they took with them three former emperors of the Northern Court—Kōgon, Kōmyō, and Sukō, together with Naohito.[93] Although this was surely not the intent of the Southern Court soldiers, they destroyed the Kyōgoku school by depriving it of its last imperial patrons.[94] From this time on until the nineteenth century the court unswervingly favored the Nijō school.

The *Shin'yōshū*

Critics generally agree that the *Fūgashū* was the last important imperial collection: the reputation of the four more compiled by Nijō poets is dismal, though some good poets were represented.[95] There were numerous vicissitudes in the warfare of the second half of the fourteenth century, but the Northern Court—the senior line—was most often in control of the capital. The Nijō poets found a way of accommodating themselves with the senior line, though it had previously favored the Kyōgoku-Reizei poets, and subsequently flourished in the capital. Among the Nijō poets four priests—Ton'a (1289–1372), Jōben (c. 1256–c. 1343), Keiun (c. 1295–c. 1370), and Kenkō (c. 1253–c. 1352)—were renowned as the Four Deva Kings of the Waka.[96] The poems of these men are never less than competent, and occasionally they have charm, as in this waka by Jōben in the *Shin Zoku Kokinshū*:

ukimi ni mo	Did it perhaps
chigiri arite ya	pledge to stay this night with me
yadoruran	despite my sad state?
namida itowanu	The moonlight on my sleeves
sode no tsukikage	shows no aversion to my tears.[97]

But poems of literary interest are rare in the imperial collections of the time, though the private collections of these poets are of greater value.

The only collection of the late fourteenth century that is still read (though even then to a very limited extent) is the *Shin'yōshū* (Collection of New Leaves, 1381), compiled by Prince Munenaga (1311–1385?), the eighth son of Godaigo and chief general of Godaigo's forces, who fought valiantly in various parts of the country, especially in the mountainous province of Shinano. His talents as a waka poet, early displayed, may have been nurtured by his mother, a daughter of the poet Nijō Tameyo. One unusual feature of this collection is that all the poems were by contemporaries. The poets were all associated with the Southern Court.

The compilation of the *Shin'yōshū* seems to have been inspired by indignation that poems by persons associated with the Southern Court had been excluded from the fourteenth-century imperial collections. The neglect was understandable in the case of the *Fūgashū*, since it was compiled by the Kyōgoku school, but the Nijō compilers of later collections had no less adamantly refused to include poems by men of their own school because, despite their poetic orthodoxy, they were fighting against the Kyoto court.

The *Shin'yōshū*, despite this unusual background, was closely modeled on earlier collections: it was in twenty books divided in the customary manner into seasonal, travel, love, and other poetic subjects. Even readers resigned to the probability that many poems in the *Shin'yōshū* will closely resemble those in collections compiled under more tranquil circumstances are likely to hope that at least some poems will be imbued with genuine feeling. It is hard to imagine that nothing would be reflected of the experiences of the authors, who had been forced to live in the mountains, far from the capital, where they experienced hardships that went beyond disappointment over the falling of cherry blossoms or the loneliness of an autumn dusk; but the rewards of the *Shin'yōshū* are limited.

The preface (in Japanese), written by Prince Munenaga, makes brief reference to the background: "Toward the beginning of the Genkō era [1331–33] within Akitsushima [a poetic name for Japan] the sound of the waves was not quiet. In the region of the Kasuga plain the light of beacon fires was often seen, but before long what had been disturbed was controlled, and a return was made to the proper Way. Afterward, the administration of rites in the palace returned to the old paths, and the people of the land again enjoyed the far-spreading imperial bounty. The emperor ruled the country entirely according to the principle of subduing the wicked and destroying the rebellious, but it seems to be the way of the world that what is once well-ruled will again become disordered. . . ."[98] The events referred to in this passage are Godaigo's revolt against the Hōjō regents, the subsequent warfare, the reestablishment of imperial authority during the Kemmu Restoration, and the collapse of imperial rule in Kyoto. Munenaga felt obliged to maintain the decorum and indirection of Ki no Tsurayuki's preface to the *Kokinshū*; but if suggestion is a legitimate and even admirable way of evoking regret over the coming of old age or the realization that one is no longer loved, it is grossly inadequate in this particular context. To say of the outbreak of Godaigo's momentous struggle to restore imperial authority merely that "the sound of waves was not quiet" (*nami no oto shizuka narazu*) is ludicrously restrained.

Prince Munenaga is generally considered to have been the most accomplished poet of the *Shin'yōshū*. He also compiled a collection of his own work, *Rikashū* (Damson Blossom Collection, 1371), some of the poems being the same as in the *Shin'yōshū*. The prose prefaces to Munenaga's poems are usually far more affecting than the poems themselves. He led a wildly romantic life, which could easily have provided a poet writing in a less intractable form than the waka with material for poetry of intense and varied emotions. In 1326, at the age of fourteen, Munenaga became a priest at the Tendai monastery on Mount Hiei and rapidly rose in the Buddhist hierarchy. Five years later, when his father, the Emperor Godaigo, staged his abortive revolt against the Hōjō regents, Munenaga descended from Mount Hiei with a band of armed priests to aid in the fighting. After the defeat of Godaigo's forces Munenaga was banished to the province of Sanuki. When Godaigo returned from exile in 1333, Munenaga led his troops into Kyoto. After the victory, he resumed his life as a monk on Mount Hiei. In 1336 Ashikaga Takauji's army drove Godaigo from the capital, and for a time he took refuge with his son on Mount Hiei. Once again, Munenaga returned to the laity to serve as a general, and for the next thirty-five years he led the Southern Court resistance to the Ashikaga family and the Northern Court. In 1374 the aged Munenaga withdrew from his stronghold in the province of Shinano and went to Yoshino, where he spent his time mainly in composing poetry. But again, at the age of sixty-five, he was ordered to take command of loyalist forces in Shinano, where he remained until 1380. In 1381 he compiled the *Shin'yōshū*. This is the last appearance of Munenaga in the chronicles of the time, but there is reason to believe that he died at the age of seventy-three in 1385 in command of an army, this time in the eastern provinces.

Munenaga's long career of loyalist devotion to the cause of the Southern Court and the many vicissitudes he suffered have caused some Japanese scholars to liken him to Tu Fu, but when we compare the war poems of the great Chinese poet with Munenaga's, we are likely to be stunned by the inadequacy of the latter, an inadequacy more of the medium than of the poet. Consider, for example, the poem Munenaga wrote in 1338 on his first visit to Yoshino, after his army had been disastrously defeated in the east. A relative in the capital, Nijō Tamesada

(1293–1360), had sent him a poem urging Munenaga to leave Yoshino and return to Kyoto. He replied:

furusato wa	Yes, it is true,
koishiku to te mo	I long for my home of old,
mi Yoshino no	But how can I desert
hana no sakari wo	Holy Yoshino, now that
ikaga misuten[99]	The cherries are in full bloom?

By implication, of course, Munenaga is saying in the poem that he will not abandon the cause of Godaigo in order to live a more agreeable life in the capital. The poem is graceful, if not distinguished; but if we try to imagine the response Tu Fu would have made to anyone urging him to desert to the opposing side, we can see how inadequate Munenaga's well-bred reply was. The weight of conventional poetic expression (especially for a Nijō poet) apparently made it impossible even for a talented poet to present a more full-blooded statement of his emotions.

At times Munenaga's genteel idiom becomes almost frivolous in view of the circumstances. In the same year as the previous poem he was sailing in a convoy across Ise Bay. The preface to his poem continues, "We intended to proceed to Tōtōmi, but while we were in the Sea of Tenryū, as I believe the place is called, the wind and waves became exceedingly rough, and for two or three days we drifted, unable to make shore. The other ships in the convoy all sank at one place or another, and our ship just barely made it to the harbor of Shiroha, borne there by the waves. Hardly knowing what we did, we managed to bring our ship to shore, but all night long we felt miserable in our sea-drenched clothes." After such a preface we are prepared for a poem of stark intensity, but instead we find:

ikade hosu	I have no idea
mono to mo shirazu	How to dry the clothes I wear:
toma yakata	In a rush-thatched hut
katashiku sode no	The sleeve I spread out wrinkles
yoru no uranami[100]	In the night waves from the bay.

It is clear that Munenaga spent an uncomfortable night in the hut, but what were his feelings when he saw the ships bearing his companions sink? Or his own on miraculously getting ashore? The preface tells us a little, but the poem itself, even allowing that wet sleeves always suggest tears, is hopelessly inadequate. The use of *katashiku sode* (single sleeve spread out) is hackneyed; and the pivot word *yoru*, which means both "wrinkle" (as the predicate for "sleeve") and "night" (as a modifier for "waves"), though it adds some content to the poem, is inappropriately clever.

Munenaga's poem on the death of the Emperor Godaigo reveals more genuine feeling, but here, too, the use of hackneyed imagery weakens the effect. Once again, the preface is more powerful than the poem: "Faint reports had reached us that the former emperor had passed away on the sixteenth day of the eighth month of 1339, but being completely unable to believe that these reports were true, we spent days of uncertainty. Yet all the rumors that reached us, from whatever quarter, spoke of the same tragic event, and we had no choice in the end but to accept them. Even then, we felt as though it were a dream, and our dwellings deep in the mountains, lonely enough even without such tidings, seemed more forlorn than ever. Toward the end of the ninth month, when the skies were more lowering than usual and the showers of tears that fell among us were unceasing, it occurred to me that the leaves in Yoshino must have been dyed a thousand times over in tears of blood, as had our own, and I sent a message to Lord Suketsugu, the intendant, urging him not to let the maple leaves scatter, and to instruct others to the same effect. I took the opportunity to enclose some tinted leaves from Ii Castle."[101] The poem follows:

omou ni mo	I realize now
nao iro asaki	That these autumn maple leaves
momiji kana	Are still pale of hue;
sonata no yama wa	How the rains must have fallen
ikaga shigururu	In the mountains where you are!

The prose is both more moving and more suggestive than the poem. The prose relates Munenaga's initial disbelief that his father, so long the central figure of the Southern Court, could have died, his terrible grief when the truth became inescapable, and his concern lest, with the death of Godaigo, the Yoshino forces would scatter like autumn maple leaves. By contrast, the poem relies on the conceit that the grief which inspired his tears has made his tears redder (they are tears of blood) even than the autumn leaves he is sending with his letter; at the same time, he imagines that the grief must be still greater in Yoshino.

There can be no doubting Munenaga's sincerity, but the form and traditions of the waka made it difficult, perhaps impossible, for him to be convincing. For centuries the subject matter of the poems composed at the court had been restricted almost exclusively to the appreciation of the seasons or the remembrances of unhappy love affairs. The waka could evoke such emotions poignantly; the subject and the form of the poetry were perfectly matched. But when the poets of the Southern Court were faced with the necessity of expressing unfamiliar and powerful themes, they became tongue-tied.

Munenaga's case is striking because he was a talented poet, though critics have also singled out for praise Munenaga's disciple, the Buddhist monk Kōun (also known by his lay name, Kazan'in Nagachika, (1347–1429).[102] Kōun, more fortunate than Munenaga, lived to see the reunification of the country in 1392 and moved back to the capital, where he frequented poetry gatherings attended by the shoguns. His poetry, in the Nijō tradition, is pleasant but unmemorable:

shigeriau	Beneath the new green
sakura ga shita no	in the shade of a cherry tree,
yūsuzumi	I take the evening cool—
haru wa ukarishi	waiting for the breezes
kaze no mataruru	that upset me last spring.[103]

The poem probably means exactly what it says. One might have wished for an allegorical meaning, but apparently there is none.

Of the other *Shin'yōshū* poets the most impressive are three emperors who lived in Yoshino—Godaigo, Gomurakami, and Chōkei. The collection as a whole is a disappointment for most modern readers, but in times of war and crisis Japanese have found inspiration in poems—and especially in the prefaces—that evoke the heroism of the Southern Court and its defenders.[104]

Shōtetsu (1381–1459)

The priest Shōtetsu was the last important waka poet of the Muromachi period. It might even be argued that he was the last major poet before the twentieth century who chose to express himself in the waka. In Shōtetsu's time the waka had been displaced by renga as the poetic medium of the most important poets, and during the Tokugawa period the haiku would be the dominant poetic form mainly because of Bashō, the greatest poet of the era. Shōtetsu belonged to the tradition of the court poets of the past, and he wrote his poems on the customary themes, but exceptional skill enabled him to create individual poetry. He was unusually prolific: he lost twenty thousand poems when his hermitage was destroyed by fire in 1432, but managed to write another eleven thousand waka that are preserved in his *Sōkonshū* (Grass Roots Collection), probably the largest collection of waka by any recognized poet.

Shōtetsu came originally from a military family in the province of Bitchū, but was taken while still a boy to Kyoto. In *Shōtetsu Monogatari* (Tales of Shōtetsu, c. 1450),[105] a work that mixes autobiography and criticism, he related that he showed aptitude for composing poetry even as a small child, and that his first poem was written on a leaf offered to the gods as part of the celebration of the Tanabata Festival.[106] When he was fourteen another priest, discovering that Shōtetsu enjoyed writing poetry, suggested that they visit an elderly magistrate (*bugyō*) called Jibu,[107] or Civil Administrator, who lived nearby in Kyoto and was known as a lover of poetry. After some hesitation (he was embarrassed to be seen because his forelock had been shaved),[108] Shōtetsu allowed himself to be taken to the magistrate's house. Here is his account of what happened:

> The Lay Priest and Civil Administrator,[109] at the time a venerable, white-haired gentleman more than eighty years old, came out to meet us. He told me, "These days one never hears of children composing poetry, but when I was young it used to be quite common. How charming of you! I have a poetry gathering every month on the twenty-fifth. Please do attend. Here are the subjects for this month." So saying, he himself wrote down the topics for me. There were three, each written with four Chinese characters: idle moon[110] late at night, distant geese over twilight mountains, and a love affair not followed by a next-morning letter. This happened at the beginning of the eighth month.
>
> On the twenty-fifth I went to attend the meeting. Inside, Reizei no Tamemasa [the great-great-grandson of Teika and the head of the Reizei school] and Reizei no Tamekuni[111] sat in one place of honor, and the former governor of Kyūshū in the other. Behind them were their close retainers and my host's family, over twenty persons in all, seated impressively in order of rank. I had arrived late, so I was shown to the central place of honor.[112] Embarrassing though it was, that is where I took my place. The governor was at the time a lay priest, over eighty years of age, and he sat there wearing a robe without the usual black hems and a sash with a long tassel.
>
> My poem on the topic "idle moon late at night" was:

itazura ni	How light the sky is
fukeyuku sora no	This night as to no avail,
kage nare ya	It grows ever later—
hitori nagamuru	All alone, I stare up at
aki no yo no tsuki	The moon of an autumn night.

My poem on the wild geese concluded, as I recall:

yama no ha ni	At the mountain edge
hitotsura miyuru	A whole chain is visible—
hatsukari no koe	The voices of the first wild geese.

I have forgotten the first part of the poem. I do not remember my poem on love either.

I learned how to compose poetry, thanks to my frequent appearances at such sessions from then on. I was fourteen years old at the time.[113] Afterwards, when I was in the service of the resident prince at Nara, I was the senior page at a memorial service conducted in the Lecture Hall on Mount Hiei.[114] I was so busy with this and other duties that I stopped writing poetry for a time. Later, after my father died,[115] I again ventured to appear at poetry gatherings and resumed writing poetry. I filled thirty-six notebooks with poems composed from the time of the meeting at the Jibu's place. There must have been over twenty thousand poems. They all went up in flames at Imakumano. I have completed somewhat under ten thousand poems since then.[116]

If we can believe this account, written nearly sixty years after some of the events described, Shōtetsu even as a boy of fourteen was able to compose poetry with sufficient skill to be a welcome visitor at gatherings attended by the outstanding poets of the day. Perhaps his youthful encounter with Reizei Tamemasa decided Shōtetsu to compose poetry in the manner of the Reizei school. However, a much more important influence was exerted by Imagawa Ryōshun (1326–1414?), a daimyo and poet whose essays on poetry defended the liberal tradition of the Reizei school against the Nijō poets.

Only about one hundred poems by Ryōshun survive,[117] none of great interest though they have been praised for their honest, *Man'yōshū* simplicity. His writings on poetry, most of them composed when he was in his eighties,[118] suggest the kind of influence he had over Shōtetsu. *Ryōshun Isshi Den* (Biography of Ryōshun for His Son), written in 1409, when he was eighty-three, contains a mixture of autobiography and poetic criticism that may have served as a model for *Tales of Shōtetsu*. Near the beginning we find these recollections:

> When I was twelve or thirteen my grandmother Kōun'in said to me, "It is disgraceful for a boy like you not to compose poetry. Put your mind to it, and regardless of whether it is good or bad, keep composing . . . I began to teach your father how to write poetry from the time when he was seven or eight. Any son who does not continue the accomplishment of his father is not worth talking about."[119]

Ryōshun elsewhere recorded two other experiences that led him to compose poetry. The first occurred in 1341:

> I must have been sixteen when I saw in a vision Lord Tsunenobu.[120] He told me that people must definitely compose poetry. I watched and listened, not knowing if this was a dream or reality, and it stirred in me an even greater desire to write poetry.[121]

In 1345 another experience helped to shape his course as a poet: he read a poem by Reizei Tamehide that profoundly moved him.

nasake aru	In this world of ours
tomo koso kataki	Friends who are sympathetic
yo narikere	Are truly hard to find:
hitori ame kiku	Alone, I listen to the rain
aki no yosugara[122]	All through the long autumn night.

Ryōshun was so impressed that he decided to become a disciple of the Reizei school. He was struck, first of all, by the word *nasake* with which the poem begins. This word was always avoided by Nijō poets because it could refer to sexual relations. Ryōshun was also moved by the unspoken implication of the poem: if the speaker had had a kind friend, the friend would surely have invited him to go somewhere, and he would not have had to spend the night listening to the dreary rain.[123]

Ryōshun's most interesting opinions concern language. Like other Reizei poets, he insisted on the poet's freedom to choose whatever words he preferred, in contrast to the strict observance of poetic diction required of members of the Nijō school. "What do the teachings mean that command us to use only old words? 'Forbidden words' should refer only to those that seem peculiar in the context in which they are placed.

Why should we avoid using a word, even if it has never before appeared in poetry, providing it is not unpleasant to the ears?"[124] He favored straightforward expression: "The essence of poetry is to describe things as they are, without decoration." He believed that the simple language of the *Man'yōshū* should be the inspiration for poets of his own time, and that it was only in the centuries after the *Man'yōshū* that poets first fell into the error of decorating their works.[125] His special esteem for the *Man'yōshū* was what one might expect of a military man; but his preference for unadorned simplicity seems not to have affected his devotion to Teika and the *Shin Kokinshū*.

Perhaps Ryōshun's most famous statement on poetry was:

> Man cannot exist without thoughts and words. Why then should it be difficult for him to express his thoughts with his mouth? If, for example, he thinks, "Brrr—how cold it is!" he will say, "I wish I had a jacket" or "I wish I could warm myself by a fire" and each of these is poetry.[126]

Ryōshun believed that the emotion (*kokoro*) that gave rise to a poem was more important than words (*kotoba*), and if the emotion was strong enough (even the emotion induced by a chilly room), the words became poetry of themselves. This conviction led him to attack the Nijō poets, especially Ton'a, who always emphasized the importance of the words. Sometimes he became quite intemperate, and he did not hesitate to declare that among the poems of Ton'a "seven or eight out of ten poems borrow more than half their words from old poems."[127] His main reason for writing his various works of criticism in old age seems to have been to protect and encourage Reizei Tamemasa, the young head of the Reizei school. No doubt he also communicated these views to Shōtetsu, who revered Ryōshun as his teacher.

Shōtetsu, though an important poet, is remembered most of all for his work of criticism and autobiography, *Tales of Shōtetsu*. The typical manner adopted by Shōtetsu in this work is to present a waka and follow it with a close analysis of its components. The following is the first part of what is perhaps the best-known passage:

FALLING BLOSSOMS

sakura chiru	They blossomed only
yo no ma no hana no	To fall in the space of a night,
yume no uchi ni	In the space of a dream;

yagate magirenu	All that remains as before
mine no shirakumo	Are white clouds over the peak.

This is a poem in the yūgen style. What we call yūgen is something within the mind that cannot be expressed in words. The quality of yūgen may be suggested by the sight of thin clouds veiling the moon or autumn fog hanging over the crimson leaves on a mountainside. If one is asked where in these sights is the yūgen, one cannot answer. It is not surprising that a person who fails to understand this is likely to prefer the sight of the moon shining brightly in a cloudless sky. It is quite impossible to explain wherein lies the interest or the wonder of yūgen.

The words "in the space of a dream; all that remains as before" were derived from a poem composed by Genji. Genji, when he meets Fujitsubo, says

mite mo mata	We meet now, but rare
au yo mare naru	Will be the nights we meet again.
yume no uchi ni	Would that this poor frame
yagate magiruru	Might dissolve, just as it is,
ukimi to mo gana	Into the world of the dream.

This, too, was in the yūgen style.[128]

Shōtetsu's conception of yūgen was the key to his poetry and to his criticism of poetry. He likened the effect of yūgen in poetry to mist that partly conceals the bare meanings of words, lending them mysterious ambiguity. To achieve this effect, words were sometimes omitted from poems, even words necessary for ready comprehension, and the difficulty of the poem that resulted was justified in terms of the elusive depths hinted at by the ambiguity. Shōtetsu gave, as an example of a poem whose meaning was not immediately apparent because one line had been deliberately omitted, the celebrated waka by Ariwara no Narihira from the *Kokinshū* (already quoted above):

tsuki ya aranu	Is that not the moon,
haru ya mukashi no	And is the spring not the spring
haru naranu	Of a year ago?

wa ga mi hitotsu wa	This body of mine alone,
moto no mi shite	Remains as it was before.[129]

He commented: "Unless one understands the implications, there is nothing interesting about the poem. The poem was composed when, remembering how in the spring of the previous year he had met the Nijō empress, he went to the western pavilion. What he meant to say was, 'Is that not the moon, and is not the spring the same as before: I am unchanged, but the person I met then is not here tonight.'"[130]

Shōtetsu's poetry is difficult because he deliberately defied normal syntax in order to achieve a richness of meaning. He gave an elaborate exegesis of one of his poems:

watarikane	Even clouds hesitate.
kumo mo yūbe wo	They still struggle this evening
nao tadoru	To cross over the bridge:
ato naki yuki no	A path to the peak in snow
mine no kakehashi	Without a single footprint.

> It is most improbable that clouds would have trouble passing over trackless snow. However, it is the general practice in waka composition to impart feelings to insentient things. The fact is, clouds are constantly crossing the sky, morning and night. But when I looked out as evening came to the mountains covered in snow, the drifts of fallen snow were so white that I thought the clouds might not even realize evening had come, and they might hesitate to cross trackless paths, but in fact they went by serenely. If one examines a scene carefully in this way, there really is something about the clouds that suggests they might have trouble crossing. It also occurred to me that the clouds might hesitate to cross when there were no human footprints in the snow along a mountain path as dangerous as a hanging bridge.[131]

Shōtetsu went on to defend the unnatural syntax of the poem in terms of the greater force it gave. His exegesis of the poem concluded, "A poem that does not spell out everything is a good poem."

Tales of Shōtetsu opens with the flat statement "Anyone who follows the way of poetry and criticizes Teika will not enjoy the blessings of the gods but will incur their punishment."[132] His reverence for Teika cannot be questioned, but his poems do not much resemble those of his avowed master. One senses instead that Shōtetsu fretted over the limitations of the waka. His disciples included renga poets, and Shōtetsu himself might have found renga a more congenial medium. He attempted to compensate for the brevity of the waka by resorting to suggestion, and he managed to cram into thirty-one syllables a surprising number of images or ideas. Teika had also composed dense poems, but he never was as arcane in his images as Shōtetsu in his poem on clouds over the snow. Shōtetsu, like Poe, would probably have been satisfied to convey "a suggestive indefiniteness of vague and therefore of spiritual effect."

Shōtetsu's yūgen was closer to that of Shunzei than of Teika, for whom the word seems to have meant surpassing charm above all. It differed also (as we shall see) from the yūgen of Zeami, as employed in his essays on Nō, where the primary meaning seems to have been elegance. Shōtetsu meant a kind of symbolism, achieved by using ambiguous but suggestive language, affording the reader the possibility of an experience that transcends words. In this respect Shōtetsu may be said to have gone beyond his avowed master Teika, and to have enunciated one of the most important ideals of the medieval aesthetic. The same preference for suggestion and mystery could be found in the monochrome paintings of the Muromachi period, the tea ceremony, and the gardens of stone and pebbles that are closer to ink sketches than to natural vegetation.

These different arts were all influenced by aesthetic beliefs associated with Zen Buddhism which, in the fourteenth and fifteenth centuries especially, acquired dominant importance among writers and artists. Shōtetsu, a Zen monk, wrote many religious poems whose inspiration came from Zen Buddhism, such as:

tera wa aredo	There is a temple,
mukashi no mama no	But, unaltered from the past,
kazari naki	The mountain becomes
hotoke to narite	A Buddha without trappings,
yama zo aseyuku	And its color fades away.

This poem, composed in 1452, when Shōtetsu was seventy-one, is a difficult but characteristic expression of Zen belief: the temple exists and Shōtetsu has often sat there in meditation, but the temple is not itself of importance; the achievement of Buddhahood is the reason for the temple's existence. On the other hand, the mountain on which the temple stands has attained the eternal essence of Buddha, though (unlike the temple) it is bare of adornment.[133] Shōtetsu's Buddhist poem is unlike any in the *Kokinshū* and later court anthologies. It comes dangerously close to bursting the seams of the waka, and suggests also the kanshi being written by the Zen monks of the Five Mountains at about the same time.

There were waka poets after Shōtetsu, but their names are hardly remembered. A few late Tokugawa waka poets are still of interest,[134] but it was not until the twentieth century that the waka was reborn as a vital medium for the communication of genuinely felt joys and griefs.

Notes

1. I have decided, following Japanese usage, to omit the particle *no* between the surnames and personal names of persons of the Kamakura period and later; there are, however, exceptions. One commonly encounters names of Kamakura figures with the *no*, e.g., Minamoto no Sanetomo; and the names of some Japanese, even as late as the Tokugawa period, usually include the *no*, e.g., Kamo no Mabuchi and Ki no Kaion.
2. The Hōjō family, to which Yoritomo's wife Masako belonged, soon acquired the same kind of control over the shogun that the Fujiwara family exercised over the emperor. This was especially true when the shogun was a minor. The official name of the position occupied by the Hōjō "regents" was *shikken*, or "administrator." For a fuller account of the Hōjō, see George Sansom, *A History of Japan to 1334*, pp. 371–437.
3. Among the many works written about Sanetomo, one might cite the novel *Udaijin Sanetomo* (1943) by Dazai Osamu (see *Dawn to the West*, I, pp. 1051–52, for an account of this work); the modern Nō play *Sanetomo* (1943) by Toki Zemmaro; and the wartime essays of Kobayashi Hideo. *Sanetomo Shuppan* (1973) by Yamazaki Masakazu is a more recent play based on Sanetomo's life.
4. See Saitō Mokichi, *Kinkai Waka Shū*, p. 113.
5. This collection was translated and commented on by Robert H. Brower and Earl Miner in their *Fujiwara Teika's Superior Poems of Our Time*.
6. *Ibid.*, p. 41.
7. *Ibid.*, p. 44. The era name Kampei is more commonly read as Kampyō. The era itself lasted from 888 to 897.
8. This is poem 144 in Sanetomo's collection *Kinkaishū*. See Higuchi Yoshimaro, *Kinkai Waka Shū*, p. 50, for this poem and two honka. Saitō (*Kinkai*, p. 117) gives five possible honka.
9. *Shūishū* 124.
10. Saitō, *Kinkai*, pp. 117–18.

11. The title means literally "Collection of Golden Locust Waka," locust being the tree (*enju* in Japanese) sometimes translated as "pagoda tree" or "Chinese scholar tree." Sasaki Nobutsuna, the celebrated scholar of Japanese poetry, interpreted "golden" as referring to Kamakura (because the word *kama* is written with the metal radical), and *kai* or *kaimon*, "locust tree," a word used in ancient China for the three highest ranks of minister. *Kinkai* would therefore mean "the Kamakura great minister" or the shogun. However, the title *Kinkai Waka Shū* was not given to the collection until long afterward, perhaps not until the Muromachi period. See Kojima Yoshio, "Kaisetsu" to *Kinkai Waka Shū* in Kazamaki Keijirō and Kojima Yoshio, *Sankashū, Kinkai Waka Shū*, p. 297. *Kinkai Waka Shū* contains from 663 to 749 waka, depending on the text.
12. Other volumes devoted to waka poetry are collections by many poets such as the *Kokinshū* and *Shin Kokinshū*.
13. Sasaki Yukitsuna, *Chūsei no Kajintachi*, p. 114. Sasaki estimated that about 60 of the 663 poems in *Kinkai Waka Shū* show the influence of the *Man'yōshū*. Sasaki did not take into account the additional 56 poems by Sanetomo, not included in *Kinkai Waka Shū* but later collected by someone who used the pseudonym Ryūei Akai. The identity of this person is unknown, but it has been suggested that he was Ashikaga Yoshimasa who from 1450 to 1458 held the position of *ryūei akai*, *ryūei* meaning "shogun" and *akai* being a Chinese name for the office of *dainagon*. Some of Sanetomo's most highly rated poems are found in the collection of Ryūei Akai. In addition, 40 other poems by Sanetomo are found in various sources such as *Mirror of the East*. See Higuchi, *Kinkai*, pp. 258–61.
14. What he actually gave was a circle, rather than a star, but I have used a more familiar sign of approbation. Mabuchi gave one circle to about 150 poems and a double circle, his highest mark of approbation, to 22.
15. *Kinkai Waka Shū* 210. Higuchi, *Kinkai*, p. 68. For Mabuchi's comment see Matsumura Eiichi, *Minamoto Sanetomo Meika Hyōshaku*, p. 115.
16. *Kokinshū* 406. Abe no Nakamaro, in China, yearned to be back amid familiar scenery in Japan.
17. *Shin Kokinshū* 1499. Although the poem seems to be no more than an expression of impatience over the slowness of the moon to appear, it has been interpreted as an indirect expression over slowness of promotion.
18. *Kinkai Waka Shū* 244. Higuchi, *Kinkai*, p. 77.
19. See above, p. 125, for another translation of the poem.
20. *Kinkai Waka Shū* 639. See Higuchi, *Kinkai*, p. 183, also Matsumura, *Minamoto*, pp. 191–92. Kojima (in Kazamaki and Kojima, *Sankashū*, p. 441) gives an account of the reputation of this particular poem. Despite Kamo no Mabuchi's praise, Itō Sachio (more recently) criticized it. Still later men, notably Kawada Jun, praised it so enthusiastically that it is now generally recognized as one of Sanetomo's finest poems.
21. Matsumura, *Minamoto*, p. 191. The quoted poem is *Man'yōshū*, XIII:3238.

The "Sea of Ōmi" was a poetic name for Lake Biwa. Mabuchi somewhat misquotes the original.

22. Kobayashi Hideo found it "an extremely tragic poem," and Yoshimoto Takaaki interpreted it as an "unbelievably nihilistic poem." See Sasaki Yukitsuna, *Chūsei*, p. 119. Sasaki also noted that when Sanetomo first got a glimpse of the superb panorama from the heights, he did not say that it was beautiful or magnificent, but focused his attention on a small island, producing an effect of loneliness rather than grandeur.
23. *Kinkai* 348, in Kazamaki and Kojima, *Sankashū*, p. 373. See also Higuchi, *Kinkai*, p. 197. This poem was not in the original *Kinkai Waka Shū* but in a seventeenth-century supplement. For a comment on the poem, see Robert H. Brower and Earl Miner, *Japanese Court Poetry*, p. 331.
24. Hisamatsu Sen'ichi, *Chūsei Waka Shi*, p. 142.
25. This account of the circumstances leading up to the submission of the *Shin Chokusenshū* is taken from Ōtori Kazuma, *Shin Chokusen Waka Shū Kochūshaku to sono Kenkyū*, I, p. 5. The most detailed account of these circumstances is found in Kyūsojin Hitaku and Higuchi Yoshimaro, "Kaidai," in *Shin Chokusen Waka Shū*, pp. 203–12.
26. In contrast to the literally dozens of commented editions of the *Shin Kokinshū*, there is not a single such edition of the *Shin Chokusenshū*, and scholars have seldom discussed its poetry.
27. The collection acquired the nickname of "Uji River Collection" (*Ujigawa-shū*), supposedly by way of reference to a poem by Hitomaro (*Shin Kokinshū* 1648) that mentions soldiers (*mononofu*) and the Uji River; but even if this reference is incorrect, the name Uji River was likely to recall the rivalry, described in *The Tale of the Heike*, between two soldiers as to who could cross the river first. See Ishihara Kiyoshi, *Chūsei Bungakuron no Kōkyū*, p. 21.
28. After Sanetomo died without heirs in 1219, he was succeeded as shogun by Yoritsune, a son of the kampaku Michiie, the head of the Kujō branch of the Fujiwara family. Among the Kyoto nobles, the Kujō and Saionji families were the most sympathetic to the shogunate. Teika was related to the Kujō family, and his eldest son, Tameie, was married to the daughter of the important shogunate official Utsunomiya Yoritsuna. For a detailed account of these relationships, see Kazamaki Keijirō, "Shin Chokusenshū," pp. 14–20.
29. For a table showing comparative numbers of poems in the two collections by different poets, see Kazamaki, "Shin Chokusenshū," p. 9.
30. *Ibid.*, p. 21.
31. Ōtori, *Shin*, I, p. 8. She made this statement in 1252 in a letter she sent to Teika's son Tameie. She objected also to the absence of even one poem by the three exiled emperors—Gotoba, Tsuchimikado, and Juntoku. She may also have been annoyed that the number of her own poems selected

was reduced from twenty-nine in the *Shin Kokinshū* to nine in the *Shin Chokusenshū*.

32. *Ibid.*, p. 6. This statement is found in his preface to *Shoku Gosen Mokuroku*.
33. See Morimoto Motoko (ed.), *Izayoi Nikki*, *Yoru no Tsuru*, p. 215. Abutsu did not like the *Shin Kokinshū* because, she wrote, it had "made the configurations of poetry bad again." Her highest praise was accorded to the *Shoku Gosenshū*, the tenth imperial collection, compiled by her husband Tameie.
34. Ōtori, *Shin*, I, p. 339. This is poem 198.
35. Quoted in *ibid.* p. 19. This statement appeared originally in Motoori's *Ashiwake no Obune*. For further information on Motoori as a critic of Japanese poetry, see my *World Within Walls*, pp. 322–30.
36. It was not considered to be an important collection until 1926 when Toki Zemmaro published his *Sakushabetsu Man'yō Igo*, a selection of poems from the twenty-one imperial collections. Toki gave considerable space to three Kyōgoku poets—Tamekane, the Emperor Fushimi, and the Empress Eifukumon'in—much to the surprise of scholars of the time who had taken the word of the Nijō poets that the Kyōgoku poets were of no importance. Toki's views were expanded in later years by other scholars of the waka, and he himself wrote a valuable study of Kyōgoku Tamekane, the most recent edition of which is called *Shinshū Kyōgoku Tamekane*. See Iwasa Miyoko, *Kyōgoku-ha Kajin no Kenkyū*, pp. 5–6.
37. Although this seems to have been his desire, the poems rarely suggest those in the *Man'yōshū*, which was imperfectly known at the time.
38. The diary *Towazugatari* (The Confessions of Lady Nijō) contains vivid descriptions of one aspect of their fraternal relations—their sexual involvement with the same woman.
39. For an account in English of the succession dispute, see Sansom, *Japan to 1334*, pp. 461–67; also (in greater detail) pp. 476–84. The senior line is commonly known as the Jimyō-in, and the junior line as Daigaku-ji, from the temples where the emperors Gofukakusa and Gouda respectively lived after they had entered Buddhist orders.
40. For an account of Abutsu's diaries, *Utatane* (Fitful Slumbers) and *Izayoi Nikki* (The Diary of the Waning Moon), see pp. 835–38.
41. By this time the surname Fujiwara had become so common among the nobility, and the names within a given branch of the family were often so similar (Tameie, Tameuji, Tamekane, and so on), that another name, usually the name of the place in the capital where the founder of a branch line lived, came to serve as a surname. This was not the official name, however, and the same man might therefore be known both as Fujiwara Tamesuke and Reizei Tamesuke or Fujiwara Tameyo and Nijō Tameyo.
42. The cause of Tamekane's arrest and exile is by no means clear. Some historians believed that it was because of the clash that had occurred

between Tamekane and Saionji Sanekane, but Inoue Muneo in *Chūsei Kadanshi no Kenkyū*, I, p. 43, gives convincing reasons for doubting this. According to the account (dated 1332) in the diary *Hanazono-in Gyoki* (quoted by Inoue, p. 43), Tamekane was slandered by "colleagues" (*hōbai*).

43. For poems by Tameyo in both collections (and unfriendly judgments of Tameyo by the author), see Hisamatsu, *Chūsei*, pp. 227–29. Hisamatsu concluded his discussion of Tameyo, "In short, as a poet Tameyo was mediocre."
44. Translation by Steven D. Carter in *Waiting for the Wind*, p. 155. Carter notes that this poem (*Shin Gosenshū* 151) was an allusive variation on *Kokinshū* 625 by Mibu no Tadamine.
45. Carter's *Waiting* contains a good sampling of such poetry.
46. Gofukakusa, Kameyama, Gouda, Fushimi, and Gofushimi.
47. For an unbearably detailed account of these sessions, see Inoue, *Chūsei*, I, pp. 106–20.
48. *Ibid.*, p. 150.
49. *Ibid.*, p. 151.
50. *Ibid.*, p. 154.
51. I have taken the dates 1311 for the command from Fushimi and 1312 for the completion from Inoue, *Chūsei Kadanshi*, I, p. 156. These are the same dates given by Tsugita Kasumi in his authoritative, "*Gyokuyōshu* no Seiritsu to sono Denrai," pp. 571–72, but he believed that the *Gyokuyōshū* was revised and augmented in 1313. Robert N. Huey in *Kyōgoku Tamekane*, p. 56, accepted these dates. However, Earl Miner and his fellow editors of *The Princeton Companion to Classical Japanese Literature*, p. 159, stated that the command to Tamekane came in 1312 and the compilation was completed in the following year. Toki Zemmaro, in *Shinshū Kyōgoku Tamekane*, pp. 286–87, gave 1311 as the year of the command to Tamekane but 1313 as the year of presentation. These contradictions originated in the discrepancies found in the various documents of the period. See Araki Yoshio, *Chūsei Bungaku no Keisei to Hatten*, p. 105.
52. See Bower and Miner, *Japanese*, p. 485.
53. Huey, *Kyōgoku*, p. 57.
54. See my *Dawn to the West*, II, pp. 38–41, for an account of his contributions to the modern tanka.
55. Toki Zemmaro, *Kyōgoku Tamekane*, pp. 239–40.
56. There is a translation by Robert N. Huey and Susan Matisoff, "*Tamekanekyō Wakashō*: Lord Tamekane's Notes on Poetry." The work is discussed by Huey in *Kyōgoku*, pp. 63–75.
57. *Gyokuyōshū* 832. Translation in Carter, *Waiting*, p. 99. See also Brower and Miner, *Japanese*, p. 366. (They use a text that has *sukunasa* instead of *sukunaki*, yielding a somewhat different meaning.)
58. *Gyokuyōshū* 1010. Another translation by Huey in *Kyōgoku*, p. 110; also Brower and Miner, *Japanese*, p. 372. See also Toki, *Kyōgoku*, pp. 30–31.

59. Windows of course appeared elsewhere in Kamakura poetry, but almost always as open windows through which one saw nature outside or heard bird calls, not as closed surfaces against which hail would rattle.
60. Toki (in *Kyōgoku*, p. 30) noted that poets of the Kyōgoku school aimed at the effect of bringing together in a poem *sei* (quiet) and *dō* (active).
61. See Hisamatsu Sen'ichi et al., *Nihon Bungaku Shi: Chūsei*, p. 57.
62. The practice of ji-amari by Kyōgoku poets is the subject of Hamaguchi Hiroaki's "Gyokuyō Waka Shū no Hyōgen." The subject is also considered at length by Huey in *Kyōgoku*, pp. 89–98. Huey stressed the function of the extra syllables in various examples of Tamekane's poetry. In the present instance, the line *neya no ue wa* can either be read as six syllables or, running the *o* of *no* and the *u* of *ue* together, as five syllables. In other instances the ji-amari is unmistakable.
63. *Gyokuyōshū* 83. Translation by Carter in *Waiting*, p. 98. For another translation see Huey, *Kyōgoku*, p. 126. For a discussion of the relation to *Gyokuyōshū* poetry and Sung poetry see Konishi Jin'ichi, "Gyokuyō Jidai to Sōshi," p. 171–80. For further comments on this poem see Toki, *Kyōgoku*, p. 14. Toki pointed out that the poem is an allusive variation on one by Ōtomo no Yakamochi, *Man'yōshū*, XIX:4139, and suggested that this is an example of the attempt of the *Gyokuyōshū* poets to go back beyond the *Shin Kokinshū* to the basic nature (*honshitsu*) of waka expression.
64. My translation in *Essays in Idleness*, p. 136.
65. *Gyokuyōshū* 628. Another translation by Huey in *Kyōgoku*, p. 83. Huey also gives a poem by Tameie that ends with the same words *meguru aki no inazuma*, and suggests that Fushimi's poem is "close enough to Tameie's to be an allusive variation." Fushimi's poem, however, is distinctly superior to Tameie's. See also Ueda Hideo, "Gyokuyōshu Fūgashū Kōgi," in *Senshū Kōgi-hen*.
66. *Fūgashū* 566. For another translation, see Brower and Miner, *Japanese*, p. 373.
67. *Gyokuyōshū* 2154. Another translation by Huey in *Kyōgoku*, p. 83. See also Ueda, "Gyokuyōshū," pp. 438–39, for an interpretation of the poem.
68. See my *World Within Walls*, p. 89.
69. *Gyokuyōshū* 713. Konishi, "Gyokuyō," p. 165. The translation is by Carter in *Waiting*, p. 129.
70. Konishi, "Gyokuyō," p. 153.
71. *Ibid.*, pp. 153–55, gives examples of the love poetry in the *Gyokuyōshū*. He recognizes that love poetry without images can also be found in earlier collections, but insists that the proportion is far greater in the *Gyokuyōshū* and *Fūgashū*. Huey (in *Kyōgoku*, p. 141) disagrees with Brower and Miner who, following Konishi, maintained that a lack of imagery characterized the love poetry of the Kyōgoku school.
72. *Gyokuyōshū* 1390. Translation by Carter in *Waiting*, p. 130.

73. Translation from Brower and Miner, *Japanese*, p. 386. Original text is *Fūgashū* 1297.
74. *Gyokuyōshū* 1569. See Konishi, "Gyokuyō," p. 159. Another translation with analysis of the poem is in Brower and Miner, *Japanese*, p. 381.
75. Konishi, "Gyokuyō," p. 166. See also Tsugita Kasumi, "Gyokuyō, Fūgashū no Uta no Tokushitsu."
76. See Iwasa Miyoko, *Eifukumon'in*, p. 32.
77. *Gyokuyōshū* 1704. Translation by Carter in *Waiting*, p. 144. See Iwasa, *Eifukumon'in*, pp. 110–11.
78. Brower and Miner, *Japanese*, p. 379.
79. *Gyokuyōshū* 1464. For commentary see Iwasa Miyoko, *Eifukumon'in*, p. 104.
80. See Brower and Miner, *Japanese*, pp. 378–79, where they discuss poets who "tended to divide a poem into two units, or sometimes more, whose integration was less one of common tonal elements than of an intensity of feeling reflected in a rich verse texture."
81. *Gyokuyōshū* 925. Another translation by Carter in *Waiting*, p. 143. For commentary, see Iwasa Miyoko, *Eifukumon'in*, p. 96; also Ueda, "Gyokuyō," p. 434.
82. There are several variant titles for this diary, including *Hanazono-in Gyoki* (see note 42). I have chosen the title given in the authoritative *Kokusho Sōmokuroku*. Excerpts from the diary translated into English, along with an interpretation of the contents are given by George Sansom in *A History of Japan: 1334–1615*, pp. 127–40.
83. For an account of the warfare, see pp. 875–78.
84. For an account of the Kemmu Restoration, see H. Paul Varley, *Imperial Restoration in Medieval Japan*. A briefer description is given by Sansom in *Japan: 1334–1615*, pp. 22–42.
85. The prefaces are given by Tsugita Kasumi and Iwasa Miyoko in *Fūga Waka Shū*, pp. 47–52; also in Nishino Taeko, *Kōgon-in*, pp. 57–60.
86. For an account of the reasons why specialists in the *Fūgashū* tend to believe that Kōgon was the compiler, see Tsugita and Iwasa, *Fūga*, pp. 20–22.
87. For a description of his final instructions, see Iwasa Miyoko, *Eifukumon'in*, pp. 65–66. Also Nishino, *Kōgon-in*, pp. 245–46.
88. Thirty-one of his poems were included in the *Fūgashū*, twenty in the *Shin Senzaishū*, fifteen in the *Shin Shūishū*, seven in the *Shin Goshūishū*, and two in the *Shin Zokukokinshū* (the last of the chokusenshū).
89. *Fūgashū* 1787. For another translation, see Carter, *Waiting*, p. 220. See Nishino, *Kōgon-in*, pp. 90–92, for a commentary.
90. *Fūgashū* 870. For another translation, see Carter, *Waiting*, p. 219. The word *fusuma* in the third line is given in kanji meaning "quilts" or "bedding" in Tsugita and Iwasa, *Fūga*, p. 189, but Nishino (*Kōgon-in*, p. 77) takes *fusuma* to be a homonym meaning interior partitions like *shōji*. The poem seems to be a honka-dori variation on one by the Emperor

Gotoba in *Shoku Gosenshū* (1251): *yo wo samumi / neya no fusuma no / sayuru ni mo / waraya no kaze wo / omoi koso yare.*

91. See Tsugita and Iwasa, *Fūga*, pp. 5–7. For a good general discussion of the characteristics of the *Gyokuyōshū* and *Fūgashū*, see Tsugita, "Gyokuyō."
92. *Fūgashū* 720. Translation by Carter in *Waiting*, p. 219. Commentary by Nishino in *Kōgon-in*, pp. 76–77.
93. For a more detailed account of what occurred, see Varley, *Imperial*, pp. 115–16.
94. See Inoue, *Chūsei*, p. 512.
95. For example, the priest Ton'a, a poet of some distinction, completed the editing of the nineteenth collection, the *Shin Shūishū*, after the editor, Fujiwara Tameaki, died. The Japanese preface to the twentieth collection, the *Shin Goshūishū*, was written by Nijō Yoshimoto, a pupil of Ton'a, who was a key figure in the development of renga though not an important waka poet. Both Japanese and Chinese prefaces to the twenty-first (and last) collection, the *Shin Zokukokinshū*, were written by Ichijō Kaneyoshi, one of the chief scholars and critics of the fifteenth century. But the contributions of these distinguished men did not diminish the dreariness of the collections as a whole.
96. Originally, the priest Nōyo (c. 1260–?), a truly obscure poet, was one of the Four Deva Kings, but by the time of Shōtetsu he was replaced by Keiun. See Inoue, *Chūsei*, pp. 305–7. English translations of waka by the (latter) Four Deva Kings are given by Carter in *Waiting*, pp. 164–201.
97. *Shin Zokukokinshū* 2036. Translation by Carter in *Waiting*, p. 186.
98. Text in Iwasa Tadashi, *Shin'yō Waka Shū*, p. 13. See also Saitō Kazuhiro, *Kōchū Shin'yōshū*, p. 1.
99. Saitō Kazuhiro, *Kōchū*, pp. 22–23; Iwasa Tadashi, *Shin'yō*, p. 36. Another translation by Carter in *Waiting*, p. 247.
100. Yoneyama Muneomi, *Rikashū Hyōchū*, pp. 154–55. See also Kawada Jun, *Yoshino-chō no Hika*, pp. 322–23.
101. Kawada, *Yoshino-chō*, pp. 326–27 (from *Rikashū*). The poem, with a somewhat shorter preface, appears in the *Shin'yōshū*; see Saitō Kazuhiro, *Kōchū*, p. 220.
102. Dates from Ogi Takashi, *Shin'yō Waka Shū Hombun to Kenkyū*, p. 487.
103. *Shin'yōshū* 239. See Saitō, *Kōchū*, p. 42. Translation by Carter in *Waiting*, p. 261.
104. It is surely no coincidence that the *Shin'yōshū* entered the Iwanami Bunko series in 1940. Kawada's book on the tragic poetry of Yoshino was published in 1944, and Iwasa's edition of the text in 1945.

    Typical praise for the collection is given by Numazawa Tatsuo in "Shin'yō Waka Shū Kōgi," p. 457: "The value of this collection is extremely high. It goes without saying that there is none among the hundreds of private anthologies that can compare with it, but even among the twenty-one imperial collections it stands out; and among the fourteen imperial collections of the Kamakura and Muromachi periods, leaving the *Shin Kokinshū* out of consideration for the moment, it is fully worthy to represent these periods, along with the *Gyokuyō* and *Fūgashū*. It is not like the rest of the collections, most of which did nothing more than imitate the *Kokinshū*."

105. The complete translation of this work by Robert H. Brower was published under the title *Conversations with Shōtetsu*. This immaculate work of scholarship is further enhanced by an extensive introduction and notes by Steven D. Carter.

106. Tanabata was the Japanese name given to the Chinese festival that celebrated the meeting of two stars (the Herd Boy and the Weaver Girl) on the seventh night of the seventh moon. Today poems are written on paper slips that are attached to stalks of bamboo.

107. The identity of this man has not been determined. Hisamatsu Sen'ichi and Nishio Minoru, *Karon Shū*, *Nōgakuron Shū*, p. 197, suggested that Jibu might have been a way of referring to Imagawa Ryōshun, noting that Shōtetsu said of both that they were over eighty, but more recent research has shown that Ryōshun was probably not there on the occasion Shōtetsu described. Jibu, though an official title, seems to be used here as a personal name. Shōtetsu, writing many years after the event, seems to have confused memories. See Inada Toshinori, *Shōtetsu no Kenkyū*, pp. 34–35 and 163–64, for a careful examination of the evidence.

108. Perhaps this means that he had recently become a Buddhist priest. The date of Shōtetsu's entering orders is not known.

109. Jibu was a general appellation of officers of the *jibushō*, which was rendered by R. K. Reischauer as "Ministry of Civil Administration."

110. *Kangetsu* was a technical term for the moon at a time of year when the farmers are idle, as opposed, say, to "harvest moon." In the poem that he composed on this subject Shōtetsu used the image to suggest the moon on a night that brought no meeting, no matter how late it might become—an "idle" moon of another kind.

111. Reizei Tamemasa's name is usually read as Tametada, but I have followed the pronunciation given by Fukuda Hideichi in *Chūsei Wakashi no Kenkyū*, p. 853. Tamemasa (1361–1417) was actually the son of Tamekuni, but because Tamekuni entered Buddhist orders in 1371, he was ineligible to succeed as head of the school. Shortly before Tamekuni's father (Tamemasa's grandfather) Tamehide (1306?–1372) died, Tamemasa was adopted as his heir, making Tamemasa and Tamekuni brothers. See Hisamatsu and Nishio, *Karon Shū*, pp. 171, 197. For Tamemasa, see Inoue, *Chūsei*, II, pp. 47–48.

112. Presumably, the other guests had modestly declined to sit in the *yokoza*, the place at the head of the table.

113. By Japanese count; only thirteen by Western reckoning.

114. The Lecture Hall (*kōdō*) was one of the buildings of the monastery Enryaku-ji on Mount Hiei, called here Muroyama.
115. In 1403, when Shōtetsu was twenty-one.
116. Translation from my *Some Japanese Portraits*, pp. 44–45. Original text in Hisamatsu and Nishio, *Karon Shū*, p. 197.
117. Araki Hisashi in *Imagawa Ryōshun no Kenkyū*, pp. 393–404 gives 113 poems, of which 5 appeared in chokusenshū, 8 in uta-awase, and the rest in essays on poetry, diaries, and so on. Some poems are incomplete in their quoted form. Hisamatsu (in *Chūsei*, p. 298), citing Araki among other authorities, seems to favor 98 poems.
118. Araki Hisashi (*Imagawa*, pp. 33–34) gives the names of eleven works. The earliest was written when Ryōshun was sixty-six, but eight were written in his eighties.
119. Sasaki Nobutsuna (ed.), *Nihon Kagaku Taikei*, V, p. 177.
120. Minamoto no Tsunenobu, a late Heian poet whose original style undoubtedly impressed Ryōshun. In his own day he was unpopular because he departed from the conventions, but in later times his poems were much praised.
121. Quoted by Araki Hisashi, *Imagawa*, p. 13. Ryōshun says he was sixteen, but he was fifteen by Western calculation.
122. The poem is found in Ryōshun's book of criticism *Rakusho Roken*. I have used the text prepared by Mizukami Kashizō in *Gengo to Bungei*, Sept. 1959, p. 68. See also Sasaki Nobutsuna, *Nihon Kagaku Taikei*, V, p. 202. For another translation see Carter, *Waiting*, p. 230.
123. This is the explanation given by Shōtetsu in *Tales of Shōtetsu*. See Hisamatsu and Nishio, *Karon Shū* p. 181.
124. Imagawa Ryōshun, "Wakadokoro e Fushin Jōjō," quoted in Sasaki Nobutsuna, *Nihon Kagaku Shi*, p. 166.
125. Quoted in Sasaki, *Nihon Kagaku Shi*, p. 158.
126. From Ryōshun's "Gonjinshū," quoted by Sasaki Nobutsuna in *Nihon Kagaku Shi*, p. 158.
127. From his "Wakadokoro e Fushin Jōjō." See Sasaki Nobutsuna, *Nihon Kagaku Taikei*, V, p. 172.
128. This is part II, section 77 of *Tales of Shōtetsu*. Text in Hisamatsu and Nishio, *Karon Shū*, p. 224. Translation, slightly modified, from my *Some Japanese Portraits*, pp. 48–49. The poem from *The Tale of Genji* is in the "Waka Murasaki" chapter. See the translation by Edward Seidensticker, *The Tale of Genji*, I, p. 98.
129. *Kokinshū* 747. For a discussion of the poem, see above, p. 226.
130. Hisamatsu and Nishio, *Karon Shū*, p. 173.
131. *Ibid.*, p. 172. Not only is the poem difficult to understand but the explanation compounds the difficulties. The modern explanation of Shōtetsu's poem, given by Fujihira Hideo (in Sasaki Yukitsuna, *Chūsei*, pp. 212–13),

is even longer and almost as obscure. For another translation of the poem, see Steven D. Carter, *Traditional Japanese Poetry*, p. 299.

132. Hisamatsu and Nishio, *Karon Shū*, p. 166.
133. Poem and explanation both derived from Koyama Keiichi, *Shōtetsu Ron*, pp. 237–39.
134. See my *World Within Walls*, pp. 494–506.

Bibliography

Note: All Japanese books, except as otherwise noted, were pubished in Tokyo.

Araki Hisashi. *Imagawa Ryōshun no Kenkyū*. Kasama Shoin, 1977.

Araki Yoshio. *Chūsei Bungaku no Keisei to Hatten*. Kyoto: Minerva Shobō, 1957.

Brower, Robert H. *Conversatons with Shōtetsu*. Ann Arbor, Mich.: Center for Japanese Studies, The University of Michigan, 1992.

———. "Ex-Emperor Go-Toba's Secret Teachings," *Harvard Journal of Asiatic Studies* 32, 1972.

Brower, Robert H., and Earl Miner. *Fujiwara Teika's Superior Poems of Our Time*. Stanford, Calif.: Stanford University Press, 1967.

———. *Japanese Court Poetry*. Stanford, Calif.: Stanford University Press, 1961.

Carter, Steven D. *Traditional Japanese Poetry*. Stanford, Calif.: Stanford University Press, 1991.

———. *Waiting for the Wind*. New York: Columbia University Press, 1989.

Fukuda Hideichi. *Chūsei Wakashi no Kenkyū*. Kadokawa Shoten, 1972.

Fukuda Yūsaku. *Teika Karon to sono Shūhen*. Kasama Shoin, 1974.

Hamaguchi Hiroaki. "Gyokuyō Waka Shū no Hyōgen," *Kokugo to Kokubungaku*, April 1969.

Higuchi Yoshimaro. *Kinkai Waka Shū*, in Shinchō Nihon Koten Shūsei series. Shinchōsha, 1981.

Hisamatsu Sen'ichi. *Chūsei Waka Shi*. Tōkyōdō, 1961.

Hisamatsu Sen'ichi and Nishio Minoru. *Karon Shū*, *Nōgakuron Shū*, in Nihon Koten Bungaku Taikei series. Iwanami Shoten, 1961.

Hisamatsu Sen'ichi et al. *Nihon Bungaku Shi: Chūsei*. Shibundō, 1955.

Hisamatsu Sen'ichi, Yokozawa Saburō, Shuzui Kenji, and Yasuda Ayao. *Geijutsuron Shū*, in Koten Nihon Bungaku Zenshū series. Chikuma Shobō, 1967.

Huey, Robert N. *Kyōgoku Tamekane*. Stanford, Calif.: Stanford University Press, 1989.

Huey, Robert N., and Susan Matisoff (trans.). "*Tamekanekyō Wakashō*: Lord Tamekane's Notes on Poetry," *Monumenta Nipponica* 40:2 (Summer 1985).

Inada Toshinori. *Shōtetsu no Kenkyū*. Kasama Shoin, 1978.

Inoue Muneo. *Chūsei Kadanshi no Kenkyū*, 2 vols. (Nambokuchōhen). Meiji Shoin, 1965.

Ishida Yoshisada. *Ton'a, Keiun*. Sanseidō, 1943.

Ishihara Kiyoshi. *Chūsei Bungakuron no Kōkyū*. Kyōto: Rinsen Shoten, 1988.

Iwasa Miyoko. *Eifukumon'in*. Kasama Shoin, 1976.

———. *Kyōgoku-ha Kajin no Kenkyū*. Kasama Shoin, 1974.

Iwasa Tadashi. *Shin'yō Waka Shū*, in Iwanami Bunko series. Iwanami Shoten, 1940.

Kawada Jun. *Yoshino-cho no Hika*. Daiichi Shobō, 1944.

Kawazoe Shōji. *Imagawa Ryōshun*. Yoshikawa Kōbunkan, 1964.

Kazamaki Keijirō, "Shin Chokusenshū," *Kokugo Kokubun*, vol. VIII, no. 3, March 1938.

Kazamaki Keijirō and Kojima Yoshio. *Sankashū, Kinkai Waka Shū*, in Nihon Koten Bungaku Taikei series. Iwanami Shoten, 1961.

Keene, Donald. *Down to the West*, 2 vols. New York: Holt, Rinehart and Winston, 1984.

———. *Essays in Idleness*. New York: Columbia University Press, 1967.

———. *Some Japanese Portraits*. Tokyo: Kodansha International, 1978.

———. *World Within Walls*. New York: Holt, Rinehart and Winston, 1976.

Keene, Donald (trans.). *Essays in Idleness: The Tsurezuregusa of Kenkō*. New York: Columbia University Press, 1967.

Kibune Shigeaki. *Shoku Gosen Waka Shū Zenchūshaku*. Kyōto: Daigakudō Shoten, 1989.

Konishi Jin'ichi. "Gyokuyō Jidai to Sōshi," in Jōkō Kan'ichi (ed.), *Chūsei Bungaku no Sekai*. Iwanami Shoten, 1960.

Koyama Keiichi. *Imagawa Ryōshun: sono Bushidō to Bungaku*. Sanseidō, 1944.

———. *Shōtetsu Ron*. Sanseidō, 1942.

Kyūsojin Hitaku and Higuchi Yoshimaro (eds.). *Shin Chokusen Waka Shū*, in Iwanami Bunko series. Iwanami Shoten, 1961.

Mass, Jeffrey P. *Court and Bakufu in Japan*. New Haven, Conn.: Yale University Press, 1982.

Matsumura Eiichi. *Minamoto Sanetomo Meika Hyōshaku*. Hibonkaku, 1934.

Miner, Earl, Hiroko Odagiri, and Robert E. Morrell. *The Princeton Companion to Classical Japanese Literature*. Princeton, N.J.: Princeton University Press, 1985.

Morimoto Motoko (ed.). *Izayoi Nikki, Yoru no Tsuru*, in Kōdansha Gakujutsu Bunko series. Kōdansha, 1979.

Nippon Gakujutsu Shinkōkai (trans.). *The Man'yōshū*. New York: Columbia University Press, 1965.

Nishino Taeko. *Kōgon-in*. Kokubunsha, 1988.

Nōtoru Damu Seishin Daigaku Kokubungaku Kenkyūshitsu Koten Sōsho Kankōkai (ed.). *Sōkonshū*. Okayama, 1973.

Numazawa Tatsuo. "Shin'yō Waka Shū Kōgi," in *Tanka Kōza*, III. Kaizōsha, 1932.

Ogi Takashi. *Shin'yō Waka Shū Hombun to Kenkyū*. Kasama Shoin, 1984.

Ōtori Kazuma. *Shin Chokusen Waka Shū Kochūshaku to sono Kenkyū*, 2 vols. Kyoto: Shibunkaku, 1986.

Saitō Kazuhiro. *Kōchū Shin'yōshū*. Nihon Dempō Tsūshin Sha, 1945.

Saitō Mokichi. *Kinkai Waka Shū*, in Nihon Koten Zensho series. Asahi Shimbun Sha, 1950.

Saitō Yōko. "Fujiwara Teika Kenkyū," *Nihon Bungaku*, no. 16, 1961.

Sansom, George. *A History of Japan to 1334*. Stanford, Calif.: Stanford University Press, 1958.

———. *A History of Japan: 1334–1615*. Stanford, Calif.: Stanford University Press, 1961.

Sasaki Nobutsuna. *Nihon Kagaku Shi*. Hakubunkan, 1910.

———. (ed.) *Nihon Kagaku Taikei*, V. Kazama Shobō, 1957.

Sasaki Yukitsuna. *Chūsei no Kajintachi*. Nihon Hōsō Shuppan Kyōkai, 1976.

Seidensticker, Edward. *The Tale of Genji*, 2 vols. New York: Alfred A. Knopf, 1976.

Senshū Kōgi-hen, in Tanka Kōza series, vol. 5. Kaizōsha, 1932.

Toki Zemmaro. *Kyōgoku Tamekane*. Chikuma Shobō, 1971.

———. *Shinshū Kyōgoku Tamekane*. Kadokawa Shoten, 1968.

Tsugita Kasumi. "Gyokuyō, Fūgashū no Uta no Tokushitsu," in *Nishō Gakusha Daigaku Sōritsu Hachijū Shūnen Kinen Ronshū*. Nishō Gakusha Daigaku, 1957.

———. "Gyokuyōshū no Seiritsu to sono Denrai," in *Bungaku*, vol. IX, no. 5, May 1941.

Tsugita Kasumi and Iwasa Miyoko. *Fūga Waka Shū*. Miyai Shoten, 1974.

Varley, H. Paul. *Imperial Restoration in Medieval Japan*. New York: Columbia University Press, 1971.

Yoneyama Muneomi. *Rikashū Hyōchū*. Furukawa Shuppanbu, 1935.

19. BUDDHIST WRITINGS OF THE KAMAKURA PERIOD

There was a great upsurge of religious belief during the Kamakura period, and many varieties of literature reveal the omnipresent influence of Buddhism. During the five centuries from the time that Buddhism first took hold in Japan, its role in the creation of literature had continued to grow. It is true that the various sects at times engaged in unseemly sectarian quarrels and even violence, but such doctrinal matters seldom appear in works of literature. Common to all sects was an awareness of the transience of worldly things; a belief in rebirth and transmigration; in causes from past lives resulting in effects in the present life; and in the existence of a heaven and hell. These concepts were reflected in literature, as obvious facts rather than as religious doctrines. Different sects paid homage to different divinities of the Buddhist pantheon, but whether believers placed their trust in the compassion of Kannon, or in the vow of Amida to save all men, the religion brought comfort in time of adversity, and the awe and gratitude the Japanese felt were often expressed in their writings.

Even literary works that may seem to owe little to Buddhist tradition were usually colored by these beliefs. We are likely to remember *The Tale of Genji* in terms of the peerless hero and the loveliness of the world surrounding him, but we should not forget that again and again Genji expressed his conviction that the beauty of this world was not enough and his determination to quit the evanescent world for the eternal world of Buddhist truth. To the end he did not take this step, but others in the novel, including emperors and their consorts, exchanged their brilliant robes for somber priestly garb. Again, the various accounts of the warfare of the twelfth century are remembered in terms of the deeds of bravery they describe; but the heroes in their last moments generally expressed not defiance of the enemy but reliance on the saving grace of

Buddha. The poetry, too, was increasingly colored by an awareness of the illusory nature of wordly pleasures.

Needless to say, *The Tale of Genji* and the other celebrated works of Heian prose and poetry were not written with the intent of proselytizing the readers. It is hard to imagine anyone being impelled by a reading of *The Tale of Genji* to "abandon the world." Some notable writings in fact had for their principal objective the dissemination of Buddhism, but they possess little literary interest. The priest Genshin's *Ōjō Yōshū* (The Essentials of Salvation, 985), one of the best-known works of this kind, contains a lengthy description of heaven and hell, but Genshin was unfortunately no Dante: his work was cast in unpoetic kambun, and his chief interest seems to have been the specific punishments appropriate for different sinners, ranging down from people who have pushed nuns off cliffs to merchants who watered their sake. None of the people suffering in Genshin's hell or rejoicing in his heaven is even named, much less characterized. The reader is unlikely to remember more of *The Essentials of Salvation* than the ingenious tortures that Genshin lovingly described.[1]

Mahayana Buddhism, as practiced in China and Japan, favored artistic depiction of principles of the faith as a means of making abstruse doctrines more easily intelligible. Shingon Buddhism, one of the chief Mahayana sects, placed particular reliance on art and accepted literature as a *hōben*, or expedient for gaining salvation.[2] Po Chü-i, a devout Buddhist, had expressed the belief that "wild words and fancy language,"[3] though not in themselves of value, could suggest higher truths, and this served as a justification for secular literature, even when the truths they conveyed remained hidden to the naked eye.

The Buddhist literature of the Kamakura period is varied. There are, first of all, the sermons and sayings of religious leaders, sometimes so memorably expressed that they can be treated as literature; tales in the tradition of the setsuwa of the Heian period; waka poetry and essays by monks; diaries of priests who traveled to sacred places or who lived in remote hermitages; and works of poetry and prose in Chinese. These categories are not of equal literary importance, but they all testify to the importance of the role Buddhism played.

Buddhist Sermons

The Buddhism of the Kamakura period is usually discussed in terms of the new sects: Jōdo (Pure Land) Buddhism, especially the Shin branch founded by Shinran (1173–1262); the Nichiren or Hokke (Lotus Sutra) Buddhism named after the prophet-priest Nichiren (1222–1282); and Zen Buddhism—both the Rinzai branch of Eisai (1141–1215) and the Sōtō branch of Dōgen (1200–1253). The older sects of Buddhism—Tendai, Shingon, and the various Nara sects—enjoyed a revival during the Kamakura period and had important leaders,[4] but in retrospect it now seems clear that the new sects exerted a greater influence over later Japanese literature.

Of the many works credited to priests of this period, one is of particular importance, *Tannishō* (Lamentations over Divergences),[5] compiled by Shinran's disciple Yuien-bō. *Tannishō* is a short work in eighteen sections, each devoted to some statement by Shinran, either an explanation of Jōdo Buddhism or else a correction of the mistaken opinion of some other priest—the "divergences" he lamented. The work concludes with a postscript by Yuien-bō and several appended notes.[6]

The first half of the work, in which Shinran voiced his basic convictions, is more interesting than the series of rebuttals to heresies that make up the second half. Some of Shinran's dicta are justly famous, notably the opening of the third section: "Even a good person can achieve birth in the Pure Land; how much truer this is for an evil person." The statement seems paradoxical, but Shinran was quite in earnest. Before explaining what he meant, he cited the more conventional, "Even an evil person can achieve birth in the Pure Land; how much truer this is for a good person." This accords better with common sense, but in fact it does not take into account the most important principle of Shinran's faith, the vow of Amida Buddha to save all those who call his name. If a man is good and aware of his own goodness, he may suppose that his good works will ensure birth in paradise; but the bad man, knowing he has no hope of gaining paradise except by the intercession of Amida, will call his name. The good man relies on his own strength (*jiriki*), but this will inevitably prove insufficient; the bad man relies on the strength of another (*tariki*) because he *knows* his own strength will not save him, and he will be saved by Amida.

The fifth section is equally striking:

> I have never said the Name even once for the repose of my departed father and mother. For all living things have been my parents and brothers and sisters in the course of countless lives in many states of existence. Upon attaining Buddhahood in the next life, I must save every one of them.
>
> Were saying the Name indeed a good act in which a person

> strove through his own powers, then he might direct the merit thus gained toward saving his father and mother. But this is not the case. If, however, he simply abandons such self-power (*jiriki*) and quickly attains enlightenment in the Pure Land, he will be able to save all beings with transcendent powers and compassionate means . . . beginning with those with whom his life is deeply bound.[7]

The saying of the name of Amida Buddha in the formula *Namu Amida Butsu* became in Shinran's day the most common expression of religious faith, and appears again and again in later literature. Hōnen (1133–1212), the founder of the Jōdo sect, began about 1175 to advocate the calling of the name of Amida Buddha (*nembutsu*) as the sole way to gain salvation. This doctrine was eagerly received at a time when the country was torn by warfare and it was feared that the world had reached the predicted last phase of the Buddhist Law (*mappō*), when people could neither comprehend nor practice the teachings of the Buddha.[8] In such a period no one could be strong enough to earn salvation himself; the only hope of birth in paradise was by beseeching the help of Amida. But it should not be thought that saying the nembutsu constituted a good deed, for that would be "self-power" (jiriki) and the essence of the nembutsu is dependence not on the self but on Amida's saving grace.[9] Hōnen had urged people to recite the nembutsu as often as possible,[10] and believed that it was necessary to say it aloud,[11] but Shinran was sure that saying the nembutsu only once, whether aloud or to oneself, was sufficient.[12] Hōnen did not ignore the traditional Buddhist learning and had many disciples, but Shinran told those who sought to become his followers:

> Each of you has crossed the borders of more than ten provinces to come to see me, undeterred by concern for your bodily safety, solely to inquire about the way to birth in the land of bliss. But if you imagine in me some special knowledge of a way to birth other than the nembutsu or a familiarity with the writings that teach it, you are greatly mistaken. If that is the case, you would do better to visit the many eminent scholars in Nara or on Mount Hiei and inquire fully of them about the essentials for birth.[13]

It might seem excessively easy for a person to achieve birth in paradise merely by saying (or even only thinking) the nembutsu once in a lifetime, but of course the invocation of Amida's name must be fully meant and absolutely sincere. It is an act of faith, an acknowledgment on the part of the person who pronounces the syllables *na-mu-a-mi-da-bu-tsu* that he is incapable of saving himself, that his only hope of salvation is the intercession of Amida Buddha. It is difficult for anyone to admit his nullity, the insignificance of all he has done in his lifetime. Building temples or offering copies of the sacred writings to the temples had always been considered to be acts of merit that would promote salvation, but Shinran insisted, "Even though one offer not even a single sheet of paper or half a sen toward the dharma (Buddhist Law), if one casts up one's heart to Other Power (*tariki*) and one's *shinjin* [faith in Amida] is deep, one is in accord with the fundamental intent of the Vow."[14]

Tannishō is today probably the best-known work by any Japanese Buddhist. Its chief appeal is the portrait it presents of Shinran himself in his strikingly individual comments; his every phrase has inspired believers. However, as far as we can tell, the work was virtually unknown for over six centuries after Yuien-bō committed it to paper. Kiyozawa Manshi (1863–1903), a priest of the Shin sect, first called the attention of the world to a work that hitherto had been kept secret by the monks of the Hongan-ji; they feared that its apparent tolerance of evil might induce the ignorant, trusting that Amida would forgive them, to commit sins.[15] But Shinran, in a memorable passage of *Tannishō*, explained the existence of good and evil in terms of karma from previous lives:

> Good thoughts arise in us through the prompting of past good, and we come to think and do evil through the working of karmic evil. The late master [Hōnen] said, "Know that not one evil act is done—even if no more than a particle of dust on the tip of a hair of rabbit's fur or sheep's wool—but has its cause in past karma."
>
> The master once asked, "Yuien-bō, do you believe what I say?"
>
> "Yes, I do."
>
> "Then, will you do exactly what I ask you?" he said, laying stress on his words.
>
> I humbly affirmed that I would, whereupon he said, "Would you be willing, for example, to kill a thousand people? If you are, your birth in the Pure Land is assured."
>
> To this I responded, "Even if this is your command, I doubt that I am capable of killing even one person."
>
> "Then how can you say you will do exactly what Shinran asks of you?"
>
> He continued, "You should realize from this that if everything were simply a matter of will, when I told you to kill a thousand

> people in order to achieve rebirth, you would have immediately set about killing. But you have not the karmic cause that would enable you to harm even one person. It is not that you refrain from killing because your heart is good. In the same way, a person may not wish to harm anyone and yet end up by killing a hundred or a thousand people."[16]

The only way to escape one's karma was to throw oneself on the mercy of Amida Buddha. The same message is found in the writings of Hōnen and of the peripatetic Ippen (1239–1289), who urged the people wherever he went to join with him in dancing and singing together in praise of Amida. A more literary expression of the same beliefs is found in *Ichigon Hōdan* (Brief Sayings of the Great Teachers), a collection of the sayings of various nembutsu practitioners and hermits. Neither the compiler nor the date of compilation of *Brief Sayings* has been determined, though it has been conjectured that it might have been Kyōbutsu (also known as Kyōbutsu-bō), a priest who appears in about a third of the episodes of the collection.[17]

On the whole, the book makes dull reading for anyone who is not a student of medieval Buddhism,[18] and many sections consist of only a few lines. The following sections are longer and more interesting than most:

> When the Abbot Myōhen of Kōya was returning from a pilgrimage to Zenkō-ji,[19] he paid a visit to the holy man Hōnen. The abbot asked him, "How may one free oneself from the cycle of death and birth?" The holy man replied, "By saying the nembutsu." Myōhen asked him next, "Yes, of course that is true. But when deluded passions arise within us, what are we to do?" Hōnen answered, "Even if deluded passions arise, the strength of the Original Vow will enable one to achieve birth [in the Pure Land]." Myōhen left, saying that he had been fully persuaded. Hōnen murmured, "The man who hopes to be reborn [in the Pure Land] without ever having been troubled by confused passions is like someone who thinks he will say the nembutsu after first gouging out the eyes and cutting off the nose he was born with."[20]

In this episode Hōnen was mocking people who hoped to gain salvation without a struggle or who would say the nembutsu only after they had deprived themselves of the sources of temptation. The following passage deals with a basic question: if one may gain salvation merely by saying the nembutsu with a devout heart, what use is there in reading books by the great teachers of the Jōdo faith?

> Kyōbutsu-bō said, "People say that learning is useless to priests who have given up the world,[21] but it is a question of degree. Those with scholarly ability should, as a matter of form, at least glance through *The Essentials of Salvation*, taking in the words if not the meanings. Turning the pages once in a while will help them to understand why this transient world of life and death is to be hated, and why we should place our trust in the nembutsu and rebirth. . . . But saying that one should study definitely does not mean that one should entertain ambitions of understanding every single word and phrase of *The Essentials of Salvation* from cover to cover. . . . It is quite enough to have opened the book and skimmed over the most important parts. Once one has grasped this technique, it will serve as a starting point for advance on the path toward the future life. . . .
>
> "Learning is especially valuable because it enables one to benefit others by persuading them to have faith. But if with even this modicum of learning one becomes puffed up with one's own importance or one seeks to gain recognition as a scholar, one should cease one's studies altogether. Nothing is more foolish than making a poison out of what should be a medicine. . . .
>
> "However, if a person is not naturally endowed with such intellectual capacity, he should devote himself wholeheartedly to the nembutsu, and not attempt to gain even this modicum of learning. If he is assiduous in intoning the nembutsu and in other acts, he will not be at variance with the basic intent of our teachings."[22]

The attitude expressed is anti-intellectual, but Kyōbutsu's opinion was not necessarily shared by all believers in Jōdo Buddhism; it was a logical extension of the supreme importance accorded to the recitation of the simple invocation to Amida Buddha.

Zen Buddhism, which, like Jōdo Buddhism, emerged into prominence in Japan during the thirteenth century, was known for its iconoclastic attitude with respect to the sacred writings. The painting by the thirteenth-century painter Liang K'ai of a Zen master tearing up a sutra[23] is probably the most vivid representation of the Zen distrust (or scorn) of authority. But, contrary to the impression created by this painting or by many of the sayings of the Zen masters that insist on nonverbal and nonliterary transmission of Zen beliefs, there is a large body of writings by the masters. *Shōbō Genzō* (The Eye and Treasury of the True Law)[24] was the name given to the collection of discourses and essays composed in Japanese between 1232 and 1253 by Dōgen, generally considered to have been the greatest Japanese master of Zen.

Dōgen was born into the highest aristocracy as the son of the court poet and statesman Minamoto no Michichika. On his father's side he was closely related to the imperial house, and on his mother's side to the Fujiwara regents. He lost his father when he was two years old and his mother five years later. He early showed such promise in his studies that the regent of the time considered adopting Dōgen and preparing him for a career as a statesman, but the boy's heart was set on religion, and at the age of twelve he entered Buddhist orders on Mount Hiei. At fifteen he felt so dissatisfied with the Tendai teachings on a critical point[25] that he went to study with Eisai,[26] a monk originally of the Tendai sect who had twice traveled to China where he studied the Zen teachings. Unfortunately, Eisai died almost immediately afterward, and Dōgen studied instead with Eisai's disciple Myōzen (1184–1225). In 1223 Myōzen took Dōgen with him to China, where both men studied with a master of the Sōtō (Ts'ao Tung) sect of Zen Buddhism. Myōzen died while in China, and Dōgen took his bones back to Japan when he returned in 1227.

After his return, Dōgen lived some years at the Kennin-ji in Kyoto, but, distressed by the lax ways into which the monks of this temple had fallen, and feeling that nothing remained of the spirit of Eisai, he went to live in a hermitage. In 1233 he moved to an abandoned temple, where he attracted a continually growing number of followers. In 1236 he opened a new temple called Kōshōhōrin-ji, the first independent Zen monastery in Japan.[27] The monks of Mount Hiei began to harass Dōgen and his followers, and attempted to burn his monastery. He accepted an invitation from the daimyo of Echizen to establish a monastery in that province and left the capital in 1243. The temple he founded was called Eihei-ji,[28] and became the central temple of the Sōtō sect.

As a religious teacher, Dōgen stressed above all the importance of sitting in meditation. The Rinzai sect of Zen, which had emerged into prominence at this time, also practiced sitting in meditation, but relied especially on the use of koans, or riddles, for gaining enlightenment.[29] Dōgen's chief work, *Shōbō Genzō*, is exceptionally difficult to understand. An American philosopher, despairing of ever understanding the text, asked a Japanese specialist in the writings of Dōgen why he had written in Japanese, rather than Chinese, the normal language of Buddhist and philosophical treatises. He was told, "Dōgen did not write the *Shōbōgenzō* in Japanese instead of Chinese. No other Japanese before or after Dōgen wrote in the language of the *Shōbōgenzō*. It is Dōgen's own language."[30] The difficulties are such that not even experts who have devoted much of their lives to studying *Shōbō Genzō* feel confident that they can explain it.[31] One authority has suggested the attraction, as well as the difficulty, of Dōgen's language in terms of "reshuffling the Chinese lexical components of a given phrase or expression." He continued, "The transposition of linguistic elements is intended to suggest that they are as dynamic and versatile as reality itself in their infinitely variegated configurations and possibilities."[32]

Shōbō Genzō is a work of profundity, but apart from its striking use of similes and metaphors it is not of great literary interest. It provides evidence that even though Zen emphasizes nonverbal means of gaining enlightenment, language could also be employed to illustrate the truths of Buddhism. The traditional beginning of Zen was traced back to the moment when Shakyamuni Buddha held up an udumbara blossom and winked, in this way directly transmitting the Law (dharma) to Mahākāshyapa. All of the seven Buddhas of the past, including Shakyamuni and the patriarchs who came after him, transmitted the Law to their successors in the same manner; it was the actualization of their enlightenment.[33] Dōgen denied, however, the view current among some monks of the time that this was the only way of transmitting the Law: did not Shakyamuni, after first twirling the flower and winking, utter the words, "I possess the Eye and Treasury of the True Law and the Serene Mind of Nirvana. I now bestow it on Mahākāshyapa"?[34] If language were not a legitimate means of communication, Shakyamuni need not have spoken. This reasoning could serve as a justification for such Zen texts as *Shōbō Genzō*.

Only a person deeply familiar with Buddhist philosophy could profitably read so difficult a work. Dōgen's thought was communicated in much easier to understand language in *Shōbō Genzō Zuimonki* (Record of Things Heard Concerning the Eye and Treasury of the True Law), the account by his disciple Ejō (1198–1280) of sayings of Dōgen he had heard on various occasions. Sometimes Dōgen's distrust of book learning approaches Shinran's,[35] but his insistence on jiriki could not be further removed from Shinran's total dependence on Amida. A few excerpts will suggest the tone of the *Zuimonki*:

> One day in casual conversation he told me, "A student of Zen must not fret himself over clothing and food. Our country is small and remote, but in the distant past as today, it has been celebrated for both exoteric and esoteric doctrines. Of the scholars who are likely

to be remembered even by future generations, I have never heard of even one who enjoyed an abundance of clothing and food. . . . How much truer this is of the practitioners of our Way: they abandon all thought of getting ahead in this world and run after nothing. How could such people ever be prosperous? In the Zen temples of the Great Sung Country,[36] even though these are the latter days of the Law, there are thousands and even tens of thousands of students, some from afar, others from nearby regions, and nearly all of them are poor. However, they do not complain of this; they worry only about the difficulty of obtaining enlightenment. Some climb to the tops of temple towers[37] to sit in meditation, others remain below under the eaves of the temple halls, practicing the Way in a silence that suggests they might be in mourning for their parents."[38]

A devotion to poverty was not unique to Zen, but it typified the indifference to worldly goods or fame on the part of the Zen believer. Members of the samurai class of the Kamakura period were especially receptive to such tenets and to the rigid discipline of sitting in meditation, even if they were unable to understand the highest reaches of Dōgen's philosophy. The emphasis on simplicity and even poverty in the tea ceremony, the bare monochromes of the landscape paintings inspired by Zen, and the austere Nō stage all evoke the rejection of abundance taught by Dōgen.

Other sections of the *Zuimonki* are in a lighter vein:

The Chancellor from Uji[39] went one day to the boiler room[40] for the bath and watched as men lighted the fires. The boiler man called out, "Who are you? What do you mean by charging into the boiler room of the palace without a word of explanation?" The Chancellor, after having been chased out, took off the mean clothes he had been wearing and, changing to a magnificent robe befitting his office, went back to the boiler room. The man in charge, seeing him coming from a distance, ran off in alarm. At this, the Chancellor hung his robe on a pole and paid it homage. When someone asked what he was doing, he replied, "The respect people pay me is not due to any virtue of mine. It's all because of this costume." The fool respects other people for the same reason. And it is true, too, of the respect paid the sutras—it's only for the words.[41]

Such anecdotes bring us to the border of literature, even though *Zuimonki* is not as a whole literary in intent. The influence of Buddhism on the literature of the Kamakura and Muromachi periods was incalculably great, but the philosophical tenets of a particular sect tended to remain within the temple walls and rarely affected society as a whole. It was through popularizations, both of the kind represented by *Zuimonki* and by the Buddhist setsuwa, that Buddhist doctrine filtered down to the general public and enriched the literature.

Kamo no Chōmei (1155–1216)

Kamo no Chōmei, an important compiler of Buddhist setsuwa literature, was also a distinguished poet and critic of poetry, but he is known today above all for his essay *Hōjōki* (An Account of My Hut),[42] written in 1212. In this short work he enunciated with great beauty of style his conviction that a hermitage was the only possible refuge from a world of disasters. Throughout the work Chōmei used the image of the house to represent the vanity of wordly attachments, describing on the one hand the grief of those who lost their houses in an earthquake, conflagration, or whirlwind, and on the other the joy of the hermit whose hut is so temporary and so unpretentious that it would not bother him even if it were destroyed.

The opening of *An Account of My Hut* is one of the most celebrated passages of Japanese literature:

> The flow of the river is ceaseless and its water is never the same. The bubbles that float in the pools, now vanishing, now forming, are not of long duration: so in the world are man and his dwellings. It might be imagined that the houses great and small, that vie roof against proud roof in the capital, remain unchanged from one generation to the next, but when we examine whether or not this is true, how few are the houses that were there of old. Some were burnt last year and only since rebuilt. Great houses have crumbled into hovels, and those who dwell in them have fallen no less. The city is the same, the people as numerous as ever, but of those I used to know, a bare one or two in twenty remain. They die in the morning, they are born in the evening, like foam on the water.
>
> Whence does he come, where does he go, man that is born and dies? We know not. For whose benefit does he torment himself in building houses that last but a moment, for what reason is his eye delighted by them? This too we do not know. Which will be first to go, the master or his dwelling? One might just as well ask this

> of the dew on the morning-glory. Perhaps the dew may fall and the flower remain—remain only to be withered by the morning sun. Or the flower may fade before the dew evaporates, but even if the dew does not evaporate, it never waits until evening.[43]

Apart from the recurrent use of the house as a metaphor for the fortunes of the people who inhabit them, other stylistic features, such as the parallel constructions (a sure sign of Chinese influence), stand out. The last two sentences quoted above, beginning with "Perhaps the dew may fall," are, in the original:

Aru wa tsuyu ochite hana nokoreri. Nokoru to iedomo asahi ni karenu. Aru wa hana shibomite tsuyu nao kiezu. Kiezu to iedomo yūbe wo matsu koto nashi.

The parallelism is as precise as in Chinese *p'ien wen*, but it does not give an impression of heaviness. The repetition of the verb *shirazu* (we do not know) at the head of two earlier sentences in the passage violates normal Japanese word order (the verb should come at the end of the sentence), but it is stylistically effective; by placing the verb in this exposed position, Chōmei emphasized the rhetorical nature of the questions he asked.

Another stylistic feature is the repeated use of hysteron protoron—a reversal of the natural order—as in "The bubbles that float in the pools, now vanishing, now forming" or "They die in the morning, they are born in the evening." The effect of this device is to suggest the rapidity of the changes and, again, the uncertainty of both the natural order and the works of man.

The main burden of the introductory section is its insistence on impermanence, the most fundamental of Buddhist beliefs. The word *mujō* (impermanence) occurs toward the end of this section in the phrase *shu to sumika to mujō wo arasou sama* (the way the master and the dwelling vie for impermanence);[44] *mujō* is a key word to the understanding of much of the literature of the time and not only works of a specifically Buddhist character.

Following the introduction, Chōmei cited examples of disasters that convinced him of the undependability of this world: the great fire of 1177, the whirlwind of 1180, the famine of 1181 and 1182, and the earthquake of 1185. Each of these is narrated with the vividness of someone who had actually witnessed the disasters he described. Again and again Chōmei referred to the destruction of houses, the symbols of human vanity; he concluded after his account of the great fire, "Of all the follies of human endeavor, none is more pointless than expending treasure and spirit to build houses in so dangerous a place as the capital." Again, after describing the whirlwind, he declared, "Not only were many houses damaged or destroyed, but countless people were hurt or crippled while repairing them." During the famine "as even firewood grew scarce, those without other resources broke up their own houses and took the wood to sell in the market." After the earthquake, "not a single mansion, pagoda, or shrine was left whole."

One of the disasters enumerated by Chōmei was caused not by the forces of nature but by the will of a tyrant: Taira no Kiyomori, wishing to have the capital closer to the Taira naval strongholds, moved it by decree from Kyoto, where it had remained for almost four hundred years, to Fukuhara on the shore of the Inland Sea. Although this decision caused immense consternation, there was no possibility of protesting the actions of a despot, "and everyone moved, from the Emperor, his ministers, and the nobility on down. Of all those who served at the court, not a soul was left behind. Those who had ambitions of office or favors to ask of the Emperor were eager to be the first to move. Only those who, having lost all chance of success, were superfluous in the world, remained behind, although most unhappily."[45] In this instance, too, the houses were eloquent witnesses of the disaster. Some people abandoned their houses in the old capital, others attempted to take their houses with them: "Houses were dismantled and floated down the Yodo River, and the capital turned to empty fields before one's eyes."

One disaster that Chōmei failed to mention probably caused more hardship than the whirlwind or the earthquake—the warfare between the Taira and Minamoto clans that broke out in 1181, the year of the famine. Perhaps Chōmei feared that mention of political matters would be improper in an essay of this kind, but by implication he had already compared the present day, when the rulers showed no compassion for their subjects, with the distant past when the Emperor Nintoku, seeing how little smoke was rising from the kitchen fires of the people, remitted taxes. Chōmei commented, "This was because he loved his people and sought to help them. If we compare present conditions with those in ancient times, we can see how great is the difference."[46] Perhaps also (though this is only a conjecture) Chōmei rejoiced over the downfall of the Taira, but thought it might weaken the force of his arguments in favor of "leaving the world" if he lightened with an expression of pleasure the otherwise unbroken gloom of his narration of life in the world.

Chōmei followed his description of the various disasters with a section on "hardships of life in the world." He wrote, "When a man of no great standing happens to live next door to a powerful lord, however happy he may be, he cannot celebrate too loudly; however grief-stricken, he cannot raise his voice in lamentation. He is uneasy no matter what he does; in his every action he trembles like a swallow approaching a falcon's nest."[47]

This is accomplished writing but (unlike the accounts of the disasters) it need not have come from Chōmei's own experience. Indeed, the language is so close to that of the tenth-century *Record of the Pond Pavilion* by Yoshishige no Yasutane, an essay written in kambun, that surely there must have been direct influence.[48] Here is the parallel passage to the one by Chōmei quoted above:

> Then there are the humble folk who live in the shadow of some powerful family: their roof is broken but they don't dare to thatch it, their wall collapses but they don't dare build it up again; happy, they can't open their mouths and give a loud laugh; grieving, they can't lift up their voices and wail; coming and going always in fear, hearts and minds never at rest, they're like little sparrows in the presence of hawks and falcons.[49]

An Account of My Hut presents next a brief autobiographical sketch of the circumstances that impelled Chōmei to "leave the world." Once again, the house is the image used to chronicle his steady disenchantment with society. He related that, after growing up in the house of his great-grandmother, unspecified misfortunes caused him to leave that house: "Many things led me to live in seclusion, and finally, unable to remain in my ancestral home, in my thirties I built after my own plans a little cottage. It was a bare tenth of the size of the house in which I had lived."[50] Chōmei was disappointed over not having been appointed after his father's death to the hereditary office of his ancestors at the Kamo Shrine, and probably lacked the means to maintain a large establishment. It was here that Chōmei, in his fiftieth year, "became a priest and turned his back on the world." It may seem strange that someone who had been reared in a Shintō family, and who himself hoped to be appointed an official of a Shintō shrine, should have become a Buddhist priest, but at the time no contradiction was felt between the two religions.

The last and longest section of *An Account of My Hut* is devoted to the description of how Chōmei at last found peace. The section opens:

> Now that I have reached the age of sixty and my life seems about to evaporate like the dew, I have fashioned a lodging for the last

> leaves of my years. It is a hut where, perhaps, a traveller might spend a single night; it is like the cocoon spun by an aged silkworm. This hut is not even a hundredth the size of the cottage where I spent my middle years.[51]

The imagery is entirely Buddhist: the quickly evaporating dew was a familiar metaphor for life; the hut where the traveler might spend a single night was similarly used as a metaphor for human beings passing only a brief time in this world before moving on to another stage of existence; and the phrase "the cocoon spun by an aged silkworm," effective though it is, had already appeared in the Buddhist-inspired *Record of the Pond Pavilion*.[52]

Needless to say, Chōmei was not guilty of plagiarism when he borrowed imagery. The underlying conception—the discovery of a refuge in a hut far from the city—owed much to Yasutane, but far from concealing his source, Chōmei probably hoped that readers would recognize it and admire his adroit variation on the theme of another man, rather in the manner of honka-dori. Yasutane himself had borrowed from prose pieces by Po Chü-i.[53] Chōmei, following in Yasutane's footsteps, took refuge in a hermitage, and his thoughts naturally turned to Yasutane's description when he attempted to convey how he had found peace.

Discovering a refuge from the passions and confusion of this world in a hermitage is common to the histories of many faiths. Sometimes the hermit chooses to live in the desert where there is nothing to tempt him, or in a forbidding mountain region where his only food is the nuts and berries he picks from the trees. Chōmei, however, chose for his retreat a particularly lovely part of Japan. He says he did not consult diviners to ascertain whether or not the site was auspicious, implying that one spot was as good as another, but it is obvious that he delighted in his surroundings. Not only were the vistas south of Lake Biwa beautiful, but everything reminded him of old poetry:

> If the evening is still, in the moonlight that fills the window I long for old friends, or wet my sleeve with tears at the cries of the monkeys. Fireflies in the grass thickets might be mistaken for fishing-lights off the island of Maki; the dawn rains sound like autumn storms blowing through the leaves. And when I hear the pheasants' cries, I wonder if they are calling their father or mother; when the wild deer of the mountain approach me unafraid, I realize how far I am from the world. And when sometimes, as is the wont of old

age, I waken in the middle of the night, I stir up the buried embers and make them companions in solitude.[54]

Even if we do not look up the sources of each allusion, the tone of the writing makes it clear that it *is* an allusion. To cite one example, here is a poem composed by Saigyō on Mount Kōya:

yama fukami	Deep in the mountains,
naruru kasegi no	So deep the deer, unafraid,
kejikasa ni	Come close up to me,
yo ni tōzakaru	I can tell just how far
hodo zo shiraruru[55]	I have left the world behind.

Chōmei saw himself not only as a hermit but as a poet. His house was a bare ten feet square (*hōjō*), and he fashioned it in such a way that it could easily be dismantled. The furnishings were extremely simple: a few shelves for his meager possessions, paintings of Amida and other buddhas and bodhisattvas, a desk, a brazier for burning brushwood. He also laid out a small garden where he grew herbs.

Chōmei seems to have deliberately planned to prevent himself from feeling attachment to his hut: "Only in a hut built for the moment can one live without fears," he wrote. But after five years spent amid scenery that gave him endless pleasure, in a hut that exactly fitted him like the little shell that a hermit crab chooses as his habitation, knowing his own size, he could not help but develop feelings of attachment: "This lonely house is but a tiny hut, but somehow I love it." And he reached the sad conclusion: "It is a sin for me now to love my little hut, and my attachment to solitude may also be a hindrance to enlightenment."[56] He told himself that although he had fled the world to live in a mountain forest in order to discipline his mind and practice the Way, "In spite of your monk's appearance, your heart is stained with impurity. Your hut may take after Vimalakīrti's, but you preserve the Law even worse that Suddhipanthaka."[57] He had no reply to offer to these and other self-accusations: "All I could do was to use my tongue to recite two or three times the nembutsu, however unacceptable from a defiled heart."

An Account of My Hut is a superbly written example of zuihitsu. Of course, the composition itself is anything but random; the successive disasters that Chōmei witnessed and described build up inexorably to his withdrawal from human society, but the conclusion is unexpected: instead of expressing joy over his triumph over vain pretenses and his assured birth in the Pure Land, he confesses that he has in fact been unable to sever his ties to the world. His hut is tiny, but he loves it, and his "only desire for this life is to see the beauty of the seasons." Even such attachments, remote though they are from the getting and spending of life in the capital, were bound to be hindrances in the path of enlightenment.

Chōmei had the honesty to record what he considered to be the ultimate failure of his attempt to free himself of worldly attachment. He seems less candid with respect to another matter: although he gives the impression of never having returned to the life he knew in the past once he had found peace in his hut, the year before he wrote *An Account of My Hut* he traveled to Kamakura at the invitation of the shogun, Sanetomo, and gave him instruction in composing poetry. This development, though in no way shameful, contradicts Chōmei's self-portrait: the reader may feel disappointed by seeming disingenuousness, as other readers have felt on discovering how close Walden Pond was to the civilization Thoreau had rejected.

Leaving such matters aside, it must be said that *An Account of My Hut* is perhaps the most perfect work of literature composed in Japanese under the strong influence of Buddhism. The style is surpassingly beautiful, accommodating Chinese influences in structure and vocabulary without a trace of awkwardness, and preserving the effortless lyrical flow of traditional Japanese prose. Each of the disasters described is made vivid by a graphically presented incident: the great conflagration fanned by the wind that carried the flames over two or three streets, leaving the houses in between untouched and the people in them feeling as though they were caught in a nightmare; the removal of the capital by the river thick with dismantled houses; the earthquake by the uncontrollable wailing of a normally impassive samurai when his child was crushed under a wall. Chōmei probably did not strive for literary effects, but his training not only as a priest but as a poet made him sensitive to the varied sights he had witnessed and gave him the stylistic control necessary to communicate his vision in a manner so vivid that it still moves readers as much as it did those for whom it was first composed.

Chōmei's achievements as a poet and as a critic of poetry are discussed above, but his compilation of Buddhist tales called *Hosshinshū* (A Collection to Promote Religious Awakening)[58] is of direct concern here. The standard text consists of 102 tales divided into eight chapters.[59] Chōmei's preface opens with a sentence quoted from the Nirvana Sutra: "There is something that Buddha taught: Even if you may become the teacher of your heart (*kokoro*), you must not let your heart be your teacher." This warning against yielding to one's emotions and insistence on the necessity for self-control is a key theme in the stories related in the work.[60] More interesting for us are the personal remarks by Chōmei about his reasons for compiling the collection:

> In view of the shallowness of my heart, I have not attempted especially to seek profound religious truths, but have done no more than gather together things I casually happened to see or hear, and have privately kept them by my side. I mean, when I saw wise deeds, even though I knew I could never equal them, they became the occasion for wishing I were capable of such deeds; when I saw foolish deeds, I made them an instrument for improving myself. . . . Who, I wonder, will take these stories seriously? . . . I have been stirred by idle tales I happened to hear on my travels, and I hope only that they will stir in my heart a modicum of religious awakening [*hosshin*].[61]

Hosshinshū has a basically different intent from that of other collections of Buddhist tales: Chōmei did not merely gather together stories of people who had achieved a religious awakening in the hope of edifying readers; he hoped that the act of compilation might help him to achieve an awakening. He did not urge other people to believe these tales. One remembers the statement in *An Account of My Hut*: "I do not prescribe my way of life to men enjoying happiness and wealth, but have related my experiences merely to show the differences between my former and present life."

Although (as scholars have demonstrated)[62] the preface and later sections of *Hosshinshū* borrowed words and ideas from *The Essentials of Salvation*, the closest connections are with *An Account of My Hut*. As yet, however, no conclusive evidence has been uncovered as to which work Chōmei wrote first. It was long believed that he completed *Hosshinshū* shortly before his death in 1216, but the similarity in mood to that of *An Account of My Hut* has led some to infer that Chōmei may have written the two works about the same time.[63]

Chōmei's preface also described what guided him in making his selection of tales. He excluded tales related in India and China because they were "too far away." He also excluded stories about buddhas and bodhisattvas because they were too exalted for someone of his modest attainments. The stories, then, were all set in Japan,[64] and dealt with monks and priests of this world and not superhuman beings. In order to emphasize the everyday aspect of the stories, the tone was made deliberately colloquial, evidence also that these were tales Chōmei had heard and that were not from written sources.

The tales are mildly interesting, but in no way comparable in effect to *An Account of My Hut*. As we might expect of Buddhist tales, especially those written under the influence of *The Essentials of Salvation*, they generally describe the blissful deaths (*ōjō*) of men who had spent their lives in prayer and austerities. Occasionally, a figure will stand out, as in the story of Butsumyō, presented as an appendix to the story of the holy man of the Tennō-ji:

> To every person he met he invariably performed obeisance, saying, "Fisherman or monk, man or woman—clear and pure," and that was how he came by his name. Not a soul who saw him but thought him no more than an ill-omened, disagreeable creature; but there must have been something special about him, for he was on good terms with the holy man named Ashōbō. He would borrow the most unlikely sutras and treatises from him and, unbeknownst to anyone, carry them off in the bosom of his robe, always returning them after a few days. He died, seated as for meditation, on top of a crumbling embankment, facing the West with his hands devoutly clasped.[65]

Not all the stories in *Hosshinshū* describe priests who at the close of their lives achieve religious awakening. One story, for example, tells of a priest who had long since retired from his duties at the Yakushi-ji, the great temple in Nara, because of old age. When he heard, however, than an important post in the administration of the temple had fallen vacant, he decided to apply for the job. His disciples attempted to dissuade him, saying it was unbecoming for a man of his age to entertain such aspirations. He refused to listen to them, and the disciples, despairing of changing the old priest's mind by their arguments, decided to invent a dream which the priest would interpret as an augury of ill fortune if he continued in his plan. One disciple was chosen to tell the old man about a dream in which demons prepare a cauldron in which to boil him alive. They supposed this would frighten him into giving up his unseemly ambition, but the old man interpreted the dream in an entirely favorable way, grinning from ear to ear to show his delight. The moral is ironic:

> This man had risen to the rank of *risshi*[66] because of his learning, but for him at seventy to have rejoiced over this dream shows the depth of his greed. There is absolutely no comparison between him and the ignorant old man of the previous story who was able to gain enlightenment through his own strength.[67]

It is difficult to imagine how such a story could have helped Kamo no Chōmei to achieve a religious awakening. However, the cauldron for boiling sinners harked back to *The Essentials of Salvation*, and the account of a priest's failure to gain enlightenment might serve as a warning. Later readers were probably amused rather than edified by the tale. *Hosshinshū* was possibly the first work of Japanese prose to have been introduced to the West: the Portuguese missionary and scholar João Rodrigues in his *Arte da Lingoa de Iapam* (1604–1608) quoted over ten passages from the work as examples of Japanese grammar. It is surprising, considering the extremely bad relations that prevailed between Christians and Buddhists at that time, that Rodrigues should have chosen so many examples from a Buddhist work (including passages praising the Buddha), but perhaps he thought missionaries should be familiar with their "enemies."[68] The citations by Rodrigues also provide evidence that *Hosshinshū* was widely known at the beginning of the seventeenth century.

Companion of a Quiet Life

Keisei (1189–1268), the Tendai priest who wrote *Kankyo no Tomo* (Companion of a Quiet Life, 1222),[69] was a member of the Kujō branch of the aristocratic Fujiwara family, the son of the Regent and Prime Minister Yoshitsune. As an infant he was dropped by his wet nurse, and he grew up with a crooked spine; this seems to have been why he later entered Buddhist orders, though the sudden death of his father may have contributed to the decision. After studying with the celebrated monk Myōe (1173–1232), Keisei went to live in a hermitage west of the capital. He left the hermitage to travel to China in 1217, returning to Japan after a relatively short stay of about a year. While in China, Keisei met a "southern barbarian" (a Persian) who wrote at his request an inscription for Myōe, a worshiper of Shakyamuni, the historical Buddha.

The story Keisei chose to head *Companion of a Quiet Life* seems to reflect both his experiences in China and the long-standing wish of Myōe to travel to India, the land where Shakyamuni Buddha was born. This story concerns Prince Shinnyo, the third son of the Emperor Heizei, who after entering Buddhist orders studied with various teachers including Kūkai. Not satisfied with what he could learn in Japan, he journeyed to China in 862, where he discovered to his disappointment that Buddhism was on the decline. He set out on foot for India, though he was over eighty years old. Various Chinese and Koreans had successfully made the journey, but Shinnyo was the first Japanese to attempt to reach India. Unfortunately, however, he was eaten by a tiger.

At the conclusion of the tale Keisei explained why, unlike Chōmei in *Hosshinshū*, he had not attempted to relate in his collection stories about persons whose biographies had already been written:[70] he feared that he might be criticized (as Chōmei had been) for attempting to improve on the old accounts.[71] These words make it evident how conscious Keisei was of writing in the tradition of *Hosshinshū*.[72]

Many tales in *Companion of a Quiet Life*, in keeping with the title, are about hermits. In this respect, too, we can detect the influence of Chōmei. Keisei described in one of the essays appended to his tales why he had decided to live in a "grass hut" (*sōan*), as a hermitage was called: "I thought I would build just for myself a humble hut of grass at the foot of some mountain where no one would find fault with me, and that I would live with quails as my only companions. And if that place should become unlivable, I would be free to go wherever else I pleased and hide myself there."[73] Apparently, however, Keisei's hermitage was anything but deserted: he received gifts of food and clothing from his family, and courtiers found his retreat a congenial place to compose poetry.[74] Keisei was even able to obtain books from abroad,[75] but the hermits who figure in his tales do not readily admit others to their remote dwellings, and they lead lives untouched by worldly attachments.

The special interest of *Companion of a Quiet Life* is to be found in four of the thirty-two tales, those that describe in vivid detail the Tendai practice of contemplating pollution. In the first of them[76] a young man, who attends a holy man of Mount Hiei as his servant though he is actually a priest, disappears each night and does not return until dawn. People at the temple suspect that he must be frequenting prostitutes in Sakamoto, the town below Mount Hiei, and one night a holy man has someone secretly follow the young priest. To his surprise, the priest goes not to the town but to a deserted area of Kyoto where corpses were abandoned. The priest approaches a putrefying corpse, indescribably loathsome, and remains there all through the night weeping, now shutting, now opening his eyes as he prays. When he hears the early morning sounds, the priest wipes away his tears and returns to Mount Hiei.

The holy man on learning what took place regrets having suspected the young priest of sinful behavior, and henceforth no longer treats him as an ordinary person. One morning, when nobody else is about, the holy man reveals that he knows the young priest's secret. At first the priest denies he has performed a meritorious action, but the holy man presses him to display the special powers he has undoubtedly acquired from his contemplation of pollution (*fujōkan*). The young priest thereupon puts a lid over a bowl of rice gruel and contemplates it. After a few moments he removes the lid. The rice gruel has turned into a mass of white worms. The holy man, weeping over the prodigy, begs the young man to guide him to salvation.[77]

The contemplation of pollution, especially the rotting of a corpse, was believed to aid in the realization of the falsity of outward appearances. The man who falls in love with a beautiful woman comes to understand that the beauty he loves will rot away as horribly as the corpse before him. Chih-k'ai (538–597), the founder of Tendai Buddhism, wrote, "If even an ignorant man goes to the side of a grave mound and contemplates a bloated and putrid corpse, it will be easy for him to achieve meditation."[78] The lesson of the contemplation of pollution is horrifying, but it is unforgettable.

Keisei was not, on the whole, a skillful writer. However interesting a tale, the effect is likely to be weakened by the lengthy moral, usually a commentary delivered in his own voice, with which it closes. Scholars have suggested that Keisei wrote mainly for women readers. The second of the two books consists almost exclusively of tales about women, and the style of the narration is more gracious than in other setsuwa collections, as if Keisei hoped that by adding poetic embellishments he would make his work appealing to women.[79]

Companion of a Quiet Life stands stylistically midway between two better-known setsuwa collections, *Hosshinshū* and *Senjūshō* (Selection of Tales), the latter traditionally attributed to the priest and poet Saigyō.[80]

SENJŪSHŌ

The postscript to *Senjūshō* states that it was written in the firt moon of 1183 at a hermitage of the Zentsū-ji in the province of Sanuki. This, to anyone familiar with the life of Saigyō, would immediately suggest that he was the author.[81] The postscript is a forgery, but the persistent attribution of *Senjūshō* to Saigyō was made plausible by the person of the narrator of many tales, a man who shared many of Saigyō's qualities: he was a priest and poet, a constant traveler, a lover of solitude, a man who sought to flee the world. Although the materials in the tales are sometimes anachronistic, they are all close enough to Saigyō's time for the mistakes to be overlooked by all but specialists. The association of the work with the great poet enhanced its popularity over the centuries. Even the Portuguese missionaries were familiar with the work, as we know from the praise bestowed on it by João Rodrigues. However, as far back as the middle of the seventeenth century scholars pointed out the contradictions between the known facts of Saigyō's life and the account of him in *Senjūshō*, and in recent times the attribution has been thoroughly discredited.[82]

The elimination of Saigyō has not brought us any closer to discovering the real author or authors. As for the time of compilation, various clues in the text strongly suggest that the author of *Senjūshō* knew *Companion of a Quiet Life* and borrowed from it.[83] This would place the time of compilation about the middle of the thirteenth century.

Two main lines of texts exist, one much longer than the other. It was at first generally believed that the shorter text was the original version, and that the longer one had been padded with later accretions, but critical opinion has shifted, and the longer version (consisting of 121 tales) is now considered to be the original state.[84] The tales are divided into nine books, the eighth of which stands out. Most of the tales in the other books are provided with epilogues in which Buddhist morality is preached, often at greater length than the tale itself, but the tales in the eighth book are presented for the most part without overt preaching; in this book poetry is the central concern, and the context is sometimes completely secular. These tales are certainly more appealing to modern readers than the more orthodox stories, though less typical of the collection.

Senjūshō enjoyed great popularity up until the late Tokugawa period, as we know from the numerous editions and the frequent references to the collection in later works. One tale was especially famous, the encounter of Saigyō and the courtesan of Eguchi. The story itself is not of unusual interest, but the striking combination of the hermit Saigyō, a man who had turned his back on worldly pleasure, and a woman who sold herself to men who craved pleasure, cast a spell over generations of readers. This is how the tale opens:

> I once passed through Eguchi, some time after the twentieth of the ninth month. Both the north and south banks of the river were

crowded with the houses of the town. The inhabitants' fickle hearts were preoccupied with the comings and goings of travellers' boats; gazing at the town, I thought how sadly ephemeral were the lives its residents led.

Just then an unseasonably wintry wind darkened the sky, and I went up to a simple cottage to seek shelter until the weather cleared. The woman who owned the place showed no sign of granting my request. I recited a verse that came to mind,

yo no naka wo	Indeed it may be hard
itou made koso	To reject
katakarame	The world,
kari no yadori wo	But you begrudge
oshimu kimi kana	A temporary lodging.

The prostitute replied sadly,

ie wo izuru	Seeing that you were one
hito to shi mireba	Who had left his home,[85]
kari no yado ni	I only thought
kokoro tomu na to	Your mind should not dwell
omou bakari zo	On temporary lodgings.[86]

Although I had intended to shelter there only briefly, for the duration of a shower, her poem was so interesting I stayed all night.[87]

Identification of the speaker as Saigyō, even if there were no other clues, would be clear from the quoted poem, which appears in *Sankashū* (Mountain Hut Collection), together with the response from the courtesan of Eguchi. The Nō play *Eguchi*, often attributed to Kan'ami, has this exchange of poems as its central incident. In the second part of the play the courtesan reveals herself in her true form, as the bodhisattva Fugen. In *The Narrow Road of Oku*, Bashō included an episode of talking with prostitutes who had spent the night at the same inn. The diary kept by Sora, Bashō's companion on the journey, does not mention the incident, leading to the suspicion that Bashō invented the episode, possibly under the influence of the tale.

The story, up to the point quoted above, possesses sufficient interest for us to understand why generations of Japanese remembered the courtesan of Eguchi. The association of prostitution and enlightenment goes back at least as far as the tale in the Flower Wreath Sutra (*Kegon-kyō*) of the courtesan Vasumitra who led men to enlightenment by the promise of sensual pleasures.[88] There is also an intriguing ambiguity in the priest Saigyō's having spent a night in a prostitute's quarters. But the remainder of the tale is likely to dampen the enthusiasm of the modern reader: the courtesan of Eguchi relates her story in a mixture of the most conventional and banal language of Buddhist and poetic tradition. The tale concludes with a barrage of hackneyed poetic imagery: "Whether there is autumn wind rustling the reeds, a storm disordering the leaves deep in the mountains, or autumn rain mixing with the leaves, when one is pensive it is the evening sky that calls forth tears. When we listen at dawn to the monkeys' lonely cries by a tall pine tree, or hear the calling of migrating geese, one's mind becomes clear and tears overflow."[89]

Needless to say, it was in order to relate the Buddhist moral lessons at the end that these anecdotes were related, and readers in the past were probably not bored by oft-repeated sentiments or by literary phraseology they had often heard before. They seem not to have craved an exciting climax or a "punch line." The repetition of poetic clichés was perhaps even welcomed as a reassuringly familiar theme, and one can imagine listeners joining in the recitation of a sonorous declaration of the undependability of this world.

Many tales in *Senjūshō* began promisingly—for example, the one that opens with Saigyō' assembling human bones to make a living man[90]—but not one manages to carry the story to a satisfying conclusion. All this suggests is what we knew before: the primary intent of the compilers of Buddhist tales was not literary. They borrowed interesting anecdotes as "accommodations" (*hōben*) that would enable them to persuade listeners or readers (who might not otherwise listen to Buddhist homilies) that they must give heed to their salvation.

Sand and Pebbles

The last major collection of Buddhist tales of the Kamakura period was *Shasekishū* (Sand and Pebbles),[91] compiled between 1279 and 1283 by the priest Mujū Ichien (1226–1312).[92] The marked tendency observable in *Senjūshō* to stress the Buddhist lessons of the tales, at the expense of literary effectiveness, is even more noticeable in *Sand and Pebbles*, where the story is often subordinated to the moral.

Sand and Pebbles is a voluminous work consisting of 153 chapters in ten books, each book consisting of tales devoted to a particular theme. The first book contains stories relating to Mujū's belief that the Japanese gods are local manifestations of the buddhas and bodhisattvas, a doctrine otherwise known as *honji suijaku* ("original substance manifests traces").[93] The second book treats miracles performed by various buddhas and bodhisattvas, and each of the subsequent books has a theme of religious or moral (not necessarily Buddhist) importance. The fifth book, of special literary interest, discusses the function of poetry in promoting enlightenment.

The collection opens with Mujū's preface, in which he explains his purpose in compiling *Sand and Pebbles*:

> Coarse words and refined expressions both proceed from the First Principle, nor are the everyday affairs of life at variance with the True Reality. Through the wanton sport of wild words and specious phrases, I wish to bring people into the marvelous Way of the Buddha's teaching; and with unpretentious examples taken from the common ordinary affairs of life I should like to illustrate the profound significance of this splendid doctrine.[94]

Mujū was here justifying the use of coarse, mundane stories in order to convey the wonderful truths of Buddhism to people who might not be able to appreciate a more philosophical presentation. "Wild words and specious phrases" (*kyōgen kigyo*) had a similar meaning; colorful language often induces people to absorb painlessly lessons that they otherwise would not understand. Earlier collections of Buddhist setsuwa had depended largely on anecdotes from antiquity that were sometimes set in India and other distant places, but Mujū's stories are most often about fairly recent people living in Japan, and the language is much closer to the colloquial than was customary. He compared what he did to people who find gold in sand or who polish pebbles until they look like gems; this was the meaning of the title.

Behind his readiness to use materials of every sort, no matter how humble, was his conviction (also expressed in the preface) that "There is not just one method for entering the Way, the causes and conditions for enlightenment being many." A man or woman could enter the Way as the result of a trivial experience, or of reading an anecdote that seemed to be devoid of religious significance. Mujū's attitude contrasted especially with those exhibited by the new religious leaders of the Kamakura period. Unlike Shinran, who insisted that calling upon Amida was the *only* way to gain salvation, or Nichiren, who made the same claim for the Lotus Sutra, Mujū, who had studied both Tendai and Zen Buddhism, was willing to accept the manifold accommodations Buddha made to human frailties.[95]

In this spirit, Mujū was able to accept the existence of the Shintō gods, as intermediaries for Japanese in approaching the Buddhist truths. An anecdote in the first book relates how a devotee of Jōdo Buddhism was punished for having slighted the gods, sure that believers in Amida need not concern themselves with any other deity. The man is stricken, and when his mother begs a Shintō priestess to intercede on his behalf, the offended god, speaking through the priestess, recalls the man's impious words and declares, "I am a Transformation Body of the Eleven-Faced Kannon. If one relies on the Original Vow of Amida, my primordial form, and calls upon his name with an upright heart, how endearing do I consider this, how precious! But how can such a dirty, defiled, and unrighteous mind be worthy of the Original Vow?"[96]

Mujū believed that Japanese poetry, no less than the Japanese gods, was a manifestation in Japan of eternal religious truth. He wrote,

> When we consider *waka* as a means to religious realization, we see that it has the virtue of serenity and peace, of putting a stop to the distractions and undisciplined movements of the mind. With a few words, it encompasses its sentiment. This is the very nature of mystic verses or *dhārani*.
>
> The gods of Japan are Manifest Traces, the unexcelled Transformation Bodies of buddhas and bodhisattvas. The god Susa-no-o initiated composition in thirty-one syllables with the "many-layered fence at Izumo."[97] The *dhārani* of India are simply the words used by the people of that country which the Buddha took and interpreted as mystic formulas. . . . Had the Buddha appeared in Japan, he would simply have used Japanese for mystic verses.[98]

Mujū also concurred in the belief expressed by Ki no Tsurayuki in the preface to the *Kokinshū* that poetry could move the gods. He wrote, "Likewise the gods, greatly admiring a man's poetry, will grant his wish. The efficacy of Japanese poetry and the nature of mystic verse are in every respect to be understood as identical with *dhārani*."[99] Mujū was not the first to have applied Tendai religious ideals to justify the existence of poetry,[100] but he gave it authority. The religious importance of the waka would be proclaimed in various Nō plays, and was implicitly accepted by many of its practitioners.

Mujū lived in a world that was believed by contemporaries to be afflicted by the ignorance and corruption of mappō. Again and again he lamented the decline in religious practices. It was true that more people than ever "fled the world" to live in hermitages, but Mujū questioned their devotion to truth: "The recluse of old imbued his heart with the Buddha's Law and set aside the myriad matters of the world, while in the present age men . . . only bear the name of 'recluse' (*tonsei*), but do not know its reality. Year after year we see an increasing number of people who escape the world simply to get ahead in life and in spite of the fact that they have no religious aspiration at all."[101]

Mujū compiled another setsuwa collection, *Zōtanshū* (Collection of Casual Digressions), completed in 1305,[102] but his chief literary work was undoubtedly *Sand and Pebbles*. It is the last important example of Buddhist setsuwa.

Buddhist Poetry

The tradition of Buddhist priests and laymen composing poetry goes back to the eighth century if not earlier, but the first imperially sponsored collection of waka poetry to include a section devoted specifically to Buddhist poetry (*shakkyōka*) was the *Goshūishū*, compiled in 1086.[103] The authors included not only priests but men and women of the court and commoners. This waka is attributed to the courtesan Miyaki:

Tsu no kuni no	What kind of thing
Naniwa no koto ka	Is not within the Law,
nori naranu	Even at Naniwa in Tsu?
asobitawabure	I have heard the Law applied
made to koso kike	Even to gambling and sex.[104]

One book of the *Shin Kokinshū*, containing sixty-three poems, is devoted to shakkyōka. These poems on the whole lack the appeal of the well-known poems of this great collection, most of them being little more than paraphrases of teachings from the Lotus Sutra and other Buddhist texts; but in others the Buddhist themes are so completely accommodated to the traditional imagery of the waka as to be unrecognizable as Buddhist unless read in conjunction with the explanation in the preface. The following waka is by Princess Shokushi:

shizuka naru	In the quiet
akatsuki goto ni	Each day before the dawning

miwataseba	When I gaze round me,
mada fukaki yo no	How saddening that still
yume zo kanashiki	The deep night's dream persists.

We might guess from the last two lines that Shikoshu's sadness comes from something more than mere observation of the darkness before the dawn, but the kotobagaki (prose preface) makes her intent clear: "Among one hundred poems on the theme of 'every morning at dawn he enters into quiet meditation.'" This is a reference to a phrase in *Emmei Jizōkyō*, a sutra that relates how the bodhisattva Jizō vowed to prolong the lives of (and otherwise benefit) those who turned to him. The speaker of the poem, then, is Jizō, who expresses grief that human beings have not yet awakened from the darkness of the "deep night" of ignorance and delusion. But the speaker is also Princess Shokushi, whose dream, from which she is still not able to free herself, fills her with sadness.[105]

Buddhist poetry was not always so difficult. *Ryōjin Hishō* (Secret Selection of Dust on the Beams),[106] a collection of some 566 poems compiled about 1170 by the Emperor Goshirakawa, contains many popular songs on Buddhist, Shintō, and secular themes. The most typical of the varieties of song found in *Ryōjin Hishō* is the imayō (new-style tunes), usually eight or twelve lines consisting of alternating lines of seven and five syllables each. The collection had been lost, but in 1911 the surviving fragments (about a tenth of the original twenty books) were discovered. Buddhist poems constitute a major part of the extant poems. Some, almost devoid of poetic quality, are little more than versifications of lines from the Lotus Sutra and other sacred writings, or else statements of the principles of a particular sect, as in the following example:

hotoke wa samazama ni	Buddhas there are
imasedomo	Of many kinds,
makoto wa ichibutsu	But in truth, they say,
nari to ka ya	There is only one.
Yakushi mo Mida mo	Yakushi and Mida both
Shaka Miroku mo	Shaka and Miroku too
sanagara Dainichi	Are none other than Dainichi
to koso kike	Or so I have been told.[107]

This hymn is clearly in praise of Dainichi, but others in the collection praise Amida, Jizō, Kannon, and various lesser Buddhist divinities. The pleasing rhythms of these hymns make it easy to imagine believers singing them, but they possess little literary interest. The secular poems in *Ryōjin Hishō* are far more interesting, and they account for the popularity of the collection today. Arthur Waley's translations of *Ryōjin Hishō* poems, published in 1921, were their first introduction to the West. They include such delightful poems as:

mae mae katatsuburi	Dance, dance, Mr. Snail!
mawanu mono naraba	If you won't I shall leave you
muma no ko ya	For the little horse,
ushi no ko ni	For the little ox
kuesaseten	To tread under his hoof,
fumiwaraseten	To trample to bits.
makoto ni utsukushiku	But if quite prettily
mautaraba	You dance your dance,
hana no sono made	To a garden of flowers
asobasen	I will carry you to play.[108]

The irregular metrics of the poem suggest it was composed to fit existing music. It is a children's song, though attempts have been made to extract from it a specifically Buddhist meaning.[109] Other poems, though seemingly irreverent, no doubt have antecedents in religious writings:

chihayaburu kami	Oh gods almighty!
kami ni mashimasu	If gods indeed you are,
mono naraba	Take pity on me;
aware to oboshimese	For even the gods were once
kami mo mukashi wa	Such men as we.[110]
hito zo kashi	

There are no clues to the authors of these poems. It is conceivable that they were composed by Buddhist priests, despite the levity of some verses and the sexual overtones of others. It had been customary ever since the age of the *Kokinshū* for priests to participate in poem competitions at which they were required to compose poems on set themes, even of romantic love, though they were not appropriate to men of their calling. There are similar poems in the *Shin Kokinshū*, but the poems by priests in that collection are generally somber rather than gallant. On the other hand, some waka of Myōe, the leader of the revival of the Kegon sect,[111] are so marked by nature imagery that they may seem to be without religious significance.[112] The poems in the *Ryōjin Hishō* are not as accomplished as those by Myōe (or by the court poets of the day), but their subjects and expression have a delightful unconventionality and have not lost their appeal. They suggest that all was not gloom even at a time when the world was believed to have entered the latter days of the Buddhist Law.

Notes

1. *Ōjō Yōshū* was translated by A. K. Reischauer in "Genshin's Ōjōyōshū."
2. The use of *hōben* (*upāya* in Sanskrit) is well discussed by William R. LaFleur in *The Karma of Words*, pp. 84–87, in terms of the Lotus Sutra. He preferred to translate *hōben* as "modes," as in his version of a passage from the sutra in which "the World Honored One" tells a disciple, "Since becoming a Buddha, I, in a variety of modes and through many kinds of metaphors, have been conversing and preaching very widely, thus in countless ways leading living beings and helping them abandon their attachments."
3. In Japanese, *kyōgen kigyo*. Po made the statement in 839, when presenting a copy of his poetry to a Buddhist library. See LaFleur, *Karma*, p. 8, for a discussion of the term.
4. This is the subject of Robert E. Morrell's *Early Kamakura Buddhism: A Minority Report*. He discusses in particular four priests: Jien (Tendai), Myōe (Kegon), Jōkei (Hossō), and Kakukai (Shingon).
5. I shall refer to the work by its Japanese rather than its translated title because that is how it is known even outside Japan.
6. The Japanese text of *Tannishō*, together with a free and a literal translation into English, is given in Dennis Hirota, *Tannishō: A Primer*. The text, together with a translation into modern Japanese and copious notes, can be found in Gorai Shigeru, *Bukkyō Bungaku*, pp. 23–137.
7. Hirota, *Tannishō*, p. 25.
8. Many people were convinced that the mappō period had commenced in 1052. Not all Buddhists, however, accepted this view. Dōgen insisted that it was no less possible than in the past to understand and practice Buddhism. See LaFleur, *Karma*, p. 3.
9. Hirota, *Tannishō*, p. 26.
10. See Harper Havelock Coates and Ryūgaku Ishizuka, *Hōnen the Buddhist Saint*, p. 441, where Hōnen is quoted: "You should continuously call upon the sacred name, and so you should do it without interruption. It would be a good thing to think of it say three times during mealtime, and if you always thus keep it in mind, even though you do not succeed in repeating it sixty or a hundred thousand times, it may still be called

continuous." For a discussion of whether the nembutsu had to be said many times or if only once was sufficient, see Alfred Bloom, *Shinran's Gospel of Pure Grace*, pp. 20–22.

11. Coates and Ishizuka, *Hōnen*, p. 725.
12. See Ryusaku Tsunoda et al., *Sources of Japanese Tradition*, p. 210.
13. Hirota, *Tannishō*, p. 22. See also Gorai, *Bukkyō Bungaku*, pp. 35–40.
14. Hirota, *Tannishō*, p. 41.
15. Gorai, *Bukkyō Bungaku*, p. 34.
16. *Ibid.*, pp. 80–81. See also the translation by Hirota in *Tannishō*, p. 33.
17. See Gorai, *Bukkyō Bungaku*, pp. 147–48; also Miyasaka Yūshō, *Kana Hōgo Shū*, pp. 21–23. Mita Zenshin in 1953 attributed the work to the poet Ton'a, but even though this attribution was based on an exhaustive study of the evidence, it does not appear to have been adopted by later scholars. The work has tentatively been dated between 1287 (the date of the death of the priest Jishin, mentioned in the text) and 1350, the conjectured date of the death of Kenkō, who quoted *Brief Sayings* in section 98 of *Essays in Idleness*.

    Virtually all that is known about Kyōbutsu is that he seems to have been a disciple of both Hōnen and Myōzen. (See Miyasaka, *Kana*, p. 191.) He is mentioned in *Shasekishū*, where he is identified as a holy man of Mount Kōya who was a native of Makabe in modern Ibaraki Prefecture (see Miyasaka Yūshō, *Shasekishū*, p. 186; also Robert E. Morrell, *Sand and Pebbles*, p. 255.) If Kyōbutsu really was the compiler of *Brief Sayings* and was also a disciple of Myōzen, he must either have been a child when he became a disciple or else he compiled the work when he was very, very old. Gorai suggested (*Bukkyō Bungaku*, pp. 202–3) that Kyōbutsu was probably a contemporary of Shinran; but if the earliest possible date for the compilation was 1287, this was twenty-four years after Shinran's death (and fifty-three years after the death of Myōzen). Obviously, the date and the author of the work are still not known.
18. This judgment may be unfair. Kobayashi Hideo opened his most celebrated work "Mujō to iu koto" (The Fact of Evanescence) with the quotation of an episode from *Brief Sayings*. See *Dawn to the West*, II, p. 605. The episode is given in Miyasaka, *Kana*, p. 204.
19. The great temple in Nagano, now used for worship by both the Tendai and Jōdo sects.
20. Miyasaka, *Kana*, p. 186. See also Yanase Kazuo, *Ichigon Hōdan*, pp. 20–21, 78. There is a retelling of the anecdote in Coates and Ishizuka, *Hōnen*, pp. 318–19.
21. Meaning a priest who lives in a hermitage, rather than in a temple or monastery.
22. Gorai, *Bukkyō Bungaku*, pp. 221–22. The texts given by Miyasaka in *Kana*, pp. 195–96, and by Yanase in *Ichigon Hōdan*, pp. 36–38, 93–94, are somewhat different.

23. This painting has often been reproduced. In Jan Fontein and Money L. Hickman, *Zen Painting and Calligraphy*, it is figure 6.
24. The title has been rendered into English in many ways, none of them graceful. I have given here the translation of Nishiyama Kōsen in *Shōbōgenzō*, I, p. 117.
25. The point was: "Both the exoteric and esoteric schools teach that all beings possess Buddha-nature and original enlightenment. If that is so, why do all the Buddhas of the three worlds arouse the Buddha-seeking mind and search for enlightenment through practice?" (Nishiyama, *Shōbōgenzō*, I, p. xiii.)
26. His name is also pronounced Yōsai.
27. See Nishiyama, *Shōbōgenzō*, I, p. xviii.
28. When the temple was completed in 1244, Dōgen at first called it Daibutsu-ji, but in 1245 he changed the name to Eihei-ji, Eihei (Ying-p'ing) being the period of Chinese history when Buddhism first entered the country.
29. Dōgen did not deny the value of the kōan, though he gave much greater emphasis to *zazen* (meditation).
30. Quoted by Thomas P. Kasulis in "The Incomparable Philosopher: Dōgen on How to Read the *Shōbōgenzō*," p. 90.
31. See Gorai, *Bukkyō Bungaku*, p. 233.
32. Hee-Jin Kim, " 'The Reason of Words and Letters': Dōgen and Kōan Language," in William R. LaFleur, ed., *Dōgen Studies*, p. 61.
33. Nishiyama, *Shōbōgenzō*, I, p. 117.
34. *Ibid.*
35. See, for example, Nishio Minoru et al., *Shōbō Genzō, Shōbō Genzō Zuimonki*, I, p. 5. The translation by Thomas Cleary is, "Extensive study and broad learning is something that cannot succeed. You should firmly resolve to give it up altogether. Only in respect to one task should you learn the ancient standards of mental discipline. Seek out the footsteps of past masters, wholeheartedly apply effort to one practice, and avoid any pretense of being a teacher of others or a past master." Thomas Cleary, *Record of Things Heard from the Treasury of the Eye of the True Teachings*, p. 4.
36. During the Sung dynasty (960–1279) China was known as Sung; the "Great" in the name conveyed the dynasty's high opinion of itself.
37. Probably the *shōrō* (bell tower) or *kurō* (drum tower) of a Zen temple.
38. Nishio et al., *Shōbō Genzō*, pp. 319–20. See also Gorai, *Gukkyō Bungaku*, pp. 238–39, and the translation by Cleary, *Record*, pp. 116–17.
39. A reference to the kampaku Fujiwara no Yorimichi, who acquired this name because he built at Uji the magnificent temple Byōdō-in.
40. A kind of cauldron used for baths. Either a lid was placed over the mouth of the cauldron, creating a kind of steam bath, or else hot water was transferred from the "boiler" to a wooden tub in which people bathed.
41. Nishio et al., *Shōbō Genzō*, p. 327. See also Gorai, *Bukkyō Bungaku*, pp. 247–48, and the translation by Cleary, *Record*, p. 123. Virtually the same

anecdotes would be told many years later of the wayward Zen monk Ikkyū Sōjun. Although the comment is attributed in this instance to the nobleman Yorimichi rather than to a Zen monk, the point is that only a fool takes the outer garments a man is wearing for the man himself. Evidently, the man in the boiler room judged people by what they wore rather than by their personal dignity, and that was why Yorimichi sardonically bowed before his robe.

42. The title means literally, "Account of One *Jō* Square." A *jō* was about ten feet, and *hōjō* came to designate a hut ten feet square, following the account of the Chinese pilgrim Wang Hsüan-ts'e who, en route to India in A.D. 660, passed the ruins of the hut where the Buddhist layman-sage Vimalakīrti had instructed 32,000 disciples and debated with Mañjuśrī. Later, *hōjō* came to designate the abbot's quarters in a Zen temple. This kind of hōjō was much bigger than a hermitage, but in theory the abbot, like Vimalakīrti, resided in a hut only ten feet square. See Martin Collcutt, *Five Mountains: The Rinzai Zen Monastic Institution in Medieval Japan*, pp. 197–201, for a description of the abbot's building and its history. Kamo no Chōmei used the term for his hut in accordance with the original meaning.
43. My translation in *Anthology of Japanese Literature*, pp. 197–98. Text in Nishio Minoru, *Hōjōki, Tsurezuregusa*, pp. 23–24.
44. Freely translated above as "Which will be first to go, the master or his dwelling?"
45. My translation in *Anthology*, pp. 199–200.
46. *Ibid.*, p. 201.
47. *Ibid.*, p. 205.
48. See above, pp. 347–48.
49. Translation by Burton Watson in *Japanese Literature in Chinese*, I, p. 59.
50. Keene, *Anthology*, p. 205.
51. *Ibid.*, p. 206.
52. Watson, *Japanese*, I, p. 64.
53. *Ibid.*, p. 211.
54. Keene, *Anthology*, p. 209.
55. *Sankashū* 1207. See Kazamaki Keijirō and Kojima Yoshio, *Sankashū, Kinkai Waka Shū*, p. 212.
56. *Ibid.*, p. 211.
57. For Vimalakīrti, see above, note 42. Suddhipanthaka (Handoku in Japanese) was the most stupid of the disciples of Buddha. See LaFleur, *Karma*, pp. 113–15.
58. The title might more literally be rendered as "Awakening of Faith Collection." Because both English translations are so awkward, I shall refer to the work by its Japanese title, as Marian Ury did in her translation of sections of the work.
59. A shorter version (*ihon*) with only sixty-four tales was apparently compiled

somewhat earlier than the rufubon version which is now accepted as authoritative. See Kishi Shōzō, "Kaisetsu," in Nishio Kōichi and Kishi Shōzō, *Chūsei Setsuwa Shū*, pp. 131–32, for a comparison of the two texts. Translations of ten stories are given in Marian Ury, "Recluses and Eccentric Monks: Tales from the *Hosshinshū* by Kamo no Chōmei."

60. Kishi, "Kaisetsu," p. 145, says, "An attitude of special attention to *kokoro* runs through the entire *Hosshinshū* from beginning to end."
61. Kishi and Nishio, *Chūsei*, pp. 142–43.
62. See, for example, Aoyama Katsuya, *Kamo no Chōmei no Setsuwa Sekai*, pp. 7–22.
63. See Nishio and Kishi, *Chūsei*, p. 148. Kishi, in his "Kaisetsu," p. 130, produced evidence that *Hosshinshū* was compiled between 1208 and 1213.
64. As a matter of fact, two stories (numbers 24 and 25) deal with India and China, but they could be considered appendages to stories about Japan. See Nishio and Kishi, *Chūsei*, p. 148.
65. Translation by Ury in "Recluses," p. 169.
66. "Master of discipline," a priestly officer of the fifth rank.
67. This is story 35 (the tenth story in Book III). I have used the text of Nishio and Kishi, *Chūsei*, pp. 210–11.
68. Passages from *Hosshinshū* quoted by Rodrigues are given and analyzed by Yanase Kazuo in *Hosshinshū Kenkyū*, pp. 26–31. For the contents of *Arte da Lingoa de Iapam*, see Michael Cooper, *Rodrigues the Interpreter*, pp. 224–33.
69. Some scholars question the attribution to Keisei, but it is generally accepted. A convincing case for the attribution was made by Nagai Yoshinori in *Nihon Bukkyō Bungaku Kenkyū*, pp. 155–69.
70. A reference to various accounts of holy men who had attained enlightenment. Fifteen persons treated in these biographies also appeared in *Hosshinshū*. See Minobe Shigekatsu, *Kankyo no Tomo*, pp. 68, 170.
71. Minobe, *Kankyo*, pp. 68–69.
72. For a discussion of the influence of *Hosshinshū* on *Kankyo no Tomo*, see Harada Kōzō, "'Kankyo no Tomo' Kikō to Keisei no Sōan Seikatsu," pp. 44–47, 59. Harada believed that Keisei began to compile *Kankyo no Tomo* only a few months after Chōmei's death in 1216, and that he closely modeled his work on *Hosshinshū*.
73. Minobe, *Kankyo*, pp. 74–75. This passage occurs at the end of the story of the Abbot Gempin.
74. Harada, "Kankyo," p. 51.
75. Minobe, *Kankyo*, p. 75.
76. This tale was summarized by Tanizaki Jun'ichirō in his novel *Shōshō Shigemoto no Haha* (The Mother of the Captain Shigemoto). For an English translation by Edward Seidensticker of this portion of the novel, see my *Modern Japanese Literature*, pp. 391–94.
77. Minobe, *Kankyo*, pp. 111–14. This is Book I, tale 19.

78. Paraphrased by Keisei (Minobe, *Kankyo*, p. 114). "Achieve meditation" is an inadequate stab at a translation of *kannen jōju*. It seems to refer to the Tendai belief in "meditation" (*kannen*) on Amida through which one attains the supreme bliss (*gokuraku*) of Buddhahood in this very body (*sokushin jōbutsu*). See Morrell, *Early*, p. 141.
79. See Minobe, *Kankyo*, pp. 4–5.
80. Biographical and other materials concerning Saigyō are found on pp. 676–81. I shall refer to the work by its Japanese title. *Selection of Tales* is nondescript; and the only study of the work in English, by Jean Moore, used the Japanese title.
81. Saigyō's connection with Sanuki is attested by the account in *Tale of the Disturbance in Hōgen* of how he visited the grave of the Emperor Sutoku at Shiramine in Sanuki. See above, p. 620.
82. See Nishio Kōichi, "Kaisetsu," in *Senjūshō*, pp. 346–63, where he lists forty-one examples of errors in the text that make it impossible for it to be the work of Saigyō. See also Nishio Kōichi, *Setsuwa Bungaku Shōkō*, pp. 233–39.
83. Minobe, *Kankyo*, pp. 39–48, noted many resemblances, not only in the tales but in the appended morals.
84. Nishio Kōichi, "Kaisetsu," p. 336. The theory that the *kōhon* (longer text) was the original text and the shorter text (*ryakuhon*) a selection from the longer one, was first proposed by Kobayashi Tadao in 1942.
85. A priest was often described as a *shukke*, meaning one who had left his home to enter the path of the Buddha.
86. "Temporary lodgings" was a Buddhist way of referring to this world, a temporary stop on the way to the eternal world of Amida Buddha.
87. Translation by Jean Moore, "*Senjūshō*: Buddhist Tales of Renunciation," pp. 168–69. Text in Nishio Kōichi, *Senjūshō*, pp. 294–95.
88. See Robert E. Morrell, "Mirror for Women: Mujū Ichien's *Tsuma Kagami*," p. 57.
89. Translation by Moore, "*Senjūshō*," p. 171. Text in Nishio Kōichi, *Senjūshō*, p. 298.
90. Translated by Royall Tyler in *Japanese Tales*, pp. 68–70.
91. There is a translation into English of a substantial part of the work by Morrell in *Sand and Pebbles*. He summarizes tales he does not translate in full. There is also a French translation by Hartmut O. Rotermund in *Collection de sable et de pierres*.
92. The best account in English of Mujū's life is given by Morrell in *Sand*, pp. 13–33.
93. For a discussion of honji suijaku in English, see Tsunoda et al., *Sources*, pp. 268–70. A much more extensive treatment is found in Alicia Matsunaga, *The Buddhist Philosophy of Assimilation*. The oldest example of honji suijaku thought in Japan dates from 937, when two gods were declared to be local manifestations of bodhisattvas.

94. Translation by Morrell in *Sand*, p. 71. Text in Watanabe Tsunaya, *Shasekishū*, p. 57. The "First Principle" is Ultimate Reality, and the whole phrase from the Nirvana Sutra (*Daihatsu Nehangyō*).
95. Morrell, *Sand*, p. 60.
96. This is anecdote 10 in Book I. Translation by Morrell in *Sand*, pp. 97–99. Text in Watanabe, *Shasekishū*, pp. 83–85.
97. A reference to the poem in the *Kojiki* attributed to the god. See p. 43.
98. Translation by Morrell in *Sand*, pp. 163–64. Text in Watanabe, *Shasekishū*, pp. 222–23.
99. Morrell, *Sand*, p. 165; Watanabe, *Shasekishū*, p. 224.
100. See Robert H. Brower and Earl Miner, *Japanese Court Poetry*, p. 257, where the Tendai practice of *shikan* ("concentration and insight") was equated with the aesthetic ideal of grasping the "real significance" or "essence" of an experience by concentrating on a given topic.
101. Morrell, *Sand*, p. 135. Watanabe, *Shasekishū*, p. 163.
102. Some stories from this collection are translated by Morrell in *Sand*, pp. 275–80. A study of the relations of *Zōtanshū* to other setsuwa collections is given by Shimura Kunihiro in *Chūsei Setsuwa Bungaku Kenkyū Josetsu*, pp. 266–83.
103. Only 19 of the 1,220 poems in *Goshūishū* are found in this section.
104. Translation by Robert E. Morrell in "The Buddhist Poetry in the *Goshūishū*," p. 100. This is poem 1199 in the collection. The preface to the poem states that the officiating priest seemed dubious about the propriety of accepting Miyaki's offering of money for a Sutra-Copying Ceremony. Her reply, in the form of this poem, declares that "all phenomena participate in true reality."
105. *Shin Kokinshū* 1970. I have followed the interpretation of Minemura Fumito in *Shin Kokin Waka Shū*, p. 586.
106. This strange appellation for a collection of poetry is explained in the text: "The reason why [this work] has been called *Secret Selection of Dust on the Beams* is that Yü Kung and Han Ê, who lived long ago, had such wondrously beautiful voices that no one could match them. People who heard them sing were so moved that they could not hold back the tears. The dust on beams rose up to the echoes of their singing voices and did not settle for three days." (From Konishi Jin'ichi, *Ryōjin Hishō Kō*, pp. 207–8. Konishi suggested that this was a later interpellation.) The two Chinese renowned for their voices are described in various works of antiquity including *Lieh Tzu*.
107. Konishi, *Ryōjin*, pp. 204–5. This is poem 19 of the collection. Konishi believed that the poem was an expression of Tendai esoteric beliefs. With respect to Yakushi (the Healing Buddha), Mida (Amida), and Miroku (the Buddha of the Future), Tendai and Shingon beliefs would have been the same, but Shingon believers differentiated between Shaka (Shakyamuni) and Dainichi (Vairochana).

108. *Ryōjin Hishō* 408. Translation by Arthur Waley, quoted in my *Anthology*, p. 168. See Konishi, *Ryōjin*, p. 501; also Kawaguchi Hisao and Shida Nobuyoshi, *Wakan Rōei Shū, Ryōjin Hishō*, p. 417.
109. See Konishi, *Ryōjin*, p. 502, where he quotes Yamada Yoshio who had found similarities between this poem and one by the priest Jakuren that described a snail that was stepped on by a calf. Konishi disagreed; he believed it was a children's song and not an example of honka-dori.
110. *Ryōjin Hishō* 447. Translation by Waley in my *Anthology*, p. 169. See Kawaguchi and Shida, *Wakan*, p. 232, for statements in earlier literature, both canonical and secular, to the effect that Buddha himself was once a human being. This is the corollary of the more frequently expressed belief that all living creatures possess the Buddha nature.
111. For a discussion of Myōe and translations of some of his writings, see Morrell, *Kamakura*, pp. 44–65.
112. Myōe's best-known waka is: *Aka aka ya / aka aka aka ya / aka aka ya / aka aka aka ya / aka aka ya tsuki*. (Yoshihara, *Myōe*, pp. 159–60.) The meaning is approximately, "Bright bright ah / bright bright bright ah / bright bright bright ah / bright bright ah / bright bright ah the moon." Kawabata Yasunari in his Nobel Prize acceptance speech quoted this poem because of the profound sense of wonder he detected. Myōe was exceptionally fond of the moon, but the moon was of course a familiar Buddhist image for enlightenment.

    Myōe's poetry is treated by Yoshihara Shikeko in *Myōe Shōnin Kashū no Kenkyū*, and by the same writer in "Myōe Shōnin no Waka," in Bukkyō Bungaku Kenkyūkai, *Bukkyō Bungaku Kenkyū*, XI, pp. 103–39. His poems were included in various chokusenshū, beginning with the *Shin Chokusenshū*, in which five poems appear.

Bibliography

Note: All Japanese books, except as otherwise noted, were published in Tokyo.

Aoyama Katsuya. *Kamo no Chōmei no Setsuwa Sekai*. Ōfūsha, 1984.

Bloom, Alfred. *Shinran's Gospel of Pure Grace*. Tucson: The University of Arizona Press, 1965.

Brower, Robert H., and Earl Miner. *Japanese Court Poetry*. Stanford, Calif.: Stanford University Press, 1961.

Bukkyō Bungaku Kenkyūkai (ed.). *Bukkyō Bungaku Kenkyū*. Kyoto: Hōzōkan, 1972–76.

Cleary, Thomas. *Record of Things Heard from the Treasury of the Eye of the True Teachings*. Boulder, Colo.: Prajñā Press, 1980.

Coates, Harper Havelock, and Ryugaku Ishizuka. *Honen the Buddhist Saint.* Tokyo: Kodokaku, 1930.

Collcutt, Martin. *Five Mountains: The Rinzai Zen Monastic Institution in Medieval Japan.* Cambridge, Mass.: Harvard University Press, 1974.

Cooper, Michael. *Rodrigues the Interpreter.* New York: Weatherhill, 1974.

Fontein, Jan, and Money Hickman. *Zen Painting and Calligraphy.* Boston: Museum of Fine Arts, 1970.

Gorai Shigeru. *Bukkyō Bungaku*, in Kanshō Nihon Koten Bungaku series. Kadokawa Shoten, 1977.

Harada Kōzō. " 'Kankyo no Tomo' Kikō to Keisei no Sōan Seikatsu," in Bukkyō Bungaku Kenkyūkai (ed.), *Bukkyō Bungaku Kenkyū*, II. Kyoto: Hōzōkan, 1976.

Hare, Thomas Blenman. "Reading Kamo no Chōmei," *Harvard Journal of Asiatic Studies* 49:1, 1989.

Hirota, Dennis. *Tannishō: A Primer.* Kyoto: Ryūkoku University, 1982.

Kasulis, Thomas P. "The Incomparable Philosopher: Dōgen on How to Read the *Shōbōgenzō*," in William R. LaFleur (ed.), *Dōgen Studies.* Honolulu: University of Hawaii Press, 1985.

Kawaguchi Hisao and Shida Nobuyoshi. *Wakan Rōei Shū*, *Ryōjin Hishō*, in Nihon Koten Bungaku Taikei series. Iwanami Shoten, 1965.

Kazamaki Keijirō and Kojima Yoshio. *Sankashū, Kinkai Waka Shū*, in Nihon Koten Bungaku Taikei series. Iwanami Shoten, 1961.

Keene, Donald. *Anthology of Japanese Literature.* New York: Grove Press, 1955.

———. *Modern Japanese Literature.* New York: Grove Press, 1956.

Konishi Jin'ichi. *Ryōjin Hishō*, in Nihon Koten Zensho series. Asahi Shimbun Sha, 1953.

———. *Ryōjin Hishō Kō.* Sanseidō, 1941.

LaFleur, William R. (ed.). *Dōgen Studies.* Honolulu: University of Hawaii Press, 1985.

———. *The Karma of Words.* Berkeley: University of California Press, 1983.

Matsunaga, Alicia. *The Buddhist Philosophy of Assimilation—the Historical Development of the* Honji-Suijaku *Theory.* Tokyo: Sophia University Press, 1969.

Miller, Roy Andrew. *"The Footprints of the Buddha": an Eighth-Century Old Japanese Poetic Sequence.* New Haven: American Oriental Society, 1975.

Minemura Fumito. *Shin Kokin Waka Shū*, in Nihon Koten Bungaku Zenshū series. Shōgakukan, 1974.

Minobe Shigekatsu. *Kankyo no Tomo.* Miyai Shoten, 1974.

Miyasaka Yūshō. *Kana Hōgo Shū*, in Nihon Koten Bungaku Taikei series. Iwanami Shoten, 1964.

———. *Shasekishū*, in Nihon Koten Bungaku Taikei series. Iwanami Shoten, 1966.

Moore, Jean. "*Senjūshō*: Buddhist Tales of Renunciation," *Monumenta Nipponica* 41:2, 1986.

Morrell, Robert E. "The Buddhist Poetry in the *Goshūishū*," *Monumenta Nipponica* 28:1, 1973.

———. *Early Kamakura Buddhism: A Minority Report.* Berkeley: Asian Humanities Press, 1987.

———. "Mirror for Women: Mujū Ichien's *Tsuma Kagami*," *Monumenta Nipponica* 35:1, 1980.

———. *Sand and Pebbles (Shasekishū).* Albany: State University of New York Press, 1985.

Nagai Yoshinori. *Nihon Bukkyō Bungaku Kenkyū.* Toshima Shobō, 1966.

Nishio Kōichi. *Senjūshō*, in Iwanami Bunko series. Iwanami Shoten, 1970.

———. *Setsuwa Bungaku Shōkō.* Kyōiku Shuppan, 1985.

Nishio Kōichi and Kishi Shōzō. *Chūsei Setsuwa Shū.* Kadokawa Shoten, 1977.

Nishio Minoru. *Hōjōki, Tsurezuregusa*, in Nihon Koten Bungaku Taikei series. Iwanami Shoten, 1957.

Nishio Minoru, Kagamishima Genryū, et al. *Shōbō Genzō, Shōbō Genzō Zuimonki*, in Nihon Koten Bungaku Taikei series. Iwanami Shoten, 1965.

Nishiyama Kōsen. *Shōbōgenzō*, I. Nakayama Shobō, 1975.

Reischauer, A. K. "Genshin's Ōjōyōshū," *Translations of the Asiatic Society of Japan*, second series, VII, Dec. 1930.

Rotermund, Harmut O. *Collection de sable et de pierres (Shasekishū).* Paris: Gallimard, 1979.

Shimura Kunihiro. *Chūsei Setsuwa Bungaku Kenkyū Josetsu.* Ōfūsha, 1974.

Tsunoda, Ryusaku, Wm. Theodore de Bary, and Donald Keene. *Sources of Japanese Tradition.* New York: Columbia University Press, 1958.

Tyler, Royall. *Japanese Tales.* New York: Pantheon, 1987.

Ury, Marian. "Recluses and Eccentric Monks: Tales from the *Hosshinshū* by Kamo no Chōmei," *Monumenta Nipponica* 27:2, 1972.

Watanabe Tsunaya. *Shasekishū*, in Nihon Koten Bungaku Taikei series. Iwanami Shoten, 1966.

Watson, Burton. *Japanese Literature in Chinese*, 2 vols. New York: Columbia University Press, 1975.

Yanase Kazuo. *Hosshinshū Kenkyū.* Katō Chūdōkan, 1975.

———. *Ichigon Hōdan*, in Kadokawa Bunko series. Kadokawa Shoten, 1970.

Yoshihara Shikeko. *Myōe Shōnin Kashū no Kenkyū.* Ōfūsha, 1976.

20.
COURTLY FICTION OF THE KAMAKURA PERIOD

The reputation of the works of fiction composed during the Kamakura period in the tradition of the Heian monogatari is by no means high. Few scholars are attracted to what seems to be a barren field, certainly when compared to the war tales or setsuwa of the same period, and even they are likely to opine that the later examples of courtly fiction are so greatly indebted to *The Tale of Genji* as to be little more than copies. Every instance of influence from *The Tale of Genji* on these works has been painstakingly traced, but the extraordinary dissimilarities are generally passed over in silence or stated without comment, as if the scholar were rather embarrassed to discover that not everything could be explained in terms of imitation. No doubt it is frustrating to deal with works of literature that are known, even before they are read, to be inferior to *The Tale of Genji* or even to the fiction of the late Heian period. The incomplete state of the texts of some of the best monogatari of the Kamakura period also makes it difficult for the rare enthusiast to claim that his particular discovery is *almost* as good as Murasaki Shikibu's masterpiece.

Other problems of a more technical nature are involved when discussing the courtly fiction of the Kamakura period. As is true of the monogatari of the late Heian period, the surviving texts are not dated, and our only sources of information about when the works of courtly fiction of this period were written are *Story Without a Name* and the *Fūyōshū* (Wind and Leaves Collection), an anthology of poems that originally had appeared in monogatari.[1] Internal evidence is even harder to obtain. The writers of courtly fiction deliberately avoided the use of new words or grammatical constructions, rather in the manner that most waka poets for a millennium avoided words that had not been mentioned in the *Kokinshū*, and there are virtually no allusions to contemporary events or to developments in Buddhism. Works of courtly fiction of the

Kamakura period are for this reason often referred to as *giko monogatari* (archaic fiction), though the appropriateness of this term has been questioned.[2]

The establishment of the shogun's court in Kamakura deeply affected the nobility, whether they remained behind in the old Heian capital or attempted to improve their situation by going elsewhere. Power was now in the hands of the military, and there are descriptions in writings of the time of how the aristocrats were obliged to fawn on their erstwhile servants. The nobles experienced severe economic hardships especially during the warfare of the late twelfth century; but little in the traditional fiction produced at the court indicates what important political changes had occurred in the lives of the authors. It is quite possible, however, that some of the lost works whose titles we know from *Story Without a Name* or the *Fūyōshū* more clearly revealed than any surviving work that a new age had begun in literature as well as in the domain of politics.[3]

Works in the courtly tradition of the Kamakura period are for this reason, perhaps even more than for their old-fashioned style, considered to be pseudoclassical. The term is used to mean that the authors were pretending to be writing in an earlier (and happier) age. Not even the Heian courtly fiction had been really faithful to its time. Who would guess when reading *The Tale of Genji* or *Wakefulness at Night* that while their authors were evoking the beauty of a society free from any hint of disorder and ruled by canons of taste rather than by laws, the capital was overrun by bandits who threatened the property and even the lives of the aristocrats?[4] All the same, the Heian writers persuade us of the truth of their romanticized portrayal of their society. The Kamakura writers, despite their lavish descriptions of the beauty of the world they portray, were not so successful. Indeed, the feature that most clearly distinguishes the court fiction of the Kamakura period is the prominence of deviations—conscious or otherwise—from the cult of beauty that had characterized the Heian literature during its heyday.

The decline in the morals of the Heian aristocracy, a conspicuous element in this loss of beauty, began long before the shogunate capital was established in Kamakura.[5] Yet it is hard to escape the impression that signs of decadence among the aristocrats, evident much earlier, grew increasingly pronounced. *The Confessions of Lady Nijō*, a diary written toward the close of the Kamakura period, is evidence of the degree of promiscuity that existed at the court. The nobles were deprived by the rising power of the military of almost everything but their titles, and in inverse proportion to the court's loss of importance as the central organ of administration, ceremony and precedents became not merely guides to the correct performance of court activities but matters of the most intense concern.

For many aristocrats of this period, especially the women, *The Tale of Genji* was not only a beautiful novel but a faithful portrayal of a glorious age of the court, which they sadly contrasted with their own reduced circumstances. In their attempt to preserve the culture of their ancestors, these nobles consecrated themselves to waka poetry with such fervor that it became all but a religion. But it was in the fiction, rather than the poetry, that the pervasive decadence is most clearly revealed.

With a very few exceptions, the writers of the Kamakura courtly fiction are unknown, but we know from the example of Fujiwara Teika that men not only read but composed monogatari. The intended readers, however, were probably still ladies of the court, and the loving evocations of the Heian past were for their delectation. Repetitions of thematic materials from *The Tale of Genji* would not have distressed such readers; on the contrary, they probably gave the kind of pleasure they knew in poetry from honka-dori. One critic wrote of the Kamakura period monogatari *Koke no Koromo* (The Moss-Colored Robe), a work usually dismissed as being wholly derivative, "It was definitely not that the author of this monogatari copied earlier monogatari in the hope of giving form to his work; rather, it is clear that he strongly hoped that readers would, as they read, perceive both the links with and the differences that separated it from the existing body of monogatari."[6] The same is true of many other monogatari of the period, notably Teika's.

The Tale of the Matsura Palace

Teika's sole surviving work of fiction is the unfinished *Matsuranomiya Monogatari* (The Tale of the Matsura Palace), though he probably wrote others. Our best clues to the authorship and dating come from a brief passage in *Story Without a Name*, where it states, "The many works composed by Teika, the lesser captain, are so exclusively concerned with creating atmosphere that they are utterly lacking in verisimilitude. The poems in *The Tale of the Matsura Palace* are exactly like those in the *Man'yōshū*, and the plot brings to mind *The Hollow Tree*."[7] We know that *Story Without a Name* was written in 1200 or 1201, and Teika held the office of *shōshō* (lesser captain) from 1189 to 1202, strong evidence that he wrote *The Tale of the Matsura Palace* between 1189 and 1201.[8]

It might seem that an extended work by a recognized, even worshiped master of Japanese poetry would command wide attention, but *The Tale of the Matsura Palace* has been little studied. The unfinished state of the work undoubtedly has contributed to the neglect, but interest in Teika's writings is largely restricted to his poetry and criticism, and his novel has therefore been as little read as the plays of Browning or Tennyson. The work has been described as an exercise in literary composition: the poems (as the lady of *Story Without a Name* stated) recall those in the *Man'yōshū*, at least in the first book, though elsewhere Teika experimented with later styles of waka. He borrowed directly from *The Tale of the Hollow Tree* when creating his hero and in the emphasis he gave to music as a central element of the plot. He was probably indebted also to *The Tale of the Hamamatsu Middle Counselor* for setting much of the story in China. It is clear that Teika was not merely recounting an entertaining tale but demonstrating his familiarity with the literature of the past and his ability to write in a variety of styles.

One influence is conspicuous by its absence—that of *The Tale of Genji*. Teika deliberately set his work in the distant past, before the capital was established at Nara (and, naturally, before *The Tale of Genji*). It opens, "Long ago, when the capital was at Fujiwara, Tachibana no Fuyuaki, a major counselor of the Senior Third Rank who also served as general of the Palace Guards, had an only son by the Imperial Princess Asuka."[9] The Fujiwara capital lasted for three reigns, from 694 to 710, immediately before Nara was made the first permanent capital. The title *chūe no taishō* (rendered here as "general of the Palace Guards") is found in the *Man'yōshū* and other early documents, but no longer existed in the Heian period; it served to confirm the period of the work.[10]

Teika, by going back to the *Man'yōshū* and *The Tale of the Hollow Tree*, was in effect refusing the possibility of influence from the later *Tale of Genji*. Perhaps Teika was attempting to return in his work to a more vigorous period of Japanese history; it certainly stands apart from more typical examples of archaic fiction which insist on the beauty and sensitivity of the heroes to the exclusion of specifically masculine traits. But, of course, even the act of refusing influence revealed how profoundly conscious Teika was of *The Tale of Genji* at every stage of writing his book.

Ben no Shōshō, the hero of *The Tale of the Matsura Palace*, displayed outstanding qualities even as a small boy. We are told that he excelled others in his looks and, as he grew up, it became apparent that he was no less remarkable in intelligence and disposition. When the boy was seven, he demonstrated his proficiency at composing poetry in Chinese. The emperor, hearing of this prodigy, summoned him and set a topic for a poem as a test of his ability; the boy, without the least hesitation, composed a splendid poem on the assigned topic. He later studied stringed and wind instruments, and soon was able to play even the most difficult pieces better than his teacher.

Thus far, we have been given more or less the standard description of the hero of a Heian monogatari. The first departure from convention comes with the statement that Ben no Shōshō, unlike most young men, was severely disciplined in his habits and seemed uninterested in romance. The self-discipline would serve him well later in the novel, when he (in contrast to the heroes of Heian court fiction) is required to demonstrate his prowess on the battlefield; but the lack of interest in romance is only apparent. As a matter of fact, he is deeply in love with the Princess Kannabi, and desperately wants to make her his wife. The princess offers no encouragement. When he summons up the courage to reach inside her screen-of-state and take her hand, she tries to escape, and to the poem he sends describing his burning love she sends a frosty reply in which she expresses doubt that he is really consumed in the flames of passion for her.

Soon afterward Shōshō is ordered by the emperor to proceed to China as second in command of an embassy. (This has the effect of confirming that the tale took place prior to 838, when the last embassy to China was sent.) His parents worry about the dangerous journey, but are aware also that it is a signal honor that their son has been chosen. Shōshō is unhappy because Princess Kannabi has been taken into the palace, and has quickly become the emperor's favorite; but at the farewell banquet for members of the embassy, he receives a poem from Kannabi urging him to return safely to Japan. She says her heart will go with him, the first kind words he has received.

He departs for the "border"—the harbor of Matsura in Kyūshū from which the embassy is to sail for China. His mother insists on accompanying him, and declares that she will stay there until he returns. Although the mother's decision to remain in Matsura is not one of the central incidents of the work, for some reason the palace (*miya*) she built at Matsura appears in the title.

After a voyage lasting just a week, the ship bearing the Japanese embassy arrives at Ningpo,[11] the traditional port through which Japanese visitors entered China. They are welcomed by local officials with whom they exchange poems in Chinese. Apart from poetry, everything in China is unfamiliar, but the Japanese are impressed by the quality of the officials even in a place so remote from the capital; China is evidently a country of great culture.[12]

When the Japanese reach the capital, they are granted an audience by the emperor. The members of the Japanese embassy join their hosts in making music and composing poetry. The emperor is pleased with Shōshō, and insists that the young man (he was then seventeen) remain by his side. Some at the court are annoyed by Shōshō's mastery of every art, which quite puts the Chinese to shame, and others remonstrate with the emperor, pointing out how unusual it is for a foreigner, especially one so young, to be admitted to the presence of the emperor; but the emperor puts an end to the discussion by citing the instance of a foreigner favored by the ancient Emperor Han Wu-ti.

No less than *The Hamamatsu Middle Counselor*, this tale insists on the Japanese mastery of Chinese culture: there was no diminution of Japanese esteem for China as the source of their higher culture, even though diplomatic contacts had long been broken, but they evidently liked to believe (at this time as much later) that they, rather than the Chinese themselves, were the heirs to the great traditions of the past.

Shōshō also reveals his moral superiority. The emperor arranges for beautiful dancing girls to entertain Shōshō, but the latter, showing no sign of being tempted, spends his nights alone. The emperor is impressed: he had not expected a Japanese to display such self-control.[13]

Although Shōshō is resolved not to commit any lapses while in China, he is finally led into temptation, not by a beautiful face but by music. He hears the sound of a *kin* (Chinese zither) being played, so magnificently that he searches until he finds the player, an old man of eighty. The old man expresses joy over seeing a Japanese, and in a scene that recalls Kūkai's account of his first meeting with Hui-kuo, his teacher, declares that he knew Shōshō would visit him that night.[14] He also reveals that there is a kin player even superior to himself, the Princess Hua-yang, and he urges Shōshō to study with her.

Shōshō finds his way to the princess's mountain retreat, guided by the sound of her music. He is dazzled by his first glimpse; compared to her, the dancing girls who had entertained him look like so many clay dolls, and even Princess Kannabi seems no more than a country wench.[15] Princess Hua-yang teaches him a secret piece, and they commemorate the occasion by exchanging poems, both in Chinese (not quoted) and Japanese. Her waka is:

kumo ni fuku	That man who has come
kaze mo oyabanu	To visit over the waves
namiji yori	Unreached even by

toikon hito wa	The winds that blow in the clouds—
sora ni shiriniki	I knew of him in heaven.

Ben no Shōshō replies:

kumo no hoka	Did I ever know
tō tsu sakai no	Parting of such great sorrow
kunibito mo	Even when I left
mata ka bakari no	Someone from that far-off land
wakare ya wa seshi[16]	Far beyond the realm of clouds?

The princess tells Shōshō how she was taught to play the kin by an immortal who descended from heaven the night of the harvest moon. At their second meeting she teaches him the remainder of the secret pieces, but reveals she has not long to live. In the meantime, the emperor falls ill. He predicts his own death and unrest in the country, but takes comfort from Shōshō's physiognomy, which bears the signs of one who will calm disorder in the country. He also foresees Shōshō's safe return to Japan. Shōshō has a final meeting with Princess Hua-yang. She promises that if he really loves her and never forgets her she will join him in her next life. She gives him a crystal bead, urging him never to let it out of his possession. Once back in Japan, he should go to the Hatsuse Temple and for twenty-one days perform the customary observances before the statue of Kannon. If he does exactly as she describes, they will be reunited.

Soon afterward the princess dies. Her kin soars into the sky, returning to its source. The death of the emperor follows the princess's. The country is grief-stricken, but soon a quarrel breaks out over the succession to the throne between adherents of the infant crown prince and those of Prince Yen, the younger brother of the late emperor. The forces of Prince Yen are so much stronger that many at the court desert the crown prince. Various plotters are exposed and executed. (This may be another attempt on Teika's part to confirm the period of the tale; no one is put to death in a Heian monogatari.) The empress mother flees with the crown prince, but desertions swell the forces of Prince Yen day by day, and there is nowhere to hide but an abandoned temple. Teika's experiences during the fighting of the 1180s may have inspired these descriptions of warfare, but it has been suggested that he was also influenced by accounts he had read of the rebellion of An Lu-shan in 756.[17]

The empress mother assembles the few ministers who are still loyal and asks for their counsels, but they are all terrified by the prospect of encountering the enemy general, Yü-wen Hui,[18] who is described as looking like a man but having the heart of a tiger. In desperation, the empress asks the help of Ben no Shōshō: she has heard that although Japan is a small country its men are brave and it enjoys the protection of the gods.[19] Shōshō has had absolutely no experience of war, but he cannot abandon the empress; he agrees to defend China.

Shōshō's army numbers only some fifty or sixty men, but he prays for help to the buddhas and gods of his country. He really needs help: the enemy numbers some thirty thousand men. There follows an account of the fighting quite without precedent in courtly fiction. Shōshō orders his men to set fires on all sides of the enemy; caught by surprise, the traitors flee toward the sea, where Shōshō confronts the enemy general. He fires an arrow that passes through Yü-wen Hui's armor, but this tiger of a man not only continues to fight but surrounds Shōshō with his men. It seems as if the Japanese will surely perish, but suddenly four men who look exactly like Shōshō and are mounted on identical horses with identical fittings come to protect him. Yü-wen Hui falls back only to be surrounded by five more identical men who slash him down.[20] His army of thirty thousand men, intimidated by this prodigy, loses its will to fight.

Several other battles, described in some detail, bring complete victory to the loyalist forces. Shōshō, having accomplished his mission, deferentially returns to the empress his office of commanding general, saying he is young, inexperienced, and a foreigner.[21] The empress refuses his resignation. The whole country is now at peace. The traitors have been punished and prosperity has returned. The empress feels that she should really turn over state affairs to Shōshō, but she knows that he desires to return to Japan. He agrees to allow the empress, who is most reluctant to let him go, to fix the time of his departure.

At first the empress makes Shōshō nostalgic for his mother, but their relationship imperceptibly changes. She sings him a Japanese poem about the moon, eliciting from the author the query, "Granted she was very intelligent, how did she happen to learn an old Japanese poem? He must have only *thought* he heard the words."[22] This curious aside seems to anticipate a question from the reader, but it also enhances the mysterious charm of the empress.

It does not come as a surprise that at the outset of Shōshō's next affair, with a mysterious woman who lives in the mountains, music once again serves as a go-between, but even more than music, her marvelous fragrance characterizes the woman. He spends the night with her, but she does not vouchsafe a word, and she will not permit him to see her clearly. The only clue is her fragrance, which reminds him of the empress's. Shortly before he is to return to Japan, the lady explains the mystery: all that has happened, including the revolt of Yü-wen Hui, was foreordained in heaven. She herself was sent from heaven, charged with reestablishing peace, but she could not do this unaided. It was arranged in heaven that a martial man, born in Japan, and protected by the god Sumiyoshi, would come to her rescue. All went well, she says, until she fell in love with Shōshō, with whom she had been intimate in a previous life. Now she not only resembled a mortal woman but shared a mortal woman's feelings. Her lapse would surely be punished when she returned to heaven.[23]

Soon afterward Shōshō takes a tearful leave of the empress. Teika, having decided perhaps that he had written long enough in this vein, resorted to a device familiar to him from his work as the editor of old manuscripts: he provided a note, supposedly in the original manuscript, to the effect that at this point some pages had been lost because the string of the binding got broken.[24] The homeward journey is briefly described. True to her word, Shōshō's mother is still waiting for him at Matsura. The Japanese emperor is overjoyed to have Shōshō back, and bestows on him a title equivalent to the one he received in China.

Shōshō hurries to the Hatsuse Temple, fulfilling his promise to Princess Hua-yang. She reappears, and his love is rekindled. He does not forget the empress, but he has unfortunately lost all interest in Princess Kannabi, who is puzzled by his lack of ardor. He and Hua-yang are happily joined in love, but the empress makes another appearance, and one day Hua-yang not only catches a whiff of the empress's scent but notices his eyes are red with weeping. Her suspicions are aroused. He attempts to reassure her, but she seems inconsolable.

At this point the novel ends. Teika appended an additional note explaining that pages had been lost, and two false postscripts, one dating the manuscript the third year of Jōkan (A.D. 861) and quoting a poem by Po Chü-i, the second (supposedly by a later person) questioning the authenticity of the poem. These pedantic touches are not without interest in themselves, but, more than anything else, they suggest that Teika was at a loss how to finish his story. Ben no Shōshō has three women in his life, and it is clear that each expects to be his only love. How will he console poor Kannabi? Will Hua-yang settle down in Japan? Is the empress waiting for him in heaven? These questions were fated never to be answered.

Teika's work in its unfinished state cannot be called a success, but he was able to write a monogatari that avoided influence from *The Tale of Genji*. It is not clear, however, *why* he was so determined to escape this influence. Perhaps an aggressively masculine temperament made him impatient with the delicacy of Murasaki Shikibu. Perhaps also distaste for the prevailing ways of the aristocracy of his day made him nostalgic for the distant past when courtiers excelled not only with their writing brushes but with bows and arrows. *The Tale of the Matsura Palace* stands outside the mainstream of Kamakura court fiction. The style is that of the Heian monogatari, an impression strengthened by the many poems scattered through the text, but the story itself provides incontestable proof that not all monogatari written after *The Tale of Genji* conformed to its manner or contents.

Parting at Dawn

Ariake no Wakare (Parting at Dawn) seems a more typical example of court fiction of the Kamakura period, but perhaps it belongs to the late Heian rather than the Kamakura period: we have virtually no information concerning either the time of composition or the author. It is discussed in *Story Without a Name* as a "contemporary tale" (*ima no yo no monogatari*), suggesting that it had been written not long before 1200. The same work praised the easy-to-read style, but disapproved of the supernatural events in the narration.[25] The high regard for *Parting at Dawn* in the eyes of the thirteenth-century critics is indicated by the inclusion in the *Fūyōshū* of twenty of its poems, next in number after *Wakefulness at Night*. A modern critic praised its "fresh, literary fragrance," which he contrasted with the "lifeless imitations" found in other monogatari of the period.[26]

The title of the work is derived from the celebrated waka by Mibu no Tadamine (fl. 898–920) in the *Kokinshū* (and in the popular collection *Hyakunin Isshu*):

ariake no	Ever since parting
tsure naku mieshi	When the daybreak moon appeared
wakare yori	Heartless in the sky,
akatsuki bakari	Nothing has been so gloomy
uki mono wa nashi	As the hour before the dawn.

This poem is quoted five times in the course of the work, but it is not clear to which parting it refers.[27] One commentator, on the basis of the quotation of a poem as the title, suggested that the unknown author was someone close to Teika.[28] Mention in the text of "somebody who climbed a mountain in the moonlight"[29] in order to obtain instruction in secret works of music may be a reference to Ben no Shōshō in *The Tale of the Matsura Palace*, a further link to Teika. Connections also suggest themselves with *If I Could Only Change Them*; both works have for the central character a person who pretends to be of the opposite sex. But *Parting at Dawn* also contains supernatural elements—the ones criticized in *Story Without a Name*—that seem to belong to folk traditions rather than those of the court.

The story opens in a manner familiar ever since *The Tale of the Bamboo Cutter*: a husband and wife, long childless, pray to the gods (and consult doctors of yin-yang divination) in the hopes that a child will be born to them. Their prayers are answered, but a daughter, rather than a son, is born, and this is a disappointment because a daughter cannot continue the family line. The couple decides, in response to an oracle sent by the gods, to raise the daughter as a son. As the story opens the "son" is sixteen or seventeen and has just been promoted to the position of *udaishō*, or general of the Right, and is known by that name. Like the other heroes of court romances, he is extremely beautiful and plays various musical instruments superbly. His only fault (apart from his rather short stature) is his apparent lack of interest in women. His father, Sadaijin, gives out that Udaishō has a younger sister who remains at home because she is too shy to appear before people. The emperor, though he has a consort and various concubines, has not had a child. He thinks that perhaps another wife is needed, and asks Sadaijin to send his daughter to court. Sadaijin refuses, alleging the extreme shyness of the girl.

Thus far we have the making of a court romance along the lines of *If I Could Only Change Them*, and it does not require a literary detective to predict that sooner or later Udaishō will resume his rightful sex and become his own sister. But we are at this point confronted with an unfamiliar element: the young general is gifted with the power to make himself invisible, and has a habit of visiting people without their knowledge.[30] His ability to pass freely into other people's bedrooms leads to the discovery that his uncle, Sadaishō, has conceived an improper love for his stepdaughter. Udaishō also peeps in on several other bedrooms. In one he sees a repulsive old prince who has been admitted by the father of the young lady whose favors he craves, in another bedroom the same prince's wife is lying with the profligate Sammi no Chūjō.

Udaishō also takes advantage of his invisibility to eavesdrop on a conversation of some women who are gossiping about him. They blame his failure to marry on excessive religious piety, and wonder if he is waiting for an angel to appear before he consents to marry.[31] One senses a ripe corruption in the sexual mores of these court dignitaries.

Sadaishō's wife is not aware that her husband is having an affair with her daughter, so it comes as a shock to learn that the daughter is pregnant. The girl, deeply ashamed, wants to die, and her parents are alarmed to think of the gossip that will surely spread concerning this unexampled case of a woman having a child by her stepfather. Udaishō, once again slipping unobserved into someone else's house, offers to lead the unhappy girl to a safe place. Having nowhere else to turn, she accepts, though she does not know who he might be. Udaishō takes her home and explains the situation to his father, who agrees to allow the girl to become Udaishō's wife.

The wife, who has been given the name Tai no Ue, gives birth to a son. This means that Sadaijin now has a male heir who can succeed as head of the family. Udaishō wants to reveal his true sex, but his father fears that this will annul the benefit of at last having a successor. Udaishō is naturally unable to consummate the marriage, but explains to Tai no Ue that this is because he does not propose to remain long in this world. For all his masculine ways, however, Udaishō must disappear for several days each month during his period. The promiscuous Sammi no Chūjō takes advantage of Udaishō's absence to seduce Tai no Ue. When Udaishō returns he notices Tai no Ue is disturbingly distant. He suspects something has happened and, making himself invisible, reads the letter Sammi no Chūjō sent Tai no Ue after their night together. She is pregnant once again, but Udaishō is ready to forgive her. His parents still refuse to allow him either to reveal his sex or enter Buddhist orders.

Soon afterward the emperor has a strange dream in which he learns that the son born to Sadaijin after years of childlessness is really a daughter. He summons Udaishō, intending to ask about the meaning of the dream, and is struck for the first time by the young man's incomparable beauty. He takes Udaishō's hand and pulls him down beside him. The emperor unties the knots in Udaishō's clothes. Udaishō weeps, but this only excites the emperor the more. Only then does he make the discovery that Udaishō is a woman. After they have lain together Udaishō puts on men's robes and is once again masculine in manner.

He begs his parents to let him live as a woman, but they are reluctant to lose the privileges they have enjoyed thanks to the position of their "son." Udaishō can wait no longer. He informs his wife of his decision to "leave the world," and soon afterward his death is reported. Everyone grieves. The emperor even considers abdicating, but he remembers the younger sister of Udaishō and commands that she be brought to the palace. After a bare four or five months since the announcement of "his" death Udaishō's hair has grown so much it is now the same length as his height.

Udaishō, renamed Himegimi (the princess), must lead a totally different life. She may no longer play the flute, an instrument reserved for men, but she now is at liberty to read fiction (*sōshi*), formerly beneath her dignity. Her knowledge of Chinese is no longer of use, composing poetry in Chinese being considered unladylike. Himegimi is proclaimed as empress, but she indicates in a waka that becoming empress means nothing to someone who has already known high office as a man. The narrator, in an aside, asks why she should have thought so little of the honor of becoming empress.[32]

The second book of *Parting at Dawn* is devoted mainly to Sadaijin, the supposed son of Udaishō and Tai no Ue. He is of an *irogonomi* (sensual) nature, seeking sexual gratification everywhere, even among women of the lower classes. The one woman before whom he feels any constraint is the now-retired empress, who arouses his passionate attachment though he supposes she is his aunt. One of Sadaijin's adventures takes him to the house of the old prince whose lovemaking had been observed by Udaishō. The prince's wife has been jilted by her lover, leaving her with a daughter who is now about fifteen. Sadaijin is attracted initially to the girl, but he happens to see the mother, who looks young for her age, and she attracts him even more. He debates with himself whether to marry the girl or become the mother's lover, and decides in favor of the latter. He spends the night with the mother and has a parting at dawn which is not marked by the usual tender regrets but by the question he puts himself: "Why did I do it?" (*Ika ni shitsuru koto zo.*)[33]

The affair drags on. He dutifully writes day-after letters, but she cannot help fearing she will be deserted. She no longer worries about gossip, but he does, and always arranges to depart before dawn. Her husband, the prince, pays her a visit, but she detests him and pulls her clothes over her head, refusing to utter a word. At this point the author describes the faces of the prince and his wife, a rare instance in classical Japanese literature:

> The prince's complexion, as one might expect of one of his birth, was extremely fair. His eyes, nose, mouth, and high cheekbones were

> massive in the old style, and he had a splendid beard. His long chin and imposing features were rather flushed, no doubt because he had been weeping with rage. One glance at his wife served to increase his rage, and he wept all the more bitterly. The woman, looking not in the least her great age,[34] was very elegant, quite short but rather plump, and her hair hung most attractively over the forehead, framing her eyebrows delightfully. Her mouth had charm, and her whole appearance was such that any man would have been delighted to be with her.[35]

The prince manages to keep Sadaijin's letters from reaching his wife, inducing an aversion to her husband so intense that she refuses food or drink, preferring death to life with her husband. Sadaijin, still hopelessly in love with the retired empress, visits her. He finds her looking at some pictures, and her ladies have scattered storybooks around the room. The description gives a vivid though momentary glimpse of what it was like in the women's quarters of the palace. The empress chides Sadaijin for his failure to marry, suggesting the daughter of the minister of the Right as a suitable wife, and warning him that he will acquire a bad reputation unless he marries. Sadaijin replies that he does not think he has long to live, and that he would feel sorry for any woman who married him. He is unable to confess that the cause of his unhappiness is his hopeless love for the empress herself.

Sadaijin has another romance (which is developed later in the work) before he meets Ōigimi, the daughter of the minister of the Right. He is attracted to her beauty, but there is something cold and reserved about her that makes him think that she would be unlikely to comfort him when he was depressed. He yields nevertheless to pressure, especially from his grandfather (the father of Udaishō), and the marriage is announced. Only then does he learn that his mistress, the prince's wife, is the aunt of the bride. She is enraged that Sadaijin has been so insensitive as to choose for his bride someone so closely related.

Soon afterward a *mono no ke* (evil spirit) attacks the retired empress, and is subdued by a holy man from Mount Hiei with the greatest difficulty. Sadaijin takes another bride, this one the daughter of the minister of the Center; the empress, who had long worried about his celibate state, is delighted that he should now have two such distinguished wives, but the prince's wife is distraught with rage. Sadaijin's first wife is attacked by the mono no ke. She is no longer haughty but gentle in the face of this affliction. She falls into a coma and her face, altered by pain, now looks exactly like that of the prince's wife. The mono no ke, speaking through a child, declares that she will kill everyone loved by Sadaijin and, true to her word, now afflicts Sadaijin's second wife as well as the first. They are saved only by the death of the prince's wife. Still further complications, mainly involving the secret of Sadaijin's birth, prolong the work before it breaks off, either not quite finished or with the original ending lost.

It is easy to trace influences from earlier literature, especially *The Tale of Genji*, on *Parting at Dawn*. For example, the aloof daughter of the minister of the Right, Sadaijin's first wife, inevitably recalls Aoi, and the vengeful mono no ke who possesses the wife is similar to Lady Rokujō. But the portrayal of the prince's wife is strikingly unlike that of the aristocratic Rokujō; she is promiscuous, a harridan, and (unlike Rokujō whose "living ghost" unwittingly torments Aoi) she consciously resolves to wreak vengeance on anyone with whom Sadaijin has become intimate. It is possible to feel sorry for Rokujō, as anyone who has seen the Nō play *Nonomiya* knows, but the prince's wife is beyond redemption. The other resemblances to *The Tale of Genji* are similarly undercut by jarring elements that make one wonder if the intent might not have been parody rather than imitation. One senses everywhere in the work a corruption of the spirit that makes these aristocrats seem both familiar and contemptible, though occasionally, as in the domestic scene between the former Udaishō and her husband the emperor, when she pinches him in the course of a little tiff, the familiarity may be rather endearing. But, no matter how indulgently read, this is a far cry from the world of *The Tale of Genji*.

The pretense of Udaishō that she is a man recalls not *The Tale of Genji* but *If I Could Only Change Them*. Here again, however, there is an important difference. Udaishō is neither temperamentally nor sexually inclined to be a man, but is brought up as one by her parents for their own motives. She excels in arts specifically associated with men, like playing the flute or composing poems in Chinese, but this is the result of her education, not of her own tastes. When it finally seems possible for her to resume her true sex, her parents object because this will cost them the special privileges they enjoy thanks to their high-ranking son. The motivation for changing sex in *If I Could Only Change Them*, at least in its present version, is ludicrously weak, as one realizes from the ease with which the brother and sister adapt to their new roles, but it is plausible in *Parting at Dawn*.[36]

One source for *Parting at Dawn* may have been a monogatari of the eleventh century, the lost *Kakuremino* (The Invisible-Making Cape). Udaishō's ability to pass unperceived into people's houses probably owed much to the magic cape of the earlier work, but all that remains of *The Invisible-Making Cape* is the severe judgment passed on the work by the ladies of *Story Without a Name*[37] and the prefatory note to a poem in the *Fūyōshū* stating that it was composed when the hero "concealing his appearance went around to various places."[38] The childishness of the invisible man/woman is at once a throwback to the past and a foretaste of the fantasy typical of medieval fiction.

Although it undoubtedly reflects a more decadent society than that portrayed in the fiction of the mid-Heian period, *Parting at Dawn* is consistently of interest, and even promises at times to become an important work of literature. The characters, particularly the disagreeable ones like Sadaijin, come alive, and their base motives and actions contrast so strongly with those of characters in the mid-Heian monogatari as to send a thrill of recognition through modern readers. The promise of literary distinction is not fulfilled, largely because of the inadequacy of the central character, Udaishō, but *Parting at Dawn* nevertheless lingers in the memory as a most distinctive example of archaistic fiction.

The Princess in Search of Herself

The decadence apparent in such works as *Parting at Dawn* is given even more explicit statement in *Wagami ni tadoru Himegimi* (The Princess in Search of Herself). This work, unusually long for courtly fiction of its time, has about sixty characters, and the action takes place over a period of some forty-five years. It was unknown until 1933 when the first article describing its contents was published in a scholarly journal. The text was not printed until 1956 and even then, because of the unusual difficulty in making sense of the vaguely worded, stylistically unattractive sentences, it was known only to a handful of scholars. Two annotated editions[39] appeared in the 1980s, and some enthusiasts now claim that it is the finest of all the pseudoclassical tales.[40]

The cumbersome title originates in a waka composed by a lady,[41] the account of whose life was intended to unify the story. Soon after the work begins we are told of her determination to uncover the secret of her birth, epitomized in this waka:

ika ni shite	By what trick of fate
arishi yukue wo	Am I obliged to search for
sazo to dani	Even the faintest

wagami ni tadoru	Clues into the vanished past
chigiri nariken[42]	To discover who I am?

Clues to the date of composition are the usual ones: it is not mentioned in *Story Without a Name*, evidence that it was written after 1200, but seven waka are quoted in the *Fūyōshū*, proof that it existed prior to 1271. There is a special problem, however: all of the quoted waka occur in the first four of the eight books, suggesting either that the work had not yet been completed or else that the editors of the *Fūyōshū* did not have access to the full text. In either case, it seems possible the work was written at about this time.[43] No strong candidate has emerged as the author of *The Princess*, but it is generally agreed that it was probably a woman. Tokumitsu Sumio listed five necessary qualifications of the author: (1) she must have been in a position to write a work of fiction between 1245 and 1271; (2) she must have been well versed in palace ceremonies and usages and have personally experienced life at the court; (3) she must have been thoroughly acquainted with *The Tale of Genji* and *The Tale of Sagoromo*; (4) she must have been an accomplished poet though an inexperienced writer of prose; and (5) she must have desired the realization of the ideal of monarchical rule based on cooperation of the imperial family with the Fujiwara regents.[44] After examining, in the light of these qualifications, the credentials of four outstanding women writers of the thirteenth century, he came to the conclusion that Ben no Naishi, a court lady known chiefly for her diary, was the most likely author, but he put forward her name without much confidence.[45] In short, the author of the story is unknown.

Another problem in the composition is the total blank of seventeen years between Books III and IV, suggesting that part of the text may be missing. Furthermore, Book VI is chronologically unrelated to the surrounding chapters, recalling the "parallel" (*narabi*) chapters of *The Tale of Genji*, and inducing some scholars to believe that it may have been written later. However, it is now generally believed that one person wrote the entire work, in its present order, and that no large sections of the manuscript have been lost.

The Princess as a whole is difficult to summarize. Although one expects that the Otowa princess and her search for her identity will be the main subject, she is not a central figure, and we learn her secret in the course of the very first book: she is the child born of the illicit union between the kampaku and the empress, and at the end of the first book, after the death of the empress, the kampaku invites the princess to live at one of his houses. This would seem to solve all the problems posed by the uncertainty of the princess about her birth, but many new complications occur, notably the various liaisons formed by men and women of the court.

Book VI is undoubtedly the most interesting section of the work. Laborious efforts have been given to tracing the influence of *The Tale of Genji* on other parts of the work, but this section stands apart from any other surviving example of court fiction. It is the story of the former *saigū*, or high priestess of Ise. As Book VI opens there is a change of reign in the capital. This automatically involved a change also in the high priestess, and the princess who had been serving in this capacity returns to the capital. She discovers that she has nowhere to go: her mother is dead and her house is occupied by the mother's younger sister, Dainagon no Kimi, who has become a nun. The priestess's father, the Cloistered Emperor Saga, now living outside the city in a remote place, does not like the idea of sharing his house with someone he hardly knows. The cloistered emperor asks Dainagon no Kimi to take her in, and she does so with evident reluctance, fearing that the wayward behavior of the high priestess (of which she has had a glimpse) will reflect on her own reputation. Her house is in a bad state of repairs and remote from the city.

We learn that Japan is now ruled by an empress, the half-sister of the high priestess. No empress had ruled in her own right since the end of the Nara period, over four hundred years before. Was this an archaic touch, similar to those in *The Tale of the Matsura Palace*, and intended to indicate that this was not a tale about the Heian period? Or was the author, a woman, merely engaging in a bit of fantasy about a time when women wielded the highest power? In any case, the empress is portrayed as an ideal ruler—learned in the classics of both Japan and China,[46] artistic, compassionate, and always fair in her governing of the nation.

Udaishō, a high-ranking official whose love for the empress (who has not married) was rebuffed, thinks he will divert himself with the former high priestess, reasoning that she probably resembles her half-sister. One rainy night he goes to her house and peeps in through the dilapidated screens. Four or five young women are flushed with the game they are playing, but no one looking like the mistress of the household is to be seen. Finally Udaishō makes out two women in the adjoining room. Although it is summer, the women have pulled their robes over their heads, and they are lying there, embraced so tightly he wonders that they can breathe. He hears their groans and supposes something extremely sad afflicts them, only for them to burst into seemingly uncontrollable laughter. Udaishō is baffled: the women are clearly doing something, but he cannot tell what it is. This should at least have aroused his curiosity but, not wishing to become involved in other people's affairs, he leaves without pursuing the matter.[47]

The story goes back to the time when the high priestess was still at Ise. She doted on a certain lady named Chūjō, and the two women were inseparable, day and night, laughing and crying together. After the high priestess returned to the capital another young woman, Kozaishō, was attracted to her service, and soon she received the passionate attentions of the high priestess.

Soon after discovering that the high priestess has a new favorite, Chūjō startles people by shrieking and throwing herself on the ground, crying that she is afraid of a mono no ke. Kozaishō, recognizing that jealousy has caused Chūjō's outburst, tries to calm Chūjō by assuring her that she does not intend to serve the high priestess any longer. She declares, "I am I!" (*ware wa ware*),[48] meaning, it would seem, that she intends to look out for her own interests, a most individualistic utterance for a character in a work of courtly fiction. Despite this reassurance, the mono no ke invariably makes an appearance whenever Kozaishō goes to the high priestess's room.

One day her brother, Hyōe no Suke, calls. He peeps under the curtained enclosure and sees two women locked in an embrace. He gives up his attempts to help her, henceforth sending only letters. Evidently, Kozaishō found it more difficult than she had anticipated to break relations with the high priestess.

A lady named Shindayū in the high priestess's entourage, envious of the attentions other women receive, attempts to ingratiate herself. As she is praying for divine assistance, the high priestess suddenly rouses herself from sleep and sends a maid to Chūjō's room to ascertain what she is wearing. The maid reports that Chūjō is dressed in pale blue, at which the high priestess cries out, "How horrible! It's just what I thought she would be wearing!" She has dreamed that a woman dressed in blue was tormenting her. We have already been told that Chūjō has begun to practice black magic.[49]

Shindayū, finding the opportunity she has been waiting for, offers to get a medium to interpret the dream. She soon returns with one who declares that a woman in blue has driven seven nails into a doll; the nails must be removed or the high priestess is doomed.[50] Shindayū finds the doll and removes the nails; the high priestess at once recovers. Shindayū is rewarded for her quick work by being chosen as her mistress's constant companion.

The book concludes with the former high priestess living in comfort and enjoying great prestige by favor of her half-sister, the empress. Her house is now so impressive that nobody rides past it without dismounting, and pedestrians carry their footwear as they go by. Guards throw stones at people who do not show proper respect.

In a rare aside (*sōshiji*) the author tells us why she wrote about these women: it was to show how their own natures, but also the force of circumstances, determined their fates. If Chūjō hadn't revealed her jealousy, she might have lived happily with the high priestess. All the other characters live to a ripe old age.[51]

There could hardly be a more unexpected conclusion to the account of the doings in the former high priestess's house; it strains the imagination to conceive of the people involved living happily ever after. One thing is certain: their story owes very little to the tale of the Shining Prince. The only time Genji's name appears is by way of contrast with an indescribably stupid, conceited dwarf who was formerly Chūjō's lover: the narrator remarks, "I pity poor Genji being made the subject of such a comparison!"[52]

Everything in this section of *The Princess in Search of Herself* is so described that we are likely to find the events not only decadent but ugly. Much as the empress is praised, we might admire her more if she chastised rather than rewarded her wayward half-sister. The whole of the work is not in this vein, but the story of the former high priestess of Ise reveals how far the monogatari had wandered from the path of *The Tale of Genji*.

A Tale of Unspoken Yearning

Iwade Shinobu Monogatari (A Tale of Unspoken Yearning) is one of the most impressive works of Kamakura period courtly fiction. Unfortunately, only the first two of the eight books have survived intact, and we know the rest of the story from extracts from the text that were included in a later book by way of providing background for the quoted 382 poems. The work seems to have enjoyed a considerable reputation in its day, as we can judge from the inclusion in the *Fūyōshū* of thirty-four of its poems, the fifth-largest total from any monogatari.[53] The date of composition has not been determined, but various clues suggest that *Unspoken Yearning* was written between 1235 and 1251.[54] Virtually nothing is known about the author, but for various reasons it has tentatively been suggested that the work was written by a woman, possibly the granddaughter of Shunzei.[55] The title seems to refer to the secret love of Nii no Chūjō for the empress.

As usual, resemblances to *The Tale of Genji* have been discovered. First of all, there is obviously close similarity between the elderly prince in *Unspoken Yearning*, who has entered Buddhist orders and lives in Fushimi with his two daughters, and Prince Hachi and his two daughters at Uji in *The Tale of Genji*. The visits of Naidaijin, the chief male character, to the princesses at Fushimi also recall those of Kaoru to Uji. One can only assume this was deliberate; the author of *Unspoken Yearning* recreated a familiar situation only to give it an entirely new meaning. The prince in Fushimi, sensing that he has not much longer to live, begs Naidaijin to take the older daughter as one of his wives, and Naidaijin, who has been living quite happily with his wife, the First Princess, reluctantly complies, seemingly out of pity for the old man. The girl, Ōigimi, is beautiful, and Naidaijin, who at first could not muster much interest in her, on occasion toys with the thought of bringing her to his palace; but in the end she is taken by the emperor himself. The surface resemblances between the Fushimi princesses and the Uji princesses become ironic; unlike Ōigimi in *The Tale of Genji* who rebuffs all attempts to win her, this Ōigimi is passed from man to man. The other similarities between the two works are confined mainly to the surface, as if the author of *Unspoken Yearning* borrowed materials from Murasaki Shikibu mainly as themes on which to create her new variations.

One of the rare scholars who have devoted much attention to *Unspoken Yearning* wrote, "It has often been said that monogatari of this kind written in the Heian and Kamakura periods did not venture one step beyond imitation of *The Tale of Genji*, and the present monogatari is no exception. However, in the precision of the descriptions and the elegant flow of the language, the exactness of the correspondence between what has gone before and what happens afterward, and in the smooth development of the plot, it is one of the outstanding examples of the novel (*shōsetsu*). I wonder if it does not rank first among the monogatari composed from the late Heian period into the Kamakura period?"[56]

Unspoken Yearning is a memorable example of courtly fiction. One is tempted to call it a novel if only because the author's control of the materials goes beyond what one expects of a mere storyteller. The supernatural is not a conspicuous element in the narration [57] and the most important incident, the false rumor that Naidaijin is neglecting his wife in favor of another woman, requires no suspension of disbelief. The characters are all unmistakable human beings, and there is little doubt that this would rank among the major achievements of Japanese traditional fiction if the entire text had survived.

The work opens with a description of the beauty of the garden at Ichijō-in, the palace of Naidaijin.[58] His wife, the First Princess (Ippon-nomiya), looks out on the garden without much pleasure, remembering the past when she lived in the Imperial Palace and could admire the cherry blossoms there. At that moment a messenger arrives from the palace. It is Nii no Chūjō, a boy of fourteen or fifteen whose unspoken love for the princess runs through the work. He catches a glimpse of her face, normally hidden behind curtains, and feels great perturbation, but controls his feelings long enough to say that the flowers are a gift from the crown prince. A letter from the prince is attached to the spray of cherry blossoms. Even as the princess examines the letter, her husband, Naidaijin, enters. He cuts a splendid figure, a worthy match for the princess in his appearance. He asks about the letter, an invitation to the palace from the crown prince to see the cherry blossoms. Although the princess would like nothing better than to go to the palace, she shrugs off the letter with a few words: "What a bore!"[59]

The characters of the principal figures in the book have been presented in a few paragraphs: the princess has never forgotten her life in the palace and regrets her marriage to a commoner, no matter how splendid; her husband, Naidaijin, loves her and fears no rivals; and the youthful Chūjō, unable to voice his love for the princess, is filled with envy of Naidaijin.

The story then reverts to a description of Naidaijin's antecedents. His father, the former emperor, had had many children, but some died young, others took Buddhist vows, and there was no one to succeed him on the throne. He abdicated in favor of his brother, at the same time taking as his concubine a lady-in-waiting whom he loved. Shortly before their union was blessed by a child, he fell mortally ill. Realizing that he would not live long enough to see the child, he asked the kampaku to marry the lady-in-waiting and to raise the child as his own. The kampaku agreed, and soon afterward the emperor died.[60]

The lady-in-waiting was extremely grieved, but (as the text informs us) one does not die of grief.[61] She vowed to become a nun as soon as her child was born, but this wish was also frustrated, and in the end she became, as the emperor had wished, the wife of the kampaku, who treated her with every kindness. The child she bore was the future Naidaijin. Although his real father was an emperor, he was the acknowledged son of the kampaku and as such was a commoner.

The First Princess, the daughter of the reigning emperor, was incomparably beautiful and gifted. She was raised by her doting parents with the utmost care, but somehow (not explained in the text) Naidaijin found a crack in the defenses surrounding her bedroom. After one meeting, both the princess and Naidaijin fell into a wasting ailment stemming from their love. Eventually the cause was discovered, and the emperor reluctantly agreed to their marriage. After the wedding, the princess moved from the palace to Naidaijin's house, the Ichijō-in.

The narration now shifts to the subject of Chūjō, whom we have seen as the youthful bearer of a branch of cherry blossoms from the palace. His mother was born while her father, the present emperor, was still crown prince and only fourteen years old; the baby's mother was sixteen. Both of Chūjō's parents died within a short time, and the orphaned boy grew up in the palace where he distinguished himself in all the standard artistic accomplishments of a courtier.

These pedigrees, though not without interest in themselves, are necessary above all as underpinning for the developments that ensue, and represent a departure from the casual character introductions more usual in a monogatari. One is tempted to interpret them as explanations of the temperaments inherited by Naidaijin and Chūjō from their different parents; in any case, we understand their characters better because of what we know of their antecedents, and the failures of their marriages echo their parents' failures. We are clearly meant to be interested in these characters as individuals and not merely as figures in a romance.

Because the First Princess is the wife of Naidaijin, there is no possibility that Chūjō's secret love will ever be fulfilled, and in his dejection he prays the gods to free him from this attachment. He is consoled by another woman,[62] who, though the daughter of a prince, has none of the demure modesty associated with women of her class; she has in fact had relations with Naidaijin, the emperor, and various other dignitaries.

One night when Chūjō is with this lady, Naidaijin passes her house and recalls his visits before his marriage. He notices through a break in the crumbling wall around the old house a man's carriage and, out of curiosity, he goes in, wondering who the visitor might be. He overhears voices, and recognizes Chūjō's. Thinking it would be fun to catch him in this compromising situation, Naidaijin lingers. The woman does not wish to let Chūjō go, but finally he makes his escape, only for Naidaijin to grasp his arm as if he were apprehending a criminal. Chūjō explains that he stopped at the house to see the tinted autumn leaves. Naidaijin teases him, "The two of you were so closely pressed together there was no chance any autumn leaves would come between you."[63] Chūjō is provoked into taunting Naidaijin for his philandering, to which

Naidaijin truthfully replies that since his marriage he has not been interested in any woman except his wife. What began as a prank on Naidaijin's part develops into an unpleasant quarrel.

Naidaijin loves his wife, but he does not really understand her. He is not aware, for example, how much she misses her old life. She muses to herself that if only she had married as her father intended she need never have left the palace. Not being able to see the emperor whenever she chooses makes her feel as if she now inhabits a totally different realm.[64] Chūjō's infatuation with the First Princess is such that he cannot seriously consider marrying anyone else, though every person of consequence would like nothing better than to have him as a son-in-law. He maintains so gloomy a mien that, in the hope of cheering him, the retired emperor offers him the use of a charming little house where he can entertain lady friends in privacy, but Chūjō rarely stays there. Indeed, he outwardly seems to have lost interest in women.

The birth of a baby boy to the First Princess crowns Naidaijin's happiness. But one day he catches her as she is writing a letter that she hides as soon as she sees him. It is not a letter to a lover, as at first he fears, but to her father, in response to one he sent her describing his loneliness in the palace without her. Her reply relates her unhappiness in two poems, of which the second is: "At first I grieved and lamented, supposing it must be an unhappy dream, but I doubt I would be so wretched, even if I had died within that dream."[65]

Naidaijin is stunned by this revelation. At first he blames himself for not having noticed anything, then he expresses anger at the emperor's words, citing instances of happy marriages between members of the imperial family and commoners. He wonders if she ever loved him, supposes she finds it painful even to think that their relations as man and wife will last through two lifetimes. He is all but carried away by his arguments, only to break down into tears as he looks at the incredibly lovely woman who is his wife. She first murmurs that she never intended him to see the letter, but finally becomes so exasperated with his rhetoric that she says with venom in her voice, "How happy I would be if you would kindly shut up!"[66] He offers to stop the argument if she will promise never to write such things again, and the scene ends with his saying, "I'm sure you must be sleepy," and inviting her to bed.

The argument has a curiously modern flavor. The resolution is what one would expect, but the fact remains that the First Princess is not happy in her husband's house. When the occasion comes for her to return to the palace she does not hesitate. The occasion is provided by a rumor that reaches the ears of the retired emperor that Naidaijin has fallen in love with another woman whom he treats with greater care than his wife. The woman in question is the older of two sisters whose mother has died and who live with their father, a lay priest, in Fushimi, as described above. Naidaijin, in the course of a visit to the father, peeps in on the sisters. The younger sister, a girl of thirteen or fourteen, looks as if she would one day make a fine wife for somebody, but the older sister is enchanting. She even resembles the First Princess.

Naidaijin's second visit to Fushimi is undoubtedly inspired by attraction for Ōigimi, the older sister, but it does not occur to him anything serious might come of his visit. However, no sooner does he arrive than the girls' father asks bluntly, "If it's all the same to you, how about tonight? I gather it's marked a lucky day in the calendar."[67] Naidaijin is persuaded. That night when he gets back home, contrary to his normal practice he does not hurry to the room of the First Princess. The next day, however, he decides to tell her what happened the previous night, reasoning that if he does not tell her somebody else will. He hides nothing, but insists that he has made a clean break with his past and that what happened in Fushimi was only a momentary aberration.

As if to prove his contention, Naidaijin does not go back to Fushimi, much to the distress of Ōigimi and her father. The First Princess is not bitter over what has happened; indeed, she shows no reaction whatsoever. Her only conscious wish is to be back in the palace. A heavy snowfall on the night that Naidaijin is making one of his infrequent visits to Fushimi makes the princess long for the shelter provided by her parents. When Naidaijin returns, he explains his absence in terms of worry over the health of the old prince-priest (who dies soon afterward).

At this time the First Princess is expecting another baby. In the midst of the delivery, which is delayed and difficult, a mono no ke makes its presence felt. The First Princess, terribly afflicted by the evil spirit, loses consciousness and finally stops breathing, but is revived by the prayers of a holy man. The mono no ke identifies herself as the deceased mother of Ōigimi, come to wreak vengeance for the unkind treatment her daughter has received. She is eventually driven away and a baby girl is safely born.

Soon afterward rumors reach the ears of the retired emperor to the effect that Naidaijin has not only been unfaithful to the First Princess but has grossly neglected her. His first thought is to take his daughter back. He decides that her son should stay with Naidaijin but that she should take the daughter with her to his palace. The First Princess accepts this command with no show of hesitation or resistance. She is sure she must not disobey her father; even if he commanded her to go and live among savages on the frontier she would have no choice but to obey. Naidaijin returns just as she is about to leave for the palace. He accepts her statement that she is going only for a short visit. He has no idea why the retired emperor has sent for his daughter, but when she fails to answer his letters he realizes that something must have gone wrong. He reasons that somebody must have lied about his actions, for he can find no fault in himself that would have occasioned this step. When he goes to the palace to see his wife his request is refused, but in a touching scene his infant daughter is brought to him.

This is more or less where the text of the two surviving books of *Unspoken Yearning* ends, though we have summaries of the rest. Even in its unfinished state it is a particularly affecting tale with many moments that strike a contemporary reader by the realism of the details. Of particular interest is the account of the terrible effects of a false rumor. Courtly fiction abounds in mentions of the obsessive dread of what people might think, even on the part of characters whose social position should make them indifferent to common gossip. But here the retired emperor not only believes the rumor but takes back his daughter and prevents her husband from seeing her. The compliance of the First Princess, even though it destroys her marriage, suggests that her love for Naidaijin was never strong enough to cause her to forget the privileged life she once led. Naidaijin is helpless to combat the rumor and will eventually take up with some other woman.

Unlike those monogatari of the Kamakura period that startle by the unconventionality of the actions of the characters, *Unspoken Yearning* describes people of the court society who suffer not because of the ambivalence of their sexual relations nor because of the machinations of evil adversaries but because the author believed that suffering is the normal condition of sensitive human beings. Even though the author borrowed little from *The Tale of Genji*, she seems to have shared the sensibilities of Murasaki Shikibu.

The Tale of Sumiyoshi

One last work of Kamakura fiction, the only one that was ever widely read, presents special problems of dating. There are over one hundred variant texts of the present version of *Sumiyoshi Monogatari* (The Tale of Sumiyoshi),[68] and strong evidence indicates that the monogatari of the same name mentioned in *The Tale of Genji* was still a different work, probably dating back to the end of the tenth century. The present *Tale of Sumiyoshi* undoubtedly has links with the earlier work of that name, but it is even more closely associated with the many later stories on the theme of the suffering of a young girl at the hands of her wicked stepmother. This theme was treated in the early monogatari *The Tale of Ochikubo*, and presumably there are connections, though very remote, to the body of similar stories in other countries, notably *Cinderella*. The cruel stepmother figures in the literature of almost every country. Some have suggested that *Cinderella* is a nature myth, Cinderella being the dawn oppressed by the night clouds (the cruel stepmother) who is finally rescued by the sun (the prince who marries her). But others claim that the suffering undergone by a girl at the hands of a stepmother and her eventual triumph is a rite of passage, the feminine equivalent of the exile of the prince who returns to triumph over his foes.[69]

The present version of *The Tale of Sumiyoshi* probably dates from the second or third decade of the thirteenth century.[70] Perhaps, as has been claimed, there was not much basic difference between the earlier and later versions of the tale,[71] but details had to be modified in response to the changes in marriage customs among the nobility. As long as a man (in the Heian manner) maintained wives in separate establishments there was not much likelihood of stepmothers inflicting hardships on the man's children by another wife. This fact of Heian marital life persuaded various eminent scholars that stories of cruel stepmothers attributed to the Heian period must have been forgeries, composed at a later time when, monogamy having become usual, the possibility of a cruel stepmother became much stronger.[72] The largest number of stepchild stories dates from the Muromachi period.[73]

The Tale of Sumiyoshi is unusual in that the two daughters of the wicked stepmother are on good terms with Himegimi, the stepchild. But the attempt of the stepmother to discredit the girl in the eyes of her father (and of the world) by introducing a man—a dissolute priest—into her room recalls a similar scene in *The Tale of Ochikubo*.[74]

The Tale of Sumiyoshi is given what literary interest it possesses by the account of the efforts of Chūjō, the officer who has fallen in love with Himegimi, to marry her. His first attempt is frustrated by the stepmother, who tricks him into marrying one of her own daughters. The stepmother decides to have Himegimi marry an elderly gentleman, but the girl escapes, taking refuge in Sumiyoshi where she hides and plans to become a nun. Chūjō prays at the Hase Temple for a divine revelation of her whereabouts and learns that she is in Sumiyoshi. He tracks her down with great effort, and at last finds and weds her. Before long he is promoted to be kampaku, and he and his bride flourish. The stepmother dies in disgrace, mourned by no one.

Perhaps the most effective passage in the work is the description of Chūjō's journey to Sumiyoshi in search of Himegimi. He goes on foot, dressed in white like a pilgrim, accompanied by only a single retainer. That night Himegimi sees him in a dream, struggling over the mountains, sleeping in the fields. She tells Jijū, her confidante, about the dream, which Jijū at once recognizes as a "true dream," and we learn,

> Chūjō was not accustomed to such exertions, and blood oozed from his beautiful, white feet. It seemed so unlikely he would ever reach his destination that even passersby stared at him. Toward dusk he reached a place where he could see, through breaks in the pines on the shore, waves rising in the distant sea. Here and there were reed-thatched cottages, and boats trolling along the coast cutting seaweed, and to his surprise he saw smoke rising from salt kilns. Even when he had come up quite close he still did not know where he was. Dejected, he threw himself under a pine and was resting there when he noticed a boy of about ten gathering dried pine branches.
>
> He called to the boy, "Where do you live? And what is this place called?" The boy answered, "This is Sumiyoshi. I live very near here." "I am delighted to hear it," said Chūjō. "Are there people of consequence living around here?" The boy answered, "There's the chief priest of the shrine." Chūjō asked, "Is there anywhere around here where people from the capital are living?" "Some nuns from the capital live at a place called Suminoe."
>
> Chūjō asked detailed questions about Suminoe, but when he got there he found only a lonely-looking hut built by an inlet of the sea. The moon shone faintly through the trees. He could not see anyone likely to respond to his questions, and the whole place looked exceedingly forlorn. The sun had already gone down, and he stood dejectedly under a pine which he addressed in tears, "If you were only a human being, there are things I would ask you."[75]

The passage is memorable because of such effective touches as Chūjō's feet bleeding because he is not accustomed to wearing straw sandals or the boy's thinking first of the priest of the shrine when asked if any people of consequence are living nearby. The descriptions of the coast along the Inland Sea, though not romanticized, are appealing; a little later in the story Chūjō admires the scenery because it is so unlike the landscapes near the capital. But for readers of the time the most noteworthy element in this passage was probably the boy, who (as commentators inform us) was not simply a local child but a messenger sent by the Kannon of the Hase Temple to guide Chūjō, or perhaps even the god of the Sumiyoshi Shrine himself. Versions of the tale composed in the Muromachi period were likely to contain religious elements absent from the original stepmother stories and only first adumbrated at this time. *The Tale of Sumiyoshi* in its present version suggests how the tradition of court fiction would imperceptibly give way to the popular fiction of a later age.

It is difficult, however, to generalize about possible trends in the fiction of the Kamakura period if only because the dating of the texts is so uncertain. We cannot even be sure that the best works have survived from the period; indeed, the mutilated *Unspoken Yearning* is unquestionably superior to the Heian romance *If I Could Only Change Them*, which survives more or less intact; and more poems from *Kaze ni tsurenaki Monogatari* (The Pitiless Winds), which survives only in fragments, were included in the *Fūyōshū* than from *Wakefulness at Night* or from *The Hamamatsu Middle Counselor*.[76] Again, we also have only vague indications about the readership of the surviving texts, and this means that the apparent changes—such as an increase in religious elements—may equally well have represented a response to the changed tastes of the same audience or else an attempt to appeal to a new audience by including such themes.

Whatever our conclusions may be about the value of the works produced during the last stage in the development of courtly fiction, it is difficult to concur in the judgment that they were little more than imitations of *The Tale of Genji* or that they betrayed a want of creative imagination.[77] None of the later works of courtly fiction compares with *The Tale of Genji*, but this may be rather like saying that no later British writer of tragedies can compare with Shakespeare. The Kamakura examples of courtly fiction are worth reading because their memorable parts so little resemble *The Tale of Genji*. Their attraction is intermittent, and we must sometimes put up with tedious passages of conventional description that imitated the least attractive features of the Heian monogatari, but at their best they give startling insights into the life of a court that had passed the zenith of its glory.

Notes

This chapter is a somewhat revised version of an article that originally appeared in *Monumenta Nipponica* 44:1 (1989), under the title "A Neglected Chapter: Courtly Fiction of the Kamakura Period."

1. For *Story Without a Name*, see above, pp. 517–18. The compilation of the *Fūyō Waka Shū* (to give the work its full title) was ordered in 1271 by the consort of the Emperor Gosaga, and was probably completed not long afterward. It consists of 1,410 poems, all drawn from monogatari. Of the two hundred monogatari from which it quotes poems, only about twenty survive. (For more information in English, see Earl Miner, Hiroko Odagiri, and Robert E. Morell, *The Princeton Companion to Classical Japanese Literature*, p. 156.)
2. See, for example, Ogi Takashi, *Kamakura Jidai Monogatari no Kenkyū*, p. 51, where he insists that the term *giko monogatari* is used properly only of works written in archaic language by scholars of National Learning during the Tokugawa period. Ogi quotes on the same page Kazamaki Keijirō's statement that it is impossible to distinguish between monogatari of the Heian and Kamakura periods.
3. Imai Gen'e (in "Ōchō Monogatari no Shūen," pp. 20–21) cited various scholars who had expressed the belief that Fujiwara Teika's novel *The Tale of the Matsura Palace* contained political criticism, the result of his experiences during the warfare of the 1180s; but Imai considered that such passages were incidental to the basic *mugen* (dream-fantasy) tone of the work.
4. Ogi (*Kamakura*, pp. 54–55) quotes Hara Katsurō's description of the real appearance of the city of Heian. Robbers roamed the street not only at night but in broad daylight and sometimes penetrated even into the Imperial Palace.
5. See above, pp. 515–16.
6. Kannotō Akio, "Kamakura Jidai no Monogatari," in Nihon Bungaku Kyōkai (ed.), *Nihon Bungaku Kōza*, IV, p. 171.
7. Kuwabara Hiroshi, *Mumyō Zōshi*, p. 98. See also Michele Marra, "*Mumyōzōshi*," p. 418. The statement that the poems were "exactly like" those in the *Man'yōshū* is evidence that the author of *Story Without a Name* thought the poems did *not* resemble those in *The Tale of Genji*; similarly, the resemblances noted with *The Tale of the Hollow Tree* meant that the plot seemed unlike that of *Genji*. *The Tale of the Matsura Palace* is the only work so clearly differentiated from *Genji*.
8. At one time doubts were expressed about the authorship, but it is not seriously questioned any longer. See Hagitani Boku, *Matsuranomiya Monogatari*, p. 293.
9. *Ibid.*, p. 9.

10. *Ibid.* Hagitani states that this title was in fact not used during the Fujiwara period; but in any case it suggested a bureaucracy unlike that of the Heian period. The other indications of when the work took place are vague and sometimes contradictory, but they always point to a period prior to the beginning of the tenth century.
11. Teika, once again insisting on the antiquity of his tale, uses the old name for the port, Ming-chou.
12. Hagitani, *Matsuranomiya*, p. 23.
13. *Ibid.*, p. 26. The original reads: "*Kano kuni no hito wa omoishi yori mo mame narikeri.*"
14. It is unlikely Teika had read Kūkai's *Shōrai Mokuroku*, in which the meeting is described, but he was surely aware that other Japanese priests (including Jōjin) had so favorably impressed the Chinese that they were never allowed to return to Japan.
15. Hagitani, *Matsuranomiya*, p. 32.
16. *Ibid.*, p. 33.
17. *Ibid.*, p. 45.
18. *Ibid.*, p. 48. Yu-wen Hui is not a historical personage but, as Hagitani points out, several men with the same surname appear in Chinese histories. All of them were foreigners who were naturalized as Chinese; this may be an indication that the intended model was An Lu-shan.
19. Needless to say, the Chinese in real life (or in their own literature) did not often praise the Japanese in these terms.
20. We later learn that Shōshō's mysterious clones have been sent by the Japanese gods.
21. Hagitani, *Matsuranomiya*, p. 62.
22. *Ibid.*, p. 71.
23. *Ibid.*, pp. 107–9.
24. *Ibid.*, p. 115.
25. Kuwabara, *Mumyō Zōshi*, pp. 98–99. The ladies of *Story Without a Name* consistently found fault with works that contained supernatural or implausible events. They also disapproved of scenes of violence, discussions of political matters, or inelegant language.
26. Ishikawa Tōru, quoted by Ōtsuki Osamu in *Ariake no Wakare*, p. 489.
27. See Ōtsuki, *Ariake*, p. 491. He suggests it might refer to the parting of the emperor and the lady general.
28. *Ibid.*, p. 499.
29. *Ibid.*, pp. 112–13.
30. For a brief study of the ability of characters in Heian fiction to make themselves invisible or transform themselves, see Inaga Keiji, " 'Kakuremi' to 'Henkei' Josetsu," in Chūko Bengaku Kenkyūkai (ed.), *Heian Kōki*, pp. 1–16.
31. Ōtsuki, *Ariake*, p. 69.
32. *Ibid.*, p. 202.

33. *Ibid.*, p. 256.
34. She was in her early forties.
35. Ōtsuki, *Ariake*, pp. 262–64.
36. I am reminded of *Arabella*, the opera by Richard Strauss, in which the younger sister is obliged to dress and act like a man in order to improve her sister's chances of making an advantageous marriage.
37. See Kuwabara, *Mumyō Zōshi*, p. 82, where it says, "The materials of *The Invisible-Making Cape* are so unusual, the book ought to be worth reading, but there are just too many things that one wishes weren't there. The language is exceedingly old-fashioned, and the poems are so bad that it is quite put in the shade if it is compared to *If I Could Only Change Them*. That is why so few people read it anymore."
38. Inaga Keiji, "San'itsu monogatari" in Ichiko Teiji (ed.), *Nihon Bungaku Zenshi: Chūko*, p. 383.
39. Tokumitsu Sumio, *Wagami ni tadoru Himegimi Monogatari Zenchūshaku*, and Imai Gen'e, *Wagami ni tadoru Himegimi*.
40. Imai Gen'e, *Wagami*, I, p. 151.
41. I shall refer to her hereafter as the Otowa princess, one of her titles, rather than "the Princess in search of her own identity," the nickname commonly used by Japanese commentators.
42. My interpretation of this difficult poem mainly follows that given by Imai Gen'e in *Wagami*, I, p. 38. Tokumitsu, *Wagami*, p. 19, scorns to explain the poem. Imai (p. 40) cannot resist quoting a section of the "Niou" chapter of *The Tale of Genji* which, he says, is being imitated in the poem. It is the passage where Kaoru, tormented by doubts concerning his identity, asks himself, *"Ika narikeru koto ni ka wa. Nan no chigiri nite, kō yasukaranu omoisoitaru mi ni shimo nariideteken."* (Quoted from Ishida Jōji and Shimizu Yoshiko (eds.), *Genji Monogatari*, VI, p. 167.) Edward Seidensticker's translation renders this: "He could only brood in solitude and ask what missteps in a former life could explain the painful doubts with which he had grown up." Edward Seidensticker (trans.), *The Tale of Genji*, II, p. 737.
43. Imai Gen'e, *Wagami*, I, p. 175, dates the work between 1268 and 1271. Tokumitsu, *Wagami*, pp. 6–7, gives the various explanations of why the quoted poems are from only the first four books.
44. Tokumitsu, *Wagami*, p. 10.
45. *Ibid.*, pp. 10–12.
46. Imai Gen'e, *Wagami*, V, 105.
47. *Ibid.*, pp. 11–13.
48. *Ibid.*, p. 44.
49. *Ibid.*, p. 80.
50. *Ibid.*, p. 82.
51. *Ibid.*, pp. 127–28.
52. *Ibid.*, p. 127.

53. The four monogatari with the largest number of poems included in the *Fūyōshū* are, in descending order, *The Tale of Genji*, *The Tale of the Hollow Tree*, *The Tale of Sagoromo*, and *The Pitiless Winds*. Only the opening chapters of the last-named work survive. See Ogi, *Kamakura*, pp. 292–312.
54. These are the dates of the submission to the emperor of the text of the anthology *Shin Chokusenshū* (1235) and the completion of the *Shoku Gosenshū* (1251). Poems from these collections are quoted in *Unspoken Yearning*. See Ogi Takashi, *Iwade Shinobu Monogatari Hombun to Kenkyū*, p. 39.
55. *Ibid*., p. 47.
56. Ogi, *Kamakura*, pp. 203–4.
57. It is true that Ipponnomiya seems to die in childbirth, the victim of a mono no ke, only to be revived by the prayers of a holy man (Ogi, *Iwade*, p. 355); but the reader is likely to obtain the impression that the resuscitation was due to natural rather than supernatural means. The mono no ke, in any case, was a familiar visitor, mentioned in almost every monogatari of the period, and accepted as a reality.
58. I call him by this name throughout, though in fact this is a title by which he is known only in part of the book; elsewhere his "name" changes as he rises in the hierarchy. At this point in the narration he is actually called Taishō.
59. Ogi, *Iwade*, p. 138.
60. *Ibid*., p. 143.
61. This surprisingly cool-headed statement is derived from *Gyokuyōshū* 1827 by Shunzei (but earlier found in his private collection). I have followed Ogi's interpretation of *uki ni kiesenu* in *Iwade*, p. 146.
62. She is characterized by Ogi, in *Iwade*, p. 50, as a "flapper" (*furappā*)!
63. *Ibid*., p. 218. There is a pun on *hima*, meaning the space between two people but also leisure; the poem means that there was no *hima* between the robes of Chūjō and the woman, and there was also no *hima* for Chūjō to admire the red leaves.
64. *Ibid*., p. 224.
65. *Ibid*., p. 237.
66. *Ibid*., p. 243. The original is: *"Ima wa, notamaiyamitaraba, ika ni ureshikaran."*
67. *Ibid*., p. 295.
68. There is a translation by Harold Parlett in "The Sumiyoshi Monogatari," pp. 37–123.
69. See Mitani Kuniaki, *Monogatari Bungaku no Hōhō*, I, pp. 373–91, for an eloquent presentation of this interpretation of *The Tale of Sumiyoshi*. He believed that Heian period stepmother stories were particularly rich in elements connected with the rite of passage of a girl into womanhood (p. 378): for example, the cellar where Ochikubo is confined represents the chamber where a girl was kept during her first menstruation.
70. Takeyama Takaaki in *Sumiyoshi Monogatari*, p. 101, gives several theories

of dating, including one that dates the revised version of the tale between 1219 and 1221, and another between 1202 and 1251. Inaga Keiji in Fujii Sadakazu and Inaga Keiji, *Ochikubo Monogatari, Sumiyoshi Monogatari*, p. 447ff, considered the work in three stages: the old text (*kohon*), the new edition (*shimpan*), and the revised edition (*kaisaku*). The old text would have been written at some time during the second half of the tenth century; the new edition at the end of the tenth century; and the revised edition at the end of the Heian or beginning of the Kamakura period.

71. Inaga suggested that revisions to the original version of *The Tale of Sumiyoshi* were made as early as 985–987; but even if some revisions go back to that time, others surely were made much later. For a brief discussion of the question, see Yoshiyama Hiroki, "Monogatari no Kaisaku," in Ii Haruki, *Monogatari Bungaku no Keifu*, pp. 164–66.
72. See Mitani, *Monogatari*, I, p. 380. The eminent scholar Origuchi Shinobu was one among those who considered *The Tale of Ochikubo*, *The Tale of Sumiyoshi*, and all other Heian stories of cruel stepmothers to be forgeries of the Kamakura period. For an excellent discussion of Heian marital life, see William H. McCullough, "Japanese Marriage Institutions in the Heian Period."
73. See Ikeda Yasaburō, *Bungaku to Minzokugaku*, pp. 42–189, for a comprehensive account of the theme of the mistreated stepchild in Japanese literature.
74. Takeyama, *Sumiyoshi*, pp. 40–41. See also Fujii and Inaga, *Ochikubo Monogatari, Sumiyoshi Monogatari*, pp. 316ff. For the *Ochikubo* reference, see above, p. 447.
75. Takeyama, *Sumiyoshi*, pp. 70–72. For a different text of the work, see Fujii and Inaga, *Ochikubo*, pp. 334–35. Chūjō's remark addressed to the pine is an altered version of *Kokinshū* 906: "Princess pine [*himematsu*] on the shore at Sumiyoshi, if you were only a human being I would ask you just how old you are."
76. For a good account of what is known about *The Pitiless Winds*, see Ogi, *Kamakura*, pp. 292–312.
77. This thesis is developed by Ichiko Teiji in *Chūsei Shōsetsu to sono Shūhen*, pp. 12ff.

Bibliography

Note: All Japanese books, except as otherwise noted, were published in Tokyo.

Chūko Bungaku Kenkyūkai (ed.) *Heian Kōki: Monogatari to Rekishi Monogatari*. Kasama Shoin, 1982.

Fujii Sadakazu and Inaga Keiji. *Ochikubo Monogatari, Sumiyoshi Monogatari*, in Shin Nihon Koten Bungaku Taikei series. Iwanami Shoten, 1989.

Hagitani Boku. *Matsuranomiya Monogatari.* Kadokawa Shoten, 1970.
Ichiko Teiji. *Chūsei Shōsetsu to sono Shūhen.* Tōkyō Daigaku Shuppankai, 1981.
———. *Nihon Bungaku Zenshi: Chūko.* Gakutōsha, 1978.
Ii Haruki. *Monogatari Bungaku no Keifu.* Kyoto: Sekai Shisōsha, 1986.
Ikeda Yasaburō. *Bungaku to Minzokugaku.* Iwasaki Bijutsusha, 1966.
Imai Gen'e. "Ōchō Monogatari no Shūen," *Kokugo to Kokubungaku* 31:10, 1954.
———. *Wagami ni tadoru Himegimi*, 7 vols. Ōfūsha, 1983.
Imai Takuji. *Monogatari Bungaku no Kenkyū: Kōki Monogatari.* Waseda Daigaku Shuppanbu, 1977.
Ishida Jōji and Shimizu Yoshiko (eds.). *Genji Monogatari*, in Shinchō Nihon Koten Bungaku Shūsei series. Shinchōsha, 1982.
Kannotō Akio. "Kamakura Jidai no Monogatari: 'Koke no Koromo' no Hōhō to Tokushitsu," in Nihon Bungaku Kyōkai (ed.), *Nihon Bungaku Kōza*, IV.
Kuwabara Hiroshi. *Chūsei Monogatari no Kisoteki Kenkyū.* Kazama Shobō, 1969.
———. *Mumyō Zōshi*, in Shinchō Nihon Koten Shūsei series. Shinchōsha, 1976.
Kyūsojin Hitaku. *Koke no Koromo*, 2 vols., in Koten Bunko series. Koten Bunko, 1954.
Lammers, Wayne P. *The Tale of Matsura: Fujiwara Teika's Experiment in Fiction.* Ann Arbor, Mich.: Center for Japanese Studies, University of Michigan, 1992.
Marra, Michele. *"Mumyōzōshi," Monumenta Nipponica* 39:2–4, 1984.
McCullough, William H. "Japanese Marriage Institutions in the Heian Period," *Harvard Journal of Asiatic Studies* 27, 1967.
Miner, Earl, Hiroko Odagiri, and Robert E. Morrell. *The Princeton Companion to Classical Japanese Literature*. Princeton, N.J.: Princeton University Press, 1985.
Mitani Eiichi and Imai Gen'e. *Tsutsumi Chūnagon Monogatari, Torikaebaya Monogatari*, in Kanshō Nihon Koten Bungaku series. Kadokawa Shoten, 1976.
Mitani Kuniaki. *Monogatari Bungaku no Hōhō*, 2 vols. Yūseidō, 1989.
Mulhern, Chieko Irie. "Cinderella and the Jesuits: An *Otogi-zōshi* Cycle as Christian Literature," *Monumenta Nipponica* 34:4, 1979.
Nihon Bungaku Kyōkai (ed.). *Nihon Bungaku Kōza*, IV. Taishūkan Shoten, 1987.
Ogi Takashi. *Iwade Shinobu Monogatari: Hombun to Kenkyū*. Kasama Shoin, 1977.
———. *Kamakura Jidai Monogatari no Kenkyū*. Yūseidō, 1984.
Ōtsuki Osamu. *Ariake no Wakare no Kenkyū*. Ōfūsha, 1969.
Parlett, Harold. "The Sumiyoshi Monogatari," *Transactions of the Asiatic Society of Japan* 29:1, 1901.
Raz, Jacob. "Popular Entertainment and Politics," *Monumenta Nipponica* 40:3, 1985.

Seidensticker, Edward. *The Tale of Genji*, 2 vols. New York: Alfred A. Knopf, 1976.

Seki Tsunenobu. *Ama no Karu Mo.* Yūbun Shoin, 1991.

Takeyama Takaaki. *Sumiyoshi Monogatari.* Yūseidō, 1987.

Tokumitsu Sumio. *Wagami ni tadoru Himegimi Monogatari Zenchūshaku*. Yūseidō, 1980.

Tsunoda, Ryusaku, Wm. Theodore de Bary, and Donald Keene. *Sources of Japanese Tradition*. New York: Columbia University Press, 1958.

21. DIARIES OF THE KAMAKURA PERIOD

The tradition of keeping diaries, begun in the Heian period, was maintained during the following centuries even after the emperor's court in Kyoto, the locus of most Heian diaries, had lost much of its authority. Some diaries, like those typical of the Heian period, were occupied mainly with descriptions of life at the court, but there were also many Kamakura-period diaries devoted to travel, either by pilgrims making their way to sacred sites or by litigants journeying from Kyoto to Kamakura to place petitions for the recovery of property and other suits before the law courts of the shogun.

No sharp line of demarcation can be drawn, however, between Heian and Kamakura diaries; some of the best-known examples from the late twelfth and early thirteenth centuries straddle both periods. As before, men tended to keep their diaries in Chinese, though diaries written by men in Japanese became more numerous; and the diaries of greatest literary interest continued to be those by women of the court.

One can easily form the impression on reading histories of the period that with the establishment of the shogunate in Kamakura the court in Kyoto suffered a mortal wound that left it with only a semblance of its former glory; but the diaries of the court ladies do not confirm this impression. Their descriptions of days filled with poetry-making and music seldom suggest that any diminution had occurred in the amenities enjoyed by the aristocrats. On the contrary, the diary entries maintain an air of such unruffled elegance that it is hard to remember that the years between the victory of the Minamoto in 1185 and the overthrow of the shogunate by the Emperor Godaigo in 1333 were troubled by rebellions, famine, earthquakes, and other calamities. The two abortive invasions by the Mongols in 1274 and 1281 were the worst but by no means the only perils that people at the court experienced. It is hard to imagine how they could have been so unaffected by these events that the pages of their diaries are devoted mainly to descriptions of the exquisite shadings of the robes worn by the ladies and gentlemen. Only those accounts kept at the very beginning and end of the period reveal how warfare affected the lives of the aristocrats.

The Poetic Memoirs of Lady Daibu

Kenreimon'in Ukyō no Daibu no Shū[1] (The Poetic Memoirs of Lady Daibu), the most affecting of the diaries that treat the end of the Heian and the beginning of the Kamakura periods, opens in 1174, when the Emperor Takakura is on the throne and the Taira family is in its heyday; it ends almost fifty years later with the poems she exchanged with Teika in 1232. On that occasion Teika informed her that he was compiling a new imperially sponsored collection of poetry (the *Shin Chokusenshū*) and asked if she had anything suitable to be included. He also asked under what name she would like to be known, to which she answered, "Just as I was known in the old days."[2] Her reply indicated that, despite all the time that had elapsed since the downfall of the Taira, she still considered that she was in their service.

Although the literary interest lies almost entirely in the prose sections, where Lady Daibu relates the backgrounds of her poems, she probably thought of the work as a collection of poetry. The poems are not of first quality, but they are nevertheless moving because of the circumstances under which they were composed. *The Poetic Memoirs* opens with an evocation of the brilliance of the court of the Emperor Takakura and his Empress Tokuko on the first day of the new year, 1174. "The two of them were, of course, always imposing, but on that day he in his formal attire and she in full court dress seemed to me quite dazzling, and as I watched from a passageway I felt in my heart:

kumo no ue ni	Here above the clouds
kakaru tsukihi no	I gaze upon the brilliance
hikari miru	Of such a sun and such a moon,
mi no chigiri sae	And I can only feel
ureshi to zo omou	How blissful is this fate of mine."[3]

This poem of unclouded joy has painfully ironic overtones: Takakura would die seven years later at the age of twenty, and his empress, the future Kenreimon'in, rescued against her will from the sea at Dannoura where her son, the boy Emperor Antoku, drowned, would end her days at the lonely convent Jakkō-in.

At first Lady Daibu observed the splendor of the court without becoming involved in the flirtations that formed the principal subject of gossip but, quite contrary to her intentions, she too acquired a lover: "Among the many men who used to mingle with us at all times of day and night, just like other ladies-in-waiting, there was one in particular who made approaches to me, though after seeing and hearing of other people's unhappy love affairs I felt I ought not to let anything of the sort happen to me. Destiny, however, is not to be avoided, and in spite of my resolve, I also came to know love's miseries."[4]

Lady Daibu's first affair was with Taira no Sukemori (1161?–1185), a son of Taira no Shigemori and grandson of Kiyomori. Sukemori was married and probably younger than Lady Daibu. From the commencement of their affair, her poems acquire a depth, a tragic dimension quite lacking in her earlier poetry. She did not disclose her lover's identity in the diary, but she supplied unmistakable clues, naming his father and the places he visited in his official capacity. She obviously fell deeply in love with Sukemori. She recalled, "One morning at my own home, as the snow lay thick, I was looking out at the unkempt garden and distractedly murmuring the lines 'The person who will come today,' when [Sukemori] appeared, unannounced, through the garden gate. . . . He looked so much smarter than I did, so splendid, that I can never forget it. Though the years and months have gone by, it seems so recent in my heart that the pain still haunts me."[5]

These words not only suggest the depth of her love for Sukemori but make it clear that she wrote this "diary" entry years after the events she described, perhaps as late as 1232, the year of the last datable entry.[6] Lady Daibu's love for Sukemori colored the rest of her life, but before long she acquired a new lover, Fujiwara no Takanobu (1142–1205), a poet and painter who is rememberd today especially for his superb portraits of Minamoto no Yoritomo and Taira no Shigemori. Her new lover may have been chiefly an agreeable companion; he certainly does not seem to have caused any change in her relations with Sukemori.

The second half of *The Poetic Memoirs* opens in an entirely different manner from the first half. In 1183 the Taira forces abandoned the capital after being defeated by Kiso no Yoshinaka. Sukemori had to leave with the other Taira supporters; before he left, he told her, "I have renounced all attachments to this world."[7] In the past this probably would have meant that he had decided to become a monk, but the new meaning was that he was sure he would be killed in battle and had prepared himself spiritually. She herself considered taking a nun's vows, or even committing suicide, but decided against such precipitate actions. However, in the next spring she heard terrible reports after the battle of Ichinotani that "great numbers of my friends had been killed, and that their heads were being paraded through the streets of the capital."[8] Taira no Shigemori, the father of her lover, had earlier figured in the diary as an amusing man who entertained the ladies of the palace with his stories. Now he had been taken prisoner at Ichinotani and brought back to the capital, to be turned over to the Nara monks for execution as punishment for having led the forces that burned the Tōdai-ji. One after another the Taira perished in the warfare. She wrote, "Whenever I meet anyone these days, I can only think what truly superior figures the Taira were."[9] Finally, in the spring of 1185, she learned that Sukemori was dead.

Several years later Lady Daibu, who had left the court after the defeat of the Taira, was persuaded to return, though it was now dominated by the Minamoto family, who had killed the Taira men she loved. She could not keep from contrasting unfavorably the Minamoto nobles to the Taira nobles she remembered: "Those whom I had known in the old days as courtiers of no great eminence were now in the highest ranks, and I could not help imagining how things might have been if Sukemori had only lived."[10]

The Poetic Memoirs of Lady Daibu conveys more poignantly than any other work of its period the pathos of defeat. The reader may find himself skipping the rather conventional waka to reach the continuation of the narrative, but the work as a whole lingers in the memory.

Chronicle of the Bright Moon

No diary of the late Heian and early Kamakura periods is as rich in literary and historical materials as *Meigetsuki* (Chronicle of the Bright Moon), kept by Fujiwara Teika between the years 1180 and 1235.[11] Even in its present state, marred by many gaps in the entries, some extending for years, it is an invaluable day-to-day account of life at the court during a period of dramatic changes in some of which Teika himself participated. Teika kept the diary in Chinese, as we might expect of a courtier, though perhaps not of one whose life was so closely involved with Japanese poetry. The original text is not easy to read, and many entries are of little interest except to those especially intrigued by matters of court routine; this adverse combination of language and content no doubt explains why such an important work has been so little studied.[12] A few oft-quoted entries are all that most readers know about the diary, despite Teika's exalted reputation as a poet and arbiter of poetic taste.

The literary value of *Chronicle of the Bright Moon* is impaired by the same factors that account for the restricted interest of the work. Teika's Chinese is not only difficult but is likely to cause the reader to imagine with irritation how much more enjoyable as literature the diary would have been if only Teika had kept it in Japanese. Occasionally, when he is particularly irritated over some rebuff or pleased by some gesture of recognition of his talent, Teika's emotions are so powerful that they transcend the barrier of the artificial language with its special rhetoric. It sometimes happens, too, that an entry which is as a whole of considerable interest may be weakened by unnecessary information. Teika was clearly not attempting to achieve literary elegance when he set down his account of each day.

Perhaps the worst fault of his diary as far as a modern reader is concerned is that Teika tells us so little about his private life. Unlike the court ladies who described their emotions so poignantly that we have no trouble in empathizing with them, or unlike Teika himself in his poetry, he is niggardly of words when it comes to feelings other than rage or satisfaction. We know from historical sources the name of his official consort, and we know also that he had twenty-seven children, but the various women in his life—the mothers of all those children—are not mentioned in his diary.

The nature of his relations with the celebrated poet Princess Shokushi, the relationship we would most like to know about, is never disclosed. In an entry for the third day of the first month of 1181 he mentions in the course of an account of people he called on that day, "I visited the former high priestess at Sanjō. (Today was my first visit. It was at her request. The fragrance of incense was pervasive.)"[13] Princess Shokushi had served as the high priestess of the Kamo Shrine, and it is clear that she was the person Teika visited. But only the mention of the fragrance suggests that it might have been more than a formal visit. Most of his subsequent visits to Princess Shokushi over the following years state no more than that he called at her residence. But in 1200, the year before Shokushi died, he visited her thirty-six times, and on two occasions noted in his diary that he did not leave until late at night.[14] It is tempting to imagine that, as in the Nō play *Teika*, these two great poets were lovers, but if they were, it makes it all the more disappointing that Teika had not a word to say about their affair. Perhaps he feared that others might read the diary; an affair between a noble not of the highest rank and an imperial princess might have reflected adversely on her virtue. On the other hand, Teika's utter recklessness when denouncing his enemies among the powerful statesmen makes it seem improbable he would have exercised such caution in the case of a love affair. We shall probably never know much more about Teika's personal life than what he chose to describe in *Chronicle of the Bright Moon*.

By far the best-known passage in the entire diary occurs in an entry dated the fourth year of the Jishō era (1180), when Teika was eighteen: "Reports of disturbances and punitive expeditions fill one's ears, but I pay them no attention. The red banners and the expeditions against the traitors are no concern of mine."[15] Even if, as has been suggested, this entry was actually written many years later, it reflects Teika's chosen indifference to the mundane matters that occupy most men. This, inevitably, was something of a pose: he could not escape involvement in the power struggles at the court, as we know from his relations with the Cloistered Emperor Gotoba.

Teika's diary covering the period when the two men saw each other regularly declared in unconditional superlatives his high opinion of the quality of Gotoba's poetry, though of course his praise must have been affected in some degree by the poet's exalted station. But for a rank amateur—unlike Teika, a professional poet who had been composing waka ever since he was a child—Gotoba was extraordinarily talented, and Teika in his diary again and again expressed his admiration: "Summoned early this morning, I entered His Majesty's presence, where I was commanded to examine his recent poetic compositions. When I opened the manuscript, it brought me a voice of gold and jade. At present there is absolutely nobody, high or low, who can touch him. Each and every poem is astonishing. I could not hold back the tears of joy."[16]

In 1201 Gotoba asked Teika to accompany him on a pilgrimage to Kumano. Teika was ecstatic that of all the many courtiers he had been selected to accompany the former sovereign. He declared in his diary that this was an honor beyond his deserts, though he also worried that his physical condition might not be equal to the difficult journey. (Two years earlier, when Gotoba had made one of his over thirty pilgrimages to Kumano, many of those in his party had fallen ill on the way, and courtiers were wary of invitations to accompany Gotoba, who seems to have had an unusually robust constitution, on subsequent pilgrimages.)[17] The journey involved not only worship at Kumano, at the time more favored even than Ise as a destination for an imperial pilgrimage, but at the many small shrines on the way. The party set out at dawn each day and traveled all day long for some twenty days. At some places the pilgrims were entertained by biwa hōshi, by bouts of sumo, and by shirabyōshi. There were many occasions for composing poems, as we know from the quotations in Teika's diary.

Teika described the same journey in another diary, *Gotoba-in Kumano Gokō Ki* (Account of the Visit of the Cloistered Emperor Gotoba to Kumano), also written in Chinese. This diary lacks the numerous outbursts of admiration for Gotoba's poems found in *Chronicle of the Bright Moon*, and Teika expressed no pleasure in the sights along the way, suggesting that the hardships of the journey had affected his spirits. Or perhaps the diary was composed later, after relations between the two men had cooled. They seem to have been on excellent terms at the time of the journey, despite Teika's silence; and in 1203, on the occasion of the ninetieth birthday[18] of Teika's father, Shunzei, Gotoba staged a huge birthday party at the Poetry Bureau he had established by way of preparation for compiling the *Shin Kokinshū*. This event is described in various other diaries,[19] but Teika wrote nothing in his diary that day, perhaps because he found the sight of his tottering old father too painful to describe. All the same, the lavishness of the celebration was proof of Gotoba's special respect not only for Shunzei but for Teika.

The first signs of a break between Gotoba and Teika did not surface until 1207, when Gotoba rejected one of the poems Teika had composed to be inscribed on a screen. By this time Teika had become fully aware of his own importance as a poet, and he was not accustomed to having his poems rejected. Years later Gotoba, after explaining why he had rejected the poem, mentioned that Teika had gone about mocking his judgment. From this point on their once-cordial relations continued to deteriorate until the final break in 1220, when (as we have seen) Teika, in response to importunate demands that he appear at court on the anniversary of his mother's death, composed two waka that indirectly expressed his resentment.[20]

There is a gap in the extant text of *Chronicle of the Bright Moon* between 1219 and 1225. This means we lack Teika's account of his break with Gotoba. We also lack his account of an even more important event, the Jōkyū Rebellion of 1221, when Gotoba and his son Juntoku unsuccessfully attempted to overthrow the Hōjō regents.[21] Gotoba was subsequently exiled to the Oki islands. Teika, who enjoyed friendly relations with the shogunate, had at one time served as a tutor in poetry to the third shogun, Sanetomo. When the extant diary resumes in 1225, Teika was back in the imperial favor, but the emperor this time was a prince chosen by the shogunate to replace Gotoba and his sons. On New Year's

Day of 1225 Teika joyfully wrote that "ignorant monarchs had been succeeded by a sage king," referring to an example in ancient China.[22] But if he expected peace and prosperity would follow, he was sadly deceived. The next years were marked instead by epidemics and famine. In 1230, after a summer so cold that snow fell in several provinces, Teika wrote in his diary, "Today I had my servants dig up the garden (the north one) and plant wheat. Even if we only grow a little, it will sustain our hunger in a bad year. Don't make fun of me! What other stratagem does a poor old man have?"[23]

The famine continued into the next year. Teika's diary mentions the dead bodies that filled the streets, and the stench that had gradually reached his house. It is small wonder that he wrote little poetry, but writing the diary must have been his most important activity. He nowhere stated why he kept writing day after day, despite his many ailments, but presumably it was to benefit his descendants by providing them with a detailed record of what happened in the past, and enabling them in this way to serve with authority at the court. The title *Chronicle of the Bright Moon* is something of a puzzle, considering the generally dark tone of the diary. The word *meigetsu* (bright moon) appears again and again in the entries for 1180 and 1181.[24] If these were in fact added much later, as scholars have suggested, mentions of the bright moon may have been intended to explain the title. However, in his *Maigetsushō* (Monthly Notes) Teika mentioned having given the same title, *Meigetsuki*, to a work of poetic criticism inspired by an auspicious dream he had of the spring moon while staying at the shrine of Sumiyoshi, the god of poetry.[25] Such a title would serve equally well for this diary in which he recorded the experiences of a lifetime of poetry.

Journey Along the Seacoast Road

Of the other surviving diaries by men of the Kamakura period, whether written in Chinese or Japanese, only one is of such exceptional literary value that it must be discussed, though the others all contain at least a few passages of interest.[26] The exception is *Kaidōki* (Journey Along the Seacoast Road), the account by an unknown man of his journey from Kyoto to Kamakura in 1223. The author states at the outset why he decided to make the journey: he had heard many glowing reports of the wonders of the new city of Kamakura, and he decided, when a favorable opportunity arose, to see the sights for himself. Although he tells us that he became a Buddhist priest shortly before leaving Kyoto, his motivation in traveling to Kamakura was by no means as serious as that of people of the same era who, as acts of penance or thanksgiving, made journeys to distant places that could be reached only after experiencing many hardships on the way.[27] All the same, this was no mere excursion: the author confesses that his despair over the failure of his life (he was about fifty at the time) had been so intense that he had considered suicide, and only his inability to throw himself into a pond had kept him from dying. Travel in his case was not a diversion, but an escape.

He was eager to get away from Kyoto not merely because he was curious about Kamakura but because his mother had lapsed into second childhood. It must have been painful to be with her, but hardly had he reached Kamakura than he felt obliged to rush back to Kyoto. He wrote, "I have an old mother in the capital. She has returned to infancy and longs for her foolish son."[28] His relations with his mother constantly preyed on his mind. He wondered if his neglect of his mother was the result of some sin committed in a previous existence: "Long ago, in my prime, I trusted in the future and prayed to heaven, but now, in my declining years, I think of the retribution from former lives and I hate myself."[29] He seems to have made the journey to escape for a while the heartrending spectacle of his mother reduced to senescence, but his conscience woud not let him remain in the city that was the object of his journey.

The most striking feature of *Journey Along the Seacoast Road* is its style. It is a new kind of Japanese known as *wakan konkō*, or "mixed Japanese and Chinese."[30] Although the language is basically Japanese, a large proportion of the words are of Chinese origin, and sometimes the sentence structure also shows marked Chinese influence. This gives a ponderous tone to the sentences, rather like English written with a heavy admixture of words of Latin origin; but the tone is appropriate to the somber content. The most affecting parts of the narrative refer to places along the way to Kamakura associated with the ill-fated Jōkyū Rebellion of 1221. The author professed admiration for the victors, the Hōjō regents, but he commiserated with those who had died in the effort to overthrow the rule of the regents, especially Nakamikado Muneyuki, the most brilliant member of Gotoba's entourage, who was captured and carried off toward Kamakura. At various stops he expected to be killed, and he composed a poem at each that he left on a pillar of the house where he stayed. The author of the diary, following Muneyuki's path, imagined his agony at each stop, until at last he reached the place where Muneyuki was actually put to death.

Journey Along the Seacoast Road, though it contains some lovely passages of description, is a thorny work. The style reflects the turbulence in the author's thoughts as he attempted to understand who he was and why he existed in a world in which he seemed to have no place. Unlike most travelers of this time or later, he did not repeat the clichés about the "famous places" he passed on his journey, but instead commented ironically, "Places one has often heard about do not necessarily appeal to the eye." He made no attempt to ingratiate himself with the readers—whoever they may have been—he anticipated for his diary, but his honesty and the seriousness with which he faced the world compel our admiration.

Tōkan Kikō (A Journey East of the Barrier) has often been paired with *Journey Along the Seacoast Road*, and some scholars have suggested that both diaries were composed by the same man. The resemblances, however, are slight. *A Journey East of the Barrier* is notable for its graceful Japanese prose, unencumbered by the Chinese rhetoric of the earlier work. The author, not at all like his tormented predecessor, was a gentleman of leisure who lived in the capital and followed "a path of life like most other people." For unknown reasons, he set out on a journey to the east in the autumn of 1242. He informs us that he kept his diary because "I thought that if I set down the various sights that had struck my eyes and the experiences that lingered in my memory, if anybody in the future still remembered such things with nostalgia, my account would of itself provide them with a memento."[31] It is baffling why this charmingly written though lightweight work has been traditionally associated with the dark *Journey Along the Seacoast Road*, but it is not difficult to imagine why its style and manner should have influenced the writing of similar diaries during the centuries to come.

The Diaries of Abutsu

The diaries of the nun Abutsu (d. 1283) seem to represent two ages of this literary form: *Utatane* (Fitful Slumbers), written when she was seventeen or eighteen, is in the tradition of the diary of the Heian court lady, but *Izayoi Nikki* (The Diary of the Waning Moon), the description of a journey from Kyoto to Kamakura taken late in her life, belongs to the new tradition of the Kamakura travel account. Of the two, *Fitful Slumbers* is literarily superior, at least when judged by our standards, but *The Diary of the Waning Moon* has attracted far more scholarly attention over the centuries.

Fitful Slumbers is the story of an unhappy love affair. The writer had her first affair with a man in the spring of a certain year (possibly 1240), but it is now the autumn, and his visits have become infrequent. As she lies awake at night she broods over her unhappiness, though she knows that brooding can do her no good. Perhaps, she thinks, writing a diary will bring relief.

Abutsu's lover was a married man and belonged to a class so much superior to her own that she could not hope, even after his wife died, that he would marry her. Like the author of *The Sarashina Diary*, Abutsu lived in two worlds, one of reality and the other of *The Tale of Genji*. Her intensely romantic feelings for a man who probably considered her to be only of passing interest probably reflected an unconscious hope that he would be like Genji, who never forgot or deserted a woman he had once loved. However, at the end of the year, Abutsu's lover ceased altogether to visit her.

Abutsu related in the diary that one night, as she sat in the moonlight thinking of him, tears came into her eyes, blotting out the moonlight, and at that moment she had a vision of Buddha. She thought for the first time that perhaps becoming a nun might bring her comfort. A month or so later, one night when everyone was asleep, she cut her hair, a gesture symbolizing her entering into Buddhist orders, and set out in the dark for a convent in a distant part of the capital. It started to rain, and soon her clothes, which were not intended for such excursions, were soaking wet, but Abutsu, with the determination she would reveal later in life, trudged on until the dawn. Two young women—country girls, as she inferred from their accents—found her and took her to the convent.

At first, the regular activities of the convent took her mind off her own misfortunes, but it was not long before she started to think of her lover again. She had taken refuge in the convent not to find Buddha but to forget the lover, and in this she failed. She wrote him, but his reply, alluding to his fear of what people might think, was cold. A poem she composed at the time indicates that her love for the man was tinged with contempt.

Not long afterward Abutsu left the convent, saying she was unwell and did not wish to cause any trouble. As she left the convent, by an extraordinary coincidence, her lover's carriage passed. She recognized his outriders, but made no sign. She never saw him again. Later, she went to live in the country at the house of her foster father, but she could not bear the place, and soon found an excuse to return to the capital. The diary concludes with a poem:

ware yori wa Though these words are sure
hisashikarubeki To last longer than myself,
ato naredo Even if he sees them,
shinobanu hito wa The man who has no love for me
aware to mo mieji Is not likely to be moved.[32]

The details of Abutsu's life after she returned to the capital are not clear, but she seems to have married twice. Her second husband was Fujiwara Tameie, Teika's son, with whom she had three sons. When Tameie died in 1275, there was uncertainty about which of his sons—Tameuji, his eldest son by an earlier marriage, or Tamesuke, Abutsu's second son—would succeed to his estate. Tameie's last will and testament named Tamesuke as his successor, but Tameuji, disregarding the will, took possession of the estate for himself. Abutsu decided to seek justice in the courts at Kamakura. *The Diary of the Waning Moon* is the account of her journey.[33]

One's opinion of the literary worth of the diary is likely to depend on one's evaluation of the eighty-eight waka and one chōka contained in the text. Each sight along the way inspired a poem that is generally marked by proficiency in such techniques of the waka as *kakekotoba, engo,* and *honka-dori*. The prose is also highly involved, as the opening words will suggest:

> Children today never dream that the title of the book discovered long ago in a wall has anything to do with them. Although what was written down by his brush, "from the hillside fields of arrowroot," is absolutely definite, the admonitions of a parent have been to no avail.[34]

In this passage Abutsu is complaining that Tameuji has disobeyed his father's instructions. He ignores the *Classic of Filial Piety* (the book found in a wall after the literary persecution of the first emperor of the Ch'in dynasty in the third century B.C.), acting as if its teachings were no concern of his, and has appropriated the estate his father meant to leave to Tamesuke. The phrase "from the hillside fields of arrowroot" is mainly decorative, though it is connected to the main text by poetic allusions. This kind of writing appealed to Japanese who could easily recognize the meanings hidden behind the involuted language, but a reader today might read the entire text of *The Diary of the Waning Moon* without becoming aware of the central theme, Abutsu's determination to secure the disputed manor at Hosokawa for her son Tamesuke.

At only one point in the narration do we sense behind the armor in which Abutsu now clad herself that there was still something of the girl who had written *Fitful Slumbers*. When she reached Hamamatsu, where she had spent an unhappy month at the home of her foster father after leaving the convent, she remembered the place with a nostalgia we might not expect of the mature Abutsu, and sent for the children and grandchildren of the people she knew in Hamamatsu so many years before.[35] She reached Kamakura without further incident, only to wait there fruitlessly for a favorable verdict. Thirty years after her death Tamasuke was at last awarded the disputed estate.

Abutsu also appears in the diary of Asukai Masaari (1241–1301), the fifth-generation descendant of a family that had continuously served the court as masters of kemari. He himself attained high rank at the court, mainly because of his proficiency at kemari, but he was also a scholar of Japanese poetry and prose. A diary entry for 1269, written while he was recuperating from an illness at Saga (northwest of Kyoto), states that he had made the acquaintance of Abutsu's husband, Tameie. He wrote, "His family and mine had known each other for generations, so we came to meet from time to time in a friendly way. He lent me *The Tosa Diary*, *The Murasaki Shikibu Diary*, *The Sarashina Diary*, *The Gossamer Years*, and other books. The authors being women, they wrote in *kana*. . . . Though I am a man, I intend to use *kana*, because there are precedents in this country. Even *The Tales of Ise* was written in Japanese script. Of course, when one is writing about formal matters, Chinese is to be preferred, and for this reason, I myself have used Chinese when writing in that vein. But when writing about poetry and suchlike matters, I have thought it preferable to use *kana*, and I shall continue to do so, adding to my account events of the past as I remember them."[36]

This passage provides invaluable information about two aspects of diary literature: the first is Masaari's statement that he borrowed the manuscripts of four diaries, firm evidence that the Heian diaries by this time circulated as works of literature and were consulted by persons intending to write literary diaries of their own, much as prospective novelists prepared themselves by reading *The Tale of Genji*; the second gives the justification for men keeping diaries in Japanese during the Kamakura period. The four diaries Masaari mentioned are the very ones that a modern reader would most likely choose among the Heian diaries, further evidence that they had attained the status of classics.

Masaari mentions later on that, when he paid a visit to the Cloistered Emperor Gofukakusa, the latter, "unlocking his storeroom, took out a number of old diaries written in *kana* and, since he knew I had long wanted to see them, he urged me to do so."[37]

Manuscripts were valuable possessions. Quite apart from their extrinsic value, those of the kind Teika's sons inherited contained priceless revelations of the secret teachings of the masters of the past, and were treasured by the possessors as proof they had special qualifications for teaching others.[38] Masaari was probably given access to these manuscripts because of the prestige of his family; but his diary provides evidence that he was passionately devoted to Heian literature. Tameie, impressed by the devotion to his studies of a man better known as an expert kemari player, inducted him into the secret traditions of the *Kokinshū*.

Masaari also studied *The Tale of Genji* with Abutsu in 1269. They read together the entire work in twenty-six sessions that extended for somewhat over two months. After each session sake was served, and a more informal atmosphere prevailed. On one occasion Abutsu called Masaari close to her curtained enclosure, and told him about the love of poetry that was shared by her own and her husband's ancestors. She continued, "It was wonderful how they used to enjoy themselves by indulging this way in conversations about the charm of the old novels. People nowadays are not like that any more, but you make me feel you are a person of long ago."[39]

The trembling girl who had written *Fitful Slumbers* was hard to recognize in the resolutely determined woman who went to do battle for her son at the courts in Kamakura, and the devil-may-care young man whose earlier diaries told of spending the night drinking with friends or disporting himself with prostitutes does not resemble the scholar who regularly went to Abutsu's house to hear her lectures; but somewhere deep within them a mutual love for the poetry and prose of the Heian past had brought together even such dissimiliar diarists.

The Diary of Lady Ben

Ben no Naishi Nikki (The Diary of Lady Ben) was probably written by a court lady soon after she retired from service in 1259. We do not know how old she was at this time, nor her reasons for giving up her life at the court (though the abdication of the Emperor Gofukakusa in that year may have been a contributing cause), but her diary is unusual in the precision with which she dated the entries. The prevailingly cheerful tone also sets off this diary from most diaries kept by court ladies, written in moods of bittersweet nostalgia. Lady Ben rarely looked back at the past: she was interested in whatever was new and in fashion. She described the latest dances and songs and even (in gory detail) a cockfight.

Perhaps the most typical entry in the diary relates how, after she had served as a court emissary to a festival, she suddenly felt an urge to see her sister at the Women's Ceremonial Office, and asked that her carriage be driven there. Her escort refused, saying it was too late to take such a roundabout route, but she insisted, saying it was the custom for the emissary to call at that place after the festival. Obviously, she had invented the "custom" on the spur of the moment, but she convinced the man, who yielded, saying, "Well, if there really is such a precedent . . ." When the carriage reached the office it was so late that the gatekeeper was reluctant to let them in. This time Lady Ben's escort, by now persuaded that there really was such a custom, scolded the gatekeeper for his ignorance, much to Lady Ben's amusement. The Japanese fondness for citing precedents has seldom been mocked with such charm.[40]

Perhaps the best-known episode in the diary occurred in the first month of 1251, on the day when Full Moon rice gruel was served in the palace. One element in the festivities consisted in hitting people on the behind with sticks. The emperor commanded the ladies of the court to watch for a chance to hit Tameuji (Abutsu's stepson), but Tameuji got in the first blow, whacking Lady Shōshō when she moved her curtains a bit. Two days later Shōshō got her revenge with the assistance of the retired emperor, who kept the stick hidden under his cloak. Shōsho sprang on the unsuspecting Tameuji as he was bowing respectfully to the retired emperor, and she hit him so hard that the stick nearly broke.[41]

The element of fun in this and other passages in the diary is typical of Lady Ben. Her diary lacks the intensity we find in the other diaries of court ladies, but the humor is welcome because it is so rare. There must have been other ladies at the court who were as charmingly frivolous as Lady Ben, but they seem not to have kept diaries.

The Diary of Lady Nakatsukasa

Nakatsukasa no Naishi no Nikki (The Diary of Lady Nakatsukasa) has often been discussed by critics in terms of its gloomy atmosphere. In comparison to the frivolous Lady Ben, with whom she is frequently paired, Lady Nakatsukasa may indeed seem in her diary to reflect a tragic awareness of the passing of beauty, but there is no gloom; her delight in the world around her is what makes the diary memorable. An early entry in this diary (which describes life at the court between 1280 and 1292) suggests its characteristic tone:

> The rain, which had fallen since dusk, cleared up as it grew late, and the moonlight, shining so brightly that the sky itself seemed different, was lovely. People came from the crown prince's palace to enjoy the moon. The enchanting mist in the air, the dew still sparkling unclouded, and the cries of the insects, singing in their different voices, all combined to produce an unforgettable impression. Drops of dew, shivering heartbreakingly as the wind caught them, gave a special light to the pine branches. They looked like precious jewels of the Buddha, and I thought that not even the jewel of the Buddha at Sagano could be more beautiful.

onozukara	It did not take long
shibashi mo kienu	For them to vanish of themselves.
tanomi ka wa	Can one depend on them?
nokibe no matsu ni	The drops of white dew hanging
kakaru shiratsuyu	On the pine trees by the eaves.[42]

There is perhaps nothing remarkable about this passage, but it perfectly conveys the emotions evoked by an autumn evening. The poem reveals Lady Nakatsukasa's poignant awareness of the transitory nature of such beauty, but this is not a rejection of the ephemeral charms of this world in the manner of Buddhist writers who spurned it because their hearts were set on the eternal beauty of the world to come. Lady Nakatsukasa loved the beautiful things of this world, though their perishability induced tears. Yet perishability itself was a necessary condition of beauty, as the priest Kenkō would write about fifty years later.[43]

The prevailing impression one receives from Nakatsukasa's diary is of an exquisitely refined court whose members delighted in playing and listening to music, especially music heard while in a boat in the moonlight. It is tempting to quote passage after passage: her descriptions of evenings spent making music are without exception lovely. The problem is not that the diary is despondent but that it presents so attractive a picture of court life that the reader may wonder: were there no instances of rivalry among the courtiers? no harsh exchanges of words? no women seduced against their will? We know, as a matter of fact, from *The Confessions of Lady Nijō* that all these ugly elements were present, but Nakatsukasa did not wish to write about such matters. She was not making a confession and had no intention of exposing the seamier side of court life. But she could not bear the thought that the beauty she had witnessed might someday be forgotten.

Nakatsukasa was not interested in politics. She did not even mention the abortive Mongol invasion of 1281, and paid no attention to court gossip. She seems to have sensed, however, that the world she had known would not last much longer, and in her diary she preserved it for all time.

The Confessions of Lady Nijō

Towazugatari, the title of the diary in which Lady Nijō recorded events from 1271 to 1306, means literally "A Tale Nobody Asked For." This unpromising title has been more happily rendered by the translator as *The Confessions of Lady Nijō*.[44] The unique manuscript of the work was discovered in 1940,[45] but since then it has gained recognition as one of the major works of Japanese literature.

The diary opens on New Year's Day of 1271. That day Koga Masatada, a distinguished official and poet, served the traditional spiced wine to the Retired Emperor Gofukakusa.[46] After he had become quite inebriated, the retired emperor murmured to Masatada, "Let the wild goose of the fields come to me this spring." This allusion to a poem in *Tales of Ise* meant that the retired emperor wanted Masatada to send him his daughter, Nijō, who would be fourteen (thirteen by Western reckoning) that spring. Masatada was far from being insulted by this proposal; in fact, he was absolutely delighted at the prospect of forming such a connection with the imperial family.

Ten days later, Nijō was summoned home by her father's command. She was surprised to see how lavishly the house had been decorated and asked the reason. Her father told her that the retired emperor would be stopping here in order to avoid travel in a prohibited direction, and he urged her to do exactly what he would ask of her. Nijō fell asleep, and when she opened her eyes the retired emperor was lying beside her. He told her he had loved her ever since she was a small child, but she could only weep by way of response. He did not attempt to force her that night, but the next night he came to her room again, and this time he treated her so mercilessly that her gowns were torn to shreds.

She wrote, "By the time I had nothing more to lose I despised my own existence."[47]

She had been raped with the connivance of her own father by a man she trusted. The rape may have been less upsetting to people at the court in Nijō's day than it is to us. Had not the peerless Genji done much the same to his young ward, Murasaki? And did not Murasaki's resentment soon give way to love for Genji? Genji's behavior probably seemed to most readers to be not only forgivable but inevitable. The shock to Nijō was real, but by the time she was seeing off the retired emperor after their night together, she discovered that her indignation had dissipated. She wrote, "I felt more attracted to him than ever before, and I wondered uneasily where these new feelings had come from."[48] She would make similar comments after several other encounters with men, each time expressing surprise that her feelings of revulsion had inexplicably changed into something like affection.

Nijō had four children, one by Gofukakusa, another by the first of her two main lovers (the one she referred to in the diary as "Snow at Daybreak"), and the remaining two by the man she loved most of all, an eminent priest whom she gave the nickname of "Moon at Dawn." The acquisition of these lovers did not cause any crisis in her relations with Gofukakusa; in fact, they became more intimate than ever, though each was fully aware of the infidelities of the other. Gofukakusa at times even arranged for Nijō to give herself to men. In the most shocking incident of the diary, a man seized Nijō's sleeve in the dark. She managed to escape, but the next night, while she was massaging Gofukakusa, the same man called through the door that he would like to see her for a moment. She continues, "The Retired Emperor then whispered to me, 'Hurry up, go. You have nothing to worry about.' I was so embarrassed I wanted to die. Then His Majesty reached out, and seizing my hand, he pulled me up. Without intending it, I was compelled to go."[49]

Nijō and the man made love in the next room, separated from the retired emperor only by a paper partition. "Though he feigned sleep I was wretchedly aware that he was listening," she commented. The next night the same man returned, and the retired emperor again urged Nijō to go to him. His action suggests not so much generosity as contempt for her as a woman (as well as his own voyeurism), but Nijō, with her incredible candor, concluded this chapter of the diary with a description of the departure of the lover of the previous nights in these terms: "For some reason I gazed after my visitor's carriage as though I regretted our parting. When, I wonder, did such feelings arise in my own heart?"[50]

Nijō's deepest emotions were aroused by the priest she called "Moon at Dawn." He was a half-brother of Gofukakusa, and was otherwise known as the Cloistered Prince Shōjo. One evening, after he had been praying at the palace for Gofukakusa's recovery from illness, he followed Nijō into a small room, where he told her, "Even when we walk in paths of darkness we are guided by the Lord Buddha."[51] He embraced her, and insisted that she come to him after the final service that night. She recalled, "My heart was not entirely possessed by love, and yet late that night, seen by no one, I slipped out and went to him." From then on they met almost every night.

One day, after Gofukakusa had summoned the priest, he was called away, and "Moon at Dawn" seized the opportunity to tell Nijō how much he yearned for her. The retired emperor returned unexpectedly soon and stood behind a partition, listening to the complaints of "Moon at Dawn," who thought Nijō did not return his love. Far from being upset to hear these protestations, Gofukakusa urged Nijō to be kinder to his half-brother and in this way to free him of his attachment. She remarked, "I wonder why he was not feeling aggrieved."[52]

The fourth of the five books of *The Confessions of Lady Nijō* opens with the abrupt disclosure that Nijō had become a nun and was about to leave the capital on a pilgrimage. Even after putting on a nun's somber habit, she continued to think of the past, especially of the love Gofukakusa had shown her. Unable to keep these memories to herself, she decided to write what she called *itazuragoto*, "a piece of mischief."

The style of Nijō's diary on the surface resembles that of the diaries kept by women of the Heian court three hundred years before. The text opens with a *makurakotoba* that leads into mention of the rising of the spring mists, as in countless other examples of poetry and prose; but it does not take Nijō long to leave behind these conventional flourishes and to enter into her startlingly frank account of her life. On occasion she quotes lines from the *Kokinshū* and other imperial collections, and her diary is interspersed with poems of her own composition, but these touches of elegance are not what make her confessions memorable. No doubt there is artistry in the presentation of her experiences, but it is the experiences themselves and the candor with which she relates them that give *The Confessions of Lady Nijō* its unique appeal. For example, after she has been raped by Gofukakusa, she composed this poem:

kokoro yori	It was not my wish
hoka ni tokenuru	That he should untie the strings
shita hibo no	Of my underclothes.

ika naru fushi ni On what occasions will this
ukina nagasan Stir up rumors I am wanton?

The subject matter is unconventional, but the poem itself is hardly beautiful. Even more striking than the poem is her appended comment (presumably written years later): "I continued to brood in this manner, but it is most surprising I still maintained such composure."[53] Her ability to see herself objectively is one of the most memorable features of the work.

The immediate impulse for writing these confessions may have been the need Nijō felt to record her pilgrimages to the various holy sites described in the last two books, but the first three books do not suggest she repented of her sins. She seems to hide nothing, and this induces us to accept without question her account not only of herself but of life at the court, especially the amorous intrigues in which emperors, chancellors, high-ranking courtiers, and priests all participated. She also mentions (but in parts of the diary one tends to forget) evenings of music-making and composing poetry, the aspect of court life Lady Nakatsukasa so beautifully evoked. Neither she nor Nijō can be trusted fully as a court chronicler, but each provides an unforgettable portrait of the author.

Account of the Takemuki Palace

Takemuki ga Ki (Account of the Takemuki Palace) is the diary kept between 1329 and 1349 by the court lady Hino Nako.[54] It is not as artistically satisfying as the diaries of other court ladies, but it has the melancholy importance of being the last of a tradition begun with *The Gossamer Years*. The name refers to the palace where Nako lived when she wrote the latter half of the work.

The first of the two books of the diary is devoted mainly to the love shared by Nako and Saionji Kimmune before they were torn apart by the warfare waged by adherents of the Southern Court and the Northern Court. After the rather stiffly written opening, a highly dramatic incident is reported: the disappearance from his palace of the Emperor Godaigo, taking with him the imperial regalia. It will be recalled that this action, which took place in the eighth month of 1331, initiated the bitter conflict between the Southern Court (Godaigo's adherents) and the Northern Court (the faction of the Emperor Kōgon, placed on the throne by the shogunate). Nako's family was deeply involved in the conflict: one uncle,

Hino Suketomo, colluded with Godaigo and was executed by the shogunate, but Nako's husband and most of her family were supporters of the Northern Court.

The first book of the diary contains detailed descriptions of festivals and entertainments at the palace. Her account of the coronation of the Emperor Kōgon in 1332, probably written years after the event, recalled the splendor of the occasion:[55] "The sight of His Majesty in his formal robes and jeweled headdress, his sceptre held at precisely the right angle, added an extraordinary dignity. . . . The smoke rising from the incense burners seemed to be the same color as the clouds, and I thought I heard someone say that even in China they would be able to tell that a new reign had begun in Japan."[56] Nako had an extraordinary memory for precisely what each person had worn on this occasion. One may gather from the diary with what mixed emotions she recalled in later years the magnificence of the coronation, with its exotic "Chinese" decorations, persuading her that even in China people would learn of so auspicious an event; but by the time she wrote these words, she knew how turbulent the new reign would be.

Soon afterward, Nako met Saionji Kimmune, and from then on there are mentions in the diary of seeing him "at the usual place," presumably somewhere away from the court. Their happiness was interrupted early in 1333 when news reached them that Godaigo had escaped from his place of exile in the Oki islands and was on his way to the capital. People flocked to the court to hear the latest rumors, and the streets were so jammed that the lovers were unable to meet. The Emperor Kōgon and the two retired emperors moved to the headquarters of the shogunate at Rokuhara, to be under the protection of the military. Nako went there because she was reluctant to leave the emperor without any ladies-in-waiting to serve him.

Nako was appalled by what she saw at Rokuhara, especially "to see savages so close at hand." The word "savages" (*ebisu*) referred not to foreign barbarians but to armed warriors from Kamakura; it suggests how frightening she found their military attire. Kimmune sent her a message saying he had managed to arrange a meeting. They spent the night together, and were loth to admit that daybreak had come:

> The sight of the dawn brightening the sky surely would have been moving even if today had not had any special significance, but at the thought that this was our last time, as we confusedly sensed the terrible pathos of love, we knew that whether we left or stayed there we could only be all the more forlorn.[57]

On the seventh day of the fifth month the Southern Court army surrounded Rokuhara and set the place afire. Nako's house was nearby, and she could all but see her lover trying to escape in the smoke. She learned that he had succeeded in making his way to the east. Two weeks later the Emperor Kōgon and the others of the Northern Court were brought back to Kyoto. Nako discovered that her father and eldest brother were now wearing priests' robes. Kimmune also wished to become a priest, but the retired emperors ordered him to abandon this thought. At the end of the first book Nako and Kimmune are at a loss what to do. She wrote, "I wonder if there is still anything left for me to relate in this pointless account that nobody asked to hear."[58]

The second volume opens with a description of the ceremony during which her son, Sanetoshi, ate fish for the first time. He was two years old, and the diary takes him up to the age of fourteen, when he had already received the title of middle captain and middle counselor of the Third Rank. The second volume is far less dramatic than the first. Kimmune is already dead, but the manner of his death, related in the *Taiheiki*, is not given in the diary, understandably, considering the dreadful circumstances. Kimmune was betrayed by his younger brother and arrested in the sixth month of 1335. The Southern Court officials decided to exile him to the province of Izumo. The night before his departure Nako secretly went to his place of confinement. She found him in a tiny cell, trussed and unable to move. He gave her for their unborn child, as a memento of the father the child would never see, some secret pieces for the biwa and an amulet. Kimmune was then turned over to Nawa Nagatoshi, the governor of Hōki, in preparation for his departure the next morning at dawn. Nako watched from behind a fence as Kimmune was dragged to the central gate. Just as he was about to be shoved into a palanquin, an official called out, "Quickly [*haya*]!" and Nagatoshi, supposing this meant he should dispose of Kimmune quickly, forced him to the ground, drew his sword, and cut off Kimmune's head, all within sight of Nako.[59]

We are likely to regret that Nako in her diary did not describe this and other tragic sights she witnessed, but perhaps the vocabulary and manner she inherited from the Heian diarists did not permit her to describe such violence. Probably she wrote the diary not for posterity but for her son Sanetoshi, to tell him about his parents before he was born. Regardless of the literary value of this diary, it powerfully suggests what it was like to live in an age of great turbulence. But the absence of diaries by women of the following two centuries suggests that worse was yet to come. The kind of education and leisure that even an unhappy woman like Nako enjoyed would be denied to most women during the age of warfare.

Notes

1. The title means literally, "Collection of the Kenreimon'in Superintendent of the Right-hand Half of the Capital." Kenreimon'in was the name given to the Empress Tokuko, the consort of the Emperor Takakura, after she entered Buddhist orders; the author of the diary served Kenreimon'in and was therefore known by her name. It has been suggested that her father was the superintendent of the Right-hand Half of the Capital, and she took his title, a not uncommon practice, but there is no record of his ever having held this office.
2. Translation by Phillip Tudor Harries in *The Poetic Memoirs of Lady Daibu*, p. 285; text in Itoga Kimie, *Kenreimon'in Ukyō no Daibu no Shū*, p. 16.
3. Translation by Harries, *Poetic Memoirs*, p. 79; text in Itoga, *Kenreimon'in*, pp. 9–10
4. Harries, *Poetic Memoirs*, p. 111; Itoga, *Kenreimon'in*, p. 33.
5. Harries, *Poetic Memoirs*, p. 141; Itoga, *Kenreimon'in*, p. 57.
6. For further information on dating (and on many other matters concerning the work), see the introduction by Harries to *Poetic Memoirs*. The dating of the diary is discussed on pages 20–27 of the introduction.
7. Harries, *Poetic Memoirs*, p. 191; Itoga, *Kenreimon'in*, p. 98.
8. Harries, *Poetic Memoirs*, p. 197; Itoga, *Kenreimon'in*, p. 103.
9. Harries, *Poetic Memoirs*, p. 199; Itoga, *Kenreimon'in*, p. 105.
10. Harries, *Poetic Memoirs*, p. 261; Itoga, *Kenreimon'in*, p. 151.
11. The authenticity of the early entries was questioned by Tsuji Hikosaburō who, on the basis of the study of the handwriting, concluded that Teika added these entries late in life. See Tsuji Hikosaburō, *Fujiwara Teika Meigetsuki no Kenkyū*, pp. 94–99. If this opinion is accepted, the earliest entries date from 1188.
12. Two volumes of a more or less popular nature have appeared in recent years, *Teika Meigetsuki Shishō* and *Teika Meigetsuki Shishō Zokuhen*, both by Hotta Yoshie. (I shall refer to these books as Hotta I and Hotta II.) Hotta, in I, p. 15, gave a typical entry from *Chronicle of the Bright Moon* (for the eleventh day of the third month of 1202) and followed it with the comment (p. 16) that except for the mention of the bright moonlight at the opening, the entry is unmitigatedly dreary and prolix. But even such an entry, for all its lack of literary interest, effectively conveys how frantically busy Teika was that day, and his detailed descriptions of costumes suggest the brightness of colors at the court.

13. Imagawa Fumio, *Kundoku Meigetsuki*, I, 21. See also Hotta I, pp. 29–51. This entry is from the period whose dating Tsuji Hikosaburō found suspect; but it is perhaps even more affecting if Teika in old age recalled his first meeting with Shokushi in these terms.
14. See Hotta I, p. 153. Shokushi died in the first month of 1201, but this month is missing from the present text of *Chronicle of the Bright Moon* and Teika did not later refer to her death.
15. Text in Imagawa, *Kundoku*, I, p. 19. For further discussion of this passage, see Keene, *Travelers of a Hundred Ages*, p. 95.
16. Imagawa, *Kundoku*, I, p. 263. See also Hotta I, p. 154.
17. See Hotta I, p. 160. Text in Imagawa, *Kundoku*, I, pp. 144, 267.
18. Only eighty-nine by Western count; Shunzei was born in 1114.
19. For example, the diary of Minamoto Ienaga. See my *Travelers*, p. 106.
20. See above, pp. 670–71. Hotta II, pp. 112–15, gives a good explanation of why Gotoba was so annoyed with the poems.
21. See above, p. 672.
22. Imagawa, *Kundoku*, IV, p. 73.
23. *Ibid.*, V, p. 192.
24. Hotta I, p. 38, considers the title, but comes to no conclusion as to why Teika called his diary by that name.
25. For a translation, see Robert H. Brower, "Fujiwara Teika's *Maigetsushō*," p. 422. Brower translated *meigetsu* as "full moon." See also Brower's comments (p. 405) on the poetic treatise *Meigetsuki*. Text of *Monthly Notes* in Hisamatsu Sen'ichi and Nishio Minoru. *Karon Shū, Nōgakuron Shū*, p. 136. See also *ibid.*, p. 258.
26. The diaries in Japanese are discussed in my *Travelers*, pp. 103–28 and 141–44.
27. Interesting European parallels to the medieval Japanese pilgrimages are described in Donald R. Howard's *Writers & Pilgrims*. There was, however, no Japanese holy site that had quite the authority of Jerusalem as a destination for a pilgrimage.
28. Quoted in my *Travelers*, pp. 116–17. Text in Noro Tadasu, *Kaidōki Shinchū*, p. 208.
29. Keene, *Travelers*, p. 117. Text in Noro, *Kaidōki Shinchū*, p. 205.
30. A detailed discussion of the style, especially its indebtedness to the Chinese *shiroku benreitai* or "parallel prose" of the Six Dynasties, is given by Tamai Kōsuke in *Nikki Bungaku no Kenkyū*, pp. 460–65.
31. Keene, *Travelers*, p. 127. Text in Kasamatsu Yoshio, *Tōkan Kikō Shinshaku*, pp. 5–6
32. Translation in Keene, *Travelers*, p. 135. Text in Tsugita Kasumi, *Utatane Zenchūshaku*, p. 121.
33. There is a complete translation of the diary by Edwin O. Reischauer in Edwin O. Reischauer and Joseph K. Yamagiwa, *Translations from Early Japanese Literature*.

34. Translation in Keene, *Travelers*, p. 138. Text in Morimoto Motoko, *Izayoi Nikki, Yoru no Tsuru*, p. 15.
35. Text in Morimoto, *Izayoi*, p. 73. See Reischauer and Yamagiwa, *Translations*, p. 74.
36. Translation in Keene, *Travelers*, pp. 141–42. Text in Mizukawa Yoshio in *Asukai Masaari Nikki Zenshaku*, pp. 43–48.
37. Keene, *Travelers*, p. 142; Mizukawa, *Asukai*, pp. 44–49.
38. The possession of scrolls that reveal secret information on techniques of performance still contributes to the authority of the *iemoto* (head) of some schools of Nō.
39. Translation from Keene, *Travelers*, p. 144. Text in Mizukawa, *Asukai*, pp. 61–65.
40. See Keene, *Travelers*, p. 146. Text in Tamai Kōsuke, *Ben no Naishi Nikki Shinchū*, p. 24.
41. Keene, *Travelers*, p. 148. Tamai, *Ben no Naishi*, pp. 230–32.
42. Keene, *Travelers*, pp. 149–50; original text in Tamai Kōsuke, *Nakatsukasa no Naishi Nikki Shinchū*, p. 8. The statue of Shakyamuni Buddha at a temple in Saga (or Sagano), to the northwest of Kyoto, was believed to be of Indian origin and the closest approximation of the historical Buddha's appearance. The jewel, here called *nyoihōju*, could bring the possessor whatever he desired.
43. See below, pp. 859–60.
44. This is the name Karen Brazell gave her translation, first published in 1973. The translation by Wilfrid Whitehouse and Eizo Yanagisawa is equally free: *Lady Nijō's Own Story*.
45. It was discovered by Yamagishi Tokuhei, a scholar of Japanese literature. The stringencies of wartime publication delayed the appearance of a printed version of the text until 1950, and an annotated edition was not published until 1966.
46. Gofukakusa (1243–1304; reigned 1246–59) abdicated in favor of his brother Kameyama (1249–1305; reigned 1259–74). In 1271, when the work opens, Gofukakusa was twenty-eight.
47. Brazell, *Confessions*, p. 8; text in Tomikura Tokujirō, *Towazugatari*, p. 210.
48. Brazell, *Confessions*, p. 9; Tomikura, *Towazugatari*, p. 210.
49. Brazell, *Confessions*, p. 118; Tomikura, *Towazugatari*, p. 284.
50. Brazell, *Confessions*, p. 120; Tomikura, *Towazugatari*, p. 284.
51. Brazell, *Confessions*, p. 80; Tomikura, *Towazugatari*, p. 258.
52. Brazell, *Confessions*, p. 124; Tomikura, *Towazugatari*, p. 287.
53. Tomikura, *Towazugatari*, p. 210. See also Brazell, *Confessions*, pp. 8–9.
54. The reading of her name is not certain. Scholars tend to call her Meishi, using the Sino-Japanese pronunciation of the characters; but we can be quite sure she was *not* called Meishi, and she *might* have been called Nako.
55. The occasion is described in quite other terms in *The Clear Mirror*; see below, pp. 902–3.

56. Mizukawa Yoshio, *Takemuki ga Ki Zenshaku*, p. 55.
57. *Ibid.*, p. 125.
58. *Ibid.*, p. 140.
59. Yamashita Hiroaki, *Taiheiki*, II, p. 280.

Bibliography

Note: All Japanese books, except as otherwise noted, were published in Tokyo.

Brazell, Karen. *The Confessions of Lady Nijō*. Garden City, N.Y.: Doubleday, 1973.

Brower, Robert H. *Fujiwara Teika's Hundred-Poem Sequence of the Shōji Era, 1200*. Tokyo: Sophia University, 1978.

———. "Fujiwara Teika's *Maigetsushō*," *Monumenta Nipponica* 40:4, Winter 1985.

Fukuda Hideichi. *Towazugatari*, in Shinchō Nihon Koten Shūsei series. Shinchōsha, 1978.

Fukuda Hideichi and H. E. Plutschow. *Nihon Kikō Bungaku Benran*. Musashino Shoin, 1975.

Harries, Phillip Tudor. *The Poetic Memoirs of Lady Daibu*. Stanford, Calif.: Stanford University Press, 1980.

Hisamatsu Sen'ichi and Nishio Minoru. *Karon Shū, Nōgakuron Shū*, in Nihon Koten Bungaku Taikei series. Iwanami Shoten, 1961.

Hotta Yoshie. *Teika Meigetsuki Shishō*. Shinshōsha, 1986.

———. *Teika Meigetsuki Shishō Zokuhen*. Shinchōsha, 1988.

Howard, Donald R. *Writers & Pilgrims*. Berkeley: University of California Press, 1980.

Imagawa Fumio. *Kundoku Meigetsuki*, 6 vols. Kawade Shobō Shinsha, 1977–79.

Itoga Kimie. *Kenreimon'in Ukyō no Daibu no Shū*, in Shinchō Nihon Koten Shūsei series. Shinchōsha, 1979.

Kasamatsu Yoshio. *Tōkan Kikō Shinshaku*. Daidōkan Shoten, 1940.

Keene, Donald. *Travelers of a Hundred Ages*. New York: Henry Holt, 1989.

Mizukawa Yoshio. *Asukai Masaari Nikki Zenshaku*. Kazama Shobō, 1985.

———. *Takemuki ga Ki Zenshaku*. Kazama Shobō, 1972.

Morimoto Motoko. *Izayoi Nikki, Yoru no Tsuru*, in Kōdansha Gakujutsu Bunko series. Kōdansha, 1979.

Murayama Shūichi. *Meigetsuki*. Kyōto: Kōtō Shoin, 1947.

Noro Tadasu. *Kaidōki Shinchū*. Ikuei Shoin, 1935. (Reprint published by Geirinsha in 1977.)

Plutschow, Herbert Eugen. *Four Japanese Travel Diaries of the Middle Ages*. Ithaca, N.Y.: Cornell University East Asia Papers, 1981.

———. *Tabi suru Nihonjin*. Musashino Shoin, 1983.

Reischauer, Edwin O., and Joseph K. Yamagiwa. *Translations from Early Japanese Literature*. Cambridge, Mass.: Harvard University Press, 1951.

Tamai Kōsuke. *Ben no Naishi Nikki Shinchū*. Taishūkan Shoten, 1966.

———. *Nakatsukasa no Naishi Nikki Shinchū*. Taishūkan Shoten, 1958.

———. *Nikki Bungaku no Kenkyū*. Hanawa Shobō, 1971.

———. *Towazugatari Kenkyū Taisei*. Meiji Shoin, 1971.

Tomikura Tokujirō. *Towazugatari*. Chikuma Shobō, 1966.

Tsugita Kasumi. *Utatane Zenchūshaku*, in Kōdansha Gakujutsu Bunko series. Kōdansha, 1978.

Tsuji Hikosaburō. *Fujiwara Teika Meigetsuki no Kenkyū*. Yoshikawa Kōbunkan, 1977.

Whitehouse, Wilfrid, and Eizo Yanagisawa. *Lady Nijō's Own Story*. Tokyo: Charles E. Tuttle, 1974.

Yamashita Hiroaki. *Taiheiki*, II, in Shinchō Nihon Koten Shūsei series. Shinchōsha, 1980.

22.
ESSAYS IN IDLENESS

Tsurezuregusa (Essays in Idleness) is a *zuihitsu* collection—essays that range in length from a single sentence to a few pages. The dating of the work poses problems, but it is generally believed that it was written between 1329 and 1331.[1] This was not a propitious time for a work of reflection and comment. In 1331 the Emperor Godaigo staged a revolt against the Hōjō family, the de facto rulers of Japan, and in the following year he was exiled, only to return in 1333 and overthrow the Hōjō rule. These events and the many incidents that presaged them created great anxiety among the educated classes, but they hardly ruffle the surface of *Essays in Idleness*. It is an expression neither of sorrow over troubled times nor of joy over the temporary successes of one or another party; it is instead a work of timeless relevance, a splendid example of Japanese meditative style.

The author is known by his Buddhist name, Kenkō, but sometimes also by his lay name of Urabe Kaneyoshi or else as Yoshida Kaneyoshi, from the associations of his family with the Yoshida Shrine in Kyoto.[2] Kenkō lived from 1283 to about 1352.[3] He came from a long line of Shintō officials,[4] but the Shintō connections were broken in the time of his grandfather. His father was a court official, as was one elder brother; another brother was a high-ranking Buddhist priest (*daisōjō*). Kenkō himself as a young man served at the court of the Emperor Gonijō (1285–1308). He became a priest after the death of this emperor, but nothing suggests Gonijō's death was the cause; dissatisfaction with worldly life had probably accumulated within him and led to his decision. He took the tonsure in 1313 on Mount Hiei and spent some years there before returning to Kyoto.[5]

During his lifetime Kenkō was known as a poet of the conservative Nijō school. Nijō Yoshimoto, the chief Nijō poet of the next generation, wrote that Kenkō was one of the three outstanding poets of the Teiwa era (1345–1350).[6] He added that "people considered him somewhat inferior to the others, but his poems were widely quoted."[7] Kenkō spent most of his life in the capital, where he took part in poetry gatherings regularly, even though the times were hardly conducive to poetry-making. His indifference to politics is suggested by the readiness with which he shifted allegiance from régime to régime—from Godaigo to Kōgon, the emperor installed by the Hōjō regents in 1331; then back to Godaigo when he returned in triumph from Oki in 1333; then from Godaigo to the Ashikaga shoguns in 1336, when Godaigo was again driven into exile. He associated with the new overlords, notably Kō no Moronao (d. 1351), a violent warrior who desired the trappings of culture. A passage in the *Taiheiki* relates that Kenkō even wrote love letters for Moronao.[8] Kenkō lived for a time in the Kantō region (in the present Kanagawa Prefecture), a fact that explains the surprising number of episodes in *Essays in Idleness* set in that part of Japan.[9]

Kenkō would probably not be remembered at all if he had not written *Essays in Idleness*, but the work seems to have been little known during his lifetime. For many years the account given by Sanjōnishi Saneeda (1511–1579) of the discovery of the text was generally accepted. This stated that Kenkō had from time to time written down his thoughts on scraps of paper that he pasted to the walls of his cottage. The poet and general Imagawa Ryōshun, learning of this after Kenkō's death, carefully removed the many scraps and arranged them in their present order.[10] Nobody believes this anymore, but the story suggests that *Essays in Idleness* was unknown for some years and had to be rediscovered. The oldest surviving text, dated 1431, is in the hand of Shōtetsu, a disciple of Ryōshun.[11] Variant texts exist, but the differences are not major, and it is now generally agreed that the work was composed in the present order.[12] The title, derived from words in the brief introductory passage, also seems to date from Shōtetsu's time, but the present division of the text into a preface and 243 numbered episodes can be traced back only to the seventeenth century.

Essays in Idleness is now almost universally accepted as one of two Japanese masterpieces of the zuihitsu genre, along with *The Pillow Book of Sei Shōnagon*. The two works treat a wide variety of subjects, seemingly in no particular order, and both are distinguished by the unusual clarity of the author's observations. There are also many obvious differences: *The Pillow Book* was written by a court lady who delighted in every piece of gossip that came her way, but *Essays in Idleness* was by a Buddhist priest who, though much concerned with things of this world, was ultimately devoted to religious truth. Sei Shōnagon is often cruelly witty and delights in exposing the ridiculous; Kenkō has humor, but it is not so much the flashing repartee that might be exchanged by men and women at the court as the amusing anecdotes old cronies might relate to one another. Her perceptions are sharp if not profound; his are generally linked with some statement of Buddhist belief. Yet it is clear that Kenkō knew *The Pillow Book* and in a few places imitated it.[13]

One important strain in *Essays in Idleness*, entirely absent from *The Pillow Book*, is the conviction that the world is steadily growing worse. Sei Shōnagon, scorning the crudities of the past, desired above all to be informed of the latest fashions, sure that such knowledge was more important than being an expert on precedents; but for Kenkō, writing in an age that saw itself as doomed to undergo the misery of mappō, when men could no longer hope to save themselves, the least important tradition of the past was a precious survival that had to be preserved, regardless of its intrinsic merits. He wrote,

> In all things I yearn for the past. Modern fashions seem to keep growing more and more debased. I find that even among the splendid pieces of furniture built by our master cabinetmakers, those in the old forms are the most pleasing. And as for writing letters, surviving scraps from the past reveal how superb the phrasing used to be. The ordinary spoken language has also steadily coarsened. People used to say "raise the carriage shafts" or "trim the lamp wick," but people today say "raise it" or "trim it."[14]

Kenkō at times more specifically referred to the widespread belief in mappō: "They speak of the degenerate, final phase of the world, yet how splendid is the ancient atmosphere, uncontaminated by the world, that still prevails within the palace walls."[15]

The Imperial Palace was splendid to the degree that it had remained untouched by change:

> When construction of the present palace had been completed, the buildings were inspected by experts on court usage, who pronounced them free of faults anywhere. The day for the emperor to move to the new palace was already near when the Abbess Genki examined it and declared, "The half-moon window in the Kan'in palace was rounder and without a frame." This was an impressive feat of memory. The window in the new palace, peaked at the top, had a wooden border. This mistake was later corrected.[16]

We may wonder why it was felt necessary to go to all the trouble and expense of replacing an unimportant window, but for Kenkō, as for the Abbess Genki, a window whose shape was at variance, however slightly, with the old traditions reflected the degeneracy of the age; it certainly was not a sign of progress. Kenkō was equally unhappy when punishments meted out to offenders varied with tradition: "Nobody is left who knows the proper manner of hanging a quiver before the house of a man in disgrace with His Majesty."[17] Again, he lamented, "A criminal being flogged with rods is placed on a torture rack. Today no one knows the shape of the rack nor the manner of attaching the criminal."[18]

Kenkō's clinging to tradition is likely to suggest an attachment to the things of this world unbecoming a true monk. At the time he made the decision to "leave the world" he was writing poems that reveal a disenchantment commonly found in the writings of the medieval monks. Unlike Saigyō and the other hermit-poets, however, he left his retreat on Mount Hiei to resume his life in the city, and became deeply involved with its activities. Although he often describes the pleasures of solitude, he does not seem to have courted it assiduously, and only five of his 243 episodes are devoted to nature, the traditional solace of the hermit. Instead, he displayed unflagging interest in whatever was happening in the world around him:

> Along about the Ōchō era [1311–1312] there was a rumor that a man from Ise had brought to the capital a woman who had turned into a demon, and for twenty days or more people of the downtown and Shirakawa areas wandered here and there day after day, hoping for a glimpse of the demon. . . . One day, as I was on my way from Higashiyama to the neighborhood of Agui, I saw a crowd of people running from Shijō and above, all headed north. They were shouting that the demon had been seen at the corner of Ichijō and Muromachi. I looked off in that direction from where I was, near Imadegawa. . . . I thought it unlikely the rumor could be completely groundless, and sent a man to investigate, but he could find nobody who had actually seen the demon. . . . Some time afterward, people in all walks of life came down with an illness that lasted two or three days, and some wondered if the false rumors about the demons had been a portent of the epidemic.[19]

As this passage reveals, Kenkō's daily round of activities took him into the city, where he mingled with the crowds, and to some degree shared their emotions. When, for example, he says, "I thought it unlikely the rumor could be completely groundless . . ." we may be surprised that this man, whose voice usually seems so modern, should have accepted as truth an implausible rumor. But if at such moments we sense the distance in time separating us from Kenkō, they make the immediacy of the rest of his views all the more astonishing.

Despite his daily contacts with the world, and despite the interest he displayed in secular behavior and secular aesthetics, Kenkō has often been treated as a recluse in the tradition of the medieval monks who turned their backs on the world. Ishida Yoshisada, an authority on the subject of hermits and recluses, declared that if one confined oneself to *Essays in Idleness*, Kenkō's life provided a perfect example of what it meant to be a recluse.[20] He analyzed Kenkō's qualifications in these terms:

> The first requirement of the recluse is a fundamental realization of the transience (*mujō*) of life; Kenkō's awareness of transience might even be said to have been excessive. Faith and a sense of beauty are the second requirement of the aesthetic recluse, and Kenkō was completely possessed of both. It was normal for the recluse not to draw his faith from the established Buddhist sects, but to consider that it was sufficient to have Buddhist religious aspirations; in this respect as well Kenkō entirely lived up to the requirement. The third requirement of the recluse was that he love solitude and seek tranquility, and Kenkō more than amply fulfilled this requirement too.[21]

Ishida had no trouble in finding passages in *Essays in Idleness* to confirm this analysis, but the reader is likely to receive a quite different impression from the work. It is true that from time to time Kenkō states with conviction his belief that the world is mutable and not to be depended on—"The world is as unstable as the pools and shallows of Asuka River. Times change and things disappear: joy and sorrow come and go; a place that once thrived turns into an uninhabited moor; a house may remain unaltered, but its occupants will have changed."[22] But Kenkō was far from being a recluse in the manner of Saigyō or of Kamo no Chōmei, and he was much too involved with this world to renounce it for a hermitage. Unlike Chōmei, who wondered apprehensively if his fondness for his hut, simple though it was, was not a sin and if his attachment to its solitude might not be a hindrance to salvation,

Kenkō devoted considerable attention to what makes for a comfortable house:

> A house should be built with the summer in mind. In winter it is possible to live anywhere, but a badly made house is unbearable when it gets hot. . . . People agree that a house which has plenty of spare room is attractive to look at and may be put to many different uses.[23]

Kenkō did not forget the principle of impermanence when he discussed what made for an agreeable place to live, but the focus of his attention was the house itself rather than its ephemeral nature:

> A house, I know, is but a temporary abode, but how delightful it is to find one that has harmonious proportions and a pleasant atmosphere. One feels somehow that even moonlight, when it shines into the quiet domicile of a person of taste, is more affecting than elsewhere. A house, though it may not be in the current fashion or elaborately decorated, will appeal to us by its unassuming beauty—a grove of trees with an indefinably ancient look; a garden where plants, growing of their own accord, have a special charm; a verandah and an open-work wooden fence of interesting construction; and a few personal effects left carelessly lying about, giving the place an air of having been lived in. A house which multitudes of workmen have polished with every care, where strange and rare Chinese and Japanese furnishings are displayed, and even the grasses and trees of the garden have been trained unnaturally, is ugly to look at and most depressing. How could anyone live for long in such a place? The most casual glance will suggest how likely such a house is to turn in a moment to smoke.[24]

The last sentence reflects Kenkō's Buddhist conviction that the things of this world do not last, but the emphasis is on the futility of overly decorating one's house, not on the transitory nature of *all* dwellings.

This episode of *Essays in Idleness* is important also for its statement of aesthetic preferences that were formulated by Kenkō but have been true of the best Japanese taste over the centuries. The richly appointed house has usually been considered in the West to be both beautiful and agreeable to live in, and gardens where "the grasses and trees . . . have been trained unnaturally" still draw visitors to the stately houses of

Europe. Even in Japan, the polychromed carvings of the Tokugawa mausoleum at Nikkō are evidence that the West has enjoyed no monopoly of garish decoration. But, Kenkō asked rhetorically, who could live for long in such a place?

Simplicity was not the only aesthetic ideal put forward by Kenkō in *Essays in Idleness*. His preference for irregularity (as opposed to uniformity or symmetry) is even more striking:

> People often say that a set of books looks ugly if all volumes are not in the same format, but I was impressed to hear the Abbot Kōyū say, "It is typical of the unintelligent man to insist on assembling complete sets of everything. Imperfect sets are better."
>
> In everything, no matter what it may be, uniformity is undesirable. Leaving something incomplete makes it interesting, and gives one the feeling that there is room for growth. Someone once told me, "Even when building an imperial palace, they always leave one place unfinished."[25]

Irregularity seems to have been an unconscious preference of the Japanese from early in their history, as we can deduce from the waka (five lines in either five or seven syllables each) and from the asymmetrical paintings and pottery especially prized by the Japanese—though most other peoples have delighted in symmetry, parallelism, and other devices for achieving aesthetic balance.[26]

But perhaps the most striking aesthetic preference voiced by Kenkō in *Essays in Idleness* was his advocacy of suggestion, as opposed to climactic expression:

> Are we to look at cherry blossoms only in full bloom, the moon only when it is cloudless? To long for the moon while looking on the rain, to lower the blinds and be unaware of the passing of spring—these are even more deeply moving. Branches about to blossom or gardens strewn with faded flowers are worthier of our admiration. . . .
>
> In all things, it is the beginnings and ends that are interesting. Does the love between men and women refer only to the moments when they are in each other's arms? The man who grieves over a love affair broken off before it was fulfilled, who bewails empty vows, who spends long autumn nights alone, who lets his thoughts wander to distant skies, who yearns for the past in a dilapidated house—such a man truly knows what love means.

> The moon that appears close to dawn after we have long waited for it moves us more profoundly than the full moon shining cloudless over a thousand leagues. . . .
>
> And are we to look at the moon and the cherry blossoms with our eyes alone? How much more evocative and pleasing it is to think about the spring without stirring from the house, to dream of the moonlight though we remain in our room![27]

Suggestion that can convey more than what is visible or otherwise apprehended is a conspicuous feature not only of Japanese literature but of all the Japanese arts. Not very much can be stated in the bare thirty-one syllables of a waka (or the even shorter haiku), but suggestion can expand the content to encompass a whole world; similarly, the Nō actor, who performs on a stage without scenery, is able, merely by taking a few steps, to suggest that he is on a long journey, though this would be unconvincing in a more realistic theater. It was not only because the forms of expression were restricted that the Japanese turned to suggestion; as Kenkō indicated in the passage cited above, suggestion was preferred to a faithful approximation of actual experience, which is bound to be finite; and perhaps there really were people who shut themselves up in their rooms in order to savor in their imaginations beauty beyond that of the reality of the spring or of the moon.

Similarly, Kenkō's preference for beginnings and ends stems from an awareness that they can evoke more than the central experience. "Branches about to blossom or gardens strewn with fallen flowers" suggest what is to come or what has been, but cherry blossoms in full bloom leave nothing to the imagination; they are splendidly and uniquely themselves. There is a limit also to the variety of expressions of joy that happily united lovers might utter, but the hopes of anticipated love or regret over a love affair that has ended are without limits; this may be why so few of the innumerable love poems in the Japanese anthologies of waka describe fulfilled love.[28]

The point where Kenkō's religious and aesthetic views came closest together was his insistence on impermanence as an essential element of beauty. Certain passages from *Essays in Idleness* help to make this clear:

> If man were never to fade away like the dews of Adashino, never to vanish like the smoke over Toribeyama,[29] but lingered on forever in this world, how things would lose their power to move us! The most precious thing in life is its uncertainty.[30]

The uncertainty of life has often been bewailed by poets, whether in East or West. When Buddhists spoke of mujō, it was usually with a sigh. Perhaps Kenkō was the first to express the conviction that perishability was a necessary element of beauty; but earlier Japanese, even if they never formulated this principle in words, prized the quickly scattered cherry blossoms more than hardier flowers and sensed the poignance that impermanence imparted to beauty. The passage of time, though inevitably regretted by once beautiful women as they looked into their mirrors, could also impart beauty to objects from the past:

> Somebody once remarked that thin silk was not satisfactory as a scroll wrapping because it was so easily torn. Ton'a[31] replied, "It is only after the silk wrapper has frayed at top and bottom, and the mother-of-pearl has fallen from the roller that a scroll looks beautiful." This demonstrated the excellent taste of the man.[32]

It is for such observations that we turn to *Essays in Idleness*. Some of the episodes are trivial or fussily pedantic, others are mutually contradictory, but the impression left by the whole is of a wonderfully civilized, extremely perceptive man, who did not feel it was beneath him to offer practical advice from time to time. Although he lived in an age of violent changes, he chose not to describe any of the political developments or even how his own way of life might have been affected by them. His book has been read in many ways ever since its rediscovery,[33] but perhaps it is best read as a guide to Japanese taste as Kenkō understood its traditions and formed its future. It can also be read as a manual of gentlemanly conduct. Again and again Kenkō describes how he thinks a gentleman should behave:

> When a person who has always been extremely close appears on a particular occasion reserved and formal toward you, some people undoubtedly will say, "Why act that way now, after all these years?" But I feel sure that such behavior shows sincerity and breeding.
>
> On the other hand, I am sure I should feel equally attracted if someone with whom I am on distant terms should choose on some occasion to speak to me with utter frankness.[34]

> How boring it is when you meet a man after a long separation and he insists on relating at interminable length everything that has happened to him in the meantime. Even if the man is an intimate, somebody you know extremely well, how can you but feel a certain

reserve on meeting him again after a time? The vulgar sort of person, even if he goes on a brief excursion somewhere, is breathless with excitement as he relates as matters of great interest everything that has happened to him. When the well-bred man tells a story he addresses himself to one person, even if many people are present, though the others, too, listen, naturally. . . . You can judge a person's breeding by whether he is quite impassive even when he tells an amusing story, or laughs a great deal when relating a matter of no interest.[35]

A man should avoid displaying deep familiarity with any subject. Can one imagine a well-bred man talking with the air of a know-it-all, even about a matter with which he is in fact familiar? . . . It is impressive when a man is always slow to speak, even on subjects that he knows thoroughly, and does not speak at all unless questioned.[36]

Kenkō's concern with gentlemanly behavior may seem inappropriate in one who has "renounced the world," but since he had chosen to live among other people, rather than on some lonely mountainside, his association with others formed tastes within him as strong as those of a purely aesthetic nature. He obviously did not hate society—it is not difficult to imagine him in the role of a French or Italian abbé at some eighteenth-century court—but in the end a social life, however engaging, was not enough. For all his involvement with other people, he was sincere in his professions of Buddhist belief as well as in his fundamental solitude:

The pleasantest of all diversions is to sit alone under the lamp, a book spread out before you, and to make friends with people of a distant past you have never known.[37]

I wonder what feelings inspire a man to complain of "having nothing to do." I am happiest when I have nothing to distract me and I am completely alone.[38]

Kenkō's pleasure in solitude was not necessarily because it gave him time to immerse himself in the sacred texts of Buddhism. None of the books he chose as his companions in the lamplight was specifically Buddhist in content, and two—the sayings of Lao Tzu and the writings of Chuang Tzu—were Taoist, rather than Buddhist. He also mentioned his pleasure in reading waka poetry. For Kenkō a man's most important act was to take the Great Step and become a priest, but this did not signify that the man was henceforth to consecrate himself solely to reading Buddhist texts. He must be aware that the impermanence of the world is a source of beauty, though it also brings death.

> A man should bear firmly in mind that death is always threatening, and never for an instant forget it. If he does this, why should the impurities bred in him by this world not grow lighter, and his heart not develop an earnest resolve to cultivate the Way of the Buddha?[39]

Again,

> A man who has determined to take the Great Step should leave unresolved all plans for disposing of urgent or worrisome business.
>
> Some men think, "I'll wait a bit longer, until I take care of this matter," or "I might as well dispose of that business first," or "People will surely laugh at me if I leave such and such as it stands. I'll arrange things now so that there won't be any future criticism," or "I've managed to survive all these years. I'll wait till that matter is cleared up. It won't take long. I mustn't be hasty." But if you think in such terms the day for taking the Great Step will never come, for you will keep discovering more and more unavoidable problems, and there never will be a time when you run out of unfinished business.[40]

There was a categorical difference between the man who had taken the Great Step and one who, though his heart was set on obtaining enlightenment, went on living with his family and mingling in society:

> Once a man has entered the Way of the Buddha and turned his back on the world, even supposing he has desires, they cannot possibly resemble the deep-seated cravings of men in power. How much expense to society are his paper bedclothes, his hempen robe, a bowl of food, and some millet broth? His wants are easily met, his heart quickly satisfied. . . . It is desirable somehow to make a break from this world so that one may benefit from having been born a man. The man who surrenders himself to his desires and neglects the path of enlightenment is hardly any different from the brute beasts.[41]

Kenkō, even after entering Buddhist orders, maintained his affection for the deluded creature called man; but in his heart he knew that this step was of paramount significance, and counted far more than any momentary diversion. All the same, we cannot but rejoice that he committed to paper not only his religious convictions but his undiminished affection for the world around him.

Notes

1. The generally accepted dates are those proposed by Tachibana Jun'ichi in 1947. He offered two hypotheses, the first dating the work 1330–1331, the second dating it 1329–1331. He arrived at these dates by tracing every historical event mentioned in the work and by determining exactly when people mentioned in the work by their titles actually held those titles. Mitsutada, the major counselor and chief of the board of censors mentioned in section 102, was appointed to this post in 1330; the section must therefore have been written after that date. The Muryōju Hall which, according to section 25, was still standing, was destroyed by a fire in 1331; the work must have been completed before that happened. The whole of the work, then, would have been written while Godaigo was emperor, between 1330 and 1331. Tachibana later responded to criticism that one year was too short a time to have composed *Essays in Idleness* by allowing the possibility that Kenkō began writing in 1329. However, in section 103 Saionji Kin'akira is described as being a major counselor, an office he did not attain until 1336. This fact encouraged other scholars to attempt to disprove Tachibana's chronology. Yasuraoka Kōsaku believed that *Essays in Idleness* was written in two parts, the first corresponding to the introduction and thirty-two sections, the second the remainder of the work. The first part would have been written in 1319, the second part from 1330 to 1331; then, at some time after 1336, when Kenkō put the two parts together, he made corrections and additions. See Kubota Jun, "*Tsurezuregusa*, sono Sakusha to Jidai," in Satake Akihiro and Kubota Jun, *Hōjōki, Tsurezuregusa*, pp. 394–95. Nagazumi Yasuaki, rejecting Tachibana's theory, spoke of the great strides made in scholarship of *Essays in Idleness* since the war, and declared that "it has now become clear that *Essays in Idleness* was not written in the brief space of a year, but that it was written and augmented over a period of at least a dozen, but perhaps even more years after 1330–31." (Nagazumi Yasuaki, "Kaisetsu," in Kanda Hideo and Nagazumi Yasuaki, *Hōjoki, Tsurezuregusa*, p. 364.) Kubota Jun, writing after Nagazumi, obviously did not consider the matter settled.

2. The first person to identify Kenkō as the author was the priest Shōtetsu in his *Tales of Shōtetsu*. (See Hisamatsu Sen'ichi and Nishio Minoru, *Karon Shū*, *Nōgakuron Shū*, pp. 187–88, where Shōtetsu identifies a well-known passage from *Essays in Idleness* as being by Kenkō.) Shōtetsu also called attention to the fact that Kenkō, contrary to usual practice, kept his lay name Kaneyoshi when he became a priest, though he gave the characters their Sino-Japanese reading of Kenkō. See *ibid*. See also the translation by Robert H. Brower, *Conversations with Shōtetsu*, pp. 95–96. An excellent short account of the known biographical data of Kenkō is found in Fukuda Hideichi, *Chūsei Bungaku Ronkō*, pp. 248–50.
3. The date of his death was usually given as 1350, but documents have been discovered that prove he was alive as late as 1352. See Kubota, *"Tsurezuregusa,"* p. 393.
4. A genealogy, derived from *Urabe-ke Keizu* and *Sompi Bummyaku*, is given by Nagazumi in his "Kaisetsu" to Kanda and Nagazumi, *Hōjōki*, *Tsurezuregusa*, p. 375.
5. It was traditionally believed that Kenkō became a priest after the death of the Emperor Gouda, whom he also served, but this theory is even less plausible: it is now clear that Kenkō entered orders eleven years before the death of Gouda in 1324. Kubota, in *"Tsurezuregusa,"* pp. 379–80, gave further evidence why this view is unacceptable; but in 1967, when I wrote the introduction to my translation of *Essays in Idleness*, I repeated the traditional account, first presented by Shōtetsu in *Tales of Shōtetsu*. (See Hisamatsu and Nishio, *Karon Shū*, p. 188). Saitō Kiyoe in *Namboku-chō Jidai Bungaku Tsūshi* also gave this account, but noted (p. 21) that it was "not necessarily" established.
6. Translations of fourteen poems by Kenkō are given in Steven D. Carter, *Waiting for the Wind*, pp. 176–83.
7. Quoted by Kubota in *"Tsurezuregusa,"* p. 387. Shōtetsu called him one of the "four heavenly kings" (*shitennō*) among the disciples of Nijō Tameyo, along with Ton'a, Keiun, and Jōben. (See Hisamatsu and Nishio, *Karon Shū*, p. 188.)
8. Kubota believed that this anecdote should not be dismissed out of hand as fiction: Kenkō's collected poems include some written on behalf of other people. See Kubota, *"Tsurezuregusa,"* p. 391.
9. Carter (in *Waiting*, p. 178) gives a translation of a poem written by Kenkō while living within sight of Mount Fuji.
10. Sugimoto Hidetarō in *Tsurezuregusa* was at special pains to trace the continuity from one episode to the next. It had long been recognized that certain groups of episodes had mutual connections, and it was argued that no one except the author could have arranged the work in the present order, but Sugimoto was exceptional in the rigorousness with which he demonstrated the links between successive episodes.
11. This text is the one used by Kubota Jun in his annotated edition of the

Shin Nihon Koten Bungaku Taikei series. He notes in *"Tsurezuregusa,"* p. 398 of Satake and Kubota, *Hōjōki*, that all other commentated editions have used the later text of Karasumaru Mitsuhiro (1579–1638).

12. See Fukuda, *Chūsei*, p. 251.
13. *Ibid.*, p. 246.
14. From section 22. Text in Satake and Kubota, *Hōjōki*, p. 100. Translation is from my *Essays in Idleness*, p. 23.
15. From section 23. Text in Satake and Kubota, *Hōjōki*, p. 101. Translation in *Essays in Idleness*, p. 23.
16. Section 33. Satake and Kubota, *Hōjōki*, p. 111. Translation from *Essays in Idleness*, pp. 32–33. Sugimoto in *Tsurezuregusa*, pp. 77–82, discusses the function of this window, which served as a kind of peephole, and gives photographs of the window in the present Kyoto Gosho. Its shape was called *kushigata*, or "comb shape," because it looked like an old-fashioned Japanese comb, which resembles a half-moon.
17. Section 203. Satake and Kubota, *Hōjōki*, p. 276. Translation in *Essays in Idleness*, p. 170.
18. Section 204. Text in Satake and Kubota, *Hōjōki*, pp. 276–77. Translation in *Essays in Idleness*, p. 171.
19. Section 50. Text in Satake and Kubota, *Hōjōki*, pp. 126–27, except for the place-name Agui, which they render as Ago. Agui is given by Miki Sumito in *Tsurezuregusa*, II, p. 37. Translation from *Essays in Idleness*, pp. 43–44.
20. Ishida Yoshisada, *Inja no Bungaku*, p. 164.
21. *Ibid.*
22. Section 25. Text in Satake and Kubota, *Hōjōki*, p. 103. Translation from *Essays in Idleness*, p. 25.
23. Section 55. Text in Satake and Kubota, *Hōjōki*, p. 133. Translation from *Essays in Idleness*, pp. 50–51.
24. Section 10. Text in Satake and Kubota, *Hōjōki*, pp. 86–87. Translation from *Essays in Idleness*, p. 10.
25. Section 82. Text in Satake and Kubota, *Hōjōki*, pp. 158–59. Text in *Essays in Idleness*, pp. 70–71.
26. For a further discussion of this point, see my *Landscapes and Portraits*, pp. 18–20; also, my *Pleasures of Japanese Literature*, pp. 10–13.
27. Section 137. Text in Satake and Kubota, *Hōjōki*, pp. 212–24. Translation from *Essays in Idleness*, pp. 115–18.
28. For further meditations on this theme, see my *Pleasures*, pp. 8–10.
29. Adashino was the name of a graveyard in Kyoto. The word *adashi* (impermanent) contained in the place-name accounted for the frequent mention of Adashino in poetry as a symbol of impermanence. The dew was also used with that meaning. Toribeyama is still the chief graveyard of Kyoto. Mention of smoke indicates that bodies were cremated there.
30. Section 7. Text in Satake and Kubota, *Hōjōki*, p. 83. Translation from *Essays in Idleness*, p. 7.

31. Ton'a was a distinguished poet as well as a monk of the Jishū sect of Jōdo Buddhism.
32. Section 82. Text in Satake and Kubota, *Hōjōki*, p. 158. Translation from *Essays in Idleness*, p. 70.
33. The haiku poet Matsunaga Teitoku (1571–1653) offered a public lecture on *Essays in Idleness* in 1603, and his commentary on the work, called *Nagusamigusa*, though prepared largely at this time, was published in 1652. Until the time of Teitoku *Essays in Idleness* had been read only by a comparatively few specialists, but it became one of the most important works in education during the Tokugawa period. See Shigematsu Nobuhiro, "Tsurezuregusa Kenkyūshi," pp. 63–111.
34. Section 37. Text in Sataka and Kubota, *Hōjōki*, p. 113. Translation from *Essays in Idleness*, p. 34.
35. Section 56. Satake and Kubota, *Hōjōki*, pp. 133–34. *Essays in Idleness*, p. 51.
36. Section 79. Satake and Kubota, *Hōjōki*, p. 156. *Essays in Idleness*, pp. 68–69.
37. Section 13. Satake and Kubota, *Hōjōki*, p. 90. *Essays in Idleness*, p. 12.
38. Section 75. Satake and Kubota, *Hōjōki*, pp. 152–53. *Essays in Idleness*, p. 66.
39. Section 49. Satake and Kubota, *Hōjōki*, pp. 125–26. *Essays in Idleness*, p. 43.
40. Section 59. Satake and Kubota, *Hōjōki*, p. 137. *Essays in Idleness*, pp. 53–54.
41. Section 58. Satake and Kubota, *Hōjōki*, pp. 136–37. *Essays in Idleness*, p. 53.

Bibliography

Note: All Japanese books, except as otherwise noted, were published in Tokyo.

Brower, Robert H. *Conversations with Shōtetsu*. Ann Arbor: Center for Japanese Studies, University of Michigan, 1992.

Carter, Steven D. *Waiting for the Wind*. New York: Columbia University Press, 1989.

Fukuda Hideichi. *Chūsei Bungaku Ronkō*. Meiji Shoin, 1975.

Hisamatsu Sen'ichi and Nishio Minoru. *Karon Shū, Nōgakuron Shū*, in Nihon Koten Bungaku Taikei series. Iwanami Shoten, 1961.

Ishida Mizumaro. *Nihon Koten Bungaku to Bukkyō*. Chikuma Shobō, 1988.

Ishida Yoshisada. *Chūsei Sōan no Bungaku*. Kitazawa Tosho Shuppan, 1970.

———. *Inja no Bungaku*. Hanawa Shobō, 1969.

Kanda Hideo and Nagazumi Yasuaki. *Hōjōki, Tsurezuregusa*, in Kan'yaku Nihon no Koten series. Shōgakukan, 1986.

Keene, Donald. *Landscapes and Portraits*. Tokyo: Kodansha International, 1971.

———. *The Pleasures of Japanese Literature*. New York: Columbia University Press, 1988.

——— (trans). *Essays in Idleness*. New York: Columbia University Press, 1967.

Kidō Saizō. *Chūsei Bungaku Shiron*. Meiji Shoin, 1984.

Miki Sumito. *Tsurezuregusa*, 4 vols., in Kōdansha Gakujutsu Bunko series. Kōdansha, 1982.

Saitō Kiyoe. *Namboku-chō Jidai Bungaku Tsūshi*. Furukawa Shobō, 1972.

Satake Akihiro and Kubota Jun. *Hōjōki, Tsurezuregusa*, in Shin Nihon Koten Bungaku Taikei series. Iwanami Shoten, 1989.

Shigematsu Nobuhiro. "Tsurezuregusa Kenkyūshi," *Kokugo to Kokubungaku* 6:6, June 1929.

Sugimoto Hidetarō. *Tsurezuregusa*. Iwanami Shoten, 1987.

23. MEDIEVAL WAR TALES

The darkness of the Japanese middle ages is most perfectly conveyed by war tales that describe the battles fought during the Kamakura and Muromachi periods. The styles of these accounts vary greatly, from stiff compositions in kambun to graceful, even poetic writings in the manner of the "mirrors" of history; but regardless of the style, they are tragic evocations of the misery of defeat, rather than paeans to victory. The events are narrated not in terms of the sweep of battle scenes but in the details of individuals entrapped in circumstances that they are powerless to alter; the tales tend to be remembered as stories of people, good and bad, rather than as accounts of dynastic struggles. Even the most factual tales contain passages that were seemingly intended to enhance their appeal for readers or possibly for people who listened to sung or declaimed recitations of the texts.[1]

Some tales are so fanciful as to read like works of fiction rather than of history, and the delineation of the historical figures in others anticipates the dramas of later times in which they would appear; but the war tales were probably accepted as historical fact by all except the most scholarly. Undoubtedly *The Tale of the Heike* influenced the composition of these later works, and though none of them matched its grandeur, the *Taiheiki* rivals *The Tale of the Heike* in its success in creating heroes for the Japanese people.

The term "medieval war tales," as used here, refers to works written between the thirteenth and early fifteenth centuries.[2] Among them, the chronicles depict, more or less faithfully, the events of warfare, and the historical romances freely mix fiction with the facts, introduce the supernatural, or enter into the thoughts of the characters in the manner of fiction rather than of history.

Chronicles

Jōkyūki

The rebellion that began in the third year of Jōkyū (1221), when the Retired Emperor Gotoba attempted to assert his supremacy over the Kamakura shogunate, is described in *Jōkyūki* (Record of Jōkyū). Various accounts known by this title were set down during the thirteenth century and later, but neither their authors nor the dates of composition are known. The oldest text apparently dates from between 1230 and 1240, and the more widely distributed *rufubon* (vulgate) text from about 1250.[3] These different texts were not variants on any single original source; although they bear the same title, each was independently composed and the materials and manner of presentation are quite dissimilar one from another; they are alike only in their main subject, the Jōkyū Rebellion. Variations on the rufubon text continued to be composed until late in the sixteenth century.[4]

The immediate cause of the disturbance is generally said to have been Gotoba's anger with the shogunate over two estates[5] that he wished to give to his favorite, a *shirabyōshi* named Kamegiku. The steward (*jitō*) of the estates refused to turn them over to Gotoba, whereupon he ordered Hōjō Yoshitoki (1163–1224), the shogunal regent (*shikken*), to replace the steward. Yoshitoki refused, and this was the signal for Gotoba to begin preparations for an attack on Yoshitoki and the shogunate.[6] Gotoba's forces were from the outset greatly inferior in numbers to the shogunate's, but Gotoba seemed confident of success. Probably he was counting on there being confusion and disarray within the shogunate following the assassination of Minamoto Sanetomo, the third shogun, in 1219. But Gotoba underestimated the iron will of Hōjō Masako (1157–1225), the widow of Minamoto Yoritomo, and of her brother Yoshitoki, who kept the shogunate forces under firm control.

The actual fighting began when Gotoba's men attacked the residence of Iga Mitsusue, the constable (*shugo*) stationed in Kyoto by the shogunate to keep an eye on the throne. Gotoba's forces were victorious in this initial combat, but all the reader is likely to retain of this first of many scenes of conflict in *Jōkyūki* is the story of Mitsusue's son.

Once the fighting began, most of Mitsusue's men deserted him because in the capital (though nowhere else) Gotoba's forces were far stronger than the shogunate's. He was finally left with only twenty-seven men, one of them his fourteen-year-old son, who had only recently had his *gembuku* ceremony.[7] Mitsusue urged the son to flee as quickly as possible. "You are still a child, only fourteen. I don't know what would happen if you got involved in the fighting. The best thing would be for you to take advantage of your youth to make your escape. Have seven or eight boys of your age who are familiar with the lay of the land accompany you." Mitsusue himself was resolved to "expose his corpse" in the capital. He urged the boy not to be impatient: when he was seventeen or eighteen, there would be occasions enough to recall what had happened and to demonstrate his mettle. The boy, however, begged his father to allow him to stay by his side to the end, and Mitsusue, gazing at his son in tears, reluctantly agreed.

The boy took an active part in the ensuing fight, even firing an arrow at the man who at one time planned to take him as a son-in-law; but when there seemed to be no sense in prolonging the struggle, Mitsusue ordered his son to commit suicide. "I don't know how to commit suicide," the boy said. "Just cut your belly," Mitsusue replied, but the boy, after making several awkward attempts, seemed unlikely to succeed. "Then, jump into the fire!" his father commanded. The boy rushed toward the flames, but each time he felt the heat against his face, he helplessly turned back. Mitsusue's eyes clouded over at the realization that, for all his courage, the boy was incapable of killing himself. He took the boy on his lap, and gazed with love at his brave and devoted son, but the enemy kept coming closer. Finally, Mitsusue, unable to delay any longer, cut off his son's head. He threw the head and the boy's body into the flames. He then intoned the invocation to Amida, and, slashing his belly, jumped into the flames after his son.[8]

It is for such moments that we remember *Jōkyūki*. In this instance, the author seems to be sympathizing with the forces of the shogunate, but only because they are the victims; in later sections, when troops loyal to Gotoba are hunted down by the overwhelmingly strong shogunate forces, the author's sympathy shifts to the losing side.

Various of the battles described in *Jōkyūki* are made memorable by poignant moments of individual tragedy, but the inevitable repetitiousness of the many combats makes for tedious reading, though less so in the rufubon text than in the others. The long lists of the names of warriors have a sonorous roll, but it is hard to remember more than a few of the names, and those mainly because their owners performed some deed that was distinctly not of valor.

The combatants included Buddhist monks from the Kōfuku-ji in Nara and from Mount Hiei, who apparently did not scruple about taking life, provided it was human life. In one memorable moment of the warfare a warrior-priest armed with a spear was crossing a bridge when an arrow passing through the big toe of his left foot nailed him to the spot. He struggled to free himself but was unable to move until another priest slashed off the toe.[9] Kakushin, the Nara priest who cut off his friend's toe, reappears later, after Gotoba's forces have been crushingly defeated. The passage is an example of the *Jōkyūki* at its most vivid:

> Dogo Kakushin, a priest from Nara, after fighting furiously, seemed to have decided that further struggle was useless, and fled the field followed by some thirty mounted men. Kakushin, a fast man on the ground, did not let the men on horses get close. He ran into the priest's quarters of the Mimuroto Temple, and saw there a white-haired priest who looked as if he might be the master of the temple. Kakushin stripped off his armor and deposited it before the priest. He found a razor, and taking a water jar out onto the verandah, he shaved his head. When the enemy soldiers arrived presently, they found the old priest standing vacantly beside the armor, and supposing that he was the man they were looking for, forced him to the floor and cut off his head. It was a heartless thing to have done. Kakushin later made his escape to Nara.[10]

Such moments are certainly more memorable than the repetitious scenes of battle, or the numerous accounts of suicides after the final defeat, but the *Jōkyūki* stands or falls as the account of Gotoba, a brilliant but erratic man who attempted to behave as an absolute ruler though he lacked the necessary military power. The rufubon text of *Jōkyūki* opens:

> The eighty-second emperor was called Gotoba. Because he died in the province of Oki, he was also known as the Oki emperor. He was the grandson of Emperor Goshirakawa and the fourth son of Emperor Takakura. On the twentieth day of the eighth month of 1183 he ascended the throne at the age of four, and no doubt because he studied literature and music[11] throughout the fifteen years of his reign, his waka poetry blossomed and his compositions in Chinese bore fruit.
>
> However, he later abdicated in favor of his eldest son. From that time on, he associated intimately with base-born persons, sitting shoulder-to-shoulder with them, legs crossed. He neglected his consort and the palace ladies of exalted birth, and frequented instead women of the lowest class. He turned his back on the correct prin-

> ciples of government of the sage kings and the saintly rulers, and indulged himself perversely in the martial arts.[12]

The text says little about Gotoba's love of poetry, and nothing about the poetry competitions he sponsored nor about his having commissioned the compilation of the *Shin Kokinshū*; instead, it offers as the cause of the ill-fated Jōkyū Rebellion the undesirable relations he formed with members of the lower classes, notably the dancer Kamegiku who, after being mentioned as the immediate cause of the conflict, does not appear again until the very end of the work, when she accompanies Gotoba into exile in the Oki islands. Gotoba also figures mainly at the beginning and end of *Jōkyūki*. His lapses from kingly rule, described at the very opening, are the causes of his downfall and exile, much as the arrogance of Kiyomori, evoked in the opening lines of *The Tale of the Heike*, has its counterpart at the end in the humility of his daughter, the shabbily dressed nun Kenreimon'in, the last of the Taira.

Gotoba is portrayed in *Jōkyūki* as a ruler who must pay the price of unkingly behavior; but his suffering ultimately makes him worthy of our compassion. After his total defeat, he was commanded by the shogunate to shave his head and put on the dark robes of a priest; but as a last memento of how he looked when he was the emperor, he had a portrait painted that he sent to his aged mother.[13] On the journey to Oki he was accompanied by a handful of retainers and women, their fewness of numbers making a painful contrast with his former excursions. When they passed the Minase Palace, a place Gotoba had particularly loved, he thought, "If only this were my destination!" When they reached Akashi, he asked where they were. Told the name of the place (which means "bright"), he composed the poem:

miyako wo ba	The capital, when
kurayami ni koso	I left it, was enshrouded
idashikado	In the dark of night,
tsuki wa Akashi no	But now the moon has come out
ura ni kinikeri[14]	On the Bay of Shining Light.

To this, his mistress Kamegiku replied:

tsukikage wa	The light of the moon
sakoso Akashi no	Is truly bright at the Bay
ura naredo	Of Shining Light, but

kumoi no aki zo	I still feel a yearning
nao mo koishiki[15]	For autumn within the clouds.

From this point on, and especially after he reached Oki, Gotoba's poems acquired an intensity not found in his earlier compositions,[16] and this capricious, cruel, ambitious man is transformed into a poet whose griefs stir us so greatly as to make us forget he had only himself to blame for his suffering. His son Juntoku was exiled to Sado under circumstances that are almost equally tragic, and he too turned to poetry for comfort. We are perhaps most likely to remember Juntoku at the moment when he must take leave of the people who have accompanied him from the capital: it is a wrench for him to part even from the men who have borne his palanquin, a recognition of the devotion of menials that Juntoku would probably not have displayed if he himself had not suffered.[17]

Gotoba's eldest son, Tsuchimikado, was not involved in the Jōkyū Rebellion. The shogunate, aware of the bitter resentment he felt when his father forced him to abdicate in order to put Juntoku, his favorite son, on the throne, did not intend to punish him. But Tsuchimikado insisted on being exiled, so that he would not be guilty of a lack of filial piety by remaining in the capital while his father suffered exile. He was accordingly sent to the province of Tosa, but his quarters were so wretched that he was allowed to move to neighboring Awa.[18]

The shogunate was evidently reluctant to shed the blood of members of the imperial family, but there was no such reluctance about killing others, even if they had no part in the rebellion; the last pages of *Jōkyūki* are filled with the accounts of small children who are put to death for the sins of their fathers. *Jōkyūki* concludes with a summation of the authors' observations:

> What kind of year was the third of Jōkyū [1221] that three emperors and two princes should have been sent into distant banishment, and nobles and members of the imperial army should have suffered death and exile? And what kind of place was our country that there were no ministers who knew gratitude and no soldiers who knew shame? Although the office of emperor of Japan was created by the Great Goddess Amaterasu and the Great Bodhisattva Hachiman[19] even a wise ruler has difficulty maintaining himself if he employs traitorous ministers; and even if wise ministers are in the service of a ruler who is wicked, it is difficult to govern the country. When the emperor was angry, he punished blameless persons. When the emperor was

joyful, he rewarded even the disloyal. That is why heaven did not side with him. He issued edicts to all corners of the land, and dispatched envoys to the different provinces, but no one obeyed him. . . .[20]

The conclusion is Confucian in tone, and it can hardly be doubted that the author believed Gotoba was responsible for the disasters that befell not only himself but the whole country. Yet, whether or not this was his intent, his evocation of the exile of three emperors creates in the reader a sense of tragedy that goes beyond Confucian lessons.

The Taiheiki

The lengthiest historical work of the Muromachi period—indeed, one of the lengthiest of all Japanese literary works—is the *Taiheiki* (Record of Great Peace) in forty books. Despite its title, the *Taiheiki* describes a period of about fifty years of almost unbroken warfare.[21] It has been suggested[22] that the title may have meant "Chronicle of Great Pacification," but even if the ultimate goal of the many people (over two thousand) who appear in the pages of this work was pacification of the country, extremely little space is devoted to the pursuit of peace. Probably the title refers to the very last event described, the assumption by Hosokawa Yoriyuki of the post of shogunate deputy (*kanrei*) in 1367, an event that seemed to promise an end to the wars. If that was the author's hope, he was sadly deluded—the fighting soon resumed—but he unquestionably desired peace, and it would not have been unnatural to express this desire in a title that implied peace had at last been achieved.[23] By an odd coincidence, this was just the time of the Hundred Years War in Europe. For Japan, no less than for Europe, it was a "calamitous century," to use Barbara Tuchman's phrase.

The *Taiheiki*, a chronicle of this period of warfare, is an important historical document, but it is given literary quality by the style, the choice of materials, and the characterization of the principal figures. Certain sections of particular dramatic effectiveness are widely known anthology pieces, while others make dull reading. It is remembered above all for its heroes, especially Kusunoki Masashige and Nitta Yoshisada, both paragons of devotion to the loyalist cause of the Emperor Godaigo (reigned 1318–1339). The key military figure, Ashikaga Takauji, is less effectively portrayed, perhaps because the author could not make up his mind how to treat a man whose martial genius was negated by his betrayal of the imperial cause.[24]

The *Taiheiki* opens with the steps taken by Godaigo to wrest control of the country from the Hōjō family, who had ruled since the death of Sanetomo as regents for the shoguns in Kamakura. His first plot to overthrow the shogunate and rule in his own right was uncovered in 1324, but he himself was not accused of complicity. In 1331 he instigated a second plot, more serious than the first, but this too was unsuccessful, and Godaigo was obliged to flee to Nara in order to escape the shogunate troops. He held out for another year, but in the meantime the shogunate set up a rival emperor in the capital. As we have seen, the division between the Northern Court, supported by the shogunate, and the Southern Court of Godaigo and his successors would last (with brief intermissions) until the end of the century.[25]

Godaigo was captured in 1332 and exiled by the shogunate to the Oki islands, but his son, Prince Morinaga, managed to arouse loyalist sentiment, and several heroes, notably Kusunoki Masashige (d. 1336), fought for Godaigo, winning victories against great odds.[26] In 1333 Godaigo escaped from Oki and landed in Honshū, the signal for the commencement of a civil war. At this point Ashikaga Takauji (1305–1358), the Kamakura general sent to suppress the rebellion, deserted to Godaigo's side and captured Kyoto in Godaigo's name. Another loyalist general, Nitta Yoshisada (1301–1338), marched on Kamakura and destroyed the shogunate. These events led to what is known as the Kemmu Restoration of 1333, when Godaigo ruled without interference from either a shogun or a retired emperor.[27]

The Kemmu Restoration lasted only three years before Godaigo was once again compelled to flee Kyoto, this time for the mountainous region of Yoshino, where the Southern Court established its capital. The failure of the Restoration is attributed from the opening paragraph of the *Taiheiki* to Godaigo's lapses from the kingly virtues, just as it attributed the somewhat earlier downfall of the Hōjō regents to Hōjō Takatoki's wanton behavior:[28]

> During the reign of the Emperor Godaigo, the ninety-fifth of the line of mortal emperors begun with the Emperor Jimmu, there was a person called Taira no Takatoki,[29] a military official who was the governor of Sagami. At this time, he who was above disregarded the sovereignly virtues, and he who was below was deficient in decorum.[30] From then on the land within the four seas was greatly

> disturbed, and not one day passed peacefully. It is now forty years since watch fires obscured the heavens and war cries made the ground tremble, and no one can enjoy a full span of life. And there is nowhere for the people to rest their limbs in peace.[31]

The collapse of Godaigo's regime was brought about by various causes, chief of which was Ashikaga Takauji's second change of allegiance; this time he deserted Godaigo with the intent of establishing himself as the real ruler of the country. This act of treachery accounts for the dismal reputation of Takauji over the centuries, despite his undoubted ability and also despite the failure of Godaigo's policies. For a time the loyalist armies under Kusunoki Masashige and Nitta Yoshisada were able to hold their own against Takauji, and even forced him to retreat to Kyūshū, but he returned with an army that was vastly superior in numbers to the loyalists' and defeated Masashige and Yoshisada at Minatogawa, near the modern Kōbe, in 1336. Masashige and his brother perished by stabbing each other to death. Before he died, Masashige uttered words that became immortal, "I wish I could be reborn seven times as the same human being so I could destroy the enemies of the court."[32]

Nitta Yoshisada, driven from the field at Minatogawa, nevertheless remained loyal to Godaigo until his death in battle in 1338. Masashige and Yoshisada, especially the former, become known as models of absolute loyalty, and the *Taiheiki* has enjoyed great popularity over the centuries, especially in times of upsurges of national feeling.[33] The solemn language lent itself to recitation, and the scenes of parting and death especially have become part of the heritage of every Japanese, no matter how resolutely opposed to martial display. Masashige, a steadfast loyalist but in every other way, too, a truly admirable man, is one of the two or three most famous Japanese heroes.

The reputation of Godaigo has varied more, ranging from the admiration traditionally accorded to emperors who confronted subjects who had dared to infringe royal authority, to criticism for his foolish policies, especially during the period of the Kemmu Restoration. For example, Godaigo chose for his new reign-name Kemmu, used in China by the Emperor Kuang-wu (6 B.C.–A.D. 57) after crushing the rebel Wang Mang and founding the Latter Han dynasty. The insistence on this particular reign-name was typical of Godaigo's unrelenting desire to restore the past glory of the imperial household (in the manner of Kuang-wu); and he refused to take into consideration the complaint that reign-names which included the word *mu* (military) presaged military disorders. (This particuliar belief proved to be no mere superstition.) Again, in his eagerness to restore the Heian past, he decided to rebuild the Imperial Palace, which had been destroyed by fire in 1177 and not since rebuilt. The country was exhausted from long warfare and could not afford such expenditure, but Godaigo was not to be swerved. The revolt of Ashikaga Takauji prevented the realization of Godaigo's dream, but this was not Godaigo's only extravagance, and his favorites lived in the utmost luxury.

Perhaps his most serious fault, however, lay in not recognizing the contribution of his son, Prince Morinaga, to the Restoration. Godaigo, apparently fearing that Morinaga had ambitions of reigning in his place, urged him to resume his life as a monk, which he had interrupted in order to fight his father's battles. The Prince of the Great Pagoda, as Morinaga was known, was eventually turned over to Takauji by Godaigo and died a miserable death, hating his father even more than the enemy.[34]

Such disastrous mistakes of judgment resulted in Godaigo's being driven from the capital to his lonely mountain retreat at Yoshino. Godaigo in adversity again commands sympathy, though the hardships of life as an exile seem not to have taught him humility: just before he died he asked that he be known posthumously as Godaigo, or Daigo the Second, in emulation of the first Daigo, an emperor of the Heian period who had ruled without interference from his subjects.[35] It is said that he died with a copy of the Lotus Sutra in his left hand and a sword in his right. His distrust of everything new and his incessant attempts to move back the clock four hundred years kept him from benefiting either himself or the country during his brief hour of triumph.

After the death of Godaigo in 1339, the fighting continued, as the *Taiheiki* records. It may seem surprising that the Southern Court was able to hold out so long against superior military forces, but there were divisions among the leaders of the adherents of the Northern Court, and at times the military advantage seemed to be turning in favor of the Southern Court. In 1350 Ashikaga Tadayoshi (1306–1352), then engaged in a bitter dispute with his brother Takauji, submitted to the Southern Court, and in the next year Takauji did the same. This might have ended the conflict (there was in fact a truce), but the chief administrator of the Southern Court, Kitabatake Chikafusa (1293–1353) was so insistent that only the emperors of the Southern Court should be recognized as legitimate that there was no possibility of compromise. The Southern Court unilaterally broke the truce by invading Kyoto and capturing three Northern Court sovereigns.[36] Chikafusa is remembered today for his *Jinnō Shōtoki* (A Chronicle of Gods and Sovereigns, 1339–

1343), a work devoted to expounding the principles of legitimacy in the imperial succession. He is critically described in the *Taiheiki* particularly because of the airs of importance he gave himself,[37] but he is perhaps the last memorable figure in the long procession of warriors who appear in the chronicle.

The *Taiheiki* was apparently written between 1371 and 1374.[38] Our chief clue to the authorship is an entry in the diary of Tōin Kinsada, a nobleman who is known especially as the compiler of the important genealogical work *Sompi Bummyaku*.[39] On the third day of the fifth month of 1374, he wrote, "I understand that on the twenty-eighth of last month Kojima *hōshi* passed away. He was the author of the *Taiheiki*, which has enjoyed such popularity throughout the country in recent years. He was of humble birth, it is true, but he had the reputation of being a master. Truly regrettable."[40]

The meaning of these brief comments has been debated over the years. The first problem is the significance of *hōshi*, a term that normally designated a priest, but was also used for such persons as *biwa hōshi*. Some recited *The Tale of the Heike*, but others amused people who paid them with tales of their own invention, songs, and other displays of talent. Scholarly opinion is divided between those who believe Kojima had actually taken priestly vows, and those who, giving emphasis to Kinsada's words "he was of humble birth," assert that he was a menial, perhaps little more than a slave, who eked out a living by amusing his master.[41] Still others insist that even if an entertainer known as Kojima *hōshi* played an important role in the compilation of sections of the *Taiheiki*, such as the accounts of battles, he must have received help when recounting Confucian doctrines and Chinese historical materials, both prominent in the work.

Another clue to the authorship is found in *Nan Taiheiki* (Anti-*Taiheiki*, 1402), a work by the soldier-scholar Imagawa Ryōshun in which the following incident is related: "A long time ago Echin, the high priest of the Hosshō-ji, brought to the Tōji-ji the thirty-odd volumes of this chronicle that were ready, and showed them to Nishikikōji-dono [Ashikaga Tadayoshi], who had them read by Gen'e *hōin*. There were so many upsetting things and mistakes that he said, 'Even from my brief acquaintance with the work, I can tell there are many errors, more than I should have expected. Many things will have to be added or deleted, and in the meantime, take care that the contents are not divulged.' Later, the rewriting was suspended, but in recent times it has been resumed."[42]

This incident apparently took place about 1350. It has been interpreted as meaning that Echin was in fact responsible for the compilation of the *Taiheiki*. This thesis is plausible, if only because the Hosshō-ji, the temple to which Echin belonged, was known as a place frequented by entertainers, itinerant priests, intellectuals, and others who for some reason were at odds with the government.[43] It is not clear from the above passage what Ashikaga Tadayoshi found so objectionable in the *Taiheiki* manuscript he was shown, but elsewhere Imagawa Ryōshun, a partisan of the Ashikaga shoguns, accused the work of being prejudiced in favor of the court—that is, the side of the Emperor Godaigo and his successors.[44] Ryōshun was moved to write *Nan Taiheiki* out of indignation over the treatment given his side. He objected specifically to the statement in the *Taiheiki* that Ashikaga Takauji surrendered to the Emperor Godaigo when it became evident that the cause of the Hōjō regents was doomed. Ryōshun insisted that this was untrue and demanded that the statement be expunged from the *Taiheiki*. As a matter of fact, it is not found in any surviving text, evidence that it was at some stage pruned of remarks that were offensive to the Ashikaga shoguns.[45]

The unsatisfactory conclusion to the various attempts that have been made to determine the author of the *Taiheiki* is that we still do not know if one man—Kojima *hōshi* or Echin or someone else—or a large number of people over a long period of time compiled the work. On the whole, the style is consistent throughout, suggesting a single editor if not a single author. The work is written in a mixed style, combining Japanese syntax with a strongly Chinese vocabulary.[46]

The philosophical background, however, is not uniform throughout the *Taiheiki*. Unlike *The Tale of the Heike*, which begins with a typically Buddhist evocation of the impermanence of all things, the *Taiheiki* opens with a passage in Chinese briefly setting forth the Confucian theory of kingship, citing precedents from Chinese history to illustrate the thesis that when a king (or emperor) lacks virtue he will not be able to preserve his throne. The first eleven of the forty books are Confucian also in their emphasis on the benefits or misfortunes that accrue from actions in this world (and not in some previous existence), and in their insistence on the importance of history as a guide to rulers. The shift from a prevailingly Confucian to a Buddhist ideology becomes conspicuous with the account of the death of Kusunoki Masashige, as if the author was at a loss to explain, except in terms of causes over which people in this life have no control, why a man who was blameless should have been defeated in battle by moral inferiors. From this point on the *Taiheiki* becomes increasingly Buddhist, invariably attributing happiness or misery in this life to causes in previous lives. The change of viewpoint does not necessarily mean that a different author is writing;

it is more likely that the worsening situation demanded a different philosophical attitude.[47]

The narrative of the *Taiheiki* is again and again interrupted by Chinese anecdotes that are in some way related to the Japanese events being described. These confirm the thesis of the author that it is possible to learn from history, providing evidence that similar events recur in different countries. Early in the first book there is the account of a group of conspirators, relaxing together in undress and sharing the pleasures of liquor and female company. They send for the learned monk Gen'e and ask him for a lecture on the Chinese philosopher Han Yü (768–825) so that it will be supposed they have gathered for literary purposes. Gen'e, who has not the least idea he is party to a conspiracy, chooses as the subject of his lecture a section of Han Yü's writings describing how he was sent into exile by an emperor whom he had angered with his attacks on Buddhism. The account of someone driven into exile rings inauspiciously in the ears of the conspirators, who no doubt secretly fear this might be their own fate, and they interrupt Gen'e's lecture. They ask him to lecture instead on one of the Chinese military classics.[48]

Gen'e was prevented from lecturing on Han Yü's exile, but this did not keep the author of the *Taiheiki* from launching into a long anecdote about Han Yü and his nephew, a Taoist adept, and their sorrowful parting when Han Yü went into exile. Usually the Chinese anecdotes introduced into the text have greater relevance than in this instance, but the reason for including them was essentially the same: to dignify the events in Japan with Chinese antecedents, as the French revolutionaries dignified themselves and their actions by references to Roman antiquity.

The *Taiheiki* was long accepted as a factual description of stirring events of the fourteenth century, but by the Meiji period some scholars began to deny its value as history.[49] The best-known passages provided the easiest targets for the rationalists. For example, the *Taiheiki* relates how Godaigo, at a time when he desperately needed someone who could lead his forces against the shogunate, dreamed of a great tree with its branches stretching to the south. A crowd of dignitaries had gathered, but one seat that faced south was left empty. Two children who appeared in the dream informed Godaigo that the seat was for him. (It was traditional for the ruler to sit facing south.) Godaigo awakened at this point and, mulling over the meaning of the dream, decided that the tree must be a *kusunoki* (camphor tree) because the Chinese character for that tree is written with a combination of elements meaning "tree" and "south." He made inquiries and discovered there was someone named

Kusunoki Masashige, as yet little known but imperially descended, and born after his mother had an auspicious dream. Godaigo summoned the man and appointed him commander of his forces.[50]

It is easy to imagine the doubts that such a passage would arouse in anyone who believed that history is a science. Not only is oneiromancy suspect, but there is reason to believe that Godaigo was acquainted with Masashige long before he had his prophetic dream. According to *The Clear Mirror*, Godaigo had depended on Masashige from the very outset of his struggle against the shogunate.[51] Faced with such problems of historiography, the Meiji rationalists rejected the *Taiheiki* altogether as a source of information. Modern scholars, showing greater generosity, believe that the *Taiheiki* possesses more of the characteristics of a work of history than, say, *The Tale of the Heike*, and that it is less prejudiced than other histories of its time.[52]

The main problem with interpreting the *Taiheiki*, at least before 1945, was that, for all its criticism of Godaigo, it obviously considers that he, rather than the emperor chosen by Ashikaga Takauji, was the rightful sovereign. Yet the later Japanese emperors were descended from the emperors of the Northern and not the Southern Court. During the Tokugawa period *Dai Nihon Shi* (The History of Great Japan) declared that only the Southern Court was legitimate. In the Meiji period it became more common to recognize both courts, but, at the very end of the Meiji period and continuing until 1945, the Southern Court was once again treated by most historians as the sole legitimate line.[53]

Regardless of such political problems, and regardless too of how seriously the *Taiheiki* should be taken as a work of history, its popularity never waned, and there can hardly be a Japanese who does not know something about the events depicted in its pages, whether Godaigo's dream, Kusunoki Masashige's death at Minatogawa, or Nitta Yoshisada's prayer to the dragon god and his throwing of his gold-mounted sword into the sea. Masashige especially has inspired affection and even worship.

The *Taiheiki* is second only to *The Tale of the Heike* as an evocation of the martial ideals that long were central to Japanese tradition, but as a work of literature it is not nearly so compelling. The innumerable digressions, no doubt of greater interest to people of the fourteenth century than to contemporary readers, tend to dampen whatever excitement the main story may arouse. It is easy to accept the theory that, unlike *The Tale of the Heike*, which was recited to musical accompaniment by blind storytellers, the *Taiheiki* was communicated mainly in the form of sermons.[54] The long interruptions to the narrative perhaps represent preachers' attempts to drum home a lesson, even if this deprived the work of the lyrical quality found in *The Tale of the Heike*. Many passages in the *Taiheiki* have been traced to sources in *The Tale of the Heike*, but the effect is almost always different; a world of poetry has been turned into prose. Perhaps the most important lesson is given late in the work by an old priest:

> In recent times control over the country was taken by the military, and their rule lasted for eleven generations, from Yoritomo to Takatoki. It was not necessarily in keeping with basic principles that lowborn persons, no better than barbarians, should have been the chief figures in the land, but in this age of deterioration, nothing can be done to remedy the situation. The times and the events are not governed solely by the assumptions of this world. Subjects killing their lords and children killing their fathers are but aspects of a world where disputes are settled by force, a world where those below overturn those above (*gekokujō*). Even the nobles, the flowers of society, and even the ruler, the emperor himself, have lost their power, and lowly, base soldiers rule the land within the four seas.[55]

The phrase *gekokujō* would be used to describe the whole of society from this time until the establishment of peace under the Tokugawa family in the seventeenth century. The idea of gekokujō—the overturn of the social order—appeals to many readers today, especially those who are not attracted by the haughty ways of the Heian aristocracy, but for most people of the time gekokujō was not an embryonic stirring of democracy but the cause of disorder, looting, and death. And to explain this phenomenon the priests expounded the familiar doctrine that the world had entered the period of mappō, when men are sunk in such depravity that they can no longer benefit by the teachings of the Buddha. A passage like the one quoted above, though in no way literary, conveys much of what life was like in an age of perpetual warfare.

Though the *Taiheiki* has this interest, it suffers from the lack of a single, controlling theme of the kind that joins the beginning and end of *The Tale of the Heike*. It might be argued that the failure to achieve peace constitutes a central theme, but we do not remember this as we read the *Taiheiki*, the way we remember that the theme of *The Tale of the Heike* is the fall of the Taira. We miss, too, the electrifying moments in *The Tale of the Heike* when a person suddenly comes alive, not simply as a figure in a tapestry but as an individual—when, for example, Awa no Naiji, who has given up the world to become a nun, weeps at the realization that she has become so old and ugly that her former lover, Goshirakawa, no longer recognizes her.

The *Taiheiki* is a flawed work, but the survival of its heroes in the memories of the Japanese, and the frequency with which later writers turned to its pages for inspiration, make it clear that its reputation is no accident. Its appeal is episodic, but it has proved to be unforgettable.

Meitokuki

None of the later Muromachi war chronicles approaches the *Taiheiki* in scope or in fame, but *Meitokuki*, the account of a rebellion during the Meitoku era by members of the Yamana family against the Ashikaga shogunate, is far more than a bare chronicle of the events; among the many accounts of warfare of the period it comes closest to matching the literary quality of the *Taiheiki*, flawed though that is.

The rebellion that took place at the end of the twelfth month of the second year of the Meitoku era[56] was one of many such incidents during the turbulent course of the Muromachi period. The actual fighting lasted only one day. Yamana Ujikiyo (1344–1391), the governor of Mutsu and the central figure in the attempt to overthrow the rule of Ashikaga Yoshimitsu, died in the fighting, and his son-in-law Yamana Mitsuyuki (d. 1395), the governor of Harima, who had fled to the province of Izumo after the failure of the rebellion, surrendered to the shogunate in the spring of 1392. The total effect of the fighting was the consolidation of power in the hands of Yoshimitsu, who had deliberately provoked the powerful and troublesome Yamana family into staging the unsuccessful revolt.

If *Meitokuki* had resembled the various other accounts of warfare during the Muromachi period,[57] the revolt of Yamana Ujikiyo against the shogunate would surely have been totally forgotten; insofar as the era-name Meitoku means anything to an educated Japanese, it is likely to be because of this work of literature. The author of *Meitokuki* is not known, but he was probably a priest, and the work itself seems to have been originally written not long after the events it describes. An entry for 1416 in *Kammon Gyoki*, the diary kept between 1416 and 1448 by Prince Sadafusa (1372–1456), states: "The other day a storytelling priest (*monogatari sō*) was summoned for a recitation. He narrated part of the story of the rebellion of Yamana Ōshū. It was interesting."[58] The author of *Meitokuki* was also likely to have been a "storytelling priest" who, like other priests who recited the *Taiheiki*, made a living by giving dramatic recitations. An afterword to the manuscript, dated 1396, states that the author revised and augmented his text.

Meitokuki was written mainly in the same mixture of Japanese and Chinese as the *Taiheiki*, but the most lyrical sections, two *michiyuki*, are in the *gabun*, or "elegant," style of pure Japanese. It is a curiously affecting work whose interest far exceeds the historical importance of the materials, and it deserves more extensive consideration than it has received. One authority on medieval literature said of *Meitokuki* that it combines the lyricism of *The Tale of the Heike* with the realistic tone of the *Taiheiki*.[59]

Meitokuki opens with an encomium of the glorious peace that the Ashikaga shoguns had brought to Japan: ever since Takauji assumed power some sixty years earlier, the world had relaxed under the benign influence of his military virtue; the people rejoiced in his enlightened rule; martial conflicts had ceased; the waves in the four seas had abated; and the winds in all quarters were calm.[60] It takes a moment for the reader to realize that the author is describing the period of the division of the country into the Northern and Southern courts, a time when Japan was torn by almost constant warfare. The point of these introductory remarks is to establish a contrast between the tranquil rule of the country by the Ashikaga family and the rude interruption in the long-abiding peace aroused by the sinister plot of the Yamana family. The author could not have been wholly sincere in his evocation of a happy Japan during the second half of the fourteenth century, but he unequivocably revealed himself as a partisan of the shogunate, and it was in this capacity that he wrote his history.

The most moving sections of *Meitokuki* are, however, not those acclaiming the victory of the shogunate but those describing the deaths of the members of the Yamana family; we remember them as we remember the chapters of *The Tale of the Heike* devoted to the deaths of the Taira warriors. The account of the death of Yamana Kojirō recalls the death of Atsumori:

> Up until a little while before, Yamana Kojirō had been accompanied by seven mounted warriors, but five of them had been killed and the other two had disappeared. Now five enemy horsemen bore down on him and in the clash his horse was shot from under him. He fell from the horse on his left side, and it seemed as though he would imminently be killed when Kanō Heigo, the son of Kojirō's wet nurse, rode up from somewhere, and jumping from his mount,

called out, "Here, ride this horse!" No sooner had he seated Kojirō on the horse than the enemy, not wasting a moment, came at him. He cried out his name: "I am Kanō Heigo Tokikazu. My master lost his horse and would have been killed. To save him I let him have mine. Now I am ready to die fighting. Please tell people later on what happened."

He cut down two of the enemy horsemen only in turn to be struck dead. Seeing what had happened, Kojirō galloped to the spot, intending to fight to the death, when Ōshū's voice, faintly intoning his last *nembutsu*, reached his ears. After fending off the enemy horsemen engaging him, Kojirō managed to get a good look at Ōshū, and saw that he had by this time been killed and his head cut off. "This is the end," he thought. Still seated on the horse, he threw away his broadsword and, unsheathing his dirk, leaped down onto Ōshū's corpse. "Kojirō is coming with you!" he cried, and clinging to the sleeve of Ōshū's armor, prepared to slash his own abdomen. At this moment a man named Kawasaki Taitō, a retainer of [Isshiki] Sakyōdayū [Akinori], threw himself on Kojirō, tore off his helmet, unfastened the visor and, holding him by the hair, turned his face upward. He saw then that Kojirō was a youth of fifteen or sixteen, extremely handsome and noble of features. His sword was poised for the kill, but he could not bring himself to take Kojirō's head.

"Who are you?" he asked. "Tell me your name. I would like to save you, if I can." Kojirō responded, "Even if I told you my name, I am so unimportant I am sure nobody would recognize it. But if you take my head and tell people this is the head of someone who died fighting and who never for a moment left the side of his general, and then you ask who I am, someone surely will remember me." The faint sound of his voice murmuring the nembutsu under his breath could be heard. He said not another word.

Moved, Taitō wanted somehow to take Kojirō alive, but on second thought he realized that even if he saved the youth, there was no telling what might happen later on, considering he was obviously a person of rank. With feelings of helplessness, as if he were regretting the fall of blossoms too weak to withstand the storm wind, he cut off Kojirō's head. When he questioned people, they told him the youth was Tatsufusa, the nephew of Ōshū whom he had adopted as his son and deeply loved. He could easily imagine this might be so, recalling the manner of Kojirō's death and the elegance of his appearance, and it made him feel all the sadder.[61]

Kojirō makes a less striking figure than Atsumori who, lying on his back under the point of Kumagai's sword, snarls back insolent rejoinders to Kumagai's solicitous questions, but he is no less affecting. The loyalty Kanō Heigo displayed in yielding his horse to Kojirō, when he might easily have galloped from the scene, is given a touchingly "human" dimension when he asks the enemy who is about to kill him to tell others how gallantly he died, and Kojirō, too, wants to be remembered for his devotion to Ōshū, the leader of the ill-fated rebellion.

The most memorable section of *Meitokuki* describes the last days of Ujikiyo's widow. On learning that he died in battle, she decides to join him. People urge her to become a nun instead, but she pays no attention to them, awaiting only an opportunity to kill herself. She stabs herself while on a journey. The wound is not fatal, and she can still be saved, but she will not touch the medicine her attendants offer and refuses even to drink water, determined to die. Two of her sons, learning of the attempted suicide, go to see her. They have become priests, in this way escaping punishment for their part in the rebellion.

The brothers meet the widow's attendant and tell her of their desire to see their mother once again, even though they are aware their behavior has been shameful. The attendant urges the mother to see her sons and take the medicine, sure that this will make her feel better, but the old woman is adamant:

> The widow shut her eyes that had been opened a little, staring up at the ceiling and, shaking her head, said in tears, "It is shameful for them to ask such a thing. Just think! They, the sons of a man who was a soldier by profession, sons over twenty years of age, went to the battlefield with their father and then, after seeing him killed before their eyes, ran away! Having nowhere else to turn, they became priests. This was so appalling, on top of all the other grief I have had to bear, that I tried to commit suicide, something no woman has ever done before.[62] How dare they ask to see their mother, now when she is already on the point of death? This is too much to ask of a mother, whose love should be stronger than a father's. Even supposing they had not been born in such a house, they should surely not have deserted an undoubted father. And they should each of them reflect how much truer this is of the behavior of men who are born into a family of soldiers. An adopted son would have behaved better. Kojirō died in battle, loudly praised by friends and foes alike. My joy over what he did is inseparable from my shame over their behavior. Never again in this lifetime will I allow myself

to be seen by such cowards, just because they are my sons. I am much too agitated now to listen to anything more." So saying, she pulled her robe over her head, and uttered not another word.[63]

Ōshū's widow, with a dignity and scorn worthy of a Roman matron, refuses to see her sons. One can all but hear her command, "Come back with your shields or on them!" Japanese women are usually depicted in literature of this period or earlier as gentle but weak creatures, prey to their emotions. A few women were strong-willed enough to take their own lives, but not in the manner of Ōshū's widow, who plunged a dagger into herself as a man might. She is the emblematic samurai wife, one of a number of wives and mothers who figure importantly in the work.[64]

Such moments establish the claims of *Meitokuki* to be recognized as a work of literature, though the work as a whole is also of exceptional interest among the many chronicles of warfare of the Muromachi period.[65]

Historical Romances

The Tale of the Soga Brothers

A conspicuous feature of the literature of the middle ages was the dissemination to the public of tales of warfare by men and women who dressed in the habits of priests or nuns even if they had not entered Buddhist orders. But the religious element in such recitations was probably greater than a modern reader would suspect from the texts. The fear of *goryō*, vengeful spirits of the dead whose wrath could be appeased only by recitation of their deeds, probably accounted for the popularity enjoyed over the centuries by the same few tales about the warfare and vendettas of the past, and may help to explain the continuing sympathy for the losers.[66] It was believed that if these spirits were neglected they might wreak vengeance on the rice harvest.

The recitations were generally accompanied by a drum or the biwa that not only commented on sung or declaimed passages but helped the performers, many of whom were blind, to follow the written texts. Entertainers ranged all over the country, performing at inns where they diverted weary travelers, at local festivals, or wherever else they were likely to be welcomed.[67] A particular group of entertainers normally recited only one text: *Soga Monogatari* (The Tale of the Soga Brothers), for example, was recited by blind women (known as *goze*) and for this reason was known as "a work of literature related by women,"[68] though it is the story of a vendetta, far removed both in tone and content from the typical women's literature of the Heian period. In the process of narrating a work, entertainers often made variations on the original text, to keep audiences from becoming bored with familiar tales; but it should be remembered that the basis of the recitations was always a written text. The recitations were not, as in some societies, the creations of illiterates.[69]

The oldest surviving text of *The Tale of the Soga Brothers* is in a kind of Chinese: that is, a page of this text consists entirely of Chinese characters, with none of the usual admixture of Japanese kana. If one examines the text more closely, however, one will see many small markings next to the characters that make it possible to read it as Japanese. The *manabon,* or "true-writing" (Chinese) text, as opposed to the *kanabon*, or Japanese text of the next century, is believed to have been set down at the beginning of the fourteenth century. It seems to have been preceded by a text, also in Chinese, composed early in the thirteenth century. Before that was the first version, probably a bare narration in Japanese of the vendetta, written only a short time after the events.[70] The oldest manabon was very likely written by priests of the area of Hakone and Izu, and the emphasis on events that took place in the Kantō (eastern) region around Hakone is characteristic of this text; it contrasts with the many earlier writings set in or around the old capital. The use of a mock-Chinese style is found in other works of the time, even folktales that would more naturally have been composed in Japanese.[71]

The kanabon is the best-known version. It seems to have been created in Kyoto during the fifteenth century.[72] Although much easier for a contemporary Japanese to read than the manabon, the narration is frequently (and irritatingly) interrupted by some forty long anecdotes from Chinese, Japanese, or Buddhist sources that relate only tangentially to the main story and take up about one quarter of the work. It is in twelve books, as opposed to the ten books of the manabon.

The vendetta of the Soga brothers, Jūrō and Gorō, carried out against the man who slew their father, is known to almost every Japanese, but from later versions of the tale or from the many adaptations for the stage, rather than from the original *Tale of the Soga Brothers*. Kabuki dramatists were traditionally expected to produce a new play each year about the brothers, each with some novel twist or change of emphasis that distinguished it from previous versions, and the theater season in

Tokyo regularly opened with one of these plays. The personalities of the brothers lent themselves to dramatization: Jūrō, the older, is fair-complexioned, prudent, and susceptible to feminine charms; whereas his brother Gorō is ruddy-faced, impetuous, and powerful rather than sensitive. Again and again the brothers, faced with the same predicament, behave quite differently, in accordance with the inborn nature of each.

The plot is simple, though there are many ramifications of detail. In the first book we learn of the bad relations that existed between Kudō no Sukechika, the grandfather of the Soga brothers, and his cousin, Kudō no Suketsugu.[73] When their grandfather, Suketaka, died he left one of his three estates to Suketsugu, officially an adopted son but in fact Suketaka's illegitimate child with his daughter-in-law. Sukechika, the son of Suketaka's eldest son, was enraged that Suketsugu should inherit the estate, and attempted repeatedly but unsuccessfully to prevent by legal means the execution of the will. When he failed, he turned to magic, persuading a priest to place a curse on Suketsugu. The curse was effective: Suketsugu fell ill and presently died. He was unaware to the end of the cause of his illness, and trustingly asked his cousin, Sukechika, to look after his sons. Sukechika gladly accepted, telling himself that this was a magnificent opportunity to deprive the boys of the estate their father inherited.

Anyone who has read only this much would be likely to suppose that if there was to be a vendetta, it would be carried out by a son of Suketsugu who wished to punish Sukechika, the agent of his father's death. Nothing said about Sukechika commends him to us, whereas Suketsune, the son of Suketsugu, is depicted as a man of taste and elegance. Our sympathy with Suketsune increases: after he is grown and marries Sukechika's daughter, he discovers for the first time that he has been swindled out of his inheritance by Sukechika. He attempts to recover the estate in court, but is foiled by Sukechika, who bribes the magistrates. Eventually, however, the estate is divided between Sukechika and Suketsune.

Up until this point Suketsune has behaved with perfect decorum, and one would hardly expect that such a man would be the object of a vendetta, but the shock of being deprived of half of his rightful inheritance causes him to think of revenge, even of killing Sukechika. The latter, not the most amiable of men, exacerbates the situation by taking back Suketsune's wife (his own daughter) and bestowing her on another man. Sukechika also contrives successfully to keep Suketsune from obtaining any of the income from his half of the estate. Suketsune, who has lost his wife, house, and money, now seriously plots with his retainers to kill Sukechika. At this point the narrative is interrupted by the story of Ch'u Chiu and Ch'eng Ying, two ancient Chinese friends who contrived to restore the throne to the rightful king. This interlude is followed by a lengthy account of sumo wrestling among participants in a hunt, a section so rich in details that it has documentary importance for the history of sumo, though hardly germane to the narrative. The author at least seems ready to describe the chief incident of the hunt, the murder of Sukeyasu, the son of Sukechika and father of Jūrō and Gorō, but not before he has told the story of the Chinese wizard Fei Ch'ang-fang who ascended to heaven on a crane. Finally, the author remembers he has a story to tell, and relates how Suketsune's men ambushed and killed Sukeyasu, whose last words were the request that those who hear his words will look after his two children, Jūrō and Gorō.

When word of Sukeyasu's death reaches his widow, she addresses her two little sons in these words: "If a baby still in the womb can understand its mother's words, how much more so should you boys, being five and three, understand what I have to say. When you become fifteen and thirteen years old, slay your father's enemy and show me his head."[74] The younger son is too small to understand her words, but Jūrō declares that when he has grown up he will indeed cut off the head of his father's enemy.

Much of the remainder of the work is devoted to the unwavering efforts of the two boys to avenge their father's death. In the third book Minamoto Yoritomo, who has cause to hate Sukechika, the boys' grandfather, is persuaded to order their execution, but they are spared after Hatakeyama Shigetada argues in their defense. Yoritomo recalls that it was because his own life was spared by the Taira that they were destroyed, and fears that the same will happen to his family if he allows the two grandsons of Sukechika to live. But Shigetada insists that it was because the Taira were wicked, and not because they spared his life, that they fell, and Yoritomo relents.

The boys are determined to avenge their father's death at all costs. Their father, Sukeyasu, is hardly mentioned and we know little of his character; but their grandfather was an unmitigated scoundrel. We might suppose this fact would dampen their ardor when they were old enough to understand the situation, but the obligation of loyalty was absolute, transcending good or bad, and his sons would probably have felt duty-bound to kill their father's enemy even if they realized the father had been a fiend, thereby fulfilling the Confucian injunction that one must not live under the same heaven as the enemy of one's father.

It is notable also that the actions of Jūrō and Gorō came to be held up as unparalleled examples of filial behavior even though they, as former adherents of the Taira family, were enemies of Yoritomo. In the ninth book the Soga brothers finally succeed (with the help of a sympathetic watchman) in penetrating Suketsune's quarters one night after a drinking party and satisfy their long-cherished ambition by killing him. Ōtōnai, a retainer of Suketsune, awakens at this point and, in a revolting scene, Gorō cuts Ōtōnai into four pieces. Then, we are told,

> Gorō looked at the remains of Ōtōnai and composed this poem:
>
> | | |
> |---|---|
> | *muma wa hoe* | Horses are mooing |
> | *ushi wa inanaku* | And oxen neigh in a world |
> | *sakasama ni* | Turned topsy-turvy; |
> | *shijū no otoko* | Here, a man of forty years |
> | *yotsu ni narikeri* | Has become a boy of four! |
>
> "A fine poem!" Jūrō exclaimed loudly. "I might have spent my entire life composing poems, but never could I have produced a poem like that! Such a fine poem deserves to be included in an imperial anthology. Now that we have achieved our goal, we need not feel constrained." They burst into raucous laughter as they left Suketsune's quarters.[75]

There is something nasty about the vendetta from beginning to end, at least as it is described in the kanabon. Even if one feels vicarious satisfaction when the brothers achieve their life's ambition, one might also wish the occasion had been marked by a bit more solemnity. The brutal poem Gorō composed after slicing into quarters a man who is not even his enemy, and the raucous laughter of the brothers, may have been exactly true of soldiers of the age, but the manabon was surely right in omitting the poem and the laughter. The manabon is indeed exceptional in the dignity it imparts not only to the avenging brothers but to their victims. For example, the grief of Suketsune's wife when she receives her husband's mutilated corpse is fully conveyed, though it is not even mentioned by the kanabon which, reducing everybody to cardboard heroes and villains, deprives the characters of their humanity.[76] But this may be why the kanabon provided Kabuki with so many plays:[77] there is no room in Kabuki for villains with whom one can sympathize; a villain must be unconditionally hateful.

Perhaps the most attractive person in the story is Jūrō's mistress, the courtesan Tora, the illegitimate daughter of a nobleman and the proprietress of a brothel in Ōiso. She is described in terms that indicate the old court culture still survived even in an age of warriors:

> She applied herself to the study of poetry, following the traditions of Hitomaro and Akahito. She was moved deeply by the tales of Narihira and Prince Genji.[78] In spring she was touched by the sight of branches of cherries laden with blossoms, blending with the mist, and by the call of wild geese hidden in the clouds. In autumn she was saddened by the beauty of the moon, the violence of a stormy night, and the sky at daybreak filled with billowing clouds. The cries of deer and insects moved her, as did the forlorn sight of the lonely hut of a guard watching over rice fields.[79]

Tora's aesthetic preferences are so hackneyed as to approach parody, but her true character is displayed not in her choice of reading matter but in her devotion to her lover, Jūrō. Gorō also has a lover, the courtesan Shōshō from Togeshi, but she is given far less attention than Tora. The two women reveal the depth of their loyalty to the men they love by becoming nuns after Jūrō dies fighting and Gorō is executed. The last two books of the kanabon are devoted to descriptions of the pilgrimages the two former courtesans make to different parts of the country to pray for the repose of the Soga brothers.

The Tale of the Soga Brothers is incompetently written and seriously marred by the many digressions, but the story of the vendetta was irresistible. Many adaptations were made for the Nō, Kabuki, and Bunraku theaters.[80] The contrasting personalities of the two brothers lent themselves to representation on the stage, and each of the main episodes of the work, especially in the kanabon, possessed dramatic elements that cried out for performance. *The Tale of the Soga Brothers* is not in itself of much literary significance, but it would provide Japanese writers of future centuries with material for innumerable adaptations.

Yoshitsune

The best known and most admired of all Japanese heroes is undoubtedly Minamoto Yoshitsune (1159–1189), the younger brother of Minamoto Yoritomo, the founder of the Kamakura shogunate. Ivan Morris, who devoted a chapter to Yoshitsune in his book *The Nobility of Failure*, wrote of him,

> Though Yoshitsune made not the slightest contribution to the advancement of society or culture, he is one of the most illustrious and beloved personalities in Japanese history.... Yoshitsune's historical fame is due mainly to his military achievements, but the real reason for his lasting popularity as a hero is that his brief career was shaped in a dramatic parabola of the type that most appeals to the Japanese imagination: after suddenly soaring to success he was undone at the very height of his glory and plummeted to total disaster, a victim of his own sincerity, outwitted by men more worldly and politic than himself and betrayed by those whom he had trusted.[81]

Yoshitsune's brilliant victories during the fighting between the Minamoto and the Taira would have earned him an immortal reputation even if he had done nothing else during his short life. But, as Morris so effectively pointed out, he won a place in the hearts of Japanese by being defeated and destroyed by his brother Yoritomo who, despite his far more important and constructive role in Japanese history, has never been an object of popular affection. Sympathy for the underdog in Japan came to be called *hōgan-biiki*, meaning "partiality to the *hōgan*" (*hōgan* having been one of Yoshitsune's titles);[82] and the glorification of Yoshitsune, found in innumerable books and works for the theater, exemplified this sympathy.[83]

Probably the most famous of the romances associated with Yoshitsune is the war tale *Gikeiki* (Yoshitsune).[84] The author is unknown, and the time of composition, a subject of much speculation ever since Tokugawa-period scholars of national literature first began to worry about such matters, is now generally believed to have been the late fourteenth or early fifteenth century.[85] The disjointed nature of the narration makes it seem probable that *Yoshitsune* was compiled over a period of years by several authors or author-performers.[86] The text is written in a style similar to that of *The Tale of the Heike*—Japanese with many Chinese loanwords. Although there is no documentary evidence that *Yoshitsune* was "performed" in the manner of *The Tale of the Heike*, scholars have conjectured, in view of the generally colloquial nature of the text, that it was recited if not actually chanted to musical accompaniment.[87] It would not be surprising if performers, hoping to please their patrons, added materials that associated the patrons' ancestors with the heroes of the past, but there are far fewer textual variants than for *The Tale of the Heike*.[88]

The most striking feature of *Yoshitsune* is the almost total avoidance of references to the historical parts of Yoshitsune's career. It has little more to say about his dazzling victories in the three major battles of the war with the Taira than: "In the third year of Juei [1184], Yoshitsune went to the capital and drove out the Heike. By fighting valiantly at Ichi-no-tani, Yashima, and Dan-no-ura, he crushed the enemy completely."[89] The first three chapters of *Yoshitsune* are devoted instead to the hero's youth, about which almost nothing factual is known, and the last five chapters to his tragic end after his brother Yoritomo, heeding the malicious gossip of his aide Kajiwara Kagetoki, decided that Yoshitsune was plotting to seize control of the government and therefore had to be killed. Some authorities have suggested that the author of *Yoshitsune* deliberately refrained from describing the central part of his career because it had already been so well treated in *The Tale of the Heike*. Be that as it may, there is almost nothing historically verifiable in this seeming work of history.

The bulk of the work describes Yoshitsune's narrow escapes from assassins and other hostile persons suborned by his brother. His flight from the capital took him to the Inland Sea, where a terrible storm nearly destroyed him and his men, to the Yoshino mountains (and later to Nara) where they were harassed by the armed monks of various temples, and finally to Michinoku in the north where Yoshitsune sought protection from the lord of the domain, Fujiwara Hidehira. During these peregrinations Yoshitsune was accompanied by fewer than a dozen retainers, headed by his lieutenant, Musashibō Benkei, a man of prodigious strength who served and revered Yoshitsune after having been defeated in a duel by the seemingly frail youth. Again and again in their flight Yoshitsune, Benkei, and the others of the little band were confronted by enemies who had been warned of their approach, but they always managed to overcome the superior numbers by the boldness of their attacks or the ingenuity of their stratagems.

Eventually Yoshitsune and the others reached Hiraizumi, the chief city of Hidehira's domain. After months of terrible hardships, they were at last safe, but this respite did not last very long. Their protector, Hidehira, died at the end of 1188. On his deathbed he predicted that Yoritomo would attempt to win the support of his heirs by promising them rich rewards in return for the head of Yoshitsune, but he commanded them not to waver in their protection. Soon afterward, however, Yoritomo persuaded the Retired Emperor Goshirakawa to issue a command calling for the execution of Yoshitsune, and Hidehira's son Yasuhira, able to justify treachery as the duty of a loyal subject, gladly obeyed.

Yasuhira with a force of some five hundred horsemen[90] attacked the stronghold at Takadachi held by Yoshitsune and ten followers. One by one Yoshitsune's men were killed, but not before each had disposed of five or ten of the enemy. Finally, only two of Yoshitsune's retainers were left—Benkei, who, though mortally wounded, held off vast numbers in order to give Yoshitsune time to commit suicide, and the aged Kanefusa, who was entrusted with the heartrending task of killing Yoshitsune's wife and children and then setting fire to the building containing the corpses of Yoshitsune and his family. Yoshitsune committed seppuku in a particularly spectacular and gory manner, and the flames lit by Kanefusa cheated the enemy of his remains.

Yasuhira's treachery brought him none of the benefits he expected. Yoritomo, who had often plotted Yoshitsune's death, now expressed outrage that his brother had been treated in so unseemly a fashion, and sent a punitive expedition to take Yasuhira's head. *Yoshitsune* concludes with the warning that those who violate the deathbed commands of their fathers will be punished by the gods.[91]

The basic materials of *Yoshitsune* are exciting, and the text contains passages of literary interest, but the work as a whole is curiously unmoving because of its painful lack of artistry. The contrast with *The Tale of the Heike*, the finest of the war tales, could not be more striking. For all its episodic nature, the main theme of *The Tale of the Heike*, the destruction of the overweening Taira family, is never forgotten; but *Yoshitsune* is so disjointedly episodic as to lead the reader to suspect that there was no editorial control over the whole. For example, we are told that when Yoshitsune began his flight from his brother's forces,

> [B]eing of a warmhearted nature he had been on intimate terms with some twenty-four ladies during his sojourn in the capital, and of these he had brought along a number of elegant beauties who were his special favorites, including the daughters of the Taira Great Counselor, the Koga Minister of State, the Karahashi Great Counselor, and the Torikai Middle Counselor. The feminine party in the ship numbered eleven in all, including Shizuka and four other *shirabyōshi* dancers.[92]

After the disastrous storm and the battle with enemy ships in the Bay of Daimotsu, "the ladies were put ashore. All but one were sent back—the daughter of the Taira Great Counselor of Second Rank with Suruga Jirō, the daughter of the Koga Minister of State with Kisanta, and the rest with kinsmen or other connections. With Shizuka, his particular favorite, Yoshitsune journeyed from Daimotsu to Watanabe. . . ."[93]

Shizuka is the only woman accorded special attention until (at the end of the sixth chapter) she becomes a nun. It therefore comes as a great surprise to the reader when, near the opening of the seventh chapter, we are suddenly told of Yoshitsune's wife, the daughter of the late Koga minister of state. She has twice been mentioned, but only just barely and in connection with other favorites of Yoshitsune, and it is not even remotely suggested that she was his *kita no kata*, or legal spouse. Nothing prepares the reader for Yoshitsune's decision (which he passes on to Benkei) to take the wife on the journey. Benkei is reluctant, knowing that having a woman in the party will slow their flight, but he finally consents, reasoning that if Yoshitsune is not permitted to take his wife with him, he will have to make do with some coarse eastern woman once they arrive in Michinoku. From this point on the wife (disguised as a page) and her aged guardian, Gon-no-kami Kanefusa, figure prominently in the narrative. (It has been suggested that stories relating to the wife and Kanefusa were added to the existing Yoshitsune legends by a storyteller in the service of the Koga family.)[94] Near the end of the work, after Yoshitsune has committed seppuku, there is another surprise: we are introduced for the first time to Yoshitsune's five-year-old son, without any indication of the boy's mother, or explanation of how he happened to be present with his nurse in Yoshitsune's remote stronghold.

Such awkwardness in the narration was perhaps inevitable in a sprawling work, but in the absence of an overarching theme that might unify the disparate elements, the effect is a series of barely connected events. Even the characters are inconsistently drawn: the charmingly insolent, all-conquering Yoshitsune of the first three books gives way without transition to the moody fugitive of the remainder of the work, and sometimes his behavior undercuts what we are meant to believe is the desperate urgency of his situation. For example, on their journey north from the province of Echizen, the fugitives are faced with a serious setback when they are unable to find a ship to take them to Dewa. This is certainly no time for delay, but we are told:

> "Even though it isn't quite on our way, I should like to see Heisenji Temple. It is one of the most famous places in this province," said Yoshitsune. His warriors did not welcome the excursion, but they set off obediently, journeying monotonously through a dismal world of rain and wind until they reached the temple's Kannon Hall.[95]

In the process of expanding Yoshitsune's story the author seems to have indiscriminately taken in originally unrelated materials, and he lacked the literary skill to graft them successfully onto the body of the work; they remain to the end digressions that cripple the narration.

One unusual feature of *Yoshitsune* is that it does not include the many supernatural legends about Yoshitsune.[96] The reader searches in vain for the familiar tale of how Yoshitsune, when still a boy and known as Ushiwaka, was instructed in the martial arts by the *tengu* of Kurama, or for the weird happenings in the Nō plays, like the angry ghost of Taira no Tomomori rising from the waves to hurl imprecations at Yoshitsune's ship. It is not clear why the supernatural was excluded, especially when one considers how importantly it figures in the Nō plays of roughly the same period; it is a rare instance of consistency in a series of basically unrelated anecdotes.[97]

The chief literary importance of *Yoshitsune* is the influence it exerted over works in various genres. It is difficult to be sure which way the influence went in the case of Nō plays, the *Kōwaka*[98], and other literary works of the same general period as *Yoshitsune*, but there can be no doubt of its influence on the drama and historical fiction of the Tokugawa period.[99]

The most famous work for the theater based on the Yoshitsune legends is probably *Kanjinchō* (The Subscription List), a Kabuki play derived from the Nō *Ataka*. Almost all the elements of this play can be found in *Yoshitsune*, but anyone familiar with *Kanjinchō* who reads the source passages in *Yoshitsune* is bound to be disappointed by the account, at once meager and repetitious, of the same events. The climax of *Kanjinchō* is the moment when Benkei, in order to draw suspicion from Yoshitsune (who is disguised as a porter), has no choice but to lift his hand against his master. This action is superbly dramatic, and it is echoed by an equally affecting moment when, after Yoshitsune's followers have successfully passed through the barrier, Benkei bows in profound apology for having struck Yoshitsune, to which the latter responds by lifting his hand in a gesture that signifies he forgives what under other circumstances would have been an impermissible breach of feudal etiquette.

In *Yoshitsune* the fugitives pass without untoward incident through the Ataka Barrier, but later are stopped twice. On the first occasion, when a ferryman is suspicious of Yoshitsune, "Benkei leaped angrily onto the gunwale of the boat, seized his master's arm, hoisted him over his shoulder, and jumped to the beach. Then he dumped him roughly onto the sand and with a fan which he pulled from his waist began to beat him so mercilessly that the onlookers averted their eyes."[100] There is more than a hint of sadism in this description, and when Benkei later begs pardon, crying, "I shall be punished by everybody—gods, bodhisattvas, and men. Forgive me, Great Bodhisattva Hachiman!"[101] he exhibits none of the dignity of Benkei in the Kabuki play. Worse, a few pages later, when the party reaches the heavily fortified Nenju Barrier, Benkei once again beats Yoshitsune:

> Benkei made up Yoshitsune to resemble a porter monk, loaded two panniers on his back, and started forward, beating him smartly with a big switch and shouting, "Get along, monk!"
>
> "What has he done to make you treat him so harshly?" the barrier guards asked.[102]

One beating of his master, performed in *Kanjinchō* with the greatest reluctance by Benkei, is dramatically effective, but the two beatings in *Yoshitsune* are less dramatic than brutal.

And yet if we decide that *Yoshitsune* is of negligible literary value we shall be guilty of ignoring its importance for Japanese over the centuries. When Bashō and his companion Sora traveled to the north on the journey described in *The Narrow Road of Oku*, they again and again recalled Yoshitsune and his men, most notably at Hiraizumi:

> The three generations of glory of the Fujiwara of Hiraizumi vanished in the space of a dream. The ruins of the Great Gate are two miles this side of the castle; where once Hidehira's mansion stood are now fields, and only the Golden Cockerel Mountain remains as in former days.
>
> We first climbed up to Takadachi, from where we could see the Kitagami, a big river that flows down from Nambu. . . . Here Yoshitsune once fortified himself with some picked retainers, but his great glory turned in a moment into this wilderness of grass. "Countries may fall, but their rivers and mountains remain. When spring comes to the castle, the grass turns green again."[103] These lines went through my head as I sat on the ground, my bamboo hat spread under me. There I sat weeping, unaware of the passage of time.

natsukusa ya	The summer grasses—
tsuwamonodomo ga	For many brave warriors
yume no ato	The aftermath of dreams.

Bashō

unohana ni	In the verbena
Kanefusa miyuru	I can see Kanefusa—
shiraga kana	Behold his white locks![104]

SORA

The legends of Yoshitsune still live in the hearts of Japanese and provide materials for new works of literature. *Yoshitsune* is itself not of great interest, despite the occasional exciting episode but, more than any other literary work, it created the image of a national hero.

The Clear Mirror

Masukagami (The Clear Mirror), the fourth of the surviving "mirrors" of Japanese history,[105] is the most poetic. Each of the chapters bears a title derived from the words of a poem, and the meaning of *Masukagami*, the intentionally ambiguous title of the whole, is explained by poems. The first is spoken in the introductory chapter by the old nun whose narration of her memories provides the material of the work:

oroka naru	All that will appear
kokoro ya mien	In the mirror's clarity
masukagami	Is my foolish heart;
furuki sugata ni	It adds to the old writings,
tachi wa oyobade	But cannot touch their grandeur.

The word *masu* is used to mean both the verb "to add to" and the noun *masumi*, or "perfect clarity." The nun promises that her tale, for all its failings, will add to the earlier "mirrors," and will be clear and without deceit.

The setting of the introductory chapter is the Seiryō-ji, a temple in the Saga area of Kyoto famous for its statue of Shakyamuni Buddha. An unidentified man, on a visit of worship, sees there an old nun leaning on a stick who is having trouble making her way as far as the temple. He approaches and, striking up a conversation with her, learns that she is well over one hundred years old. He is a student of old poetry, and has been yearning to meet someone who could tell him about the past. The old nun, giving him a toothless smile, modestly replies that she really does not remember anything worth transmitting to another person, but he persists, reminding her that the recollections related by some old people at the Urin Temple long ago had turned into a book that was now widely read, "a *Nihon Shoki* in simple Japanese" (*kana no Nihongi*).[106] He refers here specifically to *The Great Mirror*, but later mentions the other "mirrors," all of which were written in kana, unlike the official histories of Japan, composed in difficult-to-read Chinese.

The old nun is eventually persuaded, and she relates her reminiscences of the past, extending from the birth of the Emperor Gotoba in 1180 to the Emperor Godaigo's return from exile in 1333. Obviously, not even a centenarian could have memories that encompass so long a period, and at no point does the nun suggest how she happens to know intimate details of the lives of the august personages she describes. No doubt readers accepted such implausibilities in the narration as part of the conventions of "mirrors" of history.

Once the narrator of the work has been established as an old nun, the interlocutor virtually disappears from the work, and the nun herself only rarely says anything that reminds us of her identity. The convention of an old person's recalling the past was useful in that it allowed for a conversational style,[107] for the inclusion of poetic episodes even if they were not of historical importance, and for an essentially literary and dramatic structure that gave greater shape to the materials than was possible in more factual war chronicles such as the *Taiheiki*.

Scholars are now more or less agreed that Nijō Yoshimoto was the author of *The Clear Mirror*[108] although he is not identified as such in any document of the period. Yoshimoto was a noted renga poet and edited *Tsukuba Shū*, the most important collection of renga; if he was indeed the author of *The Clear Mirror*, this would explain the conspicuously poetic tone. Internal evidence concerning the date of composition of the work is scanty. It must have been written after 1338, the year of the last datable event in the text, and before 1376, the year of the oldest manuscript. Most believe *The Clear Mirror* was written between 1368 and 1376, but dates as late as 1427 have been proposed.[109]

The Clear Mirror, unlike the *Taiheiki*, makes no pretense of impartiality. The author is clearly on the side of the emperors and the nobles whenever conflict arises between them and the military, and the work contains none of the criticism of Gotoba and Godaigo found in other sources. The author ended *The Clear Mirror* with Godaigo's return to the capital from exile in Oki, sparing himself the necessity of enumerating the mistakes that would be made by Godaigo during the Kemmu Restoration.

Although *The Clear Mirror* also treats the reigns of the emperors in between Gotoba and Godaigo, including the profligate brothers Gofukakusa and Kameyama, the heart of the work is surely the accounts of the two exiled monarchs. Gotoba's arrival on the desolate island where he would spend the last nineteen years of his life is described in these terms:

> The place where he was to live was in the interior of the island, far from the village and other habitations. It was at some distance from the sea. The house was in the shadow of a mountain, protected by a towering great boulder. It was simply fashioned, the merest pretext of a dwelling. Indeed, the place looked makeshift, reminiscent of "even a brushwood hut is only for a little while"[110] in its pinewood pillars and corridor roofed with reeds. But, although it was severely plain, the house had been built with a certain charm. Yet when he recalled his Minase Palace, it seemed like a dream. The view over the water, stretching out into the distance as far as his eyes could see, made him feel that everything, even "more than two thousand miles away,"[111] was within his ken, and he realized the truth of the Chinese poet's lines as never before. When he heard the roar of the wind fiercely blowing in from the sea, he murmured the words:[112]
>
> | | |
> |---|---|
> | *ware koso wa* | I am none other |
> | *niishimamori yo* | Than the new island guardian! |
> | *Oki no umi no* | You savage sea winds |
> | *araki namikaze* | Over the waves at Oki, |
> | *kokoro shite fuke*[113] | Have a heart and blow gently! |

This passage, as numerous critics have pointed out, was derived from the description of Genji's place of exile in the "Suma" chapter of *The Tale of Genji*: "Looking back toward the city, he saw that the mountains were enshrouded in mist. It was as though he had indeed come 'three thousand leagues'.... Genji's new house was some distance from the coast, in mountains utterly lonely and desolate.... The grass-roofed cottages, the reed-roofed galleries—or so they seemed—were interesting enough in their way. It was a dwelling proper to a remote littoral, and different from any he had known."[114] The author turned to *The Tale of Genji* in part because he knew the work extremely well and passages came into his mind apropos of almost any experience; but it also provided him with an evocative account of a prince's exile. Probably when he set about writing this section of *The Clear Mirror* the only firm piece of evidence available about Gotoba's place of exile was the poem; the rest was invented or else borrowed from *The Tale of Genji*.

The Tale of Genji was not the only literary work borrowed by the author of *The Clear Mirror*. The account of the birth in 1243 of the future Emperor Gofukakusa was probably indebted to similar descriptions in both the diary of Murasaki Shikibu and *A Tale of Flowering Fortunes*.[115] Paraphrases of passages found in other works of Heian and Kamakura literature have been carefully traced. Perhaps the closest examples of borrowing were from *The Confessions of Lady Nijō*, the diary kept from 1271 to 1306 by the lover and accomplice of the Emperor Gofukakusa. Although this diary survived for centuries in a single manuscript, it was probably available to someone of Nijō Yoshimoto's importance.[116] The borrowings from *The Confessions of Lady Nijō* are by no means word for word, and the author of *The Clear Mirror* was far more discreet than Lady Nijō when it came to relating such matters as Gofukakusa's affair with his half-sister, an affair in which Nijō was obliged to serve as go-between.[117] (He chose not to include the ineffable comment Gofukakusa made the morning after he had raped the former high priestess: "The cherry blossoms were lovely, but the branch was fragile and the flowers too easily picked," meaning that rape did not give him much of a thrill unless his victim resisted.)[118]

Such borrowings from primarily literary works suggest that the author of *The Clear Mirror* aimed at effects of a kind not considered by the author of, say, the *Taiheiki*. The literarily most distinguished section is the chapter "Kume no Sarayama."[119] It opens in this way:

> The spring of 1332 had come.[120] The beginning of the first year of the new reign[121] was surprisingly festive. The new emperor, being young and handsome, lent a special brilliance to everything, and the palace ceremonies were performed in exact observance of tradition. On the occasions of official functions, and even on quite ordinary days, there was so dense a press of carriages before the palace and the residences of the cloistered sovereigns,[122] which were situated within the same area, that it was scarcely possible to move, but among all those who thronged to the court, there was not a single familiar face.
>
> The former emperor[123] was still held captive at Rokuhara. Along about the second month, when the skies were serene and lightly veiled in mist, and the gently blowing spring breezes brought from the eaves the nostalgic fragrance of plum blossoms, so melancholy was his cast of mind that even the clear notes of the song thrush sounded harshly in his ears. The comparison is rather peculiar, but one could not help thinking of some neglected court lady in the women's palace at the Chinese court.[124] Perhaps it was with the

intent of consoling him, now that the lengthening of the days made it all the harder for him to pass his time, that the empress sent him his lute (*biwa*), together with this poem written on a scrap of paper:

omoiyare	Turn your thoughts to me,
chiri no mi tsumoru	And behold these, my tears,
yotsu no o ni	Too thick to brush away;
harai ni aezu	They fell on the strings of the lute
kakaru namida wo	When I saw how thick the dust lay.[125]

The melancholy state of mind of the emperor was intensified by thoughts of the fate suffered by Gotoba a little more than a century earlier. He finally was informed that he would have to leave for Oki on the seventh day of the third moon.

> It may well be imagined how great was the emperor's consternation when he learned that the dreaded moment was now at hand. Great were the lamentations also of the empress and the princes, and those who were in attendance on him could not conceal their grief. He attempted to keep others from seeing how distressed he was, but in spite of himself tears welled up, which he concealed as best he could. Whenever he recollected what had happened to the former emperor, he realized how unlikely it was that he himself would ever return to govern the country again. He lived in the conviction that everything had now come to an end, and he ceaselessly lamented that his sorrows were due not to the wickedness of others, but had all been imposed on him from a previous existence.[126]

Godaigo's passage through the city of Kyoto is rendered the more poignant for modern readers by the fact that the street names have not changed, and one can follow his course step by step. The superb description makes it possible also to visualize the crowds along the way watching as an emperor started his long journey into exile:

> From Rokuhara they proceeded westward along Shichijō, and then turned southward at Ōmiya. The imperial carriage halted before the Eastern Temple, apparently to permit the emperor a brief moment of prayer. The carriages of spectators jammed the streets. Even ladies of quality, in wide-brimmed hats and tucked-up robes,[127] mingled with the pedestrians. Young and old, nuns, priests, and even wretched woodcutters and hunters from the mountains thronged

> the place, as thick as bamboos in a forest. Just to see them all wiping their eyes and sniffling made one feel that no worse calamity could occur in this sorrowful world. It must have been the same when the Emperor Sutoku was sent to Sanuki or when the Emperor Gotoba was exiled to Oki, but those events I know of only by report, not having witnessed them myself. It seemed to me that this was the first time anything so appalling had occurred. Even insignificant or base people who had never before looked upon the emperor were bewildered and dumbfounded by the pathos of today's leave-taking.
>
> The emperor lifted the blinds of his carriage a little and gazed around him as though not to let a blade of grass or a tree escape his eyes. The soldiers of the escort, not being made of stone or wood, could be seen to wet the sleeves of their armor with their tears. The emperor looked back until the treetops of the capital disappeared from sight. He still wondered if it might after all be just a dream.[128]

The vividness of the description suggests that the narrator actually witnessed the scene, an impression confirmed by her admission that she knows of the exile of two earlier sovereigns only by report. Much of this account, however, could only be imagined, perhaps with the aid of *The Tale of Genji*.[129] Godaigo's journey undoubtedly took place, but it was literature rather than the reports of witnesses that enabled the author to know his emotions. Godaigo's dejection on reaching Oki moves us by the details even more than the tragic situation:

> Nothing remained in the way of relics of the former exile. There was only a handful of houses and, in the distance, a village where the fishermen burned seaweed for salt. When he cast his eyes over this most miserable view, all thought of himself fled, and his mind went back to long-ago events. Sympathy and indignation welled up within him as he tried to imagine what it must have been like for that emperor to have ended his days in such a place, and he realized that his own exile stemmed from a desire to fulfill a few of the aspirations of his ancestor. Countless thoughts pursued him: he wondered whether the former emperor in his grave was now taking pity on him.[130]

In a brilliant dramatic touch, the author interrupts this account of the gloom and the drabness of Godaigo's place of exile with a description of the festivities attending the coronation of the new emperor, only to return to another aspect of his grief:

On the twenty-second day of the third month the coronation procession took place in the capital, dazzling everyone by its splendor. The cloistered soverigns, Gofushimi and Hanazono,[131] who rode together, stopped their carriage by the Taiken Gate to watch the procession. Everything had been arranged with the greatest care and went off beautifully.

But, if the truth be known, the Emperor Godaigo's consort was sunken in grief, as she had been since their parting, and never raised her head. Her grief was understandable: added to the unhappiness caused by distant separation, pangs in her heart troubled her unremittingly. Without emotion, as if it were happening to someone quite remote, she received the news that her title of empress had been taken from her, and a name as a nun bestowed.[132]

Once again, the pervading gloom is interrupted by a brief account of festivity in the capital:

This year there was an imperial procession to the Kamo Festival, which was so unusual that people devoted the utmost care to the sightseeing carriages, and the stands along the way were built with greater splendor than ever before. The deputies of the reigning and cloistered sovereigns vied with one another as to who would present the most stunning appearance. . . . The courtiers and the young men of noble families—all those who were privileged to wear the forbidden colors—escorted their majesties in bright and elegant attire. Even their attendants were so splendidly dressed as to suggest a bouquet of flowers. From the carriages the sleeves of court ladies' robes in every color—wisteria, azalea, verbena, carnation, and iris—overflowed in a most gay and charming manner.

When the festival was over and things had quieted down, all those nobles who had been seriously implicated as partisans of the Emperor Godaigo were sent to distant exile.[133]

The poetry of Godaigo, though not rated nearly so high as Gotoba's, acquires a powerfully moving quality because of the circumstances it reflects, and the portrait of the man that emerges from the pages of *The Clear Mirror* is unforgettable. It is not necessary to admire Godaigo in order to empathize with a monarch who is driven into lonely exile. Read together with the last chapter in *The Clear Mirror*, which describes his triumphant return to the capital, his sufferings seem mythic, the trials a hero must undergo to prove himself worthy of final victory; and the readers' foreknowledge of this victory may give ironic overtones to the celebrations in the capital of the régime of the rival emperor. But readers will also know, though *The Clear Mirror* ends before this point, that Godaigo's triumph in the Kemmu Restoration was short-lived, and that he was doomed to die an exile. These different layers of time help to give dramatic depth to *The Clear Mirror*. By no means an objective history, it is nonetheless a masterpiece of *rekishi monogatari* (historical tale), a genre that ever since *The Story of Masakado* has occupied an important place in the imaginations of the Japanese.

Notes

1. There is reason to believe that some of the later war tales, notably the *Taiheiki*, were recited (at least in excerpts) in the manner of *The Tale of the Heike*, but there is extremely little documentary evidence. See Nagazumi Yasuaki, *Chūsei Bungaku no Kanōsei*, pp. 409–17.
2. I have confined my account to works of apparent literary intent; others, though of historical importance, will not be discussed. Writings that describe the warfare of the latter part of the sixteenth century are treated in chapter 29. *Mirror of the East*, compiled in the second half of the thirteenth century, contains some interesting parallels to the material in this chapter, but the text as a whole possesses little literary value.
3. See Matsubayashi Yasuaki, *Shintei Jōkyūki*, p. 26. Matsubayashi, quoting the article by Masuda Shū, "Jōkyūki—Kaiko to Tembō," states why Masuda believed the rufubon text was composed after 1246. On the same page he also quotes an article by Sugiyama Tsuguko in the 1970 issue of *Gunki to Katarimono*, giving her reasons for believing that the Jikōji text of *Jōkyūki*, the oldest, dates from between 1230 and 1240. Matsubayashi (in "Kōbu no Kassenki," p. 114) states his own opinion: the Jikōji text was originally written soon after the disturbance, but put into its present form between 1230 and 1240.
4. Matsubayashi, *Shintei,* p. 29, gives the reason (the deferential attitude toward the Ashikaga family) for believing that the Maeda text must date from the fourteenth century. See also Matsubayashi, "Kōbu no Kassenki," pp. 115–16. Matsubayashi (*Shintei*, p. 30) relates why *Jōkyū Heiranki*, the best-known version of the text, has been dated between 1590 and 1606.
5. The estates were at Nagae and Kurahashi in the province of Settsu. For text, see Matsubayashi, *Shintei*, p. 55.
6. According to the rufubon text (Matsubayashi, *Shintei*, p. 57), Gotoba summoned men from fourteen provinces in the Kinki and nearby regions, ostensibly to take part in a mounted archery (*yabusame*) contest.

7. He was fourteen by Japanese, but only thirteen by Western count. Before the gembuku initiation ceremony he was known by the boy's name of Juō, but afterward was usually called Mitsutsuna.
8. Matsubayashi, *Shintei*, pp. 62–68.
9. *Ibid*., p. 109.
10. *Ibid*., p. 120.
11. The meaning of the term *geinō* is uncertain. If the author's source was the chronicle *Rokudai Shōji Ki* (c. 1224), the term, as used of Gotoba in that work, meant the literary and martial arts; but *Kimpishō*, the study of court usages and precedents compiled about 1225 by Gotoba's son Juntoku, defined *geinō* as the literary and musical arts. See *ibid*., p. 148.
12. *Ibid*., p. 46. It should be noted that the Jukōji text of *Jōkyūki*, the oldest, opens in a totally dissimilar manner, with a dreary account of the origins of Buddhism and of the ancient history of Japan. See the English translation by William H. McCullough, "Shōkyūki," pp. 169–175.
13. Matsubayashi, *Shintei*, p. 135. The portrait was painted by Fujiwara Nobuzane, the son of the even more celebrated portrait painter Takanobu.
14. *Ibid*., p. 137.
15. The word *kumoi* means literally "cloud dwelling," but it was used to mean the palace, and the people who lived in the palace were similarly referred to as *kumo no ue bito* ("people above the clouds"). Kamegiku is saying that although the moonlight is bright over Akashi Bay, she still yearns for the palace, where the moon was hidden by clouds.
16. For examples of these later poems, see chapter 17, p. 675.
17. Matsubayashi, *Shintei*, p. 138.
18. *Ibid*., pp. 144–45.
19. Two of the chief Shintō divinities, though Hachiman was given a Buddhist title.
20. Matsubayashi, *Shintei*, p. 146.
21. The unsuitability of the title to the contents was noted as early as the beginning of the Tokugawa period, when it was suggested that the title was satirically applied or that calling things by their antonyms (for example, referring to sickness as "pleasure") was a common play on words; but the deadly seriousness of the work makes it unlikely that the compiler jested when giving a title. See Hasegawa Tadashi, "Gekokujō no Sekai," pp. 38–39.
22. For example, by Helen Craig McCullough in her translation, *The Taiheiki*, p. xvii.
23. Fukuda Hideichi, in his *Chūsei Bungaku Ronkō*, p. 419, reached the conclusion that the central theme (*shudai*) of the work was the author's desire for peace, and that was why he gave the work its seemingly paradoxical title.
24. In the 1930s, a period of militant nationalism, Takauji was "relegated to

the status of the most loathsome of traitors in Japanese history." See H. Paul Varley, *Imperial Restoration in Medieval Japan*, p. 186

25. In 1392 Ashikaga Yoshimitsu persuaded the emperor of the Southern Court to return to Kyoto, with the understanding that succession to the throne would henceforth alternate between the Northern and Southern courts. This in fact did not happen; succession to the throne was entirely in the line of the Northern Court.
26. If we can believe the *Taiheiki*, Masashige had only some seven hundred horesemen against Ashikaga Tadayoshi's 500,000 at the battle of Minatogawa, where he met his end. Obviously, the numbers are exaggerated, here and elsewhere in the *Taiheiki*.
27. Varley's *Imperial Restoration* is a study of this period.
28. The insane fondness of Hōjō Takatoki (1303–1333) for dogfights (he kept thousands of dogs in Kamakura for this purpose) and for *dengaku*, a form of entertainment resembling Nō, was often given as the main cause of his downfall.
29. Hōjō Takatoki, called Taira here because his family stemmed from a branch of the Taira family.
30. The commentated editions I have consulted all state that *kami* refers to Godaigo, and I have accordingly translated the sentence in this matter. However, Yamashita notes that although Godaigo is here taxed for his "disregard of sovereignly virtues" (*kami kimi no toku ni somuki*), criticism is leveled at Takatoki and not at Godaigo, certainly in what follows immediately. Criticism of Godaigo does not really begin until the Kemmu Restoration.
31. Yamashita Hiroaki (ed.), *Taiheiki*, I, p. 16. See also the translation by Helen Craig McCullough, *The Taiheiki*, p. 3.
32. The statement was taken up by patriots over the centuries, often with meanings rather different from Masashige's. The best-known version is the phrase *shichishō hōkoku* ("[with] seven lives repay the country"), meaning that it would take seven lives to repay adequately one's indebtedness to Japan. This interpretation apparently goes back no further than the Meiji period. See Uwayokote Masataka, "Taiheiki no Shisō," in Nagazumi Yamaki, *Taiheiki no Sekai*, pp. 105–7.
33. For an extended (and well-written) account of Masashige's life and reputation, see Ivan Morris, *The Nobility of Failure*, pp. 106–42.
34. See the account by Uwayokote Masataka, "Buke yori mo kimi ga urameshi," in Nagazumi, *Taiheiki*, pp. 72–75. The statement that Morinaga had "murmured to himself that he felt more bitter toward His Majesty than toward the military" is found originally in *Baishōron*. (For this work, see below, note 45.)
35. Uwayokote Masataka, "Godaigo," in Nagazumi, *Taiheiki*, pp. 114–19. It was customary for sovereigns who had died in distant places, especially in exile, to have the character *toku* (virtue) in their posthumous names,

as in the cases of Sutoku, Antoku, and Juntoku, but Godaigo preferred to be known not as a victim but as an emulator of a great ancestor.

36. See H. Paul Varley, *A Chronicle of Gods and Sovereigns: Jinnō Shōtōki of Kitabatake Chikafusa*, pp. 6–7. See also Sakurai Yoshirō, "Taiheiki to Jinnō Shōtōki," in Nagazumi, *Taiheiki*, p. 264.
37. See Sakurai Yoshirō, "Taiheiki," p. 269. The passage occurs in Book XXX of the *Taiheiki*.
38. These are the figures given by Nagazumi in *Taiheiki*, p. 328. Earlier in the same book (p. 36) he more cautiously suggested the composition took place between 1368 and 1374.
39. The title means something like "Ramifications of Noble and Base [Families]." The "noble" families are restricted to those directly descended from the imperial family; the "base" families included the Minamoto, Taira, Tachibana, and other exalted families with connections to the imperial family, plus the various branches of the Fujiwara family that are said to have descended from the gods.
40. See, for example, Nagazumi, *Taiheiki*, p. 319. See also the translation by Helen Craig McCullough, *The Taiheiki*, pp. xvii–xviii. She cites the original text, *Tōin Kinsada Nikki*.
41. A summary of the different views on the identity of Kojima *hōshi* is given in Yokoi Kiyoshi, *Chūsei wo ikita Hitobito*, pp. 134–37. Wakamori Tarō was of the opinion that Kojima was a *yamabushi* (mountain priest) from Kojima in Bizen (the modern Okayama Prefecture), an important center of yamabushi activity. One problem with this explanation, as Yokoi points out, is that if Kojima lived and died in Bizen, it would be most unlikely that Tōin Kinsada would have learned of his death so quickly. A second theory, associated especially with Hayashiya Tatsusaburō, is that Kojima *hōshi* was from the base class (*semmin*), condemned to live in ghettoes known as *sanjo*. There were performers known variously as *sanjo shōmoji*, *sanjo ommyōji*, *sanjo hōshi*, and so on. The question here is whether Tōin Kinsada when he wrote "humble birth" (*hisen no ki*) meant someone of the lowest social class, or merely someone of a class lower than his own.
42. Text and interpretation as given by Hasegawa in "Gekokujō," p. 36.
43. See *ibid.*, p. 37.
44. See Uwayokote Masataka, "Rekishisho toshite no Taiheiki," in Nagazumi, *Taiheiki*, p. 59. Also Uwayokote Masataka, "Okoreru Kokoro aredo, Reigi midari narazu," in *ibid.*, p. 127.
45. See Nagazumi Yasuaki, "Taiheiki no Seiritsu to Sakusha," in Nagazumi, *Taiheiki*, pp. 321–22. The events of the period are otherwise described in *Baishōron*, a historical tale written by an unknown author about 1350. It is obviously prejudiced in favor of the Hosokawa family and therefore in favor of the Ashikaga shoguns whom the Hosokawa served. This work, of minor literary importance, is described in *Nihon Koten Bungaku Daijiten*, V, pp. 33–34.

46. Most modern texts, in order to make the *Taiheiki* more accessible to readers without special knowledge of the *wakan konkō*, rearrange the text (without changing the words, however) in the normal order of Japanese. For a better idea of the crowded look of the pages of the original, the reader should consult Okami Masao, *Taiheiki*, 2 vols., in Kadokawa Bunko. This text, with extraordinarily copious notes, unfortunately covers only the first fourteen books of the *Taiheiki*.
47. Fukuda Hideichi, in *Chūsei*, p. 436, expressed the view that the philosophical background of the *Taiheiki* was far less Buddhist than that of *The Tale of the Heike*.
48. The four works they ask for, *Wu-tzu*, *Sun-tzu*, *Liu-t'ao*, and *San-lüeh*, purported to be ancient writings by Chinese masters of military strategy, but all four were forgeries. They were (not surprisingly) popular in an age of warfare, and influenced the *Taiheiki* and other martial tales. See Yamashita, *Taiheiki*, I, p. 31; also Helen Craig McCullough, *The Taiheiki*, pp. 14–18.
49. This view was first expounded in 1891 by Kume Kunitake in his article "*Taiheiki* wa shigaku ni eki nashi" (The *Taiheiki* is of no use to the study of history), published in the magazine *Shigaku Zasshi*. See Uwayokote Masataka, "Rekishisho toshite no *Taiheiki*," in Nagazumi, *Taiheiki*, pp. 50–54. Kume, whose diary *Beiō Kairan Jikki* is the best of the early Meiji period descriptions of travels in the West, seems to have drawn on his experiences abroad when framing his attacks on the *Taiheiki*. For example, he declared that when he read the account of the gathering of the conspirators at which scantily clad women served, "It was exactly like a brothel in Paris, and the obscenity of the naked women, lined up and dressed in lace like the whores for sale, made me want to shut the book after one reading." (Quoted by Uwayokote in "Rekishisho," p. 57.) In 1892 Kume lost his position as a professor at Tokyo University because an article he wrote on the origins of Shintō had enraged devout believers.
50. The account is given in Book III. See Yamashita, *Taiheiki*, I, pp. 111–114. For a translation, see Helen Craig McCullough, *The Taiheiki*, pp. 67–69.
51. See Oka Kazuo, *Masukagami*, pp. 318–19, where it states, "Soldiers from Yamato, Kawachi, Iga, Ise, and other places had gathered at Kasagi Castle. Among them was a man named Kusunoki Hyōe Masashige, whom he had depended on from the very beginning. A daring and bold-spirited man, he had strongly fortified the area around his own castle in the province of Kawachi, and was prepared to look after the emperor here if his present residence became dangerous."
52. See Uwayokote, "Rekishisho," pp. 50, 62. See also Uwayokote Masataka, "Nitta Yoshisada" (in Nagazumi, *Taiheiki*), p. 128. He states that *Baishōron* and *Nan Taiheiki*, both Northern Court works, distort historical fact more than the *Taiheiki*.
53. See Varley, *Imperial Restoration*, pp. 124–55, for an account of the changing

views of the past. Uwayokote, "Rekishisho," pp. 58–59, also gives an account of the shifts of opinions regarding legitimacy.

54. See Sugimoto Keizaburō, *Gunki Monogatari no Sekai*, pp. 147–49. But see also Nagazumi, *Chūsei*, p. 409, for musical notations found in sections of certain versions of the text.
55. Quoted by Nagazumi Yasuaki, "*Taiheiki* no Shisō," in Nagazumi, *Taiheiki*, pp. 339–40.
56. In 1391 according to the lunar calendar or 1392 according to the solar calendar.
57. The best known is undoubtedly *Ōninki*, the account of the Ōnin War. It has been translated in part by H. Paul Varley in *The Ōnin War*. The events described in this work are far more exciting and memorable than those in *Meitokuki*, but it possesses no literary interest. The literary qualities of *Ōninki* and other diaries describing the warfare are discussed by Sugimoto in *Gunki*, pp. 385–405. The Kakitsu disturbance of 1441, during which Akamatsu Mitsusuke killed the shogun Ashikaga Yoshinori, also provided ample material for a historical tale, but *Kakitsu Monogatari* is disappointing, in part because it is so clearly an attempt to exonerate Mitsusuke from blame. For a discussion of the text, see Wada Hidemichi, "*Kakitsu Monogatari* no Keisei."
58. Quoted by Tomikura Tokujirō in his "Kaidai" to *Meitokuki*, p. 178. Prince Sadafusa was also known as Gosukō-in. He was the grandson of the Emperor Sukō. Yamana Ōshū refers to Yamana Ujikiyo, a former governor of Ōshū. Ōshū was otherwise known as Mutsu, and consisted of the five provinces at the northern end of the island of Honshū.
59. *Ibid*., p. 180.
60. *Ibid*., p. 13.
61. *Ibid*., pp. 94–96. The text seems to be corrupt in places, but I believe that the meaning is more or less as given.
62. Obviously, women had committed suicide, but not in the manner of a man on the battlefield.
63. Tomikura, *Meitokuki*, pp. 120–21.
64. See Sugimoto, *Gunki*, p. 372. He lists the main characters of the different episodes, including four women.
65. *Meitokuki* was the source of the Nō play *Kobayashi*, written not long after the events described, probably by Miyamasu.
66. Takahashi Nobuyuki, "Sōsetsu" in Okami Masao and Kadokawa Gen'yoshi, *Taiheiki, Soga Monogatari, Gikeiki*, p. 188.
67. A stimulating account of the different types of performances is given by Barbara Ruch in "Medieval Jongleurs and the Making of a National Literature."
68. See Takahashi, "Sōsetsu," p. 188; also Thomas J. Cogan (trans.), *The Tale of the Soga Brothers*, p. xxxviii. Fukuda Akira, in *Chūsei Katarimono Bungei*, pp. 48–60, terms this "literature recited by mediums" (*fushuku*).

69. This point is emphasized by Ruch in "Medieval Jongleurs," p. 286.

70. Takahashi, "Sōsetsu," p. 184. Takahashi quotes a passage in the manabon text of *The Tale of the Soga Brothers* stating that a copy of it was sent to China along with one of *The Tale of the Heike*. The Chinese, reading it, were so struck with admiration by the description of Hōjō Masako that they exclaimed, "We have heard Japan is a small country; is it possible such a wise woman lives there?" It is most unlikely that these two works were sent to China, and even more improbable that any Chinese praised Masako in these terms; the passage was probably no more than a literary flourish intended to persuade an audience that Masako was admired even by the Chinese, but it strongly suggests that the two works were composed in a language that the Chinese could understand.

71. Takahashi, "Sōsetsu," p. 183, gives as examples of other works in this style *Shintōshū*, *Gempei Tōsō-roku*, and *Daitō Monogatari*.

72. The manabon version seems to have been virtually unknown in Kyoto, as we can gather from the fact that it exercised extremely little influence on such literary forms as the Nō plays and the *kōwaka* dance recitations, both products of the Kyoto culture. See Amano Fumio, "Denkiteki Sekai e no Keisha," p. 144.

73. The relationship is unusually complicated. Officially, Suketsugu was the son of Itō no Suketaka's stepdaughter, and Sukechika was the son of his eldest son. This more or less makes them cousins. However, the text informs us that Suketsugu was actually the son of Suketaka, who had paid secret visits to his daughter-in-law. If this is accepted, Suketsugu was the uncle, rather than the cousin, of Sukechika. For textual reference in the kanabon to the irregular relations of Suketaka and his stepdaughter, see Ichiko Teiji and Ōshima Tatehiko, *Soga Monogatari*, p. 55; also Cogan, *The Tale*, p. 8. The same relationship was reported in the manabon; see Okami and Kadokawa, *Taiheiki*, p. 205.

74. Translation in Cogan, *The Tale*, p. 40; original text in Ichiko and Ōshima, *Soga*, p. 94. Sukeyasu is referred to in the latter text as Kawazu no Saburō Sukeshige, and in the manabon as Kawazu no Saburō Sukemichi. However, works of history give Sukeyasu, and that no doubt is why Cogan rendered the name as Sukeyasu throughout.

75. Translation by Cogan (except for the poem which is my version) in *The Tale*, p. 233. Original text in Ichiko and Ōshima, *Soga*, p. 352. The manabon text does not specify Ōtōnai was quartered and does not contain the poem. (See Okami and Kadokawa, *Taiheiki*, p. 255.)

76. See Amano, "Denkiteki," pp. 145–46, for excerpts from the manabon that illustrate this point.

77. Among the Kabuki plays *Sukeroku Yukari no Edozakura* and *Ya no Ne* are perhaps the best known. For the latter play, see Laurence Kominz, "*Ya no Ne*; The Genesis of a Kabuki *Aragoto* Classic."

78. Hitomaro and Akahito were, of course, two leading *Man'yōshū* poets;

Narihira was the hero of *Tales of Ise*, and Genji of *The Tale of Genji*. There was nothing unorthodox about Tora's literary tastes.

79. Translation in Cogan, *The Tale*, p. 111. The translation is free—necessarily so, because the text is highly poetic and elliptical. Original kanabon text in Ichiko and Ōshima, *Soga*, p. 194.
80. For a list of the nineteen Nō plays based on *The Tale of the Soga Brothers*, together with brief summaries of each, see Cogan, *The Tale*, pp. xxxiii–xxxv. Summaries of eight Kabuki and Bunraku plays with the name Soga at the head of the title are found in *Nihon Koten Bungaku Daijiten*, IV, pp. 37–41, and there are many other plays (such as *Yotsugi Soga*) that were derived from *The Tale of the Soga Brothers* but are not given in this entry of *Nihon Koten Bungaku Daijiten* because their titles begin with a word other than Soga.
81. Morris, *The Nobility*, p. 67.
82. *Hōgan* or *hangan* was a position of the third rank within the *kebiishi*, or imperial police. In this instance (and in many others) it was purely an honorary title and did not involve any duties.
83. The first known use of the term was in 1638, but it probably existed from early in the sixteenth century. See Kajihara Masaaki, "Kaisetsu," in his edition of *Gikeiki*, pp. 6–7.
84. *Yoshitsune* is the title of the complete translation of *Gikeiki* by Helen Craig McCullough. *Gikei* is the Sino-Japanese rendering of the name Yoshitsune, and *ki* means "record." The use of the Sino-Japanese pronunciation of a man's name is found as early as *Shōmonki* (The Story of Masakado), and (closer to Yoshitsune's time) there are the examples of Shunzei and Teika, commonly used instead of Toshinari and Sadaie as pronunciations of these poets' names.
85. For a summary of the various theories concerning the time of composition, see Kajihara, "Kaisetsu," pp. 16–18. The most persuasive attempt to date the play was probably that of Amano in "Denkiteki," pp. 155–59. Amano concluded, on the basis of the failure of *Yoshitsune* to include the Yoshitsune legend found in the Nō play *Settai*, that it must have been compiled before the play was first performed; Amano thought it was "highly probable" the play was written before 1430, and this provides a date by which *Yoshitsune* would have been compiled. The rufubon text of *Yoshitsune*, compiled during the Tokugawa period, includes the *Settai* legend.
86. I shall refer below to "the author," even though I recognize the probability that there was more than one author, in order to avoid the necessity of saying each time "the author or authors." I should note, however, that not all scholars are agreed that *Yoshitsune* was written by more than one author, and some more recent authorities, such as Amano (in "Denkiteki," p. 159), accept the view that one author wrote the entire work.

    By "author-performer" I mean someone—probably a *zatō* (blind priest) in the case of *Yoshitsune*—who recited the text before an audience and in the process of reciting may have made additions of his own invention. It was suggested by Kadokawa Gen'yoshi that the identification of Yoshitsune's wife as a member of the Koga family, and the close association of the Koga retainer Kanefusa with Yoshitsune at the end of his life, neither supported by historical evidence, was owing to the patronage of the storyteller by the Koga family. See Fukuda Akira, *Chūsei*, p. 66.

87. See Kajihara, *Gikeiki*, pp. 26–28.
88. Helen Craig McCullough, who used the text (based on a movable wooden print edition of the early seventeenth century) given by Okami Masao in *Gikeiki*, stated (p. 5): "All known texts of *Yoshitsune (Gikeiki)* are substantially the same; there are no important variants." This is a matter of degree: although all texts are *generally* the same, there are many points of difference, not all of them minor. The edition given by Kajiwara Masaaki in the Nihon Koten Bungaku Zenshū series is a text (the Tanaka-bon) first given scholarly attention in 1947–48 but not printed until 1965. Kajiwara believed that this text is the most complete and has the fewest errors. See Kajihara, *Gikeiki*, pp. 31–35, for a discussion of the various texts. It differs significantly from the text given by Okami, but was not available at the time McCullough made her translation.
89. Translation by Helen Craig McCullough in *Yoshitsune*, p. 134. Text in Kajihara, *Gikeiki*, p. 193.
90. Following the text in Kajihara, *Gikeiki*, p. 482. The text used by McCullough in her translation (*Yoshitsune*, p. 285) gives thirty thousand!
91. The text used by McCullough ends (*Yoshitsune*, p. 294) with an appropriately Confucian sentiment: "Nothing is so important in a warrior as loyalty and filial piety."
92. Translation in Helen Craig McCullough, *Yoshitsune*, pp. 157–58. The text given by Kajihara in *Gikeiki*, pp. 239–40, does not mention Shizuka's name, but states that there were five shirabyōshi.
93. McCullough translation, *Yoshitsune*, p. 165. Text in Kajihara, *Gikeiki*, p. 253.
94. See above, note 86.
95. Translation by Helen Craig McCullough, *Yoshitsune*, p. 255. The text given by Kajihara in *Gikeiki*, pp. 439–40, is rather different: "They stayed for three days in the capital, and he [Yoshitsune] thought he would like to visit the Heisen-ji, a place famous in this province. The members of the party were not pleased with this, but since it was his command, they arrived that day at the Kannon Hall of the Heisen-ji. The wind and rain were fierce, and his wife was not feeling well."
96. There is one exception: in the sea of Dannoura, Benkei shoots down a sinister cloud that is formed of the malevolent spirits of the Taira dead.
97. Every critic I have read has insisted that *Yoshitsune* is *not* merely a series of tales about Yoshitsune; but there is a general reluctance to discuss the clumsy transitions, repetitions, and inconsistencies in characterization that

hopelessly mar the literary quality. See, for example, Sugimoto, *Gunki*, pp. 266–67. Fukuda Akira in *Chūsei*, p. 63, suggested that the unsatisfactory ending (at least for modern readers) was part of a consistent pattern within the work of presenting comparatively raw materials leading to the violent death of the hero without making any attempt to achieve literary finish. Amano ("Denkiteki," p. 159–61) found a unifying element in the author's frequent use of proverbs and similes. It has no doubt proved difficult to pass an unfavorable judgment on the literary merits of a work that has enjoyed popularity over the centuries. Helen Craig McCullough believed that "the work deserves kinder treatment than it ordinarily receives." *Yoshitsune* has certainly not lacked admirers among postwar scholars, though I do not happen to be one of them.

98. See below, pp. 1153–55, for a treatment of these chanted and danced playlets on martial themes.
99. For a comprehensive account of legends in the Muromachi period, see Helen Craig McCullough, *Yoshitsune*, pp. 36–66. See also Kajihara, *Gikeiki*, pp. 29–30.
100. Helen Craig McCullough, *Yoshitsune*, pp. 262–63.
101. *Ibid*, p. 263
102. *Ibid*, pp. 268–69.
103. This is a quotation of two famous lines by Tu Fu.
104. Text in Imoto Nōichi et al, *Matsuo Bashō Shū*, pp. 364–65. Translation adapted from my *Anthology of Japanese Literature*, p. 369.
105. The three previous "mirrors" (*kagami*) were *The Great Mirror*, *The New Mirror*, and *The Water Mirror*. For a description of these works, see chapter 14. One other mirror, *Yayotsugi*, preceded *The Clear Mirror*. It treated the reigns of two sovereigns—Takakura (the eightieth) and Antoku (the eighty-first), but this work was lost, presumably during the Muromachi period. In the Tokugawa period Arakida Reijo (1732–1806) filled in the gap in the chronology with her *Tsuki no Yukue* (1771). She followed the tradition of the various "mirrors" by inventing a centenarian who described events of a past which by this time was exceedingly distant.
106. Iwasa Tadashi, et al., *Jinnō Shōtōki, Masukagami*, p. 248. In this volume Tokieda and Kidō edited the section on *Masukagami*. I shall refer to it below as Tokieda and Kidō, *Masukagami*.
107. Although the text is entirely related in the words of the old nun, she speaks not the colloquial language of the fourteenth century but a Heian-style language reminiscent of *The Tale of Genji*.
108. See Yamagishi Tokutei and Suzuki Kazuo, *Ōkagami, Masukagami*, pp. 186–88, for a discussion of the criteria used in determining the author, such as the period when he was active, his prejudice in favor of the nobility rather than the military, and his cultural background. The most unusual qualification for the author was that he be a supporter of the Nortern rather than the Southern Court; if he had been living in the Yoshino

mountains he would not have had access to the documents needed in writing the work. In every respect Yoshimoto seems more likely to have been the author than any other well-known figure of the period.

109. For a discussion of the various theories of the date of composition, see Yamagishi and Suzuki, *Ōkagami, Masukagami*, pp. 185–86; also, the article "*Masukagami*" by Kidō Saizō in *Nihon Koten Bungaku Daijiten*, V, p. 520. Inoue Muneo, whose *Masukagami Zen'yakuchū* appeared the year before the volume of *Nihon Koten Bungaku Daijiten* containing Kidō's article, gave his reasons in II, pp. 389–94, for believing *The Clear Mirror* was written between 1338 and 1358.

110. Quotation of part of the poem by Saigyō (*Shin Kokinshū* 1778): "If there is nowhere for me to live, I won't live anywhere; in this world even a brushwood hut is only for a little while." Saigyō has found he can no longer live even in the traditional brushwood hut of a hermit. He will henceforth be without a dwelling; but, after all, one is not very long in this world. The poem is quoted to suggest how frail and flimsy the house on Oki seemed to one who had hitherto lived in palaces.

111. An allusion to a famous poem by Po Chü-i that includes the lines, "On the night of the fifteenth [of the eighth month], in the light of the moon as it first appears, I long for old friends, more than two thousand miles away." These lines move Gotoba as never before.

112. "Murmured the words" is my addition. The text gives only the poem, without any indication of whether he wrote it down, recited it to someone else, or murmured it to himself. I have chosen the last of these possibilities because some verb is needed in English.

113. Tokieda and Kidō, *Masukagami*, p. 279.

114. Translation by Edward G. Seidensticker in *The Tale of Genji*, I, pp. 230–31.

115. See Tokieda and Kidō, *Masukagami*, pp. 299–301; also Yamagishi and Suzuki, *Ōkagami, Masukagami*, pp. 231–36.

116. Possibly there were other manuscripts that were destroyed during the warfare.

117. The borrowings from *The Confessions of Lady Nijō* are the subject of the article by Matsumoto Yasushi, "*Masukagami* to *Towazugatari*," in Yamagishi and Suzuki, *Ōkagami, Masukagami*, pp. 355–64. On pp. 358–59 Matsumoto gives parallel passages from the two works. The half-sister of Gofukakusa was Gaishi, the daughter of the Emperor Gosaga and former high priestess of Ise. She was also indirectly related to Nijō: her grandmother was at one time the wife of Nijō's grandfather, but later married another man (Toshimori), and the daughter by the marriage was Nijō's mother. The brief affair between Gofukakusa and Gaishi is described in Fukuda Hideichi, *Towazugatari*, pp. 78–82. See also the English translation by Karen Brazell, *The Confessions of Lady Nijō*, pp. 56–61. Muramatsu Hiroshi in *Rekishi Monogatari*, pp. 274–82, discusses various

sources of *The Clear Mirror*, including *Godai Teiō Monogatari*, a fourteenth-century historical tale that covers five reigns extending from 1221 to 1272, and *The Diary of Lady Ben*, but concludes that the only irrefutable instance of borrowing is from *The Confessions of Lady Nijō*. I have treated that work on pp. 841–44.

118. Fukuda Hideichi, *Towazugatari*, p. 81.

119. The sixteenth of the seventeen chapters. The title is derived from a poem by the Emperor Godaigo: *Kiki okishi* / Kume no Sarayama / *koeyukan* / *michi to wa kanete* / *omoi yawa seshi*. The meaning of the poem is: "I had heard of Kume no Sarayama, but did I ever dream in the past that one day I would take the road over the mountains?" Kume no Sarayama was an utamakura in the province of Mimasaka (the modern Okayama Prefecture). The chapter was no doubt given this name to convey Godaigo's surprise and grief that he saw a place known to him from poetry but only on the way to exile.

120. The text says "the second year of Genkō." Genkō was the reign-name used at this time by Godaigo and his adherents. When Kōgon was crowned in the fourth month of that year his court began to use a different reign-name, Shōkei. The use of Godaigo's reign-name may suggest the author belonged to his faction, but the year began as the second of Genkō for everyone. It is possible, too, as Tokieda and Kidō suggest (*Jinnō Shōtoki, Masukagami*, p. 227), that the author—assuming he was Nijō Yoshimoto—was personally much attached to Godaigo even though he was a member of the Northern Court. Certainly the portrait of Godaigo in this chapter of *The Clear Mirror* must have been intended to arouse sympathy.

121. This refers to the reign of the Emperor Kōgon (1331–1333). Kōgon, a descendant of the Emperor Gofukakusa, was a member of the Jimyō-in line of the imperial family. It was the policy of the Kamakura shogunate to alternate succession to the throne between this line and the Daikaku-ji line (of which Godaigo was a member), descended from Kameyama, the younger brother of Gofukakusa. Kōgon was crown prince at the time of Godaigo's attempted coup. He was placed on the throne by Ashikaga Takauji as Godaigo's successsor. Godaigo, however, did not abdicate, but continued to consider himself the reigning sovereign. Kōgon abdicated when Godaigo returned from exile.

122. At the time two emperors who had abdicated and entered Buddhist orders were living in the capital—Gofushimi (1288–1336) and Hanazono (1297–1348).

123. Although the author clearly sympathized with Godaigo, who had not abdicated, he evidently felt obliged to describe him as the "former emperor" because Kōgon had officially ascended the throne.

124. *Jōyōjin* probably refers to the court ladies who were neglected by the Emperor Hsüan Tsung because of his infatuation with the celebrated Yang Kuei-fei. "The White-haired Palace Lady," the poem by Po Chü-

i, refers to the fate of these women doomed to wait for a summons from the emperor until they were old and gray. See Tokieda and Kidō, *Masukagami*, p. 457.

125. My translation from *Anthology of Japanese Literature*, pp. 242–43, slightly modified. Text in Inoue, *Masukagami*, II, pp. 244–47.
126. Tokieda and Kidō, *Masukagami*, p. 458; also Inoue, *Masukagami*, p. 249. Translation from Keene, *Anthology*, p. 244.
127. *Tsubo-sōzoku* wa a traveling costume worn by women of the upper class during the Heian and Kamakura periods. The basketlike hats covered the head, and hems of the long robe were held up by a cord that kept them from touching the ground. See Ivan Morris, *The Pillow Book of Sei Shōnagon*, II, p. 36, for his explanation of this costume.
128. Tokieda and Kidō, *Masukagami*, 459–60; also Inoue, *Masukagami*, II, pp. 252–55. Translation modified from Keene, *Anthology*, pp. 245–46.
129. See Yamagishi and Suzuki, *Ōkagami, Masukagami*, p. 275, where it is suggested that the description of Godaigo's exile owed much to the "Suma" and "Akashi" chapters of *The Tale of Genji*.
130. Tokieda and Kidō, *Masukagami*, p. 465; also Inoue, *Masukagami*, II, pp. 280–84. Translation adapted from Keene, *Anthology*, p. 250.
131. In the text they are in fact referred to by titles—*hon'in* (main retired sovereign) for Gofushimi, and *shin'in* (new retired sovereign) for Hanazono.
132. Tokieda and Kidō, *Masukagami*, p. 466; also Inoue, *Masukagami*, II, pp. 286–88. Translation adapted from Keene, *Anthology*, p. 250.
133. Tokieda and Kidō, *Masukagami*, p. 469; also Inoue, *Masukagami*, II, pp. 300–2. Translation in Keene, *Anthology*, p. 252.

Bibliography

Note: All Japanese books, except as otherwise noted, were published in Tokyo.

Amano Fumio. "Denkiteki na Sekai e no Keisha," in Kitagawa Tadahiko (ed.), *Gunki Monogatari no Keifu*. Kyoto: Sekai Shisōsha, 1985.

Brazell, Karen. *The Confessions of Lady Nijō*. Garden City, N.Y.: Doubleday, 1973.

Cogan, Thomas J. *The Tale of the Soga Brothers*. Tokyo: University of Tokyo Press, 1987.

Fukuda Akira. *Chūsei Katarimono Bungei*. Miyai Shoten, 1981.

Fukada Hideichi. *Chūsei Bungaku Ronkō*. Meiji Shoin, 1975.

———. *Towazugatari*, in Shinchō Nihon Koten Shūsei series. Shinchōsha, 1978.

Hasegawa Tadashi, "Gekokujō no Sekai," in Okami Masao and Hayashiya Tatsusaburō, *Bungaku no Gekokujō*, in Nihon Bungaku no Rekishi series. Kadokawa Shoten, 1967.

Ichiko Teiji and Ōshima Tatehiko. *Soga Monogatari*, in Nihon Koten Bungaku Taikei series. Iwanami Shoten, 1966.

Imoto Nōichi, Hori Nobuo, and Muramatsu Tomotsugu. *Matsuo Bashō Shū*, in Nihon Koten Bungaku Zenshū series. Shōgakukan, 1972.

Inoue Muneo. *Masukagami Zen'yakuchū*, 2 vols., in Kōdansha Gakujutsu Bunko series. Kōdansha, 1983.

Iwasa Tadashi, Tokieda Motoki, and Kidō Saizō. *Jinnō Shōtōki, Masukagami*, in Nihon Koten Bungaku Taikei series. Iwanami Shoten, 1965.

Kajihara Masaaki (ed.). *Gikeiki*, in Nihon Koten Bungaku Zenshū series. Shōgakukan, 1971.

Keene, Donald. *Anthology of Japanese Literature*. New York: Grove Press, 1955.

Kidō Saizō. Chūsei Bungaku *Shiron*. Meiji Shoin, 1984.

Kitagawa Tadahiko. *Gunkimono no Keifu*. Kyoto: Gendai Shisō Sha, 1985.

Kominz, Laurence. "*Ya no Ne*; The Genesis of a Kabuki *Aragoto* Classic," *Monumenta Nipponica* 38:4, 1983.

Masuda Shū. "Jōkyūki—Kaiko to Tembō," *Kokugo to Kokubungaku* 37:4, April 1960.

Matsubayashi Yasuaki. "Kōbu no Kassenki," in Kitagawa Tadahiko, *Gunkimono no Keifu*.

———. *Shintei Jōkyūki*. Gendai Shichō Sha, 1982.

Matsumura Hiroshi. *Rekishi Monogatari*. Hanawa Shobō, 1979.

McCullough, Helen Craig. *The Taiheiki*. New York: Columbia University Press, 1959.

———. *Yoshitsune*. Stanford, Calif.: Stanford University Press, 1966.

McCullough, William H. "*Shōkyūki*: An Account of the Shōkyu War of 1221," *Monumenta Nipponica* 19:1–2, 3–4, 1964.

Mills, Douglas E. "*Soga Monogatari, Shintōshū* and the Taketori Legend," *Monumenta Nipponica* 30:1, 1975.

Morris, Ivan. *The Nobility of Failure*. New York: Holt, Rinehart and Winston, 1975.

Nagazumi Yasuaki. *Chūsei Bungaku no Kanōsei*. Iwanami Shoten, 1977.

Nagazumi Yasuaki, Uwayokote Masataka, and Sakurai Yoshirō. *Taiheiki no Sekai*. Nihon Hōsō Shuppan Kyōkai, 1987.

Nihon Koten Bungaku Daijiten, 6 vols. Iwanami Shoten, 1983–85.

Oka Kazuo. *Masukagami* in Nihon Koten Zensho series. Asahi Shimbun Sha, 1948.

Okami Masao (ed.). *Taiheiki*, 2 vols., in Kadokawa Bunko series. Kadokawa Shoten, 1975–82.

Okami Masao and Kadokawa Gen'yoshi. *Taiheiki, Soga Monogatari, Gikeiki*, in Kanshō Nihon Koten Bungaku series. Kadokawa Shoten, 1976.

Ruch, Barbara. "Medieval Jongleurs and the Making of a National Literature," in John Whitney Hall and Toyoda Takeshi, *Japan in the Muromachi Age*. Berkeley: University of California Press, 1977.

Seidensticker, Edward G. *The Tale of Genji*, 2 vols. New York: Alfred A. Knopf, 1976.

Sugimoto Keizaburō. *Gunki Monogatari no Sekai*. Meicho Kankōkai, 1985.

Varley, H. Paul. *A Chronicle of Gods and Sovereigns: Jinnō Shōtoki of Kitabatake Chikafusa*. New York: Columbia University Press, 1980.

———. *Imperial Restoration in Medieval Japan*. New York: Columbia University Press, 1971.

———. *The Ōnin War*. New York: Columbia University Press, 1967.

Yamagishi Tokuhei and Suzuki Kazuo. *Ōkagami, Masukagami*, in Kanshō Nihon Koten Bungaku series. Kadokawa Shoten, 1976.

Yamashita Hiroaki (ed.) *Taiheiki*, 5 vols., in Shinchō Nihon Koten Shūsei series. Shinchōsha, 1977.

Yokoi Kiyoshi. *Chūsei wo ikita Hitobito*. Kyoto: Minerva Shobō, 1981.

24. RENGA

The Muromachi period is not known for its waka poetry, though (as we have seen) Shōtetsu gave it a sunset glow with his criticism as well as his poetry. It is clear that, with rare exceptions, the waka did not attract the best poets of the day. *Renga* (linked verse) was far more important; indeed, it was the representative poetic form of the age.[1]

Renga did not originate at this time. Renga poets, in an effort to impart dignity to a genre of humble origins, regularly traced the history of renga all the way back to a passage in the *Kojiki* in which a poem is composed by two persons, Prince Yamato-takeru and an old man. The prince asked,

Niibari	How many nights
Tsukuba wo sugite	Have I slept since passing
iku yo ka netsuru	Niibari and Tsukuba?

To this the old man replied:

kaganabete	Counted on my fingers,
yo ni wa kokonoyo	The nights figure up as nine,
hi ni wa tōka wo	And the days amount to ten.[2]

The exchange is in the form of two *kata-uta*, each of three lines of 5, 7, and 7 syllables, though the first line of the prince's poem is a syllable short.[3] The two half-poems, put together, approximate a *sedōka*, but the question and answer are so prosaic they can hardly be said to constitute a poem. Renga poets of later centuries nevertheless revered this exchange as the first ancestor of their art, and the mention of the place-name Tsukuba in the prince's half-poem gave rise to the elegant circumlocution of "the Way of Tsukuba" as a name for the art of renga.[4]

Other instances of a single poem composed by two people are found in the *Man'yōshū* and in *Tales of Ise*.[5] The composition of short renga—normally, a waka composed by two people—developed by the middle of the Heian period into a social pastime. One person would present a riddle in the form of a *maeku* (first half-poem), and another solved it with a *tsukeku* (added half-poem). The more complicated or absurd the premise of the maeku, the greater the achievement of anyone who could make sense of it by appending two lines. Numerous anecdotes describe how a particularly brilliant rejoinder impressed people at a gathering.[6] The wit displayed in the tsukeku often took the form of a pun or play on words; mention, say, of a bow in the maeku all but invited a tsukeku containing the noun *haru* (spring), a homonym of the verb *haru*, "to draw a bow." Japanese lends itself easily to puns because of its many homonyms.

Renga received its first official recognition when a renga section was included in the *Kin'yōshū*, compiled between 1124 and 1127. The eighteen pairs of half-poems constitute a representative selection of the worst in short renga composition, as a sample may suggest. The maeku by the priest Raikei bears the headnote:

"On seeing peach blossoms at Momozono [Peach Garden]."

Momozono no	Look! the peach blossoms
momo no hana koso	In the garden of peaches
sakinikere	Have burst into bloom.

The tsukeku by Ōe no Kin'yori[7] (d. 1040) accordingly refers to Umezu (Plum Tree Ford):

Umezu no mume wa	I wonder if the plum blossoms
chiri ya shinuran[8]	At Plum Tree Ford have scattered.

The point of this exchange is that each of the place-names contains the name of the blossom particularly associated with the place. Kin'yori's query about the fate of the plum blossoms reveals he was aware that peach blossoms open later than plum blossoms.

Another maeku (by one Tamesuke) bears the headnote: "On seeing the island of Shika in Tsukushi."

tsurenaku tateru	See the island of Shika
shika no shima kana	That stands aloof like a deer.

The tsukeku (by Kunisada) is in 5, 7, and 5 syllables, an instance of the longer "half" of the poem following the shorter "half" of 7 and 7 syllables.

yumihari no	Unruffled even
tsuki no iru ni mo	By the crescent moon that drops
odorokade[9]	Like a spent arrow.

These two "links" contain puns that expand their meaning. *Shika* is the name of an island, known in poetry since the *Man'yōshū*, but is also a homonym of the usual word for "deer." *Yumihari*, literally "bow drawn," refers to the bowlike shape of the crescent moon. This meaning occasions the pun on *iru*, meaning (with reference to a bow) "to shoot an arrow," but (with reference to the moon) "to sink beyond the horizon."

Nothing is harder to appreciate in translation than a pun, and no doubt it is unfair to subject the short renga, which so heavily depended for effect on puns and similar witticisms, to the kind of explication appropriate for the mature renga, but the impression of inanity given by these verses is not misleading. Renga would probably have remained at this level, of no more artistic significance than riddles or guessing games, had it not been for two developments: the increase in the number of "links" from the original two, in this way destroying the original conception of renga as a single waka composed by two people; and the adoption of the enlarged renga as a means of expression by poets and scholars who had been stimulated by the possibilities of the new form.

The beginnings of the "chain renga" (*kusari renga*) is traditionally traced back to an event recorded in the historical tale *The New Mirror*. In an account of the pleasures of music and poetry at the court of Prince Arihito (1103–1147), a man of such artistic talent and dazzling good looks as to bring to mind Prince Genji, we are told:

> On still another occasion, when someone[10] came out with the following verse,
>
> | | |
> |---|---|
> | *Nara no miyako wo* | Turn your thoughts for a moment |
> | *omoi koso yare* | To the capital at Nara— |
>
> the general [Arihito] responded,
>
> | | |
> |---|---|
> | *yaezakura* | Yes, the double cherries |
> | *aki no momiji ya* | Are lovely, but tell me about |
> | *ika naran* | The red autumn leaves. |

When he had added this verse, Echigo no Menoto in turn added,

shigururu tabi ni	Every time the rain sweeps down
iro ya kasanaru	The colors grow the brighter.

Her rejoinder was praised long afterward. This kind of thing happened very often.[11]

Once poets were no longer obliged to confine their linked verses to the thirty-one syllables of a waka, there was no reason why they could not prolong their renga-making to thirty or fifty or even a hundred links. By the middle of the twelfth century renga in fifty links were being regularly composed,[12] but the standard number of links in a renga sequence was eventually established at one hundred, probably on the analogy of the hundred-poem sequences of waka or the hundred-round uta-awase. By 1333, as we know from the description in the *Taiheiki*, a renga sequence in ten thousand links had been composed.[13] Initially at least, the element of play remained the dominant factor even in the expanded renga: the clever rejoinder, the play on words that gave a new twist to the meaning of the previous verse, and the quickness to catch an allusion were prized more than beauty of expression.

The situation changed when the court poets became actively interested in renga composition. By this time, elaborate rules for the composition of waka had been framed, and it was therefore natural for poets to enhance the new art with equally demanding rules to be observed by participants in renga sessions. The two most important rules were the *fushimono* and *sari-kirai*.

The fushimono were set topics. At the beginning of a renga session the topic would be announced in terms, for example, of "mountain something" or else "something mountain." If the former, every verse, regardless of its overall content, had to contain a word that could be added to the word "mountain" and still make sense, such as "valley" to form "mountain valley" or "spring" to form "mountain spring"; if the latter, the word would precede mountain, on the lines of "snowy mountain," "moonlit mountain," and the like. The necessity of observing the fushimono made renga composition more interesting, as rules make any game more interesting, and the fushimono also imparted a kind of unity to the sequence; even if the successive links were otherwise unrelated, they all shared a connection (however remote) with the assigned topic. By the beginning of the fourteenth century there were dictionaries of fushimono vocabulary to help renga poets. As many as two hundred examples of words that could be used before or after the thirty or so recognized fushimono were listed.[14] Long after their original purposes had come to be fulfilled by more effective poetic means, a fushimono, like the title of a poem, continued to head each renga sequence. Sometimes the fushimono was decided on *after* all the links had been composed, more or less as an afterthought![15]

The principle of *sari-kirai*, literally "avoidance and dislike," had the opposite purpose to the unifying function of the fushimono: it was instituted in order to keep renga sequences from appearing like single, uninterrupted poems that might have been written by one person.[16] In the case of the seasons, for example, it was decreed that spring and autumn could be treated in as many as five successive links, but summer and winter in no more than three. This meant that although the first three links of a sequence might state directly or by metaphor that the season described was spring, presently the season might shift to autumn or winter. It might be imagined that an abrupt shifting of the seasons would create contradictions that would destroy the unity of a renga sequence; in fact, however, only the links immediately before and immediately after a given link needed to be taken into consideration, and when the season changed a "neutral" link between the two seasons kept them from clashing, much as, in a horizontal scroll depicting different seasons, golden clouds separate the seasonally changed vegetation. Renga was a chain, each link of which fitted smoothly and strongly into the link on either side, but connections between more remote links were deliberately avoided. Observance of sari-kirai ensured that the content of a renga sequence would shift in many directions and remain unpredictable until the last link had been forged.

The principle of sari-kirai was also applied in forbidding the use of synonyms or associated words. Poets of waka or haiku generally observed the same rule, if only because the poems they wrote were so short they could not waste any syllables with unnecessary repetitions. A renga sequence was much longer, but any two links could be considered a poem,[17] and as such it was bound to obey the same rules as the waka in avoiding verbal repetitions.

The manuscript of a renga session, recorded by a scribe, was written on a fixed number of sheets of paper folded in a prescribed manner. In the case of a sequence in one hundred links, four sheets were used, in the following manner: Sheet One, 22 verses (8 on the front side and 14 on the back); Sheet Two, 28 verses (14 on each side); Sheet Three, 28 verses (14 on each side); and Sheet Four, 22 verses (14 on the front side and 8 on the back).[18] Some words could be mentioned only once on a given side of a sheet, others not before the second or third side, still others only once in the entire manuscript.

The rules kept multiplying until there were so many that poets had trouble remembering them all. On one recorded occasion, newly framed rules were hung on the wall to help the participants,[19] but even that proved insufficient, and eventually no renga session was complete without a judge who was thoroughly versed in the rules and could instantly point out transgressions.

We might suppose that the proliferation of rules would have made spontaneous expression impossible, but as Wordswoth wrote of the sonnet,

In truth the prison unto which we doom
Ourselves no prison is: and hence for me,
In sundry moods, 'twas pastime to be bound
Within the Sonnet's scanty plot of ground;
Pleased if some souls (for such there needs must be)
Who have felt the weight of too much liberty,
Should find brief solace there, as I have found.

Nijō Yoshimoto (1320–1388)

The chief figure in the elevation of renga from a game to a demanding and artistically important art was Nijō Yoshimoto, a noble of the highest rank who rose in 1346 to be kampaku and head of the Fujiwara clan.[20] Yoshimoto was a waka poet of some distinction. His early training was in the conservative waka of the Nijō school, and at one time he studied under Ton'a, the leading Nijō poet of the day. Yoshimoto did not neglect waka composition, even after he became the preeminent theoretician of renga. More than sixty of his waka were included in imperial collections, and he also produced several treatises on the art of the waka. It is safe to say, however, that he would be forgotten as a poet if he had not also devoted himself to renga. He was a pupil of the renga master Kyūsei[21] (1282?–1376?), a *jige* (commoner) poet, and under Kyūsei's tutelage he acquired authority as an expert on renga. Yoshimoto saw no contradiction in composing both waka and renga, believing that renga was a "miscellaneous" form of waka[22] and not an unrelated genre.

It is not clear just when Yoshimoto began the study of renga, but probably it was while he was still in his teens, under the influence of his father, an enthusiastic amateur practitioner. By the time he was in his early twenties, Yoshimoto himself was sponsoring large-scale renga sessions.[23] In the meantime, in 1336, when he was sixteen, he had made a critical decision of a nonliterary nature that affected the rest of his life: he decided to remain in the capital rather than follow his former master, the Emperor Godaigo, into the mountains of Yoshino. When Ashikaga Takauji marched into Kyoto he brought with him the prince he had decided to install as the new emperor. The enthronement ceremony of the Emperor Kōmyō was carried out at Yoshimoto's residence, and from this time on Yoshimoto's fortunes would be closely linked with those of the Northern Court. He served six emperors of that court, four times in the highest position of chancellor or regent, and he shared its vicissitudes, fleeing or returning to the capital as the fortunes of the war dictated.

In 1345, in his twenty-sixth year, Yoshimoto completed the oldest surviving textbook of renga composition, *Hekirenshō*, better known in the revised version called *Renri Hishō*.[24] In an afterword Yoshimoto stated that he had written the work in response to a query from someone living in the country about the nature of renga. He modestly avowed that (because of his ignorance) everything he had written was mistaken; but he had been so moved by the devotion to renga of his interrogator that he had willingly exposed himself to the ridicule of others by setting forth his views on the subject. He hoped, however, that the man in the country would soon find a master teacher and toss away these mistaken opinions.[25]

Yoshimoto here and elsewhere in *Renri Hishō* insisted that the ability to compose renga successfully came from two factors: the poet's inborn qualities, and the experience of composing renga with superior poets. He continued,

> Renga arises from within one's heart and must be learned for oneself. There is absolutely no need to learn from master teachers. One should constantly seek out occasions for composing renga with accomplished poets. . . . To practice renga solely at gatherings of incompetent poets is worse than not practicing at all. This is something one must be careful about while one is a beginner. It is also why the renga of even skilled poets suffers if they live in the hinterland, for however short a time. . . . The only way to improve as a poet is to practice with superior poets and acquire experience at attending sessions. In addition, one should gain inspiration by perusing the three collec-

tions,[26] *The Tale of Genji*, *Tales of Ise*, books of utamakura,[27] and suchlike works.[28]

Yoshimoto was especially concerned with the problems facing beginners in renga composition:

> While one is still a beginner one should not ponder too much one's verses. As is true also for the other arts, it is better to express one's first thoughts as they come, rather than mull over the pros and cons, which can lead only to confusion. However, when a good many outsiders and other accomplished poets are present at a session, the beginner should hesitate somewhat to speak out. Even after he has become skillful at composing renga, he will find it difficult to decide on the spot whether a given verse of his own is good or bad. It frequently happens that even when the poet himself thinks a verse is poor, the judge may award it high marks for its skill. This is not a sign of incompetence on the judge's part, nor is it proof that the poet cannot tell his good from his bad verses. It occurs simply because at a certain moment a particular verse just happens to have caught the judge's fancy.[29]

Advice to beginners in renga appears also in Yoshimoto's later works of renga criticism. In *Tsukuba Mondō* (Questions and Answers on Renga), he recognized that poetic ability was likely to be inborn, quoting various Chinese philosophers on the subject,[30] but he was surprisingly open-minded concerning what class of people might compose renga. He himself, in a manner hardly typical of waka poets on the day, associated with plebeian poets, notably his own teacher, Kyūsei, whom he revered despite his humble origins. Yoshimoto insisted that neither high birth nor scholarship was necessary to an aspiring renga poet:

> If a beginner's renga is bad, it will do him no good to worry himself about scholarship or the regulations on words to be avoided. Practice is the best way to improve one's renga. If a poet's renga is still not interesting, even after he has memorized the *Man'yōshū*, the *Kokinshū*, and all the later collections, acquiring knowledge will be like counting the jewels belonging to a neighbor. On the other hand, even if a man cannot read a single character, if his renga is competent, he will surely feel that he has obtained the jewels for himself.[31] After all, the poems of a dancer and a courtesan appear in the *Man'yōshū* and the *Kokinshū*, and there are even beggar's songs among the old

verses. In all of these cases, recognition came about because their poems were admired. After one's renga has become interesting is the best time to acquire learning.[32]

Such passages are the chief attraction for modern readers in Yoshimoto's critical works, but *Renri Hishō* was probably read in its time mainly for its practical guidance, rather than for its philosophy. It opens with a brief account of the history of renga, beginning with an example from the *Man'yōshū* of a waka composed jointly by a nun (the first seventeen syllables) and Ōtomo no Yakamochi (the remaining fourteen syllables).[33] This is followed by more general remarks on how one sets about learning renga, points to be observed by beginners, the language of renga, the technicalities of composition (such as the fushimono), the conduct of renga sessions, and finally, a consideration of what constitutes a link between one verse and the next. The second part of *Renri Hishō* gives specific directions as to which words can be used only once in a hundred-link session, which twice, which three times, and so on. Yoshimoto's prescriptions would be followed by renga poets of even much later times.[34] A typical directive enumerates which words can be used only once in a hundred-link sequence:

> Young shoots, wisteria, kerria roses, azaleas, and irises in the category of plants.
>
> Deer, monkeys, song thrushes, cuckoos, fireflies, cicadas, evening cicadas, cherry shells (but cherry blossoms can be used in addition), and unknown insects in the category of animate things.
>
> Long ago, ancient times, evening, yesterday, spring rains, evening showers, passing showers, early rain, storm winds, hiding places, water conduits, hanging bridges, morning sunlight, sunset, morning moon, evening moon. These are all words of secondary significance and should be used only once.[35]

Even if one recognizes that the repeated use of certain words, especially unusual or particularly vivid words, would harm a poetic sequence (or, indeed, any literary composition), Yoshimoto's designation of words that can be used only once in a hundred links is bound to seem arbitrary. Perhaps the rules of *any* game are likely to seem arbitrary, but Yoshimoto was clearly aiming at something more elevated than a mere game. His prescriptions would be unquestioningly followed by practitioners of renga of his day and altered in later times only after much deliberation. Yoshimoto enhanced the artistic quality of renga by the emphasis he gave to conscious artistic creation, as opposed to the flashes of wit that had earlier passed for skill in renga.

Yoshimoto's later texts of renga composition are of even greater interest. *Tsukuba Mondō*, written between 1357 and 1372, stands out among Yoshimoto's critical works in its literary, almost novelistic quality, both in the style and in having an old man narrate his views on renga in a conversational manner, recalling the similar device in such historical tales as *The Great Mirror*. Unlike his other discussions of renga, here Yoshimoto, instead of responding to questions about renga, is asking another person, an old man who knows more about renga than himself, about the art.

Yoshimoto begins with the question of whether or not renga is unique to Japan. The old man answers that it is not; the Buddhist hymns (*ge*) provide an Indian example of the art, and in China there is *lien-chü* (*renku*). The next questions concern the historical development of renga in Japan, and the old man responds with the usual examples from the *Kojiki* and the *Man'yōshū*, as well as from more recent collections of poetry. Another line of questioning relates to the uses of renga: does it help to foster good government or to achieve salvation for the poet in the world after death? As we might expect, the old man supplies examples that demonstrate renga is indeed of great efficacy in promoting both good government and salvation. He is sure that every syllable in a renga sequence must conform to morality and cites the numbers of holy men who devoted their lives to renga. Not only ordinary human beings, but the buddhas of past and present have all composed poetry; and of the different varieties of poetry, renga with its frequent shifts of subject and mood most closely corresponds to the mortal world itself.[36]

Another aspect of the religious significance of renga can be surmised from the frequency with which sequences were offered to temples and shrines. Renga manuscripts might bring recovery from illness or victory in battle. In 1471 a *hokku* (opening verse) offered by Sōgi to the Mishima Shrine in Izu was credited with having effected the miraculous cure of a child; and in 1504 Sōchō offered at the same shrine a renga sequence in a thousand links to assure the victory of the daimyo he served.[37] In *Tsukuba Mondō* Yoshimoto mentioned that two of the great religious leaders of recent times, Bukkoku Kokushi (1241–1316) and Musō Kokushi (1275–1351), both composed renga "day and night" and no doubt this was of benefit to them.[38] Yoshimoto himself was not a priest, but the prominence he gave in *Tsukuba Mondō* to the religious significance of renga indicates that he shared a belief in its special powers.[39]

The fact that one could offer renga to the Buddha or to a Shintō divinity in the hopes of obtaining worldly benefits suggests the practical value of renga composition. Yoshimoto, unlike the typical waka poets, did not look back to some golden age of poetry; the present world was his concern. As a member of the Nijō school, he was conservative when it came to waka and followed its poetic diction, essentially the two thousand words that occur in the poetry of the *Kokinshū*. On the whole, Yoshimoto preferred the traditional vocabulary even in renga, but he believed that renga should not be bound by the other conventions of the waka (such as honka-dori): "As the times change, so styles also change, and there is no need to defend the old ways. One should accept the common preferences and, instead of insisting on narrow prejudices, respect the leading poets of our time and current usage."[40] He insisted that a poem that was not of interest to the general public was worthless, regardless of how correctly orthodox it might be.[41] Although he does not say so in so many words, Yoshimoto was in effect encouraging poets to take up renga, rather than waka with its constricting conventions.

He turned his attention next in *Tsukuba Mondō* to the flow of a renga sequence. The renga composed for the first sheet of the manuscript should be marked by quiet beauty (*yūgen*), but from the second sheet some liveliness was desirable, and the verses on the third and fourth sheets should contain the most striking materials of the sequence. As in Japanese music, a progression from *jo* (slow introduction) to *ha* (development) to *kyū* (climax) should be observed in renga; the first sheet of manuscript corresponded to jo, the second to ha, and the third and fourth to kyū.[42]

Yoshimoto shifted his discussion at this point to a basic aspect of renga, the manner of combining striking verses with plainer ones within a sequence.[43] The compilers of the *Shin Kokinshū* had believed it was important to maintain a smooth flow of imagery, seasonal references, and tone from one poem to the next in the collection, even though this necessitated including quite ordinary poems to serve as bridges between the indisputable masterpieces; if only masterpieces had been included, they might not have fitted together as "links" in a chain of associations.[44]

The Japanese language itself seems to have a preference for long sentences that seem reluctant to end,[45] and even when the sentences do in fact end, there is usually a smooth transition to the next one, rather than the beginning of a new paragraph. In renga, of course, transitions from one link to the next are of crucial importance; one might call renga an art of transitions. As Yoshimoto was aware, a verse that was in itself brilliant might be undesirable from the point of view of an entire sequence if, because of its brilliance, transition to the next verse was made difficult. He wrote,

> In general, it must be accounted a sign of superior renga when [only] two or three striking verses are included in a session otherwise consisting of ground verses of unobtrusive character. How could every single verse be noteworthy? The people of the past used to say that one should mix impressive poems only here and there among the ground poems making up a sequence of one hundred waka.[46]

Yoshimoto next considered the individual verses of a renga sequence. The *hokku*, the opening verse, was by far the most important. If the hokku was a failure, the whole sequence would be a failure, irrespective of the quality of subsequent verses. Yoshimoto did not enter into details on the desirable content of a hokku, but later men did. Mokujiki Ōgo (1536–1608) declared in his book of renga rules that the hokku should not be at variance with the scenery of the place (whether mountains or the sea dominated) and should convey its appearance at the time of composition (whether cherry blossoms or autumn leaves were falling). It should also allude to the prevailing atmospheric phenomena such as the wind, clouds, mist, fog, rain, dew, frost, snow, heat, cold, and phase of the moon. However, he added, the hokku must seem spontaneous; "it is not interesting if it seems to have been prepared beforehand."[48] The *wakiku*, or second verse, echoed the season of the hokku and matched it in meaning, but it had to advance the progress of the sequence. The wakiku almost always ended with a noun, and if there was allusive variation in the hokku, the wakiku also had to contain one. The *daisan*, or third verse, marked a first shift away from the mood of the first two verses. It normally concluded with *-te*, the participial form of a verb. Later verses in a sequence were also governed by rules, notably that of sari-kirai, but they were not quite so demanding as the first three verses.

Yoshimoto gave attention not only to the content of a renga sequence but to the decorum that should be observed at a gathering:

> Once the place of the gathering has been decided, the scribe first comes forth, kneels beside the round mat, then (after obtaining the host's permission) sits down on it, opens the writing set, takes out the sheets of paper and folds them, places them before him, and prepares the ink. Next, he takes up the brushes, examines them, wets with the ink only two of them, moistens the brush he is to use, removes the back of the brush stand, and puts it on the floor. He

> waits for a signal from the host, at which he writes the first character of the title. After the hokku has been produced, he should confer with the most accomplished person present with respect to the fushimono and then write it down. The scribe should begin writing the first page with the hokku, read it aloud, then intone it. He should be thoroughly informed on matters concerning things to be avoided (*kiraimono*), and should explain them in the event of contraventions.[48]

The elaborate etiquette of such a gathering was a far cry from the renga sessions that had been popular before Yoshimoto's day, and which continued to enjoy popularity away from the court. Such sessions were apt to turn into gambling bouts at which participants bet on the number of points the judge would award to successive verses. At times renga gatherings were forbidden by local authorities because of the undesirable riffraff they attracted. Even when the renga sessions did not lead to open gambling, prizes were commonly awarded for the best verses.[49] In the fifteenth and sixteenth centuries, when renga masters, driven from the capital by warfare, traveled to distant parts of the country to receive hospitality from local warlords, they normally followed a session of serious renga (no doubt just as painful for the renga masters as for their badly educated pupils) with more cheerful, often bawdy, renga helped along by sake. Konishi Jin'ichi commented on one session held at the Imperial Palace in 1480 in the presence of the Emperor Gotsuchimikado, the former Chancellor Ichijō Kaneyoshi, the then Chancellor Konoe Masaie, and various other notables, that it is difficult to tell whether the main object of the gathering was renga or sake.[50]

Regardless of the nature of the poetry composed, however, renga was by its very nature a group endeavor. It is tempting to imagine that the possibility of joining with other people in making poetry, on whatever level, was particularly appealing in an age of warfare when men more commonly met to kill; but even if this cannot be proved, the composition of poetry as a communal undertaking has without question continued to exert a special attraction on the Japanese, as we know not only from the haikai style of renga popular during the Tokugawa period but from the many twentieth-century associations of tanka and haiku poets who regularly meet to compose together under the supervision of an admired poet, and who publish their poems in the magazine edited by the poet. Indeed, it has been argued that all traditional Japanese literature is in some sense the literature of a group, or at least of multiple authorship. The waka addressed by a man to a woman who had attracted him was indeed his own composition, but it generally included allusions to the poetry of the past that he was sure she would recognize because she also belonged to a *za* (or group) of poets, which composed poetry based on a shared knowledge of that past. The woman's reply to the man's poem would not only answer it in its own terms but match it, often in such a way as to suggest a dialogue poem or even two stanzas of the same poem. Prose was also communally shared. People in one romance were often compared to those in another, and the diarists traveled mainly from one utamakura to another, associating themselves with the travelers of the past.

But of all the literary arts, the one most easily discussed as *za no bungaku*,[51] the literature of the group, is renga. It is true that some poets composed whole renga sequences by themselves, but even when such sequences were of high literary quality, a solo renga (*dokugin*) forfeited the possibility of unexpected responses.[52] Yoshimoto believed that seven or eight participants was an ideal number for renga; if too few people took part the sequence was not likely to go well.[53] Of course, the participants could not be a random group of poets. A za was a group of poets who shared a communality of spirit that was fostered by a respect for the literature of the past. This did not necessarily involve any loss of individuality on the part of the participants, though it is true that nobody deliberately tried to be unlike the others. Yoshimoto compared renga to Nō, another art carried on by a za.[54] The Nō actors who performed a play belonged to the same za and were accustomed to working together, but this did not eliminate their individual, though usually unconscious, characteristics as actors; and the audiences for Nō (now as in the past) consisted largely of people who themselves had studied the singing of the texts and the performing of the dances, establishing a far closer relationship between themselves and the actors than is common in European theater. In the case of renga, too, the ideal reader was one who had actually had the experience of creating renga; only such a reader would be able to fully understand and (more important) enjoy the shifting associations.

Two styles of renga composition were practiced. The first and literarily far more important was the *ushin*, or serious renga, the second the *mushin*, or comic renga. Few examples of mushin renga survive, no doubt because the poets did not think it worth wasting paper and ink to record the quips that passed for verse; but extant manuscripts of thousands of ushin renga sessions have yet to be printed, and perhaps never will be, considering the general lack of interest in renga today.

Yoshimoto's most important work was probably *Tsukuba Shū* (Tsukuba Collection), compiled in 1356 with Kyūsei. It is in twenty books, the standard number for imperially sponsored collections, and was evidently intended to impart to renga the same kind of dignity that the *Kokinshū* had brought to the waka. He largely succeeded in this effort: in the following year *Tsukuba Shū* was honored by being classed as the "next after" (*jun*) an imperial collection of waka. The *Tsukuba Shū* consists of 1,993 pairs of verses arranged so as to demonstrate how the second verse successfully linked with the first. Only the authors of the tsukeku are identified, a clear sign that skill in linking onto an existing verse (of whatever quality) was more important than the intrinsic literary value of the verses. Book XIX contains twenty-four examples of *wakan* (Japanese verse linked to five-character lines in Chinese), and various miscellaneous poems. Book XX is devoted to hokku.

Kyūsei, Yoshimoto's collaborator, is represented by 118 verses, the largest number, followed by Yoshimoto himself with 79. The manner of the collection may be suggested by a few examples. The first bears the prefatory note, "Among the hundred links composed at a renga session held in his house when he was minister of the Right."[55]

hana osoge naru	Spring in a mountain village
yamazato no haru	Where the blossoms seem so late.
kore wo miyo	But just look at this—
kasumi ni nokoru	Lingering in vernal mist,
matsu no yuki[56]	Snow on the pine trees.

In response to the conventional maeku, which mentions the slowness of spring flowers to reach the mountains, Yoshimoto points out the beauty of a tardy spring, when early mist hovers over the winter's lingering snow. The tsukeku shifts the mood from the forlorn aspect of a village, forgotten by the spring, to the discovery of a beauty visible nowhere else, a sight of such charm that cherry blossoms seem unnecessary. In another tsukeku Yoshimoto responded to an evocation of particular phenomena with a conceptualization:

yama wa shika no ne	In the hills, the cries of deer,
no ni wa naku mushi	In the fields, the piping insects.
mono goto ni	In every single thing
kanashiki ka na ya	What sadness meets the senses
aki no kure[57]	This autumn evening!

Another, more complex linkage is found in Kyūsei's tsukeku to a spring maeku:

inochi wa shirazu	Human life is uncertain,
hi koso nagakere	But how long the days in spring!
shiratsuyu no	Rain is falling now
tama no o yanagi	On the strings of white jewels—
ame furite[58]	Dew on the willows.

The maeku is perhaps spoken by an old man, who contrasts the uncertainty of his life, which may end at any moment, with the unhurried calm of a spring day. In the tsukeku Kyūsei responded to the uncertainty of life by mention of *tama no o* (a string of jewels), a metaphor for the easily broken thread of life, and to the length of the spring days by mention of the willow, a tree whose twigs were often used by waka poets as metaphors for great length. Kyūsei's tsukeku not only continued the description of a spring scene but responded to both elements of the maeku.

In *Renri Hishō* Yoshimoto distinguished fifteen varieties of linkage—simple meaning, overtones, language, allusion, place-names, and so on.[59] *Tsukuba Shū* is in a sense a series of demonstrations of exactly how these different linkages were performed. Yoshimoto naturally could not foresee that a time would come when people would stop wanting to compose renga. He was confident that *Tsukuba Shū* would serve as a model: "This work has been selected as an imperial collection and includes many different kinds of links. I am sure that people of future times will for this reason regard the present with awe."[60]

One does not often find in the history of Japanese literature such confidence in the value of contemporary writings, but for Yoshimoto the present moment was the most important. He insisted that renga did not take into account the past or future, only the present and the challenge to compose a response to another's verse. Unlike the waka poets who attached such importance to their art that they staked their life on a single poem and were so wounded by criticism as to die of grief,[61] renga poets were too absorbed with the task immediately before them to think of anything else.[62] Renga for Yoshimoto was a source of joy untroubled by the bothersome traditions that had grown up around the waka.

Nijō Yoshimoto was an extraordinary figure. Though he must have been obliged to spend most of each day dealing with official business, he somehow found time to devote long hours to poetry, especially renga. Together with Kyūsei, he compiled *Ōan Shinshiki* (New Rules of the Ōan Era, 1372), which served for seventy years as the standard rulebook for renga composition.[63] Yoshimoto's own renga did not rank with the finest examples of this genre, but his successors, building on his work, would make of renga one of the most distinctive genres of Japanese literature.

The Age of Ichijō Kaneyoshi (1402–1481)[64]

Renga did not flourish during the years following Yoshimoto's death in 1388. It has even been said that the twenty or thirty years afterward are a blank in renga history. This does not mean that renga suffered any drastic loss of popularity. On the contrary, many renga sessions were held in the capital, and poets of the time did not doubt that they were faithfully continuing the art developed by Yoshimoto and his teachers. But there were no masters, and later generations of renga poets considered that the renga composed at this time represented the degradation of a once noble art. The blame for the decline in the quality of renga was often placed on Shūa (d. 1377?), a former pupil of Kyūsei, who was accused of having so completely forgotten the teachings of his master as to be interested only in impressing people by his cleverness; it was averred that the links he contributed to renga sequences dazzled the ignorant but at the cost of destroying the harmony of the whole.

Shūa was in fact a thoroughly competent poet, as we know from his active participation in various important renga sessions;[65] and his style enjoyed great popularity in the years after Kyūsei's death. The special appeal of his work lay in his skill in capturing every last association (*yoriai*) found in the preceding verses (maeku) with his continuing links (tsukeku). The manner in which he and Kyūsei came to differ in their styles is illustrated by the tsukeku they gave to the same maeku by Nijō Yoshimoto:[66]

matsu aru kata ni	Are those cicadas singing
semi ya nakuran	Off there where the pine trees grow?

Kyūsei's tsukeku was:

yamamizu no	The sound of mountain
nagaruru oto wa	Water flowing resembles
ame ni nite	The sound of the rain.

Shūa's tsukeku was:

ame kaze wo	In the mountain shade
morogoe ni kiku	He hears the mingled voices
yamagakure	Of the rain and wind.

Shinkei, over a hundred years later (in 1468), added this verse:

ki naru ha wa	The yellowing leaves
sono no kozue ni	On treetops in the garden
saki ochite[67]	Are the first to fall.

Kyūsei's tsukeku is at once the simplest and the most effective of the three. Mention of *semi* (cicadas) in the maeku evoked the association of *semi-shigure*, a dinning of cicadas that was synesthetically compared to a drizzling rain (*shigure*), and this led Kyūsei to think of rain itself; from rain his thoughts moved to mountain water. Together with the maeku, Kyūsei's tsukeku means something like: "Are those cicadas singing off where the pine trees grow? No, it is a mountain stream flowing through the pine forest, its sound like rain or perhaps like 'cicada rain.' "

Shūa was even more ingenious. Mention of pines (*matsu*) in the maeku evoked for him the association with pine wind (*matsukaze*), and *semi* with *semi-shigure* (as it did for Kyūsei as well). But he added a new subject to the sequence, someone living in solitude in the shade of a mountain who listens to the varied "voices" of the rain and wind. Shūa managed to carry over in his tsukeku both images of the maeku—the pines (represented by the pine wind) and the cicadas (represented by the "cicada rain")—and even added a human element. Such virtuosity appealed to his contemporaries, but it brought on him the charge of superficial ingenuity from some modern commentators.[68]

Shinkei's tsukeku was inspired by a phrase in a Chinese poem contained in *Wakan Rōei Shū*, "Cicadas sing in the yellow leaves."[69] Shinkei explained, however, "The cicadas had been singing in the leaves of the autumn trees, but after the leaves fell, they moved to the pines." He admitted that he was not entirely pleased with his own verse, but blamed this on the maeku, saying it was so ungraceful he could not possibly add a decent tsukeku.

It is not hard to imagine why ingenuity of Shūa's kind should have been popular in his day and afterward, or why more traditional renga masters resented this popularity. His style was bitterly attacked years later by Shinkei, the haughtiest of the renga masters, who likened the debasement of the art of renga by Shūa and his followers to the triumph of the fiendish Chinese emperors Chieh and Chou over the virtuous Yao and Shun.[70]

During the transitional period from 1388 until the middle of the fifteenth century, there were few poets of significance, and the art threatened to revert to its origins as a literary game; but this long slump was followed by an extraordinary revival of renga composition and works of renga criticism. Perhaps the badness of the bad period was exaggerated by the poets of the revival who, pleased with their own consecration to the art of renga, were harsh when they discussed their predecessors. Shinkei, for example, wrote of Bontō (1349–1425?),[71] a military man who, though originally a pupil of Yoshimoto, had been much influenced by Shūa, "Bontō's verses overlook the heart of the preceding links; his only concern is to make his own verses interesting."[72]

Shinkei's comment was surprising in view of Bontō's expressed views on the subject: "The previous verse is to renga what the topic is to a waka. . . . However hard one many try to compose a waka, if one has a poor grasp of the topic, many errors will result, and what one writes will not be a waka. With renga, too, if one does not have a good idea how to attach one's link to the previous verse it will not be renga."[73] Bontō's chief fault in the eyes of his successors may have been that he left the capital and the pursuit of renga for about twenty years, beginning in his fifties when he took the tonsure as a Buddhist priest. During this time he roamed in various parts of the country. When eventually he returned to the capital about 1420 and attempted to resume his life as a renga poet, his compositions were severely criticized, perhaps because his style had remained intact while the style of poets in the capital had undergone many changes.[74] Shinkei again and again wrote in unfriendly terms about "country people" (*inaka hotori no hito*), contrasting their simplistic understanding of renga with his own profound commitment to the art. Perhaps that was the reason why he wrote disparagingly of Bontō, at least some of the time.

It is hard to date the revival of renga, but it could be argued that it began in 1452 when Ichijō Kaneyoshi, the grandson of Nijō Yoshimoto, collaborated with the renga master Takayama Sōzei (c. 1386–1455) to produce *Shinshiki Kon'an* (New Views on the New Rules), a revision of Yoshimoto's code of renga composition of 1372. In Steven D. Carter's words, "These new rules became the basis for serious *renga* composition throughout the latter part of the fifteenth century."[75] Most of the new rules consist of additions to the various categories established by Yoshimoto; for example, under the category of "Things That May Appear as Many as Four Times in a Hundred-Link Sequence," Kaneyoshi added: "Shrine (twice in the context of Shintō, twice meaning 'imperial residence.' But one of these instances should involve a Famous Place)."[76] Such changes in the rules undoubtedly meant more to renga poets than we can easily appreciate, but far more important than *what* Kaneyoshi changed was the fact that the highest official in the country was actively interested in renga composition. The patronage given to the art by such a man earned for Kaneyoshi the reputation of being a second Yoshimoto, though he was by no means so distinguished a poet, and renga composition again assumed a dominant role in the literary society of the time.

Kaneyoshi's career in many ways parallels that of his grandfather. Born into the highest rank of the aristocracy, he became minister of the interior at the age of nineteen, minister of the Right at twenty-two, and kampaku at forty-five. As a young man he displayed considerable talent for waka composition, and his learning was also exceptional for the time. He wrote both the Japanese and Chinese prefaces to the last imperial collection of waka, *Shin Shokukokinshū* (1439). Kaneyoshi also served many times as the judge of poem competitions, but none of his own waka or his criticism of other people's is read today; his standard of excellence was the work of Fujiwara Teika, and he was convinced that any deviation from Teika's views was heresy. He is remembered as a man of impressive scholarship, but not as a poet.

Kaneyoshi produced a large number of books, including important studies of the Heian classics, most notably *Kachō Yojō* (Overtones of Flowers and Birds, 1472), a commentary on *The Tale of Genji*. He delivered lectures to the nobility at his house from 1444 on *The Tale of Genji* and other Heian texts. Unlike earlier commentators, who had confined their explanations to items of vocabulary, Kaneyoshi gave ample consideration to the meaning of whole passages in the text, profiting by his exceptional knowledge of court ceremonial and precedents to clarify customs that had become obscure in the centuries since Murasaki's time. His views on *The Tale of Genji* are no longer of much interest, but his advocacy of the work greatly contributed to its popularity during the Muromachi period.

It is not clear when Kaneyoshi first became interested in renga composition, but probably it was after meeting Sōzei, his future collaborator. Sōzei, originally of the samurai class, had served the powerful Yamana family in the province of Tajima, and he maintained these connections until the end of his life, even though in the meanwhile he had become a priest on Mount Kōya.[77] He studied waka with Shōtetsu and renga with Bontō, and demonstrated proficiency in both. In particular, the renga he composed during sessions held in 1445 attracted such favorable attention that three years later the shogun, Ashikaga Yoshinori, named him the "administrator of the renga meeting place" (*kaisho bugyō*) at the Kitano Shrine,[78] and also "renga teacher" (*renga sōshō*), the highest positions a renga poet could obtain.[79] It was probably after he received this recognition that Sōzei went to visit Kaneyoshi.

The combination of these two men—a gifted poet and the outstanding intellectual of the day—ensured that a revival of renga could occur under the most favorable conditions, but they were not together for long. Sōzei left the capital in 1454 after Yamana Sōzen, whose troops had fought against the shogun, was ordered to retire to his domain in Tajima. Sōzei followed his protector into exile, where he died the following year.

Sōzei's renga, though enhanced by the yūgen he had learned from Shōtetsu, is not so highly regarded today, mainly because of its ingenuity, suggesting that renga was still something of a game for him. The following tsukeku typifies his art:

ura ka omote ka	Is it inside or outside?
koromo to mo nashi	Maybe a cloak, perhaps not.
shinonome no	In the faint glimmer
ashita no yama no	As day breaks on the mountain,
usugasumi[80]	A pale swathe of mist.

Sōzei's tsukeku interprets the "cloak" of the maeku as mist that seems to clothe the mountain at daybreak, when there is still not enough light to discern whether one sees the outside or the lining of the "cloak." The maeku is extremely vague, and it was clever of Sōzei to make sense of it by identifying the cloak as early morning mist, but there is little depth in such a verse. All the same, Sōzei supplied a necessary link in the chain of poets from Kyūsei to the masters of the 1460s and 1470s. Shinkei praised Sōzei, along with Chiun (d. 1448), as "masters the likes of whom will probably not be born for another two or three hundred years,"[81] and credited the two men with the revival of renga in recent years;[82] but he also criticized Sōzei in these terms:

> If one examines his poetry carefully, one will see that for all his devotion to the art, he was a man of the mundane world through and through. He was a warrior by disposition, and grew up surrounded day and night by the crudities of the world of soldiers and

> weapons. He had absolutely no conception of the transience and changes of the world, no inclination to study and practice the Buddhist Law. Perhaps because he lacked even a particle of such interest, his skill was entirely technical, and there is no imagination, no overtones, no compassion in his verses. He composed not one decent love poem, but only crude verses that are absolutely devoid of ushin or yūgen. Shōtetsu frequently said the same thing.[83]

Shinkei's feelings toward Sōzei, a man who long had enjoyed the protection of a warlord, may also have been influenced by the disgust he felt on witnessing the destruction of the capital by the military during the Ōnin War. Shinkei wrote the first of the three letters that make up *Tokorodokoro Hentō* (Replies to This and That) in 1466, the year before the war actually broke out, and the last in 1470, at the height of the fighting. He fled the capital in 1468 and did not return until 1473.

The archetypal figure of the intellectual during the Ōnin War was Ichijō Kaneyoshi. Although he had known only the privileged life of an aristocrat until this time, he was suddenly faced with danger and even, for a time, with starvation. In his *Fude no Susabi* (The Consolation of the Brush), written in 1469 when he was living in Nara as a refugee from the warfare with his son, the abbot of a temple, he described the destruction of his most valuable possession, the library that had been passed down in his family for generations:

> Every single one of all the temples in the East Hills and West Hills that had stood, a perfect beehive of rooftiles ranged alongside rooftiles, was set afire and destroyed, and now not a blade of green grass was left, only clouds blotting out the whole. If one looks into the cause of what has happened, it is clear that it was nothing that should have developed into such a disturbance. People who yesterday were as close as father and son today tried to kill each other, behaving as if they were confronting tigers or wolves. . . . The time had come for the destruction of the Buddhist Law and the temporal law, and it seemed as though the merciful gods of the various heavens had exhausted their power to help. Now that it had become a struggle between dragons and tigers, the fighting would not quiet down until both friends and enemies had perished. . . . For a time I found a place to stay in the area of Kujō, where I pondered all that had happened, but before long the place went up in smoke and was left an ashen wasteland. My library, probably because the building was roofed with tiles and had earthen walls, managed to escape the

> flames, but bandits of the neighborhood, supposing that there must be money inside, soon broke their way in. They scattered the hundreds of boxes that had been the haunt of bookworms, and not one volume was left of all the Japanese and Chinese works that had been passed down in my family for over ten generations. I felt exactly like an old crane forced to leave its nest, or a blind man who has lost his stick. And as for renga, I had always regretted that no collection preserved the works that had been composed since the *Tsukuba Shū*, and I had made up my mind to collect as many compositions of recent times as came to my attention. I gave this manuscript the title of *Shingyoku Shū*[84] and had begun to copy out the text in twenty volumes. But this, too, was scattered somewhere, and I have no idea where it might be now.[85]

Kaneyoshi remained in exile a total of ten years, five of them in Nara. He resigned as kampaku in 1470, and spent his time writing and lecturing on the classics. This was his most productive period as a writer, and because of his presence, Nara, which for centuries had been largely deserted except by priests, became the cultural center of the whole country. Many nobles, escaping from the war-torn capital, went to join Kaneyoshi in Nara, and he, freed from his duties at court and enjoying the comforts of the great monastery Kōfuku-ji, devoted himself to the study of *The Tale of Genji* and other classics, corrected examples of renga sent to him, wrote prefaces to other people's books, and kept up a lively correspondence. During his years of exile he was helped materially by the renga master Sōgi, whom he had earlier befriended. It was ironic that Kaneyoshi, a member of a most distinguished noble family, should have depended on Sōgi, a man of the humblest origins, but such shifts in fortunes were not uncommon during an age characterized as *gekokujō*, those underneath conquering those above.

It would be easier to sympathize with Kaneyoshi had he not been such an extremely vain man. He compared himself to Sugawara no Michizane, pointing out three respects in which he was superior to the god of literature.[86] His achievements did not confirm he was entitled to such an honor, though he was clearly the outstanding scholar of the age and, it might be argued, the last high-ranking aristocrat to contribute significantly to the creation of Japanese literature.

Shinkei (1406–1475)

Shinkei, though he has not enjoyed the fame of Sōgi, his younger contemporary, was one of the two or three finest renga poets of all time. He came from samurai stock, but entered the Buddhist priesthood as a small child and spent the rest of his life in orders, rising eventually to the high rank of acting archbishop (*gonsōzu*). His early literary training was in the waka, which he studied with Shōtetsu. He later recalled that when Shōtetsu died in 1459, "Although I had served him day and night for thirty years, I could not remember a single thing he had said and had never achieved the smallest degree of enlightenment. Now that my teacher was no more, I felt like stamping my feet in vexation."[87] This statement was presumably an example of self-effacing modesty: Shinkei's poetry, both waka and renga, showed how much he had in fact benefited by Shōtetsu's guidance.[88] But the death of Shōtetsu apparently convinced Shinkei that the waka was also dead; he wrote,

> In recent times the art of the waka has been completely abandoned, and I therefore thought I would try to study and clarify this art of the renga as sincerely as I could, in the hope that I might embody in renga at least some fragments of the teachings of waka, soften the hearts of soldiers and rustics, and transmit its feelings to people of later ages.[89]

It is not clear with whom Shinkei studied renga, but as early as 1433 he was taking part in such events as the ten-thousand-link renga offered at the Kitano Shrine under the sponsorship of Ashikaga Yoshinori. In 1447 Shinkei, along with several outstanding renga poets of the day (including Sōzei and Chiun), composed the *Anegakōji Imashimmei Hyakuin* (One Hundred Verses Composed at the Imashimmei Shrine in Anegakōji).[90]

There are gaps of many years separating the known events in Shinkei's poetic career. Perhaps they were occasioned by the ill health of which he early complained, or it may be that his priestly duties kept him from composing poetry. In 1463 Shinkei wrote his best-known work of criticism, *Sasamegoto* (Whisperings),[91] which established his importance among the renga poets of the day. His chief contribution to renga was the Buddhist religiosity that he brought to a previously secular art.

Sasamegoto is cast in a familiar form of renga criticism, the question and answer. Probably Shinkei composed not only the answers but the questions. A typical section discusses the importance of yūgen, a critical term in the appreciation of renga. The overall meaning of this difficult section seems to be that true yūgen—that is to say, true beauty of expression—is not a surface manifestation, as people of Shinkei's day supposed, but lies in the heart of the poet. It is difficult to find equivalents for Shinkei's key terms, and in the following passage I have had to translate certain Japanese words in several quite different ways:

> Question. Is it correct to keep the style of yūgen central in one's mind as one cultivates this art?
>
> Answer. People of the past used to say that *yūgen* should pervade the form [*sugata*] of every verse. It is the most essential thing for anyone who practices the art. However, what people in the past understood by *yūgen* would seem to be far removed from what most people today suppose it means. People of the past seem to have considered that the heart was where the most important aspects of *yūgen* were to be found, but most people today think it refers to a gentility of surface [*sugata*]. Perfect beauty [*en*] is difficult to achieve within one's heart [*kokoro*]. Many people try to improve their external appearance, but only the solitary individual can improve his mind [*kokoro*]. That is why the poems which the people of the past considered to be in the *yūgen* style are not easy to understand these days.[92]

The word *kokoro*, as always, is difficult, corresponding to both mind and heart in English. *Sugata* usually means "form," but in poetic criticism often is closer to "overall tone." *Yūgen* varied in meaning with the time and the person who used the term; the characters with which the word is written literally mean "mysterious darkness," but often *yūgen* meant "charm" or "elegance" rather than anything more profound. Not all of Shinkei's pronouncements are so hard to translate, but he was a difficult poet and critic and demanded the most of all who practiced the art of renga, as the following may suggest:

> Question: Why is it that the verses by a poet who has attained the highest realm of expression should become increasingly difficult to understand?
>
> Answer. Our predecessors have discussed this matter. It is to be expected that ordinary people who have ears only for the verse that has just been linked should find it difficult to understand the mind of a man for whom the study and practice [of this art] involve not disregarding the meaning of every previous verse and every single

> particle. He keeps the whole of the hundred links in mind, constantly going back and forth, considering links that skip a verse [*uchikoshi*] or repeat an earlier theme [*tōrin'e*], and he gives careful thought even to the link that the next man is likely to append to his own verse.[93]

Obviously, it was beyond the average practitioner of renga to follow the example of the master conjured up by Shinkei in this section of his work. Only a person who devoted his every faculty to the art with a consecration no less than that devoted to a religion could satisfy Shinkei's description of a master of renga. His study of Zen philosophy led him to demand exalted ideals for the art that went far beyond the lyrical impulses of earlier masters or the pleasure in the game that probably still induced people to take part in renga sessions. Shinkei often discussed renga in Buddhist or Confucian terms, citing the "ten virtues" or the "seven treasures" of the art, or tracing parallels between the three bodies of the Buddha and the three kinds of understanding of renga.[94]

The effect of such prescriptions was to impart to renga a forbidding dignity and grandeur. It is unlikely that people of his time understood his purpose. The renga composed at the court still contained a strong element of play, and Shinkei seems not to have participated in more than a handful of official sessions. Unlike Sōzei, Shūa, Sōgi, and various other renga masters, he was never appointed as the Kitano "administrator" of renga. In short, he seems to have been relatively little known in his own time.[95] For his part, Shinkei had only contempt for the rank and file of amateur renga poets. In *Sasamegoto* he used the words "country people" as a term of abuse, and *tomogara* (the masses) was equally pejorative. When queried about the belief, common in China (and in Europe), that great poetry should be intelligible even to a peasant, his answer was unambiguous:

> Someone asked, "They say that a waka or renga accords with the true way of poetry when it is enjoyable even to the humblest, most barbarous peasant. What do you think of that?"
>
> No art worthy of the name is intelligible to persons of shallow understanding who have not mastered it. No doubt even the most untalented and ignorant person may be pleased by closely related verses[96] and a banal style, but it is inconceivable that anyone only vaguely familiar with the art could understand poetry of an elevated and profoundly beautiful nature.[97]

By Shinkei's time the history of renga was long enough for him to be able, like Teika prescribing the correct way to learn waka, to urge renga poets to learn from the masters of the past. Without study of the old models, he asserted, it is impossible to become an accomplished poet. On the other hand, study of the wrong models permanently impairs a poet. Shinkei told the story of a man who asked a famous *shakuhachi* player to admit him as his pupil. "Can you already play the shakuhachi?" the master asked. The would-be pupil replied, "I have practiced a little." To this the master responded, "Then I can't teach you." Shinkei concluded, "From this one may see that it is impossible to straighten a mind that has once entered an incorrect path, however briefly."[98]

Shinkei's preference in waka was for the style of the *Shin Kokinshū*, not too surprising in a pupil of Shōtetsu's. He recalled that Shōtetsu had often said, "It is true that I studied with Lord [Reizei] Tamehide and [Imagawa] Ryōshun, but in waka I look to the hearts of Teika and Jichin for direct guidance. I feel no nostalgia for the worn-out remnants of the Nijō and Reizei schools."[99] Shinkei, looking back on the period of the *Shin Kokinshū*, felt it was a time of prodigies, when waka poetry "fell into place." "It was indeed an age when Buddha himself appeared in the world of this art. [The poets included] the Emperor Gotoba, Fujiwara no Yoshitsune, the priest Jichin, Shunzei, Teika, Ietaka, Saigyō, Jakuren. And among the poets of recent times, the 'bones' [*fūkotsu*] of Shōtetsu provide the best model for the careful study and practice of this art."[100]

Shinkei made little distinction between the waka and renga; his reason for devoting himself mainly to renga was, he wrote on several occasions, because the art of waka was neglected in his time. He considered renga not (as some renga poets did) as an independent art that had its own ancient roots, but as the appropriate form of poetry for an age that was sadly unlike the ages of the past when waka had flourished.

The qualities that most attracted Shinkei to the poetry of the *Shin Kokinshū* or of the Chinese masters was what he called *take takaku hiekōri*, literally, "lofty and chilled to ice." Loftiness is an easily recognized ideal, but the chill of poetry, as opposed to warmth, has not often been espoused. Shinkei explained this conception in the following terms:

> The greatest of the Chinese poets, Tu Fu, during the course of his lifetime composed poems only about his grief, and it may be said that his life was one of grief. Hsü Hun during his whole career composed poems only about water, three thousand of them. Truly,

> there is nothing so deeply moving, so cool and refreshing as water. At mention of "the waters of spring" one's heart becomes relaxed and a vision comes before one's eyes, somehow moving. In summer at the source of pure water, near a spring, the water is chilly and cold. At the words "the waters of autumn" the heart becomes chilled and clear. And nothing is so exquisite as ice. Again, is it not delightful, exquisitely beautiful, when of a morning a harvested field is coated with a thin sheet of ice, when icicles hang by cypress-bark eaves, or when the dew and frost on the grasses and trees in a withered field have turned to ice?[101]

Shinkei's literary preferences are otherwise stated in *Sasamegoto*: "This Way takes evanescence and lamentation as the aim of both word and heart."[102] Shinkei's poetry is prevailingly dark. The austerity of expression—the iciness, to use his word—grew naturally from his love of the poetry of the *Shin Kokinshū* and of Shōtetsu. It reflected his Buddhist conviction of the sadness and transience of the world, and may also have been fostered by his dislike of the frivolous or overly ingenious renga of his immediate predecessors; but increasingly it seemed to be a judgment on the age in which he lived. In the fourth month of 1467, shortly before the outbreak of the Ōnin War, he left the capital on what he supposed would be a journey of a few months at most, but by the time he reached Shinagawa, outside the newly created town of Edo, the warfare in the capital had become so intense that he abandoned all thought of returning. In the years that followed, up until his death in 1475, he lived mainly in the area of Edo. In 1468 he wrote *Hitorigoto* (Talking to Myself), a book of renga criticism that is interesting for the autobiographical elements, especially his account of the fighting he had witnessed.

In Edo he continued to compose both waka and renga, participating on several occasions in gatherings sponsored by the local military, including Ōta Dōkan (1432–1486), whose castle at Edo, built in 1457, is considered to have formed the nucleus of the city now called Tokyo. Much of Shinkei's time seems to have been spent bringing the civilizing art of poetry to the local warriors—soothing their fierce spirits, in the old phrase. The terrible warfare of the period had at least this one compensation: poets who were obliged to flee from the capital came to make their living by teaching renga to uncultured military men, thereby spreading to the provinces the culture that had been confined to the capital. The craze for composing renga extended to every part of the country; and even in the capital, where the emperor and the shogun

Ashikaga Yoshimasa did their best to forget that people were being killed and houses destroyed a few steps away, the craze raged unabated during the worst of the fighting. Most of the renga composed was of the mushin, or unliterary, style. Shinkei did not relish this development:

> The renga I have heard recently in country districts have none of the earmarks of a disciplined, conscious art. The poets seem to be in a state of utter confusion.
>
> Yes, one might say that ever since such amateurs have grown so numerous, the art of writing noble, deeply felt poetry seems to have become extinct. Renga has become nothing more than a glib chattering, and all mental discipline has vanished without a trace. That is why when one passes along the roads or the marketplaces one's ears are assailed by the sounds of thousand-verse or ten-thousand-verse compositions, and even the rare persons who have some real acquaintance with the art use this knowledge solely as a means of earning a living. Day after day, night after night, they engage in indiscriminate composition together. Our times would seem to correspond to the age of stultification and final decline of the art. . . . Renga is in such a state that neither Buddha nor Confucius nor Hitomaro can save it.[103]

Shinkei's contributions to renga stand apart from the mainstream of fifteenth-century composition.[104] Although he was devoted to the principles of renga and did not consciously violate the rules, his verses are marked by an individuality that is rare in renga. Konishi wrote that in any renga sequence in which Shinkei took part, his verses stand out and leave a special impression; if one concealed the names of the authors, only Shinkei's verses would be identifiable. He stated, "I believe that Shinkei's stanzas are of unmatched greatness. Sōgi also writes outstanding stanzas, but if one considers stanzas alone, it is Shinkei's that one would judge to excel by the profound effect they have on us."[105]

Individuality was not prized as such by renga masters. Perfect conformity to the rules, grace of language, richness of overtones—the importance of these and other qualities was stressed in contemporary discussions of renga, but the renga masters seem never to have considered it desirable for the participating poets to speak with distinctive voices. Shinkei once stated, "The supreme renga is like a drink of plain boiled water. It has no particular flavor, but one never wearies of it, no matter when one tastes it."[106] Surely he did not intend his verses to stand out from the others, but his perceptions of the world had greater depth and intensity than those of other renga masters, even the most distinguished, and this difference revealed itself in his poetry.

Perhaps Shinkei's finest achievement as a renga poet is found in his solo sequence *Yama-nani Hyakuin*.[107] It opens:

hototogisu	To have heard a cuckoo—
kikishi wa mono ka	What's so special about that?
Fuji no yuki	The snow on Fuji.
kumo mo tomaranu	There is such cool in the sky
sora no suzushisa	Not even the clouds linger.
tsuki kiyoki	In the purity
hikari ni yoru wa	Of the light of the moon
kaze miete	The wind can be seen.

The translation does not remotely suggest the beauty and grandeur of these three verses. The season of the hokku is summer, as we know from mention of the hototogisu, the bird most typically associated with that season. It was so unusual to hear one in the capital that people might boast of it, but the lingering snow on Fuji seems far more beautiful to the poet. Within a mere seventeen syllables the imagery shifts from sound to sight, from a bird so inconspicuous that it is rarely seen to the towering mass of Fuji. The second verse moves laterally with the clouds over the clear sky—itself a surprise in summer, when it so often rains. The cool in the sky is of course welcome in this season. The third verse shifts the season to autumn, as we know from mention of the moon, and the cool of the second verse is no longer pleasant relief from the summer heat but the cool brought by the first winds of autumn, which are not only felt but seen in the movement of the clouds over the sky.[108]

It is not surprising, in view of Shinkei's expressed disdain for catering to popular tastes, that his renga is not so immediately appealing as Sōgi's. It tends to be admired by the few, those who can fully grasp the achievement made possible by his mastery of language and extraordinary sensitivity to poetic beauty.

Sōgi (1421–1502)

Shinkei's relations with Sōgi are not entirely clear, but judging from Shinkei's letter of 1470, Sōgi must have been his pupil for years. In the winter of 1468 they joined with several other poets in Shinagawa to compose the sequence *Nanibito Hyakuin*,[109] and they later met at the same place a number of times. But the clearest evidence of Sōgi's admiration for Shinkei is found in the collection *Shinsen Tsukuba Shū* (New Tsukuba Collection) which Sōgi (and Kensai) edited in 1495: more verses by Shinkei than any other poet were included. Sōgi singled out one hokku by Shinkei for his highest praise:

"Among the poems in a thousand-verse sequence composed when I visited the Great Shrine of Ise:"

hi no mikage	Holy light of the sun—
hana ni nioeru	A morning fragrant with
ashita kana[110]	The scent of blossoms.

Sōgi in his *Azuma Mondō* (Questions and Answers in the East, 1470?) wrote of Shinkei's verse: "This hokku was apparently composed among a thousand verses offered to the Great Shrine of Ise. This, I feel, is a perfect poem. How many hokku have been composed since ancient times before the Great Shrine! And how foolish it would be to compare any of them to this masterpiece."[111] The generosity of the praise bespeaks genuine admiration, but Sōgi and Shinkei had basically different sensibilities, no doubt because of their dissimilar backgrounds.

We have little information about Sōgi before his fortieth year, despite the efforts of biographers over the centuries. Neither his family name nor his place of origin is known for certain, but it is generally believed that he came from the lower classes, perhaps even from outcasts.[112] In earlier times it would have been virtually unthinkable for someone of this background to rise in the world, but in an age of gekokujō, anything was possible.

We can gather from bits of evidence in his later writings that in his twenties Sōgi entered the Shōkoku-ji, a major Zen temple in the capital. Probably he first became interested in renga while living at the temple, and his adoption as a protégé by Ichijō Kaneyoshi suggests that he displayed unusual talent in this art.[113] A fruitful relationship between the two men continued until Kaneyoshi's death in 1482. Sōgi was tutored by Kaneyoshi in the traditions of the waka and of court ritual, and he received special instruction in *The Tale of Genji*. He also studied waka with Asukai Masachika (1416–1490) and Tō no Tsuneyori, the latter revered as the founder of the *Kokin Denju*, or secret traditions of the transmission of the *Kokinshū*. If one recalls the reluctance of the court poets to admit Kamo no Chōmei, a member of a rather distinguished family, to their number, it is striking that the humbly born Sōgi should have counted among his teachers the great nobles of the country. In later years, when his reputation had been made, warlords all over the country vied for the privilege of having Sōgi stay at their castles.

The training he received in the classics undoubtedly imparted authority and fluency to his compositions, whether waka or renga, but it also exerted a conservative, even inhibiting influence. Sōgi's own selection of his best work, the verses he included in *Shinsen Tsukuba Shū*, would not be the ones a modern critic would choose; they show him at his most ingenious, in the vein of the *Kokinshū*, rather than as deeply moving. It seems likely that Sōgi escaped the fate of becoming a conventionally competent poet of the Nijō school mainly because so much of his life was spent outside the capital. From 1466 to 1472, during the worst of the Ōnin War, he traveled and lived mainly in the eastern region of the country; it was there that he studied the *Kokinshū* with Tō no Tsuneyori, then living at Mishima in Izu, and these studies were crowned by Sōgi's commentary on the *Kokinshū*, completed in 1471. While in the east, Sōgi associated with military leaders and joined with them in renga composition. It was at this time that he wrote his first important critical work on renga, *Azuma Mondō*. By the end of his stay in the east he had emerged as a renga poet of the first order; clearly, prolonged contacts with poets who were not of the court tradition had enriched Sōgi's work.

Sōgi returned to Kyoto in the spring of 1472. His residence in the capital, known as Shūgyoku-an, became a center of literary activity and remained such for about thirty years. Sōgi conducted waka and renga sessions, lectured on *The Tale of Genji* and other classics, compiled the *Shinsen Tsukuba Shū*, and gave training to his disciples, including Shōhaku and Sōchō. His first important collection of renga, *Wasuregusa* (Day Lilies), compiled about 1473, included verses composed while in the east and some from even earlier.

Sōgi was one of the great traveler-poets, like Saigyō before him and Bashō two hundred years later. His travels were in part inspired by the desire to see with his own eyes the famous sites of poetry, and in his critical works he devoted considerable attention to the importance of verses on "famous places." During the course of his lifetime Sōgi made many lengthy journeys, seven times to the province of Echigo on the Japan Sea coast (where he was the guest of the warlord Uesugi Fusasada), twice to Yamaguchi at the western end of Honshū (at the invitation of

Ōuchi Masahiro), and to Kyūshū in 1480, a trip commemorated in his travel diary *Tsukushi no Michi no Ki* (Journey Along the Tsukushi Road).[114]

Sōgi's reason for traveling to distant Kyūshū is succinctly stated in the diary:

> My decision to depend on a single, lofty tree proved to be efficacious: from its shade the dew of generosity was shed abundantly on the grasses below. The months and days passed quickly and, to my heart's delight, in numerous sessions of poetry on many different occasions, and soon it was the ninth month. Many invitations came to visit the cedars of Kashii and the pines of Iki, and, moved by gratitude, I made up my mind to undertake the journey.[115]

The "lofty tree" upon whom Sōgi depended was Ōuchi Masahiro (d. 1495), one of the most powerful warlords in the country; his kindness ("dew") enabled Sōgi and various other refugee poets from the capital to live comfortably in Yamaguchi, and he thereby transformed a cultural desert into a center of literary and artistic creation. At the time Masahiro controlled the Shimonoseki Strait, and one of his vassals made arrangements with people in Kyūshū (called Tsukushi, its old name, by Sōgi) for Sōgi's travels to places of interest in the area.

These travels helped to establish his great renown, and Sōgi became the only renga poet whose name was known to the general public. At one time "Sōgi's mosquito netting" was as familiar a reference as the beds in which Queen Elizabeth or George Washington are alleged to have slept. In *Saikaku Nagori no Tomo* (Saikaku's Parting With Friends, 1699) a renga teacher says, "I am of no importance myself, but one year, when Sōgi the renga master was traveling through the provinces in search of truth, by a curious coincidence we stayed at the same inn in Okabe on the Tōkaidō, and I slept under the same mosquito netting with him."[116]

Sōgi's reputation as a poet is based mainly on two or three renga sequences. The most famous of all renga sequences, *Minase Sangin* (Three Poets at Minase), was composed by Sōgi with Shōhaku and Sōchō on the twenty-second day of the first month of 1488. Minase, a village west of Kyoto, had been the site of a favorite palace of the Emperor Gotoba, and the day on which the three poets gathered was the anniversary of his death. The sequence in one hundred verses, offered to the memory of one of the great figures of Japanese poetry, demonstrated Sōgi's mastery of the medium at the height of his powers. The sequence began with Sōgi:

yuki nagare	Snow yet remaining,
yamamoto kasumu	The mountain slopes are misty—
yūbe kana	It is evening.

Direct reference is made to the well-known waka by Gotoba in the *Shin Kokinshū*:

miwataseba	When I gaze far off
yamamoto kasumu	The mountain slopes are misty
Minasegawa	Minase River—
yūbe wa aki to	Why did I ever supoose
nani omoiken	Evenings were best in autumn?

Sōgi's hokku pays tribute to Gotoba the poet. At the same time, it reveals by the allusion that the site of the compositon was the Minase River, and satisfies the requirements of a hokku by indicating the season (early spring, when the mountains still covered with snow turn misty in the first warmth of the spring), the time of day (evening), the prevailing aspect of the scene (mountains and river), and the mood (serenity and majesty). The successive links also conformed to the renga code as established at the time of Nijō Yoshimoto, but are imbued with a fresheness of expression. The second verse was by Shōhaku:

yuku mizu tōku	Far away the water flows
ume niou sato	Past the plum-scented village.

The second link, as prescribed, ends with a noun and continues the mood and season of the first, but it also supplies additional details: it tells us that the river, frozen during the winter, has melted, and plum blossoms have opened on lower ground. Sōchō supplied the third link:

kawakaze ni	In the river breeze
hitomura yanagi	A cluster of willow trees—
haru miete	Spring reveals itself.

The season (spring) is continued, as required by the code, to a third link, as is mention of water. The river breeze, stirring the willows, calls attention to their springtime green. This link ends in *-te*, a participle, also in keeping with the code. The fourth link was by Sōgi:

fune sasu oto mo	The sound of a boat being poled,
shiruki akegata	Clear in the early dawning.

Although the hokku stated that it was evening, the time has been deliberately shifted to early morning, following the principle of change. In renga composition only the verse immediately before needs to be taken into consideration; a reference to an earlier link was in fact undesirable. The fourth link changed the time of day, but did not suggest any particular season, and it is therefore possible to combine the third and fourth links to form a waka about the scenery of a spring dawn:

kawakaze ni	In the river breeze
hitomura yanagi	A cluster of willow trees—
haru miete	Spring reveals itself.
fune sasu oto mo	The sound of a boat being poled
shiruki akegata	Clear in the early dawning.

The seasonless fourth link, when joined to the following verse, could equally well allow for a seasonal shift. The water imagery, however, was continued. The fifth link was by Shōhaku:

tsuki ya nao	The moon—does it still
kiri wataru yo ni	In the fog-enshrouded night
nokururan	Hover in the sky?

The season has now been changed to autumn, as we know from mention of the moon and fog, two phenomena conventionally associated with autumn. The time of day is still dawn, as stated in the previous link, but the meaning of the fourth link has changed when combined with the fifth link from a spring to an autumn scene. The fourth and fifth links together make a poem that tells of a foggy autumn morning when one cannot even be sure the moon still lingers in the sky, and the only clear thing is the sound of an invisible boat being poled in the river. The shift of scenery and mood was prized by renga poets; it guaranteed the freedom of associative references that is at the heart of the genre.[117]

The hundred links composed at Minase included some of Buddhist content, others of love, others still on scenes of poverty and death. One link by Sōgi suggested the misery of Kyoto during the Ōnin War:

kusaki sae	Even plants and trees
furuki miyako no	Share the bitter memories
urami ni te	Of the old capital.

The note of despair makes this link more affecting than others that are conventional in their evocations of nature. A series on poverty[118] has a similar appeal though these verses are atypical, too, in that they lack seasonal words or mention of features of the landscape. The hundredth (and last) link of *Three Poets at Minase*, quiet in tone, has overtones of an auspicious nature, suitable for a work that was dedicated to an emperor, though rather incongruous in a time of terrible war.[119]

Three years later, in the winter of 1491, the same three poets met at the hot springs of Arima in Settsu province where they composed the hundred links of *Yuyama Sangin* (Three Poets at Yuyama).[120] Some critics admire this sequence even more than *Three Poets at Minase*, in part because of the relaxed atmosphere induced in the poets by bathing in the hot springs. Other critics believe that Sōgi's solo renga sequences, notably the one composed in 1492, represent the acme of his art.[121]

Sōgi's contributions to renga were not confined to his poetry. His renga criticism, especially *Oi no Susami* (A Diversion of Old Age, 1479),[122] provides practical discussion of the different techniques of linking verses; but these works, like his renga, are impersonal[123] and leave little impression of what Sōgi was like as a human being. His emotions are revealed only indirectly, as in his commentary on a link by Shinkei. Another person had given the maeku:

wa ga furusato to	The birds are chirping as if
tori zo saezuru	The old town belonged to them.

Shinkei added the verse:

ta ga ueshi	Who planted these trees?
kozue no nobe ni	In the fields, by the treetops,
kasumuran	The spring mists hover.

Sōgi commented:

> The old town has been completely devastated. The only sign of spring is the mist in the trees that somebody planted, but there is no trace now in the fields of whoever it was, and only the birds consider the treetops as home. He [Shinkei], surveying the scene,

imparted "feeling" to the previous verse. The effect of the link is striking and deeply moving.[124]

Sōgi did not take the trouble to indicate that the "old town" (*furusato*) was the capital, or that mention of fields meant that where houses once stood there were now open spaces. But the fact that he felt it necessary to supply a commentary (and that almost every renga sequence of importance has been provided with at least one old commentary and usually more) suggests how difficult renga was to understand even for professionals. A twentieth-century reader may be intrigued by the possibility in renga of multiple streams of consciousness creating a single literary work,[125] but it is not easy to feel poetic excitement when renga is read in a modern commentated edition, much less in a translation. The staggering skill displayed by Sōgi and his colleagues will be apparent to anyone who takes the trouble to follow a sequence link by link, but unless the reader has had personal experience composing renga, the text is likely to be an exhausting test of his attention.[126]

Sōgi's colleagues at Minase and Yuyama, Shōhaku and Sōchō, were both skilled poets. Apart from his poetry, not much is remembered about the personality of Shōhaku (1443–1527) except that he was so fond of peonies that he took the name Botanka (Peony Flower) as his sobriquet and that he enjoyed drinking sake;[127] but Sōchō emerges quite distinctly from his writings.

Sōchō (1448–1532)

Commentators agree that Sōchō, though a good poet, was the least accomplished of the three who met at Minase;[128] but by the time the poets met again at Yuyama, Sōchō had largely closed the gap separating him from the other two men. After Sōgi's death in 1502, he was probably the most accomplished renga poet. Most of his poetry was in the manner of his teacher, relying on suggestion and simplicity of expression, and only occasionally revealing that he was more interested in human affairs than in nature. Unlike Sōgi, however, he did not compose waka, though he was, of course, familiar with the standard collections.[129] Sōchō traveled all over the country, in the tradition of Sōgi, but the only places mentioned in his renga were those sanctioned by the old lists of utamakura.[130]

It might be imagined from the content of Sōchō's renga that he belonged to some conservative family of poets, but he was in fact the son of a swordsmith from the province of Suruga. In 1467 he entered

Buddhist orders. He described his ordination in terms that indicate his sect of Buddhism was Shingon, but his notebooks are otherwise dotted with references to the Daitoku-ji, a Zen monastery in Kyoto, and to the Shūon-an, the hermitage where the Zen priest Ikkyū lived and died. Sōchō does not mention when he first met Ikkyū, but from 1476, when Ikkyū was eighty-two years old, until his death five years later, Sōchō spent as much time as possible with him. This influence dominated the rest of Sōchō's life, and showed itself in a defiance of convention that contrasted with his orthodoxy in renga composition. Like Ikkyū, who delighted in shocking his fellow priests with overt references to his sexual exploits and who loathed above all the mealy-mouthed hypocrisy of venal priests, Sōchō openly admitted that he had had two children by a washerwoman, and there was a salacious side to his writings, especially the comic poetry of his late years. Sōchō is important not only as an adept follower of Sōgi but as a predecessor of the haikai (comic) style of renga that began in the sixteenth century. He and Yamazaki Sōkan, the traditional founder of *haikai no renga* as it was known, on occasion composed poetry together.[131]

Sōchō emerges from his notebook *Sōchō Shuki* as a far more distinct personality than Sōgi or Shōhaku, but this involves a problem: how to reconcile the uninhibited life Sōchō led with the formal correctness of his renga. The explanation is undoubtedly that Sōchō was a professional who could compose to order. The military were an important source of income through most of his life, and he was able to join with them in renga sessions of the most orthodox variety or (after the formal session was over and the drinks were served) of the most ribald variety, according to their wishes.[132] His notebook includes some of the mushin (comic) renga Sōchō and his associates composed. These are the only surviving examples, but they provide a bridge to the haikai poetry of the following century and even to the poetry of Bashō.

Notes

1. I shall refer to renga by the Japanese term, rather than a translation, because it is familiar outside Japan by that name.
2. Translation from Donald Keene, "The Comic Tradition in Renga," in John Whitney Hall and Toyoda Takeshi, *Japan in the Muromachi Age*, p. 243. See also Donald L. Philippi (trans.), *Kojiki*, p. 242.
3. The kata-uta, as its name "half-poem" suggests, could be either the first

half of a waka (5, 7, and 5 syllables) or the first half of a sedōka, an archaic poetic form consisting of 5, 7, 7, plus 5, 7, 7 syllables. In the eighteenth century Takebe Ayatari unsuccessfully attempted to revive the kata-uta. See Keene, *World Within Walls*, p. 378.

4. The first important collection of renga (1356) was called *Tsukuba Shū*, and the next most important collection, *Shinsen Tsukuba Shū* (1495).
5. See Keene, "Comic Tradition," pp. 244–45.
6. See, for example, Okuno Isao, *Rengashi*, pp. 12–18. These anecdotes are related in such works as *Toshiyori Zuinō* by Minamoto no Toshiyori, *Kikigakishū* by Saigyō, and *Shasekishū* by Mujū Ichien.
7. The name looks as if it should be read Kinsuke, but I have adopted the reading given in *Nihon Koten Bungaku Daijiten*, I, p. 420.
8. Kawamura Teruo, Kashiwagi Yoshio, and Kudō Shigenori, *Kin'yō Waka Shū, Shika Waka Shū, p.* 193.
9. *Ibid.*, p. 196.
10. Identified as Fujiwara no Kinnori (1103–1160). See Okuno Isao, *Rengashi*, p. 23.
11. Text in Takehana Isao, *Imakagami*, III, pp. 259–60. I have based my translation on his interpretation of the poetry, given on pp. 261–63. For a quite different explanation, see Okuno Isao, *Rengashi*, p. 23. The puzzling mention of *yaezakura* (the double cherries) in Arihito's verse is explained by Takehana in terms of a poem by Ise no Taifu that praises the cherry blossoms in Nara. Arihito is saying that (because of the poem) he already knows about the cherry blossoms in Nara, but he is wondering about the autumn leaves, the other conventionally admired sight of nature. This seems a preferable interpretation to the more obvious "How are the double cherry blossoms (of the spring) and the red leaves of the autumn?"

    Fujiwara no Kinnori was a high-ranking statesman, a few of whose poems were included in the *Kin'yōshū* and later collections. The known facts about Echigo no menoto are exhaustively presented by Takehana on pp. 263–68. Kawamura (in *Kinyō Waka Shū*, p. xxvii) identifies her simply as the daughter of Fujiwara no Suetsuna, the governor of Echigo, who became the wife of Fujiwara no Sadayori and later the wet nurse (menoto) of Prince Arihito. Five of her poems are included in the *Kin'yōshū*.
12. See Ijichi Tetsuo, *Renga no Sekai*, pp. 110–11. Ijichi quotes from *Kokon Chōmonjū* an anecdote datable about 1165 that gives one link from what was apparently a series of forty-seven or possibly fifty links, each one opening with a successive syllable of the *i-ro-ha* "alphabet."
13. This sequence in ten thousand links probably consisted of ten thousand-link sessions. The participants, the defenders of Chihaya Castle, diverted themselves in this way during the tedious days of a long siege. The number of people who took part is not known, but there were presumably very

many; the object was to cheer as many people as possible. According to the *Taiheiki*, they were guided by professional renga masters brought in from the capital. For the text, see Okami Masao (ed.), *Taiheiki*, I, p. 241; also Yamashita Hiroaki (ed.), *Taiheiki*, I, pp. 302–3. Translation by Helen Craig McCullough in *The Taiheiki*, p. 184.

14. Okuno Isao, *Rengashi*, p. 26. He refers specifically to a book known as *Nosaka-bon Fushimono Shū*, a section of which is reproduced on p. 27.
15. So stated by Shinkei in his *Hitorigoto* (1468). Quoted by Okuno Isao, *Rengashi*, p. 30.
16. The similar Chinese poetic form, the *lien-chü*, composed by several poets, evolved in the direction of producing a poem that might have been the work of a single person. For an example, see Cyril Birch, *Anthology of Chinese Literature*, p. 265.
17. Either as a waka in the usual 5, 7, 5, 7, and 7 syllables, or else a poem that otherwise did not exist in 7, 7, 5, 7, and 5 syllables. The translations of renga in Earl Miner's *Japanese Linked Poetry* are all arranged in the form of five-line verses.
18. This information is quoted from Steven D. Carter, *The Road to Komatsubara*, p. 39.
19. This was at the Hase-dera, a temple in Yamato province, in 1468. See Okuno Isao, *Rengashi*, p. 32.
20. For Yoshimoto's other literary activities, see pp. 974–76.
21. The name is more commonly read as Gusai, and Kyūsai is also found, but (as usual) I have followed *Nihon Koten Bungaku Daijiten*.
22. Text in Kidō Saizō and Imoto Nōichi, *Rengaron Shū, Hairon Shū*, p. 35. Yoshimoto's words were *Renga wa uta no zattai nari*. This has been translated by Carter in *The Road*, p. 9, as "Linked verse is one of the miscellaneous styles of *uta*." Reference was being made to a passage in the Chinese preface to the *Kokinshū*. The translation by Leonard Grzanka in Laurel Rasplica Rodd, *Kokinshū*, p. 380, rendered the word *zattai* as "diverse forms." Yoshimoto, following the *Kokinshū* preface, considered that renga, like the chōka or sedōka, was a variant form of waka.
23. See Kidō Saizō, *Nijō Yoshimoto no Kenkyū*, pp. 31–32. A headnote in *Tsukuba Shū*, the collection of renga compiled by Yoshimoto, says of a link by Kyūsei, "Composed at a one-thousand-link session at the house of the kampaku when he was minister of the interior." (See Ijichi Tetsuo, *Renga Shū*, p. 124.) Yoshimoto served as minister of the interior (*naidaijin*) from 1340 to 1343.
24. Carter (*The Road*, p. 280) rendered *Hekirenshō* as "Some Warped Ideas on Linked Verse." *Renri Hishō* probably meant "A Secret Selection of Renga Principles," but *renri* was also used of branches that twine together, a metaphor for abiding love, and (in this context) perhaps also for the art of renga itself.
25. Kidō and Imoto, *Rengaron*, p. 46.

26. The first three imperially sponsored collections of waka—the *Kokinshū*, *Gosenshū*, and *Shūishū*.
27. Places that have inspired poets of the past.
28. Kidō and Imoto, *Rengaron*, p. 37. In *Tsukuba Mondō* Yoshimoto on the one hand discouraged beginners from imitating the language or events related in such ancient works as the *Man'yōshū* (p. 85); but he urged advanced practitioners of renga to study the *Man'yōshū* as "the roots of the uta" (p. 93).
29. Kidō and Imoto, *Rengaron*, p. 38.
30. *Ibid.*, p. 83. The Chinese philosophers included Mencius, Hsün Tzu, and Yang Chu.
31. Yoshimoto seems to be referring to persons who compose poetry orally, like the old man who composed the "first renga" with Yamato-takeru.
32. Kidō and Imoto, *Rengaron*, p. 116. This quotation comes from *Jūmon Saihishō* (Most Secret Comments on Ten Questions), one of Nijō Yoshimoto's last works, written in 1383.
33. *Man'yōshū* 1635. For a translation of this joint effort, together with comments, see Keene, "Comic Tradition," p. 244.
34. Yoshimoto's directives for renga usage were quoted in *Renga Shinshiki Tsuika narabi ni Shinshiki Kin'an tō* (The New Rules of Linked Verse, with Additions, New Ideas on the New Rules, and Other Comments) compiled in 1501 by Shōhaku (1443–1527). This work has been translated by Carter in *The Road*, pp. 41–72. Shōhaku's quotations from Yoshimoto's writings are mainly from *Renri Hishō*.
35. Text in Kidō and Imoto, *Rengaron*, p. 57. The last phrase (mentioning secondary words) seems to refer to words that, unlike "moon" (which can be mentioned several times), are not of primary importance; this category included such words as "morning moon" or "evening moon," which were less important than the unqualified "moon." See also Carter, *The Road*, pp. 43–44.
36. Kidō and Imoto, *Rengaron*, pp. 81–83.
37. Konishi Jin'ichi, *Sōgi*, pp. 18, 21.
38. *Ibid*, p. 82.
39. The religious associations of renga were by no means confined to Buddhism. *Ise Jingū Shinkan Renga no Kenkyū* by Okuno Jun'ichi is an important study of renga composed by Shintō priests at the Great Shrine of Ise.
40. Kidō and Imoto, *Rengaron*, p. 36. This quotation is from *Renri Hishō*.
41. *Ibid.*, p. 113.
42. *Ibid.*, p. 86. In a Nō play, however, the ha section is usually the longest, often more than the jo and kyū combined. Other works of renga criticism give different proportions for the three tempi. See Carter, *The Road*, p. 93.
43. Miner in *Japanese*, p. 362, following Konishi, distinguished four grades of

impressiveness in renga verse: ji or Ground; jimon or Ground-Design; monji or Design-Ground; and mon, Design. The four different varieties are discussed more fully by Miner on pp. 72–76. Nijō Yoshimoto used various terms in *Tsukuba Mondō* to designate the difference between verses that create a stong impression and those that provide the fundamental ground of the sequence. At this point in his discussion (p. 87) he used *ji*, *ji renga*, and *ji uta* for the plain verses, and *shūitsu* for the striking ones.

44. This matter was discussed by Konishi Jin'ichi in his article "Association and Progression: Principles of Integration in Anthologies and Sequences of Japanese Court Poetry, A.D. 900–1350."
45. For a modern example of this tendency, see my *Dawn to the West*, II, p. 976.
46. Kidō and Imoto, *Rengaron*, p. 87. For a detailed discussion of "design" and "ground" poems, see Carter, *The Road*, pp. 95–100.
47. From Mokujiki Ōgo, *Mugonshō* (Wordless Notes, 1958), quoted by Yamada Yoshio in *Renga Gaisetsu*, p. 49.
48. Kidō and Imoto, *Rengaron*, p. 103.
49. The story is given in section 89 of *Essays in Idleness* of a priest who had won prizes in renga. For a translation, see Keene, *Essays in Idleness*, pp. 75–76.
50. Konishi, *Sōgi*, p. 76.
51. For an excellent study of this activity, see Ogata Tsutomu, *Za no Bungaku*. See also Tanaka Hiroshi, *Chūsei Bungakuron Kenkyū*, pp. 393–415, for a discussion of the formation of za. Hayashiya Tatsusaburō, "Za no Kankyō," is especially valuable for the za of the performing arts.
52. For a discussion of solo renga, see Carter, *The Road*, p. 101.
53. Kidō and Imoto, *Rengaron*, p. 92.
54. *Ibid.*, p. 113. Konishi, in *Sōgi*, pp. 105–7, called attention to the striking similarity of vocabulary in criticism concerning the two arts.
55. Yoshimoto was minister of the Right (Udaijin) between 1343 and 1347.
56. Text in Ijichi, *Renga Shū*, p. 149. This text differs somewhat from that given by Fukui Kyūzō in *Tsukuba Shū*, I, p. 40.
57. Ijichi, *Renga Shū*, p. 151; Fukui, *Tsukuba*, I, p. 116.
58. Ijichi, *Renga Shū*, pp. 110–11. The text given by Fukui in *Tsukuba*, I, p. 56, is somewhat different.
59. See Kidō and Imoto, *Rengaron*, p. 41.
60. *Ibid.*, p. 79. The quotation is from *Tsukuba Mondō*.
61. These examples refer to Minamoto no Yorizane, who prayed for inspiration in waka even at the cost of his life, and Fujiwara no Nagayoshi who, when his poetry was criticized by Fujiwara no Kintō, took ill and died. These anecdotes are related in *Fukuro Zōshi*. See Kidō and Imoto, *Rengaron*, pp. 82–83, notes.
62. *Ibid.*
63. See Carter, *The Road*, pp. 33–34.

64. His personal name is more commonly read as Kanera, but Kaneyoshi is preferred by *Nihon Koten Bungaku Daijiten*. Nagashima Fukutarō in *Ichijō Kanera*, p. 26, noted that there was no documentary evidence for either pronunciation, but he chose Kanera.
65. Shūa was represented by only 22 verses in *Tsukuba Shū*, as compared to 126 by Kyūsei. At the time of the *Bunna Senku* renga sequence, composed at Yoshimoto's house in 1355, the year before the compilation of *Tsukuba Shū*, Shūa contributed 56 verses to 104 by Kyūsei, an indication that he was catching up to his teacher; and fifteen years later 168 verses by Shūa to 178 by Kyūsei were included in *Murasakino Senku*, suggesting that by 1370 he had attained nearly equal standing. (See Ijichi, *Renga no Sekai*, pp. 227–40, for an extended description of Shūa's art.)
66. These are contained in *Jikō Shūa Hyakuban Renga-awase* (a later version which included tsukeku by Shinkei is known as *Kyūsei Shūa Shinkei Renga-awase*.) The examples I have chosen, however, come from Okuno Isao, *Rengashi*.
67. Okuno Isao, *Rengashi*, pp. 80–81.
68. This comment is by Okuno Isao in *Rengashi*, p. 81.
69. The phrase is from selection 194 in the collection, two lines of a poem by Hsü Hun. The full line (of which Shinkei quoted the first part) is: "Cicadas are singing in the yellow leaves; it is autumn in the palace of Han." See Kawaguchi Hisao, *Wakan Rōei Shū*, p. 152.
70. Quoted by Araki Yoshio in *Muromachi Jidai Bungaku Shi*, I, pp. 557–58. Shinkei's original work, *Oi no Kurigoto*, was written about 1475. Chieh and Chou were the last rulers of the Hsia and Shang dynasties respectively. Chiehs' cruelty disgusted his subjects, one of whom raised a successful rebellion against him in c. 1776 B.C. Chou, even more tyrannical than Chieh, was forced to commit suicide c. 1122 B.C. by nobles who could no longer endure his misdeeds. Yao and his son-in-law Shun were legendary rulers of the twenty-fourth century B.C. who served as models of kingly virtue and wisdom over the centuries. Shinkei is saying that Shūa was as guilty as Chieh and Chou of corrupting the virtuous efforts of his predecessors.
71. Bontō (or Bontōan) was his name as a Buddhist priest and renga master. His lay name is generally given as Asayama Kojirō Morotsuna. After studying waka composition with Reizei Tamehide, he turned to renga, studying at first with Nijō Yoshimoto, later with Shūa. Although his military and political duties took up much of his time, he gained recognition as a talented renga poet while still in his thirties. He was friendly with Imagawa Ryōshun, one of Ashikaga Yoshimitsu's chief lieutenants, who likewise studied both waka and renga. Ryōshun's activities as a renga poet are discussed by Kawazoe Shōji in *Imagawa Ryōshun*, pp. 43–46, 188–96.
72. Quotation from Shinkei's "Tokorodokoro Hentō." Text in Ijichi Tetsuo,

Rengaron Shū, I, p. 327. Shinkei was not always so unkind to Bontō. In his earliest and best-known work of renga criticism, *Sasamegoto* (1463), he wrote, "From the Ōei period [1394–1428] Bontō seemed like the guiding light [*tomoshibi*] of this art." (Text in Kidō and Imoto, *Rengaron*, p. 163.)

73. Bontōan, "Chōtanshō" (1390), in Ijichi, *Rengaron*, I, p. 159.
74. This theory is advanced by Okuno Isao, *Rengashi*, p. 92.
75. Carter, *The Road*, p. 35.
76. *Ibid.*, pp. 50–51.
77. For a detailed study of Sōzei, see Ijichi, *Renga no Sekai*, pp. 257–90. See also Thomas W. Hare, "Linked Verse at Imashinmei Shrine," pp. 170–72.
78. The Kitano Shrine, also known as Kitano Temmangū, is sacred to the memory of Sugawara no Michizane, the god of literature. Poetry was regularly offered to Michizane when praying for divine favors. The annual ceremony of offering renga to the shrine was known as *hōraku renga*.
79. For a convenient explanation of *renga sōshō* and related terms, see Okami Masao and Hayashiya Tatsusaburō, *Nihon Bungaku no Rekishi*, VI, pp. 288–90.
80. Ijichi, *Renga Shū*, p. 177.
81. Shinkei, "Tokorodokoro Hentō," p. 314.
82. *Ibid.*, p. 308.
83. *Ibid.*, pp. 308–9. See Ijichi, *Renga no Sekai*, pp. 283–85 for more specific criticism by Shinkei of Sōzei's renga. See also Hare, "Linked Verse," p. 174.
84. New Jewels Collection.
85. Ichijō Kaneyoshi, "Fude no Susabi," in Ijichi, *Rengaron Shū*, I, pp. 283–84.
86. The three respects were (1) he had attained a higher court position; (2) his family was superior; and (3) Michizane knew of Chinese literature only that of the Han and T'ang, and Japanese literature only before the Engi era, whereas he knew much later writings! (See Nagashima Fukutarō, *Ichijō Kanera*, p. 97.)
87. From *Hitorigoto* (Soliloquy, 1468), quoted in Okuno Isao, *Rengashi*, p. 103.
88. For Shōtetsu's contribution to the formation of Shinkei's poetic art, see Miner, *Japanese*, pp. 23–26.
89. From *Oi no Kurigoto* (c. 1475), quoted in Okuno Isao, *Rengashi*, p. 103. Mention of his desire to "soften (*yawarageru*) the hearts of soldiers" of course is an allusion to Tsurayuki's preface to the *Kokinshū*.
90. The whole of this sequence has been translated by Hare in "Linked Verse," pp. 177–208. Text in Kaneko Kinjirō, Teruoka Yasutaka, and Nakamura Toshisada, *Renga Haikai Shū*, p. 124–46.
91. There is a partial translation of this work by Dennis Hirota, "In Practice of the Way: *Sasamegoto*, An Instruction Book in Linked Verse."

92. Text in Kidō and Imoto, *Rengaron*, p. 126.
93. *Ibid.*, p. 150.
94. *Ibid.*, p. 201. The three levels of renga were (1) verses that are so easily intelligible that even the most stupid practitioner can understand them, corresponding to the transformational body of the Buddha (*nirmanakāya*); (2) those intelligible only to persons of intelligence and discrimination, corresponding to the rewarding body (*sambhogakāya*); and (3) those that are so mysterious and obscure as to be intelligible only to those deeply immersed in the discipline of the art, corresponding to the body of principle (*dharmakāya*).
95. See Shimazu Tadao, *Rengashi no Kenkyū*, p. 150.
96. In the original, *shinku*, a term meaning a verse that stems closely from the previous verse. Shinkei thought such verses inferior to *soku*, verses whose connections with the previous verses were indirect and not so easy to appreciate.
97. Kidō and Imoto, *Rengaron*, p. 143.
98. *Ibid.*, p. 142.
99. Shimazu Tadao (ed.), "Hitorigoto," in Hayashiya Tatsusaburō, *Kodai Chūsei Geijutsuron*, p. 417.
100. *Ibid.*, p. 415.
101. From "Hitorigoto." Text edited by Shimazu in Hayashiya, *Kodai*, p. 469. For a commentary on this passage, see Shinoda Hajime, *Shinkei*, p. 95.
102. Translation by Carter in *The Road*, p. 174. Original text in Kidō and Imoto, *Rengaron*, p. 139. Shinkei goes on to say that it should be the function of "this Way" (renga) for participants to discuss together the deeply moving qualities of all things, to mollify the hearts of warriors, no matter how savage, and to set forth the principles of a transient world.
103. Kidō and Imoto, *Rengaron*, pp. 162–63.
104. It is not clear whether or not he ever met Ichijō Kaneyoshi, the guiding spirit in the world of renga at the time. He did not participate in the best-known renga sequences, but his solo sequences (dokugin), perhaps Shinkei's finest compositions, fall into this category. A solo sequence was private, rather than public, and in this sense it stood apart from the conception of renga as *za no bungaku*.
105. Konishi, *Sōgi*, p. 52. I have given the quotation as translated by Miner in *Japanese*, p. 29. The word translated as "stanza" is *tsukeku*.
106. From Kensai, "Shinkei Sōzu Teikun" (1488), quoted by Shimazu in *Rengashi no Kenkyū*, p. 146.
107. The title means literally "One Hundred Verses on Mountain Something." "Mountain Something" is, of course, a fushimono.
108. The interpretation of these verses is derived largely from Shinoda, *Shinkei*, pp. 116–17. Shinoda, a scholar primarily of English literature, expressed the profoundest admiration for these opening lines of Shinkei's sequence.

109. The title means literally "One Hundred Verses on Something Man," "something man" having been the fushimono of the hokku. The sequence is discussed by Shinoda in *Shinkei*, pp. 189–213.
110. Text in Ijichi, *Renga Shū*, p. 259.
111. Sōgi, "Azuma Mondō," in Kidō and Imoto, *Rengaron*, p. 220. Sōgi's praise is likely to seem excessive to a reader of the English translation, but the original is indeed worthy of the highest praise. *Hi no mikage* refers to the sunlight visible that morning, but also to the Sun Goddess, who is worshiped at Ise. Reference is probably also made to *Shin Kokinshū* 1877, a poem by Saigyō that concludes *hi no mikage kana*, evoking the splendor of the Great Shrine. The "blossoms" of Shinkei's verse are, of course, cherry blossoms, though they actually have no scent; the place is so holy as to create the illusion of some wondrous fragrance. The verb *nioeru* can also mean "to be bright," and that is probably intended, too; the blossoms glow in the morning sunlight. The effect is one of brightness and cleanness appropriate to the Great Shrine.
112. According to one theory he was the son of a *gigaku* performer. His surname is often given as Iio.
113. See Okuno Isao, *Rengashi*, p. 143. Okuno believed that it was through Sōzei that Sōgi was first introduced to Kaneyoshi's "cultural sphere." The adoption probably took place in Sōgi's early thirties.
114. This diary has been translated by Eileen Kato under the title "Pilgrimage to Dazaifu." I have described the work in *Travelers of a Hundred Ages*, pp. 223–27.
115. From Keene, *Travelers*, p. 223. Text in Kaneko Kinjirō, *Sōgi Tabi no Ki Shichū*, p. 33.
116. See Imoto Nōichi, *Sōgi*, p. 1.
117. I have followed the text given in Konishi, *Sōgi*, pp. 178–81, though I have not translated all of his explanation. For more details, see Miner, *Japanese*, pp. 184–87.
118. Links 31 to 34.
119. Konishi (in *Sōgi*, p. 234) suggests that the auspicious note was intended to evoke and praise not the reigning sovereign but Gotoba. The link, which lends itself badly to translation, means something like "For all human beings / There is a proper path to tread."
120. There is a complete translation by Steven D. Carter, *Three Poets at Yuyama*. Carter and *Nihon Koten Bungaku Daijiten* give the reading Yuyama, but Yunoyama is preferred by most scholars who have written on the subject.
121. The sequence of 1499, *Sōgi Dokugin Nanibito Hyakuin*, is translated in full with a commentary by Miner in *Japanese*, pp. 234–71. Konishi (*Sōgi*, p. 54) is among the critics who believe that the highest beauty of renga is found in this sequence. Sōgi's less-famous solo sequence of 1492, *Entoku Yonen Sōgi Dokugin Nanimichi Hyakuin*, has been translated with an extensive commentary by Carter in *The Road*, pp. 117–65.

122. The complete text, together with a commentary, is given in *Nose Asaji Chosakushū*, VII, pp. 379–559. Excerpts, with modern-language translations, are given in Fukuda Hideichi, Shimazu Tadao, and Itō Masayoshi, *Chūsei Hyōron Shū*, pp. 135–212.
123. The impersonality of renga is illuminatingly discussed by Konishi in *Sōgi*, p. 104ff.
124. Text in Fukuda et al., *Chūsei*, pp. 139–40. Also *Nose Asaji Chosakushū*, VII, pp. 409–10.
125. The volume *Renga* published by Gallimard in 1971 contains poetry by four poets—Octavio Paz (Mexican), Jacques Ribaud (French), Edoardo Sanguineti (Italian), and Charles Tomlinson (English)—each composing in his own language according to a code of renga invented by the four men.
126. Anyone who wishes to test himself in this manner is urged to read Carter's excellent translation and study of Sōgi's solo sequence of 1492 in *The Road*, pp. 117–79.
127. He is also remembered for his book of rules of renga, *Renga Shinshiki Tsuika Narabi ni Shinshiki Kin'anto*, translated by Steven D. Carter as "The New Rules of Linked Verse, With Additions, Suggestions for a New Day, and Other Comments" (in "Rules, Rules, and more Rules: Shōhaku's *Renga* Rulebook of 1501," p. 587). Anyone who *really* wishes to learn the rules of renga should consult Carter's article. The text translated by Carter was originally by Nijō Yoshimoto, with criticism by Ichijō Kaneyoshi and comments by Shōhaku. See also note 34.
128. See, for example, Miner, *Japanese*, pp. 46–47.
129. See Oda Takuji, *Renga Bungei Ron*, p. 57ff, for an analysis of Sōchō's renga in terms of their conformity not only to the rules of renga but to the poetic diction of the waka.
130. See Oda, *Renga*, p. 60.
131. See my *World Within Walls*, pp. 12–16; also "Comic Tradition," pp. 274–77.
132. For Sōchō's associations with the *kokujin* (local warriors) in particular, see H. Mack Horton, "Saiokuken Sōchō and the Linked-Verse Business," pp. 63–70. This article, based largely on *Sōchō Shuki*, provides a valuable account of how renga masters made a living.

Bibliography

Note: All Japanese books, except as otherwise noted, were published in Tokyo.

Araki Yoshio. *Muromachi Jidai Bungaku Shi*, I. Kyoto: Jimbun Shoin, 1944.

Birch, Cyril. *Anthology of Chinese Literature*. New York: Grove Press, 1965.

Carter, Steven D. *The Road to Komatsubara*. Cambridge, Mass.: Harvard University Press, 1987.

———. "Rules, Rules, and More Rules: Shōhaku's *Renga* Rulebook of 1501," *Harvard Journal of Asiatic Studies* 43:2, 1983.

———. *Three Poets at Yuyama*. Berkeley: Institute of East Asian Studies, 1983.

Fukuda Hideichi, Shimazu Tadao, and Itō Masayoshi. *Chūsei Hyōron Shū*, in Kanshō Nihon Koten Bungaku series. Kadokawa Shoten, 1976.

Fukui Kyūzō. *Minase Sangin Hyōshaku*. Kazama Shobō, 1954.

———. *Tsukuba Shū*, 2 vols., in Nihon Koten Zensho series. Asahi Shimbun Sha, 1951.

Hare, Thomas W. "Linked Verse at Imashinmei Shrine," *Monumenta Nipponica* 34:2, 1979.

Hayashiya Tatsusaburō. *Kodai Chūsei Geijutsuron*, in Nihon Shisō Taikei series. Iwanami Shoten, 1973.

———. "Za no Kankyō," in Hayashiya Tatsusaburō (ed.), *Nihon Geinōshi Ron*. Kyoto: Tankōsha, 1986.

Hirota, Dennis. "In Practice of the Way: *Sasamegoto*, An Instruction Book in Linked Verse," *Chanoyu Quarterly*, vol. 19 (1978).

Horton, H. Mack. "Saiokuken Sōchō and the Linked-Verse Business," *The Transactions of the Asiatic Society of Japan*, Fourth Series, 1, 1986.

Ijichi Tetsuo. *Renga no Sekai*. Yoshikawa Kōbunkan, 1967.

———. *Rengaron Shū*, 2 vols., in Iwanami Bunko series. Iwanami Shoten, 1953–56.

———. *Renga Shū*, in Nihon Koten Bungaku Taikei series. Iwanami Shoten, 1960.

Imoto Nōichi. *Sōgi*, Kyoto: Tankōsha, 1974.

Itō Kei. *Shin Hokuchō no Hito to Bungaku*. Miyai Shoten, 1979.

Kaneko Kinjirō. *Rengaron no Kenkyū*. Ōfūsha, 1984.

———. *Rengashi Kensai Den Kō*. Ōfūsha, 1962.

———. *Sōgi Sakuhin Shū*. Ōfūsha, 1963.

———. *Sōgi Tabi no Ki Shichū*. Ōfūsha, 1970.

Kaneko Kinjirō, Teruoka Yasutaka, and Nakamura Toshisada. *Renga Haikai Shū*, in Nihon Koten Bungaku Zenshū series. Shōgakukan, 1974.

Kato, Eileen. "Pilgrimage to Dazaifu," *Monumenta Nipponica* 34:3, 1979.

Kawaguchi Hisao. *Wakan Rōei Shū*, in Kōdansha Gakujutsu Bunko series. Kōdansha, 1982.

Kawamura Teruo, Kashiwagi Yoshio, and Kudō Shigenori. *Kin'yō Waka Shū, Shika Waka Shū*, in Shin Nihon Koten Bungaku Taikei series. Iwanami Shoten, 1989.

Kawazoe Shōji. *Imagawa Ryōshun*, in Jimbutsu Sōsho series. Yoshikawa Kōbunkan, 1964.

Keene, Donald. *Anthology of Japanese Literature*. New York: Grove Press, 1955.

———. "The Comic Tradition in Renga," in John W. Hall and Toyoda Takeshi, *Japan in the Muromachi Age*. Berkeley: University of California Press, 1977.

——— (trans.). *Essays in Idleness*. New York: Columbia University Press, 1967.

———. "Jōha, a Sixteenth-Century Poet of Linked Verse," in George Elison and Bardwell L. Smith (eds.), *Warlords, Artists, and Commoners*. Honolulu: University of Hawaii Press, 1981.

———. *Travelers of a Hundred Ages*. New York: Henry Holt, 1989.

———. *World Within Walls*. New York: Henry Holt, 1976.

Kidō Saizō. *Chūsei Bungaku Shiron*. Meiji Shoin, 1984.

———. *Nijō Yoshimoto no Kenkyū*. Ōfūsha, 1987.

———. *Rengashi Ronkō*, 2 vols. Meiji Shoin, 1973.

Kidō Saizō and Imoto Nōichi. *Rengaron Shū, Hairon Shū*, in Nihon Koten Bungaku Taikei series. Iwanami Shoten, 1961.

Konishi Jin'ichi. "Association and Progression: Principles of Integration in Anthologies and Sequences of Japanese Court Poetry, A.D. 900–1350," *Harvard Journal of Asiatic Studies* 21 (1958).

———. *Sōgi*. Chikuma Shobō, 1971.

McCullough, Helen Craig (trans.). *The Taiheiki*. New York: Columbia University Press, 1959.

Miner, Earl. *Japanese Linked Poetry*. Princeton, N.J.: Princeton University Press, 1979.

Nagafuji Yasushi. *Chūsei Nihon Bungaku to Jikan Ishiki*. Miraisha, 1984.

Nagashima Fukutarō. *Ichijō Kanera*, in Jimbutsu Sōsho series. Yoshikawa Kōbunkan, 1959.

Nihon Koten Bungaku Daijiten, 6 vols. Iwanami Shoten, 1983–85.

Nose Asaji Chosakushū, VII. Kyoto: Shibunkaku, 1982.

Oda Takuji. *Renga Bungei Ron*. Kyoto: Kōtō Shoin, 1947.

Ogata Tsutomu. *Za no Bungaku*. Kadokawa Shoten, 1973.

Okami Masao (ed.). *Taiheiki*, 2 vols., in Kadokawa Bunko series. Kadokawa Shoten, 1975–82.

Okami Masao and Hayashiya Tatsusaburō (eds.). *Nihon Bungaku no Rekishi*, VI. Kadokawa Shoten, 1967.

Okuno Isao. *Rengashi*. Hyōronsha, 1986.

Okuno Jun'ichi. *Ise Jingū Shinkan Renga no Kenkyū*. Nihon Gakujutsu Shinkōkai, 1975.

Ozaki Yūjirō, Shimazu Tadao, and Satake Akihiro. *Wago to Kango to no Aida*. Chikuma Shobō, 1985.

Philippi, Donald L. (trans.). *Kojiki*. Tokyo: University of Tokyo Press, 1968.

Ramirez-Christensen, Esperanza. "The Essential Parameters of Linked Verse," *Harvard Journal of Asiatic Studies* 41:2, 1981.

Rodd, Laurel Rasplica (trans.). *Kokinshū*. Princeton, N.J.: Princeton University Press, 1984.

Sasaki Nobutsuna. *Nihon Kagaku Shi*. Hakubunkan, 1918.

Shimazu Tadao. *Rengashi no Kenkyū*. Kadokawa Shoten, 1969.

———. *Rengashū*, in Shinchō Nihon Koten Shūsei series. Shinchōsha, 1979.

Shinoda Hajime. *Shinkei*. Chikuma Shobō, 1987.

Takehana Isao. *Imakagami*, 3 vols., in Kōdansha Gakujutsu Bunko series. Kōdansha, 1984.

Tanaka Hiroshi. *Chūsei Bungakuron Kenkyū*. Hanawa Shobō, 1980.

Yamada Yoshio. *Renga Gaisetsu*. Iwanami Shoten, 1937.

Yamashita Hiroaki (ed.). *Taiheiki*, 5 vols., in Shinchō Nihon Koten Shūsei series. Shinchōsha, 1977–88.

25. DIARIES AND OTHER PROSE OF THE MUROMACHI PERIOD

The most memorable diaries of this period were written by priests and soldiers. Courtiers also kept diaries, but most of them, though often of historical interest, were composed in unliterary kambun. Women of the court had dominated in creating and continuing the tradition of diary literature ever since the Heian period, but that tradition came to an end about 1350 with *Account of the Takemuki Palace*, and the subjectivity that had been its chief distinction also disappeared. While male diarists of the Heian and Kamakura periods who wrote in Japanese had usually followed the introspective models established by the women, the Muromachi diarists, though certainly not indifferent to literary expression, rarely chose to reveal their innermost feelings. At best their diaries were permeated by an elegiac tone occasioned by the contrast between the sight of the desolate ruins of temples, put to the torch during the warfare, and the magic of old names and places, familiar from poems celebrating their glory.

Diaries

Account of a Pilgrimage to the Great Shrine at Ise

Ise Daijingū Sankeiki (Account of a Pilgrimage to the Great Shrine at Ise) describes the visit of the priest Saka Jūbutsu in 1342. It is not surprising that Jūbutsu, a Buddhist priest, should have made a pilgrimage to a Shintō shrine; at the time it was normal to believe simultaneously in the two religions, though their tenets were contradictory. As early as 768 a Buddhist temple had been erected nearby the Great Shrine of Ise, the holiest site of Shintō, and elsewhere in the country the same man was often the resident priest of both a Shintō shrine and a Buddhist temple, presiding over ceremonies held at each. The principle of *honji suijaku* ("original substances manifest their traces") fostered the belief that the Shintō gods were manifestations in Japan of the original Buddhist divinities.[1] The Japanese turned to the gods of Shintō for help in their present lives, and to Buddhism for salvation after death.

Most of *Account of a Pilgrimage to the Great Shrine at Ise* is devoted to Jūbutsu's conversations with Watarai Ieyuki, the chief priest of the Outer Shrine. Jūbutsu, far from voicing objections to Ieyuki's exposition of Shintō doctrine, seems to have been unconditionally impressed. One even senses a note of desperation in the readiness with which he accepts the wisdom of Shintō, as explained by Ieyuki, and one wonders if he will not in the end abandon his own religion in favor of Shintō. But Jūbutsu remained profoundly Buddhist in his outlook; what he sought from Shintō was consolation for his griefs in this world. The most affecting parts of the diary are his descriptions of the desolation of the landscapes he saw on his journey to Ise:

> After I passed the purification hall on the Kushida River, it became apparent how terribly the southern part of this province has been devastated ever since the country fell into disorder. Even in places where bamboo groves or stands of shady trees grew thickly, one could see on approaching that there were no houses. At breaks in the *susuki* grass and lemongrass, a newly cut path was visible, with many withered stumps along the way. When I asked a man I chanced to meet about the place, he answered that this was what had happened to neglected rice fields. His words made me feel all the sadder that the world should have changed so much.
>
> I arrived at the residence of the High Priestess. There were what looked like the remains of old earthen walls, and here and there were tall bushes and trees. The torii had fallen over and the pillars lying across the road were so completely rotted that, if a person did not actually know what they were, he would pass them by without a second glance, supposing they were merely fallen trees.[2]

This is the atmosphere characteristic of many Muromachi diaries. Jūbutsu's account is typical also in that it describes a journey. Travel during the medieval period, though difficult because of the unsettled state of the country, was undertaken for both religious and secular motives. The belief that visiting holy places brought spiritual blessings was as pervasive in Japan as in Europe of the same time. Some destinations of pilgrimages, notably Ise and Izumo, were specifically Shintō in character; others, such as Mount Kōya or the great temple Zenkō-ji, were Buddhist. To pray at one of these sites was believed to be more efficacious than at shrines or temples that lacked their special aura, and the hardships endured on the way also enhanced the merit that accrued from the pilgrimage.

Travels to Secular Sites

Shrines and temples were not the only destinations of travelers of this time. Many went to secular sites, inspired chiefly by the desire to see the places that had inspired the poetry of the past. When a diarist arrived, say, at the site of the Fuwa Barrier, whose desolate remains had been evoked by the poets of hundreds of years before, he could participate in their experience and share their emotions. It did not much matter whether or not anything was left of the Fuwa Barrier; to stand in the place where the poets of the past had stood was sufficiently rewarding and inspiring. Even if one arrived at the wrong season, when the flowers associated with a particular place were not in bloom, one could imagine how they must look in these surroundings, as someone arriving at a time when poppies are not in bloom in Flanders fields can imagine them.

The travels of the poet-priest Saigyō in particular inspired later men to follow in his footsteps, seeking what he sought, to use Bashō's phrase. Kawabata Yasunari once explained this phenomenon in these terms: "It is part of the discipline of the different arts of Japan, as well as a guidepost to the spirit, for a man to make his way in the footsteps of his predecessors, journeying a hundred times to the famous places and old sites, but not to waste time traipsing over unknown mountains and rivers."[3] Sōgi, some five hundred years before Kawabata, had said the same thing more succinctly in a diary: "It was not a famous place, so I took no special note of it."[4]

An utamakura on inspection may prove to be highly disappointing to the eye, but seen across the poetry written about the place it never failed to stir poets of later times. The Tama River at Noda, for example, is an insignificant stream, but beside it stands a small forest of stone monuments inscribed with poems about the river composed by men who were attracted by its mention in a poem by Nōin (another poet-priest famous for his travels) included in the *Shin Kokinshū*. To visit such a place was for a poet a means of drawing on the strength of tradition to revitalize his own poetry.

The other secular attractions were headed by Mount Fuji. Everyone knew about this mountain, the tallest and most beautiful in Japan, and it was a common desire to see it at least once in a lifetime. When someone of the exalted status of the shogun decided to visit Mount Fuji, he naturally traveled with a large entourage that included poets who would commemorate the journey in poetry and often in a diary. The same was true of visits to Itsukushima, the island in the Inland Sea where Taira no Kiyomori had built a magnificent shrine that is celebrated more for the beauty of the site than for its holiness. The cherry blossoms at Yoshino attracted still other diarists.

Some destinations were imposed on the diarists by the urgencies of war. The Ōnin War (1467–1477) in particular drove poets from the capital to refuge in distant parts of the country, but again and again in their diaries one finds wistful memories of the capital; the highest praise they could give to a local site was to say that it resembled one in Kyoto. The many diaries of the Kamakura period that describe travels on the road between the capital and Kamakura had made the sights along the way familiar, but diarists of the Muromachi period went much farther afield, even as far as Kyūshū, as is evidenced by Sōgi's *Journey Along the Tsukushi Road*.

The most affecting diaries of the Muromachi period, naturally enough, are those written by unhappy men. Their unhappiness may stem from the misery of living as a refugee in some mountain village far from the capital, as in the case of Nijō Yoshimoto, or from the losses suffered as the result of the warfare, as in the case of his grandson Ichijō Kaneyoshi, or from purely personal causes, as in the case of the renga master Sōgi. None of these diaries was written from day to day in the manner of the diaries in kambun written by members of the court; they were composed after the experiences had been slowly filtered through the diarist's literary sensibility, leaving only the matters of lasting interest. No doubt if the entries were written at the close of each day there would be much more about the routine of daily life and much less about the author's reflections on the sad times in which he lived.

Reciting Poetry to Myself at Ojima

Ojima no Kuchizusami (Reciting Poetry to Myself at Ojima) is the account by Nijō Yoshimoto of a journey from the capital to Ojima in the province of Mino in 1353. The journey was definitely not inspired by any desire to visit famous utamakura; Yoshimoto was summoned to Ojima where the Emperor Gokōgon and members of his court had temporarily established themselves while waiting for the army of Ashikaga Takauji to rescue them. The Japanese poets are deservedly famous for their appreciation of nature, but it has generally been nature as seen in a garden or in some suitably poetic spot not too far from the capital, but Yoshimoto discovered what nature, uncultivated by human hands, was really like:

> I was unfamiliar with scenery of this kind. There was not a break in the clouds that hung heavily over the mountains to left and right. Truly, nothing is so heartrending as such a place as this. No words can convey the look of these remote mountains, especially in autumn, and the indescribable pathos of the landscape squashed in between the hills.[5]

The language recalls another lonely place of exile, Genji's at Suma, but Yoshimoto's description was no mere pastiche. It rained without letup and the "temporary capital" was shut in by clouds and fog. Of course, it rained in the capital, too, and clouds and fog were frequently mentioned in poetry, but there was nothing poetic about rain or clouds in the mountains.

It was not only the uncongenial weather that depressed Yoshimoto. The enforced living in cramped quarters and the danger of enemy attack had totally changed the appearance of the courtiers. Everyone was now in "barbarian clothes" (Yoshimoto's term for military costume), and the nobles looked more like soldiers than poets as they awaited the arrival of Ashikaga Takauji. Under normal circumstances the men of the court would not have deigned to associate with such a man, but when everyone was dressed for combat, even a "barbarian" could be their savior. Takauji has usually been portrayed in works of popular history as a most unattractive character, a villain who was responsible for the deaths of the loyalist heroes Kusunoki Masashige and Nitta Yoshisada, but for Yoshimoto and the others in the mountains he provided their only chance of returning to the capital.[6]

After many false rumors about his arrival, Takauji finally appeared with his men, to the immense joy of Gokōgon and his court. Yoshimoto, despite himself, dwelt lovingly on details of Takauji's armor. Takauji presented Gokōgon with some horses, a gift that would not have made much sense in the capital, where nobles traveled in carts pulled by oxen;

yet now many nobles, if not the emperor himself, knew how to ride a horse, and the gift was welcomed. But when Takauji's son captured the capital and the members of the Northern Court were able to return, they chose to dress themselves in their court finery, rather than armor, and they were a great attraction for sightseers along the way.

Yoshimoto's diary concludes on a joyful note. He relates that the emperor himself had inscribed the title for his diary, which he had kept because he feared that, with the return to the capital and the restoration of normal court life, people might forget the hardships suffered in the mountains. But his optimism was misplaced. In the following year Takauji's forces were driven from the capital by Southern Court armies, and once again Gokōgon and the others had to find a place of refuge. A year later they recovered the capital, only to find it, after all the fighting, in ruins. At this distance from the events it hardly matters which side held the capital in a given year, but the repeated battles for possession of the city destroyed much of the heritage from the past, and these battles by no means ended with the reunification of the country in 1392.

Account of Fujikawa

The most distinguished of the diarists who described the Ōnin War was Yoshimoto's grandson Ichijō Kaneyoshi.[7] *Fujikawa no Ki* (Account of Fujikawa), written in 1473, is only one of his depictions of the most senseless war in Japanese history. The diary relates Kaneyoshi's journey to the province of Mino to express his gratitude to the provincial constable (*shugo*) for having supplied him with food during his years of privation. He repeatedly refers to the changes that have been brought about by the terrible war. When, for example, he reached the Fuwa Barrier, the dilapidated state of which had been mourned by generations of diarists, he followed tradition to the extent of meditating on the evanescence of things; but he had actually seen with his own eyes far worse destruction than any imagined by earlier poets who had visited this famous utamakura.

The impression a modern reader is likely to receive from Kaneyoshi's diary (as from his grandfather's) is of a civilized man bewildered by the changes in society and the negation of the cultural values that had been the foundation of his life. Modern critics often discuss with admiration the vitality of those below in shaking off the domination of the upper classes, and it is gratifying that from this time on commoners figure importantly in the creation of literature;[8] but it is hard not to sympathize with Kaneyoshi when he saw his library going up in flames and ignorant soldiers (the most conspicuous practitioners of *gekokujō*) destroying the accumulated learning of the past.

Kaneyoshi's diary covers a period of about three weeks, from his departure to his return to his place of refuge in Nara. The form closely follows that of his grandfather's *Reciting Poetry to Myself*. There are no fewer than eighty-eight waka on the various utamakura along the way and similar subjects. For example, on reaching the Ishiyama Temple, sacred to Kannon of infinite mercy, he composed the poem:

sawagitatsu	Even in times disturbed
yo ni mo ugokanu	As ours, Stone Mountain remains
Ishiyama wa	Unmoving as stone—
ge ni aigataki	How truly wonderful to find
chikai narikeri	The promise of salvation.

Here, Stone Mountain is not only the translation of the name *Ishiyama* but stands for Kannon's promise, firm as stone, to save mankind.

The journey brought remembrances not only of the poets who had traveled the same route but also of battles fought in the region both in the distant past and, more recently, during the fighting between the Northern and Southern courts. The journey did not lack amenities. Kaneyoshi mentions waka and renga gatherings and a performance of *sarugaku* by local actors that favorably impressed him.[9] The poems of the journey included not only waka but kanshi, composed in the company of Buddhist priests. He even had time to watch cormorant fishing. The journey, despite frequent mentions of hardships, was clearly not without consolations. But his stay in Mino was interrupted by news of political significance:

> Fourteenth [of the fifth month, 1473]. I returned to Kagamishima. I had hoped to see all the famous places and old sites in the province, taking advantage of this unexpected journey away from the capital, but I have received word that Hosokawa Katsumoto[10] passed away on the eleventh of this month. If this has indeed happened to the chief of the Eastern Army, there are likely once again to be uprisings on the frontier at this juncture. I doubt therefore I can carry out my travels as planned, so although "our next meeting is far off," "the road ahead will surely be distant."[11] I hastened to report the news to the abbot and whipped my horse on the return journey.[12]

The appeal of Kaneyoshi's diary is mainly in the poetry. The experiences of the journey were so unlike those known to the court poets of the past, who rarely stirred from the capital, that they could not be described in the customary poetic diction. The following poem, composed at a place called Musa, a homonym of a word for soldier,[13] is not an example of Kaneyoshi's poetry at its best, but, coming from a member of an ancient family, it is surprising:

mononofu no	Before the gauntlet
yugake wa tate zo	Of the warrior even
nabiku naru	Shields bend in defeat:
mube koso Musa no	How fitting the name Musa
na wa nokorikere[14]	Still preserves the soldiers' fame!

Surely Kaneyoshi would never have written such a poem if not for the warfare and if not, more specifically, for the experiences of his journey.

Sōgi's Diaries

Sōgi's achievements as a renga master made him the outstanding literary figure of the late fifteenth century. His diaries reflect the extent of his celebrity.

In an age when renga masters were constantly on the move from one part of the country to another, Sōgi stands out as probably the most given to travel.[16] Only two of his many journeys were recorded in diaries. The first, *Shirakawa Kikō* (Journey to Shirakawa), is devoted to the relatively short journey he made toward the end of 1488 to Shirakawa by way of Tsukuba and Nikkō. In the following year he went to Ise and then on to Nara where he visited Kaneyoshi.

It may be wondered why Sōgi felt impelled to travel so much. One reason is evident: the year of his journey to Shirakawa, 1482, was the second year of the Ōnin War, the year when Kaneyoshi fled to Nara, and a good time for anyone to be out of the capital. However, Sōgi's travels had begun long before this disaster. Under circumstances that remain obscure, he became acquainted with various of the daimyos in the east of the country, and spent seven years there, beginning in 1466, making occasional journeys to Echigo and Shinano where he had other patrons. It was safer to be in the provinces than in the capital and Sōgi could live more graciously in the castle of some daimyo than in his thatch-covered retreat in Kyoto.

It was not only physical comfort that Sōgi craved. Like every other traveler of the age, he wanted to see the utamakura, and the main purpose of his journey to Shirakawa was to climb Mount Tsukuba on the way. As a renga poet he honored as the first manifestation of his art the poem in the *Kojiki* in which Prince Yamato-takeru asked about Tsukuba.

When Sōgi reached the Shirakawa Barrier, his ultimate destination on this journey, he was deeply moved by the solemn atmosphere that pervaded the place, and described the dilapidated shrine at the barrier in these terms:

> Moss served for its eaves, and maples made its fence, and in place of sacred streamers, ivy hung before the altar. At the thought that now only cold winds came to make offerings here, I could not check the tears of emotion. I imagined how deeply Kanemori and Nōin must have been moved and, although I hesitated to compose a poem that would be so much rubble when compared with their masterpieces, my thoughts were too many to keep to myself.[17]

Sōgi composed two waka on this occasion. The second was:

yuku sue no	I do not expect
na woba tanomazu	The future to bring me fame,
kokoro wo ya	But I hope to keep
yoyo ni todomen	Future poets from forgetting
Shirakawa no seki	Shirakawa Barrier.

Sōgi is saying here that although his own poem on the Shirakawa Barrier cannot compare with those composed by the great poets of the past, he hopes that it will help to keep poets of future ages from forgetting the utamakura that had inspired so many poems. It is probably no exaggeration to say that it was in order to compose this poem that Sōgi made a dangerous journey in time of war.

Journey Along the Tsukushi Road is no less affecting as the poetic account of a journey even though there were virtually no utamakura in northern Kyūshū for Sōgi to admire. In place of utamakura, Sōgi sometimes referred to evocations of the scenery in the *Man'yōshū*, sometimes to historical personages (like Sugawara no Michizane) who lived for a time in Kyūshū, but most often by summoning up remembrances of similar places he himself had visited or knew through literature, especially *The Tale of Genji*. His greatest pleasure in travel came from the recollections of the old writings that the places he passed stirred in him.[18] A passage such as the following suggests how he contrived to write a literary diary without the convenient props of utamakura:

> As we passed on by Utsura Hama, I could see the Cape of Kane and Ōshima; I remembered those olden days and the reciting of "I shall not forget." I recalled to mind, too, the many interesting associations of the island of Shiga, and I thought sadly of the story of Shōni's daughters and the poem with "Whom do they long for?" said to have been composed by them at Ōshima.[19]

"I shall not forget" (*ware wa wasureji*) comes from an anonymous poem in the *Man'yōshū* that mentions the Cape of Kane (*kane no misaki*). "Whom do they long for?" (*tare wo kou to ka*) was derived from a poem in the "Tamakazura" chapter of *The Tale of Genji*,

> To whom might it be that the thoughts of these sailors turn,
> Sadly singing off the Ōshima strand?[20]

"Shōni's daughters" refers to two girls, one the daughter of Shōni, an official, and the other Tamakazura, who had been left in the care of Shōni's wife, her nurse.

Such allusive writing is tiresome to unravel and unlikely to add much to the pleasure of a modern reader, but for Sōgi it was essential to give overtones and importance to every place mentioned; an associationless mountain was no more than one of innumerable such mountains in Japan and hardly worth mentioning. He wrote elsewhere in the diary, "The many hills, islands, and places within view seemed close enough to touch and there was not one that was not famous."[21]

There are few personal thoughts expressed in the diary. For the most part Sōgi contented himself with describing what he observed. Undoubtedly it saddened him to see the desolation that had been left in the wake of warfare that had extended to Kyūshū, but one does not often receive the impression that a comment was either like or unlike Sōgi. The most affecting part of the work, however, gives us a sudden unforgettable glimpse of a particular man:

> The winds were rough and the waves billowed high. Disconsolately I watched the little fishes gaily leaping out of the water. I realized

that even they must live in great fear of the bigger fishes that inhabit the ocean depths, and so I did not envy them. Again, when I saw a shell being carried to and fro by the waves, I observed that when it approached the shore and was far from the great ocean it did not grieve, nor did it rejoice when it was drawn back into the sea again. All living species are of a sadness beyond compare. The world we live in, whether in pleasure or in pain, is ultimately a place of lamentation. Since I am one who understands this philosophy very well, I reflected that the only thing to be envied was this empty shell.[22]

Sōgi, the most famous poet of the age, feted wherever he went by the great nobles and generals, says the only thing he envies is an empty shell, indifferent to pleasure or pain. For a moment we see the man himself. It is so startling in the light of the rest of the diary, or indeed of all of Sōgi's writings, including his renga, that we may wonder if he was not in fact alluding to some text that has yet to be uncovered.[23]

What made Sōgi unhappy? Perhaps it was, as he says, his awareness of the human condition: all of us live in sadness. If one searches for something more concrete that might have depressed him, it too may be found in *Journey Along the Tsukushi Road:* "It is useless to practice the Way of Japanese poetry unless one is born into one of the great families of poets or else one is of noble birth."[24] Sōgi was acclaimed as a renga poet, but he may have been resentful that his humble birth kept him from gaining recognition as a master of the waka, the only poetic art blessed by the Japanese gods. A lesser man might have been satisfied with having been inducted into the mysteries of the *Kokinshū*, but Sōgi seems to have craved the supreme accolade of recognition as one of the company of Tsurayuki, Shunzei, Teika, and the rest, and this was denied him by his birth.

Sōchō's Notebook

Among Sōgi's many disciples, the closest was probably Sōchō.[25] Their relations, begun in 1466, when Sōchō was only seventeen, lasted until Sōgi's death in 1502. Sōchō accompanied Sōgi on his final journey and was at his side when Sōgi died. His account, *Sōgi Shūen no Ki*, opens as the two men start on another journey together. Sōgi had no expectation of returning to the capital alive, but was resolved to die on his travels, like Saigyō in Japan or Tu Fu in China before him. Sōchō seems to have been reluctant to make one more journey; perhaps by this time he had become weary of being the companion of anyone, even a revered teacher, who was so obsessed with travel.

Sōgi had always enjoyed robust good health, and this was what made his incessant journeys possible. Ironically, his final, serious illness started while he was taking a cure at the hot springs in Ikaho. He was unaccustomed to being ill and this seems to have made him a bad patient, but the stops on the journey became more frequent and longer. His physical condition, however, did not prevent Sōgi from composing renga wherever he and Sōchō went, but a gloomy tone pervades many of his verses.

In the seventh month of 1502 Sōgi suffered a rheumatic seizure, and the alarmed Sōchō arranged for a palanquin to bear him to the next inn. They continued their journey to Yumoto, at the foot of the Hakone mountains. That night Sōgi seemed to be suffering in his sleep, and Sōchō awakened him. Sōgi said he had been dreaming of Teika. He murmured a verse from a sequence composed not long before:

nagamuru tsuki ni	Along with the moon I gaze on,
tachi zo ukaruru	I rise and float in the sky.

Sōgi then said, "I have trouble adding a link. All of you, try to supply one." Sōchō continued, "Even as he spoke in these jesting tones, his breathing ceased, like a lamp that goes out."[26]

Sōchō's most characteristic work is his diary *Sōchō Shuki* (Sōchō's Notebook), written between 1522 and 1527.[27] It is obvious from its pages how temperamentally dissimilar he and Sōgi were. Sōgi's humor, rarely displayed in surviving texts, is not an important element in our appraisal of the man, but of all the materials included in Sōchō's grab bag of a diary, those of greatest literary interest are the humorous poems composed by himself and his friends.[28] These verses have no merit if judged by the lofty ideals of renga as expounded by Shinkei and Sōgi; they are entirely comic in conception, and rely for effect not on richness of overtones but on the crude humor of the double entendre.[29]

Sōchō's Notebook is by no means devoted solely to amusing poetry. There are many descriptions of warfare and fortifications, some so detailed as to suggest that Sōchō may have taken advantage of the freedom with which Buddhist priests could travel even in time of war to act as a spy for the daimyo of his native province, Suruga. The style throughout is resolutely prosaic in the manner of a real diary, rather than in the literary manner more typical of the diaries of earlier poets. Sōchō does not seem to have had any particular readers in mind, and that may be why he seldom indicates why a man of his age felt impelled to travel so often in a country that was torn by warfare. Perhaps the simplest explanation is that he never lost his interest in people and landscapes. He evinced to the end a joy in living, despite his constant insistence that he longed for death. Writing early in the sixteenth century, he anticipated the writers of a hundred years later in his absorption with the floating world.

Religious and Secular Tales

The principal collection of religious tales of the Muromachi period was the *Shintōshū* (Collection of the Way of the Gods), compiled in the late fourteenth century.[30] One might expect from the title that these tales would all deal with the Shintō gods, but in fact the prevailing religious belief is the medieval fusion of Shintō and Buddhism. The earliest mention of the Shintō gods being given titles as *bosatsu* (bodhisattvas) goes back to 782 when the deity Hachiman acquired a "bosatsu name." In 937 the deity of the Kasuga Shrine, speaking through an oracle, declared, "I am already a bosatsu, but the Court has not yet given me any bosatsu name." When asked what bosatsu name he should be given, he replied, "Jihi Mangyō Bosatsu," or "Bodhisattva Complete in Mercy's Works."[31] In this way he proclaimed himself to be a manifestation in Japan of the "original substance" of a Buddhist divinity.

During the Kamakura period the identifications between Japanese deities and their prototypes in India were carried out mainly by Shingon priests. Sometimes the identifications were almost automatic: for example, Dainichi (Vairochana Buddha), whose name is written with characters meaning "great sun," was naturally associated with the sun goddess Amaterasu.[32] The identification of Amida Buddha as the "original substance" of the Shintō god of war Hachiman was not quite so obvious, and the reasons for associating other Shintō deities with the various bodhisattvas were often equally unconvincing.[33] By the end of the Kamakura period twelve Buddhist divinities[34] had been identified as the "original substances" of the Shintō gods enshrined at such centers of Shintō belief as Kumano, Usa, and Hiyoshi, and they became the objects of popular worship.[35]

The first important collection of tales based on the combined faith of Shintō and Buddhism was *Kasuga Gongen Genki* (The Miracles of the Kasuga Deity). It was compiled at the end of the Kamakura period by Kakuen (1277–1340), a monk at the Kōfuku-ji, the great temple that from its foundation at the beginning of the eighth century was intimately associated with the Kasuga Shrine. Although the work is better known for the magnificent illustrations by Takashina Takakane (fl. 1309–1330) than for the text, it is not without literary interest, quite apart from its importance as a document of syncretistic belief. Each of the episodes relates some oracle or prodigy related to the Kasuga deity.[36] Many of these episodes are likely to strike a non-Japanese reader as lacking in point, but the oracles of the Kasuga deity justify their being narrated, regardless of whether or not they have the piquance of, say, *Tales of Times Now Past.* The oracular message is sometimes conveyed in a dream, sometimes by a medium, sometimes by an old man or child who bears the divine words.[37] Almost any episode will serve as well as another to suggest the manner of *The Miracles of the Kasuga Deity*, but one concerning Egyō, a monk at the Ichijō-in abbacy of the Kōfuku-ji monastery, is typical:

> Hōin Egyō of Shūnan'in [a temple founded by Egyō] had plumbed the depths of the Two Wisdoms,[38] and stood as a model for the whole Temple. So fine a scholar was he that he had no need to blush before the sages of the past.
>
> Once Egyō lay as though dead from evening until the hour of the Serpent the following morning. After he revived he was asked what had happened. "I was summoned to the palace of King Enma,"[39] he replied, "and so I made my way there. King Enma ordered me to read the Lotus Sutra, so I did."
>
> In his youth, Egyō was disappointed in a little quarrel over an estate, and secretly thought of leaving the Temple. Then the Daimyōjin told him in a dream, "I had planned to have you serve Me as Deputy Superintendent. Why do I now hear that because of some trifling difficulty you wish to leave the Temple?" Egyō completely gave up the idea after that, and did in the end come to serve as Deputy Superintendent.[40]

The episode as it stands is not satisfactory in literary terms. The last paragraph explains why Egyō was asked to read the Lotus Sutra, but what the reader expects is some overt reaction to his visit to the world of the dead. The point of the episode is that it was thanks to the oracle from the Kasuga deity that Egyō, abandoning his plan to leave the temple, became so learned that he was asked by King Enma himself to read the sutra. Some of the episodes, especially those devoted to Myōe, are longer and have greater literary value, but the collection as a whole is of interest chiefly to scholars of Japanese religion.

The Miracles of the Kasuga Deity is written throughout in Japanese, as befitting a collection that describes a Shintō deity, but the *Shintōshū* is in kambun. The use of kambun suggests (as was true long ago of *Account of Miracles in Japan*) that the texts were intended to be used in proselytizing. The collection consists of fifty tales of short and medium length, each beginning with a brief account of a certain divinity, followed by a story that may at first seem unrelated to the opening, and ending with a connection being established between the story and the divinity. The story of the Kumano deity opens in this fashion:

> I shall tell you about the Kumano deity (*gongen*). Both En no Gyōja and Baramon Sōjō[41] believed in the honji of the Kumano deity. According to the history of the Kumano shrine, the god descended from the sky in the Year of the Tiger onto Ōmine at Hikone in the westerly province of Buzen in Japan, following the traces of the prince who had come from the holy mountain in China. His appearance was that of an octagonal pillar of crystal, and he stood three feet and six inches in height. Later, he wandered here and there in quest of a place to settle, and after long months and years spent in this manner he at last manifested himself as the Kumano deity.[42]

Following other details of the wonders of the deity, the author enters into the story of King Zenzai, the ruler of an Indian kingdom, whose palace was so extensive that it took seven days and nights to walk around its periphery, and forty-two days to traverse all the corridors. Each of his thousand consorts lived in a palace of her own. The least favored in looks was the Lady of the Palace of Five Marks of Decline,[43] and the king so rarely visited her that her palace had fallen into ruin. But the lady prayed fervently to a statue of the Thousand-Armed Kannon and a miracle was granted: she was transformed into a woman of radiant beauty.

The king, entranced by this metamorphosis, spent all of his time with the lady, much to the annoyance of his 999 other consorts. The king had never had a son, and he prayed that this lady would bear him one. His prayers were heard, and she was soon great with child. But (the narrator warns us with a quotation from the Flower Wreath Sutra) women are messengers from hell who have often destroyed the seed of the Buddha; though in appearance they resemble bodhisattvas, in their hearts they are like *Yasha* (devils).[44]

The homily prepares us for the evil deeds of the spurned 999 consorts. They suborn with rich gifts a physiognomist, directing him to predict that the child born to the Lady of the Palace of Five Marks of Decline will be a monster with nine legs and eight faces, and that his body will emit flames that will consume the capital and all the rest of the realm.

The king is naturally perturbed, but he declares that he wants to see his child anyway. The 999 ladies, disappointed in the king's tolerance, adopt a second stratagem. They assemble 999 unusually tall old women and dress them up so that they seem to have nine legs and eight faces, and have them beat drums. This goes on for five nights. The palace ladies say that the Lady of the Palace of Five Marks of Decline is the cause of this unseemly noise and insist she must be moved from the capital. The king weakly agrees.

Some brutal soldiers are deputized to escort the lady, supposedly to a safe place; but actually, they are under orders from the unaccommodating 999 to take her to Devil's Ravine and kill her there. The lady, whose feet had never before trodden the earth, is forced to walk barefoot. When informed she must die, she prays to Kannon for a miraculous delivery of her child, though she is only five months into pregnancy. Kannon hears her prayer, and the lady gives birth to a marvelously beautiful boy. Even as she is suckling the baby, a hard-hearted soldier beheads her. The headless corpse continues to nurture the baby, her love proving stronger than death.

Twelve tigers, attracted by the smell of fresh blood and eager for a meal, approach the beheaded mother, but at the sight of the baby suckling at her breast, they are struck with pity, and stand guard over them. In the meantime, Kiken, a holy man who lives a long distance away, receives a mysterious oracle to the effect that King Zenzai's son is being reared by twelve tigers. He hurries to the spot indicated by the oracle and finds the child playing with the tigers. The holy man addresses the tigers, first praising them for their acuity (though they are brute beasts) in having detected the ten marks of majesty in the child. He asks their permission to take the child to the king, and the tigers graciously agree.

The holy man and the little prince travel through the air to the palace of the king. He is surprised to see them drop from the sky, and even more surprised when the saint tells him of the conspiracy of the infamous 999 and the death of the Lady of the Palace of Five Marks of Decline. The king declares that he had known all along of the wickedness of women, but he never supposed they would be guilty of anything quite so dreadful. He sends for his carriage, fashioned of solid gold, and boards it together with the prince and the holy man. Not knowing where to go, he resorts to divination. He throws five swords into the air, resolved to go wherever they land. All five fall in Japan, the first in the land of Kii, near the site of the Kumano Shrines, the rest at strategically located places in Kyūshū, Mutsu (at the northern end of Honshū), the island of Awaji, and Mount Daisen near the Japan Sea coast.

At this point the narrative returns to the Kumano deity. An account is given of the principal shrines and of the Buddhist ancestry of each. King Zenzai himself rules over the entire complex of shrines, but the Lady of the Palace of Five Marks of Decline, their son, and the holy man Kiken each becomes the guardian divinity of one of the shrines. The wicked 999 ladies follow the king as far as Kumano, but he gives them short shrift, and presently they turn into red bugs. The story continues with a description of the connections between the Kumano deity and the mandalas, and concludes with the statement that the Kumano deity is first among the gods who protect the *naishidokoro*, the sanctuary in the palace where the divine mirror, one of the three imperial regalia, is enshrined.

Other stories in the *Shintōshū* follow this pattern, presenting at the beginning and end such theological matters as the relations between the various gods and buddhas, but devoting most of the space to a tale of general interest. This particular tale was closely derived from a sutra,[45] though the ending—the king and his entourage going to Kumano—was obviously a Japanese addition.

Listening to or reading such a tale could bring great benefits. In *Kumano no Honji,* an *otogi-zōshi* (tale of the Muromachi period) that relates the same story in a more concentrated and artistic manner, we are told, "If one hears this story once, it is the same as going to Kumano once, and people who read this story twice receive the same benefits as if they had visited the deity twice. If those who are prevented by circumstances from making the long journey read this story and listen to the explanation of the sacred text (*sekkyō*), it will be the same as if they had made the pilgrimage themselves. Their action will turn bad karma into good, and the believer, escaping the pains of the Three Ways and the Eight Obstacles, will without doubt find his way to the Pure Land."[46]

It is easy to imagine the tales in the *Shintōshū* being delivered to an audience of pious but badly educated people. The performer might be either a man or a woman, though in the case of stories involving the Kumano deity it was more likely to have been a woman, one of the

Kumano *bikuni* (nuns) who figured prominently in the dissemination of such tales.[47] Because of the benefits that were believed to accrue from listening to such recitations, some of the faithful would probably have listened to even the most boring accounts, but the performers attempted to reach as wide a public as possible. Often their recitations were enhanced by pictures, whether horizontal scrolls, hanging scrolls, or illustrated books; *e-toki,* or "explanation of pictures," was a favored means of communicating Shintō or Buddhist beliefs during the medieval period, and still survives vestigially. Stories about distant India or about events of remote antiquity could be given immediacy by the vivid descriptions of the storytellers and the visual presence of the divinities in the paintings displayed.

The *Shintōshū* seems to have been compiled between 1352 and 1360, as we can gather from various hints in the text. Probably, however, it represents a final recension of stories that had been related orally in the form of sermons for many years. At the head of each of the ten books the words "Written by Agui" appear, but there is virtually nothing in the text that suggests a connection with the Agui, a kind of dormitory for Tendai priests in the city of Kyoto. Priests of the Agui were celebrated for the dramatic nature of their preaching (*shōdō*), and the texts they used had literary quality.[48] Kishi Shōzō, an authority on literature of this period, offered the suggestion that the *Shintōshū* may have been compiled from a much larger collection of sermon materials that had been amassed over the years by the chief priests of the Agui. These materials consisted of excerpts from the sutras, statements of Shintō belief, histories of shrines and temples, and explanations of the Buddhist divinities and their Shintō avatars. From among them (some in kambun and others in Japanese) a priest of the Agui selected those with the best literary style.[49] Close resemblances in style and content with *The Tale of the Soga Brothers* suggest that the author of the monogatari and of some of the tales may have been the same man, possibly a priest from Hakone, the geographical region common to both.

The literary value of these and similar works of religious inspiration is not high, though they are certainly interesting for other reasons. But every so often, in the midst of an improbable or even fantastic account of a miraculous event, one's attention will be caught by a detail or a phrase that startles by its "human" reality. It is not hard at such moments to imagine the effects the recitations and the display of pictures might have had on audiences all over Japan. Barbara Ruch wrote of the dissemination of these tales by itinerant performers as "the making of a national literature," a literature known to everyone, learned or illiterate, who had come within range of the narrators' voices or seen the crudely illustrated pamphlets that communicated in writing and pictures the tales of the two great religions miraculously fused into one.

Courtly Fiction

The chief interest of the archaistic tales composed during the Muromachi period is that the authors, indifferent to their own times, kept on writing about the relatively short period in the past when the Heian aristocracy flowered. The plots are by no means uniform, but the unvarying setting and even the Heian titles (minister of the Left, middle counselor, lesser general, and the like) by which the characters are known produce a general impression of sameness. The repeated use of familiar patterns in the characters and situations, the paucity of overt action, and above all the bittersweet mood that pervades works of this genre no doubt reflected the fondness of readers for variations on well-known themes. The lovers portrayed in one of these tales of court life are rarely together at the end of the work, and even if consolation is offered by a devoted child or second spouse, the prevailing impression is of mono no aware. The preference for a sad ending contrasts with the tastes of readers elsewhere. Northrop Frye wrote, "One of the things that comedy and romance as a whole are about, clearly, is the unending, irrational, absurd persistence of the human impulse to struggle, survive, and where possible escape. It is perhaps worth noting how intense is the desire of most readers of romance for the happy ending."[50] It is hard to think of anyone who struggles to survive in a medieval Japanese romance, though an escape (not, however, of the kind found in European romances) was provided by Buddhist monasteries where the world and its preoccupations could be forgotten.

Many Muromachi period romances were unknown until their discovery in the twentieth century, and most of them have yet to be given the benefit of an annotated edition. If the great classics of Heian literature had perished in the warfare that ravaged the great collections of manuscripts and only these works survived, they would undoubtedly be treated with much greater respect, for some have considerable merit; but even their names are now unknown to all but a handful of specialists.

Perhaps the best known of the Muromachi[51] romances is *Shinobine Monogatari* (The Tale of Shinobine). The original version, of which a few poems are preserved in the collection *Fūyōshū*,[52] was probably written toward the end of the Heian period. These poems do not appear in the extant version, and there are various other indications that the reworking of the text did not consist (as was often true of Muromachi adaptations of Heian monogatari) merely of a condensation of the plot.[53] The *Shinobine* of the title is at once a poetic word for "silent weeping" and the name of the heroine. In other monogatari a woman is known by such a nickname only after it has appeared in one of her poems or the author has used the word in describing the character, but there is no antecedent for the nickname in the present *Tale of Shinobine*. Probably the original text had one,[54] and probably, too (judging from the prominence of her name in the title), the heroine was of greater importance to the whole story than in the existing version, where the hero, the handsome and gifted Kintsune, is the central figure. The changes may have been made to shorten a text that seemed excessively long-winded to a later generation of readers, but it may also have been inspired by a specifically medieval concern for Buddhist salvation.

The Tale of Shinobine opens in a manner familiar from *The Tale of Genji* and other Heian romances. Kintsune, the hero, is the son of the minister of the Center, who is among the most distinguished men of the realm, and his younger sister is the consort of the crown prince. One autumn day, having gone to see the colored leaves at Sagano, he happens to hear the sounds of a koto being played most exquisitely. He sends his companion to discover who might be playing, concealing himself behind a fence. Eventually he plucks up the courage to peep inside. Kintsune sees several women looking at some picture books, a familiar scene in early fiction. One of the women is revealed to be the koto player, and Kintsune is attracted by her extraordinary beauty. His presence is detected by the rare perfume he uses (another echo of *The Tale of Genji*), and he hastily beats a retreat, but he cannot endure the thought of not meeting her. He asks his man to request lodgings for the night from a nun, the companion of the lady, under the pretense that they have lost their way. Once inside the house, Kintsune insists on being presented. The nun, recognizing him as the peerless Shii no Shōshō (lesser captain of the Fourth Rank), is persuaded, and Kintsune eventually spends the night with the lady, who is henceforth referred to as Shinobine, though up to this point she has not indulged in secret weeping.

Kintsune falls passionately in love. He arranges for Shinobine and the nun to move to a house near his own, much to the disappointment of his father, who has other, more ambitious plans for his son. In the next year Shinobine gives birth to a boy, and the happiness of the couple is at its height; but Kintsune's father, determined that his son will rise in the world, commands him to marry the daughter of the powerful Sadaishō. The father announces a wedding day and states his intention of rearing Shinobine's child at his home. Kintsune breaks the news to Shinobine, and with much grief on both sides, he takes the child away.

Kintsune's predicament is genuine. He loves Shinobine, but he cannot bring himself to oppose his father. When the father urges him to pay the ritual three visits to Sadaishō's daughter, as a sign that they are married, he complies, but the first sight of the woman who is to be his wife chills him: she has a broad forehead and big eyes and "though she might appear beautiful to her own father, she was certainly no match for the lady he had left behind." All the same, he goes through with the visits; but these are the last attentions he pays his wife. Instead, he secretly takes his child to see its mother, Shinobine, and discovers that his love is in no way diminished.

Although he neglects his wife, his marital connection brings Kintsune rapid advancement, as his father had hoped, and he is considered to be the most promising young member of the court. But when he decides to build a more suitable dwelling for Shinobine, his father, who considers this a betrayal of Kintsune's wife, interferes. He intercepts a letter from Kintsune to Shinobine, and substitutes a note which has the effect of making her leave the vicinity. However, her companion, the nun, knows a high-born lady who secures for Shinobine a place at the court. Before long, she attracts the attention of the emperor, and he favors her with his love. One day Kintsune, who has searched in vain for Shinobine, plays his flute at court. Shinobine, recognizing his distinctive tone, is unable to control her agitation. The emperor, guessing the cause, permits her to meet Kintsune. He is still in love with Shinobine, but feels he cannot stand in the way of the emperor, and announces his intention of entering Buddhist orders. He returns to his house, bids farewell to his wife and son, then goes to Mount Hiei where he is initiated as a monk.

Shinobine in time gives birth to the emperor's son, who is at once designated as the crown prince. Her son by Kintsune rises spectacularly, but he never neglects to visit his father on Mount Hiei. The emperor abdicates in favor of the crown prince, and Shinobine's son by Kintsune, now a middle counselor, makes a happy marriage with a princess of the highest rank.

The story ends happily, but the overall tone is melancholy. Perhaps Kintsune has found peace and a kind of happiness in the monastery, but the reader is likely to think of him with pity, a man torn from the woman he loves. Shinobine is established as the empress, and her son succeeds to the throne, but there is no indication that this brings her joy. Most striking in terms of the narration is the absence of dreams or fantasies, an almost inescapable plot device in tales of the period. The story is related in believable, everyday detail, as if the author had invented nothing but had merely recounted a quite ordinary series of events. The only person who might be called a villain is Kintsune's father, but even his disagreeable actions are inspired not by a craving for personal gain but by anxiety over the welfare of his son. The story lacks the intensity and dimensions of tragedy, but leaves a poignant aftertaste of sadness.

The Tale of Shinobine is moving not because of the novelistic elements—Kintsune's being attracted by the sounds of Shinobine's koto or her recognizing his presence by his wondrous flute-playing—but because of the understated portrayal of the characters. At the end of the story nobody is happy, and yet each has achieved what under other circumstances might be interpreted as fulfillment.

The *otogi-zōshi Shigure*, written later in the Muromachi period, is very similar in plot,[55] but there are differences in the narrative that suggest how much time has elapsed between the two works. In *The Tale of Shinobine* the lovers meet at Sagano, in the manner of a Heian romance, after Kintsune has heard the sounds of Shinobine's koto; in *Shigure* they meet by chance in the bustle of the crowd at the Kiyomizu Temple when the heroine is caught in a sudden rainstorm, and the hero lends her his umbrella.[56] The transition from the monogatari to the otogi-zōshi could hardly be more striking.

Despite the many changes in Japanese society between the eleventh century, when the courtly romance was perfected, and the sixteenth century, when it finally ceased to be of importance, it retained its hold on members of the aristocracy, who sought to identify themselves with people of the Heian past they knew from romances. But the endless warfare and the general impoverishment of the aristocrats at the end of the sixteenth century apparently had the effect of making it impossible for them to bridge the widened gap between themselves and their ancestors. The meeting of Chūjō, the hero of *Shigure*, and the beautiful daughter of the late Sanjō middle counselor at a popular place of worship, rather than a mountain retreat, suggests that even the aristocrats had come to feel that the world they lived in could no longer be ignored in favor of the past. This change in the story would be developed even more conspicuously in the literature of the seventeenth century: one of the first *kana zōshi* (the characteristic tales of that era), and a forerunner of the popular romance, also opens with the first meeting of lovers at the Kiyomizu Temple. But this is not a tale of "once upon a time"—we are informed that the meeting occurred in 1604, just eight years before publication of the work.[57] The traditions of the courtly romance were in this way extended into the modern world.

Notes

1. For further discussion of the effect of the synthesis between Shintō and Buddhism on literary composition, see H. E. Plutschow, *Chaos and Cosmos*, pp. 145–99. The philosophical background of the synthesis is the subject of *The Buddhist Philosophy of Assimilation* by Alicia Matsunaga. The union of the two religions is embodied in the stories in the *Shintōshū* (see below, pp. 985–88).
2. Quoted from the translation in my *Travelers of a Hundred Ages*, pp. 179–80. The original text is found in Katō Genchi, *Kenkyū Hyōshaku: Saka-ō Daijingū Sankeiki*, p. 3.
3. See *Dawn to the West*, I, p. 822. The original text is found in *Kawabata Yasunari Zenshū*, XXIII, p. 407.
4. From his diary *Journey Along the Tsukushi Road* (1480). In the original: *Meisho naraneba shiite kokoro tomorazu.* See Kaneko Kinjirō, *Sōgi Tabi no Ki Shichū*, p. 92; also the translation by Eileen Kato, "Pilgrimage to Dazaifu," p. 364.
5. Quoted in Keene, *Travelers*, p. 188. Text in Fukuda Hideichi et al., *Chūsei Nikki Kikō Shū*, p. 370.
6. It may only be an accident of the transmission of texts, but the surviving diaries that treat the era of the two courts were almost all by adherents of the Northern Court.
7. He is also known as Kanera, but I have followed the reading preferred by the *Nihon Koten Bungaku Daijiten.*
8. I am speaking, naturally, only of known authors; it is quite likely that creators of the stories in *Tales of Times Now Past* and later collections of setsuwa bungaku were commoners, but it is only from this time that we know the names of commoners who wrote important works of poetry and prose.
9. Fukuda Hideichi et al., *Chūsei*, pp. 392–93.
10. The text gives his full name and title: Hosokawa Ukyō no Daibu Katsumoto Ason.
11. A quotation from a kanshi by Ōe no Asatsuna, poem 632 in *Wakan Rōei*

Shū. See Kawaguchi Hisao, *Wakan Rōei Shū*, p. 475. The meaning here seems to be that although Kaneyoshi realizes he may not have another chance to visit the old sites, he was afraid of being caught up in the fighting while he was sightseeing, far from his protectors.

12. Fukuda Hideichi et al., *Chūsei*, p. 394.
13. More commonly, *musha*.
14. Fukuda Hideichi et al., *Chūsei*, p. 400.
15. See above, pp. 950–57.
16. There is a book on the travels of renga poets at this time, *Rengashi to Kikō* by Kaneko Kinjirō. The frontispiece, appropriately, is a picture of Sōgi dressed for travel and riding a horse. Sōgi's travels are specifically treated on pp. 124–50. See also above, pp. 952–53.
17. Translation from Keene, *Travelers*, p. 221. Both Kanemori and Nōin were well-known poets of the Heian period who composed poems on the subject of Shirakawa Barrier.
18. Sōgi says in the diary, "That is how it is on a journey. Even though the affairs of the world are a source of grief, one consoles oneself recalling the old poems that have come down through the generations." Translation in Eileen Kato, "Pilgrimage," p. 364. Original text in Kaneko, *Sōgi*, p. 91.
19. Translation by Eileen Kato in "Pilgrimage," pp. 363–64. Text in Kaneko, *Sōgi*, p. 91.
20. Translation by Edward G. Seidensticker in *The Tale of Genji*, I, p. 388.
21. Translation by Eileen Kato in "Pilgrimage," p. 360. Text in Kaneko, *Sōgi*, p. 82.
22. Translation by Eileen Kato in "Pilgrimage," p. 362. Original text in Kaneko, *Sōgi*, p. 88.
23. Kaneko (in *Sōgi*, p. 90) records his search for a source for the little fishes fearing the big ones, as much as to indicate that *every* comment by Sōgi must have had a source.
24. Kaneko, *Sōgi*, p. 92. See also Eileen Kato, "Pilgrimage," p. 364.
25. For further details concerning Sōchō, see above, pp. 957–58.
26. I have drawn this description of *Sōgi Shūen no Ki* from my *Travelers*, pp. 228–32. The text is given in Kaneko, *Sōgi*, pp. 103–25.
27. The notebook provided H. Mack Horton with the materials for his very interesting article, "Saiokuken Sōchō and the Linked-Verse Business."
28. For more about Yamazaki Sōkan, with whom Sōchō composed comic renga, see *World Within Walls*, pp. 12–19. Little is known about Sōkan's life, but he is revered as the founder of *haikai no renga*, and his name is associated with *Inu Tsukuba Shū*, the first collection devoted to that genre.
29. For some examples in translation, see my article, "The Comic Tradition in Renga," pp. 274–76.
30. Dates corresponding to 1354 and 1358 occur in the text, and it is believed

that the original version of the collection was compiled not long afterward, but the extant text seems to have been compiled at the beginning of the fifteenth century. The rufubon text probably dates to the late fifteenth century. See the article by Murakami Manabu, "Shintōshū," in *Nihon Koten Bungaku Daijiten*, III, p. 499.

31. This passage occurs in section 1.2 of *Kasuga Gongen Genki*, translated by Royall Tyler in *The Miracles of the Kasuga Deity*, p. 165.
32. However, Amaterasu was also identified as the "manifested trace" of the Jūichimen (Eleven-headed) Kannon. See *ibid.*, p. 117.
33. Sometimes it happened that religious factions made different identifications of the honji of the Shintō gods. See *ibid.*, p. 104.
34. These were (in Japanese pronunciation) Dainichi, Amida, Shaka, Yakushi, Monju, Fugen, Jizō, Miroku, Kannon, Seishi, Kokūzō, and Fudō. These constitute twelve of the thirteen Buddhist divinities who "presided" over the thirteen memorial services for the dead ranging in time from one week to thirty-three years after the death.
35. See Kishi Shōzō, "Kaisetsu," in his edition of *Shintōshū*, p. 295.
36. The number and sex of this deity (*daimyōjin*) is by no means clear. At times four (or five) different deities, one of them female, are distinguished, but in general a single male deity seems to be intended. The Japanese language does not distinguish singular from plural or masculine from feminine, and it is only when translating into an Indo-European language that it is necessary to decide on the number and sex of the deity. The four "sanctuaries" and the Wakamiya Shrine all form part of the deity, but as Tyler pointed out (pp. 112–13), "The *Genki* contains no hint that the various aspects of Kasuga no Daimyōjin have a collective life apart from the divinity's acts of communication with humans."
37. See Tyler, *The Miracles*, pp. 96–97, for a listing under various categories of the different kinds of bearers of oracles.
38. *Nimyō*, the last of the *gomyō* ("five wisdoms"), which are: languages; the arts and crafts including mathematics; medicine; logic; and Buddhist doctrine. The nimyō were essential fields of study at Kōfuku-ji.
39. The reigning deity of the world of the dead. The romanization of the name is often Emma.
40. Translation (including note 19) from Tyler, *The Miracles*, p. 205. This is episode 11.1 in Tyler's numbering. He divided (on the basis of content) the ninety-three sections of text mentioned in the original table of contents into seventy-two numbered tales.
41. En no Gyōja (634–?), a semilegendary figure, was traditionally considered to have been the founder of *shugendō*, the mountain ascetic cult whose members are known as yamabushi. The ascetic practices they performed were in order to acquire magic powers that could aid the community.

    Baramon Sōjō (704–760) was an Indian priest who came to Japan in

736 and subsequently took a leading role in the ceremonies attending the dedication of the Great Buddha at the Tōdai-ji in 752.

42. Kishi, *Shintōshū*, p. 3.
43. *Gosuiden*, the Palace of Five Marks of Decline, refers to the last incarnation of a heavenly being, when sweat, bad odor, and so on mark its decline from celestial status. It was not an auspicious name for a palace.
44. Kishi, *Shintōshū*, p. 6.
45. *Senda Okkoku-ō Kyō*, contained in vol. 14 of *Taishō Shinshū Daizōkyō*. See *Nihon Koten Bungaku Daijiten*, II, pp. 297–98.
46. Quoted by Kishi in his "Kaisetsu" to *Shintōshū*, p. 293.
47. For an account in English of the Kumano bikuni, see Barbara Ruch, "Medieval Jongleurs and the Making of a National Literature," pp. 299–304.
48. Kishi, "Kaisetsu," pp. 303–4.
49. *Ibid.*, pp. 307–8.
50. Northrop Frye, *The Secular Scripture*, p. 136.
51. Many Japanese scholars are careful to distinguish between writings of the Namboku-chō—the period from 1336 to 1392 when the rule of the country was divided between the Southern and Northern courts—and the Muromachi period proper, from 1392 to 1573. There are legitimate reasons for making this distinction, but I have preferred to follow the more traditional periodization according to which the Muromachi period began in 1333 with the fall of the Kamakura shogunate and ended in 1573 when Oda Nobunaga expelled the last Ashikaga shogun from the capital.
52. For the importance of *Fūyōshū* in dating works of courtly fiction, see above, p. 789.
53. An example of a medieval "revision" (kaisaku) of a Heian text is the Nakamura-bon text of *Wakefulness at Night*, a summary and adaptation that has the special significance of enabling us to know what happened in the missing volumes of the Heian text.
54. See Koyama Hiroshi (ed.), *Nihon Bungaku Shinshi (Chūsei)*, p. 130; also Kannotō Akio, "Shinobine Monogatari no Isō," p. 118.
55. Kannotō in his "Shinobine" treats *Shigure* as no more than an adaptation of *The Tale of Shinobine*, and traces the development of themes from the lost *Shinobine* to the extant text of *Shigure*. But not all scholars have accepted his thesis.
56. See the article by Kuwabara Hiroshi in *Nihon Koten Bungaku Daijiten*, III, p. 170.
57. For further details, see *World Within Walls*, pp. 150–51.

Bibliography

Note: All Japanese books, except as otherwise noted, were published in Tokyo.

Frye, Northrop. *The Secular Scripture.* Cambridge, Mass.: Harvard University Press, 1976.

Fukuda Akira. *Chūsei Katarimono Bungei.* Miyai Shoten, 1981.

Fukuda Hideichi. *Chūsei Bungaku Ronkō.* Meiji Shoin, 1975.

Fukuda Hideichi, Iwasa Miyoko, Kawazoe Shōji et al. *Chūsei Nikki Kikō Shū*, in Shin Nihon Koten Bungaku Taikei series. Iwanami Shoten, 1990.

Horton, H. Mack. "Saiokuken Sōchō and the Linked-Verse Business," *Transactions of the Asiatic Society of Japan*, Fourth Series, 1, 1986.

Imatani Akira. "Sengokuki Gunki Bungaku no Kyokō to Jijitsu," *Bungaku* 53:10, 1985.

Itō Kei. *Shin Hokuchō no Hito to Bungaku.* Miyai Shoten, 1979.

Kaneko Kinjirō. *Rengashi to Kikō.* Ōfūsha, 1990.

———. *Sōgi Tabi no ki Shichū.* Ōfūsha, 1970.

Kannotō Akio. "Shinobine Monogatari no Isō," in Nihon Bungaku Kenkyū Shiryō Kankōkai (ed.), *Otogi Zōshi.* Yūseidō, 1985.

Kato, Eileen. "Pilgrimage to Dazaifu," *Monumenta Nipponica* 34:3, 1979.

Katō Genchi. *Kenkyū Hyōshaku: Saka-ō Daijingū Sankeiki.* Fuzambō, 1939.

Kawabata Yasunari Zenshū, 35 vols. Shinchōsha, 1980–83.

Kawaguchi Hisao. *Wakan Rōei Shū*, in Kōdansha Gakujutsu Bunko series. Kōdansha, 1982.

Keene, Donald. "The Comic Tradition in Renga," in John Whitney Hall and Toyoda Takeshi (eds.), *Japan in the Muromachi Age.* Berkeley: University of California Press, 1977.

———. *Travelers of a Hundred Ages.* New York: Henry Holt, 1989.

Kidō Saizō. *Chūsei Bungaku Shiron.* Meiji Shoin, 1984.

Kishi Shōzō (ed.) *Shintōshū*, in Tōyō Bunko series. Heibonsha, 1967.

Koyama Hiroshi (ed.). *Nihon Bungaku Shinshi (Chūsei).* Shibundō, 1990.

Kubota Jun and Kitagawa Tadahiko. *Chūsei no Bungaku.* Yūhikaku, 1976.

Matsumura Yasushi. *Chūsei Joryū Nikki Bungaku no Kenkyū.* Meiji Shoin, 1983.

Matsunaga, Alicia. *The Buddhist Philosophy of Assimilation—the Historical Development of the Honji-Suijaku Theory.* Tokyo: Sophia University Press, 1969.

Mitani Eiichi (ed.). *Taikei Monogatari Bungakushi*, IV. Yūseidō, 1989.

Murakami Manabu. "Shintōshū no Sekai," *Kokubungaku Kaishaku to Kanshō* 52:9, 1987.

Nihon Koten Bungaku Daijiten, 6 vols. Iwanami Shoten, 1983–85.

Plutschow, H. E. *Chaos and Cosmos.* Leiden: Brill, 1990.

Plutschow, Herbert, and Hideichi Fukuda. *Four Japanese Travel Diaries of the Middle Ages.* Ithaca, N.Y.: Cornell University East Asia Papers, 1981.

Ruch, Barbara. "Medieval Jongleurs and the Making of a National Literature," in John Whitney Hall and Toyoda Takeshi (eds.) *Japan in the Muromachi Age.* Berkeley: University of California Press, 1977.

———. *Mō Hitotsu no Chūseizō.* Kyoto: Shibunkaku, 1991.

Seidensticker, Edward. *The Tale of Genji*, 2 vols. New York: Alfred A. Knopf, 1976.

Tomikura Tokujirō. *Meitokuki*, in Iwanami Bunko series. Iwanami Shoten, 1941.

Tyler, Royall. *The Miracles of the Kasuga Deity.* New York: Columbia University Press, 1990.

Varley, H. Paul. *A Chronicle of Gods and Sovereigns: Jinnō Shōtōki of Kitabatake Chikafusa.* New York: Columbia University Press, 1980.

26. NŌ AND KYŌGEN AS LITERATURE

The culture of the Muromachi period, as the activities of renga poets and professional storytellers demonstrated, was by no means confined to the capital or to the aristocracy. During the course of the warfare that began in the 1330s and continued with few pauses until late in the sixteenth century, almost everything that had survived in the capital of the manuscripts, works of art, and architecture of the Heian period was destroyed. The court nobles, the patrons of culture since its inception in Japan, were reduced to powerlessness by the rise of the military, and could contribute little to the new culture except the dignity of their names and their special knowledge of old traditions. Their place as patrons was taken partly by commoners in the villages who paid storytellers and other performers to entertain them, but principally by the new aristocracy—the shogun and his court in the capital, and the daimyos in their castle towns throughout the country.

The movement of culture went in both directions: warfare drove renga masters from the capital to the provinces where they taught their art, but it also occasioned rustic entertainments in the capital—perhaps brought back from temporary places of exile by men from the capital who had enjoyed such performances. In whichever direction the movement went, it was beneficial to the art—on the one hand, it freed renga from excessive reliance on courtly traditions, and on the other, it helped to purge the emerging Nō theater of the crudities of amateur theatricals.

The arts of the period were discrete, but there were resemblances in their ideals and sometimes their realization. This was true even of the nonliterary arts. The understatement (one is tempted to say symbolism) in the gestures of Nō was echoed in the tea ceremony, the monochrome landscape paintings, the rituals of Zen Buddhism. The vocabulary is also similar: *yūgen,* the mysterious depths sought by the practitioners of renga, was equally an ideal of Nō; and *hie* (chill) defined

Zeami's plays that treated old age as much as it did the renga of Shinkei.

The materials used by performing artists of the Muromachi period were also similar. The principal sources of the Nō plays were incidents related in *The Tale of the Heike,* and this was true, of course, of the professional storytellers who recited and sang the glory of the heroes of the past. Though the Nō theater is likely to impress modern audiences as a supremely aristocratic form of drama, many of the plays were based on folktales or on the legends that had grown up around shrines and temples in the countryside. Shinkei professed haughty contempt for anything smelling of rusticity, but other renga masters (notably those who took part in composing *Three Poets at Minase*) incorporated in their verses their experiences when traveling across landscapes unmarked by a single utamakura.

Nō

Of the literary arts of the Muromachi period, none is more impressive than Nō; yet it has only been in the relatively recent past that these plays have come to be considered works of literature. In terms of the literature as a whole, plays of literary interest were a late development,[1] and even after they had attained their full flowering, the texts were seldom praised in terms of poetic beauty that might be appreciated by a reader no less than by a spectator. Performance—whether by professionals on a stage or by amateurs intoning the texts for their own pleasure—was the chief and virtually the only aspect of the plays to elicit comment. The texts of the Nō plays, the oldest surviving form of Japanese drama, tended to be dismissed as no more than patchworks of quotations from the old poetry and romances; and the high reputation of individual works was in recognition of their success on the stage, rather than a tribute to the dramatists' understanding of the human heart or to the magnificence of their poetry. The singing and the dancing in Nō plays were of such importance that the texts were often considered to be hardly more than libretti. This attitude stemmed from the older traditions of nonliterary theater—performances that were either without words or used them merely as props for the movements on stage.

Scholars have increasingly insisted that Nō cannot be understood without reference to the music and dance, and considerable attention has been devoted, especially in recent years, to the musical structure of the plays.[2] This opinion is welcome: a full understanding of a Nō play does indeed require an awareness of how song and choreography enhance its meaning. However, recognition of how much more there is to a Nō play than the bare texts should not prevent us from considering the plays as literature any more than the loss of the musical and dramatic elements of the Greek dramas has prevented readers from being deeply affected by these expressions of the human condition.[3] The discussion here will be limited to an examination of the plays as literary texts.[4]

Historical Background

The oldest recorded Japanese entertainments were the *gigaku* dances first imported from China in A.D. 612. Gigaku survives today only in the vestigial form of the *shishimai*, or lion dance, a popular feature of New Year celebrations, but over 220 gigaku masks have been preserved from the seventh and eighth centuries, evidence of its variety and popularity. Fragmentary records indicate that a gigaku performance began with a procession of the actors, some masked as birds and beasts, others as barbarians with un-Japanese features, and they were accompanied by musicians who played flutes, drums, and gongs. From time to time the procession halted and dances were performed. These dances, ultimately perhaps of Indian, or possibly even Greek origins,[5] contained mimetic elements, some comic or even indecent, but there seems not to have been any dialogue.

The Japanese court of the Nara period, eager to import and assimilate anything produced by the great civilization of China, sponsored performances of gigaku, and youths were commanded to perfect themselves in the art. The high point in gigaku history occurred in 752, on the occasion of the ceremonies marking the "opening of the eyes" of the Great Buddha at the Tōdai-ji, when sixty gigaku artists performed. Half a century later only two men were qualified as gigaku performers.[6] In the meantime, the court had learned of a more decorous Chinese entertainment, the stately *bugaku* dances. Two varieties of bugaku were introduced, the *samai* (or "left" dances) from China, and the *umai* (or "right" dances) from Korea.[7] The bugaku dances depicted such scenes as the triumphal return of a king from war or the effects of liquor on a party of frolicsome demons, and they were accompanied by *gagaku*, a beautiful and complex orchestral music.[8] The samai and umai dances were distinguished by the coloring of the costumes and the musical instruments employed in the accompaniment. There was still no spoken or sung dialogue, though *kami-uta*[9] (god songs) and other ancient songs accompanied some performances. Bugaku would influence Nō not so much in its costumes, masks, or dances as in its organization into three musical sections of increasingly rapid tempo—*jo* (introduction), *ha* (development), and *kyū* (fast conclusion). A few Nō plays include dances in the bugaku style, usually to suggest the exotic world of China.

Bugaku was a fully mature art when first introduced to Japan, and because its alien characteristics were faithfully preserved, it has survived as ritual performances that can be repeated but not developed. By the end of the twelfth century, the period when Nō was first emerging as a theatrical art, bugaku had become established as part of the ceremonials at the Imperial Palace and Shintō shrines.

Sangaku, a much humbler form of entertainment, was introduced from China along with bugaku. It consisted of acrobatics, juggling, sleight-of-hand, puppet-operating, and stunts of various kinds. A picture of one stunt survives: a girl wearing high clogs crosses a rope strung between poles balanced on the chins of two cavorting men, and the girl juggles as she walks.[10] There were also sangaku playlets whose subjects were mentioned by Fujiwara no Akihira in *A New Account of Sarugaku*[11] as part of his account of a day spent by a family watching a performance.[12] These may have been little more than brief skits, but they presumably included dialogue.

There were mimetic elements also in the indigenous *kagura* dances performed by *miko* (priestesses) at Shintō shrines, but the native entertainment that contributed most to the formation of Nō was *dengaku* (field music), originally the songs and dances peasants offered to the gods as part of agricultural celebrations. The earliest mention of dengaku goes back to 998, and there are scattered references to dengaku in diaries and other documents from then until the middle of the fourteenth century.[13] Almost every mention, beginning with the first (in the official history *Nihon Kiryaku*), is in connection with an account of disorder that involved rioting and slaughter. Presumably dengaku was sometimes performed without incidents of violence, but on such occasions it did not attract the attention of historians. Surviving documents do not describe how dengaku was performed when it was first introduced to the capital from the country, but its deleterious effects on public order suggest that it consisted of dances that involved not only the performers but the spectators in a kind of mass hysteria that tended to culminate in bloodshed. The riots in 1096, at the time of dengaku performances, were on such a scale as to cause some historians to describe them as a turning point in the history of Japanese society.[14] Virtually everyone, from the emperor on down, seems to have been infected with the dengaku craze.[15]

By Hōjō Takatoki's time, however, dengaku had evolved beyond the wild dances described in the early accounts. Elements of sangaku, such as the juggling of balls and swords, enhanced the dengaku performances, and a musical beat was provided by hip drums and rattles. The costumes, formerly simple, became lavish, no doubt in keeping with the tastes of audiences that included aristocrats.

No surviving evidence indicates whether or not the dengaku actors of Takatoki's time performed texts that might be described as literary, but by the end of the fourteenth century such texts certainly existed. In 1375 Zeami, then a boy of twelve, went to Nara to see a performance of dengaku by the master actor Kiami. Even fifty years later he still recalled how Kiami had delivered certain lines.[16] Kiami has sometimes been credited with having created *Matsukaze*, the most beautiful of the Nō plays.[17] It appears that dengaku (often called *dengaku nō*) and sarugaku[18] (or *sarugaku nō*),[19] the direct ancestor of the Nō, developed along parallel lines and much influence passed between the two. Dengaku seems to have achieved artistic distinction more quickly, but failed to keep pace with sarugaku, perhaps because of the historical accident that it had no outstanding performers during the crucial period when Kannami and Zeami were developing Nō into a great dramatic art.

Ennen was another early form of entertainment that influenced sarugaku. The name *ennen* means "prolonging life," and the art probably originated as ceremonies of prayer for the long life of some exalted person; but as early as 1100 the ennen prayers were followed by dances, and ennen[20] eventually came to mean an entertainment performed by priests at the conclusion of a religious ceremony. At first, dances by boys were the most characteristic feature of ennen,[21] but gradually dramatic elements were incorporated. For some years it was a matter of dispute as to whether or not ennen was older than sarugaku, but it is now generally agreed that it provided an important formative influence, and that it was closer in structure to sarugaku nō than any other performing art of the time.[22]

Not all aspects of ennen were taken over by Nō. An account of an ennen performance at the Kōfuku-ji in 1429 indicates that plays in highly poetic language were staged with ornate sets. Ennen provided Nō with models of how old poetry and quotations from religious and secular literature, Chinese as well as Japanese, might impart dignity and beauty to the language.[23] Even if the language influenced Nō, the sets clearly did not: Nō was performed on bare stages with only a pine painted on the back wall for scenery.

It is not clear exactly when texts of indisputably literary value were first performed. It is hard to imagine that the only predecessors of the superb texts of Kannami and Zeami, early masters of the art, were plays with dialogue improvised by the actors; but—with one exception—not a single play or even line from a play can be shown to antedate the works of these two men. The exception is the ritual play *Okina* (The Old Man), still performed, especially at New Year or at the beginning of a festive season of plays.

Okina

Okina apparently dates from the late twelfth or early thirteenth century, but it underwent various changes during the two centuries before it reached its present form. Originally (as we know from the surviving masks and other evidence), it consisted of a series of dances performed by spell-working priests (*shushi*)[24] of the Kōfuku-ji in Nara taking the roles of three old men, known as Chichi-no-jō, Okina, and Samban Sarugaku.[25] The Kōfuku-ji, together with the associated Kasuga Shrine, figured importantly in the early history of Nō, and the ancient ties with the Kasuga Shrine are epitomized by the painting of a huge pine tree on the wall at the back of every Nō stage, said to be the Yōgō Pine at the Kasuga Shrine before which the plays were originally presented.

Later, two dances were added to the original three of *Okina*, one called Tsuyu-harai (Brushing Off the Dew), danced by a boy, and the other danced by Emmei Kaja, a youth.[26] Still later, in Zeami's time, the dances were reduced to three—Tsuyu-harai (later known as Senzai), danced by a young Nō actor; Okina, danced by a senior Nō actor; and Sambasō, danced by a Kyōgen actor. A unique feature of *Okina* is the presence of the mask bearer, an actor who carries a box containing the mask to be worn by the Okina actor, and who (in full view of the audience) helps the actor to put on the mask.

Okina as currently performed is without a plot or specifically dramatic elements, but it may originally have been a kind of Buddhist sermon.[27] The Okina mask, unique among those used in Nō, has a movable jaw, and the expressivity of this mask, the face of a benevolent old man, contributes to the festivity of a performance. The text, largely unintelligible, begins with the intoned syllables *tō tō tarari*, words uttered by a god that the actor, like a medium, pronounces but does not understand.

Desperate scholars have attempted to trace these words even in unlikely sources, but without success; probably they are corruptions of brief passages from the sutras. At moments, though generally not for long, the fog that obscures the text lifts and intelligible phrases are communicated in the form of *kami-uta*, cast roughly in the form of the four-line *imayō*, or of the irregular lines of the even older *saibara*, folk songs dating back to the Nara period or earlier.[28]

Okina stands by itself among the plays of the Nō repertory. It does not belong to any of the five categories into which the plays have been divided, and the roles are not designated as *shite*, *waki*, and so on in the usual manner. As currently performed, the play consists of five dances—two by Senzai, a Nō actor, usually chosen for his good looks, who dances without a mask; followed by Okina, who dances after first putting on his mask, which he removes at the conclusion of the dance; and finally, by the two dances of Sambasō, performed by a Kyōgen actor, first without and later with a mask. The intelligible portions of the text are typified by the words Senzai sings in his second dance: "May this place last a thousand ages! We shall serve you a thousand autumns. The roar is the water from the falls. The sun shines but never ends. *Tōtari aryū dōdō.*"

Sambasō's first dance is punctuated by the actor's meaningless cries of *yo*, *hon*, *ho*, which contribute to the lively rhythms of the dance. The second dance of Sambasō, performed while shaking a small bell that accentuates the rhythm of his movements, is particularly effective.[29] Nose Asaji, the great historian of Nō, believed that when the shushi lost their authority and the sarugaku players became more important, the latter came to perform Sambasō's dance.[30] At a still later stage, when the dances of Chichi-no-jō and Okina were taken over by the sarugaku (Nō) actors, they allowed Kyōgen actors to perform Sambasō's dances.

There is obviously an immense gap between *Okina* and even the simplest of the Nō plays by Kannami. No doubt there were intermediate developments—texts that marked a transition from the world of the gods who appear in *Okina* to the world of the mortals who appear in Kannami's most characteristic plays.[31] These intermediate texts would presumably have been of religious inspiration, intended to convey doctrinal truths in a form appealing even to illiterates.

The materials for the Nō plays, even from this early period, seem to have been drawn from both literary and folk sources. It is not always clear which was more important: a play like Kannami's *Motomezuka* (The Sought-for Grave), derived ultimately from a poem in the *Man'yōshū*, may have been influenced by the telling of the same story in *Tales of Yamato*, but then again, it may have been directly inspired by Kannami's hearing a local legend while his troupe was on tour.[32]

Kannami (1333–1384)[33]

Since so little is known about the earliest forms of what is now called Nō, scholars usually trace the creation of this theater no farther back than the realistic plays of Kannami, the first master of the art. He was born in the province of Iga, but founded his troupe (*za*), at first known as Yūsaki but later as Kanze, in the area of Nara, where the troupe participated in services at the Kasuga Shrine along with three other companies of actors.

The nature of the repertory is not clear, but we know the names of some dengaku masters whose works he adapted. His own surviving plays are few in number, but they have been highly praised for reflecting the new importance of the common people. It is assumed that it was to please badly educated audiences in the countryside, rather than aristocrats in the capital, that Kannami composed these earliest extant Nō plays. Judging from the name *sarugaku*, by which Nō was generally known, a term written with characters meaning "monkey music," the early repertory probably emphasized *monomane* (imitation) rather than dramatic effect. "Monkey music" may have been an appropriate designation for the early skits, but not for Kannami's plays, let alone those of his son, Zeami.[34]

Kannami's texts are varied, ranging from the simple but dramatically effective *Jinen Koji* (Jinen the Priest) to the superb *Sotoba Komachi* (Komachi at the Stupa). In general, critics who discuss the works of Kannami give greatest attention to the conflicts, scenes of madness, and other specifically dramatic elements in his plays, contrasting them with the remote, otherworldly plays of Zeami. Kannami's typical works contain few references to the literature of the past. In his later plays (assuming that the more literary works came later) he relies no less than Zeami on allusions to enrich the text, but when writing for rustic audiences his aim was probably less elegance than intelligibility, even to poorly educated audiences. Kannami's chief stylistic contribution to Nō was the *kuse*, a section of the play sung by the chorus to irregular meter during which the main subject of the play is narrated.[35]

There is reason to believe that the plays were performed realistically and rather briskly, taking no more than thirty to forty minutes, though present-day performances of the same works require at least twice as much time. The language was on the whole fairly close to the contemporary colloquial. Masks, props, and costumes were at once more realistic and more elaborate than those used today, in order to persuade audiences that the actors were really the people they portrayed. The purpose of performing the plays was primarily not religious, even when staged within the grounds of a temple, but economic—to provide a living for the actors. By Kannami's time the actors had banded into troupes, four of which survive to this day.[36]

Although *Jinen Koji* is considered to be by Kannami, there is evidence that Zeami altered the text. Zeami in his critical writings expressed unbounded admiration for every aspect of Kannami's art—as an actor, playwright, and musician—but he also believed that it was necessary to rewrite old plays in order to accord with the tastes of new audiences. This process of adapting old plays continued long after Zeami's time, probably until the plays were printed late in the sixteenth century.[37] The changes sometimes consisted of the addition of a single passage, but might have been more extensive. Because Zeami's style was so much more literary and involved than Kannami's, a section of a play by Kannami that is noticeably literary in its allusions and contains wordplay and other rhetorical devices is apt to be by Zeami.[38]

Jinen Koji clearly belongs to an earlier age than Zeami's but it exhibits many of the characteristic features of Nō. The parts are known not by the names of persons but by types. The chief character, called the *shite* or "doer," in this play is Jinen the Priest.[39] The shite in many plays is accompanied by a *tsure* (companion).[40] The secondary character, or *waki* ("man at the side"), is in *Jinen Koji* a slave trader. A waki can also be accompanied by a tsure, called the *waki-zure*, a minor role. There is a child actor (*kokata*),[41] who in this play takes the part of a girl. Finally, there is the *ai*, or Kyōgen actor (designated as a "man before the gate"), a commoner who lives near the temple where the action opens. In addition, there is a chorus. Unlike the choruses in a Greek drama, which are identified as "Elders of Thebes" or "Women of Troy" and so on, the Nō chorus has no identity; it generally speaks for the shite, often when the latter is performing a dance, but occasionally it also voices comments, not in its own person but as disembodied truths.

Jinen Koji opens as the ai tells us who he is. He addresses an unseen crowd, urging the people to be present on the final day of the week-long sermons of Jinen the priest. The language used by the ai is known as *sōrōbun*, *sōrō* being the copula found in the prose sections of the Nō plays and in other writings of the Muromachi period.[42] The ai's first sentence follows a set pattern typical of the *nanori*, or "self-introduction," in Nō:

Kayō ni sōrō mono wa, Higashiyama Ungoji no atari ni sumaitsukamatsuru mono ni te sōrō.[43]

(The person before you is a person who lives in the vicinity of the Ungo-ji [a temple] in Higashiyama [a section of Kyoto].)

The parts of a play in sōrō-bun, though seldom of literary interest, are delivered in an incantatory manner that helps to create the special, solemn atmosphere of the Nō theater. Although the sōrō-bun sections of a Nō text are stylized and not the colloquial language, they are relatively easy to understand; this may be why a play like *Jinen Koji*, probably first performed before plebeian audiences, contains so much sōrō-bun and so little good poetry.

The ai withdraws to the back of the stage after his little speech, and the shite enters. His opening words are addressed to unseen worshipers at the temple:

Ungoji zōei no fuda mesaresōrae. (Buy a ticket for the repair of the Ungo-ji!)

He then sings the first passage of the play in poetry, beginning with the lines:

1. *yūbe no sora no*	"In the evening sky,
2. *kumoidera*	A temple within the clouds;
3. *tsuki matsu hodo no*	To comfort you,
4. *nagusame ni*	While you await the moonrise,
5. *seppō ichiza*	I shall deliver
6. *noben to te*	A sermon on the holy law."
7. *dōshi kōza ni*	So saying, he climbs
8. *agari*	To the preacher's lofty seat,
9. *hotsugan no kane*	And rings a bell,
10. *uchinarashi*	Before he intones his vow.

This passage on the whole follows the traditional poetic meter of the Nō plays, an alternation of lines in seven and five syllables. Exceptions to the metrics occur, notably in the eighth line, perhaps in order to fit the music, but an alternation of seven and five syllables constitutes the basic pattern of the poetry, and departures are relatively few.[44] The vocabulary consists mainly of words of Japanese origin, but includes the Buddhist terms *dōshi kōza* and *hotsugan* derived from Chinese; such words impart a variety and strength of sound to the poetry of Nō not possible in poetry composed entirely in the softer native Japanese. Mention of "a temple within the clouds" is an indirect way of referring to the Ungo-ji, the temple where the action occurs.[45] The clouds in turn suggest the moon: the temple is now hidden by clouds, but presently the moon (a familiar Buddhist image for enlightenment) will show itself in the sky.

The most unusual feature of the passage in terms of European dramaturgy is the speaker's description of his own actions, beginning with line 7. On occasion the chorus may speak in the first person the thoughts of the shite, but it also happens (as here) that the actor describes or comments on his own actions, as if he were observing himself from a distance. A clear-cut division of the roles among persons who voice only their own thoughts or emotions, such as we find in European plays, was not observed in Nō.[46]

The emphasis in *Jinen Koji* is not on the poetry or the atmosphere but on the plot. It is the account of how Jinen, a priest known for his songs and dances, saves a girl who has sold herself into slavery in order to buy the robe she offers the temple in the name of her dead parents. Jinen, learning that slave traders have taken the girl off to the north, follows them. He catches up to them at Lake Biwa, where he discovers that the men have bound and gagged the girl, who lies helpless at the bottom of a boat.[47] Jinen demands that the slave traders turn over the girl to him in return for the robe. They at first refuse, but in the end yield to Jinen's impassioned plea and agree to release the girl, provided he perform his songs and dances. At the conclusion Jinen rescues the girl and they return to the capital together.

The most striking feature of *Jinen Koji*, in comparison to more famous plays of the Nō repertory, is its realism. The characters are all people of this world, not ghosts who are drawn back to the scenes of their earthly life. The role of the waki is generally that of a priest or high-ranking courtier, but here he is a slave trader, a member of a demeaning profession. Although conflict rarely occurs in other plays between the shite and the waki, whose function is not to oppose the shite but merely to ask the questions the audience might ask, in *Jinen Koji* the conflict between Jinen and the slave trader for possession of the girl is the central element of the plot. The sung parts of the play, though they observe the rules of prosody, are similarly realistic and appropriate to the social status of the characters. In other plays, even fisherwomen quote poetry from the past and their utterances are likely to be filled with dazzling poetic imagery, but here the poetry is only slightly more elevated than the prose. In other plays, too, songs and dances usually occur as representations of the deepest feelings of the characters, without explanation and without even being identified as song or dance; but Jinen's dances, in response to the demand of the slave traders, are clearly just that, and not a projection of his emotions.

One can imagine that in early performances the villainy of the slave trader was emphasized by the actors, and that the pious girl bound and gagged at the bottom of a boat elicited the compassion of the audience. Probably, though, the dances at the end constituted the chief appeal of the play. These were not likely to have been the slowly executed, complex dances typical of the later Nō but lively prancing to the beat of the small drum Jinen carries suspended from his neck.

We do not know to how great a degree Zeami revised this particular play by his father.[48] He may have introduced into *Jinen Koji* the few passages of literary quality, hoping in this way to win the approbation of the audiences before whom he appeared (members of the court of the shogun Ashikaga Yoshimitsu), for a play originally written for entirely different audiences. In contrast to *Jinen Koji*, most of the other plays attributed to Kannami—those identified as works by Kannami in the critical writings of Zeami—are anything but simple in their present state. Then again, Zeami may have revised these plays so extensively that only isolated passages retain the imprint of Kannami's dramaturgy.

The play *Sotoba Komachi* is attributed to Kannami,[49] but a glance at the text reveals at once how little it resembles *Jinen Koji.* The magnificent poetry creates a profoundly moving atmosphere, and although there is sufficient interest in the plot to retain the attention of the audience, the character of Komachi herself, rather than the events, gives the play its unique interest. It will be recalled that Ono no Komachi was a major poet of the ninth century, and some of her poems are included in the play; but more important than the historical Komachi are the legends that grew up around her, particularly those relating to her unkind treatment of her would-be lover, Fukakusa no Shōshō. Komachi refused to accept him unless he visited her on one hundred consecutive nights. On the hundredth night he died, and as punishment for her cruelty Komachi was condemned to live a hundred years, her beauty ravaged by age, and her mind obsessed by memories of her dead lover.

Even a bare recitation of the materials should suggest how far removed this play is from the world of *Jinen Koji*, but various elements in the structure have confirmed critics in their belief that *Sotoba Komachi* was written by Kannami. For example, in the first part of the play Komachi engages the waki and his companion, Shingon priests, in a verbal duel over the significance of a *sotoba* (stupa), a piece of wood that marks a grave. The priests insist that Komachi must not sit on the stupa because it represents Buddha himself, but she counters their arguments with Zen iconoclasm, so persuasively that in the end the priests bow in homage before her. The opposition between the shite and the waki is more typical of Kannami than of Zeami, and the arguments exchanged between them have recalled to some critics the satirical humor of Kyōgen.[50] The language in which the contrasting opinions of Komachi and the priests are expressed is close to the colloquial, another feature of Kannami's, but not of Zeami's, plays.[51]

The priests, having been defeated in their theological dispute with the old beggar woman, ask her name, and she reveals that she is Komachi, the daugher of Ono no Yoshizane, the governor of Dewa. There follows a dialogue between the priests and Komachi contrasting her former beauty and her present wretched appearance. The priests sing:

How sad to think that you were she.
Exquisite Komachi
The brightest flower long ago
Her dark brows arched
Her face bright-powdered always
When cedar-scented halls could scarce contain
Her damask robes.[52]

The sudden shift in mood from the witty repartee of Komachi's exchanges with the priests to the bittersweet recollections of the days of her beauty has been interpreted as a special feature of the syle of Kannami, not shared by Zeami.[53] However, there is nothing jarring in this shift; rather, the wit and the beauty are both integral parts of the legend of Komachi. The loss of beauty and the degradation in the world are quickly evoked in exchanges with the chorus:

Komachi: "Oh shameful in the dawning light
These silted seaweed locks that of a hundred years
Now lack but one."[54]
Chorus: What do you have in the bag at your waist?
Komachi: Death today or hunger tomorrow.
Only some beans I've put in my bag.
Chorus: And in the bundle on your back?
Komachi: A soiled and dusty robe.

Chorus: And in the basket on your arm?
Komachi: Sagittaries black and white.
Chorus: Tattered coat
Komachi: Broken hat
Chorus: Can scarcely hide her face.[55]

Komachi's description of her present misery abruptly breaks off. She reveals that when begging fails she is seized by madness. Immediately afterward, in a changed voice, she calls out, *Nō mono tabe*, *nō osō nō* (Hey! Give me something, you priests!). The priests ask her what she wants, to which she replies, "Take me to Komachi!" The first priest, astonished, cries out, "You *are* Komachi! Why do you say such crazy things?" Komachi answers:

No. Komachi was beautiful.
Many letters came, many messages
Thick as rain from a summer sky
But she made no answer, even once,
Even an empty word.
Age is her retribution now.
Oh, I love her!
I love her![56]

Komachi, possessed by the spirit of her dead lover, Fukakusa no Shōshō, describes the agony of the ninety-nine nights he visited her house, in rain and wind and even when the snow lay deep. On the last night he felt dizziness and pain as he made his accustomed journey, and he died before he could enjoy his promised reward. Komachi's temporary madness under the spell of her lover's possession has also been cited as proof that Kannami was the author of the play; such madness figures prominently in works attributed to him.[57] The play ends as the chorus, speaking for Komachi, declares,

It was his unsatisfied love possessed me so
His anger that turned my wits.
In the face of this I will pray
For life in the worlds to come
The sands of goodness I will pile
Into a towering hill.
Before the golden, gentle Buddha I will lay

Poems as my flowers
Entering in the Way
Entering in the Way.[58]

In view of the evidence, beginning with Zeami's attribution of *Sotoba Komachi* to Kannami, it is difficult to dispute the authorship, but it is puzzling all the same that two of the only four plays confidently attributed to Kannami[59] should be as dissimilar as *Jinen Koji* and *Sotoba Komachi.* Perhaps they were written at different stages of Kannami's career, the former while he performed mainly before rustic audiences, the latter after his troupe had come to enjoy the patronage of the shogun, Ashikaga Yoshimitsu. This is only a conjecture, since none of the plays is dated. Another possibility is that Zeami considerably revised the original play by Kannami. We know of one revision, mentioned by Zeami in *Sarugaku Dangi*, a compilation of his views on the art of the Nō made by his son Motoyoshi:

> Originally the Nō play *Sotoba Komachi* was an extremely long play. From the line "who is that who passes by" the actor chants at great length. Later in the play, Komachi, because the god of Tamatsushima [the deity of poetry] is enshrined nearby, makes an offering to that spirit, at which point a raven, representing the deity of the shrine appears. . . .These days, however, the entire scene has been eliminated.[60]

Probably it was Zeami himself who eliminated the scene, and he may also have refashioned the rest of the text to meet the tastes of his patrons. The actor who originally performed as the raven established a reputation for his skill in the role, but it is hard to imagine how an actor dressed to resemble a raven could appear in this play without destroying the prevailing mood. Perhaps Kannami's original version, less elevated in tone than the present text, more easily accommodated the raven.

Sotoba Komachi is an example of a *genzaimono*, or "contemporary" play. Komachi lived many years before the composition of the play, which was obviously not contemporary in the usual sense, but the waki and shite are contemporaries, in contrast to the *mugen*, or "dream-unreality" plays (more typical of Zeami), in which the waki, a person of the present day, encounters someone—a ghost in reality—who belongs to the past, a time remote from his own. Probably the mainstays of Kannami's repertory were the genzaimono, easier to understand and more obviously dramatic than the mugen plays. He continued to tour the provinces even after Nō had come to enjoy the protection of the shogun, apparently reluctant to give up his old ways. He died in the province of Suruga.

Zeami (1363–1443)[61]

Ever since the Muromachi period Zeami has been considered to be the supreme exemplar of the art of Nō. This opinion has been much strengthened in the twentieth century as the result of the discovery of the treatises in which Zeami, with great intelligence and precision, discussed every aspect of his craft. Zeami himself always spoke of his father Kannami as the supreme master of Nō, but Kannami's fame has tended to be obscured by that of his even more brilliant son. Zeami's life was unhappy, especially during his declining years, but by the time Nō was established as its official "music" by the Tokugawa shogunate, his place in the world of Nō was secure, and many plays of uncertain authorship were attributed to him in order to give them greater prestige. The various lists that identify the authors of Nō plays (made as long ago as the Muromachi period) contain numerous discrepancies,[62] but more than half of the 240 plays in the standard repertory used to be credited to Zeami.[63] The number has gradually been whittled down since 1945 by scholars who have applied increasingly rigorous standards; only plays mentioned by Zeami in his critical writings are now accepted as definitely his. This has left some thirty to forty plays.[64]

The publication in 1944 of the manuscripts of six plays in Zeami's own hand, discovered in a temple in Nara Prefecture, brought home to scholars another problem involved in discussing the texts. It had previously been assumed that the five schools of Nō had faithfully preserved the texts of the plays unchanged over the centuries, but the newly discovered manuscripts revealed that changes, some of major proportions, had occurred between the early fifteenth century when Zeami penned the manuscripts and the early seventeenth century when the plays were printed and became fossilized.[65] Unfortunately, none of the plays transcribed in Zeami's manuscripts is by himself, but presumably his plays also suffered alterations by later Nō dramatists.[66]

Another important discovery made in the twentieth century was of the treatises written by Zeami on the art of Nō. In 1909 the scholar Yoshida Tōgo published sixteen of these treatises, hitherto kept secret by the various schools of Nō.[67] Other treatises came to light in the 1930s and 1940s, and in 1963, the year when the six hundredth anniversary of Zeami's birth was celebrated, the last of the discoveries was published, for a total of twenty-one treatises. These publications more than ever confirmed the importance of Zeami as the outstanding figure in the history of Nō.

Our oldest item of biographical data for Zeami refers to an event of 1374,[68] when he was eleven years old (twelve by Japanese reckoning). The youthful shogun Ashikaga Yoshimitsu, seventeen that year, attended a performance of Nō at the Imakumano Shrine in Kyoto. This was the first time he had ever seen Nō, and he was entranced by the skill of Kannami and by the beauty of Zeami. From then on, Yoshimitsu accorded the troupe generous protection, raising Nō to a privileged status similar to that already enjoyed by dengaku; and before long Nō had displaced dengaku in the favor of the shogunate. This enabled the actors to remain in the capital, though formerly they had spent most of each year traveling from temple to temple to give performances at local festivals. Zeami's own stage experiences seem to have been confined to the capital.

Yoshimitsu's fondness for Zeami was described in 1378 in the diary kept by an irritated nobleman. At the time of the Gion Festival that year a special stand had been erected for the shogun to watch the procession. The nobleman wrote, "The shogun was accompanied by a boy, a Yamato sarugaku player, who watched the festival from the shogun's box. The shogun, who has for some time bestowed his affection on this boy, shared the same mat and passed him food from his own plate. These sarugaku performers are no better than beggars, but because this boy waits on the shogun and enjoys his esteem, everyone seeks his favor. Those who give the boy presents ingratiate themselves with the shogun. The daimyos and others vie to offer him gifts at enormous expense. A most distressing state of affairs."[69]

Despite this characterization of sarugaku actors as "beggers," Yoshimitsu's patronage brought the actors financial security and the advantages (including educational) of living in the capital. It assured them also of an audience capable of understanding the loftiest expressions of the dramatist's imagination. Kannami was probably set in his ways by the time that Yoshimitsu accorded his patronage, and continued to perform for rustic audiences. Zeami was therefore encouraged to create works whose appeal was restricted to audiences with the requisite education and tastes. He was aware of his good fortune: in *Sarugaku Dangi*, the conversations of the art of Nō recorded by his son, Motoyoshi, he twice predicted that his play *Kinuta* would not be fully appreciated by audiences of future times.[70] It had been more usual for writers to hope that future generations would recognize the value of works that were in advance of their time, but Zeami was sure that future audiences would not possess the sensitivity exhibited by Yoshimitsu.

Nō developed under Yoshimitsu's aegis into a theater for the connoisseur. Passages in the texts are sometimes so complex as to defy parsing; in such cases the reader (or the spectator) can only intuit what is meant. The obscurity arises in part because of the many varieties of word-play used to impart depth and richness to the text. These include engo,[71] kakekotoba, and joshi. If these features of the style were nothing more than a display of virtuosity in the use of language, they would quickly become tedious, but the impression one is likely to receive from the text of one of the great plays, say *Matsukaze*, is of inexhaustible riches in the language that reveal themselves only with repeated readings.[72]

The texts are further enhanced by quotations from the poetry of Japan and China. The notes to a well-annotated edition of the play are likely to cause the reader to wonder how spectators, especially those at first performances, could have caught all the allusions. Probably most spectators did not; but Zeami, sure that at least a few of those present would recognize the sources of his allusions, made no compromise with popular taste, let alone with ignorance.

It has been argued that Zeami's plays were not in the mainstream of Nō composition.[73] The only Nō dramatist who followed his style was his son-in-law Komparu Zenchiku (1405–1468?); most later dramatists wrote instead in the popular, openly dramatic vein of the early Kannami. In part this may have been a matter of individual talent and temperament, but it also reflected the tastes of the successive shoguns. Yoshimitsu died in 1408. He was succeeded as shogun by Ashikaga Yoshimochi (1386–1428), who preferred the dengaku actor Zōami to Zeami. Yoshimochi was in turn succeeded by Yoshinori (1394–1441), who favored Zeami's nephew On'ami (1398–1467). Neither of Yoshimitsu's successors had his refined tastes, and Zeami, who continued to write in the style he had perfected with Yoshimitsu's backing, fell out of favor.[74] In the end, however, Zeami triumphed: his plays count among the glories of Japanese literature, and the style he created, poles apart from the realism of almost all other playwrights of Nō, prevails today in performances. The masks (much less realistic than those used by his predecessors), the costumes (splendid even when the actor is playing the role of a fisherwoman), the bare setting, and the insignificant props all attest to the triumph of Zeami's art of nonrealism.

The term most often associated with Zeami's art is yūgen. Zeami himself used the word in different senses, ranging from "elegance" of speech or appearance to "mysterious depth." Yūgen is difficult to define, but one has little trouble identifying it in the texts or in performance. It may be the moment at the end of *Nonomiya* (The Shrine in the Fields) when Rokujō hesitates before passing through the torii that stands as a gate between this world and the next, or it may be at any moment in a climactic dance that epitomizes the deepest emotions of the shite. Or it may be the incredibly beautiful ending of *Matsukaze*, when Matsukaze and her sister Murasame disappear, leaving only the wind in the pines and the autumn rain, the meaning of their names. Even though the term yūgen was used originally to describe any display of elegance, even at kemari, when used of Zeami's plays it came to designate the indefinable beauty toward which Nō is pointed in language, music, and dance.

Jo, Ha, Kyū

Zeami's critical writings are especially insistent on the principle of *jo, ha,* and *kyū*, the three successive tempi observed in the composition and performance of a play. The three contrasting tempi are not of equal length. The jo (introduction), slow in tempo and usually not of great emotional intensity, is normally only one section long, as contrasted with the three of ha (the development), during which the main matter of the play is presented. The three sections of the development are followed by a single section of kyū (the rapid finale). There is also a progression of jo, ha, and kyū in sustained utterances within each part of a play; and the style and tempo of the dances are determined by the section of a play (whether jo, ha, or kyū) in which they are performed.

The Five Categories of Plays

Apart from the division into jo, ha, and kyū within each play, a program of five plays is arranged along the same lines: the first play,[75] which treats the gods and their legends, is in the deliberate tempo of the jo; the second, third, and fourth plays, corresponding to the ha sections of a single play, exhibit mounting dramatic complexity; and the fifth play, the kyū component, is often about demons and is performed with the greatest intensity of movement. It became traditional during the Tokugawa period to present a program of five Nō plays, sometimes preceded by *Okina* or concluded with an additional dance play, arranged in the order of jo, ha, and kyū. At one time a full program also included four Kyōgen between the Nō, all performed on a single day. A program that includes in the proper order works of jo, ha, and kyū intensity should surely leave the audience with feelings of satisfaction, but it is also exhausting, and contemporary spectators are reluctant to sit through ten or more hours of drama. In any case, a "complete" program of five plays, though intelligible in terms of Zeami's principles, was probably a relatively late development.[76]

Plays of the first category are generally the least interesting as works of dramatic literature. Often they are devoted to the history of a shrine and the miracles attributed to its divinity. Presumably, this is the oldest variety of Nō, the kind of play that Kannami and his predecessors performed at the festivals of shrines in the countryside, and great attention is devoted to persuading the audience of the special holiness of a particular site. The characters, being divine, are generally remote, and the poetry rarely rises to the emotional heights found in other plays. Only a few plays of the first category are of such beauty as to rank as popular favorites (for example, *Takasago*), but it would be unthinkable to eliminate them from the repertory because, more than the plays of any other category, they create the special atmosphere of Nō—slow, solemn, and distant, but somehow auspicious.[77]

Zeami's most characteristic plays are those of the second category, the *shuramono*—plays about military men who are doomed after death to torment in the hell of warring ghosts. It may seem strange that plays about warriors should be placed between those about gods and those about women (the third category) in the jo, ha, kyū progression, but Zeami's critical writings make it clear that he considered the world of the shuramono to be an extension of the jo part of a program, a continuation of the atmosphere evoked by plays about the gods.[78]

The shuramono at the same time anticipated the elegance of the plays about women. Zeami wrote, "If you take a famous character from the Genji or the Heike and bring out the connection between him and poetry and music, then—so long as the play itself is well written—it will be more interesting than anything else."[79] One remembers in Zeami's shuramono the artistic tastes of the heroes at least as much as their martial prowess—Tadanori who braved death in the hope of having a poem included in an imperial anthology, Atsumori who carried a flute in his armor, Sanemori who wore a red brocade robe into battle. Zeami wrote at least five of the best-known sixteen shuramono plays, and possibly as many as twelve.[80] The shuramono written in the age after Zeami—for example, *Kanehira*—contain far more graphic descriptions of the horrors of battle than any play by Zeami. For this reason (and also because the text of *Kanehira* borrows word-for-word long passages from *The Tale of the Heike*, contrary to Zeami's usual practice)[81] the attribution of this play to Zeami is no longer accepted. It would be hard to justify considering such a shuramono as an extension of the jo section of the jo, ha, kyū sequence.

Zeami's special contribution to the form of the Nō was the creation of the *fukushiki mugen nō*, a modern term that means literally "compound dream-unreality Nō." All but one of his shuramono are in this form. *Atsumori*, a typical example, is in two scenes. In the first the waki, identified as the priest Renshō, encounters the shite, a villager who is first seen reaping grain along with his companions. Renshō, hearing a flute, asks a reaper (the shite) who played it. All the reapers but one, the same man the priest questioned, then leave. The man asks the priest to pray for him, but without giving his name, he too disappears.

In the second scene, following an interval in which a "man of the place," a Kyōgen actor, tells the story of Atsumori and the man who killed him, Kumagai no Jirō Naozane, the shite reappears, this time in his true form as the young Heike general Atsumori, wearing the splendid armor in which he perished. He reenacts the tragic last moments of his life. His resentment over defeat, which he cannot forget, has caused him to return to this world as a ghost. At the climax of Atsumori's narration of the final combat with Kumagai, he cries out and lifts his sword to strike Renshō, none other than his enemy Kumagai, who took the tonsure in order to pray for Atsumori's release from attachment to this world. The two men are reconciled, and it is predicted that they will be reborn on the same lotus in paradise.

The two layers of time in a fukushiki mugen play not only impart greater complexity than is possible in the more realistic genzaimono, plays of "contemporary" life in one scene, but enable the spectator (or reader) to feel that a work consisting of no more than six or seven pages of text has provided a complete theatrical experience. The tension between the two parts of a mugen Nō play resembles that between the two elements—eternal and momentary—in the best haiku, which likewise provide the possibility of creating a world from the barest of suggestions.

The interval narrations (ai) between the two parts of the play (with a few exceptions) are not of great interest, and some members of the audience today take advantage of this break to enjoy a cigarette in the corridors. A pause is, however, essential to the mugen play, providing the time needed for the shite to change mask and costume, and sometimes even identity, as in the popular *Funa Benkei* (Benkei in the Boat), where the shite of the first part is the dancer Shizuka, but in the second the menacing ghost of the warrior Tomomori, who rises from the waves of the Inland Sea. The interval narrations may also have afforded audiences the pleasure of oratory in a country without the tradition of a forum where speeches might be heard. They also explain in relatively easy-to-understand language the events and background of the first half of the play. But perhaps the most important function of the speech of the Kyōgen actor during the interval is to keep a mugen play from splitting into two unrelated halves. The narrator helps the audience to recognize that the humble person of the first scene is a temporary manifestation of the shite who appears in his true form in the second scene.

The most important source for Zeami's shuramono was *The Tale of the Heike*. The warrior was one of the three basic Nō roles he singled out for consideration in his critical work *Sandō* (The Three Ways).[82] He stated, "If, for example, the play is to be created around a famous general of the Genji or the Heike, you should take special care to write the story just as it appears in *The Tale of the Heike*."[83] These words should not suggest that Zeami merely arranged selected passages of *The Tale of the Heike* in the form of a play;[84] despite his injunction to playwrights to remain faithful to their sources, especially *The Tale of the Heike*, he seems to have felt free to modify the texts to suit his dramatic purposes. Moreover, he chose from his source chiefly figures who attracted him, men who met their death in battle rather than those who were victorious. *Yashima* is a rare play by Zeami about a victorious hero, but his hero exhibits none of the exultation found in the source; instead, Zeami gives a graphic description of the torment Yoshitsune suffers in the *shura* hell where men who fought in this world are doomed to reenact their murderous deeds.[85]

The third play in the program, often referred to as *kazuramono*, or "wig piece," has a woman for the shite. Two works of this category, *Matsukaze* and *Yuya*, are often said to be the "rice bowl" of Nō actors because of their central importance to the repertory. Plays of the third category are less likely than shuramono to be in the form of fukushiki mugen, probably because only one play in this mode is indisputably by Zeami, *Izutsu* (The Well-Curb). Complexity akin to that of the double identity in a mugen play is provided in some kazuramono by moments of "madness," when the shite imagines she is her lover. In *Izutsu* the daughter of Aritsune, putting on the court robe and cap of her lover, Narihira, goes to the well-curb (*izutsu*) where as children she and Narihira had compared their heights, and looks at her reflection in the water.

mireba natsukashi ya	She looks—how sweet the memory
warenagara natsukashi ya	Sweet the memory, though of herself,
bōfū hakurei no sugata wa	This ghost in her dead husband's form:
shibomeru hana no	A withered flower,
iro nōte	Its color vanished,
nioi nokorite	Perfume only lingering.
Ariwara no tera no kane mo	The bell of the Ariwara Temple too
honobono to akureba	Tolls dimly at the break of day.
furudera no	Over the old temple,
matsukaze ya	The wind through the pines,
bashōba no	The rustle of plantain leaves,
yume mo yaburete	Broken easily as dreams;
samenikeri	Awakened,
yume wa yabure	The dream is broken,
akenikeri	The day has dawned.[86]

The most beautiful of the plays about women is *Matsukaze.* It is usually credited to Kannami, even by scholars who believe that uncomplicated language and clear-cut action are the hallmarks of Kannami's style, though it is conceded that Zeami revised the text.[87] The story is simple: a priest on his travels takes shelter for the night at the hut of two sisters, Matsukaze and Murasame. The sisters eke out a living by dipping brine from which salt is extracted. Their references to events in the distant past arouse the priest's curiosity, and he asks the sisters who they really are. They reveal that they are the ghosts of fisher girls who, many years before, were loved by the nobleman Yukihira. After he returned to the capital they heard that he had died. All they still possess of him are the court hat and hunting cloak he left as a memento.

Matsukaze puts on the hat and cloak. She imagines that the pine she sees is Yukihira himself, and she remembers the poem in which he promised to return if he heard she "pined"[88] for him. Her yearning for Yukihira induces momentary madness, but the sisters recall that they are no more than ghosts, tormented by attachment to the world. They ask the priest to pray for them and then disappear, leaving only a memory of the autumn rain (*murasame*) that fell the previous night and the wind in the pines (*matsukaze*).

The one "action" in the usual theatrical sense occurs when Matsukaze imagines she sees her dead lover. The performance of the madness is in no way realistic, but it is affecting when Matsukaze persuades Murasame, who had chided her sister for the deluding sin of passion that made her mistake a pine tree for Yukihira, that the pine is their lover, and he has returned as he promised. The sisters share the "madness," for they both loved Yukihira. It makes no sense to ask (as a Western reader might) whether Yukihira was equally in love with both sisters or favored Matsukaze. Murasame, as the companion (tsure) of Matsukaze, serves chiefly to give resonance to her sister's longing; this is true even when, momentarily, she rebukes Matsukaze's delusion.

The plot is hardly more than a framework for the magnificent poetry and for Matsukaze's dance. *Matsukaze* is a mugen play: the sisters are ghosts who appear before the priest, the only member of this world. As in *Izutsu*, the change of costumes (when Matsukaze puts on Yukihira's robe) creates an effect similar to the fukushiki of the shuramono, transforming the fisher girl into a court lady. What lingers in the mind of the reader, however, is the language. Many phrases and even fairly long passages were borrowed from *The Tale of Genji*, using descriptions that related to Genji's exile on the coast at Suma (and, earlier, Yukihira's) to evoke the loneliness of the lives of the two sisters.

Matsukaze sings,

1. The autumn winds are sad.
2. When the Middle Counselor Yukihira
3. Lived here back a little from the sea,
4. They inspired the poem,
5. "Salt winds blowing from the mountain pass . . ."
6. On the beach, night after night,
7. Waves thunder at our door;
8. And on our long walks to the village
9. We've no companions but the moon.
10. Our toil, like all of life, is dreary,
11. But none could be more bleak than ours.
12. A skiff cannot cross the sea,
13. Nor we this dream world.
14. Do we exist, even?
15. Like foam on the salt sea,
16. We draw a cart, friendless and alone,
17. Poor fisher girls whose sleeves are wet

18. With endless spray, and tears
19. From our hearts' unanswered longing.[89]

A comparison of the text of the first nine lines of the *sashi*[90] section with the relevant passage in *The Tale of Genji* reveals the closeness of the borrowing:

(Matsukaze). Kokorozukushi no akikaze ni, umi wa sukoshi tōkeredomo, kano Yukihira no chūnagon, seki fukikoyuru to nagametamau urawa no nami no yoruyoru wa, ge ni oto chikaki ama no ie, satobanare naru kayoiji no, tsuki yori hoka wa tomo mo nashi.[91]

(The Tale of Genji). Suma ni wa, itodo kokorozukushi no akikaze ni, umi wa sukoshi tōkeredo, Yukihira no chūnagon no, seki fukikoyuru to iiken uranami, yoruyoru wa ge ni ito chikaku kikoete, matanaku aware naru mono wa, kakaru tokoro no aki narikeri.[92]

Apart from the modifications in the original text made in order to fit the normal pattern of alternating lines in seven and five syllables,[93] the main difference is in the final phrases. The beautiful ending of the passage in *The Tale of Genji*, "autumn, in such a place as this, is incomparably moving," was not included in this section of the text of *Matsukaze*, but it occurs a little later, toward the conclusion of the following passage sung by the chorus:

1. Endlessly familiar, still how lovely
2. The twilight at Suma!
3. The fishermen cry out in muffled voices;
4. At sea the small boats loom dimly.
5. Across the faintly glowing face of the moon
6. Flights of wild geese streak,
7. And plovers flock below along the shore.
8. Fall gales and stiff sea winds:
9. These are things, in such a place,
10. That truly belong to autumn.
11. But oh, the terrible, lonely nights![94]

Images borrowed from the "Suma" chapter of *The Tale of Genji* include the voices of the fishermen, the face of the moon, and the line of wild geese.[95] But this was not simple expropriation of an earlier text. The language in *Matsukaze* is far more concentrated and richer than that in *The Tale of Genji;* almost every phrase is related to the one it follows and the one it preceeds by poetic or verbal associations. For example, the text in lines 4 and 5 are bound together by the shared words *kasuka naru* ("which are faint"):[96]

oki ni chiisaki isaribune no
kage kasuka naru tsuki no kao

Almost every phrase has literary overtones, whether derived from *The Tale of Genji* or some other work. The density of the text is further intensified by the intricate word-play. The opening of the passage contains a kakekotoba:

narete mo suma *no*
yūmagure

The word *suma* with what goes before is part of the verb *sumu*, "to live," but it is also the place-name Suma. Line 3 of the translation given above is, in the original:

ama no yobikoe
kasuka ni te

The corresponding words in *The Tale of Genji* are different: *Oki yori funadomo utainonoshirite kogiyuku nado mo kikoyu.* (He could hear the fishermen singing as they rowed their boats toward shore from the open sea.)

The difference is not simply one of language; the mood created by the words is entirely dissimilar. The voices of the fishermen raised in lusty song contrast with Genji's gloomy state of mind, though at other times would probably sound cheerful; but in *Matsukaze* the sounds of their voices are faint and far from the world of Yukihira and the sisters he loved. The words *ama no yobikoe* are not from *The Tale of Genji* but from a poem in the *Man'yōshū*.[97]

Allusion to another work usually strengthened the expression in a passage of Nō by giving it additional resonance, but sometimes the allusion brought ironical contrast. Perhaps the most extreme instance occurs during Matsukaze's "mad" dance:

"Awake or asleep,
From my pillow, from the foot of my bed,
Love rushes in upon me."
Helplessly I sink down,
Weeping in agony.[98]

Matsukaze's grief is unmistakable, but the poem she is quoting in the first three lines of the above passage is a comic (haikai) verse from the *Kokinshū*:

makura yori	From my pillow
ato yori koi no	And from the foot of my bed
semekureba	Love comes pursuing;
sen kata namida	Helpless and in tears I stay
tokonaka ni oru[99]	In the middle of the bed.

The use of an incongruously amusing verse resembles the contrast between Ophelia's distraught state and the ditties she sings before she drowns.

Another complexity in the texts of Nō is the intrusion of phrases that are not syntactically related to the rest of the sentences. Lines 6 and 7 (though joined in translation for smoother reading to the rest of the text by the verbs "streak" and "flock") in the original are grammatically unrelated to anything else:

kari no sugata ya	The forms of the wild geese
tomo chidori	The cluster of plovers

The juxtaposition of such images is typical of the Nō, but not easy to bring off in translation. Ezra Pound, in his version of *Kakitsubata*, managed the effect superbly:[100]

SPIRIT

The flitting snow before the flowers:
The butterfly flying.

CHORUS

The nightingales fly in the willow tree:
The pieces of gold flying.[101]

Matsukaze contains numerous other examples of allusion and other poetic devices.[102] It should not be supposed, however, that the text represents virtuosity for its own sake, or that it is a Japanese equivalent of euphuism. The impression given by the text of *Matsukaze* and other masterpieces of the Nō theater is of associations revealing themselves subconsciously, the moods of the characters being reinforced by remembered scraps of the poetry of the past or verbal associations that may sometimes seem irrelevant but contribute to the extraordinarily concentrated effect of the poety. Matsukaze and Murasame appear in the play before an itinerant priest at a particular time, but no doubt they have rehearsed many times before the fate that brought them, fisher girls, to the attention of a great noble who left them to grieve on a lonely shore when he returned to the capital. Repetition of their emotions has pared away anything superfluous in their words; instead, the associations impart to each utterance different layers of meaning. *Matsukaze* is one of the marvels of Japanese poetry. It is worth learning Japanese to read it.

Yuya,[103] another favorite play, is set at the end of the Heian period, and the source seems to be a variant text of *The Tale of the Heike*.[104] The plot is strikingly realistic. The tyrannical Taira no Munemori plans to view the cherry blossoms at Kiyomizu in the capital with his mistress Yuya. She, however, has received word from home that her mother is seriously ill, and begs to be allowed to return to the mother's side. Munemori, refusing her request, insists that she accompany him. After they have reached Kiyomizu, Yuya dances for Munemori. She also composes a poem that so impresses him that he finally allows her to go to her mother.[105] Unlike many Nō plays of the third category, *Yuya* is without suggestion of the supernatural and, although the play is set several centuries before the time of composition, no emphasis is given to the remoteness in time from the audience. What keeps *Yuya* from being considered a genzaimono, and the source of its appeal, is the lyrical emphasis given to the beauty of the spring; it might even be said that the spring is the central character of the play.[106]

The mysterious beauty known as yūgen is most perfectly evoked in plays of the third category. Although the ideal of yūgen is closely associated with Zeami, the two plays that are most imbued with this quality, *Matsukaze* and *Yuya*, are ironically attributed to other men. His only important successor as a playwright of yūgen was Komparu Zenchiku, the author of such plays as *Ugetsu, Yōkihi*, and *Bashō*, all of the third category, as well as treatises on the art of Nō that rank in a class with Zeami's.[107]

Plays of the fourth category fall under two distinct headings, *kyōjomono* (madwomen plays) and genzaimono. It is easy to imagine that the madwomen plays might have developed from the sections in plays like *Matsukaze* or *Sotoba Komachi* where the shite, a woman, has the illusion that she sees her dead lover or even that she is the lover. The interest in mad people is otherwise demonstrated by the surprising number of plays about them, perhaps because it was believed they were in communication with the world of the dead.

Among the madwomen plays there are two distinct varieties—plays in which the woman is actually (though perhaps only temporarily) insane, and those in which she is obsessed rather than mad. In *Hanjo* the shite, a courtesan named Hanago, is grief-stricken because her lover has broken his promise and failed to return. She waits for him, day after day and month after month, unable to think of anything else, so distraught that when he eventually does return she at first does not recognize him. But when he shows her the fan she gave him as a keepsake, she is restored to her senses, and the play ends happily with their reunion.[108]

A "madwoman" of the obsessed variety is the shite in *Sumida-gawa* (The Sumida River) by Zeami's son, Motomasa. A woman who lives in the capital has suffered the loss of her son, abducted by slave traders, and she wanders around the country looking for him. Her obsession with this search earns her the name of a madwoman, but her speech and actions until the last scene in no way suggest madness. In that scene, one of the most powerful in the Nō repertory, the woman is at last led to the place where her son is buried, and she claws at the earth, seeking to uncover his body for a last look. The child appears before her in a vision, only to disappear with the coming of the dawn, leaving her in desolate loneliness.[109]

The appeal of these and similar plays lies in their human interest. The Nō actors are at pains to avoid seeming "theatrical," and their version of *Sumida-gawa* is far less overtly "human" than the one performed by Kabuki actors; but the audience's empathy with the mother much more closely resembles that accorded to a Kabuki play or even a modern drama than the response to a remotely beautiful play like *Matsukaze.* The reader's reactions are likely to be similar or even stronger; the moment when the voice of the dead child is heard among the other voices reciting the invocation to Amida Buddha is electrifying when one reads it, but it may be difficult to hear in actual performance.

The place of the genzaimono at the end of the ha section of the program of five plays is as a natural development from the realism of a play like *Yuya*. Most of the genzaimono owe their appeal to openly theatrical qualities. A play like *Ashikari* (The Reed Cutter)[110] is affecting as a story of the love of husband and wife, though it has none of the deeper overtones of the great plays of the second and third categories.

A number of genzaimono are devoted to incidents in the warfare between the Taira and the Minamoto, and others still to the vengeance exacted by the Soga brothers on their father's enemy. The dramatist Miyamasu is credited with having written many of these plays, though almost nothing is known about the man or his background.[111] Old records seem to indicate that he took secondary roles in plays by other men, which is perhaps the reason the waki and tsure roles in his plays are more fully developed than in Zeami's. Miyamasu's plays on the whole are distinctly more dramatic than others in the repertory. The dialogue, at times colloquial, is both vivid and believable as the utterances of military men. Unlike the typical plays of Zeami, in which no more than two or three characters appear, those by Miyamasu sometimes have large casts, as many as fourteen or fifteen actors crowding the stage. The plays also contain important roles for kokata, perhaps in order to take advantage of the sentimental interest that children arouse in an audience. The interval scenes (ai) in some of Miyamasu's plays (for example, *Eboshi-ori*) are distinctive in that they possess dramatic interest and are not mere narrations.

The plays of Miyamasu may well have enjoyed greater popularity than Zeami's, not only in his own time but much later; it is otherwise difficult to explain why so many have been preserved. But their popularity inevitably suffered when faced with the competition of Kabuki performances that mined the same vein much deeper. Other realistic plays of the fourth category approach Kabuki even more closely than do Miyamasu's. The most popular of the later dramatists was Kanze Nobumitsu (1435–1516), the author of such highly dramatic plays as *Ataka, Momijigari, Rashōmon*, and the original version of *Dōjō-ji*, the most exciting work of the repertory.

Dōjō-ji is the tale of a priest who, to placate a young girl who has fallen in love with him, promises to return to her one day. When he breaks this promise, the girl, transformed into a serpent of jealousy, pursues him to the temple Dōjō-ji. He hides within the great temple bell, only for the serpent to coil herself around it and with the flames of her hatred roast him to death. The Nō play begins with the erection of a new bell to take the place of the one that was melted. For fear that the serpent may again intervene, orders are given that no woman be admitted to the ceremony for the inauguration of the bell. A shirabyōshi manages to persuade the priests guarding the bell that she is no ordinary woman, and she lulls them to sleep with a weird dance called *rambyōshi*, the only example in Nō, which is accompanied by the eerie cries of the player of the kotsuzumi drum. She leaps inside the new bell and conceals herself. When the priest returns, his prayers draw her from the bell. Now turned into a demon, she yields to his exorcism, plunges into the waters of the Hidaka River, and disappears.

The prop used for the bell, suspended from the ceiling on a pulley, has a lead frame and is the heaviest used in the Nō theater. If dropped too soon by the stage assistants, it can fracture the actor's leg as he leaps up into the bell. While inside the bell, the actor changes from the costume and mask of a dancer to those of a terrifying demon. The play succeeds less because of the text or even the dramatic situation than because of the music and especially the rambyōshi, the series of stamping dances performed in all four directions.[112] *Dōjō-ji* creates an unforgettable impression in performance, though the text itself is of only moderate interest.

Nobumitsu also wrote several of the most popular plays of the fifth category, the *kiri nō*, or final Nō, in which a demon has the principal role.[113] *Funa Bunkei* is not only frequently performed in Japan but is an obvious choice whenever troupes of Nō actors perform abroad: its dramatic tensions are readily intelligible even to foreigners with no acquaintance with Nō or any other form of Japanese theater. This might suggest that it is an inferior or at least atypical play, but this judgment would be unfair: *Funa Benkei* is not typical (the shite of the first part is not the same person as the shite of the second part), but when Tomomori, transformed into a demon of hatred for his enemies, threatens the boat in which Yoshitsune and his followers are fleeing, the atmosphere is entirely appropriate for a play of this category. The most striking feature of the play, however, is the exceptionally interesting ai scene in which the boatman suggests by his cries of alarm and his gestures his consternation over the fierce waves battering the boat. From among these waves Tomomori, now a demon, emerges, implacable in his hatred of the Minamoto.

In other plays of the fifth category (such as *Yamamba* [Mountain Hag]), a woman whose appearance in the first part in no way suggests she might be a demon in disguise reveals her true ferocity in the second part. The final dance (*shimai*) of the last play should represent the highest crest reached by the successive kyū sections of the entire program.

Kanze Nagatoshi (1488–1541) also wrote several plays in the yūgen style, including the lovely *Yugyō Yanagi*.[114] Komparu Zempō (1454–?), the grandson of Zenchiku, also wrote one yūgen play, *Hatsuyuki*, and surely some of the anonymous yūgen plays must also have been composed in the sixteenth century. But the emphasis at the time was on increased dramatic tension, large casts,[115] and spectactular effects. The division of the roles into shite, waki, tsure, and so on became arbitrary, often depending on the traditions of a particular school of Nō rather than on the nature of the characters.

Nō plays continued to be composed in the late sixteenth century,[116] and some were written (generally for a single performance) as late as the twentieth century; but Nō attained its apogee in the fifteenth century, and although in later centuries it enjoyed the protection of the shogunate and continued to be performed on stages at temples and shrines situated even in remote parts of the country, it ceased to grow. The fall in 1867 of its long-time patron, the shogunate, dealt Nō what seemed to be a deathblow, but it miraculously recovered. Its imminent demise, often predicted during the years after the defeat in 1945, was not only averted, but Nō came to enjoy even greater popularity than before, mainly because well-to-do amateurs enjoyed displaying their skill at singing and dancing the texts, a mark of social refinement. New theaters have been built, and outdoor performances are popular in the summer. The texts and the history of Nō continue to attract scholars, some of whom give adequate consideration to the literary importance of the plays.[117]

Kyōgen

The name *Kyōgen* is derived from the phrase *kyōgen kigyo*, meaning literally, "wild words and fancy language."[118] The term, first used by the great Chinese poet Po Chü-i to designate the worldly writings that he had come to reject in favor of Buddhist truths, acquired a rather different sense in Japan and came to mean that even works which seem to serve no higher purpose than to amuse may provide the impetus for gaining salvation.[119] Literature and art, even of a secular nature, such as the stories in *Tales of Times Now Past*, had earlier been tolerated as *hōben*, or expedients, for inculcating painlessly the principles of Buddhism. The term *kyōgen kigyo* was used in several Nō plays for songs and dances as well as fancy language. For example, in the play *Tōgan Koji* the young priest Tōgan Koji guides others to the teachings of the Buddha not by his preaching but by his singing and dancing. He declares, "Truly, these too, like 'wild words and fancy language,' can turn into teachings that bring salvation. As we enter the path of truth where the wheel of his Law rolls, let us sing these songs that are flowers of the human heart, for even they can be guides."[120]

It is not clear from existing sources when and how Kyōgen acquired its name. The art itself may have originated not as a stage performance but as recitations rather in the manner of present-day *rakugo*.[121] The earliest reference to what seem to be Kyōgen performers occurs in a document dated 1350, where mention is made of *okashi hōshi* ("funny priests"), who seem distinct from both sarugaku (Nō) and dengaku actors. These "funny priests" entertained audiences with their adroitly delivered monologues, and before long they acquired *ado*, or "partners," who served as foils.

Early Performances of Kyōgen

The early Kyōgen plays were probably skits that lasted no more than ten or fifteen minutes.[122] The title of one such play is given in a document dated 1352.[123] The plots may ultimately have been derived from written sources, [124] but they in turn may have been little more than transcriptions of folktales or extemporaneous recitations.[125] A few plays have been attributed to particular authors, notably the priest Gen'e (1269?–1350), but even granting that the plots were probably improved and their expression refined by educated persons, who were very likely priests, it makes little sense to search for authors before texts were first printed in the seventeenth century.[126] The plays are not uniform in tone, and some are decidedly less humorous than others, but many passages recur from play to play, and we are likely to be struck more by the similarities than by individual differences of style.

By Zeami's time a program, when performed in a public place, consisted of three Nō plays and two Kyōgen plays, but sometimes as many as ten plays might be performed on a single day at the house of a noble.[127] It is clear from Zeami's account that Nō and Kyōgen were performed on the same stage, but he does not mention whether or not they were presented in any particular order. The earliest reference to the alternation of Kyōgen and Nō plays, in the manner now observed, appears in a document of 1464,[128] though the practice may have started earlier. The inclusion of humorous, realistic plays at regular intervals in a program may have been originally intended as a concession to those in the audience who could not appreciate the lofty poetic expression of Nō, and may have made it easier for Zeami to present elsewhere in the programs plays of great complexity intended for the discriminating few. Possibly Zeami believed that both Nō and Kyōgen contributed to the same end, Buddhist enlightenment, though the means they employed were entirely different.

The Kyōgen actors appeared not only in independent plays but also as narrators of the ai. Often the waki, after a tantalizing conversation with the mysterious shite of the first scene, asks a "man of the place" what he knows of the person he has encountered. The man, usually after making a modest disclaimer of any special information, thereupon launches into a lengthy account of a famous battle or of a woman deserted by her lover or of the unusual custom observed in a certain village. Although the narration of the "man of the place" is delivered by a Kyōgen actor, it is not in the least comic; perhaps these speeches reflect the eloquence, rather than the humor, of the early Kyōgen performers. Kyōgen actors also take minor (but occasionally fairly important) parts within a Nō play; in such instances, too, there is normally no display of humor, but in a few late plays the ai contributes to the dramatic interest of the whole, including elements of humor.

Zeami on Kyōgen

It is not clear from existing documents which of these functions of the Kyōgen actor was the oldest,[129] but the two arts—Nō and Kyōgen—developed in close relationship from the fifteenth century on. Zeami had relatively little to say about Kyōgen in his various treatises, but he devoted one section of *Shūdōsho* (Learning the Way) to the Kyōgen actors:

> The functions of *kyōgen* actors: it is well known that their method of creating amusement for the audiences in the form of a comic interlude involves the use either of some impromptu materials chosen at the moment, or of some interesting incidents taken from old stories. On the other hand, when these actors take part in an actual *nō* play, their function does not involve any need to amuse the audience. Rather, they are to explain the circumstances and the plot of the play that the audience is in the process of witnessing.[130]

Zeami reveals in these words that impromptu materials formed a basic part of the dialogue and actions of the Kyōgen plays. However, we may suppose that lines or scenes in Kyōgen that had proved effective with audiences were retained in future performances of the same skits, and gradually the purely extemporaneous elements of the plays diminished until nowadays every inflection of the voice and every bodily movement is prescribed. The "interesting incidents from the old stories" probably refers to humorous anecdotes that had by Zeami's time become standard parts of the repertory of the Kyōgen actors.

The Texts of Kyōgen

The oldest texts of Kyōgen are the some 240 plays set down in 1642 by Ōkura Yaemon Toraaki (1597–1662), who was also the first Kyōgen actor to relate, in the manner of Zeami, his theories on the art of Kyōgen.[131] The Toraaki texts were antedated by a volume of summaries of Kyōgen made in the late sixteenth century.[132] The summaries (of 104 plays) range from four or five lines to about twenty lines each. Only the bare outlines, key phrases, and songs are given, evidence that the dialogue was largely improvised. The numerous kana misspellings and mistaken characters indicate that the writer was badly educated. The plays themselves, thus rendered, are likely to baffle a modern reader. For example, the well-known *Busu* is summarized in this manner:

> A priest comes forward and summons two men. He says he is going somewhere and leaves them to look after the place. In the back room there is some *busu* (poison). He tells them that if they open it to have a look it will kill them. They say they understand. The two men are curious and take a look. They eat up all the sugar. Then they tear up an inscribed painting and break a *temmoku* tea bowl. They weep. The priest comes and, seeing them, asks what has happened. Dialogue. We ate one mouthful and still we did not die. We ate two mouthfuls and we still didn't die. Three mouthfuls, four mouthfuls, five mouthfuls, six mouthfuls—even after we'd licked and ate a whole ten mouthfuls, we still couldn't die. Marvellous! Final stamping of the feet.[133]

It is hard to imagine from this account that *Busu* is one of the masterpieces of the Kyōgen repertory. Only if one knows how the play is performed today can one understand why, for example, the two men destroy the painting and the bowl; but their action, together with the description of the number of mouthfuls of sugar the men ate, forms the core around which the play was created. *Busu*, in its present version, tells how a man, about to go on a journey, leaves his two servants, Tarōkaja and Jirōkaja, in charge of his house. He warns them that there is some busu, a deadly poison, in the backroom, and urges them to stay as far away from it as possible. Even if the wind blowing from its direction touches them it will kill them. Once the master has left, the servants decide to have a look at the busu, despite the danger. They fan vigorously from their side so that the wind will not strike them. When they at last uncover the busu, Tarōkaja is seized with a longing to eat it. Jirōkaja tries in vain to stop him. Tarōkaja then discovers that the busu is in fact sugar, and the two men eat it all up. Now they must face the wrath of the master. Tarōkaja tells Jirōkaja to tear up the painting in the alcove. Jirōkaja complies, then the two men join to smash the master's treasured bowl. The master returns and finds the men weeping. Tarōkaja relates that, to pass the time while waiting for the master's return, he and Jirōkaja wrestled. In the course of their wrestling, the painting and the bowl were accidentally destroyed. They decided to commit suicide by eating the busu, but strangely enough, they did not die.[134]

The effectiveness of *Busu* in performance depends largely on the skill of the actors in conveying curiosity and fear as they approach the mysterious cask of busu, in their manner of greedily devouring the sugar, in Tarōkaja's ingenious scheme for justifying their actions, and finally, in the prolonged account of their fruitless efforts to kill themselves by taking one mouthful after another of the deadly poison. Unlike most Kyōgen plays, however, the success of *Busu* does not depend solely on the skill of the actors. The story itself was deemed sufficiently interesting for it to appear in later collections of anecdotes, and many people know it even if they have never seen a performance of Kyōgen.

It would be idle to pretend, however, that this (or any other Kyōgen play), for all its interest as a story or for all the opportunities it provides for master actors to display their comic gifts, is of the quality of one of the great Nō plays, in the manner that *As You Like It* might be said to be worthy of comparison with one of Shakespeare's tragedies. The language of the Kyōgen plays falls agreeably on the ears, as delivered by the actors in rhythmic patterns with ringing voices and clear enunciation, and the copula verb *gozaru* that ends many sentences gives a distinctive tone to the language as a whole. The words themselves, however, are ordinary. One of the pleasures of Kyōgen, in fact, is to hear an essentially uninteresting line, delivered first in the pompous tones of the master, and then (perhaps in the form of a question) in the humble accents of his servant. There is pleasure even in the stereotyped phrase with which most Kyōgen conclude—*yarumai zo, yarumai zo* (You won't get away with it!).

The Language of Kyōgen

The contrast between the language of Nō and that of Kyōgen is emphasized by the delivery. The Nō actor, even when he is not wearing a mask (which naturally interferes with the clarity of his words), speaks or sings in a muffled voice that makes it extremely difficult for those who do not already know the texts or who are not looking at a text before them to understand the poetry. In Kyōgen not a syllable is slurred or prolonged for musical effect. A few archaisms, as the sound change of such words as *itashite* to *itaite*, present problems of comprehension at first, but a Kyōgen audience has no need to look at a libretto while watching a performance.

Scholars of recent years who have annotated texts of Kyōgen frequently make use of the Japanese-Portuguese dictionary of 1603. This dictionary is a priceless source of information on the pronunciation of words and their meanings at the end of the sixteenth century—in general, the period when Kyōgen achieved maturity, as we know from the Tenshō texts. But probably the language of the plays as they are now performed is closer to that of the late seventeenth century, the time of the Toraaki texts, or even later. As long as improvisation was a feature of the performances, it was natural that the language change with different actors and certainly with the passage of time. The Nō texts were printed and used in instruction from the early seventeenth century, but Kyōgen (until recent years, in any case) continued to be taught orally, with the teacher pronouncing one sentence again and again until the pupil could repeat it with exactly the same inflections. Small differences can be detected in the wording even of actors of the same school, and when it comes to the texts used by the three schools of Kyōgen—Ōkura, Izumi, and Sagi—the differences are enormous.

The Humor of Kyōgen

It seems likely that many of the early Kyōgen plays were parodies of the tragedies they followed, rather in the manner of the Italian theater of the eighteenth century.[135] Very few of the Kyōgen that are currently performed are parodies, but *Esashi Jūō* (The Bird Catcher in Hades) clearly satirizes the Nō *Utō* (Birds of Sorrow). In the Nō play a hunter is tormented in hell for having slaughtered many birds; in the Kyōgen a bird catcher, who is about to be punished in hell for his taking of life, offers some roasted birds to the king of hell, who finds them so delicious he sends the bird catcher back to earth to catch more birds.[136] *Tsūen* is a parody of the Nō play *Yorimasa*, not only in the plot but in the musical accompaniment. But parodies of Nō no longer form a prominent element in the Kyōgen repertory.

The humor of Kyōgen depends much less on parody than on the contest of wills between master and servant, husband and wife, priest and layman. Since the Kyōgen are comedies, we can be fairly sure that in disputes between servant and master, the servant will somehow gain the upper hand; it would not be much of a comedy if a play concluded with the master righteously punishing an impudent servant. This point is often overlooked by critics who detect in the Kyōgen plays the voices of the common people protesting against the despotic acts of their masters. No doubt commoners in the audience felt satisfaction when the typical daimyo of a Kyōgen play was discomfited, as commoners in France were pleased by the cleverness of the servants in a comedy by Molière. But this does not explain why aristocrats in the audience not only permitted but enjoyed plays that portrayed the ruling class so unattractively. Just as the Parisian aristocracy was unlikely to feel class solidarity with the foolish *petit marquis* of a Molière farce and could laugh at his pretensions and countrified ways, the audience at the shogun's court could laugh at the rustic daimyo who wished to compose renga or who was in such financial straits that he had to send his servant to cadge sake from a merchant. The rulers of Japan certainly did not feel threatened by the irreverent attitudes displayed by Tarōkaja, the clever servant, toward his ill-tempered, pretentious, or simply foolish master.[137]

Some Kyōgen plays overstepped the limits of acceptable satire and were quickly dropped, but the main thrust of censorship during the Tokugawa period, when Kyōgen, along with Nō, was afforded official protection and encouragement, was against indecency.[138] In comparison with European farces, the humor of Kyōgen is surprisingly free of risqué, let alone salacious, elements. The samurai evidently found it easier to tolerate humor directed at their class than erotic representation.

Another element found in European farces that is almost entirely missing from Kyōgen is the comic foreigner or, for that matter, the person from the country who speaks a peculiar dialect. *Tō-zumō* (Wrestling in China) is one of only two or three plays in the repertory that has foreigners in the cast. This play tells of a Japanese wrestler who travels to China where he takes on members of the court, including the emperor, in bouts of wrestling. Naturally, he is victorious in every instance. The humor of this play is partly in the outlandish costumes worn by the actors performing as the Chinese characters, but mainly in the weird noises that they utter in place of human speech. It is surprising that greater use was not made of this familiar feature of farce in other countries, but no doubt this was because the Japanese had so little experience of foreigners. As for regional accents, there is no attempt in Kyōgen (or, naturally, in Nō) to suggest that people from the Tōhoku region or from Kyūshū speak differently from those in the capital, though it would have been easy to make fun of rustic pronunciation.

If people in the capital differ from those in the hinterland it is in their citified cunning. In *Suehirogari* (The Fan), a pompous daimyo sends his servant Tarōkaja to the capital to buy for him an especially good fan to celebrate the New Year. Instead of using an ordinary word for "fan," however, he tells Tarōkaja to buy a *suehirogari*, meaning literally, "spreading out at the end," a descriptive word for a folding fan but also a felicitous term suggesting greater and greater good fortune. He gives varous specifications for the fan he wants—the number of ribs, the kind of paper, the design, and so on. Tarōkaja, who has no idea what a suehirogari might be, goes to the capital where a clever shopkeeper sells him an umbrella that corresponds in every particular with the requirements of the daimyo. When Tarōkaja returns with an umbrella instead of a fan, his master is at first furious, but the man who sold the umbrella taught Tarōkaja an infectious ditty that he guaranteed would improve the master's humor if ever he became out of sorts. Sure enough, the song cheers the enraged daimyo and in the end he and Tarōkaja join in a happy song and dance. The humorous situation is created not because *suehirogari* is a dialectal expression, but because it is a foolish affectation. The city man takes advantage of the ignorance of the man from the country, but he also provides him with the means of restoring the master's humor.

The Categories of Kyōgen

Suehirogari is an example of a *waki kyōgen*: that is, a Kyōgen of a felicitous nature with a happy ending which corresponds to the *waki nō*, the most dignified and felicitous part of the Nō repertory. The Kyōgen repertory is generally divided into eleven categories, their content varying slightly according to the school:[139] in addition to the waki kyōgen, there are plays about daimyos, *shōmyō*,[140] sons-in-law, women, devils, *yamabushi*, priests, blind men, miscellaneous subjects, and secret works.[141] These categories do not necessarily convey the contents of the plays. For example, the central figure in the shōmyō plays is generally not the pompous samurai but Tarōkaja, his servant. Little distinguishes the character of one Tarōkaja from another, though sometimes (as in *Suehirogari*) he does not display the quick-wittedness we expect of him.

Plays about women almost always portray them unfavorably, as termagants who (sometimes with just cause) make their husbands miserable with their complaints and jealousy. The actors who play the parts of women often seem to have been chosen for their burliness and aggressively masculine faces. Masks are worn to *increase* the ugliness of the features, and the only touches of femininity are the costumes and a towel wrapped around the actor's head in an approximation of a woman's hairdo. The most common exclamation of the woman is probably *haradachi ya*—"I am furious!"

Priests do not fare much better than women in the Kyōgen devoted to them. In *Shūron* (A Theological Dispute) two priests, one of the Nichiren and the other of the Jōdo sect, returning to the capital from pilgrimages to sites holy to their two sects, accidentally meet on the road. At first each is delighted to have a companion on the journey, but when they discover they belong to hostile sects, each expresses, at first in polite language, his aversion for the other's beliefs and his disinclination to continue traveling together. The Nichiren priest declares his convictions with the vehemence characteristic of his sect, but when they reach an inn, the more sophisticated Jōdo priest, secretly pleased to have such an interesting companion (who makes the journey seem shorter), requests one room for both of them. The enraged Nichiren priest demands separate rooms, but finally consents to spend the night in a theological dispute. Their disagreement moves from proclamations of the tenets of their sects to name-calling, and in the concluding scene each dances, shouting all the while the ritual formula of his sect—*Rengekyō*! or *Namōda*![142] At the end, the dancing and the chanting become so heated that each man gets confused and unwittingly calls out the invocation of the wrong sect. When they realize what has happened, they laugh, and recall that there is scriptural evidence for believing that the two sects are not, after all, incompatible.

This is perhaps the most attractive Kyōgen about priests. Another variety of priest, the *yamabushi*, famed for their magical spells, are often treated as braggarts and impostors, whose pretenses are comically exposed. But the attacks are not ill-tempered or even serious, any more than those against women. Perhaps women and priests were so frequently made the butts of the humor of Kyōgen because everybody realized that, for all their faults, the world could not exist without them.

Shintō gods and even devils also appear in the plays, treating the human beings with easy familiarity, sometimes even giving them presents. There is none of the awe that surrounds such divinities in the Nō plays.

The humor in Kyōgen is sometimes touched with pathos. This is true particularly of the plays about *zatō* (blind men). In *Tsukimi Zatō* (The Blind Man Views the Moon), for example, a blind man, attracted by the sounds of autumnal insects, goes out into the fields to enjoy the moonlight, even though he cannot see it. A man from the capital joins the blind man, and the two sing and dance together under the moon, the blind man somehow sensing the moonlight. The man from the capital goes off, only to be struck by a sudden impulse to torment the blind man. He returns, knocks down the blind man, and beats him with his stick. After he has left, the blind man, groping for the stick, reflects on the differences between people—some are as kind as the man with whom he sang, others are as cruel as his assailant. The play ends not in the usual manner, with one man chasing off another, nor with a stamping of the feet, but with a sneeze, traditional in plays with a bittersweet ending.

A few of the plays contain so little humor that they hardly seem to belong in the Kyōgen repertory.[143] In others, like *Buaku*, one of the daimyo plays, the humor of the ending is insufficient to make us forget the chillingly unhumorous events earlier on. In this play a daimyo commands his servant Tarōkaja to kill another servant, Buaku, because he is lazy and escapes work by pretending to be ill. Tarōkaja protests this harsh punishment, but the daimyo is implacable, and Tarōkaja has no choice. The daimyo lends his sword to Tarōkaja, who finds Buaku. But when he unsheathes the sword, he realizes he is unable to kill the helpless Buaku, and allows him to escape. He informs the daimyo that his command has been carried out. By accident, however, the daimyo sees Buaku at the Kiyomizu Temple, where he has gone to thank Buddha for his escape. With Tarōkaja's connivance, Buaku pretends to be a ghost, and frightens the daimyo by telling him that he has met the daimyo's father in hell, and that the father has ordered the daimyo to accompany Buaku to the land of the dead. The daimyo beats a retreat. The play ends more or less cheerfully with Buaku, grateful to Tarōkaja for the narrow escape, preparing to run away; but it is hard to forget the malevolence of the daimyo for whom the taking of a man's life is of so little consequence that he can ask his servant to do it.[144]

Few of the plays contain the darkness or the complexity of *Buaku*. It demands great skill on the part of all three actors, but *Buaku* is not one of the plays that the actors themselves rank at the top of their repertory. *Hanago* is traditionally considered to be the summit of Kyōgen, the supreme test of a master actor,[145] but it is in the nature of a farce, so much enjoyed by audiences that it is frequently played on the Kabuki stage as well.[146] Obviously, the difficulties of performing roles in Kyōgen can be appreciated fully only by a professional actor, but as literature *Buaku* leaves a deeper impression than any other Kyōgen play.

The Schools of Kyōgen

As late as the middle of the Meiji period there were three schools of Kyōgen. Each had an impressive pedigree dating back to the foundations of the art. The Ōkura school, for example, traced its origins to Gen'e. The Sagi school, which ceased to exist after the death of its last *iemoto* (head of the school) in 1895, boasted an impressive genealogy that went back to the beginning of the Muromachi period, though it seems likely that the first five iemoto were "invented" at the beginning of the seventeenth century.[147] The Izumi school similarly traced its founding back to the time of the shogun Ashikaga Yoshimasa at the end of the fifteenth century, but the first historically verifiable iemoto probably lived toward the end of the sixteenth century.[148]

The Ōkura and Sagi schools both served the Tokugawa shogunate and had their "headquarters" in Edo; but the Izumi school, which now ranks with the Ōkura school, was in the service of the Owari and Kaga clans, and therefore of lesser importance. However, only the Izumi school enjoyed the privilege of appearing at the Imperial Palace in Kyoto, presumably because the "semiprofessional" status of the actors seemed preferable to out-and-out professionals.[149]

The fact that there were three schools of Kyōgen, each with its own texts, is of greater importance to the scholar of the literature of the Japanese theater than the five schools of Nō.[150] The contrast between the Ōkura and Izumi schools is not confined to the wording: the rhythms of the delivery are dissimilar, and sometimes the effect produced on the audience by a given play may differ because the emphasis is on different sections of the text. One finds everywhere lingering examples of the improvised nature of the dialogue in the past when the actors freely altered or augmented the bare outlines of the plays given in the Tenshō texts. The versions taught by the three schools were not printed until the Meiji era, by which time the differences had come to be emphasized as an important part of the traditions of each school. There are records from the seventeenth century of actors of different schools appearing together in the same play, but this would be difficult today, unless many compromises were made.

The Kyōgen plays provide invaluable glimpses of the society of Japan in the sixteenth and early seventeenth centuries and the humor, though perhaps less evident to the reader than to the spectator, rings true often enough to excite our smiles across time and great distance.

Notes

1. The earliest plays of literary interest, those by Kannami, were written a full five hundred years after the *Man'yōshū*.
2. Thomas Blenman Hare's *Zeami Style* is an excellent example of this approach, inspired in the first instance by the work of Yokomichi Mario on the *shōdan*, the basic unit of Nō texts and performance.

   The music of Nō itself was derived from various sources, including the Buddhist chants known as *shōmyō* and the "party songs" (*enkyoku*) of the medieval period. *Gagaku* music was also used in several of the plays. For further treatment of this subject, see Yokomichi Mario, *Nōgeki no Kenkyū*, pp. 255–90.
3. Similarities between the Greek tragedies and Nō, noted for many years, have been discussed with authority by Mae J. Smethurst in *The Artistry of Aeschylus and Zeami*. She mentions in the introduction to her book (p. 3), "There is no question, for example, that early productions of both nō and Greek tragedy involved outdoor theaters, small all-male casts of actors, choruses, instrumentalists, masks, dancing, and other strikingly similar features." Her study of the Nō plays gives great importance to the structural elements of the songs, much in the manner of Hare's *Zeami's Style.*

   The difference in the appreciation of Greek tragedies and Nō (the latter being rarely considered as literature) is discussed by Tashiro Keiichirō in *Yōkyoku wo Yomu*, pp. 3–5.
4. Readers who are interested in the musical and choreographic aspects of Nō should consult the works mentioned in notes 2 and 3. I should like to recommend in addition the books by Monica Bethe and Karen Brazell, *Dance in the Nō Theatre* and *Nō as Performance: An Analysis of the Kuse Scene of "Yamamba."* Yokomichi Mario's pioneering work on the shōdan has been presented by Frank Hoff and Willi Flindt in *The Life Structure of Noh.* There are many descriptions in Japanese of the performance of the Nō plays, some of which are listed in the Bibliography. For a study of another aspect of the Nō theater, the audiences, Jacob Raz's *Audience and Actors* should be consulted.

As far as the texts themselves are concerned, each of the five schools of *shite* (Kanze, Hōshō, Komparu, Kongō, and Kita) has its own version of the plays. The textual differences occur chiefly in the spoken parts; the sung parts—the poetry—are more or less the same from school to school. The repertories of the five schools are not identical. The Kanze school has the most extensive repertory and, because this is also the school with the greatest popularity, the Kanze texts are generally used in the standard collections of Japanese literature. The texts of the Komparu school are the fewest in number, but they are considered to be the oldest by some scholars; for this reason the Komparu texts were chosen by the editors of the Nihon Koten Bungaku Zensho series. Naturally, each school is convinced that its texts are the most authentic. The matter is further complicated by the existence of still other texts used by the *waki* actors of the Shimogakari Hōshō, Takayasu, and Fukuō schools. In performance, the waki usually yields to the shite's text in exchanges of dialogue, but follows the text of his own school at other places in the plays.

5. Noma Seiroku, *Nihon Kamen Shi*, p. 84.
6. P. G. O'Neill, *Early Nō Drama, Its Background, Character, and Development*, p. 2.
7. The samai included dances from India, the Champa kingdom of Indochina, and even Bali. The umai included dances not only from the three kingdoms of Korea but from the country of Po-hai in the region of Manchuria. See Gunji Masakatsu, *Kabuki Nyūmon*, pp. 36–37. Our knowledge of the variety of these dances comes mainly from such legal works as *Ryō no Gige* (833) in which regulations for performers were set forth.
8. For brief accounts of the various pieces performed by the bugaku dancers, see Jingū Shichō Gagaku Shūbu (ed.), *Bugaku Kaisetsu*, pp. 7–34. This work states (p. 6) that about thirty samai dances and over twenty umai are still performed.
9. Also read as *shinka*.
10. The picture is reproduced in Shigematsu Akihisa (ed.), *Shin Sarugakki, Unshū Shōsoku*, p. 28. It appeared originally in *Shinzei Kogaku-zu*, a book of pictures of bugaku probably compiled toward the end of the Heian period. The picture shows three women, one climbing up the rope to a horizontally stretched section, a second on the horizontal rope, and the third descending the rope on the other side. All three are juggling, but it is not clear whether these are three different women or one woman at three different stages of a performance.
11. See above, pp. 349–50, for an account of this work.
12. Shigematsu, *Shin*, p. 8. It is difficult to tell from the cryptic descriptions of the contents what these playlets were about. Shigematsu, pp. 10–11, bravely attempts to explicate. One of the easier to understand themes is: "The nun Myōkō begs for diapers," no doubt meaning that she had broken her vow of chastity and given birth to a baby.

13. See Moriya Takeshi, *Chūsei Geinō no Genzō*, pp. 17–24.
14. This was, for example, the opinion of Hara Katsurō, expressed in his well-known *Nihon Chūsei Shi* (1906). He believed that the riots marked the beginning of the transition from antiquity to the middle ages. See Moriya, *Chūsei*, p. 7.
15. See chapter 23, note 28. See also, for example, the account in Book V of the *Taiheiki*, "On the Indulgence of the Lay Priest of Sagami in Dengaku and Dogfights." (Yamashita Hiroaki, *Taiheiki*, I, pp. 212–16.)
16. These recollections are given in *Sarugaku Dangi*, his conversations with his son Motoyoshi about the art of Nō. Text in Omote Akira and Katō Shūichi, *Zeami, Zenchiku*, pp. 261–62. Omote and Katō point out (pp. 498–99) that "twelve" was a slip of memory: Zeami was actually thirteen by Japanese reckoning (though twelve by Western reckoning). See Hare, *Zeami's Style*. p. 20.
17. For the authorship of *Matsukaze*, see Itō Masayoshi, *Yōkyoku Shū*, III, pp. 483–85. He discusses the possibility that Kiami's play *Shiokumi* was the original version of *Matsukaze*, and concedes that Zeami probably followed its general outlines; however, he concludes by expressing agreement with the view advanced by Kōsai Tsutomu that although the characters and the language owed much to Kiami's play, *Matsukaze* should be considered as an entirely new creation of Zeami. (See Kōsai Tsutomu, *Nōgaku Shinkō*, p. 129.) Other plays by Zeami, such as *Aridōshi*, are believed to have been much indebted to Kiami, especially for the music. See Itō, *Yōkyoku Shū*, I, p. 403.
18. The final *n* in certain loanwords from the Chinese (such as the *san* in *sangaku*) was changed to *-ru, -mu,* or *-bu*. *Sarugaku* came to be understood as meaning "monkey" (*saru*) music.
19. The nature of the differences between dengaku and sarugaku is by no means clear; but presumably sarugaku included more of the acrobatics, juggling, and so on of sangaku.
20. I shall use the term *ennen* throughout, but Japanese scholars often distinguish *ennen nō, ennen furyū*, and *ennen geinō*. See Ueki Yukinobu, "Nō Keiseizen no Sarugaku," p. 1, for the three terms on one page. It is hard to find a description of the differences that separated the three. The best short description of ennen I have found is the one by Frank Hoff in *Kodansha Encyclopedia of Japan*, II, pp. 218–19.
21. This tradition survives in the ennen performed at Mōtsu-ji, notably in the dances "Hana-ori" and "Kara-byōshi."
22. For a concise discussion of the issues involved, see Amano Fumio, "Ennen Furyū," in Geinōshi Kenkyūkai, *Nihon Geinōshi*, II, pp. 234–36. See also Kitagawa Tadahiko, *Kannami no Geiryū*, pp. 154–60. Kitagawa stated his belief (p. 160) that the close relations between ennen furyū and *waki nō* was an established fact, and gave compelling evidence to prove this.
23. See O'Neill, *Early*, pp. 99–100. Ennen texts, usually in stiff Chinese, did

not lend themselves readily to dramatic performances. (See Nose Asaji, *Nōgaku Genryū Kō*, p. 380. See also Nose, *Nōgaku*, pp. 420ff, for a discussion of the reciprocal relations of the *kaikō* in ennen and Nō.) The kaikō, literally "opening the mouth," was the opening section of an ennen performance, which began with an auspicious description of events in China, followed by a lighter passage in which word-play (*shūku*) was a prominent feature. The waki nō took over the general tone of the ennen description, but usually shifted the scene and the materials to Japan. Word-play, usually not for humorous purposes, became characteristic of the Nō texts.

24. The word is also pronounced *jushi* or *zushi*, and sometimes referred to as *noronji*. It originally designated priests who recited *darani* and worked spells, but later came to refer to priests who performed songs and dances after the conclusion of religious services with the intention of making the meaning of the magical rites more intelligible to worshipers. Even in the early days of songs and dances by shushi the performers wore splendid costumes, as we know from a comment made by Fujiwara no Michizane, recorded in *Ōkagami*. (See Helen Craig McCullough, *Ōkagami*, p. 211.) The best-known element of the performances was the *hashiri*, a rapid and energetic circumabulation of the main altar by priests carrrying swords and bells.

25. The three roles were equated with the Buddha, Monju (Manjusri), and Miroku (Maitreya) respectively in a document dated 1126. If this document is genuine, it contains the oldest known reference to *Okina;* but various authorities have insisted it is a forgery. The oldest indisputable reference to *Okina* occurs in a document dated 1283 that relates how priests of the Kōfuku-ji in Nara performed a series of dances including those of the three old men. See Yamaji Kōzō, *Okina no Za*, pp. 144–46.

26. *Ibid.*, p. 146. The source of this information is a document of 1349 describing the dances at the Wakamiya Festival of the Kasuga Shrine in Nara. On this occasion shrine priestesses (miko) performed two sarugaku nō and shrine officials (*negi*) performed two dengaku nō. *Okina* was danced by the miko in the order of Tsuyu-harai, Okina, Samban Sarugaku, Kajakō, Chichi-no-jō.

27. See Nose, *Nōgaku*, pp. 164–70.

28. For imayō see above, pp. 777–78. The sixty extant saibara, translated as "horse-readying music," are briefly discussed by Robert H. Brower and Earl Miner in *Japanese Court Poetry*, p. 510. The texts are found in Tsuchihashi Yutaka and Konishi Jin'ichi, *Kodai Kayōshū*, pp. 380–415. Konishi elsewhere (in his *History of Japanese Literature*, I, pp. 268–69), wrote of the *Ōuta*, or great songs of the court, "The saibara are a somewhat older group, dating in general from the eighth century, and containing a considerable number of works believed to come from the seventh century." He notes (p. 269, n. 5) that a reference in the *Sandai Jitsuroku* for 23-X-859 records that Princess Hiroi was skilled in saibara, suggesting that

saibara music had come into being by the beginning of the ninth century at the latest.

29. Photographs of a performance of *Okina* are given in my *Nō: the Classical Theatre of Japan*, pp. 93–98.
30. Nose, *Nōgaku*, p. 184.
31. The question of which plays of Kannami are "characteristic" will be discussed below; I refer here to such plays as *Jinen Koji, Yoshino Shizuka,* and *Kayoi Komachi*, which have a lively dramatic quality. See Kitagawa, *Kannami*, p. 49. Authorship of *Kayoi Komachi* is unclear; although Zeami himself attributed it to Kannami, he noted that Kannami had revised an existing play by the *shōdō* (proselytizing) monks of Mount Hiei that had already been performed by Komparu Gon-no-kami at Tōnomine. Kannami's revised version was in turn revised by Zeami. See Itō, *Yōkyoku Shū*, pp. 431–32; also Omote and Katō, *Zeami*, p. 291, and the translation by J. Thomas Rimer and Yamazaki Masakazu, *On the Art of the Nō Drama*, p. 222.
32. See Kitagawa Tadahiko, "Yōkyoku Kyōgen to Setsuwa Bungaku," pp. 155–60. Kitagawa emphasized the importance of the setsuwa element.
33. The name is also read Kan'ami, and he is also sometimes referred to by his full name, Kanze Kan'ami Kiyotsugu. Other dates have been proposed for his birth and death.
34. In Zeami's time the writing of the word *saru* was changed from the unflattering ideograph for "monkey" to one which, though pronounced *saru* when used as one of the twelve signs of the zodiac, normally meant "to speak reverently."
35. For an account in English of the kuse and the *kusemai* which preceded it, see O'Neill, *Early*, pp. 42–52. Although Kannami invented the kuse, most of the plays attributed to him lack a kuse section, and it was not until Zeami's time that inclusion of a kuse became regular. Only nine of the plays attributed to Zeami lack a kuse section. See Kitagawa, *Kannami*, p. 122, 124.
36. Kannami himself founded the Yūzaki troupe, which developed into the Kanze school. Three other troupes, active at that time, survive to this day: Tobi (or Tohi), Emai, and Sakato, the ancestors of the Hōshō, Komparu, and Kongō schools respectively. The fifth school of Nō, Kita, was not founded until the sixteenth century.
37. These were the celebrated texts printed from movable types by Honnami Kōetsu (1558–1637).
38. For example, we know from evidence in Zeami's works that the *rongi* section of *Kayoi Komachi*, a highly involved passage in which Komachi describes the flowers and fruits she carries with her, was added by Zeami.
39. It was argued by Nogami Toyoichirō, a specialist in Nō drama (and in European literature) that the shite is the *only* person of importance in a Nō play. In general this is true, but there are obvious exceptions, especially

in the plays of Kannami, Miyamasu, and the later Nō dramatists. But even among Zeami's works, there is a conflict between the shite and the tsure in *Kiyotsune.* In some of the late Nō plays, such as *Tanikō* or *Chōryō*, the part of the shite is relatively insignificant when compared to that of the waki. Perhaps such plays were written by request of a waki actor who had become tired of being little more than "a man at the side" and wanted more attention.

40. One or more tsure may appear in a play. Normally, the role of the tsure is unimportant, but in some plays (such as *Kayoi Komachi*) there is a conflict between the shite and tsure, and in others (such as *Shunkan*) one or more tsure will contribute an essential element to a play.
41. The kokata plays the roles not only of children (whether boys or girls) but also of adults, notably in plays where there is a romantic interest involved. For example, in order to keep *Funa Benkei* from seeming unattractively mundane, the role of the hero Yoshitsune (who is accompanied by his mistress, Shizuka) is performed by a kokata; but in *Shōzon* it is Shizuka who is performed by a child. In both cases the intent is to preserve an element of unreality in the relationship between the lovers. In still other plays, where it might seem sacrilegious to have a mature actor take the role of an emperor, the role is played by a child.
42. The verb *sōrō* was a contraction of *saburau*, to serve. Although examples of the verb occur even in very early Heian texts, it was first used commonly in the late twelfth century, notably in *The Tale of the Heike.* From this time on it was often used by military men especially as a polite variant on the common verbs *aru* or *iru*, presumably because it was so much easier to use the one verb *sōrō* than the elaborate honorifics of the court. In the Nō plays female characters generally employ the original form *saburau*, but men use *sōrō*. Most of the utterances of the waki conclude with the prolonged, mournful vowels of *sōrō.* The verb *sōrō* continued to be used in formal letters until after 1945, when it disappeared in the postwar educational reforms.
43. This and other quotations from the text of *Jinen Koji* are taken from Itō, *Yōkyoku Shū*, II, pp. 131–42.
44. The kusemai section of a play is particularly free in its metrics because it follows closely the special melodic rhythms of the original accompaniment. See O'Neill, *Early*, pp. 42–52.
45. Ungo-ji and *kumoidera* (in the second line) have similar meanings; the former is in the Sino-Japanese and the latter in the pure Japanese pronunciation.
46. The ambiguity was increased by the frequent lack of a subject in a Japanese sentence; the meaning of an utterance varied, depending on how one interpreted the implied subject. This was true also of renga, a poetic art that undoubtedly affected the expression of Nō.
47. Needless to say, current performances do not depict this scene realistically.

48. The best description of the text of *Jinen Koji* and its modifications is given by Itō in *Yōkyoku Shū*, II, pp. 448–51. Itō treats the play as one originally composed by Kannami but modified by Zeami. He also gives documentary evidence concerning the historical Jinen Koji, the model of the character in the play, suggesting that Kannami took over the dances and musical instruments (the *sasara* and *kakko*) from the historical Jinen's performances. The texts of the play performed by the *kamigakari* schools (Kanze and Hōshō) differ considerably from those performed by the *shimogakari* schools (Komparu, Kongō, and Kita), the latter being closer to the original form of the play.
49. Zeami himself (in *Sarugaku Dangi*) credited to Kannami three plays, *Sotoba Komachi, Jinen Koji*, and *Kayoi Komachi.* See Omote and Katō, *Zeami*, p. 291. Translation in Rimer and Yamazaki, *On the Art*, p. 222.
50. See Yokomichi Mario and Omote Akira, *Yōkyoku Shū*, I, p. 81, where the arguments (and especially the puns) are said to be similar to those in the Kyōgen *Shūron*. Kitagawa (in *Kannami*, p. 245) makes the same comparison, and states that the questions and answers in *Sotoba Komachi* can be considered as belonging to the tradition of verbal play. Elsewhere in the same book (p. 63), Kitagawa expresses the opinion that the vivid colloquialisms were originally intended to be comic, though the manner of performance adopted since Zeami's time has obscured the comic intent.
51. See Kitagawa, *Kannami*, p. 21. Kitagawa (p. 113) cites seven characteristics of plays by Kannami, as enunciated by two earlier authorities of Nō, Kobayashi Shizuo and Nogami Toyoichirō: (1) they draw their materials from a world close to the spectators of the time; (2) they combine drama and elements of music and dance; (3) their structure is free; (4) there are few quotations of old poems; (5) they use colloquial language and contain traces of popular songs; (6) the dialogue is skillful; and (7) there is humor.
52. Translation by Sam Houston Brock in Donald Keene, *Anthology of Japanese Literature*, p. 268. Original text in Yokomichi and Omote, *Yōkyoku Shū*, I, p. 86.
53. Yokomichi and Omote, *Yōkyoku Shū*, I, p. 81.
54. In part, this is a quotation of a poem in *Tales of Ise.* Helen Craig McCullough translates this poem as: "The lady with thinnning hair— / But a year short / Of a hundred— / Must be longing for me, / For I seem to see her face." (McCullough, *Tales of Ise*, p. 110.) For original text, see Watanabe Minoru, *Ise Monogatari*, p. 76. The word *tsukumogami*, translated by Brock as "silted seaweed locks" and by McCullough as "thinning hair," is unclear. There is a variety of seaweed known as *tsukumo*, and this might refer to the old woman's unkempt locks. The word *tsukumo* is sometimes written with characters meaning "ninety-nine," Komachi's age. Watanabe prefers to think of the term as a kind of calligraphic pun: taking the character for "one" away from the character for "hundred"

leaves the character for "white," and the meaning is therefore "white hair."

55. Translation by Brock in Keene, *Anthology*, pp. 268–69. Text in Yokomichi and Omote, *Yōkyoku Shū*, I, pp. 86–87.
56. Translation by Brock in Keene, *Anthology*, p. 269. Text in Yokomichi and Omote, *Yōkyoku Shū*, I, p. 87.
57. Another example of madness resulting from possession by the spirit of another person is found in *Matsukaze*, attributed to Kannami. See Kitagawa, *Kannami*, p. 183.
58. Translation by Brock in Keene, *Anthology*, p. 270. The translation is free but captures the spirit of the original. "The sands of goodness" refers to a statement found in the Lotus Sutra and other works to the effect that by piling up small deeds of goodness one achieves union with the Buddha. The last lines are the repeated declaration of *satori no michi ni irō yo* (I shall enter the path of enlightenment!). Text in Yokomichi and Omote, *Yōkyoku Shū*, I, p. 88.
59. The four, according to Kitagawa (in *Kannami*, p. 112), are: *Furu, Sotoba Komoachi, Jinen Koji*, and *Kayoi Komachi*. However, Kannami is usually credited with such plays as *Kinsatsu*, *Yoshino Shizuka*, *Eguchi*, and *Motomezuka*, as well as with *Matsukaze*, a work that also bears the imprint of Zeami's revisions.
60. Translation by Rimer and Yamazaki in *On the Art*, p. 215. Text in Omote and Katō, *Zeami*, p. 287.
61. In works published before about 1950 the pronunciation of the name is usually given as Seami, but Zeami is now universally preferred. The pronunciation was determined in part by observing that three generations of Nō actors had the names *Kan'*ami (or Kannami), *Ze*ami, and *On'*ami, the first syllables of the three names spelling out Kanzeon. The date of Zeami's death has been disputed, some authorities preferring 1444. His full name was Zeami Motokiyo.
62. For an invaluable discussion of the problem of authorship of the Nō plays, see Konishi Jin'ichi, "New Approaches to the Study of the Nō Drama," especially pp. 5–7. For example, the play *Shōkun* is attributed to Zeami by *Nōhon Sakusha Chūmon, Kokayō Sakusha Kō,* and *Jikaden Shō*, but to Komparu Zenchiku by *Komparu Hachizaemon Kakiage* and *Nihyakujūban Utai Mokuroku;* but Konishi concludes that it is actually not by either dramatist.
63. Nogami Toyoichirō, *Zeami Motokiyo*, p. 71.
64. Hare, in *Zeami's Style*, pp. 44–47, lists "Works specifically identified as Zeami's," "Works that can be considered Zeami's," "Works revised by Zeami," and "Works of uncertain authorship." Some "works" are only songs and not plays, others have disappeared. There are fewer than forty works in Hare's first two categories. Surprisingly, several works that are indisputably by Zeami are not in the current repertory of any school,

perhaps because the music has been lost. Other works, though probably by Zeami, are rarely or even never performed, because they lack popularity with the performers and audiences.

65. See Konishi, "New Approaches," p. 8, for the changes that were made to the plays *Unrin'in* and *Yoroboshi*. In the latter play, for example, the original text had at least seven characters, though the version now performed has only three.

66. Ienaga Saburō in *Sarugaku Nō no Shisōshiteki Kōsatsu*, pp. 7–64, describes how alterations were made in the texts of various Nō plays during the "fifteen-year war" of the 1930s and 1940s in order to accord with the patriotic sentiments of the day.

67. For a succinct presentation of Yoshida's discovery, see Omote Akira, "Zeami to Zenchiku no Densho," in Omote and Katō, *Zeami*, pp. 549–50. Omote mentions (p. 549) a few copies of Zeami treatises made during the Tokugawa period and circulated among friends of the possessors of the manuscripts.

68. The date has been much debated ever since Omote Akira in 1963 proposed 1375 instead. He based this date on Zeami's statement that at the age of twelve (by Japanese count) he had seen Kiami perform in Nara, the same age as when he himself appeared at Imakumano. The only year he could have seen Kiami at the Kasuga Shrine was 1375; therefore, he must have been twelve in 1375, rather than 1374. However, Ijichi Tetsuo in 1967 published an extract from the diary *Fuchiki* of the Retired Emperor Sukō, which gives Zeami's age in 1378 as sixteen; this would make him twelve in 1374, the traditional date. In that case, Omote argued, Zeami must have made a mistake about his own age either about the time he performed in Imakumano or about the time he saw Kiami perform. Omote continued to believe that 1375 was correct for the Imakumano performance. See Omote and Katō, *Zeami*, pp. 498–99. The recent (1986) study, *Zeami* by Dōmoto Masaki, gives 1375 (p. 123).

69. Translation from my *Some Japanese Portraits*, p. 38. The original text is given on p. 211 of the same book. This extract is from *Gogumaiki*, the diary of Sanjō Kintada, which has entries from 1361 to 1383.

70. See Omote and Katō, *Zeami*, pp. 265, 287. Translation by Rimer and Yamazaki in *On the Art*, pp. 180 and 215. Zeami also stated that it was unlikely anyone in the future would write plays like his *Saigyō-zakura* and *Akoya no Matsu*. (Rimer, p. 214; Omote and Katō, p. 286.)

71. In Zeami's case the engo were not only conscious but gave an underlying unity to the text. The first person to mention this was W. B. Yeats in *Certain Noble Plays of Japan* (1915). See also my *Nō*, p. 54.

72. For a discussion of these and other stylistic features of the texts of Nō, see Smethurst, *The Artistry*, pp. 153–59 (with reference to a passage in *Matsukaze*) and pp. 166ff (with reference to *Sanemori*). The glossary in

Hare's *Zeami's Style* (pp. 291–300) provides definitions of such terms and explanations of their use.

73. See Kitagawa, *Kannami*, p. 221 where he speaks of the "isolation" of Zeami. He states (p. 220) that even Zeami's son Motomasa was in the tradition of Kannami, his grandfather, rather than of his father.
74. See Kitagawa, *Kannami*, p. 31.
75. It is known as the *waki nō*, from its position in a program "at the side" (*waki*) of *Okina*, the play traditionally performed at the opening of a series of plays.
76. Gotō Hajime in *Zoku Nōgaku no Kigen*, pp. 392–94, considered the various theories that have been offered concerning the *gobandate* of Nō. He concludes that at least the *idea* was known by 1512, though actual performances in keeping with the five categories probably do not antedate the Tokugawa period.
77. For an analysis of *Takasago*, see my *Nō*, pp. 55–57; also (at much greater length) Hare, *Zeami's Style*, pp. 69–103.
78. See Omote and Katō, *Zeami*, p. 90. In his treatise *Kakyō* (The Mirror Held to the Flower) Zeami wrote, "The sarugaku plays of the second category differ in character from the waki [first category] plays. They have a firm basis in an original source and give an impression of strength, but they should be performed in a graceful manner. Although they differ in character from the waki plays, they still are not elaborate, and this is not the point in the program to display the utmost techniques. For that reason these plays should retain in performance the atmosphere of the jo." Another translation by Rimer and Yamazaki in *On the Art*, pp. 83–84.

    See also William R. LaFleur, *The Karma of Words*, pp. 120–21, where in his discussion of the *rokudō* (the *gati* of the six-course system) he discusses why the *ashura* plays should appear second on the program even though in the basic paradigm they occupy the third slot, below that of the human. He writes, "First, as Paul Mus has shown, the location of the ashura in the sequence of gati is strikingly inexact in the texts of the tradition: some place it in the second position because the ashura are thought of as titans, brothers (though rivals) of the gods. In power they rank above human beings. Inasmuch as they are *warring* beings, however, they deserve rather less than great respect in a Buddhist system of values. Thus, if the plays about ashura seem somewhat anomalously placed in the nō progression, it is the reflection of a great deal of ambiguity and vacillation in the received tradition."
79. Translation by Hare in *Zeami's Style*, p. 185. Text (from *Fūshikaden*) in Omote and Katō, *Zeami*, p. 24. Another translation in Rimer and Yamazaki, *On the Art*, p. 15. The words translated as "poetry and music" are *kachō fūgetsu*, literally "flowers and birds, the wind and the moon," a familiar term for natural beauty but here used for the different arts.

80. Hare, *Zeami's Style*, p. 185.
81. See Itō, "Meikyoku Kaidai," in *Yōkyoku Shū*, I, p. 431.
82. The other two are the old person and the woman. For an extended discussion of the three roles see Hare, *Zeami's Style*, pp. 65–224.
83. Translation in Hare, *Zeami's Style*, p. 186. Text in Omote and Katō, *Zeami*, p. 138. Another translation in Rimer and Yamazaki, *On the Art*, p. 155. *Sandō* is sometimes called *Nōsakusho* (Book of Nō Composition).
84. Yamashita Hiroaki, in "Namboku-chō Dōranki no Bungaku—Gunki" (quoted in Kitagawa, *Kannami*, p. 198), expressed the belief that Zeami was urging dramatists of Nō to preserve the "aesthetic world" (*biteki sekai*) of *The Tale of the Heike*, not its language or structure. Zeami remained close to his source in *Sanemori*, but in other plays based on *The Tale of the Heike* he conspicuously departed from the original text.
85. Yashima was the scene of one of the three great battles of the Gempei War. The Minamoto under Yoshitsune were victorious. There is no suggestion in *The Tale of the Heike* that Yoshitsune agonized (as in the play) over being obliged to kill. His retrieval of a lost bow, an important part of the narration in *Yashima*, is described briefly in *The Tale of the Heike*: " 'Let it go,' the warriors urged, but he finally retrieved it and rode back to the shore laughing." (Translation by Helen Craig McCullough, *The Tale of the Heike*, p. 370.) The laughing Yoshitsune has no place in *Yashima*.
86. Translation from my *Nō*, p. 59.
87. It has also been suggested that *Matsukaze* should be considered the product of three generations of dramatists: Kiami (a master of dengaku), Kannami, and Zeami. For Kiami, see above, p. 1003. See also Kitagawa, *Kannami*, p. 166.
88. The verb *matsu* (to wait for) is the homonym of the noun *matsu* (the pine), providing the rare chance for a similar pun in English on "pine."
89. Translation by Royall Tyler in my *Twenty Plays of the Nō Theatre*, pp. 22–23.
90. A section (shōdan) of a play delivered in a manner resembling recitative in opera. Hare (*Zeami's Style*, p. 299) wrote of the sashi, "Because they have neither a strong underlying rhythm nor a melismatic melody, they are among the most readily intelligible shōdan in noh and are used when it is particularly important that the audience grasp the precise meaning of the text."
91. Text in Itō, *Yōkyoku Shū*, III, pp. 240–41.
92. Text in Ishida Jōji and Shimizu Yoshiko. *Genji Monogatari*, II, pp. 236–37. For a translation, see Edward Seidensticker, *The Tale of Genji*, I, p. 235.
93. In the sashi section of the play some lines are in irregular meter.
94. Translation by Tyler in my *Twenty Plays*, pp. 23–24. Text in Itō, *Yōkyoku Shū*, III, p. 242.
95. See Ishida and Shimizu, *Genji Monogatari*, II, p. 239, for text. Seidenstick-

er's translation (*Genji*, I, p. 237) is: "From offshore came the voices of fishermen raised in song. The barely visible boats were like little seafowl on an utterly lonely sea, and as he brushed away a tear induced by the splashing of oars and the calls of wild geese overhead, the white of his hand against the jet black of his rosary was enough to bring comfort to men who had left their families behind."

96. This is not quite the same thing as a kakekotoba, which changes in meaning when applied to what follows. Here the meaning remains the same, referring both to the small boats that are faintly visible in the offing and the faintly bright face of the moon.
97. See Itō, *Yōkyoku Shū*, III, p. 242, note 2.
98. Translation by Tyler in my *Twenty Plays*, p. 30; original in Itō, *Yōkyoku Shū*, III, p. 247.
99. *Kokinshū* 1023. Text in Okumura Tsuneya, *Kokin Waka Shū*, p. 351.
100. The lines in the original are: *Kazen ni chō mau / fumpun taru yuki / Ryūshō ni uguisu tobu / hempen taru kin.* (See Itō, *Yōkyoku Shū,* I, p. 265.
101. Ezra Pound, *The Translations of Ezra Pound*, p. 339.
102. Smethurst in *The Artistry,* pp. 153–58, analyzes the rongi section of *Matsukaze.* She concludes her discussion (p. 158) with: "I have pointed to the author's use of such features of Japanese poetic style as enken, kakekotoba (a kind of paronomasia), *ren'in* (alliteration), anaphora, repetition of words, engo (words associated in meaning), words contrasted in meaning, and joshi (preface), as well as more or less explicit allusions to other poetry."
103. The author is unknown, but there is a strong possibility that it was Komparu Zenchiku. See Itō, *Yōkyoku Shū*, III, p. 506.
104. See Tashiro, *Yōkyoku*, pp. 60–65, for a discussion of the *Hyakunijūkuhon* text, particularly with reference to the historical Taira no Munemori, who is the waki in the play. Tashiro quotes (pp. 62–63) the relevant section of the text.
105. Tashiro, in *Yōkyoku*, pp. 38–139, presents a detailed analysis of *Yuya* as literature.
106. *Ibid.*, p. 66.
107. The texts of Zenchiku's treatises (unfortunately, without any notes) are given by Omote and Katō in *Zeami.* Zenchiku's theories are discussed by Konishi Jin'ichi in *Nōgakuron Kenkyū*, especially pp. 240–71. For a brief study of Zenchiku's writings, see Benito Ortolani, "Zenchiku's Aesthetics of the Nō Theatre." Ortolani quotes the English translations made by Asaji Nobori in "Zenchiku's Philosophy of Noh Drama," included in *Hiroshima Bunkyō Joshi Daigaku Kenkyū Kiyō* (1960).
108. Translation by Tyler in my *Twenty Plays*, pp. 133–42.
109. Translation in Nippon Gakujutsu Shinkōkai, *Japanese Noh Drama*, I.
110. Translation by James A. O'Brien in my *Twenty Plays*, pp. 150–62.
111. The most detailed treatment of Miyamasu is found in Kitagawa, *Kan-*

nami, pp. 78–104. On pp. 88–89 he gives lists of thirty-five plays that have been attributed to Miyamasu. Kitagawa is ready to accept them all, in principle, as having been written by him.

112. There is a translation of the play in my *Twenty Plays*, pp. 241–51.

113. It is not always apparent why a play in which the shite is a demon is nevertheless considered to belong to the fourth category. This is true, for example, of *Dōjō-ji* and *Aoi no Ue*, described as *shūnenmono*, plays in which the shite's vindictive emotions provide the impetus for the drama. On the other hand, *Tanikō*, in which the demon has a minor (and benevolent) role, is considered to be of the fifth category. Obviously, the works were not designated by category by their original authors, and later men sometimes had difficulty in fitting them into the five categories.

114. Translated by Janine Beichman in my *Twenty Plays*, pp. 223–34, as "The Priest and the Willow."

115. In the plays *Shōzon* and *Chikatō* by Nagatoshi nine characters appear, and there are thirteen in his *Kasui*. *Chikatō* has four principal characters, each given a display scene in the manner of an Italian opera. *Kasui*, not currently performed, features many changes of scene and prodigies. See my *Nō*, p. 61. For texts, see Yokomichi and Omote, *Yōkyoku Shū*, II, pp. 195–225.

116. See below, pp. 1150–53.

117. I am thinking especially of Tashiro's *Yōkyoku*.

118. For a discussion of this term, see Etsuko Terasaki, "Wild Words and Specious Phrases: *Kyōgen Kigo* in the Nō Play *Jinen Koji*."

119. The term *kyōgen kigyo* occurs in a prose passage by Po Chü-i written in 840 at the Hsiang-shan Temple in Lo-yang. Several close friends had recently died, and he resolved to abandon the "wild words and fancy language" of poetry and henceforth to compose hymns in praise of the Buddha. The Japanese, believing that poetry also could serve to bring about illumination, did not renounce "wild words and fancy language." See Tachibana Hideki, *Haku Kyoi Kenkyū*, pp. 379–83. It is likely that the term entered the Japanese language by way of an excerpt from his prose that appears in *Wakan Rōei Shū* (selection 588). Kawaguchi Hisao's translation of the passage into modern Japanese can be rendered in English: "I have in this life composed worldly works of literature and committed the error of captivating others with my beautiful language. I earnestly hope to put an end to such sins and to turn my future literary activity to praise for the Buddhist Law, in the hope it may prove the impetus for explaining his truth." (Kawaguchi Hisao and Shida Nobuyoshi, *Wakan Rōei Shū, Ryōjin Hishō*, p. 200.)

Perhaps the earliest use of the term in Japanese writing is found in poem 222 of *Ryōjin Hishō*, which opens, "*Kyōgen kigyo no ayamachi wa . . .*" See *ibid.*, p. 383.

120. Sanari Kentarō. *Yōkyoku Taikan*, IV, p. 2170.

121. This was the theory of Kitagawa Tadahiko, first presented in his "Kyōgen Nō no Keisei," p. 16. He further expressed the belief that impromptu, humorous recitations were the source not only of the early Kyōgen but of early Nō and dengaku. (He gives on p. 21 a diagram of these relationships.)

   Rakugo are humorous monologues delivered with great expression by professional raconteurs that usually lead to an unexpected and amusing conclusion known as the *ochi* or *raku*. Raconteurs probably served the feudal lords of medieval Japan in much the manner that jesters served the courts of Europe. During the kinsei period they came to perform professionally before commoners as well. Anrakuan Sakuden (1554–1642) left a collection of over one thousand humorous stories. See *World Within Walls*, p. 154.

122. For calculations of the length of time needed to perform a Kyōgen in the early period, see Koyama Hiroshi et al., *Kyōgen no Sekai*, pp. 13–15. Basing his findings on the number of Nō and Kyōgen performed on a single day, he concuded that a Nō play took some thirty to fifty minutes and a Kyōgen "about fifteen minutes at the longest."

123. See Yonekura Toshiaki, *Warambegusa Kenkyū*, pp. 2, 6. A temple record mentions a Kyōgen play, *Yamabushi Seppō*.

124. This is the opinion of Taguchi Kazuo, presented in diagrammatic form in *Kyōgen Ronkō*, p. 147. He gives the scriptural text *(kyōten)* developing into setsuwa that in turn branch off into Kyōgen on the one hand and "old tales" (mukashibanashi) on the other. He believed that although it was commonly assumed that it was difficult to posit a direct connection between a setsuwa and a Kyōgen, quite a few Kyōgen in fact originated in this manner.

125. For example, *Busu*, one of the most popular works of the Kyōgen repertory, relates essentially the same story as an anecdote in *Shasekishū*, a setsuwa collection of the Kamakura period. For a translation, see Robert E. Morrell, *Sand and Pebbles*, p. 222. The original text is found in Watanabe Tsunaya, *Shasekishū*, p. 346; it is episode 11 in Book VIII of the work. Another variant of the story appears in *Ikkyū Kantō-banashi* (1672), a collection of tales about the witty priest Ikkyū. But Taguchi (*Kyōgen Ronkō*, pp. 146–47) thought it more likely that the Kyōgen was derived from a mukashibanashi than from *Shasekishū*. This view was shared by Kitagawa, expressed in "Yōkyoku Kyōgen," pp. 167–70. He believed that the play, originally about priests, was transformed because of the ending (inappropriate for a play about priests) into a daimyo play, and subsequently into a shōmyō play in order to give greater importance to the characters Tarōkaja and Jirōkaja.

126. This is the conclusion of Kitagawa Tadahiko and Yasuda Akira in *Kyōgen Shū*, p. 397. In 1721, the head (*iemoto*) of the Ōkura school presented to the shogunate a list of plays arranged by authors. He credited

fifty-nine plays to Gen'e and seventy-six to two men, Komparu Shirojirō and Uji Yatarō. Another twenty-three plays were listed as anonymous. Modern scholars are divided on the credibility of these attributions. For the lists and various opinions, see Matsumoto Kamematsu, *Kyōgen Rikugi no Kenkyū*, pp. 52–56.

127. Zeami mentions this in *Shūdōsho*. See translation by Rimer and Yamazaki, *On the Art*, pp. 170–71. Original text in Omote and Katō, *Zeami*, p. 239.
128. Kitagawa ("Kyōgen," p. 24) quotes from *Tadasugawara Kanjin Sarugaku*.
129. This was the opinion of, for example, Koyama Hiroshi, "Kyōgen no Koten," p. 264.
130. Translation from Rimer and Yamazaki, *On the Art*, p. 170. Text in Omote and Katō, *Zeami*, p. 239. The passage is difficult, and not all scholars are in agreement on the meaning of some phrases.
131. Toraaki's theories are contained in his *Warambegusa*, written between 1651 and 1660. They are exhaustively discussed by Yonekura in *Warambegusa Kenkyū*. The text consists partly of anecdotes about the great Kyōgen actors of the past, partly of recommendations on how to perform specific plays.
132. This book, first published in 1940, is known as *Tenshō Kyōgenbon* from the date, the sixth year of Tenshō (1578), found at the conclusion of the manuscript. However, doubts have been expressed about the authenticity of the date, which is in a different hand from the rest of the manuscript: it may have been added after the text (meaning that the text is earlier than 1578), or it may have been added in later years by the owner to lend prestige to a more recent text. See Nonomura Kaizō and Furukawa Hisashi, *Kyōgen Shū*, II, pp. 211–12. The entire text of *Tenshō Kyōgenbon* is given in this volume.
133. Nonomura and Furukawa, *Kyōgen*, II, p. 266.
134. This summary is based on the text given by Sasano Ken in *Nō Kyōgen*, II, pp. 118–25. The Toraaki text, given by Ikeda Hiroshi and Kitahara Yasuo in *Ōkura Toraaki-bon Kyōgen no Kenkyū*, I, pp. 270–72, is quite different in wording and much shorter, but it contains the essential elements, including the *"Hitokuchi kuedomo shinare mo sezu . . ."* passage found in the Tenshō summary.
135. See Vernon Lee, *Studies of the Eighteenth Century in Italy*, pp. 171–72, where she writes, "Metastasio wrote not only the tragic play itself but wrote also two little comic interludes, according to the illogical jumbling fashion which prevails whenever an art is adolescent. After the curtain had fallen upon the intensely tragic Dido upbraiding the stately and statuesque Aeneas, it rose upon Signorina Santa Marchesini, as a prima donna, quarrelling with the stage tailors about the length of her train, and interrupted by the arrival of a famous buffo as Nibbio, a ridiculous manager from the Canary Islands . . . [It was the] turning of everything into ridicule fearlessly, from the certainty that as soon as the tragedy

was resumed people would weep as much at the originals of the caricatures as they had laughed at the caricature itself."

136. For translations of both works, see my *Anthology*, pp. 271–85 and pp. 301–4. Taguchi (in *Kyōgen Ronkō*, p. 28) suggests that originally Kyōgen were "paired" with Nō plays and performed together.

137. Various explanations have been offered by Japanese scholars for the tolerance by the samurai class of the humor in Kyōgen. Yanagita Kunio (in *Teihon Yanagita Kunio Shū*, VII, pp. 245–47) attributed it to the fact that although as a class the samurai detested lying and underhanded acts, these were performed in Kyōgen not to conquer an enemy but to raise laughter, and there clearly was no malicious intent behind them. Taguchi (*Kyōgen Ronkō*, p. 25), accepting this theory, gave examples from *Zōdanshū*, an early fourteenth-century setsuwa collection, to show that satire directed at the upper classes was forgiven when the intent was humorous.

138. The play *Tsuratogi* (The Face Polisher), no longer in the repertory, apparently contained overt suggestions of sexual acts. Other indecent Kyōgen were probably never set down on paper and have therefore totally disappeared. See Taguchi, *Kyōgen Ronkō*, pp. 102–14.

139. For lists of the categories determined by the three schools (Ōkura, Izumi, and Sagi) see Matsumoto, *Kyōgen*, pp. 144–45. Various scholars have proposed additional categories. *Kyōgen Sambyakuban Shū*, edited by Nonomura Kaizō and Andō Tsunejirō, for long the best collection of texts of the Izumi school, listed twenty-seven categories (see *ibid.* pp. 151–53).

140. A lesser daimyo, but in Kyōgen often simply the "master" (*shū*), a man who has a servant named Tarōkaja. The master may be in debt to the liquor store, but he still maintains his pompous manner when ordering Tarōkaja to perform his errands.

141. Secret works *(naraimono)* were those that required special permission and instruction. The three highest naraimono of the Ōkura school repertory are *Tanuki no Harazutsumi, Hanago,* and *Tsurigitsune.*

142. *Rengekyō* (Lotus Sutra) is invoked by Nichiren sect believers with the words *Namu Myōhō Rengekyō*; Jōdo believers called *Namu Amida Butsu*, here abbreviated to *Namōda*.

143. An example is *Keimyō*, a play about a boy who saves the life of his father.

144. There is a translation by Shio Sakanishi in *Kyōgen*, pp. 35–40. Satake Akihiro (in *Gekokujō no Bungaku*, pp. 114–36) presents a brilliant but not altogether convincing explanation for why the daimyo is so incensed with Buaku as to command his death.

145. This is stated, for example, by Miyake Tōkurō in *Kyōgen Kanshō*, p. 83. He says that it is treated more seriously *(omoku)* even than *Tsurigitsune*, a play whose secrets of performance are taught by a master actor to only one of his sons and to no one else. *Hanago* is the story of a married man who acquires a mistress named Hanago. The wife is suspicious, and in

order to escape her watchful eyes, he says he will engage in Zen meditation, a hood over his head to shut out the mundane world. He commands Tarōkaja to sit in his place, and leaves happily for Hanago's place. The wife goes to the meditation hall, moved (she says) by sympathy for the husband. She tears off the hood and discovers Tarōkaja. She then puts on the hood and sits in meditation. When the husband returns, he recounts his delightful evening with Hanago, only for the wife to remove the hood.

146. The Kabuki play is called *Migawari Zazen*.

147. The best study of the founding of the three schools is contained in Kobayashi Seki, *Kyōgenshi Kenkyū*, pp. 1–79. Kobayashi gives (p. 30), as the first firm date for the Sagi school, documentary evidence that in 1614 this school was attached to the Kanze school of Nō as its Kyōgen component. Nothing in records of the Muromachi period substantiates the claim that the men named by the Sagi school as its first five iemoto had any connection with the actors.

148. *Ibid.*, p. 68.

149. The term *tesarugaku* was used of performances by actors who did not belong to one of the four recognized schools of Nō. These actors, though their status was officially that of farmers, probably performed Nō with considerable skill, and because they were officially amateurs, they were preferred by the court in Kyoto to actors tainted by professionalism. The court bestowed on these actors court appellations *(zuryōgō)* that gave them the privilege of appearing at the court or in the houses of the nobility. Needless to say, these titles were mere formalities and did not involve palace duties. The practice of giving such appellations to performers of Jōruri is said to have begun in 1577 and has continued to our day.

150. The differences between the Ōkura and Izumi school versions of the play *Akutarō* are discussed by Taguchi in *Kyōgen Ronkō*, pp. 129–40.

Bibliography

Note: All Japanese books, except as otherwise noted, were published in Tokyo.

Bethe, Monica, and Karen Brazell. *Dance in the Nō Theatre*. 3 vols. Ithaca, N.Y.: Cornell University East Asia Papers, 1982.

———. *Nō as Performance: An Analysis of the Kuse Scene of "Yamamba."* Ithaca, N.Y.: Cornell University East Asia Papers, 1978.

Brazell, Karen (ed.). *Twelve Plays of the Noh and Kyōgen Theaters*. Ithaca, N.Y.: Cornell University East Asia Program, 1988.

Brower, Robert H., and Earl Miner. *Japanese Court Poetry*. Stanford, Calif.: Stanford University Press, 1961.

Dōmoto Masaki. *Engekijin Zeami*. Nihon Hōsō Shuppan Kyōkai, 1990.
———. *Zeami*. Geki Shobō, 1986.
Geinōshi Kenkyūkai. *Nihon Geinōshi*, II. Hōsei Daigaku Shuppankyoku, 1982.
Goff, Janet. *Noh Drama and The Tale of Genji*. Princeton, N.J.: Princeton University Press, 1991.
Gotō Hajime. *Nōgaku no Kigen*. Mokujisha, 1975.
———. *Nō no Keisei to Zeami*. Mokujisha, 1966.
———. *Zoku Nōgaku no Kigen*. Mokujisha, 1981.
Gunji Masakatsu. *Kabuki Nyūmon*. Bokuyōsha, 1990.
Hare, Thomas Blenman. *Zeami's Style*. Stanford, Calif.: Stanford University Press, 1986.
Hayashiya Tatsusaburō. *Chūsei Geinōshi no Kenkyū*. Iwanami Shoten, 1960.
Hirakawa Sukehiro. *Yōkyoku no Shi to Seiyō no Shi*. Asahi Shimbun Sha, 1975.
Hoff, Frank, and Willi Flindt. *The Life Structure of Noh*. Racine, Wis.: Concerned Theatre Japan, 1973.
Honda Yasuji. *Ennen Shiryō*. Nōgaku Shorin, 1948.
Ichiko Teiji and Ōshima Tateki. *Nihon no Setsuwa*, IV. Tōkyō Bijutsu, 1974.
Ienaga Saburō. *Sarugaku Nō no Shisōshiteki Kōsatsu*. Hōsei Daigaku Shuppankyoku, 1980.
Ikeda Hiroshi and Kitahara Yasuo. *Ōkura Toraaki-bon Kyōgen no Kenkyū*, 3 vols. Hyōgensha, 1972–83.
Ishida Jōji and Shimizu Yoshiko. *Genji Monogatari*, 8 vols., in Shinchō Nihon Koten Shūsei series. Shinchōsha, 1976–85.
Itō Masayoshi. *Yōkyoku Shū*, 3 vols., in Shinchō Nihon Koten Shūsei series. Shinchōsha, 1983–88.
Jingū Shichō Gagaku Shūbu (ed.). *Bugaku Kaisetsu*. Shintō Bunka Kai, 1955.
Kawaguchi Hisao and Shida Nobuyoshi. *Wakan Rōei Shū, Ryōjin Hishō*, in Nihon Koten Bungaku Taikei series. Iwanami Shoten, 1965.
Keene, Donald. *Anthology of Japanese Literature*. New York: Grove Press, 1955.
———. *Nō: the Classical Theatre of Japan*. Tokyo: Kodansha International, 1966.
———. *Some Japanese Portraits*. Tokyo: Kodansha International, 1978.
———. *Twenty Plays of the Nō Theatre*. New York: Columbia University Press, 1970.
Kitagawa Tadahiko. *Kannami no Geiryū*. Miyai Shoten, 1978.
———. "Kyōgen Nō no Keisei," *Kokugo Kokubun*, vol. 28, no. 2, February 1959.
———. "Kyōgen Sozai toshite no Minkan Setsuwa," *Ritsumeikan Bungaku* 240, June 1965.
———. "Yōkyoku Kyōgen to Setsuwa Bungaku," in Ichiko Teiji and Ōshima Tateki, *Nihon no Setsuwa*, IV.
———. *Zeami*. Chūō Kōron Sha, 1972.
Kitagawa Tadahiko and Yasuda Akira. *Kyōgen Shū*, in Kan'yaku Nihon no Koten series. Shōgakukan, 1985. (Ōkura texts of the Shigeyama family.)
Kobayashi Seki. *Kyōgenshi Kenkyū*. Wan'ya Shoten, 1974.
Kobayashi Shizuo. *Zeami*. Hinoki Shoten, 1958.

Konishi, Jin'ichi. *A History of Japanese Literature*, I, translated by Aileen Gatten and Nicholas Teele. Princeton, N. J.: Princeton University Press, 1984.

———. "New Approaches to the Study of the Nō Drama," *Tōkyō Kyōiku Daigaku Bungakubu Kiyō*, no. 5, 1960.

———. *Nōgakuron Kenkyū*. Hanawa Shobō, 1961.

———. *Zeami Jūrokubu Shū*, in Gendaigoyaku Nihon Koten Bungaku Zenshū series. Kawade Shobō, 1954.

Kōsai Tsutomu. *Nōgaku Shinkō*. Hinoki Shoten, 1972.

———. *Zeami Shinkō*. Wan'ya Shoten, 1962.

Koyama Hiroshi. "Kyōgen no Hensen," *Bungaku* 24:7, July 1956.

———. "Kyōgen no Koten," in *Yōkyoku, Kyōgen*, in Nihon Bungaku Kenkyū Shiryō Sōsho series, 1981.

———. *Kyōgen Shū*, 2 vols. in Nihon Koten Bungaku Taikei series. Iwanami Shoten, 1960. (Ōkura School texts.)

———. *Nihon Bungaku Shinshi (Chūsei)*. Shibundō, 1990.

Koyama Hiroshi and Kitagawa Tadahiko. *Yōkyoku, Kyōgen*, in Kanshō Nihon Koten Bungaku series. Kadokawa Shoten, 1977.

Koyama Hiroshi, Taguchi Kazuo, and Hashimoto Asao. *Kyōgen no Sekai*, vol. V of the Iwanami Kōza Nō Kyōgen series. Iwanami Shoten, 1987.

LaFleur, William R. *The Karma of Words*. Berkeley: University of California Press, 1983.

Lee, Vernon. *Studies of the Eighteenth Century in Italy*. London: 1880.

Masuda Shōzō. *Nō no Hyōgen*. Chūō Kōron Sha, 1971.

Matsuda Tamotsu. *Waka to Yōkyoku Kō*. Ōfūsha, 1987.

Matsumoto Kamematsu. *Kyōgen Rikugi no Kenkyū*. Wan'ya Shoten, 1962.

McCullough, Helen Craig. *Ōkagami*. Princeton, N.J.: Princeton University Press, 1980.

———. *The Tale of the Heike*. Stanford, Calif.: Stanford University Press, 1988.

———. *Tales of Ise*. Stanford, Calif.: Stanford University Press, 1968.

Miyake Tōkurō. *Kyōgen Kanshō*. Wan'ya Shoten, 1943.

Moriya Takeshi. *Chūsei Geinō no Genzō*. Kyoto: Tankōsha, 1985.

———. *Geinō to Chinkon*. Shunjūsha, 1988.

———. *Nihon Chūsei e no Shiza*. Nihon Hōsō Shuppankai, 1984.

Morrell, Robert E. *Sand and Pebbles*. Albany: State University of New York Press, 1985.

Nihon Bungaku Kenkyū Shiryō Kankōkai. *Yōkyoku, Kyōgen*. Yūseidō, 1981.

Nippon Gakujutsu Shinkōkai (ed.). *Japanese Noh Drama*, 3 vols., 1955–60.

Nogami Toyoichirō. *Zeami Motokiyo*. Sōgensha, 1938.

Noma Seiroku. *Nihon Kamen Shi*. Geibun Shoin, 1943.

Nomura Hachirō. *Kyōgenki*, 3 vols. in Yūhōdō Bunko series. Yūhōdō, 1926. (Izumi School texts, somewhat abbreviated.)

Nonomura Kaizō and Andō Tsunejirō. *Kyōgen Sambyakuban Shū*, 2 vols. Fuzambō, 1938–42.

Nonomura Kaizō and Furukawa Hisashi. *Kyōgen Shū*, 3 vols. in Nihon

Koten Zensho series. Asahi Shimbun Sha, 1953–56. (Sagi School texts.)
Nose Asaji. *Nōgaku Genryū Kō*. Iwanami Shoten, 1938.
Okumura Tsuneya. *Kokin Waka Shū*, in Shinchō Nihon Koten Shūsei series. Shinchōsha, 1978.
Omote Akira. *Nōgakushi Shinkō*, 2 vols. Wan'ya Shoten, 1979, 1986.
Omote Akira and Katō Shūichi. *Zeami, Zenchiku*, in Nihon Shisō Taikei series. Iwanami Shoten, 1974.
O'Neill, P. G. *Early Nō Drama, Its Background, Character, and Development*. London: Lund Humphries, 1958.
Ortolani, Benito. "Zenchiku's Aesthetics of the Nō Theatre," *Riverdale Studies* 3, 1976.
Peri, Noël. *Le Nō*. Tokio: Maison Franco-Japonaise, 1944.
Pound, Ezra. *The Translations of Ezra Pound*. London: Faber and Faber, 1970.
Raz, Jacob. *Audience and Actors: A Study of Their Interaction in the Japanese Traditional Theatre*. Leiden: E. J. Brill, 1983.
Renondeau, Gaston. *Nô*, 2 vols. Tokio: Maison Franco-Japonaise, 1954.
Rimer, J. Thomas, and Yamazaki Masakazu. *On the Art of the Nō Drama: The Major Treatises of Zeami*. Princeton, N.J.: Princeton University Press, 1984.
Sagara Tōru. *Zeami no Uchū*. Perikan Sha, 1990.
Sakanishi, Shio. *Kyōgen*. Boston: Marshall Jones Company, 1938.
Sanari Kentarō. *Yōkyoku Taikan*, 7 vols. Meiji Shoin, 1954.
Sasano Ken. *Nō Kyōgen*, 3 vols., in Iwanami Bunko series. Iwanami Shoten, 1942–43. (Ōkura School texts of Ōkura Yaemon Torahiro.)
———. "Nō Kyōgen no Seikei," *Kokugo to Kokubungaku* 17: 11, November 1940.
Satake Akihiro. *Gekokujō no Bungaku*. Chikuma Shobō, 1967.
Satoi Rokurō. *Yōkyoku Bungaku*. Kyoto: Kawara Shoten, 1966.
Seidensticker, Edward. *The Tale of Genji*, 2 vols. New York: Alfred A. Knopf, 1976.
Shigematsu Akihisa (ed.). *Shin Sarugakki, Unshū Shōsoku*, in Koten Bunko series. Gendai Shichō Sha, 1982.
Sieffert, René. *La tradition secrète du Nō*. Paris: Gallimard, 1960.
Smethurst, Mae J. *The Artistry of Aeschylus and Zeami*. Princeton, N.J.: Princeton University Press, 1989.
Tachibana Hideki. *Haku Kyoi Kenkyū*. Kyoto: Sekai Shisō Sha, 1971.
Taguchi Kazuo. *Kyogen Ronkō*. Miyai Shoten, 1977.
Tamba, Akira. *The Musical Structure of Nō*. Tokyo: Tōkai University Press, 1981.
Tanaka Hiroshi. *Chūsei Bungakuron Kenkyū*. Hanawa Shobō, 1969.
Tani Hiroshi. *Chūsei Bungaku no Tassei*. San'ichi Shobō, 1962.
Tashiro Keiichirō. *Yōkyoku wo Yomu*. Asahi Shimbun Sha, 1987.
Terasaki, Etsuko. "Wild Words and Specious Phrases: *Kyōgen Kigo* in the Nō Play *Jinen Koji*," *Harvard Journal of Asiatic Studies* 49:2, 1989.
Torii Akio. *Chinkon no Chūsei*. Perikan Sha, 1989.
Tsuchihashi Yutaka and Konishi Jin'ichi. *Kodai Kayōshū*, in Nihon Koten Bungaku Taikei series. Iwanami Shoten, 1957.

Tyler, Royall. "Buddhism in Noh," *Japanese Journal of Religious Studies* 14:1, March 1987.

——— *Granny Mountains: A Second Cycle of Nō Plays*. Ithaca, N.Y.: Cornell University East Asia Papers, 1978.

———. *Japanese Nō Dramas*. London: Penguin, 1992.

———. *Pining Wind: A Cycle of Nō Plays*. Ithaca, N.Y.: Cornell University East Asia Papers, 1978.

Ueki Yukinobu. "Nō Keiseizen no Sarugaku," in Nihon Bungaku Kenkyū Shiryō Kankōkai, *Yōkyoku, Kyōgen*.

Watanabe Minoru. *Ise Monogatari*, in Shinchō Nihon Koten Shūsei series. Shinchōsha, 1976.

Watanabe Tsunaya. *Shasekishū*, in Nihon Koten Bungaku Taikei series. Iwanami Shoten, 1966.

Yamaji Kōzō. *Okina no Za*. Heibonsha, 1990.

Yamashita Hiroaki. *Taiheiki*, I, in Shinchō Nihon Koten Shūsei series. Shinchōsha, 1977.

Yanagita Kunio. *Teihon Yanagita Kunio Shū*, VII. Chikuma Shobū, 1962.

Yokomichi Mario. *Nōgeki no Kenkyū*. Iwanami Shoten, 1986.

Yokomichi Mario and Omote Akira. *Yōkyoku Shū*, 2 vols. Iwanami Shoten, 1960–63.

Yonekura Toshiaki. *Warambegusa Kenkyū*. Kazama Shobō, 1973.

27. LITERATURE OF THE FIVE MOUNTAINS

During the Muromachi period there was an impressive growth of scholarship in Chinese studies. This development began during the latter part of the Kamakura period, and was closely related to the popularity, especially among the upper ranks of samurai, of Zen Buddhism. Shogunate officials were probably attracted both by the self-reliance—the insistence that each person must find enlightenment for himself—characteristic of Zen, as well as by the fact that Zen, having only recently been introduced, was not intimately associated with the aristocracy, as were other sects of Buddhism, notably Tendai and Shingon.

Although Zen Buddhism emphasized intuitive, immediate apprehension of Buddhahood, rather than the study of religious texts, Zen was not without writings of its own,[1] and the Japanese priests who went to study Zen in China sometimes acquired a command not only of spoken Chinese but also of the literary expression typical of Chinese intellectuals.

The Kanazawa Bunko, a library of Chinese books founded about 1275 in Kamakura by Hōjō Sanetoki (1225–1276), reflected the interest of the shogunate in Chinese studies. Another, even more celebrated library was at the Ashikaga Gakkō (Ashikaga School), founded before 1440 by Uesugi Norizane (d. 1466). Instruction at this school was given by Zen priests, but they were forbidden to lecture on Buddhist texts; it was intended that the content of the instruction be secular, in the Confucian classics and other works of history and philosophy.[2]

Impetus for the growth of Chinese studies was stimulated by the renewal of trade between Japan and China at the beginning of the Muromachi period. From 1342 the Chinese government permitted Japanese merchant ships to enter Chinese ports, though no Japanese embassies had visited the Chinese court since 894, when Sugawara no Michizane had succeeded in terminating the traditional missions. With the reopening of trade with China, the major Zen temples of Kyoto eagerly sent commercial delegations to China, and monks attached to these delegations sometimes remained in China to study. The ships sent by the Tenryū-ji in Kyoto were especially important; the temple was authorized by the shogunate to engage in foreign trade as a means of raising funds, and the shogunate even agreed to protect the ships from pirates in return for a share of the profits. This was tantamount to official Japanese recognition of the existence of trade with China and eventually led to a resumption of diplomatic relations.

In 1401 Ashikaga Yoshimitsu sent a mission to Ming China requesting the renewal of amicable relations. The Chinese were glad to comply, both because they were always pleased to receive expressions of fealty from the surrounding barbarians and because they long had been troubled by the depredations of Japanese pirates and hoped that Yoshimitsu would be able to suppress them. Yoshimitsu, for his part, was entranced with Chinese ways, and gratefully accepted the title of "King of Japan" from the Chinese court.[3] He studied Chinese literature and invited masters of Chinese poetry like the Zen priests Gidō Shūshin and Zekkai Chūshin to lecture before him. Yoshimitsu's enthusiasm for things Chinese greatly fostered the growth of Chinese studies during the early Muromachi period.

Most of the writings by Zen monks who studied Chinese at this time were religious or philosophical, but they also composed many poems and works of artistic prose. Their writings are generally known as Gozan Bungaku, or Literature of the Five Mountains. The word "mountain" had by convention designated a temple in China, because temples were often situated on mountains, and was adopted with that meaning by the Japanese even though their temples might be on flat ground inside the city. There were five great Zen temples (later six) in Kyoto, and a similar number in Kamakura, which remained centers of learning throughout a period when warfare and civil disorder often made serious study of any kind difficult.

The creation of the Literature of the Five Mountains is sometimes credited to the Chinese monk I-shan I-ning (1247–1317), known to the Japanese as Ichizan Ichinei, who arrived in Japan in 1299 as an emissary from the Yüan (Mongol dynasty) Emperor Shih Tsung. I-shan I-ning, at first suspected of being a Mongol spy, was arrested and kept under confinement, but his great learning eventually won the confidence of the regent (*shikken*) Hōjō Sadatoki (1271–1311), who appointed him as abbot of the Kenchō-ji and Engaku-ji in Kamakura and later of the Nanzen-ji in Kyoto. His reputation was so high that many more monks flocked to the Engaku-ji than could be accommodated, and in order to determine the best students he instituted examinations in the composition of kanshi in the style of the Zen masters.[4] I-shan I-ning's disciples included Musō Soseki (1275–1351), the outstanding Zen priest of the age,[5] and Sesson Yūbai (1290–1346), the first important poet of the Five Mountains.

Sesson's life was unusually colorful. At the age of seventeen, after study with I-shan I-ning in Kamakura and later at the Kennin-ji, one of the most important temples in Kyoto, he sailed for China, where he visited the celebrated monasteries, paid his respects to the learned Zen priests of the day, and studied poetry and calligraphy as well as Buddhism. However, in 1313 he was arrested on charges of being a Japanese spy by the Mongol authorities, who were planning another invasion of Japan, and he was condemned to death. Just before he was to be executed, he recited the poem composed under similar circumstances by the Chinese monk Wu-hsüeh Tsu-yüan (Mugaku Sogen, 1226–1286), who narrowly escaped execution and later became a refugee in Japan. This display of apt erudition so impressed the prison warden that he obtained a stay of execution for Sesson. Sent back to prison, he composed four additional poems, each having for its first line one taken from Mugaku Sogen's original poem.[6] The four poems may suggest why Sesson's poetry has been described as "metaphysical":

In heaven and earth, no ground to plant my single staff,
but I can hide this body where no trace will be found.
At midnight the wooden man mounts his horse of stone,
crashing through a hundred, a thousand folds of encircling iron.

I delight that man is nothing, all things nothing,
a thousand worlds complete in my one cage.
Blame forgotten, mind demolished, a three-Zen joy—
who says Devadatta is in hell?[7]

Wonderful, this three-foot sword of the Great Yüan,[8]
sparkling with cold frost over ten thousand miles.
Though the skull go dry, these eyes will see again.
My white gem worth a string of cities has never had a flaw.

Like lightning it flashes through the shadows, severing the spring wind;
The god of nothingness bleeds crimson, streaming.

Mount Sumeru to my amazement turns upside down.[9]
I will dive, disappear into the stem of the lotus.[10]

Sesson's poems are likely to recall to Western readers the imagery of English seventeenth-century poetry, or T. S. Eliot's evocation of John Webster:

Webster was much possessed of death
And saw the skull beneath the skin;
And breastless creatures under ground
Leaned back with a lipless grin.

Daffodil bulbs instead of balls
Stared from the sockets of the eyes!
He knew that thought clings round dead limbs
Tightening its lusts and luxuries.[11]

Some metaphysical images, like those of the skull and the empty eye sockets, are common to Sesson and the English poets, and we may also recall this passage from *Doctor Faustus* as we read the last of Sesson's four poems:

The stars move still, time runs, the clock will strike,
The Devil will come, and Faustus must be damned.
O, I'll leap up to my God! Who pulls me down?
See, see where Christ's blood streams in the firmament!

Sesson's are among the few poems composed by Japanese before the twentieth century that are likely to evoke such memories of European poetry of the past. Within the Japanese context they are atypical, and the Five Mountains poems as a whole, virtually ignored for centuries, are still not much admired by Japanese scholars, especially those who are deeply familiar with Chinese prosody.

Konishi Jin'ichi found the translations by Burton Watson more interesting as poetry than the originals, and enumerated Sesson's failings as a poet: (1) his failure to observe the prescribed tonal patterns makes his poems rhythmically unpleasant; (2) the language of his poems is unrefined; (3) the construction is weak; and (4) the imagery is stereotyped.[12] These are major objections and not lightly made, but Western readers, even if ignorant of the background and meaning of the poems, are likely to be moved by such images as a wooden man mounting a steed of stone at midnight—unfamiliar imagery that stimulates fresh perceptions.[13] It is probably sufficient for the uninitiated to sense behind the four poems the poet's fearless disregard of temporal power and his confidence in ultimate triumph.

Not all of the Five Mountains poetry is in this vein; most poems, in fact, treat quite ordinary, generally pleasant, daily experiences. The "temperature" of the poems tends to be low, not intense in the manner of Sesson's, and many echo Chinese models so closely that we have difficulty in deciding what is Japanese about them.[14] Those that mention places in Japan where the priests traveled or describe scenery that seems distinctly Japanese rather than Chinese tend to be more interesting than those about landscapes in China, whether seen during the poet's travels or only imagined.

Sesson did not return to Japan until 1329, having spent twenty-two years in China.[15] By this time, he may have been more Chinese than Japanese, but he had not forgotten his country, as the following poem suggests:

YEARNING FOR MY FRIEND ON AN AUTUMN NIGHT

I'm by origin a man of the southeast,
And I constantly long for a guest from the southeast;
How will this splendid evening be endured?
Deserted, the rural walks by the city wall.
Dew lies on the chrysanthemums, permeates the garden;
Wind rustles the branches, flutters the drifting leaves.
I hum to myself, but you, dear friend, do not come,
And the bright moon shines in vain in an empty sky.[16]

In this poem Sesson used "southeast" for Japan, a Sinocentric term that suggests Japan is no more than a region of China, but his reference to the Japanese friend he misses reveals that this stern man, reputed never to have smiled, had a gentler side that made him feel homesick for people he once knew in Japan. Another poem, also written in China, expressed longing for his mother:

DAY LILIES

When the spring breeze from the marshland penetrates
the grass roots,
In whose garden do they fail to plant day lilies?

My distant yearning has not a day's surcease from grief
As I wonder if, her white hair loose, all alone she leans
against the gate.[17]

The day lily, a plant known in Japan as *wasuregusa*, or "grass of forgetfulness," was believed to have the property of enabling people to forget grief. The plant was also used metaphorically for a mother because it was frequently planted in northern exposures, near the part of the house where the women of a family lived. This poem of Sesson's, in which he imagines how his mother must be longing for his return, may have inspired the story of how, after he returned from China, he unsuccessfully searched everywhere for her, only to discover her one day quite by chance when he was thrown from his horse and went to ask at a nearby cottage for water with which to wash the mud from his clothes.[18]

Back in Japan, Sesson founded two temples and served as the abbot of several others, including the Kennin-ji. His poetic works were gathered in the collection *Binga Shū*, named after Min and O, two mountains near Ch'eng-tu in Ssu-ch'uan where he had been exiled. It was appropriate for him to have given his collection a title referring to Chinese landscapes: most of Sesson's poems were composed in China, and even after his return, they continued to be mainly on Chinese themes. Sesson had no trouble in writing poetry in classical Chinese, the language of the Buddhist texts he read, and probably the medium in which he communicated with Chinese people in regions where dialects made comprehension of the spoken language difficult. Perhaps his Japanese had even become rather rusty during his long stay abroad. In his case composing poetry in Chinese was neither (in the manner of kanshi writers of earlier times) a proof of erudition nor an affectation.

The verse forms employed by Sesson in the examples given above were the most typical of the Five Mountains poetry: the four-line poem ("cutoff lines"; Chinese *chüeh-chü*, Japanese *zekku*) and the eight-line poem ("regulated verse"; Chinese *lü-shih*, Japanese *risshi*). Each line of either variety of poem had five or seven characters, and there were complicated rules concerning rhyme and tonal patterns which the Japanese generally obeyed with the aid of manuals of kanshi composition. The popularity of the four-line poem with Japanese kanshi poets has sometimes been explained in terms of its brevity, which had the same appeal as a waka, epitomizing in a relatively few words a perception or experience. But perhaps a more important reason why the Zen priests of the Five Mountains found the shorter verse forms attractive was that the words of a *chüeh-chü* often referred to unspoken truths, like a finger pointing at the moon. Many Five Mountains poems seem on the surface to be without religious significance, hardly more than description of landscapes that might equally well have been depicted in an ink painting. Sometimes the poems in fact contain no deeper meaning; but in many, the words have overtones and associations that give religious meaning to the descriptions.[19]

The poetry and the painting of the Zen monks were closely related. Many poems, like the following example by Ichū Tsūjo (1349–1429), were intended to be inscribed on paintings:

ABOUT A PAINTING

Two old fishermen on the river bank in spring,
Their boats made fast, walk on the soft sand.
They've started to chat—whatever about?
They're planning to go see the plum trees in bloom.[20]

This simple, even banal poem has been analyzed in these terms: "In the foreground are several willows by the edge of a river. That is where the boat is tied up. In the middle ground two old men who look like fishermen are standing and talking. In the distance plum blossoms are faintly visible. The time is afternoon, probably early in the afternoon when the sun is still high. The first two lines depict the quiet movement of the little boats gently rocking in the river and of the two old men; it is a leisurely scene of a river in spring with fishermen. The language of these two lines is specific and creates a clear description. The last two lines depict the action of the two old men in going home. Here, the words . . . are general, and convey the haziness of the distant landscape. . . . A real scene unfolds itself before one's eyes."[21]

Not all of the elements described in this analysis are mentioned in the poem itself, but the subject was so familiar in painting that, whether or not a poem mentioned willow trees, for example, they were easily supplied by the reader. After reading a dozen or so poems in this mood, one's attention is likely to wander, but the superior Five Mountains poets could make even familiar subjects seem new, as this poem by Kokan Shiren (1278–1345) may suggest:

BOAT IN THE MOONLIGHT

Floating on the moon, my monk's boat winds through the reeds.
Tide's going out, the boy shouts, urging me back to the temple,

And village folk, thinking that a fishing boat's come in,
Scramble over the sand spit trying to buy fish from me.[22]

The cry of the servant boy warns the monk that dawn is near and that he must return to the temple. The poem concludes with the misapprehension of the village people who suppose that any boat rowed to shore at dawn must have fish for sale; a monk, of course, would not take life, even a fish's, and this particular monk has been too absorbed with the moonlight to think of anything else.

Two among the Five Mountains poets have been singled out for special attention, Gidō Shūshin and Zekkai Chūshin. It has often been said that Gidō excelled in kambun. and Zekkai in kanshi. This view may be correct, but in his own day Gidō's poems were as highly rated as his prose, and today none of his prose is still read for literary pleasure, though his poetry retains its charm.[23] The poems are accomplished and free of technical flaws, as an anecdote suggests: when a Japanese visitor to China showed his hosts some poems by Gidō they supposed they had been written by a Chinese, the highest compliment they could offer.[24]

Gidō Shūshin (1325–1388)

Gidō, the son and grandson of scholars of Confucian philosophy and Zen, is said to have begun his study of the Lotus Sutra and various Confucian classics in 1331, at the age of six. In the following year he found in the family storehouse a copy of *Rinzai-roku*, a basic text of the Rinzai school of Zen,[25] and read it, much to the astonishment of his parents. At thirteen, shocked by the sudden death of a relative, Gidō had his head shaved, and in 1339 he was ordained as a Tendai monk on Mount Hiei. Increasingly attracted to Zen, he went two years later to Kyoto to study with Musō Soseki. He intended to visit China for study in 1342, but illness prevented him on this occasion and he never had another chance to go. Instead, he remained in Kyoto, where he studied with Musō at the Tenryū-ji. His earliest specifically literary work dates from 1347 when he compiled a collection of *chüeh-chü* by Chinese Zen monks of the Sung dynasty.

In 1359 Ashikaga Motouji (1340–1367), the youthful commandant of the eastern region, asked Musō to send his best disciple to Kamakura, and Gidō was chosen. He spent twenty-one years at the Engaku-ji and other temples in Kamakura where he composed much of his poetry. Gidō was summoned back to Kyoto in 1380 by Ashikaga Yoshimitsu as the abbot of the Kennin-ji. That year he delivered lectures to Yoshimitsu on *The Doctrine of the Mean*, one of the Four Books of Confucianism, and in later years also lectured on *The Analects*. His most impressive intellectual achievement in Kyoto, however, was probably not his lectures on the Confucian texts but his success in converting Yoshimitsu to Zen Buddhism.[26] In 1386 Gidō became the abbot of the Nanzen-ji; in the same year Yoshimitsu, reordering the rankings of the Zen temples in Kyoto and Kamakura, placed the Nanzen-ji in a special category above all the rest.[27] Gidō died in 1388.

Gidō was an exceptionally prolific writer: he is credited with 1,739 poems and 476 works in prose including prefaces, inscriptions, and commentaries. By far the largest number of poems are *chüeh-chü* in lines of seven characters.[28] Despite all this literary activity, Gidō in principle disapproved of priests' spending their time composing poetry instead of in meditation. A poem he "humorously presented" to the regent, Nijō Yoshimoto, expressed this view:

> The minor art of poetry isn't worth a copper—
> Best just to sit silently in Zen meditation;
> "Wild words and ornate speech" don't cease to violate Buddha's
>   Law
> Just because he died two thousand years ago![29]

As Martin Collcutt noted, Gidō in his diary "stressed the ideal of the stern, frugal, meditation-centered Zen monastic life. His vigorous advocacy of *zazen* and repeated strictures against literary activities and pomp and luxury, however, suggest that the ideal was already eroding in practice."[30] Gidō himself commanded some disciples, who had failed to attend a lecture on a Buddhist text because they had been busy writing poetry, to desist these secular activities at once, threatening otherwise to confiscate all the non-Buddhist writings in their possession.[31] But he himself continued to write poetry, earning a rebuke from an abbot, though for a different reason: the abbot thought Gidō was too much of an amateur and had not devoted enough time to studying poetry![32] The Chinese learning that Zen priests acquired brought with it a commitment to the composition of poetry as the mark of an educated man, and even though the monks' poetry more often consisted of descriptions of nature than hymns to the Buddha, most of them obviously considered that writing poetry did not conflict with their calling.

Gidō's poems and prose were collected in twenty books under the title *Kūgeshū*, literally "Sky Flowers Collection." The title apparently refers to his faulty vision, "sky flowers" meaning the spots he saw before his eyes; the word was derived from a passage in the Lankāvatāra Sutra: "It is like a person with a cataract who sees spots in the air—when the cataract is removed, the spots disappear."[33] Gidō wrote a number of poems referring to this ailment:[34]

Year after year on this day I used to yearn to detain the spring glory;
How often did I dash off a poem I planned to polish in my thatched hut!
Today the plum blossoms will surely smile at me:
My eyes are too dim now to see their royal splendor.[35]

Despite his ailment, Gidō led a long and active life. His poetry, though largely conventional and perhaps not the product of a genuinely poetic spirit,[36] is often diverting, occasionally moving. The poems concerned with Zen teachings are by no means pious homilies, but sometimes (in the Zen manner) deny the possibility of logical explanation of doctrines. The following poem is entitled "In Response to a Request to 'Explain the Secret Teaching' ":

If I explained aloud, then it wouldn't be a true explanation,
And if I transmitted it on paper, then where would be the secret?
At a western window on a rainy autumn night,
White hair in the guttering lamplight, asleep facing the bed . . .[37]

The second two lines do not seem to follow from the first two, but they contain an allusion to *Pi-yen-lu*, or *Hekiganroku* in Japanese, a book of Zen *kōan* (riddles) compiled by Yüan-wu K'o-ch'in (1063–1135).[38] Riddle 17 goes: "A monk asked Hsiang-lin, 'What was the meaning of Bodhidharma's coming from the West?' Hsiang-lin said, 'To meditate a long time and get tired.' "[39] Gidō, asked to explain the secret teaching, refuses; he describes instead how he looks when he is asleep, tired after his studies, much as Hsiang-lin, when asked why Bodhidharma came all the way from India to China, where he neither taught nor wrote books, replied that he simply wanted to sit in Zen meditation until he got tired. This response, like those to most Zen parables, is unlikely to satisfy people unfamiliar with Zen. A more easily comprehensible Buddhist poem is Gidō's "To Show to My Disciples on the Eighth Day of the Twelfth Month":

When age overtakes, it is hard to achieve the Way;
When sickness comes, it is wearisome to leave the temple.

Can I, even so, save all other sentient beings?
And there is countless more to suffer in this world.
When he awoke from sleep a star hung low over his door;
As the sky brightened, snow hid the gate bar.
I, from a great distance, feel sorry for the old man with curly hair:
Barefoot, he went down the precipitous mountain.[40]

No explanation is likely to help one to understand the poem on Bodhidharma, but with the aid of a commentary it is relatively easy to understand this poem about Shakyamuni, the historical Buddha. The title indicates that it was composed on the day when a service was conducted to celebrate the anniversary of Shakyamuni's having attained enlightenment after six years of meditation in the Himalayas. The poem opens with a description of Gidō's own condition: he is too old and debilitated to achieve the path of enlightenment, and he finds it wearisome even to perform the austerities expected of priests. How, then, can he save the sentient beings of the world from suffering? To save others is difficult, but it is even more difficult to surmount the innumerable worldly hardships in the path of enlightenment. Gidō finally imagines (or perhaps recalls) a painting depicting Shakyamuni immediately after he attained enlightenment, and describes himself, far off in Japan, having watched with pity as the barefoot Shakyamuni descended the snow-covered mountain.

In another poem, addressed to a young monk who was about to leave for China, he even more strongly urged the necessity of a priest to expose himself to danger:

It is ten years now since first we met;
Where do you plan to go after we part?
If you go into the sea, you must plumb its depths;
If you climb the mountains, you must not fear its dangers.
In the dragon's palace the clouds stretch out;
In the tiger's lair the mist hangs heavy.
Go! and do not turn back your head—
Green youth too soon gives way to wispy hairs.[41]

Such sentiments may arouse irreverent recollections of Mabel in *The Pirates of Penzance*, who urges the policemen, "Go to death and go to slaughter!" But probably Gidō did not *really* mean to expose the monk to such dangers!

Zekkai Chūshin (1336–1405)

Zekkai, the greatest of the Five Mountains poets, by contrast wrote hardly any poetry expressing Buddhist convictions or even advice on how to deal with the problems of life in this world; most of his poems are occasional, presented to some friend who was about to depart on a journey, or composed in response to another man's poem.[42] By no means as prolific as Gidō, he left only 163 poems and 38 prose compositions.[43]

Zekkai, like Gidō, was a native of Tosa. At the age of twelve he entered the Tenryū-ji in Kyoto, and in the following year his head was shaved, signifying he was now an acolyte. Even as a boy he had shown skill at composing Chinese poetry; his talent was recognized by Musō Soseki when he visited Tosa, and after Zekkai entered the Tenryū-ji he studied with the great priest. Musō administered the rites of ordination when Zekkai at the age of fifteen became a full-fledged priest. After the death of Musō in 1351, Zekkai (together with Gidō) went to study with Ryūzan Tokken (1284–1358) at the Kennin-ji. Ryūzan, having spent forty-four years in China, was familiar with recent developments in Chinese poetic composition, and Zekkai probably studied kanshi with him; but not a single poem by Zekkai composed prior to his journey to China survives.

In 1368 Zekkai sailed to China in the company of various other monks including his friend Jorin Ryōsa.[44] Their purpose (unlike that of some monks of the Tenryū-ji who went to China to engage in trade) was to study poetry as well as Buddhist doctrine.[45] The Yüan (or Mongol) dynasty had been overthrown by the native Ming dynasty earlier in the same year, but order had been reestablished and Zekkai seems to have experienced no special difficulties in his travels. He went to Hang-chou where he met, at the Chung-t'ien Temple, Ch'üan Shih (1318–1391),[46] one of the important Zen priest-poets of the time. Ch'üan Shih was impressed by the Japanese: the story (similar to that of Kūkai and his master Hui-kuo)[47] is told that the priest took one look at him and instantly recognized his extraordinary abilities. Ch'üan Shih was the teacher of Kao Ch'i (1336–1374), often ranked as the foremost poet of the entire Ming dynasty, but Kao Ch'i unfortunately was no longer at the Chung-t'ien Temple and Zekkai never met him. In 1371, when Ch'üan Shih was appointed the abbot of one of the Five Mountains temples of China, he chose Zekkai to occupy the office of the chief seat (*shuso*),[48] a signal honor, especially for a foreigner.

In 1376 Zekkai and his friend Jorin were invited to Nanking (the Ming capital) by the Emperor Ming T'ai-tzu and Zekkai was asked about the content of Buddhist services. His replies apparently pleased the emperor. Later, the emperor, after showing Zekkai some Japanese paintings, asked him to compose a kanshi about Kumano. This was Zekkai's poem:

Before the peak of Kumano stands Hsü Fu's shrine;
The mountain abounds in herbs thanks to the rains.
Now the billowing waves of the sea are calm;
A favorable wind blows ten thousand miles; it's time he went home.[49]

According to traditional accounts, the first emperor of the Ch'in (259–210 B.C.), the creator of the unified empire of China, sent the diviner Hsü Fu to search for a medicine of immortality. He set sail for the east, accompanied by three thousand boys and girls of good family, and never returned to China. One version of the legend has it that he ended up in Japan. The poem has been accordingly interpreted as meaning that Hsü Fu should now return to China because the waves of the sea are calm (there are no disturbances in China) and there is a favorable wind.[50] Even if that is the surface meaning, it is likely that Zekkai was indirectly asking the emperor's permission to return to Japan. As we know from the instances of Ennin and other Japanese priests who resided for a long time in China, the Chinese were often exceedingly reluctant to let such learned men go. In this case, however, the emperor of China was pleased with Zekkai's impromptu poem and composed a reply using the same rhymes. After bestowing rich presents on Zekkai and Jorin, he granted them permission to return to Japan.

Zekkai and Jorin left for Japan some months later, but it is not clear precisely when. A poem written in 1377 about Akamagaseki (an old name for the Strait of Shimonoseki) suggests that he must have passed this historically famous site not long before:

The scene before me brings sorrow night and day:
A cold tide battering the red walls,
Among weird crags and fantastic boulders, a temple in the clouds,
Between the new moon and the setting sun, boats on the sea.
A hundred thousand valiant warriors have turned to empty silence,
Three thousand swordsmen are gone forever;
Heroes' bones rot in a soil of shields and lances—
Thinking of them, I lean on the balustrade, watch the white gulls.[51]

Zekkai's poem evokes the naval engagement in 1185 at Dannoura in the Strait of Shimonoseki, the last battle in the war between the Taira and the Minamoto (which resulted in the destruction of the Taira).[52] The "hundred thousand valiant warriors" of the poem[53] probably refers to the Minamoto, who much outnumbered the Taira on this occasion. The "new moon and the setting sun" probably describes what Zekkai himself saw, rather than the conditions when the battle was fought two hundred years before. Victors and vanquished, soldiers loyal to the crown (the Minamoto) and those who betrayed it (the Taira) have all disappeared, but they return to Zekkai as he gazes out on the scene. One recalls Bashō's immortal haiku, composed as he gazed, some three hundred years later, at the site of another battle of the distant past.[54]

Although Zekkai's poem was composed in Japan and described a momentous occasion of Japanese history, the expression owes little or nothing to Japanese poetic tradition. Mention of the "red walls" (cliffs) may recall the famous prose poems by Su Tung-p'o,[55] but even if there was no specific allusion to Su's poetry, the description of a scene viewed from a moving boat, the mention of "weird crags and fantastic boulders" and a "temple in the clouds" suggests the Yangtse gorges rather than the Strait of Shimonoseki. Zekkai might have found in the *Man'yōshū* a treatment in Japanese poetry of death in battle, but it is unlikely he knew the chōka. He used the Chinese language as his medium of expression and saw Japanese landscapes and even Japanese history through the eyes of the Chinese poets.

Zekkai returned to Japan to discover that not only was the country torn by warfare, but even within the Rinzai branch of Zen there were bitter divisions. During the following years he sometimes left Kyoto for a hermitage in the mountains, but generally returned to the city before long in response to the request of some military man who had founded a temple and wished Zekkai to be its abbot. Ashikaga Motouji, Akamatsu Yoshinori, Hosokawa Yoriyuki, and Ashikaga Yoshimitsu were among the military leaders who were not only impressed by his piety and learning but sought his advice on secular matters as well. He was especially close to Yoshimitsu, though their relationship was not always harmonious. In 1384 Zekkai irritated him with a piece of overly blunt advice (the nature of this advice is not known) and was ordered to leave the capital. For a while he hid in a remote temple in the province of Settsu, where he wrote this poem:

Worldly matters have always involved many uncertainties;
I realized this from the start, as clearly as now.

In green mountains I live secluded under thatched eaves;
I do not let the white clouds know my heart.[56]

From Settsu, Zekkai moved to the island of Shikoku, where he served as the abbot of a temple built by Hosokawa Yoriyuki (1329–1392) in the province of Awa. It is said that the only possession he carried with him was a copy of the poetry of Tu Fu.[57] Yoshimitsu, having changed his mind about Zekkai (apparently as the result of Gidō's intercession), now summoned him back, but Zekkai refused, alleging he was unwell. A second missive from Yoshimitsu induced him to return to the capital, where he was appointed abbot of the Ashikaga family temple, Tōji-in, succeeding Gidō. After Gidō's death in 1388, Zekkai became one of Yoshimitsu's chief advisers. At the time of the Meitoku Rebellion of Yamana Ujikiyo in 1391, Yoshimitsu is said to have gone into battle wearing Zekkai's Zen robes and to have attributed his victory to their miraculous power.[58] In 1399 Zekkai was sent as Yoshimitsu's emissary to the rebellious Ōuchi Yoshihiro, but his peacemaking efforts were unsuccessful, and Yoshihiro was killed in battle the same year. In 1401, when Zekkai was sixty-five, Yoshimitsu appointed him abbot of the Shōkoku-ji, sumultaneously raising the rank of that temple to first among the Five Mountains. Zekkai served concomitantly as the abbot of the Rokuon-ji, the temple founded by Yoshimitsu, more popularly known as Kinkaku-ji. Probably these activities kept him from composing much poetry during the latter part of his life. Zekkai died at the Shōkoku-ji in 1405 in his seventieth year. Four years later he was honored with the title *kokushi*, "teacher of the nation."

Banri Shūkyū (1428–1502)

Perhaps the most interesting feature of the Five Mountains poetry is the description of ordinary daily life given by some of the poets, mainly those who had not visited China. The sometime monk Banri Shūkyū recorded incidents in his life with startling directness:

FISH-OIL LAMP AT A ROADSIDE INN

Oil squeezed from fish guts makes the lamp burn strange,
A hazy light in a dim room reeking of fish.

Midnight, can't sleep, try to trim the lamp—
And the tiny glow is buried in a real fog.[59]

WOMEN LADLING BRINE ON THE BEACH

Brine ladlers—ugly women, black as crows,
Scrabbling with both hands at the salt that fills the sand;
They couldn't understand the wretched karma:
Yonder, buried in lime-smoke, tiny hovels on the bay.[60]

FOR A BATH AT KAKEZUKA THEY CHARGED 100 PIECES

Boat arrives at Kakezuka—out of my travelling clothes,
But 100 pieces of copper to get into the bath!
Seafood meal gritty with sand, food completely tasteless,
Wind strikes the nostrils with the reek of fishermen's huts . . .[61]

Not only were the waka poets uninterested in such scenes but the poetic diction did not contain the language needed to describe oil pressed from fish guts, brine ladlers, a gritty seafood meal. Poetry in this vein seems to owe extremely little to tradition, whether Chinese or Japanese, but in one important sense it is more faithful to tradition than the more frequently praised poems of Gidō, Zekkai, and the other pillars of Five Mountains poetry: like the great Chinese poets of the past, Banri wrote about his experiences with freedom and vigor and seeming indifference to conventional conceptions of poetic beauty.

The rare scholars who have treated Banri's poetry have experienced no difficulty in finding faults.[62] As with Sesson, it is easier to appreciate his poems in translation than in the original, where faults of construction, rhyme, tones, and so on obscure the interest of the content. The mundane concerns expressed in Banri's poems have been judged unbecoming in a Zen priest, and probably for this reason they are often excluded from collections of Five Mountains poetry.[63] As David Pollack wrote of the poetry of Banri's late years, "Banri's poems became progressively more eccentric as he grew older, often written in a 'Chinese' so Japanese that it sometimes seems a sort of pidgin, fraught with literary allusions that refer more frequently to Japanese sources than to Chinese."[64] It is precisely this "defect" of referring to Japanese, rather than Chinese, events and people that gives immediacy to Banri's poetry, and his failings of diction are easily forgiven by those who are not specialists in Chinese poetic practice.

The latter part of Banri's life was greatly affected by the Ōnin War that caused Banri to leave the monastic life, marry, and have children. He was involved also with the temporal masters of Japan, notably Ōta Dōkan, the traditional founder of the city of Edo. After Dōkan was assassinated, Banri left for the province of Mino where he had earlier built a retreat, and that was where he died. His poems convey perfectly the character of the author—individual, cranky, probably intolerant of other people's views, but unmistakably himself.

Ikkyū Sōjun (1394–1481)

The most famous kanshi poet of the time, Ikkyū Sōjun, was, strictly speaking, not a Five Mountains poet. Even schoolchildren in Japan know the name of Ikkyū-san, a mischievous, lovable priest about whom many anecdotes are related.[65] Most of these anecdotes have little or no basis in fact, but that does not matter: Ikkyū has come to embody all the most endearing aspects of Zen priests.

According to traditional accounts, Ikkyū was born on New Year's Day of 1394, a son of the Emperor Gokomatsu and a palace lady. Sceptics have expressed doubts about his royal birth, but good reasons to accept this tradition can be found both in the works of Ikkyū's contemporaries and in his own poems.[66] When Ikkyū was five years old he was sent as an acolyte to the Ankoku-ji, a secondary temple of the Five Mountains system in Kyoto, and during the rest of his life he appears to have had few contacts with his father, though it is reported that Gokomatsu summoned Ikkyū when on his deathbed.

As a child Ikkyū showed exceptional quickness at learning; he began his study of the Vimalakīrti Sutra at eleven and Chinese poetry in the following year. By the time he was fourteen he had established something of a reputation as a poet and demonstrated an exceptional devotion to Buddhist studies that contrasts with his later notoriety as a profligate. After four years of study under a hermit monk of unusually pure disposition,[67] Ikkyū was cut adrift by his master's death in 1414. He spent a week in meditation at the Ishiyama Temple by the shores of

Lake Biwa but, failing to obtain consolation, decided to commit suicide by throwing himself into the lake. He was saved at the last moment by the arrival of a messenger sent by his mother.[68]

Ikkyū decided at this point to become the disciple of Kasō Sōdon (1352–1428), a Zen master known for the unremitting severity of his discipline. Kasō, following the Zen tradition begun by Bodhidharma (who accepted Hui-kuo as his disciple only when he had demonstrated the strength of his resolve by cutting off his arm), at first barred the gate to his temple at Katada on the shore of Lake Biwa, and refused to let Ikkyū in. Ikkyū persisted, never going far from the gate and sleeping at night in an empty boat nearby. One day Kasō left the temple to perform a service in the village. Noticing Ikkyū still waiting by the gate, he ordered an attendant to throw water on him. Ikkyū was still waiting when Kasō returned; this time Kasō admitted him to the temple. Ikkyū spent the next three years studying under Kasō, leading a life of extreme austerity. One night in the summer of 1420, when he was twenty-six, he experienced enlightenment (satori) after hearing the cawing of a crow, and he felt that all uncertainties had melted away.

This period of Ikkyū's life provides an extraordinary contrast with the life he led in later years when, flagrantly disregarding the rules of priestly conduct, he openly gave himself to sensual pleasures. In 1440, when services for the thirteenth anniversary of Kasō's death were held at the Daitoku-ji, the monastery with which Ikkyū was most closely associated, parishioners had assembled from the prosperous port city of Sakai, bearing lavish presents for the occasion. Ikkyū was annoyed by what he took for unseemly commotion at a ceremony honoring his revered master and decided to leave. He composed two poems, one he left on the temple wall, making an inventory (in conformance with regulations) of the articles belonging to the temple that he was leaving behind, and the other for Yōsō Sōi (1376–1458), the abbot of the Daitoku-ji at the time. Yōsō was Ikkyū's greatest enemy, and again and again Ikkyū reviled him as a poisonous snake, a seducer, and a leper. The first poem was the inventory:

I've left behind the temple belongings I used;
And hung my wooden spoon and bamboo plate on the east wall.
I have never craved useless furnishings around me;
For years on my journeys a straw coat and hat have been my style.[69]

The poem addressed to Yōsō was naturally more provocative:

For ten days in this temple my mind's been in turmoil.
My feet are entangled in endless red strings.
If some day you get around to looking for me,
Try the fish shop, the wine parlor, or the brothel.[70]

The "ten days" of the first line refer to the time Ikkyū was the abbot of a branch temple at the Daitoku-ji. The "red strings" *(kōshisen)* of the second line is a key expression in Ikkyū's poetry. Here it seems to mean connections with the mundane world, but elsewhere it can refer to ties of physical desire. The primary Zen meaning was apparently the thread-like red lines of the capillaries on the soles of a newborn baby's feet; these are gradually effaced and, in the case of priests who go forth on long journeys, the lines become totally invisible as the skin thickens under the soles of the feet. The soles of the feet of a person who has not yet freed himself from worldly ties are likely still to show the telltale red threads.[71] The main thrust of the poem, however, is in the last lines: Ikkyū defiantly announces that he is fleeing the temple, polluted by vulgar commercial transactions, for the sanctity of the fish shop (though priests were forbidden to eat meat or fish), the wine parlor (though liquor was also forbidden), or (most shockingly) the brothel.

Ikkyū's collection *Kyōunshū*, literally "Crazy Cloud Collection,"[72] contains many poems describing his indulgence in fleshly pleasures. He wrote of one attempt to free himself of this addiction:

TWO POEMS ON LIVING IN THE MOUNTAINS

Ten years in the licensed quarter, and I still couldn't exhaust the pleasures;
But I forced myself to live in these empty mountains and dark valleys.
The view is fine, but clouds blot out the whole thirty thousand miles,
And those winds over the roof from the tall pines grate on my ears.[73]

Crazy Cloud is truly Daitō's heir;
But how could these lonely haunts and dark mountains be called holy?
I think back on long-ago nights of music and sex—
A young man of the world, I tipped the sake cask.[74]

The contrast between the first and second couplets of this poem is like that in the previous poem: living in the mountains, Ikkyū finds the silence oppressive and not conducive to the practice of Zen. He recalls nostalgically nights spent in the brothels. The world *fūryū*, translated here as "elegant," appears very frequently in Ikkyū's poetry; it has several distinct meanings, including refined elegance in the manner of the old Chinese poets, fleshly attraction, a state of transcendence of fleshly desire (the religious meaning), and a quiet pleasure in the beauty of nature.[75] Ikkyū's conviction that he is the heir to the teachings of Daitō (1282–1337), the great Zen master and founder of the Daitoku-ji, is proclaimed in other poems. But in his best-known poem on his spiritual ancestry, the one inscribed on the portrait of Ikkyū by Bokusai,[76] he insisted that he alone transmitted the Zen of the Chinese master Sung-yüan (1132–1202):

> None of Kasō's posterity knows Zen;
> But who before Crazy Cloud's face dares expound
> Zen?
> For thirty years it has been heavy on my shoulders:
> Alone I have borne the burden of Sung-yüan's Zen.[77]

Ikkyū on occasion contrasted the material decline of the Five Mountains temples with the prosperity of the Daitoku-ji (not one of the Five Mountains), but he saw no reason to rejoice:

> The Mountain Forest prospers, the Five Mountains languish,
> But there are only corrupt priests, no decent master.
> I would like to take a pole and become a fisherman,
> But of late a contrary wind blows over rivers and lakes.[78]

"Contrary wind" seems to refer to the unfriendly reception given to Ikkyū's refusal to conform by the other priests at the Daitoku-ji. In another poem he rejected their concern with the rules:

RED THREADS ON THE SOLES OF FEET

> Those who keep the commandments become donkeys, those who break
> them, men.
> Rules of every kind, many as Ganges' sands, play havoc with the spirit;
> The newborn babe bears the lines of marital ties,
> But how many springs do red blossoms open and fall?[79]

In this poem Ikkyū seems to be contrasting the artificial, constricting rules imposed by men with the naturalness of the flowers. Donkeys do not break the commandments against killing, lying, and so on; only man can break the commandments he has imposed on himself. The red lines on a baby's feet show its destiny: here, the meaning seems to be closer to the usual Chinese interpretation of *kōshisen* as physical ties rather than the Zen doctrine of lines that are erased by the seeker of enlightenment after years of austerities.

Other poems evoke the destruction brought about by the Ōnin War and the hardly less hateful conflicts between temple and temple or within a single temple. Physical pleasure seems to have been Ikkyū's refuge from the torment of a world against which he constantly struggled:

THE BROTHEL

To sleep with a beautiful woman—what a deep river of love!
Upstairs in the brothel the old Zen priest is singing.
He's had all the pleasure of embraces and kisses,
With never a thought of throwing himself into the flames.[80]

The last line refers to the self-sacrificing faith of the monks who, not fearing death, threw themselves into fires. Ikkyū (no doubt the monk of the poem) denies he possesses that spirit.

The most affecting of Ikkyū's poems on women are those relating to Mori, a blind musician. They first met in 1470 when Ikkyū, then seventy-six, heard Mori (who was about forty) sing. By the next year she had moved to Ikkyū's temple to live with him. Ikkyū wrote some twenty poems about Mori, all of them affecting, including:

The most elegant beauty of her generation,
Her love songs and charming party tunes are the newest.
When she sings the dimples in her lovely face break my heart;
It is spring in the long-ago forest of apricot trees.[81]

Blind Mori every night accompanies my songs;
Deep under the covers mandarin ducks whisper anew.
Her mouth promises Miroku's dawn of deliverance,
Her dwelling is the full spring of the ancient Buddhas.[82]

After the tree withered and the leaves fell, spring returned;
The old trunk has flowered, old promises are renewed.
Mori—if I should forget how much I owe you,
May I be a brute beast through all eternity![83]

Reading Ikkyū's poems of hatred directed at the corruption of the Zen establishment, or his poems of love directed at Mori, leaves no room for doubt that they were fully meant; one is not tempted to search for Chinese antecedents to the poems, though some undoubtedly existed. Ikkyū himself at times repented of the violence of some of the denunciations in his poems:

> With spears of words how many men I have murdered!
> With odes and quatrains my brush has reviled my fellows.
> In hell I'll be torn to pieces for the sins of my tongue;
> In the world of the dead I won't escape the flaming carriage.[84]

But readers today can only rejoice that someone who lived five centuries ago communicated his passion with such intensity that we probably know him better than any Japanese poet who ever chose the kanshi as his medium of expression.

The achievements of the Five Mountains poets were considerable. Their poetry commanded the respect even of the Chinese, and some of their poems still impress, whether because of the evocations of natural beauty, the religious content, or the surprising individuality. Undoubtedly, too, the kanshi of the Five Mountains poets helped to lay the foundation for the works in this genre by poets of the Tokugawa period, when the kanshi again flourished. But it is hard to imagine anyone turning for pleasure to these poems, in preference to those by Tu Fu, Po Chü-i, Su Tung-p'o, or the other great Chinese. Nor is their appeal comparable to that of the major poets of the waka, renga, or haiku. Their poetry, because written in a foreign language, has become in the last century increasingly difficult for Japanese to understand, and has accordingly remained on the periphery of studies of Japanese literature.

Notes

1. For the writings of Dōgen, see above, pp. 755–59.
2. The regulations issued in 1440 by Uesugi Norizane stated that the books to be studied were the Four Books, the Six Classics, Lao Tzu, Chuang Tzu, *Shih Chi*, and the *Wen Hsüan*. Although Zen priests not only taught

at the school but administered it, they were not allowed to teach Zen. See Okada Masayuki, *Nihon Kambungaku Shi*, p. 369. The library of the school permitted borrowing, and we even possess a list of regulations for users of the library dated 1439, including an admonition against marking passages with black or red ink, suggesting that the books were actively used. The text of the regulations is given by Okada on pp. 369–70.

3. For translations of the letters Yoshimitsu received from the Ming court, see Wang Yi T'ung, *Official Relations between China and Japan*, p. 22.
4. Martin Collcutt, *Five Mountains*, p. 74. See also David Pollack, *The Fracture of Meaning*, p. 122.
5. For an account of Musō Soseki, see Pollack, *Fracture*, pp. 121–33; also Akamatsu Toshihide and Philip Yampolsky, "Muromachi Zen and the Gozan System," in John Whitney Hall and Toyoda Takeshi, *Japan in the Muromachi Age*, pp. 322–24.
6. The four poems, translated by Burton Watson, were first given in my *Anthology of Japanese Literature*, p. 312.
7. Devadatta, who attempted to kill the Buddha, represents the epitome of evil.
8. Yüan was the name taken by the Mongols for their dynasty.
9. The central mountain of the Buddhist universe.
10. Translation by Burton Watson in Hiroaki Sato and Burton Watson, *From the Country of Eight Islands*, p. 230.
11. These are the opening lines of T. S. Eliot, "Whispers of Immortality." They are quoted by Konishi Jin'ichi in "Gozanshi no Hyōgen," p. 17.
12. Konishi, "Gozanshi," pp. 20–23.
13. It may be also that the translator, in choosing among possible English equivalents for the Chinese words, unconsciously adopted expressions familiar from his readings in European poetry.
14. The question of what is Japanese in the Chinese poems by Zen monks is well discussed by Pollack in *Fracture*, pp. 120ff.
15. This account of Sesson Yūbai's life is derived from Okada, *Nihon*, pp. 313–14.
16. Translation by Marian Ury in *Poems of the Five Mountains*, p. 35. Original poem in Yamagishi Tokuhei, *Gozan Bungaku Shū, Edo Kanshi Shū*, p. 75.
17. Yamagishi, *Gozan*, p. 76. Also Saitō Shō, *Nihon Kanshi*, pp. 181–82.
18. This story is related in Saitō Shō, *Nihon Kanshi*, p. 180.
19. David Pollack (in *Zen Poems of the Five Mountains*, p. 11) wrote, "While any object might thus be emblematic of Zen principles, certain objects and activities were so charged with symbolic meaning through regular association with Zen ideas that they came in time to constitute a sort of code language. Because of the almost automatic association of words with certain Zen referents, Zen poetry can often be interpreted on two independent levels of meaning in a way that is 'metaphysical' in much the same sense that the word is applied to the poetry of seventeenth-century England."

He also gave a list of some words that frequently appear in Five Mountains poems together with their associations, including: "maple leaves: the illusory world of discriminations based on sensory perceptions of such things as the brilliant 'colors' of maple leaves in autumn."

20. Translation by Ury in *Poems*, p. 129. Original text in Yamagishi, *Gozan*, pp. 125–26.
21. Yamagishi, *Gozan*, p. 411.
22. Translation by Pollack in *Zen*, p. 99. Original text in Yamagishi, *Gozan*, p. 63.
23. I shall not consider the kambun written by Gidō or any other Gozan author. The problem in reading kambun is well described by Terada Tōru, *Gidō Shūshin, Zekkai Chūshin*, pp. 69ff. Terada contrasted the reading of poetry and prose in other languages, where prose was easier to understand than poetry, with the tendency of kambun to be far more difficult than kanshi. This was not simply because prose written in Chinese was likely to contain difficult characters that had to be looked up in a dictionary; the Japanese who wrote kambun did not intend it to be read for pleasure. Kanshi might describe the poet's appreciation of nature and other engaging topics, but kambun was restricted to the poet's convictions and was not consciously literary.
24. Praise of a similarly patronizing nature was bestowed on Zekkai Chūshin by a Chinese Zen monk who wrote in the colophon to the collected poems of Zekkai how astonished he was that the poetry bore no trace of Japanese influence. See Pollack, *Fracture*, p. 120.
25. Much of our knowledge of Gidō comes from his diary, *Kūge Rōshi Nichiyō Kūfu Ryakushū*, which covers the period 1325–1388. Although it is called a "diary," much of it was obviously written long after the events. The text, given by Tsuji Zennosuke in his work of the same name, is in kambun, not annotated in any way; however, Tsuji supplied a very useful index and a study of Gidō. The biographical material concerning Gidō given here comes from this source.
26. See Usui Nobuyoshi, *Ashikaga Yoshimitsu*, pp. 205–13.
27. See Collcutt, *Five Mountains*, p. 110, for a table showing the rankings of the six Kyoto and five Kamakura monasteries. Nanzen-ji was *gozan no jō* (superior *gozan*).
28. For a breakdown in the different kinds of poems written by Gidō, see Okada, *Nihon*, p. 342. Gidō wrote 1,003 seven-character *chüeh-chü*.
29. Translation by Pollack in *Fracture*, p. 134. (Pollack gives a slightly different version in *Zen* p. 53.) For "wild words and ornate speech" (kyōgen kigyo), see above, p. 1030.
30. Collcutt, *Five Mountains*, p. 100.
31. Pollock, *Fracture*, p. 135, quoting a passage from Gidō's diary for the twenty-eighth day of the ninth month of 1371.
32. *Ibid.*, p. 136. The abbot of this anecdote of 1354 was Ryūzan Tokken.

33. Translated by Pollack in *Zen*, p. 150.
34. See Terada, *Gidō*, pp. 19–26.
35. *Ibid.*, p. 26.
36. Terada Tōru was a particularly severe judge of Gidō's poetry, partly because he believed that Gidō lacked natural lyric impulses and tended to portray a bleak and charmless world, but also because he was a sycophant who sought above all his own security. See *ibid.*, pp. 33–37.
37. Pollack, *Zen*, p. 26.
38. There is an English translation by R.D.M. Shaw entitled *The Blue Cliff Records*. The title has also been translated as *Record of the Green Rock Room* by Earl Miner et al. in *The Princeton Companion to Classical Japanese Literature*, p. 392.
39. Translation slightly modified from Pollack, *Zen*, p. 26.
40. Text and notes in Yamagishi, *Gozan*, p. 107. Other translations by Ury in *Poems*, p. 98, and by Pollack in *Zen*, p. 47.
41. Saitō Shō, *Nihon Kanshi*, p. 188.
42. See Saitō Kiyoe, *Insen no Bungaku*, p. 73.
43. Okada, *Nihon*, p. 356. Of his poems, sixty-seven were seven-character *lü-shih* and fifty-two were seven-character *chüeh-chü*.
44. Jorin and Zekkai had studied together at the Tenryū-ji under Shun'oku Myōha (1311–1388), the religious adviser to Ashikaga Yoshimitsu. For Shun'oku Myōha, see Collcutt, *Five Mountains*, p. 119. A brief account of Jorin is given by Okada in *Nihon*, p. 362; also Tamamura Takeji, *Gozan Bungaku*, p. 194. Jorin's dates are not known.
45. See Saitō Kiyoe, *Insen*, p. 72. According to Saitō, Zekkai was especially drawn to the style of two Yüan poets, Chao Meng-fu (1254–1322) and Yang Wei-chen (1296–1370).
46. Ch'üan Shih was more commonly known in China as Tsung Le.
47. See above, pp. 185–87.
48. Collcutt (in *Five Mountains*, p. 238) wrote about this office, "The chief seat *(shuso)* derived his title from his place next to the abbot on the meditation platforms. He was the principal monk in the hall and the leader of meditation."
49. Text in Terada, *Gidō*, p. 135; also Yamagishi, *Gozan*, p. 116. Another translation in Ury, *Poems*, p. 113.
50. This is the interpretation of Yamagishi, but Terada takes the last line to mean "it's time I went home." The story of Hsü Fu and the three thousand boys and girls is given in the *Shih Chi* of Ssu-ma Ch'ien. See Burton Watson, *Records of the Grand Historian of China*, II, p. 375.
51. Translation by Pollack in *Zen*, p. 105. Text in Terada, *Gidō*, p. 247.
52. See above, p. 634.
53. In the translation the term *gigun* is rendered "valiant warriors," but it means literally "just army," an epithet that could be appropriately given

only to an army that was fighting for a cause approved of by the emperor, in this case the Minamoto. See Terada, *Gidō*, p. 247.

54. See p. 898; see also *World Within Walls*, pp. 104–5.
55. Translated by Burton Watson in *Su Tung-p'o*, pp. 87–93.
56. Text in Kitamura Sawakichi, *Gozan Bungakushi Kō*, p. 388; also Terada, *Gidō*, p. 272.
57. Inokuchi Atsushi, *Nihon Kanshi*, I, p. 96.
58. Kitamura, *Gozan*, p. 291.
59. Translation by Pollack in *Zen*, p. 51. For a short biography of Banri, see *ibid.*, pp. 145–46.
60. *Ibid.*, p. 85.
61. *Ibid.*, p. 122.
62. See Kageki Hideo, *Gozan Shishi no Kenkyū*, pp. 460–61, where he summarizes and comments on faults in Banri's kanshi that were pointed out by Tamamura Takeji.
63. For example, not a single poem by Banri was included by the editor of the volume devoted to Gozan Bungaku in the Nihon Koten Bungaku Taikei volume. Banri is not represented, either, in the Shin'yaku Kambun Taikei volume edited by Inokuchi, *Nihon Kanshi*; and he is dealt with summarily (less than a page without any poems quoted) by Kitamura in *Gozan*. Kageki (*Gozan*, p. 470) ended his comparatively detailed description of Banri's career with the query, "Is the present writer the only person for whom Banri's playful attitude toward literature arouses distaste?"
64. Pollack, *Zen*, p. 146. See also his comments on Banri in *Fracture*, pp. 189–92.
65. *Ikkyū-banashi*, or tales about Ikkyū, have been told in many forms and have even been performed on television. Needless to say, the more scabrous events of Ikkyū's life do not figure in books or television programs meant for children. James H. Sanford has translated a selection of Tokugawa-period tales about Ikkyū in his *Zen-Man Ikkyū*, pp. 250–96. Paraphrases of similar stories are given by Jon Carter Covell in *Unraveling Zen's Red Thread*, pp. 289–99. These stories were first printed during the Tokugawa period, but some may have circulated orally even within Ikkyū's lifetime. *Ikkyū Gaikotsu* (Ikkyū's Skeletons) was one of the rare nonscriptural texts to have been printed during the Muromachi period.
66. See Sanford, *Zen-Man*, pp. 9–11.
67. For a description of the master, Ken'ō, see Sanford, *Zen-Man*, pp. 14–19. Ken'ō was a member of the Myōshin-ji school of Rinzai Zen, which was outside the Gozan system. The Zen of Myōshin-ji and Daitoku-ji would later be distinguished from Gozan Zen and called Ōtōkan Zen, a name derived from elements in the names of the three founders, Dai*ō*, Dai*tō*, and *Kan*zan.
68. The timely arrival of the messenger was described in *Ikkyū Oshō Nempu* (Chronicle of Ikkyū) by his disciple Bokusai. (For a translation of this

section of the *Chronicle*, see Sanford, *Zen-Man*, pp. 79–80.) There is no evidence to show that this event did *not* occur, but the account is so dramatically arranged that some doubt its veracity.

69. Text in Hirano Sōjō, *Kyōunshū Zenshaku*, I, pp. 81–82. Other translations by Sonja Arntzen in *Ikkyū and the Crazy Cloud Anthology*, p. 24; Sanford, *Zen-Man*, pp. 47–48; Donald Keene, *Landscapes and Portraits*, p. 235. The poem is difficult. Hirano's modern-language translation represents an attempt to grasp the poem as a coherent whole, but it creates other problems. His version goes, "I have left in the hut all the temple treasures, possessions, and the like, and have hung the ladle *(shaku)* and plate *(zaru)* on the east wall. I, who have spent many years in quiet regions by the seacoast, living a life without any fixed abode, have no need of such useless appurtenances." Perhaps that is what Ikkyū meant, but it is strange that he singled out such humble objects as a rice ladle and a bamboo plate as typifying the temple treasures. Sanford, aware of this problem, translated the first two lines as " 'interesting donations' are dragged into the hermitage; / They decorate the east wall with wooden ladles and rustic baskets." But the words "interesting donations," "dragged into," and "decorate" are not in the original. Arntzen changes the attitude of the speaker from someone who is reporting what he has left in his hermitage to someone asking another person to remove the objects and put them in some other hermitage: "Take the everyday things, place them in the hermitage. Wooden ladles, bamboo baskets hanging on the east wall . . ." None of the translations faces the problem of why "east wall" (if that is what it means) is *hekitō*, rather than *tōheki*, the normal form. The above may suggest the problems of interpreting many of Ikkyū's poems.

70. Text in Hirano, *Kyōunshū*, I, p. 82. Other translations in Arntzen, *Ikkyū*, p. 25; Sanford, *Zen-Man*, p. 48; Keene, *Landscapes*, p. 235.

71. I have derived this explanation from Hirano, *Kyōunshū*, I, p. 23. In his modern-language translation of this poem, however, he gives for the second line, "*Watakushi wa dōmo bonnō ga sukoshi ōsugiru yō da*." (I seem to have a little too many worldly afflictions.) This is what is known as a free translation. Covell gave her book the title *Unraveling Zen's Red Thread*, an indication of the importance she attached to the term, but her explanation of *kōshisen* on pp. 82–83 does not suggest the variety of meanings found in Ikkyū's poems, concentrating instead on the use of the term as "a metaphor for a stream of sexual desires." In this particular poem the meaning does not seem to be sexual desire but worldly involvement.

72. The word *unsui*, literally "cloud water," was used of itinerant priests who wandered like clouds or flowing water, and it is possible that the title of the collection meant "Crazy Priest Anthology."

73. Text in Hirano, *Kyōunshū*, I, p. 89. Other translations in Arntzen, *Ikkyū*, p. 99; Satō and Watson, *From the Country*, p. 232; also Keene, *Landscapes*, p. 235.

74. Text in Hirano, *Kyōunshū*, I, pp. 86–87. Hirano notes that it is difficult to find a single thread of meaning running through the whole poem. Another translation in Arntzen, *Ikkyū*, p. 99.
75. See the interesting article by Okamatsu Kazuo, "Ikkyū Sōjun ni okeru Fūryū no Kōzō," in Akiyama Ken (ed.), *Chūsei Bungaku no Kenkyū*, pp. 287–304. Okamatsu calculated (p. 287) that the word *fūryū* occurred 53 times in the 560 poems and other works in *Kyōunshū*, and 73 times in the 304 poems in the sequel collection, *Zoku Kyōunshū*.
76. See my essay, "The Portrait of Ikkyū," in *Landscapes*, pp. 231–32.
77. Text in Hirano, *Kyōunshū*, I, pp. 126–27. Another translation in Arntzen, *Ikkyū*, p. 113; also Sanford, *Zen-Man*, p. 56; Keene, *Landscapes*, p. 232.
78. Text in Hirano, *Kyōunshū*, I, p. 167. Another translation in Arntzen, *Ikkyū*, p. 123. In another poem in *Kyōunshū* (Hirano, I, p. 269) Ikkyū declared there were no Zen masters left in China either. "Mountain Forest" *(sanrin)* seems to designate temples situated away from the center of the city.
79. Text in Hirano, *Kyōunshū*, I, p. 123. Another translation in Arntzen, *Ikkyū*, p. 113; also Keene, *Landscapes*, pp. 236–37.
80. Text in Hirano, *Kyōunshū*, I, p. 139. Another translation in Arntzen, *Ikkyū*, p. 144; also, Keene, *Landscapes*, pp. 235–36.
81. *Kyōunshū* 547. Text in Karaki Junzō, *Chūsei no Bungaku*, p. 249. The last line says literally the "T'ien-pao forest." "T'ien-pao" refers to the Chinese era, 742–755, that marked the high point of poetry of the T'ang dynasty. Another translation in Sanford, *Zen-Man*, p. 163.
82. *Kyōunshū* 537. Text in Karaki, *Chūsei*, p. 249. Another translation in Arntzen, *Ikkyū*, p. 158; also Sato and Watson, *From the Country*, p. 233.
83. *Kyōunshū* 543. Text in Karaki, *Chūsei*, p. 249. Another translation in Arntzen, *Ikkyū*, p. 162; also Sato and Watson, *From the Country*, p. 233.
84. Text in Hirano, *Kyōunshū*, I, p. 240. Translation in Keene, *Landscapes*, p. 237. "Odes" is a rough translation of *ge* (*gāthā* in Sanskrit), a Buddhist hymn; "quatrains" translates *chüeh-chü (zekku)*.

Bibliography

Note: All Japanese books, except otherwise noted, were published in Tokyo.

Akiyama Ken (ed.). *Chūsei Bungaku no Kenkyū*. Tōkyō Daigaku Shuppankai, 1972.

Arntzen, Sonja. *Ikkyū and the Crazy Cloud Anthology*. Tokyo: University of Tokyo Press, 1986.

———. *Ikkyū Sōjun: A Zen Monk and His Poetry.* Bellingham: Western Washington State College, 1973.

Collcutt, Martin. *Five Mountains.* Cambridge, Mass.: Harvard University Press, 1981.

Covell, Jon Carter. *Unraveling Zen's Red Thread.* Elizabeth, N.J.: Hollym International Corp., 1980.

Eliot, T. S. *Collected Poems.* New York: Harcourt, Brace and Company, 1936.

Hall, John Whitney, and Toyoda Takeshi. *Japan in the Muromachi Age.* Berkeley: University of California Press, 1977.

Hirano Sōjō. *Kyōunshū Zenshaku,* I. Shunjūsha, 1976.

Inokuchi Atsushi. *Nihon Kanshi,* I. Meiji Shoin, 1972.

Kageki Hideo. *Gozan Shishi no Kenkyū.* Kasama Shoin, 1977.

Kaneko Matabei. "*Kyōunshū,*" *Kokubungaku Kaishaku to Kanshō* 29:12, 1964.

Karaki Junzō. *Chūsei no Bungaku.* Chikuma Shobō, 1965.

Keene, Donald. *Anthology of Japanese Literature.* New York: Grove Press, 1955.

———. *Landscapes and Portraits.* Tokyo: Kodansha International, 1971.

Kitamura Sawakichi. *Gozan Bungakushi Kō.* Fuzambō, 1941.

Konishi Jin'ichi. "Gozanshi no Hyōgen: Sesson Yūbai to Keijijōshi," *Bungaku Gogaku* 58, 1970.

Miner, Earl, Hiroko Odagiri, and Robert Morrell. *The Princeton Companion to Classical Japanese Literature.* Princeton, N. J.: Princeton University Press, 1985.

Nishida Masayoshi. *Ikkyū.* Kōdansha, 1977.

Okada Masayuki. *Nihon Kambungaku Shi* (rev. ed.). Yoshikawa Kōbunkan, 1954.

Pollack, David. *The Fracture of Meaning.* Princeton, N. J.: Princeton University Press, 1986.

———. *Zen Poems of the Five Mountains.* New York: The Crossroad Publishing Company, 1985.

Saitō Kiyoe. *Insen no Bungaku.* Musashino Shoin, 1963.

Saitō Shō. *Nihon Kanshi.* Shun'yōdō, 1937.

Sanford, James H. *Zen-Man Ikkyū.* Chico, Calif.: Scholars Press, 1981.

Sato, Hiroaki, and Burton Watson. *From the Country of Eight Islands.* Garden City, N.Y.: Anchor Press, 1981.

Shaw, R.D.M. *The Blue Cliff Records.* London: Michael Joseph, 1961.

Tamamura Takeji. *Gozan Bungaku.* Shibundō, 1966.

Terada Tōru. *Gidō Shūshin, Zekkai Chūshin.* Chikuma Shobō, 1977.

Tsuji Zennosuke. *Kūge Rōshi Nichiyō Kūfu Ryakushū.* Taiyōsha, 1942.

Ury, Marian. *Poems of the Five Mountains.* Tokyo: Mushinsha, 1977.

Usui Nobuyoshi. *Ashikaga Yoshimitsu.* Yoshikawa Kōbunkan, 1960.

Varley, H. Paul. *The Ōnin War: History of Its Origins and Background.* New York: Columbia University Press, 1967.

Wang Yi T'ung. *Official Relations between China and Japan.* Cambridge, Mass.: Harvard University Press, 1953.

Watson, Burton. *Records of the Grand Historian of China,* 2 vols. New York: Columbia University Press, 1961.

———. *Su Tung-p'o.* New York: Columbia University Press, 1965.

Yamagishi Tokuhei. *Gozan Bungaku Shū, Edo Kanshi Shū*, in Nihon Koten Bungaku Taikei series. Iwanami Shoten, 1966.

Yanagida Seizan. *Ikkyū Kyōunshū: Mukei no Uta*, 2 vols., in Zen no Koten series. Kōdansha, 1977.

———. *Ikkyū: Kyōunshū no Sekai.* Kyoto: Jimbun Shoin, 1980.

28. MUROMACHI FICTION: OTOGI-ZŌSHI

The traditions of Heian fiction, and especially of *The Tale of Genji*, were not forgotten during the Muromachi period. Not only was *The Tale of Genji* itself made the subject of learned commentaries by members of the emperor's court but, along with various handbooks to the celebrated classic, it was perused even by badly educated warriors who were determined to become cultured. The typical fiction of the Muromachi period, however, did not much resemble *The Tale of Genji*: it was shorter, closer in language to its time, and more apt to describe priests, soldiers, or commoners than courtiers who preserved the traditions of the world of the Shining Prince. There was little influence from the courtly fiction of the Kamakura period, but the stories about soldiers often derived inspiration from *The Tale of the Heike* and similar works.

These short stories are generally known today as *otogi-zōshi*, a term that originally meant "tales of a companion"—"companions" (*otogi*) having been those who entertained their superiors with recitations and other spoken or sung performances.[1] The term *otogi* acquired its present meaning early in the eighteenth century when a collection of twenty-three medieval tales was published in Osaka under the title *Otogi Bunko* (Companion Library);[2] the individual stories of this collection became known as otogi-zōshi, a term used later for most of the fiction written during the Muromachi and early Tokugawa periods.[3]

Over four hundred of these stories survive. Only one can be dated precisely; the dates proposed for the others vary in some cases by as much as two hundred years. Authorship is equally uncertain; only the one dated story can be confidently credited to a particular man, and even this identification is not illuminating because the author is otherwise unknown.[4] A few tales have been attributed to such celebrated writers of the Muromachi period as the poets Nijō Yoshimoto and Ichijō Kaneyoshi or to the priests Gen'e and Ikkyū.[5]

The otogi-zōshi are not stylistically distinguished. The same images occur innumerable times: the appearance of beautiful women almost invariably evoked comparison to cherry blossoms and tinted autumn leaves, and if these women were likened to famous beauties of the past, it was always to the same three or four Chinese or Japanese ladies.[6] Stereotyped phrases and descriptions recur from tale to tale and are sometimes repeated within the same work. The texts, though mercifully easier to read than most other examples of premodern literature, lack individuality of expression; it is hard to imagine that an accomplished writer like Kaneyoshi could have penned such compositions.[7]

It was no doubt because of their lack of stylistic distinction that the Muromachi stories were seldom considered by scholars of Japanese literature of the past, and even in recent times the greatest efforts have been devoted to transcribing the texts and collating variants, rather than to discussing their literary worth or placing these stories within Japanese literary traditions. Relatively few of the sources of the stories have been identified apart from those that unquestionably borrowed their themes from well-known Japanese or Chinese works or that resemble extant folktales. Perhaps it has not seemed worth the trouble to trace the antecedents of stories of uncertain intrinsic literary value.[8] However, interest of quite another kind was shown in the otogi-zōshi during the postwar years. At a time when the democratization of Japan was much on people's minds the tales were praised as examples of "literature of the common people";[9] later (as the Japanese became more absorbed with their particular place in the world), they were acclaimed as "literature of the Japanese people."[10] But regardless of how commentators have interpreted the otogi-zōshi, their attention has usually been focused on the twenty-three stories of the original *Otogi Bunko* collection, and the bulk of the stories remains inaccessible to the general reader.

The stories have been divided into various categories in the hope of bringing order to an otherwise unmanageable mass of texts.[11] Ichiko Teiji, whose scholarly work has exercised the greatest influence, proposed six categories of subjects—the aristocracy, the priesthood, the military, the common people, foreign countries, and nonhuman beings. Not every story can be easily fitted into one of these categories, and some fit almost equally well into several. Even within the same category, moreover, there may be a great range of subjects; for this reason Ichiko was obliged to establish subcategories; for example, among stories treating the priesthood he distinguished those about young acolytes, corrupt priests who had violated the commandments, priests whose faith had been awakened by some extraordinary experience, and great priests of the past. Tales about the avatars of the various Buddhist or Shintō divinities formed still another subcategory of "the priesthood." A simpler division might be equally satisfactory: the nobility, the priesthood, the military, and the commoners.[12]

Tales of the Nobility

The otogi-zōshi that treat the lives of the nobility are generally the least praised by scholars who discuss fiction of the Muromachi period. These tales say little, except inadvertently, about the lives of the mass of people of their time. They are cast in an idiom that seldom suggests how much the Japanese language had changed in the course of the three hundred years since the Heian romances were written and are all too frequently devoted to matters that were more effectively treated in earlier fiction. But some of these stories about the nobility have enough charm to keep them from being dismissed as mere copies of *The Tale of Genji*.

Utatane no Sōshi (A Tale of Fugitive Dreams) has traditionally (but uncertainly) been attributed to a daughter of the courtier and poet Asukai Masachika (1417–1490).[13] An inscription on the box containing one of the surviving manuscripts, in the form of an *emakimono*, or hand scroll, credits the illustrations and calligraphy to two men who were otherwise active in the middle of the fifteenth century.[14] This seems to date the manuscript, though not necessarily the text, a pastiche of a Heian romance whose content hardly suggests the turbulence of Japan in the fifteenth century. Perhaps it most clearly reveals its time in the wistfulness of its evocations of the court in former days.

A Tale of Fugitive Dreams opens with the celebrated poem by Ono no Komachi:

utatane ni	Ever since I saw
koishiki hito wo	The man who is dear to me
miteshi yori	While I was napping,
yume chō mono wa	I have begun to believe
tanomi someteki	The things that people call dreams.

The poem is appropriate as the epigraph for a work whose plot is unfolded mainly in the form of dreams. In Japanese poetry dreams were normally considered to be the opposite pole to reality and therefore unworthy of trust, but the heroine of this story (like Komachi before her) came to believe in them.

The lady is the daughter of an important court official. Although he has had many children by his various wives and concubines, he dotes so much on this particular daughter that he is unwilling to send her to court where, even if she is fortunate enough to enjoy the emperor's favors, she will surely be subjected to the jealousy and intrigues of other palace ladies. The daughter grows into a woman of exceptional beauty and accomplishments, but she is lonely. Her mother would have searched for a suitable husband, but the mother is dead, and her father is so preoccupied with court business that he tends to forget about her. The lady spends her days in brooding and in boredom.

One day in the rainy season the lady is whiling away the time by playing her koto. She wearily puts aside the instrument, and before she knows it she has dozed off. In her dream someone brings her a spray of wisteria to which a letter written on lavender paper has been attached. It contains this poem:

omoine ni	More insubstantial
miru yume yori mo	Than phantoms seen only in
hakanaki wa	A dream of longing:
shiranu utsutsu no	The face of one who is real
yoso no omokage[15]	But distant and a stranger.

She awakes before she can discover who sent her the letter, but her thoughts keep returning to the dream. She induces herself to fall asleep again, and this time she sees before her the man who wrote the poem, a splendidly attired young gentleman whose appearance is so radiant that she wonders if "even the Shining Genji one reads about in that old story could be a match for this man."[16] The gentleman takes her hand and chides her for not having vouchsafed a word in response to his poem, and he reminds her of the terrible consequences of rejected love. But just as she prepares to answer him, a cock crows and the gentleman says he must leave. Once again she awakes, still ignorant of the identity of her dream suitor.

The lady falls into a despondent state that is not relieved by the prayers of the priests summoned by her worried father. Her half-brother, a priest of the Ishiyama-dera, suggests that the lady pray at the temple to the deity Kannon, who grants to believers whatever they desire,[17] and the lady sets out on foot, imitating Tamakazura in *The Tale of Genji* who had refused a carriage when she made a pilgrimage to Hatsuse, believing that the more arduous the journey, the more likely her prayers would be answered.

Once she is surrounded by the holy atmosphere of the temple the lady recalls that it was in this very temple that Murasaki Shikibu wrote *The Tale of Genji*.[18] At that moment she hears from the next room men's voices; one of them, to her astonishment, is exactly like the voice of the man of her dream. In the course of the conversation the man (identified as Sadaishō) reveals that he had come to the temple in the hope of obtaining relief from the torment aroused by a dream. The lady peeps into the room. Peeping through a fence or hedge (*kaima-miru*) is a familiar device in Heian literature, but this is a rare instance of a woman's taking a covert look at a man.

As Sadaishō tells his companions about his dream, he recalls a passage in *The Tale of Genji*;[19] like the lady, he is reenacting *Genji*. He describes the beautiful woman of his dream and his unhappiness over not being able to meet her.

The lady spends the night by the crack in the door, looking at and listening to the man she loves. But when morning comes she decides that there is no seemly way for her to reveal her identity,[20] nor can she possibly forget him. She has no choice but to place her trust in Kannon and in the life to come.

A messenger arrives from the aged nurse of her elder brother, a priest. The nurse has heard that the lady is in the vicinity. The lady decides to visit her, but as she and her women are crossing a bridge, she suddenly throws herself into the river. The women shriek for help. Providentially, a boat is passing and the lady is rescued. Aboard the boat, as we might have guessed, is Sadaishō. Seeing her in the flesh for the first time, he is dazzled by her beauty, even more striking than in the dream, and she, overcome with joy, forgets her embarrassment. They are united and, we are told, their descendants prosper mightily. The story concludes with a brief apology from the author for having wasted good ink in writing so inadequate an account of the wonders of fate.

The author of *A Tale of Fugitive Dreams* was in no sense attempting to hide his indebtedness to *The Tale of Genji*; on the contrary, he was at pains to call attention to parallel situations. All the same, this wispy romance bears little resemblance to its great predecessor. It is not merely a matter of scale; unlike Murasaki Shikibu, this author used only the most conventional expressions when describing his hero and heroine, and we are likely to remember the tale not in terms of the characters but of its dreamlike atmosphere or perhaps its pictorial beauty. Several enchanting emakimono confirm this impression: the people depicted seem to have their eyes shut throughout, as if they walk in their sleep.

The paintings are even more successful than the prose in conveying the fragile beauty of the story.[21]

This is by no means the only instance of the illustrations of an otogi-zōshi being of superior aesthetic quality to the works they illustrate. Many tales survive only in booklets that were bought and preserved primarily for their illustrations. These brightly colored volumes are known as Nara Ehon, or Nara picture books.[22] They were produced in the sixteenth and seventeenth centuries, mainly for the amusement of the upper classes, whether as bridal gifts or merely as tasteful decorations for empty bookshelves; but their popularity waned when inexpensive illustrated printed books began to appear in the seventeenth century.[23]

Hitomotogiku (A Single Chrysanthemum), a tale of the nobility in the form of a Nara picture book, recounts (like many otogi-zōshi about the nobility) the cruelties of a wicked stepmother; but it is unusual in that there are two victims, a brother and a sister, rather than a single Cinderella in the tradition of the stepmother stories of the Heian and Kamakura periods.[24] The boy (like Genji) is exiled, and the girl (like Ochikubo) is shut up in a wretched house, but despite these Heian touches, the work betrays its Muromachi origins in such passages as the account of a pilgrimage to Kiyomizu-dera, another temple sacred to Kannon. Worship of Kannon was certainly not new, but during the Muromachi period pilgrimages to the thirty-three temples sacred to Kannon became a craze.[25]

Iwaya[26] (The Hut in the Rocks), another work of the same genre, features an even more hateful stepmother. The story, set in the ninth century, relates the hardships endured by Tainoya,[27] the daughter of Middle Counselor Korenaka. Her mother died when she was still a child, and her father remarried two years later. The new wife had a daughter of her own, a year older than Tainoya, and this made Korenaka suppose that she would extend to Tainoya the affection she felt for her own daughter. However (as we might have predicted), the stepmother resents Korenaka's seeming partiality for Tainoya, and resolves to get rid of her.

In Tainoya's thirteenth year Korenaka is appointed the vice-governor of the Dazaifu in Kyūshū. He decides to take his family with him, and the stepmother sees a golden opportunity for getting rid of Tainoya. She summons the daughter's tutor, Tadaie, who assures her there is no task, however difficult, that he would not perform for her. The stepmother orders Tadaie to abduct and drown the girl on the way to Kyūshū.

The obedient Tadaie manages to abduct Tainoya, but she is so lovely he finds it almost impossible to kill her. Steeling himself, he tells the girl to say her prayers, but as she prays his resolution falters once again; instead of killing Tainoya, he abandons her on a rock off the coast of the island of Awaji.

When the others discover that Tainoya is missing, they can only suppose that she has drowned. Tainoya, however, is rescued by fishermen and lives in their remote village for four years until a nobleman, shipwrecked in a storm, accidentally discovers her and, entranced by her beauty, takes her to the capital.

This unusually long otogi-zōshi goes on to describe the jealousy Tainoya's beauty arouses among the palace ladies, the tests to which she is subjected by them in the hope of revealing her uncouth background, and finally her joy when she is reunited with her father and acclaimed at court as the fairest and most accomplished lady of the land. At the end the wicked stepmother (who has already suffered a bout of madness, attributed to spirit possession) loses her senses completely and dies, and the fisherman who rescued Tainoya is rewarded by being elevated to the rank of daimyo.

The Hut in the Rocks is far more literary than most other otogi-zōshi, possibly an indication that it followed closely a lost Heian romance. As so often in these stories, there is mention of Prince Genji, in this case in connection with his travels along the coast of the Inland Sea from Suma to Akashi.[28] The principal characters are more persuasively drawn than in most tales, and even minor figures are sometimes characterized so successfully in a few words as to leave a distinct impression.

Other stories about the nobility are devoted to such historical figures of the Heian court as Ono no Komachi and Izumi Shikibu. Both women are portrayed in terms of their sensual natures. *Izumi Shikibu* opens in this manner:

> Not so long ago, during the reign of the Emperor Ichijō, there was in our fair capital a beautiful courtesan named Izumi Shikibu. There was in the palace a man named Tachibana no Yasumasa. From the time that Yasumasa was in his nineteenth year and Izumi Shikibu in her thirteenth, an extraordinary bond was formed between them. Their feelings ran deep, and in the spring of her fourteenth year she gave birth to a baby boy. At night, as they murmured together, pillows side by side, how ashamed she must have felt! She abandoned the baby on the Gojō Bridge. She wrote a poem on the hems of the

narrow-sleeved kimono of pale blue lined with crimson the baby wore, and left beside him an unsheathed dagger.[29] A townsman found the baby and, after rearing him, sent him up Mount Hiei."[30]

The boy grows to maturity at the Tendai monastery on Mount Hiei, where he develops into such an extraordinary scholar that even as a youth he is celebrated not only in the monastery but throughout the whole country. When Tōmei, as he is called, is in his eighteenth year he is summoned to the palace to give sermons on the Lotus Sutra. A wind is blowing through the courtyard as he lectures, and two or three times the blinds are lifted by the wind, revealing a beautiful young woman of about thirty years of age who is sitting within, intently listening to his sermon. (This scene recalls the one in *The Tale of Genji* when a cat on a leash knocks aside the curtains hiding the Third Princess, permitting Kashiwagi to see her.) From the first glimpse, Tōmei falls in love with the woman, and when he returns to his cell, he can think of nothing but her. Yearning to see her again, he hits on the plan of gaining access to the palace by pretending to be a tangerine peddler. (During the Heian period it would have been quite unthinkable for a peddler to wander into the palace, but times had evidently changed.) The lady sends a servant with twenty coppers to buy some tangerines, and Tōmei gives her twenty tangerines which he counts out in the form of twenty love poems.[31] The astonished servant asks how it happens that a man of his talents became a peddler, and he answers with the cryptic word *furifuri*. Word of the strange peddler gets around the palace, and the emperor orders that he be trailed when he leaves.

The servant reports to her mistress what has happened. Izumi Shikibu at once recognizes the allusion to a poem describing a woman whose tears fell like rain *(furifuri)* because of unrequited love. Recalling the unhappy fate of Ono no Komachi, who was cruel to her would-be lover, she goes to Tōmei's lodgings. He is overjoyed and the two spend the night together. The next morning, when she is about to leave, she happens to notice Tōmei's little dagger and asks about it. He tells how it was found with him after he was abandoned as a baby on the Gojō Bridge. The lady asks him how old he is, what clothes he was wearing when he was abandoned, and what poem was written on his infant clothes. She produces the scabbard of the dagger, and reveals that she has kept it on her person ever since she abandoned her baby. They realize to their horror that they are mother and son. But Izumi Shikibu, unlike Jocasta, is not suicidal; instead, she intuitively understands that she had to be shocked into following the path of the Buddha. She leaves the same night for a temple where she spends the rest of her life in prayer. The story concludes with a somewhat altered version of one of Izumi Shikibu's best-known poems:

kuraki yori	I came from darkness
kuraki yamiji ni	To be born in the darkness
umarekite	Of an obscure path;
sayaka ni terase	Oh, shine on me most brightly,
yama no ha no tsuki[32]	Moon at the edge of the hill.

The religious ending of this story is characteristic of the otogi-zōshi, many of which conclude with the protagonist fleeing the "burning house" of this world and entering Buddhist orders. In Izumi Shikibu's case, the realization that she has committed incest leads her to take a step that she might not have otherwise considered or would have postponed indefinitely. In other cases, the intentional commission of a crime, even murder, provides the impetus for gaining salvation; repentance and prayer can win forgiveness.

Other otogi-zōshi about the nobility follow traditions of the monogatari so closely that it is almost impossible to detect anything that is specifically of their time, though the clumsiness of the style and the construction often gives away the late composition. Yet however derivative these stories about the nobility may be, they are certainly more effective as literature than the mass of otogi-zōshi. The emphasis in these stories is not so much on the love shared by the characters as on the obstacles that keep them apart; perhaps this is their most distinctive feature. But the classicizing attitude of the authors, who seem to have felt that the world they actually lived in was not worth describing, kept their works from enjoying the popularity of even inartistic tales that better reflected their own times.

Tales of the Buddhist Priesthood

The Buddhist temples played so large a part in the lives of people of the Muromachi period that it is not surprising many of the otogi-zōshi describe priests, temples, or the avatars of the various Buddhist divinities. Among the tales of the priesthood, two subcategories proposed by Ichiko, those that described *chigo* (acolytes) and those that are devoted to the events which caused some priest to experience *hosshin tonsei* (awakening of the faith and escape from this world), were of particular literary importance.

Seven of the nine surviving stories about chigo relate how monks fell in love with boys—some acolytes at their temples, others merely visitors. It was, of course, prohibited for monks to marry or to have sexual relations with women, and for that reason some sought erotic pleasure in the company of boys of fifteen or sixteen. This, too, was a sin, but probably not quite as shameful to people of the time as consorting with women. In the otogi-zōshi the love of monks for boys is usually reciprocated, and is not portrayed in terms of decadence or immorality; rather, these attachments (though attachments to *anything* in this world were undesirable) are praised as the direct causes of enlightenment. At the end of a chigo story the boy is likely to be revealed as having been in reality a buddha who came into the world to guide the monk on the true path of salvation.

The best known of the chigo stories is *Aki no Yo no Nagamonogatari* (A Long Tale for an Autumn Night).[33] This late Kamakura or early Muromachi work tells the story of Sensai, a learned and artistically accomplished priest who lived at the end of the Heian period.[34] Sensai was known in his own time especially because of the great golden statue of Amida Buddha erected in the Ungo-ji, the temple in the Higashiyama area with which he was long associated.[35] Poems by Sensai were included in the *Shin Kokinshū* and later imperial anthologies, and he enjoyed a following as a leading Jōdo cleric of his day.

A Long Tale was written in the episodic manner of an emakimono with shifts of scene that lend themselves to pictorial depiction. Despite its title, it is not especially long even by the standards of the average otogi-zōshi (it is only about twenty-five pages in a modern edition). The story opens with an account of Sensai, then known as Keikai, a priest who has gained recognition as a master of sacred and profane knowledge and even of the military arts, but is nevertheless dissatisfied with his life. He has begun to wonder if all of his efforts to gain Buddhist enlightenment had not in the final analysis been inspired by his hopes of winning fame and profit. He makes up his mind to withdraw from human society and seek truth in a solitary hut in the mountains.

Before he leaves for this retreat, Keikai goes to the Ishiyama-dera where he plans to spend seventeen days and nights praying for Kannon's help in achieving enlightenment. On the seventh night he sees in a dream a beautiful young man standing beneath a cherry tree that sheds blossoms over him. Keikai interprets this vision as a sign that his prayers have been answered; and instead of going off to a hut in the mountains, he enters the monastery on Mount Hiei. He can think of nothing but the youth who appeared in his dream, though it hardly seems possible anyone so beautiful could exist in this world.

One day when Keikai is passing by the great Mii-dera, not far from Mount Hiei, he is caught in a sudden rain and decides to take shelter. As he nears the gate he sees the boy who appeared in his dream, standing under a magnificent cherry tree and breaking off a branch from which blossoms cascade like snow.

Keikai falls madly in love with the youth, and eventually is able to spend one night with him, but the boy, Umewaka, mysteriously disappears. He has been abducted by a *tengu* and shut up in a cave. The priests of the Mii-dera, not knowing this, suppose that Umewaka has been stolen from them by Keikai, a monk from the hated Enryaku-ji. Their fury aroused, two thousand monks from the Mii-dera attack their rivals, only to be met by a vastly superior force from the Enryaku-ji. The Mii-dera is once again destroyed.

In the cave where he is kept prisoner by the tengu, Umewaka hears about the burning of the Mii-dera, and learns that it was in order to foment discord between the two temples that the mischief-making tengu abducted him. Umewaka and his servant manage to escape, aided by a storm god, but the thought that he was responsible for the destruction of the temple and the loss of many lives weighs on Umewaka, and he throws himself from a bridge into Lake Biwa. Keikai is desolated, but Shinra Daimyōjin, the Shintō god who protects the Mii-dera, manifests himself and reveals that Umewaka was in reality the Kannon of the Ishiyama-dera who, in order to bring enlightenment to Keikai, had taken the form of the beautiful youth. Keikai, at last free of all worldly attachment, changes his name to Sensai as a sign he is a new man, and goes to live in a mountain retreat. The poem he wrote on the wall of his hut was of such surpassing beauty that it was later included in the *Shin Kokinshū*.

A Long Tale for an Autumn Night describes a priest who actually lived, and a historical event, the burning of the Mii-dera. It is at least possible that Sensai loved an acolyte of the rival temple: indeed, one professedly historical record of the fighting between the monks from the two temples stated that the Mii-dera was burned in 1181 as the result of the hostility aroused by the disappearance of a boy loved by Keikai.[36] But even if the historicity of a few elements in the story can be demonstrated, the rest is fiction, inspired by the legends that grew up around Sensai after his death.[37] The intervention of the tengu and

Shinra Daimyōjin makes it evident that the author's main purpose in relating the tale was to persuade readers that enlightenment can be attained in unexpected ways.

The author of *A Long Tale* was traditionally identified as the priest Gen'e. Modern scholars for a time rejected the attribution for want of hard evidence, only for it to be revived in recent years, mainly because of the discovery of the oldest-known text of *A Long Tale*, dated 1377, on the reverse of a manuscript of the *Taiheiki*, which was long supposed to be (in part) by Gen'e.[38] Perhaps Gen'e actually witnessed the last burning of the Mii-dera in 1319, and recalled it in his story. However, the appeal of this tale obviously does not lie in its documentary value but in the exceptionally moving and well expressed narrative. We cannot take seriously the machinations of goblins, but it is possible to believe in Keikai's love for the boy Umewaka, and the tale is far more appealingly narrated than most of the otogi-zōshi. This first work of Japanese literature devoted chiefly to a description of homosexual love is one of the most artistic. Scholars have suggested that the author—Gen'e or whoever it was—may have been attempting to justify, by revealing that Umewaka was a manifestation of Kannon, the love he personally had felt for a beautiful boy.[39] Such loves were evidently common in monasteries, but if they had not been clothed in the poetic expression of *A Long Tale* and the other chigo tales, they would probably not have been preserved in later times when the loves of priests were no longer of much interest.

The chigo tales generally have plots that (in all but the crucial respect of the sex of the beloved) closely resemble more conventional stories of romantic love. The first meeting of a priest with the boy is accidental, but after one glimpse the priest falls helplessly in love; he discovers to his great joy that the love is shared; against their inclinations, the lovers are separated, leading to the death of one of them; the survivor spends his remaining days in prayers for the lover he has lost. In *Matsuhoura Monogatari* (The Tale of Matsuhoura), for example, a priest and the boy he loves are separated by the son of the prime minister, who has himself fallen in love with the boy. He sends the priest into exile on the island of Awaji in order to get rid of the rival, but the boy does not respond to the other man's affection. Resolved to follow the priest into exile, the boy escapes and reaches Awaji, only to learn that the priest has died. In despair, he shaves his head and, in his sixteenth year, becomes a monk on Mount Kōya.[40]

The language of the chigo tales is generally poetic, in the manner of the Heian novels rather than that of most otogi-zōshi. This passage from *Toribeyama Monogatari* (The Tale of Mount Toribe) may suggest the mood:

> One night he secretly made his way into the house where the boy lived. A perfume that seemed a part of the place lingered pervasively in the air, making him all but exclaim that he had reached the land of a living Buddha. He peeped in through the door, which had been left slightly ajar. A screen depicting swirling cherry blossoms and red leaves stood around the boy who was quietly bending over a pile of picture books that he had spread open in the dim light of a lamp, a faint fragrance emanating from his tumbling stray locks. He was like the dawn when blossoms are heavy with dew or an evening landscape when willows incline with the wind, incomparably more lovely than when the priest first saw him in the northern hills. He pushed open the door and went in. The serene charm with which the boy greeted him made him wonder if this might not be an unfinished dream, but he went up beside him, tears as much of pain as of joy starting to his eyes. The look on the boy's face as he shyly turned away might be likened to a spray of autumn clover, the blossoms heavy with dew. It need hardly be said how touching, how lovely he was—it quite made the priest lose all sense of reality, and the melancholy to which he was prey was completely swept away in the night they spent together.[41]

Phrase after phrase echoes the Heian classics. The scene of their meeting is written with grace and sensitivity, but we know from the outset that the pledges of love they exchange that night cannot last very long; this gives greater poignance to the Buddhist belief with which the work is colored throughout—that the world we live in is not to be depended on. The priest and the boy continue to write even after they part, but the boy wastes away with loneliness. At first he refuses to disclose the cause of his grief, but one day, moved by an old servant's devotion, he reveals the secret of his love. The servant informs the boy's parents, who agree to send for the priest and allow him to live with the boy. As soon as the priest receives word of the parents' decision, he sets out for the boy's house; on the way, however, another letter reaches him, this one telling of the boy's death. The priest builds a hut by Mount Toribe, the site of the boy's funeral pyre, where he spends his remaining days in prayer.

If some of the chigo tales are similar in expression to the tales about the nobility, others are close to the tales of the military, suggesting once again the difficulty of assigning works to a particular category. *Gemmu Monogatari*[42] (The Tale of Gemmu) is once again the story of a priest who has fallen in love with a young man, but Hanamatsu is somewhat older than the boys in the other stories, and though he responds to Gemmu's love, his heart is set on vengeance for his father. Hanamatsu and Gemmu meet intimately only in Gemmu's dreams. He learns that Hanamatsu successfully killed his father's enemy only to be killed by another man. Stunned by this revelation, he goes to Mount Kōya, where he gives himself to prayers for his dead lover.

On the first anniversary of Hanamatsu's death Gemmu attends a special service in the Founder's Hall, where he notices a young priest praying with unusual fervor. Moved by curiosity, Gemmu asks the other priest why he has entered orders so young. The priest reveals that he is the son of the slain man. He killed his father's assailant; but when he examined the body of the man he had killed, Hanamatsu's beauty had moved him to an awareness of the brevity and undependability of human life. He had come to Mount Kōya to pray for Hanamatsu's repose. The two men realize that it was because of Hanamatsu that they had both experienced an awakening of faith. We are told that they spent the rest of their lives on the mountain in prayer, and the story concludes with the revelation that Hanamatsu was a reincarnation of the divinity Mañjuśri, who had assumed human form in order to bring about the salvation of the two men.[43]

Another variety of tale about priests, one of particular literary importance, is the confession of what had induced men and women to "abandon the world" and devote themselves to Buddhist prayer and meditation. People of the middle ages believed that if one became a priest or nun it would wipe out all one's sins on earth and promote rebirth in paradise. Most people of the aristocratic or warrior class in their old age or when they suffered a severe illness shaved their heads, took vows of ordination, and assumed the dark robes of the Buddhist clergy.[44] Even a man like Taira no Kiyomori, whose life of violence hardly promised salvation, became a priest late in life; but it was less common for a man in his prime to enter Buddhist orders. Some of the most affecting otogi-zōshi describe what led relatively young people of dissimilar backgrounds to take the Great Step.

The best of these stories and, indeed, the story often rated as the finest of all the otogi-zōshi is *Sannin Hōshi* (The Three Priests).[45] The setting is Mount Kōya, as so often in these tales. Three priests come together by chance from the various places on the mountain where they have their abodes, and one of them in the course of a conversation suggests, "Let us each confess to the others why he has abandoned the world. This can surely do no harm, for they say that confession reduces the sins."[46]

The first priest to speak is a man in his early forties. Despite his torn robes and haggard face, something of the aristocrat lingers about his appearance. He recalls how when he was young and known as Kasuya no Shirozaemon, he was in the service of the shogun Ashikaga Takauji. On one occasion he accompanied Takauji to the house of Lord Nijō,[47] where he saw a court lady who was so extraordinarily beautiful that he fell desperately in love. Unable to think of anything but the lady, for days he refused all nourishment. The shogun, worried about Kasuya's condition, sent his personal physician to examine the young man. The physician diagnosed Kasuya's malady as love. The shogun thereupon sent Kasuya's closest friend to find out who had aroused this passion in Kasuya, and the friend, discovering the name of the lady, reported this to the shogun, who did what he could to promote Kasuya's suit.

All went well, but one night, when Kasuya had left the lady to worship at a shrine, he heard people gossiping about a court lady who had been killed by a robber who tore off her clothes. As he listened, a terrible presentiment came over him, and he rushed out to learn what had happened. His worst fears were realized: not only had his beloved been killed without mercy, but even her hair had been sheared off by the robber. In horror and despair, Kasuya became a monk that very night. For the past twenty years he has lived on the mountain, praying for her repose.

> The next priest to speak was a man of about fifty. He stood six feet tall, had a protruding Adam's apple, angular chin, prominent cheekbones that gave the face a forbidding expression, thick lips, large eyes and nose. He was dark complexioned and had an extremely heavy frame. Above his tattered robes he wore a stole tucked into his cloak. As he spoke he fingered a large rosary. "I should like to be the next to tell my story," he said. The others urged him to begin at once. He said, "Strange to relate, it was I who killed the lady!"[48]

At the words Kasuya starts up, ready to kill the man who murdered his beloved, but Aragorō, the second priest, begs him to remain calm until he has finished his story. Aragorō relates that he began his life of crime at the age of eight and was twelve when he first killed a man. But in the year that he killed the woman Kasuya loved, his luck had turned and he had failed to commit even one successful robbery. His wife and children were without food or clothing, and his wife nagged at him to bring home some money. In desperation Aragorō went out that night and waited for someone to pass. A radiantly beautiful court lady accompanied by two maids went by and he ran after them. The maids escaped, but the lady stood her ground. Aragorō demanded all her clothes, including her underrobe, and when she refused he killed and stripped her.

His wife was delighted with the loot, but asked how old the victim was. "Seventeen or eighteen," replied Aragorō, at which the wife rushed outside without a word of explanation. After a while she returned, saying, "You are really much too magnanimous a robber. As long as you are committing a crime you should try to make the most of it. I just went to cut off her hair. My own is rather thin, but if I twist hers into plaits it will really look beautiful. I wouldn't change it for the robes."[49]

Aragorō, filled with disgust and revulsion, reflected on his life of crime, and understood that if he continued he would not escape the torments of hell. "To go on in this way committing grievous sins, dragging out a meaningless existence, not realizing the hollowness and futility of my life, seemed revolting even to me. And now the monstrous behavior of my wife had struck me dumb with horror. I repented bitterly that I had slept with such a woman, that our lives had been joined." That very night he went to see the monk Gen'e, became his disciple, and soon afterward climbed up Mount Kōya. He offers now to let Kasuya kill him, in whatever way he chooses, but Kasuya realizes that the lady must have been a manifestation of a bodhisattva who came into the world to save both men. "If this had not happened, would we have become priests, turned our backs on the world, and placed our hopes in the incomparable bliss of paradise? This is our joy within sorrow, and from this day forth I shall be grateful for the event that has made us companions in seeking the Way."

The story of the third of the priests, disappointingly, is not connected with those of Kasuya and Aragorō. The high reputation of *The Three Priests* is due to the unexpected dovetailing of the first two narrations (though a similar effect is found in *The Tale of Gemmu*), and to the brief but unforgettable portrait of Aragorō's wife. The ending of the story recalls Shinran's paradox, "Even the good person can be saved"; and Aragorō, for all his unspeakable acts of wickedness, will be saved because he has thrown himself on Buddha's mercy. This was certainly an appropriate conclusion for a tale about priests, but it was also used to conclude many other works; however artfully they might narrate their stories, however many amusing or frightening events they might include to capture the attention of readers, a didactic intent was generally close to the hearts of those who composed the otogi-zōshi.

Tales of the Military

The Muromachi period was marked by almost incessant warfare, and much of the fiction composed during the age, as we might expect, described the military. Some otōgi-zōshi rehearse the mighty deeds of the heroes of the war between the Taira and the Minamoto, others are devoted to their immediate descendants or else to warriors of a somewhat later generation, but surprisingly few tales are about more recent events. The repulsion of the two invasions of the Mongols in 1274 and 1281 should have provided materials for stories celebrating the Japanese heroes and the *kamikaze*, but they inspired hardly a single literary work.[50] Godaigo's abortive revolt, his exile to Oki and later triumphant return, and, above all, the heroism of Kusunoki Masashige are the kind of subjects that would have attracted European writers of poetry and prose, but the Japanese authors, fearing perhaps official disapproval, avoided mention of the military and political events of their own times. When not set in the distant past, the stories are usually no more precisely dated than *mukashi* (a long time ago).

Although vague with respect to time, the tales are usually quite precise as to where the action took place. Unlike the Heian and Kamakura stories, they are prevailingly set in the hinterland rather than in the capital, reflecting the establishment of centers of culture in many parts of the country.[51] Writers who had been driven from the capital by the warfare of the fifteenth century took refuge with local potentates, bringing with them the culture of the capital. They may have felt obliged to mention in their compositions the legends and traditions of the places where they had taken refuge.

The otogi-zōshi that treat the military class were probably intended to please samurai who enjoyed hearing or reading about the heroic deeds of the past. Ichiko distinguished three main varieties of military tales: those about heroes who vanquished monsters; those concerned with the warfare between the Minamoto and the Taira; and those that describe succession disputes and vendettas among the military families of the provinces.

Stories about heroes who conquered supernatural creatures go back as far as the *Kojiki*, where we find the story of the god Susano-o and the monstrous serpent. The best-known otogi-zōshi, both in terms of its lasting popularity through the centuries and its influence on later literature, is probably *Shuten Dōji*.[52] This rather lengthy tale describes the triumph of the hero Minamoto Raikō and his five friends over a demon who has been abducting and devouring beautiful young ladies. Their victory is not unaided: before they set out for Ōe-yama where the demon has his stronghold the heroes pray at three shrines,[53] and the gods of these shrines lend their help at critical moments. When the gods first appear (in the guise of three old men), they tell the heroes about the sake-loving demon Shuten Dōji, and supply them with a magical liquor which, if consumed by demons, will prevent them from flying, but if consumed by men is a medicine. The old men also give the heroes star-crested helmets that they must wear when they kill Shuten Dōji.

The six heroes make their way to Shuten Dōji's hideout. When the other demons first see Raikō and his friends, they are delighted: they have not had any human beings to eat in quite a while, and these men will make a fine dinner. But they dare not eat the men without first obtaining permission from their master. The heroes, brought before Shuten Dōji, identify themselves as *yamabushi* who have lost their way. They say they would like to offer him some special sake. At the mention of sake Shuten Dōji's interest is aroused, and he invites the six men to drink with him. The liquor he serves is blood squeezed from human beings, and as appetizers there are human arms and thighs. Shuten Dōji offers Raikō a cup of this wine, which he cheerfully drains. Entering into the spirit of the occasion, Raikō slices off some of the meat and eats it, smacking his lips. Watanabe Tsuna does the same. Shuten Dōji is surprised that priests should so readily drink and eat the rather special fare of his table, but Raikō informs him that it is their duty to eat whatever anyone out of kindness bestows on them even if it is not entirely to their taste.

Now it is Raikō's turn to offer entertainment. Shuten Dōji and the other demons gladly drink and become inebriated on the sake provided. Shuten Dōji retires to his bedchamber, perhaps to sleep off the effects of the liquor, but once again the three gods intercede, fastening Shuten Dōji's arms and legs to posts in four directions. The gods instruct the heroes how best to decapitate Shuten Dōji and the lesser demons. In a scene of joyful carnage, Raikō and his associates do precisely as told. They rescue the many maidens who have been captured by the ogres and bring them back to the court where the emperor welcomes the heroes and bestows splendid rewards. They all live happily ever after.

The other heroes on Raikō's team were celebrated in stories of their own, and some also slew monsters.[54] They were not the only men credited with such feats. *Tawara Tōda Monogatari* relates how the hero Tawara Tōda Hidesato killed the giant centipede of Mikami Mountain; in the second part of the tale Hidesato disposed of a mere human being, the would-be usurper Taira no Masakado.[55] Sometimes the hero instead of killing a female monster marries her, discovering her true identity only when, about to give birth, she resumes her "real" appearance as a serpent.[56]

The bravery of these heroes is never in question, but they always benefit from divine intervention, and sometimes even a man who is not a renowned hero triumphs because he carries a magic sword presented by the gods.[57] It is curious all the same that in an age of warfare, when there was no shortage of heroism, the storytellers felt obliged to provide divine help for their heroes, some of them bearing the names of historical personages.

The otogi-zōshi about heroes and the descendants of the heroes of the wars between the Minamoto and the Taira are more appealing and certainly of greater literary value. Two in particular stand out, *Yokobue no Sōshi* (The Story of Yokobue)[58] and *Ko Atsumori* (Little Atsumori).

The Story of Yokobue is not concerned with warfare or the suppression of demons though its hero, Takiguchi,[59] is a soldier. He falls in love with Yokobue, a lady in the entourage of the Empress Kenreimon'in. His love is reciprocated, and he wishes to marry Yokobue, but his father, pointing out that she comes from an unimportant family,[60] insists that he break all ties with her at once. Unwilling to disobey his father, but unable to dismiss Yokobue, Takiguchi takes Buddhist vows and enters a temple. Yokobue, at first supposing he has deserted her, is heartbroken, but when she discovers he is at a temple rushes there. She begs for a glimpse of him, but he yields only to the extent of speaking to her briefly from behind a door. In despair, she drowns herself. Takiguchi finds her body and, after burying her ashes, climbs Mount Kōya, to live the rest of his life in its silence.

The Story of Yokobue illustrates the difficulty of assigning works to a particular category: although about a military man, it portrays the world of the aristocracy, and the hero at the end becomes a priest. Needless to say, readers remember the work not in terms of the category to which it belongs but as a story of a tragic love. The essential elements were already present in *The Tale of the Heike*,[61] but the story, as expanded in the otogi-zōshi version, is even more affecting.

Little Atsumori[62] is also derived from *The Tale of the Heike*, but only indirectly. The account of the death of the young general Taira no

Atsumori at the hands of the Minamoto soldier Kumagai Naozane is one of the unforgettable incidents of *The Tale of the Heike*, and doubtless readers desired to know what happened afterward; *Little Atsumori*, like the Nō play *Ikuta Atsumori*, is about the next generation. *The Tale of the Heike* makes no mention of a wife of Atsumori, let alone a son, but the otogi-zōshi states that the wife was seven months pregnant at the time of Atsumori's death. When the baby was born she feared for its life; the victorious Minamoto were determined to eradicate every male Taira. At a loss what to do, she abandoned the baby by the wayside together with a sword, hoping that some kindly person, recognizing the child's superior lineage from the sword, would rear him. The celebrated priest Hōnen, on his way to a ceremony at the Kamo Shrine, heard the baby's cries and took him in his arms. He left the baby with a nurse, and arranged for him to have a suitable education.

Kumagai, at the time a monk at Hōnen's temple, happens to see the child. Struck by his extraordinary resemblance to Atsumori, he asks him about his family. The boy replies, "I was an orphan without father or mother, but the Holy Man found me and saved me." Then, bursting into tears, he asks, "Why do all other children have fathers and mothers and I have none? I have never had a father or a mother." When the boy asked Hōnen the same question, he was told to think of Hōnen himself as both father and mother.

The boy, increasingly unhappy because he knows nothing of his real parents, stops eating and refuses even to drink water. The boy's condition is such that Hōnen decides to track down the boy's parents even if this means that the boy may be killed as a Taira; it is better for him to know his parents than to go on living in ignorance. The boy loses consciousness and it seems as if he must surely die, but just at this time a beautiful young woman, dressed in magnificent robes, arrives at the temple. Seeing the sick child, she reveals that she is his mother.

The boy opens his eyes at his mother's words, seemingly brought back to life. He understands that Atsumori is dead, but he yearns to see him all the same. He goes to the Kamo Shrine and prays for one hundred days that the god grant his wish. On the hundredth day an old man appears and tells the boy that Atsumori is at Ikuta in the province of Settsu. The boy, though in pitifully weakened condition, goes to Ikuta, where he sees an aristocratic-looking young man praying at the shrine. The man asks the boy who he is, and when he replies that he is the son of Atsumori, the man bursts into tears. He is Atsumori. He draws the boy to him, removes his rain-soaked clothes, and then tells him the circumstances of his death. Atsumori describes also the torments of hell, and urges the boy to accumulate merit on earth and in this way lighten the torment his father suffers. The boy begs Atsumori to persuade Emma, the king of hell, to let him take his father's place in the netherworld. Atsumori weeps at these words and strokes the hair of his son, who lies with his head in Atsumori's lap. He writes a poem and gives it to the boy, only to disappear with the approach of the dawn.

When the boy awakens he finds a human bone, and realizing that this must be a relic of his father, takes it along with Atsumori's poem to his mother in the capital. Stunned by these relics, she exchanges the beautiful robes of a court lady for the somber habit of a nun, and builds a shrine to Atsumori where she intends to spend the rest of her days in prayer. At first she is reluctant to part with her son, but she realizes that having this living keepsake of Atsumori by her can only increase the pain she must bear, and she sends the boy back to Hōnen. Alone in the hut she has built, she prays for Atsumori's repose.

Although *Little Atsumori* has its ultimate source in *The Tale of the Heike*, its appeal does not stem from its references to warfare. The story moves us because each detail of the description—for example, when Atsumori removes his son's wet clothes—is at once believable and affecting. The characters are also believable in a way not often encountered in literature of this time. When Hōnen decides it would be better for the boy to be dead rather than live in perpetual uncertainty about his parents, we may not agree about the correctness of his opinion, but psychologically it rings true; and when the boy begs his father to persuade the king of hell to allow him to take his father's place, we can be sure that this is not a formal gesture of filial piety but his real emotion. The otogi-zōshi, though they contain many passages that convey genuine emotions, do not often rise to this level of literary distinction.

A number of otogi-zōshi are about another hero of *The Tale of the Heike*, Minamoto Yoshitsune. The best known of these tales is *Jōruri Jūnidan Sōshi* (The Story of Jōruri in Twelve Episodes),[63] which recounts Yoshitsune's meeting and love affair with Lady Jōruri while on his flight to the north of Japan. The original *Otogi Bunko* included another tale about Yoshitsune, *Onzōshi Shimawatari* (Yoshitsune's Crossing to the Islands), which relates his journey to the islands north of Japan where he encounters a king of devils and is rescued by a beautiful princess. These stories are of interest to modern readers mainly as examples of the fascination that Yoshitsune continued to exert over the Japanese.

One more military tale should be mentioned, *Akimichi*. Despite its pedestrian style, the story is unforgettable. It is set in the Kamakura period, and the hero, Yamaguchi Akimichi, is a samurai whose consuming wish is to avenge his father, who was murdered by the brigand Kanayama Hachirozaemon; but even though Akimichi is brave and resourceful, he is unable to discover the whereabouts of Kanayama's secret stronghold. As a last resort, Akimichi asks his beautiful wife to gain access to Kanayama by pretending she is a prostitute. At first she is horrified at the thought of surrendering her chastity to another man, even for a noble purpose, but in the end, as a samurai wife, she yields to her husband's imploration.

The plan is successful. Kanayama, despite his extreme suspicion of outsiders, is captivated by the wife's beauty and takes her as his mistress. For a year and a half she waits for some carelessness that will give Akimichi the chance to strike, but Kanayama never relaxes his vigilance. In the meantime, she gives birth to Kanayama's son. The wife's most important task is to discover the location of his secret cave in the mountains. Kanayama killed all the laborers who built the place, and no one except himself knows the way. The wife feigns illness in the hope that Kanayama, who by this time dotes on her, will care for her at his hideout and, just as she hoped, he takes her there.

The first chance to attack Kanayama occurs while he is off in a distant province. The wife guides Akimichi to the cave, where he waits. When Kanayama returns he again takes the wife to the cave, but his suspicions are aroused by every slight indication that an outsider may have found his way there. The wife manages to give a plausible explanation for each sign that Akimichi has penetrated the stronghold, but when they reach the cave Kanayama, just to be sure no one is there, throws a dummy inside to see if some enemy, mistaking the dummy for himself, will attack it. Just as Akimichi, falling into the trap, raises his sword to strike, a chorus of voices is heard. These are the voices of all the people Kanayama has killed. Akimichi holds back his sword and Kanayama, reassured, enters the cave where he is killed.

Now that Akimichi has avenged his father, he plans to revert to his old life, but his wife refuses to live with him; her sacrifice has changed her too much. Abandoning both her husband and her child by Kanayama, she becomes a nun. Akimichi also enters Buddhist orders, leaving Kanayama's child as the heir to the Yamaguchi family.[64]

Akimichi is an exceptionally well narrated tale. Nothing is known about the sources, though there are somewhat similar stories of people who disguised themselves as menials in order to penetrate an enemy's defenses.[65] The special interest of the story, however, is not Akimichi's vendetta but his wife. It was an unimaginable disgrace for a samurai's wife to have an illegitimate child, and this was one reason why she could not resume her life with her husband. Even more important, she could not forget that Kanayama was the father of her child, and she felt obliged to pray for his repose; although he was a cruel and violent man, he had trusted and loved her. The conclusion is ironic: as the result of the successful vendetta, Kanayama's son becomes the heir of Akimichi.

Vendetta stories occupy an important place in medieval Japanese literature; *The Tale of the Soga Brothers* is perhaps the best-known example. The theme is developed in later literature, notably in *Chūshingura*, but the ending of *Akimichi* is not like that of more typical vendetta stories—a shout of triumph to celebrate the taking of the enemy's head. Akimichi has carried out his plan, but it has cost him his wife and his own position in society. There is no mention of joy when he enters the path of the Buddha; instead, we are left with the impression that the success of the vendetta was ultimately meaningless.

Tales of Commoners

Many of the twenty-three tales in *Otogi Bunko*, the first collection of otogi-zōshi, are (at least in some sense) about commoners. Even fables that recount the doings of monkeys, cats, mice, and other creatures hardly differ from the tales of human beings; they wear Japanese clothes, behave exactly like human beings of the time, and express themselves in familiar imagery when they write their love letters or bewail their distinctly human griefs.[66]

Bunshō Sōshi (The Tale of Bunshō),[67] the first tale in *Otogi Bunko*, may seem to the reader more like a European than a Japanese tale. Bunshō, the hero, is a menial who diligently serves the high priest of the Kashima Shrine in the province of Hitachi. The high priest, thinking perhaps to test him, tells Bunda (as Bunshō is then called) that he is dissatisfied with him, and urges him to seek employment elsewhere. Bunda accepts the priest's decision and apprentices himself to a saltmaker. He works so hard that before long he is rewarded with two salt kilns of his own. Throwing himself into the work, Bunda produces and sells salt of unusually high quality, and his customers, sure that it brings long life, buy his salt in great quantities. In this way he becomes rich, and as a sign of his prosperity, he takes a new name, Bunshō Tsuneoka.[68]

Even though Bunshō has become exceedingly prosperous, with no fewer than eighty-three storehouses and ninety houses, his wife is childless and she is by now over forty. At the suggestion of the high priest of the Kashima Shrine, she observes abstinence and prays at the shrine. The god grants her a child. (Many otogi-zōshi are about *mōshigo*, children born in response to prayers addressed to a god or buddha.) Bunshō is disappointed that it is a daughter. The wife tries again, and gives birth to a second child, but it too is a daughter.

Bunshō is unhappy not to have a male heir, but the two girls are extraordinarily beautiful. The high priest, learning of their beauty, asks for the girls as wives for his sons, but the girls absolutely refuse. They are equally unresponsive when the governor of the province, a noble from the capital, asks for one of the daughters. The disappointed governor gives up his post to return to the capital. He tells the son of the kampaku, a captain, about his experience, and this young man instantly falls in love from the description of their beauty. The pangs of unrequited love turn into a wasting illness that arouses the consternation of his family. Two friends, learning the cause of his malady, propose that they all go to Hitachi disguised as merchants, and the captain accepts with delight.

When they reach Bunshō's mansion, a maid comes out to ask what these merchants have brought with them. This is the occasion for a long enumeration of silken goods of many different colors and patterns. (Enumeration is one of the typical stylistic devices of the otogi-zōshi.) Bunshō, intrigued by these unusual merchants, invites them into his house and drinks with them. The captain offers presents to Bunshō's daughters, one of which hides a sheet of exquisite paper exquisitely inscribed with an exquisite poem. Naturally, she is interested.

At a concert that night given by the captain and his friends, a gust of wind lifts the bamboo blinds, revealing the ladies seated behind—another echo of the famous cat on a leash of *The Tale of Genji*. The captain and Bunshō's older daughter exchange glances. That night he makes his way to her room and they are soon joined in ties of love. The next day he abandons his disguise and attires himself in his court costume, not neglecting to blacken his teeth and darken his eyebrows. When Bunshō learns the true identity of the merchant, he is all but wild with joy. He cries, "My son-in-law is a prince, and the prince is my son-in-law!" (*Mukodono wa denka zo, denka wa mukodono yo!*)

The captain takes his bride with him to the capital, where his parents offer her boundless affection, sure that she is not merely the daughter of someone named Bunshō but a manifestation on earth of a heavenly being. Not long afterward, the emperor, having heard that Bunshō's second daughter is even lovelier than her sister, sends for her. Bunshō is desolate at the thought of being deprived of the company of both his daughters, but the emperor solves this by commanding not only the daughter but Bunshō and his wife to come to the capital. The girl before long is made a consort and gives birth to an imperial prince. Bunshō is appointed a major counselor and his wife is known as Lady of the Second Rank. They live happily ever afterward, each one of them attaining an age of at least one hundred years. The final sentence urges everyone to read this tale as the first, felicitous act of the new year.

The Tale of Bunshō is not artistically told. The language is ordinary and there are many repetitions of words and phrases. The one section that reveals literary intent (of a kind) is the tedious description of the fabrics offered for sale by the pretended merchants. The plot is also filled with implausibilities, whether the amazing success of a salt merchant or the unexplained antipathy of his daughters for the various candidates for their hands. The lovesickness of the captain has been interpreted in terms of the well-known trope of the prince, forced to leave the capital for the country, who finds a woman to love despite the unpromising surroundings,[69] but surely nobody ever fell that gravely ill over a woman he had never seen. The honors heaped on Bunshō and his family are without parallel in Japanese fact or fiction. And, finally, we may have trouble believing that every member of the family lived to be over one hundred years.

It is precisely because one improbability is piled on another in this way that *The Tale of Bunshō* appealed to readers of its day and is still of interest to us. Bunshō's success may recall the diligent merchants described by the seventeenth-century novelist Ihara Saikaku,[70] but not even his most worthy merchant was rewarded by having his daughter marry the emperor or himself becoming a major counselor, one of the highest offices of the land. In the Muromachi period it seems to have been possible at least to dream of such glory coming to a man who had started his career as a saltmaker. This, perhaps, is an example of the spirit of *gekokujō*, often invoked as the essence of the culture of an age of constant warfare. The point is emphasized when Bunshō's daughters reject the sons of a high-ranking Shintō priest and various members of the samurai class and the nobility in favor of a man whom the older daughter supposes to be a merchant. This is an obvious instance of wish fulfillment, but perhaps when *The Tale of Bunshō* was first written there was at least a glimmering hope that the fairest maiden in the land, regardless of her father's occupation, might marry Prince Charming, in the manner of a European fairy tale.[71]

Saru Genji Sōshi (The Tale of Monkey Genji) concerns a sardine peddler with the peculiar name of Monkey Genji. He has succeeded to the sardine business of his father-in-law who had entered Buddhist orders and become a priest on familiar terms with great landholders and members of the shogun's family. Monkey Genji goes to the capital, where he roams the streets crying, "Here's Monkey Genji from Akogi Bay in Ise, buy your sardines from me!"[72] This unusual greeting appeals to people of the capital and they buy his sardines in such quantities that before long he becomes quite rich. One day, as he is crossing the Gojō Bridge, a palanquin with reed blinds passes him. Just then a wind from the river lifts the blinds, permitting Monkey Genji to get a glimpse of the beautiful woman inside. He falls in love from that first glance, and can think of nothing but the lady. Tormented by his unrequited love, he wastes away.

His father-in-law, the priest, when he learns the cause of Monkey Genji's sickness, bursts out laughing, "I have never before heard of a sardine seller falling in love! Under no circumstances let other people hear about this." Monkey Genji counters with an instance of a fishmonger who won the love of a court lady. The priest grudgingly concedes that the example is apt, but insists that one glance is not enough to make a man fall in love, to which Monkey Genji responds with quotations from *The Tale of Genji*, including (predictably) the instance of Kashiwagi's infatuation with the Third Princess, aroused by a single glimpse. The father-in-law is again impressed, but objects that Monkey Genji does not even know the name of the woman. Monkey Genji reveals that he has investigated and found out that her name is Keiga, to which the father-in-law replies that she is the most famous courtesan in the capital, a favorite of the greatest lords of the land. He suggests that Monkey Genji disguise himself as a daimyo. The only problem is that a daimyo always travels with a great entourage. Monkey Genji has thought of that: he will suitably disguise two or three hundred of his fellow sardine vendors.

The plan works. The resourceful Monkey Genji, disguised as the daimyo of Utsunomiya, is entertained at a teahouse by a dozen or more courtesans including Keiga. She visits him at his lodgings where they spend the night together. However, her suspicions are aroused by his plebeian manner after he has been drinking, and in his sleep he sings his sardine seller's song. He responds to her suspicions that he is a false daimyo by citing examples from Heian literature to explain his actions and his murmuring in his sleep. Keiga is convinced that no sardine monger could possibly know so much about classical poetry and she accords Monkey Genji her favors. The conclusion is that in love there is neither high nor low. Monkey Genji takes his bride back to Akogi

Bay where they and their descendants prosper. And all this was brought about by Monkey Genji's knowledge of poetry; one can see just how important poetry is!

The successful courtship by a sardine seller for the hand of the most beautiful woman in the capital is another dream-fantasy, but there is a strong and appealing suggestion of egalitarianism. Anyone, even a man with so humble a profession, can not only become rich but can pass as a daimyo if he puts his mind to memorizing poetry.

Many other stories about commoners are worth describing, sometimes because of an ingenious development in the plot, sometimes because the underlying thought is refreshingly freer than in writings of earlier or later times. It is possible to find in these stories many examples of gekokujō, but this did not mean simply that the lower classes triumphed over the classes above; rather than a triumph that involved destruction, it was (as in the case of Monkey Genji) a conquest of the culture that formerly had been the exclusive possession of the nobles. Saikaku would warn of the dangers of a merchant's forgetting the proper way of life for merchants and aping his betters by trying to absorb their culture, and the government during the Tokugawa period frequently attempted by imposing sumptuary laws to keep the merchants from displaying their wealth; but in the otogi-zōshi no such caution is urged. Monkey Genji's knowledge of poetry, far from hindering him in his profession, was the source of his success. The stories are prevailingly optimistic; surprisingly so, considering that they were composed during an age of warfare and destruction.

The otogi-zōshi had another importance. They (or similar works derived from these stories) include the first Japanese stories for children (*otogi-banashi*).[73] Every Japanese child knows at least a few of the stories such as *Urashima Tarō*, the Japanese Rip van Winkle, who sojourned in the palace of the Dragon King only to discover when he returned to Japan that he had spent a whole lifetime under the sea; or *Issun Bōshi*, the Tom Thumb of Japan, only one inch tall but nevertheless a hero; or *Tsuru no Sōshi*, the story of the crane who is rescued by a man and, out of gratitude, transforms herself into a woman and becomes his wife. Otogi-zōshi adapted from such Chinese classics as the *Twenty-four Examples of Filial Piety* or from the Indian Jataka tales were also used in the education of children. Other stories that were not suitable as reading matter for children reached them orally in the form of folktales; sometimes it is hard to be sure which came first, the oral or the written tale.[74]

The otogi-zōshi drew on many sources, some as yet not ascertained, and in turn supplied materials for the literature and drama even of recent times.[75] The long neglect of the genre by most scholars has ended, and it seems likely that discoveries of new works will further enrich our knowledge of the fiction of the Muromachi period.[76]

Notes

1. The exact meaning of *togi* (the initial *o* is an honorific) is not clear. For an examination of evidence concerning use of this word, see Ichiko Teiji, *Chūsei Shōsetsu no Kenkyū*, pp. 2–24. (This work will henceforth be referred to as *Chūsei Kenkyū*.) See also Ichiko Teiji, *Chūsei Bungaku no Shūhen*, pp. 58–70, where Ichiko gives thirty-two examples of the use of the word *togi* or *otogi* prior to the seventeenth century; there are innumerable examples from the seventeenth century on. (This work will henceforth be referred to as *Chūsei Shūhen*.) The oldest known use of the term *otogi* occurs in *Story Without a Name*, written between 1196 and 1202. The earliest uses are in the sense of a companion, with overtones of the pleasure afforded by agreeable company.
2. The exact date of publication is unknown, but it has reasonably been conjectured that it was between 1688 and 1730. See Ichiko, *Chūsei Kenkyū*, p. 15; also Barbara Ruch, "Origins of *The Companion Library*," p. 593. Tokuda Kazuo, in " 'Otogi Bunko' Kankō Zengo," convincingly argues that the collection published by Shibuya Seiemon about 1720 was a reprint of a horizontal format, illustrated book (*yokonaga tanroku-bon*) published about 1675. The distinguishing feature of *tanroku-bon* was the hand-colored illustrations in vermilion and green. David Chibbett wrote of them, "Though a disaster aesthetically, achieving only a sad parody of Tosa color schemes, *tanroku-bon* are much prized in Japan on account of their rarity" (*The History of Japanese Printing and Book Illustration*, p. 119).
3. The appropriateness of the term *otogi-zōshi* has often been questioned. Ichiko Teiji preferred *chūsei shōsetsu* (medieval stories); Yokoyama Shigeru, the compiler of the most important collection of these tales, called them *muromachi monogatari*, and the compilers of the most recent collection (in the Shin Nihon Koten Bungaku Taikei series) adopted this term; but still other scholars, stressing the brevity of the stories, as compared to the Heian and Kamakura period romances, have referred to them as *tampen shōsetsu*, or short stories. Despite these attempts to find a more accurate way than otogi-zōshi of designating the tales, the term continues to be used not only by scholars but by the general reading public.

   Fujikake Kazuyoshi in *Muromachi-ki Monogatari no Kinseiteki Tenkai*, p. 6, discusses the use of the "narrow meaning" of *otogi-zōshi* (that is, the collection published by Shibukawa Seiemon in Osaka about 1720) and the "broad meaning" (that is, a general term for short stories composed in the Muromachi period or in the same manner in the early Tokugawa period). Fujikake also (p. 11) notes that the oldest known use of the term *otogi-zōshi* in the "broad meaning" is found in a work published in 1802 by Ozaki Masayoshi (1755–1827), a scholar of Japanese literature.

4. The work (*Hikketsu no Monogatari*) is signed Ihō and dated the twelfth year of Bummei (1480); a note appended to the work and dated 1517 identifies Ihō as the priestly name of Ishii Yasunaga. Yasunaga's name and crest appear in a book compiled about 1532, from which it has been inferred that he must have been a person of some importance; but nothing else is known about him. See Ichiko, *Chūsei Kenkyū*, pp. 388–89. Also Ruch, "Origins," p. 595.
5. Ichiko Teiji, for long the reigning authority on otogi-zōshi, was inclined to accept the attribution to Ichijō Kaneyoshi of several stories because he possessed the requisite knowledge of waka poetry, Buddhism, traditional customs and usages, music, and so on displayed in these stories (see Ichiko, *Chūsei Kenkyū*, pp. 390–92); but Kaneyoshi was not the only man of his time with this knowledge, and the stories do not resemble his other writings.
6. Fujikake, in *Muromachi-ki*, p. 94, stated that the stereotyped descriptions of beautiful women in the otogi-zōshi have earned them a bad reputation among scholars of literature. But the repetition of such stereotyped phrases may have helped poorly educated listeners to follow the story, and it may also have given the pleasure of recognition. Fujikake elsewhere in the same book (pp. 79–80) discussed the typical patterns of expression in the otogi-zōshi under three headings: enumeration, similes, and word-plays.
7. Scholars of the past, reluctant to admit that they did not know the author of a particular work, were apt to credit it to some celebrated literary figure, improbable though it was, and their conclusions have sometimes been accepted by later scholars who argue that there must have been *some* reason for the traditional attributions.
8. An example of what might be done in future study of the sources of the otogi-zōshi is provided by Hamanaka Osamu in "Otogi-zōshi to Chūgoku Setsuwa." Hamanaka traced a theme in the story *Urakaze*, the impregnation of a woman by the wind, in Japanese, Okinawan, and Chinese written and oral texts, as well as in the *Motif-Index of Folk Literature* of Stith Thompson. In his article "Otogi-zōshi 'Tsubo no Ishibumi' no Seiritsu," Hamanaka found the source of this tale in the Nō *Chibiki*, a play no longer in the repertory. He stressed (p. 173) the close relationships of the Nō plays to the otogi-zōshi, especially those of the *kinsei* period. An obvious instance of this close relationship is between the Nō *Ikuta Atsumori* and the otogi-zōshi *Ko Atsumori*.
9. The essay of Araki Yoshio, "Shomin Bungaku toshite no Otogi-zōshi," was published in the October 1951 issue of *Bungaku*. It is reprinted in his *Chūsei Bungaku no Keisei to Hatten*, pp. 406–23. Araki contended (p. 407) that the

fact that typical examples of otogi-zōshi, such as *Hachikazuki, Monokusa Tarō, Issun Bōshi, Urashima Tarō, Yokobue no Sōshi*, and *Shuten Dōji*, were still being read as children's stories (*dōwa*) even in contemporary Japan demonstrated they still lived as literature of the common people. For a criticism of what she calls "the concept of *shomin*-ization" of medieval literature, see Barbara Ruch, "Medieval Jongleurs and the Making of a National Literature," pp. 284–86.

10. See, for example, Ichiko, *Chūsei Kenkyū*, p. 194, where he speaks of "*kokuminteki na bungei*." Barbara Ruch in her studies of the genre has also emphasized this aspect. Ichiko believed that the heart of this "people's literature" was the tales about the military, but other scholars, like Araki Yoshio (see note 9) reserved this distinction for stories closer to the folktale tradition.
11. Seven different systems of classification made by scholars of Japanese literature are presented by Jacqueline Pigeot in her "Histoire de Yokobue," pp. 18–21.
12. My categories are close to those made by Nishizawa Masaji in *Chūsei Shōsetsu no Sekai*, p. 6. He proposed a division into: *gikomono* (stories about members of the aristocracy), otogi-zōshi (stories about commoners), and *Muromachi jidai monogatari* (stories about priests and warriors).
13. There is a complete translation of this story by Virginia Skord, called "A Tale of Brief Slumbers," in *Tales of Tears and Laughter*. Two illustrations from the emakimono in the Museum of Fine Arts in Boston have been included.
14. See Ichiko Teiji et al., *Muromachi Monogatari Shū*, p. 270. The inscription states that the illustrations were by Tosa Mitsunobu (1434–1525) and the calligraphy by Iio Mototsura (1431–1492).
15. Ichiko et al., *Muromachi*, I, p. 273. The poem states that the writer has unhappily fallen in love with a woman who is unaware of his passion, though she really exists and is not simply a figment of his imagination.
16. Ichiko et al., *Muromachi*, I, p. 275.
17. The particular manifestation of Kannon enshrined at the Ishiyama Temple was the *nyoirin* (*chintamani-chakra* in Sanskrit) Kannon, who granted what people desired. The author of *The Gossamer Years* went to Ishiyama Temple to complain of her misfortunes and ask Kannon's intercession. Her niece, the daughter of Takasue, mentions in *The Sarashina Diary* that she made a pilgrimage to Ishiyama Temple to pray for her salvation. See Ichiko et al., *Muromachi*, I, p. 278.
18. See chapter 12, page 482 and note 21.
19. In the "Akashi" chapter the old governor of Akashi, in response to a dream, sends a boat to sea. See the translation by Edward Seidensticker, *The Tale of Genji*, I, p. 251.
20. The words in Japanese are: *sasuga ni onna no saru beki koto ni shimo araneba*. . . . See Ichiko et al., *Muromachi*, I, p. 283.

21. One set of scrolls is in the Freer Gallery in Washington, another in the Museum of Fine Arts in Boston, a third in Japan. The scrolls in the American collections are in the *hakubyō-e* style: that is, they are painted in different shades of black but without color except for faint touches of red on the lips of the people depicted. For a discussion of the Boston scrolls, see Yonekura Michio, "Boston Bijutsukan-bon 'Utatane Sōshi' ni tsuite," pp. 46–55 in Shimada Shūjirō, *Shinshū Nihon Emakimono Zenshū, bekkan* 2. The same volume contains (plates 75 to 91) a reproduction of these scrolls. An emakimono in color illustrating the same story is in the possession of the Kokubungaku Kenkyū Shiryōkan in Tokyo; it seems to belong to a quite different tradition from the two black-and-white sets of scrolls.
22. The term Nara Ehon dates back only to the late Meiji period. The reason for referring to these illustrated books by the name "Nara picture books" is unclear, though various scholars have suggested reasons. See Akai Tatsurō, "Nara Ehon Kenkyū Shi," pp. 44–48; also Matsumoto Ryūshin, *Otogi-zōshi Shū*, p. 388–89.
23. For a discussion in English of the tanroku-bon, printed books with vermilion and green coloring added by hand, see Chibbett, *History*, pp. 118–19.
24. The work was translated by Jacqueline Pigeot and Keiko Kosugi with an introduction explaining its background in *Le chrysanthème solitaire*. The original illustrations (from the copy in the Bibliothèque Nationale) are reproduced in color.
25. See Pigeot and Kosugi, *Le chrysanthème*, pp. 13–15.
26. The name is also given as *Iwaya no Sōshi* or as *Tainoya-hime no Sōshi* in different versions. There are numerous textual variants, some of considerable importance. I have followed the version given by Matsumoto in *Otogi-zōshi*, pp. 145–97.
27. The name refers to the Western Pavilion (*nishi no tai*) where she lives after her father remarries.
28. Matsumoto, *Otogi-zōshi*, p. 149.
29. The dagger (*mamorigatana*) was generally carried by women inside their kimonos for protection if attacked. Toward the end of the story, Izumi Shikibu, seeing such a dagger in the possession of a man (Tōmei), expresses surprise.
30. Ichiko Teiji, *Otogi-zōshi* (NKBT), p. 312. Also Ōshima Tatehiko, *Otogi-zōshi Shū*, p. 385.
31. Each poem begins with the first syllable of a number: the first (*hitotsu*) with *hitori*, the second (*futatsu*) with *futae* and so on, going up to twentieth (*nijū*) with *nikushi*. He also gives a twenty-first to the servant who, dazzled by his accomplishment, asks for a poem for herself. See Ichiko, *Otogi-zōshi*, (NKBT), pp. 314–15. Also Ōshima, *Otogi-zōshi*, pp. 386–89.
32. For the original poem (in the *Shūishū*) and a translation, see above, p. 288.

It is obviously superior to the later version with its peculiar *kuraki yamiji*—"dark obscure path." In the original poem, inspired by the Lotus Sutra, Izumi Shikibu asks the moon (a familiar Buddhist symbol of enlightenment) to illuminate the path ahead of her into the dark. Perhaps the word *sayaka* was used in this altered version instead of *haruka* because it resembles *saya*, a scabbard.

33. There is an English translation of this story by Margaret H. Childs in *Monumenta Nipponica* 35:2, 1980. I have followed her translation of the title, but "a tale long in the telling" seems to be the original meaning of *nagamonogatari*. See Hirasawa Gorō, "Aki no Yo no Monogatari Kō," pp. 228–31. The words *aki no yo no naga* also suggest the length of the autumn night (much longer than the proverbially short summer night).
34. The date of Sensai's birth is not known, but is conjectured that it was about 1050. (See Miyaji Takakuni, "Jitsuzai Jimbutsu no Monogatarika," p. 46.) We know from an entry in *Chūyūki*, the diary kept by Fujiwara no Munetada from 1087 to 1138, that Sensai died in 1125. Sensai was for many years associated with the Ungo-ji, a temple in the Higashiyama area of Kyoto that was originally founded in 837 but subsequently allowed to fall into ruins. It is stated in *Honchō Kōsō Den* (1702), a series of biographies of eminent Japanese priests, that Sensai reconsecrated the Ungo-ji about 1124. (Quoted in Hirasawa, "Aki," p. 232.) Other documents indicate that Sensai and various waka poets (including the well-known Fujiwara no Mototoshi and Minamoto no Toshiyori) joined in composing uta-awase at the Ungo-ji in 1116. (See Miyaji, "Jitsuzai," pp. 47–48.)
35. Miyaji (in "Jitsuzai," p. 48) suggested that it was because of Sensai's fame in the middle ages as the holy man who had erected the great statue that he was chosen as the hero of *A Long Tale*.
36. *Sammon Mii Kakushitsu no Okori*, p. 246. This work, though included in the Shiseki Shūran series, is of dubious historical value. It has not been dated, but clearly is later than *A Long Tale*, which it quotes.
37. This is the thesis of Miyaji in his interesting article "Jitsuzai."
38. See Hirasawa, "Aki," pp. 263–94. Hirasawa, who gives pages of parallel texts of the *Taiheiki* and *A Long Tale*, insists on the similarity of style, language, and structure, and declares (p. 273) that it is "incontrovertible" that there is a close relationship between the two works.
39. See, for example, Nishizawa, *Chūsei Shōsetsu*, pp. 38–39.
40. Text in Shinkō Gunsho Ruijū series, vol. XIV, pp. 152–60.
41. *Toribeyama Monogatari*, p. 145.
42. There is a complete translation by Margaret Helen Childs in *Rethinking Sorrow: Revelatory Tales of Late Medieval Japan*.
43. Text in Zoku Gunsho Ruijū series, *kan* 509, pp. 395–411.
44. See Ichiko, *Chūsei Kenkyū*, p. 146.
45. There is a complete translation of this tale by Childs in *Rethinking Sorrow*.
46. Translation from Donald Keene, *Anthology of Japanese Literature*, p. 322.

Text in Nishizawa Masaji, *Meihen Otogi-zōshi*, p. 19. Also Ichiko, *Otogi-zōshi* (NKBT), p. 434.

47. Perhaps Nijō Yoshimoto.
48. Translation in Keene, *Anthology*, p. 327. Text in Nishizawa, *Meihen*, pp. 27–28.
49. Translation in Keene, *Anthology*, p. 330. Text in Nishizawa, *Meihen*, pp. 33–34.
50. See Kawazoe Shōji, *Chūsei Bungei no Chihōshi*, pp. 68–85, for a consideration of the treatment of the Mongol invasions in literary writing. *The Clear Mirror* was one of the few works that even touched on the events.
51. The development of literary cultures in different parts of the country during the Muromachi period is the subject of Kawazoe's *Chūsei*.
52. *Shuten Dōji* is the name of a demon, but *shuten* means "sake drinking" and *dōji* means "lad." Both terms apply to the demon, and in the work he is sometimes called simply *dōji*. In the story *Ibuki Dōji* it says that he acquired this name because of his fondness for sake; he was previously known as Ibuki Dōji. (See Ichiko et al., *Muromachi*, I, p. 197. Also Shimazu Hisamoto, *Zoku Otogi-zōshi*, p. 156.) It should be noted, however, that *shuten dōji* was probably a corruption of the original *sute dōji*, meaning an abandoned child, and referring to the old legend of a monstrous child born after thirty-three months (or more!) in its mother's womb, and abandoned when its strangeness became apparent. For a discussion of the name and the legend, see Satake Akihiro, *Shuten Dōji Ibun*, pp. 34–37.

    Satake elsewhere in his study (p. 94) mentioned the extraordinary popularity of the Shuten Dōji stories, as evidenced in the innumerable copies of the work scattered over the country.
53. Raikō (Yorimitsu) and Hōshō (Yasumasa) pray at the Iwashimizu Hachiman Shrine; Watanabe Tsuna and Sakata Kintoki at the Sumiyoshi Shrine; and Usui Sadamitsu and Urabe Suetake at the shrines of Kumano. For text, see Ōshima, *Otogi*, pp. 447–48.
54. For example, Watanabe Tsuna killed the demon of the Rashōmon. Sakata Kintoki, usually known by his boyhood name of Kintarō, was credited with similar exploits.
55. Text in Matsumoto, *Otogi*, pp. 89–142.
56. See Ichiko, *Chūsei Kenkyū*, pp. 215–19. He says of *Tamura no Sōshi* (The Story of Tamura), which features a serpent bride, that it is the most typical of the medieval stories about demon-quelling.
57. Ichiko, *Chūsei Kenkyū*, p. 220. Reference is being made particularly to *Yukionna Monogatari* (The Tale of the Snow Woman).
58. There is a beautiful translation into French by Pigeot in "Histoire de Yokobue."
59. Strictly speaking, Takiguchi was not his name but his office; he was a member of the Imperial Palace Guard of the sovereign's private office.
60. In some versions of the story Yokobue's mother is said to be the proprietress

of a brothel. See Pigeot, "Histoire de Yokobue," p. 87, for the translation from the Nagato-bon text of *The Tale of the Heike*.

61. Text in Takagi Ichinosuke et al., *Heike Monogatari*, II, p. 268.
62. The title *Ko Atsumori* is difficult to translate. In context, it means "the son of Atsumori," but *ko* before a noun usually means "small," and in the story we see the son only as a boy.
63. Text in Matsumoto, *Otogi*, pp. 11–74. I have discussed this work (under a slightly different title) in *World Within Walls,* pp. 235–36.
64. The text is given in Nishizawa, *Meihen*, pp. 174–201. Nishizawa analyzed the work in *Chūsei*, pp. 44–76. There is a translation by Margaret Childs in *Monumenta Nipponica* 42:3, 1987.
65. See Nishizawa, *Chūsei*, pp. 49–50.
66. The delightful *Fukurō* (The Owl) (not in *Otogi Bunko*, however) contains a love letter from the owl to a bullfinch, with immensely long sentences cast into alternating phrases in seven and five syllables and replete with kakekotoba: *"Irie ni chikaki amaobune, kogarete mono ya omouran, nani shi kimi wo mi Kumano no, Otonashigawa no fuchise ni mo shizumihatsubeki to omoedomo, kimi ni nagori ya oshidori no. . . ."* Text in Fujii Shiei (ed.), *Otogi-zōshi*, p. 543.
67. There is a complete English translation by James T. Araki, "*Bunshō Sōshi*: The Tale of Bunshō, the Saltmaker." Text in Ōshima, *Otogi*, pp. 41–75.
68. Bunshō was the name of an era (nengō) from 1466 to 1467. This may be a clue to the time of composition of the story; Araki (p. 244) notes that at a conference the noted book dealer Sorimachi Shigeo said that there was a text dated 1466, but that no one Araki knew had actually examined it. Tsuneoka is a fictitious place-name, but there have been attempts to identify it with a salt-producing area of the coast of present-day Ibaraki Prefecture. We are to believe that the menial Bunda has no surname, but when he became rich he took Bunshō as his surname and Tsuneoka as his personal name.
69. See Ichiko Teiji, "Bunshō Sōshi," in Ichiko Teiji and Noma Kōshin, *Otogi-zōshi, Kana-zōshi*, p. 15. Well-known noblemen who find love in the country include Genji (with the Lady of Akashi) and Yoshitsune (with Lady Jōruri).
70. For a description of the *chōnin-mono* of Saikaku, see my *World Within Walls*, pp. 196–204.
71. Chieko Irie Mulhern in her interesting article "Cinderella and the Jesuits: An *Otogizōshi* Cycle as Christian Literature" concluded (p. 446) that three tales about stepmothers were "Jesuit literature authored by the Japanese Christians in collaboration with the Italian missionaries for the purpose of glorifying Christian daimyo and ladies, edifying the faithful, and propagating the gospel of love and endurance in the face of persecution in the early seventeenth century." It is unlikely that anyone will attempt to prove that *The Tale of Bunshō* was written under the influence of European literature, but its sources have been sought in regional histories and in the

folktales remembered by very old people who live near the coast of Ibaraki, where Bunda was supposed to have made his fortune in salt. Different conclusions were advanced by three scholars: (1) the tale was first invented by priests of the Kashima Shrine, where the New Year is celebrated with offerings of salt, to transmit the wonders of salt to later generations when their descendants made a living from salt rather than as priests of the shrine; (2) the tale expresses the merchant ethos of medieval Japan; and (3) the tale was first told by prostitutes who yearned to attain the worldly success of Bunshō's daughters. (These theories are presented by Ōshima Tatehiko in "Bunda Chōja no Densetsu to sono Kiban.")

72. Text in Ōshima, *Otogi*, p. 204.
73. See Ichiko Teiji, "Otogi-zōshi to Kinsei no Jidō Yomimono," p. 230. Ichiko says that almost nothing that might be called reading matter or literature for children existed before the Muromachi period.
74. The oral transmission of tales was the subject of many books by Yanagita Kunio, for example *Monogatari to Katarimono*.
75. To give two examples: the most popular postwar play, *Yūzuru* (Twilight Crane, 1949) by Kinoshita Junji was based on *Tsuru no Sōshi*; and Mishima Yukio's *Iwashi-uri Koi no Hikiami* (The Sardine Seller and the Dragnet of Love, 1954) was based on *The Tale of Monkey Genji*.
76. The international conference on Nara Ehon (Nara Ehon Kokusai Kenkyūkai) held in London, Dublin, and New York in 1978 and in Tokyo in 1979 did much to bring together scholars not only of Nara Ehon but of otogi-zōshi and of the religion and art of the period. It also led to the publication of several valuable volumes of essays, including *Otogi-zōshi no Sekai*, which gives the most complete finder's list of the locations of surviving manuscripts of otogi-zōshi and an equally complete bibliography of printed texts and studies.

Bibliography

Note: All Japanese books, except as otherwise noted, were published in Tokyo.

Akai Tatsurō. "Nara Ehon Kenkyū Shi," in Nara Ehon Kokusai Kenkyū Kaigi (ed.), *Otogi-zōshi no Sekai*.

Araki, James T. "*Bunshō Sōshi*: The Tale of Bunshō, the Saltmaker," *Monumenta Nipponica* 38:3, 1983.

Araki Yoshio. *Chūsei Bungaku no Keisei to Hatten*. Kyoto: Minerva Shobō, 1957.

Chibbett, David. *The History of Japanese Printing and Book Illustration*. Tokyo: Kodansha International, 1977.

Childs, Margaret H[elen]. "*Chigo monogatari*: Love Stories or Buddhist Sermons?" *Monumenta Nipponica* 35:2, 1980.

———. *Rethinking Sorrow: Revelatory Tales of Late Medieval Japan*. Ann Arbor: Center for Japanese Studies, The University of Michigan, 1991.

Fujii Shiei (Otoo) (ed.). *Otogi-zōshi*, in Yūhōdō Bunko series. Yūhōdō, 1926.

Fujikake Kazuyoshi. *Muromachi-ki Monogatari no Kinseiteki Tenkai*. Osaka: Izumi Shoin, 1987.

Gemmu Monogatari in *kan* 509, Zoku Gunsho Ruijū series. Zoku Gunsho Ruijū Kansei Kai, 1924.

Gotō Tanji. *Chūsei Kokubungaku Kenkyū*. Isobe Kōyōdō, 1943.

Hamanaka Osamu. "Otogi-zōshi to Chūgoku Setsuwa," in Wakan Hikaku Bungaku Kai (ed.), *Chūsei Bungaku to Kambungaku*, II. Kyūko Shoin, 1987.

———. "Otogi-zōshi 'Tsubo no Ishibumi' no Seiritsu," in Nihon Bungaku Kenkyū Shiryō Kankōkai (ed.), *Otogi-zōshi*. Yūseidō, 1985.

Hirasawa Gorō. "Aki no Yo no Nagamonogatari Kō," *Shidō Bunko Ronshū* 3, 1964.

Ichiko Teiji. *Chūsei Shōsetsu no Kenkyū*. Tōkyō Daigaku Shuppankai, 1955.

———. *Chūsei Shōsetsu no Shūhen*. Tōkyō Daigaku Shuppankai, 1981.

———. *Otogi-zōshi*, 2 vols., in Iwanami Bunko series. Iwanami Shoten, 1985–86.

———. *Otogi-zōshi*, in Nihon Koten Bungaku Taikei series. Iwanami Shoten, 1958.

———. "Otogi-zōshi to Kinsei no Jidō Yomimono," *Kokubungaku Kaishaku to Kanshō* 50:11, 1985.

Ichiko Teiji, Akiya Osamu, Sawai Taizō, Tajima Kazuo, and Tokuda Kazuo. *Muromachi Monogatari Shū*, 2 vols., in Shin Nihon Koten Bungaku Taikei series. Iwanami Shoten, 1989.

Ichiko Teiji and Noma Kōshin. *Otogi-zōshi, Kana-zōshi*, in Nihon Koten Kanshō Kōza series. Kadokawa Shoten, 1963.

Kawazoe Shōji. *Chūsei Bungei no Chihōshi*. Heibonsha, 1982.

Keene, Donald. *Anthology of Japanese Literature*. New York, Grove Press, 1955.

———. *World Within Walls*. New York: Holt, Rinehart and Winston, 1976.

Kishi Shōzō. *Shintōshū*, in Tōyō Bunko series. Heibonsha, 1967.

Matsuhoura Monogatari in *kan* 311, Shinkō Gunsho Ruijū series, XIV. Naigai Shoseki Kabushiki Kaisha, 1928.

Matsumoto Ryūshin. *Otogi-zōshi Shū*, in Shinchō Nihon Koten Shūsei series. Shinchōsha, 1980.

Miyaji Takakuni. "Jitsuzai Jimbutsu no Monogatarika," *Kokugakuin Zasshi* 62, January 1961.

Mulhern, Chieko Irie. "Cinderella and the Jesuits: an *Otogizōshi* Cycle as Christian Literature," *Monumenta Nipponica* 34:4, 1979.

Nara Ehon Kokusai Kenkyū Kaigi. *Otogi-zōshi no Sekai*. Sanseidō, 1982.

Nihon Bungaku Kenkyū Shiryō Kankōkai. *Otogi-zōshi*. Yūseidō, 1985.

Nishizawa Masaji. *Chūsei Shōsetsu no Sekai*. Miyai Shoten, 1982.

———. *Meihen Otogi-zōshi*. Kasama Shoin, 1978.

Ōshima Tatehiko. "Bunda Chōja no Densetsu to sono Kiban," *Kokugo to Kokubungaku* 57:5, 1980.

———. *Otogi-zōshi Shū*, in Nihon Koten Bungaku Zenshū series. Shōgakukan, 1974.

Pigeot, Jacqueline. "Histoire de Yokobue (Yokobue no sōshi)," *Bulletin de la Maison Franco-Japonaise*, Nouvelle Série, 9:2, 1972.

Pigeot, Jacqueline, and Keiko Kosugi. *Le chrysanthème solitaire*. Paris: Bibliothèque Nationale, 1984.

Ruch, Barbara. "Medieval Jongleurs and the Making of a National Literature," in John W. Hall and Toyoda Takeshi (eds.), *Japan in the Muromachi Age*. Berkeley, University of California Press, 1977.

———. *Mō Hitotsu no Chūseizō*. Kyoto: Shibunkaku, 1991.

———. "Origins of *The Companion Library*: An Anthology of Medieval Japanese Stories," *Journal of Asian Studies* 30:3, 1971.

———. *Otogi Bunko and Short Stories of the Muromachi Period*. Unpublished dissertation, Columbia University, 1965.

Sammon Mii Kakushitsu no Okori, in Shintei Zōho Shiseki Shūran series. Kyoto: Rinsen Shoten, 1967.

Satake Akihiro. *Shuten Dōji Ibun*. Heibonsha, 1977.

Seidensticker, Edward. *The Tale of Genji*, 2 vols. New York: Alfred A. Knopf, 1976.

Shimada Shūjirō. *Shinshū Nihon Emakimono Zenshū, bekkan* 2. Kadokawa Shoten, 1981.

Shimauchi Keiji. *Otogi-zōshi no Seishin Shi*. Perikan Sha, 1988

Shimazu Hisamoto. *Zoku Otogi-zōshi*, in Iwanami Bunko series. Iwanami Shoten, 1956.

Skord, Virginia. *Tales of Tears and Laughter: Short Fiction of Medieval Japan*. Honolulu: University of Hawaii Press, 1991.

Takagi Ichinosuke, Ozawa Masao, et al. *Heike Monogatari*, 2 vols., in Nihon Koten Bungaku Taikei series. Iwanami Shoten, 1960.

Tokuda Kazuo. "'Otogi Bunko' Kankō Zengo," *Kokubungaku Kaishaku to Kanshō* 50:11, 1985.

———. "Otogi-zōshi Nijūshi Kō Tanjō Zenya," in Wakan Hikaku Bungaku Kai (ed.), *Chūsei Bungaku to Kambungaku*, II. Kyūko Shoin, 1987.

Toribeyama Monogatari, in *kan* 311, Shinkō Gunsho Ruijū series, XIV. Naigai Shoseki Kabushiki Kaisha, 1928.

Yanagita Kunio. *Monogatari to Katarimono*. Kadokawa Shoten, 1975.

29.
THE LATE SIXTEENTH CENTURY

The last forty years of the sixteenth century are generally known as the Azuchi-Momoyama period.[1] Azuchi was the site of the castle built in 1576 near the shores of Lake Biwa by Oda Nobunaga (1534–1582); and Toyotomi Hideyoshi (1537–1598), Nobunaga's successor as the de facto ruler of the country, built his castle at Momoyama, south of Kyoto. These two events, symbolic of major steps in the unification of Japan after a century of warfare and division, were of the greatest military and political significance, but the literature of the period was notable less for achievements than for ends and beginnings. Some genres of the medieval period, such as renga and Nō, enjoyed a final flowering before disappearing as media for serious composition, while others, like Jōruri and Kabuki, the chief dramatic arts of the Tokugawa period, trace their crude beginnings to this time. Rapid and sometimes cataclysmic changes of fortune were characteristic of the period, and writers who depended on the patronage of the military had to accommodate themselves again and again to the tastes of new masters. It is small wonder that the literature showed little sustained development, but it has exceptional variety.

Waka Poetry

For most Japanese of the late sixteenth century (as had been true for many centuries) poetry was the chief literary art. Poetry had almost always meant the waka, but in this period the waka was moribund. Its fusty traditions were preserved by the aristocrats in Kyoto and also by generals (and other military men) who were eager to demonstrate by a mastery of the form that they were not barbarians. By this time, however, the various schools that had long dominated waka composition were dead. The last important family of poets, the Asukai, had served the Ashikaga shoguns since the time of Yoshinori, but their minor contributions to the development of the waka had ended. No court-sponsored anthology had been compiled for over a century. Waka gatherings were still regularly held at the palace and the poets composed poems on the usual assigned topics, but the conventions were exhausted. There were two possible ways of recovering the dignity and vitality of the waka—either (in the manner of the eighteenth-century poets) by renewing it at its sources in the *Man'yōshū*, or else (in the manner of the twentieth-century poets) giving it new life by using the old form to communicate contemporary thought in contemporary language. But none of the poets of the late sixteenth century made more than feeble efforts in either direction.

The diary of the poet and antiquarian Yamashina Tokitsugu (1507–1579),[2] an important source of information on the artistic life of the time, frequently mentions the composition of waka at the court. He described, for example, a poetry gathering in the Imperial Palace in the second month of 1560, followed two days later by a similar one at the Minase Palace. On the latter occasion the prescribed topics were "returning wild geese," "waiting love," and "travel through the fields." His own poem on the first topic was:

Koshiji ni mo	Even in Koshiji
Yoshino no hana ya	The blossoms of Yoshino
niouran	Will surely smell sweet:
miyako no haru ni	See the wild geese returning
kaeru karigane[3]	To spring in the capital.

Tokitsugu relied on a thoroughly established cliché of Japanese poetry: wild geese, flying north in the spring, were traditionally believed to bear messages with them. In this case, the geese, which have already been seen in the capital on their way north, will bear the scent of the Yoshino cherry blossoms all the way to Koshiji. The place-name Koshiji was probably chosen because of its assocation with *kosu*, the verb "to cross over"; the geese were believed to cross that part of the Japan Sea coast on their way north. The fact that cherry blossoms have no fragrance is irrelevant. Tokitsugu demonstrated with this waka that even when he had nothing to say, he could say it gracefully.

Fuller quotation of the poems composed on this occasion would only confirm the impression that *nobody* had anything to say at the monthly poetry meetings. Perhaps it might be fairer to the poets to suggest instead that, living in turbulent times and ever fearful that some new catastrophe might destroy their way of life, they found comfort and refuge in the abiding strength of clichés. Even if some poet of the time had miraculously thought of a way of giving new life to such topics as "song thrushes announce the spring" or "cranes dwell in the pine trees" or "spring colors float in the water," he would probably not have been so contemptuous of tradition as to compose a poem without a single cliché.

Araki Yoshio (1890–1969), the chief authority on the literature of this period, believed that the two most typical varieties of waka of the sixteenth century were the satirical *kyōka* (literally, "wild poems") and the *jisei*, valedictory poems to the world, especially those composed by men before committing suicide. Like other poems that depend on puns and other kinds of word-play for effect, a kyōka is difficult to translate, but one example may suggest its sardonic nature and the kind of knowledge that is necessary in order to appreciate fully the humor. This is an anonymous poem composed in Kyoto mocking (and deploring) the deer hunts staged by Toyotomi Hidetsugi, the sanguinary nephew of Hideyoshi, on Mount Hiei. Although hunting was prohibited on the sacred mountain, the sound of rifle fire could be heard in the city night after night. Hidetsugi's offense was particularly grievous because less than a year had elapsed since the death of the Retired Cloistered Emperor Ōgimachi in 1593; out of deference to the deceased sovereign, he should have refrained from taking life. Hidetsugi had been appointed kampaku in 1591. This position was familiarly known as *sesshō kampaku* because, when the emperor was a minor, the person who performed the duties of kampaku was known as *sesshō*, or regent; more to the point here is the fact that a homonym of *sesshō* means "to take life."

in no gosho	Since his is a hunt
tamuke no tame no	In memory of the late
kari nareba	Cloistered emperor,
kore wo sesshō	They call him the murderous
kampaku to iu[4]	Regent and chancellor.

The tedious explication deprives this poem of whatever humor it may possess, suggesting how much more perishable humor is than tragedy. The tragic poems composed during the sixteenth century by men on the battlefield or on the point of death are not necessarily superior in terms of literary skill than the kyōka, but sometimes they move us. In 1580, for example, when Hideyoshi, by command of Oda Nobunaga, was besieging the castle of Miki in the province of Harima, Bessho

Nagaharu, the lord of the castle, decided to surrender on condition that the lives of his men be spared. Nagaharu, then twenty-six, committed suicide, and his wife followed him in death. Each composed a jisei. Nagaharu's was:

ima wa tada	Now nothing is left
urami mo arazu	Even of hostility
morobito no	When I consider
inochi ni kawaru	That I sacrifice my life
wagami to omoeba	To save those of many men.

His wife's poem was:

morotomo ni	How happy I am
kiehatsuru koso	We shall vanish together
ureshikere	At the same moment
okure sakidatsu	In this world where usually
narai naru yo wo	One dies before the other.[5]

Sometimes the jisei reveal more pathos than heroism. Ikeda Izumi, realizing that his situation in Itami Castle was hopeless, wrote:

tsuyu no mi no	Even if my body
kiete mo kokoro	Disappears like the dew
nokoriyuku	My heart will linger,
nani to ka naran	Wondering what can be done
midorigo no sue	To look after my children.

Soon after composing this poem, Izumi loaded his gun and blew his brains out.[6]

We know the contexts of many poems of this era from the prose descriptions in which they are set. Even when the poems were inspired by disasters unimagined by the poets of the *Kokinshū*, the imagery was likely to be conventional; but a poem of slight intrinsic interest might be made memorable by the circumstances of composition. The following waka, by Ōtomo Yoshiaki (1502–1550), was composed after he had killed in battle Tachibana Nagatoshi, the lord of Tachibana Castle in the province of Chikuzen. When Yoshiaki formally inspected Nagatoshi's head, the open eyes seemed to glare at him. Yoshiaki composed a poem that induced the head to close its eyes:

Tachibana wa	Tachibana has
mukashi otoko to	Now been transformed into
narinikeri	A man of long ago.
uikaburi suru	He must feel as if he had
kokochi koso sure[7]	First put on an adult's hat.

The words *mukashi otoko* ("man of long ago") immediately evoke memories of Ariwara no Narihira and *Tales of Ise*, as does *uikaburi*, the hat worn by a boy at his induction into manhood, mentioned in the first sentence of *Tales of Ise*. Perhaps Tachibana, the name of a distinguished aristocratic family, was used with ironic overtones, contrasting the courtly world of Narihira with the bloodthirsty reality of sixteenth-century Japan. The poem, even when analyzed into its component parts, is hardly more than a flash of grisly wit, but the head inspection (*kubi jikken*), familiar from Kabuki plays, and the glaring eyes of the severed head make the poem far more memorable than many technically superior waka of the Nijō or Reizei schools.

During this age of strife, poems often served religious or pedagogical purposes in the form of easily memorized homilies. The *dōka*, as they were called, usually took the form of the waka. Most of these dōka have slight literary interest, but occasionally one stands out because of its striking images:

mi hitotsu ni	On my single body
hashi wo narabete	Carrion birds are arrayed,
motsu tori ya	Beak alongside beak:
ware wo tsutsukite	I am sure they will succeed
koroshihatsuran[8]	In peck-pecking me to death.[9]

The poem, though metrically in the form of a waka, has nothing of the traditional elegance of expression. It is an allegory, representing Japan as a body that is being pecked to death by predatory birds—the contesting armies. Allegory is by no means unknown in Japanese poetry,[10] but it is rare to find a poem that can be interpreted *only* as allegory.

Most of the examples of sixteenth-century waka given above lay so far outside the mainstream that they were probably unknown to the major poets of the time. The recognized poets, being more conventional, are considerably less interesting to a modern reader. The chief waka poet at the court during the early part of the sixteenth century was Sanjōnishi Sanetaka (1455–1537). Although not of the highest nobility, he served three emperors, and rose to be minister of the center (*nai-*

daijin). In a time of war, when the nobles in the capital lived in relative poverty and it was often impossible for the emperor to hold court ceremonies because of insufficient funds, the study of the Heian classics became a refuge from the present. Sanetaka attended lectures given by Sōgi on *The Tale of Genji, Tales of Ise*, and other texts, and took part in what might be called a joint research project on *The Tale of Genji* together with Sōgi, Shōhaku, Sōchō, Kensai, and other renga poets.[11]

The knowledge Sanetaka acquired of the classics not only enhanced his position at the court, but benefited him financially: military men were willing to pay handsomely for copies of famous literary works in the hand of a nobleman. Sanetaka in turn depended on his mentor, Sōgi, for introductions to such men and for other direct and indirect financial support. Aristocrats have often been the patrons of artists, but this is an instance of an artist who was a nobleman's patron. Sanetaka was especially indebted to Sōgi for induction into the mysteries of the *Kokinshū*.[12] After Sōgi's death, he became the guardian of its traditions, another source of prestige and income.

Sanetaka's erudition extended to Chinese literary and philosophical texts, especially those of the greatest interest to the Japanese, such as *The Collected Works of Po Chü-i, Meng Ch'iu*, and *Wen Hsüan*.[13] He often participated in sessions at which lines of Chinese and Japanese poems were alternately linked,[14] and his extensive diary, begun in 1474 when he was nineteen, was kept in Chinese. Sanetaka's diary,[15] though not of literary distinction, is a major source of information on the life led by the aristocrats of his day and is the only work for which he is still remembered.[16] His waka, essentially of the Nijō school, rarely rise above the level of clichés. His renga compositions were of higher quality, and his commentary on *The Tale of Genji* is of some interest; but these works do not account for the respect he enjoys as the outstanding intellectual of his day.[17] His reputation owes much to the contrast he and his scholarship made with the chaotic conditions prevalent in the country. Repeated incidents of burglary and arson were common in the capital, even in the Imperial Palace, as we know from Sanetaka's diary. It was definitely not an atmosphere conducive to study, and most of the members of the aristocracy turned to drink, gambling, and theatricals (chiefly Nō) in the attempt to keep their minds from dwelling on the grim conditions in the world around them.[18] Others sought comfort in religion, and various religious crazes swept through the country.[19]

Sanetaka managed to keep at his books despite the extremely unfavorable conditions. Indeed, his diary shows an almost ostentatious indifference to the warfare plaguing the country, but he devoted the greatest possible attention to poetry gatherings in the palace and similar matters. He was best known to his contemporaries as a calligrapher, as we know from the frequent commissions he received to copy both Buddhist and secular texts. His income from such commissions gradually increased until it exceeded his income from all other sources, including his country estates.[20] This was no small achievement for a member of the court at a time when the emperor and his family depended on the goodwill of the shogun and other military leaders even for subsistence. The Emperor Gokashiwabara, who ascended the throne in 1500, had to wait twenty-one years for his coronation because there was never enough money to hold the ceremonies.

In 1509 sections of *The Tale of Genji* from the brush of Gokashiwabara were sent as presents to ladies of the Imagawa family in Suruga and the Asakura family in Echizen in the hope (fulfilled) of receiving monetary offerings. Sometimes the emperor resorted to more desperate expedients for raising funds: samples of his calligraphy were hung outside his screen-of-state in the Imperial Palace to advertise that they were available for purchase.[21] Sanetaka seems to have done better than the emperor, but even Sanetaka, for all his connections with the provincial military, was obliged by financial necessity to sell his most precious possession, a complete set of *The Tale of Genji*.[22] Yet neither despair over the world nor personal hardship ever caused him to abandon his studies of the old literature. It has been suggested that with Sanetaka the medieval literary traditions came to an end.[23] The nobility would never again occupy the position of being the focal point of literary activity, and even the traditions of medieval poetry, notably renga, all but terminated with the deaths of Shōhaku and Sōchō. When Sanetaka died at the age of eighty-two he must have felt that the world was rapidly approaching its final days, as the prophets had insistently but mistakenly proclaimed some centuries before.

The most distinguished waka poet of the last years of the sixteenth century, Hosokawa Yūsai (1534–1610), was consecrated to the preservation of the traditions of Japanese poetry, and worshiped the memory of Fujiwara Teika. His poems themselves, in the style of the Nijō school,[24] are unmemorable, but it is noteworthy that a daimyo, who often saw service in battle and helped to restore the fortunes of the Hosokawa family after the disastrous Ōnin War, was so prominent a poet.

Yūsai, the fourth son of the shogun Ashikaga Yoshiharu,[25] had been adopted into the Hosokawa family. As a youth he showed unusual interest in poetry, at first in renga, later mainly in waka. He studied waka composition with Sanjōnishi Saneki (1511–1579), the grandson of

Sanetaka, and in 1575 was inducted by Saneki into the *Kokin Denju*, the secret traditions of the *Kokinshū*. It was highly unusual for these traditions to be transmitted to someone who was not of the nobility, but Saneki, sixty-four at the time, apparently feared that he might die before his young son could comprehend the mysteries, and thought that Yūsai, though not a noble, was the best vehicle for teachings that otherwise might perish. The most jealously guarded privilege of the nobility passed in this way to the samurai class.

In 1600, before Yūsai inducted Prince Tomohito (the younger brother of the Emperor Goyōzei) into the mysteries, he first asked the authorization of Tokugawa Ieyasu. Later in the same year, when Yūsai was besieged at Tanabe Castle in his fiefdom of Tango, Goyōzei, fearing that the secrets of the *Kokinshū* might die with Yūsai, sent off high officials to the castle with instructions that they receive the *Kokin Denju*. When this imperial command was transmitted to the armies inside and outside the castle, the fighting at once abated.[26] After the ceremony of transmission had been completed, the officials sent word to the attacking general that Yūsai must now be considered to be the emperor's teacher, since he had transmitted the *Kokin Denju* to surrogates of the emperor. The attacking general was commanded to lift the siege at once; if he did not, he would be considered an enemy of the court. Faced with this threat, the general lifted the siege. Both friends and enemies of Yūsai evidently believed that the *Kokin Denju* was more important than military victory.

In 1582, after Oda Nobunaga, whom Yūsai had served, was assassinated by Akechi Mitsuhide, Yūsai entered Buddhist orders; but this did not prevent him from becoming a member of the literary circle surrounding Toyotomi Hideyoshi, and he frequently took part in renga sessions. On one occasion, when Yūsai was composing renga with Hideyoshi and Satomura Jōha (1524–1602), Hideyoshi supplied the hokku:

okuyama ni	Deep in the mountains,
momiji fumiwakete	As I tramp through maple leaves,
naku hotaru	A firefly sings.

Yūsai at once added a second verse, but somebody in the gathering murmured that fireflies do not sing. Jōha agreed with this criticism, much to Hideyoshi's annoyance, but Yūsai insisted there was textual authority for saying that fireflies sang, and he quoted an ancient poem:

Musashino no	In Musashi Plain
shino wo tabanete	Where the falling rain comes down
furu ame ni	Like spears of bamboo grass,
hotaru yori hoka	Apart from the fireflies
naku mushi mo nashi	Not an insect is singing.

Hideyoshi's good humor was restored, and he praised Yūsai's deep understanding of renga. Later, when Jōha went to visit him, Yūsai expressed surprise that a master of renga had been so lacking in human feelings, and admitted that he had made up the "ancient poem" on the spot in order to relieve the tension![27]

Yūsai's waka, especially those composed during the latter part of his life, are collected in *Shūmyō Shū* (Collection of the Wonders of Nature).[28] Many of the poems have titles or headnotes explaining the circumstances under which they were composed, and when these introductions consist of more than a few words they are generally more interesting than the poems themselves. Yūsai's poems are most often merely stale variations on the traditional themes of Nijō poetry, but he also displayed, far too often, irritating farcicality in the puns and other word-plays with which he decorated his works. Here is an example of Yūsai at his most characteristic:

"In 1597, hearing that Shōzan was unwell, I left for Ōzaka by boat on the night of the fifteenth of the eighth month. At the inlet of Mishima I stopped the boat and gazed at the moon visible through the reeds.

tare ka mata	Who in the future
koyoi no tsuki wo	Seeing the moon of tonight
Mishima-e no	In Mishima bay[29]
ashi no shinobi ni	Will give himself to longing
mono omouran[30]	In the shadow of these reeds?"

The poem begins with what seems to be a parody of Shunzei's famous lines:

tare ka mata	Who in the future
hanatachibana ni	Will recall me in the scent
omoiden	Of orange blossoms
ware mo mukashi no	When I, too, shall have become
hito to narinaba[31]	A person of long ago?

Yūsai could not resist the opportunity to include a *kakekotoba* on the *mi* of the place-name Mishima, meaning "see" with what precedes. *Ashi no shinobi* suggests *shinobi-ashi*, meaning "on tiptoes," though *ashi* is written with the character meaning "reed." *Shinobi*, "hiding" or "secret," also meant "longing," and it suggests *shinobu*, the name of a kind of fern. Probably Yūsai did not intend all these possible word-plays, but after reading a dozen or more of his waka one hesitates to rule out any possibility of a pun.

Yūsai was not an important poet, but he was revered, even by members of the court, as the possessor of the secrets of the *Kokinshū*, and he associated not only with the remnants of the poetic schools of the past but with the younger poets (like Matsunaga Teitoku) who would create the new poetry, especially haikai. He also held the key to the revival of the waka in the next century: he owned a manuscript of the *Man'yōshū*, and interested his disciples in studying the text, which had long since become obscure. The rediscovery of the *Man'yōshū* would give a moment of new life to a variety of poetry that had seemed thoroughly exhausted.

Renga Poetry

Renga was the chief poetic art of sixteenth-century Japan, and its practitioners did not doubt that its glory would be long lasting. In 1568, when Oda Nobunaga entered Kyoto with Ashikaga Yoshiaki, his choice as shogun, reports spread through the city that Nobunaga was a monster "more terrifying than any demon," and people trembled at the horrid fate that awaited them.[32] The renga master Satomura Jōha, always eager to be on the winning side, hurried to the Tōfuku-ji, the temple that served as Nobunaga's headquarters, and offered him a pair of fans, reciting these verses:

nihon te ni iru	Oh, the joy I feel this day
kyō no yorokobi	You take in your hands these two fans.

The point of these lines is the pun on *nihon*, meaning "two fans," but also "Japan." Jōha was seeking to please Nobunaga by expressing his joy that Japan had a new master. Nobunaga, not known as a literary man, responded instantly:

maiasobu	These fans are meant
chiyo yorozuyo no	For joyous dances of a thousand,
ōgi ni te	Nay, ten thousand ages.

Word of his unexpected skill in renga composition quickly spread. Oze Hoan's *Shinchō Ki* (Life of Nobunaga) follows its account of the exchange of renga with this passage:

> Throughout the capital, old and young were speechless with astonishment when they learned this. People had supposed that because this man was a fierce warrior he would be just as violent as Kiso no Yoshinaka when he burst into the capital in 1183; but Nobunaga seemed to be gentle and refined. They were comforted to think that things were likely to go easily, and everyone breathed a sigh of relief.[33]

The passage, taken from a biography of Nobunaga published in 1622, is not a contemporary source, and as a whole cannot be accepted as a work of history, but the political and social functions of renga at the time could hardly have been better conveyed.

Nobunaga's partner in this exchange of linked verse, Satomura Jōha, was not only the finest renga poet of the age but probably its most distinguished literary figure, regardless of genre. His poetry is no longer read except by specialists, it is true, but it is of a literary quality unmatched by the work of any contemporary waka poet, essayist, or playwright. The man himself would attract the attention of authors of later times who found in him the emblematic figure of the artist who managed to rise in the world by ingratiating himself with one or more tyrants.[34]

Jōha was born in Nara, the son of a temple servant at the Ichijō-in. This was a humble occupation, but probably not without influence within the temple, perhaps the most richly endowed abbacy of the great Kōfuku-ji Monastery. Jōha received a good education despite his lowly background. He began at an early age to study renga with a wealthy townsman, a silk dealer who was also an amateur renga poet.[35] After the death of his father when Jōha was twelve, he became an acolyte (*kasshiki*) at the temple, where he was taught not only the Buddhist scriptures but classical literature. He maintained his interest in renga and met renga masters who visited the Kōfuku-ji. That was probably how he happened to meet Shūkei (1470–1544), a leading renga poet of the day, in 1542. Jōha that year was formally ordained as a priest, but he seems not to have been satisfied with his prospects. Even within the Buddhist temples, despite the possibilities they offered for talented men of humble birth to rise to high position, family background was not ignored. Jōha probably judged that he would not achieve eminence as a priest, and decided to become a renga master instead. When Shūkei returned to Kyoto, he took Jōha with him.

Jōha was fortunate to have been accepted as a pupil by Shūkei, and learned from him not only the rules of linked verse, but the formalities of conducting a renga session. The earliest mention of Jōha in accounts of renga states that he was the scribe of a session held in 1545, the year after Shūkei's death. Jōha chose as his next teacher Satomura Shōkyū (1510–1552). The leading figure in the world of renga after Shūkei's death was Tani Sōboku (d. 1545), but Jōha for some reason chose to study under Shōkyū instead. This proved to be another stroke of good fortune, for Sōboku died the year after Shūkei, leaving Shōkyū as the leading renga poet; Jōha remained his pupil for seven or eight years. The process of becoming a professional renga poet took years, but Jōha was sustained by his ambition. He told his disciple Matsunaga Teitoku what had prompted him to become a renga master:

> A man who fails to make a name for himself by the time he is thirty will never succeed in this life. I examined my prospects carefully, and it seemed to me that becoming a renga master would be an easy way to get ahead. After all, at renga gatherings even artisans and merchants sit side-by-side with members of the nobility.[36]

Nothing suggests that Jōha, even as a youth, felt deep emotions that demanded to be expressed in poetry. It seems likely that if he could have thought of some other easier and surer way to get ahead in the world than by becoming a renga master, he would have chosen it without hesitation. He was a thoroughly professional poet with a quick intelligence that permitted him to follow another man's link smoothly, and his knowledge of the rules of renga was flawless; but one looks in vain in his writings on the art of renga for anything resembling the breathtaking insights into the nature of poetic expression in the renga criticism of Shinkei. Jōha, for all his fame and skill, is usually praised for his lack of faults, rather than for the beauty of his expression.

At first, advancement was so slow that Jōha even considered abandoning renga, but gradually he began to build up a reputation. He had a rival in Tani Sōyō (1526–1563), the son of Sōboku. Sōyō not only enjoyed the advantage of having been born into a celebrated family of renga poets, but he possessed greater talent. At a renga session in one hundred links, the first time Jōha composed poetry with poets in the capital, he contributed only six links to eleven by Sōyō, an indication of their relative standing.

In 1552 Shōkyū died at the age of forty-two. Jōha was now almost at the top of the ladder of renga poets; only Sōyō still ranked higher. Jōha became the head of the Satomura school of renga and in this capacity participated in poetry gatherings of the nobility; his dream of sitting beside men of high birth had come true. He made his living by teaching renga composition, chiefly to members of the samurai class, and also pursued his studies of the waka, no doubt in emulation of the court poets. Jōha became intimate with members of the Konoe and Sanjōnishi families, both of impeccable descent, and was especially close to Sanjōnishi Kin'eda (1487–1563), the second son of Sanetaka, but the latter refused to give Jōha instruction in the secret traditions of the *Kokinshū* on the grounds that his interest in the traditions was commercial.[37]

Despite this rebuff, Jōha became a frequent visitor to the Sanjōnishi mansion. In the spring of 1553, when Sanjōnishi Kin'eda journeyed to Yoshino to admire the cherry blossoms, he took Jōha along. At the outset of his diary *Yoshino-mōde no Ki* (Record of a Pilgrimage to Yoshino), Kin'eda described his companion in these terms: "Jōha is deeply committed to the art of renga. Lately, he has been living in the capital, where he has been a constant visitor, day and night. He is well acquainted with byways in the province of Yamato, and has urged me to see the blossoms at Yoshino."[38]

The most interesting feature of this diary, which is given over mainly to descriptions of temples, places mentioned in poetry, and the cherry blossoms at various sites, is the unspoken fact that the son of a temple servant was associating familiarly with a great noble. Jōha was certainly astute in his choice of profession: only the mastery of an artistic skill could have enabled him to climb so high.

Toward the end of 1563 Kin'eda died at the age of seventy-six. The grief-stricken Jōha composed a solo thousand-link sequence in honor of his late mentor and friend. It began:

toshigoto no	How bitter I feel
hana naranu yo no	At a world where this flower
urami kana	Will not bloom each year.
furinishi ato mo	Even amid the ruins
niwa no harukusa	Spring grasses in the garden.
yama no ha no	I can see the dew—
usuyuki nokoru	The remains of the thin snow
tsuyu miete[39]	On the mountain edge.

In the same year, 1563, Tani Sōyō died at thirty-seven. Jōha had never quite displaced Sōyō as the leading renga poet, but death, once again, removed a rival. The lucky Jōha was now the single figure at the apex of the hierarchy of renga poets.

In 1565 the shogun, Ashikaga Yoshiteru, was murdered by two warlords, one of whom (Matsunaga Hisahide) had been Jōha's patron. The scarcity of literary compositions by Jōha at this time suggests he might have been busy with behind-the-scenes activities. His special influence with the military and court officials had resulted in his being approached by dignitaries from the provinces who wished to be invited to poetry gatherings in the capital, and no doubt these visitors paid Jōha well. For that matter, Jōha apparently felt no hesitation about serving as a kind of pander to nobles who wished to sell the aura of their names to rich bumpkins attracted by the old culture.

In 1566 the younger brother of the assassinated shogun Yoshiteru, Ashikaga Yoshiaki, returned to the laity from the Buddhist priesthood and attempted to restore the dignity of the shogunate, but the warfare continued. Jōha, unaffected by the vicissitudes of society, led a life of refined pleasures more luxurious than the emperor's, and proudly invited noblemen to his spacious residence.[40] A party he gave in the fourth month of 1566 was attended by literary men of the highest ranks. On this occasion Jōha displayed to the guests his collection of rare manuscripts and entertained them with music and an elaborate feast.

Jōha's income was derived chiefly from the fees he charged to correct renga composed by amateurs who sought his guidance. He delivered private lectures on classical texts, and this, too, brought in money. Undoubtedly his highest fees were for his manuals of the secrets of renga composition, written to special order. Far from taking refuge from the turmoil of the world in a mountain retreat, Jōha lived in the city, surrounded by admirers. He married twice, even though he had entered Buddhist orders.

The year 1567 was marked by desperate fighting. The countryside was torn by warfare and there was no central authority in the capital. This was the year Jōha chose to fulfill his cherished dream of visiting Mount Fuji. Though he came within sight of the fighting, he himself was unscathed, and his diary rarely indicates even that he was traveling through dangerous country. He mentions at one point, however, that he was forced to turn back because Oda Nobunaga's army was attacking the nearby castle of Nagashima, held by the fanatical Ikkō sect. Even while desperate fighting was in progress at Nagashima, Jōha and his hosts enjoyed their feasting and poetry-making. But he wrote in his diary, "Some time after midnight I happened to look to the west, and I saw that Nagashima Castle had fallen, and many fires set. The light was bright as day, so I got up out of bed." He composed this waka:

tabi makura	A traveler's pillow—
yumeji tanomu ni	I had set forth on a path of dreams,
aki no yo no	But now I shall spend
tsuki ni akasan	This night of autumn moonlight
matsukaze no sato[41]	In a village of pine winds.

It would be hard to guess the circumstances that had inspired this innocuous waka. Jōha closely associated with the men who burned cities, but he was indifferent to everything except his personal advancement. In 1568 Nobunaga entered Kyoto. This was the occasion on which he and Jōha exchanged links of renga, the beginning of their friendly relations. Jōha also began to cultivate the company of other military leaders, including Hosokawa Yūsai, the literary daimyo, and Akechi Mitsuhide, Nobunaga's lieutenant, who was a devoted amateur of renga. Mitsuhide, unlike Nobunaga, had wide cultural interests, and was especially fond of the tea ceremony, but he was something of a brute himself. In 1582 he assassinated Nobunaga at the Honnō-ji, a temple in Kyoto. A few days earlier he had joined with Jōha and other poets in composing a hundred-link renga sequence.

After the assassination Jōha was interrogated by Toyotomi Hideyoshi about his role. He admitted that he had suspected Mitsuhide might be planning such an attack, but insisted that it would have been improper to disclose a mere intuition. He not only persuaded Hideyoshi of his lack of complicity in the attempted coup, but became Hideyoshi's renga master, and eventually his adviser on all cultural matters. As early as 1578 Hideyoshi had joined Jōha in composing a thousand-link sequence to pray for victory over the Mōri family. Jōha, nothing if not impartial in his choice of renga partners, a few months later composed renga with a Mōri retainer, and in 1580 presented Mōri Motoyasu with a manual of renga composition.[42] He began his most important work of renga theory, *Renga Shihōshō* (Book of the Supreme Treasure of Renga), at the request of Akechi Mitsuhide, but presented it on completion to Mitsuhide's archenemy, Hideyoshi, along with a fulsome preface acclaiming the new master of Japan.[43]

Jōha enjoyed friendly relations also with Hideyoshi's nephew,

Hidetsugi, a man who (in George Sansom's words) "lived a vicious life, performed no useful function, and was so brutal that he was known as "Sesshō Kampaku, the Murdering Regent."[44] But this friendship proved to be a costly mistake: in 1595, Hidetsugi fell from Hideyoshi's favor and was ordered to commit suicide. Hideyoshi's wrath extended to Hidetsugi's wife, two small children, and thirty-five concubines, all of whom were put to death.

Jōha was one of only three men associated with Hidetsugi who were not obliged to commit seppuku. Instead, he was confined at the Miidera. His stipend was terminated, and his house and property were confiscated. Jōha was pardoned in the autumn of 1597 and returned to the capital; soon he was actively taking part in renga gatherings and regained his old supremacy. In the spring of 1598 he accompanied Hideyoshi on an excursion to Daigo to see the cherry blossoms. He had been forgiven.

Jōha, despite his worldliness and the lack of depth in much of his poetry, thought of renga not merely as an easy way to make a living but also as a noble calling. His eager cultivation of the military leaders of the day is not endearing, but was perhaps inevitable. A waka poet could live in solitude; but renga by its very nature required the poet to join with others in creating a sequence. It is unfortunate that Jōha tended to choose his companions for their rank rather than their poetic talent; for this reason he is remembered (if at all) for his political involvement, rather than for his renga. All the same, he was the last of the important poets of serious renga.

Popular Songs

The oldest examples of Japanese songs are contained in the *Kojiki* and other early texts. Some were included in *Kinkafu* (Songs to Koto Accompaniment), probably compiled early in the ninth century.[45] Various other types of song, such as *kagura-uta*, *saibara*, and *azuma-uta*, were sung and often danced as part of religious observations in ancient Japan, as we know from mentions in the official Six Histories. The texts of the songs are seldom of literary interest: repetition of phrases, dictated probably by the music or by the movements of a dance, the intrusion of irrelevant details, and the seeming lack of unity of conception make it difficult to enjoy them as poetry.

In contrast to such songs were those of secular content, many of which could be appreciated in written form. The word *uta*, the common word for "song," also denoted the waka, perhaps because it was possible to sing any waka to a fixed melody, as we know today from the annual poetry competitions held in the presence of the emperor at which the prizewinning waka are sung. Possibly the poets of the *Man'yōshū* sang their compositions, but the Heian poet who sent a note to his beloved that included a waka probably did not expect her to sing it. The poem was still called an *uta*, but it had an independent existence in writing. Orally performed folk songs continued to be heard long after the waka had come to be transmitted in writing. *Ryōjin Hishō*, the anthology of folk and popular poetry compiled in the twelfth century, is the finest such collection. The next major period of collecting popular and folk songs was the sixteenth century.

The *Kanginshū* (Collection for Quiet Singing)[46] was compiled in 1518. The work (in the tradition of the *Kokinshū*) has two prefaces, the first in Chinese and the second in Japanese, but the preface writers provided few clues to their identity. The Japanese preface opens: "I am one who has abandoned the world. I have spent more than ten years watching the snows of successive winters accumulate at my window, here in a hut I built for its distant view of Fuji."[47] The self-identification of the compiler as a priest who lived within sight of Mount Fuji led some to attribute the work to the renga poet Sōchō, whose hut was in Suruga; but problems reconciling the date of compilation with the facts of Sōchō's life have forced more recent scholars to conclude that the compiler is unknown. The Chinese preface is equally uninformative.

The collection consists of 311 poems, the same number as in the Chinese *Shih Ching* (as the compiler pointed out in the Japanese preface). The poems are labeled according to the category of song to which each belongs: 231 are *ko-uta* (short songs), 48 *Yamato-bushi* (Yamato tunes), 10 *dengaku-bushi*, 8 *sōka*,[48] and the remaining 14 belong to four other categories. These figures indicate that the compiler's intent was primarily to make a collection of ko-uta and Yamato-bushi, rather than a comprehensive anthology of the different varieties of song performed in his day.

Unlike the waka, the ko-uta have no single, fixed form, doubtless because they were originally sung to melodies of different lengths and rhythms. The most common example is in four lines of 7, 5, 7, and 5 syllables, resembling the imayō of the Heian period. Others are in the form of a waka less the first line—7, 5, 7, and 7 syllables. Still others are in 7, 7, 7, and 5 syllables or 7, 7, 7, and 7 syllables, or contain irregular lines of 3 or 4 syllables. The Yamato-bushi, passages from Nō plays, are considerably longer than the ko-uta and for the most part of a totally different, somewhat tragic nature.[49]. The main interest of the *Kanginshū* is in the ko-uta which, even if not of uniformly high quality as poetry, are pleasingly unconventional, and reflect ordinary life much better than waka of the period. The care given to arranging the poems under various topics such as "young shoots," "summer nights," "love by the waterside," or "autumn at the Shrine in the Fields" has suggested to critics that the compiler was probably a renga poet, a thesis borne out by the skill with which one poem leads to another. The following sequence of ko-uta is about pillows:

toga mo nai shakuhachi wo
makura ni katari to nageatete mo
sabishi ya hitorine[50]

I slammed my shakuhachi,
Though it was not to blame,
against my pillow.
How lonely it is to sleep alone!

hitoyo koneba tote
toga mo naki makura wo
tate na nage ni
yoko na nage ni
nayo na makura yo
nayo makura[51]

He hasn't come one night
But the pillow is not to blame
So don't throw it up in the air
And don't throw it sideways
You poor pillow,
Poor pillow!

hike yo tamakura
kimakura ni mo otoru tamakura

Take that arm of yours away!
Your arm's a worse pillow than a
block of wood

Takao no wajō no
Takao no wajō no, tamakura[52]

You priest from Takao,
You priest from Takao, on
whose arm I sleep.

kuru kuru kuru to wa, makura
koso shire
nō makura
mono iō ni wa
shōshi no makura[53]

He's come and come again, the
pillow knows it.
How about it, pillow?
If you tell anybody else,
That'll be the end of me, pillow.

The love songs are deservedly the most popular. Unlike the love poetry of the imperial collections, tinged with the grief of the love that has not been realized or the melancholy of love that has faded, the ko-uta on love in the *Kanginshū* not only convey the transience of love but also its joy:

amari mitasa ni	I wanted so badly to see you
soto kakurete hashite kita	I crept out and ran all the way
mazu hanasai nō	But first let me go—
hanashite mono wo iwasai nō	Let me go, I've something to tell you—
sozoro itōshūte	I'm so crazy about you
nan to shō zo nō[54]	I simply don't know what to do.

Translation of these poems is only approximate because of the ambiguity of the original texts, which were meant to be sung rather than parsed.[55] The many onomatopoetic refrains are particularly hard to convey. Yet even in translation, and certainly in the original, the freshness of the language can hardly be missed. Even the expressions of disenchantment are delightful. Many poems in the *Man'yōshū* and later had described the poet sleeping with his head on the arm of his beloved, giving piquance to the *Kanginshū* poem that opens with the command, "Take that arm of yours away!" Again, the first and second poems in the pillow sequence are universally intelligible in terms of the speaker venting her anger and frustration not on the cause of her suffering but on an innocent flute or pillow, a more endearingly "human" moment than those conjured up by the many waka that tristfully lament the beloved's neglect.[56] The last of the pillow poems echoes a famous one in the *Kokinshū*:

wa ga koi wa	Is it possible
hito shirurame ya	He knows how much I love him?
shikitae no	Perhaps my pillow,
makura nomi koso	Only my woven pillow,
shiraba shirurame[57]	Knows this secret of my heart.

The *Kokinshū* poem indicates that although the woman has told no one of her love, the pillow, into which she has wept many times, may have divined it from her tears. The pillow is personified to the extent that it can understand its owner's emotions; but in the *Kanginshū* song the speaker addresses the pillow with familiarity, as if it were a coconspirator.

The unexpected attitudes and the colloquial tone of its language give the *Kanginshū* special charm. Even though the exact meaning of many poems is no longer clear—they might be more easily understood if sung and delivered with gestures—they are superbly evocative. The lovers of the past come alive, briefly but poignantly, in each fragmentary little song. Among the poems in the *Kanginshū*, only the ko-uta have attracted special attention, but the collection as a whole has been enthusiastically praised by poets and scholars alike, especially in recent years.[58] Japanese poetry, long considered the special demesne of the aristocracy, is revealed in its pages to be the property of the entire people.[59]

Several similar collections of ko-uta were compiled during the late sixteenth century. *Sōan Ko-uta Shū* (Sōan's Collection of Ko-uta), first published in 1931, contains 220 poems, all of them ko-uta. Neither the identity of Sōan nor the date of compilation has yet been determined, though it is believed that the collection dates from the last two decades of the sixteenth century, in between the *Kanginshū* and *Ryūdatsu Ko-uta* (Ryūdatsu's Ko-uta), with which it shares about a fifth of its songs.

Ryūdatsu Ko-uta was compiled by Takasabu Ryūdatsu (1527–1611), a merchant from the city of Sakai who was also a master of ko-uta song and on occasion gave command performances before Nobunaga and Hideyoshi. The songs in *Ryūdatsu Ko-uta*—unlike those in the *Kanginshū*, composed by people of all classes of society, or *Sōan Ko-uta Shū*, almost exclusively songs of the common people—are distinctly urbane and polished.[60] The collection contains 514 ko-uta, many of them about love. Some texts were by Ryūdatsu himself, but for the most part he probably took existing poems and supplied them with new musical settings.[61] Many of the songs are in the rhythm of 7, 7, 7, and 5 syllables, which would be the most typical form of songs of the Tokugawa period, and the accompaniment to the songs was provided by the samisen, another indication that *Ryūdatsu Ko-uta* serves as a bridge between medieval and premodern song.

The collection, *Tauezōshi* (A Collection of Rice-Planting Songs),[62] was also compiled during the Azuchi-Momoyama period. These are true folk songs, typical of those sung while men and women were planting rice in the middle ages, but unusual in the richness of their content. Ko-uta figure prominently also in Kyōgen;[63] some Kyōgen are even constructed around a series of songs, evidence of their popularity and the closeness of their association with the common people.

Drama

Various dramatic entertainments developed during the sixteenth century, especially in the Azuchi-Momoyama period. The warfare led to the breakup of the court society that had patronized the Nō, and forced the actors to return to the provinces, where their art had originated.

In order to please spectators who did not possess the knowledge of the literature of the past that could be assumed of audiences in the capital, they performed newly composed Nō plays that featured greater action (and less poetry) than the plays of Zeami's time. It is noteworthy that each class had come to crave theatrical performances that accorded with its own tastes. For example, the Kōwaka, ballad-dramas, that mainly treat the war between the Taira and the Minamoto, were created for samurai audiences in the sixteenth century. The introduction of the samisen from the Ryūkyū Islands in the middle of the century led to a new style of singing, and eventually to a new dramatic entertainment, Jōruri, that appealed primarily to townsmen. Finally, influences from Europe, introduced to the Japanese by missionaries, may have helped to stimulate another new kind of theater, Kabuki. These various developments enjoyed reciprocal influences: each variety of drama during the sixteenth century borrowed from the others, and together they attested in performance to the birth of a new society.

Nō Drama

The Nō had attained its highest development in the fourteenth and fifteenth centuries, and by the beginning of the Tokugawa period was in the process of becoming the repertory drama that it is today. But there was one last spurt of creativity in the sixteenth century as the Nō actors attempted to regain the popularity with the common people they had forfeited when they accepted the patronage of the Muromachi shoguns.

The emblematic figure of this last period of Nō as an art capable of new developments was the dramatist and actor Kanze Nagatoshi, the son of the better-known Kanze Nobumitsu.[64] Only one of Nagatoshi's plays is still regularly performed, *Shōzon*, based on a section of *The Tale of the Heike* describing how the treachery of Tosabō Shōzon was exposed and he was put to death. The first thing one is likely to notice on examining the text of *Shōzon* is that it is not clear whether the shite is the villainous Shōzon or the avenging Benkei; it depends on whether in performance Shōzon's lying oath of loyalty is read by Shōzon himself or by Benkei. The two men are antagonists in the same sense that this can be said of a European play; the waki is definitely not a "man at the side" who merely asks questions of the protagonist. The cast of *Shōzon* is exceptionally large; apart from the shite and waki, there is a kokata who appears as Shizuka, four tsure, all of whom are named, and two Kyōgen roles. In performance, there is even more to startle the spectator who knows only the Nō plays of Zeami's time. In the second part, for example, an actor does a front somersault from the *hashigakari* (passageway) onto the stage, and another on being killed falls perpendicularly backward without relaxing his body, miraculously not cracking his skull.[65]

The cast of *Kasui* (River Waters), a play by Nagatoshi that is no longer performed, includes not only the shite and waki but nine tsure and two Kyōgen actors. This play has many changes of scene, and its plot shifts from the fable of a dragon princess who dries up a river in order to compel the Chinese court to provide her with a husband, to the more realistic scene of the courtier who volunteers to marry her, to a strange scene in which a great drum sounds of itself, presaging war, and finally to a battle scene in which the Chinese emperor, aided by the dragon king, is victorious. *Chikatō*, another play by Nagatoshi that has dropped from the repertory, is perhaps the most extreme example of his unconventionality. The usual divisions into categories of actors—shite, waki, tsure, and so on—have become meaningless. The principal character, a child, is sometimes considered to be the shite, sometimes only a kokata. Chikatō, who gives his name to the play, is perhaps the shite, but perhaps only a tsure. It is not clear, for that matter, whether the minor characters are companions of the shite or of the waki. There are four principal characters, each of whom is given a display scene, rather in the manner of an old-fashioned Italian opera. The texts of the plays are resolutely prosaic, though the sung passages on occasion include such clichés of the poetry of the past as the tear-soaked sleeve.

There is no evidence as to whether these plays, created in order to please audiences who could not follow the difficult poetry and the barely enunciated plots of the great Nō dramas, were successful. Surviving records of sixteenth-century performances indicate that the most often staged works were the relatively static classics, but these records do not take into account performances away from the capital. The fossilization of the Nō during the Tokugawa period and, above all, the development of new forms of dramatic entertainment that were of greater mass appeal than even the plays of Nagatoshi, tended to deprive his plays of their popularity, as we can infer from the number that are no longer performed.

One further development in Nō occurred at the end of the sixteenth century: Toyotomi Hideyoshi commanded his panegyrist Ōmura Yūko (1536?–1596) to write a series of Nō plays about himself. Traditionally, the Nō plays had been set at a considerable distance in time from the events they portrayed. Even works of the category *genzaimono*, "contemporary plays," were not set in the present; the word *genzai* (present) meant that the events depicted took place in the time of the waki, who meets not ghosts from the past but his contemporaries. The plays closest to the present of the audience itself were from at least a century earlier. But Hideyoshi wanted plays describing himself and his achievements, shrinking the distance in time to nothing. Yūko naturally complied.

Ōmura Yūko was no mere hack writer. He began his career as a scholar of Zen Buddhism, and later extended his studies to include waka, renga, and the Japanese classics. He was so proficient at these different studies that he eventually acquired the reputation of being the foremost authority on non-Buddhist literature.[66] In 1578, when Hideyoshi was about to attack Yūko's native place, Miki in Banshū province, he asked Yūko to come along as the official chronicler. Yūko's account of the siege of Miki Castle, *Banshū Go Seibatsu no Koto* (The Conquest of Banshū), is a moving account of how the defenders of the castle perished.[67] It was the first of an impressive series of chronicles of Hideyoshi's exploits known under the collective title of *Tenshō Ki*. After Hideyoshi established himself as the ruler of Japan in 1582, Yūko became a central figure in his inner circle of *otogishū*, entertainers and advisers on cultural matters. In the manner of a poet laureate, he wrote congratulatory pieces on such subjects as the recovery from illness of Hideyoshi's mother or the birth of his son Tsurumatsu.

Perhaps Yūko's most lasting literary monument was the ten Nō plays[68] he wrote by order of Hideyoshi, an enthusiastic amateur performer of Nō who did not hesitate to perform even the most difficult roles. The waki nō[69] *Yoshino-mōde* (A Pilgrimage to Yoshino) evokes the visit of Hideyoshi to Yoshino in the second month of 1594. According to a contemporary account, on that occasion "Lord Hideyoshi had on his usual false whiskers, wore false eyebrows, and had his teeth blackened. The persons accompanying him [they included Ōmura Yūko and Satomura Jōha] were all dressed with the utmost magnificence, each trying to outdo the other, and created so splendid a sight that crowds assembled to watch them."[70] Once the party reached Yoshino a poetry gathering was held.

Yoshino-mōde opened with the waki, a courtier in the service of the present emperor, relating the great deeds of Hideyoshi: "He rules our country as he sees fit, has pacified the three kingdoms of Korea, and has further acceded to entreaties for peace from China. Having accomplished these mighty deeds, he has returned and built a great palace in the village of Fushimi in Yamashiro province. And now, this spring, he is making a pilgrimage to Yoshino to admire the cherry blossoms. I go to serve him."[71] In the second part of the play the god Zaō Gongen appears, and after relating the history of the shrine at Yoshino, promises to protect Hideyoshi on his return to the capital.

The second play of the series, *Shibata-uchi* (The Slaying of Shibata), relates Hideyoshi's exploits in defeating Shibata Katsuie; the shite, the ghost of Shibata, describes how he triumphantly led his forces into Ōmi province and seemed about to win a great battle when "Hideyoshi himself came riding up against us, and tens of thousands on my side, slashed down by his sword, fled the field, unable to withstand him."[72] Hideyoshi performed the role of the shite in another second-category play, *Akechi-uchi* (The Slaying of Akechi). It dramatizes the vengeance he wreaked on Akechi Mitsuhide for having murdered Oda Nobunaga. The play concludes with the slaying of Mitsuhide and a paean of praise for Hideyoshi's loyalty to his master. This was an unconventional ending for a Nō play, but it is easy to imagine Hideyoshi's self-satisfaction as he acted out his own glorious deeds.[73]

Hōjō, based on Yūko's chronicle "Odawara Gojin," another section of his *Tenshō Ki*, describes how a Zen priest encounters the ghosts of Hōjō Ujimasa and his brother Ujinao. They relate how Hideyoshi besieged their castle at Odawara, and how they committed suicide. The dialogue between the priest and the brothers includes statements of Zen doctrine, but ends with predictions of Hideyoshi's future triumphs that will carry his rule even to the Kuril Islands.

The shite of the third-category, or woman play, *Kōya-mōde* (Pilgrimage to Kōya), is none other than Hideyoshi's mother. The play opens with a man in Hideyoshi's service climbing Mount Kōya to offer flowers at the grave of the mother. She appears first as an aged nun, but in the second scene reveals herself as a bodhisattva of song and dance, and performs a bugaku dance. The play concludes like the others with praise for Hideyoshi, in this case specifically for his filial piety.

Kōya-mōde was performed while Hideyoshi and his party were actually staying on Mount Kōya. It is reported that during the final dance of the play, black clouds suddenly covered the sky, the earth trembled, and lightning flashed in the sky. These ominous signs were attributed to the fact that a flute and drums had been played during the performance, in disregard of Kōbō Daishi's interdiction on music-making on the holy mountain. Even the fearless Hideyoshi felt it prudent to hurry down the mountain after such an expression of supernatural displeasure.[74]

Toyokuni-mōde (Pilgrimage to the Toyokuni Shrine), written by an unknown dramatist after Hideyoshi's death, provides a fitting conclusion to the series, presenting him as the god Toyokuni Daimyōjin. The tsure is Yūgeki, a Chinese general, who arrives with tribute offerings for the god, declaring that Toyokuni Daimyōjin is worshiped not only in Japan but in China.

Although Ōmura Yūko's plays are likely to seem in synopsis no more than sycophantic tributes to a despot, they are actually among the most successful examples of "new Nō." Yūko had no special training in Nō, but his inborn literary gifts and his knowledge of the poetry of the past enabled him to create plays that were more than pastiches. On the whole, he adhered closely to the formal structure and traditional language. It must have seemed strange to the first audiences to see people they knew (or even themselves) represented by actors who spoke a poetic language that was certainly not their own, but such conventions are not hard to accept after a few minutes. The failure of these plays to hold the stage was probably due to their closeness to Hideyoshi. The death of Hideyoshi and the defeat of the forces loyal to his son made it highly unlikely that plays which proclaim Hideyoshi's glory would be revived in the Tokugawa period, and they have seldom been discussed since.[75] Ōmura Yūko's success in pleasing his master ultimately deprived him of the fame that his writings might otherwise have brought him.

From time to time in the following centuries Nō plays were written, but none managed to secure a place in the repertory. During the Tokugawa period Nō was elevated into a stately, even ritual art that served as the official "music" for the shogunate which, in the Confucian tradition, believed that rites and music promoted stable government. The protection of the shogunate ensured that Nō would not perish despite the popularity of newer theatrical arts, but it was at the sacrifice of its vitality.

Kōwaka

Several Kōwaka, ballad-dramas that were popular with the samurai class, were also composed by order of Hideyoshi to celebrate his feats.[76] The practitioners of Kōwaka, anxious to establish its antiquity and dignity, were fond of tracing its origins back to Momonoi Naoaki (1393?–1470?), the grandson of an illustrious daimyo, who had been known in his youth as Kōwakamaru.[77] Perhaps some connection existed between this man and the creation of Kōwaka, but he is more likely to have been a patron than a composer of ballads, a demeaning profession.[78] James Araki, the author of an important study of the "ballad-drama," as he called Kōwaka, believed that the existing Kōwaka texts were not used for performances prior to the middle of the sixteenth century.[79]

Kōwaka has also been traced to the *kusemai*, a section of the Nō play in irregular meter that usually narrated the central dramatic incident of the story; but as Araki noted, "The kusemai changed considerably during the fifteenth and sixteenth centuries, and a comparison of the kusemai of Zeami's time and what was called kusemai after the 1530's reveals that they were similar only in name."[80] In short, there is no evidence that kusemai or any other early texts served as libretti for Kōwaka. Kōwaka still survives vestigially in one village in Kyūshū, but in the seventeenth century it ceased to be of literary or dramatic importance, and its survival is something of a miracle.[81]

Little information survives on how Kōwaka was originally performed. It seems to have owed its popularity to the beautiful voices and dances of the performers, rather than to dramatic presentation, and the plays were performed not in theaters but in temples, mansions of the great, and even in the Imperial Palace. Later on, the Kōwaka performers adopted elements of more popular stage entertainments, but (perhaps because they preferred to think of themselves as samurai, rather than as actors) they never succeeded in winning the audiences of Jōruri or Kabuki. Kōwaka performances today are recited in a cadenced monotone that sometimes rises to melody, but there is no mimetic action, and hardly any choreographic movement beyond a rhythmic strut.[82] Unlike Nō, however, the delivery is clear and meant to be intelligible.

Most of the fifty or so extant Kōwaka texts are derived from *The Tale of the Heike* and *The Tale of the Soga Brothers*. Yoshitsune, who figures in so many other works of medieval literature, is the hero of twenty of these plays, and thirteen more deal with other persons in *The Tale of the Heike*. The Soga brothers appear in another seven. The rest of the repertory is of miscellaneous origins.[83] Apart from two works based on the writings of Ōmura Yūko, the authors of these texts are unknown.[84] Even when the stories borrow from the same sources as the Nō plays, they are consistently less dramatic. They tend to be prolix, but even so, they sometimes deliberately omit what should be the climax of a story, assuming it will be familiar to the spectator.[85] The element of drama is much attenuated, though the materials contain every potential for drama.[86]

It may be wondered why so undramatic and so conspicuously unamusing a form of entertainment should have enjoyed popularity. A well-known anecdote tells how Oda Nobunaga performed the Kōwaka version of *Atsumori* in 1560 on the eve of a crucial battle, and he later extended his patronage to the actors. Probably his interest in Kōwaka went beyond simple entertainment; he may have believed that the solemn recitation of a Kōwaka drama would identify him with the great warriors of the past. These heroes had all perished, it is true, but Nobunaga accepted their tragedy along with their glory. Or perhaps the brevity and uncertainty of life made him resolve to make the most of it while he could.

Kōwaka was of particular appeal to the samurai class. The solemnity of the language and the unrelieved seriousness of the events were congenial to their belief in their special destiny as the guardians of society. The eloquence of the delivery of the texts may also have moved audiences more than similar recitations would move people today. In a society where there was little or no occasion for oratory, it must have been deeply affecting to hear actors who spoke so eloquently of tragic matters. A similar pleasure was to be had from some of the *ai-kyōgen*, notably the battle narration from *Yashima*, often performed as an independent work. The visual appeal of Kōwaka tended to diminish over time because of the increased emphasis on the samurailike dignity of the art; by the beginning of the seventeenth century, as we know from João Rodrigues,[87] performances were declaimed rather than danced. The achievements of the heroes of the past still stirred Japanese of the seventeenth century and later, but Kōwaka possessed neither the grandeur of Nō nor the mimetic excitement of Kabuki, and gradually lost its hold even on the samurai class, whose favor the Kōwaka actors had so sedulously cultivated.

Other Dramatic Entertainments

The second half of the sixteenth century was the seedbed for the most important varieties of theater for the next three hundred years. None of the works performed by the Jōruri, *sekkyō-bushi*, or Kabuki troupes of the time survive, and we can only guess what they may have been like from the texts that began to be published in the seventeenth century.[88]

The sudden emergence of these different theatrical forms at more or less the same time may have been no more than coincidence. For example, the combination of the three elements—texts, puppets, and musical accompaniment—that constitute Jōruri (later known as Bunraku), took place at the end of the sixteenth century; but puppets had been known in Japan for five hundred years, and the narratives, initially at least, were mainly about Yoshitsune and his beloved Lady Jōruri, figures from the distant past. The crucial factor in the creation of Jōruri at this time was probably the introduction from the Ryūkyū Islands of the samisen, an instrument with so penetrating a sound that it could be heard over the voice of a chanter narrating the story. The introduction of the samisen at this time was probably related to the awakened Japanese interest in the islands to the south and Southeast Asia.

There is also a possibility that European influence affected the development of both Jōruri and Kabuki.[89] Letters from the missionaries mention performances of plays based on biblical themes that were staged in the churches. It is not clear what form these performances took, but the introduction of themes that were totally unlike any in Japanese or Chinese literature may well have affected intending playwrights. The biblical plays have not survived, but one curious play of a somewhat later date, *Amida no Munewari* (The Riven Breast of Amida), first performed by the puppets in 1614, has suggested specifically Christian influence. The work, though nominally set in India, is entirely Japanese in its details. It tells of a rich man who is so confident that his money can buy him every happiness that, for the pleasure of it, he decides to do wicked things instead of good, and persuades his wife to join him. Their wicked acts are directed in particular against Buddhism; they burn temples, refuse alms to priests, and in other ways delight in doing evil. Shakyamuni Buddha, disturbed by the influence of the couple on other people, determines to punish them. He assembles his disciples and orders them to fetch demons from hell. They return with some three hundred who eventually destroy the rich man's treasures, kill his servants, and pour molten iron down the throats of the once-arrogant couple. Buddha, however, commands the devils to spare their two children, a boy and a girl.

The remaining acts of the play are devoted to the tribulations suffered by the children. In the sixth and final act the girl, who was born in the same year, month, day, and hour as the ailing child of a certain rich man, is sacrificed in order to cure his illness: her liver is torn from her body and fed to the sick boy, who immediately recovers. That night, the boy's attendants go to examine the dead girl's body. They discover her and her brother sleeping peacefully, hand in hand. Beside them, a statue of Amida Buddha is streaming blood from a terrible rent in its chest, and it is apparent to all that Amida has offered his own liver to save the girl. People gather from everywhere to pay homage before the mutilated, blood-stained statue.

Although this play at first glance may not seem to show any Christian influence, one notes that Shakyamuni Buddha, not in the least resembling the all-compassionate deity found in other Buddhist writings, initially behaves rather like Jehovah, and the rich man's suffering may recall Job's. The Amida Buddha of the last act, however, is more like Christ; nothing in earlier Japanese descriptions of Amida accounts for the scene of people worshiping a holy image streaming with blood in the manner of European (especially Iberian) representations of Christ on the cross. Amida's sacrifice of himself to save the girl also suggests Christ's saving of mankind. It is not possible to prove there was direct influence, but we can recognize the great difference between the deity here described and the traditional portrayals of Amida in his Western Paradise. Christian art was certainly well enough known in Japan at the time to account for this unusual Amida.[90] But even if Kabuki and Jōruri were indebted to European influences in their earliest period, very little remained of these influences in later years.

Sekkyō was originally (as the literal meaning of the name indicates) an "explanation of the sutras" given to musical accompaniment by a priest at a temple.[91] Such explanations were intended for illiterates who could not read the commentaries on the sacred works of Buddhism for themselves and would not listen to a sermon unless it was interestingly delivered. The musical accompaniment, intended to heighten the dramatic effect of the stories of miracles and the powers of karma, was at first the sasara, an instrument consisting of thin strips of bamboo that the performer rubbed with a stick, causing a rhythmic rattle that accentuated the delivery of the text. There are records as far back as the fourteenth century of such performances. The Nō play *Jinen Koji* has for its chief character a priest who not only delivers a sermon to sasara accompaniment but also sings and dances.

The main effect on the audience of the sekkyō plays, even in the early days, was probably to induce tears, as we can gather from surviving paintings of performances of a later date.[92] At first the performers of Sekkyō were probably priests, but later, as some men began to attract audiences by the skill of their recitations, the performers became professionals who, in order to elicit donations from the audience, heightened the effects of their performances with gestures and music. That may be how it happened, early in the seventeenth century, that the Sekkyō performers adopted the samisen and the puppets from Jōruri in the hope of drawing still larger audiences. The texts of the old Jōruri plays were largely borrowed from Sekkyō,[93] but the latter in turn had borrowed from Kōwaka, as can be inferred from the existence of a Sekkyō version of *Yuriwaka Daijin* (The Minister Yuriwaka), the tale allegedly borrowed from *The Odyssey*.[94]

Although the Sekkyō repertory grew in the seventeenth century, the staples of Sekkyō performances remained five works that already existed by the Azuchi-Momayama period—*Karukaya, Sanshō Dayū, Oguri, Shintokumaru*, and *Aigo no Waka*. These works would be modified over the years by Sekkyō performers and adapted for the Jōruri and Kabuki stages, but their lasting appeal for the Japanese has not been confined to the theater. Some, especially *Sanshō Dayū*, have become established, especially since the Meiji period, as part of the common heritage of the medieval past, in the form of children's stories and even films.

Kabuki undoubtedly had its origins in entertainments of the Azuchi-Momoyama period, but it is usually traced back no further than to Okuni, the priestess of the Izumo Shrine who brought her troupe to Kyoto in 1603. It was (and remains) far less literary than Jōruri, depending on the charm or the dramatic skill of the actors to win the favor of the audience even for works that were too trivial to be printed.

More important than the differences in these three kinds of entertainment was the fact that for the first time there were many theaters attended by anyone who could buy a ticket. The Momoyama-period screens showing scenes within and without the capital often depict clusters of small theaters where audiences happily watch the plays of their choice. After the long period of warfare Kyoto had become a city again, and this time a city not only of the aristocrats or even of the samurai but of everyone who lived there.

Prose Writings

Prose did not thrive during the last part of the sixteenth century, though it was the time when the *kana zōshi*, the characteristic tales of the seventeenth century, were being incubated.[95] Perhaps the most important development of this period was the demise of the monogatari, the staple of prose writing since the early Heian period. This does not mean, of course, that no later works of fiction were ever called monogatari; quite to the contrary, even writers of the twentieth century on occasion called their novels "monogatari," especially when they were set in the distant past.[96] But the monogatari, as the term was used of the court fiction of the Heian or of the archaistic fiction (*giko monogatari*) of the Kamakura and Muromachi periods, by the end of the sixteenth century had breathed its last gasp.

The most striking prose writings of the period were probably the biographies of Oda Nobunaga and Toyotomi Hideyoshi. Autobiography, usually called "diaries," had a long history in Japan, but biography had never developed as in China. Of course, one can consider *The Tale of the Heike* as a biography of Taira no Kiyomori and his family, and *Gikeiki* pretends to be a biography of Minamoto no Yoshitsune, but the impression received from these works is of a romance in which characters, named for historical prototypes but by no means faithfully portrayed, figure in episodes that have dramatic rather than historical significance. It is hard to believe, for example, when reading *The Tale of the Heike* that water poured onto the feverish body of Taira no Kiyomori actually turned to flames, but such details reveal the extremes to which the author went in order to satisfy the expectations of readers who believed in divine punishment.

The biographies of Nobunaga and Hideyoshi also glorified their subjects, but the aim of the authors was to heighten the importance of actual deeds, not to capture the attention of readers with invented prodigies. These histories are intermittently interesting, though the accounts of one battle after another inevitably become repetitious, and the names of the defeated generals do not linger in the memory. An even more serious failing is the inability of the authors to paint convincing portraits of their subjects, let alone create characters in the round. The inadequacy of their portrayals is apparent from the description of Nobunaga in a letter written in 1569 by the missionary and historian Luis Frois (1532–1597):

> A tall man, thin, scantly bearded, with a very clear voice, much given to the practice of arms, hardy, fond of the exercise of justice, & of mercy, proud, a lover of honor to the uttermost, very secretive in what he determines, extremely shrewd in the stratagems of war, little if at all subject to the reproof, & counsel of his subordinates, feared, & revered by all to an extreme degree. Does not drink wine. He is a severe master: treats all the Kings and Princes of Iapan with scorn, & speaks to them over his shoulder as though to inferiors, & is completely obeyed by all as their absolute lord. He is a man of good understanding, & clear judgment, despising the *Cámis* & *Fotoquès*, & all the rest of that breed of idols, & all the heathen superstitions.[97]

In one paragraph Frois painted a far more memorable portrait of Nobunaga than Ōta Gyūichi achieved in his lengthy *Shinchō-ko Ki* or Oze Hoan in his even more extensive *Shinchō Ki*, though occasionally an anecdote will catch fire by a single detail or unexpected action. For example, we are told that at the funeral services for his father in 1549 Nobunaga, dressed peculiarly for the occasion, went up to the altar to offer incense in the traditional manner, only to take up a handful of incense and throw it in the direction of the funeral tablet, to the astonishment and dismay of all.[98] The gesture probably was intended to reflect Nobunaga's disbelief in Buddhism, even at the age of fifteen, but it is even more indicative of his refusal to comply with the etiquette expected of warriors of his class. A Buddhist priest from Kyūshū who happened to be present reportedly exclaimed on seeing Nobunaga's gesture that he was destined to possess the country. But such dramatic passages are infrequent.

The anecdotes related about Nobunaga tend to emphasize a few of his traits, notably his bravery. Hoan described in *Shinchō Ki* how on one occasion Nobunaga set out to relieve the defenders of a certain castle. He and his men got close enough to the castle to hear the sounds of the fighting, but a river in flood prevented them from going to the relief of the besieged forces:

> Lord Nobunaga, tense with anxiety, felt the sweat ooze in his clenched hands that trembled so violently he could not keep his horse steady. His looks inspired confidence, but there seemed to be absolutely no way to cross the river. The sounds of guns and arrows and the war cries of friends and foes could be heard without letup. "I can't stay here. It will mean I am deserting Daigaku. If I'm to drown in the river, well, I'll drown." He called to his men, "Let's make it across!" He plunged his horse into the river, and his men followed him, each eager to be first. It was a time when it was all but impossible to get across without a boat, but such was his bravery that nothing seemed impossible, and they made it safely to the opposite shore.[99]

The first of the biographies of Nobunaga, *Shinchō-kō Ki* by Ōta Gyūichi, was probably completed by 1598. It describes events from 1568, when Nobunaga headed for Kyoto with the shogun Ashikaga Yoshiaki, until 1582 when he was killed at the Honnō-ji by Akechi Mitsuhide. The text was originally composed in kambun, but seems to have been intended to be read aloud to persons who wished to learn of the great achievements of its hero.[100]

Shinchō Ki[101] by Oze Hoan was not published until 1622, but most of the work was probably completed by 1611. It was intended to supplement the material in Ōta Gyūichi's biography of Nobunaga, which Hoan termed "crude and truncated."[102] The text is in Japanese and shows that some attempt was made to achieve stylistic distinction. Its aim seems to have been not so much a glorification of Nobunaga as a revelation of how Nobunaga's deeds accorded with the higher principles of government. Oze Hoan also published (in 1634?) *Taikō Ki*, a biography of Toyotomi Hideyoshi.[103] Even more clearly than in his biography of Nobunaga, he judged his subject in terms of Confucian principles; but the interest of the work is in the factual information he supplied about a most remarkable man.

Tenshō Ki, the account written by Ōmura Yūko between 1580 and 1590 of the battles fought and won by Hideyoshi, is less a biography than a panegyric, but it rises at times to literary heights not attained by other works of this genre. Biography still had a long way to go before it attained the literary distinction of Aubrey or Boswell, but it had made a promising start.

European Influence

One unprecedented development affected the composition of literature: the arrival of Europeans in the middle of the sixteenth century. The first Europeans known to have reached Japan were some Portuguese sailors who arrived at the southern island of Tanegashima aboard a Chinese ship in 1542. These early visitors were followed by many more Portuguese and Spaniards, and later also by British, Dutch, and other Europeans. Most of the Iberians were either soldiers or priests; the soldiers carried the guns with which they had conquered far-flung territories in Africa, Asia, and the Americas; the priests brought the crosses that were the sign of their faith and of their mission to spread their religion throughout the world. The English and Dutch, who were Protestants, did not show the same crusading zeal, but confined their activities mainly to trade.

Among the European cultural influences that entered Japan as the result of the proselytizing efforts of the missionaries were painting in the Western manner, mainly of religious scenes,[104] and the Gregorian chant.[105] Literary influences were much more restricted. The priests, whose chief task was to communicate the mysteries of the Christian religion to the Japanese, had no reason to introduce the masterpieces of European literature. Almost all the translations made into Japanese at this time were of religious texts, and when Christianity was prohibited under penalty of death in the 1630s such books were either destroyed or hidden. Extremely few copies survive.[106] One of the rare secular works to be translated was *Aesop's Fables*, in a version made from Latin into Japanese in 1593 and published by the Jesuits in Amakusa. A later translation into Japanese, made in 1639, was better known; although it did not circulate freely, it inspired several Japanese works of the seventeenth century.[107] In the late eighteenth century the eccentric painter and essayist Shiba Kōkan found a copy of the translation of *Aesop's Fables* in the library of a daimyo, and made fresh versions and adaptations of some of the fables.[108] Translations were also made of Cicero's *De Amicitia* and of Euclid's *Elements*, but these works, kept secret, had no influence on the writing of Japanese literature.

Finally, there was one European story that somehow seems to have made its way independently to Japan, where it was imitated and adopted: *The Odyssey*.[109] It is hard to imagine under what circumstances a Portuguese priest might have taken the trouble to narrate the adventures of Ulysses to Japanese acquaintances, and it is equally difficult to imagine that the story was transmitted solely by word of mouth across the breadth of Asia; yet if, as is widely believed, *The Odyssey* reached Japan, it must have been by one or both routes.

The Japanese work that most clearly suggests the influence of *The Odyssey, Yuriwaka Daijin*, tells of Yuriwaka,[110] a warrior who was chosen to head Japanese forces in the war against the Mongols. His ships scored a great victory at sea over the Mongol fleet, but on the way back to Japan he was abandoned on a desert island by command of a treacherous subordinate. By the time the gods enabled Yuriwaka to return to Japan, the years on the island had much altered his appearance, and he was not recognized. The villainous subordinate had in the meanwhile attempted to marry Yuriwaka's wife, asserting that her husband was dead, but the wife insisted that she must first transcribe a Buddhist text a thousand times. Yuriwaka returned, flexed and strung an iron bow, and killed the suitor. Yuriwaka and his wife were then reunited.[111]

The resemblances to *The Odyssey* are obvious, but many Japanese scholars have insisted that these resemblances are no more than coincidences, and that sources existed within the Buddhist or Shintō traditions for all the events related in the story.[112] If, as was first suggested by Tsubouchi Shōyō in 1906,[113] the narrative *Yuriwaka Daijin* was derived from *The Odyssey*, the transmission would have had to occur during a very short period during the early years of the Portuguese presence in Japan. James Araki concluded that the story was passed on to the Japanese by Juan Fernandez, the interpreter of Francis Xavier, between November 1550, when Xavier arrived in the city of Yamaguchi, and February 1551, when *Yuriwaka Daijin* was first recited by Kōwaka performers in Kyoto.[114] But even if Fernandez was capable of narrating in Japanese the story of Ulysses, it is hard to imagine that within three months it had not only spread from Yamaguchi to the capital but had been transformed into a story of a war with the Mongols.

There is another problem: one famous episode of *The Odyssey*, the story of Polyphemus and his cave, which does not appear in *Yuriwaka Daijin*, is found in a secular Chinese work of the tenth century and (much later) in an eighteenth century Japanese account by a man who heard the story in Nagasaki.[115] Both Chinese and Japanese versions are brief, and they differ in details, but they seem clearly to have been derived from the same source, *The Odyssey*.[116] This suggests that the Yuriwaka stories reached Japan in the same manner, traveling from the shores of the Mediterranean across the breadth of Asia to the Chinese court and eventually to the Chinese merchants in Nagasaki.

Regardless of how *The Odyssey* reached Japan, or whether or not it actually got there, Japan in the sixteenth century was open to such influences from abroad. Not only did Europeans and Chinese visit and reside in the country, but Japanese traveled abroad. Some, especially converts to Christianity, went as far as Rome, and others sailed to Southeast Asia, where "Japan towns" were founded in Thailand and elsewhere.[117] This openness to the rest of the world, strikingly unlike the isolationism that prevailed during the period of seclusion (*sakoku*) that followed, suggests how close Japanese literature came to developing along quite different lines. The influences of the literatures of Europe that so profoundly affected Japanese writers of the nineteenth and twentieth centuries would surely have been easier to assimilate in the climate that prevailed three hundred years earlier. It is clear from the letters of the European missionaries of the Azuchi-Momoyama period that they considered Japanese civilization to be at least as advanced as their own, and it is not unreasonable to suppose that if the Japanese had chosen to participate in the literary movements of sixteenth-century Europe they could have produced works of quality rivaling those of their mentors. They chose instead, for political and not literary reasons, to reject European influence and to enter on a period of isolation, when contacts with the rest of the world were severely limited. This decision, by turning the Japanese in on themselves, contributed to the creation of the distinctive literature of the Tokugawa period, including the novels of Saikaku, the plays of Chikamatsu, and the haiku poetry of Bashō. It deprived them, however, of the fertilizing influences from abroad that normally enrich a country's writers, and forced them to look back to their own past when in need of fresh inspiration. Fortunately, as we have seen, their patrimony was generous—a thousand years of literary works in every genre, including some that rank high among the masterpieces of the world.

Notes

1. The exact date of the beginning of the Azuchi period is a matter of dispute. Oda Nobunaga's first major victory was won at Okehazama in 1560. His conquest of Gifu, where he established his residence, took place in 1567, and in the following year he occupied Kyoto. In 1573 he drove the shogun, Ashikaga Yoshiaki, from Kyoto into exile. Any one of these dates (1560, 1567, 1568, and 1573) could be used as a starting point for the new era. I shall generally use 1560 in this discussion. The Momoyama period begins shortly after the death of Nobunaga in 1582, when his lieutenant, Hideyoshi, avenged Nobunaga's death and established himself as the chief military figure in the country. The Azuchi-Momoyama period ended in 1600 with the victory of the forces of Tokugawa Ieyasu at the Battle of Sekigahara, but some historians prolong it to 1615, the date of the fall of Osaka Castle to the Tokugawa forces. This chapter will be devoted chiefly to literature written between 1560 and 1600, but I shall not hesitate to discuss literary events of importance to this period even if they occurred somewhat earlier or later.
2. The diary, known as *Tokitsugu Gyōki*, covers the period 1527–1576. It is written in a strictly factual, unengaging style of kambun. Tokitsugu's son Yamashina Tokitsune (1543–1611) kept a diary (*Tokitsune Gyōki*) between the years 1576 and 1608. Its style is equally dreary, but it contains valuable information on contemporary Nō. Both men wrote their diaries on the backs of letters they had received (and in Tokitsugu's case, on the backs of prescriptions for medicine), suggesting that paper was a valuable commodity even for the aristocracy.
3. Quoted in Araki Yoshio, *Azuchi Momoyama Jidai Bungaku Shi*, p. 25.
4. Araki Yoshio, *Azuchi*, pp. 34–35.
5. Translations from Keene, *Some Japanese Portraits,* pp. 66–67. Text in Araki Yoshio, *Azuchi*, pp. 34–35, 147. On page 34 Araki gives Nagaharu's age at death as twenty-six (Japanese count), on page 147 as twenty-three. The

latter figure is also given by Kawada Jun in *Sengoku Jidai Waka Shū*, p. 156. However, I have followed a more recent work, the edition by Okuno Takahiro and Iwasawa Yoshiko of *Shinchō-kō Ki*, p. 532, which gives Nagaharu's dates as 1554–1580.

6. Okuno and Iwasawa, *Shinchō-kō Ki*, p. 295.
7. Text in Kawada, *Sengoku*, p. 114. The poem and its explanation appeared originally in *Ōtomo-kō Goke Oboegaki*.
8. Kawada, *Sengoku*, p. 31. This poem was written during the Ōnin War. Kawada suggested that it might have been composed by the author of the chronicle *Ōnin Ryakki*.
9. For other translations of this poem, see Keene, *Anthology of Japanese Literature*, p. 27.
10. See Robert H. Brower and Earl Miner, *Japanese Court Poetry*, especially pp. 16–17, 387–89.
11. See Haga Kōshirō, *Sanjōnishi Sanetaka*, pp. 47–48, 53, 57, 59, 72–73, for mentions of lectures on Japanese and Chinese classics. For the "joint research project" held in 1492, see p. 81.
12. The transmission of this secret information did not take place all at once. In 1489 Sōgi inducted Sanjōnishi Sanetaka into the first stage of the mysteries, and in the following year he received further instruction. Not until 1501 was the induction completed. See Haga, *Sanjōnishi*, pp. 57, 65, 111.
13. He also attended lectures on the Confucian Four Books, the *Tso Chuan*, the *History of the Han Dynasty*, the *Shih Chi*, the collection of poetry *San T'i Shih*, the poetry of Wu Shan-k'u and Su Tung-p'o, the *I-ching* (Book of Changes), and various Buddhist sutras known in their Chinese versions.
14. This variety of linked verse was known as *wakan, wa* standing for Japan and *kan* for China.
15. It is known as *Sanetaka-kō Ki*.
16. Sanetaka's diary supplied the material for a classic of modern Japanese historiography, *Higashiyama Jidai ni okeru Ichi Shinshin no Seikatsu*, by Hara Katsurō (1871–1923).
17. Haga, *Sanjōnishi*, p. 187, describes the respect in which Sanetaka was held as *tōdai saikō no bunkajin* (literally, "the highest man of culture of the time").
18. For incidents of such activities at the court, see *ibid.*, pp. 19, 55, 77.
19. For religious vogues of the time, see *ibid.*, pp. 68, 102, and 131. They included *hayari-botoke*, miraculous manifestations of the Buddha at one temple after another; *goryōsha*, angry ghosts who had to be appeased; and *Bon odori*, dances performed in connection with the Bon Festival (Urabon'e) honoring the spirits of ancestors.
20. See *ibid.*, pp. 188–89, for specific fees that he received in 1523. Making copies of *The Tale of Genji* was his chief source of such fees.
21. *Ibid.*, p. 159.

22. *Ibid.*, p. 179. The purchaser was Hatakeyama Yoshifusa, the governor of Noto.
23. In *ibid.*, pp. 191–250, Haga gives an account of what he calls "the end of ancient and medieval things" (*kodai, chūseiteki na mono no shūen*).
24. See *World Within Walls*, pp. 304–7, for an account of Hosokawa Yūsai and his influence on the waka poetry of the early Tokugawa period.
25. I have followed the account of Hosokawa Yūsai by Hayashi Tatsuya in *Nihon Koten Bungaku Daijiten*, V, pp. 457–58. Other sources (as Hayashi acknowledges) state that Yūsai's father was Mitsubuchi Harukazu, an adviser to several shoguns.
26. For further deatils see Keene, *Some Japanese Portraits*, pp. 73–74.
27. See *ibid.*, pp. 76–77, for a fuller account of Yūsai's success in mollifying Hideyoshi.
28. There is a modern edition edited by Tsuchida Masao in the Koten Bunko series. *Shūmyō Shū* contains, in addition to the waka, two diaries by Yūsai, *Kyūshū Michi no Ki*, and *Tōgokujin Michi no Ki*. There is a total of 817 waka in the collection, including those in the diaries.
29. Mishima-e was an old name for the lower reaches of the Yodo River near Ōzaka (the modern Osaka). The reeds (*ashi*) in the river at this point were often mentioned in poetry.
30. Tsuchida, *Shūmyō Shū*, p. 98.
31. *Shin Kokinshū* 238.
32. See my essay "Jōha, a Sixteenth-Century Poet of Linked Verse," in George Elison and Bardwell L. Smith (eds.), *Warlords, Artists, and Commoners*, pp. 124–25. The original source of this information is Oze Hoan's biography of Nobunaga, *Shinchō Ki*. See Kangōri Amane (ed.), *Shinchō Ki*, I, pp. 87–88
33. Kangōri, *Shinchō Ki*, I, p. 88. See also Araki, *Azuchi*, p. 344.
34. Perhaps the most notable appearance of Jōha in a later work of literature is the play *Mitsuhide to Shōha* (1926) by Masumune Hakuchō. He portrayed Jōha (whom he mistakenly called Shōha) as a cowardly and sycophantic man who betrayed his patron Mitsuhide.
35. Biographical data have been derived from Odaka Toshio, *Aru Rengashi no Shōgai*, pp. 16–21. My essay "Jōha," from which I have directly quoted here, contains more detailed information on Jōha's life.
36. From Matsunaga Teitoku's *Taionki*, edited by Odaka Toshio in *Taionki, Oritaku Shiba no Ki, Rantō Kotohajime*, p. 63.
37. Odaka, *Aru Rengashi*, p. 46.
38. Sanjōnishi Kin'eda, *Yoshino Mōde no Ki*, in Nihon Kikōbun Shūsei series, III, p. 197. For a discussion of this diary, see my *Travelers of a Hundred Ages*, pp. 242–46.
39. Text in Fukui Kyūzō, *Renga no Shiteki Kenkyū*, I, p. 238. See note 19 on page 311 of Elison and Smith, *Warlords*.
40. Odaka, *Aru Rengashi*, p. 83.

41. Satomura Jōha, *Fujimi no Michi no Ki*, in Nihon Kikōbun Shūsei series, III, p. 242. See also my *Some Japanese Portraits*, p. 59.
42. Odaka, *Aru Rengashi*, p. 143. See also Elison and Smith, *Warlords*, p. 127.
43. Araki Yoshio, *Azuchi*, pp. 351–52.
44. George Sansom, *A History of Japan: 1334–1615*, p. 41. See above, p. 1131.
45. The text of *Kinkafu* was discovered in 1924 by Sasaki Nobutsuna. A postscript states that the manuscript (the only one extant) was copied in 981 by Ō no Yasuki, a master of great song (*ōutashi*), and it has been conjectured that the collection was originally compiled in the early Heian period, probably about 810. The work consists of texts of songs, given in the *Man'yōgana*, together with musical notations for the singer's voice and for the koto. There are twenty-one poems, one of which, however, is different from another only in the musical notation. There are also brief notes on sources of the songs. Thirteen of the twenty-one poems are found only in this collection.
46. The origin of the title was discussed by Asano Kenji in his introduction (*kaisetsu*) to his edition *Shintei Chūsei Kayō Shū*, pp. 7–8. He noted that the name of the collection does not appear in any book catalogue prior to the nineteenth century; it was only in the Meiji era that the work attracted attention, starting with an essay by Takano Tatsuyuki in *Teikoku Bungaku* for August 1906.
47. Text in Kitagawa Tadahiko, *Kanginshū, Sōan Ko-uta Shū*, p. 16. A man "who has abandoned the world" is, of course, a Buddhist priest. The yearly accumulation of snow was a conventional way of alluding to the passage of time, but it may have referred to Chinese tales of scholars who studied by reflected light from the snow or by the light of fireflies.
48. *Sōka* (or *sōga*) was a kind of song that was popular especially with the samurai class during the two hundred years or so from the end of the Kamakura period up to the Azuchi-Momoyama period. It was known as sōka (fast song) because the tempo was considerably faster than in earlier songs (like the saibara) or recitations, though the texts themselves were comparatively long. Sōka were often absorbed into the texts of the Nō plays, particularly the kuse sections.
49. See, for example, the translations by Frank Hoff of poems 99 and 100 in *Like a Boat in a Storm: A Century of Song in Japan*, pp. 65–66. These are passages taken from Komparu Zenchiku's Nō play *Bashō*, which in turn quoted Chinese poetry.
50. Poem 177. Text in Kitagawa, *Kanginshū*, p. 98.
51. Poem 178. Kitagawa, *Kanginshū*, p. 99.
52. Poem 179. Kitagawa, *Kanginshū*, pp. 99–100.
53. Poem 180. Kitagawa, *Kanginshū*, p. 100.
54. Poem 282. Kitagawa, *Kanginshū*, p. 146. Poem 164 in *Sōan Ko-uta Shō* (Kitagawa, p. 208) is a shortened form of the same song.
55. There is a complete translation of the *Kanginshū* by Frank Hoff in *Like*

a Boat. His translations are fluent and effective, but are quite free, as will be apparent when they are compared with my (equally free) translations.

56. I am reminded of the poem by Ishikawa Takuboku that concludes, "Who will you strike / With that luckless fist— / Your friend? your self? / Or the innocent pillar at your side?" (Translated in my *Modern Japanese Literature*, p. 204.)
57. *Kokinshū* 504. It is anonymous.
58. For example, the preface by Ōoka Makoto to Hoff's *Like a Boat* expresses his admiration for the open hedonism of the *Kanginshū* (p. 10) and his hope that the translation "may one day share something of the significance in English-speaking countries with Fitzgerald's translation of the *Rubaiyat*" (p. 14). In his own works on Japanese poetry Ōoka has often described the special attraction of *Kanginshū* poetry; see, for example, his *Koi no Uta* (pp. 169–85) and *Nihon Shiika Kikō* (pp. 204–7), where he gives favorite ko-uta from the *Kanginshū* along with his high appraisal of the collection. For an appreciation of the work by a contemporary novelist, see Hata Kōhei, *Kanginshū: Koshin to Ren'ai no Kayō*.
59. The popularity of the ko-uta during the sixteenth century is attested by many sources. Oda Nobunaga, not the most artistic of men, is reported not only to have been fond of ko-uta but to have composed one. Toyotomi Hideyoshi's praise for ko-uta has also been preserved. The popularity of ko-uta spread to the aristocracy, as we know from court diaries of the time. See Kitagawa, *Kanginshū*, p. 244.
60. See *Nihon Koten Bungaku Daijiten*, VI, p. 227.
61. This is the theory of Kitagawa given in *Kanginshū*, p. 252.
62. The collection has been translated by Frank Hoff under the title *The Genial Seed*.
63. Only two songs in the *Kanginshū* are labeled as *Kyōgen Kayō*, but this may be an accident of the compilation. Kitagawa emphasizes the importance of ko-uta in Kyōgen by beginning his discussion of the *Kanginshū* with summaries of two Kyōgen, *Narugo* and *Mizukumi*, in which many ko-uta are used in the course of the play. See Kitagawa, *Kanginshū,* pp. 229–40.
64. Nobumitsu wrote some of the most popular plays of the entire Nō repertory, including *Funa Benkei, Momijigari*, and *Yūgyō Yanagi*, and revised others, including *Dōjōji* and *Ataka*. He has nevertheless attracted curiously little attention from scholars of Nō.
65. These actions are performed by actors of the Kongō school; not all schools are quite so dramatic.
66. For an account of Ōmura Yūko in English, see my *Some Japanese Portraits*, pp. 63–70.
67. For a fuller description of the contents of Yūko's work, see my *Some Japanese Portraits*, pp. 65–67. The poems by Bessho Nagaharu and his

wife, quoted above on p. 1132, were written just before Miki Castle fell to Hideyoshi.

68. Only five of these plays have been preserved. The music for the plays was composed by Komparu Yasuteru (1549–1621), a sixth-generation descendant of Komparu Zenchiku and the head of the Komparu school at the time. The texts of the five plays are included in Nonomura Kaizō, *Yōkyoku Sambyakugojūban Shū*.
69. The plays are not designated by category, and not every scholar would agree with my divisions. See Hata Hisashi, "Kinsaku Nō, Kindai Nō, Gendai Nō no Sakusha to Sakuhin," pp. 304–5. Hata seems to consider *Kōya-mōde* as a first-category play; in that case there is no third-category play in the sequence.
70. Araki Yoshio, *Azuchi*, p. 391, quoting *Hoan Taikōki*.
71. *Ibid.*; full text in Nonomura, *Yōkyoku*, p. 675.
72. Nonomura, *Yōkyoku*, p. 687.
73. The concluding passage is given in Araki, *Azuchi*, p. 395. See also Nonomura, *Yōkyoku*, p. 685.
74. Araki Yoshio, *Azuchi*, pp. 399–400, from *Hoan Taikōki*.
75. The first recorded revival of any of these plays took place in 1898, on the 300th anniversary of Hideyoshi's death when *Shibata-uchi* was performed. Contemporary reviews were surprisingly favorable. See Hata Hisashi, "Kinsaku Nō," pp. 305–6. In 1989 *Akechi-uchi* was successfully revived in connection with the film *Rikyū*, directed by Teshigahara Hiroshi. See the article by Matsuoka Shimpei, "Hakken Tanoshii Nō no Fukkyoku Būmu," p. 11.
76. For summaries of two Kōwaka based on texts by Ōmura Yūko, *Miki* and *Honnōji*, see James T. Araki, *The Ballad-Drama of Medieval Japan*, pp. 148–49. Hideyoshi's command was given to three Kōwaka performers to use materials in two parts of *Tenshō Ki* in making texts for which they supplied the music. See Araki Shigeru, "Kaisetsu, Kaidai," in Araki, Ikeda, and Yamamoto, *Kōwaka-mai*, I, p. 352.
77. For genealogical information, see James T. Araki, *The Ballad-Drama*, pp. 19–26.
78. The name Kōwaka, like the similar names Kōfuku and Kōgiku, was used by performers of entertainments in Wakasa and Echizen (the seat of the Momonoi family), where the art is believed to have originated. See Anzako Iwao, "Maimai to Kōwaka"; also Araki Shigeru, "Kaisetsu, Kaidai," p. 344.
79. James T. Araki, *The Ballad-Drama*, p. 69.
80. *Ibid.*, p. 71.
81. Its survival in the village of Ōe in Fukuoka Prefecture was discovered in 1907 by the drama scholar Tatsuno Tatsuyuki (1876–1948). A detailed description of contemporary performances is given by James T. Araki in *The Ballad-Drama*, pp. 80–108. Kōwaka was sometimes known as *maimai*

(dance-dance), and perhaps *Kōwaka* and *maimai* originally designated the same art, but the former came to be associated with the samurai class. The performers in Ōe Village still consider they are preserving samurai tradition; but maimai, never losing its humble origins, became an entertainment for the lower classes during the seventeenth century.

82. *Ibid.*, p. 87.
83. In addition to the two Kōwaka about Hideyoshi, mentioned above, there are two about Fujiwara no Kamatari (614–669), another about the Chinese hero Chang Liang, a love story, a retelling of the story of Izanagi and Izanami creating the islands of Japan, and *Yuriwaka Daijin*, described on p. 1162.
84. Fukuda Akira in *Chūsei Katarimono Bungei*, p. 103, quotes from *Kōwaka Keizu no koto* in support of his belief that the performers composed the texts themselves, but he admits there are difficulties in this interpretation.
85. For example, in *Togashi*, a Kōwaka with the same plot as the Nō *Ataka* or the Kabuki *Kanjinchō*, the work concludes with Benkei's reading from a blank page what he claims is the subscription list of gifts for rebuilding the Tōdai-ji; he is praised for this action, but we are not informed whether or not Togashi believes Benkei's, the climax of the incident. See James T. Araki, *The Ballad-Drama*, p. 112.
86. *Ibid.*, pp. 150–71, gives a translation of the Kōwaka *Atsumori.*
87. Muroki Yatarō in his article "Kōwakamai," in *Nihon Koten Bungaku Daijiten*, II, p. 528, cites a statement in *Arte da Lingoa de Iapam* by Rodrigues as evidence that by this time Kōwaka was being recited and no longer danced. Anzako Iwao in "Maimai to Kōwaka" quotes other passages in the same work, evidence of Rodrigues's familiarity with Kōwaka. For Rodrigues's interest in other aspects of Japanese literature, see Michael Cooper, *Rodrigues the Interpreter*, pp. 230–37; also Michael Cooper, "The Muse Described."
88. For the early history of Jōruri and Kabuki, see *World Within Walls*, pp. 230–41.
89. This is the subject of the study of Thomas F. Leims, *Die Entstehung des Kabuki*.
90. For a more detailed description of *Amida no Munewari* see my *Bunraku*, pp. 45–47. There are also complete translations by C. J. Dunn of two versions of the play in *The Early Japanese Puppet Drama*, pp. 112–34.
91. For a concise presentation of the background of Sekkyō and a discussion of the principal texts, see Susan Matisoff, *The Legend of Semimaru*, pp. 113–23.
92. The appropriate sections of such paintings are given by Iwasaki Takeo (in *Sanshō Dayū Kō*, p. 20) and Muroki Yatarō (*Sekkyō Shū*, p. 397). Both show a man, dressed in a patterned kimono rather than priestly robes, who stands under a large parasol, presumably reciting, while a small group of spectators, some of them weeping, listen. A section of the "Funaki

Screen," showing theaters in the dried bed of the Kamo River at Shijō in Kyoto about 1600, is reproduced in Elison and Smith, *Warlords*, p. 140; unfortunately, the photograph is so blurred that it is hard to recognize in the painting what Frank Hoff says about it on the preceding page.

93. Araki Yoshio, *Azuchi*, p. 485, lists the *ko-jōruri* texts derived from sekkyō-bushi, including *Amida no Munewari, Sanshō Dayū, Shintokumaru, Karukaya Dōshin, Aigo no Waka*, and *Shinoda-zuma*. These were the basic texts of the old Jōruri, an indication of how difficult it is to distinguish between the two theaters.
94. The influence of Kōwaka on Sekkyō was noticed by the Confucian philosopher Dazai Shundai (1680–1747) in his *Dokugo*. See Iwasaki, *Sanshō*, p. 19. For annotated texts of Sekkyō, see Muroki, *Sekkyō Shū*, which includes six of the best-known works. Muroki's "kaisetsu" gives a good general background. For *Yuriwaka Daijin*, see page 1162.
95. For kana zōshi, see *World Within Walls*, pp. 149–64.
96. I am thinking of such works as Ishikawa Jun's "Shion Monogatari," published in 1956.
97. Translation by George Elison in his essay "The Cross and the Sword," in Elison and Smith, *Warlords*, p. 66. The letter, sent by Frois to P. Belchior de Figueiredo, SJ, was dated "Miyako, 1 June 1569." The word *Cámis* refers to the *kami*, or gods, of Shintō, and *Fotoquès* to *Hotoke*, or the Buddha.
98. Kangōri, *Shinchō Ki*, I, p. 40.
99. *Ibid.*, pp. 50–51. "Daigaku" refers to Sakuma Daigaku, one of Nobunaga's lieutenants.
100. See Okuno and Iwasawa, *Shinchō-kō Ki*, p. 5.
101. The title is slightly different from Ōta Gyūichi's work, omitting the word *kō*, or "lord."
102. Kangōri, *Shinchō Ki*, I, p. 14.
103. The text, edited by Kuwata Tadachika, appeared in the Iwanami Bunko in 1944 and was reprinted in 1984.
104. The Kobe Municipal Museum has a celebrated collection (formerly known as the Ikenaga Collection) of *namban bijutsu*, "art of the southern barbarians." Most of the examples were probably painted by Japanese.
105. The music survived vestigially until the twentieth century as the *orashio* (oratio) sung by the hidden Christians (*kakure-kirishitan*) of the Gotō archipelago. The original melodies had been lost by this time, and the words of the hymns reduced to meaningless gibberish. The *kokyū*, a bowed musical instrument that became popular about this time, was generally believed to have been introduced from China, but Professor David Waterhouse has shown that the instrument was actually a rebec, introduced by the Portuguese.
106. The curious work *Honkyō Gaihen* (1806) by the Shintō revivalist Hirata

Atsutane (1776–1843) borrowed from at least three Christian works written in Chinese by Jesuit priests: *The Ten Chapters of an Eccentric* (1608), *The True Meaning of Christianity* (1603), and *Seven Conquests* (1614) by Didacus de Pantoja. For a discussion of what Hirata borrowed, see Donald Keene, *The Japanese Discovery of Europe, 1720–1730*, pp. 164–69. Hirata presumably borrowed these prohibited books from scholars in Mito, where there was a collection of Christian books and objects.

107. See *World Within Walls*, pp. 158–60.

108. See Keene, *The Japanese Discovery*, pp. 73–74.

109. Another story, telling of a woman's love for her stepson, in the manner of Phaedra and Hippolytus, is found in Japanese works of literature of the middle ages and afterward, notably the Sekkyō plays *Shintokumaru* and *Aigo no Waka* and the Jōruri play *Sesshū Gappō ga Tsuji*. However, the resemblances may be coincidental. See my article, "The Hippolytus Triangle, East and West," in *Yearbook of Comparative and General Literature*, no. 11 (supplement), 1962.

110. The first part (*yuri*) of the name Yuriwaka suggests it was derived from Ulysses. The earliest extant version of the name is the variant Yurikusawaka, seemingly from Ulixes, the Latin name for the hero. See James T. Araki, "Yuriwaka and Ulysses: The Homeric Epics at the Court of Ōuchi Yoshitaka," pp. 14–17.

111. The text is given in Araki Shigeru et al., *Kōwaka-mai*, I, pp. 113–38. This is the Kōwaka version.

112. See Araki Shigeru, "Kaisetsu, Kaidai," pp. 366–69, in Araki Shigeru et al., *Kōwaka-mai*, I.

113. Tsubouchi's article was published in the January 1906 issue of *Waseda Bungaku*. A summary of his article is given by Araki Yoshio in *Azuchi*, pp. 467–69.

114. James T. Araki, "Yuriwaka," pp. 32–35. The performance at the court in Kyoto of the dance-play (kōwaka-mai) *Yuriwaka Daijin* in the first month of 1551 was recorded in *Tokitsugu Gyōki*, the diary of Yamashina Tokitsugu. See Araki Yoshio, *Azuchi*, p. 471. Araki doubted that the material of *The Odyssey* could have been made into a theatrical work so quickly after it was first introduced. However, after considering also *Yuriwaka Sekkyō*, the Sekkyō play based on the same story, he found so many close similarities between it and *The Odyssey* that he reluctantly reached the conclusion that Tsubouchi was right, after all.

115. Russell Maeth published in 1986 the article "On the Supposed Fragment of Homer Discovered in a Chinese Text of the Tenth Century: *Taiping guangji*, 481.4, and *Odyssey*, ix, 105–542." He expressed the belief that the Chinese scholar Yang Xianyi "did, indeed, discover a fragment of the *Odyssey* in a Chinese text of the tenth century."

The Japanese source is a work by Hirazawa Kyokuzan, a samurai who visited Nagasaki in 1774. See Keene, *The Japanese Discovery*, p. 74.

116. The Japanese account is longer and more detailed, evidence that it was not derived from *Taiping guangji*.
117. Yamada Nagamasa (?–1630), the best known of the Japanese adventurers who resided in Southeast Asia, became the leader of the Japanese town (Nihommachi) in the Siamese capital, Ayuthia. Other Japanese went to Cochin China, Annam, Luzon, Cambodia, and Taiwan with permission of the Japanese government. This was the so-called *shuinsen bōeki* (vermilion-seal ship trade). The system of granting licenses with vermilion seals to persons authorized to travel abroad and engage in commerce began as early as 1593 and continued until 1635.

Bibliography

Note: All Japanese books, except as otherwise noted, were published in Tokyo.

Anzako Iwao. "Maimai to Kōwaka," *Kinsei Minzoku* 39, February, 1966.

Araki, James T. *The Ballad-Drama of Medieval Japan*. Berkeley: University of California Press, 1964.

———. "Yuriwaka and Ulysses: The Homeric Epic at the Court of Ōuchi Yoshitaka," *Monumenta Nipponica* 33:1, 1978.

Araki Shigeru, Ikeda Hiroshi, and Yamamoto Kichizō. *Kōwaka-mai*, 3 vols., in Tōyō Bunko series. Heibonsha, 1979–83.

Araki Yoshio. *Azuchi Momoyama Jidai Bungaku Shi*. Kadokawa Shoten, 1969.

Asano Kenji. *Shintei Chūsei Kayō Shū*, in Nihon Koten Zensho series. Asahi Shimbun Sha, 1973.

———. *Shintei Kanginshū*, in Iwanami Bunko series. Iwanami Shoten, 1989.

Brower, Robert H., and Earl Miner. *Japanese Court Poetry*. Stanford, Calif.: Stanford University Press, 1961.

Cooper, Michael. "The Muse Described," *Monumenta Nipponica* 26:1–2, 1971.

———. *Rodrigues the Interpreter*. New York: Weatherhill, 1974.

Dunn, C. J. *The Early Japanese Puppet Drama*. London: Luzac, 1966.

Elison, George, and Bardwell L. Smith. *Warlords, Artists, and Commoners*. Honolulu: University of Hawaii Press, 1981.

Fukuda Akira. *Chūsei Katarimono Bungei*. Miyai Shoten, 1981.

Fukui Kyūzō. *Renga no Shiteki Kenkyū*, 2 vols. Seibidō Shoten, 1930.

Haga Kōshirō. *Sanjōnishi Sanetaka*, in Jimbutsu Sōsho series. Yoshikawa Kōbunkan, 1960.

Hara Katsurō. *Higashiyama Jidai ni okeru Ichi Shinshin no Seikatsu*. Chikuma Shobō, 1967.

Hata Hisashi. "Kinsaku Nō, Kindai Nō, Gendai Nō no Sakusha to Sakuhin," in Yokomichi Mario, Nishino Haruo, and Hata Hisashi, *Nō no Sakusha to Sakuhin*.

Hata Kōhei. *Kanginshū: Koshin to Ren'ai no Kayō*. Nihon Hōsō Shuppan Kyōkai, 1982.

Hoff, Frank. "City and Country: Song and the Performing Arts in Sixteenth-Century Japan," in Elison and Smith, *Warlords, Artists and Commoners*.

———. *The Genial Seed*. New York: Mushinsha-Grossman, 1971.

———. *Like a Boat in a Storm: A Century of Song in Japan*. Hiroshima: Bunka Hyōron Shuppan, 1982.

Iwasaki Takeo. *Sanshō Dayū Kō*. Heibonsha, 1973.

———. *Zoku Sanshō Dayū Kō*. Heibonsha, 1978.

Kangōri Amane (ed.). *Shinchō Ki*, 2 vols. Kyoto: Gendai Shisō Sha, 1981.

Kawada Jun. *Sengoku Jidai Waka Shū*. Kyoto: Kōchō Shorin, 1943.

Keene, Donald. *Bunraku*. Tokyo: Kodansha International, 1965.

———. *The Japanese Discovery of Europe, 1720–1830*. Stanford, Calif.: Stanford University Press, 1969.

———. *Modern Japanese Literature*. New York: Grove Press, 1956.

———. *Some Japanese Portraits*. Tokyo: Kodansha International, 1978.

———. *Travelers of a Hundred Ages*. New York: Henry Holt, 1989.

Kitagawa Tadahiko. *Kanginshū, Sōan Ko-uta Shū*, in Shinchō Nihon Koten Shūsei series. Shinchōsha, 1982.

Kubota Jun and Kitagawa Tadahiko. *Chūsei no Bungaku*, in Nihon Bungakushi series, III. Yūhikaku, 1976.

Leims, Thomas F. *Die Entstehung des Kabuki*. Leiden: E. J. Brill, 1990.

Maeth, Russell. "On the Supposed Fragment of Homer Discovered in a Chinese Text of the Tenth Century: *Taiping guangji*, 481.4, and *Odyssey*, ix, 105–542," *Estudios de Asia y Africa* 21:2, 1986.

Matisoff, Susan. *The Legend of Semimaru*. New York: Columbia University Press, 1978.

Matsuoka Shimpei. "Hakken Tanoshii Nō no Fukkyoku Būmu," *Asahi Shimbun*, June 24, 1991 (evening ed.).

Muroki Yatarō. *Sekkyō Shū*, in Shinchō Nihon Koten Shūsei series. Shinchōsha, 1977.

Nihon Koten Bungaku Daijiten, 6 vols. Iwanami Shoten, 1983–85.

Nonomura Kaizō. *Yōkyoku Sambyakugojūban Shū*, in Nihon Meicho Zenshū series. Kōbunsha, 1928.

Odaka Toshio. *Aru Rengashi no Shōgai*. Shibundō, 1967.

———. *Taionki, Oritaku Shiba no Ki, Rantō Kotohajime*, in Nihon Koten Bungaku Taikei series. Iwanami Shoten, 1964.

Okami Masao and Hayashiya Tatsusaburō. *Nihon Bungaku no Rekishi*, VI. Kadokawa Shoten, 1967.

Okuno Takahiro and Iwasawa Yoshiko (eds.). *Shinchō-kō Ki*, in Kadokawa Bunko series. Kadokawa Shoten, 1969.

Ōoka Makoto. *Koi no Uta*. Kōdansha, 1985.

———. *Nihon Shiika Kikō*. Shinchōsha, 1978.

Sanjōnishi Kin'eda. *Yoshino Mōde no Ki*, in Nihon Kikōbun Shūsei series, III. Nihon Tosho Sentā, 1979.
Sansom, George. *A History of Japan: 1334–1615*. London: Cresset Press, 1961.
Shimmura Izuru. *Isoho Monogatari*, in Iwanami Bunko series. Iwanami Shoten, 1939.
Tsuchida Masao (ed.). *Shūmyō Shū*, in Koten Bunko series. Koten Bunko, 1969.
Yokomichi Mario, Nishino Haruo, and Hata Hisashi. *Nō no Sakusha to Sakuhin*, in Iwanami Kōza: Nō Kyōgen series. Iwanami Shoten, 1987.

Glossary

ai-kyōgen. Also called *ai*. A scene played between the two parts of a Nō play. Usually consists of a Kyōgen actor, known as "the man of the place," who, in response to the request of the *waki*, relates the circumstances behind the appearance of the *shite* in the first part.

aware. The moving qualities of the sights and experiences of the world.

biwa. A stringed musical instrument, somewhat resembling in shape the mandolin. Used as an accompaniment for dramatic recitations in the middle ages.

bosatsu. A bodhisattva.

bugaku. The stately dances performed to the accompaniment of *gagaku* music.

bunjin. A literatus. The ideal "gentleman," especially during the Tokugawa period.

butsumei. Poems that include "hidden words" by means of puns. Literally, "names of things." Also known as *mono no na*.

chōka. A long poem of indeterminate length, consisting of alternating lines in five and seven syllables with a final extra line in seven syllables. Most skillfully used by the *Man'yōshū* poets.

chokusenshū. A collection of poetry (mainly *waka*) compiled by command of a sovereign.

chōnin. A townsman. This class did not enjoy many privileges until the Tokugawa period.

chūgū. The meaning of this term varied somewhat according to the period, but it generally designated an empress, the consort of an emperor.

chūnagon. A "middle counselor."

dai. Topics of *waka* poetry, such as the seasons.

daisaku. A poem composed for another person.

daruma-uta. A term expressing dislike or contempt for difficult poems; used specifically of some of Teika's poems.

Dazaifu. One of several military stations. The most important was in northern Kyūshū.

dengaku. Literally, "field music." A kind of drama, originally performed by peasants in order to please the gods, later developed into an art that rivaled Nō.

dōka. A religious or didactic song, used especially of those composed in the middle ages.

engo. A "related word." In order to give unity to a poetic composition a poet might choose from among various synonyms one related to his subject. Thus, with *tsuyu* (dew) the word *okidokoro* (rather than some synonym) was likely to be used to mean a "place to stay" because the verb *oku* also was used of dew "settling."

ennen. A kind of play, resembling Nō, that was performed at temples in the Kamakura period. The name means "prolong life," suggesting ennen was originally an offering to the gods made in the hope of prolonging someone's life.

fu. A Chinese form of rhymed prose. Burton Watson, who translated many examples, called the form "rhyme-prose."

fudoki. A gazetteer, especially those made early in the Nara period.

gabun. "Elegant prose." Used especially of the pseudo-archaic compositions of the Tokugawa period.

gagaku. The orchestral music that often serves to accompany *bugaku* dance-plays.

gekokujō. "Those underneath overcoming those above"—a phenomenon described especially in the writings of the late middle ages.

gembuku. A boy's coming-of-age ceremony.

genzaimono. A Nō play without supernatural elements. The persons encountered by the *waki* belong to the same period as himself; hence the name, "present-day work."

gigaku. The earliest form of ritual dances, imported from China for performance at the court during the Nara period. Superseded by *bugaku*.

giko monogatari. "Archaistic fiction." Used especially of the fiction written during the Kamakura and Muromachi periods in imitation of the Heian tales.

gongen. A bodhisattva who manifests himself in Japan as a Shintō divinity in order to save people.

gunki monogatari. Martial tales that describe warfare of the late Heian period.

haikai no renga. The comic style of renga that gave birth to the haikai poetry of the Tokugawa period.

hakama. The trousers of a formal Japanese costume.

hanka. An "envoy" to a *Man'yōshū* poem. One or more of these envoys, in the form of a *waka*, was appended to a *chōka*.

hiragana. The flowing style of *kana* writing. Lends itself to graceful calligraphy, and is used today to record Japanese words, as opposed to importations.

hōben. Originally, an expedient used by the Buddha and the bodhisattvas to save human beings by adapting the teachings to fit individual capacities. Later, a justification for literature as a painless means of spreading doctrine.

hōin. A general term denoting a Buddhist priest, used during the middle ages and later.

honji suijaku. Literally, "original substance manifests traces," used to mean that the buddhas had manifested themselves in Japan as Shintō deities.

honka-dori. "Allusive variation"—the borrowing of some elements of an earlier poem in making a new poem, a feature especially of *Shin Kokinshū* and later *waka* poetry.

hōshi. A priest; however, it sometimes designated anyone who dressed as a priest even if he was a professional entertainer. *Biwa hōshi* were such entertainers who played the *biwa*.

hyakushu. A sequence of one hundred poems. The celebrated *Hyakunin Isshu* is such a sequence, though it lacks the connections between one poem and the next characteristic of the best hyakushu.

iemoto. The head of a school of Nō, Kyōgen, and many other traditional Japanese arts.

imayō. "New style"—popular songs of the late Heian period, usually sung by *shirabyōshi*. They were in four lines, each containing seven plus five syllables. *Ryōjin Hishō* contains many such imayō.

ji-amari. "Excess syllables"—said of a line in a *waka* with more than the normal five or seven syllables.

jiriki. "Self-efforts"—a belief that one can save oneself by one's good works and other efforts, typical of Zen Buddhism.

jisei. A farewell verse to the world, usually composed immediately before a person dies.

Jōdo. The Pure Land—the paradise of Amida Buddha. Believers in Jōdo Buddhism pray that Amida will receive them in this paradise.

jo, ha, kyū. The three tempi of a Nō play—slow, fast, and very fast. The *ha* section contains the development of the plot of the play and is much longer than either of the other two.

jokotoba. Same as *joshi* or *jo*.

joshi. (Also called *jo*.) The "preface" to a poem consisting of one or more lines, often related to what follows not by sense but by an association or word-play.

kagami. A mirror, and by extension, a kind of history that "mirrors" the past.

kagura. Sacred dances performed at Shintō shrines.

kakekotoba. A word that differs in meaning depending on the word it follows and precedes; sometimes also a portmanteau word.

kambun (or *kanbun*). Prose written in classical Chinese.

kampaku. The "chancellor"—the highest position to which a person not of the imperial family could rise.

kan. A scroll or volume of a longer work.

kana. The syllabary used to record the sounds of Japanese. Two forms, the flowing *hiragana* and the severer *katakana*, are used.

kanshi. A poem composed in classical Chinese.

kana zōshi. A work of fiction written mainly in words of Japanese origin and transcribed mainly in *kana*.

kata-uta. A "half-poem" consisting of the first three lines of a *sedōka* (5-7-7 syllables). Of importance in the *Man'yōshū* and other early poetry, and revived unsuccessfully in the Tokugawa period.

kemari. "Kickball." A kind of football played by courtiers in the Heian period and afterward that survives vestigially.

kin. A stringed musical instrument imported from China.

kinsei. The premodern period, from 1600 to 1867.

kōgō. Empress, the consort of an emperor. In some periods there was both a *kōgō* and a *chūgū*, both considered to be empresses.

kokata. The role of a child in a Nō play.

kokoro. As a term of *waka* criticism, it meant the affective quality of a poem.

koto. A stringed instrument; sometimes translated as "zither."

kotoba. "Words"—the language used in a poem to express the poet's feelings.

kotobagaki. A preface to a poem, often expressing the circumstances under which the poem was composed.

kunimi. "Looking at the country"—a ritual act of observation performed by an emperor.

Kyōgen. The comic plays performed in conjunction with Nō. Also, the *ai-kyōgen*, the short plays or narrations performed in between the two parts of a Nō play.

kyōgen kigyo. "Wild words and fancy language"—a characterization of literature, used often when discussing literary expression as a *hōben* for enlightenment.

kyōka. A comic *waka*.

makurakotoba. A fixed epithet in five or seven syllables, used in poetry, often before place names.

mana. Chinese characters, as opposed to the *kana*.

mappō. The last period of the Buddhist Law, when people would no longer be able to understand or practice the teachings of Buddha.

menoto. Originally, a wet nurse; also used to mean a governess, and (in the case of a male) a preceptor.

monogatari. A work of fiction; literally, a "relating of things" from *mono* (things) and *katari* (relating).

mono no aware. A sensitivity to things, usually used in connection with an awareness of tragic implications.

mono no ke. An evil spirit that causes sickness or death.

mugen. A variety of Nō in which the central character (*shite*) is a spirit or ghost.

mujō. The inconstancy of the things of this world. A Buddhist principle that lay behind much poetic expression.

nembutsu. The invocation to Amida Buddha—*namu amida butsu*—pronounced by believers in Jōdoshū or Jōdo Shinshū Buddhism.

nengō. A "reign-name." Since the Meiji period there has been only one reign-name for each emperor, but in the past the *nengō* was changed in certain years of the cycle of sixty or else when unusually auspicious or ill-omened events occurred.

nikki. A diary, though many examples of this genre were written long after the events described.

nikki bungaku. "Diary literature"—the genre to which the literarily conceived diaries belong.

Nō. The classical drama, usually tragic in character. There are two main varieties: *mugen Nō*, in which the *shite* is a spirit or ghost, and *genzaimono*, in which the *shite* is a person of this world.

onryō. A vindictive spirit who returns to this world to afflict those he considers were responsible for his grief while he was alive.

otogi-zōshi. Tales composed in the Muromachi or early Tokugawa period.

p'ien wen. A form of Chinese parallelism in literary composition.

rakugo. Recitations of comic anecdotes.

renga. "Linked verse"—one of the major forms of poetic composition during the middle ages.

rensaku. A series of poems, sometimes united by a common theme.

risshi. Originally, a Buddhist priest who was especially familiar with the Buddhist Law; the third highest rank bestowed on learned priests, after *sōjō* and *sōzu*.

rufubon. A vulgate text, the most widely known version of a particular text.

sabi. The quality of appreciating loneliness, poverty, or even desolation—an ideal in poetry from the time of Fujiwara Shunzei.

sadaijin. Minister of the Left. A high-ranking office immediately below that of *dajōdaijin* (prime minister).

saigū. The imperial princess who served as the high priestess at Ise.

sakoku. "Closure of the country"—a condition that persisted during much of the Tokugawa period.

sarugaku. An early name for Nō, sometimes written with characters meaning "monkey music."

sedōka. A poem in six lines of 5-7-7-5-7-7 syllables which appears chiefly in the *Man'yōshū*.

sekkyō. Originally, an explanation of the sutras, but as the explanations became more dramatic, it turned into a pronouncedly lachrymose variety of theatrical entertainment.

semmyō. Originally, an imperial rescript written in Japanese but including words of Chinese origin. It gave rise to the mixed style of Chinese and Japanese known as *wakan konkō*.

sesshō. A regent—the name by which a *kampaku* was known when the sovereign was a minor.

setsuwa. Tales of the variety found in *Tales of Times Now Past*, especially of the late Heian and Kamakura periods.

shimai. The climactic dance of a Nō play.

Shingon. One of the principal Buddhist sects, founded in Japan by Kōbō Daishi (Kūkai).

shirabyōshi. Women dancers and entertainers, especially during late Heian and Kamakura times. They figure prominently in such works as *The Tale of the Heike*.

shite. The principal actor in a Nō play.

shōmyō. Buddhist chanting to Sanskrit or Chinese texts.

shōnagon. Lesser counselor—a fairly high rank in the court bureaucracy.

shōsetsu. "Novel"—a term borrowed from China and first used by the Japanese in the eighteenth century.

shū. "Collection," found in such titles as *Kokinshū*.

sōrōbun. A style characterized by the use of the copula verb *sōrō*. First used in the Kamakura period, it appears in the prose sections of the Nō plays and eventually became the epistolary style in use until about 1945.

sōshi. A work of fiction, found in such terms as *kana zōshi* and *ukiyo zōshi*.

sōshiji. The voice of the novelist, intruded into such texts as *The Tale of Genji*.

tanka. The classical verse form, composed in five lines of 5-7-5-7-7 syllables. More commonly called *waka* before the Meiji Restoration.

tariki. "Other's efforts"—the kind of Buddhism characterized by a belief that salvation is possible only through the intercession of Amida Buddha.

Tendai. A Buddhist sect of particular importance during the Heian period. Founded in Japan by Dengyō Daishi (Saichō).

tsure. A "companion" to the *shite* or *waki* in a Nō play.

udaijin. Minister of the Right. A high-ranking office immediately below *sadaijin* (minister of the Left).

uguisu. A songbird that is frequently mentioned in spring poems.

uta. A song, but also a poem; used interchangeably with *waka*.

uta-awase. A poem competition. Two teams (the left and right) composed poems on specified topics, and a judge awarded victory or a tie to each competing pair.

utagaki. In ancient times an exchange of poems between men and women that often led to mating.

utagatari. Talks on poetry, usually by a group of poets trying to ascertain the meaning of obscure poems.

utamakura. Generally, a place that had inspired poetry and was believed to be still capable of inspiring new poems.

uta monogatari. A work consisting of episodes centered around one or more *waka*, typified by *Tales of Ise*.

wabi. A taste for simplicity, especially in the tea ceremony.

wakan konkō. A style that mixes Japanese and Chinese words, typified by *The Tale of the Heike*, as opposed to the "pure Japanese" style of *The Tale of Genji*.

waki. The secondary actor in a Nō play, often a traveling priest.

yamabuki. A yellow flower, sometimes called a "kerria rose," that blooms late in the spring.

yamabushi. Ascetic "mountain priests" who live in remote places and practice austerities that enable them to perform miraculous cures, etc.

yūgen. "Mystery and depth"—an ideal associated especially with the Nō theater, though the term was also used for *waka* and *renga*. The connotations of the word varied considerably according to the user.

zatō. Blind entertainers; they figure importantly in several Kyōgen plays.

zuihitsu. "Following the brush"—miscellaneous essays, typified by *The Pillow Book of Sei Shōnagon* and *Essays in Idleness*.

zuryō. The provincial governor class during the Heian period, consisting of members of the middle- or lower-class aristocracy.

Selected List of Translations into English

This list does not attempt to be complete. It does not include translations that are part of longer studies, or translations of single Nō or Kyōgen plays. Works that are primarily of historical, rather than literary, interest have generally been excluded.

Works Covering Several Periods

Carter, Steven D. *Traditional Japanese Poetry.* Stanford, Calif.: Stanford University Press, 1991.

———. *Waiting for the Wind.* New York: Columbia University Press, 1989.

Keene, Donald. *Anthology of Japanese Literature.* New York: Grove Press, 1955.

McCullough, Helen Craig. *Classical Japanese Prose: An Anthology.* Stanford, Calif.: Stanford University Press, 1990.

Miner, Earl. *Japanese Poetic Diaries.* Berkeley: University of California Press, 1969.

Plutschow, Herbert, and Hideichi Fukuda. *Four Japanese Travel Diaries of the Middle Ages.* Ithaca, N.Y.: Cornell University East Asia Papers, 1981.

Reischauer, Edwin O., and Joseph K. Yamagiwa. *Translations from Early Japanese Literature.* Cambridge, Mass.: Harvard University Press, 1951.

Sato, Hiroaki, and Burton Watson. *From the Country of Eight Islands.* Garden City, N.Y.: Doubleday, 1981.

Watson, Burton. *Japanese Literature in Chinese*, 2 vols. New York: Columbia University Press, 1975–76.

Ancient and Nara Periods

"The Footprints of the Buddha": an Eighth-Century Old Japanese Poetic Sequence, trans. by Roy Andrew Miller. New Haven, Conn.: American Oriental Society, 1975.

Ko-Ji-Ki, or Record of Ancient Matters, trans. by Basil Hall Chamberlain. 2nd ed. Kōbe: J. L. Thomson, 1932.

Kojiki, trans. by Donald L. Philippi. Tokyo: University of Tokyo Press, 1968.

The Manyōshū. The Nippon Gakujutsu Shinkōkai Translation. New York: Columbia University Press, 1965.

Man'yōshū, Volume One, trans. by Ian Hideo Levy. Princeton, N.J.: Princeton University Press, 1981.

Nihongi, trans. by W. G. Aston. Reprint ed. Tokyo: Tuttle, 1972.

Heian Period

As I Crossed a Bridge of Dreams, trans. by Ivan Morris. New York: Dial Press, 1971.

The Changelings, trans. by Rosette F. Willig. Stanford, Calif.: Stanford University Press, 1983.

The Emperor Horikawa Diary, trans. by Jennifer Brewster. Honolulu: The University of Hawaii Press, 1977.

Ennin's Diary: The Record of a Pilgrimage to China in Search of the Law, trans. by Edwin O. Reischauer. New York: Ronald Press, 1955.

The Gossamer Years (Kagerō Nikki), trans. by Edward Seidensticker. Reprint ed. Tokyo: Tuttle, 1964.

The Izumi Shikibu Diary, trans. by Edwin A. Cranston. Cambridge, Mass.: Harvard University Press, 1969.

Kokinshū, trans. by Laurel Rasplica Rodd with Mary Catherine Henkenius. Princeton, N.J.: Princeton University Press, 1984.

Kokin Wakashū, trans. by Helen Craig McCullough. Stanford, Calif.: Stanford University Press, 1985.

Mirror for the Moon: A Selection of Poems by Saigyō (1118–1190), trans. by William R. LaFleur. New York: New Directions, 1978.

Murasaki Shikibu: Her Diary and Poetic Memoirs, trans. by Richard Bowring. Princeton, N.J.: Princeton University Press, 1982.

Ōkagami, The Great Mirror, trans. by Helen Craig McCullough. Princeton, N.J.: Princeton University Press, 1980.

The Pillow-Book of Sei Shōnagon, trans. by Arthur Waley. London: Allen & Unwin, 1928.

The Pillow Book of Sei Shōnagon, 2 vols., trans. by Ivan Morris. New York: Columbia University Press, 1967.

The Poetic Memoirs of Lady Daibu, trans. by Phillip Tudor Harries. Stanford, Calif.: Stanford University Press, 1980.

The Riverside Counselor's Stories, trans. by Robert L. Backus. Stanford, Calif.: Stanford University Press, 1985.

"*Takamura Monogatari*," trans. by Ward Geddes in *Monumenta Nipponica* 46:3, 1991.

A Tale of Eleventh-Century Japan: Hamamatsu Chūnagon Monogatari, trans. by Thomas H. Rohlich. Princeton, N.J.: Princeton University Press, 1983.

The Tale of Genji, trans. by Arthur Waley. One-volume edition. New York: Random House, 1960.

The Tale of Genji, trans. by Edward G. Seidensticker. New York: Alfred A. Knopf, 1976.

Tales of Ise, trans. by Helen Craig McCullough. Stanford, Calif.: Stanford University Press, 1968.

Tales of Yamato, trans. by Mildred Tahara. Honolulu: University of Hawaii Press, 1980.

Kamakura Period

The Confessions of Lady Nijō, trans. by Karen Brazell. Garden City, N.Y.: Doubleday, 1973.

"Fitful Slumbers: Nun Abutsu's *Utatane*," trans. by John R. Wallace in *Monumenta Nipponica* 43:4, 1988.

Fujiwara Teika's Hundred-Poem Sequence of the Shōji Era, trans. by Robert H. Brower. Tokyo: Sophia University, 1978.

Fujiwara Teika's Superior Poems of Our Time, trans. by Robert H. Brower and Earl Miner. Stanford, Calif.: Stanford University Press, 1967.

Lady Nijo's Own Story, trans. by Wilfrid Whitehouse and Eizo Yanagisawa. Tokyo: Charles E. Tuttle, 1974.

"Recluses and Eccentric Monks: Tales from the *Hosshinshū* by Kamo no Chōmei," trans. by Marian Ury in *Monumenta Nipponica* 27:2, 1972.

Record of Things Heard from the Treasury of the Eye of the True Teachings, trans. by Thomas Cleary. Boulder, Colo.: Prajna Press, 1990.

Sand and Pebbles (Shasekishū), trans. by Robert E. Morrell. Albany: State University of New York Press, 1985.

A Tale of Flowering Fortunes, 2 vols., trans. by William H. and Helen Craig McCullough. Stanford, Calif.: Stanford University Press, 1980.

The Tale of the Heike, trans. by Hiroshi Kitagawa and Bruce T. Tsuchida. Tokyo: University of Tokyo Press, 1975.

The Tale of the Heike, trans. by Helen Craig McCullough. Stanford, Calif.: Stanford University Press, 1988.

The Tale of Matsura: Fujiwara Teika's Experiment in Fiction, trans. by Wayne P. Lammers. Ann Arbor: Center for Japanese Studies, The University of Michigan, 1992.

"*Tamekanekyō Wakashō*," trans. by Robert N. Huey and Susan Matisoff in *Monumenta Nipponica* 40:2, 1985.

Tannishō: *A Primer*, trans. by Dennis Hirota. Kyoto: Ryūkoku University, 1982.

Muromachi Period

"*Bunshō Soshi*: The Tale of Bunshō, the Saltmaker," trans. by James T. Araki in *Monumenta Nipponica* 38:3, 1983.

Conversations with Shōtetsu, trans. by Robert H. Brower. Ann Arbor: Center for Japanese Studies, The University of Michigan, 1991.

Essays in Idleness: the Tsurezuregusa of Kenkō, trans. by Donald Keene. New York: Columbia University Press, 1967.

Granny Mountains: A Second Cycle of Nō Plays, trans. by Royall Tyler. Ithaca, N.Y.: Cornell University East Asia Papers, 1978.

Ikkyū and the Crazy Cloud Anthology, trans. by Sonja Arntzen. Tokyo: University of Tokyo Press, 1986.

Japanese Nō Dramas, trans. by Royall Tyler. London: Penguin, 1992.

Japanese Noh Drama, 3 vols., trans. by Nippon Gakujutsu Shinkōkai. Tokyo, 1955–60.

Like a Boat in a Storm: A Century of Song in Japan, trans. by Frank Hoff. Hiroshima: Bunka Hyoron, 1982.

The Nō Plays of Japan, trans. by Arthur Waley. Reprint. New York: Grove Press, 1957.

Noh Drama and The Tale of Genji, trans. by Janet Goff. Princeton, N.J.: Princeton University Press, 1991.

On the Art of the Nō Drama, trans. by J. Thomas Rimer and Yamazaki Masakazu. Princeton, N.J.: Princeton University Press, 1984.

"Pilgrimage to Dazaifu: Sōgi's *Tsukushi no Michi no Ki*," trans. by Eileen Kato in *Monumenta Nipponica* 34:3, 1979.

Pining Wind: A Cycle of Nō Plays, trans. by Royall Tyler. Ithaca, N.Y.: Cornell University East Asia Papers, 1978.

Poems of the Five Mountains, trans. by Marian Ury. Tokyo: Mushinsha, 1977.

Rethinking Sorrow: Revelatory Tales of Late Medieval Japan, trans. by Margaret Helen Childs. Ann Arbor: Center for Japanese Studies, University of Michigan, 1991.

Saka's Diary of a Pilgrimage to Ise, trans. by A. L. Sadler. Tokyo: The Meiji Japan Society, 1940.

The Tale of the Soga Brothers, trans. by Thomas J. Cogan. Tokyo: University of Tokyo Press, 1987.

The Taiheiki, trans. by Helen Craig McCullough. New York: Columbia University Press, 1959.

Tales of Tears and Laughter: Short Stories of Medieval Japan, trans. by Virginia Skord. Honolulu: University of Hawaii Press, 1991.

Twelve Plays of the Noh and Kyōgen Theaters, trans. by Karen Brazell and others. Ithaca, N.Y.: Cornell East Asian Program, 1986.

Twenty Plays of the Nō Theatre, trans. by Donald Keene and others. New York: Columbia University Press, 1970.

Yoshitsune, trans. by Helen Craig McCullough. Tokyo: University of Tokyo Press, 1966.

Zen Poems of the Five Mountains, trans. by David Pollack. New York: The Crossroad Publishing Co., 1985.

INDEX

(In general, poetry collections and plays are indexed under their Japanese titles; prose works—tales, diaries, and histories—are indexed under their English titles.)